E-Business Issues, Challenges and Opportunities for SMEs:
Driving Competitiveness

Maria Manuela Cruz-Cunha
Polytechnic Insitute of Cavado and Ave, Portugal

João Varajão
University of Trás-os-Montes e Alto Douro, Portugal

BUSINESS SCIENCE REFERENCE
Hershey · New York

Director of Editorial Content: Kristin Klinger
Director of Book Publications: Julia Mosemann
Acquisitions Editor: Lindsay Johnston
Development Editor: Dave DeRicco
Publishing Assistant: Milan Vracharich, Jr.
Typesetter: Keith Glazewski
Production Editor: Jamie Snavely
Cover Design: Lisa Tosheff

Published in the United States of America by
Business Science Reference (an imprint of IGI Global)
701 E. Chocolate Avenue
Hershey PA 17033
Tel: 717-533-8845
Fax: 717-533-8661
E-mail: cust@igi-global.com
Web site: http://www.igi-global.com/reference

Library of Congress Cataloging-in-Publication Data

E-business issues, challenges and opportunities for SMEs : driving competitiveness / Maria Manuela Cruz-Cunha and Joao Varajao, editors.
p. cm.
Includes bibliographical references and index.
Summary: "This book discusses the main issues, challenges, opportunities, and solutions related to electronic business adoption, with a special focus on SMEs"--Provided by publisher.
ISBN 978-1-61692-880-3 (hbk.) -- ISBN 978-1-61692-882-7 (ebook) 1. Small business. 2. Electronic commerce. I. Cruz-Cunha, Maria Manuela, 1964- II. Varajao, Joao, 1972- III. Title.

HD2341.E22 2011
658.8'72--dc22

2010016458

British Cataloguing in Publication Data
A Cataloguing in Publication record for this book is available from the British Library.

List of Reviewers

Adamantios Koumpis, *ALTEC S.A., Greece*
Agustin Orfila, *University Carlos III of Madrid, Spain*
Alexis Barlow, *Glasgow Caledonian University, Scotland*
Anne Smith, *Glasgow Caledonian University, Scotland*
António Trigo Ribeiro, *Instituto Superior de Contabilidade e Administração de Coimbra, Portugal*
António Tavares, *Polytechnic Institute of Cávado e do Ave, Portugal*
Beatriz Sainz de Abajo, *University of Valladolid, Spain*
Burkhardt Funk, *Leuphana University, Germany*
Ciara Heavin, *University College Cork, Ireland*
Claudia C. Cabal, *University of Quindío, Colombia*
David Lewis, *University of Massachusetts Lowell, USA*
Eduardo Escofet, *University of Holguín, Cuba*
Eduardo Galán, *University Carlos III of Madrid, Spain*
Eduardo Huerta, *Universitat Politècnica de Catalunya, Spain*
Elisabete Morais, *Instituto Politécnico de Bragança, Portugal*
Emmanuel Tadjouddine, *Xi'an Jiaotong-Liverpool University, China*
Fintan Clear, *Brunel University, UK*
Francisco J. Martínez-López, *University of Granada, Spain*

Rui Rijo, *Institute for Systems and Computers Engineering at Coimbra, Portugal*
Serdal Bayram, *Siemens, Turkey*
Simona Šarotar Žižek, *University of Maribor, Slovenia*
Stephen Burgess, *Victoria University, Australia*
Sunilkumar Manvi, *Reva Institute of Technology and Management, India*
Susan Jones, *Southwest Minnesota State University*
Susana Badillo, *Universidad Autónoma Metropolitana de México, Mexico*
Tatiana Levashova, *SPIIRAS, Russia*
Ugljesa Marjanovic, *University of Novi Sad, Serbia*
Valentina Ndou, *Università del Salento*
Vítor Fernandes, *Instituto Politécnico de Leiria, Portugal*
Vojko Potocan, *University of Maribor, Slovenia*
Yi Zhao, *Fernuniversität, Germany*
Zlatko Nedelko, *University of Maribor, Slovenia*

Table of Contents

Detailed Table of Contents

Section 1
Technological and Organizational Challenges

Section 1, "Technological and Organizational Challenges" includes seven chapters concerned with the more technological and organizational challenges, opportunities and impact of e-business.

In today's digital world the majority of companies, including small and medium-sized enterprises (SMEs) and large firms, aim to have an online presence. However, SMEs differ from large-sized companies in terms of financial and staffing resources, which have implications for the development of e-business strategies. Thus, SMEs must not only overcome these barriers but must also take care of several critical success factors (CSFs). This chapter discusses three elements (i.e., design principles, web usability and search engine optimization), which are vital to the effective design of a successful digital marketplace. The chapter discusses the importance of integrating these three elements in website design especially for SMEs.

According to the authors, it is hoped that agent mediated e-commerce will be carried out as open systems of agents interoperating among different institutions, where different auction protocols may be in use, and argue that in order to put such a scenario to work, agents will need a method to automatically verify the properties of a previously unseen auction protocol. This poses the problem of automatically

This chapter informs SME owners, developers, consultants, and academics with the reasons, means, and possibilities afforded by 21st century technology in helping SMEs to improve their operational efficiencies and discover more effective marketing strategies for their products and services. SMEs typically underutilize opportunities to enhance their efficiencies by using more complex e-Business systems, and in so doing under develop the talents of their workforce for innovation and success. This underutilization is due to a lack of exposure to leadership and HR development training. Knowing the need to learn must be a strong foundation before technological development can ensue. This chapter provides a synthesis of research and literature across several related, but seldomly connected fields - including, organizational theory, leadership, adult development and learning, 21st century learning, distance learning and human resource management. The authors attempt to communicate the need for SMEs to both develop leadership and technological program developments to implement the changes needed to compete in a marketplace that reflects rapid change and imperfect information.

Chapter 6
Open Innovation: Opportunities and Challenges for SMEs 87
Hakikur Rahman, University of Minho, Portugal

With the advent of innovative technologies and multi-dimensional researches along the setting of entrepreneurship development, philosophy, context and business handling has been transformed from being traditional to innovative. Depending on diversity and nature of the transformation, innovation has been shifted from closed to open to crowdsourcing innovation. Ranging from small entrepreneurs to corporate business houses are being immensely benefited by the innovation techniques, especially utilizing information and communication technologies. However, the road to innovation, despite being a paradigm shift is not smooth and ready for many, particularly the SME who mainly deal with the clients at the outer peripheries of the social circle. This chapter synthesizes issues of opportunities and challenges for SME by carrying out a broad literature review and synthesis, providing a few research hints to be applicable for researchers and research institutions.

Chapter 7
Organizational Readiness/Preparedness 101
Bojan Lalic, University of Novi Sad, Serbia
Ugljesa Marjanovic, University of Novi Sad, Serbia

The Internet and information technology (IT) are being used in many ways to bring benefits and to increase competitiveness to businesses and public sector organizations. Implementing innovations in an organization is a dynamic and continuous process. This chapter discusses factors and elements fundamental for overcoming business challenges that most of the organizations are facing during successful implementation of an IT initiative within an organization. However, in order for systems to be prepared for change in terms of organizational readiness, organization needs to asses and plan their organizational readiness. The chapter also presents how to assess an organization's readiness for success and how to put together an organizational readiness plan.

Section 2
New Business Models and Technological Support

The eight chapters included in Section 2, "New Business Models and Technological Support," are concerned with the potential of new technologies and tools in the support of new business models based on e-business.

In the networked world supply chain, integration and networking is being echoed in various industries as a strategic imperative solution for firms. Digital marketplaces represent one of the most powerful solutions adopted by firms to manage their supply chains and to support the networking practices among firms, especially among SMEs. In fact they enable firms to more efficiently buy, sell, and manage their supply chain processes on a global scale. However, SMEs supply chains may differ in the modalities of coordination and collaboration, in the intensity of relations between actor and more specifically in the technological infrastructure and competencies available. These factors may affect the success of digital marketplaces and their potentialities for firms networking. The chapter suggests that digital marketplaces could provide a viable model for SME networking; however, successful path toward networking requires a harmonization of digital marketplace business model with supply chain characteristics.

In modern working relations, a company can improve its business dramatically, especially with formation and performance of suitable management. An important role in the whole management of a company belongs also to management of e-business. One of the main concerns about management of e-business is how much of each e-business should be owned by each e-business participants. This is called the extent of vertical integration. But in the modern business environment, vertical integrations alone are not enough. The alternative to vertical integration is some other form of relationship, not necessarily ownership. The chapter examines the relationship between the links of the e-business in terms of the flows between the operations involved. This contribution discusses two issues: (1) How different relationships in e-business impact organization of e-business, and (2) How different organizational forms impact of e-business.

Current trends of globalization and increased competition require new forms of organization and work support. Especially in SME, the competitiveness and future market position of an enterprise is closely related to the ability of cooperating with partners in SME networks or virtual supplier organizations. In complex work processes with a number of distributed partners, high requirements with respect to competence and a lot of rules and guidelines to be obeyed; detecting and sharing knowledge among different members of networked organizations is an important issue. Based on an empirical investigation regarding the demands of SME and illustrating this demand with industrial cases, this chapter investigates two technical approaches supporting knowledge supply in networked organizations: enterprise modeling and self-organization of flexible supply networks. These approaches are presented with related work and their limits and potentials.

Enterprises, and in particular SMEs, besides having to stay agile, competitive and aware of competition, must give customers what they need (customized products or services) when they need it. The classical business paradigm (carefully studying what customers have bought in the past to predict what they will buy in the near future and derive a strategy from it) is not agile and adequate enough anymore. This chapter discusses a customer-centric business paradigm with enough agility to follow the patterns of customers' needs and the ability to customize specific needs as a variant of some pattern, turning the very low volume customer market into a viable business opportunity. The customization and corresponding production result from concrete user request and not anticipation of demand. The authors call it EaaS (Enterprise as a Service), and is particularly adequate to SMEs.

As modern economies faces its growth challenges, SME are potential agents to become strategic competitive, especially when it can be supported by information technology. A scenario composed by rapid changes in the economies, introduction of new communication and information technology and emergence of new markets forms the study background, which was proposed to analyze new business models for SMEs based on e-business concepts and how these resources, applied under strategic thinking, are increasing the SMEs' competitiveness. A case study of Brazilian e-business based SMEs is conducted, in order to understand IT application in this evolving context, examining five successful cases.

Internet and IT (information technologies) among other innovative drivers push companies to update their business models, and design stands out as an emergent issue strongly connected with innovation, which, in turn, is the main resource of the modern economy. One way to achieve innovation is through artifacts that allow the development of successful information systems in organizations. Moreover, the field of health appears as a sector with many opportunities to improve services through IT and design. Therefore, e-health comes out as one of the elements that should eventually help in the evolution of business models in health systems. In this chapter, authors present a design method of IT artifacts for e-health adapted from the method proposed by Pahl and Beitz (1995). The correctness of the design method adopted is a significant issue to generate new business models successfully or to adapt the existing ones in health systems.

These days, small businesses typically have a web presence beyond their own website, employing the services of other online providers to host details of their businesses and hopefully attract more customers to them. This chapter examines the notion of a web presence audit tool for small businesses to enable them to track the various website features that they have implemented on their own, and other, websites over time. A 'website feature' can be something as simple as listing the business address and telephone number on the website, but it can also include more advanced features such as online ordering and purchasing. The chapter discusses the specifications for such a website audit tool and suggests a relational database design for the tool. The resultant specifications are to be trialed in a number of settings before being introduced to a wider group of small businesses.

adoption is ridden with barriers and understanding these along with the benefits it offers to SMEs is important. This chapter has reviewed the existing literature of barriers and benefits of e-business adoption by SMEs to identify the various enablers that can facilitate adoption. The chapter also provides an insight into e-readiness and analyses six existing tools that are used globally to measure e-readiness. Based on a comprehensive analysis, an holistic framework (Motivation Application Measurement Support (MAMS) e-readiness assessment framework) has been proposed. The framework can be utilized as a reference to assess, design and implement a supplementary strategic approach for the assessment of e-business readiness of SMEs. Further empirical research to test, amend and improve the MAMS framework can be undertaken in the future.

This chapter aims to investigate the issues of electronic commerce activities in SME as a consequence of organizational change initiated by IT adoption. The fundamental issues influencing e-commerce practices of SMEs are their insufficiency of cognitive learning and organizational strategy, financial and distribution problems specific to SMEs, limitations of supply chain management, reluctance of organizational culture for electronic change, problems of IT usage, insufficiency of human resource, resistance of top management to organizational change as required by the adoption of information technologies, integration problems of new technologies with the existing systems, lack of confidence on the side of customers towards electronic commerce. A study of the Turkish Automotive Supplier Industry has revealed that electronic commerce has been adopted and its benefits are accepted, however, the industry has to overcome some technical and managerial difficulties to implement it more efficiently and effectively.

Technological advance of the last decades created an atmosphere in which the organizations are forced to look actively for new options for the cost reduction, in addition to, simultaneously, seeking to compete more effectively in their markets. This context requires focused, swift, more flexible and more competitive organizations which are forced, many times, to implement radical changes in the way they conduct business, employ people and use technology. Despite the recognition and the attention given to e-business over the last years, this type of business has not yet achieved a desirable maturity stage. This problem, current and stated over the last years, demands research efforts so that a solution can be

could be applied to both ways in terms of value gain to the participants. The chapter emphasizes open innovation for SMEs at the outset, by focusing transformation of innovation leading to a networked paradigm in spite of being in closed periphery, providing some overview on innovation strategies and challenges.

Preface

ABOUT THE SUBJECT

Electronic business (eBusiness) plays a central goal in the economy, facilitating the exchange of information, goods, services and payments. E-Business is not exclusive for large enterprises. It propels productivity and competitiveness and is accessible to all enterprises, and sophisticated systems like e-Marketplaces act as business integrators, potentiating business opportunities for both buyers and sellers.

eBusiness represents potential and opens opportunities to foster competitiveness, but brings in operational, tactical and strategic challenges for Small and medium enterprises (SME). This topic is gaining an increasingly relevant strategic impact on global business and the world economy, and organizations of all sort are undergoing hard investments (in cost and effort) in search of the rewarding benefits of efficiency and effectiveness that this range of solutions promise. But as we all know this is not an easy task it is not only a matter of financial investment. It is much more, as the book will show.

Responsiveness, flexibility, agility and business alignment are requirements of competitiveness that enterprises search for. And we hope that the models, proposals and studies presented and discussed in this book can contribute to highlight new ways to identify opportunities and overtake trends and challenges of eBusiness adoption and exploitation, in particular targeting SME.

The book project was born under the intention to collect the most recent developments on the organizational, technological and legal dimensions of electronic business, discuss its potential, impact, trends and challenges. This objective was met, due to the high adhesion of contributors and the quality and complementarity of the manuscripts proposed that allowed a comprehensive whole, addressing all the aspects initially previewed.

ORGANIZATION OF THE BOOK

This book is a compilation of 22 contributions to the discussion of the main issues, challenges, opportunities and developments related with e-Business, as tools for SME competitiveness, from the Technological, managerial and organizational perspectives, in a very comprehensive way, in order to disseminate current achievements and practical solutions and applications.

These 22 chapters are written by a group of 52 authors that include many internationally renowned and experienced researchers and specialists in the e-Business field and a set of younger authors, showing a promising potential for research and development. Contributions came from the five continents, and integrates contributions from academe, research institutions and industry, representing a good and comprehensive representation of the state-of-the-art approaches and developments that address the several dimensions of this fast evolutionary thematic.

"E-Business Issues Challenges and Opportunities for SMEs: Driving Competitiveness" is organized in three sections:

- **Section 1:** *Technological and Organizational Challenges* is concerned with the technological and organizational challenges, opportunities and impact of e-Business.
- **Section 2:** *New Business Models and Technological Support* addresses the potential of new technologies and tools in the support of new business models based on e-Business.
- **Section 3:** *New E-Business Frameworks* is centered on e-Business and e-Commerce barriers, readiness, constraints, and the proposal of new frameworks to enable overcoming the difficulties.

The first section, "Technological and organizational challenges" includes seven chapters concerned with the more technological and organizational challenges, opportunities and impact of e-Business, summarized below.

In today's digital world the majority of companies, including small and medium-sized enterprises (SMEs) and large firms, aim to have an online presence. However, SMEs differ from large-sized companies in terms of financial and staffing resources, which have implications for the development of e-business strategies. Thus, SMEs must not only overcome these barriers but must also take care of several critical success factors (CSFs). In this first first chapter, "Designing Digital Marketplaces for Competitive Advantage", Rathi and Given discuss three elements (design principles, web usability and search engine optimization), which are vital to the effective design of a successful digital marketplace. The chapter discusses the importance of integrating these three elements in website design especially for SMEs.

In the second chapter, " E-commerce Systems for Software Agents: Challenges and Opportunities" the authors Tadjouddine and Jiaotong hope that agent mediated e-commerce will be carried out as open systems of agents interoperating among different institutions, where different auction protocols may be in use, and argue that in order to put such a scenario to work, agents will need a method to automatically verify the properties of a previously unseen auction protocol. This poses the problem of automatically verifying desirable properties in order to trust a given auction mechanism. The chapter we discusses relevant opportunities for SMEs in addressing the issues of enabling software agents (e.g., PDAs, mobile phones) to connect to auction houses and verify desirable properties that need to hold before engaging any transactions.

In " Enhancing the Preparedness of SMEs for E-Business Opportunities by Collaborative Networks", Duin and Thoben introduce Virtual Organizations (VOs) as a special organizational form of collaborative networks of SMEs to conduct E-Business projects. VOs are normally not created from scratch, but instantiated from a strategic network or pool of enterprises, enhancing the preparedness of participating members when an E-Business opportunity occurs. The underlying strategic network acts as VO Breeding Environment (VBE). Examples from the automotive industry are illustrating the development and needs of this concept. Strategic planning is important for such a network in order to increase chances of occurring business opportunities. The chapter also discuss how scenario-oriented methods such as cross-impact analysis can be used to support a collaborative strategic planning in such networked organizations. The application of such methods allows long-term foresight and the anticipation of the right technological, financial and business oriented decisions.

SMEs have a special need to be able to collect knowhow from the global community and implement this as competence in the enterprise. E-Learning is an approach for competence development that can assist SMEs in creating a learning organization. There are different approaches to E-Learning, and amongst the most powerful ones is the application of serious games. The PRIME project conducted experiments with serious games in project business and in manufacturing and has resulted in a set of guidelines for successful implementation of games in an organization, according to Rolstadas, Andersen and Fradinho in "E-learning for SMEs - challenges, potential and impact". It is necessary to allow a learning curve and put emphasis on the social context to obtain effective learning. SMEs are advised to develop E-Learning in cooperation with academic institutions, and to use real life cases and problems for assignments.

In chapter five, "21st Century Learning Opportunities for SME Success: Maximizing Technology Tools and Lifelong Learning for Innovation and Impact", King and Foley inform SME owners, developers, consultants, and academics with the reasons, means, and possibilities afforded by 21st century technology in helping SMEs to improve their operational efficiencies and discover more effective marketing strategies for their products and services. SMEs typically underutilize opportunities to enhance their efficiencies by using more complex e-Business systems, and in so doing under develop the talents of their workforce for innovation and success. This underutilization is due to a lack of exposure to leadership and HR development training. This chapter provides a synthesis of research and literature across several related, but seldomly connected fields - including, organizational theory, leadership, adult development and learning, 21st century learning, distance learning and human resource management. The authors attempt to communicate the need for SMEs to both develop leadership and technological program developments to implement the changes needed to compete in a marketplace that reflects rapid change and imperfect information.

With the advent of innovative technologies and multi-dimensional researches along the setting of entrepreneurship development, philosophy, context and business handling has been transformed from being traditional to innovative. Depending on diversity and nature of the transformation, innovation has been shifted from closed to open to crowdsourcing innovation. Ranging from small entrepreneurs to corporate business houses are being immensely benefited by the innovation techniques, especially utilizing ICT. However, the road to innovation, despite being a paradigm shift is not smooth and ready for many, particularly the SME who mainly deal with the clients at the outer peripheries of the social circle. In "Open Innovation: Opportunities and Challenges for SMEs", Rahman synthesizes issues of opportunities and challenges for SME by carrying out a broad literature review and synthesis, providing a few research hints to be applicable for researchers and research institutions.

The Internet and IT are being used in many ways to bring benefits and to increase competitiveness to businesses and public sector organizations. The seventh chapter, "Organizational Readiness/Preparedness" by Lalic and Marjanovic, discusses factors and elements fundamental for overcoming business challenges that most of the organizations are facing during successful implementation of an IT initiative within an organization. However, in order for systems to be prepared for change in terms of organizational readiness, organization needs to asses and plan their organizational readiness. The chapter also presents how to assess an organization's readiness for success and how to put together an organizational readiness plan.

The eight chapters included in "Section 2: New business models and technological support" are concerned with the potential of new technologies and tools in the support of new business models based on e-Commerce.

Electronic Marketplaces represent one of the most powerful solutions adopted by firms to manage their supply chains and to support the networking practices among firms, especially among SMEs. In fact they enable firms to more efficiently buy, sell, and manage their supply chain processes on a global scale. However, SMEs Supply chains may differ in the modalities of coordination and collaboration, in the intensity of relations between actor and more specifically in the technological infrastructure and competencies available, factors that may affect the success of digital marketplaces and their potentialities for firms networking. In chapter 8, "Open Innovation: Opportunities and Challenges for SMEs", Ndou and Sadguy suggest that digital marketplaces could provide a viable model for SME networking; however, successful path toward networking requires a harmonization of digital marketplace business model with supply chain characteristics.

According to Potocan, Nedelko and Mulej in "What is New with Organization of E-Business: Organizational Viewpoint of the Relationships in E-business", the management of e-Business plays an important role in the whole management of a company, and one of the main concerns about management of e-business is how much of each e-business should be owned by each e-business participants. This is called the extent of vertical integration. But in the modern business environment, vertical integrations alone are not enough. The alternative to vertical integration is some other form of relationship, not necessarily ownership. The chapter examines the relationship between the links of the e-business in terms of the flows between the operations involved. This contribution discusses two issues: 1) How different relationships in e-business impact organization of e-business, and 2) How different organizational forms impact of e-business.

Current trends of globalization and increased competition require new forms of organization and work support. Especially in SME, the competitiveness and future market position of an enterprise is closely related to the ability of cooperating with partners in SME networks or virtual supplier organizations. In complex work processes with a number of distributed partners, high requirements with respect to competence and a lot of rules and guidelines to be obeyed; detecting and sharing knowledge among different members of networked organizations is an important issue. Based on an empirical investigation regarding the demands of SME and illustrating this demand with industrial cases, chapter 10, "Knowledge Supply for SME Networks: Application Cases and Selected Technical Approaches", by Smirnov, Shilov, Levashova, Carstensen and Sandkuhl investigate two technical approaches supporting knowledge supply in networked organizations: enterprise modeling and self-organization of flexible supply networks.

Besides having to stay agile, competitive and aware of competition, enterprises must give customers what they need when they need it. The classical business paradigm (carefully studying what customers have bought in the past to predict what they will buy in the near future and derive a strategy from it) is not agile and adequate enough anymore. In chapter 11, "SME as a Service", Delgado discuss a customer-centric business paradigm with enough agility to follow the patterns of customers' needs and the ability to customize specific needs as a variant of some pattern, turning the very low volume customer market into a viable business opportunity. The customization and corresponding production result from concrete user request and not anticipation of demand. The author call it EaaS (Enterprise as a Service), and is particularly adequate to SMEs.

To Jamil, Balloni and Carvalho, in "Reflecting on New Businesses Models for SMEs through Technological Application: Cases of E-Business in Brazil", as modern economies faces its growth challenges, SME are potential agents to become strategic competitive, especially when it can be supported by information technology. A scenario composed by rapid changes in the economies, introduction of new communication and information technology and emergence of new markets forms the study background, which was proposed to analyze new business models for SMEs based on e-business concepts and how these resources, applied under strategic thinking, are increasing the SMEs' competitiveness. A case study of Brazilian e-business based SMEs is conducted, in order to understand IT application in this evolving context, examining five successful cases.

Internet and IT among other innovative drivers push companies to update their business models, and design stands out as an emergent issue strongly connected with innovation, which, in turn, is the main resource of the modern economy. One way to achieve innovation is through artifacts that allow the development of successful information systems in organizations. Moreover, the field of health appears as a sector with many opportunities to improve services through IT and design. Therefore, e-health comes out as one of the elements that should eventually help in the evolution of business models in health systems. In chapter 13, "E-Health Business Models Prototyping by Incremental Design", the authors present a design method of IT artifacts for e-health adapted from the method proposed by Pahl and Beitz (1995). The correctness of the design method adopted is a significant issue to generate new business models successfully or to adapt the existing ones in health systems.

These days, small businesses typically have a web presence beyond their own website, employing the services of other online providers to host details of their businesses and hopefully attract more customers to them. This chapter examines the notion of a web presence audit tool for small businesses to enable them to track the various website features that they have implemented on their own, and other, websites over time. A 'website feature' can be something as simple as listing the business address and telephone number on the website, but it can also include more advanced features such as online ordering and purchasing. In "Specifications for a Website Audit Tool for Small Businesses", Burgess discuss the specifications for such a website audit tool and suggests a relational database design for the tool.

Businesses are aware of the popular demand for careful waste management as a high priority environmental issue and SME face greater pressure when coping with waste products, because they often lack necessary resources or expertise. E-business could offer unique opportunities both for SMEs wanting to dispose of their waste or find waste management services and for SMEs who deal with specific aspects of waste disposal itself. Chapter 15, "An Approach to Efficient Waste Management for SMEs via RBVOs" proposes an approach for locating actors involved in the transportation, disposal, recycling and reuse of waste created by SMEs. The authors' approach incorporates the notion of Request Based Virtual Organizations (RBVOs) using a Service Oriented Architecture (SOA) and an ontology for the definition of waste management requirements. The populated ontology is utilized by a Multi-Agent System which performs negotiations and forms RBVOs. This approach enables SMEs to find appropriate partners, handle waste management and gain competitive advantage in the marketplace.

A set of seven chapters are contemplated in "Section 3: New E-Business Frameworks", centered on e-Business and e-Commerce barriers, readiness, constraints, and the proposal of new frameworks to enable overcoming the difficulties.

Retail was born in 1879 with the first Five & Dime Stores. 130 years after, we still live in the era of Retail 1.5, this means, no real Quantum Leap was made in Customer Experience. However, Porfírio and Ganhão in "Retail 2.0: The Coming Up of a New Era for Retail Business in the 21st Century" strongly believe that, starting half of the first decade of the 21st Century, a new Retail Era began. The objective of the study introduced is to understand what have been done in the field of New Customer Experiences since the beginning of the Classic Retailers, and try to devise what will be the strategic implications for the future, arising from the changes foreseen in the field of retail business. The authors emphasize the emerging new trends, and try to foresee what in Social Retail and Online / Shop Customer Experience could be the mainstream for the next decade.

Chapter 17, "A Unified View of Enablers, Barriers, and Readiness of Small to Medium Enterprises for e-business Adoption", by Chugh and Gupta reviews the existing literature of barriers and benefits of e-business adoption by SMEs to identify the various enablers that can facilitate adoption. The chapter also provides an insight into e-readiness and analyses six existing tools that are used globally to measure e-readiness. Based on a comprehensive analysis, an holistic framework (Motivation Application Measurement Support (MAMS) e-readiness assessment framework) has been proposed. The framework can be utilized as a reference to assess, design and implement a supplementary strategic approach for the assessment of e-business readiness of SMEs. Further empirical research to test, amend and improve the MAMS framework can be undertaken in the future.

In chapter 18, "Issues Influencing Electronic Commerce Activities of SMEs: A Study of the Turkish Automotive Supplier Industry", Zerenler and Gözlü investigate the issues of e-commerce activities in SME as a consequence of organizational change initiated by IT adoption. The fundamental issues influencing electronic commerce practices of SMEs are their insufficiency of cognitive learning and organizational strategy, financial and distribution problems specific to SMEs, limitations of supply chain management, reluctance of organizational culture for electronic change, problems of information technologies usage, insufficiency of human resource, resistance of top management to organizational change as required by the adoption of information technologies, integration problems of new technologies with the existing systems, lack of confidence on the side of customers towards electronic commerce. A study of the Turkish Automotive Supplier Industry has revealed that e-commerce has been adopted and its benefits are accepted, however, the industry has to overcome some technical and managerial difficulties to implement it more efficiently and effectively.

Technological advance of the last decades created an atmosphere in which the organizations are forced to look actively for new options for the cost reduction, in addition to, simultaneously, seeking to compete more effectively in their markets. This context requires focused, swift, more flexible and more competitive organizations which are forced, many times, to implement radical changes in the way they conduct business, employ people and use technology. Despite the recognition and the attention given to e-business over the last years, this type of business has not yet achieved a desirable maturity stage. This problem, current and stated over the last years, demands research efforts so that a solution can be found to solve it. In "Constrains associated to e-business evolution", Morais, Pires and Gonçalves explore a range of constraints which are suggested by the literature to influence e-business evolution, so that organizations could be better equipped in anticipating any difficulties while in progress through their e-business initiatives.

A conceptual model to understand the consumer's adoption and use of certain website recommendation system is presented in the chapter; the research problem is tackled from a psychological perspective. The authors of chapter 20," An Integrative Framework on the Psychological Variables Explaining the Consumers' Use of E-Commerce-Based Recommendation Systems" base on, adapt and integrate classical theories of consumer behavior with particular theories developed in the framework of computer-mediated environments. The model proposed, along with the relations analyzed among the variables considered (a total of 16 research propositions), should be of help for recommendation systems designer and website managers, in order to work with systems more aware of the psychological process experienced by consumers when interacting with them.

Using organizational justice as a conceptual framework, Beugré in "Fairness in Virtual Teams: A Construct of E-Organizational Justice" discusses the importance of fairness in managing virtual teams, introducing a new construct, e-organizational justice, defined as employee perceptions of fairness in virtual work environments. The chapter also posits that fairness is essential to building and maintaining the cohesiveness and effectiveness of virtual teams, and ends with a discussion on e-organizational justice's implications for further research and management practice.

In the realm of technological development, innovation processes have been transformed into various forms, like open innovation, crowdsourcing innovation, or collaborative innovation. This chapter focuses on open innovation processes to reach out to the common stakeholders in the entrepreneurship system through SME. It has been observed that to provide innovative services or products to the outer periphery of the customer chain, SMEs play an important role. Hence, focusing innovation for SMEs would lead to a newer dimension of innovation research for better business and economic growth. It could be applied to both ways in terms of value gain to the participants. Rahman in "Open Innovation in SMEs: From Closed Peripheries to Networked Paradigm" emphasizes open innovation for SMEs at the outset, by focusing transformation of innovation leading to a networked paradigm in spite of being in closed periphery, providing some overview on innovation strategies and challenges.

EXPECTATIONS

Along this 22 chapters, the reader is faced with discussions and confirmation of the relevance and impact of this hot topic on enterprises (and in particular SME) competitiveness; its role in the support of new organizational models (networked, collaborative, virtual, knowledge-based, ubiquitous); discussion of drivers and barriers to e-Business development; and the presentation of state-of-the-art enabling technologies.

The book provides researchers, scholars, professionals with some of the most advanced research developments, solutions and discussions of e-Business challenges, impacts and opportunities for SME under the social, managerial and organizational dimensions. This way, is expected to be read by academics (teachers, researchers and students of several graduate and postgraduate courses) and by professionals of Information Technology, IT managers and responsible, Marketing experts, Enterprise managers (including top level managers), and also technology solutions developers.

Maria Manuela Cruz-Cunha
Polytechnic Insitute of Cavado and Ave, Portugal

João Varajão
University of Trás-os-Montes e Alto Douro, Portugal

Acknowledgment

Editing a book is a quite hard but compensating and enriching task, as it involves a set of different activities like contacts with authors and reviewers, discussion and exchange of ideas and experiences, process management, organization and integration of contents, and many other, with the permanent objective of creating a book that meets the public expectations. And this task cannot be accomplished without a great help and support from many sources. As editors we would like to acknowledge the help, support and believe of all who made possible this creation.

First of all, the edition of this book would not have been possible without the ongoing professional support of the team of professionals of IGI Global. We are grateful to Dr. Mehdi Khosrow-Pour and to Mrs. Jan Travers, Managing Director, for the opportunity and belief in this project. A very very special mention of gratitude is due to Mrs. Christine Bufton, Assistant Development Editor, and to Mr. Dave DeRicco and Mrs. Myla Harty, Editorial Assistants, for their professional support and friendly words of advisory, encouragement and prompt guidance. We also address our recognition and appreciation to all the staff at IGI Global, whose contributions throughout the process of production and making this book available all over the world was invaluable.

We are grateful to all the authors, for their insights and excellent contributions to this book. Also we are grateful the authors who simultaneously served as referees for chapters written by other authors, as well as to the external referees, for their insights, valuable contributions, prompt collaboration and constructive comments. Thank you all, authors and reviewers, you made this book! The communication and exchange of views within this truly global group of recognized individualities from the scientific domain and from industry was an enriching and exciting experience!

We are also grateful to all who accede to contribute to this project, some of them with high quality chapter proposals, but unfortunately, due to several constraints could not have seen their work published.

Thank you.

Maria Manuela Cruz-Cunha
Polytechnic Insitute of Cavado and Ave, Portugal

João Varajão
University of Trás-os-Montes e Alto Douro, Portugal

Section 1
Technological and Organizational Challenges

Chapter 1
Designing Digital Marketplaces for Competitive Advantage

Dinesh Rathi
University of Alberta, Canada

Lisa M. Given
University of Alberta, Canada

ABSTRACT

In today's digital world the majority of companies, including small and medium-sized enterprises (SMEs) and large firms, aim to have an online presence. However, SMEs differ from large-sized companies in terms of financial and staffing resources, which have implications for the development of e-business strategies. Thus, SMEs must not only overcome these barriers but must also take care of critical success factors (CSFs), including developing a good website and ensuring that their websites are listed among the top search engine results. This chapter discusses three elements (i.e., design principles, web usability and search engine optimization), which are vital to the effective design of a successful digital marketplace. The chapter discusses the importance of integrating these three elements in website design especially for SMEs.

INTRODUCTION

Consumers (or users of business services) have different types of informational and goods/services needs. There are generally two ways that individuals explore digital spaces to satisfy their perceived needs: 1) either users know of specific resources (e.g., websites where they can find the answers they need); or, users use search engines (such as Google, Altavista, Yahoo and MSN) to identify available resources in cyberspace. In cases when users rely on search engines to identify resources, users formulate a query based on their perceived needs and enter the query term(s) in the search box of the search engine. Generally, users' queries are presented in natural language and the search engines are designed to handle queries in this form (Ding, et al., 2004). A large number of published papers and books (e.g., Brin and Page (1998); Morgan and Hunt (2006)) have described details regarding how search engines work, including how users query search engines,

DOI: 10.4018/978-1-61692-880-3.ch001

Figure 1. Inter-relatedness of Website design, Usability and SEO

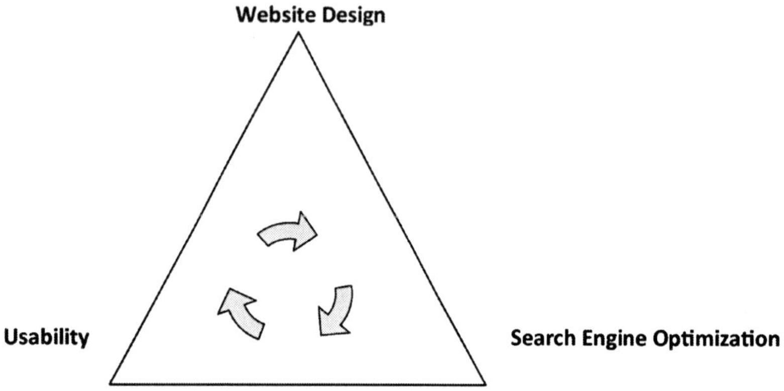

mechanisms for indexing billions of webpages, the different types of data collected from webpages (e.g., contents, title, tag and link details) and the complexities involved in webpage ranking and search engine optimization (SEO) techniques. Search engines match the indexed webpages with the user's query terms and then return results which include both paid search results (i.e., where companies have paid for ranking and placement in the search engine's results) and organic search results (i.e., where pages are retrieved based on metadata relevant to the query). The organic search results presented to the user are ordered based on relevance criteria determined by a complex page rank algorithm which uses a large number of criteria to rank the webpages. The user then explores the search results to seek answers to his/her perceived needs.

Xing and Lin (2004) reported survey results from a study conducted at the Georgia Tech University in which it was found that 85 percent of users use search engines. The findings of the study reflect the importance of search engines in identifying resources for consumers and, at the same time, highlight the value of having a website indexed by the search engine and consistently retrieved among the top ranked websites. Once users identify useful resources (i.e., websites), users will then explore these sites to satisfy perceived needs. This leads to the next issue of how well the consumer can explore the website, itself (i.e., web usability), and how easy it is for the user to complete the information-seeking activity. For example, in an e-commerce context, how easy is it for the user to search for a particular product on a company's website, place an order for that selected product and complete the sales transaction? All of these steps are dependent on the usability aspects of the website (e.g., ease of navigation; intuitive organization of information) which emanates from appropriate website design. Thus from the perspective of both search engine optimization and usability, a well-designed website is integral to ensuring consumer success in looking for web-based information and goods/services (see Figure 1).

Schmid (1999) and Meffert (2000) as cited by Schmees (2003) defined electronic market place (e-marketplace) as a place where all or some business transactions (i.e., goods, services and/or information transfer (Ordanini and Pol, 2001)) are done by using Information and Communication Technologies (ICT). According to Issa et al. (2003) electronic market places are also known as online exchanges, internet markets, digital marketplaces, virtual store, virtual marketplace, e-market, etc. Thus, in this chapter, a digital marketplace is defined as a virtual place (i.e., a website) where consumers and buyers come together to interact; it is the online space where an organization engages with its customers. A well-designed website is not only vital for successful (and satisfactory) interactions between buyers and sellers but also has implications for search engine optimization. A website is one of the critical elements in the success of any type of e-commerce models (i.e., B2B [Business-to-Business] or B2C [Business-to-Consumer] or G2C [Government-to-Citizen] or C2C [Consumer-to-Consumer]). Out of the four e-commerce models, B2B and B2C are the key models for web transactions for small to medium-sized enterprises (SMEs). It is estimated that B2B is much larger than B2C, which constitutes only 10% of all e-commerce transactions (Connor, Galvin, Evans, 2004). According to E-Stats (http://www.census.gov/retail/mrts/www/data/pdf/09Q1.pdf), e-commerce retail sales (i.e., online sales) were over $120 billion in 2007 in the United States alone. According to Aspedia.com, a study done by "*Forrester in May 2007 estimates that around $400 billion of in-store sales are influenced by the web*" (http://aspedia.net/index.php?module=pagesetter&func=viewpub&tid=4&pid=48) and, in the next five years, this value is expected to be around $1 trillion. This value represents the significance of the e-commerce activity in the business domain. The e-commerce activities are important for every type of organization (including small and medium types of organizations) in order to have wider outreach, lowering spatial and temporal barriers and increasing interactivity with customers at a relatively low cost.

However SMEs differ from large companies in many ways, which have a bearing on the adoption of e-business models for these organizations. SMEs are in a resource deficit position, as compared to large firms (Mosey, 2005), in terms of financial capabilities, technology use, availability of technologically competent employees and staff time (Tödtling and Kaufmann, 2001; Rostro and Grudzewski, 2008; Mosey, 2005; Pelham and Wilson, 1996; Hamill, 1997; Urwin, 2000; Harker and Akkeren, 2002; Hill and Wright, 2001). There are other barriers, as well, which can adversely affect the adoption of e-commerce; these include: SME managers who are not willing to take responsibility for technological changes; SME managers' and employees' misunderstandings of the importance of e-business; an overall lack of awareness of (or concerns for) the processes and different elements of e-business (e.g., technology, security, etc.); and other issues like trust and help within the organization (Simpson and Docherty, 2004). Thus, SMEs must not only overcome these barriers but must also take care of critical success factors (CSFs) in implementing an e-business strategy. Some of the identified CSFs include: having simple business processes (e.g., simple order placement, payment process, etc.); recognizing local culture and regulations; having good communication with consumers; being listed among the top search engine results (i.e., SEO); and implementing a good website design (i.e., creating a usable website) (Jennex, et al., 2004; Taylor and Murphy, 2004; Feindt, et al., 2001; Eid et al., 2002). This chapter will focus on two of these CSFs i.e., usable website design and SEO. Barnard and Wesson (2003) state that large brick-and-mortar businesses have the finances to locate themselves at a prime location and thus have competitive advantage than small businesses; however, they also argue that the Internet provides SMEs comparatively the opportunity to level the playing field. Thus, a good, usable website is a prerequisite for success (Barnard and Wesson, 2003) and is "*one of the key potential sources of competitive advantage for SMEs engaging in Internet adoptions*" (Griffin, 2004, p. 134). According to Murphy and Kielgast, (2008) who conducted research on SMEs (small hotel businesses), SMEs that have a very basic online presence and are not using their website effectively risk losing business opportunities to competitors who are able to provide a good online experience to the customers. Thus, an organization that has a well designed website (e.g. appropriate layout, usable navigation) will have a competitive advantage compared to an organization that has a website with design flaws (Elsammani, et al., 2004; Grigoroudis et al., 2008).

DIGITAL MARKETPLACE

Digital Marketplace Design

There are many reasons identified in the literature for businesses to have a digital presence. These include wider market access, competitive advantage, online distribution, connection to consumers, lower transaction costs and improved and quick consumer feedback (Iyer, 2005; O'Connor, Galvin and Evans, 2004; Wilson and Abel, 2002). Advances in internet technologies have led to a proliferation in online businesses, with low entry and exit barriers for both corporations and consumers. This has created opportunities for global expansion for even small and medium-sized companies (Wilson and Able, 2002). Thus, organizations from every domain are venturing into the digital space; however, in order to succeed in an online business model, the organization needs to design a digital marketplace which is both usable and searchable. Well designed marketplaces will be attractive, accurate and convenient for consumers (Reedy and Schullo, 2004), they will build trust with consumers (Egger, 2001), they will allow for successful online transactions (Oppenheim and Ward, 2006) and for quick response by the web manager, when needed (dellaert and kahn, 1999). Although the human-computer interaction (hci) literature highlights the importance of designing good and usable websites, in e-business this focus has been sidelined as many organizations focus on business strategies alone. There are two key aspects to building a successful digital marketplace: first, whether the website has been indexed by search engines for organic results display; and second, whether the website displayed in an organic results list is usable or not. The design concepts and usability principles discussed in this chapter are important elements of e-business strategies which are, unfortunately, not given prominence in e-business books. A well designed website can address most usability and SEO issues, which will (in turn) enhance an organization's overall business strategy.

A website is a very important element of an e-commerce business model. However, in many e-business books the importance of a well designed digital market is often discussed only briefly; this is counter-productive in planning for e-business success, as consumers experience the 4Ps (i.e., Product, Price, Place, and Promotion) of marketing at the same time and in the same place in a web-based environment (Constantinides, 2002a). A few researchers have argued strongly in favour of re-visiting the current 4Ps of marketing management in the current context of e-commerce. For example, Constantinides (2002a, 2002b) proposed a new 4S (i.e., Site, Scope, Synergy and System) web-marketing mixed model, which included *Site* design as one of the core elements for success in an e-commerce environment because the "*website is the counter, helpdesk and sales outlet where the actual commercial or non-commercial transaction takes place. Moreover for products delivered in digital form, the site fulfills even the task of the physical distributor by allowing the product delivery online*" (p. 3). With the growth and increased penetration of the internet and the subsequent expansion of business into the online domain, organizations' websites have started playing a crucial role in business. Today, websites have become an important channel to disseminate organizational promotional plans, to support and enhance the brand image of products and the organization, itself (Singh and Dalal, 1999), and to distribute products online such as software, photos, movies and music. Thus the web is becoming progressively not only a medium of communication but also an "*important component of promotional strategy*" (Geissler, et al., 2006, p. 69) and distribution strategy (Dholakia et al., 1999) for a large number of organizations.

Many online ventures have failed not because of the products that are being sold on the website but due to the poor design of the website itself. For example, one of the reasons for the failure of Boo.com was "... *its ambitious Web site, which was graphics heavy, meaning for users with a 56K modem, it could take several minutes to load"* (Wood, 2000 as presented in Shabazz, 2004, p. 123), and which created antipathy among consumers using the website. This idea is echoed by Constantinides (2002a, 2002b) who notes that there should be a particular focus on different aspects of site design, such as findability and speed, to suit users' needs. Mandel and Johnson (1999) (as presented in Fortina et al. 2002) argued that "*even minute changes in the design and configuration of the interface of a website have significant effects on consumer attitudes and intentions*" (p. 626). These effects could arise, for example, due to web changes that inadvertently result in poor usability; where an organization redesigns or changes its e-market interface it must take care to ensure that those changes do not render the website less usable from the customer's perspective. Hence it is important to consider the design of the digital marketplace so that it meets users' preferences and needs; unfortunately, this aspect of e-business is often neglected by organizations (especially small and medium-sized enterprises, where the resources to have a dedicated information technology department to support and manage effective web design may be cost prohibitive).

Poor design of a digital marketplace has an impact not only on the consumers' attitude (resulting, potentially, in a loss of business) (Oppenheim and Ward, 2006) but also on search engine optimization. The design of a good digital marketplace is not the sole determinant of the success of a business venture, but it will certainly act as one of the key "hygiene factors" outlined in Herzberg's Motivation-Hygiene Theory in Organizational Behaviour. Hygiene factors are those elements which do not give positive satisfaction, but whose absence can lead to dissatisfaction among users (Zhang, et al., 2000), resulting in a loss of business to competitors. For example, Zhang et al. (2003) identified dead links (or 'broken links') as hygiene factor because users assume that the links on the website will work but if the links are not working (i.e., are dead or broken) then users will be disappointed. Hence, organizations must strive to minimize the impact of hygiene factors on e-business. A well designed website will evoke positive emotions, perceptions and attitudes among consumers due to the "*the impact the user's attitude towards the Web site's content, advertised products, company, credibility and site usability*" can have on the business itself (Chen, 2009, p. articles/062009news.html). A recent study conducted by Geissler, et al. (2006) noted that design principles such as the home page length, graphics, links and text affect the user's perception of the website, which has a bearing on consumers' attitudes and purchase intentions. A well designed website will provide a strong visual appeal which will lead to quick judgment among users, positively affecting consumers' buying behaviors and "*influence brand perception and credibility"* (Chen, 2009, p. articles/062009news.html). According to Lindgaard et al. (2006) the visual appeal of the website can be assessed within 50 milliseconds (ms), so it is vitally important that businesses get the design right, the first time.

Large organizations with significant budgets to devote to web design often do understand (and design for) the concepts of usability and SEO optimization; however (as discussed previously), SMEs often lack the resources to implement web usability and SEO concepts. A large number of organizations fail to understand the integrated nature of the three activities (i.e., website design, SEO and usability). Often, the web designer is not aware of the impact their design will have on SEO; similarly, copywriters (i.e., website content writers) may not realize how the choice of the words, placement of the words, etc., can affect SEO and usability. This is because the designers and copywriters are, typically, not trained in usability principles and are not experts in SEO techniques. Hence, it becomes imperative that the design and development of a digital marketplace should happen in a collaborative and integrated manner, with team members with varied expertise working together, rather than in silos. A well designed marketplace can lead to competitive advantages in many ways; for example, having the website among the top ranked sites in an organic results list can lead to repeated visits by users and a greater likelihood of repeated transactions (e.g., higher sales). If users are not able to find a website in the search results, there is a greater likelihood that the user will not visit the website and the company will lose the business opportunity. However, being ranked in the top list of returned results is only half of the equation; if a user cannot navigate the website and complete the transaction, then the user will leave the website and go to a competitor's website, resulting in a gain for that competitor. In the section that follows, we will outline the central design principles that small and medium-sized enterprises should consider, followed by an overview of key usability principles and methods, including the impact of good website design on SEO techniques.

Website Design Principles

There are a large number of research papers on website design principles; different research papers have highlighted the importance of different website design elements that can make websites effective and attract users' attention in a visually appealing way, in a very short period of time. Oppenheim and Ward (2006) have identified numerous design elements, such as presentation, content, accessibility, navigation, language, transaction pages, security, privacy and authority. Liu and Arnett (2000) note the importance of information quality and playfulness in effective design. Palmer (2002) and Ranganathan and Ganapathy (2002) have noted content quality, security, privacy and navigation as central to good design. Webb and Webb (2004) have identified navigability, accuracy, security, trust and representation relevancy. Cao, et al. (2005) have outlined four main elements (and a few sub-elements) for quality evaluation of e-commerce websites, specifically, including System Quality (i.e., search, multimedia and responsiveness), Information Quality (i.e., accuracy and relevance), Service Quality (i.e., trust and empathy) and Attractiveness (i.e., playfulness). Similarly, Gehrke and Turban (1999) identified a few important website design factors and emphasized in their conclusion that "*cool stuff is on its way out. Revolving wingdings, flashing banner ads, grotesque background colors and textures, and a meaningless multitude of multimedia effects that require endless plug-ins will be extinct as electronic commerce continues to advance"* (p. 6-7). Interestingly, although the latter paper was published a decade ago, many e-business websites continue to privilege "cool stuff" while ignoring many of these key principles of quality design, which customers crave. E-business must embrace the principles of effective design and move away from flashy trends in web design, which often do not satisfy customers' web-based needs.

The findings of these research projects have been compiled and summarized in a number of guides, including U.S. Department of Health and Human Services (2006 ed.) that is available at the website www.usability.gov, '*an official U.S. Government Web site managed by the U.S. Department of Health & Human Services'*. A comprehensive and detailed description of key design principles and practical solutions are presented on this site, which was developed based on findings from different domains, including "cognitive psychology, computer science, human factors, technical communication, and usability" (http://www.usability.gov/pdfs/guidelines.html). The following are identified as high level elements for website design:

- **Design Process and Details**: e.g., identifying website goals and detailed users' requirements;
- **Accessibility**: e.g., support for assistive technologies and presenting webpages in text only format;
- **Homepage**: e.g., designing a website to allow home page access from any page of the website;
- **Page Layout**: e.g., organization and structuring pages for easy and quick comprehension;
- **Navigation**: includes the ability to find information on the website by adopting consistent policies on different elements such as tabs, heading, listing, layout, layering of menus, etc.;
- **Scrolling and Paging**: e.g., designing appropriate page length for the content presented (i.e., longer page length for reading comprehension; minimizing horizontal scrolling);
- **Text Appearance**: e.g., use of familiar font size, bold, background and text color combination, font consistent across webpages;
- **Lists**: e.g., providing headings for lists and ordering elements to support quick scans of the purpose of the list;
- **Widgets**: e.g., consistent use of buttons, check boxes, drop down lists, etc.;
- **Graphics and Multimedia**: e.g., appropriate image-text ratio, size of graphics to minimize impact on downloading speed, corporate logo placement consistency;
- **Search**: e.g., having search features on the website, full website search capability, case- insensitive and natural language search support;
- **Links**: e.g., appropriate colors and labels for links, checking for dead links and relevancy of links;
- **Content and Content Organization**: e.g., placement of critical information near the top of the page; consistency and clarity of organization of information at the website, page, paragraph and list levels;
- **Heading, Titles and Labels**: e.g., use of correct HTML tags (h1, h2, p, …), appropriate and meaningful page headings, meta tags;
- **Hardware and Software Configuration**: e.g., designing the website of (all or) commonly used web browsers by the target audience, typical user connection speed;
- **Practice Web Standards**: e.g., using website design standards such xHTML standards, validations, etc.
- **Meet Accessibility Guidelines**: e.g., use alt-tags for images, avoid the use of frames, etc.

An appropriate adoption and deployment of each of these design elements will enhance the e-commerce website's usability (i.e., ease of use) and attractiveness. Some of the above-listed design elements, such as content, heading, title, content organization and page layout, will also have an impact on both usability and SEO. In the next section, we discuss usability principles and evaluation methods, followed by a section on SEO.

In addition, websites should explicitly address how customers' privacy will be maintained (e.g., how users' confidential financial information will be managed). Similarly, companies must maintain secure transactions with consumers by implementing technologies such as SET (Secure Electronic Transaction), SSL (Secure Sockets Layer) and digital ID (Gehrke and Turban, 1999) and displaying the logos and icons that represent these technologies. When consumers see a padlock icon or an "s" added to the http code, they gain an enhanced sense of security and see that it is safe to complete a transaction on that company's website.

Usability

According to Gullikson et al. (1999) the visual appearance, utility aspect (i.e., "*the ability of the web site to do functionally what it is supposed to do*" (p. 294)) and usability are the three important aspects of a well-designed website. A website should enhance visual appeal and utility while reducing usability problems, substantially. Often, website designers primarily focus on the "*look and feel*" (Gullikson et al., 1999) of a site, so that the usability aspects are ignored. ***Usability*** is about the ease with which users' interact with a system or website (Nielsen and Mack, 1994; Nielsen, 2000) as they search for information or place product orders on the web (Benbunan-Fich, 2001; Nah and Davis, 2002). There are different usability definitions proposed in the literature; for example, Matera et al., 2006 define usability as "*the extent to which a product can be used by specified users to achieve goals with effectiveness, efficiency and satisfaction in a specified context of use*" (p. 4). The most cited usability definition is from Jacob Nielsen's work; Nielsen (2003) defined usability as "*a quality attribute that assesses how easy user interfaces are to use*" and "*refers to methods for improving ease-of-use during the design process*" (p. http://www.useit.com/alertbox/20030825.html). Nielsen (2003) identified five elements of usability which include ***learnability*** (i.e., ease of use even in the first instance of interaction), ***efficiency*** (i.e., the ability to undertake an activity quickly after learning the design), ***memorability*** (i.e., the ability to undertake an activity efficiently after prolonged absence from the site), ***errors*** (i.e., the types of errors, their severity and the ability to recover from them), and ***satisfaction*** (i.e., enjoyment of the site in use).

Nielsen (2003) has also presented a few misconceptions about usability. First, usability is often considered as an expensive exercise and many corporations are not inclined to undertake it. However, the objective of the usability study dictates the cost of the exercise. In some cases, usability testing can cost many thousands of dollars; however, this is typically only if the usability project involves multiple websites, which are examined over a long period of time. However, as small and medium-sized organizations typically have small-scale websites, often with a smaller target audience than a large organization, these studies can be undertaken at a very low (or even no) cost. A low cost usability exercise could capture a large number of problems in a website, resulting in resolutions of major issues that can lead to increased sales with only a few changes to the organization's website. The rule of thumb proposed by Jacob Nielsen is that "*on average, best practices call for spending 10% of a design budget on usability*" (p. Alertbox, September 8, 2003). A second myth is that usability testing will delay a website launch; however, employing a user-centered design process throughout can minimize the impact of time needed to incorporate changes to a site, resulting in an on-time launch that will meet users' website needs. According to Maguire (2001) the design process and usability testing were originally considered independent events, but the new approach to design (as reflected, for example, in the ISO 13407 human-centred design framework) integrates these steps, so that usability is now part of the website development process. A third myth is that usability can kill creativity. However, Nielsen has been firm in noting that "*following design conventions doesn't destroy creativity*" (Nielsen, 2003, p. Alertbox, September 8, 2003); rather, finding creative solutions that support customers' intentions can enhance design creativity, while serving customers' needs. A fourth myth is that users do not need to use the website to do usability testing; i.e., that the website can be evaluated by using market research techniques such as customer satisfaction survey. According to Nielsen (2003), in actual practice, market research might not always be able to provide insight into usability issues of the website because the websites that "*look incredibly cool and compelling, yet they almost never work in actual use*" (p. Alertbox, September 8, 2003).

In the HCI literature, three different major usability methods and techniques (i.e., inquiry, testing and inspection), have been proposed (Paas and Firssova; 2004; Folmer and Bosch; 2004; Nielsen, 1994). In a ***Usability Inquiry*** method, data are collected by talking to users about their experiences with websites when they try to engage in real-life tasks. This could be done by using instruments such as questionnaires, focus groups, panel discussions and interviews (Paas and Firssova; 2004; Folmer and Bosch; 2004). In ***Usability Testing*** methods, experts evaluate how the website would support the user to complete tasks; data are collected by observing users as they engage in representative tasks on prototype models. Data collection methods include think aloud protocols, co-discovery learning, trial runs, coaching methods, etc (Nielsen, 1993; Paas and Firssova; 2004; Folmer and Bosch; 2004). In ***Usability Inspection,*** the experts play the role of users' (in addition to relying on their expert knowledge) as they review websites using various formal and informal methods; these include heuristic evaluation cognitive walkthrough, pluralistic walkthrough, feature inspection, and standard inspection (Nielsen, 1994; Paas and Firssova; 2004; Folmer and Bosch; 2004; Maguire, 2001). The most commonly used usability inspection method is heuristic evaluation and Nielsen (1994) has identified ten heuristic principles: visibility of system status; the match between the system and the real world; user control and freedom; consistency and standards; error prevention; recognition rather than recall; flexibility and efficiency of use; aesthetic and minimalist design; helping users recognize, diagnose, and recover from errors; and help and documentation (www.useit.com/papers/heuristic/heuristic_list.html). Although inspection methods can give a designer (and an organization) a clear sense of areas for development (e.g., to audit a website for its adherence to accessibility design principles), these approaches should be used in conjunction with – not, in isolation from – methods that engage real users in real web searching tasks. As experts cannot anticipate a user's potential use of a given website, it is vital to include members of the site's target audience in the web design and evaluation process, prior to launch.

A large number of studies have discussed and propagated the importance of usability, but many organizations continue to fail to understand its importance; for this reason, websites continue to be designed with usability errors (Nah and Davis, 2002, p. 98) and customers continue to be lost. The commonly identified problems on websites are poor navigability, low response times and confusing content (Nielsen, 1999; Nah and Davis, 2002). Tedeschi (1999) [as reported by Benbunan-Fich, 2001] argued that *"better usability will result in more efficient interaction between the user and the site and will increase the probability that the user will return and/or make a purchase"* (p. 151). If website usability is not addressed in the design of a site, this will lead to loss of customers and will risk the economic viability of the e-business enterprise (Nah and Davis, 2002). Nielsen (1998) cited a research report by Forrester (1998) that reflects the loss of potential business opportunities due to poor usability caused by poor website design. The author noted that there is expected to be a

> *loss of approximately 50% of the potential sales from the site as people can't find stuff" in addition to "losing repeat visits from 40% of the users who do not return to a site when their first visit resulted in a negative experience (Nielsen, 1998, p. Alertbox for October 18, 1998).*

This potential loss was confirmed by Konradt et. al (2003). The authors in their work presented an interesting finding from a study conducted by Manhartsberger and Musil (2001) in which the 100 consumers who participated were given a task to buy products from the websites; the e-business companies involved lost 63% (USD 5,645 out of USD 9,000) of the potential revenue as consumers were not able to locate the product of their choice. These studies are just a few examples that reflect the idea that poorly designed websites with poor usability can lead to loss of potential business opportunities. As Nielsen (2003) notes, "*the first law of e-commerce is that if users cannot find the product, they cannot buy it either*" (p. alertbox/20030825.html).

Search Engine Optimization (SEO)

The growth of the internet is demonstrated in the increasing number of registered domains; there were 174 million, 150 million and 120 million domains registered at the end of the third quarter of 2008, at the end of 2007 and 2006 respectively (http://www.verisign.com/domain-name-services/domain-information-center/domain-name-resources/domain-name-report-dec08.pdf). Verisign.com report has also reported that annual domain renewal is in the range of 74% to 77% for years 2006 and 2007. Thus the high renewal rate and continuous registration of new domains is leading to a crowding of the internet search space as every domain vies for a slot in the search engine results space. E-commerce websites must compete not only with the competitors from their own business domains but also with other websites (e.g., informational websites; entertainment sites) for users' attention. Research in HCI and information science demonstrates that users will reduce the cognitive load involved in searching for information by (for example) scanning only through the first page of results retrieved by search engines (Sen, 2005). Hence it becomes imperative for businesses to design a marketplace which not only adheres to website design principles and is usable, but that is also indexed by search engines so that the website will be listed among the top 20 organic search results (i.e., the first page) for a user query.

There are two major ways in which a website can be included in the search engine results. First, a business can design a search engine-friendly website, so that it will be indexed by the search engine (i.e., organic results); or, second, a business can pay the search engine company to ensure that their website is displayed in the search engine results list (i.e., paid results) (Yu and Lin. 2007). Paid results are of two types, i.e., paid inclusion and paid placement. Paid inclusion means paying the search engine to "*guarantee a web site's pages are stored in the search index*" (Moran and Hunt, 2006, p. 513); however, in this approach, there is no guarantee for a high search result ranking for the website. Paid placement, on the other hand, involves paying the search engine to show the pages of the website in the search results in response to the particular set of query (or search) terms "*regardless of how closely the page matches*" the query (or search) terms (Moran and Hunt, 2006, p. 5). For example, with paid placement the website links display as sponsored links by Google on the top of the search results or on the right side of the search result pages. The main revenue model for search engine for paid placement is CPC (cost per click) (Xing and Lin, 2004). The organic results are the "*best pages found for the words the searcher entered*" (Moran and Hunt, 2006, p. 5) by the search engine, which is commonly linked to SEO.

SEO is a technique to optimize the website so that it has a better ranking in the organic search (Moran and Hunt, 2006; Xing and Lin, 2004; Joshi and Motwani, 2006; Sen, 2005). There is always competition between paid placement and SEO but there are contradictory assessments among researchers. Sen (2005) argued that a large number of businesses do not want to invest in SEO because the organizations believe that adopting SEO strategies is more expensive than investing in paid placement; however, SEO might become more attractive to companies than paid placement if SEO costs are controlled. Xing and Lin (2004) argued that SEO is more popular than paid placement because unbiased organic results appeal more to the consumers. Also the CPC have problem of fraudulent clicks which is estimated to be in the range of 20-35% (i.e., 20-35% clicks are fraudulent) when using generic keywords (e.g., automobile, cell phones) (Quinton and Khan,

2009). Malaga (2007) compared the SEO cost vis-à-vis CPC rate for an iPod-related website; the author found that their CPC for their SEO project was $0.16 (as the website had 7500 unique visitors per month and their SEO cost was 1200, hence 1200/7500=$0.16) while the CPC rate for iPod related keywords was $0.40 and $0.30 for Google and Yahoo respectively. SEO is important because websites need to be high in the ranking in the organic search results, especially as most consumers browse top-listed websites of the organic search results (Sen, 2005) which affects traffic onto the website (Yu and Lin, 2007). The results from the survey conducted by Georgia Tech University and by the Search Engine Marketing Professional Organization (SEMPO) as reported in Xing and Lin (2004) indicate that 70% of users prefer organic results; paid listings only received about 24.6% of clicks. This was confirmed by Moran and Hunt (2006) who noted that organic search results are important because "*searchers click organic results 60 percent of the time*" (p. 5). The number of people using search engines to search and browse for information and products is constantly increasing. Hence it is important for companies involved in e-business (either in online commerce or information dissemination businesses) to include SEO strategies in the design phase for their websites because 62% of users generally examine the first page search results, only, and a very few users (less than 10%) browse the search results beyond third page of the search results (Malaga, 2008; Malaga, 2007; Zhang and Dimitroff, 2005; Yu and Lin, 2007).

There are a large number of organizations that are involved in search engine marketing, an important marketing activity in e-business. These organizations specialize in the area of SEO. In their services for SEO, these search engine marketing organizations such as Wordtracker.com, Yahoo (Small Business), Google, and Marketleap.com offer (one or more) services that include keyword analyses, word trackers (i.e., to highlight the best keywords for your website), keyword selection (i.e., choosing the right keywords for marketing), website ranking evaluation, link popularity analysis and Meta tag generators. These elements all have an impact on SEO. The SEO can be done by making changes in the website design and code (Sen, 2005; Zhang and Dimitroff, 2005; Moran and Hunt, 2006; Abel, 2002). Hence, the design of the digital marketplace requires an approach that interweaves website design principles and theories and SEO techniques in the early development stage. By incorporating SEO techniques during the design phase, the organization can save substantial amounts of money by not needing to pay SEO consultants at a later stage, to increase website traffic. According to Malaga (2007), many SEO consultants charge more than $5000 for a SEO research project.

The design elements that can affect SEO include: headings, titles, website content and content organization, tags (such as meta tags and image tags), links, as well as web standards and the design process itself (Joshi and Motwani, 2006; Moran and Hunt, 2006; Wilson and Abel, 2002; Zhang and Dimitroff, 2005; Yu and Lin, 2007; Weideman and Schwenke, 2006; Malaga, 2007). In the following paragraphs, some of the design elements that impact SEO will be discussed.

Impact of Different Design Elements on SEO

Organizations with a digital presence need to identify the website's goals (Design Process and Details) and align these with the organization's goals. This is important because this will inform the choice of a target audience for the site and an understanding of what search engine would best meet the potential customers' requirements, as different search engines have different ranking criteria and indexing strategies (Zhang and Dimitroff, 2005). By identify the goals and objectives, the organization can target particular search engines. Even though there are over 30,000 search engines in existence (Zhang and Dimitroff

2005), the three most prominent search engines (i.e., Google, Yahoo and MSN) account for over 80% of the search engine market (Malaga, 2007).

There is a crowding of cyberspace with an increasing number of websites in the digital space. Hence, search engines are working towards developing more and more innovative algorithms to better the search results. A large number of design elements can affect a site's ranking in major search engines. The design elements such as heading, title, website content and content organization have an impact on SEO as they affect keyword selection, keyword density, keyword proximity and keyword prominence. *Keyword density* (also known as keyword weight) is the ratio of the total number of times a word occurs on a page to the total count of all words in a page (Moran and Hunt, 2006; Malaga, 2007). Previously, a search engine gave importance to a term count (i.e., a page that had a higher number of instances of the query term was considered 'good'); more recently, search engines changed to examine keyword density, so that the target density should be around 7% (Moran and Hunt, 2006, p. 39). *Keyword proximity* is the distance between the query terms on a page (i.e. if the user uses more than one query term, how far are these query terms from one another on the webpage). Thus, the closer the query terms the better it is from a retrieval standpoint re: the relevance of the page to the query itself. For example, if a user employs the query terms 'cell phones', then having both the terms next to each other is better than the term 'cell' separated from the term 'phone' by a few words or in a separate paragraph (Moran and Hunt, 2006). *Keyword prominence* refers to the location of the keywords on the page (i.e. whether they are in the header, title, or top of the page) (Moran and Hunt, 2006); here, the higher the prominence of the keyword, the more likely that the page will match the relevance content of the user's query.

The quality, relevance, completeness and currency (Konradt et al., 2003) of the content are not only important factors in consumers' buying decision processes, but also have an impact on the SEO. Cole et al. (2003), Agarwal and Venkatesh (2002), and Kim and Lee (2002) [as referenced in Konradt et al. (2003)] have highlighted the importance of quality of content on websites. The quality of the content will influence the selection of keywords along with density, proximity and prominence. Wilson and Abel (2002) noted that it is important to optimize the content of the web with the appropriate choice of keywords and to ensure that those keywords are positioned in an important area of the page (i.e., top of the page); this notion was also supported by Sen (2005) who suggested that companies can improve their website page ranking by modifying the website title tag, heading tags, etc. Hence, content writers and website designers are required to work in close collaboration to ensure SEO. Content writers need to identify the important keywords which they feel reflect their business and are frequently used by consumers to identify specific business websites. For example, if a the company is in the business of online selling of cameras, content writers need to identify which keywords users will use to find websites that sell cameras. One of the keywords that users might commonly use is 'digital camera'. The company's website should have keywords 'digital' and 'camera' in close proximity to each other and on the top of the webpage. The top keywords that users use to find webpages can be identified by using online resources such as *wordtracker* (available at http://www.wordtracker.com/).

The importance of keyword density and prominence in title and main text is confirmed by the results that Zhang and Dimitroff (2005) found in their experimental study. Zhang and Dimitroff (2005) note that the website achieved a better search ranking by having the same keywords used multiple times (i.e., increasing keyword density) and also by having the same keywords both in the title and in the initial part of the full-text, which is, generally, on the top of the webpage (i.e., increasing keyword prominence) (Malaga, 2007; Zhang and Dimitroff, 2005; Curran, 2004). Yu and Lin (2007) have identified over 41 different types of tools that can be used in SEO. For example, the keyword density tool provided by SEO Chat (available at http://www.seochat.com/seo-tools/) can help both content writers and website designers, as they can make informed decisions on the choice of keywords to be included in the webpage. However, companies should also be ethical in their practices in use of SEO techniques. The use of unethical practices (e.g., artificially increasing the keyword density by using the same term multiple times in the content or changing the font color of the keyword to white so that the high visibility of the keyword does not irritate the user or alter the content flow, while increasing the term count) could lead to penalization such as "*worse placement in the SERPs* (Search Engine Result Pages) *or an outright ban from the search engine*" (Malaga 2008, p. 147; Malaga, 2007). For example, BMW used unethical practice in order to have a high page ranking for its German website in Google organic search results. The company used a technique called 'doorway page' (Malaga 2008) which means that the company had two separate sets of webpages, where one set of webpages were for indexing purposes while the other set of pages were for users to view. Google thus banned the website because the webpages that were indexed by Google were not shown to the users but were redirected to different sets of webpages.

Another element that needs to be addressed in the design process, which affects SEO, is the appropriate and effective use of meta tags and image tags. Meta-tags are the tags that provide additional data (e.g., such as keywords, description) from a page to search engines (Joshi and Motwani, 2006; Sen, 2005; Malaga, 2007; Wilson and Abel, 2002). The meta tags are part of the head element of an HTML and xHTML document, and *"are typically used to specify page description, keywords, author of the document, last modified and other metadata*" (http://w3schools.com/tags/tag_meta.asp) of HTML/xHTML page (Malet, et al., 1999). For example: <meta name="description" content= "E-business Book Chapter" /> and <meta name="keywords" content= "SEO, Usability, Digital Market, Website Design" />. "*Meta tags are important pieces of code that many search engines use to analyze, categorize and rank a website*" (http://www.mailworkz.com/tools.htm). According to Joshi and Motwani (2006), a large number of websites include important keywords in meta tags, which are crawled by search engine spiders (or crawlers). Spiders are computer programs that continuously traverse the Web and download the pages, collect webpage location information and store them on the server for indexing purpose (Heydon and Najork, 1999; http://www.kbkmarketing.com/other-seo-definitions.php). Some search engines use meta tags in page ranking while others collect the meta tag data but do not use them in page ranking (Wilson and Abel, 2002). For example, Google does not make use of meta tags in ranking of search results (http://searchenginewatch.com/2167931). In addition, other tags such as image tags (e.g., ALT) i.e., text associate with images or text in comment are indexed by some of the search engines such as Google and AltaVista (http://searchenginewatch.com). Hence designers need to pay attention in naming or commenting on the images.

Search engines such as Google use link analysis to enhance the organic search results of websites (Moran and Hunt, 2006; Sen, 2005; Weideman and Mgidana, 2004; Yu and Lin, 2007; Zhang and Dimitroff, 2005; Wilson and Able, 2002). Link analysis used by a search engine has its grounding in the Hub and Authority model, proposed by Jon Kleinberg (Kleinberg, 1999a; 1999b), which aims to harness the "*diversity roles among different types of pages*" (Kleinberg, 1999b, p. 2). Kleinberg proposed that the hubs are those pages which act as guides and resource to users by recommending them to a website which is an authority on the content; and, authorities are those pages which are the primary sources of the information. For example, www.useit.com is the authority (website) on usability and any other website providing the link to this website will be the hub for the topic. The presence of the links as well as the anchor text (i.e., label name) given to the link on the website has been identified as one of the techniques for SEO (Moran and Hunt, 2006). For example, a website (say, 'www.helloworld.com') is in the business of usability consultancy. This website has many usability related links including 'http://www.useit.com', which has the anchor text label 'Heuristic Evaluation by Jacob Nielsen'. The website (www.helloworld.com) is a 'hub' for usability and 'www.useit.com' is the 'authority' on usability (as many other websites also point to www.useit.com for usability-related concepts). Now, when a user uses the query terms 'Heuristic' and 'Nielsen', the search engines used for link analysis to rank 'www.helloworld.com' would evaluate both the link itself (www.useit.com) and the anchor text label ('Heuristic Evaluation by Jacob Nielsen'). Hence. SMEs' in designing their webpages, should consider the link analysis element and should strive to become hubs for information in their specialty area by providing links to other websites (i.e., authorities).

Finally, following the website design standards such as those proposed by W3C (World Wide Web Consortium) (www.w3.org) is a good design practice, and certainly would support in optimizing the website for search engine indexing as

the search engine spider/crawlers can easily understand the content of your page and follow all the links throughout your site. Web standards were developed with specific accessibility issues in mind and following these standards not only aids those visiting your site with visual impairment, it also helps search engine spiders understand the graphical content of your site as well. Another key component to building pages with Web standards is separating content from page structure, formatting and functionality. In doing this it helps load times, assists the search engine spiders in focusing on content and decreases the ratio of code to content (Hendrikse, 2008, p. 7-8).

CONCLUSION AND FUTURE RESEARCH DIRECTIONS

In today's digital world, firms should have an online presence and should explore the ways to harness the internet's potential to advance their business goals. The firms (whether large or small and medium-sized) should take care of critical success factors (including those discussed in this chapter) required to benefit from e-commerce. One of the critical success factors is the online presence of a business via a website. However, the mere online presence of a firm is not adequate; consumers should also be able to search the website easily and place the order quickly. Thus, the firm's website should be designed so that it is not only usable but also optimized to support search engine marketing. This requires an investment of time and human resources; although large firms generally have adequate resources (e.g., skilled manpower, technological base, and financial strength) to support their website design process, usability testing and SEO for search engine marketing, small-scale firms may have limited resources to devote to these activities. These organizations should strive to optimize their resources by carefully planning their online strategies; this includes planning well ahead before designing of the website and involving consumers throughout the design process, to manage time and finances devoted to usability, effectively. SMEs should strive to achieve multiple goals, such as usable website and optimized for search engine, in their website design phase by carefully adopting the design principles and incorporating SEO technique. A large number of usability elements and SEO techniques can be done at low cost and do not require expensive consultants to undertake these activities. All of these factors are crucial – and doable – for small and medium-sized enterprises that plan to embark on (or enhance) e-business activities. In future, we would like to examine the current practices of SMEs in terms of usability and SEO practices; i.e., how usability is being currently practiced in SMEs, what SEO techniques SMEs are using to enhance their ranking on the web, what resources (i.e., external consultants or internal expertise) SMEs are using in SEO techniques implementation. Finally, there is a need to develop a set of best practices for SMEs for designing, usable and SEO-compliant websites.

REFERENCES

Barnard, L., & Wesson, J. L. (2003). Usability issues for E-commerce in South Africa: an Empirical Investigation.*In Proceedings of SAICSIT 2003*, 258 – 267.

Benbunan-Fich, R. (2001). Using Protocol Analysis to Evaluate the Usability of a Commercial Web Site. *Information & Management*, *39*, 151–163. doi:10.1016/S0378-7206(01)00085-4

Brin, S., & Page, L. (1998). The Aanatomy of a Large-scale Hypertextual Web Search Engine, Proceedings of the Seventh International World Wide Web Conference, 30(1-7), p. 107-117.

Cao, M., Zhang, Q., & Seydel, J. (2005). B2C E-Commerce Web Site Quality: An Empirical Examination. *Industrial Management & Data Systems*, *105*(5), 645–661. doi:10.1108/02635570510600000

Chen, J. (2009). *The Impact of Aesthetics on Attitudes Towards Websites*. Retrieved from July 24, 2009 from http://usability.gov/articles/062009news.html.

Constantinides, E. (2002a). The 4S Web-Marketing Mix Model. *Electronic Commerce Research and Applications*, *1*, 57–76. doi:10.1016/S1567-4223(02)00006-6

Constantinides, E. (2002b) From Physical Marketing to Web Marketing: The Web-Marketing Mix.*Proceedings of the 35th Hawaii International Conference on System Science (HICSS)*, 7, 205-216.

Curran, K. (2004). Tips for Achieving High Positioning in the Results Pages of the Major Search Engine. *Information Technology Journal*, *3*(2), 202–205. doi:10.3923/itj.2004.202.205

Dellaert, B. G. C., & Kahn, B. E. (1999). How Tolerable is Delay? Consumer's Evaluation of Internet Web Sites after Waiting. *Journal of Interactive Marketing*, *13*, 41–54. doi:10.1002/(SICI)1520-6653(199924)13:1<41::AID-DIR4>3.0.CO;2-S

Dholakia, N., Dholakia, R. R., Laub, M., & Hwang, Y.-S. (1999). Electronic Commerce and the Transformation of Marketing, In Wolfgang, F., (Ed.), *Internet Marketing*, (pp. 55-80) Germany, Schaefer-Poeschel: Verlag.

Ding, L., Finin, T., Joshi, A., Pan, R., Cost, R. S., Pen, Y., et al. (2004). Swoogle: A Search and Metadata Engine for the Semantic Web. *Proceedings of the thirteenth ACM international conference on Information and knowledge management.* 652 - 659.

Egger, F. N. (2001). Affective Design of E-Commerce User Interfaces: How to Maximise Perceived Trustworthiness. *Proceedings of the International Conference on Affective Human Factors Design*, 317-324.

Eid, R., Trueman, M., & Ahmed, A. M. A. (2002). Cross-Industry Review of B2B Critical Success Factors. *Internet Research: Electronic Networking Applications and Policy*, *12*(2), 110–123. doi:10.1108/10662240210422495

Elsammani, Z. A., Hackney, R., & Scown, P. (2004). SMEs Adoption and Implementation Process of Websites in the Presence of Change Agents. In Al-Qirim, N. A. Y. (Ed.), *Electronic Commerce in Small to Medium-Sized Enterprises: Frameworks, Issues and Implications* (pp. 146–163). Hershey, PA: Idea Group Publishing.

Feindt, S., Jeffcoate, J., & Chappell, C. (2001). Identifying Success Factors for Rapid Growth in SME E-Commerce. *Small Business Economics*, *19*, 51–62. doi:10.1023/A:1016165825476

Folmer, E., & Bosch, J. (2004). Architecting for Usability: A Survey. *Journal of Systems and Software*, *70*(1-2), 61–78. doi:10.1016/S0164-1212(02)00159-0

Fortina, D. R., Dholakia, R. R., & Dholakia, N. (2002). Emerging Issues in Electronic Marketing: Thinking Outside the Square. *Journal of Business Research*, *55*, 623–627. doi:10.1016/S0148-2963(00)00202-2

Gehrke, D., & Turban, E. (1999). Determinants of Successful Website Design: Relative Importance and Recommendations for Effectiveness. *Proceedings of the 32nd Hawaii International Conference on System Sciences (HICSSS-32)*, 1-8.

Geissler, G. L., Zinkhan, G. N., & Watson, R. T. (2006). The Influence of Home Page Complexity on Consumer Attention, Attittudes and Purchase Intent. *Journal of Advertising*, *35*(2), 69–80.

Griffin, J. (2004). Mapping the Diffusion of the Internet Technology Cluster: An Examination of Irish SMEs. In Al-Qirim, N. A. Y. (Ed.), *Electronic Commerce in Small to Medium-Sized Enterprises: Frameworks, Issues and Implications* (pp. 128–145). Hershey, PA: Idea Group Publishing.

Grigoroudis, E., Litos, C., Moustakis, V. A., Politis, Y., & Tsironis, L. (2008). The Assessment of User-Perceived Web Quality: Application of a Satisfaction Benchmarking Approach. *European Journal of Operational Research*, *187*, 1346–1357. doi:10.1016/j.ejor.2006.09.017

Gullikson, S., Blades, R., Bragdon, M., McKibbon, S., Sparling, M., & Toms, E. G. (1999). The Impact of Information Architecture on Academic Web Site Usability. *The Electronic Library*, *17*(5), 293–303. doi:10.1108/02640479910330714

Hamill, J. (1997). The Internet and International Marketing. *International Marketing Review*, *14*(5), 300–323. doi:10.1108/02651339710184280

Harker, D., & Akkeren, J. V. (2002). Exploring the Needs of SMEs for Mobile Data Technologies: the Role of Qualitative Research Techniques. *Qualitative Market Research: An International Journal*, *5*(3), 199–209. doi:10.1108/13522750210432002

Hendrikse, M. (2008) *Search Engine Marketing 101: A Guide for Small Businesses and Not-For-Profits to Engage in Search Engine Marketing*. Retrieved from on July 25, 2009 from http://markhendrikse.com/storage/post-images/june-2009/SearchEngineMarketing101_MarkHendrikse.pdf.

Heydon, A., & Najork, M. (1999). Mercator: A Scalable, Extensible Web Crawler. *World Wide Web (Bussum)*, *2*, 219–229. doi:10.1023/A:1019213109274

Hill, J., & Wright, L. T. (2001). A Qualitative Research Agenda for Small to Medium-Sized Enterprises. *Marketing Intelligence & Planning*, *19*(6), 432–443. doi:10.1108/EUM0000000006111

Issa, R. R. A., Flood, I., & Caglasin, G. (2003). A Survey of e-Business Implementation in the US Construction Industry. In Bjork, B.(ed.), *Journal of Information Technology in Construction*, 8, 15-28.

Iyer, G. R. (2005). Global Internet Marketing Strategy: Framework and Managerial Insights. In Clarke, I. III, & Flaherty, T. (Eds.), *Advances in Electronic Marketing* (pp. 84–102). Hershey, PA: Idea Group Publishing.

Jennex, M. E., Amoroso, D., & Adelajun, O. (2004). E-Commerce Infrastructure Success Factors for Small Companies in Developing Economies. *Electronic Commerce Research*, *4*, 263–286. doi:10.1023/B:ELEC.0000027983.36409.d4

Joshi, A., & Motwani, R. (2006). Keyword Generation for Search Engine Advertising. *Sixth IEEE International Conference on Data Mining Workshops,* ICDM Workshops, 490-496.

Kleinberg, J. M. (1999a). Authoritative Sources in a Hyperlinked Environment. *Journal of the ACM*, *46*(5), 604–632. doi:10.1145/324133.324140

Kleinberg, J. M. (1999b). Hubs, Authorities, and Communities [CSUR]. *ACM Computing Surveys*, *31*(4es), 1–3. doi:10.1145/345966.345982

Konradt, U., Wandke, H., Balazs, B., & Christophersen, T. (2003). Usability in Online Shops: Scale Construction, Validation and the Influence on the Buyers' Intention and Decision. *Behaviour & Information Technology*, *22*(3), 165–174. doi:10.1080/0144929031000107072

Lindgaard, G., Fernandes, G., Dudek, C., & Brown, J. (2006). Attention Web Designers: You have 50 Milliseconds to Make a Good First Impression. *Behaviour & Information Technology*, *25*(2), 115–126. doi:10.1080/01449290500330448

Liu, C., & Arnett, K. P. (2000). Exploring the Factors Associated with Website Sucess in the Content of Electronic Commerce. *Information & Management*, *38*(10), 269–282.

Maguire, M. (2001). Methods to Support Human-Centered Design. *International Journal of Human-Computer Studies*, *55*, 587–634. doi:10.1006/ijhc.2001.0503

Malaga, R. A. (2007) The Value of Search Engine Optimization: An Action Research Project at a New E-Commerce Site. In Khosrow-Pour, M. (Ed.), *Journal of Electronic Commerce in Organizations*, 5(3), 68-82.

Malaga, R. A. (2008). Worst Practices in Search Engine Optimization. *Communications of the ACM*, *51*(12), 147–150. doi:10.1145/1409360.1409388

Malet, G., Munoz, F., Appleyard, R., & Hersh, W. (1999). A Model for Enhancing Internet Medical Document Retrieval with "Medical Core Metadata. *Journal of the American Medical Informatics Association*, *6*(2), 163–172.

Matera, M., Rizzo, F., & Carughi, G. T. (2006). Web Usability: Principles and Evaluation Methods. In Mendes, E., & Mosley, N. (Eds.), *Web Engineering* (pp. 143–180). Berlin, Heidelberg: Springer. doi:10.1007/3-540-28218-1_5

Moran, M., & Hunt, B. (2006). *Search Engine Marketing: Driving Search Traffic to Your Company's Web Site*. Upper Saddle River, NJ: IBM Press, Pearson PLC.

Mosey, S. (2005). Understanding New-to-Market Product Development in SMEs. *International Journal of Operations & Production Management*, *25*(2), 114–130. doi:10.1108/01443570510576994

Murphy, H. C., & Kielgast, C. D. (2008). Do Small and Medium-sized Hotels Exploit Search Engine Marketing? *International Journal of Contemporary Hospitality Management*, *20*(1), 90–97. doi:10.1108/09596110810848604

Nah, F. F.-H., & Davis, S. (2002). HCI Research Issues in E-commerce. *Journal of Electronic Commerce Research*, *3*, 98–113.

Nielsen, J. (1993). *Usability Engineering*. San Diego, CA: Academic Press.

Nielsen, J. (1994). Heuristic Evaluation. In Nielsen, J., & Mack, R. L. (Eds.), *Usability Inspection Methods*. New York: John Wiley & Sons.

Nielsen, J. (1994) *Usability Inspection Methods, Conference on Human Factors in Computing Systems*413-414.

Nielsen, J. (1998) *Failure of Corporate Websites*, Retrieved from July 21, 2009 from http://www.useit.com/alertbox/981018.html.

Nielsen, J. (1999) *Who Commits the Top Ten Mistakes of Web Design*?Retrieved from www.useit.com/alertbox/990307.html.

Nielsen, J. (2000). *Designing Web Usability*. Indianapolis, USA: New Riders Publishing.

Nielsen, J. (2003) *Misconceptions About Usability*. Retrieved from July 20, 2009 from http://www.useit.com/alertbox/20030908.html.

Nielsen, J. (2003). *Usability 101: Introduction to Usability*. Retrieved from July 24, 2009 from http://www.useit.com/alertbox/20030825.html.

Nielsen, J., & Mack, R. L. (1994). *Usability Inspection Methods*. New York: Wiley.

O'Connor, J., Galvin, E., & Evans, M. (2004). *Electronic Marketing: Theory and Practice for the Twenty-First Century*. London: Prentice Hall.

Oppenheim, C., & Ward, L. (2006). Evaluation of Web Sites for B2C E-commerce. *Aslib Proceedings: New Information Perspectives*, *58*(3), 237–260.

Ordanini, A., & Pol, A. (2001). Infomediation and Competitive Advantage in B2b Digital Marketplaces. *European Management Journal*, *19*(3), 276–285. doi:10.1016/S0263-2373(01)00024-X

Paas, F., & Firssova, O. (2004). Usability Evaluation of Integrated e-Learning. In Jochems, W., van Merrienboer, J., & Koper, E. J. R. (Eds.), *Integrated eLearning: Implications for Pedagogy, Technology and Organization* (pp. 112–125). London: RoutledgeFalmer.

Palmer, J. W. (2002). Web Site Usability, Design and Performance Metrics. *Information Systems Research*, *13*(2), 151–167. doi:10.1287/isre.13.2.151.88

Pelham, A. M., & Wilson, D. T. (1996). A Longitudinal Study of the Impact of Market Structure, Firm Structure, Strategy, and Market Orientation Culture on Dimensions of Small-Firm Performance. *Journal of the Academy of Marketing Science*, *24*(1), 27–43. doi:10.1007/BF02893935

Quinton, S., & Khan, M. A. (2009). Generating web site traffic: a new model for SMEs. *Direct Marketing: An International Journal*, *3*(2), 109–123. doi:10.1108/17505930910964777

Ranganathan, C., & Ganapathy, S. (2002). Key Dimensions of Business-to-Consumer Web Sites. *Information & Management*, *39*(6), 457–465. doi:10.1016/S0378-7206(01)00112-4

Reedy, J., & Schullo, S. (2004). *Electronic Marketing: Integrating Electronic Resources into the Marketing Process*. Florence, KY: Thompson Learning.

Rostro, F. R. & Grudzewski, W. M. (2008). Marketing Strategic Planning as a Source of Competitive Advantage for Mexican SMEs.*Institute of Organization and Management in Industry* ("ORGMASZ"), 1(1), 19-26.

Schmees, M. (2003). Distributed Digital Commerce. *Proceedings of the 5th International Conference on Electronic Commerce (ICEC2003)*, 131-137.

Sen, R. (2005). Optimal Search Engine Marketing Strategy. *International Journal of Electronic Commerce*, *10*(1), 9–25.

Shabazz, D. (2004). Towards a Better Understanding of e-Marketing Strategy: Past and Present. *Services Marketing Quarterly*, *26*(2), 117–130. doi:10.1300/J396v26n02_08

Simpson, M., & Docherty, A. J. (2004). E-Commerce Adoption Support and Advice for UK SMEs. *Journal of Small Business and Enterprise Development*, *11*(2), 315–328. doi:10.1108/14626000410551573

Singh, S. N., & Dalal, N. P. (1999). Web Home Pages as Advertisements. *Communications of the ACM*, *42*(8), 91–99. doi:10.1145/310930.310978

Taylor, M., & Murphy, A. (2004). SMEs and e-Business. *Journal of Small Business and Enterprise Development*, *11*(3), 280–289. doi:10.1108/14626000410551546

Tedeschi, B. (1999). On-Line Merchants Find That a Well Designed Web Site can have a Big Impact on the Bottom Line. *E-Commerce Report, New York Times*, 30 August 1999, As accessed on August 10, 2009.

Tödtling, F., & Kaufmann, A. (2001). The Role of the Region for Innovation Activities for SMEs. *European Urban and Regional Studies*, *8*(3), 203–215. doi:10.1177/096977640100800303

Urwin, S. (2000). The Internet as an Information Solution for the Small and Medium Sized Business. *Business Information Review*, *17*(3), 130–137. doi:10.1177/0266382004237647

U.S. Department of Health and Human Services. (2006 ed.) Research-Based Web Design & Usability Guidelines. Retrieved September 10, 2009, from http://www.usability.gov/pdfs/guidelines.html.

Webb, H. W., & Webb, L. A. (2004). SiteQual: An Integrated Measure of Website Quality. *Journal of Enterprise Information Management*, *17*, 430–440. doi:10.1108/17410390410566724

Weideman, M., & Mgidana, M. (2004). Website Navigation Architectures and their Effect on Website Visibility: A Literature Survey. Proceedings of SAICSIT, 292-296.

Weideman, M. & Schwenke, F. (2006).The Influence that JavaScript™ has on the Visibility of a Website to Search Engines – A Pilot Study. *Information Research*, 11(4).

Wilson, S. G., & Abel, I. (2002). So You Want to Get Involved in E-Commerce. *Industrial Marketing Management*, *21*, 85–94. doi:10.1016/S0019-8501(01)00188-2

Xing, B., & Lin, Z. (2004).The Impact of Search Engine Optimization on Online Advertising Market. *Proceedings of the 8th international Conference on Electronic Commerce*, 519-529.

Yu, W. D., & Lin, A. (2007). The Design and Implementation of a Search Engine Marketing Management System (SEMMS) Based on Service-Oriented Architecture Platform. *IEEE International Conference on e-Business Engineering*, 513-519.

Zhang, J., & Dimitroff, A. (2005). The Impact of Webpage Content Characteristics on Webpage Visibility in Search Engine Results (Part 1). *Information Processing & Management*, *41*, 665–690. doi:10.1016/j.ipm.2003.12.001

Zhang, P., Small, R. V., von Dran, G. M., & Barcellos, S. (2000). A Two Factor Theory for Website Design. *Proceedings of the 33rd Hawaii International Conference on System Sciences (HICSS),* 1, 1-10.

Chapter 2
E-Commerce Systems for Software Agents: Challenges and Opportunities

Emmanuel M. Tadjouddine
Xi'an Jiaotong-Liverpool University, China

ABSTRACT

It is hoped agent mediated e-commerce will be carried out as open systems of agents interoperating between different institutions, where different auction protocols may be in use. The authors argue that in order to put such a scenario to work, agents will need a method to automatically verify the properties of a previously unseen auction protocol. This, in turn poses the problem of automatically verifying desirable properties in order to trust a given auction mechanism. This challenge needs be addressed so that the business scenario of agent mediated e-commerce becomes a reality. In this chapter, the authors discuss salient opportunities for SMEs in addressing the issues of enabling software agents (e.g., PDAs, mobile phones) to connect to auction houses and verify desirable properties that need to hold before engaging any transactions.

INTRODUCTION

Future *agent mediated e-commerce* will involve open systems of agents interoperating between different institutions, where different protocols may be in use; the roaming agents will need to understand the rules of engagement in foreign institutions in much the same way human agents can. This implies software agents will be engaging financial transactions and entering legally binding contracts on behalf of their owners. An agent's owner must be legally responsible for his or her agent's actions. However, such *software agents* may be developed and owned by different individuals or organizations, which may have conflicting interests. As a consequence, agent owners may be reluctant to delegate tasks that may cause detrimental outcomes to an agent unless they can have a guarantee that the system has certain desirable properties. For instance, if I want my agent to bid in a web-based auction on my behalf, I will need a guarantee that my agent

DOI: 10.4018/978-1-61692-880-3.ch002

will not pay a higher price than it should because other participants are placing fictitious bids.

We can reasonably assume that electronic institutions will publish the specifications of their protocols in a high-level language specifying who can bid, in what order, and how the winners and prices are determined. A roaming agent that arrives at a foreign institution can download a protocol and analyze it in order to make a decision about whether or not to participate, and what strategy to use. The challenge now is for the roaming agent, with bounded computing resources, to be able to automatically check some desirable properties of the protocol. These properties may be related to economic or security issues of the trading platform. To give an idea of the sort of properties we have in mind, consider these questions:

- Can I *trust* my mobile phone to connect to an auction web-site in order to buy goods for the best prices available in the market?
- Can my mobile phone with limited computer resources be capable of ensuring an electronic auction such as eBay is fair and safe?
- Will my *software agent* be smart enough to interoperate between auction houses that use different communication settings and have different protocols?

The success of such agent mediated e-commerce systems will depend mainly on the ability to address the above issues, and to develop, maintain, and augment interoperable components. These pose real challenges to the computer science community and need be tackled so that we can advance our understanding about this very important area and realize the vision of *agent mediated e-commerce*.

Moreover, an important niche in e-commerce protocols is *auctions* since they usually yield to higher revenues than fixed price offerings (Zhang, 2008). *Auctions* are usually designed to have certain desirable game theoretic properties such as incentive compatibility (encouraging agents to bid truthfully), collusion-proofness (agents cannot collude to achieve a certain outcome), or false-name bidding free (agents cannot manipulate the outcome by using fictitious names). Game theoretic properties such as incentive compatibility rely on very strong assumptions; it is required that the property be common knowledge among the players, otherwise agents cannot be expected to follow any kind of recommendation (Guerin & Tadjouddine, 2006).

To illustrate these requirements, we need to bear in mind that an auction is typically defined by a winner determination algorithm; there are several in the literature, see for example (Cramton et al, 2006). This provides the winning criteria and therefore implicitly determines the optimal strategy for participating agents. These winner determination algorithms are designed with desirable properties such as truthful bidding is optimal. If an electronic *auction* house is using such a protocol, it is not sufficient for the auctioneer to claim that a truth telling strategy is optimal. The fact is that sincerity cannot be assumed in open systems. The protocol in use must be published in a standard specification language so that the bidding agents can understand its rules and verify that the auction is being implemented as advertised (Tadjouddine & Guerin, 2008).

These kinds of requirements are necessary to fully exploit the potential of e-commerce systems and to eventually achieve the vision of agent mediated e-commerce. In summary, the motivation for this work comes from the belief that verifying certain properties of a trading platform are useful to agents in open e-commerce environments only if:

- Their protocols can be published in a *machine-understandable* form.
- Their properties can be automatically verified by an agent.

These requirements need be addressed by providing a suitable specification language and associated proof procedures.

There are a certain number of opportunities related to this work too. Typically, this type of technical advances will benefit companies including SMEs deploying agent technology for e-commerce, those providing electronic devices with features likely to help with our increasingly busy life or those engaged in trading between different auction houses, where there is the potential to automate that trading. By giving certificates of desired outcomes to agent owners this work has the potential to increase the range of applications in which humans may be willing to delegate to their software agents. This may also help to fully automate trading institutions and therefore increase the efficiency and reliability of electronic marketplaces.

In this paper, we aim to address in details these challenges and argue on the opportunities related to the vision of agent-mediated e-commerce. It is hoped this work will facilitate the move from existing trading institutions to fully automated ones. The use of fully automated negotiation is expected to greatly increase the efficiency of electronic marketplaces, just as the move from traditional commerce to e-commerce has already improved efficiency on how business is carried out worldwide.

BACKGROUND

The vision of *agent-mediated e-commerce* system relies on the ability to provide trading mechanisms that are *machine understandable* so that *software agents* can verify desirable properties of the system. We therefore rely on *mechanism design*, languages allowing us to express mechanisms and formal verification.

Algorithmic Mechanism Design

Algorithmic *mechanism design* (Cramton et al, 2006, Chap. 1-2) consists in finding decision procedures that determine the outcome for the game mechanism according to some desired objective. This is in contrast with game theory, which is used to model and analyze multi-agent systems composed of selfish but rational agents. A game mechanism is simply a set of rules designed to induce a certain outcome. In agent mediated ecommerce, software agents may be engaged in financial transactions in which auction rules may be chosen to suit the features of the participants. It is not obvious to provide a mechanism that induces certain behavior of the agents in such a scenario. For example, how do we prevent agents from colluding bearing in mind it is even difficult to detect collusion between the agents in the system. We therefore restrict ourselves to models of rationality and behavior given by equilibrium concepts that are well studied in game theory *mechanism design*. For example, the objective of achieving incentive compatibility (truth-telling is an optimal strategy) can be obtained using game theory equilibrium concepts such as Nash equilibrium or dominant strategy equilibrium. In *auction* design, a well known class of incentive compatible mechanisms is the VCG (Vickrey-Clarke-Groves) mechanism, see for example (Cavallo, 2006; Cramton, 2006; Nissan & Ronen, 2000). The VCG mechanism is performed by finding

- The allocation that maximizes the social welfare,
- The pricing rule allowing each winner to benefit from a discount according to his contribution to the overall value for the auction.

Logic-Based Languages

Logic-based languages (such as temporal and first order logics and model-checking languages) are useful tools to model and reason about systems. They allow us to specify behavioral requirements of components of a system and formulate desirable properties for an individual component and the entire system. In (Tadjouddine & Guerin, 2007), a first order relational logic was used to verify incentive compatibility for auctions using Alloy (Jackson, 2000). This has shown an elegant way of modeling an auction and expressing its game-theoretic properties but it did not scale up very well since the Alloy analysis is intractable asymptotically. The Alloy analysis relies on the assumption that "negative answers tend to occur in small models already; boosting the confidence we may have in a positive answer" (Huth & Ryan, p. 143). Tractability is therefore achieved by restricting the analysis to a finite universe. The way in which this work combined game theory and logic gives us valuable insights into how game-theoretic properties such as Nash equilibrium can be formalized in logic and be verified automatically.

Our proposal of identifying key relevant properties widely expected by e-commerce users and relying on a logic based language to verify them is likely to be adequate. The important insight is to use tailored languages rather than expect a single language (e.g., temporal logic) to fit all desirable properties. Considering the growing interest in e-commerce in general as well as the recency nature of many of the work in this area, it is likely that the research problem outlined in this paper will receive a lot of attention from the industry in the near future.

Desirable Properties

The idea of agents automatically checking e-commerce properties is relatively new, so there are not many results in this area as yet. However earlier work explored the idea of verifying game-theoretic properties by using model-checking. Model checking is an attractive approach since it offers the possibility for agents to check trading mechanisms automatically. There is by now some work on verifying game equilibria (Pauly, 2005; Tadjouddine & Guerin, 2007; Tadjouddine et al, 2008). Specifically, the issues of building **trust** in multi-agent systems by verifying for example that a protocol enforces truth-telling were explored in (Osman & Robertson, 2007; Tadjouddine & Guerin, 2007; Tadjouddine et al, 2008). The computational complexity of such verification procedures are investigated in (Tadjouddine, 2007). Note that the complexity of verifying Nash equilibrium is different from that of computing one; see (Daskalakis & Papadimitriou, 2005; Chen & Deng, 2005; Chen & Deng, 2006) for more details. On one hand, it is well-known that a model-checking approach can suffer from the state space explosion problem and abstraction techniques can be used to reduce such a computational cost, see (Tadjouddine et al, 2008). However, abstraction is not a 'one size fits all' and finding a property-preserving abstraction requires some creativity from the human designer. For example, can we find an abstraction that will enable us to model check a combinatorial auction protocol regardless of the number of bidders and items? On the other hand, the work reported in (Pauly, 2005) on verifying game equilibria relies on program verification techniques. It develops proof rules based on Hoare's calculus for mechanisms that are specified in a WHILE programming language. The main advantage of this approach is that it offers the possibility of verifying large games without needing to explore every state that the system can reach; however it is not fully automatic. In this paper, we advocate the use of the *proof-carrying code* paradigm introduced in (Necula, 1997) in order to achieve the goal of enabling agents to automatically verify trading protocols.

VERIFYING E-COMMERCE SYSTEMS

The impact of e-commerce in the way we lead our daily life is evident. As we adopt new technologies, e.g., PDAs, mobile phones with features that constantly link us to entertainment, market houses, there is a need to enable these devices to make informed decisions just like humans can. We would like to argue that there are huge opportunities for SMEs to make the vision of fully automated agent-mediated e-commerce a reality. In this section, we give technical details as to how this may be implemented.

Proof-Carrying Code

Proof-Carrying Code (PCC), see (Necula, 1997), is a paradigm that enables a computer system to automatically ensure that a computer code provided by a foreign agent is safe for installation and execution. PCC is based on the idea that the complexity of ensuring code safety can be shifted from the code consumer to the code producer. The code producer must provide a proof that the code satisfies some safety rules defined by the code consumer. Safety rules are verification conditions that must hold in order to guarantee the safety of the code. Verification conditions can be, for example, that the code cannot access a forbidden memory location, the code is memory-safe or type-safe, or the code executes within well-specified time or resource usage limits. The proof of the verification conditions is encoded in a machine readable formalism to allow automatic checking by the code consumer. The formalism used to express the proof is usually in the form of logical axioms and typing rules and must be chosen so that it is tractable to check the correctness of a given proof. In the PCC paradigm, certification is about generating a formal proof that the code adheres to a well-defined safety policy and validation consists in checking the generated proof is correct by using a simple and trusted proof-checker. PCC has been applied to many areas including mobile code security (Aspinall & MacKenzie, 2005), ubiquitous computing (Barthe & Fournet, 2007), compiler certification (Leroy, 2006), or program transformation (Tadjouddine, 2008). As argued in (Necula, 1997), cryptography is weak in establishing *trust* in the system since it relies on personal authority given that trusted persons can make errors or adopt a malicious behavior occasionally. Our aim is to adapt the PCC framework into the area of agent mediated e-commerce wherein **trust** in the system is paramount.

Unifying Pcc and Mechanism Validation

Unifying PCC and mechanism validation implies that it is the responsibility of the mechanism designer to

ensure the mechanism has some desired properties by providing their proofs if requested. For a given mechanism, a certifying tool will return either nothing or a certificate that should be used by a proof-checker in order to establish a given property. In this project, our intention is to generate the certificate with the help of a verification condition generator (e.g., the Why tool, see http://why.lri.fr/) and a theorem prover such as Coq (Berthot & Casteran, 2005) or Isabelle, see http://isabelle.in.tum.de/. In this case, a buyer agent must run the proof-checker, a small and easy to certify program that checks whether the generated certificate is correct.

There are variants of the PCC framework. For example, instead of generating an entire proof, it may be sufficient for the mechanism designer to generate enough annotations or hints so that the proof can be constructed cheaply by a specialized theorem prover at the buyer agent's site.

General Setting

Generally speaking, an auction can be checked against security properties or economic properties that encourage participation of agents and discourage collusive and predatory behaviors. Collusion is a concern as participants may collude to keep the bidding values low. A predatory behavior can prevent bidders from entering the auction; the auction risks to be unprofitable for

Figure 1. Applying PCC to formally certify Auction properties

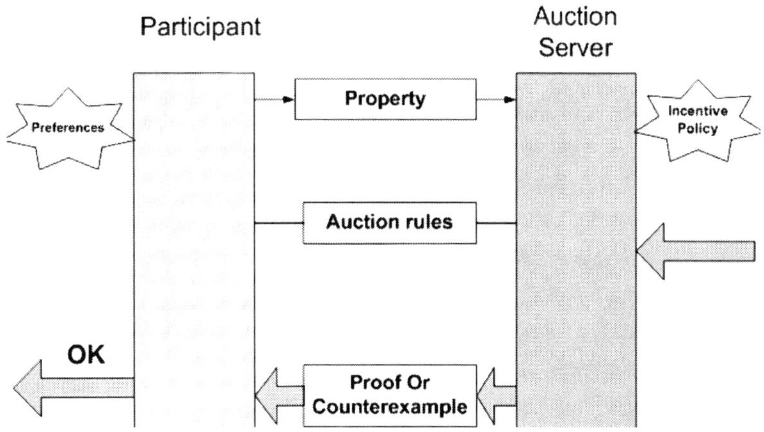

the auctioneer. In non-cooperative settings, one may be interested in game-theoretic properties that harness the ideal of truthful bidding agents or optimal revenue for the auctioneer. For an auction mechanism to be profitable, all necessary steps to ensure *trust* in the system must be taken since security or economic flaws in the system are not simply acceptable. In addition to the transactions security of the system, any claimed economic property must be proven correct and must adhere to a safety policy acceptable by the participants.

Figure 1 illustrates our PCC framework. A buyer agent downloads a computer program encoding the rules

of an auction, understand them, and requests about safety or economic properties of interest according to its preferences. The auction server has a well-defined policy of incentives e.g., the safety and economic aspects of the proposed auction rules. This is used to generate verification conditions using code analysis. A verification condition may be the auction code does not overflow, the code is type and memory safe, or some identified information is preserved.

With the help of a theorem prover, the server generates a proof that the auction code adheres to the safety policy or a counter-example invalidating a policy line. This is sent to the participant who has to verify the given proof by a simple proof-checker before submitting a bid or simulates the given counterexample. Observe that the proof generated by the server must be expressed in a formalism enabling its checking to be tractable. Although the PCC framework is simple, its implementation raises a number of practical issues that need to be resolved for its relevance and success, see http://raw.cs.berkeley.edu/pcc.html.

Issues, Controversies, Problems

The objective of this paper is to enable agents in an open e-commerce system to understand a published specification of a trading protocol, request for a digital evidence of a desired property, and then check the given evidence. To achieve this, we will need to develop the following:

1. Specifications for a set of trading policies relevant to e-commerce systems to be studied and taken into account.
2. A logic-based framework which can relate formally specified auction mechanisms to the desired properties of those auctions.
3. An extension of the PCC paradigm addressing the foundational issues for the proof development of mechanism properties by the mechanism designer as well as the checking of such proofs by the trading agent.

4. A verification environment to support automatically checking properties of a formally specified auction mechanism.

The difficulties lie primarily on how well the space of possible auctions is covered by each of these four items and how well a trading agent can reliably and efficiently ensure desired properties hold in the system. Our interest in the verification is to use Hoare-style verification techniques in a PCC setting wherein agents have limited computer resources in carrying out the verification. Once overcome, these technical challenges may lead to considerable business opportunities using the Internet from which SMEs may lead the way. The scenario may exceed that of what happen when we move from traditional commerce to electronic ones. Typically, in the present e-commerce format, humans may be cheated since they often do not bother to check the authenticity of a seller or even a product. With software agents equipped with computational resources and a network of auction houses equipped with *machine understandable* sets of trading rules, we may get closer to markets that are competitive and trustworthy.

Solutions and Recommendations

We recommend a survey of state of the art architectures for e-commerce systems such as RUBiS(see http://rubis.objectweb.org/), and then derive low-level requirements for market-based software agent systems such as the set of properties to be proven on such open multi-agent systems and the set of equilibrium concepts that are attractive for financially motivated agents (Goeree & Holt, 2003). We also need to investigate high-level requirements by searching for various models of those systems and then make a decision about which model to adopt. We will then decide on how well the low-level and high-level requirements fit together or select the most appropriate features to consider for the scenario envisaged. Eventually, we need to develop an abstraction allowing us to formalize the relevant requirements rigorously in a more or less machine-readable way.

We then need to develop scalable verification techniques for the scenarios found to be useful and profitable. Such verification may rely on existing environments based on theorem proving tools such as ESC/Java2 (see http://kind.ucd.ie/products/opensource/ESCJava2/), JACK (see http://www-sop.inria.fr/everest/soft/Jack/jack.html), Coq, or Isabelle. A survey on those verification tools will permit us to select the tool which has been deemed to be most appropriate. The main issue to be addressed at this stage is how to choose the specification language so as to express a wide range of trading policy and safety properties that ensure *trust* in the system and at the same time allow for automatic, reliable and efficient verification by agents with limited computer resources.

At the end of the day, we need to build a verification infrastructure wherein a buyer software agent can enter an auction house, understand the rules of engagement, request for evidence about a property it cares about, receive a certificate produced by the auctioneer for that property, and finally check the soundness of the produced evidence. We can start by investigating various PCC architectures given the requirements and constraints of the system. Although the concept of PCC is simple, the development of an efficient PCC architecture requires addressing the following key points:

1. **Proof development**: we need to develop logic-based foundations in order to generate certificates for the desired properties of the system.
2. **Certificate format**: we need to choose a formal language in which to express the certificate so that checking the validity of the certificate is tractable. This will require exploring trade-offs between the size of a certificate and the complexity for proof-checking. The objective is to come up with a format allowing us to represent the cer-

tificates of complex properties of interest and for which the certificate can be checked efficiently.

3. **Proof-checking**: we need to develop powerful checkers that are simple, easy to validate, and in polynomial time.

We will consider the following two scenarios:

- Each buyer agent checks the mechanism itself which we term on-device checking. A particular attention must be paid to parameters such as the certificate size and the complexity of the proof since computer resources (CPU and memory) are very limited.
- A trusted third party performs the checking on behalf of the buyer agent which we term off-device checking. This may allow for some flexibility on the available computer resources in the sense that we can connect into a powerful computer in order to perform the required checking.

FUTURE RESEARCH DIRECTIONS

The solutions we advocated earlier are perhaps starting points to be considered in order to fully realize the vision put forward in this chapter. How do we enable a small device with limited resources to understand previously unseen protocols, verify certain desirable properties and then make a decision on whether to engage into transactions or not. How those proofs should look like, what are the limits of what can be practically done with some degree of efficiency. The results of such a research can be used by SMEs to boost profits for companies just as e-commerce has achieved by moving to online trading.

In this chapter, we have focused on technical issues but legal issues need to be considered as well. Who is responsible of the software agent or robot that is roaming between auction houses? Who is responsible for the protection of that robot? What happens if the robot got destroyed? How much can human beings delegate to their software agents?

CONCLUSION

In this paper we have put forward a framework based on the *proof-carrying code* paradigm enabling an agent in an e-commerce scenario to automatically check some interesting properties of a published auction specification. A property of interest can be for example strategy-proofness (i.e. the protocol is immune to counter-speculation and strategic bidding) or revenue maximizing (i.e. the protocol yields the optimal revenue). The main lesson learnt is that while verifying e-commerce properties is feasible, it can be quite computationally difficult even for relatively simple auction types. In addition to this technical difficulty, a scenario wherein human beings own software agents and can delegate tasks (e.g., buying of selling products) to those agents, a legal framework need be implemented. This is even harder given the global nature of e-commerce systems, which can be accessed anywhere and at any time.

Given the technical challenges that need be tackled in this framework (agents are resource-bounded, protocols may be complex, some properties such as collusion-proofness can be hard to formulate), we may need to identify certain classes of auctions for which the verification of desirable properties is tractable. The outcomes of such a study will certainly benefit SMEs, which may be involved in developing safe software agents, setting up trustworthy as well as interoperable e-commerce systems. We feel this line of research can increase the competitiveness of software companies and showcase once again how the Internet is part of our daily-life.

ACKNOWLEDGMENT

The author would like Dr Frank Guerin for enlightening discussions on this work.

REFERENCES

Aspinall, D., & MacKenzie, K. (2006). Mobile resource guarantees and policies. *Construction and Analysis of Safe, Secure, and Interoperable Smart Devices (*LNCS series, Vol. 3956,pp. 16–36). New York: Springer.

Bathe, G., & Fournet, C. (2007). *Trustworthy Global Computing*. (LNCS: Vol. 4912)New York: Springer-Verlag.

Bertot, Y., & Casteran, P. (2004). *Interactive theorem proving and program development: Coq'Art: the calculus of inductive constructions. Texts in theoretical comp. science*. New York: Springer-Verlag.

Cavallo, R. (2006). Optimal decision-making with minimal waste: strategy-proof redistribution of VCG payments. In Nakashima, H. (Eds.), *Autonomous Agents and Multi-Agent Systems 2006* (pp. 882–889).

Chen, X., & Deng, X.(2005). 3-NASH is PPAD-complete. *Electronic Colloquium on Computational Complexity*, No 139.

Chen, X., & Deng, X. (2006) Settling the complexity of two-player Nash equilibrium. In FOCS 2006, 47th Annual IEEE Symposium on Foundations of Computer Science (pp. 261–272), IEEE Computer Society.

Cramton, P., Shoham, Y., & Steinberg, R. (Eds.). (2006). *Combinatorial Auctions*. Cambridge, MA: MIT Press.

Daskalakis, K., & Papadimitriou, C. H. (2005) Three-player games are hard. *Electronic Colloquium on Computational Complexity, No 139.*

Goeree, J. K., & HOLT, C. A. (2003). Stochastic game theory: For playing games not just for doing theory. *Proceedings of the National Academy of Sciences of the United States of America*, *96*(19), 10564–10567. doi:10.1073/pnas.96.19.10564

Guerin, F., & Tadjouddine, E. M. (2006) Realising common knowledge assumptions in agent auctions. *In The IEEE/WIC/ACM Int. Conf. on Intelligent Agent Technology (pp. 579–586*), IEEE Computer Society.

Huth, M. R. A., & Ryan, M. D. (2000). *Logic in Computer Science: Modelling and Reasoning about Systems*. Cambridge, UK: Cambridge University Press.

Jackson, D. (2000). Automating first-order relational logic. In *SIGSOFT Foundations of Software Engineering* (pp. 130–139). New York: ACM Press.

Leroy, X. (2006). Formal certification of a compiler back-end or: programming a compiler with a proof assistant. *ACM SIGPLAN Notices*, *41*(1), 42–54. doi:10.1145/1111320.1111042

Necula, G. C. (1997) Proof-carrying code. *In Annual Symposium on Principles of Programming Languages 1997 (pp. 106–119).New York:* ACM Press.

Nisan, N., & Ronen, A. (2000) Computationally feasible VCG mechanisms. *In the 2000 ACM Conference on Electronic Commerce (pp. 242–252),* New York: ACM Press.

Osman, N., & Robertson, D. (2007) Dynamic verification of trust in distributed open systems. *In International Joint Conference on Artificial Intelligence (pp. 1440–1445),* New York: ACM Press.

Pauly, M. (2005). Programming and verifying subgame-perfect mechanisms. *Journal of Logic and Computation*, *15*(3), 295–316. doi:10.1093/logcom/exi014

Tadjouddine, E. M. (2007) Complexity of verifying game equilibria. In B. Hans-Dieter et al (Ed.), *Vol. 4696, Lecture Notes in Artificial Intelligence (pp. 103–112)*.New York: Springer.

Tadjouddine, E. M. (2008) On formal certification of AD transformations. In C. Bischof, M. Bucker, P. Hovland, U. Naumann, and J. Utke (Ed.), *Lecture Notes in Computational Science and Engineering, Vol. 64, Advances in Automatic Differentiation (pp. 23–34),* New York: Springer.

Tadjouddine, E. M., & Guerin, F. (2007) Verifying dominant strategy equilibria in auctions. In B. Hans-Dieter et al (Ed.), *Vol. 4696, Lecture Notes in Artificial Intelligence (pp. 288–297),* New York: Springer.

Tadjouddine, E. M., Guerin, F., & Vasconcelos, W. (2008). Abstractions for model checking game-theoretic properties in auctions. In Padgham, L., Parkes, D. C., Müller, J., & Parsons, S. (Eds.), *Autonomous Agents and Multi-Agent Systems* (pp. 1613–1616). New York: ACM Press.

Zhang, P. (2008) *Uniform price auctions and fixed price offerings in IPOs: an experimental comparison*. Tech. Rep. No. 200805, Centre for Decision Research and Experimental Economics, The University of Nottingham, UK.

Chapter 3
Enhancing the Preparedness of SMEs for E-Business Opportunities by Collaborative Networks

Heiko Duin
BIBA Bremer Institut für Produktion und Logistik GmbH, Germany

Klaus-Dieter Thoben
BIBA Bremer Institut für Produktion und Logistik GmbH, Germany

ABSTRACT

This chapter introduces virtual Organisations (VOs) as a special organisational form of collaborative networks of SMEs to conduct E-Business projects. VOs are normally not created from scratch, but instantiated from a strategic network or pool of enterprises. This enhances the preparedness of participating members when an E-Business opportunity occurs. The underlying strategic network acts as a breeding environment for the VOs. Therefore, it is called a VO Breeding Environment (VBE). Examples from the automotive industry are illustrating the development and needs of this concept. Strategic planning is important for such a network in order to increase chances of occurring business opportunities. The remainder of this chapter shows how scenario-oriented methods such as cross-impact analysis can be used to support a collaborative strategic planning in such networked organisations. The application of such methods allows long-term foresight and the anticipation of the right technological, financial and business oriented decisions.

INTRODUCTION

The continuing change of producer markets towards buyer markets has a strong impact on the competition between manufacturing enterprises. As a strategic answer collaborative networks such as virtual corporations, virtual enterprises or virtual factories have been discussed since the beginning of the 90ies of last century. Many models and concepts supporting the life cycle of such organisations – consisting of the creation, operation and dissolution phases – have been developed. An important aspect in the creation

DOI: 10.4018/978-1-61692-880-3.ch003

Figure 1. Two Ways to Instantiate VOs

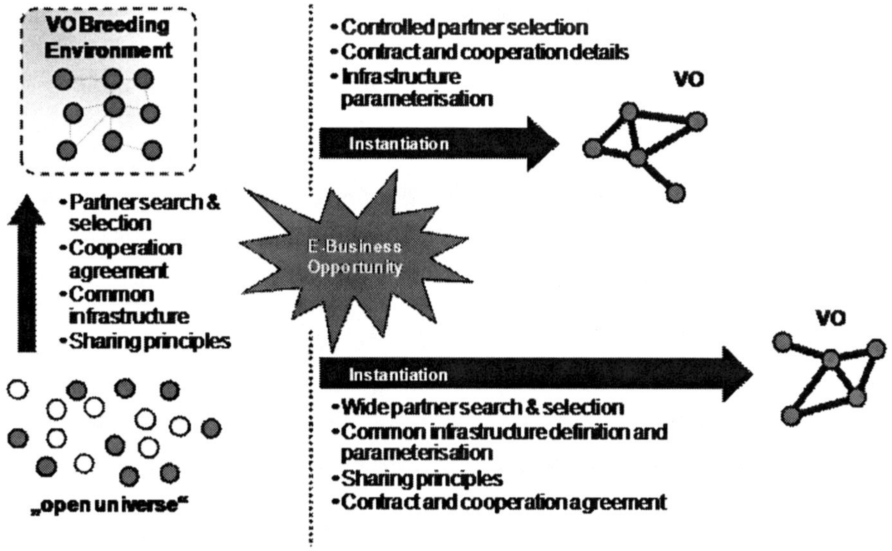

phase is strategic planning. This phase is supported by concepts of long-term networks like industrial clusters or regional networks which act as a breeding environment and which enable the short-term creation of virtual organisations. Especially this phase needs support of strategic planning which is a part of the strategic management process.

The two basic types of collaborative networks are represented by Virtual Organisations (VOs) and by Source Networks (e.g.Kürümlüoglu, Nostdal, & Karvonen, 2005):

- A **Virtual Organisation** (VO) is a temporary consortium of partners from different organisations established to fulfil a value adding task, for example a product or service to a customer. The lifetime of a VO is typically restricted: it is created for a definite task and dissolved after the task has been completed. A synonym for VO is the term Virtual Enterprise.
- A **Source/Support Network** is a more stationary, though not static, group of organisational entities which has developed a preparedness to collaborate in case of a specific task / customer demand. Another name for such a network is **Breeding Environment**.

The relationship between these two forms is that the Breeding Environment prepares the instantiation of VOs. It acts as an incubator for a VO. From the VO point of view, the VO is created when an E-Business opportunity occurs. In order to perform the actual value creation task, the VO can be created from scratch (collecting cooperating partners from an "open universe" of enterprises) or through a VO Breeding Environment (VBE, see Figure 1).

When collecting the partners for the VO from the open universe, several steps or activities have to be performed. This includes partner search and selection of the "right" partners, the definition of a common infrastructure to be used by those partners, agreement on common sharing principles and finally the collaboration needs to be fixed in a cooperation agreement resulting in a contract between all participating partners. It is obvious that this process needs a certain amount of time which may result that competitors are faster in preparing their offer.

In the second way of Figure 1 all activities which are independent from the E-Business opportunity are prepared in advance. The search and selection of partners fitting to a specific kind of E-Businesses activity results in a pool of known and trusted partners. It should be quite easy to select those partners who have the right competencies and resources to implement a VO to answer the E-Business opportunity. All partners in the pool also agree on cooperation and sharing principles and the common infrastructure to be used in the case of a VO instantiation. This saves a lot of negotiation time and enhances the speed with which such a pool can prepare an offer for an upcoming opportunity.

The remaining of this chapter is investigating the situation and needs of SME suppliers in the automotive industry. According to an Accenture study (Baier, 2007) and backed by the FAST-2015 study (Dannenberg & Kleinhans, 2005) the market of the OEMs (Original Equipment Manufacturers) is still consolidating. From 36 independent manufacturers worldwide in 1970 only 19 will still exist in 2010 (in 2006 there were 27). The same situation concerns the supplier industry: while in 2005 about 1,500 – 2,000 suppliers were delivering for an OEM, it is expected that in 2010 this number is reduced to 500 – 700. At the same time the percentage of value added by suppliers' increases from 65% to 75%.

Hüttenrauch & Baum (2008) posit ten hypothesis' concerning the future of the automotive industry. The main important ones in the context of this chapter are:

- Automotive manufacturers will transfer more and more complex tasks to their suppliers while focussing their own value creation on brand-defining modules.
- Only a few suppliers with clear business models and very high module-based competences will determine the automotive industry.
- End users are demanding new ways and more flexible concepts of mobility.

With these trends in mind it is obvious that automotive supplier SMEs do have the need of finding new business models ensure to participate the automotive value creation chain in the future. To establish a Virtual Organisation which acts as one partner (or supplier) is one solution.

As end users are demanding new ways and more flexible concepts of mobility, the product "car" will also change. Beside owning just the physical product, services ensuring availability and environmentally friendly transport become more and more important (Becker, 2006).

The objective of this chapter is to show how SMEs can enhance their preparedness for conducting E-Business projects in virtual organisations by doing two things. Firstly, the potential partners have to organise as long-term strategic networks with the objective to continuously seek for E-Business opportunities. Secondly, the strategic networks need to perform continuous strategic planning.

BACKGROUND

In order to react fast and effective in the context of the VBE as shown in Figure 1 the E-Business Opportunity needs to be analysed a little more. In difference to traditional thinking (i.e. the development and/or production of physical products) two kinds of E-Business opportunities might be distinguished:

- **Electronic Services** for businesses, administrations or consumers. As explained below, there nine different areas on which E-Business applications can be classified. Typical for each E-Business application is that there are no physical products involved. Most E-Business applications just cover the more or less administrative information exchanges within market transactions (e.g. orders and payments).

- Development and/or production of an **Extended Product**. The paradigm of the Extended Product is explained by Jansson and Thoben (2005). Extended Products can be defined as a physical product expanded by services which provide benefit(s) for the users. This is one step further than providing a solution. In such a case, it is obvious that especially services provided with the mean of the Internet represent the E-Business opportunities.

Concerning the automotive industry, the extended product can be defined as the provision of mobility. The main benefit is shifting from owning a car towards having a car at hand whenever wanted by the user. This can be realised in many ways, one example is a car sharing programme, where the members pay a monthly fee for the service of using a car at specific times. The car sharing organisation ensures the optimal size and regular maintenance and the necessary insurance of the fleet so that each member has a car at hand whenever wanted. This includes the provision of cars for specific purposes. Often members just need a 'normal' car, but sometimes there is e.g. a need for a van.

Beside the shared ownership of a vehicle fleet, there are many options to provide additional services combined with the product car. Such services can be information services like weather and traffic information, routing services or to call intention to any interesting points (POI = Point of Interest like sights or infrastructural elements like gasoline stations or motels).

Such an extended product like 'mobility' also runs through a product development process. As the OEM of cars is not in the situation to deliver all physical as well as all intangible elements of the final product, it needs to cooperate with partners. This leads to E-Business opportunities of any kind of supplier for such a kind of an extended product.

E-Business

Because of the rapid technological changes and the dynamics in the economic environment, the factor information has become more significant than the production factor. Many enterprises and other organisations have implemented business processes utilising the Internet and realizing customer relationships with the help of electronic means, i.e. Information and Communication Technology which led to coining the term Electronic Business (E-Business) (Meier & Stormer, 2009).

E-Business describes initiating, arranging, and carrying out electronic business processes, i.e. exchanging services with the help of public or private communication networks via the Internet. This is done with the objective to achieve added value. Enterprises (businesses), public institutions (administration), as well as private persons (mostly they are assumed to be consumers) can be both service providers and service consumers. What is important is that the electronic business relationship generates added value, which may take the form of either a monetary or an intangible contribution.

A commonly used typology to distinguish different forms of E-Business is to categorise the involved actors in the groups of consumers, businesses and administrations. Putting providers and consumers of E-Business services onto two different perpendicular axis results in a matrix with nine different fields of relationships:

- **Consumer-to-Consumer (C2C)**: An example is the classified advertisement of other consumer web sites on the own consumer's web site. Another example are the many social networking sites like XING.
- **Consumer-to-Business (C2B)**: Consumers offer their profiles in social networking sites which are often used by head hunters searching for qualified people for their customer enterprises.

- **Consumer-to-Administration (C2A)**: Consumers offer to verify and evaluate administrative services.
- **Business-to-Consumer (B2C)**: This is the classical area of online shops, where enterprises offer goods and services for consumers.
- **Business-to-Business (B2B)**: All electronic services concerning the supply, production and distribution of products (physical products and services) belong to this area. One example is the electronic Supply Chain Management.
- **Business-to-Administration (B2A)**: this area includes any services enterprises offer for the administration, e.g. information concerning the emission of carbon dioxide.
- **Administration-to-Consumer (A2C)**: This is the classical area of E-Government where the authorities offer services to citizens like online registration of cars, etc.
- **Administration-to-Business (A2B)**: This is another area of E-Government where the authorities offer services to businesses like the online tax declarations, etc.
- **Administration-to-Administration (A2A)**: Here the authorities offer each other services for collaboration. As an example one might think about the exchange of information on criminals between the different levels of police (national police with Interpol, etc.).

The remainder of this chapter assumes enterprises to be involved in B2B E-Business opportunities.

The life cycle of a (extended) product can be divided into three major phases. First, the Beginning-of-Life (BOL) phase deals mainly with the product development and its manufacturing. The second phase is called Middle-of-Life (MOL) dealing with all issues of product use and maintenance. Finally, the End-of-Life (EOL) phase includes everything from disassembly, re-usage and recycling of all product parts. In the following this chapter focuses on the BOL phase, i.e. product development and manufacturing of the product.

Returning to the example of the automotive industry, there are many opportunities for E-Business in the context of Supply Chain Management (SCM) and Customer Relationship Management (CRM) including E-Marketplaces, E-Procurement, E-Commerce and E-Distribution (Raisinghani et al., 2005). This view supports the manufacturing phase including procurement of parts and distribution of the final product. But the development phase also offers many opportunities of E-Business resulting in the collaborative development of the final product.

Collaborative Business

A further development of E-Business is sometimes called C-Business, where the C stands for collaboration. Collaborative Business is a business strategy which animates different partners along a value creation chain to generate additional added value by information exchange (Silberberger, 2003).

The concept of Collaborative Business has been some kind the predecessor for Collaborative Networked Organisations which are presented in the following section. The focus of Collaborative Networked Organisations is broader than the concept of Collaborative Business.

Collaborative Networked Organisations

Camarinha-Matos and Afsarmanesh (2005) propose a new scientific discipline dealing with all aspects of networks of institutions and/or persons which temporarily collaborate in order to follow a common objective. This discipline is called Collaborative Networked Organisations (CNOs).

According to Camarinha-Matos & Afsarmanesh (2006), everyone has an intuitive understanding of what collaboration is, but this concept is often confused with cooperation. This confusion reaches even a higher level when related terms such as networking, communication or coordination are considered. Although each of these concepts is an important component of collaboration, they are not equal and none is equivalent to another. An attempt to clarify these various concepts has been presented by Camarinha-Matos & Afsarmanesh (2006):

- **Networking** involves communication and information exchange resulting in mutual benefit. An example of networking is the case in which a group of entities shares information about their specific experiences concerning a specific subject. All partners benefit from the information made available and shared, but there is not necessarily a common goal or structure influencing the form and timing of individual contributions.
- **Coordination** includes in addition to the exchange of information the alignment of activities resulting in more efficient outcomes. Coordination describes the act of working harmoniously in a concerted way. It is one of the main components of collaboration. An example of coordinated activities occurs when a number of autonomous entities share some information and adjust the timing, e.g. for their lobbying activities for a new subject. Nevertheless each entity might have a different goal and use its own resources and methods.
- **Cooperation** involves above information exchange and adjustments of activities also the sharing of resources with the objective to achieve compatible or common goals. Cooperation is achieved by dividing tasks among partners. In such a case the aggregated value is the result of the addition of individual contributions to value generated by the single participants. A traditional supply chain is a good example of a cooperative process. Each participant performs its part in series of process steps in a coordinated manner. Each partners behaves following a common plan which is not defined jointly but provided by a single entity the focal organisation in the supply chain.
- Finally, **collaboration** describes a *"process in which the partners share information, resources and responsibilities to jointly plan, implement, and evaluate a program of activities to achieve a common goal"* (Camarinha-Matos & Afsarmanesh, 2006). This concept is based on the Latin word *collaborare* meaning "to work together". It implies the sharing of risks, resources, responsibilities, but also the results and rewards. Collaboration involves mutual engagement of participants to solve a problem together, which implies mutual trust. If wanted by the group they can give to an outside observer the image of a joint identity.

The same authors also provide a classification of CNOs (Camarinha-Matos & Afsarmanesh, 2008). Generally CNOs can be divided into goal oriented networks and long-term, strategic networks. The first type can be further sub-divided into continuous production driven networks (such as supply chains) and opportunity grasping networks (like extended enterprises, virtual enterprises and virtual organisations). The second type can be further sub-divided into VO Breeding Environments (VBEs) and Professional Virtual Communities. Examples for VBEs are Industry Clusters, Industrial Districts and Business Ecosystems. VBEs provide an environment for the rapid and fluid instantiation of opportunity grasping networks like VOs when opportunities arise.

Figure 2. The Life Cycle Phases of a VBE

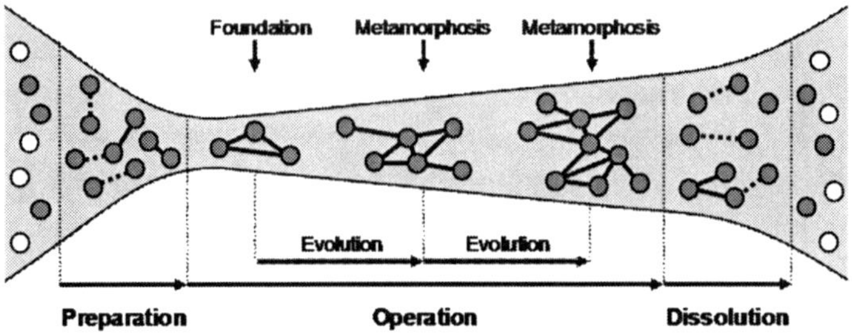

VO BREEDING ENVIRONMENT (VBE)

A Virtual Organisation Breeding Environment (VBE) can be defined as an association of organisations and related supporting institutions, adhering to a base long term cooperation agreement, and adoption of common operating principles and infrastructures, with the main goal of increasing both their chances and their preparedness towards collaboration in potential VOs (Afsarmanesh & Camarinha-Matos, 2009).

Members of the VBE must comply with the general rules and policies, e.g. adopting the common infrastructure. But, once an organisation joined the VBE, it has access and shall benefit from its bag of assets including common information, services, and tools as well as common market and distribution channels, common resources and labour pool, common VBE cultural ties and facilities to share the cost of new experiences.

The constitution of a VBE is an optimal possibility for SMEs to generate benefits through a networking strategy. The expected main benefit for enterprises engaged in automotive clusters is the involvement in strategic developments concerning their main customers, i.e. the OEMs.

VBE Life Cycle

As all CNOs, the VBE has a life cycle of the following phases: set-up, operation and dissolution. But, as the VBE is normally planned as a long-term alliance, and considering its valuable bag of assets collected during the lifetime of the VBE, its dissolution is considered as a quite unusual situation. Instead, it is much more probable that the VBE goes through another stage that is called metamorphosis, where it can evolve by changing its form and purpose. This leads to a life cycle for a VBE consisting of five major steps and phases as shown in Figure 2.

- **Preparation**. This phase includes the initiation and recruiting of the initial set of members for the VBE. In this phase strategic planning takes place. It ends with the foundation of the VBE.
- **Foundation**. This step represents the constitution and the start-up phase.
- **Evolution**. From its constitution the VBE is constantly running, i.e. identification of business opportunities, instantiation, operation and dissolution of VOs. It is assumed that this operational phase of the VBE involves some evolutionary steps like the recruitment of additional members are the release of some other members. This affects the form and the bag of assets of the VBE in an evolutionary (slow changing) style, always adapting to the requirements from its environment.
- **Metamorphosis**. This step is the revolutionary pendent to the evolution explained above. If the VBE cannot react any long appropriately to the requirements of its environment, a dramatically change concern-

ing its form and purpose is needed. This results in new strategic plans, releasing unnecessary members and recruiting new ones. After the metamorphosis the VBE has completely changed.

- **Dissolution**. If a metamorphosis cannot solve the problems the VBE will dissolute. This is the final step in the life cycle of a VBE.

A comprehensive discussion of a management system supporting the all these phases of the life cycle and the roles of actors involved is beyond the scope of this chapter and can be found elsewhere (e.g. Romero Diaz, 2007).

The need for strategic planning is most obvious during the preparation and foundation as well as while the metamorphosis takes place. Provider of the strategic planning process should be a steering committee consisting of selected members of the VBE (Duin, 2007b).

Continuous Creation of VOs

Foundation, evolution and metamorphosis of the VBE may be driven by random or in a planned and controlled way. Camarinha-Matos and Afsarmanesh (2007) do mention a long-term strategy behind the VBE, but the responsibility to develop and implement the strategy has not yet been assigned to one of the roles identified within a VBE. Duin (2007b) proposes to define a steering committee for strategic management tasks. Several other roles have already been identified including the member, administrator, opportunity broker, VO planner and coordinator (Camarinha-Matos & Afsarmanesh, 2007). The VBE Administrator is a role performed by a member organisation, which is responsible for the VBE operation and evolution, which includes promotion of cooperation among the VBE members, filling the skill/competency gaps in the VBE by searching and recruiting/inviting new organisations into the VBE and the daily management of the VBE general processes, conflict resolution, preparation of a bag of assets, and making common VBE policies, among others. The responsibility of the VBE administrator needs to be extended by strategic management tasks, when the long-term evolution and metamorphosis of the VBE should occur in a planned and controlled way.

Figure 3. Continuous Instantiation of VOs by aVBE

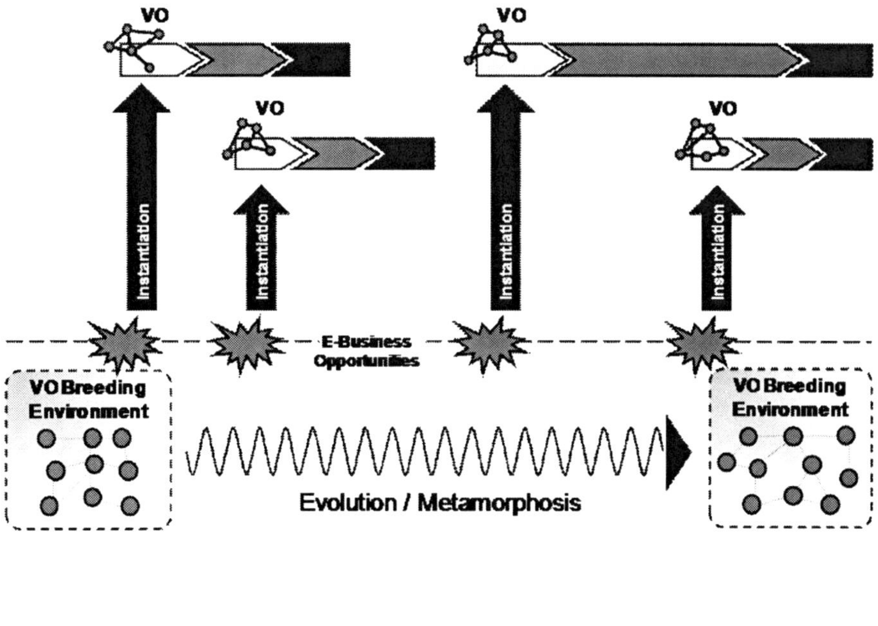

Metamorphosis and Evolution

The foundation of the VBE can be considered as a special – i.e. the first – metamorphosis in a series a metamorphosis steps. Each of these steps is central for strategic planning activities. As structure follows strategy, the strategic objectives of the network change first. The resulting change in structure represents the implementation of strategy. During the evolutionary phases of a VBE strategic controlling takes place to assure the detection of situations where radical changes within the VBE are necessary to assure long-term survival.

The evolutionary phase is characterised by small continuing events such as the gaining of new experiences during the execution of instantiated VOs or small changes in customer demands. The VBE can react with internal resources on each of these events. Only minor changes within the structure are necessary in order to adapt to these changes. As such events and the corresponding responses occur in a continuous way, the VBE is evolving in its environment.

The metamorphosis is a step to be taken as an answer to a more radical change in the environment of the VBE. Most commonly, it takes place as a response to one of the following two reasons:

- A dramatic change within the market where the VBE is operating in can be observed in terms of a change in the competitive situation (new competing VBEs may be formed). The VBE needs to sharpen their competitive profile.
- The customer driven demand of offered competencies, products or services is changing. The VBE needs to adapt to the changed customer demands. Most often this means the acquisition of new competencies.

In each case, the VBE needs to reflect on such changes in order to redefine its strategy. This includes the change of the structural and componential dimensions of the network by including new members who can fill the gaps of the needed profile. The VBE changes – in comparison to the evolutionary changes – more dramatically so that this step is called a metamorphosis.

Within the automotive industry it can be observed that the formation of collaborative networks is driven from two sides. The OEMs are interested in restructuring their Supply Chains into Supply Networks. A good example for this development is the Daimler Supplier Network (Daimler, 2009). Daimler is dividing their suppliers into three groups: (1) Strategic Partners, (2) Key Suppliers, and (3) Suppliers. The intention is to include the Strategic Partners into the strategic innovation of the OEM expecting an exceptional reliability but also offering planning security, reliability, information access, trustful collaboration and business opportunities as compensation.

Smaller suppliers – which are often SMEs – are very much interested in such close cooperation with OEMs, but are considered due to different reasons (mostly because of their size) not as reliable as necessary. The answer is the foundation of strategic networks such as VBEs in order to arise stronger and more reliable into the market. Especially in the automotive industry the industrial cluster (which is a special manifestation of a VBE) has emerged as a strategic network in the automotive industry.

Examples for VBEs

The Automotive Cluster Slovenia (ACS) was founded in November 2001 by 12 Slovenian organisations (10 enterprises, the University of Ljubljana and a regional development agency). After a period of preparation which lasted a few months, the network became operational on 14 March 2002 (ACS, 2002). Currently, the ACS counts 58 members.

All members are suppliers in the automotive industry. Their product portfolio is quite manifold reaching from simple parts like tires via interior and window systems to engine parts and gear units.

The strategic objectives of the members of the ACS include profitable growth, acquisition of new customers, common promotion and marketing campaigns, optimization of the supply chain, common development of ICT infrastructure, and common knowledge management activities (GzS/izGTM, 2008). The main objective of the cluster is to develop and sell complex parts with a high added value. In order to reach this goal a cluster-office has been established to coordinate common activities. Currently a network-wide information system is under development to streamline the interactions among the single members (Jaklic, Svetina, & Zagorsek, 2008).

Another strategic objective of the ACS is collaborative networking with other automotive clusters. The ACS is involved in the foundation of a network of clusters covering the region of south-east Europe (Busen, 2004).

Customers of the ACS include many of the big OEMs and their first-tier suppliers such as Audi, BMW, Bosch, Ford, MAN, MAGNA Steyr, Mercedes, New Holland, Opel, Renault, SAAB, VALEO, Vis-teon, and Volkswagen.

The PANAC (Pannon Automotive Cluster) was established in 2000 representing a coalition of automotive supplier of the region Pannon in the north-west of Hungary with Györ as central town (Santoro & Bifulco, 2005). Because of the nearby locations of manufacturing plants of OEMs like Opel, Suzuki and Audi many SMEs settled in that region to supply in a fest and flexible way. Currently, PANAC counts around 70 members (Grosz, 2008).

Most of the partners of PANAC are second-tier and third-tier suppliers of the region. Most of them understood relatively fast that cooperation instead of competition is more beneficial for each of those enterprises. As a consequence, PANAC was founded with the goal to offer system integration solutions to the OEMs. This allows highly flexible and configurable proposals for the customers, which in turn provides a strong negotiation position for the members. The strategic objectives of the members include the common marketing of the competences of the region, common innovation projects and the development of competitive advantages.

The cluster management is performed by a regional development agency. Specific services such as a 'Automotive-Benchmarking-Club' and common public relations and marketing activities are offered to its members. The OEMs Audi, Suzuki, and Opel are customers and members of PANAC at the same time.

STRATEGIC PLANNING IN VBES

Strategic planning as part of the strategic management process for organisations has been researched extensively during the last few decades (e.g. Mintzberg, Ahlstrand, & Lampel, 1998). The challenges as well as methods and tools to address the need of such kind of long-range planning are well understood. But, with the creation of an own unity, i.e. the collaborative network, the interference of strategic planning within the partner organisations and the network level needs further investigations.

For the following of this paper, the planning dimension is considered to be central. Planning has two main aspects: (1) Identification of the long-term (strategic) objectives of the organisation, and (2) Setting up a (strategic) action plan to be implemented by the organisation in order to reach the objectives.

Strategic Planning in the Partner Organisations

In a traditional enterprise, the forms of strategy are (Jagdev, Brennan, & Browne, 2004):

- **Corporate Strategy**: Is the overall business strategy of the enterprise based on the vision and mission. The corporate strategy guides the single business strategies.

- **Business Strategy**: The enterprise divides their activities into Strategic Business Units (SBUs). For each SBU an own strategy is developed and implemented.
- **Functional Strategy**: The functional strategies concern individual business functions and processes, e.g. human resources or marketing.

These three forms of strategy are strictly hierarchical, meaning that the functional strategies are strictly in line with their business strategies and all business strategies are compatible with the corporate strategy. The direction of governance is top down.

Common Strategic Planning on Network Level

In comparison to the hierarchical strategy structure, strategy formation in a VBE is different. The corporate level strategies are still top down, but within the VBE, the direction of governance is bottom-up. All members are responsible for strategy at the same time.

Sturm et al (2004) outline, that the process of strategic management, which is including the strategic planning, becomes a tedious and time consuming dialog in a network, because the members might have controversial interests and there is a need to find compromises and broadly accepted solutions. The preconditions, which make the execution of a strategy process in a network context to a lengthy procedure are: (1) decentralisation, and volatility of decisions, communications and resources, (2) inconsistency of interests and (3) novelty of coordination processes. This applies to open networks, but, this might not apply to VBEs due to:

- An enterprise joining a VBE has to sign a cooperation agreement. Assuming that this agreement regulates the basic responsibilities, procedures and rules of cooperation, the members shouldn't have very controversial understandings.
- The members of the VBE follow a common objective, otherwise they wouldn't join together into a VBE.

From this point of view, the VBE seems not to be that different to other forms of long-term organisations, where strategic management is – of course – an issue. And this opens the discussion, which of the traditional methods and tools of strategic planning apply best to VBEs.

Cross-Impact Analysis as Strategic Planning Aid

Scenario technique (Götze, 1993) or scenario planning (Walton, 2008) is a widely used tool for strategic planning, risk and sensitivity analysis and organisational learning. When dealing with hard (quantitative) approaches of forecasting, the result is often just one single scenario connected with a specific probability of occurrence. But, to anticipate the full range of possible future states, other approaches (like narrative storytelling, simulations with varying parameters) should be applied.

The natural time frame for scenario techniques is mid-term to long-range. Concerning the planning of the VOs to be created from a VBE two aspects are important: First, the long-range trends and developments of the VBE and its environment, which form the frame for the VOs, and second the VO itself with focus on the collaboration.

Scenario techniques are based on two principles (e.g. Gausemeier, Fink, & Schlake, 1998):

- **Systems thinking**: Organisations – in this case the VBE – must perceive their environment as a complex network of inter-related (external as well as internal) factors.

- **Multiple futures**: Organisations should not reduce their strategic thinking to exactly one prognosticated future. Instead, alternative future scenarios should be created and considered during strategic planning.

The scenario generation approach adopted by BIBA is based on causal cross-impact analysis (Krauth, Duin, & Schimmel, 1998), which has first been developed by Olaf Helmer (Helmer, 1977; Helmer, 1981). Up to now, BIBA included several enhancements to the causal cross-impact analysis method according to requirements identified during various research projects: delayed impacting, threshold impacting, expression variables and a technique for structuring and managing scenarios in a tree. BIBA implemented a cross-impact modelling and simulation software package called JCrimp, which allows the interactive set-up, simulation and evaluation of causal cross-impact models (Duin, 2007a).

The basic idea of cross-impact analysis is to get a systemic picture of the rough structure of a complex system supporting long-term planning and assessment tasks. In difference to other simulation approaches like system dynamics, causal cross-impact analysis is not used to generate prognostic data, but to analyse effects over and above a business-as-usual scenario provided by the end user.

The end-user (the steering committee, which will commonly develop the model) generates different scenarios by applying action vectors (representing different strategic options) and/or setting uncontrollable events, which might strongly influence the system under consideration. The basic elements of cross-impact analysis in the context of VBEs have been introduced by Eschenbächer and Duin (2009).

The ARCON reference model (Afsarmanesh & Camarinha-Matos, 2008) provides a sub-division of the endogenous and exogenous view on any CNO which can be used as a general modelling guideline for the cross-impact analysis. The endogenous view is divided into four dimensions:

- **Structural Dimension**. This dimension focuses on the structure or composition of the CNO regarding its constituting elements (members and their mutual interactions) and the roles as performed by the involved actors. Other characteristics of the network nodes such as the location, time, etc. are also included.
- **Componential Dimension**. This dimension addresses the tangible and intangible elements in the CNO's network as a whole including the available resources such as staff, hard- and software resources, data, information and knowledge. Note that not all of those elements are physically existing objects but represent the components the network is based of. Additionally, this dimension also covers ontology and any descriptions of the important basic information.
- **Functional Dimension**. This dimension consists of differentiating the 'base operations' potentially executed at the network level in terms of time-sequenced flows of operations (processes and procedures). This dimension is related to the operational phase of the life cycle as described above.
- **Behavioural Dimension**. This dimension involves all the principles, policies, and governance rules which determine the behaviour of the CNO and its members. This includes elements such as collaboration principles and rules of conduct, any contracts, conflict resolution policies, etc.

The exogenous view is also divided into four dimensions:

- **Market Dimension**. The marketing dimension concerns all issues related to the interactions with customers (or potential beneficiaries) on the one side and the competitors on the other side. Interaction with customers includes elements like transactions and established commitments (contracts), marketing, branding, etc. Competition related issues include market positioning, market strategy, policies, etc. Additionally, the purpose or mission of the CNO, its value proposition, and joint identity is also considered in the scope of this dimension.

- **Support Dimension**. This dimension collects all the issues related to support services which are provided by third parties. Examples are: certification services, insurance services, training, consulting, etc.
- **Societal Dimension**. This dimension covers all interactions between the network and the society in general. Even if this perspective may has a quite broad scope its purpose is the modelling of any impact the CNO potentially has on the society (e.g. effects on unemployment, sustainability, and ecological situation). This also includes any constraints and facilitating elements such as legal issues, administrative decisions, demographic development, etc.
- **Constituency Dimension**. This dimension addresses the interaction of the network with the all potentially new members. General strategic issues like the sustainability of the network, attraction factors, what creates a sense of community, or specific aspects such as rules of adhesion and specific 'marketing' policies for members, are considered here.

Table 1 shows how these dimensions can be used to structure the cross-impact model to be developed to support strategic decision making on the network level. A number of variables are defined for each dimension and inter-connected by cross-impacts in a later stage. The presentation and discussion of the complete model and its simulation results goes beyond the scope of this chapter.

The presentation and discussion of the complete model and its simulation results goes beyond the scope of this chapter, but it is further elaborated by Duin (Duin, 2008; Duin, Eschenbächer, & Thoben, 2009).

FUTURE RESEARCH DIRECTIONS

Currently the focus is changing from VBEs towards Digital Business Ecosystems (DBE) as introduced by Nachira, Dini, & Nicolai (2007). A digital ecosystem can be described as the technical infrastructure, based e.g. on a P2P distributed software technology that transports, finds, and connects services and information over a network like the Internet enabling. This allows the distribution of all the digital 'objects' present within the infrastructure. Such an 'organisms of the digital world' encompass useful digital representations that can be interpreted and processed (by computer software or humans), e.g. software applications, services, knowledge, taxonomies, folksonomies, ontologies, descriptions of skills, reputation and trust relationships, training modules, contractual

Table 1. Variables defined for Cross-Impact Analysis structured by ARCON Views

Endogenous View	Exogenous View
Structural Dimension *Number of VBE Members* *VBE Complexity*	Market Dimension *Market Share* *Competition*
Componential Dimension *Staff Capabilities* *Appropriateness of Re sources*	Support Dimension *Supporting Completeness* *Appropriateness of Supporting Institutions*
Functional Dimension *Appropriateness of Functions* *Complexity of Functions*	Societal Dimension *Society Climate Index* *Ecological Sustainability*
Behavioural Dimension *Collaboration Index* *Openness of VBE*	Constituency Dimension *Members' Satisfaction* *VBE Complexity*

frameworks, laws. A business ecosystem represents an economic community supported by a foundation of interacting organisations and individuals – the 'organisms of the business world'. This economic community produces goods and services of value for customers, who themselves are members of the ecosystem. A healthy ecosystem is in balance between cooperation and competition in a dynamic free market.

The DBE concept is currently the basic concept in ongoing projects like COIN (www.coin-ip.eu) which develops Enterprise Collaboration and Enterprise Interoperability platforms enabling open and dynamic digital business ecosystems.

Another prevailing research subject is the 'Internet of Things' which refers to a network of objects, such as cars or even parts of a car like the engine. The idea is that physical goods are represented in the Internet providing an interface which allows the exchange of information with that physical part. For an engine this can be e.g. runtime or temperature information. The implementation of such a concept would allow the definition of a new range of business opportunities including E-Business options for SMEs. In June 2009 the Commission of the European Communities communicated the 'Internet of Things – An Action Plan for Europe' (CEC, 2009).

CONCLUSION

This chapter has introduced the concepts of Virtual Organisations (VO) and their Breeding Environments (VBE). Whereas the VOs are created to respond to occurring E-Business activities, the VBE is responsible to prepare all partners for the event of occurring E-Business opportunities. The VBE is the organisational frame where strategic planning and management takes place on the network level. Furthermore, this chapter has shown how the strategic planning process could look like on the network level and the cross-impact analysis method can be applied using VBE relevant variables.

Especially for SMEs it is important to be prepared for E-Business opportunities. This can only be achieved with the right organisational structure (e.g. enterprise networks, i.e. a Collaborative Networked Organisation) and with appropriate planning and management methods and tools in place.

ACKNOWLEDGMENT

This work has been partly funded by the European Commission through IST Integrating Project COIN: COllaboration and INteroperability for networked enterprises (EU FP7 Project 216256; www.coin-ip.eu) of the 7th Framework Research Programme.

REFERENCES

ACS. (2002). *Annual Report 2002. WWW [On-line]*. Retrieved from http://www.acs-giz.si/pic/pdf/Letno-porocilo-(Annual-report)-2002.pdf.

Afsarmanesh, H., & Camarinha-Matos, L. M. (2008). The ARCON Modelling Framework. In Camarinha-Matos, L. M., & Afsarmanesh, H. (Eds.), *Collaborative Networks: Reference Modelling* (pp. 67–82). New York: Springer.

Afsarmanesh, H., & Camarinha-Matos, L. M. (2009). On the classification and management of Virtual Organisation Breeding Environments. *International Journal of Information Technology and Management*, *8*, 234–259. doi:10.1504/IJITM.2009.024604

Baier, A. (2007). *High Performance in der Automobilzulieferindustrie. WWW [On-line]*. Retrieved from http://www.automotive-rheinland.de/content/P5_accenture_270307_kurzfassung.pdf.

Becker, H. (2006). *High Noon in the Automotive Industry*. Berlin, Heidelberg: Springer.

Busen, D. (2004). The ACS to Co-Operate in Establishing the Serbian Auto Cluster. *ACS News*, *1*, 7.

Camarinha-Matos, L. M., & Afsarmanesh, H. (2005). Collaborative Networks: A New Scientific Discipline. *Journal of Intelligent Manufacturing*, *16*, 439–452. doi:10.1007/s10845-005-1656-3

Camarinha-Matos, L. M., & Afsarmanesh, H. (2006). Collaborative Networks: Value Creation in a Knowledge Society. In K. Wang, G. L. Kovacs, M. Wozny, & M. Fang (Eds.), *PROLAMAT'06: The IFIP TC 5 International Conference on Knowledge Enterprise* (pp. 26-40). Boston: Springer.

Camarinha-Matos, L. M., & Afsarmanesh, H. (2007). A Framework for Virtual Organization Creation in a Breeding Environment. *Annual Reviews in Control*, *31*, 119–135. doi:10.1016/j.arcontrol.2007.03.006

Camarinha-Matos, L. M., & Afsarmanesh, H. (2008). Classes of Collaborative Networks. In G.Putnik & M. M. Cunha (Eds.), *Encyclopedia of Networked and Virtual Organizations* (pp. 193-198). Hershey, PA: Information Science Reference (IGI Global).

CEC. (2009). *Internet of Things - An Action Plan for Europe. WWW [On-line]*. Retrieved from http://ec.europa.eu/information_society/policy/rfid/documents/commiot2009.pdf.

Daimler (2009). Daimler Supplier Network. WWW [On-line].

Dannenberg, J., & Kleinhans, C. (2005). The Coming Age of Collaboration in the Automotive Industry. *Mercer Management Journal*, *17*, 88–94.

Duin, H. (2007a). In Thoben, K.-D., Baalsrud Hauge, J., Smeds, R., & Riis, J. O. (Eds.), *Causal Cross-Impact Analysis as a Gaming Tool for Strategic Decision Making* (pp. 79–93). Aachen: Verlag Mainz.

Duin, H. (2007b). In Camarinha-Matos, L. M., Afsarmanesh, H., Novais, P., & Abalide, C. (Eds.), *Causal Cross-Impact Analysis as Strategic Planning Aid for Virtual Organisation Breeding Environments* (pp. 147–154). New York: Springer.

Duin, H. (2008). In Camarinha-Matos, L. M., & Picard, W. (Eds.), *Systemic Strategic Managment for VBEs in the Manufacturing Sector* (pp. 25–32). New York: Springer.Duin, H., Eschenbächer, J., & Thoben, K.-D. (2009). Strategische Planung in Unternehmensnetzwerken. *Industrie Management*, *25*, 9–12.

Eschenbächer, J., & Duin, H. (2009). A Forecasting Concept for Virtual Organisations Supporting SMEs. In Cruz-Cunha, M. M. (Ed.), *Enterprise Information Systems for Business Integration in SMEs: Technological, Organizational and Social Dimensions* (pp. 76–101). Hershey, PA: IGI Global.

Gausemeier, J., Fink, A., & Schlake, O. (1998). Scenario Management: An Approach to Develop Future Potentials. *Technological Forecasting and Social Change*, *59*, 111–130. doi:10.1016/S0040-1625(97)00166-2

Götze, U. (1993). *Szenario-Technik in der strategischen Unternehmensplanung*. Wiesbaden: Deutscher Universitäts-Verlag.

Grosz, A. (2008). *Intellectual Capacity Report for Pannon Automotive Cluster (PANAC). WWW [On-line]*. Retrieved from http://www.ricarda-project.org/downloads/ICR-panac.pdf.

GzS/izGTM (2008). *Introduction to Innovative Groups of Slovenia. Innovative Clusters and Technology Networks*. Chamber of Commerce Slovenia (GzS) und National Center of Clusters and Technology Networks (izGTM).

Helmer, O. (1977). Problems in Futures Research: Delphi and Causal Cross-Impact Analysis. *Futures*, *9*, 17–31. doi:10.1016/0016-3287(77)90049-0

Helmer, O. (1981). Reassessment of Cross-Impact Analysis. *Futures*, *13*, 389–400. doi:10.1016/0016-3287(81)90124-5

Hüttenrauch, M., & Baum, M. (2008). *Effiziente Vielfalt. Die dritte Revolution in der Automobilindustrie*. Berlin, Heidelberg: Springer-Verlag.

Jagdev, H. S., Brennan, A., & Browne, J. (2004). *Strategic Decision Making in Modern Manufacturing*. Boston: Kluwer Academic Publishers.

Jaklic, M., Svetina, A. C., & Zagorsek, H. (2008). Specific Responses to Universal Pressures in the Industry - Comparing European Automotive Clusters. WWW [On-line]. Retrieved from http://miha.ef.uni-lj.si/_dokumenti/wp/paper_jaklic_cotic_zagorsek.doc.

Jansson, K., & Thoben, K.-D. (2005). The Extended Products Paradigm, An Introduction. In Arai, E., Kimura, F., Goossenaerts, J., & Shirase, K. (Eds.), *Knowledge and Skill Chains in Engineering and Manufacturing. Information Infrastructure in the Era of Global Communications* (pp. 39–47). New York: Springer. doi:10.1007/0-387-23572-2_5

Krauth, J., Duin, H., & Schimmel, A. (1998). A Comparison of Tools for Strategic Simulation and Scenario Generation with Special Emphasis on 'Soft Factors'. *Simulation Practice and Theory*, *6*, 23–33. doi:10.1016/S0928-4869(97)00005-0

Kürümlüoglu, M., Nostdal, R., & Karvonen, I. (2005). Base Concepts. In Camarinha-Matos, L. M., Afsarmanesh, H., & Ollus, M. (Eds.), *Virtual Organizations. Systems and Practices* (pp. 11–28). New York: Springer. doi:10.1007/0-387-23757-7_2

Meier, A., & Stormer, H. (2009). *eBusiness & eCommerce*. Berlin, Heidelberg: Springer-Verlag.

Mintzberg, H., Ahlstrand, B., & Lampel, J. (1998). *Strategy Safari. A Guided Tour through the Wilds of Strategic Management*. New York: The Free Press.

Nachira, F., Dini, P., & Nicolai, A. (2007). A Network of Digital Business Ecosystems for Europe: Roots, Processes and Perspectives. WWW [On-line]. Retrieved from http://www.digital-ecosystems.org/book/DBE-2007.pdf.

Raisinghani, M. S., Herwick, L. B., Pulamsetti, R., Gunther, T. H., Caisan, V., & Wang, A. (2005). E-Business in the Global Automotive Industry: Key Value Propositions. In Lan, Y.-C. (Ed.), *Global Information Society. Operating Information Systems in a Dynamic Global Business Environment* (pp. 240–264). Hershey, PA: Idea Group Publishing.

Romero Diaz, D. C. (2007). *An Instantiation Methodology for Virtual Breeding Environment Management*. Master Thesis. Campus Monterrey, Mexiko.

Santoro, R., & Bifulco, A. (2005). Survey of Industriel Case Studies. In Camarinha-Matos, L. M., Afsarmanesh, H., & Ollus, M. (Eds.), *Virtual Organizations. Systems and Practices* (pp. 201–220). Berlin, Heidelberg, New York: Springer. doi:10.1007/0-387-23757-7_14

Silberberger, H. (2003). *Collaborative Business und Web Services*. Berlin, Heidelberg, New York: Springer-Verlag.

Sturm, F., Kemp, J., & Wendel de Joode, R. v. (2004). Towards Strategic Management in Collaborative Network Structures. In Camarinha-Matos, L. M., & Afsarmanesh, H. (Eds.), *Collaborative Networked Organisations. A Research Agenda for Emerging Business Models* (pp. 131–138). Boston: Kluwer Academic Publishers. doi:10.1007/1-4020-7833-1_16

Walton, J. S. (2008). Scanning Beyond the Horizon: Exploring the Ontological and Epistemological Basis for Scenario Planning. *Advances in Developing Human Resources*, *10*, 147–165. doi:10.1177/1523422307304101

Chapter 4
E-Learning for SMEs:
Challenges, Potential and Impact

Asbjorn Rolstadas
Norwegian University of Science and Technology, Norway

Bjorn Andersen
Norwegian University of Science and Technology, Norway

Manuel Fradinho
Cyntelix, The Netherlands

ABSTRACT

SMEs have a special need to be able to collect knowhow from the global community and implement this as competence in the enterprise. E-Learning is an approach for competence development that can assist SMEs in creating a learning organization. There are different approaches to E-Learning. Amongst the most powerful ones is the application of serious games. The PRIME project conducted experiments with serious games in project business and in manufacturing. This has resulted in a set of guidelines for successful implementation of games in an organization. It is necessary to allow a learning curve and put emphasis on the social context to obtain effective learning. For delivery of E-Learning the hybrid learning model is recommended. SMEs are advised to develop E-Learning in cooperation with academic institutions, and to use real life cases and problems for assignments. Delivery should be based on proven technology when used in SMEs.

INTRODUCTION

The extended enterprise is being implemented worldwide using different e-business technology. To be on the competitive arena today requires cutting-edge competence not only on the products supplied, but also in all aspects of business operation and competence development. ICT is in this respect an extremely powerful tool enabling enterprises to work globally and allowing creation of supply chains, enterprise networks, and learning communities. For SMEs this represents a challenge. SMEs have limited resources to drive this technology, but are at the same time dependent on access to the same technology. There is a special need to be able to collect knowhow from the global community and implement this as competence in the enterprise.

E-Learning is an approach for competence development that can assist SMEs in creating a

DOI: 10.4018/978-1-61692-880-3.ch004

learning organization. E-Learning allows learning at the time, place, and pace decided by the learner. It enables tailoring of learning content to the needs of the user and facilitates collaborative learning and access to expert teachers wherever they might be. Recent research from previous and on-going EU-projects (GEM, PRIME, and TARGET) has been able to demonstrate some of the power of E-Learning, or more correctly "technology-enhanced learning". Some key research findings from these projects will be presented together with a case study on practical implementations of E-Learning solutions in industry.

The GEM project developed a framework of a curriculum for manufacturing strategy. The project included a study of different delivery methods. The PRIME project used serious games to train middle management in decision making. It was tested through demonstrators for repetitive manufacturing and for project based business. The TARGET project is ongoing and is studying different learning approaches based on concepts for technology-enhanced learning (TEL).

The objectives of this chapter is to discuss different E-Learning approaches that are relevant for SMEs based on research findings from the mentioned projects and to develop an agenda for future research for competence development in SMEs using advanced ICT. It indirectly explore how SMEs can exploit E-Business by discussing how innovative E-Learning approaches can be used to facilitate transfer of knowledge and building of experience. This new knowledge and experience can in turn be leveraged by SMEs to develop and experiment with E-Business strategies.

E-LEARNING BACKGROUND

There exists a number of questionnaire-based evaluation approaches for E-Learning (Sage, 2002, U.S.I.G., 2003, Carliner, 2002, Hughes, 2003). They indicate four essential areas for evaluation (Schwesig, Rolstadås, and Thoben, 2005):

- E-Learning content - the preparation and the selection of content
- E-Learning approach - the instructional approach of the E-Learning course
- E-Learning delivery mechanism - the actual design of the learning environment
- Overall assessment- general questions, strengths and weaknesses, suggestions for improvement for the course

In this context, we will focus on E-Learning approach and delivery mechanisms.

E-Learning Approaches

Most SMEs are, in terms of organizational structure, fairly simply designed, with few departments or units. On the other hand, this means that typically employees are involved in more than one function or discipline required to run the company. In such integrated areas, decisions are taken that have a crucial influence on the competitiveness and profitability of a company. These decisions relate to questions like various strategic management tasks, product portfolio, product program, competitor strength, competition parameters, market segmentation, project planning, innovation management, process management, etc.

These integrated areas all require competences that go beyond the narrow technical competences that can be acquired easily and affordably through traditional courses or training. As complexity and dynamics in the internal and external specialization and collaborations increase, the need for training and competence development increases as well. In terms of competence development, organizations therefore have concrete needs that are not met well by traditional learning approaches:

- Reduce the time it takes an employee to acquire the necessary competences to do their job in the most efficient and effective manner;

- Change the learning context rapidly and in response to the real world;
- Facilitate knowledge sharing within an organization;
- Support a soft failure environment where mistakes have no impact on the real world, thus promoting a willingness to engage in measured risk taking, focused on achieving a high level of polished performance in the real world

The above are a response to market pressures, but society itself has also gone through changes as a result of the advances of technology. For example, the way people scan reading material has changed significantly due to the World Wide Web, thus having a significant impact on marketing strategies (Meyer, Chall, Onofrey, and Rose, 1998). With E-Learning it is no different and already there are signs that E-Learning needs to take account of the enhanced abilities of the so-called gamer generation, such as differences in cognitive processes when compared to non-gamers, which can give gamers a competitive edge in fast-changing market situations such as arise in economic downturns (Herring and Job, 2008). This has implications for organizations that need to change work environments and business practices to face new challenges. In this light games can be seen as the most recent element in E-Learning offering new and different approaches to organizations in their effort to upgrade and enhance competences.

Traditionally, problems have been seen as complicated challenges that should be solved through breaking them down into smaller and smaller chunks. Seen from the solution perspective, the solutions then emerge by solving the problems related to the smaller chunks. Largely, this reflects an analytical way of thinking. In such regimes, learning and training are also related to the smaller chunks. By training the competences behind the smaller chunks the person gradually becomes able to meet the challenges.

We experience that most modern problems are more frequently complex rather than complicated. Complex problems are messier and more ambiguous in nature; they are more connected to other and often very different problems; more likely to react in unpredictable non-linear ways; and more likely to produce unintended consequences. Most organizations have been designed to deal with a complicated rather than a complex world. Hierarchical and silo structures are perfectly designed to break problems down into more manageable fragments. They are not, however, so effective in handling high levels of complexity. For this reason many institutions and companies are now struggling to adapt to a more complex world.

The Cynefin (the word has a Welsh origin and is pronounced *kun-ev'rin*) framework proposes an association between the nature of context of problems and appropriate responses (Snowdon & Boone, 2007). The Cynefin framework consists of five domains (see figure 1 for an adapted version):

- Simple, in which the relationship between cause and effect is obvious and the appropriate approach is to Sense – Categorize – Respond
- Complicated, in which the relationship between cause and effect requires analysis or some other form of investigation and/or the application of expert knowledge,

Figure 1. The Cynefin Framework

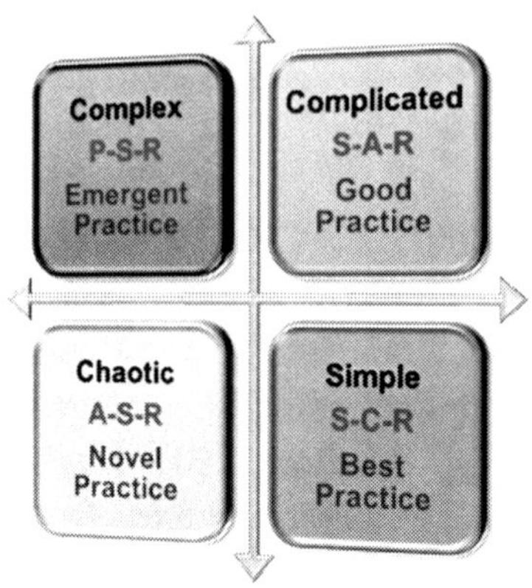

and the appropriate approach is Sense – Analyze – Respond
- Complex, in which the relationship between cause and effect can only be perceived in retrospect, but not in advance, and the appropriate approach is Probe – Sense – Respond
- Chaotic, in which there is no relationship between cause and effect at systems level, and the appropriate approach is to Act – Sense – Respond
- Disorder – in which it is unclear what type of causality exists. Disorder is in the centre of the framework. Here people will revert to their own comfort zone and choose the approach related hereto.

Each domain of the Cynefin framework represents different levels of expected achieved practice. In the simple domain, we can expect "Best Practice". In the complicated domain, we can expect "Good Practice". In the complex domain, we can expect "Emergent Practice", and in the chaotic domain, we can expect "Novel Practice".

These expectations relate to the nature of the problems. Heavily process-oriented situations, such as loan payment processing, are often simple contexts. Directives are straightforward, decisions can be easily delegated, and functions can be automated. As problems become complicated, they tend to require assistance from specialists: A car owner may know that something is wrong with his car because the engine is knocking, but he has to take it to a mechanic to diagnose the problem.

When problems become complex, the clear pattern between cause and effect disappears. We can understand why things happen only in retrospect. Instructive patterns, however, can emerge if the leader conducts experiments that are safe to fail. That is why, instead of attempting to impose a course of action, we must patiently allow the path forward to reveal itself. We need to probe first, then sense, and then respond. There is a scene in the film Apollo 13 where the astronauts encounter a crisis that moves the situation into a complex domain. A group of experts is put in a room with a mishmash of materials – bits of plastic and odds and ends that mirror the resources available to the astronauts in the flight. The team is told: This is what you have; find a solution or the astronauts will die. None of those experts knew a priori what would work. Instead, they had to let a solution emerge from the materials at hand.

In the chaotic context, searching for right answers would be pointless: The relationships between cause and effect are impossible to determine because they shift constantly, and no manageable patterns exist – only turbulence. Here we must first act to establish order, then sense where stability is present and from where it is absent, and then respond by working to transform the situation from chaos to complexity, where the identification of emerging patterns can both help prevent future crises and discern new opportunities.

The analytical learning and competence building approach that has proven efficient when dealing with simple and complicated problems proves inefficient when confronted with complex problems. In short the "probe" element is missing in traditional approaches, and the "sense" element appears to be very different when dealing with complex problems compared to complicated and simple problems.

The probe and sense elements seem to be crucial when dealing with complex problems. This is supported by a number of research results published in the past 30 years. In 1984 David Kolb published his book title "Experimental Learning" (Kolb, 1984). His claim is that we are learning by cyclic patterns of four types of activities: Concrete experience, reflective observation, abstract conceptualization, and active experimentation (see figure 2). According to Kolb it does not matter where we start - the important requirement for real learning is that one goes through the full cycle.

Though Kolb's work is aiming at the individual level there are several contributions supporting that a similar pattern is valid at the orga-

Figure 2. David Kolb's learning circle

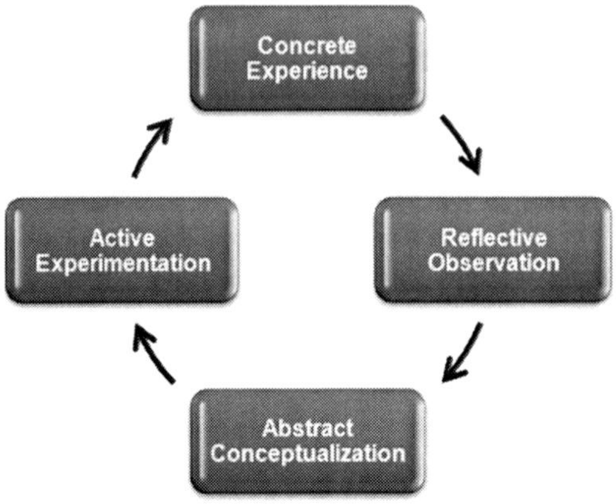

nizational level. Dorothy Leonard argues that: "The primary activities spawning organizational learning are experimentation and prototyping" (Leonard-Barton, 1995) and Argyris and Schön (1978) have introduced the notion of single-loop and double-loop learning which includes active experimentation.

Donald Schön has been studying how professionals are working very differently from novices. His point is that when people have reached a certain level of professionalism it will change their working style and they become "reflecting practitioners" (Schön, 1983). The reflective practitioner is in a constant process of thinking, reflecting, acting, and building experience – very much in line with the learning process as described by Kolb. This process is efficient for the professional person but due to the amount of tacit knowledge it is often difficult to articulate and share the results with others (Polanyi, 1967). Physical models or other model representations seem to be the most efficient means to facilitate this sharing (and learning) process (Schrage, 2000).

In his book, Serious Play, Michael Schrage (2000) praises many aspects of prototyping for speeding up processes etc. and mentions examples of great breakthroughs made by new prototyping tools. The following extracts provide exemplary viewpoints from the book:

- When talented musicians improvise, you don't look inside their minds; you listen to what they play. When talented innovators innovate, you don't listen to the specs they quote. You look at the models they've created.
- The challenge of converting uncertainty into manageable risks or opportunities explains why serious play is often the most rational behavior for innovators.
- Serious play is about improvising with the unanticipated in ways that create new value.
- Prototypes engage the organization's thinking in the explicit. They externalize thought and spark conversation.
- Prototypes force confrontation with the tyranny of trade-offs.
- The conventional wisdom that "innovation processes" drive prototype development is misleading. Empirical observations of organizations with effective innovation cultures confirm just the opposite: changes in prototypes and simulations drive the innovation process.
- Prototypes are machine tools for producing choice.

- Most companies have formal prototyping processes and informal prototyping cultures.

Schrage (2000) argues against the common assumption that "great teams make prototypes" and suggests that instead one should realize that "prototypes make great teams". The making of great teams goes beyond the individual team, but helps create teams out of people with different backgrounds by creating "shared space". Shared space is the common ground where people can meet on even terms and objectively discuss matters.

Obviously, physical and mental prototypes provide opportunities to probe and sense. They invite for questioning and challenging of conventional wisdom (March, 2006) and thereby learning and competence development can be supported.

One of the most promising, future oriented concepts of E-Learning is the use of serious games. (This concept will be described more detailed in a later section.) The game culture has been studied by Oliveira, Andersen, Oliveira, and Rolstadås (2006). They assessed the culture and its impact using a questionnaire consisting of 48 questions. The results of the survey demonstrate that the gamer generation is not as prominent in Europe as in the United States, but present nonetheless. The managers, who experienced an upbringing with the influence of digital games, demonstrated an advantage over those that did not share the same background. Throughout all the statements aimed at capturing a respondent's thoughts and motivation on particular topics, the gamers revealed an edge and advantage over those without gaming experience.

Delivery Mechanisms

Delivery of E-Learning relies heavily on Internet-based technologies (Rolstadås, 2002; Lefrere, 2007). Technology, the fast outdating of knowledge and training, the desire for just-in-time training delivery, and the continuous hunt for cost-effective methods to meet learning requirements have redefined the processes of design, development, and delivery of training and education (Urdan and Weggen, 2000). Several terms have been used to characterize the new methods of E-Learning including: technology-enhanced learning, distributed learning, online learning, and web-based learning. Many educational organizations are experimenting with E-Learning, using intranets, websites, and multimedia solutions, and a great deal has been written about the issues and problems encountered in these attempts (Hall & Snider, 2000; Urdan & Weggen, 2000; Berge, 1998). However, by giving careful consideration to the design and implementation of E-Learning, successful courses that take full advantage of the benefits enabled by the technology can be created.

Delivery of E-Learning content can be synchronous or asynchronous. The alternate use of video, audio, pictures, text, (interactive) animations, quizzes and chat, and discussion boards should assure that both styles can be covered (Rolstadås and Hussein, 2002). Whatever the choice of learning communication, the learning success heavily depends on the actual form of mediation. According to Dale (1969), passive learning activities like reading texts or watching a demonstration result in the fact that just 10% (reading) or 30% (watching) of the content is remembered afterwards. Active involvement within the learning process, like participating in a discussion, leads to the fact that the learners can remember about 70% of the related content afterwards (Dale, 1969). Accordingly, content needs to be delivered on the basis of active learning. In order to assure the appropriate employment of the mentioned design elements and the application of active learning elements, design guidelines have been used explaining the correct use of pictures and texts, (interactive) animations, quizzes, chat/messaging video, and audio. Kommers, Grabinger, and Dunlap (1996) present a number of design elements such as pictures and text, animations, quizzes, chats, messaging, video, audio, games, and laboratories that can bring maximum benefit to the learner.

A powerful concept for delivery is based on the concept of the hybrid learning published by Rolstadås and Hussein (2002). They claim that this type of mixed instructional delivery has proved to be an effective tool for enhancing the learning value for the workforce. Applying this approach may also lead to significant reduction in learning time. The hybrid solution is well suited for large organizations distributed over a large geographic area. Thus, the target group may be characterized by diverse social, cultural, and academic background. Therefore, it is important that the model enables multiple learning styles.

According to Rolstadås and Hussein (2002), the hybrid model must contain the following properties:

- Create an environment for learning that addresses multiple learning styles
- Ensure active participation and to focus on accommodating the learners' former experiences
- Enable the learners to build personal and possibly social networks
- Use information and communication technology for designing the content in order to enrich the learning experience
- Restrict the use of on-campus delivery whenever high level of interactivity between the learners themselves is required or between the learners and the content
- Availability in the form of an updated support system that assists the learners on the academic, technical, and administrative level
- Learners should be motivated and self-disciplined and using education in order to achieve clear goals.

The hybrid model is based on a mixture of on-campus plenary learning sessions (face to face), self paced learning using rich media through virtual classroom, and collaborative group work using collaborative ICT tools included in the virtual classroom.

IMPROVING BUSINESS DECISION CAPABILITY USING SERIOUS GAMES

The knowledge-based economy has redefined the rules of economic development with continual and ever-more rapid industrial and social changes. Enterprises have realized that knowledge workers are a key to a company's productivity, competitive edge, and ability to adapt to changes in markets and customers. A highly educated, well-trained, and adaptable workforce is a key element in competitiveness, productivity, and the growth of employment, thus life-long learning (Aspin and Chapman, 2000) anywhere and anytime has become a fundamental strategy of the knowledge-based organisations. This is corroborated by the report of the Task Force on Employment, chaired by Wim Kok (2004), and the Spring European Council of 2004 stressed that Europe must invest more, and more effectively, in its human capital. These recommendations are clearly guiding the revised Lisbon Knowledge Society initiative, the i2010 Strategy. However, tailoring effective E-Learning frameworks within organizations is highly challenging and its promises have not been highly successful in addressing the challenge of supporting life-long learning of knowledge workers. Within SMEs, the challenges of deploying successfully an E-Learning framework are exacerbated due to their focus on immediate business survival.

As pointed out by Romiszowski (2004), the failure of E-Learning can be associated to some common mistakes, which are rooted in the focus on the technology itself rather than on the impact of technology in the context of human-activity systems (i.e., education and training systems). A

Figure 3. The four generations of serious games according to their driving learning theories

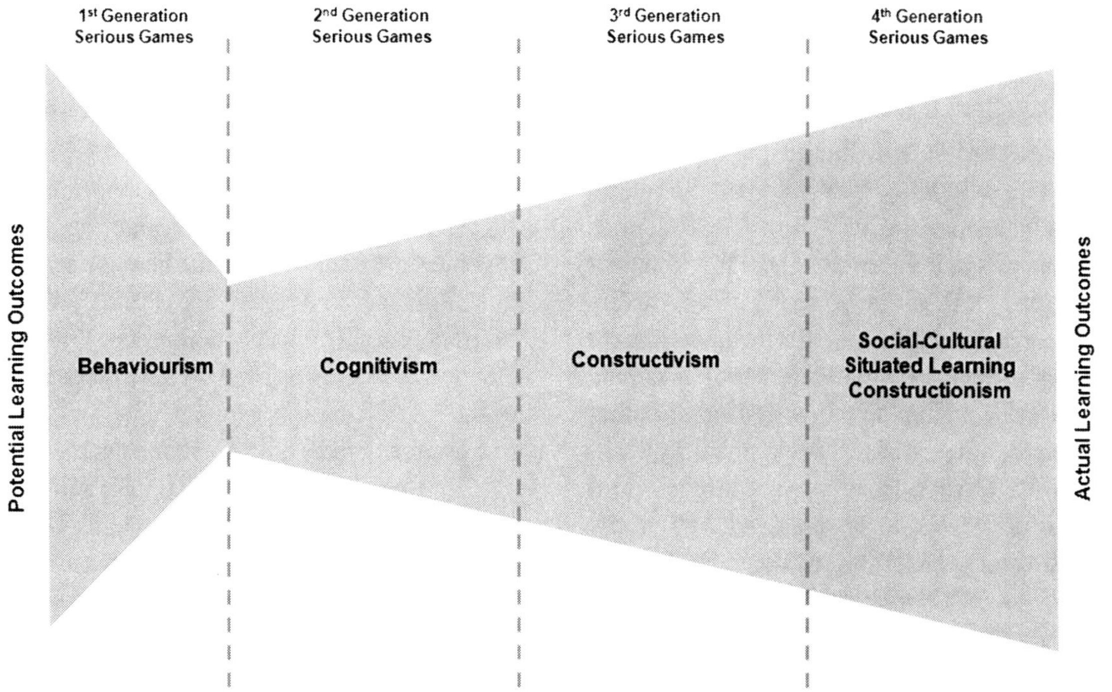

promising technological innovation in E-Learning platforms is the use of digital games, which according to Prensky (2001) introduces play into the learning process, an essential missing factor in traditional technology-enhanced learning (TEL) platforms since learning is more than education. In fact, the most common term currently in use is serious games, where the flow engagement of digital games is merged with concrete learning outcomes. Although only recently have serious games gained more prominence in mainstream learning environments, one may consider that a total of 3 generations have taken place with a 4th generation emerging (figure 3).

The first generation focused on learners acquiring designated behaviors through conditioning and reinforcements. The approach is only interested in directly observable behavior based on stimuli and response. The learning theory does not take into account that learners are different from one another and assumes that a learner acquires a skill provided it is practiced enough times. This led to the second generation where the focus shifts from the behavior to the learner and their internal cognitive constructs to represent knowledge. However, the feasibility of knowing precisely the learner's cognitive processes is limited. The third generation relies on constructivism, which still focuses on the learner, but from the outside. In this case, the learners build and constructs their knowledge by interacting with the environment and each learner acquires the knowledge in their own way. Finally, the current generation of serious games is based on situated learning where constructivism is complemented by social processes that are necessary for learners to externalize knowledge.

PRIME Case Description

Providing Real Integration in a Multi-disciplinary Environment (PRIME) is a serious game on the borderline between the 3rd and 4th generation, but exploiting some of the key strengths of cognitivism. The PRIME serious game was the result of a European IST project (FP6-016542), that aims to give business professionals in strategic manufacturing a learning environment where they can experiment with new ideas and learn the effects of their decision making. The PRIME serious game consists of a Virtual Business Environment (VBE) that defines the global business reality where users are responsible for the management of a single Business Unit (enterprise). A crucial characteristic, if not the strongest contributing factor, to learning is the feedback capability available to the learner. In addition, emotions (fun) are also connected to learning, where "people learn in direct proportion to the amount of fun they are having" (Rose and Nicholl, 1997). The VBE provides real-time feedback to all the user's interactions and being a serious game, it focuses on providing a fun and engaging environment for users. The management breakdown of a business unit is based on eight functional units: Production, Product Development, Sales, Human Resources, Strategic Marketing, Distribution, Finance and Information Systems. Associated to each functional unit is a set of operation processes that are based on an input-transformation-output model.

The block diagram of figure 4 corresponds to the PRIME conceptual model, illustrating the interplay of the global business environment and the different business units, each controlled by either a human player or an artificial stakeholder (agent).

The heart of the PRIME Concept Model is the set of Decision Flows where each flow consists of a linked graph of strategic decisions, which have far-reaching consequences for an organization and typically involve the commitment of vast resources. The decisions play out over long time frames and have significant opportunity costs. Strategic decisions often must be made under conditions of substantial uncertainty, particularly when complex policy objectives must be reformulated in the face of a dynamic, sometimes volatile strategic environment. Initial assumptions about the environment and other players may be incorrect or incomplete. The Decision Flows were shaped by applying a methodology based on Critical Incident Technique (CIT) (Flanagan, 1954) to capture the decisions supported by the PRIME Serious Game, which can be aggregated together in the following main categories: Logistics, Product Innovation and R&D, Sales and Strategic Marketing, Production, and Finance. In essence, the Decision Flows define the game play of the PRIME serious game, which is an innovative approach to defining a serious game.

The implementation of the VBE relies on a hierarchical simulation model (Duin, Oliveira, and Saffarpour, 2007), which relies on a set of well-defined Key Performance Indicators (KPIs), such as throughput, defect rate, turnover, number of sold products, etc, which are derived from the underlying measures of the simulation model. KPIs describe how the operation process is performing. An initial set of KPIs is given to the user based on the ENAPS Framework (ENAPS Consortium, 2001). The supporting simulation model is extensible, thus it is permissible for an end-user to add more KPIs.

The PRIME Serious Game is based on two game modes:

- **Corporate**. The corporate mode provides an overview of the organization and the necessary information to support high-level strategic decisions. By default, the mode is dominated by the geographical global view. This view only exists in Corporate Mode and the player may extract information on geography, demographics, macroeconomics and political systems.
- **Site**. The site mode provides fine granular detail, it is necessary for the player to switch from corporate mode into Site Mode to make localized strategic decisions.

Figure 4. PRIME Conceptual Model

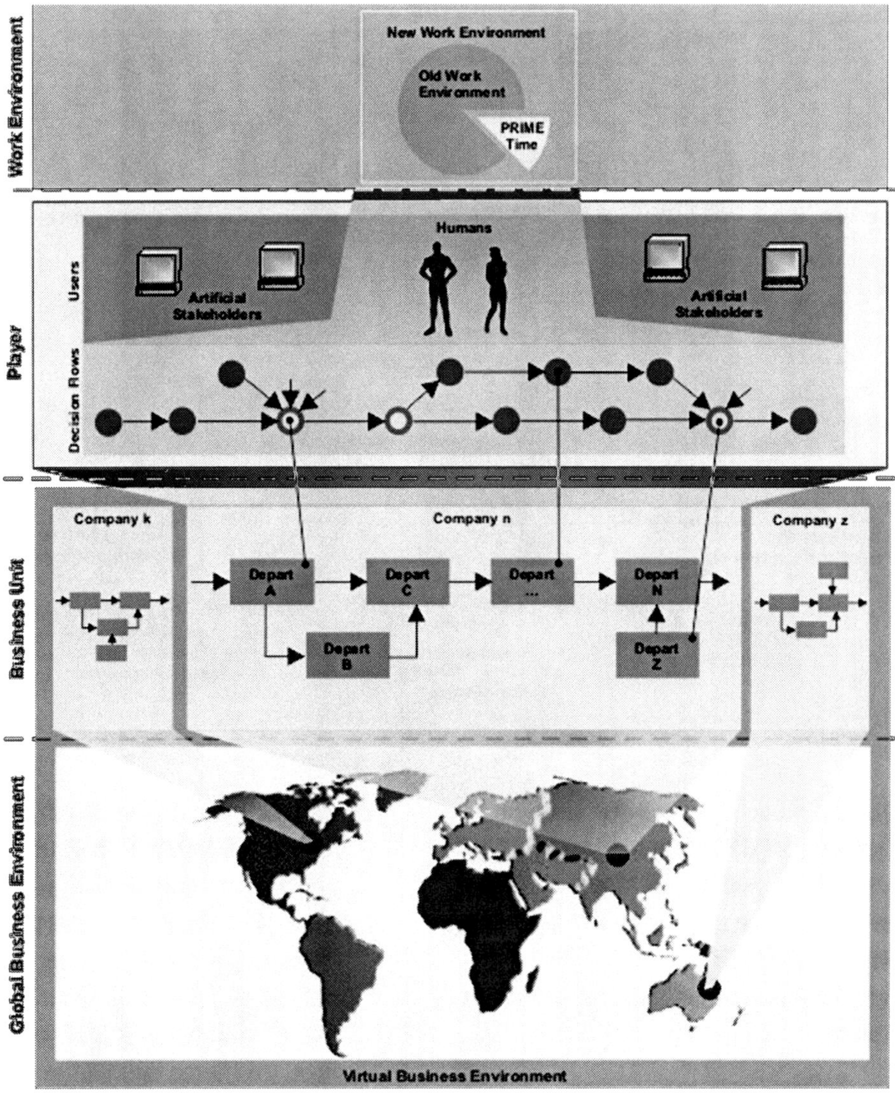

The image of figure 5 shows an example of PRIME in corporate mode. It is extracted from the prototype corresponding to the final release version of the software, which again is corresponding to a fully working prototype.

Evaluation

The PRIME serious game was evaluated in six end-user companies, from different industrial sectors and with different characteristics:

- Fiat (automotive)
- IAI (aerospace)
- Intracom (telecommunications)
- Kesz (construction)
- Lego (toy industry)
- Siemens (software)

The resulting population sample from the 6 end-user companies involved in the evaluation process yielded a total of 50 participants with different gaming experience, which revealed

Figure 5. PRIME in corporate mode

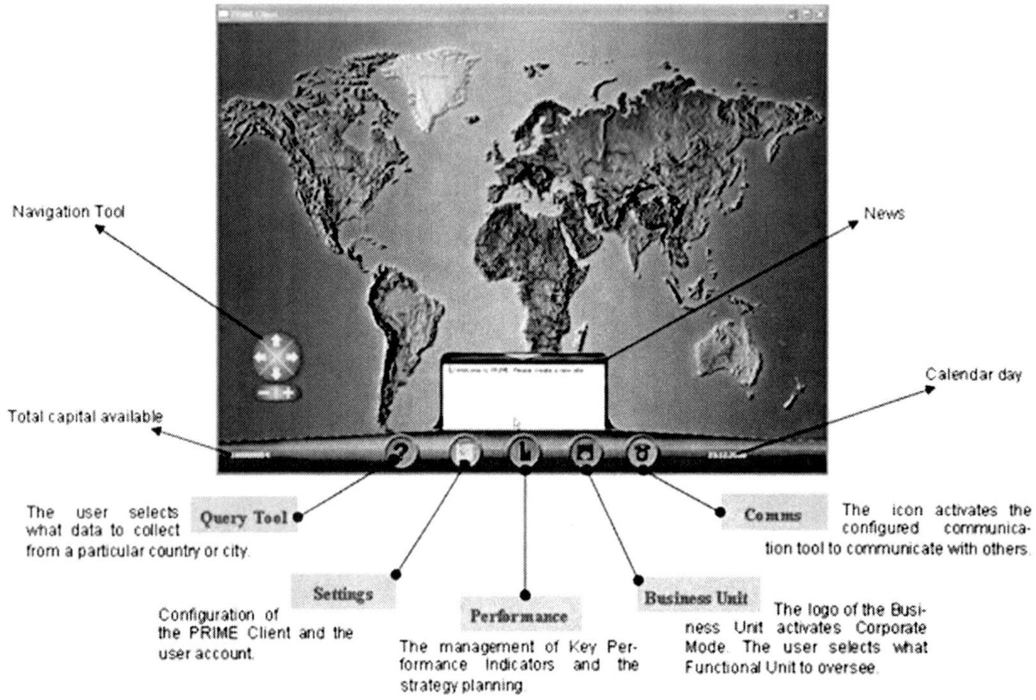

to be detrimental in tackling the learning curve associated to the PRIME serious game. 20% of the participants were players; 50% were seldom players; and 30 were not players. In average they spent 14 hours on PRIME.

The adopted evaluation methodology consisted of three phases:

- **Preparation**: This phase lasted two to three weeks and participants were encouraged to experiment with the PRIME serious game. This was necessary to tackle the learning curve and was done with the support of a moderator located locally within the organization. An underlying aim of PRIME is to facilitate the transfer of experience gained in the serious game to the real world, thus encouraging the building of the learner's repertoire. Consequently, the participant has two forms of preparation: guided-play and free-play. In the former, the participant interacted with the PRIME serious game based on tutorials that are well structured with clear aims for each case. In the case of free-play, the participant has no support or structure to their gaming sessions. During this phase, the participant was requested to log (Training Log) their opinions, difficulties, problems encountered and time spent playing the game.
- **Assessment**. At the end of the preparation phase, the participant was sufficiently familiarized with the PRIME serious game to focus on the learning process rather than any particular issue related to gameplay or game mechanics. The learner was challenged with a crafted "mission" where certain business objectives needed to be achieved within a given business context. During the process, evaluation data was collated in the form of semi-structured interviews, questionnaires, and quantitative

data resulting from in-game performance indicators. The collated data forms part of the participant's Mission Log.

- **Analysis**. All the collated data from the two previous phases was analyzed and processed to distil lessons learnt and validate the PRIME serious games.

Only a small minority of participants were mainly players (around 20%), which has an impact on the evaluation data results since there was a correlation between the gaming experience and leveraging the learning curve associated to the PRIME serious game. For the assessment phase, the participants played a crafted mission that included:

- Sales Forecasts
- Project Management
- Product Development
- Production Management
- Logistic Management

Results

Even with a period of one month, the evaluation process could not measure the success of transference of experience into the real world. Consequently, the evaluation focused on usability and user friendliness with some exploration of its potential for achieving learning outcomes.

Since the PRIME serious game was a prototype, it was plagued with some development teething issues that were eventually sorted. The great majority of the learners (66% of the participants) experienced minor problems, but these would not affect their experience. A total of 14% never experienced problems whilst 18% manifested difficulties with the PRIME serious game. However, it should be noted that those experiencing most difficulties were also those individuals who did not have any previous gaming experience. Therefore when confronted with an open system that enabled emergent outcomes, an inexperienced learner would not understand how to proceed. Unlike a behaviorist approach where a learner has a well-defined path, in our case a constructivist approach was taken where there are no clear objectives, but the learner learns by doing. This problem was more self-evident in the Assessment phase where the learner was confronted with a mission with clear objectives, but the non-gamers had serious difficulty in proceeding without the assistance of the moderator. However, after the learner had built their own internal mental model of the process, they would gradually know how to engage and interact with the PRIME serious game.

Another factor to take into account is the fact that PRIME is a serious game on strategic global manufacturing involving management, which is a very complex and interdisciplinary topic. Consequently, PRIME touches most of the aspects of the life of a company, which depending on the size of the enterprise involves the management by a large team of people with different expertise, studies, and competences. Within the population sample, none of the industrial companies were small enough to have a single individual with all the necessary expertise to manage their organization, but neither was this the objective as one design requirement was the alignment of stakeholders by carrying out role reversal.

In addition to the semi-structured interviews and questionnaires, the participants were encouraged to provide comments and feedback in written form, which were important in identifying improvements in the PRIME serious game.

All learners clearly demonstrated, and reported, to enjoy the experience of being engaged with PRIME for learning. However, it was also reported that PRIME was more beneficial when engaged with a group of learners rather than in isolation. For this reason PRIME is located on the borderline between the 3rd and 4th generation of serious games according to figure 3.

With regards to learning, it was not feasible to have an in-depth assessment that measured the transfer from serious game playing to real-life.

However, 76% of the learners reported to acquired new knowledge and gained new understanding that they otherwise didn't have. For this reason, it is not surprising that more than 80% of the learners understood the potential of PRIME as a learning delivery mechanism for global strategic manufacturing.

Recommendations

From the analysis carried out, some guidelines for the improvement of PRIME and serious games in general emerged:

1. As with most sophisticated software, irrespective of how much effort is invested into improving usability, there will always be a learning curve that needs to be tackled by learners. An effective tool to support the leaner is the use of interactive tutorials, in the absence of these; video tutorials are also useful albeit less effective.
2. Learning is more effective in a social and situated context.
3. There is a need for single user experiences where a mission is tailored to very specific tasks. This is the particular case of highly engineered processes, which resemble almost an algorithm that the learner is required to follow. These cases bring the learner a significant return on their time.
4. Learners are partial to simpler missions that require short period of time to be experienced. However, learners recognise that their utility might be limited.
5. A serious game, such as PRIME, would benefit from linking to actual learning objects that provide the theoretical background, thus enabling the learner to have deeper understanding of what would be best decisions to make.
6. In the case of PRIME, each session should have a pre-briefing and debriefing to align the learner to what is the purpose of the mission and facilitate the externalization process.

STRATEGIES FOR CORPORATE LEARNING IN SMES

Corporate learning means learning organized by an enterprise – in this case SMEs. The SME sets up the learning objectives and defines the main structure in cooperation with an academic institution. The courses are tailor-made to the enterprise although a part of each course always is generic and therefore applicable independent of a company or even an industrial sector. Examples and cases used are normally based on real data from the enterprises, and assignments address problems the enterprise encounters. Solutions to assignments can be based on company procedures, systems, and governing documentation.

We will describe a case showing an E-Learning approach. Even though the case is from a large company, the approach may be applied also to SMEs. Next some of the challenges experiences in implementing and operating E-Learning will be discussed, and at the end some recommendations are given.

Case Description

The case is a real course developed and delivered in cooperation with a company and a university. The university cooperates with two other universities in different countries bringing a global dimension into the education.

Figure 6 shows an outline of the approach selected in the case. The course was used for training experienced project managers. Participation in each course is limited to 24 persons in order to provide the best possible learning environment. The participants all have more than 10 years of industrial experience from managing projects. Therefore the approach selected is discussion-oriented and highly interactive. The participants learn from each other, and the role of the teacher

Figure 6. E-Learning approach used in case

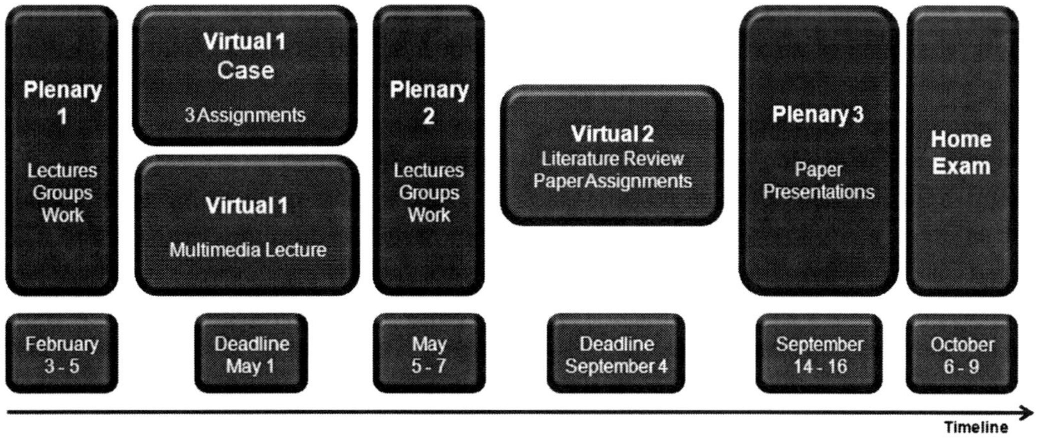

is more that of a moderator than a lecturer. The teachers are selected both from the company and the cooperating university.

As can be seen the selected approach is based on the hybrid model. There are three plenary sessions, each with three full days of face-to-face learning. The first two plenary sessions contain lectures and substantial group work and discussions. For each day, there are defined learning objectives. An electronic classroom is used for distributing handouts and reading material as well as for discussions amongst the participants and between participants and professors. The third plenary is different, as the participants will present the papers they have written in the virtual 2 assignment. Ample time is allowed to discuss each paper. This stimulates learning from each other and has proved very effective.

The first virtual session is split into two. The first part contains a case description. This is delivered using documents, slide shows, video clips, and interviews with actual stakeholders. From the case, each participant then gets three assignments that they will answer individually. The second virtual session is to write a paper according to normal academic standards. However, there is one important exception. The paper does not need to contain an original research contribution. It will be based on a problem from the company and take the form of a literature survey to find a solution to the problem or a recommendation for the company. This forces the learning to look into literature and discuss findings and alternative solutions. The problem has a "problem owner" in the company. This person serves as a mentor to the learner in addition to the supervision given by the professor. The learners work in groups of about three persons for this assignment. The paper is graded and the participants receive a certificate from the university. As already indicated, the group will have to present the results at the last plenary session.

After the third plenary session, there is a home exam to be answered individually. The exam is published in the virtual classroom and is open for three days. It represents about 6 hours of work, allowing the participant some flexibility in scheduling his or her work. All aids are permitted. The exam has the form of a case description with a number of assignments based on the case. The exam is graded and a certificate is issued by the university.

At the bottom of figure 6, a typical timeline is indicated. The course is run once every year, and is now into its fourth year.

Challenges

The authors have been engaged in a number of E-Learning courses for different customers and using different approaches. The authors have also studied a number of E-Learning courses available on the web. There are many different solutions, ranging from simple courses presenting a number of slides and running quizzes to advanced multimedia applications.

Some of the most important challenges in developing a successful solution for an SME are discussed below.

The first challenge is to create a stimulating learning environment. This means that the learner is inspired to go on seeking more and more knowledge. A prerequisite for this is that the learning environment is interactive and that the delivery methods applied varies. It is also important that the participant is continuously challenged. The level of education must be adapted to needs of the learner. It should not be too easy or too difficult, and there must be reasonable progress.

Progress of the learner is in itself a challenge. All experience shows that learning is postponed until the very last moment. At the same time research shows that learning is a process maturing over time. It is thus important to break any course into a number of sessions, and to use deadlines and tests to enforce a reasonable progress.

Although progress must be enforced, it should not be so strict that the learner is not allowed any flexibility with respect to time and place for learning. People attending courses delivered through their employer will always have to attend to their normal job in addition. Even though they may use some time for learning during work hours, all experience show that they will have to spend some of their free time for learning as well. For them to succeed and keep up motivation, they should have flexibility to fit learning into their social life in a good way.

For the supplier of the course it is a challenge to respond to the service level demanded from the learner. Using electronic classrooms, one can easily see that questions from participants come in evenings after small children's bedtime and during the weekends. For the teacher it is a challenge to always be available when the participant needs help.

Also technology may represent a challenge. Pure technical questions connected to ICT platforms, security and firewalls may be solved, but requires attention and should not be underestimated. The use of media must also be carefully considered. Video is not always the best solution. The "talking head" may appear boring and reading an article may actually result in better learning. Interactive approaches, such as using serious games, have proved very effective.

Recommendations

For an SME starting to use E-Learning for developing their competence, the authors would like to offer the following recommendations:

1. Develop the courses in cooperation with an academic partner, but make sure the learning objectives are defined by the company.
2. Use hybrid learning based on asynchronous learning for the virtual sessions. Plenary sessions are extremely important for the participants to socialize and to stimulate learning from each other.
3. Base assignments and cases on realistic data from the company.
4. Involve the most qualified people from the company in lecturing practical approaches and company policies. Let the academic partner handle the generic aspects and the theory and try to put company practice into a global generic perspective.
5. Select proven technology for the delivery methods. Such courses are not the battleground for experimenting with cutting edge solutions and for training the employees in

learning technology rather than learning content.

6. Provide adequate information on the selected approach to the participants before the first plenary session so that they can enter the learning arena well prepared.

FUTURE RESEARCH DIRECTIONS

In light of the challenges outlined earlier in this chapter, some topics for future research in the area of E-Learning can be identified:

- How to design E-Learning/technology-enhanced learning platforms that are at the same time cost effective in developing and implementing while providing tailored learning for the individual users. This is both a pedagogical and technical problem that is yet unsolved. The pedagogical issues will most likely have to be researched through exploring theories about learning models and concepts that attempt to identify learning needs of individuals (e.g., threshold concept (Meyer and Land, 2003). Technically, tailored learning can probably be realized through the use of mechanisms like serious games with tailored game scenarios, artificial mentors that aid the learners, etc. None of these issues have yet been sufficiently researched to be implemented in mature E-Learning environments.
- Learning progress measurement is another topic that is inherently difficult, but required to develop personalized and tailored learning situations. Determining the slope of the learning curve and presenting the learner with material, situations, and game scenarios that strike the required balance between a sufficient level of difficulty to both motivate and not scare off and a suitable engagement factor to keep the learner's interest necessitates the ability to measure how the learner performs in various learning situations. Beyond learning quizzes and game scores, very little exists in terms of progress measurement approaches that can be put to use. Future research must look into aspects like cognitive load theory (Sweller, 2005), psycho-physiological measurements, and game scoring principles aimed at uncovering skills and understanding.
- While electronic learning systems have been designed almost exclusively for individual learning processes, i.e., where single learners obtain material, read, solve problems, etc. using their computers, there seems to be a much higher learning potential if at least part of the learning process can be integrated into a larger community of learners. Theories like learning communities (Wenger, 1999) and knowledge ecology (Qvortrup, 2006) have approached this issue from a social sciences perspective, but very little research has been done in terms of how such theories can be exploited to make E-Learning environments more effective. The strength of various on-line forums shows some of the potential, but we have yet to learn how to stimulate such powerful forums in E-Learning applications.

CONCLUSION

Most SMEs are in terms of organizational structure fairly simply designed, with few departments or units. On the other hand, this means that typically, employees are involved in more than one function or discipline required to run the company. In such integrated areas, decisions are taken that have a crucial influence on the competitiveness and profitability of a company. It is therefore mandatory to find adequate learning processes for these organizations to take up new ideas. E-Learning can help in this respect by:

- Reducing the time it takes an employee to acquire the necessary competences
- Changing the learning context rapidly and in response to the real world
- Facilitating knowledge sharing within the organization
- Supporting a soft failure environment where mistakes have no impact on the real world.

One of the most promising, future-oriented concepts of E-Learning is the use of serious games. Studies have shown that gamers have an edge and advantage over those without gaming experience. By introducing games as a tool in the learning process, changing of behaviour and mindset are stimulated and the organization may gradually be transformed into a learning organization.

The PRIME project has experimented with serious games for project business and on-going manufacturing. The project revealed some recommended guidelines for introducing games as learning tools into an organization:

- Irrespective of how much effort is invested into improving usability, there will always be a learning curve that needs to be tackled by learners. An effective tool to support the leaner is the use of interactive tutorials.
- Learning is more effective in a social and situated context.
- There is a need for single user experiences where a mission is tailored to very specific tasks.
- Learners are partial to simpler missions that require short period of time to be experienced.
- A serious game would benefit from linking to actual learning objects that provide the theoretical background.
- Each session should have a pre-briefing and debriefing to align the learner to what is the purpose of the mission and facilitate the externalization process.

For the delivery of E-Learning content, the concept of hybrid learning is recommended. A successful implementation should follow the following guidelines:

- Develop the courses in cooperation with an academic partner.
- Use hybrid learning based on asynchronous learning for the virtual sessions.
- Base assignments and cases on realistic data from the company.
- Involve the most qualified people from the company in lecturing practical issues.
- Select proven technology for the delivery methods.
- Provide adequate information on the selected approach to the participants before the first plenary session.

There is a need for further research in three directions:

- Design of cost effective technology-enhanced learning platforms that provides tailored learning for the individual users.
- Learning progress measurement.
- Integration of the learner process into larger communities of learners.

REFERENCES

Argyris, C., & Schön, D. (1978). *Organizational Learning: A theory of action perspective*. Reading, MA: Addison-Wesley.

Aspin, D., & Chapman, J. (2000). Lifelong learning: concepts and conceptions. *International Journal of Lifelong Education*, *19*(1), 2–19. doi:10.1080/026013700293421

Berge, Z.L. (1998). Barriers to online teaching in post-secondary institutions. *Online Journal of Distance Education Administration, 1(2).*

Carliner, C. (2002). Tips for Conducting Level 1 Evaluations of Asynchronous e-Courses. *American Society for Training and Development publication What Works, March.*

Dale, E. (1969). *Audiovisual Methods in Teaching*. New York: The Dryden Press.

Duin, H., Oliveira, M., & Saffarpour, A. (2007). A Simulation Model for Virtual Manufacturing Environments for Serious Games. In Proceedings from *13th International Conference on Concurrent Enterprising: Concurrent Innovation: An Emerging Paradigm for Collaboration and Competitiveness in the Extended Enterprise.*

ENAPS Consortium. (2001). *ENAPS Indicator Model, Version 1.0*. Bremen, Germany: PRODUTEC Ingenieurgesellschaft mbH.Flanagan, J. (1954). The Critical Incident Technique. *Psychological Bulletin*, *51*(4). doi:10.1037/h0061470

Hall, B., & Snider, A. (2000). Glossary: The hottest buzz words in the industry. In Schreiber, D. A., & Berge, Z. L. (Eds.), *Distance training: How innovative organizations are using technology to maximize learning and business objectives*. San Francisco: Jossey-Bass.

Herring, T., & Job, R. (2008). The Next Generation of eLearning: Instructional Alternate Reality Games. *Online Forums*. Retrieved October 15, 2009 from http://www.elearningguild.com/olf/olfarchives/index.cfm?id=387&action=viewonly.

Hughes, J., & Atwell, G. (2003). A Framework for the Evaluation of E-Learning. In *Proceedings of European Seminars – Exploring Models and Partnerships for E-Learning in SMEs*. Retrieved February 4, 2004 from http://www.theknownet.com/ict_smes_seminars/papers/Hughes_Attwell.html.

Kok, W. (2004). *Facing the Challenge: The Lisbon strategy for growth and employment, report from the High Level Group*, available at http://europa.eu.int/growthandjobs/pdf/kok_report_en.pdf.

Kolb, D. A. (1984). *Experimental Learning – Experience as The Source of Learning and Development*. Upper Saddle River, NJ: Prentice Hall.

Kommers, P. A. M., Grabinger, S., & Dunlap, J. C. (1996). *Hypermedia Learning Environment: Introduction Design and Integration*. Mahwah, NJ: Lawrence Erlbaum Associates.

Lefrere, P. (2007). Technology to support distance education. In proceedings from *Strategies for Global Manufacturing: a European view of IMS.* Available from ftp://ftp.cordis.europa.eu/pub/ims/docs/4-6-lefrere.pdf.

Leonard-Barton, D. (1995). *Wellsprings of Knowledge – Building and sustaining the sources of innovation*. Cambridge, MA: Harvard Business School Press.

March, J. (2006). Ideas as Art. *Harvard Business Review*, (October): 83–89.

Meyer, A., & Rose, D. H. (1998). *Learning to Read in the Computer Age*. Cambridge, MA: Brookline Books.

Meyer, J. H. F., & Land, R. (2003). Threshold concepts and troublesome knowledge: Linkages to ways of thinking and practising within the disciplines. In Rust, C. (Ed.), *Improving Student Learning: Improving Student Learning Theory and Practice – Ten Years On*. Oxford: Oxford Centre for Staff and Learning Development.

Oliveira, O., Andersen, B., Oliveira, A., & Rolstadås, A. (2006). The Impact of Serious Games in the European Industry. In proceedings from the *10th Workshop on Experimental Interactive Learning in Industrial Management - IFIP WG5.7 SIG*, IFIP.

Polanyi, M. (1967). *The Tacit Dimension*. Garden City, NY: Doubleday.

Prensky, M. (2001). *Digital Game-Based Learning*. New York: McGraw Hill.

Qvortrup, L. (2006). *Knowledge, Education and Learning: E-Learning in the knowledge society*. Copenhagen: Forlaget Samfundslitteratur.

Rolstadås, A. (2002). An Example of an E-Learning Solution for an International Curriculum in Manufacturing Strategy. In Proceedings from *e-2002 Conference*.

Rolstadås, A., & Hussein, B. (2002). Hybrid Learning in Project Management – Potentials and Challenges. In Proceedings from *PMI Research Conference*, PMI.

Romiszowski, A. (2004). How's the E-Learning Baby? Factors Leading to Success or Failure of an Education Technology Innovation. *Educational Technology*, *44*(1).

Rose, C., & Nicholl, M. (1997). *Accelerated Learning for the Twenty-First Century*. New York: Delacote Press.

Sage Learning System. (2002). E-Learning Evaluation. Retrieved July 5, 2003 from http://www.sagelearning.com/papers/Evaluation%20 Forms.pdf.

Sawyer, S., & Tapia, A. (2005). The sociotechnical nature of mobile computing work: Evidence from a study of policing in the United States. *International Journal of Technology and Human Interaction*, *1*(3), 1–14.

Schön, D. (1983). *The reflective practitioner: How professionals think in action*. New York, NY: Basic Books.

Schrage, M. (2000). *Serious Play – How the Worlds Best Companies Simulate to Innovate*. Cambridge, MA: Harvard Business School Press.

Schwesig, M., Rolstadås, A., & Thoben, K.-D. (2005). An E-Learning experiment in manufacturing strategy. In proceedings from *8th IFIP World Conference on Computers in Education*, IFIP.

Snowden, D. J., & Boone, M. (2007). A Leader's Framework for Decision Making. *Harvard Business Review*, (November): 69–76.

Sweller, J. (2005). Implications of cognitive load theory for multimedia learning. In Mayer, R. E. (Ed.), *Cambridge handbook of multimedia learning*. Cambridge, MA: Cambridge University Press.

Urdan, T. A., & Weggen, C. C. (2000). *Corporate E-Learning: Exploring a new frontier*. San Francisco, CA: WR Hambrecht & Co.

U.S.I.G. (2003). Usability Special Interest Group: Usability checklist for E-Learning. Retrieved December 1, 2003 from http://www.stcsig.org/usability/resources/toolkit/E-Learning-checklist.doc.

VandenBos, G., Knapp, S., & Doe, J. (2001). Role of reference elements in the selection of resources by psychology undergraduates. [from http://jbr.org/articles.html]. *Journal of Bibliographic Research*, *5*, 117–123. Retrieved October 13, 2001.

Wenger, E. (1999). *Communities of Practice: Learning, Meaning and Identity*. Cambridge, UK: Cambridge University Press.

Chapter 5
21st Century Learning Opportunities for SME Success:
Maximizing Technology Tools and Lifelong Learning for Innovation and Impact

Kathleen P. King
University of South Florida, USA

John J Foley III
Citigroup, USA

ABSTRACT

This chapter informs SME (small and medium enterprise) owners, developers, consultants, and academics with the reasons, means, and possibilities afforded by 21st century technology in helping SMEs to improve their operational efficiencies and discover more effective marketing strategies for their products and services. With the rapid development and broad-based integration of web-based technologies across domains of communication, marketing, e-Commerce, and training, SMEs can benefit greatly by using these inexpensive tools to their advantage. SMEs typically underutilize opportunities to enhance their efficiencies by using more complex e-Business systems, and in so doing under develop the talents of their workforce for innovation and success. This underutilization is not just because of ignorance of technological capabilities, but also from a lack of exposure to leadership and HR development training. Knowing the need to learn must be a strong foundation before technological development can ensue. This chapter provides a synthesis of research and literature across several related, but seldomly connected fields - including, organizational theory, leadership, adult development and learning, 21st century learning, distance learning and human resource management. In developing this chapter, the authors are attempting to communicate the need for SMEs to both develop leadership and technological program developments to implement the changes needed to compete in a marketplace that reflects rapid change and imperfect information.

DOI: 10.4018/978-1-61692-880-3.ch005

INTRODUCTION

With the great proliferation and social adoption of web-based communication tools, e-Commerce platforms, and distance learning, SMEs are in a prime position to broaden their scope of service, increase scalability, cultivate innovation, and add to their profit margin. However, as the literature reveals, most SMEs do not know how to utilize e-Business platforms, nor are they aware of the various forms of education available to become proficient in this media. This chapter defines the current dimensions of what e-Business is, what it offers SMEs, and strategies for evaluation and possible implementation. Moreover, the chapter documents current issues and trends regarding how SMEs are, or are not, using the e-Business potential, and what the obstacles are for learning and implementing these changes. In addition, the discussion includes a review of salient limitations and risks which SMEs may review as they weigh these substantial strategic organizational opportunities. The chapter concludes with an overview of the macro level of the opportunities and recommendations for action.

In addressing options and strategies to encourage SME adoption of e-Business technology, we will build upon the literature of human resource development, business management, organizational theory, leadership, adult development, adult learning, 21st century learning and distance learning. Specifically, the chapter defines a business epistemology for the proper mix of e-knowledge and vision that are relevant for SMEs who are developing an e-Business platform. The chapter focus culminates in proposed solutions to encourage SMEs to embrace e-change, and a call for future directed research in this business challenge. The chapter begins by clarifying e-Business types and their definitions which are essential to the focus of the discussion.

Definitions

In any discussion of such emergent and evolving concepts as e-Business, it is always beneficial to define the terms used. Therefore, this section defines the types of e-Business especially pertinent to this chapter. In reviewing the academic record, uniform nomenclature to describe the various types and platforms of e-Business has not as yet been normalized; however, for our purposes:

E-Business is the umbrella term for all uses of inter-company electronic networks to connect to intra- and inter-company systems, where the use of those networks and software is to organize and transact business activities in cyberspace (Brown & Lockett, 2004, p.1; Wu & Hisa 2009, p. 95).

E-Commerce is the simplest subset of e-Business, and relates to using the internet to order and pay for products or services, plus general e-mail activities (Wu & Hisa 2009, p. 96). Most SMEs (like many individuals) already use these base skills in order to communicate and order supplies. Research on SME adoption of e-Business has shown that SMEs are fine with e-mail/e-Commerce (low to medium technology) applications, but have very little engagement in highly complex applications (Brown & Lockett, 2004, p. 1). Most e-Business definitions exclude e-Commerce from their measurements of adoption of e-Business solutions.

E-Marketplaces, also known as inter-organizational networks (IONs), use the Internet to allow for the development of many e-Business models, which results in SME aggregation via IONs. These IONs form a web of SME exchanges that reflect cooperative and competitive elements, and vary in the form of network autonomy versus dependence, based on the specific needs, trust, and control requirements demanded of each individual network of SMEs. Aggregations in these IONs can range from social networking to formal integration (Brown & Lockett, 2004, p. 2-3).

An example of the first aggregation would be an industry social media which used blogs (web sites which are easily updated and allow comments to be posted), forums (online discussion areas), wikis (collaborative websites allowing for multiparty editing of documents), etc for members to communicate and share their expertise in nuanced business matters. These aggregations serve two purposes, they make industry expertise available for all SMEs in a particular field, (rather than having expertise residing only with larger competitors), and these forums allow individual SMEs to advertise their knowledge and experience.

An example of formal aggregation sites would be ones in which members can:

- purchase supplies from an industry-aggregated catalog,
- sub-contract out portions of their workload to competitors who currently have excess capacity
- access industry websites that have product lists with price comparisons
- access industry developed back-office tracking systems for billing, payroll, etc.

E-Mobile expands e-Business to mobile computing devices. Wi-Fi networks and Bluetooth® LANs have allowed mobile devices to easily connect to local enterprise networks and the internet. This technology has allowed mobile employees to increase their range of activities and connectivity to allow them to service their customers while they are in transit or out on other business meetings. This extension of connectivity provides employees with flexibility, responsiveness and efficiency when they are not in the office (Sairamech, Goh, Stanoi, Padmanabhan, & Li, 2004, p. 651).

BACKGROUND

Why Do SMEs Need to Maximize 21st Century Learning Opportunities?

In a perfect world where SMEs have the same access to knowledge, financial and human resources, and wield the same marketing acumen as large corporations, the formation of SME aggregations and the advanced usage of e-Business applications would mirror the developments in other corporate practices. ION formation to advance sales efforts and for cost efficiencies would develop linearly. For these SMEs that adopt e-marketplaces, the cause célèbre for forming IONs in e-Business models would be to integrate suppliers, distributors, service providers and clients. These aggregations would ensure better communications with each party, and would enhance business transactions via the internet in order to produce value-added services/efficiencies for themselves and their customers.

Such e-Business networks would not just form in the ether of the internet. Motivated SMEs would link up through general intermediaries and SME targeted networks. These IONs would congeal as individual SMEs connect up to each other within structure provided by these intermediaries. Examples of e-Business intermediary networks are bCentral (Microsoft®), NetBusiness (Netscape™, etc), BizProlink, and Achilles, 2002. These platforms provide host software networks for SMEs, and would also serve as a portal to more complex e-application via consultancy services (Brown & Lockett, 2004, p. 3).

Building upon these foundational definitions of different types of e-Business, the next section describes the current applications of e-Business today. Based on a review of the literature, the practices are analyzed for trends and themes pertinent to SMEs.

The Real World: E-Business Use by SMEs Circa 2010

Based on literature review and analysis, the only SMEs that have fully engaged in highly complex applications are those that are imbedded within a client or supplier chain network, and were required to be compliant with the best practice e-Business applications of these larger companies (Xu, Rohatgi & Duan, 2007, p. 83). In effect, they were

Figure 1. E-application Complexity Effect on SME Adoption

	E-commerce (Low Complexity)	E-marketplace (High Complexity)
Perceived Benefit by SMEs	Yes	Benefit not commonly known
Organizational Costs:	Low, only need PC	High
Educational awareness	Owners are aware	Owners don't perceive value
Need for additional resources	None	More specialized employees
Need for training	Employees already trained	Significant training

Rate of Adoption by SMEs	High	Low

forced to adopt because of their captive position in an e-Business vertical chain. Also, the network that was forcing compliance would also have had the expertise to guide these SMEs through the adoption phase.

As e-Business applications become more complex, most independent SMEs are slowing in their adoption of this technology. Academics and policy makers had assumed that as large organizations implemented e-practices, that these would trickle-down down to influence the practices of SMEs. This has not transpired. The high level of application complexity has had a negative impact in SME adoption decisions (Brown & Lockett, 2004, p. 1).

Researchers on this adoption question had speculated that the internal and external critical factors that would effect whether an SME adopted complex e-Business solutions would come down to either barriers to adoption, or enablers to adoption. They speculated that these considerations would fall into 3 categories: specific perceived benefits, organizational readiness/resources, and external pressures to adopt (Levy, Powell & Worrell, 2005 p. 2). However, these generally accepted factors did not include a review of the e-Business application complexity, which appears to have a high correlation on why SMEs lag in adopting complex e-Business applications.

Government sponsors of e-Business initiatives and academia sought a more granular explanation than a simple large to small trickle-down effect, and expanded their considerations. A more nuanced explanation involves the relationship of three barriers to SME adoption of complex e-Business: access to education/information, financial and human resources, and employee training.

One way of depicting and better understanding the relationships among these concepts is illustrated in Figure 1. At the easiest levels of e-Business, SME owners and employees are self trained -from their personal experiences with e-mail, online shopping, etc. As complexity increases, SME owners are less aware of the e-benefits, and are more constrained by limited resources (financial and staffing), and are less willing to provide formal training for their employees.

Demands on SMEs

There have been many studies on the issues affecting SME adoption, most point to the limiting effects of the three barriers listed above; the education of SME owners on the benefits and applicability of e-Business solutions for their firms, limitations of funding and available personnel, and ignorance that employees training programs exist for e-Business applications. We have carefully selected six of these studies as representative of the dominant issues reviewed.

The first study examined more obvious, practical aspects of these barriers. Without intellectualizing the factors, Xu, Rohatgi, and Duan (2007) revealed that the development and implementation of e-Business technology by SMEs tends to focus only on short-term benefits (operational savings, etc.) to the detriment of long term strategic planning. This shift away from long-term planning is most likely caused by limited financial resources and employee capacity at most SMEs, which serves to impact the ability to fund and provide training due to limiting constraints. At the more basic levels of e-Business, such as e-mail and the ordering of supplies, employees teach themselves how to use the systems – it is easy. However, the more complex the application, the less likely employees will train themselves, and financial constraints prevent formal management training of these employees. Therefore, advanced applications are ignored (Xu, Rohatgi, & Duan, 2007, pp. 82-85).

In a concurring study, the relatively low rates of SME adoption of e-Business applications relates to a lack of e-Business competency, and a lack in training (Eikebrokk & Olsen, 2009. Lack of time and resources within SMEs and a general ignorance of the training available are seen as the primary barriers to organizational adoption of e-Business (Eikebrokk & Olsen, p. 7). Jeon, Han, and Lee conducted another study in South Korea in 2006 which demonstrated that the most critical determinants of SME adoption of e-Business was the vision and support of the CEO, and the dissemination of information showing business relevance of e-Business applications, as well as access to properly promoted training programs (Jeon, Han, & Lee, 2006, pp.1905-1916)

A Canadian business study, Canadian e-Business Initiative (2003), identified a barrier to SME adoption of e-Business to be a lack of technical expertise in the Canadian marketplace. Universities are producing IT specialist that are trained for the needs of Fortune 1000 companies. Since SMEs need as much business planning as technical development, IT graduates alone are not very useful to them. SMEs need employees or consultants that can design and implement turn-key e-Solution systems (Canadian e-Business Initiative, 2003, pp. 10-11). That requires specialists that can evaluate an SME's existing manual procedures toward redesign, look to identify sales and savings potentials from e-Business platforms, design the technology, train employees and implement the new process. These types of specialists are not being trained at universities currently.

In a follow-up Canadian business-sponsored report, SME adoption of e-Business solutions was found to be stalling (Canadian e-Business Initiative, 2004). While most SMEs have adopted e-Commerce, most have not adopted the more difficult integrated solutions. This report also found that most SMEs do not understand how e-Business can help them, don't have the internal capacity to implement, and that the quality of external consultants to help plan and instruct was uneven. A further concern on that last point was that SME owners felt that there were no coordinated or trusted sources of information and training.

Another study that interviewed the owners of SMEs found that most executives believe that they should pursue e-Business solutions, but that they had concerns over technical and human resource constraints (Ihlstrom & Nisson, 2003). Specifically, there was a lack of knowledge about the topic within their organization, and if anyone did have some e-knowledge, they were too busy on other

Figure 2. Owners' Perceptions of Barriers to SME E-marketplace Adoption

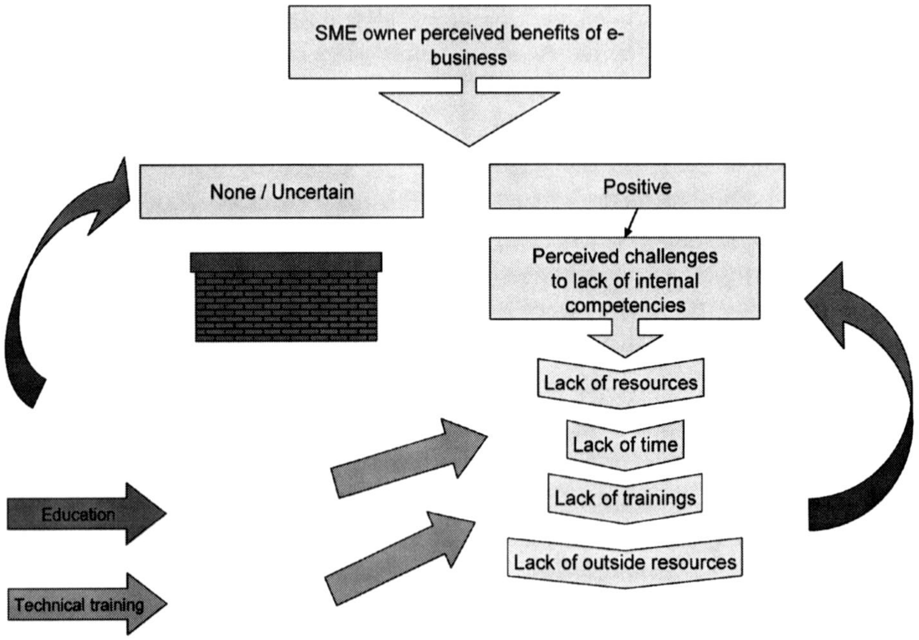

work responsibilities to be reassigned to program development (Ihlstrom & Nisson, 2003, p. 221).

In Figure 2, the findings of the above studies on issues surrounding the adoption of more complex e-marketplace applications is diagramed from the SME owners' perspective. Education to address these misconceptions is critical if SMEs are to adopt e-Business, and the degree of this education will depend on the SME owners' perception of the usefulness of e-Business to their operations. Once owners' misconceptions are addressed and e-Business plans are devised, technical training can address employee competencies.

As can be seen in this diagram, SME owners' education of the capabilities of e-marketplace applications starts at a basic level if the owners do not have any perceived value in e-Business solutions. If they do have a positive perception, then the education process would be focused on their misconceptions of the costs, lack of supports, and savings associated with e-applications. Technical training would proceed once the misconceptions were redressed.

Understanding the current practice, trends and challenges of e-Business today, provides the context for pursuing our discuss ion. However another critical building block is the theoretical framework. The next section describes the theoretical foundation which guides our discussion.

SYNTHESIZED THEORETICAL FOUNDATION

Introducing e-Business to SMEs is not just about an e-Business plan, consultations and training. The process is developed within the framework of a theoretical understanding of leadership skills, management and adult (employee) centered learning. As such, the literature can illuminate salient principles, strategies and models of addressing organizational change, training needs, human performance issues and human resource development needs for our SME e-Business process.

Leadership and Organizational Theory

Due to the very nature of SMEs, the leadership has a vast impact on the organizational climate and vision. Based on our review of the current literature, it is to be expected that SME leaders will also have vast impact on the choices, comfort level and implementation of e-Business. While leadership theories have varied greatly over the centuries, current trends are that leaders will usually adopt styles which are congruent with their personality style and social adeptness (Kouzes & Posner, 2007). That said leadership has also been encouraged to realize that different missions, situations and constituencies require different strategies and communication approaches. Being able to read the signs of the economic, political and organizational field are high on the list of skills required by successful SME leaders and entrepreneurs in any-sized organizations (Tapscott & Williams, 2006).

Human Resource Development

Concomitantly, organizational theory demonstrates that while organizational structure may be established and organized identically, leader "A" and leader "B" can create entirely differently organizational climates without changing the structure. The blend of organizational climate and structure cannot be ignored because either alone is insufficient to characterize the dynamics and environment of a specific organization. In fact, in SMEs the impact of the leader on the climate is magnified because of smaller numbers of personnel, greater interaction across ranks and cross training needs (Yorks, 2005). When people fulfill several roles in an SME, they work across departments and sectors of organizations that they may never encounter otherwise (Enriquez, 2001). Greater interpersonal communication provides abundant opportunities to influence and craft the climate of SMEs (Caffarella, 2001). Much like a potter with clay, the CEO may well have direct interaction with large percentages of the employees and able to personally control the delivery of leadership vision, intentions, favor and disfavor, and preferences, thereby molding the climate of his/her SME (Kouzes & Posner, 2007).

Business Management

The literature of business management offers several astute insights which bear on our question and need. Specifically, current practice includes global project management which successfully implements company-wide processes from product and service development, to customer service (Ahoy, 2008; Feigenbaum & Feigenbaum, 2009; Tapscott & Williams, 2001). The fundamental elements comprising this need is found in being able to design and implement data driven decision making, benchmarking, and greater accountability. The emphasis on data driven decision making and bench marking provide a foundation to guide SMEs to document, quantify and evaluate the cost of doing business via non-automated and e-Business platforms. It provides urgency for cost-benefit analysis and return on investment (ROI) in most decision making processes which can guide the CEO and leadership to the degree that they wish this information drive their organization.

In global economies which create more possibilities of fiscal uncertainty (ASTD, 2009), such evaluations become major determinants of making decisions based on real-time data rather than solely projections and expectations (ASTD & Booz Allen Hamilton, 2009). However, in the area of human performance and human resource management, data-driven decision making is imperative and needs to be not only well documented, but also consistent, must demonstrate a lack of prejudice or bias, and closely follow tax, legal and industry requirements (Wang & King, 2009; Yorks, 2005). In times of rapid legal, industry and economic change, SMEs do well to examine the ways the human resource management services as well as performance can be outsourced to large cooperatives (IONS) or web based for outsourcing (401Ks (retirement plans), payroll, employee handbooks, etc)

Adult Development

The closely related field of adult development reminds SME owners that the increased life span of our workforce means not only an aging workforce, but also a greater number of life transitions, all of which leads to a growing demand for more human resource services (Wang, & King, 2009). Whether it means upgrading credentials in order to satisfy regulations for the same job title, or changing focus of the work of the organizations due to rapid shifts in global markets or technology-driven obsolescence, training is a larger need for today's worker than ever before (ASTD, 2008, 2009). Increased numbers of SMEs cannot afford training departments and sending workers to frequent off-site (or out of town) training, which can be especially expensive and inefficient for SMEs with their smaller staffs (ASTD, 2009). Enter e-Learning, which includes not only learning on demand, but also video conferencing with inexpensive hardware and mobile learning options for staff to take continuing education credits, competency exams or updates via Blackberries®, iPhones®, or iPods®.

The adult development and career literature have indicated for years that adults are changing careers more frequently than even 20 years ago (Bjorklund &Bee, 2007). Add to this consistent trend the national and global economic changes, and businesses will experience even greater personnel turnover and changes. This pattern creates impossible demands for SMEs to handle frequent changes to benefits and industry or government related compliance issues such as, 401K plans, pensions, tax withholdings, staff information, organization wide bonding, individual employee bond compliance, individual employee licensing compliance, etc. Again the cooperative resources of an e-Source or outsource provider can be most effective in addressing these increased demands and thereby allow SME leadership and to staff focus on the business they are engaged in rather than trying to master increasingly specialized and time consuming personnel services. Electronic solutions allow these services to be integrated into a one company based employee portal (enterprise system), or web-based accounts with major providers.

Adult Learning

One of the most exciting breakthroughs to impact adult learning in the last 8 years is from the field of neuroscience and boldly contradicts of the old saying, "you can't teach an old dog new tricks". Instead, we have learned that children and adults of any age are able to create new brain neuropathways, as long as they are not cognitively impaired by disease or disability (Jensen, 2006; Willis, 2008). Furthermore, the brain remaps areas which no longer function, or functions less than optimally. Much of this development happens through simple practice as adults use their minds in moderately complex mental activity. Such activities include simple number calculations, reading different types of literature, discussions, conducting word or numerical analysis, and visually discerning differences among images or characters.

The research demonstrates that when adults, regardless of age, continue to use their minds actively and challenge them with different types of activities they are able to maintain or increase their mental alertness, and acuity (Begley & Check, 1999-2000; Willis, 2008). The message for SMEs is that all employees can continue to benefit from training, because adults are never too old to develop new skills, improve existing abilities, and master new procedures.

Adult learning theory also confirms that the multiple learning styles identified by Gardner (2006b) apply to adults. Indeed, this is likely in part why people gravitate towards different careers. While your marketing and development team will likely be highly visual intelligence and learning, bookkeepers, compliance officers, benefits personnel, technical support, and technicians are likely to be inclined towards numerical intelligence.

The current and foundational theoretical literature which has been discussed provides a framework for the discussion of how SMEs may best address the challenges of technology use and training in the 21st century. By bringing together these varied disciplines (leadership and management, business management, adult development and learning) the framing view is one of leveraging and empowering human capabilities rather than solely technological. The two cannot be isolated, and our discussion will illustrate how essential it is to understand the human capabilities in considering SMEs opportunities.

21st Century Learning and Distance Learning to Address the Opportunities

Gardner's book, *Five Minds for the Future* (2006a), is a compelling application of his original premises to current trends and the scope of the business world. This book proposes that there are 5 different types of "minds" which best meet the demands of the current workplace, technology driven society and global marketplace. Consistent with the Partnership for 21st Century Skills (2004) and The Conference Board (2009) reports of global business and workforce needs he identifies critical thinking, problem solving, creativity, and team building major characteristics.

While 21st century skills has been prevalent in k-12 schools for many years, and are now gaining attention by President Obama and Secretary of Education, Duncan's *Race to the Top* educational reform (Duncan, 2009; Obama, 2009; US Department of Education, 2009) and the broader ARRA legislation, the term has been less often applied to the workplace and human performance. However, the same skills are identified in major literature from UNESCO education initiatives and higher education reports (2009), and also professional associations such as Society of Human Resource Management (SHRM) and American Society for Training and Development (ASTD) (The Conference Board, 2009). SMEs can act on this unequivocal message by making sure the training they are securing for their leadership and staff includes the emphasis on these same skill sets and the best minds which address them for their specific industry.

Taking these theoretical underpinnings and applying them broadly to e-Business adoption, Figure 3 encapsulates a possible synthesis of best practices for management theory, adult learning, and the development of e-Business solutions.

SME SUCCESS: STRATEGIES FOR 21ST CENTURY LIFELONG LEARNING

Scenario 1: Providing Top Notch Training, For All, And Under Budget!

Up, Up and Away International (UUAI) *is a global import export company which has a virtual team of 50 employees spread across three continents. It is an exciting time as they have purchased a new software solution to increase productivity, project management and communication company-wide. However it is no small challenge to roll-out this extensive new platform across multiple sites of varied staff members. Part of the dilemma is a situation where there are several major types of equipment, settings and workflow process for different employees. For instance, just two examples reveal that while the CEO and several of the front line account executives primarily use high-end handheld devices to conduct all their work, most of the home office administrative, payroll and marketing staff are terminal based. Moreover, many of the virtual team are located in*

Figure 3. E-Business, Management, and Adult Learning

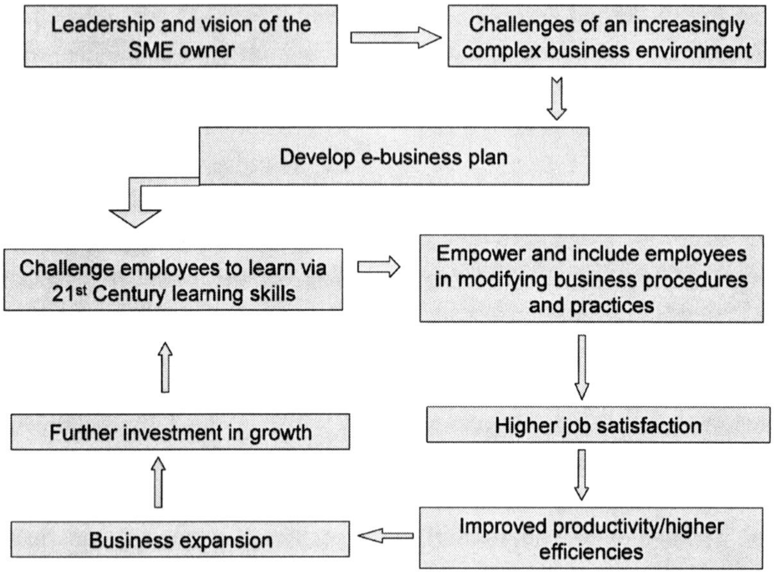

one-person offices worldwide and have entirely different hardware specifications, tasks and needs.

Many SMEs are faced with similar challenges as seen in the UUAI Scenario as they struggle to serve a wide variety of learning needs of their staff effectively, conveniently, and under budget. In smaller organizations you might only have 1 bookkeeper, instead of 5. When new software is acquired or upgraded, do you hire a specialized trainer to train one person?

As indicated in our earlier discussion, the need to support, cultivate and provide ongoing training of SME employees is paramount in sustaining organizational success. In many cases the vast resources available through e-Learning can be combined with face to face and personal instruction so that based on the urgency of the need, e-Learning might provide more immediate and cost effective assistance. In the scenario above, employees in different offices could access software and procedure tutorials on-demand via a web-based interface. In this case the SME might purchase the number of seats they need for their staff with an e-Outsource provider who has a large variety of quality self-paced software tutorials. Then they can also work with the company to develop simple presentations about company-only policies which would be proprietary to their staff.

High level technical and complex learning may be best facilitated in-person or via interactive synchronous technologies and learning experiences. While in other instances, general introductory instruction for software or hardware might successfully addresses the entire staff's needs, and may be negotiated for a reduced fee, bundled in the cost of the product purchased or in varied formats and time frames as described.

Table 1 provides a detailed chart which enumerates technology options for addressing many of these concerns and needs which are facing this familiar SME dilemma. Software, or web-based solutions, can be selected from open-source, inexpensive and enterprise categories as appropriate. However the focus is in maximizing ROI and cost-benefit results for SMEs. Readers will find this practical and informative chart of resources, benefits and limitations includes integrated e-platform solutions, remote login and tech support systems, IT help desk and dashboard solutions,

Table 1. Comparison Charts of Resources for Scenario 1: UUAI

Need	Resource	Benefits	Limitations
Integrated e-Business Platforms Examples Most have these capabilities included: • CRM • Customer • Supplier • Inventory • Accounting • eCommerce • Banking • Reports Manager • System Manager • Point of Sale **All have these benefits:** - Streamline and coordinate processes because of integration - Potential of increasing customer purchasing, retention and repeat purchases - Better, more comprehensive tracking of vital processes: inventory, client needs, banking, etc	**Interprise Solutions** http://www.interprisesolutions.com	- Fully integrated system across business, product and sales processes - Free online trial available - Extensive product information available - Many available modules, not all have to be purchased.	- Because it is an extensive software, it is not inexpensive - Time for training staff in new software needs to be set aside -Likely new/revised processes to be established and learned
	Oracle e-Business Suite http://www.oracle.com/us/products/applications/ebusiness/index.htm	-Comprehensive business performance management -Extensive integration of knowledge resources and capital - Large tech support staff and extensive product development	- High cost - Long list of included features may not be needed
	Insite Commerce http://www.insite-commerce.com	- Capable of enterprise resource planning (ERP) integration - Integrated system across business, product and sales processes - Free online demo available - Includes content management system - Online shopping cart - Order tracking - Create online product catalog	-Greater focus on eCommerce, maybe less on CRM, accounting, and inventory needs - Only a representative lead demo - Price is not published
IT Dashboard Examples - Immediate download and install - From one computer can gather information on all software and hardware assets, licenses and versions. - Helpdesk ticket system built in- keep track all requests for tech support even in your SME	**Spiceworks** www.spiceworks.com	- Open source - Free online community of users serving as detailed tech support community	- Ads posted except on paid version
	SysAidIT http://www.ilient.com/	• Free version for under 100 computers • Varied price plans available for larger organizations	• Ads posted except on paid version - Other free products including online customer service support www.sysaidcss.com/
Remote Login and Backup Examples Remote desktop control of computers to help user at another location - Remote tech support platform backup -Remote retrieval of files -Screen sharing for demonstrations, training, training	**Logmein.com** www.logmein.com	- Free version has fair number of features - Paid versions range in costs, most affordable -Client sit back and you connect to them once installed	- Requires download of software prior to use
	GoToMeeting www.gotomeeting.com	- Free version has fair number of features - Paid versions range in costs, most affordable - Paid version, setup page and then client put in code to connect	- Requires download of software prior to use
Travel Tracker Examples -Web based -Mobile device compatible (iPhone®, Blackberry®, etc) -Track flights in real time -Travel itinerary -Travel reminders/ alerts - Calendar integration	**Tripit.com** www.tripit.com	-Widget to embed and share schedule in websites, Facebook, Linked-In and more -Share access to different areas of your schedule with designated people - Integrates with other apps -Very simple to use - Space to track bonus travel points/ miles	-Free and paid versions
	World Mate www.worldmate.com/	-Travel reminders -Travel expense module available -Currency converter -World time converter -Weather reports - Video tutorials as help files -Windows Mobile, Nokia	Free and paid versions - Paid (gold) version enables reserving hotels, cars, flights from smartphone

personnel need solutions such as remote and synchronized travel trackers, and more.

Scenario 2: Going Global, Smarter with Scalable Products and Services

The amazing part of the GnuFone is that this inexpensive device allows people to interact effortlessly with family, friends and colleagues through an ear insert. This is possible because the R&D group at GnuTeam Inc. had discovered how to send video, audio and text via infrared messages to cell phones. The system was able to track what the wearer was looking at, saying and writing without further intervention as it is closely tied to the activity of the brain. More than voice activated software; this device was turning the tech community on end because user-interfaces could become obsolete. The website at GnuFone was constantly crashing because of the huge number of people logged in. It was meant to be a place where aficionados exchanged ways to maximize the use of the device, hack new features, and seek company technical support. Instead it had become the major hotspot for social interaction, file uploads and downloads, dating and collaboration. People were clamoring for additional paraphernalia and products with the GnuTeam and GnuFone brands emblazoned on them. How does a company of 100 people keep pace with global adoption?

At a time when all companies must cope with rapid changing global markets, and provide high quality products and services, while retaining their expert talent, how do SMEs compete? Scenario 2 could be every small enterprise's dream and nightmare simultaneously. Their core product gains mainstream adoption and has a wide base of users-members, but the company is racing to figure out how to increase capacity, scalability and efficiency in service, development and production quickly enough to meet demand.

Fortunately, inexpensive and free technologies provide solutions to many of these needs when used in effective ways to support staff learning, innovation and motivation. Human resources are our most valuable asset and these reports indicate how to maximize their development.

Indeed, a critical element which has been identified in the adult learning and development field is that a vibrant organization cultivates motivation (Wlodkowski, 1998). Often in times of great work-related stress, people will find support and release in discussing their needs among their colleagues with professionals form similar settings. Web based technologies and the e-collaborations provide just such possibilities as even SMEs can enable their staff to participate in group activities, services and programs. Rather than having to start separate programs for each need as it arises in the ramp up mode, instead the community based support- provides a platform for SME on-demand service to their staff. Examples of collections of training, consultative support, even counseling and benefits may be needed to handle the extra stress during this time of rapid expansion. Leaders who keep a close eye on the quality of life and health of their staff will have the opportunity to recognize early signs of excessive stress and provide access to resources. Sustaining and refreshing your talented staff is more cost efficient and beneficial to the knowledge capital of your company than seeing them burn out and leave, finding yourself forced to replace and retrain a new hire.

Furthermore an organizational climate which values individuals and dialogue provides additional support for change, and refreshment, detection of stress patterns across the organization and insight into needs, and possible recommendations. A climate of acceptance, support and dedication to each other and the organization is valuable in weathering the real struggles of even positive stress. (See Table 2.)

Regarding the technical dimensions of ramping up development, production and service e-Business provides a multitude of solutions which can integrate the diverse work responsibilities of a SME into a desktop application. Integrated

Table 2. Comparison Charts of Resources for Scenario 2

Need	Resource	Benefits	Limitations
Possible Providers for Health, Counseling Personnel Services	Trade Associations Professional Associations Chamber of Commerce	-Group rates are lower than if your company goes in solo. -Feedback from other plan participants.	
Project management software online Usually they include most of these features, and specialize with additional ones -contacts and group manager, -custom workspaces, -file management, -calendars & events, -blogs, -discussions, -chat and instant messaging, -RSS feeds, -web databases, -tasks, -reminders, -charts If your organization uses a paid version, usually these have low monthly fees- no long term contract needed	TimeStamp http://www.syntap.com/	-Simple to use -Track time on task -Set hourly rates -Add additional notes -Append new time to old files -Saved in compatible csv format -Loads quickly to startup	**-Only tracks time on task and hourly rates** **-No other project management functions**
	Basecamp.com	-Top notch project collaboration service that many top companies utilize. - Includes create and manage projects, private or public to-do lists, milestones, messaging, upload and share files, time tracking, notifications, time reporting. -Rights assignments differentiated - RSS, whiteboards, chat, calendars, assign milestones, - Design templates, activity stream, corporate branding Assign deadlines, commenting, drag and drop interface, and message boards. -Has other extras and 3rd party add-ons that integrate with it for iPhone® applications, billing and invoicing tools, planning tools, desktop widgets, etc.	-Offers a free plan that permits limited access. -Also paid version of their award winning service -30 day free trial of paid version
	Sosius http://sosius.com/	-Many features includes task automation, and access and permissions assignment - Free account has unlimited number of workspaces, unlimited users, but only 200 MB of storage space.	-Varied prices for paid plans
	GroupSwim – www.groupswim.com	-Different array of features - Groups, workspaces, discussion boards, file sharing, wikis, **semantic search, tagging, collective intelligence tools,** notifications, profiles, etc. -Free account includes has unlimited workspaces, up to 3 users, and 500 MB of storage space. - Great opportunity to growth and collaboration	May be too unusual for non-Gen Y people. -Varied prices for paid plans
	LiquidPlanner – http://www.liquidplanner.com/	- Has many features including project scheduling and analysis tools, task management, milestones, collaboration tools, personalized dashboards, resource scheduling, and more. -The free version lets you have up to 3 members, an unlimited number of projects, and 2 GB of storage space.	-Varied prices for paid plans
	Huddle http://www.huddle.net/	-Unique in respects - Integrate online collaboration, project management and document sharing using social networking principles. - Free plan will get you up to 3 workspaces, 1 GB of storage, and an unlimited number of users.	-Varied prices for paid plans

continued on following page

Table 2. continued

Need	Resource	Benefits	Limitations
Ecommerce Shopping cart – Provides two major components usually the storefront and administrative side of a shopping cart package. Basically a database backbone customized to maintain inventory tracking ad serve it up in web-based purchase catalog or listing. Includes also connection to credit card/ paypal or other credit card/online payment provider (some include connection to limited number of merchant accounts) The backbone of being able to actually conduct online transactions/buy/sell.	Mals-e http://www.mals-e.com	-Entirely free Works from their website -No install on server needed	-Very plain -Cannot be customized very much -Limited help resources
	Cartville www.cartville.com	-Works from their website -No install on server needed -Better point-and-click interface for setup -More customize options -Integrated auto responder available (see below)	-Not simple, but somewhat user friendly - Varied price plans based on options needed -30 day free trial available
	Paypal Shopping Cart www.paypal.com/shoppingcart	-Works from their website -No install on server needed -Better point-and-click interface for setup -More customize options	-Not simple, but somewhat user friendly -Varied pricing plans based on size of catalog (number of items in your list)
	Zencart www.zencart.com	-Load on your own site -Widely used by others -Big support group	-Need your own server space -Not simple to install and configure
	OScommerce www.Oscommerce.com	Load on your own site	-Need your own server space -Not simple to install and configure
	Fantastico	Load on your own site OR have it hosted on a site for you -Widely used -Several add-on options -Open source -Usually free from web host	Usually on your won server Not simple to install and configure
Ecommerce Auto-responders - Full strength auto-responders include tracking user forwarding, reading, etc. Watch out because some charge extra for survey capability while for same price it is included in others.	http://www.freeautobot.com/	Use their site and load your info Absolutely FREE	Not as user friendly to configure or use as some others Learning curve
	http://www.listmailpro.com/	-Use their site and load your info -$195 but only **one** time fee -Testimonies of ease of use -Technical support available	Varied pricing tiers Not as user friendly to configure or use as some others
	www.iContact.com	- Per month investment - Discounts when paying multiple months -All versions includes unlimited survey capability - Least expensive of paid versions - Abundant help resources, including videos	Varied pricing tiers
	www.getresponse.com	- Per month investment -Pro version includes unlimited survey capability	Varied pricing tiers
	www.constantcontact.com	- Per month investment - Discounts when paying multiple months	Varied pricing tiers
	http://www.dadamailproject.com/	Load on your own site Free version Pro version only $50 (one time fee)	Need your own server space Not as user friendly to configure or use as some others
	http://www.phplist.com/	- phplist is an open-source newsletter manager - Load on your own site	Need your own server space Pretty technical
	http://www.scripts4webmasters.com/	-Load on your own site -Free, basic, pro free -$99 -No monthly fees- as you buy to own -Inexpensive install service $	Need your own server space Not as user friendly to configure or use

continued on following page

Table 2. continued

Need	Resource	Benefits	Limitations
Ecommerce-Integrated shopping cart, autoresponder, follow-up	www.cartville.com	$29, 34, 39, 99 /month Several Integrated options: autoresponder, affiliate package, digital download capability, recurrent billing	Run off their server All features more expensive, but extensive capabilities
	http://www.1shoppingcart.com/	- $29-99/month - $3.95, 30 day trial	Need your own server space Not as user friendly to configure or use

dashboards are being used for many purposes across industries. Applications of these include free programs that cost $3000-20,000 just a few years ago. One example is a project management program that could help a team like ours help keep track of rapid changes in their processes, timelines and work assignments. Having a web-based or server-based application enables everyone to login and see the latest information, rather than chasing after files which are outdated. (See Table 2.)

Moreover, the same technologies may have modules which provide users to be able to individually and independently customize their purchasing, and community experience in a membership portal. At this time, such features can be provided by open source software hosted and configured on dedicated server space for $30-60/month. Mammoth corporations no longer have a monopoly on these valuable features. Table 1 provides a chart similar to the one for the prior scenario, but with details for technology solutions to address the specific needs detailed herein.

Connections to Training. As research has pointed out, an essential stage in designing implementation solutions for e-Business is the effort required for training. In order to swiftly and efficiently provide training, SMEs need to first communicate to employees how the new e-Business applications will help improve internal operating efficiencies and sales generation (Kouzes & Posner, 2007). This focus helps develop staff Ownership and motivation as they can see that their time and effort spent learning will have benefits for their success, professionally and fiscally (ASTD, 2009; Wang & King, 2009).

The second essential training focus is to strategize the message and means to develop SME owners' awareness of the vacuum in their training offerings and delivery methodologies (Caffarella, 2001; King, 2003). This goal can be accomplished by trainers demonstrating the application of common marketing success principles. For instance, trainers need to articulate that effectively serving staff needs applies the same principles, but produces more ROI benefits than building satisfied customers by serving *their* needs (ASTD, 2009). Moreover, a simple, specific cost benefit analysis can illustrate the ROI benefit of ideal training. This training serves the staff's and organization's needs and is characterised by being:

- targeted training content,
- delivered for rapid transfer of learning,
- designed and facilitated to address varied learning styles, support, and preferences, and
- prepared to scaffold support needs of the staff.

This synthesis of knowledge and practice regarding training for SMEs provides much needed direction in a changing world. However, without a doubt in coping with rapid changes and much technology integration, there will be limitations. The next section of our chapter explores these issues.

Limitations: Issues, and Potential Barriers

Certainly change does not come easily to any organization; however, when people realize it may provide benefit to them personally or collectively, they are more ready to invest the effort, learning, and complications (Kouzes & Posner, 2007; Wlodkowski, 1998; Yorks, 2005). Therefore, the manner in which change is introduced, discussed and experienced has an immense impact on its reception. When leaders and managers mindfully fine tune the message, process, participation in feedback opportunities, and incentives for participation, there are a multitude of benefits.

However, what limitations, issues, and barriers might be confronted also in such instances? Certainly many can arise, but this section identifies 3 areas of concern to evaluate prior to and during the process of incorporating e-Business tools in SMEs: interpersonal, processes, and growth.

Interpersonal. Our opening paragraph for this section illustrates the high stakes value of interpersonal communication skills in SMEs. Guiding an organization through change successfully is on the shoulders of the leader in SMEs more than ever. However, this process has to be supported by transparency, frequent communication, constructive feedback and positive feedback about communication, and opportunities for staff to participation in decision making at every level of the organization. When staff have a voice, even if small in change processes, when their expertise in doing their work is recognized and called upon to guide the change process, they are much more willing to follow the leader. The power of cultivating Ownership in the vision can never be overestimated. Build Ownership, and create buy-in, then your organization will work long and hard. Fail to appreciate their efforts, hours of commitment to their work, and concerns, and you will have a much more difficult and uncertain journey ahead.

Process. Another urgent need is focused on processes. In contemplating change, SME leaders must study existing processes, identify where the problems are, determine how to meet that need, and *plan* prior to implementing change. The emphasis on planning prior to implementing change cannot be overemphasized as history and headlines are replete with examples of catastrophes from lack of planning. Moreover, employees' personal memories of frustration will be unfortunate vivid reminders of the consequences of changes which did not occur smoothly. Instead, work with all levels of staff to understand and plan process transitions before, during, and after change. For example, temporary redundancy, running parallel systems to enable both old and new systems co-exist before the discontinuation of old processes (whether electronic or paper), can head off much of this disaster.

In addition, the strain on technical support during times of change might be excessive. Therefore, in planning for transition, SMEs need to negotiate upfront all technical support from vendors, or other sources, and consider how to scale this support down over time. The transition will be acutely felt at first, but if planned well, it will pass and business will be back to a steady pace, albeit quicker.

Growth. The final area is that SMEs are often caught off-guard with the surge of growth that occurs after making the shift to the integration of ebusiness technologies and platforms. The greater global reach for the marketing of their products and/or services, the expanded ability to serve global customers, may not have been anticipated in specific areas. Such areas may arise in scalability—being able to cope with large numbers of orders, with more sales people, support personnel, production timeline and capacity, and shipping volume, packaging, and costs. They also might not have anticipated how different geographic client bases might have different needs with their products and services either in different features and compatibilities, technical support, hours of availability, etc. Finally, the successful launch may also bring many suggestions for new products, large clients, new collaborations, affiliations, and partnerships. If the CEO has previously made all top level decisions, he/she might not be able to personally handle them all; instead cultivation of different levels of leadership and succession needs to be considered.

When SMEs use e-Business tools during the change process they have a much greter chance of success. e-Business tools can be effectively applied across there critical areas: interpersonal, processes, and growth. This discussion has laid the groundwork to proactively address change; the next section provides direction for solutions and recommendations within the scope of e-Business.

SOLUTIONS AND RECOMMENDATIONS

Strategy for Encouraging SMEs Adoption of E-Business Solutions

The strategy for SMEs adopting e-Business begins with the education of the SME owners on what e-Business can do for them. After that, specialists and consultants must be available to help design the e-Business plan, and introduce the e-marketplace platform. The last step is employee training.

SME owners must become aware that changes in their business and the technological environment can be first and foremost addressed using e-Business solutions. They must also be aware that these e-Solutions can help them offset these challenges, and in such ways that also improve their competitive edge. Once owners are aware of these possibilities, industry leaders will most likely see SMEs begin to migrate from low complexity e-Commerce to high complex e-Business applications.

The adoption of complex e-Business innovations requires two principal elements, development of internal and external technology, and adoption of new business models. The purpose of an e-Business model is to take advantage of new technologies (hardware and software) through a flexible market structure that then translates into business value. Business value does not just mean profits; it can mean better communications, responsiveness, cost control, etc. Once implemented, SMEs must continually restructure their resources within an e-Business model to react to ongoing industry changes.

In adopting e-applications, SME owners must be educated to understand that their new e-Business model not only requires the adoption of these new technologies, but must also lead to the destruction of old practices and capabilities. Upon adoption, old ways become obsolete (Wu & Hisa, p.105). All this involves knowledge which few SME have, and the need for continuing refinement in training as new applications develop.

After SME owners understand the potential impact of e-Business on their business, the next educational goal (after the e-specialist has created a new business plan and designed the e-platform) is to train employees in the technology and e-Procedures prior to and during the transition. All the planning and education described is important, but remember, the academic reports show that SMEs do not really implement these procedures. Evidence reveals that there is a trend of SMEs not using training resources which they can afford, are available, and/or have been developed for them. SMEs need assistance in applying the recommendations included in this chapter and further research to determine ways to improve and any barriers to overcome.

FUTURE RESEARCH

Further research is needed in examining the adoption, integration and effectiveness of e-Business in a wide variety of industry areas. Building upon literature for each industry and researching related professional associations may provide substantial leads in comprehending the industry climate, expert and demands. By better understanding the context and organizations, specific studies may be posed and conducted to identify leading trends, and best practice. Just a few questions which might prove informative for efficiency, scalability and sustainability may include

- Are there similar or different ways to introduce ecommerce across SME industries?
- Are there similar or different ways to implement ecommerce across SME industries?
- Are there similar or different ways to introduce ecommerce across SME industries?
- What are trends in each of these areas?
- What are the best practices in each of these areas?
- What are promising practices in each of these areas?
- What are emergent technologies in each of these areas?

Action research (Glanz, 1998) can be a very valuable first level research model for SMEs because it is less intensive, and may be executed by a non-expert who has been sufficiently trained. At the same time action research takes inquiry in SMEs much further than evaluations. Action research allows the staff, leader or researcher to pose a question which they will research (Glanz, 1998; Stringer, 2007). The purpose is to identify how to serve that need. Therefore a proposed solution is established, in this case it would be vetted though the organization, tested in the action research study and data gathered which can provide direction for new or revised product development, marketing approaches, organizational processes, customer service quality, etc. In the context of SMEs, action research can guide and advance data driven decision making to a more proactive level to increase creativity, efficiencies and success.

Trends

Based on our findings, with the continuation of uncertain markets, increasingly global commerce and collaboration, greater e-Business services will be adopted by successful SMEs. Therefore, how will these organizations respond? What will be the specific details and larger trends in the barriers, challenges, and new opportunities experienced? Continued research will reveal these answers. However, if these questions are pursued on the basis of interpersonal needs, skills, training and organizational change, the SMEs stand to gain much valuable information in readily usable forms. Specific trends which bear watching and tracking for impact on SME specific markets include technologies related to the delivery of more publications, media and entertainment products on-demand, web-based entertainment opportunities, green technologies, and knowledge management.

The e-Book has been the source of debate for decades now, but seems to be coming of age, more recently with Kindle DX®, Sony® Reader and the newer "Cool-er" (Pogue, 2009). Whichever of these or other devices wins the race for global social adoption and market domination; it is clear that people worldwide are ready to use technology to provide reading material. Furthermore, users *seem* to expect to be able to access video, audio, and text all in the same device and retrieve new information on demand. Like a great technological ballet we see features dance in and out of handheld devices over the years: stripped down, one-function-only devices, to the Swiss army knife of smart phones, for instance. The race continues for the next iPod®, iPhone® and Blackberry®.

Younger users' dominate the use of web-based entertainment, social media and networking, but they are also a large consumer market. Fast growing SMEs include those who have identified new and niche web-based entertainment opportunities. Netflix®, Twitter®, Hulu®, and craigslist are examples of sustained and new success in this area (MacMillan, 2009). SMEs are especially capable of making advances in this field due to their smaller size, fewer decision makers, and abilities to respond to new idea markets without having to shift the direction of a behemoth bureaucracy. Keeping a vigilante watch on emergent trends and evaluating opportunities to maximize your SMEs strengths in this market has been a wise strategy for many.

No other technology application matches the scope of information and constant use as knowledge management via the web. SMEs do well to watch the trends happening in this field and determine how their resources, expertise and strengths can be used to develop new products and services which serve the unquenchable hunger of the public for new information, false information, and on-demand information (Tapscott, & Williams, 2006). Moreover, in 2010 and beyond, users are expecting to *use and create* content. We only need to look as far as Google®, Facebook® and LinkedIn® for success stories in this area (McGrit, 2009). Therefore developing platforms, frameworks, communities, portals and spaces in which users, prospective clients or purchasers can find the information they need, manipulate in new ways and share more information there is a prime approach. Fortunately, many open source and inexpensive web-based tools exist which allow SMEs to host such communities, but why not develop your own, or develop entirely new dimensions of knowledge management and creation? The world is hungry for these experiences and you might launch the next profit making subculture, or must-have add-on feature for every SME.

CONCLUSION

What has emerged in this chapter is a clear image that SME owners lag in adopting e-Solutions for various reasons. These concerns include

- A lack of understanding of the solutions' applicability to their enterprises,
- A deep concern over the cost of development both in actual program dollars, training dollars, and higher personnel costs, and
- A belief that there is no outside help available for assistance should they decide to adopt e-Solutions.

We have also seen that innovative technology initiatives need to be developed within the framework of current theories of effective leadership skills, employee empowerment, and training in new and advanced processes. Moreover, these critical frameworks need to be supported by conclusions that a vibrant work environment motivates higher productivity.

The reality of coordinating successful SME ventures today is that increasing demands of global competition, more complex reporting requirements, and greater demand for human resource management have significantly increased the back-office cost of doing business. Giving even greater hesitation in the commitment of resources and direction is the fact that these expenses do not include the costs of increasing revenue volumes.

The misunderstanding that some SME owners have on the costs of implementing e-Business solutions is not only false, it is *inversely* false. SME owners that question cost often view business expansion in a linear fashion. When sales go up, they add one more person to the payroll. However, investing in future growth can require a high upfront investment in fixed costs – those being costs that are incurred regardless of whether the sales have yet materialized to support them. The benefit of e-Solutions is that proper implementation eats into fixed costs, existing and future, by making these fixed processes much less costly, or making them more like variable costs – that being a direct cost of sales. By joining IONs, the fixed cost nature of many back-office operations can be outsourced to collective systems, making those expenses part of current costs. The most competitive businesses in the world are those that have very low fixed costs.

SME owners must first understand that e-Business solutions will drive down their current fixed costs now. And that they will also make future growth less costly on a per unit of sales basis. By educating owners as to cost savings, the relative inexpensive investment in these platforms, and by improving support scaffolding available while developing e-platforms, more SMEs should be able to move towards adopting e-Solutions as a core component of their operations in the future.

REFERENCES

Ahoy, C. (2008). *Customer driven operations management*. New York: McGraw-Hill.

ASTD. (2009). *Learning in tough economic times*. Alexandria, VA: American Society for Training and Development.

ASTD. (2009). *2008 state of the industry report*. Alexandria, VA: American Society for Training and Development.

ASTD, & Booz Allen Hamilton (2009). *Executive development: Strategic and tactical approaches*. Alexandria, VA: American Society for Training and Development.

Begley, S., & Check, E. (12/27/99-1/3/2000). Re-wiring your gray matter. *Newsweek 135*(1), 89-31.

Bjorklund, B., & Bee, H. (2007). *Journey to adulthood* (6th ed.). Upper Saddle River: Prentice Hall.

Brown, D. H., & Lockett, N. (2004). Potential of critical e-applications for engaging SMEs in e-Business: A provider perspective. *European Journal of Information Systems*, *13*(1), 21–38. doi:10.1057/palgrave.ejis.3000480

Caffarella, R. (2001). *Planning programs for adult learners* (2nd ed.). San Francisco: Jossey-Bass.

Canadian e-Business Initiative. (2003, May). *Fast forward 4.0 growing Canada's digital economy*, pp. 1-25.

Canadian e-Business Initiative. (2004, September). *Net impact study Canada. Strategies for increasing SME engagement in the e-economy*, Retrieved August 1, 2009, from http://www.net-impactstudy.com/ca/pdf/canada-en.pdf.

Duncan, A. (2009, July 24). Education reform moon's shot. *The Washington Post*. Retrieved August 5, 2009, from http://www.washington-post.com/wp-dyn/content/article/2009/07/23/AR2009072302634.html.

Eikebrokk, T. R., & Dag, H. O. (2009). Training, competence, and business performance: Evidence in European small and medium-sized enterprises. *International Journal of E-Business Research*, *5*(1), 92–108.

Enriquez, J. (2001). *As the future catches you*. New York: Three Rivers Press.

Feigenbaum, A. V., & Feigenbaum, D. S. (2009). *The power of management innovation*. New York: McGraw-Hill.

Gardner, H. (2006a). *Five minds for the future*. Cambridge, MA: Harvard Business School Press.

Gardner, H. (2006b). *Multiple intelligences: New horizons in theory and practice*. New York: Basic Books.

Glanz, J. (1998). *Action research*. Norwood, MA: Christopher-Gordon.

Ihlstrom, C., & Malin, N. (2003). E-business adoptions by SMEs – Prerequisites and attitude of SMEs in a Swedish network. *Journal of Organizational Computing and Electronic Commerce*, *13*(3), 211–223. doi:10.1207/S15327744JOCE133&4_04

Jensen, E. (2006). *Teaching with the brain in mind* (2nd ed.). Alexandria, VA: ASCD.

Jeon, B. N., Han, S. H., & Lee, M. J. (2006). Determining factors for the adoption of e-Business: The case of SMEs in Korea. *Applied Economics*, *38*, 1905–1916. doi:10.1080/00036840500427262

King, K. P. (2003). *Keeping pace with technology: Educational technology that transforms* (*Vol. 2*). Cresskill, NJ: Hampton Press.

Kouzes, J. M., & Posner, B. Z. (2007). *The leadership challenge* (4th ed.). San Francisco: Jossey-Bass.

Levy, M., Powell, P., & Worrall, L. (2005). Strategic intent and e-Business in SMEs: Enablers and inhibitors. *Resources Management Journal*, *18*(4), 1–8.

MacMillan, D. (2009, Mar 31). Hulu attracts crowds but not ads. *Business Week*. Retrieved August 4, 2009 from http://www.businessweek.com/print/technology/content/mar2009/tc20090330_571175.htm.

McGirt, E. (2009, Mar 17). How Chris Hughes helped launch Facebook and the Barack Obama campaign. *Fast Company*. Retrieved August 4, 2009 from http://www.fastcompany.com/magazine/134/boy-wonder.html

Obama, B. (2009). President Obama on the race to the top. Retrieved August 5, 2009, from http://www.youtube.com/watch?v=VNbDv0zPBV4

Partnership for 21st Century Skills. (2004). *Learning for the 21st century*. Retrieved July 23, 2009, from http://www.21stcenturyskills.org/images/stories/otherdocs/P21_Report.pdf.

Pink, D. (2006). *A whole new mind: Why right-brainers will rule the future*. New York: Riverhead Trade.

Pogue, D. (2009, May 27). Don't quit the Kindle yet. *The New Times*. Retrieved on August 7, 2009 from http://www.nytimes.com/2009/05/28/technology/personaltech/28pogue.html

Sairamesh, J., Goh, S., Stanoi, I., Padmanabhan, S., & Li, C. S. (2004). Disconnected process, mechanisms and architecture for mobile e-Business. *Mobile Networks and Applications*, *9*, 651–662. doi:10.1023/B:MONE.0000042504.21014.61

Stringer, E. T. (2007). *Action research* (3rd ed.). Thousand Oaks, CA: Sage.

Tapscott, D., & Williams, A. D. (2006). *Wikinomics: How mass collaboration changes everything*. New York: Portfolio.

The Conference Board. (2009). *The ill-prepared U.S. workforce*. New York: The Conference Board.

UNESCO. (2009). *Improving education quality*. Retrieved July 23, 2009, from http://www.unesco.org/en/education_ar/themes/improving-education-quality/education-for-sustainable-development/strategy/learning-to-know/?0=.

US Department of Education. (2009, July 31). *Racing to the top of education*. Retrieved August 6, 2009, from http://www.ed.gov/programs/racetothetop/index.html.

Wang, V., & King, K. P. (Eds.). (2009). *Human performance models revealed in the global context*. Charlotte, NC: Information Age Publishing, Inc.

Willis, J. (2008, Feb.). Building a bridge from neuroscience to the classroom. *Phi Delta Kappan*, *89*(6), 424–427.

Wlodkowski, R. (1998). *Enhancing adult motivation to learn: A comprehensive guide for teaching all adults* (Revised ed.). San Francisco: Jossey Bass.

Wlodkowski, R., & Ginsberg, M. (1995). *Diversity and motivation: Culturally responsive teaching*. San Francisco: Jossey Bass.

Wu, J., & Hisa, T. (2008). Developing e-Business dynamic capabilities: An analysis of e-Commerce innovation from i–m, to u-commerce. *Journal of Organizational Computing and Electronic Commerce*, *18*(2), 95–111. doi:10.1080/10919390701807525

Xu, M., Rohatgi, R., & Duan, Y. (2007). E-business adoption in SMEs: Some preliminary findings from electronic components industry. *International Journal of E-Business Research*, *3*(1), 74–90.

Yorks, L. (2005). *Strategic human resource development*. Mason, OH: Thomson.

Chapter 6
Open Innovation:
Opportunities and Challenges for SMEs

Hakikur Rahman
University of Minho, Portugal

ABSTRACT

With the advent of innovative technologies and multi-dimensional researches along the setting of entrepreneurship development, philosophy, context and business handling has been transformed from being traditional to innovative. Depending on diversity and nature of the transformation, innovation has been shifted from closed to open to crowdsourcing innovation. Ranging from small entrepreneurs to corporate business houses are being immensely benefited by the innovation techniques, especially utilizing information and communication technologies. However, the road to innovation, despite being a paradigm shift is not smooth and ready for many, particularly the small and medium enterprises who mainly deal with the clients at the outer peripheries of the social circle. This chapter synthesizes issues of opportunities and challenges for small and medium enterprises by carrying out a broad literature review and synthesis. Furthermore, the chapter will provide a few research hints to be applicable for researchers and research institutions.

INTRODUCTION

Innovation relates to transformation of processes, products or services (BlessingWhite, 2006; Chason, 2008) to create additional value and wealth (Beacham, 2006; Vaitheeswaran, 2007; Barker, 2008) leading to the benefit of community (Cox, 2008). In this aspect, the real growth of the importance of innovation activities has been linked with several simultaneously affecting societal phenomena, such as easier familiarization with the globalization, obtaining benefits from deregulation and liberalization of markets, utilizing the benefits from the ICT revolution, and adopting themselves with the dynamic changes in the demand patterns (Schienstock & Hämäläinen, 2001).

However, along the roadmap of innovation, inclusion of open contexts are becoming popu-

DOI: 10.4018/978-1-61692-880-3.ch006

lar day by day. Success stories such as those of Google, Skype and Microsoft teach us at least one lesson – no one could ever know where the next big idea will be coming from! Experience shows that innovative ideas thrive when different disciplines or mindsets come together (Oxford Business School, 2008). Moreover, the contribution of the innovation systems approach to the open innovation perspective has been emphasizing the importance of external linkages for innovative success and the importance of innovation diffusion together with innovation creation. Studies on service innovations have confirmed the versatility of innovation sources. These studies have also brought up the significance of new patterns of thought and models of operation, in addition to technological innovations (Toivonen, 2004).

Business establishments have come to realize the importance of innovation for survival in a world of global competition (Sullivan, 1998; Hage, 1999). Furthermore, it has long been recognized that small and micro businesses have a vital role to play in the economy (Stanworth & Gray, 1991) with small business accounting for 99% of all businesses in the UK, and an estimated 3.7 million active businesses in 1998. Collectively, small and medium enterprises (SMEs[1]) are responsible for 65% of employment and 57% of Gross Domestic Product within the UK (Madsing, 1997; Tonge, 2001).

The scenario is the same in other European countries. SMEs in Europe comprises of about 23M€ investment market that account for 99% of all businesses and represent 2/3rd of the total employment (Renaud, 2008). But, in spite of being key contributor to the global economy accounting for approximately 50% of local and national GDP, 30% of export and 10% of FDI[2] most of the SMEs communities are lagging behind promoting their products at the national level, and at the global level (OECD, 2006).

Innovation has many effects on SMEs in various school of thoughts in terms of economics. It lead them to evolutionary economics, institutional economics, new regional economics, the economics of learning and knowledge and the economics of innovation (Lundvall, 1999). Successful innovation is crucial for business success and SME growth through innovation underpins any region's long term economic prosperity (Roper & Hewitt-Dundas, 2004). Innovation in SMEs leads to product innovation, as well as process innovation including providing impact in employment system. However, this proxy is relatively challenging, since the importance of innovations is not only due to the impact they have on employment, but also depend on other variables. Innovations have effects on other variables, such as turn-over, economic growth etc. Firms may also have made more than one innovation where the innovation-induced employment changes are counteractive, which result in little visible employment change (Nählinder, 2005).

A pioneer survey reveals that, when innovation is reported by SMEs themselves, and defined more widely in terms of service as well as manufacturing innovations, including process as well as product innovations, the frequency of product innovations seem lowest among peripheral SMEs, in aggregate form and even for both manufacturing and services treated separately (Keeble, 1997). It is a continuing debate about the role of SMEs in introducing fundamentally novel innovation than the large firms (Storey & Sykes, 1996), but they do have a greater ability to take incremental role in open innovation to niche themselves in better ambiance (Storey, 1994). Furthermore, SMEs can be a starting place of important innovations, which would then be commercialized by large firms, rendering to employment generation (Smallbone, North & Vickers, 2003).

In recent years, the contribution of SMEs to economic growth, job creation, innovation and promotion of enterprise has been widely recognized. While SMEs are important in terms of their overall share of GDP, it is also believed that many smaller firms lack both managerial and technical skills, which inhibits their effectiveness.

Therefore, improving the competitive advantage of SMEs is important to individual firms and to the national economy as a whole. (Tilley & Tonge, 2003). This study restrains within the context of opportunities and challenges of innovation for SMEs to growth effectively for providing better products and services through better processes. The study is outcome of a progressive research on influence of open innovation for SMEs development.

BACKGROUND

The term innovation means a novel way of doing something. It may refer to incremental, radical, and revolutionary changes in thinking, products, processes, or organizations[3]. Innovation, then could be defined as the creation, development and implementation of a new product, process or service, aiming at improving efficiency, effectiveness or competitive advantage (Chesbrough 2003; 2006; EIRMA, 2004). The term may apply to products, services, manufacturing processes, managerial processes or the design of an organization. It is most often viewed at a product or process level, where product innovation satisfies a customer's needs and process innovation improves efficiency and effectiveness of the organization. Innovation links to creativity and the creation of new ideas, and involves taking those new ideas and turning them into reality through invention, research and new product development[4]. Furthermore, innovation can be seen as the process that translates knowledge into economic growth and social well-being. It encompasses a series of scientific, technological, organizational, economic and commercial activities. Researches in the context of innovation are targeted towards one of these activities and may be carried out at different phases of the innovative process[5] (Chesbrough, Vanhaverbeke & West, 2006).

Open Innovation[6], a term recently added to the industries and organizations to promote open ended ideas, thoughts, processes, and researches to improve the product development, provide better services to the clients, increase efficiency and enhance value-addition. In terms of process dynamics, it incorporates accumulation of ideas, knowledge, licenses, intellectual properties, patents, and inventions (through licensing, joint ventures, spin-offs); and in terms of concept dynamics, user innovation, market innovation, cumulative innovation and distributed innovation. Open innovation emerges on issues like, in the diverse world of widely distributed knowledge, solitary enterprises cannot afford (economically and organizationally) to rely entirely on their own research and resources, but may instead collaborate, buy, lease-out or license processes or inventions (patents, intellectual properties) from other companies, organizations or institutions (Chesbrough 2003; 2006; Chesbrough, Vanhaverbeke & West, 2006). Currently, many companies are promoting open innovation and among them IBM, InnoCentive, InnovationXchange, Nerac, NineSigma, Nokia, Procter & Gamble, and Yet2.com[7] are widely renowned.

The most important benefit of open innovation to companies is that it provides an extended base of ideas and technologies. Companies look at open innovation as a close collaboration with external partners, as such customers, consumers, researchers or other people that may have an input to the future development of their company. The main motives for joining forces is to seize new business opportunities, to share risks, to pool complementary resources and to realize synergies. Companies recognize open innovation as a strategic tool to explore new growth opportunities at a lower risk. Open technology sourcing offers companies higher flexibility and responsiveness without necessarily incurring huge costs (OECD, 2008; Sousa, 2008).

Referring to the importance of innovation in SMEs, Davenport (2006:3) stated that, "Innovation is important for SMEs - a massive 60% of innovations come from the small and medium enterprise sector, and it is crucial that this total must not diminish against competing pressures in the modern market". For sake of this research, literature review will be limited to opportunities and challenges that are being faced by SMEs on the way of establishing innovation, and inclusion of SMEs into a possible discourse within the process.

OPPORTUNITIES

Open innovation targeting the SME development revolves around various issues and perspectives, in terms of product, process and service innovation (OECD, 2000a; de Jong & von Hippel, 2005; 2009; IBM, 2007; Hass & Hochrinner, 2008; Maes, 2009; van de Vrande, de Jong, Vanhaverbeke & de Rochemont, 2009) leading to increased competition, demanding customers, knowledge acquisition, and better positioning in the market (Storey, 1994; De Jong, 2006; NOUS, 2007; Lemola & Lievonen, 2008). This research would like to construct a innovation opportunities framework focusing improved business environment, better access to finance, better access to market and creation of new opportunities (see Figure 1).

It has been observed that open innovation has created various opportunities for SMEs in terms of their development, and a few are being categorized in Table 1. Henceforth, this paper would like to make a qualitative synthesis of the parameters that are put in Table 1. It will emphasize on competition, customers' demand, knowledge acquisition, product, process and service or technology innovation, and SMEs role as catalyst in the innovation processes.

Competition

In Joseph Schumpeter's (Tidd, Bessant & Pavitt, 2005:7) view competition in the domain of innovation is, "competition from the new commodity, the new technology, the new source of supply, the new type of organization. .. competition which.

Figure 1. Innovation opportunities framework

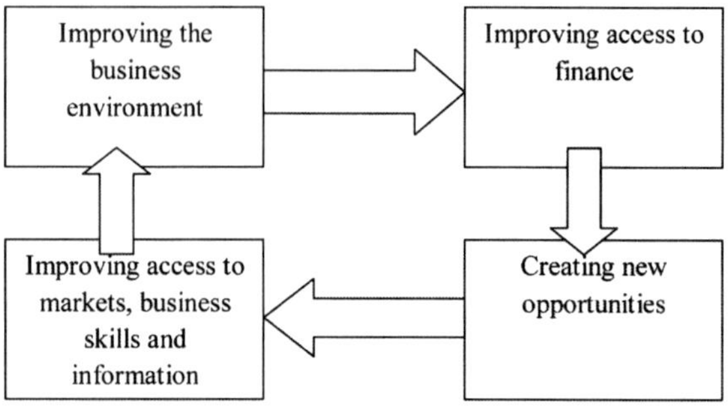

Table 1. Opportunities Associated to Open Innovation Affecting SMEs Development

Opportunities	Reference
Intense competition	De Jong, 2006; NOUS, 2007; Grama & Fotache, 2007; IFAD, 2007; Tidd, Bessant & Pavitt, 2005; BERR, 2008
More demanding customers	De Jong, 2006; BERR, 2007
Abundance of knowledge, opportunities and interactions	European Commission, 2003a; 2003b; Cosh, Fu & Hughes, 2005; Lemola & Lievonen, 2008
Easily adopt OI strategies such as inward and outward licensing and joint ventures	Fischer, 1978; Gold, 1987; Cervantes, 2009
Technological innovations	Evangelista, 2000; Tilley & Tonge, 2003; Toivonen, 2004;
Product innovation	OECD, 2000a; Nählinder, 2005; Maes, 2009; van de Vrande, de Jong, Vanhaverbeke & de Rochemont, 2009; Salavou, 2006
Process innovation	OECD, 2000a; Nählinder, 2005; Maes, 2009
Better positioning in the market	Storey, 1994; Grant, Laney & Pickett, 2002
Act as starter or catalyst	Smallbone, North & Vickers, 2003; Telemetica Institute, 2008
Enabler of employment generation	Smallbone, North & Vickers, 2003; European Commission, 1997; 2000
Ability to adopt quickly with new products	Design Council, 2005; Parrilli, 2006

.. strikes not at the margins of the profits and the outputs of the existing firms but at their foundations and their very lives". Grama & Fotache (2007) emphasized on utilization of ICT to enhance the competition within the innovation processes. IFAD (2007), however, pointed out SMEs often compete with protected public enterprises, which is a fact in many countries. But, the basis of competition has shifted from price of product to price and quality, or price, quality, choice, and others. The field has now become mature with much of the competition shifting to marginal issues like relative interest rates (Tidd, Bessant & Pavitt, 2005). Furthermore, free trade/globalization has resulted to adapt the ways of thinking to dismantle protective tariff and other barriers and, therefore, new competition basis emerges (Barnes, J. *et al.*, 2001; Kaplinsky, Morris & Readman, 2003).

Increased Customer Demand

Observing positive sales and R&D picture in various services reflects robust demand from key customers in diverse sectors, and to cope with the situation is to build a global, flexible, cost effective network and service infrastructure that can support the dynamic needs of the future customers (BERR, 2007). Furthermore, the innovation opportunity framework should have representation through clearly defined, focused services, in a cost-optimized structure and with a customer-oriented approach (FFG, 2006).

Knowledge Acquisition

Innovation involves generating, disseminating and applying knowledge. It is not a linear process, with an originator at one end and a customer at the other. There are many players involved, and they interact and influence each other in multifaceted ways. Ideas can come from anywhere and may lead to unexpected directions (Commonwealth of Australia, 2009). In this aspect, external linkages, both public (including higher education institutions) and private, benefit SME innovation. These linkages can be important sources of knowledge that directly strengthen the technological competences of the SMEs and their competitive advantage. Furthermore, collaboration with customers, suppliers, higher education institutions, even competitors, allows entrepreneurs to expand their range of expertise, develop specialist products, and achieve various other corporate objectives (Cosh, Fu & Hughes, 2005). In addition to these, the growing weight of, and policy emphasis on, innovation and knowledge as drivers of competitiveness and growth brings major opportunities for countries that are generally not considered to be at the forefront of knowledge creation or innovative capacity (Napier, Serger & Hansson, 2004).

Innovation Paradigm (Product, Process, Service, Technological Innovation)

This manuscript has touched issues like product, process and service innovation during earlier portion, and therefore, would like to emphasize on technological innovation in terms of SME development that enclave product, process and service innovations. A report of Telemetica Institute (2008) supports that, technological innovations trigger new services, better care for clients, new ways of working, and new means of exchange of ideas. Hence, understanding technological trends allows one to anticipate better on near-future possibilities for tangible problems for consumers and organizations, and in this aspect SMEs act as a catalyst of innovation promotion (Telemetica Institute, 2008). However, Conceição & Heitor (2000) have indicated that, the direct implication for innovation policies is important, but sometimes, limited role of demand at the firm level in assessing the amount of incentives for firms to introduce technological innovations hinders development of SMEs.

Table 2. Challenges Associated to Open Innovation Affecting SMEs development

Challenges	Reference
differences in organization and culture between the individual partners	Wei & Morgan, 2004; De Jong, 2006; TIEKE, 2009
Inconsistency in turn-over and pattern of economic growth	O'Sullivan, 2000; Nählinder, 2005; NOUS, 2007; Govt. of UK, 2008
Multiple innovation channels are counterproductive	Interact, 2004; Nählinder, 2005; Parrilli, 2006
Naïve in fundamental innovation	Storey & Sykes, 1996; Napier, Serger & Hansson, 2004; Hölzl, 2006a; b
Lack in managerial and technical skills (Small companies with innovative ideas have often found themselves without the capacity to develop or exploit their innovation)	Hadjimanolis, 1999; Van Hemel & Cramer, 2002; Tilley & Tonge, 2003; Del Brío & Junquera, 2003

CHALLENGES

Antti Peltomäki, the Deputy Director General of European Commission (European Communities, 2008) states that, innovation is a costly process. He reiterated further, that only one out of 3000 product ideas makes it on the market, which means that there are hundreds of unsuccessful ICT products beyond every success. Moreover, even successful products may be far from being user friendly. Surveys show that 75% of all users find their ICT tools more stressing than relaxing. In such a context, user-centric validation can play an important role in speeding up effectively the innovation process through addressing the actual user needs. OECD (2000b) finds that, most of the obstacles to growth and innovation in services are the same as in manufacturing. Insufficient access to finance and risk capital, lack of internal capacity to innovate, insufficient expertise in applying ICT and high risk are characteristically the main barriers to innovation in both sectors.

As a newly emerged field of research, open innovation for SME development deserves a prolonged and strategically developed qualitative and quantitative synthesis on literature review, including other forms of validation. However, during the early process of this research, this paper would like to carry out qualitative analytical discussion based on challenge parameters as depicted in Table 2. It is expected that within the next two quarter, this research would be able to provide some more in-depth parameters related to challenges associated to open innovation affecting SMEs development. The same inference is applied for opportunities aspects too.

Organizational and Cultural Differences

Forcing of technology is one of the main reasons behind the failure of several attempts of the SMEs to simply use ICTs effectively. Initially, awareness building activities should be introduced before taking short-term initiatives, followed by more general and long-term benefits. Furthermore, by bearing in mind that the introduction of ICTs in SMEs can bring a real modification in the way of their working environment, the introduction of ICT-based processes should take into account the specific culture of the company, especially the background of the entrepreneur and/or the managers, as well as their openness to innovation orientation (Wei and Morgan, 2004; Barba-Sánchez, Martínez-Ruiz & Jiménez-Zarco, 2007). However, doing things collectively, collaboratively and jointly is a good culture in many countries who are forerunner in open innovation for SMEs development (Callegati & Grandi, 2005; Govt. of UK, 2008; TIEKE, 2009).

Turn-Over

Innovations have effects on other variables as well, such as turn-over, economic growth etc[8], though they seem minor from outside, but these parameters affects innovation channels in the long run (Nählinder, 2005). Turn over data effects critical benchmarking indices of SMEs (European Commission, 2002), that reflects input on development contexts, as such human development (OECD, 2007), and thus excessive external turn-over of personnel should be avoided (Herstad, Bloch, Ebersberger & van de Velde, 2008).

Innovation Channels

The Open Innovation model implies that enterprises can use both internal and external ideas, technologies and knowledge to advance their innovation processes, and internal ideas can be taken to the market through external channels (e.g. spin-offs, external licensing of intellectual property) to generate additional value. This new paradigm inspires enterprises to find the most appropriate business model to commercialize new products or services, regardless of any model that exists within the enterprise or must be sought externally (Chesbrough, 2003b; De Jong, Vanhaverbeke, Kalvet & Chesbrough, 2008). In this context, utilization of new innovation channels for business cooperation are imperative (Interact, 2004), and smaller equity companies experimenting with alternative technologies creates multiple channels of innovation (Carlsson and Eliasson 2002). Often, it eliminates the need for commitment to specific technologies or R&D projects. However, problems may arise at the point of acquisition, specifically, it is critical for the acquiring firm that it gains control over not just for a specific issue but the competencies embedded in the acquired organization and its personnel (Lazonick 2007). Moreover, multiple innovation channels in SMEs are found to be counterproductive (Interact, 2004).

Technological (Fundamental) Innovation

Simple as it seems, open innovation for SME development requires a paradigm shifts from traditional processes to innovative processes, integration of skill development, knowledge development, product development to service development, system development and technology development. It requires general awareness, diagnostics, pro-active counseling, management and monitoring, empowerment of people involved, new business models and new collaborations among public, private, academic and service providers (Telemetica Institute, 2008). However, some researches argue that, in order to foster new technological sectors a fundamental change of financial systems towards more market-based finance is necessary. Furthermore, there is evidence that financial systems are not always rigid, which effect institutional configurations over time (Hölzl 2006a). Research by Ahrweiler et al. (2005) also suggests that, while institutional heterogeneity persists at the level of institutional frameworks, the differences are of decreasing relevance in knowledge-intensive industries (Holzl, 2006a; b), creating a space for other agents to act as intermediaries.

RESEARCH RECOMMENDATIONS

Innovation has become a key factor for the economic success of many countries and a prerequisite for sustainable development. Open innovation models have become an integral part of the innovation strategies and business models of companies in recent years. Innovation is increasingly based on knowledge assets beyond the boundaries of the company and co-operation has become an important way of tapping into knowledge resources outside in order to generate new ideas and bring them quickly to the market (the "outside-in" approach). At the same time companies may spin out technologies and intellectual property that they have developed internally but that are outside their core business and thus better developed and commercialized by others (the "inside-out" approach) (OECD, 2008).

Governments are paying more attention to the contribution of science and innovation to economic growth and have introduced a variety of new initiatives and reforms. Several countries, including Australia, Canada, Hungary, Ireland, South Korea and Spain, introduced comprehensive policy frameworks to guide developments in science, technology and innovation. In a number of countries, government institutions and agencies have been restructured to improve the governance of innovation systems, and at the same time policy evaluation has become more widespread. In addition to these, public research systems are being reformed to better contribute to economic and social needs, creating innovative opportunities of researches (OECD, 2002).

Moreover, the 'SME pact' foresees the positive mobilization of larger entrepreneurs or organizations (private or public) to promote innovative SME's development. Within this SME pact, programmes foster R&D-collaboration between innovative SMEs and large enterprises. If large enterprises are interested by SME's innovative products or services while still needing further development, these programmes support R&D projects that facilitate the testing and adaptation of the products and services to the specific needs of the large enterprise (Cervantes, 2009; OECD, 2007; 2008).

CONCLUSION

Innovation is a prime factor for economic success in many countries and in a complex and highly competitive global market, entrepreneurs have to innovate and develop commercially viable products and services faster than ever. To meet these new challenges, companies are adopting new approaches to their innovation strategies and processes (OECD, 2008). In a world of transformation and competition, innovating is not a luxury anymore, it is essential. All businesses need to innovate, though it may take any number of forms, from the steady refinement of established products to the leap in the unknown when an untried idea is launched. Whether introducing new technology, getting people to work in new ways or creating new products, one must innovate to survive (ACCA, 2008), which implies to SMEs equally (De Jong, 2006).

Open innovation is a paradigm that assumes that enterprises can and should use both external and internal ideas and paths to the market, when enterprises look to discover and realize innovative opportunities. The open paradigm assumes that internal ideas can also be taken to markets through external channels, outside the current businesses of the enterprise, to generate value. The Open Innovation model does not completely upset traditional policymaking to legitimize policy interventions, including spillovers, system failures and market failures, still apply equally to SMEs (De Jong, Vanhaverbeke, Kalvet & Chesbrough, 2008).

REFERENCES

ACCA. (2008). *Director's Briefing: Strategy*. UK: BHP Information Solutions Ltd.

Ahrweiler, P., Gilbert, N., & Pyka, A. (2005) Institutions matter, but ...: Organizational alignment in knowledge-based industries, the case of German and British bio-pharmaceuticals. A paper presented at the EMAEE conference in Utrecht 2005.

Barba-Sánchez, V., Martínez-Ruiz, M., & Del, P. (2007). Jiménez-Zarco, A.I. (2007). Drivers, Benefits and Challenges of ICT Adoption by Small and Medium Sized Enterprises (SMEs): A Literature Review. *Problems and Perspectives in Management*, *5*(Issue 1), 103–114.

Barker, J.E. (2008). The Foundations of Innovation, Transformation and Change, a WiKi book from the AussieInvention dot com

Barnes, J. (2001). Developing manufacturing competitiveness in South Africa. *Technovation, 21*(5). doi:10.1016/S0166-4972(00)00047-X

Beacham, J. (2006). *60 Minute Guide to Innovation: Turning Ideas Into Profit. Succeeding Through Innovation, Department of Trade and Industry*. UK: Published by TSO.

BERR. (2007). *The 2007 R&D Scoreboard, The top 850 UK and 1250 global companies by R&D investment. Department for Business Enterprise and Regulatory Reform*. UK: BERR.

BERR. (2008). *The 2008 Value Added Scoreboard, The top 800 UK and 750 European companies by Value Added: Commentary & Analysis. Department for Business Enterprise and Regulatory Reform*. UK: BERR.

BlessingWhite. (2006). *Leading Technical Professionals 2006 Report*. Princeton, NJ: BlessingWhite, Inc.

Callegati, E., & Grandi, S. (2005). Cluster dynamics and innovation in SMEs: the role of culture, Working paper No. 03/2005, International Centre for Research on the Economics of Culture, Institutions, and Creativity (EBLA), Università di Torino, Turin, Italy

Carlsson, B., & Eliasson, G. (2002). Industrial dynamics and endogenous growth. *Industry and Innovation, 10*(4), 435–455. doi:10.1080/1366271032000163676

Cervantes, M. (2009). *Open Innovation in Global Networks: Recent OECD work*, Policy issues and Open questions, a paper from Trade and Development Board Investment, Enterprise and Development Commission Multi-year expert meeting on enterprise development policies and capacity-building in science, technology and innovation, Geneva, 20–22 January 2009

Chason, M. (2008). [Center, MA, USA.]. *The Innovator, 1*(1), IXL.

Chesbrough, H. (2003). *Open Innovation: The New Imperative for Creating and Profiting from Technology*. Boston: Harvard Business School Press.

Chesbrough, H. (2006). *Open business models: How to thrive in a new innovation landscape*. Boston: Harvard Business School Press.

Chesbrough, H., Vanhaverbeke, W., & West, J. (2006). (Eds.). *Open innovation: Researching a new paradigm*. London:Oxford University Press.

Chesbrough, H. W. (2003b). The era of open innovation. *MIT Sloan Management Review, 44*(3), 35–41.

Commonwealth of Australia (2009). *Powering Ideas: An Innovation Agenda for the 21st Century*. Commonwealth of Australia 2009

Conceição, P., & Heitor, M. (2000). *Engineering and Technology for Innovation in PORTUGAL: a study on the dynamics of technological change*, A Preliminary Summary, Center for Innovation, Technology and Policy Research, Instituto Superior Tecnico, Technical University of Lisbon, available at http://in3.dem.ist.utl.pt/et2000/

Cosh, A., Fu, X., & Hughes, A. (2005). *Management Characteristics, Collaboration and Innovative Efficiency: Evidence from UK Survey Data*. Working Paper no. 311 (Cambridge: Centre for Business Research, 2005), p. 8.

Cox, G. (2008). Defining innovation: what counts in the University of Cape Town landscape? A proceedings of ascilite Melbourne 2008, Melbourne

Davenport, C. (2006). *In Beacham (2006), 60 Minute Guide to Innovation: Turning Ideas Into Profit* (p. 3). UK: Succeeding Through Innovation, Department of Trade and Industry, Published by TSO.

De Jong, J. P. J. (2006). *Open Innovation: Practice, Trends, Motives and bottlenecks in the SMEs (Meer Open Innovatie: Praktijk, Ontwikkelingen, Motieven en Knelpunten in het MKB)*. Zoetermeer: EIM.

De Jong, J. P. J., Vanhaverbeke, W., Kalvet, T., & Chesbrough, H. (2008), Policies for Open Innovation: Theory, Framework and Cases, Research project funded by VISION Era-Net, Helsinki: Finland.

De Jong, J.P.J. & von Hippel, E. (2005). *User Innovation in SMEs: Incidence and Transfer to Producers, SCALES-initiative (SCientific AnaLysis of Entrepreneurship and SMEs)*. the Netherlands Ministry of Economic Affairs.

De Jong, J. P. J., & von Hippel, E. (2009). Transfers of user process innovations to process equipment producers: A study of Dutch high-tech firms. *MIT Sloan School of Management Research Paper No. 4724-09,* March, 2009

Del Brío, J. Á., & Junquera, B. (2003, December). A review of the literature on environmental innovation management in SMEs: implications for public policies. *Technovation*, *23*(12), 939–948. doi:10.1016/S0166-4972(02)00036-6

Design Council. (2005). *National Survey of Firms*. London: Design Council.

EIRMA. (2004). *Technology Access for open innovation*. Working Group Report WG63, Eirma: Paris.

European Commission. (1997). *The European Observatory for SMEs, Fifth Annual Report, Report submitted to the Enterprise Directorate-General of the Commission of the European Communities*. European Network for SME Research, European Commission.

European Commission. (2000). *The European Observatory for SMEs, Fifth Annual Report, Report submitted to the Enterprise Directorate-General of the Commission of the European Communities*. European Network for SME Research, European Commission.

European Commission (2002). Observatory of European SMEs 2002 / No 2, SMEs in Europe, including a first glance at EU candidate countries, Report submitted to the Enterprise Directorate-General of the European Commission by: KPMG Special Services and EIM Business & Policy Research in the Netherlands in co-operation with: European Network for SME Research (ENSR), and Intomart

European Commission. (2003a), Innovation Policy in Seven Candidate Countries: The Challenges. *Final Report* Volume 1, March, Brussels.

European Commission. (2003b), Innovation Policy in Seven Candidate Countries: The Challenges. *Volume 2.7, Innovation Policy Profile: Turkey,* Brussels.

European Communities. (2008). Antti Peltomäki. In *Foreword of Living Labs for user-driven open innovation: An overview of the Living Labs Methodology, Activities and Achievements. Directorate-General for the Information Society and Media, Unit F4 New Infrastucture Paradigms and Experimental Facilities, European Commission Information Society and Media, January 2009.* Luxembourg: Office for Official Publications of the European Communities.

Evangelista, R. (2000). Sectoral Patterns of Technological Change in Services. *Economics of Innovation and New Technology*, *9*, 183–221. doi:10.1080/10438590000000008

FFG. (2006). *SME Associations in Austria: an overview*. Austria: FFG Austrian Research Promotion Agency.

Fischer, W. A. (1978). Follow-up strategies for technological growth. *California Management Review*, *21*(1), 11–20.

Gold, B. (1987). Approaches to Accelerating New Product Development. *Journal of Product Innovation Management*, *4*, 81–88. doi:10.1016/0737-6782(87)90054-3

Govt. of UK. (2008). Accelerating the SME economic engine: through transparent, simple and strategic procurement, Government of UK., Crown copyright 2008

Grama, A., & Fotache, D. (2007). ICT and ERP Applications Challenges in Romanian SMEs, ANALELE ŞTIINŢIFICE ALE UNIVERSITĂŢII „ALEXANDRU IOAN CUZA" DIN IAŞI. *Tomul LIV Ştiinţe Economice, 2007*, 23–28.

Grant, K., Laney, R., & Pickett, B. (2002). A Process of Innovation in Marketing by SME's, ANZMAC 2002 Conference Proceedings, Deakin University, Australia, pp. 2531-2538

Hadjimanolis, A. (1999). Barriers to innovation for SMEs in a small less developed country (Cyprus). Technovation, 19 (9), pp. 561-570. September 1999

Hage, J. T. (1999). Organizational Innovation and Organizational Change. *Annual Review of Sociology*, *25*, 597–622. doi:10.1146/annurev.soc.25.1.597

Hass, J., & Hochrinner, H. (2008). *Enhancing Product- and Process Innovation in SMEs through Cooperative Education, ASET Annual Conference 2008*, The Placement and Employability Professionals' Conference, 2-4 September 2008, Robbins Conference Centre, Plymouth, UK.

Herstad, S. J., Bloch, C., Ebersberger, B., & van de Velde, E. (2008). *Open innovation and globalisation: Theory, evidence and implications*. Eurostat.

Holzl, W. (2006a). *Scoping Paper*. Gazelles, Europe Innova.

Hölzl, W. (2006b). Convergence of financial systems: Towards an evolutionary perspective, Journal of Institutional Economics-3

IBM. (2007). *Service Science: The next frontier in service innovation. IBM Singapore Pte Ltd.* IBM Corporation.

IFAD. (2007). *Country strategic opportunities programme, The Republic of Moldova, International Fund for Agricultural Development (IFAD)*, Executive Board — Ninety-second Session, Rome, 11-13 December 2007

Interact (2004). Project "Embrace" Preparation and Implementation: lessons learnt and recommendations to Potential Applicants, INNOSTART National Business and Innovation Centre, a project paper submitted to European Regional Development Fund, European Union and presented at Translational INTERREG IIIB CADSES Seminar, Katowice, Poland.

Kaplinsky, R., Morris, M., & Readman, J. (2003). The globalisation of product markets and immiserising growth: lessons from the South African furniture industry. *World Development*, *30*(7), 1159–1178. doi:10.1016/S0305-750X(02)00029-3

Keeble, D. (1997). Small Firms, Innovation and Regional Development in Britain in the 1990s. *Regional Studies*, *31*(3), 281–293. doi:10.1080/00343409750134692

Lazonick, W. (2007). The stock market and innovative enterprise. *Industrial and Corporate Change*, *16*(6), 983–1035. doi:10.1093/icc/dtm030

Lemola, T., & Lievonen, J. (2008). *The role of innovation policy in fostering open innovation activities among Companies. a report from Vision Era.net*, Finland

Lundvall, B.-Å. (1999). Innovation Policy and Economic Theory. In Schienstock, G., & Kuusi, O. (Eds.), *Transformation Towards a Learning Economy. The Finnish National Fund for Research and Development - Sitra. Report no. 213*. Helsinki.

Madsing, D. (1997). *NCC presentation on the information technology initiative*. Manchester Metropolitan University, 1999

Maes, J. (2009). *SMEs' Radical Product Innovation: the Role of the Internal and External Absorptive Capacity Spheres, Job Market Paper July 2009*. Belgium: Katholieke Universiteit Leuven – Faculty of Business and Economics.

Nählinder, J. (2005). *Innovation and Employment in Services: The case of Knowledge Intensive Business Services in Sweden*, PhD Thesis, Department of Technology and Social Change, Linköping University, Sweden, Unitryck Linköping

Napier, G., Serger, S. S., & Hansson, E. W. (2004). *Strengthening Innovation and Technology Policies for SME Development in Turkey– Opportunities for Private Sector Involvement, International Organisation for Knowledge Economy and Enterprise Development*. IKED.

NOUS. (2007). Today's Knowledge Intensive SME: Where, Why and How? Discussion Paper, Department of Innovation, Industry and Regional Development, The Nous Group, Australia

O'Sullivan, M. (2000). *Contests for corporate control*. Oxford, UK: Oxford University Press Oxford Business School (2008). Introducing the Oxford Centre for Entrepreneurship and Innovation, Retail Policy Issues, The Retail Digest, Oxford SAID Business School, pp. 30-31

OECD. (2000a). Enhancing the Competitiveness of SMEs in the Global Economy: Strategies and Policies Enhancing the Competitiveness of SMEs through Innovation, *Conference for Ministers responsible for SMEs and Industry Ministers, Bologna*, Italy, 14-15 June 2000

OECD. (2000b). *OECD Science Technology and Industry Outlook 2000*. France: OECD.

OECD. (2002). *OECD Science Technology and Industry Outlook 2002*. France: OECD.

OECD. (2006). *The Athens Action Plans for Removing Barriers to SME Access to International Markets,* OECD Report, France.

OECD (2007). SME Policy Index 2007, Report on the Implementation of the European Charter for Small Enterprises in the Western Balkans, Prepared by: the European Commission Directorate General for Enterprise and Industry and the OECD Investment Compact for South East Europe. In consultation with: the European Bank for Reconstruction and Development and the European Training Foundation Published with the financial support of the European Commission and the OECD Investment Compact for South East Europe

OECD. (2008). *Open Innovation in Global Networks, a policy brief*. France: OECD.

Parrilli, M. D. (2006). A Tripartite Innovation Framework for Small Firms in Developing Regions: Key Issues for Analysis and Policy, Paper Number 2007-01, *Institute for Economic Development Policy Discussion Paper Series,* University of Birmingham, UK

Renaud, P. (2008). Open Innovation at Oseo Innovation: Example of the Passerelle Programme, a presentation at the OECD Business Symposium on Open Innovation in Global Networks, Copenhagen, 25-26 February, 2008

Roper, S., & Hewitt-Dundas, N. (2004). *Innovation, Networks and The Diffusion of Manufacturing Best Practice: A Comparison of Northern Ireland and the Republic of Ireland,* A report from Northern Ireland Economic Research Centre Queen's University of Belfast, UK.

Salavou, H. E. (2006). Exploring Product Innovativeness Determinants in SMEs, PhD Thesis, Athens University of Economics & Business, 2006

Schienstock, G., & Hämäläinen, T. (2001). Transformation of the Finnish innovation system. A network approach. The Finnish National Fund for Research and Development - Sitra. Report series No. 7. Helsinki.

Smallbone, D., North, D., & Vickers, I. (2003). The role and characteristics of SMEs in innovation. In Asheim, B. T., Isaksen, A., Nauwelaers, C., & Todtling, F. (Eds.), *Regional innovation policy for small-medium enterprises, Edward Elgar Publishing, 2003* (pp. 3–20).

Sousa, M. (2008). Open innovation models and the role of knowledge brokers, Inside Knowledge magazine, March 2008: 18-22

Stanworth, J., & Gray, C. (1991). *Bolton 20 years on: the small firm in the 1990s*. London: Paul Chapman.

Storey, D. J. (1994). *Understanding the small business sector*. London: International Thomson Business Press.

Storey, D. J., & Sykes, N. (1996). Uncertainty, Innovation and Management. In Burns, P., & Dewhurst, J. (Eds.), *Small Business and Entrepreneurship* (pp. 73–93). London: Macmillan.

Sullivan, A. (1998). Research outlays: the real bottom line: expenditures color a company's outlook. *Int. Herald Tribune* July 4-5th, pp. 15-17

Telemetica Institute. (2008). *Service innovation and ICT: Vision and ambition*. The Netherlands: Telemetica Institute.

Tidd, J., Bessant, J., & Pavitt, K. (2005). *Managing Innovation: Integrating technological, market and organizational change* (3rd ed.). John Wiley and Sons.

TIEKE. (2009). *ICT Cluster Finland Review 2009*. Finland: TIEKE Finnish Information Society Development Centre.

Tilley, F., & Tonge, J. (2003). *Introduction*. In Jones, O. & Tilley, F. (Eds.). Competitive Advantage in SME's: Organising for Innovation and Change, John Wiley & Sons

Toivonen, M. (2004). Expertise as Business: Long-term development and future prospects of knowledge-intensive business services (KIBS), Laboratory of Industrial Management, Helsinki University of Technology, Doctoral dissertation series 2004/2

Tonge, J. (2001). *A Review of Small Business Literature Part 1: Defining The Small Business*, Manchester Metropolitan University Business School Working Paper Series: WPS025, available at http://www.business.mmu.ac.uk/wps/

Vaitheeswaran. V. (2007) Special Report: Innovation. *The Economist*. Retrieved from http://www.economist.com/specialreports/displaystory.cfm?story_id=9934754

Van de Vrande, V., de Jong, J. P. J., Vanhaverbeke, W., & de Rochemont, M. (2009, june-july). Open innovation in SMEs: Trends, motives and management challenges. *Technovation*, *29*(6-7), 423–437. doi:10.1016/j.technovation.2008.10.001

Van Hemel, C., & Cramer, J. (2002, october). Barriers and stimuli for ecodesign in SMEs. *Journal of Cleaner Production*, *10*(5), 439–453. doi:10.1016/S0959-6526(02)00013-6

Wei, Y., & Morgan, N. (2004). The Supportiveness of Organizational Climate, Market Orientation, and New Product Performance in Chinese Firms. *Journal of Product Innovation Management*, *21*, 375–388. doi:10.1111/j.0737-6782.2004.00092.x

ENDNOTES

1. There is no single agreed definition of a SME. A variety of definitions are applied among OECD and APEC economies, and employee number is not the sole defined criterion. SMEs are considered to be non-subsidiary, independent firms which employ less than a given number of employees.
2. This refers to firms in the formal sector only

[3] http://en.wikipedia.org/wiki/Innovation

[4] http://www.digitalstrategy.govt.nz/Resources/Glossary-of-Key-Terms/

[5] http://www.arc.gov.au/general/glossary.htm

[6] a term promoted by Henry Chesbrough, a professor and executive director at the Center for Open Innovation at Berkeley

[7] http://en.wikipedia.org/wiki/Open_Innovation

[8] Firms may also have made more than one innovation channel, where the innovation-induced employment changes are counteractive, thus resulting in little visible employment change

Chapter 7
Organizational Readiness/ Preparedness

Bojan Lalic
University of Novi Sad, Serbia

Ugljesa Marjanovic
University of Novi Sad, Serbia

ABSTRACT

The Internet and Information Technology (IT) are being used in many ways to bring benefits and to increase competitiveness to businesses and public sector organizations. Implementing innovations in an organization is a dynamic and continuous process. This chapter discusses factors and elements fundamental for overcoming business challenges that most of the organizations are facing during successful implementation of an IT initiative within an organization. However, in order for systems to be prepared for change in terms of organizational readiness, organization needs to assess and plan their organizational readiness. It will be also presented how to assess an organization's readiness for success and how to put together an organizational readiness plan.

INTRODUCTION

„Suddenly business is not the same any more“ (Hammer, 2002). The Interent and IT jumped from „back office“ to the „front office“ further more to the main role in the play. The Internet and Information Technology (IT) are being used in many ways to bring benefits and to increase competitiveness to businesses and public sector organizations. Businesses are using the Internet and IT to form alliances, create new products and services, increase revenue and productivity, and improve customer satisfaction. Public Sector organizations are reducing costs for government and citizens, promoting economic development and improving education and healthcare through citizen-centric service delivery, while private organizations are reducing costs for their operations and accelerating the speed of product, or service, lifecycle, through consumer-centric service delivery. Organizations of all types are improving communications, collaboration, and business processes.

DOI: 10.4018/978-1-61692-880-3.ch007

Implementing innovations in an organization is a dynamic and continuous process. This chapter discusses factors and elements fundamental for overcoming business challenges that most of the organizations are facing during successful implementation of an IT initiative within an organization. Hence, in order for systems to be prepared for change in terms of organizational readiness, organization needs to asses and plan their organizational readiness.

In this chapter, we will try to present what organizational readiness means and discover what the relationship is between Information Technology governance, business planning, and project success. It will be also presented how to assess an organization's readiness for success and put together an organizational readiness plan.

Questions that will be answered are related to definition of the characteristics that prepare an organization to embark on Internet and IT initiatives, and explaination how to move organization closer toward organizational readiness.

After description of four pillars of organizational readiness four keys to IT governance will be presented and explain why the IT governance process during planning is vital to the success of IT initiatives.

VALUE OF ORGANIZATIONAL READINESS

If a simple question is raised"What makes Internet-enabled organizations successful?" the answer will be even simpler - execution. If an organization is ready to execute it implies that organization has ability to successfully plan, implement, and manage Internet-enabled strategies and initiatives, or in other words it means that organization has built its organizational readiness. In addition, another important characteristic in the approach of improvement of organizational readiness presents the fact that organizational readiness is not a one-time strategy-it is a continuous process. It is seldom either discrete or one-time event; it is overlapping activity that occurs throughout the life cycle of the organization.

Successful leaders understand the need to develop the organization, its culture, and its infrastructure. As the organization develops and executes its strategies it needs to ensure that IT strategies and initiatives are strongly linked to organizational goals and objectives and to make ongoing improvements to organizational readiness to enhance its ability to execute on IT initiatives.

What is Organizational Readiness?

Expressions, such as organizational readiness or organizational preparedness have the same meaning and they are focus more on the micro level, which is organization level. On the other hand, addition expression can be found, such as e-readiness which is more focused on macro level. "E-readiness (electronic readiness) is a measure of the degree to which a country, nation or economy may be ready, willing or prepared to obtain benefits which arise from information and communication technologies" (Dada, 2006, p. 1). This paper will attempt to carry out the concept of organizational readiness at the micro level, and to suggest ways to bridge the limitations that today's organizations are facing. The most practical definition of organizational readiness/preparedness from our stand point of view is the one proposed by Hartman, Sifonis, and Kador (2000) and refers to the "level at which an organization has optimized key attributes required to successfully implement Internet-enabled business strategies and initiatives". Without first addressing its readiness, an organization's IT initiatives may fail.

As a ninth pillar of Global Competitiveness report organizational readiness plays the crucial role not only in an organization but also in an economy of every country. "This pillar measures the agility with which an economy adopts existing technologies to enhance the productivity of its industries" (Porter & Schwab, 2008, p. 5).

Table 1. Enablers of Success

Strong execution	An organization must have the ability to identify, execute and deliver.
Metric driven	Internet-enabled capabilities are linked to organizational goals and objectives, and are measured and evaluated on a continuing basis.
Being focused on immediacy	Internet-enabled applications should be developed and deployed within three to six months. Large complex projects should be organized into smaller projects based on customer priorities and delivered phases.
A 'visioning" philosophy	Successful organizations recognize the need for continuous development and modification.
Being customer focused and technology enabled	Organizations must offer a product or service with clear value to a customer, called a customer value proposition, and focus on creating a new value through innovation.
Scalable applications/ standardized network architecture	Organizations must create technology foundations to utilize applications without creating systems that do not work together.
Being driven by vision	Organizations that communicate and act on a clear vision for the use of IT deliver greater customer value and transform processes for greater efficiency and productivity.

Jennett et al. (2003) has mentioned a similar approach to the definition of organizational readiness as a multifaceted concept that is related to planning and the workplace environment. It is crucial for every organization to understand these factors within organizational readiness in order to avoid costly implementation errors. "Readiness needs to be systematically assessed and is important for long-term success" (Jennett et al., 2003).

Hartman et al. (2000) presented four crucial areas for organizational readiness stating that organizational readiness is built on four pillars that can enhance an organization's ability to successfully implement ICT initiatives. They are:

- Leadership
- Governance
- Competencies
- Technology

Organizational readiness is a journey, not a destination. Through continuous improvement, an organization can more easily deploy and use ICT-enabled business processes that are focused, accountable, and measurable. Together, the four pillars can help drive organizational success. If the foundation of one pillar is not as strong as the others, the organization may falter on its path to long term success.

Most successful organizations demonstrate one set of characteristics, called enablers, presented in Table1, which makes an organization ready for success with IT.

Less successful organizations demonstrate a different set of characteristics, called barriers, presented in Table 2. These barriers will impact the success an organization has with IT.

FOUR PILLARS OF ORGANIZATIONAL READINESS

Leadership: The 1st Pillar of Organizational Readiness

The organization who has built in this pillar to the level of excellence has all right to say that they are an Internet leader.

Most successful organizations have strong leaders who believe in the power of IT. They understand how a move to web-based processes will create new opportunities for innovation, productivity, and efficiency. To extend processes internally and externally, this decision must be made at the executive level. The most successful organizations have strong leaders that set the vision, goals, and objectives that drive the organization to use ICT solutions in a strategic manner. These organizations understand how to change effectively, how to attract and motivate good and effective people, and how to build a strong organizational culture.

Table 2. Barriers to Success

Inadequate leadership mind-share	Failure of top management to link business strategies to achieve core goals and objectives of organization.
Build it and they will come	The illusion that customers, employees, and partners will naturally use Web-enabled applications without incentives and a solid management effort.
Inadequate execution and network architecture	Failure to build a technology foundation capable of meeting the future needs of the organization.
Partially automated responses	Failure to understand and redesign business processes creating delays and errors due to manual processes.
Islands of websites	Creating pockets of automation, often redundant and without integration.
Following the competition	Instead of developing innovative new products and services, the organization copies what their competitors are doing.
One-time-effort mentality	Building new systems and capabilities once without an effective plan to monitor and improve over time.

Strong leaders typically promote change throughout the organization, engage and empower the organization to use the Internet as a tool, view information technology as a strategic asset, and encourage and reward risk-taking in the organization. Without strong leadership, the other pillars of Organizational Readiness (even if executed well), will most likely not be enough to succeed.

For the organization to be a IT-Savvy Leaders it needs to have following leadership characteristics:

- Set new expectations and promote positive changes in the organization, highlighting accomplishments.
- Engages and empowers the organization to use the Internet as a tool.
- Are paranoid of its competition and monitor their strategic e-business initiatives closely to always stay ahead.
- Make sure that decisions and power are distributed evenly in the organization, online tools are shared, and all employees (including top management) are held accountable for results.
- Promote an Internet culture; they encourage both experimentation and initiatives that best utilize the Web.
- View information technology (IT) as a strategic transformation tool that they can use to get things done better, faster, and more effectively. They create an open environment for the sharing of information and expertise.
- Accept a certain amount of risk to gain a competitive advantage. They encourage employees to be comfortable with change and movement.

Governance: The 2nd Pillar of Organizational Readiness

The answer to the question how do we organize around Internet business leads to governance. Governance is the operating model – the glue – that holds together and defines the very nature of the organization. Governance describes the operational structure of the organization, including its authority, roles, responsibilities, and accountabilities; organizes and establishes an effective operating model, which is often the most problematic obstacle for organizations to overcome; deals with how to organize, fund, and execute IT initiatives; and means finding creative business and customer-driven ways to do this.

Leading organizations with strong IT governance models have established metrics for determining how to fund internet-enabled initiatives and for measuring the impact of those initiatives after their launch. Organizations with high organizational readiness have new governance models that focus on setting new business and interpersonal dynamics both inside and outside the organization. They rely less on established hierarchies and bureaucratic procedures. In most but not all cases, governance follows leadership.

The most successful Internet-ready organizations have developed established and flexible governance models.

Governance Characteristics of Effective Governance Models

- Establish cross-functional teams to promote collaboration across the organization and to execute initiatives throughout the organization. It helps reduce conflicts and allows the organization to be as creative as possible.
- Focus on near-term business results and tangible returns on IT investments.
- Encourage accountability for e-business success. Set up compensation and reward systems for all levels of employees.
- Actively promote the use of Web-based applications and standard tools, especially when traditional applications or manual processes might be more familiar.
- Make sure business decisions are made by business owners, with the IT department as a strategic consultant in the decision making process.
- Dictate a strong partnership between business and IT with metrics directing this partnership.

Competencies: The 3rd Pillar of Organizational Readiness

Organization competencies determine how an organization addresses a market need or achieves its purpose and provides an answer on question what capabilities do we need to compete and succeed

Organizations with strong competencies respond to customer needs and execute new programs quickly. They also develop strong partnerships with competitors and complementary organizations to help achieve their goals. Organizations who have stabile competencies react immediately to challenges such as globalization and reduce barriers to entry. Coherence, particularly in cultures where experimentation and failure is advocated, is critical for promoting successful Internet business initiatives. Strong competencies within organizations make investments in developing core competencies to create competitive advantage and customer value.

Competencies can be viewed as four primary skill sets:

1. **Strategic components** address an organization's ability to plan, adapt, and execute strategies with the agility to anticipate and drive change.
2. and 3. **Both operational and managerial competencies** provide the metrics that track successes, provide clear direction to project owners and customers, and support successful corporate culture changes.
4. **Technical competencies** address the understanding of technical foundations, tools, and how to apply them to solve business problems.

Competencies Characteristics of the Internet-savvy organization:

- Is knowledgeable and skilled on standard technology platforms, tools and applications. It is responsive and can be implemented quickly.
- Can manage multiple relationships simultaneously. It knows how and when to dissolve and form relationships or partnerships to respond to the customer facing (any part of the organization that the customer interacts with) needs.
- Understands the capabilities of an organizationally ready company, including

customer-facing, self-service (the customer can interact with the organization via the Internet), partnering, and technology competencies.

- Can handle increased complexity in the business environment. It has interrelated and fast-moving activities that adapt to changes in customer buying patterns, markets, and competition more quickly than most organizations.
- Encourages the sharing of information, which increases power across the organization. Has employees who can work on multiple tasks simultaneously, and can build networks of relationships that can shift without disrupting the business.

Technology: The 4th Pillar of Organizational Readiness

How can an organization develop or acquire a technology platform capable of supporting current and future growth?

Success with IT requires a robust enterprise-wide information technology (IT) architecture based on industry standards. A standards-based platform will enable easier external integration and faster migration to new systems over time. IT managers must be able to implement Web-based applications rapidly, without having to make improvements in the computing infrastructure. The technology pillar helps organizations acquire key technology capabilities needed for success such as security, standardization, flexibility, adaptability, scalability, and reliability. This makes it easier for employees to collaborate and develop new capabilities. Internet-ready organizations have the technology infrastructure (network services, hardware, and software) and skill competencies in place to develop, scale, and support these Internet initiatives.

Three essential Internet-ready technology elements include (a) skills – the organization is strong across all technology domains, including security and IT operations. The IT department partners closely with the organization, (b) applications – the organization's Internet-enabled solutions adapt to rapid change and are scalable and customizable for the needs of the company, its customers, suppliers, and partners, (c) infrastructure – the organization establishes and abides by a standard IT infrastructure. Backend systems are continually upgraded to meet future organizational requirements. Employees and customers can access all critical information.

Technology Characteristics

- The organization builds itself around an architecture that is robust and comprehensive. It has established organization-wide standards.
- Whenever possible, buy technology solutions, don't build them. There are other organizations that can build them better.
- Make sure that an intelligent technology infrastructure leads the development of applications. The Information Technology (IT) department should not develop applications that do not fit in with the overall technology plan.
- The organization has trained personnel on technology standards and developed flexible applications to run on standard platforms.
- The organization has a standardized, IT architecture. This enables new applications to emerge easily, cheaply, and quickly.
- Information is accessible and shared globally for a competitive advantage.

The Four Pillars in Action

This presents an example of an organization who is successfully implementing ICT initiatives based on four pillars.

With Local institutes around Serbia, Cisco Entrepreneur Institute, Training center Serbia continuously improves communications and coordination. They do this by sharing internal information via a company intranet, providing tools for coordinating calendars, and scheduling conference calls and webinars by using WebEx. Together, the four pillars of organizational readiness can help drive Training center Serbia's success. How can Training center Serbia apply the four pillars within the organization?

Leadership

To ensure strong leadership within the organization, Training center Serbia encourages an open environment for sharing information and expertise. Program managers set up a weekly webinar meeting so the managers from the local institute offices can share ideas between themselves and also with the leadership team from Training center Serbia.

Governance

Training center Serbia requires all IT-related improvement projects have a measurable benefit and measurement strategy before approving the spending. This requires that business and IT managers work together to make sure the right initiatives get funded.

Competencies

To improve management skills and business practices, Training center Serbia posted human resource policies and procedures online and added e-learning offerings to improve organizational competencies such as people management, finance, and marketing communications.

Technology

To ensure IT-efficient business operations and security, Training center Serbia upgraded a common, secure network infrastructure and web foundation that allows customer and product data to be shared by multiple business applications such as order entry, online directory, scheduling, and customer service.

IT GOVERNANCE AND PLANNING

Information Technology (IT) Governance is essential to all organization, it helps organization to manage the transactions, information, and knowledge necessary to initiate and sustain new Internet initiatives. This covers (a) four keys to IT governance, and (b) importance of IT governance planning.

According to Hartman et al. (2000) IT Governance is a board or senior management responsibility in relation to IT to ensure that:

- IT is aligned with the business or organizational strategy, or in other words, IT delivers the functionality and services in line with the organization's needs, so the organization can do what it wants to do.
- IT and new technologies enable the organization to do new things that were never possible before.
- As a result of the efficiency, partner satisfaction and loyalty also increase.
- IT-related services and functionality are delivered at the maximum economical value or in the most efficient manner. In other words, resources are used responsibly.
- All risks related to IT are known and managed and IT resources are secured.

Four Keys to IT Governance

Along with enjoying the benefits of new Internet initiatives, organization will also need to manage the risks associated with implementing new technologies. Among the organization's challenges and concerns are:

Table 3. Three Funding Models of IT

	User Discretionary	User Mandatory	IT Pays all Costs
Data-center (Servers, Middle-ware)	Non-standard undersized servers	Standardized undersized servers	Standard-ized scalable servers
Infra-struc-ture (LAN, WAN, PC, Tel)	Low standard-ization Low capability	Somewhat standardized Medium capa-bility	Highly stan-dardized High capabil-ity
Appli-cations (ERP, CRM, SCM)	High innova-tion Low standard-ization	Some innova-tion Some standard-ization	Low innova-tion High stan-dardization

- Funding: How IT obtains money to pay for people and systems, as well as align the IT strategy with the business strategy.
- Standards: How IT defines and enforces technical standards, without costs increasing and reliability suffering.
- Execution: How IT manages the entire project life-cycle, from idea origination to development to production to retirement.
- Measurement: The metrics used to ensure that IT implementation is successful.

Four Keys to IT Governance: Funding

Funding money drives behavior in organizations. The funding model used for IT has to strike a balance between cost-efficiency and innovation.

Three Funding Models

Data centers, shared infrastructure, and enterprise applications comprise the three main parts of an organization's IT systems. They can be funded in different ways. For example user discretionary, user mandatory and IT pays (presented in Table 3).

1. User Discretionary: Users can choose how much they want to spend on a particular part of IT. This provides the greatest flexibility, but at the expense of standardization as users are now fully in control.
2. User Mandatory: This is otherwise known as a "charge-back" or "tax" model. IT spends the money but charges the users for its operation. This leads to greater visibility by the business, but as there is little or no choice in what IT delivers, the business has little choice.
3. IT Pays: There is a single budget and IT has to make the tradeoff in investments in the three parts (for example, should we spend more on ERP or on the network?).

The most effective approach integrates all three funding models. For example, the business is well positioned to express requirements for the end-user applications. At the other extreme, the business has little understanding of the complex datacenter hardware and software, so IT should be the main decision maker on those technologies. In the middle, with end-user hardware (PCs, telephones, and networks), there should be some joint planning and decision-making.

Four Keys to IT Governance: Standards (presented in Table 4)

Studies have repeatedly shown that 20% of the total cost of a system is in the cost of the hardware. The remaining 80% is in the operating costs over the lifetime of that equipment. One way to reduce operating expenditure is to ensure standardization.

The standardization required for an organization will change depending on the stability of the technology. Balance between innovation and standardization is sometimes involved in the process of decision making. If an organization enforces standardization too aggressively, it can miss out on important emerging technologies.

Table 4. Example of IT Governance: Standards

Stability of the Technology	What to Do	Example
When technology is rapidly changing...	Set standards on a protocol or category.	• Network should be IP • Buy the most commonly used desktop operating system
As changes in the technology start slowing down...	Enforce stricter standardization requirements.	• Standardize on company A routers • Still buy only company B notebook computers
As technology stablizes...	Apply standardization across the organization.	• Use this configuration file • Install this version of the operating system with these settings turned on

The benefits of a standardized network can be significant and can include more reliable infrastructure, more financial savings, better IT performance, improved security, higher availability, faster deployment, and better defined priorities for processes. Once organization has standards in place, the IT department establishes these priorities across the enterprise. Only than IT resources can be allocated to work on developing new services and Web-based applications.

Four Keys to IT Governance: Execution

After examination of funding options and ways for standardization of organization's IT structure, organization is ready to execute new IT plan.

A successful implementation of the new IT structure involves setting business and IT priorities based on strategic goals, managing the cost of new technologies, and measuring business value and the success of the new technology in the organization.

Timeline will determine how quickly the IT department needs to implement each aspect of the new IT structure. Depending on requirements, some activities will take longer than others. Setting up standards and deadlines and examining the IT technology already available will accelerate organization's move to business.

Factors That Will Slow Organization Down

- Building own programs
- Customizing programs
- Using multiple vendors
- Adding people after start
- Setting unclear deadlines
- Changing success metrics
- Relying on too many decision makers

Factors to Keep Organization Moving

- Buying existing software programs
- Adapting the package to suit organization's needs
- Adding basic features only
- Driving change through small focused teams
- Setting firm deadlines
- Setting and adhering to success metrics
- Communicating effectively

Given the rapid pace of business today, especially in the economy, organizations need to implement their new IT structures as well as new business practices simultaneously. Cultivating an IT-confident organization requires constant communication from start to finish on every project.

Four Keys to IT Governance: Measurement

Organization's measurements will assess whether or not IT initiatives are in alignment with business strategies, ensure that the funding is allocated appropriately based on organizational priorities, and demonstrate that investment produced the expected results. For each activity, Key Performance Indicators (KPIs) must be defined. KPIs are measurable indicators that can be used to report the progress of the project or the new result against its pre-defined goals. Some examples of success metrics include time to delivery, project budget, application performance, user adoption, cost savings, etc.

IMPORTANCE OF IT GOVERNANCE PLANNING

Organizations are investing a lot of time, money, and resources into new networks and IT infrastructures. "Research shows that the top performing organizations generate up to 40 percent higher returns on their IT investments than their competitors with weak IT governance" (Harris, Herron, & Iwanicki, 2008, p. 60). IT governance planning is essential to ensure that these investments support Internet-enabling strategies because:

- IT is becoming more critical to operations.
- IT initiatives must link to the business strategies.
- Organizations spend more of their budgets on IT.
- Organizations need to ensure a return on their IT investment.

As business processes increasingly integrate with IT, it is vital that IT projects succeed and deliver value. In many organizations, the limiting factor in successful implementation of IT is not technology or funding, but the maturity of the IT organization's internal processes. Other challenges, such as the availability of adequate and standardized infrastructure and the ability of IT to balance its investments across the applications, shared infrastructure, and datacenter areas, are a direct consequence of the funding model used.

How to Manage Funding for IT Governance

Researching IT options and measuring results prevents organizations from over-spending or under-spending on their Internet initiatives. One of the biggest myths about IT is that the more you spend, the more value you reap from IT.

The likely reason for this is that large IT projects often fail. Projects fail for several common reasons, such as:

- Insufficient leadership
- Unclear objectives
- Moving requirements
- Long development times
- Unproven technology

IT governance issues raise multifaceted questions for organizations when they focus on new Internet initiatives.

- How the company is build to be capable of changing as quickly as the marketplace it serves?
- How the customer satisfaction is enhanced without overburdening employees?

IT plays some role in answering these questions. How big that role is varies by organization.

The Role of the IT Organization

Once strong communications and a successful partnership between the business and IT leaders have been established, organization can be evaluated how prepared the organization is, as a whole. Organizations have options available to streamline their new IT programs and to integrate IT priorities with business strategies. Adams (2003) suggested that there are seven leadership strategies for successful IT programs:

Table 5. Challenges of the IT Organization

Execution Time-frame	CIOs have an average tenure of 2-3 years
Organization	• Find, afford, and keep IT staff with skills in new technologies • Build employee morale in IT • Decide what to outsource and what to keep in the company
Funding	• Cut costs (in business and IT) • Provide value for money
Systems	• Keep legacy systems going • Remove obsolete systems • Scale systems • Migrate to new technologies • Deploy systems fasters
Influence	• Understand and exploit new technologies • Communicate business benefits/opportunities of new technologies • Gain credibility as a change agent in the corporation • Understand the inefficiencies and strengths of the corporation

1. Align IT to business strategy.
2. Make IT governance a priority.
3. Use metrics but don't let them dictate strategy.
4. Commit to a unified information architecture.
5. Create a shared business and technology leadership vision.
6. Develop IT organizational skills beyond technology.
7. Know when and how to partner.

Companies of all sizes are searching for new ways to successfully deploy complex, mission-critical, and often costly IT initiatives. Seven strategies suggested by Adams (2003) will enhance the success of those initiatives.

MOVING TOWARDS ORGANIZATIONAL READINESS

To improve organizational readiness, an organization must look for ways to improve its leadership, governance, competencies, and technology. Improvements in these four areas will allow an organization to deploy a web-enabled business strategy more successfully. There are key questions that pertain to the Leadership, Competencies, Governance, and Technology pillars that need to be asked in an organization in order to determine whether it is ready to implement Internet-enabled solutions.

Organizational Readiness Planning

What is the first step to improvement? Since organizational readiness is multifaceted concept it is necessary to be systematically assessed. This section has objective to present the importance of planning for organizational readiness and the basic steps that needs to be taken in order for organization to be prepared for this journey. Hartman et al. (2000) proposed following steps:

- Evaluation of organization's strengths and weaknesses objectively.
- Construction of the core competencies with the aim of organizational readiness improvement.
- Development of a readiness plan along with quarterly revision

Organizations must expand to keep up with the ever-changing and fast moving economy. Yet many organizations disregard planning and immediately start using the new technologies that are available. They let the technology determine the strategy and this leads to failure. Organizational readiness refers to the level at which an organization has optimized key attributes required to successfully implement Internet-enabled business strategies and initiatives.

Organizational readiness planning helps organizations:

1. create a more effective organizational culture
2. adapt quickly and easily to ongoing changes

3. identify areas of improvement
4. overcome barriers to organizational success

Improving Organizational Readiness

First step is to examine an organization in order to be found out how ready it is to implement new Internet business initiatives. After organization has assessed its readiness gaps and their importance, an Organizational Readiness plan needs to be prepared. Focus should be on strong implementation, accountability, and measurable near-term results. This plan should be a part of existing organization planning process and should be embeded in what organization already does.

Follow these steps to build a plan:

Step 1: Evaluate – Evaluation of organization's strengths and weaknesses objectively.

Step 2: Build - Construction of the core competencies with the aim of organizational readiness improvement.

Step 3: Develop – Development of a Readiness Plan. Quarterly revision of the Organizational Readiness plan.

An organization with strong organizational readiness typically has strong leadership, effective governance, and an innovative approach to the use of new technologies. The effective organization can move from strategy to planning to implementation more quickly and with greater focus and innovation. Several questions to consider include:

- Is an organization capable of dealing with rapid and ongoing change?
- Can it adapt and drive change quickly across the organization?
- Does it have the implementation competencies to execute meaningful Internet initiatives in three months or less?
- Does it have the technical competencies and resource talents to support Internet initiatives?
- Can it form and dissolve partnerships and relationships quickly to build and manage suppliers and partners?

Build Core Competencies

Organizations with strong readiness competencies are very responsive to customer needs and have the agility to execute and move quickly. More than a sum of their skills, these organizations have a culture, or at least influential departments that are more capable of reaping the benefits of Web-enabling business processes.

This culture is more inclined to combine people, process, and technology to solve problems and address opportunities. This organization is more capable of responding to new complexities such as globalization, shorter product life cycles and the entrance of new competitors due to barriers to entry.

A useful way to think about competencies is that it is an actionable concept. Following five points needs to be considered in order for an organization to build core competencies for its organizational readiness:

1. **Complexity**

   The Internet replaces physical constraints with the constraint of complexity. The new way of doing business can become even more complex because of the limited ability for humans to manage increasingly complex, interrelated, and fast-moving activities.
2. **Concurrency**

   Everything happens at the same time now. To excel in this business climate, organizations must feel comfortable with multitasking on every level.
3. **Coherence**

   Coherence defines the integrity of the organization. The organization may be extremely fluid and willing to change, but it must have a foundation and boundaries built so that it does not become chaotic. These boundaries include external (legal and regulatory rules) and internal (centered on the governance of the leaders of the organization.)

4. **Connectivity**

   Connectivity is a requirement for managing knowledge. Leaders must model how connectivity and collaboration between employees actually increases power and self-sufficiency by enforcing a value of sharing knowledge and expecting everyone else in the organization to do the same.

5. **Coordination**

   Coordination is required between an organization and established partners with well-known brand names. Partners gain the power of Internet knowledge and ability. Organization gains the support of name recognition. It's a mutually beneficial partnership both for organization and its new partner.

Develop an Organizational Readiness Plan

In order for organization to develop a plan, first needs to be determined if it can develop the ability to:

- Manage multiple relationships effectively. Successful organizations can build, manage, and dissolve relationships easily.
- Adapt easily to rapid and ongoing change. The economy changes rapidly and advantages are temporary. The ability to manage change is imperative.
- Drive change quickly across the organization. The entire organization must be willing to abandon current business practices in favor of something new.
- Identify and prioritize business opportunities. Act on favorable opportunities quickly. Spending too much time in analysis and decision-making can lead to lost opportunities.
- Execute strongly and quickly. Make meaningful changes in three months or less. Break larger projects down into segments that can be executed within three months. Abandon perfection and focus on satisfactory progress to promote speed.
- Support initiatives. Support Internet initiatives with a talented, innovative technical staff.

After assessment of an organization, which will provide the understanding the role and importance of IT governance, it is necessary for organization to assess its state of readiness, as well as creation of an Organizational Readiness Improvement Plan.

Why Assess Organizational Readiness?

Organizational readiness refers to the level at which a company or an organization has optimized the attributes required to successfully implement internet-enabled strategies and initiatives. To prepare for the move to the Internet, an organization needs to:

- Discover strengths, weaknesses, and areas of disagreement.
- Identify potential barriers to success and develop initiatives to resolve them.
- Assess progress within a structured timeline.
- Measure progress and continuously improve processes.

In-depth evaluation of the organization's strengths and weaknesses allows organization to focus its time and resources on improving weaknesses.

Characteristics of Organizational Competencies

First, organizational traits needs to be considered:

- The organization is knowledgeable and skilled on standard platforms, tools, and applications. It is responsive and can implement ruthlessly and quickly.
- The organization is able to manage multiple relationships. It also knows how and when to start and end partnerships to respond to customer needs.
- The organization understands the capabilities required for organizational readiness, including focusing on customer needs, offering self-service functions, developing strong partnerships, and increasing technology competencies.
- The organization can handle increasing complexity. It has interrelated and fast-moving activities that adapt to changes in customer buying patterns, markets, and competition more quickly than most organizations.
- The people can do multiple tasks, and can build networks of relationships that can shift without going into chaos.
- The organization encourages the sharing of information, which increases power across the organization.

Tools for Assessing Organizational Readiness

The Net Readiness Survey (NRS) is an analysis tool designed to assess an organization's ability to migrate to an Internet business model. The result of the survey tool is a scorecard containing a series of statements that relate to the four critical success factors: Leadership, Governance, Organization Competencies, and Technology.

The NRS provides recommendations in the four areas of organizational readiness based on individual or organizational inputs. These recommendations are based on the respondents' perceptions rather than "facts." Organization should evaluate and adapt the recommendations to meet the specific needs and priorities. If taken across an organization, the NRS can:

- Provide a broad strategic insight into company culture, such as how it shifts from business as usual to the new business practices.
- Produce an accurate picture of the organization's readiness.
- Provide a means of communication across the functional departments and between various levels of an organization.

Entire management team needs to be encouraged to take the NRS.

Net Readiness Survey

Young & Jude (2008) developed the Net Readiness Survey (NRS) which addresses how an organization rates its preparedness in each of the four pillars:

- Leadership
- Governance
- Competency
- Technology

To find out what an organizations strength and weakness are, diagnostic NRS needs to be taken, which is built in the Cisco Entrepreneur Institute web site (www.ciscoinstitute.net) as an online tool application as the part of their workshop content. The results will help organizations to develop a comprehensive Organizational Readiness Plan. After completion of online scorecard, Net Readiness Scorecard Overall Score can be obtained, along with a Best of Breed (BoB) number, and a scorecard graph that shows where organization is relative to the industry average.

Gap score that shows the difference between organization's score and the BoB score by subtracting average score from the BoB score can be generated. A low Gap score indicates a strength within that pillar, a higher Gap score indicates a weakness, and the highest Gap scores indicate areas of disagreement.

Overall Score: Based on answers to the questions in each pillar, scores are tallied up. It can be seen how ready an organization is by comparing organization's score to the scores in the table.
Best-of-Breed: These numbers indicate an average of the scores of most organizations in particular industry.
Graph: The graph shows the difference between organization's score and that of the Best-of-Breed score.

Net Readiness Scorecard (NRS) - What Needs to Done With the Results?

Review of the steps for assessing organization's readiness:

1. Take the NRS.
2. Evaluate organization's scores against industry Best-of-Breed scores and use the scores to identify areas of strength, weakness, and disagreement.
3. Generate a list of strengths, weaknesses, and disagreements.
4. Create an initial list of possible solutions.

Based on the Gap scores of each pillar, it can be determined some of the strengths and weaknesses in the organization. If there is a particularly high Gap score in a pillar, organization needs to try to determine what the weaknesses are. After evaluating the scores and determining the strengths, weaknesses, and areas of disagreements, it's time to consider ideas on how to address each of those elements. If taken across an organization, the NRS can provide a broad strategic insight into company culture, such as where and how it will be necessary to shift from old business practices to make way for new internet-enabled practices. Encouraging the entire management team to use the NRS will produce an accurate picture of the organization's organizational readiness. In addition, it can provide a means of communication across functional departments and between the various levels of an organization.

Create an Organizational Readiness Improvement Plan

Answering the following questions will lead to a successful Net Readiness Improvement Plan:

- Where are our issues?
- How are we at implementation?
- What is our culture?
- How do we use technology?
- What are the barriers?
- What are some projects/solutions we should implement?
- How can we measure success?

Organizational Readiness Improvement Plan

Young & Jude (2008) presented four steps to develop an improvement plan:

1. **Examine:** Examine the NRS results.
2. **List:** List the top three areas of weakness for each of the four pillars.
3. **Discuss:** Discuss the solutions and other actions that might be taken to address issues.
4. **Create a Plan:** Create a short readiness plan for each recommendation with the planning template.

CONCLUSION

This topic regularly seems to be avoided in the process of business planning but it is embedded into organization as the driving force of its competitiveness ability in successful technological transformation and ICT initiative implementation. As one of the 12 pillars of Global Competitiveness Report organizational readiness has an essential role within organization and represents e-business challenge and opportunity at the same time for every SMEs. Improving organizational readiness takes work and time, but the rewards are outstanding. The rewards are given in the satisfaction on the investments made in IT and Internet presence. If it is naturaly to check ground below fundamentals when building house, then why it is not regular to check organizational grounds for building IT infrastructure. Nowdays, Internet and network infrastructure is in the same position as the highways, bridges, and tunnels. This chapter tried to introduce organizational readiness as the tool for bridging the gap between briliant IT and Internet enebled solution and effective and efficient business usage of it in its early stage, almost before the implementation takes its role. No one can say that we are moving back with IT and Internet but how many of us can say that we are moving faster forward because we are using more than 30% of all installed engines. It is time to start to work on readiness to open chance and the door of new business age, since „Sudenlly business is not the same any more" (Hammer, 2002).

Nevertheless, there are implications for further research in this area. It would be useful to undertake empirical studies that include comparison of the organizational who are planning organizational readiness and ones they do not, in order to formulate a more refined version of the proposed model.

REFERENCES

Adams, J. E. (2003). Seven Leadership Strategies for IT Success. *IQ Magazine*. Retrieved September 1, 2009, from http://www.xynomedia.com/media/Seven_Leadership_Strategies.pdf

Dada, D. (2006). E-Readiness for Developing Countrie: Moving the Focus from the Environment to the Users. *The Electronic Journal of Information Systems in Developing Countries*, *27*(6), 1–14.

Hammer, M. (2002). *The Agenda: What Every Business Must Do to Dominate the Decade*. New York: Three Rivers Press.

Harris, M. D. S., Herron, D., & Iwanicki, S. (2008). *The Business Value of IT: Managing Risks, Optimizing Performance and Measuring Results*. New York: Auerbach Publications. doi:10.1201/9781420064759

Hartman, A., Sifonis, J., & Kador, J. (2000). *Net Ready: Strategies for Success in the E-conomy*. New York: McGraw Hill.

Jennett, P., Yeo, M., Pauls, M., & Jennifer Graham, J. (2003). Organizational readiness for telemedicine: implications for success and failure. *Journal of Telemedicine and Telecare*, *9*(Supplement 2), 27–30. .doi:10.1258/135763303322596183

Porter, M. E., & Schwab, K. (2008). *The Global Competitiveness Report 2008–2009*. Geneve: World Economic forum.

Young, M., & Jude, M. (2008). *iExec Enterprise Essentials Companion Guide*. San Jose, CA: Cisco Press

Section 2
New Business Models and Technological Support

Chapter 8
Digital Marketplaces as a Viable Model for SME Networking

Valentina Ndou
Università del Salento, Italy

Nezha Sadguy
Università del Salento, Italy

ABSTRACT

In the networked world supply chain, integration and networking is being echoed in various industries as a strategic imperative solution for firms. Firms are recognizing the power of the Internet as a platform for creating different forms of relationships and collaborations aimed to enhance value and achieve a sustainable competitive advantage. Digital Marketplaces represent one of the most powerful solutions adopted by firms to manage their supply chains and to support the networking practices among firms, especially among SMEs. In fact they enable firms to more efficiently buy, sell, and manage their supply chain processes on a global scale. However, SMEs Supply chains may differ in the modalities of coordination and collaboration, in the intensity of relations between actor and more specifically in the technological infrastructure and competencies available. These factors may affect the success of digital marketplaces and their potentialities for firms networking. The authors suggest that digital marketplaces could provide a viable model for SME networking; however, successful path toward networking requires a harmonization of digital marketplace business model with supply chain characteristics.

INTRODUCTION

The Internet technology is one of the most characterising features of current socioeconomic scenarios. This technology has been changing the interactions among people as well as the way businesses operate by enlarging the physical boundaries of the organizations and reconfiguring their structures and strategies. Therefore, we can say that the internet offers new opportunities & perspectives, as well as a great level of interactivity for firms, mainly the small and medium enterprises (SMEs).

Changes in the economic environment have sped up companies' process of focusing their activities on core competencies, outsourcing others

DOI: 10.4018/978-1-61692-880-3.ch008

to partners and therefore increasing the space for inter-organizational relations among firms in order to increase economic benefits, explore and develop new techniques of production and marketing, design, and develop new products and services.

To meet the challenges of the new competitive environments the supply chains integration is being echoed in various industries, and companies are learning that they must collaborate to compete (Bleeke and Ernst, 1993). Accordingly, different forms of relationships, collaborations and networking are being experienced among firms namely suppliers, competitors, customers, and research institutes and universities. Many forms and models of information technology solutions are being adopted by companies to facilitate the process of integration and networking with other actors of the supply chain. In fact, Digital Marketplaces represent one of the most powerful solutions adopted by firms to increase their competitiveness, support the networking practices among firms, reduce the transaction costs, enhance the economy, and perform benefits of the outsourcing. However, many of these digital marketplaces have failed to realize their core objectives because of the lack of a consistent business model that takes into account the peculiarities of small and medium enterprises and the nature of relationships that characterize and monitor their supply chains.

Thus, in this study we aim to demonstrate how the usage of digital markeplaces can build strong relationship and create a network among SME organizations. In this context, we will try to provide a viable digital marketplace model for SME that guides them toward networking approaches. Having said that, with the use of this model, it can be possible to trace the evolutionary path that the firms, participating in a digital marketplace, need to follow in order to develop progressively the necessary resources and capabilities (relational, technical and infrastructural) to enhance their competitiveness in the current digital economic landscape.

LITERATURE REVIEW

SME Networks

SME networks, identified with traditional industrial districts in Italy and clusters in other countries, have been acknowledged as successful models for SMEs. SME networks have been defined as groups of firms that combine forces to achieve competitive advantages that would be difficult to achieve individually (Mezegar, Kovacs, & Paganelli, 2000; Sherer, 2003). They have been considered as a viable model for SME competitive advantage (Hamel, 1991, Nonaka, 1994, Powell et al, 1996) and value creation through interactions that may take place within a firm and between firms. Scholars suggest that networks offer greater potential as they allow firms to access key resources such as industry information, capital, goods and services that have the potential to maintain or enhance a firm's competitive advantage (Gulati, 2000).

It is argued that through networks, SMEs can partly resolve their problems liked to size. Cooperative relationships can help firms gain competence, build resources, share risks, undertake quick market movements, and make solid investments (Malmström, 2002).

According to the social exchange theory no firm can survive by exclusively combining its internal resources, but it is always dependent on other firm's provision of resources, which causes a situation where this latter is exchanging resources with other firms. Accordingly, a network offer greater potential as they allow firms to access key resources from its environment, such as information, capital, goods, services that have the potential to maintain or enhance a firm's competitive advantage (Gulati, 2000). By building relation – specific assets, knowledge-sharing routines, and effective relational governance mechanisms into relationships, firms can leverage networks for knowledge acquisition and exploitation.

The technology enabled landscape offers new opportunities for firms networking. They create conditions for establishment of electronic networks where firms can collaborate with former competitors and potentially achieve competitive co-evolution (Ordanini & Pol, 2001). In this vein, an important trend born in various industries is the creation of digital marketplaces as a key enabler that allows SMEs to expand the potential benefits originating from linking electronically with suppliers, customers, and other business partners. In sectors such as industrial metals, chemicals, energy supply, food, construction, and automotive, "digital-marketplaces are becoming the new business venues for buying, selling and supporting to engage in the customers, products, and services" (Raisch, 2001).

These electronic markets allow firms to gain a significant contribution in creating value through low transaction costs by reducing information symmetries, increasing customer loyalty and enhancing transaction frequency, as well as by allowing firms to access other's resources increasing so the possibility of firms to acquire new knowledge (Bakos, 1997, Bakos, 1998, Kaplan and Sawhney, 2000 and Amit and Zott, 2001).

Many studies related to the use of internet ecommerce by SMEs (Daniel & Wilson & Myers 2002, Poon & Swatman 1999, Walczuch & Van Braven & Lundgren 2000) indicate growing levels of awareness and enthusiasm by SMEs, however only a small proportion of SMEs are realising substantial benefits from it. One of the major challenges faced by SMEs stems from lack of technological expertise and uncertainty about the benefits offered by e-commerce (Gengatharen and Standing, 2005).

We are of the view that to ensure SME participation and use of electronic networks solutions such as digital marketplaces, it is necessary to understand and examine the main factors affecting their adoption as well as provide appropriate business model that shows sensitivity to SMEs problems.

The Digital Marketplaces For SME

Digital Marketplaces are an integral part of conducting business online (White et al. 2007; Soh et al. 2002; Gengatharen & Standing 2005; Markus & Christiaanse 2003; Kambil & van Heck 2002; Koch 2002). Simply speaking, this application can be defined as web-based systems that link multiple businesses together for the purposes of trading or collaboration (Howard et al., 2006).

Digital marketplaces are based on the notion of electronically connecting many buyers and suppliers to a central marketspace in order to facilitate exchanges of, for example, information, goods and services (Bakos, 1991; Bakos, 1998; Grieger, 2003; Kaplan & Sawhney, 2000).

Digital Marketplaces have become increasingly used across industries and sectors, nowadays. There are different types and categories of these technological platforms. In sectors such as industrial metals, chemicals, energy supply, food, construction, and automotive, "digital marketplaces are becoming the new business venues for buying, selling, and supporting to engage in the customers, products, and services" (Raisch, 2001).

Some authors categorize them based on the functionalities they offer (Dai and Kauffman, 2002; Grieger, 2004; Rudberg et al., 2002) some based on number of owners and their role in the marketplace (Le 2005).

Three classes of marketplace ownership are commonly identified:

- Third party or public marketplaces are owned and operated by one or more independent third parties.
- Consortium marketplaces are formed by a collaboration of firms that also participate in the marketplace either as buyers or suppliers (Devine et al., 2001).
- Private marketplace is an electronic network formed by a single company to trade with its customers, its suppliers or both (Hoffman et al., 2002).

Consortium marketplaces are identified as most likely to be sustainable (Devine et al., 2001), as the founders can introduce their own customers and suppliers to the marketplace, helping the marketplace establish a viable level of transactions – a ready source of buyers and suppliers not available to third party marketplaces (White et al., 2007).

According to Kaplan and Sawhney (2000) the digital marketplaces add value through two basic functions: aggregation and matching.

The aggregation mechanism involves bringing many buyers and sellers together under one roof, which facilitates "one-stop shopping" and thus reduces transaction costs.

The matching mechanism brings buyers and sellers together to dynamically negotiate prices on a real-time basis.

Howard et al.'s (2006) argues that there are significant evidences regarding the benefits that firms could realize by using digital marketplaces in term of reductions in transaction costs, improved supplier communication, improved planning and improved audit of capability. While Rask and Kragh, (2004), classify the main benefits for participation in a digital marketplace into three main categories:

- efficiency benefits (reducing process time and cost);
- positioning benefits (improving company's competitive position);
- and legitimacy benefits (maintaining relationship with trading partners).

However, most of the implemented digital marketplaces have failed to realize their core objectives and to deliver real value for their participants. According to Bruun, Jensen, & Skovgaard (2002), many digital marketplaces have failed as they have been founded on optimism and hope rather than on attractive value propositions and solid strategies.

Evidently, the benefits that could be created via digital marketplaces have generated tremendous interest. This has led to a large number of e-marketplace initiatives rushed online without sufficient knowledge of their customers' priorities, with no distinctive offerings, and without a clear idea about how to become profitable (Wise & Morrison, 2000). In 2006 only 750 active digital marketplaces were registered on the directory of E-Market-Services compared to 2,233 e-marketplaces identified by Laseter et al in 2001. According to Bruun et al (2002) many digital marketplaces have failed as they have been founded on optimism and hope rather than on attractive value propositions and solid strategies. These failures seem to be mirrored in relatively low levels of adoption across firms as result of a number of challenges faced when it comes to the adoption of digital marketplaces.

Digital marketplaces' operators provide standardized solutions that do neither match the needs of firms nor allow this latter to exploit new technologies' potentialities. Also they ignore the fact that most industries are dominated by small and medium enterprises that are far less likely to use new technologies as result of resource poverty, limited IT infrastructure, limited knowledge and expertise with information systems.

In fact, SME encounter difficulties in using digital marketplaces due to lack in "resources and knowledge" (Cragg & King 1993; Mehrtens et al. 2001), in skill levels of business operators (Darch & Lucas. 2002; Duan, Mullins, Hamblin & Stanek, 2002), "trust in the IT industry" (Bode & Burn. 2002; van Akkeren & Cavaye. 1999), and "lack of e-commerce readiness in some industry sectors" (Lewis & Cockrill. 2002). Another obstacle which does not go without saying is the need for recognition in terms of potential to improve businesses appropriate enough to accommodate for the efforts and costs of adoption (Goode 2002; Poon 2000).

Therefore, offering simply a standard marketplace platform will result in a failure of the initiative as firms might not be prepared to use it, do not see the value proposition and hence they remain disinterested in using the platform for integration.

According to Rayport and Jaworski (2002), the process of convincing organizations to join the digital marketplace is both long and expensive, despite the economic incentive behind it On the other hand, prospective buyers and suppliers will not join the digital marketplace only on "visionary predictions of the glorious future of B2B e-trade; they must see the benefits in it right now," according to Lennstrand et al. (2001). Therefore, finding a business model that provides enough value to trading partners, to justify the effort and cost of participation is a substantial challenge associated with the creation of a digital marketplace (Rayport & Jaworski, 2002).

The success factors of a digital marketplace are determined not only by the willingness on the part of suppliers and buyers to participate in that market but also the understanding of types of relationships and dynamics of supply chains. An essential fact to take into consideration is that smaller firms do not often see themselves as part of a large supply chain. Indeed, Mentzer et al. (2001) states that relationships vary on their levels of trust, commitment, mutual dependence, organizational compatibility, vision, leadership, and top management support; the higher the levels of these elements, the closer the firms are to an integrated relationship.

In fact, trust, frequency of the transaction, complexity of the transaction, firm reputation, managerial skill, service, delivery scheduling and switching costs, are some of the factors that make strategic decisions on firms' participation in B2B e-markets more difficult (Glassberg & Merhout, 2007).

In the following sections we analyze the dynamics of supply chain relationships as an important variable to take into consideration in finding the appropriate business model for a digital marketplace that ensures SME participation.

Supply Chain Relationships

The dynamics of supply chains relationships have been discussed by several authors. Sako (1992) identified two patterns of relations, arm's length contractual relations (ACR) and obligational contractual relations (OCR), as extremes of a multidimensional spectrum of possible trading relationships.

ACR involves a single specific, discrete economic transaction. An explicit contract specifies the tasks and duties of both parties. All business exchanges are performed at arm's length to avoid undue familiarity and personal ties. Therefore, it is easy to change trading partners when the contract is terminated.

OCR, on the other hand, is more embedded in social relations between trading partners and is also characterized by a sense of mutual trust and open exchange of information. Transactions often take place without a prior formal contract. Even when tasks and duties of each partner are specified in a contract, both parties recognize an incentive to do more than expected by the trading partner. When one partner fails, there is a willingness to seek remedies rather than to shift to other partners

Different authors have since acknowledged these two end points, arms' length and integration (Larsen et al, 2003). However, the character of buyer–supplier relationships has been undergoing dramatic changes over the last decades. Industry observers and researchers have described these emerging relationships as "partnerships" or "strategic alliances," as opposed to the traditional "arm's length" type of relations (Heide and John, 1990).

Although there is a confusion as to the distinction among different collaboration, relationship type can be defined as the group or class of relationships that share common governance characteristics and operational by the three accepted categories of supply chain relationships (Bove and Johnson 2001; Golicic, Foggin, and Mentzer 2003):

- **Arm-length relationships**: Also called "open market negotiations," this is the most common type of relationship in supply chain environments. This level is characterized by little investment, hardly any information sharing and limited interaction between companies. Also on the low side are trust and commitment. Relationships at this stage are short-term, contract-based and adversarial, with several suppliers competing where price is the overriding factor. At this level, companies can easily change partners and efficiently perform routine tasks. From this starting point, companies can eventually develop a collaborative supply chain relationship if they invest a great deal of resources, cultivate trust and commitment, and share long-term strategic goals.
- **Cooperation**: This type of relationship emerged from firms' need to manage the increasingly complicated flow of information and material between organizations. At this stage, companies are more tightly tied together, sharing more information, than they would be in an extended arm-length relationship. What distinguishes this level from the previous one is fewer suppliers and longer-term supplier-customer relationships. But this relationship stage involves a shorter-term perspective and less commitment than higher levels. Also, the two key elements present at this stage - integration and interdependency - are more moderate than in coordinated or collaborative supply chain relationships.
- **Coordination**: As information technology is getting cheaper to deploy, it is becoming a defining factor in supply chain relationships. In particular, the degree of information infrastructure and sharing determines if companies are in coordinated supply chain relationships. At this level, firms' information systems are more strongly linked, and there is more emphasis on strategy. At this stage, firms engage in more joint initiatives, such as Collaborative Planning, Forecasting and Replenishment (CPRF) and Vendor Managed Inventories (VMI) to get a better handle on demand information.

WHAT VIABLE MODEL FOR DIGITAL MARKETPLACE?

Given all of the problems, is there a business model that will work?

Finding a business model that provides enough value to trading partners to justify the effort and cost of participation is also cited as a substantial challenge associated with the creation of an e-marketplace (Rayport & Jaworski, 2002).

In a recent paper Ndou and Petti (2006) have provided a multi-category of business models that a firm could chose to implement depending on the innovation degree and on the integration level they want and are able to realize.

The methodology used for clustering business models was mainly a desk research analysis, starting with determining common denominators or dimensions to be used for mapping business models. Although the most known business models taxonomies provided by Tapscott et al., (2000), Timmers (1998); and Rappa (2001) use different dimensions to categorize business models, all of them contend that companies that decide to embark on an e-Business model seek to innovate their company value through a restructuring of structures, assets, resources, products and services. They all seem to converge on two main aspects: first, the degree of *value innovation* and, second, the degree of *integration* they want to realize with their business model. Thus, the multi-category business models a firm could chose to implement differ depending on the degree of innovation and on the integration level they want and are able to realize in the contexts where they are rooted. So, if a company simply wants or can only sell and market its products/services over the Internet it

Figure 1. Business model multi-categories

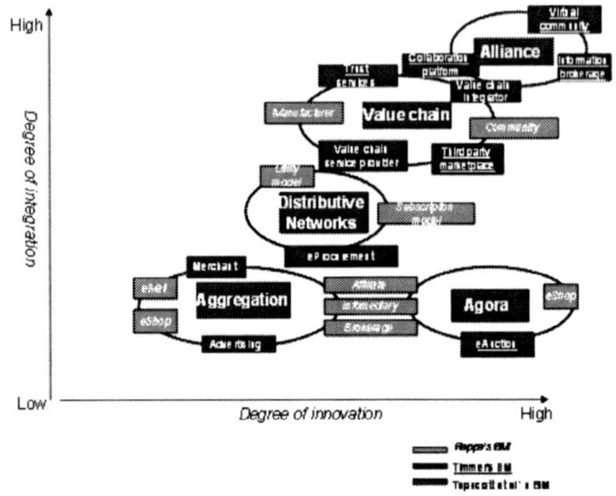

needs to simply approach an eShop, eAdvertising business model that doesn't require a high level of integration and innovation.

Having these two new dimensions, the authors proceed to realize a mapping of all types of business models, representing them in the same graph by trying to find out homogeneities and similarities among them. In particular were considered:

a. All the possible matches that could be established between molecular taxonomies of Rappa and Timmers based on their descriptions and features;
b. The insights that emerge from the comparative analysis of business models of some well-known internet companies to find out the matches among different categories (see Figure 1).

Through these steps a map of business models was constructed that allows to realize the multi-categorization of business models according to the innovation and integration level realized.

Tapscott et al's (1999) business model categories are used as meta-models as they are recognized as single, specific types of business models that describe, in a generic manner, the value in terms of innovation and integration that could be realized, the main features, the organizational structure and processes to be realized. But, in order to have a broader and detailed view of different molecular parts of business models that need to be blended together in a generic model to realize personalized and effective interface with customers, suppliers and partners, the author mapped the molecular business types around the generic categories. As Tapscott et al (1999) admit some business model subtypes need to be blended together in each generic business model. Given that "Timmers" and "Rappa" give a very detailed level of business models that can be used, the authors identify which of these molecular business models could be combined in the generic business model to effectively interact and collaborate with different stakeholders (customers, partners, suppliers etc). In this way they came up with a multi-categorization of business models provided by different authors.

This clustering has two meanings:

First, it shows which types of molecular business models could be combined in a generic business model (Tapscott taxonomy). Some molecular business models are present in almost all types of generic business models (such as the merchant, E-Shop, E-Advertising etc), but some others could be developed only when the e-Business strategy of the firm is highly innovative and its business model integrated. However, it is worth noting that moving to upper to more advanced stages doesn't mean that firms need only to develop, for example, collaboration platforms, virtual communities, knowledge communities, but the previous basic business models such as E-Shop, E-Advertising, E-Procurement are integrated and enhanced with new advanced and sophisticated services, technologies and solutions. While the upper molecular business models such as collaborative platforms, virtual communities, value chain integrator are not present in lower levels. This fact is related to the second insight that comes out of this analysis.

Second, the clustering is an evolutionary pathway, as well. That means that to pursue greater integration and innovation levels firms need to keep changing their business model, shifting toward higher levels in the graph. In higher levels more complex and sophisticated solutions, services, and technology architectures are used. Stage by stage firms will develop organisational structures, routines, assets, resources and capabilities that allow them to pursue high innovation levels. Reaching upper stages is very challenging. It requires firms to have a good base of customer data and customer relations, have strong social capital with their partners and suppliers and to have a good knowledge and technology infrastructure. Hence, the context where firms are rooted, the social and structural capital they pose are very important elements to consider in finding the business model cluster that a firm can approach and the evolutionary pathway to pursue.

We used this approach to try to find out the appropriate business model of digital marketplaces that could drive firms toward networking solutions.

THE DIGITAL MARKETPLACE BUSINESS MODEL IDENTIFICATION

The three different types of supply chain configuration need different types of digital marketplace models in order for firms to perform a stage by stage process toward higher supply chain integration and networking (Figure 2)

SME that belongs to supply chains that are mainly based on arms length relationships, are characterized by limited interaction between companies, low trust and commitment, short term relationships. As such, they tend to be disinterested on technology solutions and any digital marketplace platform which point directly to the integration of supply chain actors risks to fail. The digital marketplace in this case could serve as a context to initiate a change management

Figure 2. Digital marketplace business model

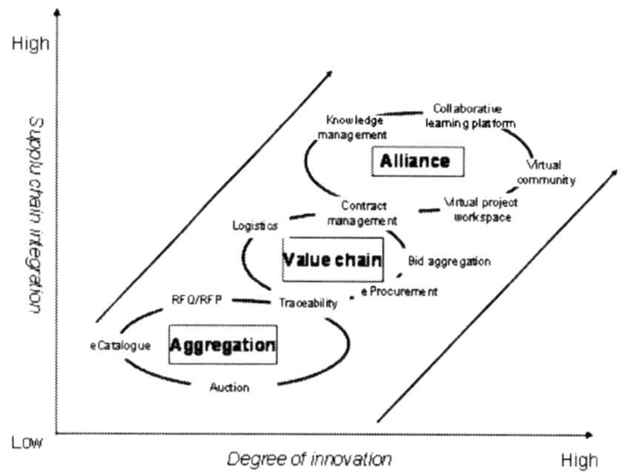

process aimed at creating, overtime, the necessary cultural, organizational, and technological prerequisites for any further intervention aimed at developing and enhancing the competitiveness of the supply chain. Thus an aggregation business model for digital marketplace is the most suitable configuration (see Figure 2). In this stage digital marketplace will serve as an aggregator of single buyers and sellers in a one single market in order to enhance products promotion and commercialization.

It is aimed at offering a one-stop procurement solution to SMEs by matching buyers and sellers through its website. Simple services such as E-Catalogue, Request for Quote/Request for Purchase, auction are suitable for firms in this stage.

Starting to use these basic services offered by digital marketplaces in this stage is an indispensable phase for creating the right conditions for pursuing an evolutionary pathway toward a cooperative or coordination configuration, as well as making SMEs aware of the potentialities and benefits of digital marketplaces for firms' networking.

For SME that are part of supply chains based on cooperative relationships and which are characterized by more strong ties, sharing more information, fewer suppliers and longer-term supplier-customer relationships, the principal role of a digital marketplace initiative should be that of reinforcing the existing relationships among different actors, creating new ones and exploiting partnerships in order to enhance services. The appropriate business model for a digital marketplace initiative is thus a value chain (see Figure 2). In these contexts, there is no need to start from aggregating and integrating, since participants are already tied in long-term relationships. Such a kind of digital marketplace empowers participants with more advanced collaborative technologies in order to connect suppliers, customers and partners in a global supply network where critical knowledge and information about demand, supply, manufacturing, and other departments and processes is shared instantaneously. More value added services could be provided at this stage such as – bid aggregation, contract management, transaction tracking, logistics, traceability etc - which permits the supply chain actors to integrate their operations and processes (Figure 2).

While in case of SME that are part of supply chains based on coordination internetworking technologies allow for the distributed management of supply chains. In these contexts the digital marketplace needs to leverage on the integrated and collaborative culture of the context (so a value chain model seems a prerequisite for such kind of models) to create distributed knowledge networks, composed by a set of dynamic linkages among diverse members who are engaged in deliberate and strategic exchanges of information, knowledge and services for design and produce both integrated and/or modular products. The appropriate business model in this case could be an alliance oriented towards setting directions, vision and standards for the offerings to which each player contributes autonomously. Networking services could be implemented in this phase such as Virtual Project Workspace (VPW) for product development teams, e-learning services, knowledge management, virtual communities (Figure 2).

CONCLUSION

New internetworking technologies have provided new tools, applications and opportunities for SME to organize and manage their activities in new and more cost-effective ways, to build and maintain relationships with the external world and to strategically position themselves in the increasing dynamic environment.

A relevant trend today is the creation of digital marketplaces as a key enabler that allows SMEs to expand the potential benefits originating from linking electronically with suppliers, customers and other business partners.

But, while the digital marketplace provides many benefits for SME and for their networking many of them have failed to deliver their values for their participants. In this paper we argue that, among all the possible explications of the failure of digital marketplace there is the negligence of the fact that firms differ in the intensity and density of interaction, the social climate and more general the readiness for internet adoption. These differentiated features influence the feasibility and the performance of digital marketplaces.

We argue that a successful digital marketplace model for SMEs of a supply chain requires an understanding of the type of relationships already existing as well as the readiness of SME to use and benefit from platforms in terms of skills, capabilities, technologies etc. The business model of a digital marketplace needs to be suited to the supply chain relationships already existing among firms. In this way the digital marketplace will serve as a context for firms to reinforce their relationships and to gradually adopt the strategic capabilities of the e-marketplace such as the ability to synchronize supply chain activities simultaneously with different participants all at the same time. It, also, plays a major role in initiating the process of capability building and coordinating the actions of a large number of interested actors.

However, starting at the right point and in the right way doesn't automatically guarantee success and competitive advantage. In today's business environment firms and supply chains need to continuously upgrade and develop organizational structures, assets and capabilities, the social and customer capital that would allow them to enhance their innovation and integration level.

SMEs that intend to enhance their value and reap the strategic advantage of their participation in digital marketplaces should be aware that their interaction with other firms requires an integration of various functional areas within an organization and coordination with external participant organizations.

In this instance, firms would need to expend resources on changing and evolving their skill sets, technological capabilities and relationships with other users of the digital marketplace, thus, generating networking patterns.

It seems reasonable to argue that firms would gradually develop the capabilities to reap the benefits of digital marketplace participation such as the ability to network with different participants as well as to synchronize with them their activities.

In terms of future research, the ideas here proposed need to be refined in further conceptual and empirical research. In particular, a longitudinal study could be undertaken to validate the evolutionary path proposed in this paper in a specific SME supply chain configuration. It will be important also to monitor the process of adoption of different stages of digital marketplaces, by analysing the time taken for firms to move from one stage to the next and the main factors that determine successful progress of firms in the evolutionary model. Also an analysis of how these factors vary across different stages of evolutionary path could also be usefully undertaken

REFERENCES

Amit, R., & Zott, C. (2001). Value Creation in E-Business. *Strategic Management Journal*, *22*, 493–520. doi:10.1002/smj.187

Bakos, J. Y. (1991). A strategic analysis of electronic marketplaces. *Management Information Systems Quarterly*, *15*(3), 295–310. doi:10.2307/249641

Bakos, J. Y. (1997). Reducing buyer search costs: implications for electronic marketplaces. *Management Science*, *43*(12), 1676–1692. doi:10.1287/mnsc.43.12.1676

Bakos, J.Y. (1998) The emerging role of electronic marketplaces on the Internet. *Common ACM*, 41 (8).35–42.

Bleeke, J., & Ernst, D. (1993). *Collaborating to Compete*. New York: John Wiley & Sons.Bode, S., & Burn, J. M. (2002). Strategies for consultancy engagement for e-business development - a case analysis of Australian SMEs. In Burgess, S. (Ed.), *Managing Information Technology in Small Business: Challenges and Solutions*. Hershey, PA: Idea Group.

Bove, L. L., & Johnson, L. W. (2001). Customer relationships with sales associates: an opportunity for retailers. *International Quarterly Journal of Marketing*, *1*(1), 135–150.

Bruun, P., Jensen, M., & Skovgaard, J. (2002). e-Marketplaces: Crafting A Winning Strategy. *European Management Journal*, *20*(3), 286–298. doi:10.1016/S0263-2373(02)00045-2

Cragg, P. B., & King, M. (1993). Small-firm computing: Motivators and inhibitors. *Management Information Systems Quarterly*, *17*(1), 47–60. doi:10.2307/249509

Dai, Q., & Kauffman, R. J. (2002a). Business Models for Internet-Based B2B Electronic Markets. *International Journal of Electronic Commerce*, *6*(4), 41–72.

Darch, H., & Lucas, T. (2002). Training as an e-commerce enabler. *Journal of Workplace Learning*, *14*(4), 148–156. doi:10.1108/13665620210427276

Devine, D. A., Dugan, C. B., Semaca, N. D., & Speicher, K. J. (2001). Building enduring consortia. *McKinsey Quarterly Special Edition*, *2*, 26–33.

Duan, Y., Mullins, R., Hamblin, D., & Stanek, S. (2002). Addressing ICT skill challenges in SMEs: Insights from three country investigations. *Journal of European Industrial Training*, *26*(8/9), 430–445. doi:10.1108/03090590210451524

Eng, T. Y. (2004). The role of e-marketplaces in supply chain management. *Industrial Marketing Management*, *33*, 97–105. doi:10.1016/S0019-8501(03)00032-4

Gengatharen, D. E., & Standing, C. (2005). A framework to assess the factors affecting success or failure of the implementation of government-supported regional e-marketplaces for SMEs. *European Journal of Information Systems*, *14*(4), 417–433. doi:10.1057/palgrave.ejis.3000551

Glassberg, C. B., & Merhout, W. J. (2007). Electronic markets hypothesis redux: Where are we now? *Communications of the ACM*, *50*(2), 51–55. doi:10.1145/1216016.1216020

Golicic, S., Foggin, L. J., & Mentzer, T. J. (2003). Relationship Magnitude and Its Role in Interorganizational Relationship Structure. *Journal of Business Logistics*, *24*(1), 57–76.

Goode, S. (2002). Management attitudes toward the World Wide Web in Australian small business. *Information Systems Management*, (Winter): 45–48. doi:10.1201/1078/43199.19.1.20020101/31475.6

Grieger, M. (2003). Electronic marketplaces: A literature review and a call for supply chain management research. *European Journal of Operational Research*, *144*, 280–294. doi:10.1016/S0377-2217(02)00394-6

Grieger, M. (2004). An empirical study of business processes across Internet-based electronic marketplaces. *Business Process Management Journal*, *10*(1), 80–100. doi:10.1108/14637150410518347

Gulati, R., Nohria, N., & Zaheer, A. (2000). Strategic Networks. *Strategic Management Journal*, *21*(3), 203–215. doi:10.1002/(SICI)1097-0266(200003)21:3<203::AID-SMJ102>3.0.CO;2-K

Hamel, G. (1991), Competition for Competence and Inter-Partner Learning within International Strategic Alliances. *Strategic Management Journal*, no. 12 (special issue), 83-103.

Heide, J. B., & John, G. (1990). Alliances in industrial purchasing: the determinants of joint action in buyer– supplier relationships. *JMR, Journal of Marketing Research*, *27*, 24–36. doi:10.2307/3172548

Hoffman, W., Keedy, J., & Roberts, K. (2002). The unexpected return of B2B. *The McKinsey Quarterly*, *3*, 97–105.

Howard, M., Vidgen, R., & Powell, P. (2006). Automotive e-hubs: exploring motivations and barriers to collaboration and interaction. *The Journal of Strategic Information Systems*, *15*(1), 51–75. doi:10.1016/j.jsis.2005.06.002

Howarth 2002; Howarth, B. (2002). E-survivors: Get 'e' or get out. *Business Review Weekly*.

Kambil, A., & van Heck, E. (2002). *Making markets. How firms can design and profit from online auctions and exchanges*. Boston: Harvard Business School Press.Kaplan, S. & Sawhney, M., (2000). E-hubs: the new B2B marketplaces. *Harvard Business Review,* 397-103.

Koch, H. (2002). Business-to-business electronic commerce marketplaces: the alliance process. *Journal of Electronic Commerce Research*, *3*(2), 67–76.

Larsen, T. S., Kotzab, H., & Grieger, M. (2003). Electronic marketplaces and supply chain relationships. *Industrial Marketing Management*, *32*, 199–210. doi:10.1016/S0019-8501(02)00263-8

Laseter, T., Long, B., & Capers, C. (2001). *B2B benchmark: the state of electronic exchanges*. Booz Allen Hamilton.

Le, T. (2005). Business-to-business electronic marketplaces: evolving business models and competitive landscapes. *International Journal of Services Technology and Management*, *6*(1), 40–53. doi:10.1504/IJSTM.2005.006543

Lewis, R., & Cockrill, A. (2002). Going global - remaining local: the impact of e-commerce on small retail firms in Wales. *International Journal of Information Management, Vol.*, *22*, 195–209. doi:10.1016/S0268-4012(02)00005-1

Malmström, M. (2002). *Acquiring Competence to Create and Sustain Competitive Advantages. A Study of four high technology firms*. Licentiate Thesis, Luleå University of Technology.

Markus, M. L., & Christiaanse, E. (2003). Adoption and impact of collaboration electronic marketplaces. *Information Systems and E-Business Management*, *1*(2), 139–155. doi:10.1007/s10257-003-0001-7

Mehrtens, J., Cragg, P. B., & Mills, A. M. (2001). A model of Internet adoption by SMEs. *Information & Management*, *39*(3), 165–176. doi:10.1016/S0378-7206(01)00086-6

Mezegar, I., Kovacs, G., & Paganelli, P. (2000). Co-operative production planning for small- and medium-sized enterprises. *International Journal of Production Economics*, *64*, 37–48. doi:10.1016/S0925-5273(99)00032-8

Ndou V., Petti C., (2006) DMS Business Models Design and Destination Configurations: Choice and Implementation Issues, *Journal of Information Technology and Tourism,* 9.(1), New York: Congizant Comm. Corp.

Nonaka, I. (1994). A dynamic theory of organisational knowledge creation. *Organization Science*, *5*(1), 14–37. doi:10.1287/orsc.5.1.14

Ordanini, A., Micelli, S., & Di Maria, E. (2004). Failure and Success of B-to-B Exchange Business Models: A Contingent Analysis of Their Performance. *European Management Journal*, *22*(3). doi:10.1016/j.emj.2004.04.013

Ordanini, A., & Pol, A. (2001). Informediation and competitive advantage in D2B digital marketplaces. *European Management Journal*, *19*(3), 276–285. doi:10.1016/S0263-2373(01)00024-X

Poon, S. (2000). Business environment and internet commerce benefit - a small business perspective. *European Journal of Information Systems*, *9*, 72–81.

Poon, S., & Swatman, P. (1999). An exploratory study of small business Internet commerce issues. *Information & Management*, *35*, 9–18. doi:10.1016/S0378-7206(98)00079-2

Porter, M. E. (2001). Strategy and the internet. *Harvard Business Review*, *79*(3), 63–78.

Powell, W. W., Koput, K. W., & Smith-Doerr, L. (1996). Inter-organizational collaboration and the locus of innovation. Network learning in Biotechnology. *Administrative Science Quarterly*, *41*, 116–145. doi:10.2307/2393988

Raisch, W. D. (2001). *The e-Marketplace: Strategies for Success in B2B eCommerce*. New York: McGraw-Hill.

Rappa, M. (2001) *Managing the digital enterprise: Business models on the Web*. Retrieved from <http://ecommerce.ncsu.edu/business_models.html>

Rask, M., & Kragh, H. (2004). Motives for e-marketplace participation: Differences and similarities between buyers and suppliers. *Electronic Markets*, *14*(4), 270–283. doi:10.1080/10196780412331311720

Rayport, J. F., & Jaworski, B. J. (2002). *Introduction to e-Commerce* (pp. 204–206). New York: McGraw-Hill.

Rudberg, M., Klingenberg, N., & Kronhamn, K. (2002). Collaborative supply chain planning using electronic marketplaces. *Integrated Manufacturing Systems, 13*(8), 596–610. doi:10.1108/09576060210448170

Sako, M. (1992). *Prices, quality and trust—interfirm relations in Britain and Japan.* Cambridge, UK: Cambridge Univ. Press. doi:10.1017/CBO9780511520723

Segev, A., Gebauer, J., & Fäber, F. (1999). Internet-based Electronic Markets. *EM - International Journal of Electronic Markets,* 9 (3), 138-146.

Sherer, S. (2003). Critical Success Factors for Manufacturing Networks as Perceived by Network Coordinators. *Journal of Small Business Management, 41*, 325–345. doi:10.1111/1540-627X.00086

Soh, C., & Markus, L. M. (2002). B2B E-Marketplaces - Interconnection Effects, Strategic Positioning, and Perfor-mance. *Systemes d'Information et Management, 7*(1), 77–103.

Stockdale, R., & Standing, C. (2003b). Increasing the adoption of electronic commerce by SMEs: Reflections from an empirical study.*4th International We-B Conference*, ECU, Perth, Australia.

Tapscott, D., Lowi, A., & Ticoll, D. (2000). *Digital Capital: Harnessing the Power of Business Webs.* Boston: Harvard Business School Press.

Timmers, P. (1998). Business Models for Electronic Markets. *Journal on Electronic Markets, 8*(2), 3–8. doi:10.1080/10196789800000016

Turban, E., King, D., Lee, J., Warkentin, M., & Chung, H. M. (2002). *Electronic Commerce - A Managerial Perspective.* Upper Saddle River, New Jersey: Prentice Hall.

Van Akkeren, J., & Cavaye, A. L. M. (1999). Factors affecting entry-level Internet technology adoption by small business in Australia - evidence from three cases. *Journal of Systems and Information Technology, 3*(2), 33–48. doi:10.1108/13287269980000747

Walczuch, R, B, Van., G, & Lundgren, H. (2000). Internet adoption barriers for small firms in The Netherlands. *European Management Journal, 18*(5), 561–572. doi:10.1016/S0263-2373(00)00045-1

White, A., Daniel, E., Ward, J., & Wilson, H. (2007). The adoption of consortium B2B e- marketplaces: An exploratory study. *The Journal of Strategic Information Systems, 16*(1), 71–103. doi:10.1016/j.jsis.2007.01.004

Wise, R., & Morrison, D. (2000). Beyond the Exchange - The Future of B2B. *Harvard Business Review*, (November-December): 86–96.

Chapter 9
What is New with Organization of E-Business:
Organizational Viewpoint of the Relationships in E-Business

Vojko Potocan
University of Maribor, Slovenia

Zlatko Nedelko
University of Maribor, Slovenia

Matjaz Mulej
University of Maribor, Slovenia

ABSTRACT

In modern working relations, a company can improve its business dramatically, especially with formation and performance of suitable management. An important role in the whole management of a company belongs also to management of e-business. A broad definition defines e-business as a business process that uses Internet (and/or any other electronic medium) as a channel to complete business transactions. One of the main concerns about management of e-business is how much of each e-business should be owned by each e-business participants. This is called the extent of vertical integration. But in the modern business environment, vertical integrations alone are not enough. The alternative to vertical integration is some other form of relationship, not necessarily ownership. Inthe authors' contribution, they will examine the relationship between the links of the e-business in terms of the flows between the operations involved. The authors use term link for all the different types of flow in exchange. This contribution discusses two issues: (1) How different relationships in e-business impact organization of e-business, and (2) How different organizational forms impact of e-business.

DOI: 10.4018/978-1-61692-880-3.ch009

INTRODUCTION

Many factors importantly influence the way in which organizations conduct their business nowadays (e.g., see Etzioni, 1997; Daft, 2003; Potocan, Kuralt, 2007; Robins, 2007; etc.). In the last decade a special attention has been focused on advancement in information-communication technology (i.e., ICT), since it has made a tremendous impact on the contemporary business practice in various ways (e.g., see Rodgers et al., 2002; Hartley, 2007; McLeod, Schell, 2007; Schermerhorn, 2009; etc.). In that frame, electronic business (e-business) has become an inescapable fact and also a powerful initiator for different kinds of improvements within organizations (e.g., see Amor, 1999; Amit, Zott, 2001; Eckersley et al., 2004; Laudon, Laudon, 2005; Laudon, Traver, 2008; etc.). E-business means different things to different people. This contribution attempts to fill in the perceived theoretical gap by developing an organizational model for understanding, defining and management of relations (and/or relationships) between entities involved in e-business. But to do that, we must first define the contents of e-business and relationships in e-business.

In theory and in business practice there is no general agreement on definition of e-business (e.g., see Timmers, 2000; Culler, Webster, 2007; Pavic et al., 2007; Turban et al., 2008; etc.). A prevailing definition defines e-business as a business process that uses Internet (and/or any other electronic medium) as a channel to complete business transactions (Swaminathan, Tayur, 2003). In literature one often sees the definition by Wu (see Wu et al., 2003), that defines e-business as the use of the Internet technologies to link customers, suppliers, business partners, and employees, employing at least one of the following: e-commerce websites that offer sales transactions, extranets and supply chains, intranets and enterprise information portals, and electronic data interchange.

For contents-related understanding of e-business it is also important to emphasize that the concept of e-business is often mixed with the concept of electronic commerce (e-commerce). In reality they are completely different concepts (e.g., see Afuah, Tucci, 2000, Rodgers et al., 2002; Beynon-Davies, 2004; Li, 2006; etc.). E-commerce focuses primarily on transaction with organization's customers (e.g. see Savole, Raisinghani, 1999; Amor, 1999; Anderson, 2000; Laudon, Traver, 2008; etc.). On the other hand e-business expands the concept of e-commerce and also includes connections of organizations with their suppliers, employees and business partners (e.g., see Rodgers et al., 2002; Budd, Harris, 2004; Li, 2006; Pavic et al., 2007; etc.). We look at the e-commerce in a broader sense, therefore we use terms e-business and e-commerce interchangeably.

E-business has some important and distinguishing characteristics (e.g., see Anderson, 2000; Laudon, Laudon, 2005; Chaffey, 2006; Daft, 2006; etc.). Laudon and Traver (2008) defined the following:

- Ubiquity – Internet (and web technology) is available everywhere (at work, at home, at official/public institutions),
- Global reach – reach of technology is boundariless, and it reaches across national boundaries, around the globe,
- Universal standards – internet standards enable interoperability among different users,
- Richness – communication channels are very rich,
- Interactivity – since the technology works by interacting with the users,
- Information density – use of technology reduces information costs and raises quality of information,
- Customization – since technology enables delivering of personalized messages to individuals as well as groups.

Many organizations recognized the importance and possible benefits from e-business in nowadays business environment in order to remain/become competitive (e.g., see Amit, Zott, 2001; Laudon, Traver, 2008; etc.). Experiences from business practice assign different benefits from engagement in e-business, such as (e.g., see Wang, 2001; Al-Mashari, 2002; Peet et al., 2002; Rodgers et al., 2002; Laudon, Laudon, 2005; McLeod, Schell, 2007; etc.):

- E-business enhances the competitiveness of the organization by lowering transaction costs in various fields in organization (e.g. less paper work);
- Improved customers satisfaction by differentiating products/services and better customer service before, during, and after sale;
- Improved relationships with partners in supply chain, especially suppliers and financial community; and
- Increased overall performances of organization, due to previously mentioned benefits, which can result in organization's increased, profit/reduced loss.

However, organizations engaging in e-business could also experience the following disadvantages (Rodgers et al., 2002; Laudon, Laudon, 2005; McLeod, Schell, 2007; Pavic et al., 2007; etc.):

- High development costs are one of the primary obstacles for engaging in e-business. Due to the complexity of e-business applications, the organization may need to restructure its current systems (e.g. new hardware, software, employee training);
- Security becomes another concern for the organization when implementing e-business, since all information is now exposed over the internet, which is vulnerable (e.g. hackers) and;
- Immature or unavailable software.

E-business therefore requires profound changes in the ways that organization conducts its business. From the firm's perspective a crucial consideration is management of relationships between entities involved in e-business.

When organizations try to adopt e-business, it also creates its own network of relationships between entities involved in e-business (e.g., see: Bensaou, Venkatraman, 1995; Gulati et al., 2000; Vlaar et al., 2006; Potocan, Kuralt, 2007). There is plenty of literature about e-business phenomenon, but from the organizational aspect little is known about type/forms of relationships among entities involved in e-business (e.g., see Ring, Vandeven, 1994; Amor, 1999; Afuah, Tucci, 2000; Kalakota, Robinson, 2001; Wu et al., 2003; Vlaar et al., 2006; etc.). Relationships among entities in e-business are mostly partially addressed (see: Bensaou, Venkatraman, 1995; Gulati et al., 2000; Johnson, Whang, 2002).

Even more, literature available to date did not provide many discussions about possible differences between types/form of relationships of e-business. An exception is, for example, discussion by Johnson and Whang (2002), which addresses relationships between entities involved in e-business (as a whole), beyond the transactions among the supply chain partners, both suppliers and customers, as an e-collaboration, but very limited and only in the frame to define their impact on the supply chain.

BACKGROUND OF RELATIONSHIPS IN E-BUSINESS

E-business can be defined in terms of its content, once its working characteristics are known and understood (e.g., see Hatch, 1997; Afuah, Tucci, 2000; Tiwana, Willianms, 2000; Beynon-Davies, 2004; Chaffey, 2006; Daft, 2006; Mullins, 2007; etc). Therefore it makes sense to first study the possible basic forms/types of working of e-business in organizations. Theory and business practice know of many different definitions of e-business working that create the basic division of e-business types (e.g., Bensaou, Venkatraman, 1995; Amit, Zott, 2001; Laudon, Traver, 2008; Daft, 2009; etc.). We can put the various models in two groups to meet the needs of our consideration.

The first group can collect models, which are defined according to the orientation of e-business activities (e.g., see Afuah, Tucci, 2000; Trombly, 2000; Chaffey, 2006; Laudon, Traver, 2008; etc.). In literature and also in business practice this group of models is prevalent. As a rule they combine different types of consumer-oriented activities and/or different types of business-oriented activities. For our further consideration we will chose from the set of models the model by Geoffrion and Krishnan (2001). With it they tried to holistically define the most important attributes of e-business working and most crucial preconditions for its working; they considered for this end its activities (i.e. consumer-oriented activities, and business-oriented activities), and its infrastructure. Their model of e-business is presented in Figure 1.

For the purpose of our work we collected in the second group models, which are defined according to the various forms of e-business applications (and also area of work in organization) (e.g., see Afuah, Tucci, 2000; Trombly, 2000; Chaffey, 2006; Laudon, Traver, 2008; etc.). Models in this group are mostly defining e-business according to the various forms of e-business applications (also including the areas of work in organization) into three categories (Johnson, Whang, 2002):

- **E-commerce** helps a network of supply chain partners to quickly and flexibly respond to changing customer demand captured over the Internet;
- **E-procurement** enables procuring of needed materials, as well as handling value-added services (e.g. transportation, warehousing) over the Internet; and
- **E-collaboration** facilitates coordination of various decisions and activities beyond transactions among the supply chain partners (i.e. both the suppliers and customers) over the Internet.

This group can also include models that are by purpose created to match the needs of consider-

Figure 1. Model of E-business

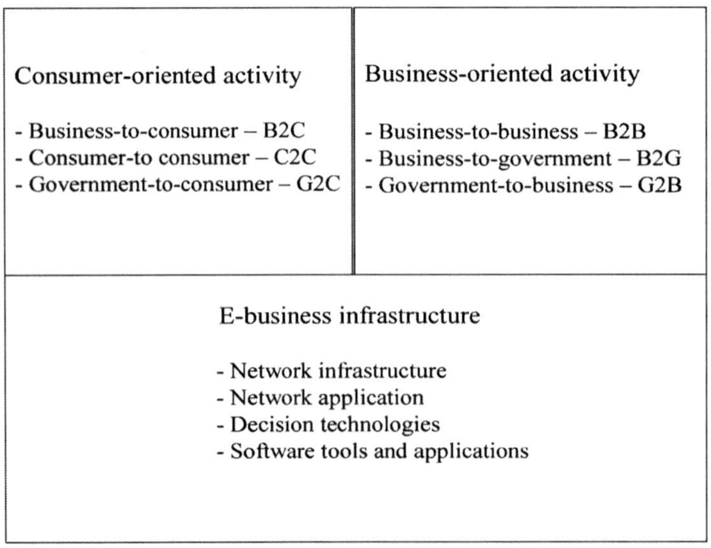

ation of transactions in e-business, e.g. the model, developed by Chaffey (2006). His model is supposed to support a more detailed consideration of attributes of relationships between consumers and producers and between producers themselves. It provides a basic classification of potential types transactions in e-business. Chaffey's model of e-business is presented in Figure 2.

There is a substantial difference between B2B and B2C e-business transactions (e.g., see Afuah, Tucci, 2000; Chaffey, 2006; Laudon, Traver, 2008; etc.). B2B transactions involve relatively few people/entities in comparison to B2C, where transactions occur between organization and end-users. The number of B2B transaction is relatively low in comparison with B2C transactions, but on the other hand B2B transactions' values are quite high, because a single B2B transaction between supplier and manufacturer could involve thousands of items and millions of dollars.

Another crucial aspect which differentiates "B2B" and "B2C" is the level of training and expertise of the people involved in transactions (e.g., see Beard, Sumner, 2004; Kim et al., 2005; Laudon, Laudon, 2005; Li, 2006; McLeod, Schell, 2007; Nedelko, 2008; etc.). In comparison to B2B transactions, B2C transactions require substantial design differences due to different level of training and expertise of people involved in transactions.

Figure 2. Taxonomy of transaction between business and consumers

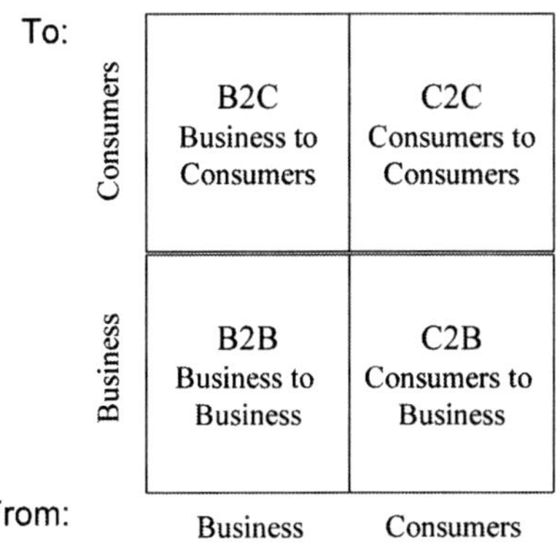

People involved in B2B transactions are usually highly trained and have a sufficient expertise in using information systems and are familiar with business processes, which are affected by transactions.

On the other hand customers in B2C transactions may have no sufficient expertise with information technology. Due to this fact web sites must offer help and instructions. Possible issues could also arise from having a slow internet connection, inappropriate navigation on site, payment security, etc.

The above main types of e-business are most commonly used in business practice. Other types of e-business are also business to employees (B2E) and electronic government (e-gov) (more about that in Laudon, Laudon, 2005; Chaffey, 2006; McLeod, Schell, 2007; etc.). Trombly (2000) defines also two other e-business models, namely: peer-to-peer (P2P), where individuals trade goods with one another (e.g. Napster); and E-marketplaces, where buyers and sellers trade their goods online (e.g. e-Bay).

Content-related cognitions about various kinds, types, and forms of e-business activities present a formal basis for further organizational consideration. But the knowledge of the basic typology of the relationships in e-business is not enough for a rather detailed insight in and definition of their organizational attributes. Using the types in an organizational consideration makes us namely face dilemmas: 1) typology of relationships of e-business can be understood differently on the bases of different content-related understanding of e-business in 2) single types of relationships of e-business can be organized in different ways.

Based on this review of references, and the reach beyond their selected frameworks, with our work we would like to shift attention from a generalized discussion about different e-business models and/or management of e-business to a more practical issue: how to organize e-business on the basis of consideration of relationships between its participants. We offer some new suggestions about: role and meaning of e-business from organizational viewpoint, different contents types of relationships in e-business, starting points of design of approapriate organization for different types of e-business relatinships, and creation of different organizational structure for the relationships in e-business.

ORGANIZATIONAL UNDERSTANDING OF E-BUSINESS

E-Business: New form of Business vs. New Concept of Business

In literature and business practice one can often hear, that implementation of e-business within established organizations usually leads to coexistence of the classical way of conducting business and e-business, whereas many new ventures are based solely on e-business (e.g., see Afuah, Tucci, 2000; Trombly, 2000; Chaffey, 2006; Mullins, 2007; Potocan, Kuralt, 2007; Laudon, Traver, 2008; etc.). On the other hand, e-business is often considered just another facet of every-day business transactions (e.g., see Adeoti-Adekeye, 1997; McLeod, Schell, 2007; Wang, 2001; Sumner, 2004; Potocan, Kuralt, 2007; etc.) or even as a pervasive channel for selling product globally (e.g., see Wang, 2001).

What is, or might be, contents of e-business from organizational viewpoint? The fast development of ICT (information and communications technologies) and the internet on one hand and hyper-competitive global economy on other hand created a new competitive landscape – one in which events and attributes change constantly and unpredictably (e.g., see Etzioni, 1997; Hatch, 1997; Daft, 2000; Potocan, 2002; Robbins, 2007; Hitt et al., 2008; Daft, 2009; Potocan, Mulej, 2009; etc.). All these conditions require organizations to transform their business from traditional business into the modern post-industrial ones, which are becoming open, flexible, innovative, and sustainable. In accordance with that, the "new economy" presents the framework for e-business implementation and working (e.g., see Hatch, 1997; Laudon, Laudon, 2005; Mullins, 2007; Laudon, Traver, 2008; etc.).

Trends that appeared due to development and increasing application of information technology, influencing the organization structure crucially, are the business globalization, change in employees structure, elimination of boundaries between parts within organizations, as well as between organizations (e.g., see Potocan, 2002; Potocan, Kuralt, 2007; Potocan, Mulej, 2009; etc.).

Organizations can significantly improve their activity with the use of the e-business. We must mentioned here, that authors use different approaches in research of e-business, be it the new form of business or new concept of business. In accordance with their intentions authors also expose different viewpoints of e-business's activity – for example organizational, managemental, informational, ethical, etc. (e.g., see Afuah, Tucci, 2000; Trombly, 2000; Chaffey, 2006; Laudon, Traver, 2008; Potocan, Mulej, 2009; etc.).

For the need of our research, different understanding (and treatment) of e-business by different authors can be divided in two basic groups (e.g., see Afuah, Tucci, 2000; Potocan, 2002; Trombly, 2000; Chaffey, 2006; Potocan, Kuralt, 2007; Laudon, Traver, 2008; Potocan, Mulej, 2009; etc.).

- The first group of researchers defines and treats e-business as a (new) stage of development of business. Different authors asume that the activity of the classical business in the modern environment must be adapted to new conditions and demands, especially concerning resources, management structure, technology, values, and knowledge. To define the characteristics of components of the new e-business various criteria are used. In the framework of continual process of development they define the basic type of business's change from the traditional business to the e-business. Evaluating the development of all important and selected attributes enables the definition of the e-business stage of the whole organization. In business practice the stage of each organization can be somewhere in the interval between the wholly traditional and wholly virtual business.

- The second group of researchers define and deal with e-business as new concept of business in the framework of global new economy. The consideration of e-business problematique by this group of authors the following is typical: 1) e-business is viewed as a concept of business, that can and does exist independently from the traditional business, 2) they pressume that the organization can work only in the e-business style, 3) they assume that the rules and principles of e-business differ from the ones of the traditional business.

In spite of all differences the approaches are mutually connected and supplement each other. The first approach enables us to understand starting points of transforming of a classical business of organizations to e-business of organizations. It focuses on research of different stages of business development and enables us to more holistically understand the development process. The second concept is focused on handling of the completely implemented e-business, as the final phase of development of the e-business activity and/or as the most developed form of the e-business activity of an organization.

Despite the differences, researchers share opinion that transforming the traditional business of organizations into e-business of organizations is not possible without innovative change of organization and management of business (e.g., see Mulej et al., 1992; Potocan, 2002; Mulej, 2007; Potocan, Kuralt, 2007; Potocan, Mulej, 2009).

What do these congnitions mean for our consideration? The known types of relationships of e-business in the above typologies give us a basis to understand e-business as a new concept of business, as e-business as a development step in e-business, or as a combination of the two. The definition of the concept of content-related understanding of e-business provides therefor for a urgent, but not sufficient precondition for a more holistic understanding of the organizational viewpoint of e-business. The latter must hence be, in addition, considered with congnitions and definitions of the attributes with crucial impact over the organizational contrent of relationships in e-business.

How to Define the Organizational Contents (and Characteristics) of Cooperation Relationships in E-Business

Successful e-business requires organizations to apply the systems approach across all stakeholders of e-business (e.g., see Afuah, Tucci, 2000; Potocan, 2002; Laudon, Laudon, 2005; Chaffey, 2006; Mullins, 2007; Potocan, Kuralt, 2007; Potocan, Mulej, 2009; etc.). When applied to e-business, the systems approach suggests that organizations must recognize the interdependence of major functional areas within, across, and between firms. In turn, the goals and objectives of individual e-business participants should be compatible with the goals and objectives of other participants in the e-business.

How does e-business change relations between e-business stakeholders? A realistic perspective is that individual participants of a e-business will compete based on the relevant capabilities of their e-business network/s, with a particular emphasis on immediately adjacent suppliers or customers (or any other members of organizational environments) (e.g., see Potocan, 2002; Potocan, Kuralt, 2007; Potocan, Mulej, 2009).

A number of key attributes are associated with e-business, including power of e-business participants (i.e. stakeholders), a long-term orientation, leveraging technology, enhanced communication across e-business, and interactivity, inter-functional, and inter-organizational coordination work (e.g., see Amit, Zott, 2001; Potocan, 2002; Daft, 2003; Vlaar et al., 2006; Potocan, Kuralt, 2007; Hitt et al., 2008; Laudon, Traver, 2008; etc.). Although each of these is discussed in the following paragraphs as discrete entities, interdependencies exist among them (e.g., see Potocan, 2002; Potocan, Kuralt, 2007).

Power ofe-businessstakeholders: E-business recognizes the power of each stakeholder and views each stakeholder as un-material assets. In recent years, a clear shift of power has moved away from the manufacturer toward the customer power. The increasing power of customers has important implications for the design and management of e-business. Because customers needs and wants change relatively quickly, e-business should be fast and agile. The 'fast' encompasses a speed/time component, while the 'agile' focuses on an organization's ability to respond to changes in demand with respect to volume and variety.

A long-term orientation: A long-term orientation tends to be predicted on relational exchanges, while a short-term orientation tends to be predicated on transactional exchanges. At a minimum, relational exchange may result in individual e-business stakeholders having to rethink (and rework) their approaches to other e-business stakeholders. We must mention here also partnerships, as long-term relationships between e-business participants. Some partnerships can be informal, while others involve ownerships. Alternatively, partnerships can be formalized by some type of contractual agreement among the various stakeholders of e-business.

Leveraging technology: It is argued that technology has been at the centre of changes taking place that affect the e-business, and that two key factors – computing power and the Internet – have sparked much of this change. With respect to the former, e-business can be made of complex entities consisting of multiple organizations, processes, and requirements. As such, attempts at ICT support e-business in an effort to maximize shareholders' wealth and/or minimize costs. However, the introduction and continued development of the ICT now allows for fast, low-cost ICT solutions to complex e-business issues.

Enhanced communications acrosse-business: Because e-business depends on huge quantities of real-time information, it is essential that this information can be seamlessly transmitted across organizations. It is also important that all members of e-business understand, that the enhanced communications across organizations depends upon both technological capabilities and willingness to share information.

Interactivity, inter-functional, and inter-organizational coordination: Until the past 30 years, managers tended to be concerned with optimizing the performance of their particular activities, particular functions, or particular organizations. By contrast, e-business requires managers to subordinate their particular activities, functions, or organizations in order to optimize the performance of their e-business. The interconnected nature of e-business suggests that optimal performance will be elusive without coordination of activities, functions, and processes. Additionally, there's little doubt that inter-organizational coordination is more challenging and difficult than either inter-functional or interactivity coordination.

The mentioned criteria enable us to define the basic attributes of relationships of e-business, that can be measured by flows of operations. Single types of operations form, when working, flows (e.g. of material, value, information, etc.), defining their attributes in a unified way.

Organizational Viewpoint of Relationships in E-Business

The relationship between the links of the e-business will be examined in more detail in terms of flows between the operations involved (e.g., see Bensaou, Venkatraman, 1995; Amit, Zott,

2001; Potocan, 2002; Daft, 2003; Vlaar et al., 2006; Potocan, Kuralt, 2007; Turban et al., 2008; Schermerhorn, 2009; etc.).

These flows may include transformed resources such as materials or transforming resources such as people or equipment. The term used to include all different types of flow is exchange. The exact nature of the relationship between the different linkages within the e-business can be viewed on a continuum which goes from highly integrated at one extreme all way to temporary and short-term trading commitments at the other.

Literature offers various divisions of relationships (For details concerning each division, see also Bensaou, Venkatraman, 1995; Timmers, 2000; Amit, Zott, 2001; Potocan, 2002; Vlaar et al., 2006; Potocan, Kuralt, 2007; Mullins, 2007; Robbins, 2007; Turban et al., 2008; Daft, 2009; etc.). We will limit our consideration to a selection from the set of various possible forms of content-related relationships of e-business as follows: integrated hierarchy, semi-hierarchy, co-contracting, coordinated contracting, coordinated review links, long-term trading commitment, medium-term trading commitment, and short-term trading commitment (e.g., see Potocan, 2002; Mullins, 2007; Potocan, Kuralt, 2007; Potocan, Mulej, 2009).

Integrated hierarchy: What is known as an integrated hierarchy is a fully vertically integrated process organization which houses all activities in the e-business from raw material source to dispatch to the end customers, as well as all their support activities on one site. In an integrated hierarchy there is no inter-company exchange of orders, information and materials because the entire e-business is "under one roof". Examples of totally vertical integrated chain are rare.

Semi-hierarchy: In a semi-hierarchy organization the firms in the e-business are owned by the same holding organization or are part of the same group, but they operate as separate business units. Both integrated hierarchy and semi-hierarchy are examples of vertical process integration, as in both cases ownership belongs to the same organizations. In semi-hierarchy, however, there is an exchange process between different organizations: materials, services and money change hands between the separate business units.

Co-contracting: Co-contracting is a term used to describe alliance between organizations which have long-term relationship (e.g. co-contracting as partnership) but which, for various reasons, do not merge, but transfer some equipment (ownership), technology, people, and information, as well as goods and services. These alliances typically do not include the whole business chain. A type of co-contracting receiving significant attention is partnership. Partnership is a long-term process and should not be viewed as an instant cost-saving exercise, but rather as an investment where future returns are possible, but only in the medium to long term.

Coordinated contracting: Coordinated contracting involves a prime contractor, who employs a set of sub-contractors, with whom a long-standing relationship exists over several contracts. They are used on a contract basis of each specific job, but between jobs there is no continuing relationship. In coordinated contracting the contractors usually provide the specification and instructions for the production of goods and services to be exchanged. It may provide materials (or other important inputs) and will usually take responsibility for planning and control of all the sub-contractors. The sub-contractors will often provide the necessary tools and equipment required for their trade or profession.

Coordinated revenue links: Coordinated revenue links are used primarily for licensing and franchising and are a form of relationship which transfers ownership to other, usually smaller, firms while still retaining a guaranteed income for the licensor or franchiser. This type of relationship is common in many services, especially those with very high customer contact. These operations need many small local sites which can be located for the convenience of their customers. Rather than managing all the sites themselves, the original owners of the service concept will license out each individual operation to separate owners.

Medium-/long-term trading commitment: It is not uncommon for businesses to trade with each other for 20 years or more, but never exchange formal long-term contracts that legally tie them together. However, where this medium- to long-term trading takes place, some commitment beyond each delivery of a different type can be made.

Short-term trading commitment: In situations where there is no interdependence beyond one order, all that is transferred between the parties to the transactions are the orders in one way and goods and services in the other. Once the good or service is delivered and payment is made, there may be no further trading between the parties. However, this short-term, price-oriented type of relationship can have a downside in terms of ongoing support and reliability.

The presented potential contents of relationships of e-business can cover all types of relationships of e-business in the framework of all conceptual approaches to consideration of e-business and on the basis of application of all criteria for definition of organizational viewpoint of e-business. Hereby we created the content-related framework for research of relationships of e-business.

From the whole problematique of organizing different types of relationships on e-business, we are going to discuss the chosen important starting points to form organizational structure supporting their work.

Basis for Design of Organizational Structure for Relationships on E-Business

Managers (or/and other influential participants) deal with two main problems when forming the organizational structures of different types of relationships in e-business. i.e.:

1. How to understand relations between strategy and structure, and
2. How to implement contingency approach for creation of e-business organizational structure

(e.g., see Lu, 1995; Etzioni, 1997; Hatch, 1997; Daft, 2000; Daft, 2006; Potocan, Kuralt, 2007; Robbins, 2007; Schermerhorn, 2009; etc.).

The first is the fact, that the structure follows the organizational strategy and reflects it (e.g., see Etzioni, 1997; Daft, 2000; Potocan, 2002; Daft, 2006; Mullins, 2007; etc.). Therefore, we cannot talk about proper structure without previous and wholly suitable and recognizable defined strategy of relationships of e-business. Thereby, the organization can choose for its chosen strategy different types of organizational structure to enable the required coordination of activities to reach its aim.

On the other hand, we can use single organizational structures in different situations which, at the same time, are suitable to satisfy different needs and demands of the organization. (e.g., see Hatch, 1997; Potocan, 2002; Daft, 2003; Mullins, 2007; Robbins, 2007; etc.). Both viewpoints of the problem – choosing the proper structure for e-business – are partly solved by the contingency approach, which is based on the presumption that by forming organizational structure, all managers have to consider specific needs and demands of the given organization and specific content-related characteristics of its work (more about contingent approach see in Etzioni, 1997; Hatch, 1997; Daft, 2000; Hitt et al., 2008).

Because of statements mentioned in organizational and management theory and business practice, general valid solutions for organization of different types of relationships in e-business do not exist (see Potocan, 2002; Potocan, Mulej, 2009).

Organizing work and the choice of the organizational structure are to a great extent independent from the chosen legal form of organizational structure. But in reality, the owners and other influential participants have direct influence on the organization and the choice of the organizational structure. The basic dilemma of managers is to search for, and assure, balance between the vertical approach (which is based on the vertical mastering) and horizontal approach (which is based on the horizontal coordination) of organizational work in accordance with the organization's needs and demands.

Vertical dealing is connected with aims of efficiency and stability. Horizontal coordination is connected with aims of success, innovation, and flexibility. Figure 3 shows the relation between the organizational structure of e-business and chosen forms of organizational structure of e-business on one hand and the organizational needs for efficiency and success of the e-business on the other.

Managers (and other influential stakeholders) therefore must improve the process of transformation of organizational structure all the time.

Another problem is creation of appropriate information support for working of the chosen organization form, which presents a selected structure and/or specific combination of structures (e.g., see Lu, 1995; Etzioni, 1997; Hatch, 1997; Daft, 2000; Daft, 2006; Potocan, Kuralt, 2007; Robbins, 2007; Schermerhorn, 2009; etc.). When an organizational form does not suit the informational needs of the given organization, its participants will not have enough information or will occupy themselves with processing unnecessary data that cannot be used as information, i.e. influentially.

The basic problem in forming a comprehensive informational flow of each organization (and structure of organizations, which are based on different relationships in e-business) is the "natural" opposition between the vertical and horizontal informational flow and informational connections that they include (Potocan, 2002; Potocan, Kuralt, 2007; Potocan, Mulej, 2009).

The vertical connections are formed (especially) to assure control over work and behavior of an organization. Horizontal connections are meant to assure and perform cooperation and coordination, which consecutively lowers (the level and extent) of control.

Figure 4 presents the relation between organizational forms and different structure approaches to its forming.

Each organization must form a structure that includes balanced integrity of vertical and hori-

Figure 3. Relationship of Structure to e-business's need for Efficiency vs. Effectiveness

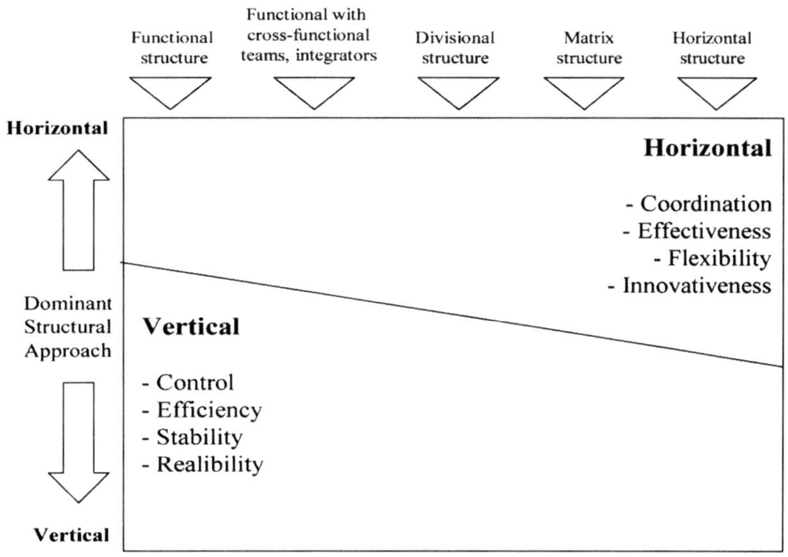

Figure 4. The relationship of organization design to vertical vs. horizontal structure

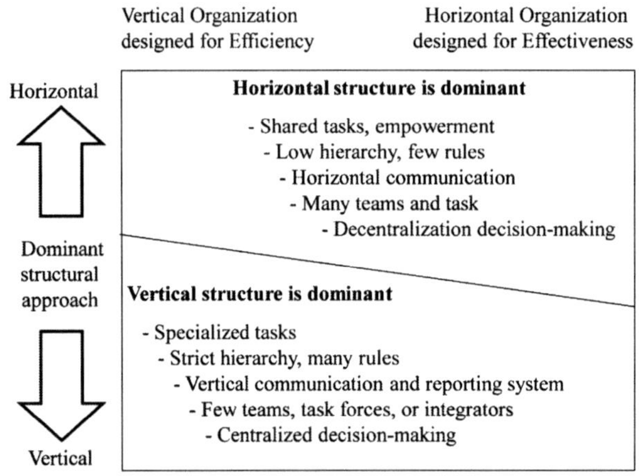

zontal informational connections. From the problematique – when discussing integrity of informational connections of an organization – we present the chosen starting points and basic characteristics of vertical and horizontal informational connections for relationships of e-business.

HOW INFORMATIONS SUPPPORT INFLUENCE ON ORGANIZATION OF RELATIONSHIPS IN E-BUSINESS

One of the main decisions in interest in e-business reads: how much of the given e-business should be owned by each participants (i.e. stakeholders) of e-business (e.g., see Bensaou, Venkatraman, 1995; Amit, Zott, 2001; Potocan, 2002; Daft, 2003; Vlaar et al., 2006; Potocan, Kuralt, 2007; Turban et al., 2008; Schermerhorn, 2009; etc.). This is called the extent of vertical integration (The alternative to vertical integration is some other form of relationship, not necessarily involving ownership. Informational connections also have an important role.)

The connections in general can be defined as showing up of communication and coordination between the organizational factors. For the needs of our discussion, (different) connections in an organization were defined as vertical and horizontal.

Vertical connections represent coordination activities on all levels (or work and behavior) of an organization from the supreme management to performers of work and are target-formed for the needs of its control. The intention of such connections is to adjust work of participants with the aims (of the management) (for example organization, type of e-business, value chain) and to give the supreme management all the needed information about the work on the lower working levels. Organizations can use for forming them different solutions, as for example: hierarchy, rules, plans, and (formal) vertical management informational systems.

Important for work organization in organizations, which work on the basis of different relationships in e-business, are especially horizontal informational connections. They enable a requisitely holistic (and relatively united) coordination of work of all participants aimed at reaching organizational aims and dismissing barriers in cooperation among (single) parts (for example of an organization, type of e-business, value chain, etc.).

Contextually, they refer to the quantity of communication and coordination by horizontal adjustment among parts of the organization. Horizontal connections (regularly) are not separately shown in the organizational scheme, although they represent an important part of the organizational structure. The organization can use – for the formation of horizontal connections – different solutions, as for example horizontal informational system, direct connection, temporary commissions, integrators and permanent groups (more about the characteristics of single solutions e.g. see Daft, 2000; Potocan, 2002; Daft, 2003; Potocan, Kuralt, 2007; etc.).

Which of the mentioned cognitions about the organizational viewpoint of consideration of relationships of e-business can be used for defining the organization and organizational structure in sigle organizations?

A Model of Organizing Relationships of E-Business

In the subchapter Basis for design of organizational structure for relationships on e-business we mentioned that it is impossible (or makes no sense) to create generally valid solutions for organization of different types of relationships in e-business. Thus, we can conclude that a more holistic model of organizational consideration of relationships of e-business can be created, matching two interdependent and interrelated preconditions:

- It defines a unified framework of consideration of relationships of e-business in different (kinds, types and forms of) organizations, and
- It enables a (bigger) comparison of considerations in different organizations (needing and able to use for their consideration a unified framework of it).

What can be unified in the model and how can we attain this unification? In order to consider the organizational viewpoint of relationships of e-business we used our theoretical cognitions and practical experiences to formulate the Process Model for designing organization (and organization structure) for relationships of E-business. The model content is shown in Figure 5.

The model presents an entity of three phases:

Figure 5. Model for designing organization (and organization structure) for relationships of E-business

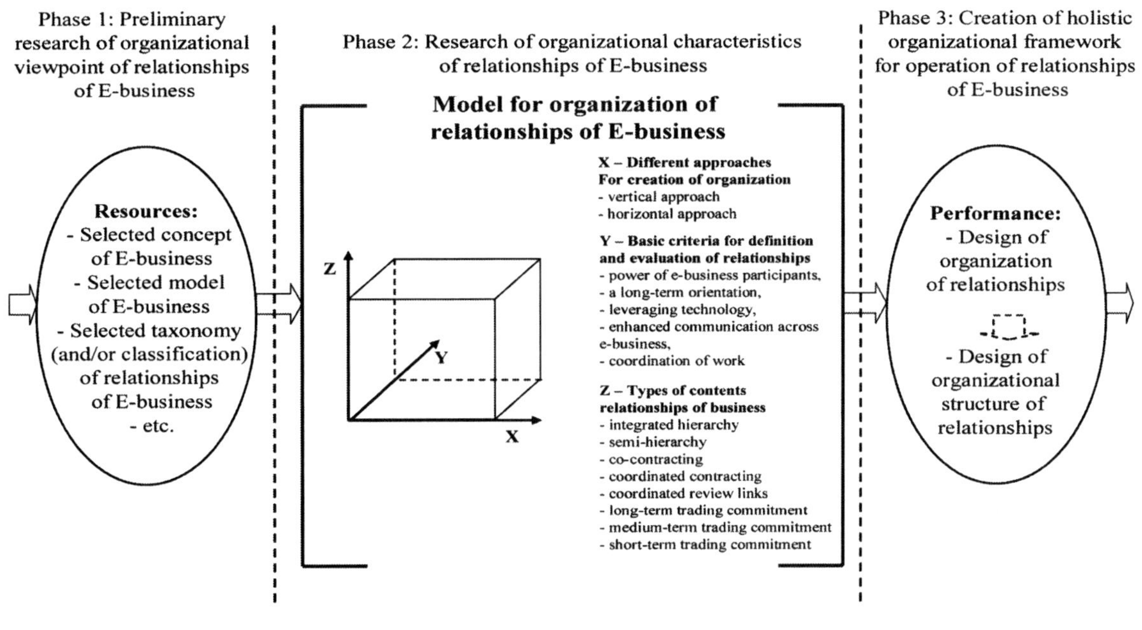

- Phase 1: Preliminary research of organizational viewpoints of relationships of e-business;
- Phase 2: Research of organizational characteristics of relationships of e-business; and
- Phase 3: Creation of a requisitely holistic organizational framework for operation of relationships of E-business.

The Phase 1 is aimed at a (requisitely) holistic definition of the area, way, and content of consideration. In this framework:

- The area definition defines the general framework for research on the basis of the foreseen selection of the: Prevailing theoretical perspectives, Driving forces, Explaining theories, and Important (and selected) domains;
- The definition of the way of consideration defines the methodological framework for the selected research on the basis of the foreseen approach (i.e. methodology), methods and techniques for consideration of the business reality.
- The definition of contents of consideration defines the general content-related framework for research. For consideration in our model we defined the general content-related framework by application of three factors: the selected concept of e-business, selected model of e-business, and selected taxonomy (and/or classification) of relationships of E-business.

In our model (Figure 5) the content of the Phase 1 is denoted with the term resources for research. The basic criteria for its definition consist of three factors. But our model can be used in two ways. The model can present a part of a (requisitely) holistic organizational consideration of business, which can (and must, if we aim at assuring its application) be based on a unified definition of the area and way of consideration. In this case, of course, there is no need for our re-definition of the area and way of consideration for research of relationships of e-business. Model can also be used with limitation to consideration of a single part and/or area of business (e.g. relationships of e-business); but in this case, of course, its specific area and way of consideration must be defined.

The central area of the process model (Figure 5) lies in the 2nd phase that is aimed at consideration of the organizational characteristics of relationships of e-business. In this phase we try to as holistically as possible learn to know, define, and systemize kinds, types, and forms of relationships of e-business from the organizational viewpoint. In working on this phase we study in synergy: Types of contents for relationships of business, Basic criteria for definition and evaluation of relationships of e-business, and different approaches for creation of organization. The basic aim and wish in this phase covers formation of groups of relationships of e-business, that possess the same or similar attributes and can therefore in the next phase make sense of organizing in a similar way and with application of the same organizational structure.

The Phase 3 (in Figure 5) is aimed at formation of a requisitely holistic organizational framework for operation of relationships of e-business. Theoretically, the Phase 3 can (and must) be done in two ways. If the enterprise wants to create a totally new or unique solution, this phase includes the following activities: innovative formation of its organizing of single types of relationships of e-business, and innovative formation of suitable organizational structure for single types of relationships of e-business. The phase 3 can also be done as a process of defining the organizing and organizational structure for the chosen types of relationships of e-business on the basis of the created basis of knowledge about the potential organizing and way of organization. In this case the organization considers the phase 3 in two steps.

- In the 1st version the knowledge about organizing and way of organization (and other knowledge, e.g. from good practices) is used to define the typology of possible organizing of working and typology of possible ways of organizing (or possible applications of various types of organizational structures) for working of relationships of e-business.
- In the 2nd version the formation of the desired organizing and way of organizing uses the given basis of knowledge.

In the business practice a separation of the presented ways of performance of the 3rd phase is possible in principle only, as a rule. In every creation of organizing and ways of organizing the given and additional knowledge is always used (available in formal and informal forms). Whether the available knowledge will be applied in a routine-loving style, i.e. by selection of an existing/known form of organizing and/or ways of organizing, or with an innovative creation of new solutions – this depends on different subjective and objective factors (e.g. situations, knowledge, values, culture, ethics, norms, etc.).

FUTURE RESEARCH DIRECTIONS

The presented model is aimed at a more unified organizational consideration of relationships of e-business. Though, it might become more usable and yield better results, if the basis of knowledge about organizing and ways of organizing of single types of relationships of e-business operation inside single (kinds, types, and/or forms of) organizations was created.

Theory and business practice know of researches on organizational attributes of organization's business relationships (including e-business). But these investigations mostly cover relationships in relations between organizations and their environments (e.g. topic of outsourcing), relations between process phases and entire process (e.g. topic of value chain), needs related to working of production (especially the mass production) in the difficult competition conditions (e.g. automotive industry).

Less many investigations tackle organizing of relationships of e-business operation of production, services, and public administration organizations aimed at matching the need for organizing them while using both the traditional and e-business. In this framework a possible research might address the development of organizing and ways of organizing in the process of transition from the traditional to e-business. Theory namely fails to offer requisitely holistic solutions concerning dynamic changing of organizing and ways of organizing under a rapid development of different forms of them. This development might demand a permanent, innovative, and flexible adaptation to new requirements and preconditions of working, including its permanent renewal of organizing and ways of organizing.

In such conditions an organizational consideration urges a requisitely holistic understanding and taking in account of the new bases of organizational working, including the systemic understanding of organization, of synergetic entity of objective and subjective organizational factors, of behavioral factors of organizational working, of cognitions from other sciences (e.g. from social sciences), etc. The organizational theory is trying to find answers to the mentioned and other open issues of the contemporary organizational working, especially inside two of its directions of development – the postmodernism and a scientific value approach.

CONCLUSION

A broad definition defines e-business as a business process that uses Internet (and/or any other electronic medium) as a channel to complete business transactions. Many different terms and concepts describe e-business; some of them overlap and describe various parts of the e-business. They present an increasing degree of integration among the e-business linkages.

The exact nature of the relationship among the different linkages within the e-business can be viewed on a continuum between the highly integrated at one extreme, and temporary and the short-term trading commitments at the other. The organization tries to define all working tasks, their mutual relationships, connections and synergies, as well as mechanisms for the suitable connection and coordination of organizational factors.

For the formation of the working structure, the organization can use various starting points. The modern conditions of work demand that organizations include into their structure the characteristics of the informational process needed for the realization of organizational aims. The organization can use the traditional or modern formation of the structure. The traditional approach to the formation of the structure is based on considering vertical informational connections. But for most organizations, the vertical connections are not enough, so they complete them up with horizontal connections.

For the formation of the organizational structure, the organization can use functional grouping, divisional grouping, grouping with more viewpoints, and horizontal grouping. Different structures in the frame of functional, divisional, and horizontal structures enable different levels of coordination and integration.

In the frame of functional and divisional structures, the management can create a requisitely holistic business support by forming all vertical and horizontal connections. In such a way, efficiency of the present vertical connections will increase and the integration of the organizational work will improve. In horizontal structures, the activities are organized horizontally around the basic (or key) working process. Most organizations form specific hybrid structures, which include characteristics of two or more structure types, on these starting points.

REFERENCES

Adeoti-Adekeye, W. (1997). The importance of management information systems. *Library Review*, *46*(5), 318–327. doi:10.1108/00242539710178452

Afuah, A., & Tucci, C. (2000). *Internet Business Models and Strategies: Text and Cases*. New York: McGraw-Hill.

Al-Mashari, M. (2002). Electronic commerce. *Benchmarking*, *9*(2), 182–189. doi:10.1108/14635770210421845

Amit, R., & Zott, C. (2001). Value creation in e-business. *Strategic Management Journal*, *22*(6-7), 493–520. doi:10.1002/smj.187

Amor, D. (1999). *E-business (R)evolution*. New York: Prentice Hall.

Anderson, D. (2000). *Managing Information Systems*. New York: Prentice Hall.

Beard, J., & Sumner, M. (2004). Seeking strategic advantage in post-net era. *The Journal of Strategic Information Systems*, *13*(2), 129–150. doi:10.1016/j.jsis.2004.02.003

Bensaou, M., & Venkatraman, N. (1995). Configurations of inter-organization relationships: A comparison between US and Japanese automakers. *Management Science*, *41*(9), 1471–1492. doi:10.1287/mnsc.41.9.1471

Beynon-Davies, P. (2004). *E-Business*. Basingstoke: Palgrave.

Budd, L., & Harris, L. (2004). *E-Economy: Rhetoric or Business Reality*. New York: Routledge.

Chaffey, D. (2006). *E-business and E-commerce Management*. New York: Financial Times.

Culler, A., & Webster, M. (2007). A model of B2B e-commerce, based on connectivity and purpose. *International Journal of Operations & Production Management*, *27*(2), 205–235. doi:10.1108/01443570710720621

Daft, R. (2000). *Management*. Orlando, FL: The Dryden Press.

Daft, R. (2003). *Organization Theory and Design*. Mason: Thomson South-Western.

Daft, R. (2006). *Understanding the theory and design of organizations*. Mason: Thomson South-Western.

Daft, R. (2009). *The New Era of Management*. Cincinnati, OH: South-Western College.

Eckersley, P., Harris, L., & Jackson, P. (2004). *E-business Fundamentals*. New York: Routledge.

Etzioni, A. (1997). *Modern Organizations*. New York: Prentice-Hall.

Geoffrion, M., & Krishnan, R. (2001). Prospects for Operations Research in the E-Business Era. *Interfaces*, *31*(2), 6–36. doi:10.1287/inte.31.2.6.10628

Gulati, R., Nohria, N., & Zaheer, A. (2000). Strategic Networks. *Strategic Management Journal*, *21*(3), 203–215. doi:10.1002/(SICI)1097-0266(200003)21:3<203::AID-SMJ102>3.0.CO;2-K

Hartley, R. (2007). *Management Mistakes and Successes*. New York: Wiley.

Hatch, M. (1997). *Organization theory: Modern, symbolic and postmodern perspectives*. Oxford: Oxford University Press.

Hitt, M., Black, S., & Porter, L. (2008). *Management*. New York: Prentice Hall.

Johnson, E., & Whang, S. (2002). E-business and supply chain management: An overview and framework. *Production and Operations Management*, *11*(4), 413–423. doi:10.1111/j.1937-5956.2002.tb00469.x

Kalakota, R., & Robinson, M. (2000). *E-Business 2.0: Roadmap for Success*. Boston: Addison-Wesley Professional.

Kim, Y., Lee, Z., & Gosain, S. (2005). Impediments to successful ERP implementation process. *Business Process Management Journal*, *11*(2), 158–170. doi:10.1108/14637150510591156

Laudon, K., & Laudon, J. (2005). *Management Information Systems*. New York: Pearson-Prentice Hall.

Laudon, K., & Traver, C. (2008). *E-Commerce: Business, Technology, Society*. New York: Pearson/Prentice-Hall.

Li, F. (2006). *What is e-business: How the internet transforms organizations*. New York: Wiley-Blackwell.

Lu, H. (1995). Managerial behaviors over MIS growth stages. *Management Decision*, *33*(7), 40–46. doi:10.1108/00251749510090575

McLeod, R., & Schell, G. (2007). *Management Information Systems*. New York: Pearson-Prentice Hall.

Mulej, M. (et al.) (1992). *Systems Theory*. Maribor: FEB.

Mulej, M. (2007). Systems Theory. *Systems Research and Behavioral Science*, *24*(3), 347–357. doi:10.1002/sres.810

Mullins, L. (2007). *Management and Organisational Behaviour*. London: Prentice Hall.

Nedelko, Z. (2008). The role and importance of groupware for teamwork. *Business Review (Federal Reserve Bank of Philadelphia)*, *10*(1), 211–217.

Pavic, S., Koh, S., Simpson, M., & Padmore, J. (2007). Could e-business create a competitive advantage in UK SMEs? *Benchmarking*, *14*(3), 1463–5771. doi:10.1108/14635770710753112

Peet, S., Brindley, C., & Ritchie, B. (2002). The EC and SME support mechanisms for e-business. *European Business Review*, *14*(5), 335–341. doi:10.1108/09555340210444185

Potocan, V. (2002). Business systems: Sustainable development and anticipatory system. *Management, 7*(1), 67–77.

Potocan, V., & Kuralt, B. (2007). Synergy in business: Some new suggestions. *The Journal of Academy of Business, 12*(1), 199–204.

Potocan, V., & Mulej, M. (2009). Business Cybernetics. *Kybernetes, 38*(1/2), 93–112. doi:10.1108/03684920910930295

Ring, P., & Vandeven, A. (1994). Development processes of cooperative interorganizational relationships. *Academy of Management, 19*(1), 90–118. doi:10.2307/258836

Robbins, S. (2007). *Organization Theory: Structures, Designs, and Applications*. New Delhi: Dorling Kindersley.

Rodgers, J., Yen, D., & Chou, D. (2002). Developing e-business. *Information Management & Computer Security, 10*(4), 84–192. doi:10.1108/09685220210436985

Savole, M., & Raisinghani, M. (1999). Identifying future trends in information technology. *Industrial Management & Data Systems, 99*(6), 247–250. doi:10.1108/02635579910253742

Schermerhorn, J. (2009). *Management*. New York: Wiley.

Sumner, M. (2004). *Enterprise Resource Planning*. New York: Pearson-Prentice Hall.

Swaminathan, M., & Tayur, R. (2003). Models for Supply Chains in E-business. *Management Science, 49*(10), 1387–1406. doi:10.1287/mnsc.49.10.1387.17309

Timmers, P. (2000). *Electronic Commerce - strategies & models for business-to-business trading*. New York: Wiley.

Tiwana, A., & Willianms, M. (2000). *The Essential Guide to Knowledge Management: E-Business and CRM Applications*. New York: Prentice Hall.

Trombly, R. (2000). E-Business Models. *Computerworld, 34*(49), 61–62.

Turban, K., McKay, D., Marshall, J., Lee, P., & Vielhand, D. (2008). *Electronic Commerce: A Managerial Perspective*. Upper Saddle River, NJ: Pearson.

Vlaar, P., Van den Bosch, F., & Volberda, H. (2006). Coping with problems of understanding in interorganizational relationships: Using as a means to make sense. *Organization Studies, 27*(11), 1617–1638. doi:10.1177/0170840606068338

Wang, S. (2001). Designing information systems for electronic business. *Industrial Management & Data Systems, 101*(6), 304–314. doi:10.1108/EUM0000000005580

Wu, F., Mahajan, V., & Balasubramanjan, S. (2003). An Analysis of E-Business Adoption and Its Impact on Business Performance. *Journal of the Academy of Marketing Science, 31*(4), 425–447. doi:10.1177/0092070303255379

Chapter 10
Knowledge Supply for SME Networks:
Application Cases and Selected Technical Approaches

Anders Carstensen
Jönköping University, Sweden

Tatiana Levashova
St. Petersburg Institute for Informatics and Automation RAS, Russia

Kurt Sandkuhl
Jönköping University, Sweden

Nikolay Shilov
St. Petersburg Institute for Informatics and Automation RAS, Russia

Alexander Smirnov
St. Petersburg Institute for Informatics and Automation RAS, Russia

ABSTRACT

Current trends of globalisation and increased competition require new forms of organisation and work support. Especially in small and medium sized enterprises (SME), the competitiveness and future market position of an enterprise is closely related to the ability of cooperating with partners in SME networks or virtual supplier organisations. In complex work processes with a number of distributed partners, high requirements with respect to competence and a lot of rules and guidelines to be obeyed; detecting and sharing knowledge among different members of networked organizations is an important issue. Based on an empirical investigation regarding the demands of SME and illustrating this demand with industrial cases, this paper investigates two technical approaches supporting knowledge supply in networked organizations: enterprise modeling and self-organisation of flexible supply networks. These approaches are presented with related work and their limits and potentials.

DOI: 10.4018/978-1-61692-880-3.ch010

INTRODUCTION

Current trends of globalisation and increased competition require new forms of organisation and work support. Especially in small and medium sized enterprises (SME), the competitiveness and future market position of an enterprise is closely related to the ability of cooperating with partners in SME networks or supplier organisations. SME networks are communities or associations of enterprises based on common economical and value-creation objectives. They pro-actively form co-operations for joint development or project work. These co-operations typically are temporary, dynamical with respect to the members, geographically distributed, flexible and quick responsive to market demands.

SMEs usually have a number of internal knowledge sources which should be used more systematically and intensively in cooperation projects. Although most knowledge exists in the heads of employees, there usually is a substantial amount of *externalised knowledge*, i.e. stored electronically in documents, databases or information systems. Furthermore, we consider *corporate knowledge* represented in work processes, organisation structures or best practices as an important knowledge asset.

All these knowledge sources are especially important in complex work processes with a number of distributed partners, high competence requirements and a lot of rules and guidelines to be obeyed. In these situations it is important to discover the exactly "right" knowledge source, to find it "in time" and to get access to it fast. Furthermore, networks with changing partners often have communication problems due to different understanding of the same term. Knowledge supply has to be more than simply installing a search engine or providing a repository for all partners. A promising approach is to use knowledge representation approaches, like ontologies and semantic nets, in order to support knowledge capturing, management and supply in organisations.

The chapter addresses the area of knowledge supply for networks of small and medium-sized enterprises based on experiences from several industrial projects. The main intention is to present requirements and challenges in SME networks based on industrial cases, propose options for IT solutions supporting these demands, and discuss potentials and limits of these options from an SME focus. The chapter will start with a section on SME demand regarding IT solutions for information and knowledge management (section 2), present two application areas related to the demand (section 3) and selected technical approaches (section 4). Finally (in section 5 and 6) the chapter reflects on the potential future development of the selected technical approaches and discuss their limits. A summary of the content and contributions will conclude the chapter.

BACKGROUND

Work in the area of knowledge supply for SME networks should be based on at least two different perspectives: the existing work on information and knowledge supply and findings about the demand of SME and SME-networks. Both subjects will be briefly described in this chapter.

Information and Knowledge Supply

This section provides background information and description of the research activities in information logistics and knowledge supply in networked organizations. Joint basis for this research are the areas of enterprise modeling and knowledge modeling, in particular concepts and approaches to describe and characterize the meaning of information objects and to model information demand.

Information Logistics

Information Logistics investigates approaches and solutions for an optimized information flow (the right information for a user's needs, just-in-time, in the right quality, to the right location) for all kinds of distributed work contexts (enterprises with several locations, networks of SMEs, geographically distributed work groups, mobile workforces, etc.)[1]. We see especially needs for supporting, organizing, and optimizing information flow in networked organizations. In comparison to logistics information management in the context of material logistics, which focuses on information related to material flows and which sometimes also is called information logistics, the perspective is to consider information as subject of logistics.

We consider an optimized information flow to be more important for SMEs than for large enterprises. SMEs usually have to act very efficiently due to very limited resources. Personnel will often have more than one role within the enterprise, with quick reaction time as part of their competitive advantage. Information flow solutions for SMEs should be based on as many pre-defined components or patterns as possible in order to reduce deployment time and costs.

Contemporary research work in information logistics includes

- method for information demand analysis in an enterprise context (Lundqvist et al. 2009),
- patterns of information demand for efficiently constructing information supply solutions (Sandkuhl, 2009),
- technologies for matching information demand and content (Lin & Sandkuhl, 2007),
- applications of solutions in an SME context, e.g. for networks of automotive suppliers (Sandkuhl, 2003) or media industries (Billig et al., 2007).

Knowledge Supply

Knowledge management is defined as a complex set of relations between people, processes and technology bound together with the cultural norms, like mentoring and knowledge sharing. Knowledge management consists of the following tasks: knowledge discovery (knowledge entry, capture tacit knowledge, etc.), knowledge engineering (knowledge base development, knowledge sharing and reuse, knowledge supply, knowledge exchange, etc.), knowledge mapping (identifying knowledge sources, indexing knowledge, making knowledge accessible, etc.).

Knowledge supply is a subfield of knowledge management responsible for delivering the right knowledge at the right time to the right person. It is paid a strong attention in the IT community since the knowledge supply has become an important success factor for companies in our information age. There is a number of works related to this area. Since the knowledge supply assumes a number of operations it is reasonable to speak about the knowledge supply process. As a result, just like in production, depending on the topology of the process operations, knowledge supply chains and knowledge supply networks are distinguished. As examples of research efforts in these areas the following ones can be mentioned. The authors of (Wang & Rong, 2007) study the knowledge supply chain taking into account the urgency required by the emergency decision support. The authors of (Suresh &Mahesh, 2008) describe the experience of building a knowledge supply chain within a company. The knowledge supply network is introduced and described in (Mak & Ramaprasad, 2003). An application of knowledge supply network to the area of collaborative design is presented in (Song et al., 2008).

SME Demand

During the last decade, an increasing number of successful cases of knowledge supply in industrial application scenarios have been reported, see e.g. (Lau & Sure, 2002) and (Sandkuhl & Billig, 2007). The majority of these cases stem from large companies, or from IT-intensive middle-sized or small enterprises. Most SMEs outside the high tech sector have probably not heard about knowledge supply solutions and approaches. Existing studies about IT use in SMEs, like (Lybaert, 1998), do not cover knowledge representation techniques sufficiently. Drawing conclusions from experiences of larger enterprises with regards to SMEs is not appropriate, as SMEs have their own characteristics (Levy et al., 2002): SMEs often belong to the "late adopters" of new technology, i.e. they prefer mature technologies, which are easy to deploy, use and maintain. SMEs show a clear preference for to a large extent standardized processes and solutions. Innovation projects in SMEs typically have to contribute to business value within a short time frame.

In 2008, a study focusing on information management and its improvement potential in SME was performed, which also investigated application potential for knowledge representation technologies[2]. The study consisted of a pilot study (questionnaire with 8 enterprises) and a survey. The survey was sent to 436 enterprises in the South of Sweden, most of them small and medium-sized enterprises, and received 164 valid responses. The sample used for the following results includes industrial SMEs from manufacturing, construction, and industrial electronics industries, which account for approximately 80% of the responses.

The study was designed in order to investigate several predefined conjectures, two of them very relevant for exploring the demand of SMEs regarding knowledge supply techniques.

The first conjecture addressed the need for supporting information search and retrieval in SMEs. Experiences from using ontologies for information structuring or in search engines show clearly that they can contribute to improving precision. Examples for work in this field can be found in (Ciravegna & Petrelli, 2006) and (Redon et al., 2007). However, the main question to discuss from an SME perspective is which approach creates the best benefit/effort ratio, i.e. substantial benefits at a reasonable price. As a considerable part of SMEs neither have Intranets or Document Management Systems, and as even the established systems have improvement potential, these improvements should be made first before starting an ontology development for a specific SME. Thus, our conclusions regarding use of ontologies for supporting information management in SMEs are

- The SMEs participating in our survey perceive a number of shortcomings in information management, like difficulties to find the right information, shortcomings in the established IT-systems or information overload. This presents an application field for ontologies.
- The use of conventional technologies should be given preference to ontologies when addressing these information management shortcomings in SMEs.

The second conjecture focused on the need for supporting document management in SME project work. 71 of 113 SMEs responded to the questions regarding project work, which indicates that many SMEs actually use project organization with documents as main means to capture results and working documents.

When analysing the data from the study, the approach of various scholars in the field was applied that the complexity of an application case is an essential parameter when deciding on improvement potential. The more complex the application scenario is, the more likely is the usefulness of IT solutions for improving information management and knowledge management. Research on projects complexity proposes to define complexity as "consisting of many varied interrelated parts", to distinguish between organisational and technological complexity, and to operationalize this in terms of "differentiation and interdependence" (Baccarini, 1996).

Evaluating the complexity of document management in projects was based on four criteria: average number of employees in a project, average number of documents per project, average duration of projects, average number of pages per document. The survey result contained 13 cases which show both, a very high degree of differentiation and interdependencies between the criteria. However, 18% of the SMEs working in project organization and 11% of all SMEs in the sample have a high project complexity, which from our perspectives is sufficient motivation to aim at supporting project document management. The result of the study is a clear indication that two application areas offer improvement potential: information management in (distributed) projects, and management of product information.

APPLICATION AREAS FOR KNOWLEDGE SUPPLY IN SME

This section will introduce two application cases for knowledge supply in SME networks: collaborative engineering and flexible supply networks.

Collaborative Engineering

Collaborative engineering aims at supporting a distributed group of engineers sharing a common collaboration objective in jointly performing an engineering task, like product design, production planning, engineering change management or development of specifications. These engineering tasks are usually knowledge-intensive activities involving different specialists in collaboration processes tailored for the engineering domain under consideration.

The collaborative engineering application case focuses on distributed product development with multi project lifecycles in a networked organization from automotive supplier industry. Main partner is the business area seat comfort of a first tier supplier, which main products are seat comfort components (seat heater, seat ventilation, lumber support and head restraint), gear shifts and commercial vehicle components.

The case is focused on development of new products in collaboration of the first tier supplier and its sub-suppliers for heating wires, seat sensors and carrier material. Development of products includes identification of system requirements based on customer requirements, functional specification, development of logical and technical architecture, co-design of electrical and mechanical components, integration testing, and production planning including production logistics, floor planning and product line planning. This process is geographically distributed involving engineers and specialists at several locations and suppliers from the region. A high percentage of seat comfort components are product families, i.e. various versions of the components exist and are maintained and further developed for different product models and different customers. General requirements regarding infrastructure and methodology are:

- to support geographical distribution and knowledge sharing between changing partners,
- to enable flexible engineering processes reflecting the dynamics of changing customer requirements,
- to coordinate a large number of parallel product development activities,
- to allow richness of variants while supporting product reuse and generalization.

Within these phases, one of the core activities is to *establish a material specification*. The material of a seat heating is an essential element of the product specification as diverse quality characteristics, the manufacturability of the product, suitability for the geometric shape and other customer requirements have to be followed and met by the material.

Establishing a material specification comprises roughly the steps of

- Preparing a draft is based on order, the product requirement specification and specific material requirements. The responsible engineer describes characteristics and limits of the material and negotiates with suppliers about contributions and feasibility.
- Testing the material is initiated by the responsible engineer when receiving the samples of the material. The test engineer conducts the test and documents the results.
- Performing process trials are conducted based on the specifications and experiences of engineers. If the results are satisfactory, the specification is prepared for releasing.
- Releasing the material specification in a specification meeting with the project manager, person responsible for production, product designer, material engineer and relevant suppliers involved.

This process illustrates the need for flexible knowledge supply both within the different locations of the first tier supplier and in the network of SME-sub-suppliers.

Flexible Supply Networks

Increasing competition makes companies change their strategies on global markets. Growing requirements to flexibility, lead time reduction or customization possibilities have caused a need to establish numerous collaborative partnerships between them. Establishment of automotive production networks is one of the consequences of these changes. Typical car manufacturers that made 75% of product components 25 years ago now make only 25% of those components and 50-70% of product cost is with suppliers. Organizations of this form use information and communication technologies to extend their boundaries and physical location and form multiple links across the boundaries to work together for a common purpose.

One of the outcomes of these changes is the growing rate of collaboration between manufacturers, their suppliers and customers. This can be explained by the fact that network-like organizations consisting of a large amount of nodes are usually more flexible and robust when compared with hierarchically organized large-scale companies.

Distributed production networks have a number of advantages when compared to vertically controlled companies, but they also pose challenges. Partnering on manufacturing and design has increased the need to integrate and share product information, from initial design to manufacturing and engineering changes, including best practices of processes and their integration over company limits. With the aim of achieving global distributed processes & functions and value chain integration & dynamic collaboration, knowledge management has become of high importance.

Together with the above advantages flexible supply networks raise a number of problems. The most important problem is coordination of the large amount of independent members of the large network. When dealing with multiple organizations and multiple processes within a complicated supply network, trying to identify and locate a member that has responsibility and/or competence in a particular part of the network can be a laborious, time-consuming process. Developing and maintaining a competence directory of all the relevant parties associated with troubleshooting and solving potential problems can significantly reduce the time. Further, linking this directory to key decision points and frequent problems can further enhance its effectiveness (Lessner & Butner, 2005).

In flexible supply networks it is important to derive and process knowledge from various sources including (adapted from (Botkin, 1999)):

- customer needs, perceptions, and motivations, etc.;

- expertise within and across the supply chain;
- best practices, technology intelligence and forecasting, systemic innovation, etc.;
- products in the marketplace, who is buying them and why, what prices they are selling at;
- what competitors are selling now and what they are planning to sell in the future.

The knowledge supply as a part of knowledge management in a flexible supply network requires interoperability at both technical and semantic levels. The interoperability at the technical level is addressed in a number of research efforts. It is usually represented by such approaches as e.g., SOA (Service-Oriented Architecture) (SOA 2007) and is based on the appropriate standards like WSDL and SOAP (Web services, 2007). The semantic level of interoperability in the production network is also paid significant attention. As an example (probably the most widely known), the Semantic Web initiative is worth mentioning (Semantic Web, 2006). The Semantic Web relies on application of ontologies for knowledge and terminology description.

The approach described in (Smirnov et al., 2009) relies on the ontological knowledge representation for its sharing. The ontology describes common entities of the enterprise systems and relationships between them. The dynamic nature of the flexible supply networks requires considering the current situation in order to provide for actual knowledge or information. For this purpose, the idea of contexts is used. Context represents additional information that helps to identify specifics of the current transaction. It defines a narrow domain that the user of the knowledge management platform works with. One more important aspect covered by the approach is the competence profiling. Profiles contain such information as the network member's capabilities and capacities, terminological specifics, preferred ways of interaction, etc.

The conceptual model of the knowledge management platform in a flexible supply network is presented in Figure 1. The ontology forms the core of the platform. It describes common entities (objects, facilities, products, processes, etc.) of the production network members and relationships between them. In order for the ontology to be of a reasonable size it includes only the most generic common entities of the participating companies. For modern decision support systems, personalized support is important. Usually it is based on application of the profiling technology. For organization of a multi-tier supply network, a company profile structure including a description of a company's responsibilities and competences is proposed. The knowledge management platform provides an access to internal data models of the network members through their competence profiles. Each user (human or an information system) works on a particular problem or scenario represented via a context that may be characterised by a particular customer order, its time, requirements, etc.

Development and application of this model were subject of the FP6 project "Intelligent Logistics for Innovative Product Technologies" (ILIPT). ILIPT aimed at developing new methods and technologies to facilitate the implementation of a new manufacturing paradigm for the European automotive industry. This new paradigm, "the 5-day car" approaches the building of 'cars to order' in a reduced time scale (ILIPT, 2006). ILIPT project addresses the conceptual and practical aspects of delivering cars to customers just in a few days after placing the order, the automotive industry's exciting and radical new business model (Stone et al, 2005).

One of the ILIPT project tasks was to develop a common knowledge management platform to support interoperability within the "5-day car" production network, thus, allowing to accumulate, share, reuse and process knowledge across the "5-day car" production network that in turn could have a dramatic impact upon increasing the

Figure 1. Conceptual model of ontology-driven knowledge management platform

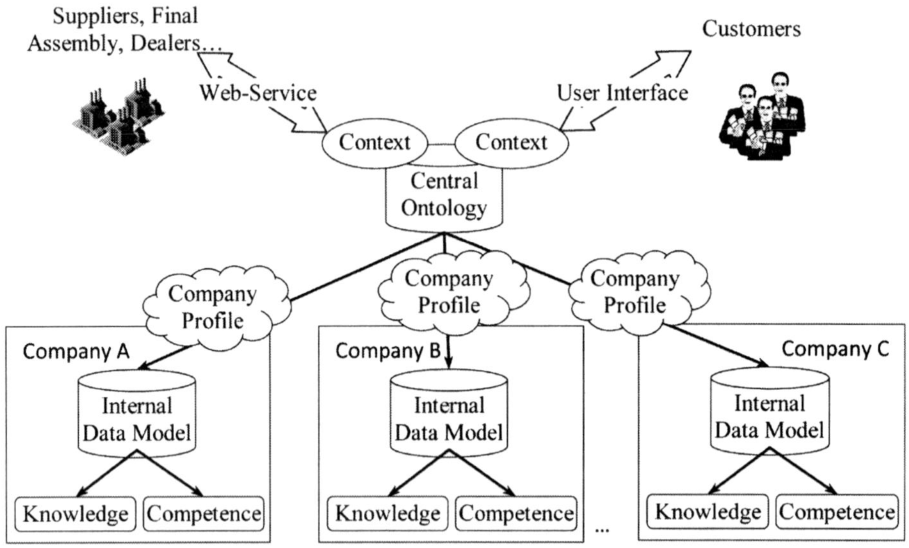

production network effectiveness and decreasing the lead time, and achieving the goal of 5 days.

The prototype of the knowledge management platform has the following components (Figure 2):

- system core,
- ontology management environment,
- knowledge content management environment.

Besides the main components some additional components (extensions) can be developed and attached. In the ILIPT project the following extensions have been implemented:

- OWL import module (importing OWL ontologies),
- contact establishing (an e-mail based system for initiating a dialog between potential supply chain members),
- competence profiling (competence profiles for supply chain members containing information to help to differentiate between BTO (Build-to-Order) and BTS (Build-to-Stock) suppliers, e.g., lead time, current free capacities, etc.).

SELECTED TECHNICAL APPROACHES

The technical approaches selected for presentation in this chapter complement each other quite well when implementing knowledge supply for

Figure 2. Components of the knowledge management platform

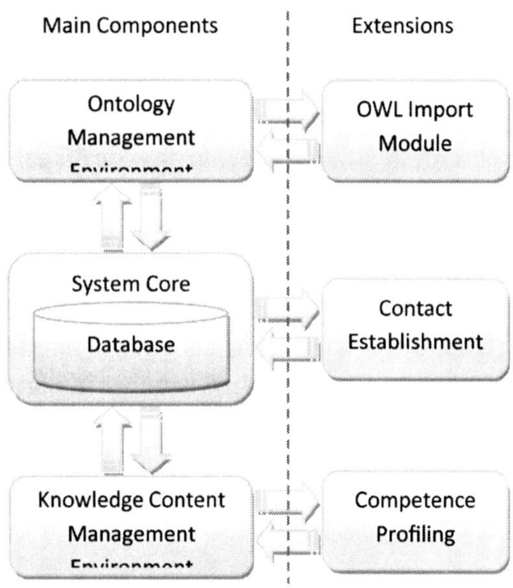

SME networks based on the industrial application scenarios presented in section 2. The first approach addresses the enterprise interoperability, which is a precondition for implementing knowledge supply. The approach presented is using a specific practice of enterprise modelling, the connector view, in order to establish interoperability, i.e. this approach is focussing on set-up time. The second approach is addressing operation time by proposing self-configuring networks, which can be both used for configuration of networks with dynamic partnerships or for creating continuity in case of services and partners dropping out unexpectedly.

Using Enterprise Modeling for Creating Enterprise Interoperability

The aim of enterprise modelling is to give the methodologies and tools to analyze the enterprise by separating different concepts, such as organisational architecture, processes, information and knowledge, functions and resources.

Several enterprise modelling frameworks exist: the Zachman Framework, CIMOSA, GRAI-GIM, PERA, ARIS, C4ISR and GERAM to mention some of the most well known.

Generalised Enterprise Reference Architecture and Methodology (GERAM) is a generalised framework based on three different enterprise modelling architectures (CIMOSA, GRAI/GIM and PERA). Since 1990 the IFIP/IFAC[3] task force has been working with the framework of GERAM, mainly to establish a set of requirements, necessary for an enterprise modelling methodology in order to perform the integration within the enterprise (IFIP-IFAC, 2003). The IFIP/IFAC task force has elevated the human- and process-oriented concepts since these aspects have long been neglected, which often has led to the "islands of automation" problems. GERAM may be used as a guiding architecture in order to set up and perform enterprise modelling, but the prime intention is to be a reference for other enterprise modelling frameworks. It is possible to diagnose the methodology, language and other architectural components of other frameworks and thereby find out what parts possibly are missing. On the other hand GERAM is intended to be the conclusion from the different existing enterprise modelling architectures and frameworks in use. The IFIP-IFAC task force is hence following what is happening within the enterprise modelling community to decide on necessary revision of GERAM. A comprehensive and extensive mapping of different frameworks towards GERAM is found in (Noran, 2003).

Different forms of cooperation between enterprises are externalised in supply chains, extended enterprises and more recently virtual enterprises. The extended enterprise (EE) is a term denoting several more or less loosely integrated companies that cooperate in order to gain mutual benefits, such as making the companies concentrate on their core business and outsourcing other activities, to make it possible to sharpen and proliferate their knowledge and skill assets in the domain of their core business (Farell, 2008). The virtual enterprise (VE) is compared to the extended enterprise characterised by a more temporary existence. It still has the same benefits in mind as the EE but has also the aim to enhance flexibility. One of the driving forces for establishing the concept of the VE is the development of information and communication technology (ICT) seen during the last two decades. Such development to be mentioned concerns techniques for e-collaboration, groupware systems, video conferencing systems and also the emerging use of web services (Fong, 2005).

The VE was studied in the GLOBEMEN project. One of the results from this project is Virtual Enterprise Reference Architecture and Methodology (VERAM) which is a further development of the GERAM framework. VERAM aim to capture the knowledge for organising VE's. In order to ease the formation of a VE it has been suggested to use an organisational structure which should include all partners that may participate in particular VE's. This has been called virtual breeding environment (VBE) and is settled in order "to establish a degree of preparedness for forming particular VE's" (Tølle & Vesterager, 2003) (Tøle & Zwegers, 2003).

Some of the major difficulties encountered for a VE are:

- establishing relationships and mutual agreements,
- sharing information, knowledge, competences, etc. between the collaborating enterprises,
- distributing business processes to optimise the work flow for the whole VE.

Related Modelling Issues

Active Knowledge Models

Enterprise knowledge modelling aims at capturing reusable knowledge of processes and products in knowledge architectures supporting work execution (Lillehagen & Karlsen, 1999). These architectures form the basis for model-based solutions, which are often represented as active knowledge models (AKM). An essential characteristic of active models vs. passive models is that "the model must be dynamic, users must be supported in changing the model to fit their local reality, enabling tailoring of the system's behaviour" (Krogstie & Jørgensen, 2004).

Variability Modelling

Complex products offering a rich set of features to their users often cause a serious challenge to their developers. Modelling and capturing this product complexity in enterprise models requires a combination of enterprise knowledge modelling and variability modelling. Two approaches for variability modelling are configurable components (Claesson, 2006) and feature modelling. Feature modelling offers capturing and visualizing of commonalities and dependencies between features and between the components providing feature implementations (Kang et al., 1990).

The Connector View Concept

One of the problems encountered when trying to model the situation of the virtual enterprise (and extended enterprise) is to capture the points of integration, i.e. the situations and entities where collaboration is taking place and what this collaboration actually consists of. The connector view concept, to be presented, has been developed with the intention to contribute to solve the problems with interconnecting business processes and give a "network-wide view" (Tøle & Zwegers, 2003) of the collaboration.

The development of the connector view concept is based on an industrial case from the automotive supplier industry. It brings together experiences from enterprise knowledge modelling, variability modelling of complex systems and enterprise interoperability.

The main idea behind the connector view concept is that if several enterprises are collaborating or have the intention to collaborate there exist mutual collaboration instances. Those instances incorporate the connection points between these enterprises. The enterprises themselves may have more or less elaborated enterprise models. The connection points between the enterprises are however in these models only partially captured, and there will exist knowledge that span across these enterprise models. By placing an intermediate model (the connector view) between the existing enterprise models it is possible to capture this knowledge.

Description of the Connector View Concept

The connector view is a model which capture collaboration elements. The collaboration element is an entity which constitute collaborative situations. It is necessary to first define the mutual goals for the collaboration, that address the particular areas of interest to be modelled in the connector view. The collaboration elements should be thoroughly described so the collaborating partners have a mutual understanding of them. To our notice these kind of models are best captured using a participative modelling approach (Stirna et al., 2007). Once the collaboration elements have been modelled it is necessary to connect these elements to existing partner enterprise models, and to model the information that is involved in the collaboration. Preferably modelled in parallel, since when trying to relate the collaboration elements to activities and other modelling elements of the existing enterprise models there is a good opportunity to reveal the information content. Also it is not always possible to find the appropriate triggering activities for the collaboration within the enterprises and it can in some cases be necessary to change the collaboration elements.

Modelling the information content in a separate *information view* makes it possible to generate a mutually agreed naming and definition of the different information concepts involved with the collaboration elements. Relating the information concepts that have been defined in the information view with the information elements, available in the existing enterprise models, gives an indication of which information is involved from the different partners and how this information is interrelated between the partners. Together with the elements in the connector view it is possible to describe how the information is used in the collaboration elements in the relationships towards the other enterprise models. It is also possible in the information view to describe which part of the information element respective partner is contributing with.

The difficulty to sometimes find the appropriate triggering activities in the existing enterprise models make it necessary to innovate these elements. It is therefore appropriate to model a *supporting view* for each collaborating partner. This view contains such modelling elements that connect with the collaboration elements. The elements in the supporting view are either an already existing part of the existing enterprise model for a collaboration partner or some new elements to be incorporated. The connector view, information view and supporting views and how they are interrelated is illustrated in a generalised model in Figure 3. Modelling the three different views is an iterative procedure. It can be necessary to further develop the collaboration elements either internally redefining them or generalising or specialising the elements (Carstensen, Sandkuhl, & Holmberg, 2008).

Figure 3. Showing in a generalised way several collaborating partners enterprise models and how the connector view, information view and supporting views for the enterprises are interrelated

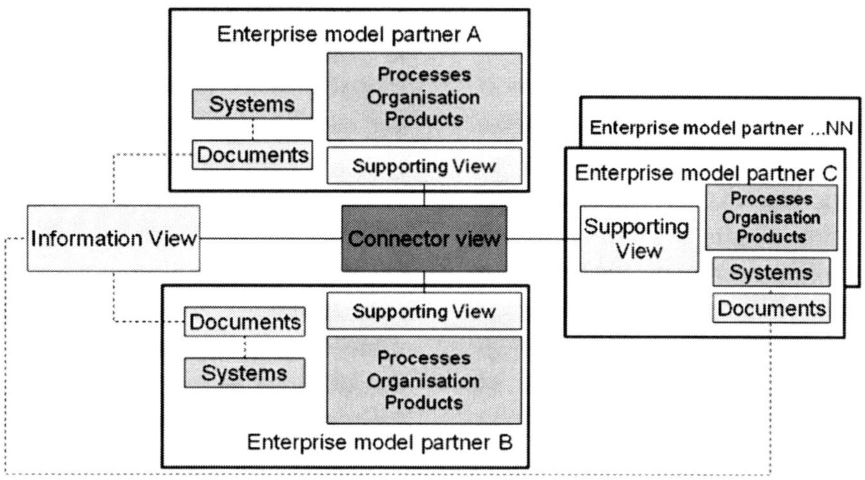

Definition of Connector View Point

In our use case there is mentioned three different views: the connector view, the information view and supporting views for each enterprise in the collaboration. In the Reference Model for Open Distributed Processing (RM-ODP) five different viewpoints, that describe how corresponding views can be modelled, are defined: the enterprise viewpoint, the information viewpoint, the computational viewpoint, the engineering viewpoint and the technological viewpoint (Putman, 2001) (ISO/IEC, 2000). Therefore there are already viewpoints in RM-ODP that describe how to model the information view and the supporting view, since the supporting view is part of the enterprise view. The connector view extends the set of viewpoints given in RM-ODP and therefore it is appropriate to define such a viewpoint (according to the ISO/IEC 42010 standard for viewpoints) (ISO/IEC, 2007). For further details see (Carstensen, Sandkuhl, & Holmberg, 2008).

Use Case for Developing the Connector View Concept

The connector view concept was developed in a use case as part of the EU-FP6 project MAPPER (Model-Adapted Process and Product Engineering). The project was active during the period 2005 until 2008 and aimed at enabling fast and flexible manufacturing in networked enterprises by providing methodology, infra structure and reusable services for collaborative engineering (Johnsen et al., 2007). The modelling process was inspired by the C3S3P methodology which distinguishes between seven stages: concept study, scaffolding, scoping, solution modelling, platform integration, piloting in real projects and performance monitoring and management. Active knowledge models, to be used in model generated and role-specific work places, which allow for collaborative capturing and modification of product knowledge, were created using the tool METIS[4] (Lillehagen & Krogstie, 2008).

In MAPPER the models were developed as active knowledge models using the mutually reflective POPS* perspective (Lillehagen, 2003) (Sandkuhl & Lillehagen, 2008):

- Process perspective (P) including work processes and tasks;
- Organisational perspective (O) including roles involved with the processes;
- Product perspective (P) including components, possibility to configure products and dependencies of the product family;
- Systems perspective (S) including IT systems supporting processes and product development;
- Further perspectives (*) depend on the purpose of the project.

The use case involves two companies (partner A and partner B). Partner A is working as a supplier towards the automotive manufacturing industry. Partner B is a supplier of wire products towards partner A. In this particular use case the intention for the collaboration was settled to improve their collaborative work on testing of materials of products for seat heating wire solutions. From both partners, one or two domain experts together with a modelling facilitator participated in several modelling sessions (Carstensen, Sandkuhl, & Holmberg, 2008).

Initially the participative modelling approach of Enterprise Knowledge Development (EKD) was adopted in order to find out the status of existing models and to balance the somewhat differing situations between the partners (Bubenko et al., 2001). This also created a good modelling atmosphere. These initial modelling attempts concentrated on creating concept and scaffolding model parts missing at partner B and models capturing what was at that time considered as important for the collaboration between the partners. However these models were later on revised and the connector view concept was included. Most of the modelling elements considered as collaborative were found to be supporting elements and instead new "real" collaboration elements were included in the connector view.

Operationalising the Connector View

The last stage in the connector viewpoint methodology is operationalising the connector view. The intention is to put the models into practical use in the collaborating enterprises. While the work with creating the models as such gives valuable knowledge it is necessary to develop the work environment for the stakeholders also. The idea was to do this by using the concept of AKM workplaces. More precisely, to use the IRTV-methodology (IRTV stands for Information Roles Tasks and Views) in the AKM-platform to create a workplace tailored for this particular use case (Carstensen, Holmberg & Sandkuhl, 2008). However while establishing the workplace it became apparent that it is necessary to find a suitable "way" of modelling the product structures. The way of solving this issue during the project work was by using several excel-sheets to capture product values and the inter relationships between them (Carstensen et al., 2009).

For the future development feature modelling is intended to be used for capturing the knowledge from the different partners and then to be integrated by using the connector view concept. Basically this idea of future development can be illustrated as in Figure 4.

Self-Organising Networks

Centralized control in complex distributed systems is not always possible: for example, supply networks consist of independent companies and do not have a central decision making unit. Thus, decentralized self-organisation of distributed independent components is a promising architecture for such kind of systems. The section will present an approach to information support for self-organisation of flexible supply networks based on such technologies as ontology management, context management, competence profiling, and Web-services.

The approach to model management of flexible supply networks presented in this section integrates efficient management of information services in the open information environment with enterprise modeling taking into account dynamic nature of the flexible supply networks. For this purpose the models proposed are actualized in accordance with the current situation. An ontological model is used in the approach to solve the problem of service heterogeneity. This model makes it possible to enable interoperability between heterogeneous information services due to provision of their common semantics (Uschold

Figure 4. A generalised view of capturing product knowledge in feature models for each collaborating enterprise and then integrating, by using the connector view, the feature models from those enterprises into a mutual feature model. Thereby externalising the shared product knowledge

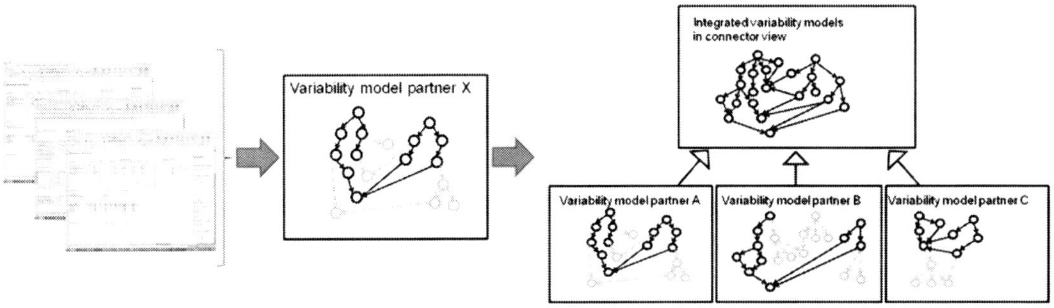

Figure 5. Generic scheme of the approach

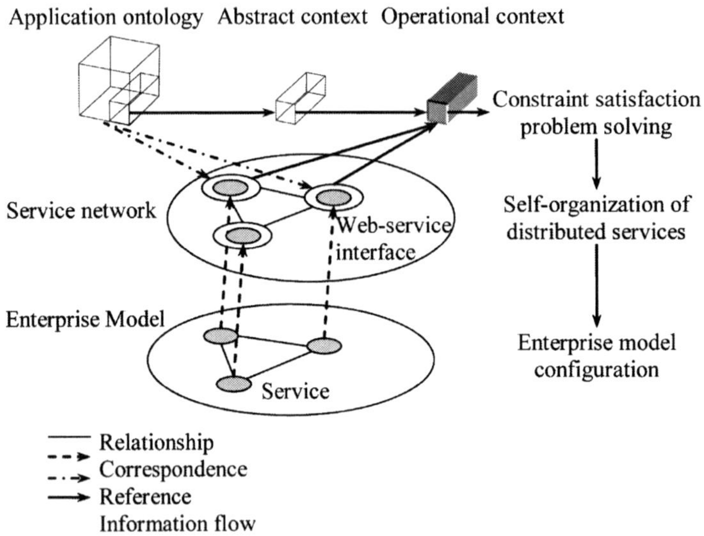

& Gruninger, 1996). Application of the context model makes it possible to reduce the amount of information to be processed. This model enables management of information relevant for the current situation (Dey, 2001). The access to the services, information acquisition, transfer, and processing (including integration) are performed via usage of the technology of Web-services.

Figure 5 represents the generic scheme of the approach. The main idea of the approach is to represent the participants (components) of the flexible supply network by sets of services provided by them. This makes it possible to replace the self-organisation of the supply network with that of distributed services. For the purpose of interoperability the services are represented by Web-services using the common notation described by the application ontology (AO). Depending on the problem considered the relevant part of the application ontology is selected forming the abstract context that, in turn, is filled with values from the sources resulting in the operational context (the model of the current situation). The operational context represents the constraint satisfaction problem that is used during self-organisation of services for problem solving.

To summarize, the general three-level scheme of the approach is shown in Figure 6. The technological base is provided by Web-services. The problem is described via object-oriented constraint networks (Smirnov et al., 2009) and the semantics is provided for by using ontologies. Semantic level provides for knowledge sharing and exchange in an enterprise model.

In the architecture (Figure 7) of the service-oriented knowledge supply, two types of Web-services are distinguished: *core Web-services* and *operational Web-services*.

The core Web-services are intended for the creation of the abstract context and for monitoring of the environment. The core Web-services comprise:

Figure 6. Three-level scheme of the proposed approach

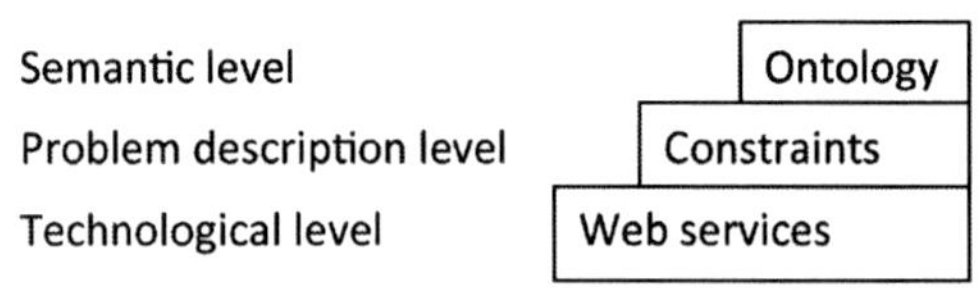

Figure 7. Service-oriented architecture

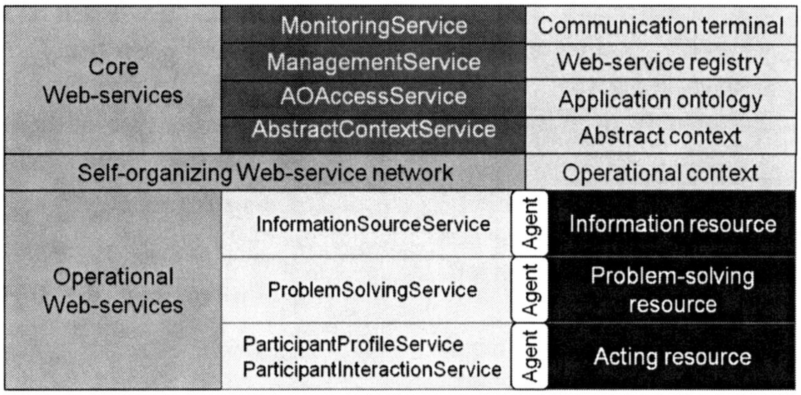

- **MonitoringService** monitors the environment, identifies the type of problems arising, and produces appropriate signal messages.
- **AOAccessService** provides access to the AO;
- **AbstractContextService** creates, stores, and reuses abstract contexts;
- **ManagementService** manages Web-services to create the abstract context. It operates with the service registry where the core services are registered.

The operational Web-services self-organize a network. To make the Web-services active components capable to self-organize an agent-based service model is used. Agents are intended to negotiate services' needs and possibilities in terms of the AO and "activate" Web-services when required. The services' needs and possibilities are respectively input and output arguments of the functions that the Web-services implement. The set of operational Web-services comprises:

- **InformationSourceService** – a set of Web-services responsible for interactions with information sources of different types and for processing information provided by these sources. The following main types of information sources are distinguished: *sensors*, *databases*, *Web-sites*, and *humans*;
- **ProblemSolvingService** – a set of Web-services responsible for problem solving.
- **ParticipantProfileService** creates, modifies, and updates profiles of the acting resources (flexible supply network participants); provides access to these profiles; collects information about the participants; in a context-based way accumulates information about the participant activities; reveals preferences of the participants;
- **ParticipantInteractionService** – a set of Web-services responsible for support of and interactions with the participants 1) providing system messages, context-sensitive help, results of problem solving to the participants, and 2) delivering information from the participants to the system.

The approach relies upon the Web-service model represented by the structure <*WS_URI*, *WS_RI*, <*WS_Function*>, *WS_Calls*, *WS_Fails*, *WS_Price*, *WS_Access_Time*, *WS_Time_In*, *WS_Owner*, *WS_Weigh*>, where

- *WS_URI* – URI of the Web-service;
- *WS_RI* – the identifier of a service;
- *WS_Function* – a set of functions the Web-service implements, for *WS_F*∈*WS_*

Function there exists a mapping f_m : *WS_Function*→C_{m_AO} so that $f_m(WS\_F)=c_{m\_AO}$, $c_{m\_AO} \in C_{m\_AO}$, where C_{m_AO} – a set of classes representing methods in the AO;

- *WS_Calls* – the number of Web-service calls;
- *WS_Fails* – the number of failed calls (if a service is associated with a supplier this parameter would allow to analyze the reliability of that supplier);
- *WS_Price* – the costs of information acquisition (the costs of the functions the Web-service implements, e.g., supplier's price of the materials);
- *WS_Access_Time* – the access time of the Web-service;
- *WS_Owner* – the owner of the Web-service;
- *WS_Weight* – the weight of the Web-service. Weight is calculated based on the access time of the Web-service, the execution times and costs of the functions the Web-service implements, and the Web-service reliability.

The element <WS_Function> is a structure: <FK: *WS_Function*, *F_IArg*, *F_D_IArg*, *F_OArg*, *F_D_OArg*>, where

- FK: *WS_Function* – the reference to the function in the Web-service model;
- *F_IArg* – a set of input arguments of the function, for $iArg \in F\_IArg$ there exists a mapping $f_{inp}:F\_IArg \rightarrow P_{m\_AO}$ so that $f_{inp}(iAgr)=p_{m\_AO}$, $p_{m\_AO} \in P_{m\_AO}$, where P_{m_AO} – a set of properties representing method arguments in the AO;
- *F_D_IArg* – a set of types of the input arguments, for *F_D_IArg* there exists a set of functions $\Phi_i:F\_D\_IArg \rightarrow D\_P_{m\_AO}$, where $D\_P_{m\_AO}$ – a set of ranges for properties P_{m_AO}, so that $\phi_i\left(diArg\right) = \left\{d_j^p \middle| d_j \in D\_P_{m\_AO}, p \in P_{m\_AO}, j \in \mathrm{N}\right\}$, $\phi_i \in \Phi_i$;
- *F_OArg* – the output argument of the function, there exists a mapping $f_{outp}:F\_OArg \rightarrow P_{m\_AO}$ so that $f_{outp}(F\_OArg)=p_{m\_AO}$, $P_{m\_AO} \in P_{m\_AO}$;
- *doArg* – the type of the output argument, for *doArg* there exists a function $\phi_o : doArg \rightarrow D\_P_{m\_AO} : doArg \rightarrow D\_P_{m\_AO}$ so that $\phi_o\left(doArg\right) = d^p \middle| d \in D\_P_{m\_AO}, p \in P_{m\_AO}$ P_{m_AO}.

One of the purposes of the Web-service model is to enable specification of alignment for class properties contained in the AO and attributes being found in Web-service descriptions.

The base for self-organization of Web-services into a network is the abstract context. To describe processes of self-organization of a service network a sequence of scenarios is proposed (Figure 8).

The first scenario describes Web-service interactions for the purpose of exchange information of services (functions) provided by a given service and the service requirements. The result of this scenario is a set of Web-services (WS_f) which can participate in self-organization of the Web-service network based on the service functionalities.

The second scenario describes interactions of the Web-services comprising the set WS_f for the purpose of determination if the services being modeled by these Web-services are projected to be available during predicted time of adequacy of the model of the current situation. The result of this scenario is a set of Web-services (WS_a) which model those services that partly or fully are available during the predicted time.

The third scenario describes interactions of the Web-services comprising the set WS_a for the purpose of self-organisation of an efficient Web-service network. The efficient network is organised based on an analysis of:

- The services that provide several functions. More expedient is considered usage

Figure 8. Scenario of self-organizing service network

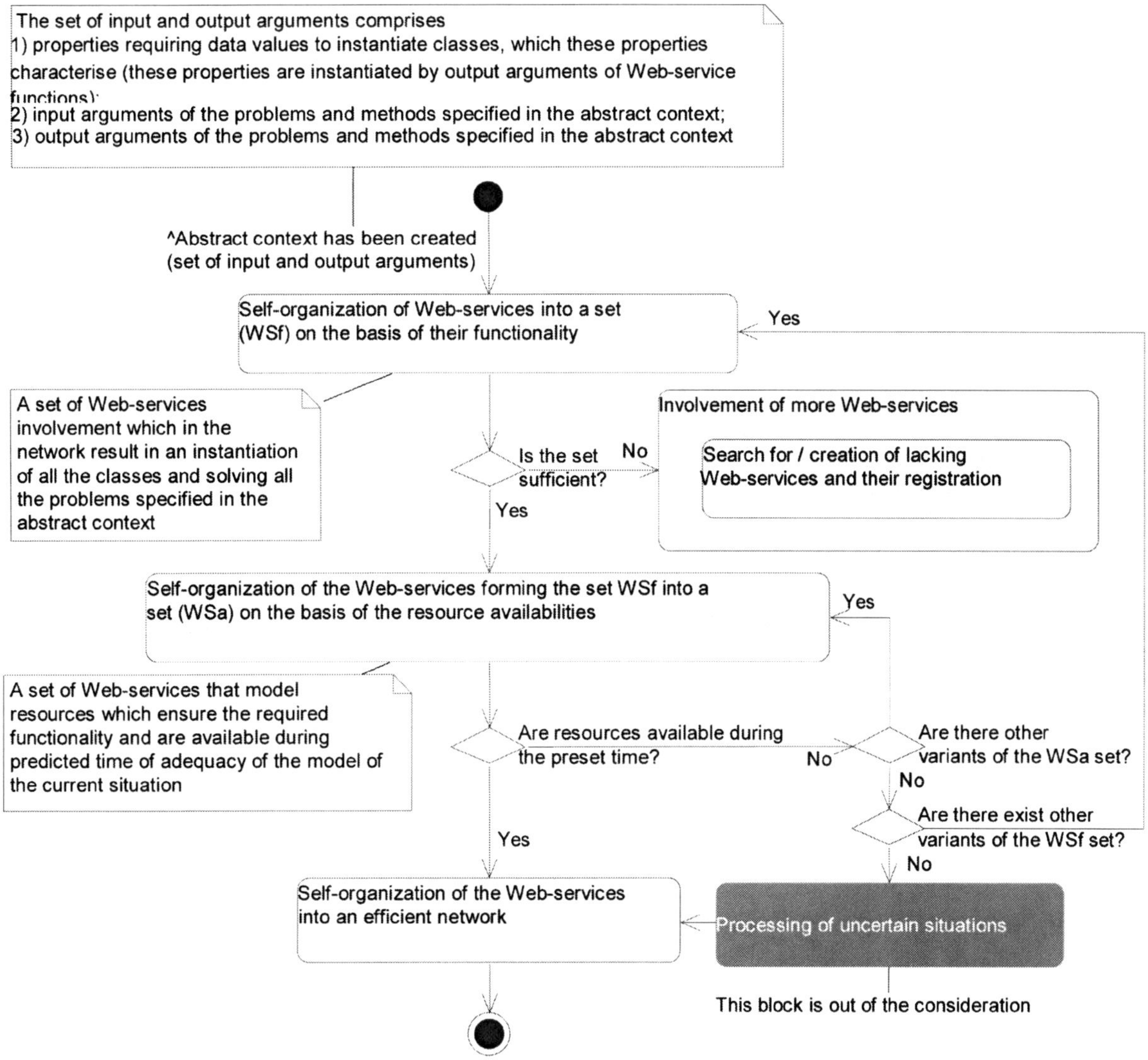

of one service that provides several functions than involvement of several services that provide the same functions separately;

- The availabilities of the services. Usage of a service that is available over the predicted time is thought of more efficient than deploy several services that are available at different times;
- The alternative services. The efficiency of usage of alternative services is determined by the weights of the Web-services that model such services.

DISCUSSION

This section will contain a discussion of the presented research efforts. The major advantages and limitations will be described and analyzed.

Potentials and Limits

As in most SME related research and development areas, the suitability and acceptance of the proposed approaches is an important question when discussing limits and potentials of technologies. SMEs have in general terms the following requirements when introducing new technologies. These requirements are based on own experiences and supported by related work, e.g. (Caussanel & Chouraqui, 1999), (Levy et al., 2002) or (Lybaert, 1998):

- SMEs usually have very limited resources and personnel with often more than one role within the enterprise. Involvement of these information workers in work processes should be as efficient as possible.
- Knowledge about information modeling and system analysis is not spread among staff members in small enterprises. This qualification issue has to be taken into account when staffing project teams and providing development aids.
- SMEs show a clear preference for proven and to a large extent standardized solutions. The approaches or products used should have a high maturity.
- The decision to introduce innovations often is influenced by large customers or general trends and standards within the work domain of the SME. Compatibility or integration with solutions of the domain leaders are supporting this decision.
- The cost for the whole life cycle of an innovation (i.e. introduction, maintenance and evolution) should be clearly defined before starting the project.
- Project risks have to be minimal, i.e. runtime of the project, development steps and efforts should bear no uncertainties.

For the proposed IT technologies introduced in section 4, the application cases in 3 show the principal applicability. However, more industrial cases are needed in order to meet all the above requirements.

The formal ontology-based domain description opens a number of potentials in various aspects of the supply networks. For example, on the basis of the formal description of possible products within the common ontology it is possible now to design new applications which offer customers better ways to find and choose the right product (Oroszi et al., 2009). Furthermore it is possible to add dependent technical data to a certain configuration (which is a set of selected properties and values). For example, a products weight can be calculated based on the properties / values selected by customer. Even more challenging are inter-product-relationships. The most common use case is the relationship between a main product and an accessory product. The dependencies between them are related to the products' individual properties and values. The depth of product-accessory relationships is basically not limited, so accessory-of-accessory combinations have to be taken into account, too. This opens new horizons for such directions as, for example, innovation democratization, which is based on involving customers into the R&D processes.

Related Work

The use of enterprise modelling approaches when developing knowledge supply solutions has been recognized since many years. Examples for areas contributing to this field are enterprise integration and enterprise knowledge modelling. Starting in the early 1990's, enterprise integration aimed at facilitating coordination of functional entities in order to contribute to fulfilment of enterprise goals (Vernadat, 1996). A recent example for interoperability frameworks was developed in the EU-FP6 ATHENA IP[5]. ATHENA developed reference architectures, methodologies and infrastructures for Interoperability of Heterogeneous Enterprise Networks (Ruggaber, 2006).

Enterprise knowledge modelling aims at capturing reusable knowledge of processes and products in knowledge architectures supporting work execution (Lillehagen & Karlsen, 1999). These architectures form the basis for model-based solutions, which often are represented as active knowledge models (Krogstie & Jørgensen, 2004). A common denominator for the above areas is the expectation that capturing and reusing organizational knowledge will contribute to the competitiveness of the enterprise.

Other research related to the work presented in this paper proposes several new paradigms for self-organisation of flexible supply network; the Sustainable District Logistics (Strati et al., 2002); self-organised collaborative supply network designed from autonomous or semi-autonomous mission-focused centres (Frayret et al., 2000); a decentralized, self-organizing real-time coordination of hospital logistics using a multi-agent system (Müller et al., 2004); regulation of intersecting material flows in complex networks (Donner et al., 2007).

Some of these issues are also considered in the framework of PLASTIC – Providing Lightweight & Adaptable Service Technology for Pervasive Information & Communication project sponsored by the EC FP6 (PLASTIC, 2006). Among other issues a service oriented approach allowing for ad hoc context awareness in pervasive environments has been developed. In the approach context-related entities – all taking the form of contextual services – are purposed to dynamically self-organize and self-adapt to optimally exploit available, possibly heterogeneous, contextual resources at the specific time and place.

SUMMARY AND FUTURE WORK

In complex work processes with a number of distributed partners, high requirements with respect to competence and a lot of rules and guidelines to be obeyed, detecting and sharing knowledge among different members of networked organizations is important. Based on an empirical investigation regarding the demands of SME and illustrating this demand with industrial cases, this paper investigated two technical approaches supporting knowledge supply in networked organizations: enterprise modeling and self-organisation of flexible supply networks. These approaches were presented with related work and their limits and potentials.

The research results showed that the proposed methodology makes it possible to provide for efficient knowledge supply in SME networks. Alignment of Web-service descriptions and the ontology allows the Web-services to exchange information about their needs and possibilities in terms of the ontology vocabulary. The ontology-based problem model represented as context provides the Web-services with awareness about the problems to be solved in the current situation and the information needed for this. As a result, the Web-services become capable to organize themselves in a service network for a common purpose of knowledge supply.

Recent activities aiming at decreasing the industrial impact on the environment have led to appearance of new research efforts towards the knowledge-based low carbon economy. As one possible future direction of the here proposed approaches can be mentioned the use of sustainable intelligent SME networks adapted for a minimal impact on the environment. Such networks do not necessary have to belong to the industrial sector but also to logistics, tourism, etc.

Furthermore, the knowledge supply approach should be validated in more application fields and evaluated in a larger number of SME and SME-networks. Candidate areas for application fields are management and control of variability in product development and engineering change management in environments with many ad-hoc changes.

For future development of operationalising the connector view the idea is that product structures can be captured using feature modelling. The collaboration elements in the connector view do not have the granularity to capture the product knowledge, which resides in documents and as tacit knowledge in the minds of the stakeholders. Using feature modelling common characteristics and dependencies between features, and between the components providing feature implementations, can be collected and visually modelled (Kang, 1990). This development would be a substantial contribution in making the aforementioned AKM workplaces operational.

ACKNOWLEDGMENT

The paper is due to research projects supported by grants # 08-07-00264, # 09-07-00436, and # 09-07-12111 of the Russian Foundation for Basic Research, and project # 213 of the research program "Intelligent information technologies, mathematical modelling, system analysis and automation" of the Russian Academy of Sciences.

REFERENCES

Baccarini, D. (1996). The concept of project complexity – a review. *International Journal of Project Management, 14*, 201–204. doi:10.1016/0263-7863(95)00093-3

Billig, A., Blomqvist, E., & Lin, F. (2007) Semantic Matching based on Enterprise Ontologies, In *Proc. of the 6th International Conference on Ontologies, DataBases, and Applications of Semantics, ODBASE 2007* (pp. 1161 – 1168)Vilamoura, Algarve, Portugal.

Botkin, J. (1999). *Smart Business: How Knowledge Communities Can Revolutionize Your Company*. Washington, DC: Free Press.

Bubenko, J. A., Jr., Persson, A., & Stirna, J. (2001). User Guide of the Knowledge Management Approach Using Enterprise Knowledge Patterns, *IST Programme project Hypermedia and Pattern Based Knowledge Management for Smart Organisations: Delivery 3*, Royal Institute of Technology (KTH) and Stockholm University, Sweden. Published October 01, 2001, at http://www.dsv.su.se/~js/ekd_user_guide.html.

Carstensen, A., Holmberg, L., & Sandkuhl, K. (2008). Supporting collaboration in an Extended Enterprise with the Connector View on Enterprise Models. In *Proceeding of First IFIP WG 8.1 Working Conference, PoEM 2008* (pp. 111 - 126). Stockholm, Sweden.

Carstensen, A., Holmberg, L., & Sandkuhl, K. (2009). Modelling Interoperability in Networked Organisations with the Connector Concept. In *Proceedings of the 13th IFAC Symposium on Information Control Problems in Manufacturing* (pp. 916 - 921). Moscow, Russia.

Carstensen, A., Sandkuhl, K., & Holmberg, L. (2008). Towards a Methodology for Modeling Interoperability Between Collaborating Enterprises. In *Proc. of the 10th International Conference on Enterprise Information Systems* (pp. 333 - 338). Barcelona, Spain.

Caussanel, J., & Chouraqui, E. (1999) Model and methodology of knowledge capitalization for small and medium sized enterprises. In *Proc. of the 12th Workshop on Knowledge Acquisition, Modeling and Management*. Banff, Alberta, Canada.

Ciravegna, F., & Petrelli, D. (2006). Annotating document content: a knowledge management perspective. *The Indexer, 25*(1), 23–27.

Claesson, A. (2006). *Product Design by Configurable Components*. Unpublished PhD dissertation, Chalmers Technical University, Sweden. Retrieved December 19, 2009, from http://www.variant.se/acthesis/

Dey, A. (2001). Understanding and Using Context. *Personal and Ubiquitous Computing Journal*, *5*(1), 4–7. doi:10.1007/s007790170019

Donner, R., Höfener, J., Lämmer, S., & Helbing, D. (2007). Dynamic Stabilization and Control of Material Flows in Traffic and Manufacturing Networks by Means of Phase Synchronization. In *Proceedings of the 3rd International Conference on Physics and Control (PHYSCON 2007)*. Potsdam, Germany. Retrieved June 02, 2009, from http://lib.physcon.ru/?item=1196.

Farell, J. (2008). What is the extended enterprise? Retrieved September 16, 2009, from http://jpfarrell.blogspot.com/2008/04/extended-enterprise.html.

Fong, M. (2005). *E-Collaborations and Virtual Organisations*. Hershey, PA: IRM Press.

Frayret, J.-M., & Cloutier, L. Montreuil., B., & D'Amours, S. (2000). A Distributed Framework for Collaborative Supply Network Integration. In L. M. Camarinha-Matos, R. J. Rabelo, & H. Afsarmanesh (Eds.), *E-Business and Virtual Enterprises* (pp. 233 – 244). New York: Springer.

IFIP/IFAC Task Force on Architectures for Enterprise Integration. (2003). The Generalized Enterprise Reference Architecture and Methodology. In Bernus, P., Nemes, L., & Schmidt, G. (Eds.), *Handbook on Enterprise Architectures* (pp. 21–63). Berlin: Springer-Verlag.

ILIPT Project Description (2006). Retrieved June 02, 2009, from http://www.ilipt.org.

ISO/IEC (2000). ISO/IEC JTC1/SC7/WG17, ISO/IEC 15414|ITU-T Recommendation X.911, Initial Committee draft; Information Technology-Open Distributed Processing-Reference Model-Enterprise Language. CD 15414.

ISO/IEC. (2007). IEEE Std 1471-2000 Recommended Practice for Architectural Description of Software Intensive Systems. ISO/IEC 42010. IEEE: 24.

Johnsen, S., et al. (2007). Model-based adaptive Product and Process Engineering. In M. Rabe, & P. Mihok (Eds.), *Ambient Intelligence Technologies for the Product Lifecycle: Results and Perspectives from European Research* (pp. 7 - 27). Fraunhofer: IRB Verlag.

Kang, K., Cohen, S., Hess, J., Novak, W., & Peterson, S. (1990). *Feature-oriented domain analysis (FODA) feasibility study*. Tech. Report CMU/SEI-90-TR-21, ADA235785. Software Engineering Institute, CMU, Pittsburgh, PA, November 1990.

Krogstie, J., & Jørgensen, H. D. (2004). Interactive Models for Supporting Networked Organizations. In [LNCS, Springer.]. *Proceedings of CAiSE, 2004*, 307–332.

Lau, T., & Sure, Y. (2002). Introducing Ontology-based Skills Management at a Language Insurance Company. In *Modellierung in der Praxis – Modellierung für die Praxis, 12*, LNI, 123 - 134.

Lesser, E., & Butner, K. (2005)... *Knowledge and the Supply Chain, Inside Supply Management*, *16*(4), 12.

Levy, M., Powell, P., & Yetton, P. (2002). The Dynamics of SME Information Systems. *Small Business Economics*, *19*(4), 341–354. doi:10.1023/A:1019654030019

Lillehagen, F. (2003). The Foundations of AKM Technology. In *Proceeding of 10th International Conference on Concurrent Engineering (CE) Conference* (pp. 619 - 629). Madeira, Portugal.

Lillehagen, F., & Karlsen, D. (1999). Visual Extended Enterprise Engineering embedding Knowledge Management, Systems Engineering and Work Execution. In *IFIP International Enterprise Modelling Conf.* Norway.

Lillehagen, F., & Krogstie, J. (2008). *Active Knowledge Modeling of Enterprises*. Springer Verlag. doi:10.1007/978-3-540-79416-5

Lin, F., & Sandkuhl, K. (2007). A New Expanding Tree Ontology Matching Method. In *Proc. of OTM 2007: 3rd International IFIP workshop on Semantic Web & Web Semantic (SWWS2007)* (pp. 1329 - 1337). Vilamoura, Algarve, Portugal, November 25—30.

Lundqvist, M., Holmquist, E., Sandkuhl, K., Seigerroth, U., & Strandesjö, J. (2009). Information Demand Context Modelling for Improved Information Flow: Experiences and Practices. In *IFIP Working Conference PoEM, The Practices of Enterprise Modelling, 2* (pp. 8 - 22). LNBIP 39, Springer Verlag.

Lybaert, N. (1998). The Information Use in a SME: its Importance and Some Elements of Influence. *Small Business Economics, 10*(2), 171–191. doi:10.1023/A:1007967721235

Mak, K-T & Ramaprasad, A. (2003). Knowledge Supply Network, *The Journal of the Operational Research Society, 54*(2), Palgrave, 175 – 183.

Müller, G., Eymann, T., Nopper, N., & Seuken, S. (2004). EMIKA System: Architecture and Prototypic Realization. In *Proc. of the IEEE Intl. Conf. on Systems, Man and Cybernetics (SMC), 6* (pp. 5621 – 5626). The Hague, The Netherlands, October 2004.

Noran, O. (2003). A Mapping of Individual Architecture Frameworks (GRAI, PERA, C4ISR, CIMOSA, Zachman, ARIS) onto GERAM. In Bernus, P., Nemes, L., & Schmidt, G. (Eds.), *Handbook on Enterprise Architecture* (pp. 65–210). Berlin, Heidelberg: Springer-Verlag.

Öhgren, A. (2009). *Towards an Ontology Development Methodology for SME.* Unpublished PhD dissertation, Linköping University, Sweden.

Oroszi, A., Jung, T., Smirnov, A., Shilov, N., & Kashevnik, A. (2009). Ontology-Driven Codification for Discrete and Modular Products [Inderscience.]. *International Journal of Product Development, 8*(2), 162–177. doi:10.1504/IJPD.2009.024186

PLASTIC. (2006). Retrieved June 2, 2009 from http://www.ist-plastic.org/.

Putman, J. R. (2001). *Architecting with RM-ODP*. Upper Saddle River, NJ: Prentice Hall.

Redon, R., Larsson, A., Leblond, R., & Longueville, B. (2007). Vivace context based search platform. In *Proceedings of the 6th International Conference CONTEXT-07*. LNCS (LNAI), *4635* (pp. 397–410). Heidelberg: Springer.

Ruggaber, R. (2006). ATHENA - Advanced Technologies for Interoperability of Heterogeneous Enterprise Networks and their Applications. In Konstantas, D., Bourrières, J.-P., Léonard, M., & Boudjlida, N. (Eds.), *Interoperability of Enterprise Software and Applications* (pp. 459–460). London: Springer. doi:10.1007/1-84628-152-0_45

Sandkuhl, K. (2003). Information Logistics Support for Collaborative Engineering. In *Proceedings DDECS 2003*, Workshop CCE´03 (pp. 60 - 67). Poznan, Poland, April 2003.

Sandkuhl, K. (2008). Information Logistics in Networked Organizations: Selected Concepts and Applications. In *Proceedings of the 9th International Conference on Enterprise Information Systems – ICEIS 2008* (pp. 43 - 54). LNBIP, Springer.

Sandkuhl, K. (in press). Supporting Collaborative Engineering with Information Supply Patterns. *Euromicro PDP*. Pisa, Italy, February 2009.

Sandkuhl, K., & Billig, A. (2007). Ontology-based Artefact Management in Automotive Electronics [IJCIM]. *International Journal of Computer Integrated Manufacturing, 20*(7), 627–638. doi:10.1080/09511920701566467

Sandkuhl, K., & Lillehagen, F. (2008). The Early Phases of Enterprise Knowledge Modelling. In *Proc. 1st IFIP WG 8.1 Working Conference, PoEM 2008* (pp. 1 - 14). Stockholm, Sweden, November 2008. LNBIP, Springer.

Semantic Web. (2006). Retrieved June 2, 2009, from http://www.semanticweb.org.

Smirnov, A., Levashova, T., & Shilov, N. (2009). Knowledge Sharing in Flexible Production Networks: A Context-Based Approach. In A. Graves, Mr. G. Stone, & Dr. J. Miemczyk (Eds.), *International Journal of Automotive Technology and Management (IJATM), 9*(1) (pp. 87-109). Onley, UK: Inderscience Publishers.

SOA. (2007). *Service-oriented architecture (SOA) definition*. Retrieved June 2, 2009, from http://www.service-architecture.com/web-services/articles/service-oriented_architecture_soa_definition.html.

Song, H., Wang, Z., Song, Y., Zhang, Y., & Zhen, L. (2008). Exploring knowledge grid for knowledge supply in the collaborative design. In *Proceedings of the IEEE International Conference on Networking, Sensing and Control ICNSC 2008* (pp. 1663 – 1667). Hainan, China.

Stirna, J., Persson, A., & Sandkuhl, K. (2007). Participative Enterprise Modeling: Experiences and Recommendations. In *19th Intl Conference in Advanced Information Systems Engineering, CAiSE 2007* (pp.546 - 560). LNCS, Berlin / Heidelberg, Springer-verlag

Stone, G., Miemczyk, J., & Esser, R. (2005). Making Build to Order a Reality: The 5-Day Car Initiative. In *Strengthening Competitiveness through Production Networks. A prospective from European ICT research projects in the field of "Enterprise Networking"* (pp. 26 – 37). European Communities.

Strati, F., et al. (2002). *Short Paper on Sustainable District Logistics*, Retrieved June 2, 2009, from the Web-site of ENSDL – The European Network for Sustainable District Logic, http://www.district-logistics.net/download/short-paper.pdf.

Suresh, J. K., & Mahesh, K. (2008). Managing the Knowledge Supply Chain at Infosys, *Knowledge Management Review, 11*(4). Retrieved June 2, 2009, from http://findarticles.com/p/articles/mi_qa5362/is_200809/ai_n30991635/.

Tøle, M. & şi Zwegers, A. (2003). Virtual Enterprise Reference Architecture and Methodology, GLOBEMEN Joint D41/D43 Deliverable (technical report). Retrieved September 15, 2009, from http://cic.vtt.fi/projects/globemen/public.htm

Tølle, M., & Vesterager, J. (2003). Developing the Business Model – A Methodology for Virtual Enterprises. In Bernus, P., Nemes, L., & Schmidt, G. (Eds.), *Handbook on Enterprise Architectures* (pp. 291–308). Berlin, Heidelberg: Springer-Verlag.

Uschold, M., & Grüninger, M. (1996). Ontologies: Principles, methods and applications. *The Knowledge Engineering Review, 11*(2), 93–155. doi:10.1017/S0269888900007797

Vernadat, F. B. (1996). *Enterprise Modelling and Integration*. Boca Raton, FL:Chapman & Hall.

Wang, Q. & Rong, L. (2007). Agile Knowledge Supply Chain for Emergency Decision-Making Support. In Shi, Y., Dick van Albada, G., Dongarra, J., & Sloot, P. M. A. (Eds.), *Computational Science - ICCS 2007. Lecture Notes in Computer Science, 4490* (pp. 178–185). New York: Springer.

Web services explained (2007). Retrieved June 2, 2009, from http://www.service-architecture.com/web-services/articles/web_services_explained.html.

ENDNOTES

1. See (Sandkuhl 2008) for an overview to the research area information logistics.
2. A more detailed description of results can be found in (Öhgren, 2009).

[3] International Federation for Automatic Control (IFAC), International Federation of Information Processing (IFIP)

[4] METIS is a methodology neutral modelling tool for visual enterprise models, See http://www.troux.com

[5] www.athena-ip.org

Chapter 11
SME as a Service

José Carlos Martins Delgado
Instituto Superior Técnico, Portugal

ABSTRACT

The market evolves at an increasingly faster pace. Enterprises, and in particular SMEs (Small and Medium Enterprises), besides having to stay agile, competitive and aware of competition, must give customers what they need (customized products or services) when they need it. The classical business paradigm (carefully studying what customers have bought in the past to predict what they will buy in the near future and derive a strategy from it) is not agile and adequate enough anymore. This chapter discusses a customer-centric business paradigm with enough agility to follow the patterns of customers' needs and the ability to customize specific needs as a variant of some pattern, turning the very low volume customer market into a viable business opportunity. The customization and corresponding production result from concrete user requests and not anticipation of demand. We call it EaaS (Enterprise as a Service) and is particularly adequate to SMEs.

INTRODUCTION

An enterprise is usually part of a value network (buying from suppliers, selling to customers and managing its own resources, Figure 1a), where it suffers three main types of risks:

- Supplier side risks (e.g., supplier discontinuing or failing to provide a product/service, betting on a supplier's technology/product that looses on the market);
- Customer side risks (customer failing to pay, no purchase orders or cancelations);
- Its own risks (bad strategy, unattractive or uncompetitive products/services, poor supplier, customer or resource management, inability to deal with supplier capacity/customer demand mismatch, insufficient or inadequate resources, hazards).

DOI: 10.4018/978-1-61692-880-3.ch011

Figure 1. Modeling an EA: (a) structure and (b) metamodel

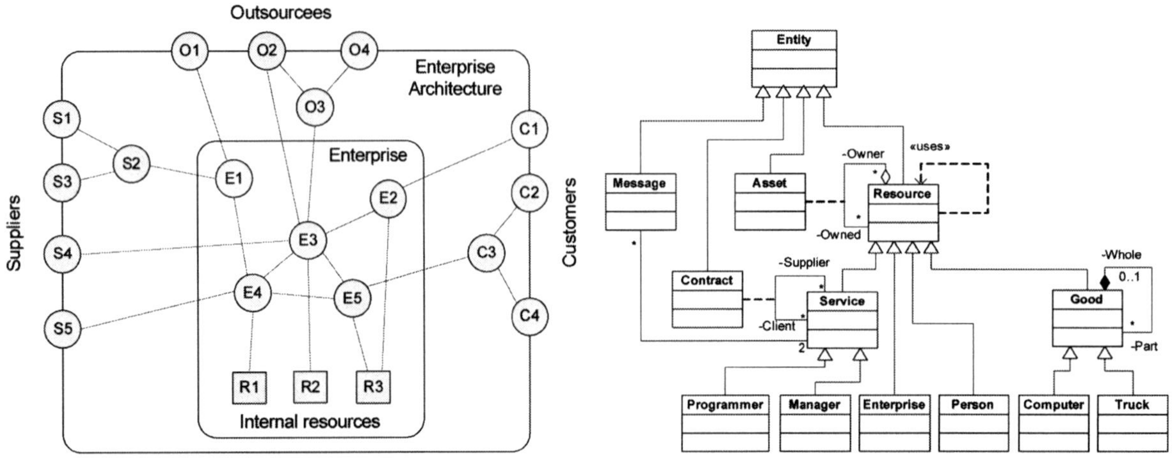

(a) (b)

Each enterprise tries to minimize these risks in various ways. One basic technique is diversification (second source suppliers, broad client base, diversified product/service offerings), but dealing with many suppliers, customers and products/services adds to entropy and entails its own costs and risks.

SMEs (Small and Medium Enterprises) are particularly vulnerable because they have limited resources and are usually neither in a position of imposing on suppliers (not enough business volume) nor of benefiting from economy of scale (most of them operate on the niche, occasional and low volume/item markets, grabbing a share of the market's long tail (Anderson, 2006) that many large enterprises don't bother with). Credibility is also a very important indicator for customers (especially the big, worthwhile ones, which are more averse to risk and prefer large enterprises as suppliers, even if their price is higher).

To be competitive, SMEs have to behave differently from large enterprises operating in the same markets, by taking approaches such as:

- Innovative products/services. Potentially very rewarding, as getting to a new market first is a huge head start, is also very risky to pull through, not to mention the difficulty of having innovative ideas and the possibility of quickly being overrun by a larger company seizing the idea with a competing product/service;
- Customized solutions, for customers that have specific requirements and cannot simply use mass products or utility services. This, however, can be man-power intensive, require significant development and management capabilities and face competition from large reconfigurable manufacturing or consulting companies;
- Adaptability. In today's fast paced world, each opportunity must be seized with efficacy, efficiency and responsiveness. This means providing the customer with the solution that is really needed (not just chewing in some ready-to-sell solution), consuming resources only as needed (TCO, Total Cost of Ownership, as low as possible) and being able to quickly restructuring the way the enterprise operates, if needed. Large companies can be slower to respond, have greater TCO and resource management (that needs to be charged to the cus-

- tomer) and be less akin to adapt to small customers.

Adaptability (the ability to change and adapt to specific or new requirements and goals) is one of the best weapons against competitors that SMEs can resort to in a sustained way. In a global survey to 1000 CEOs, IBM (2008) found out that the "change gap" (the difference between the expected needs for changes and the ability to deal with them) had almost tripled to 22% (from 8% in 2006), which leads IBM to conclude that "the ability to change quickly and successfully is becoming more critical than ever". Schekkerman (2006) asserts that "Dynamics is the only constant while adaptiveness is the natural variable". Adaptability can be characterized by:

- Its dynamicity, which depends on how fast changes can be made;
- Its flexibility, which indicates how easy it is to accomplish these changes.

Naturally, these characteristics will vary with the changes involved. In general terms, an adaptable SME (with respect to the market or competition) can be achieved with:

- Diversification. Design the enterprise architecture (EA) with as many features and scenarios as possible, since a change that is supported by the EA (such as a reconfiguration) is normally easier and faster to implement than an unexpected one. However, the EA will be more complex, will take longer to build and unanticipated changes will take a lot of time and effort;
- Agility. Design the EA as simple as possible, contemplating basically the features and scenarios that will be needed in the near future. The assumption is that a light EA will be much easier and faster to change, so that change time will be short comparatively to the rate at which new requirements arise. Recurrent changes, however, will not be as efficient.

These arguments reinforce each other and the tendency is to have a bistable situation, both when building and when changing (complexity brings sluggishness and lightness favors agility). The second route to adaptability seems clearly the best for SMEs that have to adapt to a highly variable environment, but how can we minimize the time and effort required by unanticipated changes? The objective of this chapter is to shed some light into how this can be achieved.

More important than building an efficient and highly structured EA is designing it in a way that changes are easy and quick to do, with other issues such as performance as secondary objectives. Performance can usually be compensated by using more resources, whereas lack of agility becomes an intrinsic feature that plagues the entire EA lifecycle.

Agility is inversely proportional to TCO. Implementing some functionality by invoking a service (outsourcing) rather than buying resources makes it easier to change supplier and/or the functionality itself. In fact, this chapter suggests that an enterprise's architecture should be built *a la carte*, from a menu (library) of services offered by other enterprises complemented by in-house services, rather than by traditional EA methods based on a central information model. In turn, such an enterprise can offer services to other enterprises and be part of a global service library.

This is what this chapter designates EaaS (Enterprise as a Service), or SMEaaS if we want to emphasize the SME context, although the concept and the agility it promotes can be applied to any enterprise. It is essentially a customer-centric organizational model, based on dynamic and distributed outsourcing, spurred by fast interaction channels such as the Internet, but unlike other members of the "as a service" family that now embody cloud computing (Lin, Fu, Zhu & Dasmalchi, 2009), namely SaaS (Software as a

Service), PaaS (Platform as a Service) and IaaS (Infrastructure as a Service), is not limited to IT and encompasses all aspects of a EA (including people).

The goal of EaaS is to provide a dynamic framework for EA design and maintenance, geared for change and agility, to support the needs of the customers in a customizable environment (instead of a standardized product or service offering) and in low volume markets.

BACKGROUND

A large enterprise certainly wasn't born yesterday and typically already has a working EA, established supplier network and client base, a large set of working applications and business processes with a complex data model, a substantial IT infrastructure, many human resources and a lot of other things, including very likely an extensive offer of services and/or products. This complex system took certainly much time and effort to build and suffered many errors and glitches, before achieving the current state. The main driving tenets are usually efficacy, efficiency and scalability, in its internal processes, supply network and customer relationship. Automation, interoperability and integration are very important issues. The downside of this is that non trivial changes are hard to do, because they can have a large impact on the EA, which tends to be complex and intertwined, geared for performance rather than ease of change. Large enterprises don't perform substantial EA changes frequently (by avoiding situations and market sectors where this is required).

SMEs, on the other hand, don't usually have this possibility. They have to adapt frequently in the low volume/niche sectors where they are not crushed by larger companies, either to each business opportunity, either to the larger companies they buy from or sell to. They also don't have the expertise or resources to have a large, streamlined EA. Even a medium to long-term strategy is a luxury. Therefore, the driving tenets become simplicity, adaptability and a more personal customer relationship. Being able to change a lot in a short time is an asset, in this case, and that can only be done be avoiding a strong dependency on a given system or configuration. Which doesn't mean that efficacy, quality of service and efficiency are forgotten, but adaptability has to come first.

SMEs are also more volatile. They are born and die more frequently, and may never reach the state of a mature, efficient EA. They cannot wait to build a complex EA when they start. Many enterprises began in a small garage or office, and with an incremental but sustained growth strategy (Levy & Powell, 2005) evolved into large corporations. Large initial investments should be avoided, because the early survival rate is low. SME incubators (McAdam & McAdam, 2008) perform an important role by providing (as a service) starter SMEs with resources typically owned by enterprises (facilities, equipment, administrative and technical staff, IT services, and so on), but outside their starting capabilities.

Using a resource as a service, rather than owning it, is a form of outsourcing (Ströbel, 2000) that has the following main advantages:

- For the outsourcer, it reduces the investment and the demand risk (you pay only when you need it), avoids ownership problems (maintenance and failure, for instance) and makes it a lot easier to change (solution and/or outsourcee);
- For the outsourcee, it allows better usage of the resources (shared by several outsourcers) and specialization (lower costs) in a given sector of business.

On the downside, the outsourcer incurs risks (of bad service) that may endanger its reputation before its customers. Therefore, outsourcing has been traditionally limited to well defined service types, peripheral to the outsourcer business and with competing outsourcees that have a track record of good service (such as car leasing, distribution, cleaning and catering). Outsourcing has been usually a big decision meant not to be changed frequently.

With the advent of the Internet and more recently IT virtualization (Gartner, 2008), outsourcing has become more dynamic (Wu & Park, 2009) and has pervaded the enterprises' information system itself, at the level of both the IT infrastructure and the applications. Cloud computing (Lin, Fu, Zhu & Dasmalchi, 2009) is a new IT-driven buzzword that essentially means deliverance of IT services (applications and computing power and storage) through the Internet (traditionally represented in network diagrams as a cloud). The customer uses these services, but does not (have to) know where they are physically being provided or to be aware of their management problems. The provider is able to use the scalability effect of offering the same service to many customers to improve its efficiency and reduce the service cost.

Services are becoming more and more important. The economy of developed countries is heavily service based (on the order of 70-80%) and IBM has started a movement (SSME – Service Science, Management and Engineering) towards a new vision of services as the fundamental element of enterprises and of the economy (Spohrer, Vargo, Caswell & Maglio, 2008).

To fully leverage this vision, enterprises need to have frameworks and tools that enable them to resort to services (act as outsourcers) and, at the same time, to provide services (act as outsourcees), in a much lighter and dynamic way than current EAs permit.

Building an enterprise's architecture with conventional methods (Chen, Doumeingts & Vernadat, 2008), by carefully analyzing the strategy and deriving, refining and specifying each of the subsequent architectures (business, information, application, technological) can be a tremendous task that can take one or more years and is never done (when we finish, the market and the strategy have evolved and we need to start over). And, unfortunately, the longer it takes to build, the longer it will take to change.

DESIGNING AN ENTERPRISE ARCHITECTURE (EA) FOR CHANGEABILITY

A Holistic Vision of the EA

As depicted in Figure 1a, we consider as part of the EA not only its (functional) modules (Ei) and the internal resources it owns (Ri) but also the modules that are part of the enterprise's context, which includes the suppliers (Si), outsourcees (Oi) and customers (Ci) that deal directly with the enterprise proper, and in some cases the suppliers' suppliers, outsourcees' outsourcees and customers' customers (when these relationships have a relevant impact in the enterprise). The Ei modules will have to be implemented and will manage resources Ri. The modules Si, Oi, Ci will just be used, by establishing interoperability schemas and contracts that specify the outer context of the enterprise, but are fundamental players in the enterprise's strategy.

The idea is that everything that affects the enterprise needs to be considered explicitly part of the system (EA) that models the enterprise. The modules outside the enterprise are represented by abstractions, not by implementation, but nevertheless are fundamental in designing and assessing the enterprise:

- If, for example, a distribution company fails to deliver a package to a customer, it may have to pay a compensation to the enterprise for the lost packet, but the enterprise will likely lose the customer and future orders! So, it better manage the outsourcee's performance with as much care as with one of its own modules;
- A supplier or an outsourcee today can be an insourced module tomorrow (or vice-

versa). Treating them equally as part of the system's model makes changes easier (no need to deal with several models);

- One of the enterprise's modules may act as an internal customer of another module (under activity based costing and management, for example). Using the external customer model for internal customers reduces complexity, streamlines efficiency and increases competitiveness.

The distinction between suppliers and outsourcees is more a convention than a fundamental distinction. Suppliers are part of the supply chain, whereas outsourcees can be considered enterprise modules that are being executed by a third party, eventually with less impact in the enterprise's strategy and under different contracting conditions (but nevertheless a supply model relationship).

We have a unified perspective of modules and of resources, which support their functionality. For instance, we consider human roles, computer applications and distribution services as modules, supported respectively by resources such as a person, a computer and a truck. Human roles use a browser to interact with a computer application and a cockpit to control the truck resource, for example, and have behavior that can be modeled. This unified perspective:

- Simplifies modeling the system. A human role is a first class module, able to initiate requests, execute requests made by others and be subject to usual management processes such as incident reporting, in case activity deadlines are not met. It is not a different concept;
- Favors change. The person implementing a human role may be replaced, if needed, by changing the module-resource mapping and without any changes to any of the human role relationships (such as security issues). A human role today can be replaced by a more functional or performing department or automated application, impacting other modules only insofar as its external characteristics change;
- Allows exploiting common characteristics. For instance, a redundancy solution should be foreseen in case a person gets sick, a computer crashes or a truck breaks down. Naturally, the solutions are not exactly identical, but the basic problem is the same and therefore part of the solutions will be common.

The enterprise needs essentially to deal only with the modules of other enterprises that have a direct relationship with it, since the rest of the world is hidden from the enterprise by modeling these modules with abstractions that include only the relevant details of the relationship with the enterprise. Dependencies from other aspects of these modules should be avoided, to make changes easier. However, in some cases it can be strategic to deal with more levels of the supply chain than immediate neighbors, and this should be reflected in the EA. This is the case of suppliers S1 and S3, outsourcee O4 and customers C2 and C4.

An EA should encompass all aspects of the enterprise and of the context that affects it (computer based, people-based and otherwise) and not just the enterprise's information system. The interoperability between the enterprise's modules and those it interacts with should be an integral EA design feature and not an afterword thought. The EA is not a mere documentation of how the enterprise is organized, but rather the working enterprise's architecture itself.

Services as the EA Modeling Paradigm

Figure 1b presents a simplified version of the metamodel on which we can base our vision of a service-oriented EA. The main concepts can be described as follows:

- Resource – an entity with a set of logically related capabilities that can be used by another resource. Some capabilities have finite capacity that may be depleted, partially or totally, in each use. The original capacity can usually be restored, eventually at some cost. Examples: a disk that progressively fills, a bus ticket with a limited number of uses or usage period, a programmer with N hours allocated to a project. A resource can own (be composed by) others, that become its assets. An enterprise is a resource, typically with several services and goods as its assets;
- Service – a non-material resource in which the capabilities are invoked by messages and under contract. Services can invoke other services (under a contract) and use non-service resources (typically, each non-service resource is used by one single service that manages it and may offer its capabilities to other services). Services include human roles;
- Contract – a set of clauses between two services that govern their interaction, with rights, obligations and guarantees. One service can establish several contracts with other services;
- Asset – a set of clauses that govern the ownership of a resource by another;
- Person – a physical resource that supports the implementation (is used by) a human role, such as programmer or manager. Note that a person is never an asset (owned by another resource). In terms of human resources, an enterprise's assets are the human roles and the characteristics they entail. Unfortunately, much of the expertise a person acquires while performing a role is stored exclusively in that person's head, not in the role itself, and therefore outside the EA. It can be lost to the enterprise when the person changes job. That is why knowledge management systems are so important (to bring as much as possible of the expertise back into the EA);
- Good – a resource (not necessarily physical, such as a patent, a digital key or documentation) meant to support the implementation of some service. For example, a computer supports the service of application execution and a truck supports a transportation service.

In Figure 1a, the modules are services and the internal resources are either internal services or goods. It is important to acknowledge that:

- Human roles are services and therefore first class citizens in the EA, instead of foreign entities hidden behind a browser interface. As much as possible of the human role should be modeled into the EA;
- The service ontology still depends a lot on the context, and even the word "service" means different things to different people. Some see it as a very high level economic activity and very linked to human customers (Lovelock & Wirtz, 2007), whereas others think in terms of technology and Web Services (Earl, 2005). The European Union (EU, 2006) has issued a directive requiring that certain types of economic level services offer their capabilities, at least partially, through a single point of contact, accessible electronically. Our model is completely generic and involves only the notion of capabilities that can be invoked. Both invoker and invoked services can be of any kind, nature, granularity and domain (human role, enterprise, computer application, and so on).

How do we specify behavior in the EA? There are two basic paradigms: processes (Havey, 2005) and services (Earl, 2008). They are dual and any system uses both. We can choose either of them as the main structuring and modeling paradigm

Figure 2. Main EA modeling paradigm: (a) Processes (b) Services

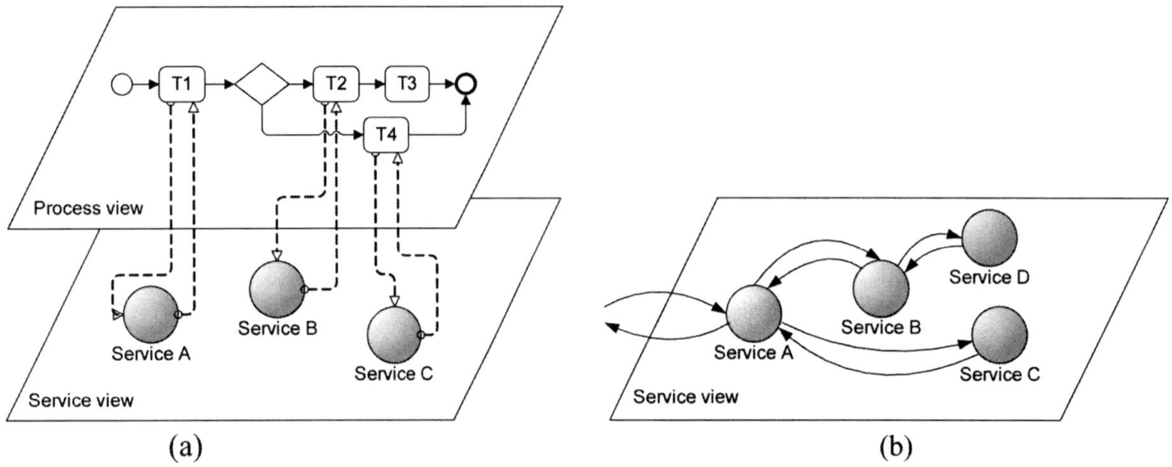

and the other as a complement to help filling in the remaining details. The relevant issue here is deciding which to use in our changeability-driven framework.

Figure 2 helps in figuring out the main differences between them. Suppose we need to describe some behavior, such as the processing of a purchase order from a customer and of all the steps involved in a sale.

The process view in Figure 2a models this operation as a process, involving some tasks (T1 through T4 and a decision) and specified in some process language, such as BPMN (Havey, 2005). Some tasks invoke services to carry out specific activities that have been wrapped into a service and made available to any process (these frequently correspond to business primitives, that is, applications programmed in Java or .Net instead of a process language). This process orchestrates (coordinates) these tasks and establishes what needs to be done, from beginning to end. Choreography is the designation of the coordination is needed between several processes (for instance, in supplier-customer cooperation).

The service paradigm is illustrated by Figure 2b, with the same operation. The tasks are now capabilities of the services. The "process" does not exist formally anymore, but has been distributed by the various services and if we look at the whole picture we still see it there. For example, the capability invoked initially in service A includes task T1 and the test. The decision leads it to invoke a capability in service B (corresponding to task T2) or in service C (task T4). Task T3 could be implemented in the same capability of service B as T3 or in another service (D), as depicted in Figure 2b.

Overall, the tasks required by the operation (whose semantics must not depend on the paradigm used to model it) are the same and get invoked in a semantically equivalent order. Each service's capability can be seen as a mini- process. If we gather all these mini-processes together, we'll get the original process. From the changeability point of view, the main differences between these two paradigms are:

- Global behavior - Processes are usually modeled after use cases (global uses of a system) and therefore tend to span across a large part of the system. Several processes will use the same service. A change in one service has potential impact in many processes. In contrast, services use the outsourcing mechanism and the information hiding principle. Consider the capability of service A that some customer invokes to place the purchase order of this example. It includes task T1 only. The subsequent two branches of the process have been outsourced to services B and C and service A knows nothing about them apart from their interface. This means that the first part of the operation is decoupled from the rest. Deciding to implement task T3 in service B or in a new service D, as in this example, is a decision that service A needs not know about (is not dependent on). The message is: don't use long processes; structure them into services instead;

- Single point of contact – An invoked service will send a reply back at the same point where it was invoked (Figure 2b). Any changes in the implementation of service A, for instance, will not affect the customer. Processes lend themselves to start at one point and finish at another. This means that communication between the process and its environment may have to be aligned in two places;
- Global state – Process based systems tend to have global state (one single database, usually). Although this seems a flexible arrangement, it does not protect one process from interference by another sharing the same state variables. It also favors a global information schema, whose changes affect potentially any process. Services behave as objects in object oriented programming and protect state inside the service that manages it;
- Behavior sharing and reuse – A processes with some part identical to another cannot easily share it. Such cases are resolved by wrapping the common part as a service.
- Behavior clustering – There is no mechanism (without services) that establishes a semantic glue between related processes, so that when requirements change the most involved processes are changed together, with a common logic. In a service, all the related capabilities and inherent state are specified together. Changes will frequently be internal to a service, instead of implying changes in several processes;
- Reality-model mismatch – Any model will be easier to change if its abstractions match the entities it models. A sale, for example, will be the result of the cooperation of several entities (workers, information system, logistics, etc). These entities are much closer to the service paradigm. Processes do not exist as real world entities.

In a sense, many of these differences are the same that motivated the evolution from unstructured to structured and then to object-oriented programming, because change was already the main concern. Structuring both behavior and state under the same abstraction, with a one-to-one mapping to the real world entities is the best way to decouple changes between different parts of the EA, so that a localized change in the enterprise does not imply changes throughout the EA. In what change is concerned, the service paradigm is much better than the process paradigm, and the way to go to make enterprises agile (Uram & Stephenson, 2005).

The problem is that the market adopts technology rather slowly, and technology evolves rather quickly. When enterprises were just starting to organize their activities by making their processes explicit, web services appeared. These started to be used merely as an interoperability mechanism, with the upper layers of the EA still as processes, and not as a basis for a truly paradigm shift. This will happen, spearheaded by cloud computing (Lin, Fu, Zhu, & Dasmalchi, 2009) at the technological level, fostered by the service-dominant logic (Spohrer, Vargo, Caswell & Maglio, 2008) as it pervades the business models and supported by the progressive evolution of ERPs towards service-orientation (Brocke, Schenk & Sonnenberg, 2009). But it will take time to become commonplace.

Figure 3. An EA lifecycle model to support changeability, with five loops

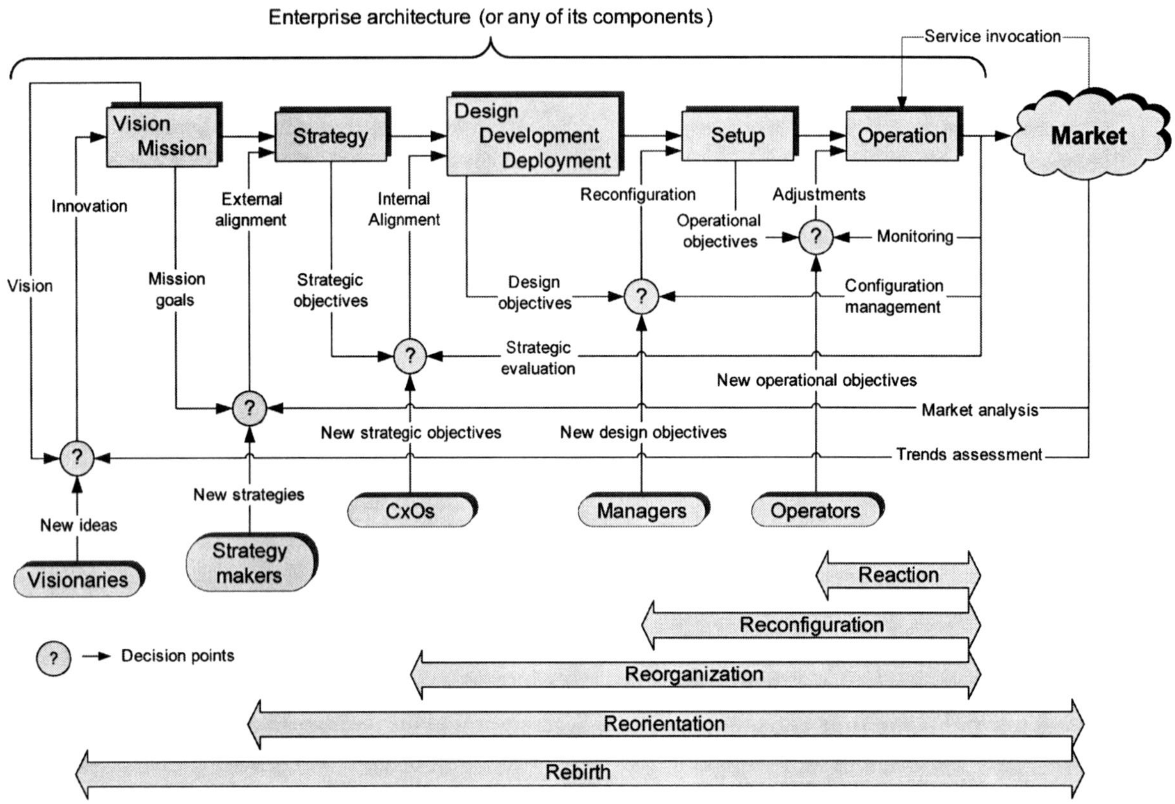

A Simple EA Changeability Model

Figure 3 depicts a basic changeability model, which can be applied to the whole EA, as it is usually conceived today, as well as to any of its components. The market represents the rest of the world, the environment of the component being modeled.

This model is maximalist, open and not prescriptive, in the sense that any component or system should go through all the stages (conceptually, at least), but the level of emphasis and detail in every stage does not have to be always identical, and we can use a different pipeline without invalidating the model's principles.

The higher the level of the component, the more important vision and strategy will be, but it must go all the way down to operations if it is meant to work. Lower level components will emphasize development and operation, but must have an underlying vision and mission as well. In the following text, "EA" should be understood as "any component or system architecture".

The basic idea is that EA changeability is achieved by a pipeline lifecycle with N loops, centered on the working EA (operation stage), but at different levels. The inner loops deal with lower levels and greater detail, whereas outer loops deal with higher levels and less detail. Each of these loops has the following structure:

1. Do whatever is necessary to build or change the EA and to make it operational;
2. Define the metrics (indicators) that we want the working EA to exhibit;
3. Measure the values of the indicators in the working EA;

4. Compare the desired values of the indicators against those measured, which indicates the EA's unalignment (with respect to these indicators);
5. If the unalignment is greater than some acceptable measure, decide what needs to be changed in the EA to reduce it;
6. Go back to step 1.

We consider the following loops (but others are possible with a pipeline in which the stages are more detailed):

- Reaction – All changes involve state only, so the cost and time to detect (monitoring) and to produce a change (of state) are usually very small. The changes are very frequent and occur as a reaction to events or to foreseeable trends, in adaptive systems. This is the loop more amenable to automation. However, and not considering self-changing systems (hard to do in complex systems), every possible change must have been included in the design;
- Reconfiguration – Some EAs, such as in the manufacturing domain, support reconfigurability (Putnik & Sluga, 2007). This is not a new EA, but involves more than merely changing state. Some of the components will be used in a different configuration or parameterization, for example to manufacture a different product in a production line. This, however, has to have been included in the EA design. Otherwise, we will need a new version, which is the next loop. A reconfiguration can be as frequent as its cost makes it effective;
- Reorganization – The current EA needs to be changed in a way that has not been included in the current design. A new version needs to be produced and deployed, that may not be completely compatible with the previous one and may imply changing other components as well;
- Reorientation – A reorientation is a profound reorganization, as result of changes in the strategy. This usually is driven by external factors, such as evolution of competitors or customers, but can also be demanded by an internal restructuring to increase competitiveness;
- Rebirth – The vision and/or mission can also suffer significant changes, driven by factors such as stiff competition, technology evolution or merges/acquisitions (change of the person fulfilling the CEO role is not infrequent). This implies changes to the EA that are so profound that, in practice, it has to be rethought and redesigned almost from scratch. This loop can also correspond to a diversification of business areas, making it necessary to build a new EA or component.

Figure 3 also indicates the typical actors involved in the change/no change decision taken at the decision points (the circles with a "?"). The strategy makers vary from entrepreneurs, in small enterprises, to a fully fledged team driven by the CEO in large enterprises.

When should a change be decided upon at a decision point? Essentially, when the deciding actor realizes that the benefit value of changing (Bc) if higher than the cost value (Cc) of the change implementation. Since the EA is not synchronized with its environment, it tends to progressively diverge from it with time (the EA unalignment grows). To realign the EA again, we will increasingly need more and more changes, and the change cost will grow. If the benefit of the change grows faster, then the change becomes cost effective and should be made (at time Tc), as illustrated in Figure 4a. If we change too early (at Tc-), the cost will outweigh the benefit. If we wait too long and change late (at Tc+), we will have lost some benefits.

If, however, the EA is complex, using diversification instead of agility to cope with changing

Figure 4. Change benefits versus cost of changes: (a) Light EA (b) Complex EA

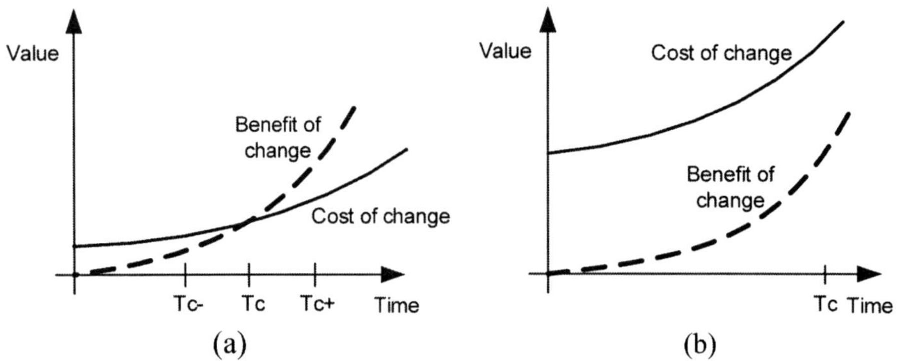

requirements, the cost of change is higher and may never be lower than the corresponding benefit, as illustrated by Figure 4b. In this case, the time to change (Tc) is determined more by the need to limit the cost of change than by its cost effectiveness. Having a light EA, including only what is currently needed but easy to change, is preferable to a complex, encompassing one, but that takes a long time and effort to change.

Note, however, that Tc is only the time at which the change is required to be in operation. The change will take time to get implemented. Suppose that we start implementing the change at Ts and deploy it at Td. We can have three cases:

- Tc ≤ Ts ≤ Td – This is a completely reactive change, since its implementation starts only after realizing that it should have been in place;
- Ts ≤ Tc ≤ Td – The change has a proactive and a reactive part. We start before Tc, but we still need some time afterwards to complete the change;
- Ts≤ Td ≤ Tc – This is a completely proactive change, since its implementation starts and finishes even before it is needed. There is no much point in having Td much before Tc.

The change delay (Td-Tc) will determine how fast the system is able to realign and accommodate a change in requirements. If its average value is small compared to the MTBC (mean time between changes), the system can be classified as very agile or even real-time.

Agility, as a desirable property, is generally associated with quick response to a changing environment (Fricke & Schulz, 2005; Patten, Whitworth, Fjermestad & Mahinda, 2005), although it has been also defined in terms of low change cost (Ganguly, Nilchiani & Farr, 2009) and proactiveness (Putnik & Sluga, 2007). We prefer to separate the several factors that characterize a change, with the following definitions related to system changes:

- Agility – An indication of the average change delay in relation to the average rate at which changes are needed ((Td-Tc)/MTBC);
- Dynamicity – An indication of the average change implementation time ((Td-Ts)/MTBC);
- Proactiveness – An indication of the average proportion of the proactive part of the change implementation time ((Tc-Ts)/(Td-Ts));
- Efficiency – An indication of the average ratio between the benefit value of a change and the corresponding implementation cost (Bc/Cc);

Agility shouldn't be dependent on implementation cost or proactiveness because it is a necessity caused essentially by external factors, such as competition or technology advances. But what the market "sees" is only whether a given enterprise responded fast enough or slowly to an evolving environment. The cost of that responsiveness or how much in advance the enterprise had to anticipate the need of change is an internal affair of that enterprise. Sometimes it is preferable to pay more for a faster solution (and be less efficient in implementing a change) just to beat the competition and gain the competitive edge of being first on the market. If time pressure is not high, then we can optimize the implementation cost instead of change delay.

It is also important to acknowledge that these indicators can be measured in each of the loops of Figure 3 but we have to consider the whole set, according to the theory of constraints (Stein, 2003). If an enterprise is very agile in strategy making (reorientation loop) but very slow in implementing and deploying changes (reorganization loop), the overall agility will hampered by this slow loop.

THE "ENTERPRISE AS A SERVICE" CONCEPT

We now draw several possible scenarios, to establish a route from a traditional EA to the EaaS concept.

The Traditional EA

By "traditional EA" we mean an EA designed and built with current frameworks and methods. It deals essentially with an information system, there is usually a global data model, processes are the main paradigm and reflect a repeatable workflow design, N-tier architecture is the norm, the strategy is typically oriented towards well typified market sectors and the goals and objectives rely essentially on past experiences and statistics as a guide for evolution.

It usually implements most of its components (outsourcing is the exception rather than the norm), internal resources abound, changes are not frequent and does not deal very well with unpredictability and risk. The EA is seen as the center of the business world, with suppliers, outsourcees and customers around it, and one of the main concerns is integration with other EAs' processes (Chen, Doumeingts & Vernadat, 2008).

The Starting and Growing EAs

A starting SME will have a very simplified structure, with the minimum of resources (one person sharing several roles, small set of equipment). To reduce the initial investment, most of these modules can be outsourced. In an extreme case, almost all could be outsourced, in which case the SME's added value would essentially be the modules' network (the idea of integration of the suppliers' products) glued with some management. This reduces the enterprise's margin (which goes to the outsourcees), but enables it to start a business and develop a client base.

If the SME survives and business grows, the enterprise is then able to acquire its own resources and to take control of a progressively number of modules, especially those more related to its core business. Those that have a smaller added value to the enterprise will remain outsourced, until business volume, specialization or some other reason justifies an investment by the enterprise to tackle its own implementation.

During initial stages, the EA and its underlying strategy are not well established and are expected to experience substantial changes, to compensate the absence of a typified customer base and to allow seizing the business opportunities. Therefore, the capability to easily change the EA and the outsourcing versus insourcing relationships will be highly valuable.

The Optimizing EA

Ideally, resources should have 100% utilization, all the time. Unfortunately, customer demand is not constant and supplier capacity is limited. One solution is to own resources planned for an average customer demand, but this translates into wasted capacity when demand is lower and will not be able to satisfy customers when demand is high. Another solution is to design the EA for dynamic, on-demand outsourcing (minimum TCO complemented with outsourcing as needed):

- When demand for a module's functionality is higher than its capacity, the requests in excess are dynamically forwarded to one or more alternative modules (with an outsourcing contract foreseeing occasional or seasonal demand);
- When the demand is lower than the module's capacity, the business model is inverted and the module can offer its excess capacity to other enterprises needing its functionality.

This way, load balancing can be achieved both at the demand and capacity ends. This is similar to microgeneration (Parker, 2009), that is becoming greenly trendy in many households and buildings. A wind turbine or a set of photovoltaic cells generate electric energy that is consumed in the building, if needed. When consumption is low, the surplus is injected into the power grid and sold to the local electricity supplier. The load balancing between consumption and generation is automatic and dynamic.

The Resilient EA

Any enterprise should have a plan B in case any of its modules or resources fails. Resources include humans, computers and other equipment. Although replacing a sick person that holds specific knowledge is much more difficult than finding an alternative to a broken truck, for example, the point is that it must be foreseen by design into the EA, and not dealt with only when it happens. Resilience is a typical topic in IT, but sometimes enterprises tend to forget that the problem is the same in every aspect of the business (including failing suppliers, outsourcees and clients).

Failures in modules usually refer to unforeseen situations or design errors, which at least should be detected and if possible compensated for any effects already made.

A typical solution for a resource failure is redundancy, either in normal use (in case of failure, only capacity is reduced) or in standby, in which case the alternative resource is only put into service when the normal one fails. In hot standby, the alternative resource exists and is reserved and ready for (almost) immediate use upon failure detection. This is generally too expensive and used only for truly critical resources. The others use warm or cold standby, in which case the situation is foreseen, what needs to be done is known but it takes increasingly longer to get the alternative solution to work. This usually implies a breach in the service provided by the failed resource, and its impact and allowed recovery time should be part of the EA design.

Redundancy can be implemented by the load balancing mechanism, although some requests may be lost or required to restart.

The Virtual EA

Gartner (2008) defines IT virtualization as "the abstraction of IT resources in a way that masks the physical nature and boundaries of those resources from resource users". But if we use "enterprise" instead of "IT", the definition still applies. Virtualization as an abstraction (hiding some features or replacing them by a seemingly equivalent one) is a universal mechanism that is not exclusive of IT or of any other knowledge domain.

In industrial environments, the traditional meaning of "virtual enterprise" has been "a temporary alliance of enterprises" (Camarinha-Matos, Afsarmanesh, Garita & Lima, 1999). In more information oriented circles, Petrie and Bussler (2003) define it as "a temporary consortium of partners and services", in which services are essentially Internet-based, and take a service centric integration perspective. Ströbel (2000) and Grefen, Aberer, Hoffner and Ludwig (2000) adopt a dynamic outsourcing approach for services, in which an enterprise dynamically discovers and enacts the services it needs to outsource, assuming the existence of an electronic market of services, with electronic descriptions and contracts to support outsourcing automation. Grefen, Mehandjiev, Kouvas, Weichhart and Eshuis (2009) go even further and use the "instant virtual enterprise" designation to emphasize the agility of a supplier network. The idea is not new (Silberschatz, 1996), but integration technologies then were not what they are today.

In the last decade, the meaning of "virtual enterprise" has evolved from a classical partnership of strategic outsourcing and collaboration, in a timescale of weeks to years, to a dynamic, cost optimizing service networks and collaborations, valid for a time span as small as a single business transaction. Cunha and Putnik (2006) describe a virtual model for manufacturing with a restructuring capability in the timeframe down to one second (at least, very fast in human terms).

Virtualization through dynamic outsourcing and reconfigurability is very important for agility and constitutes the base for the enterprise as a service. However, the automatic (or semi-automatic) design of an EA from a market of services or processes implies a loss of design control over the outcome, unless the components comply with a general semantic framework or domain defined beforehand, to ensure their compatibility when translating goals into requirements and component procurement and composition. That is why most of the examples in this area come from the manufacturing domain, in which the goals and requirements of a component are easier to express and reconfigurability of the production supply chain is a fundamental objective.

The Cloudsourcing EA

Cloudsourcing (outsourcing to the internet "cloud") is a growing trend in which outsourcing is done electronically using the Internet, either via web services or some user browser based interface. It's cloud computing (Lin, Fu, Zhu & Dasmalchi, 2009) seen from an outsourcing point of view. Although driven and still dominated by IT services, it will inevitably extend to business services and to other types of resources, such as people. Temporary job companies are already a form of cloudsourcing, but without the management dynamicity provided by information systems support and without integration with the EA design.

Cloudsourcing is essentially a service delivery model, characterized by properties such as:

- Self-service (the customer is a heavy co-producer);
- Automation (the customer does not have to deal with the management of resources, provisioning of services, application patches and updates);
- Virtualization (the customer has no notion of where and how the service is implemented);
- Elasticity (the apparent service capacity shrinks or grows dynamically as the customer requires);
- Pay-per-use (no investment upfront, no minimum consumption);
- Multi-tenancy (the resources are shared by many users, transparently, with security and load balancing, which reduces maximum capacity and hence the service costs).

Customers get relieved of many problems and details that are not their core businesses and providers can specialize and concentrate on providing the best service quality at the best price. It's the win-win situation that characterizes a good outsourcing contract.

The most popular service delivery models on the market today are:

- IaaS (Infrastructure as a Service) – The customer uses remote virtual resources (servers, storage, networks), that are managed by the provider, on top of which the customer can use his own software;
- PaaS (Platform as a Service) – The provider manages and offers both the infrastructure and platform software (operating systems, development environments), and the customer installs on it the software he developed or acquired;
- SaaS (Software as a Service) – The provider offers a fully working set of applications, platform and infrastructure, and the customer has to setup the settings (parameters, configuration) of his instantiation of the software.

There are many companies offering services in the cloud, including Google, Amazon, IBM, Microsoft and SalesForce. It should be stressed that cloudsourcing is just a form of virtualization in service outsourcing. Someone still has to design the EA and decide which components are needed. Providers offer services using an utility paradigm, which means they offer the same service (although configurable) to any customer that wants it.

The EA as a Service (EaaS)

The basic ideas behind this concept are:

- Instead of guessing what and how much the customer demand will be (designing the EA in advance), design and assemble the EA on the fly in reaction to concrete customer demand, with a high degree of customization and supporting very low ;
- Instead of considering the EA as part of a supply chain, see it as a value creator, or an adapter between what the customer wants and what other enterprises can provide;
- Instead of seeking collaboration with other enterprises, build the EA dynamically and virtually on top of a library of services, using outsourcing as the main organizational paradigm;
- Instead of investing a lot in defining an elaborate strategy, build the entire EA for agility, so that strategy is easily and quickly adaptable to our fast evolving world.

The EaaS could also be called "EA *a la carte*", the sense that a new, specialized and customized EA can be built for each business transaction (or class of transactions), with lower granularity and higher agility than traditional EAs. Unlike any of the previous scenarios, outsourcing is the main service delivery mechanism of the EaaS model and is meant to be used with all service types, including human roles.

Although SaaS seems similar to EaaS, these are two orthogonal concepts. SaaS is essentially a service delivery mechanism, whereas EaaS is an EA building paradigm. SaaS offers full applications remotely, hiding management problems, but has no idea of how an EA should be organized, and indeed current SaaS offerings (ERPs, in particular) are not that easy to configure and to integrate with other subsystems. EaaS, on the other hand, advocates lower granularity (instead of one application, it's better to use a library of smaller, customizable services) and promotes easy interoperability more than semantic integration between EA components. Agile adaptability to the customer requirements is the main tenet.

Hoeree (2009) describes several characteristics of the concept and Table 1 compares the EaaS with traditional EAs.

A more visual way of spotting differences between the two EA models is to analyze the EaaS changeability model, depicted by Figure 5, and

Table 1. Comparison between the traditional EA and the EaaS

Characteristic	Traditional EA	EaaS
Business model	• The EA is geared for mass production of standardized products or services; • Design of the production is based on the prediction of what the customer will want in the future; • The EA is one stage of a supply chain, flowing from producers to consumers; • This is a push model, in which customers will buy many identical products or use the same service many times.	• The EA is oriented towards customizability of products or services; • Production is designed and run as a response to customer demand; • The EA is a value creation adapter between what the customer needs and what other enterprises are able to provide (requests flow from consumers to producers); • This is a pull model, in which the customer gets what he wants with just-in-time production.
Business strategy	• Medium to long term, avoiding eager reactions to short-lived tendencies; • Low to medium agility; • Based on the prediction of consumer demand (both volume and characteristics); • Goal-driven; • Heavy use of past data analysis and Business Intelligence; • Typified customer market segments, usually with limits on low volume;	• Short to medium term, sensitive and adaptable to small market changes; • High agility is critical; • Based on the response to concrete customer demand (both volume and characteristics); • Opportunity-driven; • Shallow past data analysis, great attention to market opportunities; • Broad, untypified customer base, with no limits on low volume ("quantity 1" production model);
Organizational model	• Processes are the main paradigm; • Network collaboration between enterprises; • Process integration is the main collaboration objective; • Strategic outsourcing of peripheral functions only; • N-tier model, with customer on one end. • Global data model; • People treated separately.	• Based on the service paradigm; • Virtual composition of a library of services; • Decouple as much as possible, use service interoperability for the rest; • Dynamic outsourcing is the main organizational paradigm; • No tiers, customer is part of the EA and occupies a central place. • Data model local to each service; • People are unified resources.

contrast it to the traditional EA changeability model, in Figure 3.

The EaaS model divides the EA into two parts, with the customer precisely at the middle. The customer is the most important actor in the EA and where everything cycles. Again, this is a maximalist model and real cases can optimize some of the aspects. This model can be briefly explained as follows:

- **The market making part**. This involves not only assessing what the customer wants but also influencing him by showing how a customized solution can solve his problems. The EaaS must make its own customers, not just wait for them to drop by! It involves two loops:
    a. Rebirth, when new technologies, innovative ideas or competition changes appear. The EaaS develops its market vision from the gap between the customer needs and the suppliers offerings, which define the business opportunities, in particular when innovative ideas are available. Strategy, that must be light and agile, must also be attentive to competition, which has to be assumed agile as well;
    b. Reorientation. This essentially recognizes business patterns and tries to contribute to the organization and structure of the service library, to capitalize on service reuse and minimize the customization effort and implementation time. On the other hand, the customer

Figure 5. The EaaS lifecycle and changeability models

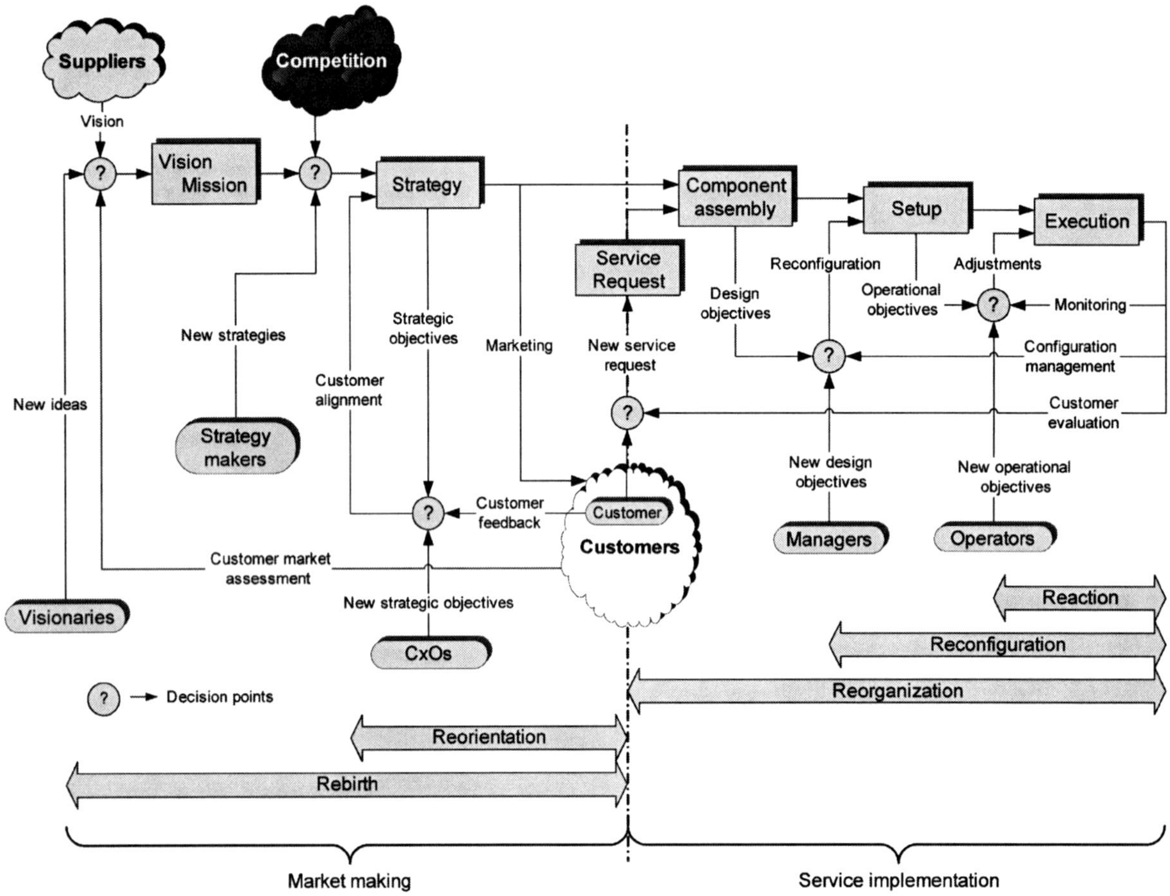

does not always know what exactly he needs, and the service library, based on proven business patterns, can be a precious help. In other words, it contributes to the mutual alignment between the service library and the customer needs.

- **The service implementation part**. The EaaS should be able to provide a new EA design for each customer request. Naturally, the most part of these requests will follow common business patterns and therefore the EAs will actually be variants of pre-established EAs adequate to those patterns. How easy it will be to adapt these patterns to concrete cases depends on how well the library is designed. For specific domains or with controlled variability, such as the manufacturing domain, semi-automatic EA design can be considered (Grefen, Mehandjiev, Kouvas, Weichhart and Eshuis, 2009). This involves the following loops:

m. Reorganization, which needs to be done in each customer request or pattern of requests. The design, development and deployment box in Figure 3 has been replaced here by an assembly box, to make it clear that this essentially involves assembling services from reusable services in the library. Adapting services and in particular developing new ones should be the exception rather than the norm;

n. Reconfiguration. Although possible in the EaaS and adequate to situations that require frequent choice among a fixed set of configurations, it is however less relevant that in traditional EAs because, given the customization environment, reorganization becomes a feasible, more flexible alternative;

o. Reaction. These is essentially the same as traditional EAs, but keep in mind that in the EaaS has not a mass production philosophy, which means that monitoring and control techniques may be made more specialized and adapted to each case.

This customer-centric approach, adapting as much as possible to the customer, whatever small the business volume is, and having the production done only when the customer requires it, is a significant business paradigm shift that makes agility the most important feature, next to quality.

Dividing the service lifecycle in two parts, one whose output is the library of services and the other that uses that library, helps in separating concerns and in shortening the lifecycle.

CONCLUSION

Enterprise agility in today's fast pacing world is a fundamental step to ensure survival and competitiveness, but achieving it with complex, conventional EAs is not very effective. We need new ways to design dynamic EAs. Using virtualization, and even dynamic outsourcing, based on a generic service market and (semi-)automatic service composition, is both hard and dangerous. Hard because services are usually complex and just being able to describe exactly what they do is already a difficult task, let alone being able to formally express its semantics and ontology, to support automated processing. Dangerous because service descriptions never include all the non-functional characteristics (risk, for instance), and even what they assert is not certified by a credible and liable authority. Therefore, automatic procurement, provisioning and invocation of services is always a shot in the dark and should only be used for well established, standardized, utility type and out-of-the-shelf services, for which alternatives are readily available.

In this respect, we should learn from the software industry, which has had the same problem for several decades now. A market of generic software components never emerged. Instead, what we have are object-oriented libraries that have proved to be the most effective way to reuse existing functionality.

What we need in the EA world are service libraries, with services structured around the most common business patterns but with the ability to be readily customized and adapted to unique situations, as required by the EaaS. These libraries need to be started by established companies or consortia, to give them credibility and a head start momentum, but enable third parties to contribute with services composed of simpler ones in the library. This will also provide standardized specifications of common services which competitors can offer alternative implementations to.

ERPs are the best base for business EAs, but they have a long time legacy of large monolithic blocks to overcome before they are readily available as service libraries. Customers are still worried about issues such as privacy, security and reliability. Nobody wants to have to stop the entire business due to a failure in the connection to the Internet that prevents employees from accessing the remote services. The problem is that enterprises and customers in general area already so interconnected and Internet dependent that, even with a local ERP, an enterprise with a broken Internet connection stops doing business, anyway. The fact is that the Internet is already a de facto infrastructure we all use, more than any other means, and the privileged channel to interconnect and outsource. The solution is then ensuring that our connection to the world is critically reliable and using correct security and privacy techniques, not avoiding dynamically outsourcing, building enterprises as a service and reaping the corresponding benefits.

REFERENCES

Anderson, C. (2006). *The Long Tail*. New York: Hyperion.

Brocke, J., Schenk, B., & Sonnenberg, C. (2009) Organizational implications of implementing service oriented ERP systems: an analysis based on new institutional economics. In Abramowicz, W. (Ed.) *12th International Conference Business Information Systems*, Poznan, Poland (252–263). Berlin, Germany: Springer-Verlag.

Camarinha-Matos, L., Afsarmanesh, H., Garita, C., & Lima, C. (1999). Hierarchical Coordination in Virtual Enterprise Infrastructures. *Journal of Intelligent & Robotic Systems*, *26*, 267–287. doi:10.1023/A:1008137110347

Chen, D., Doumeingts, G., & Vernadat, F. (2008). Architectures for enterprise integration and interoperability: Past, present and future. *Computers in Industry*, *59*, 647–659. doi:10.1016/j.compind.2007.12.016

Cunha, M., & Putnik, G. (2006). *Agile virtual enterprises: implementation and management support*. Hershey, PA: Idea Group Publishing.

Earl, T. (2005). *Service-oriented architecture: concepts, technology and design*. Upper Saddle River, NJ: Pearson Education.

Earl, T. (2008). *Principles of service design*. Boston: Pearson Education.

EU. (2006) *Directive on services in the Internal Market*. Retrieved September 3, 2009, from http://ec.europa.eu/internal_market/services/services-dir/index_en.htm.

Fricke, E., & Schulz, A. (2005). Design for changeability (DfC): Principles to enable changes in systems throughout their entire lifecycle. *Systems Engineering*, *8*(4), 342–359. doi:10.1002/sys.20039

Ganguly, A., Nilchiani, R., & Farr, J. (2009). Evaluating agility in corporate enterprises. *International Journal of Production Economics*, *118*(2), 410–423. doi:10.1016/j.ijpe.2008.12.009

Grefen, P., Aberer, K., Hoffner, Y., & Ludwig, H. (2000). CrossFlow: Cross-Organizational Workflow Management in Dynamic Virtual Enterprises, *International Journal of Computer Systems. Science & Engineering*, *5*, 277–290.

Grefen, P., Mehandjiev, N., Kouvas, G., Weichhart, G., & Eshuis, R. (2009). Dynamic business network process management in instant virtual enterprises. *Computers in Industry*, *60*(2), 86–103. doi:10.1016/j.compind.2008.06.006

Havey, M. (2005). *Essential business process modeling*. Sebastopol, CA: O'Reilly.

Hoeree, J. (2009) From Corporate Enterprise to Enterprise as a Service. *CTG Whitepaper*. Retrieved September 3, 2009, from http://www.ctg.com/PDF/From_CE_to_Eaas.pdf.

IBM. (2008). Global CEO Study: The Enterprise of the Future. *Ideias from IBM*. May 5, 2008, Retrieved September 3, 2009, from http://www.ibm.com/ibm/ideasfromibm/us/ceo/20080505/resources/IFI_05052008.pdf.

Levy, M., & Powell, P. (2005). *Strategies for growth in SMEs: the role of information systems*. Burlington, MA: Elsevier Butterworth-Heinemann.

Lin, G., Fu, D., Zhu, J., & Dasmalchi, G. (2009). Cloud Computing: IT as a Service. *IT Professional*, *11*(2), 10–13. doi:10.1109/MITP.2009.22

Lovelock, C., & Wirtz, J. (2007). *Services marketing: people, technology, strategy*. Upper Saddle River, NJ: Pearson Prentice Hall.

McAdam, M., & McAdam, R. (2008). High tech start-ups in University Science Park incubators: The relationship between the start-up's lifecycle progression and use of the incubator's resources. *Technovation*, *28*, 277–290. doi:10.1016/j.technovation.2007.07.012

Parker, D. (2009). *Microgeneration: low energy strategies for larger buildings*. Burlington, MA: Elsevier.

Patten, K., Whitworth, B., Fjermestad, J., & Mahinda, E. (2005) Leading IT flexibility: anticipation, agility and adaptability. In Romano, N. (Ed.) *Proceedings of the 11th Americas Conference on Information Systems*, Omaha, NE, 11–14, Red Hook, NY: Curran Associates, Inc.

Petrie, C., & Bussler, C. (2003). Service agents and virtual enterprises: a survey. *IEEE Internet Computing*, *7*(4), 68–78. doi:10.1109/MIC.2003.1215662

Putnik, G., & Sluga, A. (2007) Reconfigurability of manufacturing systems for agility implementation, part I: requirements and principles. In Cunha, P. & Maropoulos, P. (Eds.) *Digital Enterprise Technology: Perspectives and Future Challenges* (pp. 91-98). New York, NY: Springer Science+Business Media.

Schekkerman, J. (2006). *How to survive in the jungle of enterprise architecture frameworks*. Bloomington, IN: Trafford Publishing.

Silberschatz, A. (1996). Strategic Directions in Database Systems—Breaking Out of the Box. *ACM Computing Surveys*, *28*(4), 764–778. doi:10.1145/242223.242295

Spohrer, J., Vargo, S., Caswell, N., & Maglio, P. (2008) The Service System is the Basic Abstraction of Service Science. In Sprague Jr., R. (Ed.) *41st Hawaii International Conference on System Sciences*. Big Island, Hawaii, 104, Washington, DC: IEEE Computer Society.

Stein, E. (2003). *Re-Engineering the Manufacturing System: Applying the Theory of Constraints*. New York, NY: Marcel Dekker, Inc. doi:10.1201/9780203912508

Ströbel, M. (2000) Dynamic Outsourcing of Services, Report RZ 3236, IBM Research, Zurich Research Laboratory, Retrieved September 3, 2009, from http://www.zurich.ibm.com/~mis/publications/rz3236.

Uram, M., & Stephenson, B. (2005). Services are the Language and Building Blocks of an Agile Enterprise. In Pal, N., & Pantaleo, D. (Eds.), *The Agile Enterprise*. New York, NY: Springer. doi:10.1007/0-387-25078-6_4

Wu, L., & Park, D. (2009). Dynamic outsourcing through process modularization. *Business Process Management Journal*, *15*(2), 255–244. doi:10.1108/14637150910949461

Chapter 12
Reflecting on New Businesses Models for SMEs through Technological Application:
Cases of E-Business in Brazil

George Leal Jamil
FUMEC University, Brazil

Antonio José Balloni
Center for Information Technology (CTI), Brazil

Rodrigo Baroni de Carvalho
FUMEC University, Brazil

ABSTRACT

As modern economies faces its growth challenges, small and medium enterprises are potential agents to become strategic competitive, especially when it can be supported by information technology. A scenario composed by rapid changes in the economies, introduction of new communication and information technology and emergence of new markets forms the study background, which was proposed to analyze new business models for SMEs based on e-business concepts and how these resources, applied under strategic thinking, are increasing the SMEs' competitiveness. A case study of Brazilian e-business based SMEs is conducted, in order to understand IT application in this evolving context, examining five successful cases.

BACKGROUND

Small and medium entrepreneurship is a challenging research field. Academic studies, scientific models, business press case reports are among the numberless attempts to better understand SMEs competitive scenario. Additional motivation to understand its relevance is shown when its importance for national and transnational economies is observed, as they can be regarded as significant employers, investors and producers. In this interesting and opportune business environment we can find the application of information technology, especially those called "e-business", as an emerging paradigm for SMEs to constitute

DOI: 10.4018/978-1-61692-880-3.ch012

innovative business models in which these firms can be regarded as real alternatives for a variety of industries, offering perspectives of value aggregation, adaptive forms of market events response, integration of larger enterprise networks and working with flexibility as an answer to the rapid changes in the customer´s needs (Caron, 2003; Hua, 2007; Beneton, Balloni & Bacic, 2007).

A special concern when researching about SMEs, in order to distinguish and identify similarities in its profiles throughout the world is how to deal with regional, cultural, social, economic and educational different aspects. Complex regulatory and fiscal laws, tough competition by foreign or networked firms, immediate sensitivity to changes in the customer´s preferences, pressures to innovate, regional culture habits and intuitive organizational structures are among factors which have impact on the SMEs' strategy formulation and execution, which results in a fragmented and heterogeneous picture of entrepreneurship around the world.

It is unquestionable, however, that SMEs nowadays represent a real economic force in the world economy (Gatti & Honoratti, 2008; Maur, 2008; OECD, 2009). This fact provokes additional interest on its growth, development and competing characteristics which can be proofed by the existence of specific political and economic programs, sponsored by governments and international organizations, to promote its success and expansion. As stated before, information technology appears as another theme of increasing interest not only as a segment where software, hardware and diversified services SMEs has been successful for long time, but as a set of managerial and operational tools which can help SMEs to implement innovative business models. Unfortunately, as studies show, these implementations frequently emerge not as a result of structured plans, but as impetuous choices or entrepreneurs reaction, for example, to external competitive events. It is our main objective, in this chapter, to bring additional discussion about IT application for specific entrepreneurial arrangements, especially observing those types identified as "e-business" implemented on SMEs scenarios.

For this purpose, and considering that this text is supposed to be consulted by readers such as academic researchers and interested SMEs owners and business partners (e. g. consultants, investors, etc.) the following structure was composed: first, we briefly discuss strategy principles, in search of a rational framework for e-business choices for SMEs instead of intuitive or impulsive risky initiatives. In the second section the reality of strategic planning and execution is studied, in order to comprehend how strategy principles are or are not used for SMEs management. After understanding how these strategic decisions could define information technology adoption in SMEs, a discussion is developed about e-business and new models of entrepreneurship. In the last section, supported by that previous study, it is discussed the e-business evolution in Brazilian organizations, based on an analysis of selected cases.

Associating Strategy Basics and SMEs Business Environment

This section makes a brief study of strategy and strategic planning fundamentals. Its contribution is to review this basal ideas allowing forthcoming discussion about the main issues for a SME's owner to conduct critic managerial actions. Strategic planning, as understood by the authors, will allow SMEs' managers to implement successful IT solutions, resulting in efficient new business models (Kalakota & Robinson, 2001; Kearns & Lederer, 2003; Takeuchi & Nonaka, 2004). It is also recognized that small and medium firms constitute a heterogeneous sector throughout the world, which results in a complex business scenario with different strategic motivations, along with precarious conditions for plans design and execution. It is important to mention that only the necessary part on the vast theory of strategy that attends to the previously stated chapter objectives is discussed below. The references quoted in this section will provide directions for further studies to interested readers.

Strategy can be considered a discipline or knowledge to design a positioning for the future of an organization (Porter, 1980; Mintzberg, Lampel & Ahlstrand, 1999; Hitt, Ireland & Hoskisson, 1999). This short definition, obviously, hides important questions: Will this futuristic scenario and actions be designed as a documented plan or will it use another form of communication? Is there any standard to be adopted as organizational procedures or activities? How long this plan must be kept without changes? Is it an organizational mandatory law or can it be reviewed, negotiated? What is the role of the managers and leaders in order to conduct the execution of the plan? All of these and many other questions concerning to strategy conception are broadly studied, contested and passionately argued at least during the last seventy years.

A major debate focuses if strategy is to be deliberated, producing a definitive document or guidance which prescribes organizational functioning or, on the other hand, if it is a motivational task, intuition or form to orient abilities in order to reach defined goals. This is one focal point of this brief review, as this can be one of major dilemmas faced by small and medium entrepreneurs when a SME business is opened or during the initial days of its activity. As Porter (1980) assessed, planning a strategy is to develop a broad formula that will describe how a firm competes, what its main and immediate goals are and how to act in order to reach them. He identified this concept as "classical", referring to the works of professors Roland Christensen and Kenneth Andrews, noteworthy researchers from Harvard. This thought was also presented in a review done by Ghemawat (2006), where he also describes the successive utilization of analytical techniques to understand the surrounding external competitive environment and internal factors, considering them as forces or weaknesses to execute proposed strategies.

Here it will be considered that strategy is materialized through a structured plan or context (not essentially written, but known by the SME's owner or manager) that aims to guide an organization to a previewed scenario, specifying goals to be reached. This method is supported by that "classical" view and analyzed as a feasible attitude for SME entrepreneurs (Porter, 1980; Levi, Powell and Yetton, 2001; Mintzberg *et al.*, 2003). As it is largely discussed by authors, this view of structured strategic planning presents a first form of conception for SMEs' owners and managers, as they begin to replace usual unstructured, intuition-driven, predominantly unguided and improvised SME operation, typical in the initial days of entrepreneurship (Levi, Powell & Yetton, 2001; Ghemawat, 2006). It is not an exclusive thought, as more dynamic forms of strategic planning could be developed as a result of evolution of their abilities and experience, but is considered as a possible starting point for SMEs entrepreneurs.

Among various structured methods which have been applied for strategic studies along the last decades, some classical analytical tools or models are discussed below:

- Product / mission Matrix – Ansoff (1965) as cited from Ghemawat (2006) – determines a positioning orientation based on newness of products and organizational mission (which can be understood as an organizational commitment statement established as a mark to its existence and to develop a strategic plan). The resulting position will range from market share increase tactics applied in the actual competitive situation to a more sophisticated action to sell products and services differentiation in order to offer new aggregated value to customers.
- SWOT model – Andrews (1980), Barney (1995) – compares internal strengths and weaknesses and external signals of opportunities and threats from an organiza-

tional point of view. It was proposed in the early 1960s, consolidating various studies carried out by Harvard researchers and is largely discussed in academic and business press literature, used as a tool to start initial studies about an industry, a competitor's situation and to propose a future positioning. Its main virtue is to promote a study of both internal (strengths and weaknesses) and external (opportunities and threats) perspectives, leading to a broader strategic comprehension of a strategic positioning in a specific industry.

- Competitive forces analysis – Porter (1980), Porter (1996) – which considers the business environment as a system where five forces are exerted, driving the competition in this industry: (1) competitive rivalry expressed by peculiar factors and regulations internal to the industry, bargain power from (2) customers and (3) suppliers, threats of (4) new entrants and (5) substitution of products. Competitive forces model is certainly one of the most discussed and cited fundamentals of strategic planning, as it is simple to understand and to apply, providing a functional structure which allows a pragmatic industry analysis.
- BCG Matrix – Barney (1995), Writh, Kroll & Parnell (1998) – Proposed by the Boston Consulting Group in the end of the 1960s, attributed to researchers Bruce Henderson and Joseph Akon. It structures a bi-dimensional grid or matrix, where product and business units or product families can be compared, in terms of its commercial participation (market share) versus growth rates of this specific market. The four resulting quadrants correspond to typical strategic situations where tactics such as promotion of new investments, abandon, aggressive or defensive attitudes can be recommended. It is designed to orient business positioning for various products of a company, permitting to manage it as a portfolio of competitive aggregated value alternatives.

These remarkable propositions were applied for strategic analysis and studies for many years, being considered as standards for emerging and established markets and also used to analyze numerous real successful cases (mainly influenced by Harvard Case Study methodology), as stated by academic and business literature (Venkatraman 1989; Barney 1995; Mata, Fuerst & Barney 1995; Wright, Kroll & Parnell 1999; Hitt, Ireland & Hoskisson 2001).

Henry Mintzberg and his associated authors presented important reflections about strategy thinking and its adaptation for new market challenges (Mintzberg *et al.*, 1998; Mintzberg *et al.*, 2003). In these and other works, they reviewed those fundamentals cited earlier (models, techniques, etc.) and other renewed trends on strategic planning, grouping this reflections in nine "schools of thought", or nine ways where the organizational strategic process can be perceived, which has had expressive impact in the newest academic and scientific production about strategy. In these works it is possible to notice two main non-exclusive courses of strategic process thinking: (a) prescriptive – where the focus is on how a strategy *must be planned*, resulting in a rigorous work to generate a set of structured guides for organizational operation – or (b) descriptive – that concentrates on *how a strategy is formulated,* studying on alternatives to practice it, based on cultural, leadership, knowledge and perceptions collected by the entrepreneurs or semi-coordinated reactions from the market movements. It is interesting to note that a tenth school is discussed in Mintzberg *et al.* (1998) although it is really an indispensable view that "combines" experiences, methods and contents from the preceding nine.

Finally, another important contribution to evaluate strategic planning and execution is the resource based view (RBV) of the firm, a theory which was proposed in a seminal work by Edith Penrose, *"The theory of the growth of the firm"*, published in 1959. There, Penrose addressed the idea of observing a firm as a collection of resources, which are thought as tangible and intangible assets, encompassing, for example, capabilities, processes, information and knowledge, all under managerial control of the firm (Wernerfelt 1984; Barney 1991; Barney 1995). Strategy planning under RBV could be understood as identifying resources and positioning it to obtain sustainable competitive advantage. It is a topic that demands continuous expressive observation by researchers nowadays, especially observing that IT solutions are being discussed as competitive resources to be implemented by organizations of any type (Kearns & Shaberwal, 2007; Kearns & Shaberwal, 2007a; Yolles, 2009).

With support of RBV, many studies approached topics such as IT use, IT development and implementation, innovation and financial decisions correlating aspects like these to produce sustainable competitive advantage (Porter, 2001; Hitt *et al.,* 2001; Teng & Cummings, 2002; Caron, 2003; Kearns & Lederer, 2003; Liao, Kickul & Ma, 2009). Competitive advantage is understood as differentials offered by an organization, which are recognized by a customer in a competitive industry (Porter, 1980). If these differentials are evident and strong enough for a significant period of time, making all rivals to renounce to compete for industry leadership, we identify it as sustainable competitive advantage, a real "holy grail" of strategic planning (Porter, 1980; Porter, 1996; Barney, 1991; Barney, 1995).

As it was shown by Porter (1980) when he asserted about "explicit" and "implicit" strategic planning and principles, strategy can result in a rigorous plan or in an organized intuition by the owner or leader of a firm. These views are evidently important for our study, as SMEs competition predominantly presents non-structured conditions. They would perceive more benefits for IT application (implementing "e-business" solutions) if a plan was firstly structured and then, in a subsequent maturity level, unfold a continuous planning process to generate efficient strategic decisions based on IT application results (Levi, Powell and Yetton, 2001; Teng & Cummings, 2002; Kearns & Lederer, 2003; Liao, Kickul & Ma, 2009). This chapter aims to collaborate in promoting this evolution to SMEs entrepreneurs.

This rich analysis made by reputable scholars over the years also characterizes an opportunity aimed by the present chapter, as to analyze how strategic formulation troubled conditions in SMEs can be improved, resulting in successful use of information technology for e-business implementations.

An Overview of Small Business Strategic Processes: Standards and Difficulties

As a result of the researches about strategic planning in SMEs shows, factors as limited managers and owners planning capabilities, lack of organizational prerequisites to plan, improvised attitudes, pressures to provide fast answers to market demands and severe competitive conditions can produce difficulties for formulation and execution of plans in SMEs. These restricted conditions will affect directly the potential application of IT on SMEs, as it will be developed in the next section, when we examine suggestions of new business models.

Porter (1980) classified fragmented industries as one of the generic industrial competitive environments, being characterized as a composition of "numerous competitive organizations". This description can be used to describe typical SMEs competitive actual markets. Among these industries there are firms ranging from highly specialized markets, as software production and biotechnology, to others, acting in standardized sectors as cleaning or food distribution services. Porter (1980) also acquaints common signals of these segments as: similarity of products from different manufacturers, low bargaining power to negotiate with customers and suppliers and geographically restricted commerce. These situations can be addressed, as discussed in this section, by IT tools and systems implemented for value aggregation or geographic broadening (Levi, Powell and Yetton, 2001; Hua, 2007; Beneton, Balloni & Bacic, 2007).

To plan for this fragmented sector, Porter instructs various actions, which would be favored by IT application, as (a) decentralized management, (b) multiple low cost points of sale, (c) improvement of aggregated value by the distribution channels and (d) specialization on a type of product, selling procedures or ability to customize a product or service to specific customer desire. As stated before, such actions and goals are now largely discussed for modern SMEs, as they act not only as the main firm relating to a client, but also as a part of a more complex aggregated value chain (Porter, 2001). It is noticed that, along with other requisites, such conditions to elaborate plans are barely found in SMEs, leading to circumstances where improvised and reactive tactics are held in order to promote organizational survival in a competitive scenario (Hua, 2007; Liao, Kickul & Ma, 2009). It was debated in Porter (2001) the function of Internet employment on some industries, bringing to light a discussion of IT as an efficient builder of strategic positioning, but difficultly promoting a sustainable competitive advantage. For this reason, "Internet (or IT application) makes strategy more essential than ever", pointing how strategic thinking is relevant to obtain results from a valuable IT usage, in order, for example, to promote competitive differentiation (Porter, 2001).

According to Mintzberg *et al* (2003) strategic planning processes can be deliberated or not, and must produce a unique positioning for firms, which probably will result in pressure to innovate, consequently bringing in additional problems especially to the SMEs' managers (Caron, 2003). Those two diametrical situations can be exampled on one side by a rigorous and formal plan which orients organizational operation or, on the other, as a tactical reaction taken based on a standard industry behavior (advertisement campaigning or changing payment forms, for example).

Then, it is possible to understand, from the above, that in small and medium firms strategic processes are expected to be fast and adaptive which can result in shorter product cycles, improved time to market and rapid competitive reactions. These operations, however, are also associated to informal risky movements, strategic vulnerability (as cost mismanagement) or impossibility to learn from past experiences, as the results are overshadowed or imprecise due to lack of time or structure to correctly record and analyze it (Sergio *et al.*, 2004; Hua, 2007). Levi, Powell & Yetton (2001) considered this precarious strategic management situation as an implication for bad investments in information systems, a characteristic strategic decision, illustrating the arguments stated which present difficult circumstances for decisions in the SMEs and, clearly, affecting effective IT deployment.

Another important aspect of strategic planning analysis for SMEs is the subjective factor associated with the owner´s personality. A long and valuable discussion exists around the Entrepreneurial Orientation (EO) concept, which was defined by the remarkable researches from Covin & Slevin (1986, 1991), Zahra (1993) and Lumpkin & Dess (1996), resulting in expressive scientific debates since then. It is an attempt to associate behavioral theories with firm reactions, represented by its owners or managers, as approached in each particular study. Some of the frequent aspects considered as a background for these researches are: entrepreneurship (usually motivated by Joseph Schumpeter studies), risk taking, *proactiveness* (or actions anticipating external events, such as customers, suppliers or competitor reactions) and innovation willingness, focusing on the conceptualization of entrepreneur´s personality. A large number of studies aim to relate EO to indicators as, for example, performance measurements, concerning decision making and innovation cycle time (George, Wood Jr. & Khan, 2001), identifying it as a signal for favorable organizational results (Fernandes & Santos 2008). As those studies usually show, managers behavioral standards have an impact on the strategy formulation, along with factors such as pressure and inaccuracy to decide and implement strategic plans.

A topic frequently related to strategic planning, resource based view of a firm (RBV), results in an opportunity to observe the SMEs as a collection of resources which are managed and positioned almost directly into the market, due to their simple organizational structure and immediate intervention by the owners. IT-based systems, as stated in several studies, could result in immovable and heterogeneous resources, indicated to promote a sustained competitive advantage not by itself but as a result of strategically planned implementation (Barney, 1995; George, Wood Jr. & Khan, 2001; Kearns & Lederer, 2003; Wiklund, Patzelt & Shepherd, 2007). The standard in planning and executing strategic decisions in SMEs is focused in promoting resource applications and positioning, in to have fast short-term fast gains, which would provoke losses in terms of its cost and control.

Those cited studies and supporting researches also point out forms of strategic standards such as tactic relation in order to manage a SME, its dependency on the owner leadership and unexpected conditions of plan execution. It is necessary to reiterate that IT is frequently suggested as a solution for operational problems, as tools which may be applied in order to solve planning problems or promote immediate, impulsive reactions (Mata, Fuerst & Barney 1995; Levi, Powell & Yetton, 2001; Hua, 2007; Kearns & Shaberwal, 2007a). This situation prescribes some of those research challenges shown earlier, depicting opportunities to clarify how IT can be strategically applied in SMEs, opposing to its usage just as improvised tools.

E-Business for SMEs: Information Technology and New Entrepreneurship Models

Information technology can provide new strategic alternatives of business infrastructure that can result in revolutionary models of entrepreneurship, although its use is frequently done without strategic planning support, as discussed in the former section. It is important to note that an expressive relevance has been given to the relationship between strategic principles and restricted conditions in SMEs by authors from areas such as strategic management, IT and information systems when they analyze IT-based businesses and its potential strategic origins and repercussions (Turban, Mc Lean & Wetherbe, 2002; Kearns & Lederer, 2003; Lucas Jr., 2005; Mintzberg *et al.*, 2006, Turban, Rainer Jr. & Potter, 2007; Kearns & Shaberwal, 2007a).

As information technology can be applied in several situations in order to proportionate business activity, a large number of ways are found in competitive environments, ranging from simple office automation procedures up to complex knowledge generation tools applied to decision support systems (Porter, 2001; Jamil, 2001; Stair & Reynolds, 2003; Takeuchi & Nonaka, 2004; Mintzberg *et al.*, 2006, Turban, Rainer Jr. & Potter, 2007). According to these and other authors, e-business can be considered as IT application where distributed software and hardware, noticeably those connected through Internet infrastructure, are configured to implement any organizational business solution. Regarded both as a tool, system or process, e-business has been studied for more than a decade, turning out to be a representative research focus for global competitiveness (Ellsworth and Ellsworth, 1995; Komenar, 1997; Kalakota & Robinson, 2001; Turban, Mc Lean & Wetherbe, 2002; Lucas Jr., 2005; Turban, Rainer Jr. & Potter, 2007).

Various configurations are proposed for technology-based SMEs implementation which can constitute strategic final solutions, or "business models". From a strictly technologic point of view, forms of Internet-based implementations could be defined where a systemic (programmed, configured) function is related to any operational activity (Ellsworth & Ellsworth, 1995; Komenar, 1997; Kalakota & Robinson, 2001; Turban, Mc Lean & Wetherbe, 2002; Lucas Jr., 2005; Turban, Rainer Jr. & Potter, 2007). One common implementation, for instance, is to install IT basic infrastructure that allows an "e-commerce" (electronic commerce) for a small shopper, where products can be negotiated directly to Internet-connected customers. As stated from Kalakota & Robinson (2001) and Lucas Jr. (2005), such an implementation could overcome strategic barriers for a SME, such as geographical limitations.

Another perspective is to integrate this small network, owned by a SME, to other small networks of another firms, producing an integrated chain where a complex product or service can be offered to a customer as a final result of intensive communication, predominantly without human intervention in the operational tasks, using a model called virtual, global or networked (George, Wood Jr. & Khan, 2001; Kalakota & Robinson, 2001; Lucas Jr., 2005; Turban, Rainer Jr. & Potter, 2007). This can allow, for instance, "business-to-business" (B2B) integration, when a customer can order a product from a SME that, in fact, only accepts and treats the invoice. This final firm could pick the purchased product from a manufacturer and deliver it to the customer who only notices the interaction with the first shopper. A simple selling procedure that can integrate producer, courier, financial agents (credit card operator, banks), accounting, legal and fiscal agents and others is completely transparent, in order to attend a customer's needs (Kalakota & Robinson, 2001; Stamoulis, Kanellis & Martakos, 2002; Chen, Long & Yan, 2004; Bakos, 2005; Jamil, 2007). As processing can be divided, information also is distributed or treated collaboratively, as it is possible in sectors such as engineering design or financial consulting SMEs.

Computer networks are already a vast dynamic context where various configurations are proposed and offered as real implementation perspectives for businesses. Modern trends, as the addition of themes such as mobility – where mobile IT and communication devices are considered as active and passive network parts – tends to result in powerful alternatives which can be applied in these context, resulting in new forms of customer-seller interactions (Kalakota & Robinson, 2001; Turban, Mc Lean & Wetherbe, 2002; Lucas Jr., 2005; Bakos, 2005; Turban, Rainer Jr. & Potter, 2007; Jamil, 2007).

More concerned with managerial and decision issues, strategy and information systems researchers also present a variety of ways where those interconnected infrastructures could be assembled and presented to the user, but in this case discussing its operation. Herber, Singh and Useem (2000) cited by Mintzberg *et al.* (2006) describe, for instance: network organized, virtual, segmented, side by side, front and backwards and responsive forms. Those models can be derived from the technological composition presented above, where infrastructure flexibility allow a SME manager to implement a decision-oriented organization scheme. For instance, an e-commerce can be regarded as a virtual organization, a responsive firm that can be observed by a reseller (a SME which integrates a complex organizational network) which is allowed, for example, to implement discount promotions to customers in order to answer market changes.

Kalakota & Robinson (2001) stated other firm compositions which also can be seen as based on those technological applications, oriented to build more sophisticated services and decision support environments exemplified by customer relationship management promoters and supply chain management providers. This application also results in opportune perspectives for SMEs where they could gather and process information, in order to generate knowledge (Barney, 1991; Barney, 1995; Takeuchi & Nonaka, 2004).

The following examples illustrate a viable correspondence of strategy, tactics and technology application, which will be enhanced by Brazilian firms cases discussed in the next section, identifying a correspondent business model in each case:

a) Isolated model – where a small entrepreneur can offer products and services through Internet, together with other service providers – as Internet-based payment services or delivery firms – presenting a complete and competitive solution to customers, encompassing from product offering to final distribution or shipping. (Kalakota & Robinson, 2001; Lucas Jr., 2005; Bakos *et al.*, 2005; Turban, Rainer Jr. & Potter, 2007; Jamil, 2007). This model provides an unique form for a small business as a new entrant in a market, referring to its possible low cost, high flexibility and planned growth, resulting in a situation where plans to offer goods to distant customers can be frequently evaluated by its owners allowing increasing competition alternatives. (Kalakota & Robinson, 2001; Porter, 2001; Jamil, 2001; Mintzberg *et al.*, 2003).

Firm examples: retailers of electronic apparatus, automobile accessories, domestic appliances, books, DVDs and other end customer products.

Strategic - tactic example: One electronic customer invoice, for example, can generate information processed by an information system that identifies amounts, time and payment formats of a normal purchase by a particular client. It allows SME manager to identify customer basic interests and ways of relationships (preferred payment method, for example), qualifying SME manager to implement and promote customer-oriented tactics, resulting in increased competitive ability. (Ellsworth & Ellsworth, 1995; Komenar, 1997; Kalakota & Robinson, 2001; Bakos, 2005; Jamil, 2007)

b) Integrated to bigger value aggregated chains – in these competitive scenarios, SMEs could become partners of a complex entrepreneurial arrangement, offering specialized services or even products in intermediate points of an extensive entrepreneurial chain. Here we can identify various SMEs, some of them dealing with knowledge-based services as law, logistics, security, health care, climate prediction, commercial supply chain and so forth, others with the production of a part of a more complex assembly such as an automobile safety device or electronic gadget (Kalakota & Robinson, 2001; Stamoulis, Kanellis & Martakos, 2002; Chen, Long & Yan, 2004; Beneton, Balloni & Bacic, 2007; Jamil, 2007).

Firm examples: Logistics management (supply / delivery integration for direct point of sales – supplier connection, B2B implementation), information and knowledge-based businesses, such as marketing and strategic research offices, metal and electronic parts small and medium manufacturers that operate in a specific part production, transport of people and payloads, health insurance brokerage and services, management consulting.

Strategic-tactic example: A SME logistics supplier–consumer integration firm offers to a product management to a supermarket. This service will integrate information collected from check-out information system, ordering products directly from suppliers and fulfilling predicted customer's demands in a determined shop. It is interesting to notice that studies about customer demands turn out to be a "product" itself, as it can be offered as, for example, a consulting product, to other components of an integrated chain and even to other firms, for marketing planning.

These models can be superposed, intertwined or composed, as information technology permits flexibility in various infrastructures in order to implement business solutions. For instance, isolated firms could operate in composition or selling complementing services, transportation and supplying of goods; consulting firms could produce reports associated to some decisions such as marketing and strategic researches about products consumption.

Another special opportunity for those firms is to consider that they work with information and knowledge that is immediately perceived and absorbed by the customer's level service (Takeuchi & Nonaka, 2004; Lucas Jr., 2005; Bakos *et al.*, 2005; Turban, Rainer Jr. & Potter, 2007). Unfortunately, for the reasons discussed in the earlier section, real conditions of SMEs information technology application may prevent or difficult the perceptions on the real value generated as these contexts are spread over unplanned systems infrastructure and not correctly treated by relevant decisions. As usual, information and knowledge losses, misunderstanding or mistreatment are frequent, leading to a situation where SMEs potentials are not explored (Jamil, 2007).

BRAZIL: A CASE STUDY FOR SMALL AND MEDIUM ENTREPRENEURSHIP

Brazil has experienced a remarkable economic growth in the last twenty years, as it can be noticed from economic indicators. Noticeably, the adoption of the Real, the country's currency since March 1994, along with economic and financial regulations that allowed its definition in a globalized context, is recognized as the starting point of a new economical era (DIEESE, 1999; Ferreira, Leite & Ravaillon, 2007; IBGE, 2009; OECD, 2009).

Brazil has provoked a special interest for this study because of its recent economic development, along with occurrence of cultural and social factors which unquestionably interfered with entrepreneurship initiatives, perspectives and possibilities (IBGE, 2003; SEBRAE, 2007; IBGE, 2008). Also, geographical characteristics, perspectives of emergence of new customers, fast growing usage of information and communication technology adds special interest to our particular study, as a growing number of Brazilian users start to use Internet services every day (CGI.BR, 2009). This section intends to analyze five cases of Brazilian organizations which applied information technology in recent years, illustrating, as e-business case studies of successful entrepreneurship.

Brazilian Facts, Numbers and Indicators

Brazil has a population of approximately 191 million inhabitants, living in an area of 8.5 million km^2, with a gross domestic product of US$ 720 billion (IBGE, 2009; IPEA, 2009). Information technology, especially Internet usage for various purposes, has had a dramatic growth in the last ten years, as it can be verified at CGI.BR (2009) and IBGE (2009). According to CGI.BR (2009), the number of Brazilian Internet users has grown 17% in per year since 2004 and mobile communications users jumped from 61% in 2005, to 76% of the population in 2008. From CGI.BR (2009) we learn that computer utilization in the last 12 months (2007-2008) was reported by 42% of interviewees and Internet by 38%, with 20% informing at least one purchase via electronic commerce in the same period, pointing as main difficulties encountered: access to the Internet connection, ability to use a computer, computers and Internet provision prices and low performance of the local Internet connection. In 2007, 12% of Brazilian houses were using broadband Internet connection, mainly through private providers. These and other numbers – scholarship, GNP growth, wages increase, economic development of the less paid workers among many others – constitute the motivational background to study Brazilian cases for e-business application.

As it can be seen, it is an interesting economical scenario, where the rapid information technology diffusion, the change of the economy conditions, educational development and pressures from globalized competition, have brought special entrepreneurship demands, challenging Brazilian SMEs managers and owners to adhere to new business forms, as those supported by technology. As stated before, not only as immediate customer providers, but also as a globalized competitors (Zoschke & Lima, 2006; Henning, 2006; Gatti & Honoratti, 2008; IPEA, 2009).

Brazilian SME Cases: E-Business Application

According to the motivation presented above, an approach to five cases of e-business application in Brazilian organizations will be conducted. No real names will be informed as our main focus is to study how IT-based e-business was strategically applied in each case.

Case 1: E-Commerce Retailer

The first organization analyzed was initially proposed in 1995, by a group of entrepreneurs motivated by the rapid diffusion of electronic commerce in the USA and Europe. Their first plan was an electronic bookstore where books, CDs, DVDs and other items, usually found in physical bookstores, would be offered to customers. Inspired by the apparent success of pioneers, such as Amazon.com and Bookpol.com, a business plan was developed, which called the attention of investors that were interested in ".com" virtual businesses.

Conceived with an innovative interface, which offered a fast adaptation to the customer's needs and navigation flexibility, an expressive products catalog was initially available, with the intention of making it easier to consult and offering purchasing forms to the clients. In the early days of Brazilian Internet entrepreneurship this case was cited as the most remarkable, especially due to its efficient application of new marketing techniques as for its information systems usage and friendly commercial tactics applied. Navigating through its pages, products were easily compared, chosen and even experienced, as well as excerpts and customer opinions about books, music and video were available for analysis. Information about prices, delivery dates and payment conditions, along with the integration of logistics, financial and commercial services were very attractive to new e-business customers.

The business plan, however, had to be expressively reviewed, for marketing and financial reasons. First, the supposition made about an "Internet usage explosion" with an expressive increase of Internet users and, of course, potential customers did not occur. As it happened with many others firms around the world, difficulties found in the incipient Internet electronic commerce impacted on the expected revenues and profits, resulting in disappointing financial figures. Competitive reaction coming from competitors was also surprising as any entrepreneur, of any place and even with modest investments, could become an effective rival, implementing a functional and responsive website. As Porter (2001) noticed some years later, huge expectations attributed to the information technology infrastructure (and not particularly to its application) revealed to be delusive, as its benefits were easily reproduced. Finally, as the firm became better known in the market, its purchase volume increased significantly and since the logistics aspects were not designed for the lager quantity of customers' orders, the result was excessive delivery time and shortage of products in storage. Due to this fact, customer's frustration increased significantly, especially because the firm was not doing what was promised in the virtual negotiation of the web site.

After a severe commercial struggle that took at least two years, in order to recover from financial losses, market disbelief and logistics mistakes, several measures were taken by its managers, such as encompassing less investments on information technology and more managerial planning and approaching tactics, such as storage administration, partnership with other agents (payment and delivery firms) and strategic priority for the product lines. Today this firm is part of a major retailer group in Brazil – it was acquired in 2007 - which sells the same products lines as the original – Books, CDs, DVDs – and also electronics, computers, domestic appliances and even services as a travel agency, for instance. This experience shows, as a recommendation from this case, how the efficient application of information technology demands a solid strategic plan to deliver expressive results and that it can be integrated to other economic agents showing good growing perspectives, evolving to major business arrangements, taking advantage of the Internet's marketing possibilities.

Case 2: Electronic Banking

Internet banking in Brazil experienced an expressive evolution, reaching some of the highest levels of usage and development in the world. Although most of the Brazilian main Banks are huge enterprises, it is opportune to consider it as a case study, because of its pioneering in IT application (especially in e-banking) and important interface with SMEs. These banks offer not only essential services, as credit management, payment, loans, billing, taxes planning, etc. but even Internet hosting for clients' e-businesses, such as business to business (B2B) and business to customer (B2C). Another reason to observe banks are their relationships with financial and investment SMEs, for example: independent loan agents, stock market home brokers and financial planning (Febraban, 2009).

According Febraban (2009), approximately US$ 3 billion were invested in IT by Brazilian Banks in 2008 for nearly 24 million Internet Bank client accounts. This number shows an increase of almost 300% in this number in the last eight years. Comparatively, almost 19,100 physical agencies were reported, as 38,000 points of self-attendance services were available in various points in the country for more than 170,000 ATMs installed. Internet Banking has been a strong trend in those services, supported by a long history of successful IT investments made by Brazilian Banks, frequently in partnership with important players of the computing industry, such as IBM, Oracle, Sun, Microsoft, among many others.

For the SMEs, this technology-based Banking represents agility, flexibility and cost reduction – as some bureaucratic procedures are automatic through the services that are supplied by Internet Banking – and even possibilities of expansion of their businesses, as they can deal with customers in places where it was difficult to offer products due to the great distance. Financial and investment services were disseminated throughout the country, being done by independent or a group of consultants, small specialized firms or even departments of bigger firms, which, through e-business infrastructure and integrated with Internet Banking, can offer operations such as loan management, stock market operations, purchase and selling of governmental financial titles, among an expressive list of services.

Another interesting aspect of intensive e-business / e-Banking applied in Brazilian banks and its successful role in this market is observed when technology turns to be a differentiation advertised to customers, frequently announced as an advantage. Nowadays, mobile services are offered to be accessed by new platforms, such as PDAs, mobile smartphones and portable computers, both as for individual or enterprise clients. As a recommendation from this remarkable Internet application, Brazilian banks have been evaluating additional support for e-banking services such as safety guarantees, information systems to assist investments and on-line information about stock markets. It is strongly believed that a long successful application of IT in Brazilian banks, which resulted in a modern infrastructure and business platform, is one of the reasons of its market attractiveness even for transnational financial groups that invested and acquired some native banks in the last ten years.

Case 3: Business to Business Logistics Supplier

Logistics is an interesting theme when an immense territory with fragmented and heterogeneous markets, as in Brazilian case, is being explored. Kalakota & Robinson (2001), Bowersox, Closs and Cooper (2002) and Lucas Jr. (2005) called attention to the information technology application to integrate distribution systems in complex consumption arrays, as those found in Brazil. Here, SMEs found significant opportunities in activities such as supply management, information management (as customer behavior and demands, for example), transport, storage and others that can be carried out by an independent SME in order to attend to the supplier-customer demands in more complex organizational arrays.

For this study, a case of one small firm was selected. In the beginning, only received customer's invoices and then passed them to interested retailers. Nowadays this firm deals with more complex tasks. It was formerly a part of an automotive parts supplier, located in the southeast region of the country, specialized in delivering car parts to shops for repairs and maintenance. In 2002, this SME, started an association with an Internet service provider and began to offer its services in the Internet, with the intention of selling parts in various regions of the Brazilian territory. Orders were sent to customers using independent courier services and allowing the customer to use its payment services, associated with selected banks which offered, at that time, IT-supported billing services. This B2B supplier was initially acting only in five of the twenty-six Brazilian states.

As an evolution of this initial situation, an expansion plan was studied and proposed, which considering information technology investment as a priority. More security was added to the IT infrastructure, also including also investments in the network's capacity and improving the website's interfaces in the main plan's goals. They also aimed to add new commercial services and expand their target area, increasing it to twelve Brazilian states. These technological actions were accompanied by managerial decisions, as increasing their parts catalog and designing the new commercial services – as supply information for automotive industries, for instance – commercial team preparation and the development of new contract models, as more complex negotiations would be carried out by this firm.

The newest organization plan, delayed due to the financial world crisis, stated goals and actions in order to sign partnership contracts with manufacturers, giving priority or exclusive operation in some parts of the country, as an authentic e-business entrepreneurship, only with presence over the web and not through physical shops. Now this organization acts integrated with the automotive industry, car dealers, repair shops and other retailers, in order to distribute components, parts and accessories. Its expansion will permit to add more companies to its catalog, to offer supply services and allow future expansion, maybe including their own delivery system to final customers.

This case shows how planned movements by SMEs, with strategy-based information technology support, can result in expressive advances and integration in more complex arrays. Such marketing tactics can be considered sustainable, as new investments and management could be done with a better prediction of results, positioning the SME's competitor in a situation where it can be observed in a competitive environment and then decide how to defend and expand its role. As stated in the literature's review, investments in planned information technology investments could result in competitive growth for the SMEs, which could be isolated or integrated to bigger organizational arrangements.

Case 4: Marketing Channel

"Classifieds sections" are a traditional way to offer, negotiate and sell products and services. Almost every newspaper in the world, from the simple and small to those considered "giants" of this type of communication have a "classifieds" section, some of which have more than a hundred years, informing readers about commercial opportunities of numberless items. For a Brazilian SME it appeared to be a fair opportunity in 2001 when they initiate their business. They just informed, through a "static" web page (non-interactive, only with displayed information about characteristics, values and sellers´ contacts), advertisements of products and services. If an interested person or firm wanted to offer something in the web, this SME should be contacted – by phone! – and a paid announcement was negotiated. Practically, the only facility available for an interested costumer was the navigation using categories, which could result in a more efficient way to search for a specific offer.

This SME had a partnership with a small ISP, that took care of Internet connections and site availability, focusing its work on capturing products to sell and trying, by conventional advertisement campaigns – other newspapers and radio, mainly – to promote its service. Among the first commercial clients, the most profitable were car dealers, electronics shopkeepers, communication services and publishing firms. A simple "click dependent" billing model was adopted, something that could be considered a rudiment of modern Google-like systems, where the SME is paid for each consult done by customers and, in some cases, as occurred with real estate representatives, fees were also paid by the main dealer.

In an interesting evolution, after having a problematic first year, where results were disappointing and no reasonable plans were conceived in order to really manage the company, they decided to launch a small tabloid-sized newspaper, to be sold or delivered for free at airports, bus station and other public services places. In parallel, another effort was done to adapt the web site, continuously, launching a consulting service where Internet-based customers could have more sophisticated assistance, by chat or e-mail. Soon these two formats proved to be complementary, one informing customers about the existence of the other, resulting in the growth of both, the newspaper and the Internet service. Clearly, Internet diffusion also played a definitive role in offering the SME's service for other interested users, even in places far from its original geographic area.

Interestingly, information became a product by itself, as information about purchases, products and services negotiations, marks, payment forms, and others were processed by the SME every day, both in the web site and in the physical structure associated with the newspaper. Some consults by firms interested to start negotiating new products and services and partnership offered by older and bigger news organizations showed opportunities to the SME's managers of a marketing knowledge service, as their firm were increasingly collecting information from markets and customers. After investing in IT personnel, time had come to build an informational team (focusing market knowledge generation), which will, contracted by interested companies, analyze an expressive amount of information, through statistical methods to produce orientations for marketing actions.

Nowadays, acting both as a "classifieds" newspapers and website – as this SME kept its original actions because they still proved to be successful – they started to offer an additional and competitive service of marketing consultancy for organizations that need help for customer behavior studies. They also are now processing the classifieds sections for traditional newspapers, providing content management for this service, replacing the older structure as a third party service provider.

This case showed again the need for plans to explore opportunities in e-business environment and services integration, even in traditional sectors, using potential innovations for information-based services and the power of simple Internet solutions, not exactly to replace older services, but adapting and offering it to a growing number of interested customers.

Case 5: E-Government

The Brazilian government has implemented some of the most accessed web-based services in the world (United Nations, 2005). As Brazilian citizens and firms have to deal with complex regulatory and fiscal laws, with significant volume of documents and processes conducted by state departments, faster and simple access ways have been developed in the last years, making it easier to fulfill all mandatory obligations. A special attention was given to the federal fiscal Internet-based system, both for personal or organizational payment and information, which is one of the most used in the entire world. These web services actually support all the required interaction with citizens, such as reporting their incomes and taxes paid during a fiscal year.

Some legal documents, emitted by Brazilian government are mandatory to do real estate negotiations, goods ownership (as for cars, for example), trading, family subjects (birth certificate, marriage, divorce and others), are easily obtained through Internet-based services. Other special functions that are available to any interested citizen are governmental projects management and information or processing of public bids. As governments are always big players in the economic scenario, processes related to purchases or contracts can be followed by the Internet giving information and participation to anyone, accomplishing the desired "transparency" of public actions.

E-government in Brazil appears as special case of e-business as meaningful levels of usage are always reported. Responding to the complex legal demands and with the usually inefficient physical support by state-owned public services, the Brazilian e-government turns out to be a solution for citizens and firms, in order to follow legal determinations and being clearly informed of government actions.

CONCLUSION

E-business, considered as projects based on Internet application for businesses services, are a remarkable information technology evolution. These resources, available sometimes at low cost, wherever we are, can promote development for any business, dramatically changing its perspectives of customer interaction. Its potential range from simple automation of assistance to complex functions, as guided product choice and correspondent forms of payment and delivery. Nowadays, a large and growing number of organizations are applying e-business techniques in order to improve their position in competitive markets and their image by the customers.

This chapter first addressed the motivation to use the technology application in businesses, advancing to understand its usage under strategic planning. Strategy fundamentals were then discussed, with the purpose of studying situations where the IT could be efficiently applied, in order to achieve predetermined goals and actions planned before. Following, a discussion of constraints to plan in SMEs was done, promoting a comprehension of the real situation faced by SMEs managers or owners when they tried to design future scenarios for their firms. These two first sections presented a real basis of strategy thinking in SMEs, an essential topic to be able to interpret successful and problematic cases of the IT application.

In the following sections, a reflection about innovative business models and its repercussions in new firms were shown, approaching some forms of e-business infrastructure implementation for old and new enterprises and presenting how to interconnect it to answer strategic planned demands by firms. Finally, five Brazilian cases of e-business were analyzed, showing perspectives about how these technological tools can promote new competitive advantages for any kind of business. These cases were explored with an historical approach, looking to informing the reader about experiences, mistakes and correct actions carried out by entrepreneurs, sometimes following plans, sometimes by intuition.

E-business models continue to have excellent perspectives for the SME managers that are interested in its application to start or improve their businesses. As new technology emerges, as it happens now with the mobility and the distribution of the information systems, evolutionary forms of commerce and service can be offered, with expressive results. A final recommendation to the reader is to understand that all this technology must be designed and applied to serve feasible strategic plans that assure reasonable goals to be achieved and efficient risk management procedures. With the strategic conception, progressive business evolution is a real perspective.

REFERENCES

Andrews, K. (1980). *The concept of corporate strategy*. Homewood, USA: Dow-Jones - Irwin.

Bakos, Y., Lucas, H. C. Jr, Oh, W., Simon, G., Viswanathan, S., & Weber, B. W. (2005). The impact of E-Commerce on competition in the retail brokerage industry. *Information Systems Research*, *16*(4), 352–371. doi:10.1287/isre.1050.0064

Barney, J. (1991). Firms Resources and Sustained Competitive Advantage. *Journal of Management*, *17*(1), 99–120. doi:10.1177/014920639101700108

Barney, J. (1995). Looking inside for competitive advantage. *The Academy of Management Executive*, *9*(4), 49–61.

Beneton, E. J., Balloni, A. J., & Bacic, M. J. (n.d.). Information security in small and medium Brazilian companies. *Annals of International joint conferences on computer, information and systems, sciences and engineering.* Available at http://cisse2007online.org/ accessed on July, 2009.

Bowersox, D. J., Closs, D., & Cooper, M. B. (2002). *Supply chain logistics management*. New York: Mc Graw Hill.

Brasil. (2009). Portal do Governo Brasileiro. At www.brasil.gov.br, accessed on July, 2009.

Canada (2009). Government of Canada Internet Portal. At http://canada.gc.ca/, accessed on July, 2009.

Caron, A. (2003). *Inovações tecnológicas nas pequenas e médias empresas industriais em tempos de globalização: o caso do estado do Paraná.* Doctoral thesis, approved at Federal University of Santa Catarina, Brazil.

CGI. BR – Comitê Gestor da Internet no Brasil. (2009). *Pesquisa sobre o uso das tecnologias da Informação no Brasil.* Retrieved from http://www.cetic.br/tic/2008/index.htm on July, 2009.

Chen, I., Long, J., & Yan, T. (2004). E-Supply chain implementation strategies in a transitional economy. *International Journal of Information Technology and Decision Making*, *3*(4), 563–574. doi:10.1142/S0219622004001240

Covin, J. G., & Slevin, D. P. (1986). The development and testing of an organization-level entrepreneurship scale. In Ronstadt, R. (Ed.), *Frontiers of Entrepreneurship Research* (pp. 628–639). Wellesley: Babson College.

Covin, J. G., & Slevin, D. P. (1991). A Conceptual Model of Entrepreneurship as Firm Behaviour. *Entrepreneurship Theory and Practice.*, *16*, 7–25.

DIEESE – Departamento Intersindical de Estatística e Estudos Econômicos. (1999). *Aniversário do Real.* Retrieved on August, 2009, from http://www.dieese.org.br/esp/cju/jul99ptr.xml.

Ellsworth, J. H., & Ellsworth, M. V. (1995). *Marketing on the Internet.* Hoboken, NJ: John Wiley and Sons.

FEBRABAN – Federação Brasileira de Bancos. (2009). Retrieved from http://www.febraban.org.br on August,2009.

Fernandes, D. H., & Santos, C. P. (2008). Orientação empreendedora: um estudo sobre as conseqüências do empreendedorismo nas organizações. Retrieved on May, 2009 from www.rae.com.br/eletronica*RAE – Revista de Administração de Empresas, 7*(1), Art. 6, January / June.

Ferreira, F. H. G., Leite, P. G., & Ravaillon, M. (2007). Poverty reduction without economic growth? Explaining Brazil's poverty's dyanimcs, 1985-2004. *World Bank Policy Research Paper,* retrieved on June, 2009, from http://econ.worldbank.org/external/default/main.

Gatti, R., & Honoratti, M. (2008). Informality among Formal Fims: Firm level, Cross-Country evidence on tax compliance and access to credit. *World Bank Policy Research Working Paper*, retrieved on June, 2009, from http://econ.worldbank.org/external/default/main.

George, G., Wood Jr., R. D. & Khan, R. (2001).Networking strategy of boards: implication for small and medium-sized enterprises. *Entrepreneurship and regional development, 13*(1), 269-285.

Ghemawat, P. (2006). *Strategy and the business landscape* (2nd ed.). Boston: Prentice Hall.

Herber, J., Singh, J. V., & Useem, M. (2000). *The design of new organizational forms* (pp. 376–392). Wharton on Managing Emerging Techonologies.

Hitt, M., Bierman, L., Shimizu, K., & Kochhar, R. (2001). Directs and moderating effects of human capital on strategy and performance in professional service firms: a resource based perspective. *Academy of Management Journal, 44*(1), 13–28. doi:10.2307/3069334

Hitt, M. A., Ireland, R. D., & Hoskisson, R. E. (2001). *Strategic Management: Competitiveness and globalization* (4th ed.). London, UK: Thomson Learning.

Hua, G. B. (2007). Applying the strategic alignment model to business and ICT strategies of Singapore's small and medium-sized architecture, engineering and construction enterprises. *Construction Management and Economics, 25*, 157–169. doi:10.1080/01446190600827041

IBGE – Instituto Brasileiro de Geografia e Estatística. (2003). *As micro e pequenas empresas comerciais e de serviços no Brasil - 2001.* Rio de Janeiro, Brazil: IBGE.

IBGE – Instituto Brasileiro de Geografia e Estatística. (2008). *Demografia das empresas. Estudos e Pesquisas – Informação econômica, número 10.* Rio de Janeiro, Brazil: IBGE.

IBGE – Instituto Brasileiro de Geografia e Estatística. (2009). At www.ibge.gov.br, accessed on August, 2009.

IPEA – Instituto de Pesquisas Econômicas Aplicadas. (2009). At www.ipea.gov.br, accessed on August, 2009.

Jamil, G. L. (2001). *Repensando a TI na empresa moderna.* Rio de Janeiro, Brasil: Axcel Books.

Jamil, G. L. (2007). Comércio Eletrônico no Brasil: Tendências e oportunidades. In *Balloni, A. J. (org.) (2007) Por que Gestão em sistemas e tecnologias da informação? Segurança, inovação e sociedade* (pp. 157–201). Campinas, Brasil: Komedi.

Kalakota, R., & Robinson, M. (2001). *E-Business 2.0 – Roadmap for Success* (2nd ed.). Boston: Addison Wesley.

Kearns, G., & Shaberwal, R. (2007). Antecendents and consequences of information system planning integration. *IEEE Transactions on Engineering Management, 54*(4), 628–643. doi:10.1109/TEM.2007.906848

Kearns, G., & Shaberwal, R. (2007a). Strategic alignment between business and information technology: a knowledge-based view of behaviors, outcome and consequences. *Journal of Management Information Systems*, *23*(3), 139–162. doi:10.2753/MIS0742-1222230306

Kearns, G. S., & Lederer, A. L. (2003). A resource based view of IT alignment: how knowledge sharing creates a competitive advantage. *Decision Sciences*, *34*(1), 1–29. doi:10.1111/1540-5915.02289

Komenar, M. (1997). *Electronic Marketing*. Hoboken: John Wiley and Sons.

Levi, M., Powell, P., & Yetton, P. (2001). SMEs: aligning IS and strategic context. *Journal of Information Technology*, *16*, 133–144. doi:10.1080/02683960110063672

Liao, J., Kickul, J. R., & Ma, H. (2009). Organizational dynamic capability and innovation: an empirical examination of Internet firms. *Journal of Small Business Management*, *47*(3), 263–286. doi:10.1111/j.1540-627X.2009.00271.x

Lucas, H. C. Jr. (2005). *Information technology: strategic decision making for managers*. Hoboken: John Wiley and Sons.

Lumpkin, G. T., & Dess, G. G. (1996). Clarifying the entrepreneurial orientation construct and linking it to performance. *Academy of Management Review*, *21*(1), 135–172. doi:10.2307/258632

Mata, F. J., Fuerst, W. L. & Barney, J. B. (1995). Information technology and sustained competitive advantage: a resource-based analysis. *Management information science Quarterly*, pp. 487-505, December.

Maur, J. C. (2008). Regionalism and trade facilitation: A primer. *World Bank Policy Research Working Paper*, retrieved on July, 2009, from http://econ.worldbank.org/external/default/main.

Mintzberg, H., Lampel, J., Quinn, J. B., & Ghoshal, S. (2003). *The strategy process: concepts, contexts, cases* (4th ed.). Upper Saddle River, NJ: Prentice Hall.

Minztberg, H., Ahlstrand, B., & Lampel, J. (1998). *Strategy safari: a guided tour through the wilds of strategic management*. Washington, DC: Free Press.

OECD – Organisation for Economic Cooperation and Development. (2009). At www.oecd.org accessed on August, 2009.

Porter, M. (1980). *Competitive strategy*. New York: Free Press.

Porter, M. (1996). What is strategy? [November-December.]. *Harvard Business Review*, 61–78.

Porter, M. (2001). Strategy and the Internet. *Harvard Business Review HBR OnPoint*. Boston, USA: Harvard Business School Publishing Corporation, pp. 62-78, March.

SEBRAE – Serviço Brasileiro de apoio às pequenas e micro empresas. (2007). *Fatores condicionantes e taxas de sobrevivência e mortalidade de pequenas e médias empresas no Brasil: 2003-2005.* At http://www.biblioteca.sebrae.com.br/bds/ NT00037936.pdf accessed on March, 2009.

Sergio, R. S. G., Gomes, C. A. S., Rodrigues, C., & Boaventura, R. (2004). *Estratégias competitivas para pequenas e micro empresas: um estudo de caso.* Electronic anals of 4th Congresso de Controladoria e Contabilidade da USP, retrieved on May 2009, from http://www.congressousp.fipecafi.org/artigos42004/162.pdf.

Stair, R. M., & Reynolds, G. W. (2003). *Principles of information systems: a managerial approach* (6th ed.). Florence, KY: Cencage Learning.

Stamoulis, D., Panagiotis, K., & Martakos, D. (2002). An approach and model for assessing the business value of e-banking distribution channels: evaluation as communication services. *International Journal of Information Management*, *22*, 247–261. doi:10.1016/S0268-4012(02)00011-7

Takeuchi, H., & Nonaka, I. (2004). *Gestão do conhecimento*. Porto Alegre, Brasil: Bookman.

Teng, B. S., & Cummings, J. L. (2002). Trade-offs in managing resources and capabilities. *The Academy of Management Executive*, *16*(2), 81–91.

Turban, E., Mc Lean, E., & Wetherbe, J. (2002). *Information technology for management: transforming business in the digital economy* (3rd ed.). Hoboken, NJ: John Wiley and Sons.

Turban, E., Rainer, R. K. Jr, & Potter, R. E. (2007). *Introduction to information systems*. Hoboken, NJ: John Wiley and Sons.

United Nations –. *Global E-government readiness report* (2005). United Nations Department of Public Affairs, division of public administration and development management, retrieved on July, 2009, from http://unpan1.un.org/intradoc/groups/public/documents/un/unpan021888.pdf.

Venkatraman, N. (1989). Strategic orientation of business enterprises: the construct, dimensionality and measurement. *Management Science*, *35*(8), 942–962. doi:10.1287/mnsc.35.8.942

Wernerfelt (1984). A resource based view of a firm. *Strategic Management Journal*. 5, pp. 171-180.

White House. (2009). *United States of America Govern Internet Portal*. At www.whitehouse.gov, accessed on June, 2009.

Wiklund, J., Patzelt, H., & Shepherd, D. A. (2007). Building an integrative model of small business growth. *Small Business Economics*. Retrieved on June 2009 from http://www.springerlink.com/content/h0n5848j2330117p/fulltext.html.

Wright, P., Kroll, M. J., & Parnell, J. A. (1998). *Strategic management: concepts*. Upper Saddle River, NJ: Prentice Hall.

Yolles, M. (2009). Competitive advantage and its conceptual development. *Business Information Review*, *26*(2), 93–111. doi:10.1177/0266382109104411

Zahra, S. A. (1993). A conceptual model of entrepreneurship as firm behavior: A critique and extension. *Entrepreneurship: Theory and Practice*. Baylor University, USA. Summer.

Chapter 13
E-Health Business Models Prototyping by Incremental Design

Josep Ma. Monguet
Universitat Politècnica de Catalunya, Spain

Eduardo Huerta
Universitat Politècnica de Catalunya, Spain

Joaquín Fernández
Universitat Politècnica de Catalunya, Spain

Marco Ferruzca
Metropolitan Autonomus University, Mexico

Susana Badillo
Metropolitan Autonomus University, Mexico

ABSTRACT

Internet and IT (Information technologies) among other innovative drivers push companies to update their business models, and design stands out as an emergent issue strongly connected with innovation, which, in turn, is the main resource of the modern economy. One way to achieve innovation is through artifacts that allow the development of successful information systems in organizations. Moreover, the field of health appears as a sector with many opportunities to improve services through IT and design. Therefore, e-health comes out as one of the elements that should eventually help in the evolution of business models in health systems. In this chapter, the authors present a design method of IT artifacts for e-health adapted from the method proposed by Pahl and Beitz (1995). The correctness of the design method adopted is a significant issue to generate new business models successfully or to adapt the existing ones in health systems.

DOI: 10.4018/978-1-61692-880-3.ch013

INTRODUCTION

Many health institutions are nowadays involved in e-health projects that envision the application of internet and IT to improve their activity. This is traduced, from one side, in opportunities for multidisciplinary research and, in the other, is a chance to evolve some of the current business models in health.

E-health can become one of the main areas for e-business development in the future years, "thanks to information technologies have been touted as both a solution to rising health care costs and a way to reduce medical errors" (Adler-Milstein, 2009). In fact, IT investment is central to President Obama´s vision for health care reform in the USA and his estimates of the savings from it have been substantial (Adler-Milstein, 2009). A similar view exists in Europe where e-health is one of the central items of the European Commission Agenda. The huge investments expected all and around the world will turn e-health in a fruitful field for opportunities, where final success of many of them will depend on business models innovation.

The work presented in this chapter, based in the collaboration between health institutions, an internet company and a technical university, allow testing a methodology to design and develop internet artifacts for e-health, considering the business model evolution from the beginning.

The work is founded on the desk analysis of current paradigms of design management and relays on a field experience based in the application of the proposed methodology to a 9 e-health prototypes created during the period 2006 – 2009. The last one, a tele-rehabilitation system named E-DIS, is used to illustrate the design methodology proposed.

BACKGROUND

The E-Health Area: Expectations and Difficulties

Despite the enormous investment, both public and private, in health innovation and the magnitude of the opportunity to both do good and do well, too many efforts fail, losing billions of investor dollars along the way (Herzlinger, 2006). Innovative solutions involving internet and multimedia systems should facilitate the renovation of health care business models that are a focal aspect of problems in the health systems. ICT may help with new products and services, to develop new treatments and to improve existing ones, and it is also a tool that may improve the processes. In the e-health sector, successful innovation and the development of real health services arising from that innovation is not easy, has to be gradual, and must be connected with the evolution of health business models.

Technology in health allows record, measure, monitor, manage and provide guidance to the patient, together with the opportunity to offer care services through the Internet in real time (June Chuan Su, 2007). Telemedicine systems have enabled to maximize the collection, delivery and communication of medical information, clinical messaging, interaction with nurses and medical records (Maheu, Whitten and Allen, 2001), beside facilitates the exchange of information between doctors and patients. In short, the establishment of telemedicine systems encourages the integration of many activities in e-health clinics but also means dealing with a lot of data, information and resources (June Chuan Su, 2007). It also means having the obligation to have information systems commensurate with the importance of the task they perform. With a successful information system, allowing both to medical staff and patients to focus on other activities and, with this, translate effort and time into valuable medical resources.

The e-health sector appears as a huge market but largely untapped (European Commision, 2008). One of the main reasons for the health service providers not to invest in IT could be the lack of common standards between countries and interoperability problems. One consequence of the lack of investment is that the growth in companies supplying ICT for health sector is smaller than it could be (European Commision, 2008).

As the high risks would limit the private investments public administrations have to do extra efforts to encourage both sides of the market, offer and demand. Both in USA and Europe, the administration is expected to invest strongly in the technology sector oriented to health services for two reasons: the improvements that can be introduced into medical terms, and the money that should be saved through IT. Let's consider, for example, the adoption of electronic health records, -EHRs- by most doctors and hospitals will mean savings of up to 77 billion dollars annually in USA. Moreover, Medicare, the largest payer in the United States, has introduced the first financial incentive for doctors who adopt health IT (Adler-Milstein, 2009).

In terms of quality in providing medical services, there are still some problems arising from the adoption of technology that have not been resolved, such as the lack of integration of information systems may hamper the access of doctors and nurses to patient data. Recognizing that, the introduction of IT in health care is something that cannot be avoided. In fact, there are health care organizations who believe that gains will flow from the technology alone. For example, it is expected that practices such as adoption of electronic health records to improve the doctor's workflow, accuracy, communication with patients, access to medical history and clinical decision making (Adler-Milstein, 2009).

It is also true that, to embrace the new capabilities offered by the IT, organizations need to implement substantial changes, such as increasing training for employees and individual decision-making authority. This "flattened their hierarchies, made greater use of skilled, decentralized teams and raises incentives for team performance" (Adler-Milstein, 2009). All this represents a major challenge for organizations providing health services, because as well as making big investments, it suppose workers are skilled and opened to receive these updates. Moreover, it is natural to expect that any innovation in information systems necessarily bring economic benefits to the organization. According Hevner (et al, 2004) such information systems IT improves economic performance through the effectiveness and efficiency.

Design as an Integrative Tool for E-Health-Business Development

Design is deeply connected with innovation (Hollanders & Van Cruysen, 2009), which, in turn, is one if not the principal driver of the modern economy (Purao, 2008). One way to achieve innovation is through artifacts that allow the development of successful information systems in organizations (March et al, 2008). For the successful implementation of new information systems and IT artifacts in organizations -whether for health or any business-, design emerges as a powerful integrating agent.

From the economic point of view, we can say that products and services that are results of design are the core of the economic system. Furthermore, innovations, the main source of wealth in modern economies are precisely design changes or advances in design (Purao, 2008).

According Gui Bonsiepe (2000), the main task of design is not to produce knowledge, as many believe, but "to present" knowledge. That is, develop information systems capable of delivering knowledge in a clear way and without giving chance to second readings. This is linked to the functional task of design, in the sense of making the artifact or object efficiently make the task for which it was designed. As stated by March and Smith (in March et al, 2008), design refers to the development of artifacts that fulfill objectives.

In other words, design is the key because it extends the organizational capabilities by creating innovative artifacts (Hevner et al, 2004), constructs that allow the development of information systems in companies (March et al, 2008). These artifacts (information systems, in the case of organizations) are produced using methods like the one proposed by Pahl and Beitz in 1995, which consists in the recognition of the need, problem identification, conceptualization, preliminary and definitive solutions and the construction of the final solution.

Multidisciplinary Design

First of all, e-health-business prototypes are designed and developed in a multidisciplinary framework where internet applications design mix with health management and business in a context of knowledge management. Moreover much of the work must be done applying the appropriate research techniques. (See Figure 1)

Of the many design methods of information systems that can be found in the literature dedicated to engineering or industrial design (Christopher Alexander, 1971; Nigel Cross, 1984, Christopher Jones, 1984, etc.), the one proposed by Pahl and Beitz in 1995 seems more relevant for us and we have relied on it to develop the model for e-health-business prototyping.

Nigel Cross in 1999 classifies design methods into 2 groups: descriptive methods and prescriptive methods. The descriptive models mention the sequence of activities that occur in a design process. The prescriptive, as the name implies, prescribe a pattern of activities, that is, in addition to describing the process, they give guidelines for developing each of the phases and stages of the design process (Chaur Bernal, 2005).

The Pahl and Beitz model belongs to prescriptive models. They propose is to divide the project into different key phases: beginning with the recognition of the needs of the project and identify problems before proceeding to the first creative phase, which is known as 'conceptualization' and which sets out what will be the goal of artifact created. Once we have a clear goal, we try to propose preliminary solutions with low level of detail in the solution and closer to a sketch to the final tool. Once all stakeholders agree that the chosen is the right way, we are ready to do some more definitive solutions and finally develop the end solution, tool or artifact.

The method, as can be denoted, focuses on the so-called "embodiment design" (overall design) and for it proposes a development project by separate functional modules. This has the advantage of simplifying the analysis, but the disadvantage that can arrive to a joint proposal that can be very complex (Syed, Agarwal and Malik, 2000 in Chaur Bernal, 2005).

Figure 1. Areas of knowledge that interact to form our field of work

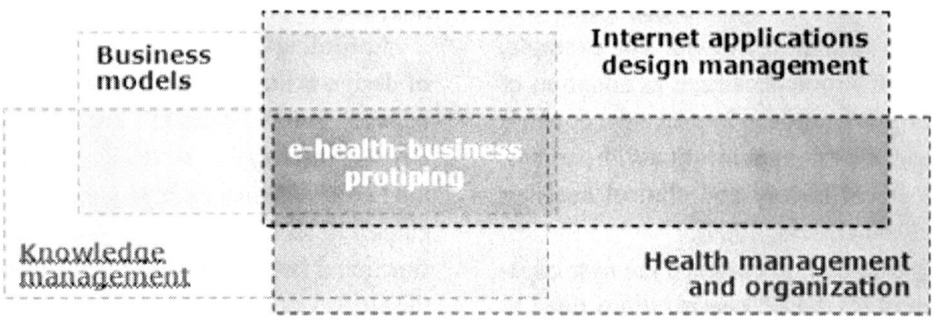

Our proposal, that has proved usefully in e-health has been developed on the basis of the Pahl and Beitz phases, but emphasising the idea that these phases cycle must be repeated iteratively as often as required. We believe that fulfilling this cycle just once, we may reach a good final solution, but incomplete or likely to receive many changes or amendments once the artifact is already being used by the end user. In each phase we incorporate as a key element the revision of the business model behind the new solution and the the participation of end users as soon and as intensively as possible.

We took inspiration from of authors such as Markus (et al, 2001) and Walls (et al, 1992) that advocate the use of prototypes in the production of artifacts as part of design research. Thus, through the process of incremental development of prototypes, the first one minimizing elements and data nearing the limit of usefulness, but fulfilling the fundamental objective of artifact. The process becomes gradual and the participation of profiles is maximized, allowing to reach a stronger final solution, complete and avoiding content, technological and use errors that reach the end user, which in our case is a patient in therapy for some disease.

MAIN FOCUS OF THE CHAPTER:

The Incremental Design Method

Collaborative Design

From the mentioned above, we propose a new method which has to be considered under the concept of collaborative design, where participants contribute to an interactive design team in order to achieve a common task by sharing experiences, ideas, resources or responsibilities (Ostergaard and Summers, 2009).

The management of design process and tasks consists in delegating them to different profiles of the team involved in the project, getting the artifacts design and the connected new business models a 100% collaborative process.

It is important to notice that once the project has begun, the client - provider relationship is a secondary factor, and from now everybody is assigned at one of the tree teams which will interact during all the design, development and implementation process according to their profile (see Table 1).

This team division is in fact nominal, because actually in a collaborative multidisciplinary team, members, information and resources can be distributed across different geographic, organizational, or time limits (Ostergaard and Summers, 2009). Particularly, the team that has worked in the prototypes is based in Spain, but with contributions from work teams installed in Portugal and Mexico.

Design Phases, Cycles and Work Flow

The method follows 5 phases and each of the phases has a cycle of 5 steps and each step has an elemental Work Flow (see Table 2).

Phases

Steps

In each of the 5 phases a cycle of 5 steps is followed. Each steps more or less relevant in each the phases as well as the phases should be repeated one or more times (see Table 3).

Table 1.

Business Team	Leading and management of the project. End-user and stakeholders relationship.
Design Team	Creative proposals, for contents and interfaces. Management of tests and assessments.
Technical Team	Implementation according to design requirements and specifications.

Table 2.

1. Problem	Identification of the need, recognizing the problem. General aim. First agreement of all stakeholders.
2. Concept	Conceptual proposal and specific aims. First agreement of all team members. First draft of the prototype and the business model
3. Proposal	Creative Proposal as a preliminary solution or as a pre-prototype. Firs to be contrasted with end users.
4. Prototype	Advanced Creative Proposal with more definition and detail. First to be tested with end users and repeated one or more times depending on the results of tests performed. Final version of the predicted business model.
5. Product/service	Final product / service, running and being used by the whole group of end users. First to apply the new business model.

Table 3.

	Idea	Leading	Relevant
1. Agreement	Is not referred to the contracts but to the fact that the people involved in the process of design and development agrees regularly on what they are doing and the focus of the work.	**Problem:** Ensuring that we share the problem to be solved in an entirely way and how this problem is an opportunity to test a new business model.	**Concept:** Ensure that the solution that is visualized meets the expectations set. **Prototype:** Ensure that the artifact complies effectively with the aims set at project beginning.
2. Documentation	Every effort should be documented to establish certain variables of knowledge management. This is for the following phases and other projects.	**Concept:** A briefing that clearly establishes the output to be obtained, the design and technical criteria as well as the framework where the system will fit when it runs.	**Proposal:** All relevant information must be known and documented. Non important data may be out.
3. Resources	Key resources must be known and be calculated in a very precise way.	**Product / service:** Description of the key resources that will be needed to develop the real system and from where these resources will come from.	**Problem:** In the first approach defines the necessary resources to meet project objectives. At this stage we know if we are able to continue the development of the project.
4. System	The system passes from its conception to its existence gradually.	**Prototype:** The artifact obtains the design and techniques features necessary to achieve the main of the project. The user should be able to interact with the artifact without problems.	**Proposal:** Is in the proposal stage where the conceptual definition of the artifact is finished and from there it will direct the project. **Product/service:** In this phase the artifact must be in optimal condition to be tested by the total number of users and to go out to the market.
5. Test	Normally, thanks to the test the agreement is closed.	**Proposal:** The key test is the one conducted with the first operative prototype, under a rigorous research protocol.	**Problem:** Testing the significance of the problem from other points of view, analyzing alternative solutions and asking to experts in the field, this should help to correct the asymmetries in the points of view of different professional profiles.

Table 4.

Phases / Steps	Agreement	Documentation	Resources	System	Test
1 Problem	Leading		Relevant		Relevant
2 Concept	Relevant	Leading			Relevant
3 Proposal		Relevant		Relevant	Leading
4 Prototype	Relevant			Leading	Relevant
5 Product/service			Leading	Relevant	Relevant

The Whole Process

All steps are present and important in all the phases of the process, for instance sometimes problems are so complex and the points of view so different that a simple graphical model should help to make in common the problem to be solved and this would be the role of the system (step n.4) in the problem phase. Anyway some of them may be highlighted as leading and as relevant steps in each phase of the process. Table 4 summarises what has been exposed previously. (See Figure 2).

The process begins with an agreement that comes from the precedent phase, except for the phase 1, **Problem**. Following the agreement is **documentation,** that specifies all the information needed in each of the phases the basic components to start producing what will be the first **prototype** of the artifact, a very preliminary version of it, in which with the minimum elements can fulfill the main objective of the project.

With the first version of the prototype we can start drawing the exploitation protocol, which ultimately will help us to know the system requirements that will be implemented in the artifact,

Figure 2. STAGES of the Incremental Design Method of Systems

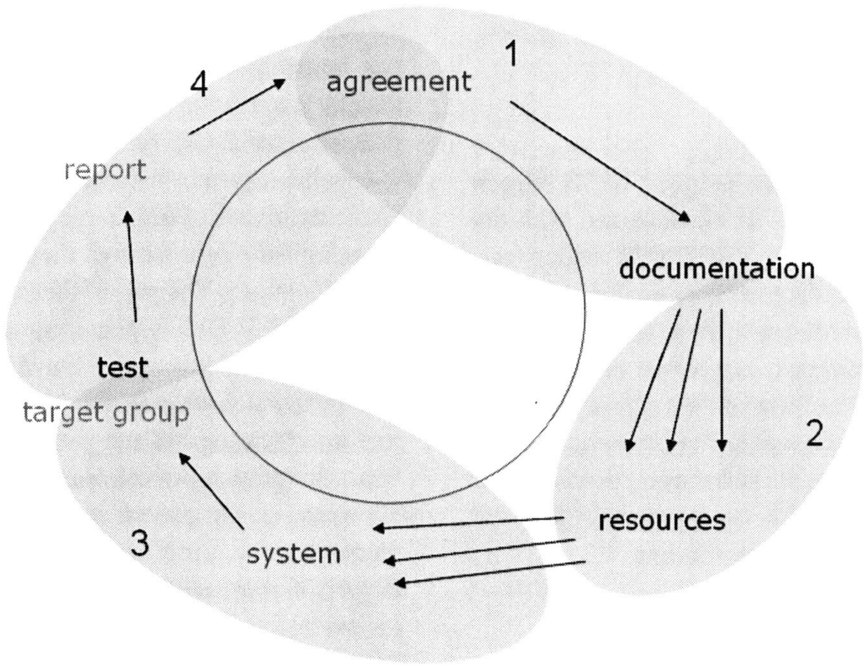

hardware or software tools that must be available by the user and/or customer and also the identification of the skills needed by the end user of the artifact to interact with him.

At this stage it is also possible to identify a first **target group** -a sample of what will be the end user audience- to serve as a real user and interact directly with the prototype. This first interaction or approach with the artifact is what we call **Test**. In it, the user should be able to comply, with the minimum elements that this first prototype offers, the overall objective of the project. Once the first test has been made, it is possible to draft a **report** with data collected in the test. With these data it is possible to reach the following **agreement** between profiles, recognize needs, specifications and details (technical, content and usage), unknown at this moment and, on that basis, advance to the next **PHASE** of the project, which increase the detail in each **STEP**, in order to make the tests with a target group with new features and which interact with a prototype artifact with a higher level of detail.

Finally it is necessary to consider that the each step in each phase follow an elemental work flow determined by four key concepts or elements: **Profile, Task, Product and Approval** (Figure 3).

Workflow Explanation

Each **PROFILE** has an assigned **TASK** in each phase of the project, which must end with the delivery of so called **PRODUCT** which varies according to the profile of each person. So, someone in the Management area will develop a document or contract, as a person of the Design area may submit a sketch design of product, a user interface or an animation. The latter concept, the **APPROVAL** consists in that every product must have the approval of the team, especially from the area manager and the team leader.

Figure 3.WorkFlow used by LAM-UPC in our diary work

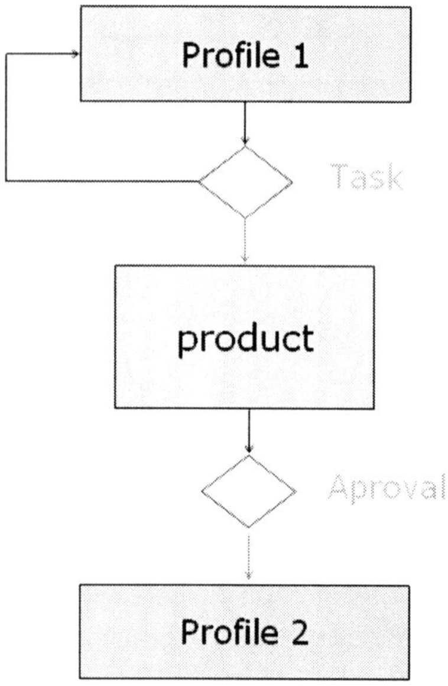

Exemplification of the Incremental Design Method of Systems: E-DIS Project

We present hereafter the instantiation of our design method in the process of design, development and implantation of E-DIS, an e-health system already in operation in the "Hospital de Sant Pau" in Barcelona. E-DIS (electronic dysphagia) is a telemedicine system that aims to change the model of the treatment of oropharyngeal dysphagia of neurological origin through the use of information technology. The part of the treatment that is replaced by E-DIS is related to oropharyngeal praxis. Patients who carry out this part of the treatment watch several videos where the doctor performs the exercises and gives specific instructions for proper performance. Once mastered the exercise, the patient records each exercise on video and sends it through the system so that the person responsible for implementing therapy review and make its recommendations (Bascuñana, et al, 2009).

The hypothesis is that use of the E-DIS system is comparable to conventional therapy in terms of patient outcomes. The E-DIS system should allow:

1) That more patients access to treatment: Is estimated that through the E-DIS system a speech therapist may review up to three times more patients at the time of a conventional session (1 hour).
2) Reduce the cost of treatment with regard to conventional therapy.
3) A clinical outcome comparable to conventional therapy.
4) The added benefit of facilitating and possibly improve the clinical work (Bascuñana, et al, 2009).

Application of Incremental Design Method

Phase 1: Problem

- **Phase 1 Aim:** Acknowledge the problem to solve, what is the target of the project and what is the aim to be met by the artifact to be developed.
- **Task Assignment:** In this phase the main task is assigned to the Business Team in conjunction with the client or partner involved in the project, who knows the need and how it should be met. The task of the Business Team is, in the first instance, to recognize if we can meet the requirements of the customer or partner and, then, identify how the project aim can be met in the most efficient possible way.
- **Implementation in the E-DIS project:** In the case of E-DIS project, the need was to facilitate the praxis to patients and to reduce costs involved in carrying out the dysphagia therapy in the hospital or medical center. The dysphagia patients are people with some degree of neurological damage and the costs of moving from home to hospital is too high. Besides, another problem is given by the inefficiency that means for medical personnel attend only 2 patients per hour at fixed schedules. Then the project aim was to create a system that would, at the beginning, to maximize the time of the therapist in patient care and, secondly, reduce the economic costs for both the patient and the health system. The initial aim was to allow the medical staff to review the exercises performed by the patient from their PC and then to provide medical advice and suggestions.
- **Conclusion:** From this point, the Design and Technical Area are able to start the creative work.

Phase 2: Concept

- **Phase 2 Aim:** Propose a conceptual solution to the problem by identifying the aims that must be reached by the artifact
- **Task Assignment:** At this phase all branches of the team collaborate, including customer or project partner, because in this phase we try to generate ideas and proposals that will form the basis of the project.
- **Implementation in the E-DIS project:** For E-DIS the conceptual proposal was simple and concrete. As a general aim we need the patient to be able to send video by Internet so the therapist could review it and decide whether the exercise was properly performed. The specific aim was to ensure proper recording of the video by the patient and its subsequent transmission. Technically, the goal was clear: We needed to record digital video, we needed the patient to attach a video file and we needed the therapist received the video in his mailbox.
- **Conclusion:** At the end of this phase, the team is confident to meet the main and

can start finding the best solutions to the problem.

Phase 3: Proposal

- **Phase 3 Aim:** The initial proposal consists in what can fulfil the main aim of the artifact with the minimum elements.
- **Task Assignment:** In this phase the tasks are divided between the Business Team, which fully meets the aim to be met by the proposal; the Design Team, which should make the user with minimal elements fulfilling the aim of the project; and the Technical Team, which should begin to identify technological needs that the project must satisfy.
- **Implementation in the E-DIS project:** In this case, we had all the tools at our fingertips. From the point of view of content, we needed the doctor to teach patients how to perform the exercise. Using a conventional video camera we filmed the doctor performing the exercises and we edit it on a DVD, which later the patient could see on his computer or on his DVD player. In a parallel way, the medical team was looking for 4 or 5 patients who form the initial target group. At this early stage they found a group of patients with different levels of neurological damage and who count with the necessary technological tools in their home. This was an Internet-connected computer equipped with a Webcam. The next stage of the Work Flow was initial testing. In these tests we noticed how the patient could see a doctor to perform the exercises and then he was able to repeat by himself or assisted by a relative or carer.

  Obviously, in patients with high neurologic damage the test outcome was less successful than in patients with low level of damage, because it is too difficult to them to keep the focus on an activity and to understand that he was undergoing tests. Thanks to these tests we were unable to determine that in those patients with high neurologic damage is essential to help a family member or assistant carer. In technical terms, we determined that the recorded video must have very special characteristics in order to be sent over the Internet without data transfer problems. With this preliminary solution we note that the project aim could meet with the minimum available elements. We get the patient not to move from his home and, with this; we get the expected cost savings. If we consider that for each therapy session the patient's family must pay an ambulance or special taxi that takes him to the hospital, spending at least 3 or 4 hours to going to the hospital, do therapy and going back to home, we believe that the aims are met favourably. From these tests was possible, with the medical team, to determine the next steps, both technical point of view -the artifact in its next version should meet certain technical requirements and interaction with the patient- and medical standpoint -to more accurately determine which patients were most suitable for further testing.
- **Conclusion:** At the end of this phase, the team is certain that the technological resources necessary to carry out the project exist.

Phase 4: Prototype

- **Phase 4 Aim:** To produce an enhanced version of the artifact, even in prototype level, but close to the final solution.
- **Task Assignment:** In this phase the most work is on the Design and Technical teams,

because it is where the artifact must to be highly developed. It is the phase that involves more work, because we passed from a solution almost sketch-level to an implementation close to the final artifact. In the stage of testing and reporting, customer or project partner must also have an important participation by providing conclusions from their views and interests.

- **Implementation in the E-DIS project:** For this phase we developed a Web application that would integrate all profiles involved in the system. We managed a database of doctor profile -responsible of general therapy-, therapist profile -manager of a group of patients- and patient profile.

  The medical team considered good the possibility of grouping the patients into 4 or 5 people and put them in charge of a therapist. The doctor responsible for the therapy plays a role of supervisor throughout the process. From a design standpoint, the application proposed a graphical user interface to enable all profiles interact seamlessly with the artifact. The whole process of exercise could be done within the application. Each person had a user name and password, and once inside, could perform tasks assigned to him. Thus the patient could come in, check which session has to perform, -of a total of 15-, review the videos that the doctor had prepared for each exercise and perform by himself/herself or assisted by a carer. Subsequently, the system allows attach and send the video made. The recorded video came directly to the profile page of the therapist to whom the patient was assigned. So, he could review the exercise performed by the patient and comment approval or tips to improve the practice face the next day of therapy.

  In this case, the target group consisted of 15 patients, again selected by the medical responsible, and the test period was 15 days in which the patient should send every day the amount of videos due to him/her. At this phase we found new problems, for example, the stress can cause an information system in people of certain age (resistance to change) and problems of use and interaction of some patients with the Web application. We note that the system should be even simpler, both in access to information as to the tasks the patient and therapist should meet within the system.

  For these findings is currently working on what would be the Phase 4.1, refining the last details of the prototype and hoping that the proposal is as close as possible to the final solution to be tested by a group of users in many much higher. It is estimated that the test may involve other hospitals locally and reach the amount of 150 patients.
- **Conclusion:** After having completed this phase, the artifact works properly in terms of technology, content and use to fulfil the aim of the project, but still presents problems to the end user on interaction and usability issues and certain levels of content still in process of definition.

Phase 5: Product/Service

- **Phase 5 Aim:** Finish defining the artifact in all design aspects.
- **Task Assignment:** At this phase again the main players are the Design and Technical team. The level of detail should reach 100% and the artifact should not present problems in any aspect. The Business

Table 5.

Project	Aim
E-SCHI	E-SCHI is a project that aims to develop a Web application that enables support in the treatment of patients with schizophrenia.
E-TONA	The E-TONA project is an application for mobile devices that allow control the diet in overweight teenagers.
E-FREN	The E-FREN project is a management system of evidence in a medical specialty.
CISMA	CISMA is a project to support decision making in primary care mental health.
E-FER	Project to support the diagnosis and treatment of wounds.
E-PARK	The E-PARK is a system to support the implementation assisted by a measurement scale of Parkinson disease.
E-COGNITIÓN	E-COGNITION is a cognitive rehabilitation system for cognitive impairment.
E-TRAN	E-TRAN is a system for monitoring transfusion.

Team must verify that the artifact fully meets the project aims and the client must approve the tool.

- **Implementation in the E-DIS project:** The E-DIS project in this moment is precisely at this phase of development. We are finishing out the details to solve the problems found in the tests of Phase 4 and the project partner for its part is determining the amount and profile of users (patients), which will be needed for the final testing stage.
- **Conclusion:** As in the prototype phase there will be a definitive approach to the final solution, it is expected that after the last test with users on a local level, the artifact is ready to be used and marketed nationally and, at best cases, globally.

Other Projects in which It was Applied the Incremental Design Method

As mentioned before, this design method has been tested on 9 projects related to knowledge management and online health. In Table 5 we can mention, beside E-DIS system, 8 prototyping experiences.

PROBLEMS

The main disadvantage of our design method is at the same time our biggest challenge in the short term. We must work on testing and validation of our proposal by the scientific community of engineering and design. In terms of operational and functional, we believe the method that we developed is consistent in the context we work and so far has brought us significant benefits, such as having the capacity to respond to different problems in the context of e-business and e - health in various projects and do so effectively and efficiently. The response to our work we found in the good relationship observed with our customers and partners in different realized and in development projects, but now we have to get the answer in scientific and research terms. It is our lack, but also the next step in our investigation.

FUTURE RESEARCH DIRECTIONS

In general terms, from our experience we believe that is possible to develop other projects to implement systems of technical support for teams to base their activities in workflows. Our experience shows that the results are favourable, so we believe that this issue can be widely developed in other work fields.

If we think in future research and application possibilities for our proposal, one of the major challenges for our team is open precisely the range of possible economic sectors where our design method of IT artifacts can be applied. So far we have concentrated on the online health sector because it represents an unexplored world with many possibilities both research and business, but we also want to test our work method in other business sectors that might be benefited by the application of information technologies in their bases of operation. A map of all sectors that can be explored can be drawn and the outlook is encouraging, because we can imagine possible e-business projects in such diverse sectors as construction and food services, but that have as a common denominator that can be affected favourably by IT from their most basic levels (Figure 4).

In this sense, we believe in the great possibilities of life "connected". We believe IT will have an important participation in almost all sectors of contemporary society. This will force companies, governments and investment sectors to change their bases and their business strategies to levels that are still unexpected. Perhaps what we know today as e-business is the only possible form of business, what we known as e-health is the only form of health and that everything around us is connected and supported by Internet and communications. In fact, someone already talks about the 'Internet of Things' and some opportunities are emerging to exploit the new network connections. Unfortunately it is not enough how the business models will be in this new era and it is very difficult to hazard something, because even the global stage comes as somewhat nebulous. Nevertheless, we believe efforts will go in that direction, to explore and exploit the use of sensors and devices that enable things are interconnected and through this to discover new business opportunities in sectors hitherto thought.

CONCLUSION

After our experience in projects in the field of e-business and e-health that have been mentioned in this chapter, the first conclusion that we propose is to highlight the importance of Design in these business areas. Design was recognized as a competitive differentiator element in the industrial production culture, but in the information age

Figure 4. Map of services which may be affected by Internet and IT

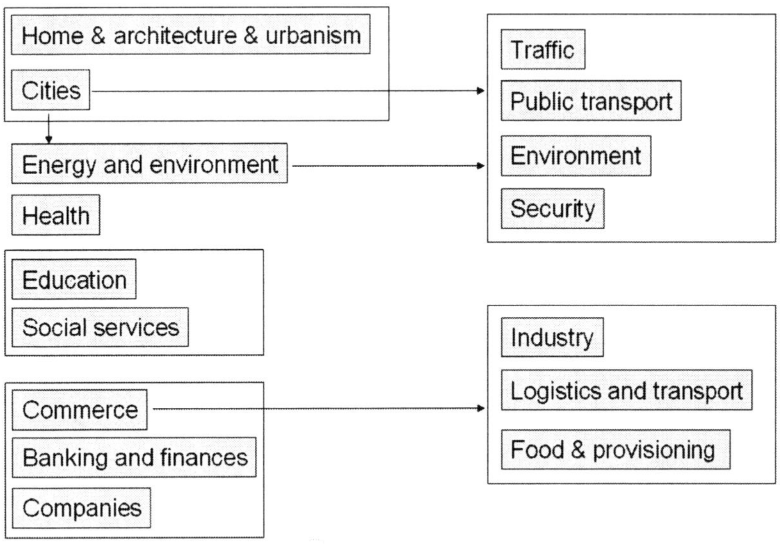

emerges as a factor of relevance when managing knowledge and developing innovative solutions in service delivery. Innovation, product of design efforts is probably the most precious resource of the modern economy, in opinion of some authors as Purao (et al, 2008).

In the quest to manage design, we presented our working method called Incremental Design Method for Systems, which until now has been tested in 9 health-related online projects. This method has been proposed with reference to the design method based on phases of Pahl and Beitz (1995), but modified according to our experience in the area of e-business and specifically in e-health. The most striking conclusion of the use of this method is the little time invested in the production of artifacts and how successful the results towards end users, to which the application comes with the bare minimum of content, technological and use errors, due to the iterative conception, design and development process.

Once we find the field that allows us to manage project development opportunities, the next step was to find the best way to manage the workflow between the different profiles that interact in the work team. The search of such a methodology has been working under the premise of "test-mistake", until we find a way to provides better results in terms of effectiveness and efficiency. The results obtained showed that in the 'time' factor we have developed artifacts and set them up using fewer hours of work -compared to previous projects with similar characteristics- and in the 'efficiency' factor we have seen that the results have been satisfactory for the 3 key players in any e-health project: Provider of technology or technological artifact, the client and the end user.

With this method based on cycles of phases that produce prototypes that increase their functionality as progress through the process, we believe that we minimizing the possibility of market failure because the artifact has passed 3 or 4 steps of testing with real users before go out to compete in the market.

We now believe that the method is mature enough to be validated by the scientific and the engineering and design community, from the point of view of science and research, and to be implemented in other business sectors, from the commercial and services point of view. These items are our biggest challenge in the near future. The publication of this chapter is our first step in that long way.

Just today we focus on the health sector, we hope to expand our research capabilities and scope and propose, from other business sectors from the large field of e-business, new views on future deliveries of reports on Internet based business.

REFERENCES

Adler-Milstein, J. (2009). Health Care Requires Big Changes to Complement New IT. *Harvard Business Review*, (April): 2009.

Bascuñana, H., Blanco, B., Rivero, Y., Monguet, J., Muñoz, J., & Sampieri, M. (March 2009). A telehealth approach to oropharyngeal dysphagia therapy; Paper presented at the 5th World Congress of International Society of Physical Medicine and Rehabilitation, Istanbul, Turkey, June 14, 2009.

Bernal, C. Jairo (2005). Diseño conceptual de productos asistido por ordenador: Un estudio analítico sobre aplicaciones y definición de la estructura básica de un nuevo programa. Doctoral dissertation, Universitat Politècnica de Catalunya, Spain.

Bonsiepe, G. (2000). Una Tecnología Cognoscitiva - De la producción de conocimientos hacia la presentación de conocimientos. Simposium Ricerca+Design, Milano, 2000.

Chuan Jun Su. (2007). *Mobile multi-agent based, distributed information platform (MADIP) for wide-area e-health monitoring; Science Direct.* Elsevier.

European Commission, Enterprise & Industry Directorate General. (2008). ICT standards in the health sector: current situation and prospects. [A Sectoral e-Business Watch study by Empirica.]. *Special Study No.*, *1*, 2008.

Herzlinger, R. (2006). Why Innovation in Health Care Is So Hard. *Harvard Business Review*, (May): 2006.

Hevner, A., March, S., Park, J., & Ram, S. (2004). Design science in information systems research. *Management Information Systems Quarterly*, *28*(1), 75–105.

Hollanders, H., & Van Cruysen, A. (2009). *Design, Creativity and Innovation: A Scoreboard Approach*. Pro Inno. Innometrics.

Maheu, M., Whitten, P., & Allen, A. (2001). *E-Health, Telehealth, and Telemedicine. A Guide to Start-up and Success*. New York: Jossey-Bass W. Wiley Company.

March, S., & Storey, V. (2008). Design science in the information systems discipline: An introduction to the special issue on design science research. *Management Information Systems Quarterly*, *32*(4), 725–730.

Ostergaard, K., & Summers, J. (2009). Development of a systematic classification and taxonomy of collaborative design activities. [London, England.]. *Journal of Engineering Design*, (February): 2009.

Pahl, G., & Beitz, W. (1995). *Engineering Design: A systematic approach; Springer Science and Business media*. London: Springer Verlag.

Purao, S; Baldwin, C.; Hevner, A; Storey, V.; Pries-Heje, J; Smith, B.; Zhu, Y. (2008). The Sciences of Design: Observations on an Emerging Field; Working Paper; Harvard Business School.

ADDITIONAL READING

Bereiter, C. (2002). Design Research for Sustained Innovation. Cognitive Studies. *Bulletin of the Japanese Cognitive Science Society*, *9*(3), 321–327.

Bertola, P., & Teixeira, J. (2002). Design as a knowledge agent: How design as a knowledge process is embedded into organizations to foster innovation. [Washington, DC: Elsevier Science Ltd.]. *Design Studies*, *24*, 2002.

Candi, M. (2007). The role of design in the development of technology-based services. [Washington, DC: Elsevier Ltd.]. *Design Studies*, 24.

Casadesus-Masanell, R., & Ricart, J. (2007) Competing through Business Models. IESE Business School, University of Navarra; Working Paper; WP no 713; November, 2007.

Chu, C.-H., & Han-Chung, C. (2007). *Business Model Innovation through Collaborative Product Development: A Case Study of Design Services in Taiwan*. Taiwan: IEEE.

Cross, N. (1989). *Engineering Design Methods*. Chichester, UK: Wiley.

Cross, N. (2007). *From a Design Science to a Design Discipline: Understanding Designerly Ways of Knowing and Thinking. Design Research Now. Essays and Selected Projects*. Berlín: Birkhäuser Verlag AG.

Johnson, M., Christensen, C., & Kagermann, H. (2008). Reinventing Your Business Model. *Harvard Business Review*, (December): 2008.

Tergan, S., & Keller, T. (Eds.). (2005). Visualizing Knowledge and Information: An Introduction; Knowledge and Information Visualization. (LNCS 3426, pp. 1 – 23,)2005. Springer-Verlag Berlin Heidelberg.

Younghwa Lee; Kozar, K. (2006); Investigating the effect of website quality on e-business success: An analytic hierarchy process (AHP) approach. Decision Support Systems. Elsevier

Youn-Kyung, L., Blevis, E., & Stolterman, E. (207) Grand Challenges in Design Research for Human-Centered Design Informatics. In D. Schuler (Ed.): Online Communities and Social Computation. HCII 2007, (LNCS 4564, pp. 106–115,) 2007. Springer-Verlag Berlin Heidelberg.

Chapter 14
Specifications for a Website Audit Tool for Small Businesses

Stephen Burgess
Victoria University, Australia

ABSTRACT

These days, small businesses typically have a web presence beyond their own website, employing the services of other online providers to host details of their businesses and hopefully attract more customers to them. This chapter examines the notion of a web presence audit tool for small businesses to enable them to track the various website features that they have implemented on their own, and other, websites over time. A 'website feature' can be something as simple as listing the business address and telephone number on the website, but it can also include more advanced features such as online ordering and purchasing. The chapter discusses the specifications for such a website audit tool and suggests a relational database design for the tool. The resultant specifications are to be trialed in a number of settings before being introduced to a wider group of small businesses.

INTRODUCTION

This chapter examines the notion of a web presence audit tool for small businesses to enable them to track the various website features that they have implemented on their own, and other, websites over time and to enable them to monitor which website features competitors are implementing. The need for such a tool has been identified by the author in a number of research studies that have shown that small businesses often 'forget' to include common website features on their website – especially after a website redesign. The chapter discusses the specifications for such a website audit tool by examining the particular types of website features and where and when they will be hosted and suggests a relational database design for the tool that would allow small businesses to track their own use of website features over time.

DOI: 10.4018/978-1-61692-880-3.ch014

BACKGROUND

Small businesses face many challenges in relation to effective website use - they are often poor planners, have limited resources (skills; finances and available time), often do not know where to source relevant expertise and are overwhelmed by having to keep the business afloat on a day to day basis (Burgess, Sellitto & Karanasios 2009). One of the tools that small businesses are increasingly turning to is a website to help them to promote their goods and communicate with customers. For instance, a recent study of small businesses in Australia (Telstra Corporation 2009) revealed that 56% of small and medium sized enterprises had a website. The proportion of businesses with a website tended to increase as the size of the business increased (for instance, 46% of businesses with 1-2 employees had a website; 72% with 5-9 employees had a website; and 84% of businesses with 20-99 employees had a website).

Each of these websites consists of a combination of 'website features'. A 'website feature' can be something as simple as listing the business address and telephone number on the website, but it can also include more advanced features such as 'Frequently Asked Questions', web logs (blogs) and online ordering and purchasing. Typically, different website features will be incorporated by businesses in different industries. Over time, small businesses often add and remove some of these features without any (apparent) logical reason. In some instances, this can be because the feature has been overlooked during a website update or redesign and has just been forgotten in the newer version of the website. This has happened with features as simple as the business telephone number - which, when forgotten, can have serious implications when a key method of contacting the business is absent from the website (Burgess, Bingley & Sellitto 2007).

There are many ways to classify website features. Jelassi and Enders (2005) have suggested that 'virtual' dimensions could be used by a business to help them select which Internet features to employ when engaging with customers. They describe the dimensions as:

- *Virtual information space* – this includes online advertising and posting business information.
- *Virtual communication space* – is where the business engages in a two-way online communication with its customers, typically through email, chat facilities or bulletin boards.
- *Virtual distribution space* – allows for the delivery of digital goods (such as online books, software) and services (such as financial advice).
- *Virtual transaction space* – allows for the acceptance of online orders and payments.

Burgess et al (2009) suggest that website features typically fall into one of five categories:

- Features that help customers to locate and/or contact the business (such as the business address and telephone number).
- Features that tell a customer about the products and services of a business (for instance, online catalogues).
- Features that help to provide added value for goods and services (such as instructions on how to use products effectively).
- Features that assist in building an online community of customers (for instance, bulletin boards, blogs or 'wikis').
- Features that allow customers to order, pay for and sometimes even receive goods online (for instance, music downloads).

Different categories of website features can assist small businesses in different ways, by improving business efficiencies, adding value to products and services and generally assisting with the promotion of the business. Website features can thus be directly related to business benefits and matched to the overall business strategy and aims (Burgess et al 2009).

MAIN FOCUS OF THE CHAPTER

As mentioned previously, part of the background for this chapter comes from research into small businesses' use of their own websites and their use of portals and directory websites to support their operations.

Issues, Controversies, Problems

Deshpande, Chandrarathna and Ginige (2002) identify the origins of auditing as being in the thirteenth century. Initially, the term 'audit' was associated with an investigation of financial matters, but more recently has been applied to other disciplines- such as a 'safety audit', 'environmental audit' and 'information systems audit'. In a study of website accessibility, Witt and McDermott (2004) conducted an *audit* of academic websites in the United Kingdom. In relation to websites, the notion of using an 'audit' to determine if a business website is meeting a set of objectives (set either internally in the business or via some external study) is gaining momentum. Desphande et al (2002) suggest that many organisations will want their websites evaluated, or audited, with the view of improving them. They suggest that a website audit could cover a range of aspects. Some of these are:

- Aesthetic appeal
- Whether page construction adheres to standards
- If the website is easy to navigate
- The policy and procedures associated with managing website security
- The method used to keep information on the website up to date.

In a study of Croatian hotel websites, Spremic, Jakovic and Bach (2008) suggest that a website audit can be used to assess the quality of a website, examining its usability (how easy the website is to use), functionality (the services that are offered on the website) and reliability (attributes, such as the level of security, that affect the level of trust of users in the website). Deshpande et al (2002) also identified a number of issues that have arisen in website auditing. These include:

- The many purposes for which websites may be built
- The lack of standard processes for developing and maintaining websites
- The lack of available tools and techniques available for development.

A website 'audit tool' that records activity at the 'website feature' level could be seen as being one of the tools which could help to fill these gaps and would allow businesses to record which website features they have implemented over time and could act as a checklist/ reminder to ensure that website features are not forgotten during major updates or redesigns. The idea for such a tool emerged when the author was interviewing experts in the small business field in relation to how small businesses can effectively plan for, implement and maintain their websites (Burgess 2008).

... interviewees mentioned the idea of archiving various parts of the business analysis – such as the content of the business web presence (and even the content of competitors' websites) over time. One interviewee even suggested that the reason for selecting various website features should be stored so that strategies over time could be reviewed. (Burgess 2008: 158)

The idea of keeping some type of record of website features had been proposed by the author beforehand. As far back as 1999, Burgess and

Table 1. The competitor comparison matrix (adapted from Burgess and Schauder 1999)

FEATURE	FIRM 1	FIRM 2	FIRM 3	FIRM 4	FIRM 5	Total
BASIC PRODUCT DETAILS						
Static product catalogue	1	1	1			3
Online product catalogue				1	1	2
Images	1	1	1	1	1	5
Prices	1	1	1	1	1	5
TRANSACTION DETAILS						
Online Ordering	1		1			2
Online Payment	1					1
INFORMATION						
About the Business	1	1				2
About Trade Shows/ Coming Events	1		1			2
Web Site Navigation screen	1		1	1		3
EXTRAS (added value)						
Frequently Asked Questions	1					1
Directions on how to use the product	1	1				2
GENERAL LINKS						
Basic Internet Feature Sites	1		1			2
Search Engines	1					1
CONTACT DETAILS						
Email	1	0.5	1	1	1	4.5
Guestbook		1				1
By Form			1			1

Schauder (1999) proposed the use of a spreadsheet to (crudely) record the website features on competitor websites for the purposes of keeping up to date with their strategies. Table 1 shows an adapted version of the *competitor comparison matrix* (as it was then labeled). In this instance, some of the website features of the five major competitors of a fictional business are shown. However, the purpose of the matrix at that stage was not as much for audit purposes, rather to see where a business was positioned according to the web activities of its competitors:

An analysis of the web sites of competitors can quickly tell a company the stage that they are at in relation to an online presence within their industry. A simple matrix can be used to document the main features of, say, a company's five major competitors, to determine where the company stands amongst its competitors in the scale ranging between early adopter and late adopter. Where a competitor already has a particular feature fully implemented on their web site, a score of one is given. Where the feature is partly implemented, a fraction is awarded... As further features become commonplace amongst competitors or on the Internet, extra rows can be added. If the firm has no Internet presence at all, a comparison table such as this can show the features which may be necessary when building the site initially. It also shows what features that may be introduced that have not been adopted by competitors where it may be possible to gain a short term competitive advantage. (Burgess 1999)

There is another need for a web presence audit tool. Small businesses can look beyond their own business website when determining what is best for them. There are now many more options available to a small business when setting up their Internet presence. Many of these are associated with portals. A portal is a special website designed to act as a gateway to give access to other related sites. Portals were originally intended to be 'base sites' that users would keep returning to after accessing these other sites, and are often seen as a starting point for specific groups of users when they access the Internet. What is special about portals is the way that these websites can be used to facilitate access to other sites that may be closely related, in the case of specialist portals, or quite diverse in the case of general portals. Portals now offer a range of services, including online transactions facilities. The possible benefits to small businesses is that the possibility now exists for small businesses to have access to website features that they may not previously have had access to because of their complexity or setup cost (Tatnall, Burgess & Singh, 2004).

Portals perform many different functions, but their main core elements (described by Eisenmann, Hallowell & Tripsas 2002) are search, content, community building, commerce and 'personal productivity' applications. The primary question for small businesses is whether portals are going to provide these services on a more cost effective or efficient basis than they could themselves, or even provide services that they are not capable of providing. This is where the choice to have a feature on a business' own website, or whether to use one of these services, is considered. For instance, some of the advantages that portals offer to small businesses are a secure environment and infrastructure for online transactions, a search and directory service and features such as blogs and message boards for enhancing community and regional relationships (Tatnall et al, 2004) – and, in many instances these are online services that small businesses are not readily able to offer themselves.

Thus, it is necessary to now consider that the online presence of a small business will often go beyond its own website to an additional presence on other websites. This can be labeled as the 'extended web' and the presence of small businesses across different types of websites to be their 'web presence' (Burgess 2006).

Summarising, small businesses now have options other than their own websites in which to build their web presence. For instance, a small accommodation business may wish to use the booking engine offered by specialised accommodation or regional portals, meaning that they can perhaps reach a wider market and will not need to concern themselves with the technology involved in online booking engines. It is not unusual for small accommodation businesses to be listed on the websites of many different online accommodation services (Bingley, Sellitto & Burgess 2009). In the case of small manufacturing firms there may be attractions in using the online shopping cart features of a regional portal or industry portal. Again, this may provide access to more customers without having to be concerned with developing the 'shopping cart' technology or becoming involved in complex negotiations to set this up on their own websites. A simpler example of an 'extended web' presence is when a small business provides its basic contact information to regional or industry portals. This can be quite inexpensive and, because the information does not change readily, is relatively easy to maintain. A more specialised example is where a business may wish to attract potential customers to a region, and realises that a regional portal has a listing of all of the tourist attractions and the latest events in the region. The business may have been thinking about introducing such a feature on their website, but if it is available elsewhere why should they repeat these on their own website? They could rely on customers seeing this information as they link to the business through the regional portal, or perhaps more realistically provide a link back to the specific page on the portal (Burgess 2008).

The role of a website audit tool becomes even more important in this environment as the website features of a small business are typically spread across a number of different websites that form part of the small business web presence. The content and existence of these website features will be reviewed and/or upgraded at different times. Sometimes this will be at the discretion of the small business, but it may also occur at the instigation of the external partner, as contracts for portal and other services expire at different times or as they review or upgrade their services. The audit tool can assist in keeping track of which website features are stored on a small business' own website and which are hosted elsewhere. Thus, when the content of a particular website feature changes (such as a telephone number or an email address) the business will know where to look in its website presence to update it. The tool can also help to keep track of the cost of these externally hosted options and when contracts are due to expire or payments come due - which can provide further assistance in planning for the online presence (Burgess 2008).

Keep it Simple

The audit tool must be easy to use by small business operators. It has already been mentioned that they face limited resources in relation to their use of websites – especially limited time and often limited technical skills – and so they do not need a tool that will complicate things even further.

One of the considerations is what level to go to when recording details about the particular website features. For instance, a quick look at Table 1 reveals a quite simple list of website features. Let us consider two of them – static product catalogue and online product catalogue. The difference between these is whether the catalogue has been manually entered via HTML or is directly connected to the business' product database. Obviously, the first is easier to set up (if there are not too many products). The second is more costly to set up, but is more flexible in that it can 'queried' by web users and will alter when the product database alters. With a static product catalogue that is not linked to a product database, the business will need to update its own product database *and* its website separately when product details change.

However, there are many more details that could be recorded here. How *much* detail is listed about products? The level of detail can range from bare details to identifying a product individually to complicated descriptions of what the product is and what it can be used for. This will differ according to the type of product being offered and the level of information the business wishes to provide for it. So – the question to ask is – does the audit tool need to record the *level* of detail associated with product listings? Probably not. The simple description as outlined in Table 1 will suffice for most businesses. This principle will be followed in the next sections.

Solutions and Recommendations: Specifications for a Small Business Web Presence Audit Tool

The first phase of the project (preliminary work for this is reported here) draws upon the author's previous work to develop the initial version of the tool. Although it is intended for the tool to eventually be developed so that it can be used online, for the purposes of demonstration during interviews (described later), the tool will initially be developed using the database program, Microsoft Access. The advantage of using Access is that once the functionality of the application is established it can be readily translated to the online environment. As MS Access is part of the Microsoft Office family of products it can operate on most standard computing environments.

Table 2. Details of the website feature classification table

Field name	Key	Description
Website classification name	P	Key identifier for the website classification
Website classification description		Description of the website classification

Table 3. Initial values of website feature classification table

Website classification name	Website classification description
Contact	Features that help customers to locate and/or contact the business
About	Features that tell a customer about the products and services of a business
Value	Features that help to provide added value for goods and services
Community	Features that assist in building an online community of customers
E-business	Features that allow customers to order, pay for and sometimes even receive goods online

Thus, it is appropriate at this stage to suggest a simple relational database design when considering the specifications of the tool. Such a design needs to consider a number of different factors as will now be discussed.

Recording the Features of the Website of a Business

A good starting point for the database is the categories of website features identified earlier in this paper. This table will contain fields that describe the broad classifications of website features as identified in Table 2. From henceforth the 'Key' column identifies the fields that comprise the primary key ('P') and any foreign keys ('F') in the table. The primary key allows unique identification of any record in the table and a foreign key is any value in a table that must match the primary key value in another table.

Initially, the values for the table will be as suggested earlier in the paper (and are listed in Table 3). Of course, the advantage of storing these classifications in a separate database table is that if there is any reason to add in a new classification it just requires a new entry in the table.

One of the suggestions of the interviewees that raised the idea of the audit tool for small businesses was that it would be able to provide a history of when the small business introduced or removed different website features to/from its website. Thus, the author felt that an 'Audit' table would serve the purpose of recording when a particular audit of website features occurred. This might occur on a regular or ad hoc basis, or even when a change to website features is made. Table 4 shows the fields contained in the Audit table.

Note that the selection of a particular date as the primary key for this table assumes that more than one audit is not carried out in a particular

Table 4. Details of the audit table

Field name	Key	Description
Audit date (dd Mth yyyy)	P	The date of the audit is used as the basis for identifying individual audits.
Reason for audit		Description of the reason for the audit.

Table 5. Typical values of audit table

Audit date	Reason for audit
10 Mar 2009	Initial audit of website features
30 Jun 2009	Regular audit of website features
15 Sep 2009	Audit due to website redesign
31 Dec 2009	Regular audit of website features

day. If the time taken to complete an audit became an issue (that is, if it took longer than one day to complete the audit and the business wished to keep a record of this) then it might be necessary to add another field to the table, such as 'End of Audit date'.

Table 5 shows some potential values of the Audit table. These values represent the initial audit, a regular audit occurring very six months and a special audit that occurred due to a website redesign.

The main database table would be the one presenting the actual website features. This is represented in Table 6.

Each website feature would have to have a website classification code assigned to it – which would match one of the codes in Table 3.

Table 7 shows the initial values of the website feature table. These have been taken from Burgess et al (2009). The list can be extended by adding further records to the table as the business considers extending its web presence. Note that under normal circumstances a business may have more than one location, or telephone number or even multiple email addresses (such as contact@businessname.com and support@businessname.com). The reader is reminded that this audit tool does not store the actual instances of these details – it is just meant to be a prompt to the small business to actually include these features (or at least *choose* not to include the feature). Note also that one particular feature may serve more than one purpose. For instance, an email form may be set up for someone to just make contact with the business, so it would fit the category of contact. However, the business may set up a second email form on its website to specifically deal with requests for product support. This would fit into the 'Value' category. Similarly, a bulletin board may be set up to encourage goodwill and discussion amongst customers ('Community') or it may be set up to deal specifically with product support ('Value'). To keep the system easy to use, it would seem logical that if one feature were used for two purposes then the most prominent classification would be selected. Again – the notion is to ensure that the feature is at *considered* for inclusion on the website.

Note the last entry in Table 7. A business may not necessarily put its own website address on its own website – but this 'feature' comes in useful later on in the development of the database when the extended web presence is examined.

One of the complications of building the audit tool will be deciding upon how to handle user-generated content (UGC), such as weblogs (or 'blogs'). UGC occurs where website users directly contribute to the content of a website and typically takes the form of text (in reviews of products or services or comments on a particular discussion point), pictures or even video. The author was involved in a study that reviewed UGC on 33 travel websites (Cox, Burgess, Sellitto & Buultjens 2008)

Table 6. Details of the website feature table

Field name	Key	Description
Website feature name	P	Key identifier for the website feature
Website feature description		Description of the website classification
Website classification code	F	Website Feature Classification

Table 7. Initial values of website feature table

Website feature name	Website feature description	Website classification code
Business name	Name of the business	About
Address	Physical location of business	Contact
Location map	Map of physical location	Contact
Telephone number	Telephone number	Contact
Fax number	Fax number	Contact
Email address	Email address	Contact
Online form	Simple form to allow customers to contact the business	Contact
Offerings	General description of products and/or services offered	About
Catalogue	Product catalogue	About
External links	Links to other websites	About
Local events	Listing of or links to events in the area	About
FAQ	Answers to Frequently asked questions about the business or its offerings	Value
Product support	Instructions on how to use products or employ services	Value
Personal product support	Personalised email form to request product support	Value
Bulletin board	To facilitate customer communication with the business and with each other	Community
Order facility	Ability to place orders or make bookings (without payment)	E-business
Online payments	Ability to make payments online	E-business
Goods download	Download of goods (such as digital music)	E-business
Website address	The URL of the business website.	About

which classified a sample of 1240 comments made on these websites into three categories:

- UGC blog (comments added by website users – which made up 45% of all comments)
- Website content (comments added by the website operators – 32% of all comments)
- Affirmation comments (comments to finish a discussion – such as 'yes', 'OK' and 'thanks' – 23% of all comments).

It is not felt by the author that the audit tool should be concerned with these categories of comments – at this stage. What it might mean is that in the near future other *Community* website features are added to reflect UGC content, which might be considered to be similar to the 'Bulletin Board' feature listed in Table 7. These could include user reviews, weblogs, picture areas and/or video diaries – or combinations of these.

In the UGC study, comments were also analysed as to whether they expressed an opinion, seeked an opinion, updated others about a specific travel destination, involved 'thinking by writing', released emotional tension or mentioned that they changed their travel plans due to participating in the blog. Clearly, the audit tool would not need to go to this level of detail.

Moving on, a table is needed to record the *instances* of website features being used at different audit times. Table 8 shows how the two tables, Audit and Website Feature, can be combined to produce a series of records that can show when a particular website feature is recorded for each

Table 8. Details of the website audit table

Field name	Key	Description
Audit date (dd Mth yyyy)	P (F)	The date of the audit is used as the basis for identifying individual audits
Website feature name	P (F)	Key identifier for the website feature
Feature status		The status of the website feature – Static or Dynamic

audit date. Note that there has been one extra field added to classify the different types of website features. It was shown in an earlier example that there was some value in having a field that recorded whether a website field was 'static' (that is, entered directly into HTML) or 'dynamic' (content automatically generated – such as from a product database or when a user enters a search that is linked to a database. The 'feature status' field can indicate whether the website feature is static or dynamic. The combination of Audit date and Website feature form the primary key for this table (representing a particular feature noted at the time of a particular audit). Note also that, individually, the audit date and website feature name are foreign keys and thus their values need to match those in the audit and website feature tables respectively.

If we use the earlier audit table (refer Table 5) as an example, our fictional business had their initial website audit on 10 March 2009. Let us assume that at this stage they had the most basic of websites – containing just contact details and some information about their offerings. The contents of the Website Audit table are shown in Table 9.

However, between this initial audit in March and the regular audit in June, the business had added in a 'frequently asked questions' page, a product catalogue (both static features) and a form to allow customers to ask for specific product support. After 30 June 2009, the Website Audit table would look similar to Table 10.

A major website redesign occurs after this. As a result, another website audit is carried out on 15 September 2009. The look of the website is improved substantially – but this is not recorded in the website audit tool as it is concerned with features and functionality – not aesthetics. However, there was some extra functionality that was added at this time that should be included in the Website audit table. The product catalogue was linked to the product database of the business and thus became 'dynamic'. Also, a real-time ordering and payment facility was added to the website. This is all reflected in Table 11.

Note that as the online product database is now automatically updated (from the business product

Table 9. Initial values of website audit table

Audit date	Website feature name	Feature status
10 Mar 2009	Business name	Static
10 Mar 2009	Address	Static
10 Mar 2009	Location map	Static
10 Mar 2009	Telephone number	Static
10 Mar 2009	Fax number	Static
10 Mar 2009	Email address	Static
10 Mar 2009	Offerings	Static

Table 10. Values of website audit table after website audit on 30 June 2009

Audit date	Website feature name	Feature status
10 Mar 2009	Business name	Static
10 Mar 2009	Address	Static
10 Mar 2009	Location map	Static
10 Mar 2009	Telephone number	Static
10 Mar 2009	Fax number	Static
10 Mar 2009	Email address	Static
10 Mar 2009	Offerings	Static
30 Jun 2009	Business name	Static
30 Jun 2009	Address	Static
30 Jun 2009	Location map	Static
30 Jun 2009	Telephone number	Static
30 Jun 2009	Fax number	Static
30 Jun 2009	Email address	Static
30 Jun 2009	Offerings	Static
30 Jun 2009	Catalogue	Static
30 Jun 2009	FAQ	Static
30 Jun 2009	Personal product support	Static

database) and the business purchase order and transactions databases are automatically updated (when a customer orders and pays for a product online), the feature status of these features can be described as 'dynamic'.

Recording the Features on the Extended Web

One of the key aspects of the audit tool is that it will not only be capable of keeping track of the website features on the business own' website, it should be capable of keeping track of where the business has features on other websites as part of its *extended web* presence – such as regional portals, industry directories and so forth. So, the first need here is to have a table that keeps track of these different service providers.

In order to consider what might be the typical website features stored on these websites, the author conducted an informal study in September 2009 of the 'extended' web presence of 20 Australian small businesses that had been studied during recent research projects. These businesses covered a wide range of areas: catering; retail; the arts; tours; accommodation; manufacturing and service areas. In order to do this, the author typed in the full name of the business (surrounded by quotation marks - for example "*business name*") into the Google search engine, and then selected the 'pages from Australia' search option. In most cases the businesses' own website was the top ranked item, or at least was very close to the top ranking. The author then searched through the various search returns that resulted, eliminating:

- Websites that contained a review of the business offerings or articles about the business (typically online newspaper articles).
- Other businesses that had listed the business as a client, or had been sponsored by the business (although it could perhaps be

Table 11. Values of website audit table after website audit on 15 September 2009

Audit date	Website feature name	Feature status
10 Mar 2009	Business name	Static
10 Mar 2009	Address	Static
10 Mar 2009	Location map	Static
10 Mar 2009	Telephone number	Static
10 Mar 2009	Fax number	Static
10 Mar 2009	Email address	Static
10 Mar 2009	Offerings	Static
30 Jun 2009	Business name	Static
30 Jun 2009	Address	Static
30 Jun 2009	Location map	Static
30 Jun 2009	Telephone number	Static
30 Jun 2009	Fax number	Static
30 Jun 2009	Email address	Static
30 Jun 2009	Offerings	Static
30 Jun 2009	Catalogue	Static
30 Jun 2009	FAQ	Static
30 Jun 2009	Personal product support	Static
15 Sep 2009	Business name	Static
15 Sep 2009	Address	Static
15 Sep 2009	Location map	Static
15 Sep 2009	Telephone number	Static
15 Sep 2009	Fax number	Static
15 Sep 2009	Email address	Static
15 Sep 2009	Offerings	Static
15 Sep 2009	Catalogue	Dynamic
15 Sep 2009	FAQ	Static
15 Sep 2009	Personal product support	Static
15 Sep 2009	Order facility	Dynamic
15 Sep 2009	Online payments	Dynamic

argued that the latter is some type of 'extended' web presence if it is planned).

- Other organisations that had used the products or services of the business and had listed this on their website (for instance, 'catered by xxxxxxx').
- Temporary listings – such as one-off events the business was involved with in some way.

Once these occurrences were ignored, what was left was typically a list of websites that the business had intentionally approached to be listed on their website and, in some cases, to use the online services they offered. The author examined between 5-10 of these 'external services' for each business. There did seem to be some patterns in relation to the types of features that businesses did prefer from other online service providers, but

Table 12. Details of the service provider table

Field name	Key	Description
Service provider	P	Key identifier for the service provider (usually the name)
Service provider description		Portal; directory
Service provider coverage		Local; State; National; International
Type of service		General; Industry; Event
Cost of service		Subscription; sign on fee'; free
Service commenced (dd Mon yyyy)		Date of commencement of the current service
Expiry of service (dd Mon yyyy)		Date of expiry of the current service ('ongoing' if no expiry date).

in some instances these may have been industry related. The types of features typically found on these sites were (in order of frequency):

- Business name
- Telephone number
- Address
- Location map
- Address of business website (URL)
- Email address
- Information about the business
- Email forms to contact the business
- Pictures of the business or its products
- Online booking/ purchasing facility (mainly for accommodation businesses and one manufacturing business).

Table 12 shows the details of the Service Provider table. Note that for each provider there is a distinction as to whether it is a portal (offering a variety of services, perhaps including online ordering and payments) or a directory service – just listing information about the business. There is also a suggestion of the level of coverage of its service – in the informal study some were just for local regions, one was 'state-wide', some were national and some were international sites. It is felt by the author that the distinction between local, state (or territory or province), national and international would fit small businesses in most areas. Next is the type of service – which may be general, industry based or instances where the service may be set up for a particular event (perhaps held just once or held regularly, such as an annual event). Finally, the cost of the service is considered. For the research, the author was mostly able to obtain this from the service providers' websites, but when practically applied the business will know the costing model from their dealings with the service provider. Lastly, the expiry date of the service is listed – this is important if the business does not wish to miss out on relisting on a particular service (for instance, if it misses or ignores reminder emails from the service to re-subscribe).

Table 13 provides some fictional values for the Service Provider table, assuming that the business started to use some free external service providers just before June 30, 2009 and then engaged a new subscription-based service during the website redesign before 15 September 2009.

So, now that the service provider details have been recorded it is possible to record the features that the business has listed with each provider. These can be recorded in the Service Provider-Website Feature table, the design of which is in Table 14.

Note that now the unique identifier for each record is made up of a combination of the date of the audit, the service provider and the particular website feature. Table 15 shows some fictional values for the service Provider- Website Features table (a portal [*'GenportA'*] and a directory service [*'LocDirA'*]. The audit on 30 June 2009 revealed

Table 13. Values of service provider table after website audit on 15 September 2009

Service Provider	Service Provider Description	Service Provider coverage	Type of Service	Cost of Service	Service commenced	Expiry of Service
GenportA	Portal	State	Industry	Free	25 Jun 2009	Ongoing
LocaldirA	Directory	Local	General	Free	25 Jun 2009	31 Jul 2010
GenportB	Portal	National	General	Subscription	15 Aug 2009	31 Aug 2010

Table 14. Details of the service provider - website feature table

Field name	Key	Description
Audit date (dd Mon yyyy)	P (F)	The date of the audit is used as the basis for identifying individual audits
Service provider	P (F)	Key identifier for the service provider (usually the name)
Website feature name	P (F)	Key identifier for the website feature
Feature status		The status of the website feature – Static or Dynamic

that two service providers were used, both with business name, location and telephone number stored, and one also with a location map. Note that the location map is considered to be 'dynamic' as it is automatically generated from the address of the business.

Note that by the time the audit on 15 September occurs that the business also subscribed to a new service provider, *GenportB*, where it has its business name, address, telephone number and website address listed, as well as having an online order and payments facility for real-time transactions. As mentioned earlier in the chapter, one typical reason that a small business will adopt these is because it does have the infrastructure or knowledge required to set one up itself.

Recording the Features of Competitors

When conducting interviews with the academics that suggested the idea of the audit tool, the interviewees were asked if they thought that there would be a need to keep a historical archive of the website features of competitors – and the answer was a clear 'no'. They felt that it was of some use to keep an eye on competitor websites at a moment in time ('now'), but that it was not an essential part of a website audit tool. Although not considered here, the possibility will remain to introduce this as part of the audit tool in the future. Of course, then a consideration would have to be given to keeping audit details of the *extended web* presence of competitors.

Recording Social Networking Websites

One challenge that has only been touched upon in this chapter is whether social networking websites, such as MySpace, Facebook and even Twitter, have a role to play as part of the audit tool. The simple fact of the matter is that some businesses, especially those that cater to younger customers, are starting up their own social networking websites that contain website features – but also allow users to generate their own content (UGC). The author feels that it will be relatively easy to amend the values in the Service Provider table (refer Table 12) to incorporate a new record for a social networking website – as has mentioned earlier about how these could be incorporated

Table 15. Values of service provider – website feature table after website audits

Audit date	Service Provider	Website feature name	Feature status
30 Jun 2009	GenportA	Business name	Static
30 Jun 2009	GenportA	Address	Static
30 Jun 2009	GenportA	Telephone number	Static
30 Jun 2009	LocalDirA	Business name	Static
30 Jun 2009	LocalDirA	Address	Static
30 Jun 2009	LocalDirA	Telephone number	Static
30 Jun 2009	LocalDirA	Location map	Dynamic
15 Sep 2009	GenportA	Business name	Static
15 Sep 2009	GenportA	Address	Static
15 Sep 2009	GenportA	Telephone number	Static
15 Sep 2009	LocalDirA	Business name	Static
15 Sep 2009	LocalDirA	Address	Static
15 Sep 2009	LocalDirA	Telephone number	Static
15 Sep 2009	LocalDirA	Location map	Dynamic
15 Sep 2009	LocalDirA	Website address	Static
15 Sep 2009	GenportB	Business name	Static
15 Sep 2009	GenportB	Address	Static
15 Sep 2009	GenportB	Telephone number	Static
15 Sep 2009	GenportB	Website address	Static
15 Sep 2009	GenportB	Order facility	Dynamic
15 Sep 2009	GenportB	Online payments	Dynamic

when they exist on the business website. There may need to be some consideration given to how UGC is handled on these websites, but such content would fall under the 'Community' classification of website features (refer Table 3).

FUTURE RESEARCH DIRECTIONS

Once the database has been developed, the second phase of the study involves interviews with academics with expertise in the applicability of information and communications technologies in small businesses. These interviews will form the basis for refinements made to the tool. Importantly, the interviews will be conducted with academics that are experts in the *practical* use of information technology by small businesses or who work closely with small businesses at an *applied* level.

Then, the modified version of the tool will be tested through its use by small businesses in a small business association that is known to the author. It is intended that initially twenty small businesses (that will have volunteered) will be exposed to the tool and asked to apply it to their business situation. They will be requested to fill in a short survey on the strengths and weakness of the tool. From this, a final version of the archival tool will be developed.

Obviously, it will not be possible to investigate long term opinions of the tool after its use over a short period of time, but it will be possible to gauge small business opinion as to the usefulness and applicability of the tool to their particular circumstances. Hopefully, monitoring and improvement of the audit tool will be ongoing with small businesses in other associations, with the audit tool eventually being implemented online.

CONCLUSION

This chapter is unusual in that much of it has been spent discussing the development of a database, a task which has been performed for many years and is not ground breaking. However, it is the context in which this database is developed that is important. The discussion surrounding the notion and development of the website presence audit tool is the major contribution of this chapter. After a discussion of website audits and the need for tools to assist in these, the specifications for the website audit tool have been developed to address a need of small businesses that has emerged due to an increasingly complex online world that not only involves the websites of small businesses, but also a series of other websites that they typically choose to have a presence on (the 'web presence').

REFERENCES

Bingley, S., Sellitto, C., & Burgess, S. (2009). The importance of third party websites: A study of small accommodation providers in Australia. *4Th International Scientific Conference "Planning for the Future - Learning from the Past: Contemporary Developments in Tourism, Travel & Hospitality"*. Rhodes Island, Greece.

Burgess, S. (2006). A model for B2C customer interactions on the web by small businesses: Adjustments for the 'Extended web'. *Grand Challenges in Technology Management: Proceedings of ISOneWorld 2006.* Las Vegas, Nevada.

Burgess, S. (2008). Determining website content for small businesses: Assisting the planning of Owner/Managers. *International Journal of Knowledge Management Studies*, *2*(1), 143–161. doi:10.1504/IJKMS.2008.016449

Burgess, S., Bingley, S., & Sellitto, C. (2007). A model for website content decisions in micro businesses. *Global Business & Economics Anthology*, *1*, 474–487.

Burgess, S., & Schauder, D. (1999). *Assisting small businesses to identify internet opportunities* (pp. 121–128). San Deigo, California: Millenial Challenges in Management Education, Cybertechnology and Leadership.

Burgess, S., Sellitto, C., & Karanasios, S. (2009). *Effective web presence solutions for small businesses: Strategies for successful implementation.* Hershey, PA: Information Science Reference.

Cox, C., Burgess, S., Sellitto, C., & Buultjens, J. (2008). *The influence of user-generated content on tourist travel behaviour*. Lismore, NSW, Australia: Australian Regional Tourism Research Centre.

Deshpande, Y., Chandrarathna, A., & Ginige, A. (2002). Web site auditing: First step towards re-engineering. *Proceedings of the 14th International Conference on Software Engineering and Knowledge Engineering(pp.* 731-737), Italy.

Eisenmann, T. R., Hallowell, R., & Tripsas, M. (2002). *Internet business models: Text and cases.* UK: McGraw-Hill Education-Europe.

Jelassi, T., & Enders, A. (2005). *Strategies for e-Business: Creating Value though Electronic and Mobile Commerce*. Upper Saddle River, NJ: Pearson Education.

Spremic, M., Jakovic, B., & Bach, M. P. (2008). Web metrics for managing quality and auditing croatian hotel web sites: Cluster analysis. *WSEAS Transactions on Systems*, *7*(3), 229–238.

Tatnall, A., Burgess, S., & Singh, M. (2004). Community and regional portals in australia: A role to play for small businesses? In Al-Qirim, N. (Ed.), *Electronic commerce in small to medium-sized enterprises: Frameworks, issues and implications* (pp. 304–320). Hershey, PA: Idea Group Publishing.

Telstra Corporation. (2009). *Sensis E:Business report: The online experience of small and medium enterprises*. Australia: Sensis.

Witt, N., & McDermott, A. (2004). Web site accessibility: What logo will we use today? *British Journal of Educational Technology*, *35*(1), 45–56. doi:10.1111/j.1467-8535.2004.00367.x

Chapter 15
An Approach to Efficient Waste Management for SMEs via RBVOs

Stamatia-Ann Katriou
ALTEC S.A., Greece

Ioannis Ignatiadis
Kingston University, UK

Garyfallos Fragidis
Technological Educational Institute of Serres, Greece

Evangelos Tolias
ALTEC S.A., Greece

Adamantios Koumpis
ALTEC S.A., Greece

ABSTRACT

Businesses are aware of the popular demand for careful waste management as a high priority environmental issue. Small and Medium-sized Enterprises (SMEs) face greater pressure when coping with waste products, because they often lack necessary resources or expertise. E-business could offer unique opportunities both for SMEs wanting to dispose of their waste or find waste management services and for SMEs who deal with specific aspects of waste disposal itself. This chapter proposes an approach for locating actors involved in the transportation, disposal, recycling and reuse of waste created by SMEs. Our approach incorporates the notion of Request Based Virtual Organizations (RBVOs) using a Service Oriented Architecture (SOA) and an ontology for the definition of waste management requirements. The populated ontology is utilized by a Multi-Agent System which performs negotiations and forms RBVOs. This approach enables SMEs to find appropriate partners, handle waste management and gain competitive advantage in the marketplace.

DOI: 10.4018/978-1-61692-880-3.ch015

INTRODUCTION

Small and Medium-sized Enterprises/Businesses (SMEs) have specific challenges and opportunities related to their waste products, namely items needed to be disposed of. Waste management in this chapter refers to the widest concept of organizing, handling, transporting, recycling and disposing responsibly of all types of waste generated by SMEs. It is now essential that interactions of SMEs both seeking and offering services related to waste management require thoughtful analysis of which partners could benefit them the most. Systems need to be devised to meet this criterion and this is one area where e-business needs to be expanded. Waste management for SMEs is now a global priority as the green movement gathers pace (Gadenne, Kennedy, & McKeiver, 2009; Hidalgo, Irusta, & Fermoso, 2008; Vives, 2006). Waste Management has now become a highly complex issue.

According to The Economist's 2009 'Special Report on Waste', the average Westerner produces over 500kg of municipal waste a year. In addition, both developed and developing countries generate vast quantities of construction and demolition debris, industrial effluent, mine tailings, sewage residue and agricultural waste (McBride, 2009). It has been estimated that the quantity of waste collected worldwide is between 2.5 and 4 billion metric tons (not including construction and demolition, mining and agricultural waste). Rich countries spend some $120 billion a year disposing of their municipal waste alone and approximately $150 billion on industrial waste (Lacoste & Chalmin, 2006). The amount of waste that countries produce tends to grow in tandem with their economies, and especially with the rate of urbanization. Waste firms see a rich future in places such as China, India and Brazil, which at present spend only about $5 billion a year collecting and treating their municipal waste. Concern about global warming should also provide a boost for the waste business. Waste is not just a substance that needs to be disposed of; it is also a potential resource. It can be burned to generate energy and new technologies turn sorted waste into fertilizer, chemicals or fuel. Paper, plastic, aluminum, etc can be recycled. Much waste can also be reused (McBride, 2009). Waste, thus, is now an opportunity for new business ventures, as well as for extra revenues or cost savings in existing enterprises.

Many businesses are becoming more aware of the popular demand for more careful waste management as a high priority environmental issue which could also be used to promote a firm's image. Business communities are responsible for large quantities and varieties of waste material. Acting in order to reduce and treat this waste appropriately can be easier for large organizations because they posses extensive resources and benefit from savings of scale. However, Small Medium Enterprises (SMEs) are in a unique situation. On the one hand they may have adopted waste management practices that are adapted to their operations. On the other hand, sometimes out of thoughtlessness and sometimes as the result of ignorance or a lack of understanding of the basic principles of effective waste management, many are content with meeting minimal requirements or restricting the adoption of such practices. Many SMEs have been found to fail to fulfill all waste management regulations due to lack of knowledge about the current environmental legislation relating to small companies (Gadenne, Kennedy, & McKeiver, 2009; Hidalgo, Irusta, & Fermoso, 2008). There is also the case of management's good will being stifled by complex problems and the barriers imposed by limited resources (Dennis et al., 2003).

Waste management is a complex and demanding issue that needs the contribution of a variety of experts to be handled successfully. Nevertheless, there is no such collaboration system supporting the management of waste in practice or in the literature. Companies and municipalities wishing to recycle, or find other ways of disposing of their waste, need to locate appropriate firms which can support them. These services can range from a simple cost effective transport company - which can collect and deliver their waste to an appropriate place - to specialized recycling companies or firms that could deal responsibly with it.

This chapter presents an integrated e-business approach for the transportation, disposal, recycling and reuse of waste generated by SMEs. This approach is designed bearing in mind the needs of an SME in finding the appropriate combination of firms that can help dispose of its waste in an environmentally friendly, efficient and cost effective manner. In order to do this they need to find and collaborate with appropriate combinations of firms. This is a difficult task due to the variety of business actors required to be involved and coordinated.

The purpose of this chapter is to outline the architectural and organizational aspects of a collaborative system for the management of waste and provide SMEs at both ends of the waste management spectrum with viable solutions and a competitive edge. We develop a generic architectural model for the collaborative management of waste in SMEs based on Service Oriented Architecture (SOA), which should be adapted to the specific situation and needs of each user. The analysis remains at a high level, leaving aside some technicalities regarding the implementation and the operation of the system in practice. We believe that the lack of similar overall approaches renders our effort not only worthy, but necessary as well.

The technological objective of this chapter is to provide an approach for the development of such systems that is based on Request Based Virtual Organizations (RBVOs). We propose the use of RBVOs by SMEs to enhance their business contacts and tackle effectively the problems outlined above. RBVOs are short-living entities that are formed to respond to business opportunities offered in electronic commerce; an RBVO is comprised of a cluster of partnering organizations that have totally replaced their vertical integration into a virtual one (Roberts, Svirskas & Matthews, 2005). Although in principle RBVOs can be used by a variety of companies small and large, their specific characteristics (demand-driven, dynamic, ad-hoc collaborations) are more applicable to the nature of SMEs. These types of companies prefer more flexible and adaptable collaborations (including those with waste management companies) as opposed to larger organizations – highly specialized with multiple competencies – whose partnerships are more strategic and long-term (Hong & Jeong, 2006).

This chapter also outlines and illustrates an ontology that serves the definition of waste management requirements. The populated ontology would be utilized by a Multi-Agent System which performs negotiations and forms the RBVOs, presenting them to the user who represents the SME. The user can then select the preferred RBVO and initiate collaboration with the proposed companies. For this purpose, the chapter will also discuss the use of Service Level Agreements (SLAs), used as a contracting mechanism amongst the partners in the selected RBVO.

CHALLENGES AND OPPORTUNITIES FOR SMES IN WASTE MANAGEMENT

Industrial activities of the past century have created serious ecological problems. Even though there are different philosophies and approaches to resolving these problems, it is necessary to organize business activities along ecologically sound principles. Waste management is a key issue because every business activity produces some waste, either hazardous or polluting to the environment. Waste management refers in general to the processes of collecting, processing, recycling or disposal of waste materials. Waste (or industrial waste) includes a wide variety of kinds, including liquids and solid waste, sewage, electronics, chemicals, commercial waste (e.g. packaging material, etc.), biodegradable waste, etc.

Even though SMEs may have relatively minor impact when examined independently, collectively their impact is great because of their large number. As a result, waste management is essential for SMEs, too. The adoption of environmental protection measures, both proactively and reactively, provides SMEs with the opportunity to meet their legal obligations, take care of and protect the natural environment and -at the same time- improve their competitive position. In this section we review the literature and outline the strategic opportunities of waste management considering the competitive advantages for SMEs. Emphasis is put on proactive views on waste management that provide strategic benefits to the firms, rather than on reactive approaches that mean merely to conform to the existing legislation.

Literature Review

The impact of business on the environment has become an issue of increasing concern since the late 1980s, particularly in western economies, with rising external pressure and internal motivation for environmental-friendly business practices. The implementation of environmental management practice is influenced by stakeholders, such as consumers, legislators, suppliers or customers and employees. Consumers, in particular, are becoming more environmentally conscious and a growing 'green market segment' seems to prefer ecologically sound products and are willing to sacrifice some economic growth for environmental protection (Shrivastava, 1995). Suppliers or customers also exercise great pressure on SMEs, especially for the establishment of environmental management systems and the adoption of certifications, such as the Eco-Management and Audit Scheme (EMAS) and ISO 14001 (Hillary, 2004). Environmental regulation leads to better environmental procedures and practices (Williamson, Lynch-Wood & Ramsay, 2006; Gadenne, Kennedy, & McKeiver, 2009) and can influence the competitive dynamics of industries by imposing new costs, investment demands and opportunities for improving production and efficiency (Shrivastava, 1995). Environmental initiatives may result from concerns expressed by employees that expect their company to behave in a socially responsible way or because of the personal preferences of the owner/manager of the firm (Gadenne, Kennedy, & McKeiver, 2009).

The adoption of environmental protection measures gives firms the opportunity to take care of and to protect the natural environment while simultaneously improving their competitive edge. Bansal and Roth (2000) suggest that companies take ecological initiatives for reasons of competitiveness (the potential to improve long-term profitability), legitimation (the desire of a firm to improve the appropriateness of its actions within an established set of regulations, norms, values, or beliefs) and social responsibility (the concern for social obligations and values). It should be noted that most of the literature has been focused on the large, usually multi-national, companies whose individual impact is apparent (Lawrence, Collins, Pavlovich & Arunachalam, 2006). For SMEs, in particular, Hillary (2004) suggests that environmental management can bring a broad range of direct benefits including: cost savings from increased resource use efficiency and waste reduction, marketing advantages, creation of a positive image and improved media coverage, improved relations with stakeholders, better supply chain relationships, lower insurance premiums and cheaper cost of finance, improved overall quality of management and increased staff commitment and motivation. Simpson et al. (2004) append that the ability of SMEs to gain a competitive advantage is thought to be related to issues of marketing, marketing research, marketing strategy, new product development, the technologies and processes and the manufacturing and operations strategy adopted.

Even though SMEs can gain a competitive advantage by adopting environmental good practices, the perceptions of SMEs and their approaches to environmental improvements reveal that there are some fundamental misunderstandings and difficulties in achieving it in practice. First of all, the majority of the surveys focusing on SMEs show that they either disregard or underestimate the competitive potential of environmental initiatives and consider the environment a 'peripheral' issue. Because of their small size and their limited knowledge, skills and resources, SMEs find difficulties responding to the challenge to improve their environmental performance (Hitchens, Clausen, Trainor, Keil & Thankappan, 2003; Collins, Lawrence, Pavlovich & Ryan, 2007). In addition, most SMEs perceive environmental protection as an extra cost or an unwelcome legal obligation with which they have to conform; many are reactive instead of proactive when dealing with environmental issues (Rutherfoord, Blackburn & Spence, 2000).

The awareness, ability, attitudes, practices and perceptions of SMEs with regard to creating competitive advantage by making environmental improvements have been reported in the literature. As recently as 2009, Revell et al. (2009) portrayed the owner-managers of small firms as: ignorant of the environmental impact of their enterprise, lacking the tools and resources to tackle environmental problems, resistant to voluntary action due to the perceived cost, time, and resources required to reduce environmental impacts, skeptical about the business benefits of sustainability and difficult to engage on anything to do with reducing their environmental impact. Simpson et al. (2004) found that SME managers do not perceive that significant benefits in the form of cost savings, competitive advantage or other can be achieved from environmental improvements. On the contrary, they considered environmental responsibility and improvement merely a financial cost. In general, the strategic potential of investment in environmental protection and the development of sustainable competitive advantages appear to be beyond the capabilities of the majority of SMEs (Simpson et al., 2004). Studer et al. (2008) suggest that the engagement of SMEs is further hampered by their limited access to relevant information and their lack of expertise to plan and implement environmental initiatives. Manufacturing SMEs seem to be more convinced than service-sector SMEs that they could gain competitive advantage through waste reduction (Simpson et al., 2004).

Several studies have identified the barriers to SME adoption of environmental practices (Hillary, 2004; Simpson et al., 2004; Revell & Rutherfoord, 2003; Rutherfoord, Blackburn & Spence 2000). The most important barriers are related to: the perception that SMEs have little individual impact on the environment, the lack of expertise and understanding of environmental issues, the increased cost of environmental practices by SMEs and the perception that little financial benefit can be gained from environmental investments. On the other hand, the key motives are related to compliance with existing legislation, social responsibility and personal commitment of individual managers.

Lawrence et al. (2006) consider that SMEs need different approaches from large firms in their effort to deal with environmental issues and they suggest seeking co-operation through networking with other SMEs and with other related organizations (e.g. research organizations, NGOs, etc). According to Collins et al. (2007) networks, with their ability to provide specialized information, mentoring and specialized support, may be a way to encourage all sustainability practices among SMEs. For example, networks can provide support to find funding and to suggest ways to deal with various environmental issues such as the reduction or recycling of waste, the implementation of new technologies or the development of new environmentally friendly products and services. In this chapter we also consider a network approach in the management of waste material, by providing a technological solution for the dynamic location and engagement of the appropriate partners that will support the handling of waste materials in every situation.

Development of Competitive Advantage through Waste Management

There are two basic theories in the business literature for acquiring competitive advantage: one is based on industrial organization theory and is expressed by the work of Porter (1980 & 1985) and the other is based on the resource-based theory of the firm (Wernerfeld, 1984; Barney, 1991).

Most of the research that relate environmental and waste management with competitive advantage for the firm derives from Porter (1980 & 1985), who suggests organizing business activities in a value chain and highlights the distinction between cost advantages and differentiation advantages. Porter (1985) suggested that value creating activities performed by the firm to design, produce, market, deliver and support a product would lead to a competitive advantage. All the primary activities with which firms create value (i.e. inbound logistics, operations, outbound logistics, marketing, sales and services) are likely to improve with the use of waste management techniques. Cost advantages can result from pollution control and pollution prevention technologies that reduce the environmental impact of the firms and from business practices that reduce the cost of production by increasing the efficiency of production processes and by reducing input and waste-disposal costs. Such practices include more efficient use of raw materials and energy, reduction of treatment costs of waste, savings from recycling activities, reduction of potential risks of environmental liability costs, reduction of logistic costs, etc. (Zutshi & Sohal, 2004). Differentiation advantages can result from improving product characteristics to be more environmentally responsible, developing new environmentally responsible products and marketing the environmental benefits of the products.

Resource-based theory views the firm as a unique - at least in some aspects - collection of productive resources that include assets, capabilities, processes and knowledge (Barney, 1991). These resources can be used to enable firms to conceive and implement strategies that improve their effectiveness and efficiency. The development of a sustained competitive advantage should be based on rare resources or on resources that result from unique historical organizational circumstances and span the whole organization. Accordingly, waste management initiatives can lead SMEs to acquire competitive advantage especially if they cannot be easily imitated by others or are implemented early. Any single waste management initiative cannot guarantee a competitive advantage for SMEs, because it can be easily imitated. SMEs should try to develop their own capabilities in establishing waste management systems and harness specialized approaches in the management of waste materials that fit best with their particular circumstances. Waste management should not only be viewed as a legal or social obligation, but as an investment that will improve the efficiency of a firm and will provide a competitive edge.

The technological solution we propose leverages the capabilities of SMEs in the handling of waste material by enabling the operation of virtual organizations that are comprised of SMEs and a variety of actors that have a role in the collection, transportation, disposal, recycling and reuse of waste created by each SME. Competitive advantages can arise from the cost improvement, the efficiency of processes and the opportunity to develop unique capabilities through the collaboration with specialized actors in waste management. For readers lacking insight into virtual organizations and other terminology a brief introduction to the technical side is provided below.

TECHNOLOGICAL BACKGROUND

Request-Based Virtual Organizations

A Virtual Organization (VO) is usually described as a network among organizations and/or individuals (Svirskas & Roberts, 2003). Therefore, it appears as a single unified organization. The benefits of VOs (cost, transaction, process and strategic) are well-documented in the literature (Bovet & Martha, 2000; Saabeel, Verduijn, Hagdorn & Kumar, 2002; Goldman, Nagel, & Preiss, 1995). However, the static nature of VOs fails to address the growing demands to locate products, services and business partners. In Government to Business (G2B) or Business to Business (B2B) contexts the above problems are more profound, due to the large potential number of collaborative partners with diverse capabilities and the lack of standardization of service description (Roberts & Svirskas, 2005). RBVOs (as a special type of VOs – more dynamic, adaptable and flexible in nature than traditional VOs) overcome this by enabling the discovery and matching of appropriate business partners.

RBVOs are short-living entities that are formed to respond to business opportunities offered by electronic commerce. According to Svriskas and Roberts, the key features of a RBVO as opposed to the "classic" VO are:

- A possibility for an enterprise to discover potential business partners *upon demand* and advertise itself in a standard way.
- *Short-lived ad-hoc* virtual formations of collaborating partners.
- *Highly dynamic* involvement of an enterprise in different e-business activities, serving different defined and advertised roles, at the same time, if needed.

As a subtype of more traditional VOs, RBVOs also inherit many of their features, i.e.:

- A cluster of geographically dispersed organizations either within regions or inter regionally.
- A range of relationships from transactional to collaborative that vary dynamically over time in response to market opportunities.
- Lower transaction costs for geographically dispersed transactions (Svirskas & Roberts, 2003).

In trying to find collaborating partners to form a RBVO, quotes from a large number of sellers can provide a good overview of the price of transactions amongst collaborating partners. However, overcoming ignorance of product/service quality and other supplier capabilities may be more difficult. RBVOs can therefore be coupled with the concept of sector specific Service Level Agreements (SLAs) to address the issue. In its most basic form, a SLA is a contract or agreement that formalizes a business relationship, or part of the relationship, between two parties (Svirskas & Roberts, 2003; Trienekens, Bouman & Zwan, 2004). SLAs are well known from the IT services provision industry (Lee & Ben-Natan, 2002), where the provision of services is measured on technical parameters like network uptime, data rate, etc. However, SLAs can also act as the regulating framework of e-collaborations among RBVO members incorporating all the business, financial and legal aspects that are essential when considering the real environment in business (Tektonidis, Ignatiadis, Katriou, Koumpis, 2008). In this case the provision of services from one partner to another within an e-collaboration is benchmarked on pre-agreed standards that are captured within an SLA (in the form of template contracts) and which reflect the partners' trading/collaborating arrangements. SLAs can then be used (manually or automatically) to monitor performance, resolve disagreements, and apply penalties (financial or otherwise) where appropriate.

Vokrinek et al. have designed an (automated) RBVO protocol which supports a flexible formation of RBVOs taking into account the use of SLAs with an emphasis on reflecting the conditions of real competitive environments. The protocol consists of three phases: (i) potential partner search, (ii) negotiation of SLAs and RBVO establishment and (iii) RBVO execution and dissolution (Vokrinek, Biba, Hodik, Vybihal, & Volf, 2007). Their results have been practically demonstrated in the "PANDA" project (co-funded by the European Union's Framework Programme 6), with a focus on RBVOs (supported by SLAs) in the European ERP industry of SMEs.

Service-Oriented Architecture

The creation and management of RBVOs inherently rely on a number of heterogeneous (in technical and business terms) partners coming together to explore and exploit synergies and collaborations. To accommodate different technical and business requirements - of current and future SMEs registered in the system - with regards to RBVO operations, it is imperative to adopt an open, adaptable and expandable architecture. It is for these reasons that a Service-Oriented Architecture (SOA) is considered in the context of the proposed system. SOA is also relevant for SMEs (Blum, Magedanz, Stein, 2007; Jardim-Goncalves, Grilo, Steiger-Garcao, 2006), and it has been argued that a SOA can be used to reduce the barriers of e-business in SMEs (Brun & Lanng, 2006).

Service-Oriented Architecture (SOA) is an architectural style in which software applications are organized as a set of loosely coupled services (Harding, 2007). The SOA paradigm enables the linking of business and computational resources (mainly organizations, applications and data) on demand. It is seen to be essential for delivering business agility and IT flexibility. It also facilitates the alignment of existing IT infrastructures to achieve internal or external enterprise connectivity, by removing redundancies, generating unified collaboration tools, and streamlining IT processes. The benefits from this approach include an increase in business agility to respond to future changes by adapting and reorganizing the existing services as well as creating new services to fit in the existing IT architecture in order to address changed business requirements. This applies to both internal operations, as well as external ones e.g. providing new services to customers or changing the way the interactions with collaborators in a supply chain are carried out. A well-executed SOA implementation can bridge the gap between enterprise architecture and business strategy, with companies achieving a closer alignment of IT with business, while in parallel implementing a robust reuse of existing technology and application code with agility and cost effectiveness (Laurent, 2007). From a business point of view, the goals of SOA are quicker time-to-market with innovative offerings, greater productivity, and reduced integration costs.

Contrary to vendor hype, SOA is not a software product, solution or technology. Rather, SOA should be viewed as a concept enabling businesses (or constellations of businesses such as in our case) to become more agile, flexible and interoperable. This is accomplished by organizing existing and new IT assets as a set of services that communicate with each other in order to form flexible processes addressing existing and future business requirements. In that sense SOA has also been termed as the 'lean manufacturing model applied to IT' (Woods, 2003). According to Marks and Bell:

SOA is a conceptual business architecture where business functionality, or application logic, is made available to SOA users, or consumers, as shared, reusable services on an IT network. "Services" in an SOA are modules of business or application functionality with exposed interfaces, and are invoked by messages (Marks & Bell, 2007).

From an architectural point of view, SOA is based on six assumptions (Brandl, 2007): applications are loosely coupled; interface transactions are stateless; interface follows the RPC (remote procedure call) model; interface is message-based; messages use XML (eXtensible Markup Language) data and interfaces may support both synchronous and asynchronous transactions. Viewed as an approach to building IT systems to match flexible business requirements, SOA connects applications across a network via a common communications protocol, allowing organizations to reuse old and future software, often with the help of Web services (Brodkin, 2007). SOA incorporates standards like SOAP (Simple Object Access Protocol) and XML, to deliver standard messaging formats and increased reuse of information assets at lower integration costs (Larrivee, 2007).

Intelligent Agents

A Service-Oriented Architecture can be complemented with Intelligent Agents for the creation and management of RBVOs. Intelligent Agents have been shown to be able to exist seamlessly within a SOA (Maximilien & Singh, 2005, Shen et al., 2007). In the domain of RBVOs, there are requirements for forming business alliances, planning long-term/short-term cooperation deals, and managing (including reconfiguration and dissolving) cooperation. Intelligent Agents (as part of a Multi-Agent System-MAS) can be assigned to represent the interest of SMEs registered in the system, which can guide the agents' behavior according to customizable business rules (e.g. I only want to find waste management companies operating locally or I am only prepared to spend a certain amount of money on recycling activities).

Implementation of agent technologies is usually based on the standards published by the Foundation for Intelligent Physical Agents (FIPA). Agent technologies show strong potential in the areas of cooperation, coordination, planning and control in the distributed environment (Marik and McFarlane, 2005). Using various negotiation techniques (such as those described by Vokrinek et al., 2007), agents are able to establish cooperation even in a competitive environment. Their dynamic reconfiguration and recommitments improve the overall service quality across the whole supply chain. Various implementations and benefits of Intelligent Agents in the supply chain (for modeling, planning, negotiation, management and reconfiguration) have already been discussed in the literature (e.g. Caridi, Cigolini & De Marco, 2005; Nissen, 2001; Fox, Barbuceanu & Teigen, 2000; Swaminathan, Smith & Sadeh, 2007). In our case, the main advantages of augmenting a Service Oriented Architecture with Intelligent Agents for supporting the formation of RBVOs are as follows:

- Private Knowledge Protection - Only company data relevant to the business operation are provided to other partners. No central database exists and the business data are not broadcasted among the whole cluster, but kept privately by each agent representing a SME.
- System robustness - Negotiation and information exchange is peer-to-peer based; therefore failure of a single part doesn't affect the rest of the system.
- Easy reconfiguration - Dynamic changes in a RBVO (e.g. partners joining or leaving) is supported by adoption of existing agents, creation of new agents, and disaffiliation of agents that are no longer exploited.
- Human Integration - Inter-agent negotiation is supported by human-based advisement, which is important in the case of business agreements.

In general, (software) agents are autonomous, which is desirable in unknown scenarios (which usually tend to appear in the real world, as in the case of waste management), where it is difficult to control directly the behavior of a business constellation (e.g. with regards to what collaborations will take place or what problems will arise during these collaborations). Even though it is possible to encapsulate some behaviors by specifying customizable business rules, agents must decide by themselves whether to execute their methods according to their goals (agents must be proactive), preferences and beliefs. In any case, human advisement is also integrated in agent operations where appropriate, to make sure that agents really represent their end users' (SMEs') needs.

THE POTENTIAL OF RBVOS FOR SMES IN WASTE MANAGEMENT

In this section we provide a general approach for the management of waste that has a wide-scope use in its implementation and a system architecture for this approach. Of course, each type of waste, according to its special characteristic, requires different handling in the processes of its waste management. However, this approach can serve as a general blueprint for the development of collaborative systems for the management of waste, which would require some specialization in order that it be disposed of in an ecologically effective manner. To illustrate the specialization of the approach, we also provide a usage example according to a specific scenario.

The main focus of this chapter is to show how RBVOs can be used in waste management to enhance the co-operability of SMEs to the advantage of other local businesses and municipalities. As RBVOs are a very recent concept this chapter focuses on a proposal and possible architectural design of a relevant system in order to stimulate discussion on ways computerization of waste management could tackle the vast problems confronting global pollution. In so doing, one enhances business opportunities within the waste management arena, by creating an evolving and competitive e-collaboration environment. Clearly, there is a need to segregate the different waste materials. These can vary enormously from solid and semi-solid forms to liquids and gases. The safety of the materials also varies widely and can include highly toxic compounds and radioactive ones. Many wastes in industrial effluent are also mixed and may be difficult to separate or need advanced systems to separate on site. A further factor to consider is the price of different waste as these vary according to season and quantities available. Another influencing factor on the price of any waste product is its open demand on the market providing commercial implications. All these factors must be considered when offering or accepting waste materials. It is these complex issues and concerns that make the use of RBVOs an attractive option as any RBVO would act like an umbrella organization to link waste producers, with waste services.

The Approach

From a functional point of view, our approach is designed bearing in mind the needs of a SME, a contracting company or a municipality in finding the appropriate combination of firms who can help dispose of its waste in an environmentally friendly and cost effective manner. At present, this remains a difficult task because a wide variety of business actors are required to be involved and coordinated, each of which undertakes a specific and highly specialized task that needs to be performed accurately and according to general standards set. A poorly selected actor performing his tasks in an inefficient and ineffective way could lead to a huge negative impact on the environment, the community and the reputation of the organizations involved.

As the green movement gathers pace, the importance of finding appropriate partners for waste management becomes more specialized. There is a need to provide a sophisticated, time saving and effective means for locating these partners. It is for these reasons that we have based our approach on the concept of RBVOs - a sophisticated form of VO. RBVOs are ideal for SMEs who wish to find suitable waste management service providers, as they allow for on-the-spot creation of a VO which can satisfy individual SME needs. The fact that RBVOs are short living, i.e. they exist for the duration of the specified task, allows for the flexibility and agility that each SME requires when addressing their unique waste management problems. Finding appropriate waste management service providers could also give SMEs a competitive advantage by opening business opportunities they had not identified, i.e. an SME could discover a company prepared to buy their waste from them.

Using RBVOs as a means of locating suitable partners, benefits the SMEs who have a mandatory obligation to dispose of their waste and need to dispose of their waste efficaciously. Using RBVOs also benefits waste management service providers - who are often themselves SMEs. RBVOs allow these organizations to advertise themselves dynamically and be paired with partners who can support them in providing better and more complete services to their customers. One further advantage of our approach, from the providers' point of view, is that knowing the types of waste that exist can stimulate new ideas for recycling, reuse or even product invention.

To simplify the agreement procedures, our approach incorporates the use of SLAs. Once a SME has selected its preferred RBVO, a contract (SLA) would need to be signed between the SME and each service provider. As well as being used in the IT services industry, SLAs can also be used as the means of defining the contractual requirements (business/financial/legal issues) between two or more partners in a RBVO context (Ignatiadis, Svirskas, Roberts & Tarabanis, 2006). This is one of the most important later trends, i.e. the shift of the goal of an SLA from being a financial and technical contract towards an instrument for the management of the customer's or collaborating partner's expectations (McBride, 1998; Passmore, 1996). In this case the parameters of the SLA to be measured are not technical like network uptime, data rate etc, but rather the quality of services that are to be provided as part of the operation of the RBVO (in this case relevant to waste management), as well as the adherence to the business, financial and legal clauses in the SLA. Financial considerations would include recycling payments, transportation costs and the costs of waste separation, if necessary.

It should be emphasized that waste management is a hugely complex issue and that this proposal does not pretend to be an absolute solution to the problems mentioned but we hope that it will open up new directions to tackle the ever increasing demand for improved waste management strategies.

The Proposed System

There are many ways to implement RBVOs, but utilizing a community of Intelligent Agents (Multi-Agent System) has shown to be a most effective method (Tektonidis, Ignatiadis, Katriou, Koumpis, 2008). In this way, the organization and functioning of the RBVO's activities are served by the Multi-Agent system that is developed to orchestrate and automate procedures and operations of RBVOs.

For the proposed system, a Service Oriented Architecture (SOA) is used. As stated earlier, the SOA paradigm enables the linking of business and computational resources - mainly organizations, applications and data on demand (Bloomberg, & Schmelzer, 2006). SOA is seen to be essential for delivering business agility and IT flexibility (Tews, 2007). The advantages of SOA can be obtained for a conglomeration of companies coming together to exploit complementary skills and competencies synergistically. Although there is no shortage of platforms for firms to collaborate online within particular industries or across industries, the advantages of adopting a SOA approach for such platforms need to be taken into consideration. This is due to the adaptability and easy reconfigurability that SOA offers which matches heterogeneous RBVO's business requirements (Tektonidis, Ignatiadis, Katriou, Koumpis, 2008). In addition, SOA has also been shown to interoperate with agent technologies (Maamar, Mostefaoui & Yahyaoui, 2005; Maximilien & Singh, 2005), which are used in the architecture described below.

Figure 1 presents the architecture of the proposed system.

The system is comprised of the following components:

- **Web platform:** A portal providing a search functionality which enables the user (an SME) to find partners (waste management service providers) who themselves might be another SME.

Figure 1. System architecture

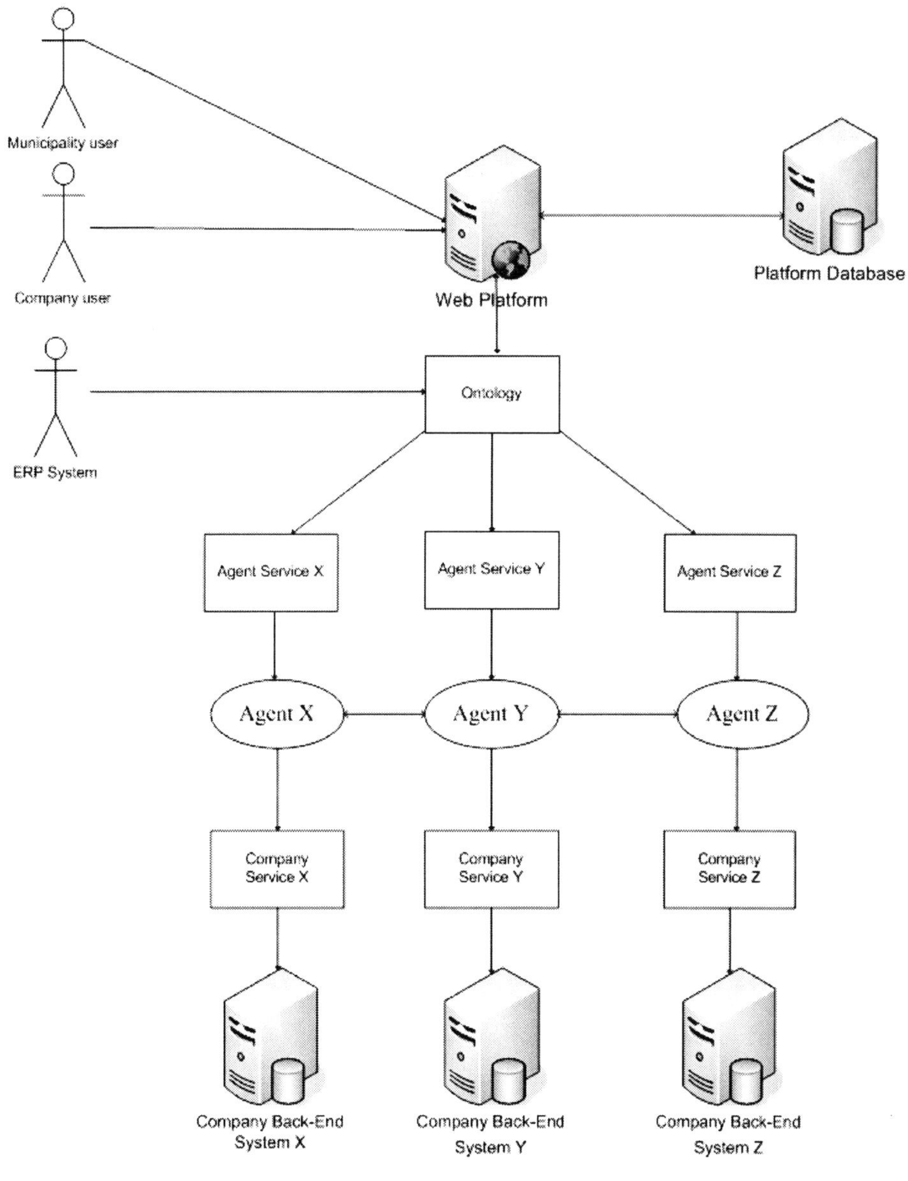

- **Directory service:** A data store with login information and user profiles which should be accessed via a web service.
- **Ontology:** A high level representation of waste related information which can be used to encapsulate the user's requirements regarding the types and amounts of substances that need to be disposed or recycled. This can include such details as the toxicity profile of the materials, transport preferences, legal issues, price options and other economic considerations, organizational details and any other information essential to disclose.
- **Agent Services:** A web service that enables the submission of a request for collaboration to the Agent and the acquisition of the list of possible RBVOs.
- **Agent:** An independent distributed instance - decision maker - which interacts with other Agents and represents a potential collaborator.
- **Company Services:** A set of simple web services that enable the SME's or municipality's Agent, to access its Information/Enterprise Resource Planning (ERP) system or private repository, i.e. Company Back-End System.
- **Company Back-End System:** Contains private information of the company such as the SME's or municipality's profile, requests for collaboration, contracts and recycling capacity it currently has available.

A Usage Scenario

Let us assume that a SME building contractor wishes to find a new cost effective way to dispose of cardboard, used batteries, canteen food waste, plastic bottles, old computers and mixed rubble. To take advantage of the proposed system, the first step would be to register as a user and have an instance of an Agent - a virtual decision maker in this example referred to as 'Agent X' - set up to represent the SME. An instance of an Agent Service would also need to be set up as an intermediary between the portal and 'Agent X' - in this example referred to as 'Agent Service X' (see Figure 1). This registration process would be required not only for SMEs and other organizations who wish to find partners for waste management, but also for the companies offering these services in order for them to be represented in the system's network by their Agents.

After logging into the system, this new user needs to complete a web form in which the type of waste which requires management is defined. The waste is categorized as sorted or mixed. For each type of waste the corresponding amount (i.e. approximate weight/volume) should be provided. Also, the location, language in which the service is required, time constraints and any other specifications would be defined in this form.

Once completed, the form can be submitted as a request to find a combination of companies within the system's network which can fulfill the tasks. An ontology would be populated with the provided information and then would be forwarded to the 'Agent Service X'.

Should the user wish to complete the aforementioned form on a frequent basis, manual insertion of values might become tiresome. For this reason a custom script could be incorporated as a means of automatically populating the ontology from specified values in the SME's ERP system. Should the SME not have an EPR system the ontology could be linked to another information system or multiple systems, if necessary.

Continuing the sequence of events, after the 'Agent Service X' has received the populated ontology, this information would be forwarded to the user's 'Agent X'. This 'Agent X' in turn would send the specifications to the other Agents (Y, Z, etc) registered in the system (i.e. those which represent waste management service providers). Each of these Agents filters the incoming specifications to see if any of the required tasks are of interest to the firm it represents.

A set of negotiations, based on each firm's private constraints and on offered prices, would be performed between the Agents, resulting in a list of suitable RBVOs. This list would finally be returned to the user who would be presented with all the possible combinations of appropriate organizations which could perform the defined tasks.

The user, in this case the SME building contractor, can now select the preferred combination of firms (RBVO), either based on price, time constraints or other criteria. Of course, once selected, contracts would need to be signed - e.g. in the form of SLAs - in order for collaboration to begin. Items of interest in the contract (SLA) would include duties and responsibilities of collaborating partners, prices to be paid for the provision (exchange) of services in the RBVO and deadlines.

The sequence of the above described scenario is presented in Figure 2.

The Intelligent Agents

Intelligent Agents are used for the formation of RBVOs in waste management collaborations. These formations arise after automated Agent negotiations, according to customizable human-specified business rules. To aid in these negotiations, publicly available information about other SMEs is used as well as an Agent's private information (i.e. that is stored in the Company's Back-End System) about the user's preferences (i.e. customizable business rules) and private information about the outcome of previous negotiations with the same Agents. As stated in the PANDA project (Tektonidis, Ignatiadis, Katriou, Koumpis, 2008), the Agents represent individual actors participating in the RBVO formation processes taking into account individual private constraints, preferences that are hidden to other actors and minimizing the disclosure of such private information. In their negotiations, agents can be guided by user-defined business rules. Agents need to decide which of these rules are applicable in each type of negotiation. Flexibility

Figure 2. Sequence of RBVO formation

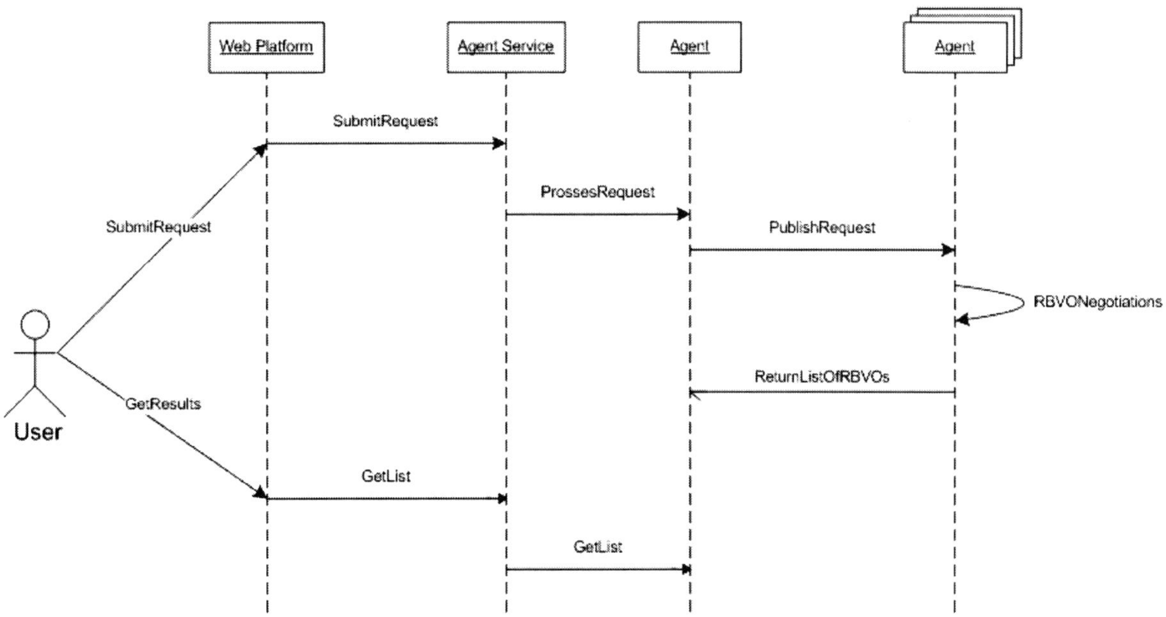

is essential when adapting and prioritizing these rules as the negotiations progress. Such rules can be set by each user to guide his/her Agent, and can be implemented using a rules engine.

Indicative user-defined business rules for the negotiation between Agents could include:

- Tolerance on price -x% to +y%.
- Prepared to wait x days for a better price.
- Prepared to pay more for the tasks to be finished sooner.
- Prepared to pay more for 'greener' outcomes.
- Wishes only to consider partners in the same region/country as the user.
- Do not want to participate in projects less than x Euros.

For example an SME construction firm wishing to dispose of rubble from a site could seek partners who would reuse their waste materials. Using a system based on the proposed architecture, the SME could set business rules for their partner search, such as the above points. The intelligent agent of the SME and the agents of other SMEs involved in the recycling trade would negotiate until an appropriate partnership for disposing of the waste was formed.

A Persistent Problem that Needs Flexible Solutions

Waste management is a persistent problem which brings controversies concerning its disposal and the issue is at constant loggerheads with the eco-movement as more mixed waste is increasingly being deposited in land fills. As fewer sites become available for these landfills ("not in my back yard, thank you") the problems involving waste management increase in complexity. Other methods of waste disposal which involve dumping are also of increasing concern; sea dumping, for example, contaminates fish stocks and shore lines.

The proposed system in this chapter is designed to use technology to assist SMEs to find the best way to reduce, recycle and reuse their waste. The approach would make searching for partners easier and would encourage greater responsibility concerning the reduction of garbage creation and disposal. This proposed system could also be of use to municipalities and even corporations. One main issue we need to confront is how to stimulate businesses, government bodies and the general population to take greater responsibility for their waste.

McBride (2009) emphasizes that subsidies are a bad idea. Governments have a role to play in the business of waste management, but it is a regulatory and supervisory one. Regarding recycling, it is useless to urge people to salvage stuff for which there are no buyers. Governments need to make sure there are markets for the materials they want collected (McBride, 2009). It is essential that incentives and opportunities are provided to motivate businesses in adopting eco-friendly attitudes towards waste management.

The proposed approach is devised to help solve waste management problems and to create a system which might encourage wider and more specialized markets for waste materials. By presenting the ideas in a proposed form we hope to open up the arena for further debate, to extend, expand or even, if necessary, re-design this scheme. Allowing SMEs and others easy access to finding quick and efficient ways to dispose of their variety of waste in an eco-friendly manner would benefit both the environment, the image of the company and its internal dynamics. The system could become a vital search and application tool for specialized state-of-the-art waste management enterprises enabling SMEs to exercise greater responsibility with their waste by selecting waste disposal firms specializing in modern utilization and recycling techniques to the benefit of all parties involved.

To improve waste management, it is vital that companies are able to collaborate with each other in the widest way possible and our proposed system could open doors to previously unforeseen collaboration potentials using virtual clusters of organizations. Examples of waste management service providers that could be sought through the system range from simple waste disposal firms to more complex ones specializing in transport and disposal systems for dangerous substances.

In addition, the system could be used to encourage start-up firms in the waste cycle process, enabling them to find companies with small waste loads and progressing to expanding their client base as their equipment and resources grow. Such start-ups might include innovative bio-fertilizer firms who could recycle human, animal and plant waste. Using an RBVO system would promote their expansion. Scientists with innovative ideas to reuse or design products from a waste source could also use the system to trace cheap raw materials.

This system would also enable firms to fine tune waste management and many of them may be stimulated to separate their waste more effectively when they realize that there are waste management service providers that can recycle, reuse or recreate something with a product which was formerly merely discarded as mixed waste. This would give both employers and employees in a firm satisfaction in knowing that their company was really eco-friendly, thus enhancing staff morale which in turn creates an environmentally friendly atmosphere for workers leading to a loyal workforce and a positive approach to green business.

FUTURE RESEARCH DIRECTIONS

In this chapter we present an approach for the development of collaborative systems for the management of waste in SMEs. We emphasize the development of a high level architecture and technological directions and described an exemplary usage scenario. As general directions for future research we single out the need to develop further the architecture outlined here by incorporating further elements (e.g. cost elements in the life cycle of waste management related to recycling, transportation of waste, etc.) and test and improve the technological solution described here. In addition, it is necessary to develop specific models and solutions for real situations that SMEs face. Such specific models could refer to specific sectors or companies or to the management of a specific type of waste (e.g. chemicals, electronics, etc.).

Waste management needs to become a more competitively driven industry to inspire present and future SMEs to be key stakeholders. Information Technology (IT) needs to be incorporated into business processes concerning waste in order to support and drive more competitive environments. Future research needs to examine how this could be accomplished.

Prices of commodities must take into account the cost of disposal of the waste items within any purchasable product ranging from soft drink bottles to old computers and carbon emissions to nuclear waste. Only when this is enforced at a transnational level there will be greater incentive for ordinary citizens to be inspired to separate and return much of the world's waste for recycling. This in turn would create enormous potential for new enterprises and open up other business opportunities. In addition, once waste is priced realistically, the proposed system would become of greater value to firms and service providers.

This could lead to the expansion of the architecture of the system which could take into account more eco-friendly ways of managing waste and other resources of the company. An 'Eco' score built into the system might spur firms to improve their style of waste disposal. The system could rate the RBVOs based on each firm's Eco considerations. For example, emissions of CO2 could be used as a basis for recommendations of the best ways of transporting the companies' waste to appropriate areas. This would require each waste management firm which registers in the system to complete its profile by providing eco-related details of its disposal methods. In cases of transport, distances would have to be calculated via a service such as Google Maps in order for emissions to be estimated.

The system could also be expanded to be a type of waste monitoring system because at present, nobody knows how much waste the world generates or what it does with this (McBride, 2009). For this purpose active government support would be required.

Research needs to be conducted on the use of Web 2.0 technologies for waste management. Designing an appropriate interface for the proposed system with Web 2.0 technologies would increase user friendliness and allow for business flexibility. Providing advice to system users through a relevant blog, twitter or other Web 2.0 services would also be an advantage, especially for SMEs who lack specialized knowledge on waste management issues.

CONCLUSION

This chapter presents a brief literature review of SMEs in relation to environmental issues of which waste management is one of increasing global concern. It also includes the competitive advantages of waste management for SMEs. An innovative approach is presented which gives a brief outline of a proposed system for decision support on selecting a combination of firms to enable cost effective, ecologically sound and efficient waste management of a SME's or other organization's waste. The complex problems faced by SMEs concerning the management of their waste is acknowledged and the solution proposed incorporates state-of-the-art technology in order to smash barriers imposed by limited resources of SMEs or confusion as to where to turn for comprehensive solutions. For readers lacking insight into virtual organizations and other terminology used in the chapter a brief introduction to the technical terminology is provided. We also demonstrate how the concept of RBVOs could be used in waste management.

A SOA based system which uses a Multi-Agent community to create RBVOs, enabling easy adaptability and reconfigurability, is illustrated. Such a simple-to-use system would notably improve the options available online for assisting the management of waste. This is an essential step in assisting SME management to find ecologically sound ways of disposing of their waste cost-effectively. The system could be a valuable pragmatic contribution towards tackling global pollution and enforcing a more competitive market for the waste industry itself. SMEs could benefit from such a scheme choosing or finding new specialist partners to dispose responsibly of each individual firm's waste. The scheme offers opportunities for the creation of new SMEs wishing to specialize in different branches of waste management as they would be supported by such an innovative system which enables them to identify potential partners. The proposed approach could also be of value to governments and larger companies. As businesses become more aware of the popular demand for careful waste management as a high priority environmental issue our proposed system in this chapter turns rhetorical demands into practical solutions which could also be used for promotional purposes to enhance a firm's image.

REFERENCES

Bansal, P., & Roth, K. (2000). Why Companies Go Green: A Model of Ecological Responsiveness. *Academy of Management Journal*, *43*(4), 717–736. doi:10.2307/1556363

Barney, J. B. (1991). Firm Resources and Sustained Competitive Advantage. *Journal of Management*, *17*(1), 99–120. doi:10.1177/014920639101700108

Bloomberg, J., & Schmelzer, R. (2006). *Service Orient or Be Doomed!: How Service Orientation Will Change Your Business*. Hoboken, NJ: Wiley.

Blum, N., Magedanz, T., & Stein, H. (2007). Service creation & delivery for SME based on SOA/IMS. In *Proceedings of the 2007 Workshop on Middleware for next-generation converged networks and applications*. ACM: New York.

Bovet, D., & Martha, J. (2000). *Value Nets: Breaking the Supply Chain to Unlock Hidden Profits*. Chichester, UK: John Wiley.

Brandl, D. (2007). SOA explained. *Control Engineering, 54*(8), 22–22.

Brodkin, J. (2007). Are SOAs saving anyone money? *New World (New Orleans, La.), 24*(28), 24–25.

Brun, M. H., & Lanng, C. (2006). Reducing barriers for e-business in SME's through an open service oriented infrastructure. In Proceedings of the 8th international conference on Electronic commerce: The new e-commerce: innovations for conquering current barriers, obstacles and limitations to conducting successful business on the internet (pp. 403-410). ACM: New York.

Caridi, M., Cigolini, R., & De Marco, D. (2005). Improving supply-chain collaboration by linking intelligent agents to CPFR. *International Journal of Production Research, 43*(20), 4191–4218. doi:10.1080/00207540500142134

Collins, E., Lawrence, S., Pavlovich, K., & Ryan, C. (2007). Business networks and the uptake of sustainability practices: the case of New Zealand. *Journal of Cleaner Production, 15*(8-9), 729–740. doi:10.1016/j.jclepro.2006.06.020

Denis, M., Lessard, P., van der Werf, P., Vitello, C., Duplessis, J., Desgagnes, N., et al. (2003). Waste Mangement Guide for Small and Medium Enterprises – Canadian Version. Editions Ruffec. http://entreprisescanada.ca/servlet/ContentServer?cid=1184867843697&lang=en&pagename=CBSC_QC%2Fdisplay&c=InfoResources. Last Verified: 2007-12-21.

Fox, M.S., Barbuceanu, M., & Teigen, R. (2000). Agent-Oriented Supply-Chain Management. *International Journal of Flexible Manufacturing Systems*, 12(2.3), 165-188.

Gadenne, D. L., Kennedy, J., & McKeiver, C. (2009). An empirical study of environmental awareness and practices in SMEs. *Journal of Business Ethics, 84*(1), 45–63. doi:10.1007/s10551-008-9672-9

Goldman, S. L., Nagel, R. N., & Preiss, K. (1995). *Agile Competitors And Virtual Organizations: Strategies For Enriching The Customer*. New York: Van Nostrand Reinhold, International Thomson Publishing.

Harding, C. (2007). An Open Marketplace for Services. *DM Review, 17*(9), 20–39.

Hidalgo, D., Irusta, R., & Fermoso, J. (2008). Generation and management of industrial waste in Small and Medium sized Enterprises. *International Journal of Environmental Technology and Management, 8*(4), 323–338. doi:10.1504/IJETM.2008.017505

Hillary, R. (2004). Environmental management systems and the smaller enterprise. *Journal of Cleaner Production, 12*(6), 561–569. doi:10.1016/j.jclepro.2003.08.006

Hitchens, D., Clausen, J., Trainor, M., Keil, M., & Thankappan, S. (2003). Competitiveness, Environmental Performance and Management of SMEs. *Greener Management International, 44*, 45–57.

Hong, P., & Jeong, J. (2006). Supply chain management practices of SMEs: from a business growth perspective. *Journal of Enterprise Information Management, 19*(3), 292–302. doi:10.1108/17410390610658478

Ignatiadis, I., Svirskas, A., Roberts, B., & Tarabanis, K. (2006). Promoting Trust in B2B Virtual Organizations through Business and Technological Infrastructures. *International Journal of Networking and Virtual Organizations, Special Issue on. Trust Development and Management in Virtual Organizations*, *3*(4), 395–411.

Jardim-Goncalves, R., Grilo, A., & Steiger-Garcao, A. (2006). Challenging the interoperability between computers in industry with MDA and SOA. *Computers in Industry*, *57*(8), 679–689. doi:10.1016/j.compind.2006.04.013

Lacoste, E., & Chalmin, P. (2006). FROM WASTE TO RESOURCE An abstract of 2006 "World Waste Survey". Retrieved July 29, 2009, from http://veoliaes.com/resource.php?id=566.

Larrivee, B. (2007). SOA: No Governance Needed. Or Is It? *AIIM E-DOC*, *21*(5), 24–25.

Laurent, W. (2007). The Importance of SOA Governance. *DM Review*, *17*(8), 38–38.

Lawrence, S. R., Collins, E., Pavlovich, K., & Arunachalam, M. (2006). Sustainability practices of SMEs: the case of NZ. *Business Strategy and the Environment*, *15*(4), 242–257. doi:10.1002/bse.533

Lee, J. J., & Ben-Natan, R. (2002). *Integrating Service Level Agreements: Optimising your OSS for SLA Delivery*. New York: Wiley.

Maamar, Z., Mostefaoui, S. K., & Yahyaoui, H. (2005). Toward an Agent-Based and Context-Oriented Approach for Web Services Composition. *IEEE Transactions on Knowledge and Data Engineering*, *17*(5), 686–697. doi:10.1109/TKDE.2005.82

Marik, V., & McFarlane, D. (2005). Industrial Adoption of the Agent-based Technologies. *IEEE Intelligent Systems*, *20*(9), 27–35. doi:10.1109/MIS.2005.11

Marks, E. A., & Bell, M. (2006). *Service-Oriented Architecture: A Planning and Implementation Guide for Business and Technology*. Hoboken, New Jersey: Wiley.

Maximilien, E. M., & Singh, M. P. (2005). *Multiagent System for Dynamic Web Services Selection.* Paper presented at The Workshop on Service-Oriented Computing and Agent-Based Engineering (SOCABE), Utrecht, The Netherlands.

McBride, D. (1998). *Successful deployment of IT Service Management in the distributed enterprise*. Hewlett-Packard Company.

McBride, E. (2009). A special report on waste. The Economist.

Nissen, M. E. (2001). Agent-Based Supply Chain Integration. *Information Technology Management*, *2*(3), 289–312. doi:10.1023/A:1011449109160

Passmore, D. (1996). Setting performance expectations. *Business Communications Review*, *26*(12), 20–22.

Porter, M. E. (1980). *Competitive Strategy*. New York: The Free Press.

Porter, M. E. (1985). *Competitive Advantage*. New York: The Free Press.

Revell, A., & Rutherfoord, R. (2003). UK Environmental Policy and the Small Firm: Broadening the focus. *Business Strategy and the Environment*, *12*, 26–35. doi:10.1002/bse.347

Revell, A., Stokes, D., & Chen, H.(2009). Small businesses and the environment: turning over a new leaf? *Business Strategy and the Environment.* Published Online: 16 Feb 2009.

Roberts, B., Svirskas, A., & Matthews, B. (2005). Request Based Virtual Organizations (RBVO): An Implementation Scenario. In L. M. Camarinha-Matos, H. Afsarmanesh, A. Ortiz (Eds.) *Collaborative Networks and Their Breeding Environments: Sixth IFIP Working Conference on VIRTUAL ENTERPRISES IFIP International Federation for Information Processing Vol. 186, 6th IFIP Working Conference on Virtual Enterprises (PRO-VE'05)* (pp. p17-24). Valencia, Spain.

Roberts, B., Svirskas, A., & Ward, J. (2005). Implementation Options for Virtual Organizations: A Peer to Peer (P2P) Approach. In: Putnik, Goran and Cunha, Maria Manuela, (eds.) *Virtual enterprise integration: technological and organizational perspectives* (pp. 400-416). Hershey PA:Idea Group Publishing.

Rutherfoord, R., Blackburn, R. A., & Spence, L. J. (2000). Environmental management and the small firm: an international comparison. *International Journal of Entrepreneurial Behavior & Research*, *6*(6), 310–326. doi:10.1108/13552550010362750

Saabeel, W., Verduijn, T. M., Hagdorn, L., & Kumar, K. (2002). A Model Of Virtual Organization: A Structure And Process Perspective. *Electronic Journal Of Organizational Virtualness*, *4*(1), 1–17.

Shen, W., Hao, Q., Wang, S., Li, Y., & Ghenniwa, H. (2007). An agent-based service-oriented integration architecture for collaborative intelligent manufacturing. *Robotics and Computer-integrated Manufacturing*, *23*(3), 315–325. doi:10.1016/j.rcim.2006.02.009

Shrivastava, P. (1995). Environmental technologies and competitive advantage. *Strategic Management Journal*, *16*(1), 183–200. doi:10.1002/smj.4250160923

Simpson, M., Taylor, N., & Barker, K. (2004). Environmental responsibility in SMEs: Does it deliver competitive advantage? *Business Strategy and the Environment*, *13*, 156–171. doi:10.1002/bse.398

Studer, S., Tsang, S., Welford, R., & Hills, P. (2008). SMEs and voluntary environmental initiatives: a study of stakeholders' perspectives in Hong Kong. *Journal of Environmental Planning and Management*, *51*(2), 285–301. doi:10.1080/09640560701865073

Svirskas, A., & Roberts, B. (2003). Towards business quality of service in virtual organisations through service level agreements and ebXML. In ISPE Conference (Ed.), *Concurrent Engineering: Vol. 1. Proceedings of the 10th ISPE International Conference on Concurrent Engineering: Research and Applications* (pp. 491-498). Taylor & Francis: Madeira, Portugal.

Swaminathan, J. M., Smith, S. F., & Sadeh, N. M. (2007). Modeling Supply Chain Dynamics: A Multiagent Approach. *Decision Sciences*, *29*(3), 607–632. doi:10.1111/j.1540-5915.1998.tb01356.x

Tektonidis, D., Ignatiadis, I., Katriou, S. A., & Koumpis, A. (June, 2008). *PANDA: Enabling RBVOs for the ERP/CRM industry using a Service Oriented Approach.* Paper presented at the 5th International Conference on Information Technology and Applications, ICITA, Cairns, Australia.

Tews, R. (2007). Beyond IT: The business value of SOA. *AIIM E-DOC*, *21*, 14–17.

Trienekens, J.J.M., & Bouman, J.J., & Zwan, Mvd. (2004). Specification of Service Level Agreements: Problems, Principles and Practices. *Software Quality Journal*, *12*, 43–57. doi:10.1023/B:SQJO.0000013358.61395.96

Vives, A. (2006). Social and Environmental Responsibility in Small and Medium Enterprises in Latin America. *Journal of Corporate Citizenship*, *21*, 39–50.

Vokrinek, J., Biba, J., Hodik, J., Vybihal, J., & Volf, P. (2009). RBVO Formation Protocol. *International Journal of Agent-Oriented Software Engineering*, *3*(2/3), 135–162. doi:10.1504/IJAOSE.2009.023634

Wernerfelt, B. (1984). The Resource-Based View of the Firm. *Strategic Management Journal*, *5*(2), 171–180. doi:10.1002/smj.4250050207

Williamson, D., Lynch-Wood, G., & Ramsay, J. (2006). Drivers of Environmental Behaviour in Manufacturing SMEs and the Implications for CSR. *Journal of Business Ethics*, *67*, 317–330. doi:10.1007/s10551-006-9187-1

Woods, D. (2003). *Enterprise Services Architecture*. Sebastopol, CA: O' Reilly.

Zutshi, A., & Sohal, A. (2004). Adoption and maintenance of environmental management systems: critical success factors. *Management of Environmental Quality An International Journal*, *15*(4), 399–419. doi:10.1108/14777830410540144

Section 3
New E-Business Frameworks

Chapter 16
Retail 2.0:
The Coming Up of a New Era for Retail Business in the 21st Century

José António Porfírio
Universidade Aberta, Portugal

Luís Ganhão
Oracle, Portugal

ABSTRACT

Retail was born in 1879 with the first Five & Dime Stores. 130 years after, we still live in the era of Retail 1.5, this means, no real Quantum Leap was made in Customer Experience. However, we strongly believe that, starting half of the first decade of the 21st Century, a new Retail Era began. This change is due to the fact that, not only Classic Retailers like Wal-Mart, Tesco and Carrefour started to look to the Persona, instead of a Person among Persons, but also eCommerce Retailers, such as Amazon or eBay showed that eCommerce Retail it's more than a Start-Up, which is something that we can observe by the continued and sustained Double Digit Revenue growths year after year. Social Retail hit the mainstream, when Time Magazine awarded Social Shopping Experience as one of the Best Inventions of 2007. The objective of the present study is to understand what have been done in the field of New Customer Experiences since the beginning of the Classic Retailers, and try to devise what will be the strategic implications for the future, arising from the changes foreseen in the field of retail business. The authors will emphasize the emerging new Trends, and try to foresee what in Social Retail and Online / Shop Customer Experience could be the mainstream for the next decade.

INTRODUCTION

Although some authors, like Drucker (1995) consider that retail was born in 18th century, in Japan, the generality of authors seems to be in accordance that, Retail Industry as we know it, was born in late 19th Century (1879) with the opening of Five & Dime store by F.W. Woolworth, which can be considered the father of Modern Retail.

Many others Five & Dime type of stores were followers until the Economic Downturn due to 1st World War and late 20's and early 30' great depression.

DOI: 10.4018/978-1-61692-880-3.ch016

After World War II we saw a new retail boom with the economy growing at a double digit rate. It was during the 50's and 60's that some of today's big name's in Retail were founded. This was the case of Sears, Wal-Mart and many others.

However, in spite of some downturns in this industry, especially in the mid 70's, Retail industry continued to Rise and Shine until today.

With the increasing needs of retailers on the management side and, in particular, regarding Logistics, we have seen during the 50´s, a significant contribution of retail business needs for the emergence of the Discipline of Supply Chain Management.

There is no doubt that the way retailers manage their business today (in the so-called retail 1.5 era) represents an important jump from the retail 1.0 era. However, we may say that today's retail megastores are an evolution but they are not really a revolution from the first Five & Dime Store.

Classic Retailers still present a growth of their revenue, but their margins are getting thinner day by day. Important traditional marketing issues like loyalty and customer retention, the reallocation of Store Space or the opening until late hours, don't work anymore. The result is a war for price in Classic Retail, with the known implications in terms of pressure for cost reduction.

Since there is not yet enough intelligence where the opportunity for profitably and the retaining of market share is most promising, Companies tend to invest into too many initiatives that produce zero or negative impact. That can prove expensive, perhaps fatal, since resources are suddenly decreasing. In this framework, getting more for less is the key for survival.

Although Social Retail is commonly misunderstood as ECommerce, it is our understanding that the Socialization of Retail will lead the future and this is a trend that we will see not only on the Web Market.

We believe that, if properly guided by strategic goals, Innovation & Technology can support the 21st Century Retailers to create this Brave New World, with the capacity to better understand Customers' Shopping Habits, help Shop Managers to know where are the "Hot and Cold corridors", to create Instant Promotions for each Customer in the Basket Case or to guarantee a real Just In Time Retail Logistics.

The objective of this study it's to devise what may be Retailers' (from Small and Medium Enterprises to Large Corporations) future, to help them to prepare strategically for the challenges that are arising, or as Gartner (2008) stated, to support why *"By 2015, more money will be spent marketing and selling to multiple anonymous online personas than marketing and selling offline".*

BACKGROUND

According to Datamonitor (2009), global hypermarkets and supercenters sector grew by 8.9% in 2008 to reach a value of $1,476.9 billion. Datamonitor states that in 2013, the global hypermarkets and supercenters sector is forecast to have a value of $1,923.8 billion, an increase of 30.3% since 2008.

The hypermarket and supercenters sector's annual growth rates fluctuated slightly over 2004-2008, but remained strong overall. The hypermarket and supercenters sector generated total revenues of $1,476.9 billion in 2008, representing a compound annual growth rate (CAGR) of 8.5% for the period spanning 2004-2008.

The performance of the sector is forecast to decelerate, with an anticipated CAGR of 5.4% for the five-year period 2008-2013, which is expected to drive the sector to a value of $1,923.8 billion by the end of 2013.

Analysts also expect that there will not be any *New Kid on the Block*, in classic retail since large corporations will benefit from scale economies. So, to create new large hypermarkets companies must invest significantly in things like purchase merchandise, premises, hire and train employees, or marketing (Datamonitor, 2009).

Classic retailers will continue to invest in cost reductions, and will continue their roadmap to have Online Stores, like Wal-Mart Sam's Club or Carrefour's Ooshop.

On the other hand, eCommerce Traders are growing. According to OneSource (2009a:44):"*one of the strongest retail performers in this year's survey was Amazon. It not only ranked as one of the fastest-growing brands, but also was the No. 1 brand, among all categories, in brand momentum, a measurement of short-term prospects. Its performance reflected the particular strength of the brand and the general growth of online, according to the study.*"

So, a Corporation that what we recognize is only a Simple Webpage was able to create a Premium Brand worldwide, through the use of innovative web marketing techniques.

It is unquestionable that Online Shopping have many benefits for the end-customer, and this is creating a permanent shift in behavior for consumers as "*consumers find that the Internet provides greater convenience, timesaving and product focus than the traditional store environment.*" (OneSource, 2009a)

At the same time it is interesting to realize, that one of the showstoppers of classic retailers growth is geography, since "*retailing remains the world's most locally based major industry (...). Almost half of the top 25 brands are largely single-market operators. Twelve derive 90% or more of their revenues from one country.*" (OneSource, 2009a).

One of the most promising tools to face these new challenges posed by this new type of consumers deriving from what has been called the "Virtual Generation" (Gartner, 2008), is CRM.

In their CRM Summit in Washington D.C. in September 2008, Gartner stated that "*unlike previous generations, Generation Virtual is not defined by age, gender, social demographic or geography – but is based on demonstrated achievement, accomplishments and an increasing preference for the use of digital media*". *(Gartner, 2008)*

We will adopt the ideas of Generation Virtual's study (Gartner, 2008), and in particular we will develop the ideas presented in its magic quadrant called Four Levels of Community Engagement, in our sub-chapter Solutions and Recommendations. For this, it is important to keep in mind the main characteristics of the so-called Generation Virtual *personas* presented in this study, that classify them into four major groups:

1. Up to 3% will be creators, providing original content. They can be advocates that promote products and services;
2. Between 3% and 10% will be contributors who add to the conversation, but don't initiate it. They can recommend products and services as customers move through a buying process, looking for purchase advise;
3. Between 10% and 20% will be opportunists, who can further contributions regarding purchasing decisions. Opportunists can add value to a conversation that's taking place while walking through a considered purchase;
4. Approximately 80% will be lurkers, essentially spectators, who reap the rewards of online community input but absorb only what is being communicated. They can still implicitly contribute and indirectly validate value from the rest of the community. All users start out as lurkers.

We strongly believe that the use of these principles and the consideration of these characteristics will help Retailers to obtain performances above average. It is our strong believe that in 2025 no Company will survive if:

a. No Generation V Creator recognizes value in Retailer, creating original content about the Company;
b. No Generation V Contributor proactively add positive remarks to already created contents (official or non-official);

Figure 1. Business volumes and growth for global hypermarkets and super centers: 2004-2008. Source: Datamonitor (2009)

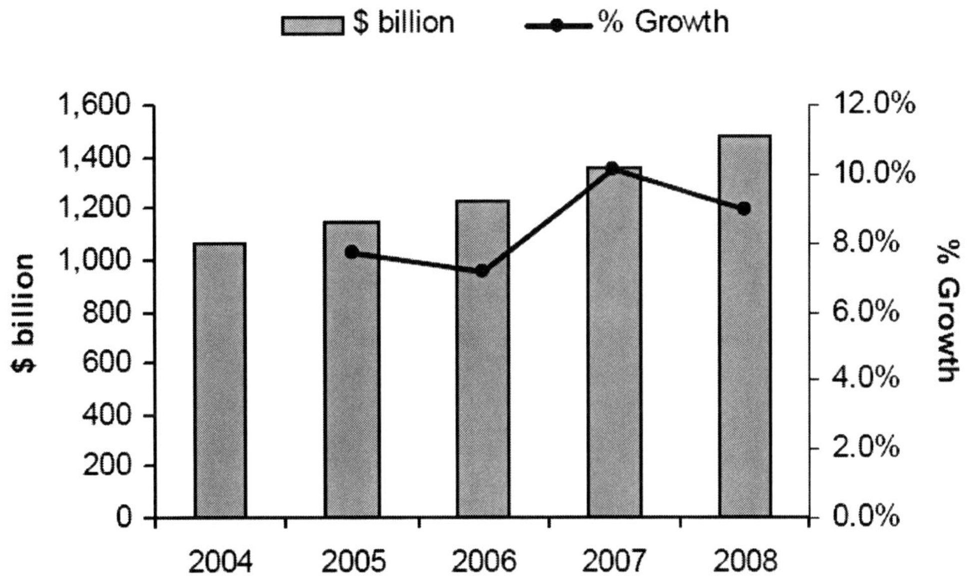

c. No Generation V Opportunist uses good remarks made by Creators and Contributors, and making the purchase, to guarantee that 80% of the futures Generation V, the Lurkers, on top of the previous good remarks, do the purchase, increasing by this way Social Retailers' Revenue Pipeline.

That is to say, the famous Silverman's principle "*It's not about the Product, it's about Customer Experience*" (Silverman, 2005) will gain a new dimension when we think about the power of web, especially if we think that the "*the secrets of the word of mouth*" will be replaced by "*the secrets of the posts on the web*" and this will produce the effect of multiplying the effects of customer experience by millions instead of a just few dozens.

MAIN FOCUS OF THE CHAPTER

Classic Retail in a Downturn

Retail business volumes have recorded a general increase during last decades. Figure 1, show the most recent evolution regarding these figures from 2004 to nowadays.

However, it is possible to see that this growth is accompanied by a general reduction in the growth rate of sales in this sector. As we can see in figure 2 (DataMonitor, 2009) analysts are forecasting a decline in Growth Revenue for classic retailers.

With a decrease of Growing Revenue, classic large retailers are forcing to maximize and revamp their revenue.

For instance, Wal-Mart is pushing itself to be number 1 retailer in several countries, and even to growth in the United States market (Oberholzer-Gee, 2006).

Figure 2. Business volumes and growth for global hypermarkets and super centers: Forecast for 2008-2013. Source: Datamonitor (2009)

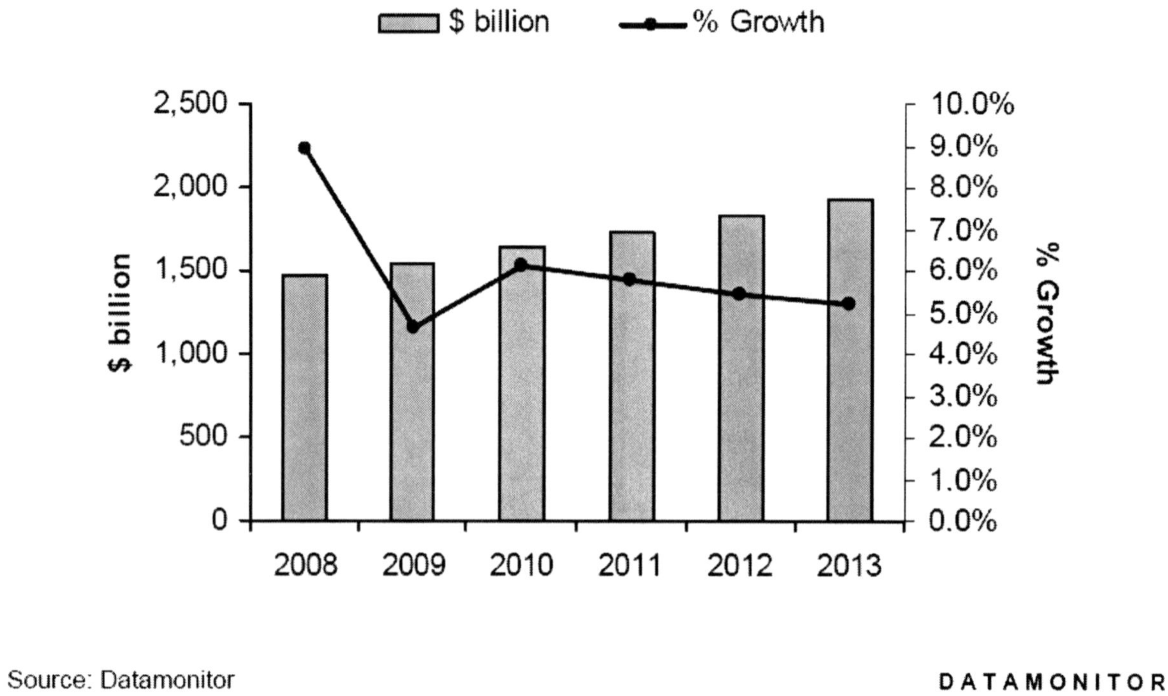

These types of expansion movements from big retailers tend to originate true storms in the geographic markets where they intend to establish for new or even just to develop their businesses. For instance, "*Wal-Mart's planned entry into California caused a storm even before the discounter opened a single supercenter. Anticipating a further decline in prices, grocery chains in southern California, where the "big three" dominated, asked their employees to bear a larger fraction of health-care costs. To be able to compete with Wal-Mart, the chains argued, stores needed to lower benefits and wages for new employees. Elsewhere in the United States, Wal-Mart's entry into new markets had dampened prices.*" (Oberholzer-Gee, 2006)

The social impacts coming up from cost reduction' efforts that are being done by giant retailers will be discussed further in this chapter. Nevertheless, it is also important to consider the slowly decease of local retailers that we are seeing in the last couple of years, mainly due to the expansion of number of shops that large retailers have. As we argued before, these facts further support the growth of Social Retail, since effectively one may say that the only true important difference between big and less big (or even small) retailers it is price. Nowadays large retailers only offer the same product at a lower cost, but they were not capable yet to offer higher customer interaction, like it seems to be the case for local retailers.

ECommerce Opportunities for Retail Giants

A different path of growth can be seen in eCommerce business.

According to Amazon's earning report, company grew more than the double compared with Classic Retail growth, as seen before. Classic retail Revenue growth was 8.5% in last year, compared with an astonishing 18% Revenue Growth (24%

on Net Sales Growth) on the eCommerce volume of business (OneSource, 2009b)

Strategically, this fact is making that, even in small countries like Portugal, large retailers (maybe the most well equipped to catch this train), are trying to surf the eCommerce wave. For instance, Continente, the largest Portuguese retailer, states that the number of Customers of Continente Online is growing around 30% plus every year, being now more that 150.000 (1,5% of all Population, almost 5% of all families) (IOL, 2008).

The eCommerce web traffic grew 10% in 2008. This phenomenon is being accompanied closely by top ten big retailers that are starting to look this channel as an important part of their development strategies and that are even showing the ability to outgrow the natural growth of the web audience. This fact is being interpreted as a sign that classic retail business is no longer considering the online as a simple add on to its classical business but, instead, they are looking at it as a crucial part of their strategy (Nielsen, 2009).

The goal of any strategy is to create value for the customer. Being value a very subjective concept, in our analysis we will try to adapt the Gartner's Virtual Generation's characteristics to the strategic principles applied to retail business and, in particular to eCommerce, in order to devise what may be the future for retail business in general and what could be the pathway for development of this business.

To serve customers means to be aware of customer's needs and expectations. Making use of the conclusions that came out from Yahoo's (2009) initiative that put together highly renewed marketers and some of the top executives of the largest UK Retailers, we may conclude that, on the side of the consumers the most important characteristics can be summarized as follows (Yahoo, 2009):

- Consumers are becoming savvier, actively seeking out bargains. In this sense, when speaking about universal customer appeal and quality, marketing and branding are being replaced for real value for money that, according to a customer's director at Sainsbury, can be summarized in the following principle: "they (customers) either see the value in their basket or they don't";
- Value for money can also be seen in terms of product's durability which can be translated in a simple indicator like "cost per usage", a concept that must be adapted to each specific product considered. For instance, Melissa Littler, marketing director at online fashion retailer Brand Alley, believes that *"consumer priority when clothes shopping is 'cost per wear'"*. This, she argues, *"is the appeal of discount designer fashion, as it is perceived as providing 'value that will last'".)*.
- Online broke geographic constraints. At the same level that we see this growing concern with value, one may state that consumers are increasingly researching products online before purchasing. According to a managing partner and head of new business and marketing at MediaCom, "Retailers need to enable consumers to travel seamlessly from online to offline stores."
- ECommerce shopping broke, somehow, with impulsive buying. Reflection started to be present before the decision to buy. MediaCom's Robinson contends that although people are thinking carefully before purchasing, 'they will invest in something if it's good value - even if it's quite a high-ticket item'. This is because consumers are prepared to invest in brands that will contribute to reinforce their ego and make them feel good
- Touch and squeeze, appealing to senses, has been replaced for reflection and projection, specially after a good system that

will alert consumers for similar or related products to buy;

- Shoppers were able to partially replace sympathy and attention of the employees by good graphics, information about products or services, and satisfaction with service, or opportunity to easy return anything that was bought by mistake.

Strategy is about value creation. And value depends on customers. So, we may say that, thinking strategically is to think about customers' whishes and expectations.

As described, retail customers' characteristics are changing, being today very different that they were in the past. Principles in eCommerce have made a type of retail very different from traditional retail functioning. The new generation of customers in retail is fuelling strategic changes in retail companies.

However, it is interesting to notice that, for some shoppers, the in-store experience and service is still playing the most influential role when choosing a retailer. One may question if retailers should ignore the in-store experience. As Jamie Davis, the creative director of Mood Media pointed out: "*Everyone seems to be looking for that point of difference(...) Clients have been coming to us and asking for extra things they can do in store and online*'" (Yahoo, 2009).

Traditionally, to create value, retailers needed to be able to pass to customers a stronger message about service, the store environment and the staff on the shop floor. But today, with the emergence of eCommerce, value creation it is not just this. We would dare to say that, besides service – whose importance might have increased – the rest of these factors are less important nowadays to the strategy of a retail company than it was before.

But this does not necessarily mean that traditional retail is dead. There will always be more conservative customers that will like to go to the stores. And for them, staff training and customer service will always be paramount if we want to talk about brand value. The main questions than it is how much time and money should retailers invest in customer service instead of business analytics and IT, especially on times where the emphasis on the bottom line is so great.

Value is also related with price, and this, in turn, is related with product availability. Retailers are, by definition, intermediaries between producers and consumers. So, the capacity to foresee what are, when it will be, and where will the consumers manifest their interests for a particular product, having at the same time the capability to deliver that product on time and place, preferably, with a peculiar interesting service associated, becomes the main difference between success and failure of retail business. And these pose very different questions compared with the traditional ones that usually pose to traditional brick and mortar retail business. This also paved the way for the astonishing increase of business analytics in retail.

All these things do not necessarily mean that business goes more and more intangible and that product became irrelevant in the overall equation. It is important to consider that the product being purchased tends to dictate the level of service required: the level of service required when someone buys a book online is very different from the necessary level of service when one buy a mobile phone using the same channel. However, when we are talking about competitors on the same product, the level of service will represent a differentiation feature between those that are competing.

In other words, it still is very important that websites used to deal with customers carry through the message that a retailer uses on the high street. Also, it is important to consider that the ease of convenience online must be intertwined with a very good and efficient service.

Moreover it is very important to have in mind that consumer's confidence on a certain product could dictate a stronger ability to buy it online, independently from the service associated by the online retailer or, as stated by the head of brand communication at John Lewis, consumer confidence is the key. '*If customer confidence in the product is high, chances are that you will buy it online. When confidence is a bit lower, consumers want to touch it and feel it, so service becomes more important.*'

In summary, eCommerce must depart from the structured experience that customers expect. And expectations are based on their experiences of the bricks and mortar's business.

Social Shopping Experience Hit the Mainstream

Web-based transactions are not just about service and ease of convenience. Being customer-centered has implicit the need to understand people's needs. To know what they have – and what they want to have – in life, it stills to be very important if one wants to do business online.

Having this in mind, management is seen nowadays, as the most important factor for competitiveness in the increasingly competitive marketplace, and it must be placed at the same level of importance of customer loyalty and retention. In this sense, expanding existing customer relationships, new customer acquisitions, and improving customer service are top management issues in business. Even important aspects like pricing optimization, business performance management and risk management tend to trail the renewed emphasis on customer. And, "*by capitalizing on high-impact business analytics, business leaders are better able to develop agile strategies that inevitably improve profitability, such as investment in innovative product development and customer retention and acquisition*" (Business Week,2009).

Being customer-centric should translate in either selling more to your existing customers or find new customers to sell to, or both. And these are the same challenges that are being put today to modern retail companies. These challenges may be faced with the help of social retail.

In its first edition of 2008, Time Magazine awarded Social Shopping Experience as the Best Invention of 2007. Social retail may be defined as "*the ability to turn conversations into sales*" or, in other words, it is "*the ability to make your customers to talk about your products and recommend them to their friends*" (socialnetit.com, 2009).

Traditionally, the volume of sales was very dependent on the capacity of employees to talk with customers that went to the shop. Modern retail and, in particular, retail based on eCommerce, replaced traditional shops by internet communication and web pages. So, one may question how we can do this in modern retail if customers do not go so often to the shops. The answer is through the use of internet tools which, at the same time, could mean to train and to adapt your employees to this new reality but also, to invest in web-based technologies. These technologies should allow knowing what each particular customer usually do and what are their needs and, at the same time, try to help him/her doing it easier, faster, cheaper to him/her and, simultaneously with more profits to you. Once he/se is happy, make sure that he/she will talk about your products and services to a friend and will recommend them. If necessary, make it available the necessary internet tools to facilitate this job.

A very interesting pilot experience in this field is using Nanette's Clothes Trade Mark associated to *Social Retailing®* IconNicholson's technology, and is being carried out at Bloomingdales (lbiiconnicholson.com/#).

Considered to be at the leading edge of retail innovation, the technology Prototype used at Bloomingdale' uses a paneled interactive mirror that provides on the spot feedback and an ambient aura animation, while beaming the experience across the websphere via live video feed.

By using proper kiosks, teens can make buying decisions together; see what others have purchased, as well as purchase items that are not in stock in the store. The technology in the store also explores the concept of user generated content. The prototype can be used instore or online and "*with Social Retailing® shoppers can get instant*

Figure 3. Bloomingdales social retail prototype. Source: http://theretailer.blogosfere.it/location/new_york/3.html

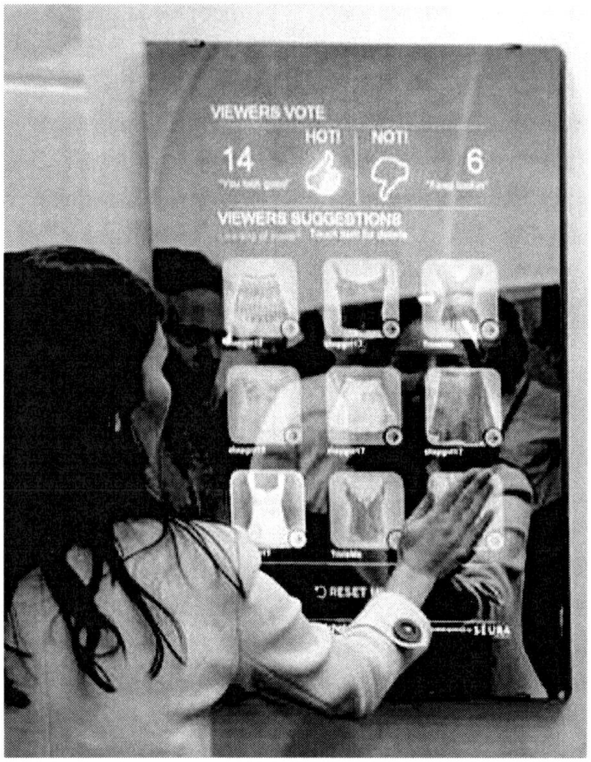

feedback from their pals or observers, anywhere in the world. Shoppers stand before an interactive mirror while their images are broadcast over the internet. Feedback is displayed on the mirror. (...) Shoppers can "try on" virtual versions of other items displayed in the mirror" (http://www.lbiiconnicholson.com/#/work/social_retailing).

Bloomingdale's idea, as pointed out by Frank Doroff, Senior Executive VP and General Merchandise Manager, is to reach today's young tech-savvy shopper, whose expectations are to be connected 24/7 with her friends even while shopping. In this sense, Social Retailing enhances that ability to connect and Bloomingdale expects to draw new, younger shoppers to their stores and to continuing to enhance its customers' shopping experience both on-and offline.

Social retail may have very important implications on the business life for second generation's retail companies in general and, in particular, for those more dependent on eCommerce, since it can be a source for:

1. Happy Customers;
2. Real Time Feedback;
3. Just in Time Supply Chain Management;
4. Answer to new buying habits and preferences;

and that is unquestionably something very beneficial, at the same time, for customers as well as the retailers themselves.

In a Manifesto published in January 2009, Peter Doyle[1] presented what have been called the ten main features regarding social retail in UK, as the following:

1. The customer is king (or queen).

2. If you can't find what you are looking for, tell us and we will find it for you.
3. If you are not satisfied, tell us and we will put it right for you.
4. We want to hear what you have to say about us – good or bad. Please talk to us.
5. Tell us when we make mistakes and we will try not to repeat them.
6. We encourage you to share your views, good or bad, on our service and our products with other shoppers and we will provide you with a place to share your views on our service and our products with us and other customers online and in our shops.
7. We sometimes rely on other companies to support our service to you, please tell us if they let you down and we will find other companies who won't.
8. Customer service is not a department.
9. We don't try to persuade you to buy things you don't need, it doesn't help anyone in the long run.
10. Every member of staff has the power to help you, please ask them questions and don't let them push you to other departments when you have a query. It's our job to communicate with every department not yours. We won't waste your valuable time.

Size of the Social Retail Market

According to Doyle (2008), one may situate the first generation of eCommerce sites in the late 90s. There we had good transactional sites, some of them with a nice good shop front and keen online shopping features, mostly pioneered by .com pure plays like Amazon.com et al.

Online sales were seen as an additional source of revenue for companies, and an alternative distribution channel. This has justified, sometimes, the creation of online departments associated with this new channel. But, the underlying management practices were still based on business as usual, that is to say, the usual brick and mortar rules of businesses.

In the above subchapter one example of Social Retail was shown, and many others already hit the High Street, but the big question is "Is there money on the table for Retailers 2.0?".

In our opinion there is still a long way for eCommerce to grow and, within eCommerce; social retail will present an increased share of the market. If there are any doubts about this, maybe we may take a look at the market figures.

ECommerce hit 250 B$ in sales during 2008 and, according to different forecasts, the overall sales on eCommerce is predicted to reach an astonishing value of 500 B$ by 2012. This means that the markets will double in 4 years, which means a Compound Aggregate Growth Rate of around 20% by year.

The 21st century has seen a very important difference in this traditional business model, starting by a new generation of web sites and web applications. Due to the tremendous development of things like social networks, online communities, blogs, reviews and forums, the discussion groups and customers became savvier and research much more online before they decide to buy anything.

This movements increased the difficulties to sale as before but, at the same time, brought new opportunities for companies once they are able to explore this new world and the expectations of the generations that live on it (Doyle, 2008). And in this scenario, social retail has definitely found its proper and autonomous way to grow.

From our point of view, social retail, if fuelled by the right technologies, will represent a big and ever increasing share of this growth once it presents the capacity to help retailers to realize new retailing innovations, waiting to delight customers, improve margins and propel profits to new heights.

ISSUES, CONTROVERSIES, PROBLEMS

In the future of retail's world there are many important discussions going on. Of these, we selected four topics which we believe will remain strategic issues for retailers' success. These topics will remain determinant to define the future position of players within this market, both for classic as well as for 2.0 generation retail companies.

Classic Retailers Costs Reduction

There is no possible good strategy for a decadent marketplace. The 21st Century Classic Retail will struggle to keep the pace with Net Margins and growing Revenue under pressure. In general, Classic Retailers are making huge efforts to lower their costs, a situation that is creating social problems in the different markets where classic big retail corporations have a huge importance in terms of employment.

For instance, although Wal-Mart damped prices in the new geographies where their market share is growing, there were also social problems involved, not only inside Wal-Mart with low benefits, "*The Company's critics alleged Wal-Mart's wage policies kept employees below the poverty line. According to these estimates, in 2003 the average pay of a sales clerk at Wal-Mart was $8.50 an hour, or about $14,000 a year, a figure that was $1,000 below the poverty line for a family of three. Low wages, the critics argued, also prevented Wal-Mart employees from participating in the company's health plan. Representative George Miller, senior Democrat on the U.S. House Committee on Education and the Workforce, estimated that Wal-Mart employees paid 42% of their health-care costs.*" (Oberholzer-Gee, 2006).

Wal-Mart also stressed existing Retailers to reduce drastically benefits from their current employees to match Wal-Mart lower prices "*In this environment, Wal-Mart's planned entry into California caused a storm even before the discounter opened a single supercenter. Anticipating a further decline in prices, grocery chains in southern California, where the big three dominated, asked their employees to bear a larger fraction of health-care costs. To be able to compete with Wal-Mart, the chains argued, stores needed to lower benefits and wages for new employees. Elsewhere in the United States, Wal-Mart's entry into new markets had dampened prices. Prices for popular items such as shampoo and laundry detergent tended to fall by 1.5% to 3% in the quarter after Wal-Mart's entry.*" (*ibidem*).

Quality of Service on Web-Channel

There are a lot of subjects regarding quality of service on the web channel. However it is known that one of the main barriers to online shopping is related with payment's security. Being a crucial subject, a major issue surrounding payment security and data privacy is the availability and implementation of a global, unified standard.

Nowadays there are too many Payment Security Standards, such as PCI DSS, EMVCo and SEPA. With globalization in place, we understand that a new order for Electronic Payments must exist.

The major issues to such a task are:

- Standardized Implementation of Existing Security Standards – aiming to release a common interpretation of existing security standards (PCI DSS, EMVCo, SEPA) and publish recommended implementation guidelines that can foster widespread compliance.
- Security of Payment Device Lifecycle – aiming to ensure security during the complete POS terminal lifecycle through an appropriate management protocol – from manufacture through deployment, field maintenance and application software upgrades and eventual end-of-life and remov-

al and secure destruction. Includes device tracking and auditing processes.
- Security Threat Analysis and Intelligence – aiming to provide education and resources to educate members and payment industry stakeholders regarding the current threats and ways to mitigate them.
- End-to-End Encryption – to create recommended implementation guidelines for the encryption of cardholder data utilizing hardware-level security before it enters the application environment.

In our opinion, these are topics that will represent very important domains of development and, at the same time, opportunities for SMEs in the eBusiness domain.

Higher Margins on WebChannel (No Fix Costs)

Another very important strategic subject is related with the cost structure of companies operating in the retail business.

When we look in detail for the Profit and Loss Figures of Classic Retailers like Wal-Mart, Tesco and Carrefour, and compare them with eCommerce Retailers like Amazon or eBay we will notice a huge difference in the level of their Fixed Costs. In general these younger companies do not present so heavy costs in important domains like:

- Shops Workforce;
- Shops Rental or Buying;
- Shops Fixed Costs (like Water, Electricity, etc);
- Supply Chain Management (since they usually do not possess own Warehouses and subcontract transportation services to deliver their products).

Nevertheless, we may observe that Social Retailers sell their products at almost the same price (eventually around 5% to 10% cheaper), than classical retailers. In spite of that, usually eCommerce's customers also need to pay for the shipment of the products.

So, it is our understanding that sooner or later, in eCommerce retailing, margins will also start to decrease, since:

- New companies will inevitably emerge, and we may expect a War for Price;
- Customers will start asking to eCommerce Retailers to lower even further their prices;
- The decrease (or disappearance) of cost of shipment will be also another customers demanding

Two or One Type of Retail in the Future

As a corollary, one of the major discussions in the market it is about the future of Retail. The main question being discussed is: "in 50 years will Classic Retail still exists?".

Even though everybody knows that futurology is hard to do, there seems to be no doubt that eCommerce and Social Retailing supported by New Technologies will develop, but that doesn't mean the end of Classic Retail, since:

- Classic Retailers will adopt also New Technologies;
- Side-by-side with technology adoption, traditional retailers will start to develop new management techniques in line with the needs arising from a new type of consumers (Generation "V" consumers);
- Consumers traditionally don't like to buy perishable products without having them on front of their eyes.

We understand that there is still a long road to go. During the 1960s the new Trend that everybody talked about was flying cars. In 2000 people believed that everyone was going to have their own "Flying Car". Evolution was as we know it.

What we mean with this comparison is that, although it seems to be no doubt about Social Retailing's growth, that doesn't necessarily mean the end of the Face-to-Face (brick-and-mortar) Large Retailers. But that does not mean that they will not face serious strategic problems for survival.

STRATEGIC IMPLICATIONS ARISING FROM RETAIL BUSINESS REVOLUTION

"*Globalization and electronic commerce present real challenges to the strategic management of business corporations*" (Wheelen and Hunger, 2008: 8) and especially to retail companies.

Twenty years ago, internet and web markets could be considered for most companies as internationalization was seen for the majority of enterprises during the 60s, that is to say, either it does not existed or, if it existed, it was carried out by a particular – usually smaller – division of the company.

If we consider traditional retail business, one may state that the offline markets where they use to work can be inefficient because they are usually fragmented and regional in nature, which is something that makes difficult and expensive for buyers and sellers to meet, to exchange information and to complete transactions. Due to this, with the exception of the big retailers, they usually offered a limited variety and breadth of goods and, they have high transaction costs due to intermediaries (Wheelen and Hunger, 2008).

With the broadband[2] development around the world, it has become much easier for a person to shop from the comfort at home. This has made that, nowadays web markets are, by their own, responsible for the existence of a lot of companies that, sometimes, supplant the traditional ones both in terms of size and in terms of profitability.

Moreover, we may observe a general trend in what web markets are replacing sales forces for many companies, and hard distribution channels are being replaced by technology and soft infrastructure based on software programs.

Even when we talk about service in retail business, it is important to differentiate traditional and new retail business. In the past, talk about service is to talk about sales force taking personally care of individual customers. However, new retail business it is not based on sales force. In new retail business, customer does not even need to ask for a salesman to consider service. Service means that customers will always know where to find the products that they need, what are their colors and sizes, and what their prices are. In this new conception of retail, service means specially to provide information (Drucker, 1995)

The dematerialization of shops must be seen together with the new classification for customers. Generation V replaced the traditional "seniors", the "baby boomers", the "generation X2" and the "generation Y". If new retailers want to become customer-centric, like it did Amazon.com with the know success that it obtained, customers can no longer be distinguished by their age but, instead, they must be considered specially by the ability they have to use IT, as well as their expectations regarding the products or services that they want to acquire.

Internet changed the way business agents interact and do business and, at the same time, changed the way companies work internally. These changes are still happening in the present and they are affecting competition in many industries by shifting competition and changing radically the value chain of the industries involved affecting the way competitive advantages are developed, maintained or loosed (Wheelen and Hunger, 2008).

First of all, when thinking about retail business, one may talk about a change in the concept of this industry. Retail is, by definition, intermediation between production and consumers. And, one of the first implications arising from the use of internet for business is precisely the idea of disintermediation (breaking down) of traditional distribution channels. Internet allows consumers to do business directly with producers making that, anything else immutable, intermediaries become useless. So, the main question arising from this trend it is: what can retailers do to break with this apparent destiny fatality?

The second idea to consider is the increase of importance given to customers. Disintermediation and the huge amount of information available to any consumer, originated by the internet, are shifting the balance of power from producers to consumers.

Traditionally, retail business pinned their hopes for the future on the creative ideas of their top merchants and marketers. However, in a much more customer-centric world, things cannot just be based on marketing and product features. "*Know the customer*" will be the "*retailing mantra (...) but it is not just knowing the customer (...) it is to anticipate and shape future demand to come as close as possible to satisfying each customer's unique needs (...) it is about tailoring the entire shopping experience to create an emotional bond with the customer*" (SAS, 2009: 6)[3].

Modern retail business can be considered as a high-technology industry. So, as pointed out by Alfred Chandler, in high technology industries, organizational strengths are mainly derived from learning capabilities (Wheelen and Hunger, 2008).

If it is true that the traditional management hits are still being very important (once operational excellence it is still a must for doing business), it is also true that companies must be capable to develop new abilities to deal with this more demanding world of consumers. That is to say that the brand, the experience or the merchandise still are key variables that help new retailers to emerge, the existing retailers to thrive, and the successful retailers to take their successes to new heights.

However, the ability to improve results is more dependent from the capacity to improve performance and, to be in the hedge of the future, companies in the field will need to develop a visionary leadership, a capacity to leverage the potentialities of information coming from the use of business analytics. Once consumers are getting more demanding, the capacity of companies to offer the right products at the right stores, at the right moment when customers demand them, at the right quantities and at the right price with the best service quality that is possible becomes crucial factors for success (SAS, 2009). These are features that could differentiate retailers and they are crucial if we want to talk about long term customer retention and satisfaction. And this calls for the intensive use of technologies as well as information (not data) obtained from it.

The use of business analytics has being seen as an important aid for business development in this framework. Business Analytics could allow retailers to increase the number of customers and to make shoppers spending more money. This should be a direct result of a bigger comprehension of customer's needs and expectations, the capacity to optimize prices and the ability to track company's performance more efficiently.

Strategy is much more than just business-as-usual. In this sense, one must consider that Business Analytics, as well as social retailing, depend heavily on technology and these are crucial aspects regarding the capacity to innovate in the retail business of the future.

Strategy means, by definition, the capacity of a company to conceive and implement a comprehensive master plan in order to achieve pre-determined objectives, by following a peculiar path of development.

Strategy should pave the way to obtain, to strengthen, or just to maintain competitive advantages that will allow the company to operate in a certain market obtaining better performance than their competitors.

Every strategy must consider the environment where the company operates and where the business develops. And one of the important aspects that came out from the increased use of internet is that knowledge is becoming a key issue for business and a real source of competitive advantage for companies. This is particularly important if we are talking about markets whose main "raw material" is information which is the case of the retail market.

In this sense, it is arguable to consider that eCommerce has obliged managers to think "outside the box" since the use of internet as an important market for most companies operated an important change in competition. One of these changes is related with time.

With internet, the competitive advantage became even a more temporary issue than it was before and this represents a big challenge for companies since any sustainable competitive advantage no longer depends on setting and following a centrally managed five-year plan. The *buzzword* associated to strategy in the new era of retail business is strategic flexibility.

The emergence of the global knowledge economy created new opportunities for companies. These opportunities are being fuelled by the fact that competitive advantage started to be primarily based on knowledge; knowledge is increasingly scattered around the world and not just based in one placed as it happened before; and the cost of distance is falling rapidly for commodities that are mobile, like capital, goods and information, which made them accessible to all (Doz et al., 2001).

In practice, strategic flexibility must be rooted in the company's critical resources (either developed to or acquired by the company) and, to be sustainable, it must be a process rooted in an environment of what specialists call a "learning organization". A learning organization can be seen as "*an organization skilled to create, acquire and transfer knowledge and, by doing this, an organization that becomes capable of modifying its environment to reflect continuously new knowledge and insights*" (Wheelen and Hunger, 2008: 9).

A learning organization is rooted in what specialists call the idea of Organizational Learning that is seen as a critical component of competition in very dynamic environment like that we are talking about. These are crucial factors for the capacity of the organization to innovate and to be capable of new product development. According to Wheelen and Hunger (2008) learning organizations are skilled at four main activities: solving problems systematically; experimenting with new approaches; learning from their own experiences and past history, as well as the experience of others; and transferring knowledge on an efficient and quick way throughout the organization.

These are characteristics that we must see in today's eCommerce organizations.

Barriers to entry in eCommerce business can be considered relatively low. The expertise of a company, from where it obtains the competitive advantage that supports their hopes for the future is based on its capacity to learn and to develop the necessary skills to be more competitive than their competitors.

In the internet markets, a small investment may allow a company to operate its own ISP and to provide eCommerce solutions and online contents to its customers[4].

At the same time, internet markets make possible to obtain scale economies by exploring a specific niche market, once it can broke the traditional geographic barriers to trade.

For strategy analysis, this meant to break with the obstructions that make any company to enter into a new market and poses a permanent pressure for companies already established in a certain market. Even the switching costs would be relatively low if we think about the dynamics involving the software industry and the need to profit permanently from the new features available from the use of new versions of specific software or even new software for a particular need. This is crucial concerning good service from the part of eCommerce companies.

Retail business in the 2.0 era is (and will be each time more) based on intangibility since the competitive origin of retail business, always considered as an intermediary between producers and consumers, lies on their capacity to transform the knowledge and learning capacity into immaterial services that, by its turn, derives very practical to the customers and can be translated into time or money. Customers must feel that it compensates to use the services offered by eCommerce retailers, instead of using the traditional sopping way.

However, due to dynamic environment and to what has been called the Hypercompetition[5] that characterizes this industry, it is not enough to have the best services, being crucial to show the ability to permanently innovate. Otherwise companies will be through out of the market, defeated by the most innovative competitors.

As Drucker said, "*retailers barely talk about reengineering. For them that sounds to much to industrial units. However, they are always redrawing their operations. In fact, most of them redesign continuously all their businesses. (...) Wal-Mart's success is largely based in the redefinition of retail business as merchandise movements, and not merchandise sales.*" (Drucker, 1995: 101).

It is widely accepted that innovation is an essential component of strategy in every market. However, due to the characteristics of retail markets, innovation may be considered as a passport for a retail company to live and one of the main competencies that derive from the organizational learning is the increased capacity of companies to innovate and to develop new products, factors that could originate a kind of barriers to entry to new competitors and so, that can sustain the performance of a company in the market for some time.

As already referred, another crucial factor for competition in today's environment for eCommerce is technology and software.

Technology plays also a very important role in many eCommerce business cases of success (where maybe the most emblematic one is Amazon.com) and, at the same time, could represent a very interesting opportunity for SMEs.

Technology could be considered either as web site's management capacity; search and customer's interaction; recommendations to customers based on data analysis concerned with their past operations; transaction processing and fulfillment service technology; etc. .

Technology can operate with proprietary software, with commercially available licensed software or both. It is up to the companies to decide whether it is useful to invest in software development or to acquire already existing software. However, they must have present that this could make the difference on service offered to their customers.

Besides software for encryption and managing of the wireless selling platform, on the operations side, eCommerce companies must assure that they have available software for accepting and validating customers' orders; to place and track orders with their suppliers; to manage and assign inventory to customers' orders; to ensure proper shipment of goods to customers (Wheelen and Hunger, 2008).

SOLUTIONS AND RECOMMENDATIONS

Classic Retailers Costs Reduction

United States ruling bodies proposed to Wal-Mart to guarantee that at least two thirds of their workforce was in Insurance Wealth Plan.

The situation in California, where some city councils were trying to avoid Wal-Mart entrance in their territories were solved with Voting on Propositions, in almost all councils people voted for the Openness of the Retail Market.

With the maturation of the market, we should expect more Mergers & Acquisitions to occur, current Classic Retailers Margins are to dim, so the only option to have a good Profit and Loss balance it is to raise Volume, since Net Margin it's impossible to growth. And eCommerce could be considered the best way to fulfill this goal. We may even expect that eCommerce will replace traditional retail businesses in importance.

Quality of Service on Web-Channel

According to IDC[6], a solution for the Security Holes in electronic payments is being studied by an International Non-Profit Organization, SPVA[7].

SPVA was founded VeriFone[8], Ingenico[9] and Hypercom[10], positions itself as the possible response to guarantee a cohesive, uniform approach to payment security for global retailers.

According to Christophe Dolique, SPVA Chairman, the work of SPVA is driving across the payment value chain. The company's mission is "*to develop an end-to-end security framework and to enhance security elements of payment solutions which protect cardholder information and defend merchants and acquirers against security breaches, while reducing fraud and lowering risk for all electronic payment stakeholders.*"

It is our understanding that the creation of Open Standards used by all retailers world-wide, being these standards completely open and not owned by any organization will be the best solutions for this situation.

FUTURE RESEARCH DIRECTIONS

There is no doubt nowadays that retail is undergoing a very important transformation. A very important issue arising from the changes, and the challenges, that we have described in previous topics concerns the implications that the retail business revolution has for the future of corporate retailers.

Some years ago, some startups try to be ahead of their time, during the eCommerce boom at the turn of the century, one of failed dot com companies was Garden.com.

In www.garden.com, consumers could enter information about where their house was located (by zip code), the color scheme of the house's exterior, and the basic layout of the yard. Based on this information the site would recommend landscape designs, plantings, and custom blended fertilizer for the area's soil characteristics.

That was a very good customer-centric company, but it went without success, since customers didn't want to pay to have bags of fertilizer shipped to their home. However, the idea was there.

Another typical case of customer Centric can also be found in a full OnShop experience, at Orthera (www.orthera.com). In an Orthera Shop, a Top-Edge Digital Scanner and Software makes all the measures and guarantee that every shoe is made perfectly to fit each foot of each *persona. E*ach shoe is delivered later at customer's home.

Puma (www.puma.com) created something similar (on the immaterial side) to Orthera in an eCommerce site. What Puma presented was a myriad of infinite possibilities to allow each customer to design their own tennis shoes. The configuration was related not only with size, color or format. Customers could chose to have a left shoe different from the right one, to have a photo or a label in their shoe, and many other options.

Another interesting approach, it is to use the information that people search on the Internet to understand what their particular interests are and understand big trends even by Geography, Age, Gender or any other desired Category.

Google launched one year ago a powerful tool that enables overall advertisers, and retailers in particular to understand what are the new Trends that people search on the Internet, and what can they expect to Growth. According to Google this new Web Tool "*provides more flexibility and functionality for advertisers and marketers to understand search behavior, and adds some cool new features like a world heat map to graphically display search volume and regional interest*" (www.google.com).

Like Google Trends[11], you can just type in a search term to see search volume patterns over time, as well as the top related and rising searches. You'll also have the ability to compare search volume trends across multiple search terms, categories

Figure 4. Interest over time and headlines for "Smartphone" in Google Insights. Source: http://www.google.com/trends

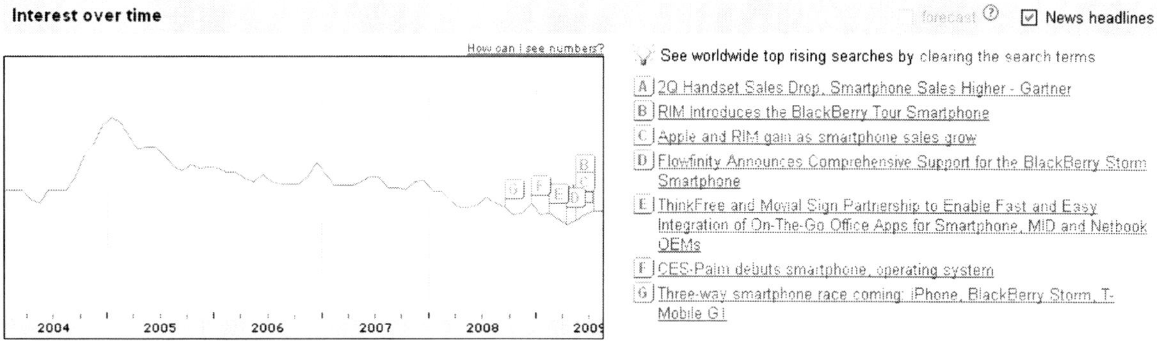

(commonly referred to as verticals), geographic regions, or specific time ranges."

As an example of the information that we can get from this website, imagine that we want Insight information for a new hot trend: the Smartphone, from 2004 to nowadays. Google will give anybody, for free, all world info regarding this topic, as we may see in Figure 4, Figure 5, and Figure 6.

With this information, a Social Retailer could start a new eCommerce Site, or an existing retailer could redirect his business, taking into consideration some interesting information, such as:

1. The new Trend is stronger in Asia;
2. Some Countries of Western Europe are also keen in this new Trend;

Figure 5. Geographic searches for "Smartphone" in Google Insights. Source: http://www.google.com/trends

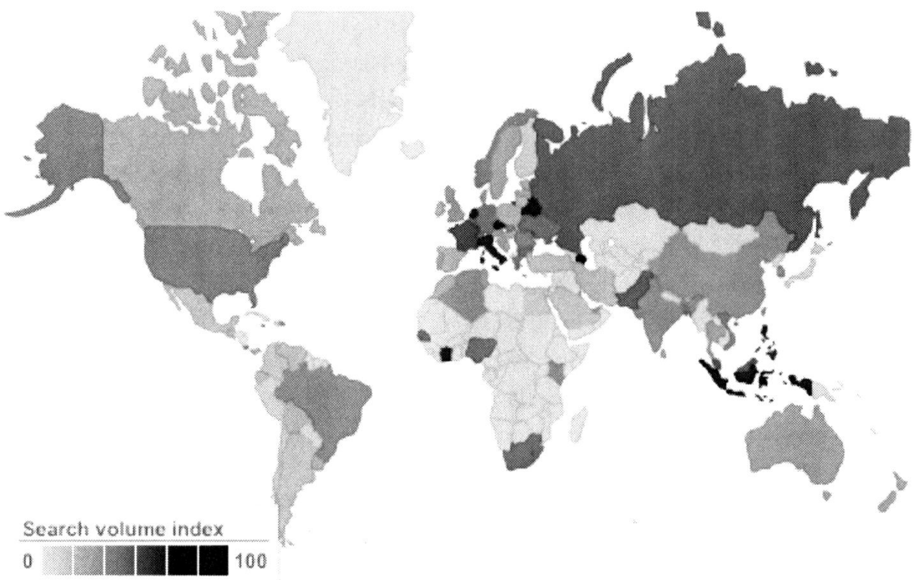

Figure 6. Expected rising searches for "Smartphone" in Google Insights. Source: http://www.google.com/trends

Rising searches

1.	htc smartphone	+850%
2.	htc	+850%
3.	blackberry smartphone	+700%
4.	best smartphone	+200%
5.	windows mobile	+160%
6.	smartphone windows mobile	+160%
7.	smartphone gps	+120%
8.	on smartphone	+70%
9.	nokia smartphone	+70%
10.	windows smartphone	+60%

3. Brazil is the only country of South America where customers are searching for Smartphone;
4. United States has an average weight in the search for Smartphone and if the Retailer wants to know more from the United States we would understand that Blackberry it's the new & hot Smartphone that Americans prefer.

CONCLUSION

Technological innovations, globalization, the continuous and improved use of ICT have changed the underlying logic of businesses. Also businesses have changed both in terms of scale, as well as pace and complexity. Some traditional businesses either will disappear or will transform radically.

As stated in the present chapter, Classic Retail is stagnating, both due to revenue stagnation as well as the incapacity shown to reduce costs and increase margins.

On the opposite side, according to eMarketer, European Union ECommerce will grow from 133b$ in 2006 to 407b$ in 2011. This represents a 200% Growth in 5 Years, or a Compound Aggregate Growth above 25% every year.

In the short-term, age, gender, class and income of individuals are less important and less rewarded than competence, motivation and effort. At the same time, we seen a general decrease in transaction costs in a new wired world where nearly ubiquitous connectivity has made new and unexpected connections with customers, talent and suppliers not only possible but easier. Also, "*digitalization has changed the economics of creating and distributing products, services, and content across a growing number of categories and has the potential to revolutionize business, managerial, and organizational models*" (Bughin et all, 2009).

Retailers will have access to new markets, since in 2030 people above 65 years old will have much higher incomes than their corresponding age group. This group will be more time online, since they will be a kind of "Generation V" members so *"Companies will need to shift from collecting personal data about individual customers toward collecting more-complete and more-relevant data around online customer behavior and influence on others. Companies will need new processes, new skills and a restructuring of how data is collected and used as they shift from demographic to psychographic insight. If companies follow a truly persona-centric approach, they can use the highly relevant information the persona leaves. Although the real person may never be known, far more intimate information of the persona's actions, personality, lifestyle habits and attitudes can be collected and exploited for business goals.*" (Gartner, 2008). This will represent not just novel businesses but also the need to use new management principles that are changing the fixed orthodoxies of the so-called Sloan-Aged companies (Bughin et all, 2009).

From our point of view, Retail 2.0 will be, not just the future but is already the present for Retail business. The results from 2009 Cyber Monday (a day known for deep discounts, advertised via email, social networks and online shopping), even in a middle of an economic recession, let us optimistic about these findings. First of all, Cyber Monday in 2009 was a success compared with previous years.

Cyber Monday happens usually after Black Friday (a classic retailers discount day), and after Thanksgiving and the traditional start to the holiday shopping season in stores. This year's Cyber Monday occurred at December 1st. Online consumers spent 887 million dollars just this day which, according to Reuters, represents a New World Record. On the words of Gian Fulgoni (comScore Chairman): "*We've seen an encouraging start to the online holiday shopping season and it would appear that retailers' aggressive and early marketing efforts have so far succeeded in persuading consumers to open their wallets online.*".

But the most interesting facts about 2009 Cyber Monday were not just the 1,6% overall sales increase, not even the average 2% increase of Amazon and other retailers' share. It was definitely the new approach that 9 million *personas* acquired products online, as shown by the facts below:

- 6% more users than in 2009;
- Average 100 dollar buy by *persona*;
- More users have logging in from home and spent more time online;
- Instead of quick browsing from work computers, users purchased more on early hours in the morning or at night after working hours. We can assume that they were browsing with relatives or friends and not just alone.

As a conclusion of the present study, we may assume that the new Consumers are really "Creators" (Saffo, 2009), that is to say people that produce and consume in the same act. In fact, today's emergent personal media platforms are making possible a society of "Creators", as shown in several examples presented below:

- Google Search (impossible two decades ago, paid one decade ago, free and fast today), it's seems free but "Creator" pays every search since he is giving away information to Adds and other Study Trends as we saw before in Google Trends. Thus, there is "*creative value flowing in both directions at the same instant*";
- Also YouTube (The "Creator" of the Man of the Year, Time Magazine 2008, WE), or even Wikipedia are examples of total interactive platforms that feed the creator's era.

In general, we may say that the Web2.0 Platforms, Interactive, Rich, Intelligent and Appealing, are no more exotic that 1950's boom of ordinary consumer goods after second world war, where the new transactions create value and the credit card replaced old wallet.

In the creator's economy, "*the most successful companies will be the ones that harness creator instincts, and the biggest winners will be the companies who harness the smallest creative acts. More people watch YouTube than post videos because creating a video is work. More people read blogs than write them because long-form writing is a hassle. Meanwhile, the telegraphic sentences of tweets, texting, and Facebook updates are becoming ubiquitous acts of creator haiku. And everyone can scribble a few words to compose a Google search, which is why Google dwarfs other creator companies.*" (Saffo, 2009).

Wrapping-Up in three bullets the findings of this chapter, we may say that:

1. Old retailers (like Wal-Mart, Marks & Spencer, etc) must adapt to the new consumers of the 21st Century or will simple vanish;
2. ECommerce companies (like eBay, Amazon, etc), that aren't yet Retailers2.0 must evolve to the new Interactive Platforms or someone will occupy their space;
3. We are pretty sure that some new Retail2.0 companies will appear in the time period of 2010 – 2015 and will become a Retail Giant by 2025, just by following the steps discussed in this study. In the words of George Silverman (2005) the retail 2.0 *"It's not about the Product, it's all about Customer Experience", or using Social Retail buzzword it is to "Sell to the Persona, not to a person".*

REFERENCES

Age, N. M. (2009). Press Release: Some Retailers see site traffic almost double. July 2009

Blog, P. S. (2009), Get Ready for a new Economic Era – The Creator Economy Beckons. Retrieved from http://whatmatters.mckinseydigital.com/internet/get-ready-for-a-new-economic-era, *consultation made in December 2, 2009*

Bughin. Jacques, Manyika, James, Roberts, Roger (2009), Beyond the Sloan Age. at http://whatmatters.mckinseydigital.com/internet/beyond-the-sloan-age, McKinsey, February, consulted at September 2009.

DataMonitor (2009). Global Hypermarkets & Super Centers, Industry Profile. March 2009

Diário, I. O. L. (2008). Clientes do Continente Online crescem 35% ao Ano. Retrieved from http://diario.iol.pt/empresas/portugal-continente-sonae-internet-continente-online-distribuicao/1005286-1728.html*consultation made in September 9, 2009*

DOYLE. Peter. (2008). eCommerce 2.0 – eCommerce next generation. Retrieved from *http://socialnetit.com*, in 25 September 2009.

Doz. Y. Santos, J., Williamson, P. (2001). *From global to Metanational: How Companies win in the knowledge economy*. Boston: Harvard Business School Press.

Drucker. P. (1995). Managing in a time of great change. *A Gestão numa Época de Grande Mudança*, translation made by Ana Paula Curado, Difusão Cultural, Lisboa.

Gartner. (2008).How to Determine Levels of Engagement for Generation Virtual. Retrieved from: http://www.gartner.com/DisplayDocument?ref=g_search&id=684508&subref=simplesearch*consultation made in September, 12, 2009.*

Google. (2009). Google Trends. Retrieved from http://www.google.com/trends*consultation made in August, 2009*

IDC. (2009). IDC Retail Insights. Retrieved from http://www.globalretail-insights.com/GRI/index.jsp*consultation made in September 12, 2009*

IDC. (n.d.). Retrieved from http://www.idc.com

Ingenico. (n.d.). Retrieved from http://www.ingenico.com/.

It, S. N. (n.d.). Retrieved from http://www.socialnetit.com

LBI. (n.d.). Retrieved from http://www.lbiiconnicholson.com/

Magazine, T. (2009). *The Best Inventions of the Year 2008*. Retrieved from http://www.time.com/time/specials/2007/article/0,28804,1677329_1678102_1678096,00.html#*consultation made in September 8, 2009*

Meer, D., Romberger, T., Favaro, K. (2006). Five Rules for Retailing in a Recession. *Harvard Business Review*, Harvard Business School, April 2009

Oberholzer-Gee. Felix (2006). Wal-Mart's Business Environment. *Harvard Business Review*, Harvard Business School, December 12, 2006.

ONESource, (2009). eBay Inc One Stop Report. August 2009

ONESource, (2009a). *Marks & Spencer One Stop Report*August 2009

ONESource, (2009b). Amazon One Stop Report. August 2009

Reuters, (2009). *Web retail a bright spot in tepid U.S. holiday season*. Retrieved from http://www.reuters.com/article/internetNews/idUSTRE5B14AP-20091202*consultation made in December 2, 2009*

SILVERMAN. G. (2005). *The Secrets of Word-of-Mouth Marketing*, Culver, CA: Amacom

SPVA. (n.d.). Retrieved from http://www.spva.org

Thome's Vincent. (2009). Social Retailing and Shoping, Virtual and Digital commerce Opportunities. Retrieved from http://www.thomevincent.com/blog/index.php?2007/08/15/349-social-retailing-and-shopping-virtual-and-digital-commerce-opportunities consultation made in September 12, 2009

Transactions, H. T. (n.d.). Retrieved from http://www.hypercom.com/.

Trends, G. (n.d.). Retrieved from http://www.google.com/trends

Verifone. (n.d.). Retrieved from http://www.verifone.com/.

Wheelen. T. L., Hunger, J. D. (2008). *Strategic Management and Business Policy*, Eleventh Edition. Upper Saddle River, NJ: Pearson International Edition, Pearson Prentice Hall.

Yahoo, (2008). "Marketing Promotion: Make me an offer", August 2009

ADDITIONAL READING

BusinessWeek Research Services. (2009). *Information is King: Business Analytics in the Age of the Downturn and the (Re)Emergence of the Customer*. at www.SAS.com, consulted in September 2009.

SAS (2009). Competing as a 21st century retailer: Maximizing profitability in a consumer-centric world, *Retail Insights*. SAS, 2009.

ENDNOTES

1 See http://socialnetit.com

2 Broadband refers to the "new" generation of high-speed transmission service of data that allow users to access to the internet and internet-related services at significantly higher speeds than by using traditional modems (Federal Communications Commission – FCC, 2003). Nowadays, with the replacement of the cable system to optical fiber system, the speed has increased dramatically which, associated with the generalization of the wireless technology is

something that represents a new revolution in data and image transfers and usage for business.

3 One may refer here the interesting initiative of Amazon.com entitled "share the love" whose main goals were to get customers to recommend products to their friends: to e-mail friends and to give them an additional 10% off on the price of the items bought.

4 Considering that fixed costs are usually considered a barrier to exist, no wonder why in internet industries one usually see a big drop rate of companies and market positions changing almost every day.

5 Hypercompetition was a concept first introduced by Richard D'Aveni. This concept supports that the markets where we see these characteristics will always be in constant disequilibrium and change which is a consequence of the frequency, the boldness, and the aggressiveness of the dynamic movements of the players. In these markets, product life cycles are even shorter and we assist to a constant entry and exit of new competitors, redefining markets' boundaries. That is to say, these are markets with a great level of uncertainty, dynamism, heterogeneity of players and hostility (Wheelen and Hunger, 2008).

6 IDC is a global provider of market intelligence, advisory services, and events for the information technology, telecommunications, and consumer technology markets (source: www.idc.com).

7 SPVA stands for "Secure POS Vendor Alliance", a non-profit organization that works with the multiple stakeholders of the payment value chain (source: www.spva.org).

8 See http://www.verifone.com/.

9 See http://www.ingenico.com/.

10 See http://www.hypercom.com/.

11 See http://www.google.com/trends.

Chapter 17
A Unified View of Enablers, Barriers, and Readiness of Small to Medium Enterprises for E-Business Adoption

Ritesh Chugh
CQUniversity Melbourne, Australia

Pramila Gupta
CQUniversity Melbourne, Australia

ABSTRACT

SMEs have been looking at expanding their market share by extending beyond their geographical boundaries and this is where electronic business has come to the forefront. The path to e-business adoption is ridden with barriers and understanding these along with the benefits it offers to SMEs is important. This chapter has reviewed the existing literature of barriers and benefits of e-business adoption by SMEs to identify the various enablers that can facilitate adoption. The chapter also provides an insight into e-readiness and analyses six existing tools that are used globally to measure e-readiness. Based on a comprehensive analysis, an holistic framework (Motivation Application Measurement Support (MAMS) e-readiness assessment framework) has been proposed. The framework can be utilized as a reference to assess, design and implement a supplementary strategic approach for the assessment of e-business readiness of SMEs. Further empirical research to test, amend and improve the MAMS framework can be undertaken in the future.

INTRODUCTION

Small to medium sized enterprises (SMEs) play an important role in any country's economy and can be considered as the backbone or engine of the national economy. The European Union has around 23 million SMEs that provide around 75 million jobs and represent 99% of all existing enterprises (European Commission, 2005). Almost 90% of the total number of businesses across the world are classed as SMEs accounting for more than 60% of employment in their countries (Hall, 2002; Organisation for Economic Cooperation

DOI: 10.4018/978-1-61692-880-3.ch017

and Development [OECD], 1997) and also account for 80% of global economic growth (Jutla et al, 2002). Australian figures are similar to the global figures with more than 95% of companies classed as SMEs (Data Monitor, 2004). In 2008, UK's Department for Business, Enterprise and Regulatory Reform reported that SMEs together accounted for 99.9 per cent of all enterprises. Internationally, approximately 99.5% of all businesses have 100 or less employees while 99.8% of all businesses have 200 or less employees (OECD, 2005). In almost every country, SMEs play a vital role in contributing towards the national economy by job creation, income generation and overall competitiveness.

SMEs, worldwide, are seen as major contributors to a nation's economy and the Gross Domestic Product (GDP) of their countries. However their contribution to the GDP has been declining over the past few years (Abernethy, 2002). With the financial turmoil that has currently engulfed most countries, this situation is unlikely to show any major improvements in the near future. The decline of SME contribution to GDP needs to be reversed by adopting some strategic goals for long term growth. To achieve long term growth, SMEs have been looking at expanding their market share by extending beyond their geographical boundaries and this is where electronic business (e-business) has come to the rescue. SMEs have been adopting e-business, in the past, for their business operations yet it needs to be adopted with more rigour and vitality to improve the situation. Undoubtedly, in today's global networked world, e-business has the potential to become a major source of competitive advantage for SMEs. Conducting business online will help to lower operational costs, allow small companies to come at par with larger competitors on an international scale, and help serve customers more efficiently.

Moving from bricks to clicks is becoming a matter of existence for most organisations today and SMEs are no exception. E-business is often touted as a global phenomenon that provides businesses with strategic advantages in the present competitive environment by enabling their processes online using Information and Communication Technologies (ICT). Thus its adoption by organisations, irrespective of their size and location, cannot be overlooked. As with the adoption of any technology, despite their benefits, the adoption of e-business by SMEs is slow and is often accompanied with various barriers. The slow adoption of e-business by SMEs can be attributed to a range of factors that include, but are not limited to, lack of physical infrastructure, high operational costs, external forces, poor guidance, lack of government support and often management who is not aware of the potential benefits of e-business. To add to these difficulties, the barriers to e-business adoption by SMEs vary between developing and developed countries, necessitating a review of these barriers. This would allow the enablers to be presented in a holistic context to promote successful adoption of e-business by SMEs globally rather than a contorted view that does not encourage and enhance universal adoption.

A disparity seems to exist in diverse empirical findings that have reported the level of adoption of e-business in SMEs (Parish et al, 2002; Ramsey et al, 2003; Xu et al, 2007). It can be argued that SMEs that do not adopt the Internet to execute their business processes will not survive. Conversely adoption may not necessarily provide a competitive advantage until it becomes part of the overall business strategy (Porter, 2001). While the problems constraining e-business adoption are considered more complex and diverse in developing countries and hinder their economic development, a range of studies have indicated that approximately one third of SMEs in the United States have yet to adopt the use of Internet technologies to conduct business (Pratt, 2002; Auger et al, 2003; Levenburg et al, 2005)

There is substantial evidence that any country's economy, whether developed or developing, is supported by SME performance and SMEs cannot be overlooked (Poon & Swatman, 1999; Jutla et al, 2002). SMEs cannot be left behind in the race of e-business adoption and need to grasp the opportunities proffered by ICT. Thus, this chapter provides an insight into the benefits, barriers and enablers of e-business for SMEs that will apply globally across multiple industries rather than being limited to a specific industry. Also, at this stage the importance of e-readiness assessments to measure the preparedness of an entity to conduct business processes in the online world cannot be forgotten. Substantial literature on SME e-business adoption is fragmented, complex and industry specific, so this chapter has been derived from the vast extant literature on SME adoption of the Internet and Internet- based technologies in executing business processes thus presenting a unified view.

The chapter begins by providing definitions of e-business and SMEs before reviewing different e-business benefits and barriers. By overcoming the identified barriers, SMEs will benefit by adopting e-business in their day-to-day activities enhancing profits by reducing operational costs. The term 'barrier' can be broadly assumed to include all requisites for e-business adoption, some easily available and some requiring special efforts from internal or external sources. The chapter then proposes key enablers that can help to resolve the barriers to encourage e-business adoption. The attention is then given to the concept of e-readiness as presented in the literature and its usefulness in assessing the preparedness for the adoption of ICT. The chapter also explores six existing e-readiness assessment tools (loosely called models or frameworks in the corresponding literature) for e-readiness that measure different sets of categories for assessing e-readiness. Due to the difference in e-business adoption in developing and developed countries, an insight into these tools is relevant for the purpose of proposing a consolidated e-readiness framework for assessing the readiness of e-business adoption with particular focus on SMEs. Review of the tools revealed that e-readiness categories relate to different levels and the nature of countries, organisations and e-business applications that have resulted in numerous but isolated studies and methods of measurements with no linkage to the barriers and enablers of e-business adoption. Subsequently, different e-readiness categories or factors of e-readiness are presented. The comprehensive analysis of existing research of e-business adoption is then used to bring the different aspects, i.e., enablers and barriers of e-business adoption by SMEs, e-readiness categories as related to the target nation or organisation together, and is presented as an e-readiness assessment framework (Motivation Application Measurement Support (MAMS) e-readiness assessment framework). The framework consolidates different e-readiness aspects and shows how they link with each other. Later in the chapter the application and usability of the framework are discussed in the context of a generic case to assess readiness for e-business adoption by SMEs. Finally, future research avenues have been recommended.

DEFINITIONS OF ELECTRONIC BUSINESS AND SMES

E-business and e-commerce are terms that are often used interchangeably. Undoubtedly e denotes 'electronic networks' or the use of Internet (i) and other information technologies to facilitate business processes. It can be argued that electronic commerce includes outward facing processes for buying and selling, involving customers, suppliers and other external stakeholders whereas electronic business, apart from outward facing processes, also includes inward facing organisational processes. Thus, electronic business refers to a larger range of processes performed electronically encompassing electronic commerce too. Various authors have provided definitions of e-commerce and e-business in isolation, however because of the seemingly gray area, a definition for e-business needs to be deduced to remove any further ambiguity at least for the purposes of this chapter. Various existing definitions for electronic commerce and electronic business have been presented below:

World Trade Organisation (WTO) has defined e-commerce as the production, distribution, marketing, sale, or delivery of goods and services by electronic means. (Baker and McKenzie, 2001)

Electronic Commerce Team of European Union has defined e-commerce as "buying and selling products or services over the Internet."(Schulze & Baumgartner, 2001, p. 7)

Poon (1999, p.114) provided a specific definition for small business Internet commerce as "the use of Internet technology and applications to support business activities of a small firm."

Currie (2000, p.7) has defined electronic business as "use of the Internet for electronic transactions, digital delivery of informational goods and services, and retail sale of tangible goods."

As evident from the above definitions and as reported by Ramsey et al (2003) and Searle (2001) there is a difference between e-commerce and e-business in terms of extent of organisational processes, technology used, and business value achieved. However the gray area has not actually ceased to exist and both the terms are still used interchangeably. Lambert (2002) has differentiated e-commerce from e-business by defining e-business as all aspects of a business where technology is imperative. Because of these variations and in the absence of a commonly agreed definition of e-business the following definition for e-business is proposed: "Buying, selling and conducting other business operations using ICT, more specifically Internet-based technologies."

Having a definition of e-business to proceed with, attention is directed to the categories of conducting business electronically. McNurlin et al (2009) have provided three important categories of working inward (Business to Employee), working outward (Business to Consumer) and working across (Business to Business). An understanding of these categories will lead to an overview of how businesses can support electronic working between the various stakeholders involved in the business ecosystem.

1. Business to Consumer encompasses buying and selling between the firm and its customers.
2. Business to Business encompasses all commercial interactions between upstream and downstream partners ie. co-suppliers, suppliers, distributors and retailers.
3. Business to employee encompasses the integration of all activities relating to employees in the firm.

The discussion in this chapter will merge all three categories and not emphasise one over the other since it is reasonable to assume that the enablers and barriers will almost overlap each category.

A review of the literature on SMEs does not provide an agreed universal definition of SMEs and a systemic problem of an accurate definition seems to exist because of the diverse nature of SMEs. Most often the classification of SMEs is based on inherent characteristics of the firm that include, but are not limited to, the number of employees in the enterprise, revenue threshold, financial assets, capital turnover and industry in which the SME operates although more often than not the main distinction is simply based on the number of employees working in the enterprise. Each of the classification has its own demerits. For example, it can be difficult to benchmark turnover across industry sectors and the turnover may not even be a true indicator of the capital invested, and financial assets can be difficult to value owing to their inconsistency and varying risk profile. The number of employees or size seems to be internationally accepted, but the difference between developing and developed countries can be large due to the varied demand/supply nature of labour. Some acceptable definitions for SMEs have been presented below to allow a more informed judgement:

European Commission (2005, p. 5) classifies SMEs as "enterprises which employ fewer than 250 persons and which have an annual turnover not exceeding 50 million euro, and/or an annual balance sheet total not exceeding 43 million euro."

The Australian Bureau of Statistics (2003) defines SMEs as firms employing less than 200 full time equivalent workers and are not subsidiaries, public companies, or incorporated bodies.

Reserve Bank of India in a 2009 circular to all scheduled commercial banks in India defined SMEs as enterprises engaged in the manufacture or production, processing or preservation of goods where the investment in plant and machinery is more than Rs.2.5 million but does not exceed Rs.100 million. A separate definition for firms engaged in the services sector has been provided that classifies SMEs as enterprises engaged in providing or rendering of services where the investment in equipment is more than Rs.1million but does not exceed Rs.50 million.

Most countries have their own definition for SMEs including quantitative or qualitative elements to better describe them and the definition becomes more important particularly for taxation purposes. The United Kingdom, Canada, Greece, Mexico and the Slovak Republic use the number of employees to make the distinction. Portugal combines the number of employees and turnover to make the distinction (OECD, 2004). Analysing some of these definitions leaves us in no doubt that there are many variables that influence an enterprise, especially SMEs, including economies of scale, market structure, the industry itself, and the regulatory environment that influences the firm. In the absence of a shared definition, it is appropriate to adhere to a definition that combines the number of employees and the annual turnover. From the existing definitions of SMEs in various countries, some qualitative and quantitative elements that may be useful in defining SMEs are presented in Table 1.

In view of the above elements, it is also worth noting that a report by OECD (2004, p. 12) mentioned that "the diversity and richness of SME characteristics, political strategies and economic conditions are unlikely to ever yield a commonly used and accepted definition of SMEs." There is a nature of impracticality in coming to a universal definition owing to the diversity of elements. For the purposes of this chapter, the revised definition by the European Commission given in 2005 has been adopted as it accounts for headcount, annual turnover, and annual balance sheet total.

Table 1. Elements of SME definition

Qualitative Elements	Quantitative Elements
• Non subsidiaries, public companies or incorporated bodies	• Number of employees
• Independently owned and managed	• Annual Turnover
	• Financial assets
	• Investment in equipment

THE BENEFITS AND BARRIERS OF E-BUSINESS ADOPTION

E-business has redefined the way business is conducted and should not be merely considered as another technology that helps in running operations. It is an innovation that has replaced the traditional way of doing business (Laudon & Laudon, 2010; Lee, 2001). The easy accessibility of the Internet and World Wide Web has transformed e-business into what used to be a complex business activity to a reasonably easy and economical means for many businesses. Various studies have shown that e-business has a significant contribution towards economic growth and competence (Forrester Research, 2005; IDC, 2004). It was pointed out earlier in the chapter that SMEs also play an important part by providing a positive contribution to a nation's economy and now the emergence of e-business has paved the way for SMEs to reach millions of customers globally.

Increased growth of e-business in recent years can be attributed towards lesser production costs and increased productivity. Now with lesser expenditures, any small business can go online; thanks to the Internet, liberalisation of telecommunications and advancement in technological segments of communications. Every firm that has adopted e-business principally depends on how it is operated, therefore it becomes necessary to edify benefits and barriers of e-business adoption to realise the true value of e-business.

Benefits of E-Business Adoption

Profiting from e-business is no longer confined to large firms with established brand names or several stores across the globe. Technical advancement has provided opportunities for SMEs to position themselves in a global market and reach worldwide customers. Most established firms now have both an offline and online presence; thus, enhancing their brand credibility and e-business provides an opportunity for SMEs to compete with the established firms by reaching out to consumers world-wide even without a physical presence. The Internet is of a global nature and has neither physical boundaries nor entry barriers creating opportunities for both small and medium sized businesses to operate on a unique platform. The ubiquitous nature of the Internet has made it an important tool of e-business for SMEs. The World Wide Web is an arena where there are no national or international barriers and regardless of company size, the Internet allows it to reach a global audience to trade their products and services.

Unswerving price, new products and services and an impressive shopping experience are the essential qualities any customer looks for while shopping (Walters & Lancaster, 1999). By providing quality products, attractive prices and services, easy to navigate sites and speedy delivery and checkouts, SMEs can build and preserve an upholding relationship with their customers. Most customers now possess the ability to conduct business anytime and anywhere with the advent of relatively inexpensive ways of communication channels like the Internet and mobiles phones. Consumers of today demand products that suit their needs and by identifying the expectations of customers in terms of value, merchandise, service, information and promotions, SMEs can target ideal customers. Thus one of the important benefits of the Internet is facilitating information transfer (Tiessen et al., 2001). The information transfer can adopt any mode and can be relevant for the stakeholders of SMEs.

It is not just about building a website, but SMEs are now able to increase their output and competence by creating practical organizations where a product can be tested for its pros and cons before representing it to their customers. SMEs can make use of the enormous influence of the Internet to promote their brands and increase sales by traffic generation. The success of SMEs not only depends on superior planning and smart management but also in realising and working towards developing a better communication relationship with clients to understand and address their needs. According to Sensis (2005), SMEs use the Internet for various purposes that include, but are not limited to, communication via email, referencing information or researching data, looking for information about products and services, banking, making and receiving payments, taking and placing orders and monitoring competition and marketing.

Past studies have indicated that firms have been using e-business for various benefits. Some important benefits of e-business adoption that are more relevant for SMEs include: direct and indirect cost savings, increased productivity, enhanced customer satisfaction and better relationships, increased competitiveness, efficient information delivery, speedy responses to customer queries, new sales and distribution channels, faster product delivery, improved organisational brand image, knowledge sharing and organisational learning through networking, relatively cheaper advertising medium, and integration of business partners in existing processes(Kaynak et al., 2005;OECD, 2004; Walczuch et al, 2000; Nath et al., 1998; Poon & Swatman, 1995; Poon & Strom,1997; Abell & Limm,1996).

Barriers of E-Business Adoption

Despite the numerous benefits from e-business adoption, SMEs are slow in its adoption and usage compared to their larger counterparts (Kartiwi & MacGregor, 2007; Ihlstrum et al, 2003; Chau & Turner, 2004) and it is mainly larger firms that are reaping the benefits of e-business (Riquelme, 2002). It is plausible that the benefits mentioned in the previous section may not have the same degree of importance for all SMEs. Various studies have been undertaken to identify the barriers that SMEs face for the adoption of e-business. Chau and Pederson (2000) have identified some of these barriers as lack of resources, complex change and implementation processes, lack of technical skills and training, poor understanding of computer technology, lack of technological and telecommunication infrastructure, initial high costs, ongoing support costs, and poor motivation. Lack of telecommunication infrastructure has also been put forth as a barrier by Sheth and Sharma (2005) and this barrier is one of the major concerns for some developing countries that are now in the process of setting up telecommunication infrastructure. The barriers become more unique for developing countries where factors such as low average income of its people, slow credit card uptake, and cultural barriers (Hawk, 2004) and initially low profits make the use of e-business technologies more uncertain. Owners of SMEs may not want to risk investing larger amounts where there are no significant profits in the short term. Apart from technology adoption problems, SMEs are also concerned with factors relating to trust, security and privacy of the transactions online, along with policies that affect online business. A study by Lawson et al. (2003) of the factors affecting adoption of e-commerce technologies by SMEs identified the top four barriers to be concern about security and privacy of transactions, cost of consultants, lack of government incentives, and lack of IT expertise. Barriers like these in developing and developed countries alike have indubitably slowed down the adoption of the Internet as a viable way of doing business. In a study by Kartiwi and MacGregor (2007) to ascertain the barriers for e-business adoption between Sweden and Indonesia, the most significant barrier reported in both countries was that e-ecommerce was not suited to the products and services offered by the surveyed SMEs. Similar views have been echoed by Hughes et al. (2003) where the products offered by the firm have been classed as unsuitable for sale on the Internet. On an alternative note, it might be worth arguing that suitability of products and services may not necessarily be a barrier to adoption of e-business since there are other important uses of e-business apart from simply buying and selling. This would call for empirical research in further studies.

Cloete et al. (2002), in their study of SME adoption of e-commerce in South Africa, have summarised a number of other additional issues that have a decapitating impact on the adoption of e-business. These issues include low adoption of e-commerce by SME customers and suppliers, high costs of e-commerce technology, legal and liability concerns, security concerns, restricted knowledge of e-commerce models and methodologies, and finally the perception that e-business does not provide any benefits to the enterprise. One of the key identified barriers in their study was lack of acquaintance and poor understanding of technology. The need to educate SMEs about the value of e-businesses cannot be underplayed and is vital. As SMEs are mostly run by owners or managers who invest on their own and are the main decision making authorities, adapting e-business largely depends on how the owners perceive e-business and its value for them. Adapting to and maintaining ICT is largely dependent on its owners' or managers' characteristics as the management of SMEs is generally centralised to a few key individuals. To add to this, it would perhaps be fit to say that a lot of SMEs lack the initiative for innovation and thus prefer to remain followers rather than becoming leaders in the adoption of e-business. Kalakota and Robinson (2001) have classified the unwillingness of managers to be responsible for technological change as one of the main barriers to e-commerce adoption. Many identified barriers in the various studies appear to be more non-technical and demonstrate general lack of knowledge of the potential benefits that the adoption of e-business can offer (Lawson et al. 2003). There is an absolute need to educate SME owners about the opportunities and benefits of adapting e-business. ICT comes at a price and not every SME is willing to adapt it owing to lack of funds, centralised decision making authorities, and the lack of necessary expertise required to maintain and update software applications. Governments need to educate and create comprehensive training programs for apprising SMEs of the importance of e-business and how its non-adoption will make them obsolete and difficult to exist in the future. As we move into the future and reflect back, is it possible to imagine the existence of enterprises without telephones?

It is evident from above that a diverse range of barriers prevent SMEs from reaping the benefits of e-business adoption and the problems seem to extrapolate for developing countries. The review described in this section has provided a clearer understanding of the benefits and barriers although the nature of the relationships between the two is not clear. It is not the intention of this chapter to explore it either, but to call for further research in this area. Without trying to assert a relationship between the benefits and barriers but drawing from the barriers, the next section proposes some key enablers that can help in promoting and directing SMEs towards the adoption of e-business.

ENABLERS OF E-BUSINESS ADOPTION

Barriers in e-business adoption can be overcome with effort, support and facilities provided by internal (organisation) and external (customers, suppliers, and government) stakeholders to gain strategic advantage. There is no doubt that governments have a vested interest in promoting SMEs as they play an important part in building a nation's economy. Governments should promote IT usage and adoption by SMEs as they form a strong foundation that is integrated into the country's economy. SMEs depend on governments for various services and the time consumed for these services can be reduced if IT practices are in place which facilitate faster connectivity and deliver reliable products and information on a wider scale. Governments should themselves adopt e-business to buy products from their domestic SMEs and thereby encourage SMEs to begin using similar technologies by providing incentives. Governments need to develop and promote policies and strategies to create facilitating conditions that benefit SMEs enabling them to adopt e-business by overcoming barriers like the lack of government incentives to SMEs.

In order to trade at both national and international levels, there need to be policies and strategies in place for businesses to set up and thrive. There is an apparent consensus that the shortage of policies to support SMEs is a very concerning barrier. Policies that regulate equal rule of law for all firms (online or offline), boast frameworks that are clear, competitive and transparent, have governing legal laws that confer equal treatment for transactions on both national and global levels are important. Tax cuts can be provided to SMEs that expend on e-business technologies.

Training and educating owners of SMEs about the potential benefits of e-business is a significant measure that needs to be addressed by the government apart from designing policies and strategies that cover issues relating to telecommunications, consumer rights, security, cyber crime, and privacy. Training will go a long way in reducing the negative perceptions and counteracting problems that SMEs business owners face, encouraging their willingness to adopt e-business. Technical training of the development, application, and support of e-business technologies can also be promoted so that the lack of skills barrier declines with time.

Technological infrastructure is one of the most crucial enablers for e-business adoption and sustenance. Telecommunications infrastructure and advancements in technology facilitate innovation, efficiency and accelerate economic growth. It is also important that the technology comes at a relatively low cost otherwise it becomes a barrier to adoption again. Nations need to promote and invest in infrastructure that supports interoperability, innovation, variety and expansion, so that it is employed by SMEs effectively. Arguably, developed countries are ahead in the adoption of technology but developing countries are leap-frogging in the implementation of newer infrastructure, which can be seen as a boon for SMEs in developing countries.

Lack of information regarding e-business benefits is one of the most common impediments hindering SMEs' inclination towards e-business. Much needed resources like research materials, websites, and practice guides for access to information regarding benefits of e-business adoption should be provided by governments. Fostering information availability across all platforms and maintaining and developing pertinent information content and rights is necessary to promote e-business awareness. Governments should provide information and assistance to companies, especially targeted to SMEs, although currently there are a variety of private companies that offer technical and business services for enterprises wanting to develop their e-business capabilities.

To draw from the discussion in this section, five enablers of e-business adoption come to the forefront: government support, e-business laws and policies, training and education, set up technological infrastructure, and adequate information.

Having identified some enablers and the barriers they help to overcome, the chapter now focuses its direction on various aspects of e-readiness that are useful to assess the readiness of a country and its organisations for the uptake of e-business. Of particular interest are the assessment categories (e.g. physical and technological infrastructures) and how these are assessed, that is, tools and methods.

E-READINESS

As evident through the review so far, e-business has a lot to offer for SMEs in developing and developed countries. In terms of relative preparedness for the adoption of e-commerce, developed countries are better prepared but nonetheless the barriers of adoption are still the same for developed countries although the seriousness of barriers may diminish for developed countries. In general, regardless of their status countries need to assess how prepared their SMEs are for adopting e-business. Owing to the nature and characteristics of SMEs, they possess unique needs for adopting e-business. To help businesses adopt ICT, various e-readiness tools have been proposed and, although the focus of most tools is on a country's e-readiness, it is important to note that the assessments can be done for any enterprise including SMEs. Bridges.org (2005) has defined e-readiness as "the ability for a region to benefit from information and communications technology". The authors of this chapter disagree with the limited inclusion of region in the definition and have proposed the following expanded definition "the ability or degree to which an enterprise, community or country is prepared to use ICT to accelerate economic growth and facilitate business". E-readiness assessments are important as they enable enterprises, communities, and countries to understand their preparedness for adoption of ICT, which will further help in benchmarking, monitoring progress and prioritising action. It is important to assess e-readiness of SMEs too, so that business benefits can be derived and inefficiencies can be overcome.

Various organisations and government bodies have developed e-readiness assessment tools to provide quantifiable and/or qualitative indices of how a country could benefit from the adoption of ICT. Over 25 different tools to assess countries' e-readiness are currently available that use a diverse range of questionnaires, statistical methods, best practices, and historical analyses (Bridges.org, 2005). Most of these existing tools provide contrasting definitions of e-readiness with different goals and objectives and the vast array of often complex tools makes choosing the right tool very difficult. Performing these assessments helps countries and their organisations plan effectively and strategically for the integration of ICT. The majority of the available tools provide definitions and validations that are related to government initiatives with no specific emphasis on the needs of SMEs. Before conducting an e-readiness assessment, it is very important that users weigh the pros and cons of each tool to ensure it meets their needs. There have been numerous studies on the diverse range of e-readiness assessment tools but these studies had their own motives and included skewed factors to complete the assessment and were not necessarily tailored for SMEs and the barriers restricting their e-readiness.

A Review of E-Readiness Assessment Tools

To understand how an assessment tool can be selected for testing e-readiness of SMEs, this section reviews existing e-readiness assessment tools by adopting a qualitative approach. The report by Bridges.org (2005) has categorised the e-readiness assessment tools into three different groups: ready-to use tools/questionnaires, case studies, and third party surveys and reports. For the purpose of this chapter and to spread the analysis a total of six tools were chosen that is, two tools from each group. The tools were randomly picked with no particular emphasis on one over the other. The tools that were analysed have been elaborated below:

Asia-Pacific Economic Cooperation (APEC) E-Commerce Readiness Assessment

APEC Telecommunications and Information working group has developed this assessment to provide a process whereby every economy can assess its own state of readiness for e-commerce and engage with the business community to set strategies to improve positioning for the digital economy (Asia-Pacific Economic Cooperation [APEC], 2000). This general framework can be applied by any economy or community. The tool builds on six indicators of e-readiness: basic infrastructure and technology, access to necessary communications services, current level and type of use of the Internet, promotion and facilitation activities, skills and human resources, and positioning for the digital economy. These six broad indicators of readiness for e-commerce have been developed into 100 multiple-choice questions that provide direction as to desirable policies that will promote e-commerce and remove barriers to electronic trade. The results of the assessment can be used to develop the most suitable strategies to overcome the barriers. The tool relies on questionnaire-based data. The results of the assessment are not intended to be scored, rather to provide a starting point in a strategic planning process for adoption of e-business (APEC, 2000). Assessment is based on opinions of individuals and there is no guide for interpreting the results of the assessment. The APEC tool is more inclined to focus on assessing government policies for e-business.

Computers System Policy Project (CSPP) Readiness Guide: For Living in the Networked World

CSPP's self assessment tool is designed to help towns, cities, counties, states, countries, or any community to determine preparedness for participation in the networked world. Communities here could include government, businesses, schools, community groups, and individual citizens, too. The guide promotes a better understanding of a community's status in a networked world. CSPP has selected five categories that are believed to be essential to capture the benefits of the networked world. The five main categories are networked infrastructure, networked access, networked applications and services, networked economy, and networked world enablers. The guide has provided a series of 23 questions that have been segregated into four progressive stages that show the e-readiness of the community under each of the five main categories. The 4 progressive stages range from a community that has a minimum of necessary technology and applications to a community that has the maximum technology and ubiquitous applications. The assessment results might yield communities that are at different stages as each category is evaluated. For example, a school might have advanced infrastructure but does not aggressively use the infrastructure for providing educational and administrative services. An overall score for the community being assessed can be estimated by averaging the scores across each category. One of the major advantages of this guide is its scalability, allowing everyone to adapt it to their needs (Computers System Policy Project [CSPP], 1998). It does not provide guidance on how to move between each of the four progressive stages of e-readiness.

Mosaic Group's Global Diffusion of the Internet (GDI) Framework

The GDI framework measures the state of Internet diffusion in an economy. Six categories to assess e-readiness are included in this framework: pervasiveness, geographic dispersion, sector absorption, connectivity infrastructure, organisational structure, and sophistication of use. Each category is ranked on a scale of zero (non-existent) to four (pervasive and highly developed)(Mosaic Group, 1998). The GDI framework does not combine the six categories to compute an overall index score for a country although Economist Intelligence Unit e-readiness rankings calculate it in their framework. The lack of an overall score makes it difficult to make adequate comparisons. There is also a mix of quantitative and qualitative data, although primarily qualitative, which makes scores open to individualistic interpretation. The GDI framework highlights a country's relative strengths and weaknesses of Internet adoption using case studies but base data is not always available or is unreliable. It does not factor in literacy levels and access issues. Sophistication of technologies is also hard to measure (Minges, 2002). GDI only focuses on Internet penetration and not on ICT adoption in general.

Association of Southeast Asian Nations (ASEAN) E-Readiness Assessment

ASEAN countries also recognise the need to develop a comprehensive collection of ICT indicators; so an e-readiness assessment was undertaken in 2001. The assessment measured the ten member countries' readiness in terms of ICT infrastructure, e-society, e-commerce, and e-government. The aim of the assessment was to provide member countries with suitable policies to promote e-commerce and an e-society. An analysis of the assessment revealed a limitation showing diversity in ICT indicators available among member countries, their surveyed elements, definitions, methodologies, and their ability to conduct the survey (Rachman, 2002). IBM was contracted to conduct the assessment for the ASEAN countries using the identified categories although IBM used their own methodology to cluster the member countries. Their methodology defines four stages in the development of an information economy; emerging, evolving, embedding, and extending (Bhatia, 2001). The four stages are a good way to classify the countries but whether IBM's methodology can be adopted by others is questionable due to copyright issues.

McConnell International (MI) Ready? Net.Go! tool

McConnell International have developed the MI Ready? Net.Go! tool that measures status and progress of a countries' e-readiness using a qualitative reference guide. The tool aims to evaluate e-readiness of countries, governments, and citizens in the networked economy. The tool has five categories: connectivity, e-leadership, information security, human capital, and e-business climate. The tool rates countries in one of the above five categories on a scale of one to three that indicate whether conditions are conducive to support e-business or not (McConnell International 2000, 2001). The MI Ready? Net.Go! tool focuses solely on economic growth but emphasises infrastructural issues.

Economist Intelligence Unit (EIU) E-Readiness Rankings 2009 Report

The EIU assesses the world's largest economies on their ability to absorb ICT and use it for economic and social benefit. The 2009 EIU rankings have covered seventy countries. The purpose of EIU's ranking is to allow governments to gauge the success of their technology initiatives against those of other countries. Over 100 separate criteria, both qualitative and quantitative, are organised into six primary categories that are weighted according to their assumed importance as influencing factors. The categories with their weightage are: connectivity and technology infrastructure (20%), business environment (15%), social and cultural environment (15%), legal environment (10%), government policy and vision (15%), and consumer and business adoption (25%). A 1-10 scoring scale is used for all indicators. Denmark has topped the 2009 rankings whilst Azerbaijan has been ranked at the 70th. Governments can use these rankings to encourage e-business adoption in their countries. The criteria are scored on their relative presence (or absence) in a country's economic, political or social environment (Economist Intelligence Unit [EIU], 2009). These rankings also provide companies that wish to trade internationally an overview of the countries' use of ICT. This assessment primarily focuses on business adoption of ICT and the large number of qualitative variables makes objective analysis very difficult.

Table 2 summarises the key assessment categories of the six tools that were analysed in this research.

An Analysis of the Investigation of the E-Readiness Tools

Despite the importance of e-readiness assessments, the existing e-readiness tools do not adequately

Table 2. Categories to measure e-readiness

E-readiness Assessment Tools			
		Categories to measure e-readiness	**Focus**
	Ready to use tools/Questionnaires		
1	Asia-Pacific Economic Cooperation (APEC) E-commerce readiness assessment	• Basic infrastructure and technology • Access to necessary communications services • Current level and type of use of the Internet • Promotion and facilitation activities • Skills and human resources • Positioning for the digital economy	National and International e-commerce readiness
2	Computers System Policy Project (CSPP) Readiness Guide: For living in the Networked World	• Networked infrastructure • Networked access • Networked applications and services • Networked economy • Networked world enablers	Existing Technology and Policy
	Case studies		
1	Mosaic Group's Global Diffusion of the Internet(GDI) framework	• Pervasiveness • Geographic dispersion • Sector absorption • Connectivity infrastructure • Organisational structure • Sophistication of use	Internet Diffusion
2	Association of Southeast Asian Nations (ASEAN) e-readiness assessment	• ICT infrastructure • e-society • e-commerce • e-government	ICT Infrastructure
	Third party surveys and reports		
1	McConnell International (MI) Ready? Net. Go! tool	• Connectivity • e-leadership • Information security • Human capital • e-business climate	e-competitiveness of countries
2	Economist Intelligence Unit (EIU) E-readiness rankings 2009 report	• Connectivity and technology infrastructure • Business environment • Social and cultural environment • Legal environment • Government policy and vision • Consumer and business adoption	Technology Initiatives

focus on SMEs and their unique characteristics particularly, in relation to overcoming the barriers. Reviewing these tools produces a general impression that there is a lot of repetition of assessment categories amongst the tools and most of them were focussed on measuring technological infrastructure although there is no doubt that it is a very important category that cannot be ignored. Also, most of the existing tools seem to focus on countries at a macro level not at a micro level e-readiness assessment for SMEs. Too many categories and sub-categories in the existing tools also make assessment cumbersome. Additionally, no tool provide any guidance on how it could be adapted, developed or extended to assess e-readiness when new paradigms and specialised applications emerge in the arena of e-business or if the focus is different from the originally intended audience. This section also assumes that "soft" categories like education and literacy are important for SMEs.

In an attempt to strike a balance between the varying categories that the above 6 tools have provided and to eliminate any existing redundancy, the following 6 categories come to the forefront that need to be assessed for SMEs. These categories are by no means exhaustive and could be expanded or narrowed depending upon the need of the assessor to overcome the barriers of specific e-business applications. The categories are:

Technological Infrastructure: Technology that is less complex, cost effective and executes the needs of companies' specific goals is seen to be vital for SMEs e-business adoption. Every business has to develop strategies to understand the impact of technology on e-business as ICT is becoming more widely used and the role of existing ICT infrastructure needs to be determined. In this category, it is important to ascertain the hardware, software and telecommunication infrastructure that exists.

Knowledge Infrastructure: Barricades to knowledge awareness have to be removed to eliminate inefficiencies resulting due to lack of knowledge. Educating and training SMEs about the inferred knowledge of e-business is essential for boosting confidence in conducting business and to eliminate any existing barriers. Assessing the literacy levels of stakeholders will also be important to help in the adoption of e-business.

Human Support: Human inventiveness has a significant contribution towards overall business efficiency. Amalgamation of company specific business practices, knowledge and technical expertise allows businesses to leverage the potential of human support in fulfilling individual customer needs in a steady and personal way. Existing human skills and expertise needs to be assessed to reap the benefits of e-business. Assessing soft skills so that e-business adoption can be achieved is of prime significance.

Government Support: SMEs need government intervention to promote, educate and provide incentives to adopt e-business. Assessment in this category will determine the contribution of governments in providing favourable environment, implementing policies that address issues related to system infrastructure and broadband use, governing laws guarding security and privacy, so that SMEs can operate and function in a fair and free market.

Internet Penetration: Assessing adoption of the Internet by customers and suppliers is of prime importance. This will enable SMEs to decide whether they should adopt e-business or not. Often such data is available from government statistical bodies. High Internet usage by customers and suppliers would mean a good indicator for SMEs, whereas low Internet adoption by customers and suppliers becomes a stumbling block to e-business adoption by SMEs.

Conduciveness: Analysis of the barriers suggested that e-business adoption depends on the products and services that the SME offers. If the product or service cannot be sold online, then it is seen as an impediment to e-business adoption. Often the products or service can be sold online but customers may not want to buy it before inspection and thus e-business turns out to be unsuitable. As mentioned earlier, it can be argued that e-business is not only about buying or selling but other important organisational processes that can be facilitated using ICT. Nevertheless, this is an important category that needs to be assessed.

MAMS E-READINESS ASSESSMENT FRAMEWORK

Comprehensive analysis of existing research of various aspects of e-business adoption and e-readiness assessment tools as discussed and reviewed in the previous sections has revealed that e-readiness assessment categories relate to different levels and nature of countries, organisations and e-business applications. Numerous but isolated studies, tools and methods of e-readiness measurements with no linkage to the barriers and enablers of e-business adoption however are

Figure 1. MAMS e-readiness assessment framework

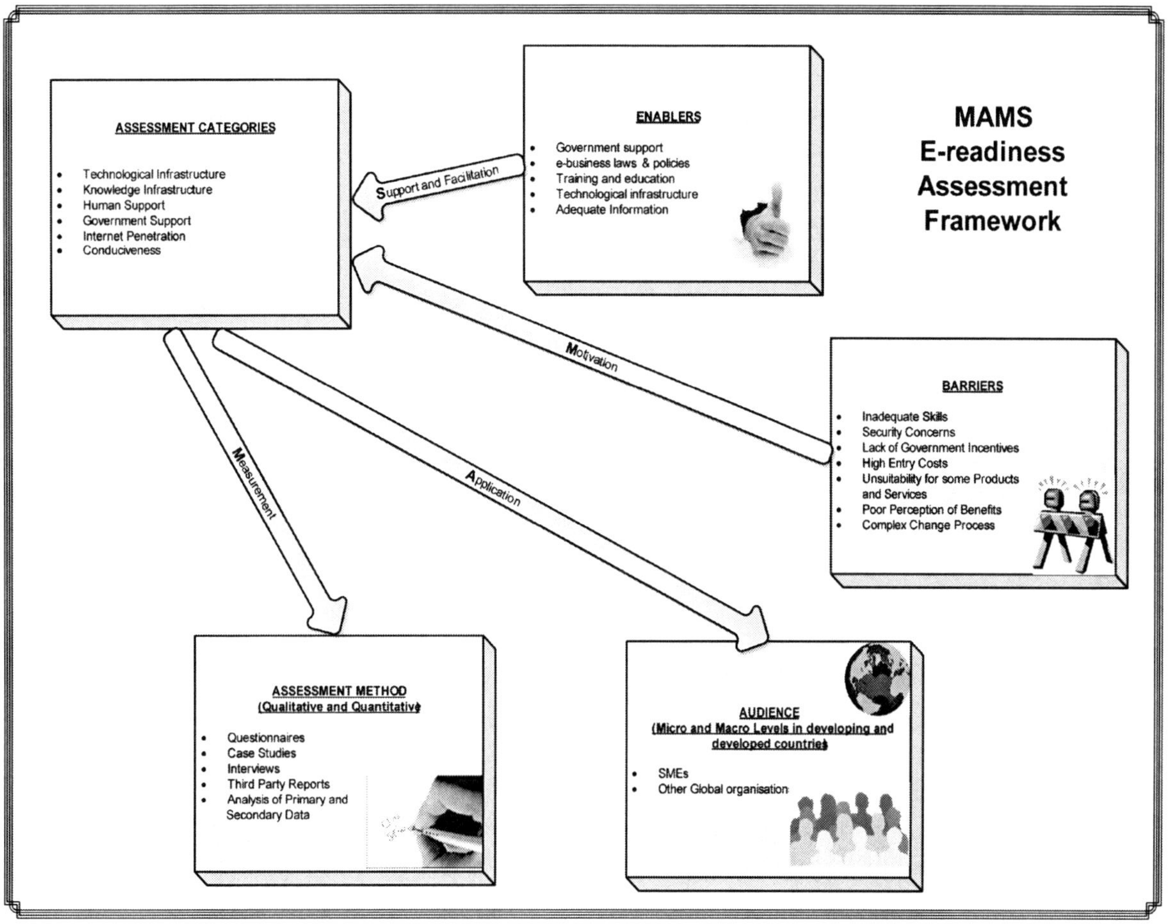

not sufficient to assess and help SMEs in finally adopting and implementing e-business for their economic growth and to win competitive advantage over their competitors.

Many research attempts have compared the tools, their approaches, the categories they measure (Bridges.org, 2005; Bui et al, 2003; Beig et al, 2007) and the target audience for e-market adoption. Such studies have only added more tools if the tool/s being investigated are found to be lacking in the categories of assessment to be measured. In contrast the research in this chapter was directed towards formulating a more generic and holistic framework for e-readiness assessment.

The proposed MAMS e-readiness assessment framework (Figure 1) links the multiple aspects of e-readiness for e-business adoption together with appropriate links. The links are abstract but logical. The most important links in the framework are inbound to and outbound from e-readiness categories that have been used to name the framework as MAMS (Motivation, Application, Measurement and Support) e-readiness assessment framework. The major components of the framework include:

- *Barriers* that make the provision of the e-readiness requirements difficult and are often the *motivation* to assess the availability and suitability of those assessment categories.
- *Enablers* that would make it possible to overcome barriers and *support and fa-*

cilitate the provision of the assessment categories.

- *Assessment methods* to assess how a business entity scores in different areas of e-readiness categories at different levels of operation (micro and macro). The existing methods provide for both qualitative and quantitative *measurements*. Some methods that could be used are questionnaires, case studies, interviews, third party reports and analysis of primary and secondary data.
- E-readiness *assessment categories* that are fundamental to e-business adoption as related to particular *application areas and audience* (can be enterprise, communities or countries).

Application of the Framework

The MAMS framework is generic in nature and is independent of the size, nature and the level of the business entity that is being assessed. It provides a comprehensive picture of readiness for e-business adoption by depicting all major components for assessing e-readiness together as a logical collection. Depending upon the scenario and the environment in which a SME operates the blocks can be populated. It is possible to identify content for each of the blocks in isolation but the major use of the framework is in linking the components together to provide an holistic view of the e-readiness assessment of an enterprise. Consequently, the framework can be utilized as a reference to assess, design and implement a supplementary strategic approach for the assessment of e-business readiness of the SME. For example, the framework can be a guide for an iterative assessment of the category by strengthening the enabling support if, in the preceding round, the category was assessed to be weak in e-readiness.

A Generic Case of E-Readiness for E-Business Adoption by SMEs

This section explains how the blocks of the framework are populated for the case of e-readiness for e-business adoption by SMEs.

Assessment Categories

As discussed in Section 5.2 SMEs must have access to technological and knowledge infrastructure, human and government support, penetration of ICT to its customers and suppliers, and conduciveness of e-business for the SMEs' products and services. Owing to the digital divide, the assessment for e-readiness can vary; nevertheless, the categories incorporated for assessment should stay the same. The categories are listed in the corresponding block in Figure 1.

Barriers and Enablers

In the case of e-business adoption by SMEs the impact of barriers may be quite impounding. Within the MAMS framework it is easy to relate barriers to assessment categories and identify if any category is missing. Before populating the blocks of barrier and enablers in Figure 1, a table is created(Table 3) to show the relationship between the six categories and the corresponding barriers from the barriers discussed in Section 3.2 along with the enablers (from Section 4.0) to alleviate the problem and further understanding. The list of barriers and enablers as extracted from Table 3 are shown in the corresponding blocks in Figure 1. Creating the links between category and the barriers will assist in identifying if any category or enabler is missing.

Assessment Methods

Some common assessment methods that could be employed to assess the categories have been shown in the framework. It is possible that more than one

Table 3. Categories, barriers, and enablers of SMEs

Categories	Barriers	Enablers
Technological Infrastructure	Security Concerns; High Entry Costs	Government Support; Set Up Technological Infrastructure; Adequate Information
Knowledge Infrastructure	Inadequate Skills; Security Concerns; Poor Perception of Benefits; Complex Change Process	Government Support; e-business Laws and Policies; Adequate Information
Human Support	Inadequate Skills	Training and Education; Adequate Information
Government Support	Lack of Government Incentives; Poor Perception of Benefits	Government Support; Adequate Information
Internet Penetration	High Entry Costs	Government Support; Set Up Technological Infrastructure; Training and Education; Adequate Information
Conduciveness	Unsuitability for some Products and Services	Training and Education; Adequate Information

of the assessment methods could be employed to help in the assessment since each method has its own pros and cons. A common application of the framework is to motivate appropriate identification and comparison of various existing tools and methods for the range of categories that can be tested. It should be accepted that one tool will not be suitable for all tests. Some tools will cover all categories that need to be assessed or if a tool is not compatible for some categories it can be extended or combined with other tools.

Following from the above discussion for the case of SMEs' assessment categories, the available tools can be reviewed and the most suitable tool for assessment of the categories can be short listed for use per se or with modifications and extensions. For example, in the case of SMEs as mentioned in Section 5.2 Soft Skills is a critical and integral part of the categories Knowledge Infrastructure and Human Support to overcome the barriers of inadequate skills, security concerns, poor perception of benefits, and complex change process. However, none of the tools reviewed in Section 5.1 provide for assessing soft skills. The tool closest to the requirement of a generic SME application is APEC e-commerce readiness assessment which would then need to be extended to include tests for Soft Skills.

The above analysis was possible with the holistic nature of the MAMS framework making it vital to consider and work with different components of the framework linked with each other and not in isolation.

LIMITATIONS AND FUTURE RESEARCH AVENUES

This is a qualitative study and further quantitative research is required to gain a clearer understanding of the barriers and enablers of e-business adoption by SMEs. It is worth noting here that this study has been informed by the extant literature of previous research on the enablers and barriers to arrive at the suggested framework. The possibility exists for further refinement of the framework after quantitative studies have been carried out. In order to develop the framework, this research has relied on hard data to capture the essence of existing tools but implementation of the framework and its testing remain open to future research. It will be interesting to apply the framework to assess e-readiness by SMEs in both developing and developed countries providing a thorough cross-country perspective.

Alternative research approaches could be used to assess the framework to improve our understanding of its usefulness and applicability. For example, the framework could be applied to different industries focussing on individual categories of e-readiness. The suggested framework is by no means exhaustive or definitive and further empirical research can be undertaken to improve it. The chapter calls for using the framework in the future for e-readiness assessments by SMEs as this would help support relative evaluations, comparisons, and improvements. The assessment categories that have been identified in the proposed framework can be further classified into sub-categories with weights assigned according to the perceived level of importance making measurement more valuable.

CONCLUSION

The importance of e-business as a critical parameter to achieve competitive advantage cannot be underemphasised. Adoption of e-business to improve operations and enhance customer satisfaction is becoming increasingly vital in today's global world and SMEs cannot afford to lag behind. In order to thrive in a competing environment, SMEs are also beginning to adopt ICT to improve their operations and accomplish many benefits. Various barriers were discussed in the chapter with an aim to facilitate the removal of the barriers by encouraging the implementation of appropriate enablers for SMEs to be e-ready. Obviously, SMEs are not necessarily prepared for the adoption of e-business so e-readiness assessments are becoming increasingly important. Assessing e-readiness is not an easy task as it relies on a large number of assessment categories and thus remains a constant challenge. Six existing tools of e-readiness were reviewed that possess their own lacunae and forte but none of them has been tailored specifically for SMEs. In this light, the MAMS e-readiness assessment framework has been proposed that provides an holistic view by putting together the assessment categories, enablers, barriers, assessment methods, and audience thereby making it easier to apply the framework for assessing e-readiness by SMEs. The proposed framework owes a lot to the pre-existing e-readiness tools that were analysed. The proposed framework, like others too, helps to present a simplified representation of reality but allows the user to adapt it to their needs to get an accurate representation of e-readiness. The proposed framework is not expected to be prescriptive but a generic guide that can be used by SMEs to assist in the assessment of their e-readiness. Alternatively, it is essential to bear in mind that integrating e-business in operations will only be beneficial to SMEs when it is incorporated into the overall business strategy so that the benefits of e-business will outweigh the disadvantages.

This chapter has its own implications in providing guidance for the adoption of e-business in SMEs to top managers and professionals. This chapter has given a concise and holistic understanding of the challenges confronting e-business adoption in SMEs and also achieved the objective of communicating barriers to a professional audience who can then apply the enablers to adopt e-business in SMEs. This generalist approach to SMEs' e-business adoption will be very pragmatic for an academic audience, particularly students.

In conclusion, it is becoming imperative to review the benefits, barriers and enablers of e-business for SMEs. SMEs play an important part in any country's economy and for any country and its organisations to move forward the adoption of e-business cannot be underplayed. It can be expected that in the future SMEs will increasingly migrate from bricks to clicks as they become more aware of the benefits of adopting e-business to facilitate their processes, particularly if their customers and suppliers are also becoming technologically savvy. In the interim, technological possibilities and opportunities are continuing to evolve and SMEs cannot afford to be left behind in joining the e-business bandwagon to achieve competitive advantage and gallop ahead into a largely unknown but bright future.

REFERENCES

Abell, W., & Limm, L. (1996). *Business Use of the Internet in New Zealand: An Exploratory Study*. Retrieved August 22, 2009, from http://ausweb.scu.edu.au/aw96/business/abell/paper.htm

Abernethy, M. (2002). SMEs: Small world order. *The Bulletin, 120*(34). Retrieved September 1, 2009, from http://bulletin.syd.ninemsn.com.au/article.aspx?id=131748

Asia-Pacific Economic Cooperation. (2000). *APEC E-Commerce Readiness Assessment Guide*. APEC Telecommunications and Information Working Group. Retrieved September 3, 2009, from http://publications.apec.org/publication-detail.php?pub_id=647

Auger, P., BarNir, A., & Gallaugher, J.M. (2003). Strategic Orientation, Competition, and Internet-Based Electronic Commerce. *Information Technology Management*, *4*(2), 139–164. doi:10.1023/A:1022942026706

Australian Bureau of Statistics. (2003). Business use of Information Technology. Canberra.

Baker and McKenzie. (2001). *Doing E-Commerce in Europe*. Hong Kong: Baker and McKenzie.

Beig, L., Montazer, G. A., & Ghavamifar, A. (2007). Adoption a proper tool for e-readiness assessment in developing countries (case studies: Iran, Turkey and Malaysia). *Journal of Knowledge Economy & Knowledge Management*, *2*, 54–69.

Bhatia, S. (2001). *e-ASEAN Readiness Assessment*. Retrieved August 15, 2009, from http://www.itu.int/asean2001/documents/pdf/Document-28.pdf

Bridges.org. (2005). *Comparison of e-readiness assessment models and tools (updated)*. Retrieved August 29, 2009, from www.bridges.org/publication/128

Bui, T. X., Sankaran, S., & Sebastian, I. S. (2003). A framework for measuring national e-readiness. *International Journal of Electronic Business*, *1*(1), 3–22. doi:10.1504/IJEB.2003.002162

Chau, S., & Pedersen, S. G. (2000). Small is Beautiful: The Emergence of New Micro Business Utilising Electronic Commerce. [Brisbane: Australia.]. *Proceedings of the Australian Conference on Information Systems*, *2000*, 1–8.

Chau, S. B., & Turner, P. (2004). An SME Experience of E-Commerce: Some Considerations for Policy Formulation in Australia. In B.J. Corbitt and NAY. Nl-Qirim (eds), *E-Business, E-Government & Small and Medium-Sized Enterprises: Opportunities and Challenges* (91-111).Hershey, PA: Idea Group Publishing.

Cloete, E., Courtney, S., & Fintz, J. (2002). Small Businesses' Acceptance and Adoption of E-Commerce in the Western-Cape Province of South-Africa. *Electronic Journal on Information Systems in Developing Countries*, *10*(4), 1–13.

Computers System Policy Project. (1998). *The CSPP Readiness Guide: For living in the Networked World*. Retrieved September 3, 2009, from http://www.cspp.org/documents/NW_Readiness_Guide.pdf

Currie, W. (2000). *The global information society*. New York: John Wiley and Sons.

Data Monitor. (2004). *SME Banking in Australia 2004*. Retrieved August 15, 2009, from http://www.researchandmarkets.com/reports/219039

Department for Business. Enterprise & Regulatory Reform. (2008). *Small and Medium-sized Enterprise (SME) Statistics for the UK and Regions 2007*, UK.

Economist Intelligence Unit. (2009). *E-readiness rankings 2009: The usage imperative.* Retrieved September 3, 2009, from http://graphics.eiu.com/pdf/E-readiness%20rankings.pdf

European Commission. (2005). *SME definition: User guide and model declaration, Enterprise and Industry Publications*. Retrieved August 20, 2009, from http://ec.europa.eu/enterprise/enterprise_policy/sme_definition/sme_user_guide.pdf

Forrester Research. (2005). *US eCommerce forecast: Online retail sales to reach $329 billion by 2010.* Retrieved August 22, 2009, from http://www.forrester.com/Research/ Document/Excerpt/0,7211,3726,00

Hall, C. (2002). *Profile of SMEs and SME issues 1990-2000*. Singapore: Asia-Pacific Economic Cooperation.

Hawk, S. (2004). A comparison of B2C e-commerce in developing countries. *Electronic Commerce Research*, *4*(3), 181–199. doi:10.1023/B:ELEC.0000027979.91972.36

Hughes, M., Golden, W., & Powell, P. (2003). Interorganisational ICT systems: the way to innovative practice for SMEs. *Journal of Small Business and Enterprise Development*, *10*(3), 277–286. doi:10.1108/14626000310489754

IDC. (2004). *IDC predicts double digit growth of Asia/Pacific Internet buyers from 2003 to 2008. IDC Australia*. Retrieved August 22, 2009, from http://www.idc.com.au/newsletters/ idcpulse/detail.asp?intID=43

Ihlström, C., Magnusson, M., Scupola, A., & Tuunainen, V. K. (2003). SME barriers to electronic commerce adoption: nothing changes-everything is new. In Gingrich, G. (Ed.), *Managing IT in Government Business & Communities* (pp. 147–163). Hershey: IGI Publishing.

Jutla, D., Bodorik, P., & Dhaliqal, J. (2002). Supporting the e-business readiness of small and medium-sized enterprises: approaches and metrics. *Internet Research: Electronic Networking Applications and Policy*, *12*(2), 139–164. doi:10.1108/10662240210422512

Kalakota, R., & Robinson, M. (2001). *E-Business 2.0: Road-map for Success*. Reading, MA: Addison-Wesley, Harlow.

Kartiwi, M., & MacGregor, R. C. (2007). Electronic commerce Adoption barriers in small to Medium-sized Enterprises (SMEs) in Developed and Developing countries: A cross-country comparison. *Journal of Electronic Commerce in Organizations*, *5*(3), 35–51.

Kaynak, E., Tatoglu, E., & Kula, V. (2005). An analysis of the factors affecting the adoption of electronic commerce by SMEs: Evidence from an emerging market. *International Marketing Review*, *22*(6), 623–640. doi:10.1108/02651330510630258

Lambert, T. (2002). *E-Commerce Answers: How to Turn Your Web Site into a Money Machine*. Upper Saddle River, NJ: Pearson Education Ltd, London.

Laudon, K. C., & Laudon, J. P. (2010). *Management Information Systems: Managing the digital firm (11th Global edn.)*. Upper Saddle River, NJ: Pearson Education.

Lawson, R., Alcock, C., Cooper, J., & Burgess, L. (2003). Factors affecting adoption of electronic technologies by SMEs: an Australian study. *Journal of Small Business and Enterprise Development*, *10*(3), 265–276. doi:10.1108/14626000310489727

Lee, C. S. (2001). An Analytical Framework for Evaluating E-commerce Business Models and Strategies. *Internet Research. Electronic Network Applications and Policy*, *11*(4), 349–359. doi:10.1108/10662240110402803

Levenburg, N. M., Schwarz, T. V., & Motwani, J. (2005). Understanding Adoption of Internet Technologies among SMEs. *Journal of Small Business Strategy*, *16*(1), 51–69.

McConnell International. (2000). *Risk E-Business: Seizing the Opportunity of Global E-Readiness*. Washington, DC: McConell International. Retrieved September 3, 2009 from http://whitepapers.zdnet.co.uk/0,1000000651,260019500p,00.htm

McConnell International. (2001). *Ready? Net. Go!Partnerships Leading the Global Economy*. Retrieved September 3, 2009 from http://www.witsa.org/papers/e-readiness2.pdf

McNurlin, B. C., Sprague, P. H. Jr, & Bui, T. (2009). *Information systems management in practice* (8th ed.). Upper Saddle River, NJ: Pearson Education.

Minges, M. (2002). Assessing e-readiness: A review of the Mosaic Methodology. *iNet Conference 2002*, Washington DC. Retrieved September 3, 2009, from http://www.itu.int/ITU-D/ict/papers/2002/inet02/MM.pdf

Mosaic Group. (1998). *The Global Diffusion of the Internet Project: An Initial Inductive Study*. Retrieved September 3, 2009, from http://mosaic.unomaha.edu/GDI1998/GDI1998.html

Nath, R., Akmanligil, M., Hjelm, K., Sakaguchi, T., & Schultz, M. (1998). Electronic commerce and the internet: issues, problems, and perspectives. *International Journal of Information Management*, *18*(2), 91–101. doi:10.1016/S0268-4012(97)00051-0

Organisation for Economic Cooperation and Development. (1997). *Small Business, Job Creation and Growth: Facts*. Paris, France: Obstacles and Best Practices.

Organisation for Economic Cooperation and Development. (2004). *SME Statistics; Towards a More Systematic Statistical Measurement of SME Behaviour*. Istanbul: Turkey.

Organisation for Economic Cooperation and Development. (2005). *OECD SME and Entrepreneurship Outlook*. OECD Publishing.

Parish, A., Kibblewhite, G., Woodley, M., & Richardson, J. (2002). The UK electronics industry e-commerce initiative-a study of the adoption of e-commerce. Retrieved August 10, 2009, from www.intellectuk.org/publications/ reports

Poon, S. (1999). Small business and Internet commerce: What are the lessons learned? In Sudweeks, F., & Romm, C. (Eds.), *Doing business on the Internet: Opportunities and pitfalls* (pp. 113–124). London, UK: Springer-Verlag.

Poon, S., & Strom, J. (1997). Small businesses use of the Internet: some realities. *Association for Information Systems Americas Conference*, Indianapolis, IN, 15–17 August. Retrieved August 10, 2009, from http://www.isoc.org/INET97/proceedings/C2/C2_1.HTM

Poon, S., & Swatman, P. M. C. (1995). The Internet for Small Businesses: An Enabling Infrastructure for Competitiveness. *Proceedings of the Fifth Internet Society Conference*, (ed.) Chon K., Hawaii, 221-231.Retrieved August 10, 2009, from http://www.isoc.org/inet95/proceedings/PAPER/126/html/paper.html

Poon, S., & Swatman, P. M. C. (1999). An exploratory study of small business Internet commerce issues. *Information & Management*, *35*(1), 9–18. doi:10.1016/S0378-7206(98)00079-2

Porter, M. E. (2001). Strategy and the Internet. *Harvard Business Review*, *79*(3), 62–78.

Pratt, J. H. (2002). *E-biz; Strategies for small business success*. US SBA Office of Advocacy. Retrieved August 10, 2009, from http://www.sba.gov/advo/research/rs220tot.pdf

Rachman, Z. M. (2002). *ASEAN e-Readiness Assessment*. Retrieved August 22, 2009, from http://unpan1.un.org/intradoc/groups/public/documents/APCITY/UNPAN011274.pdf

Ramsey, E., Ibbotson, P., Bell, J., & Gary, B. (2003). E-opportunities of service sector SMEs: An Irish cross-boarder study. *Journal of Small Business and Enterprise Development*, *10*(3), 250–264. doi:10.1108/14626000310489709

Reserve Bank of India. (2009). *Master Circular-Lending to Micro, Small, & Medium Enterprises(MSME)*. Mumbai, India: Sector.

Riquelme, H. (2002). Commercial internet adoption in China: comparing the experience of small, medium and large businesses. *Internet Research: Electronic Networking Applications and Policy*, *12*(3), 276–286. doi:10.1108/10662240210430946

Schulze, C., & Baumgartner, J. (2001). *Don't Panic, Do E-Commerce, A Beginner's Guide to European Law Affecting E-Commerce*. European Commission's Electronic Commerce Team.

Searle, J. (2001). *UK Online for business*. Retrieved August 22, 2009, from www.ncc.co.uk/ncc/Jenny_Searle.pdf

Sensis (2005). *The Online Experience of Small and Medium Enterprises*, Sensis e-business Report, Australia.

Sheth, J. N., & Sharma, A. (2005). International e-marketing: Opportunities and issues. *International Marketing Review*, *22*(6), 611–622. doi:10.1108/02651330510630249

Tiessen, J. H., Wright, R. W., & Turner, I. (2001). A model of e-commerce use by internationalizing SMEs. *Journal of International Management*, *7*(3), 211–233. doi:10.1016/S1075-4253(01)00045-X

Walczuch, R., Braven, G. V., & Lundgren, H. (2000). Internet adoption barriers for small firms in the Netherlands. *European Management Journal*, *18*(5), 561–572. doi:10.1016/S0263-2373(00)00045-1

Walters, D., & Lancaster, G. (1999). Using the Internet as a channel for commerce. *Management Decision*, *37*(10), 800–816. doi:10.1108/00251749910302908

Xu, M., Rohatgi, R., & Duan, Y. (2007). E-Business Adoption in SMEs: Some Preliminary Findings from Electronic Components Industry. *International Journal of E-Business Research*, *3*(1), 74–90.

Chapter 18
Issues Influencing Electronic Commerce Activities of SMEs:
A Study of the Turkish Automotive Supplier Industry

Muammer Zerenler
Selcuk University, Turkey

Sitki Gözlü
Istanbul Technical University, Turkey

ABSTRACT

This study aims to investigate the issues of electronic commerce activities in small and medium sized enterprises as a consequence of organizational change initiated by the adoption of information technologies. The fundamental issues influencing electronic commerce practices of SMEs are their insufficiency of cognitive learning and organizational strategy, financial and distribution problems specific to SMEs, limitations of supply chain management, reluctance of organizational culture for electronic change, problems of information technologies usage, insufficiency of human resource, resistance of top management to organizational change as required by the adoption of information technologies, integration problems of new technologies with the existing systems, lack of confidence on the side of customers towards electronic commerce. A study of the Turkish Automotive Supplier Industry has revealed that electronic commerce has been adopted and its benefits are accepted. However, the industry has to overcome some technical and managerial difficulties to implement it more efficiently and effectively.

INTRODUCTION

In societies where commercial competition is accepted as an economic system, there is a close relationship between the healthy operation of the system and the existence and power of small and medium sized enterprises (SMEs) within the system. Most SMEs positively contribute to the system since they can fulfill several functions not achieved by large enterprises (MacGregor, 2004, p. 10).

SMEs are not merely economic elements; they also have vital roles in social life. Because of the fact that SMEs spread to a large area in the country, they act as a critical power in lessening regional

DOI: 10.4018/978-1-61692-880-3.ch018

developmental differences, spreading ownership to a vast area, creating and sustaining employment opportunities, and keeping democratic life alive.

Currently, SMEs play a fundamental role in terms of employment and macro- economic balance by increasing their shares in global economy and thus enabling high levels of employment. Overall contributions of SMEs to the economy can be outlined as the following: (Kleindl, 2000, p. 75; Walczuch et al., 2000, p. 568):

- Depending on labor intensive work and efficiency in resource use, they contribute to creating employment opportunities and lessening unemployment nationwide.
- They adapt quickly and comfortably to demand changes and variations.
- They help to balance income distribution.
- They enable making decisions quickly. Since they are mostly structured as family companies, there is a tendency to make centralized decisions (Evans and Wurster, 1997, p. 72).
- In the long run, they are in a position to become manufacturers of the inputs and intermediary goods of large industrial enterprises.
- They are flexible and supportive of innovations.
- They are effective in improving life quality by providing opportunities for the socially and politically disregarded labor force, raw materials and financial sources to operate by smaller investments (Levy et al., 1999, p. 249).
- They acquire a critical role in transmitting small funds and family capital directly to investments.
- Through manufacturing inputs such as raw materials, intermediary materials, and semi-finished products consumed by large scale enterprises, they contribute to their development and also the national economy.
- They contribute significantly to increasing regional employment opportunities since they are labor intensive; therefore prevent migration from small cities to big city centers and construct a base for self development of the region within its own potential.
- By positively affecting income distribution, preventing the accumulation of capital in the hands of large industrial organizations or a minority, they increase societal income both functionally and regionally.

SMEs are also effective in providing new ideas and inventions and adopting new technologies (Kleindl, 2000, p. 76). New technologies enable SMEs to perform more creatively and flexibly with lower costs. Small enterprises are effective in transferring various technologies to national economy and in the process of modernization traditional technology or adaptation to the transferred technology; they act as a bridge between new and traditional technologies (Evans and Wurster, 1997, p. 74). On the other hand today, the rapidly increasing automation and demand for more qualified employees force SMEs to adopt new technologies. SMEs face difficulties, basically due to lack of sources, in following new technologies, acquiring technological materials, finding and employing qualified technical personnel to implement new technologies. Qualified employees generally prefer job security of large enterprises, corporate reputation, and high salaries.

The ability of SMEs to survive in a highly competitive environment depends on the extent and speed in activating the changes that will make their products and / or services noticeable and preferable. As SMEs achieve these goals in establishing and sustaining enterprise's relationship with the outer world by benefiting from the opportunities of technology, they make use of information technologies and its elements. At this point electronic commerce is helpful in achieving innovations and improvements rapidly and safely (Hawkins and Prencipe, 2000, p. 24).

SMES AND ELECTRONIC COMMERCE

While globalization and technological changes create new opportunities for SMEs, at the same time they create new risks and threats. It is considered that SMEs, due to their flexibility, can meet customer expectations more quickly and they are more advantageous than large enterprises in utilizing electronic commerce (Dandridge, 2000, p. 87; Daniel et a., 2002, p. 261). Because of competition and pressures of software providers and system integrators, several SMEs search for new ways to increase their market shares by implementing electronic commerce solutions. Besides, while large companies already have necessary personnel and financial sources to implement electronic commerce, capital limitations of SMSs restrict their investments for electronic commerce (Stansfield and Grant, 2003, p. 16).

On the basis of discussions so far, it is possible to summarize the contributions of electronic commerce to SMEs as the following. Electronic commerce enables SMEs to enter new markets and thus competition gains impetus. Since it speeds up operations and lessens demand for labor, it decreases costs. As it provides effective communication between buyers and sellers, it helps to improve service and product quality. Enhancing data share it contributes positively to the efficiency of work processes and overall economy (Eikebrokk and Olsen, 2007; Van Beveren, 2002; Levy et al., 1999).

Generally speaking, all of the contributions listed above can be deemed convincing. For instance the fact that with a lower investment SMEs can reach the markets which they can never attain through other ways seems rather feasible. Yet when this issue is discussed elaborately, the matter surfaces in a more complicated manner. Quite probably SMEs will face a difficulty in employing qualified human resources that can develop the information system within its own structure. In that case, the enterprise will be forced to employ people / companies out of the enterprise for the sales website. Employing people outside the enterprise makes it difficult to have a flexible and expandable performance applicable in their own sector. The fact that system is established / organized in a separate location will bring drawbacks in terms of updating and securing commercial safety (Dans, 2001, p.77). As it is illustrated in this scenario, several cultural, economic and commercial reasons may hinder SMEs' electronic commerce performance. Let aside all these points, it is not for certain that even a well prepared website – or other digital tools, can immediately find a market or open inaccessible markets (Liew, 2009, p.17).

Successful implementation of electronics is related to a multivariate and complicated process, which is connected with social and economic elements as much as with technical, technological, physical and legal infrastructure. In this section, the objective is to comparatively analyze the factors that affect / prevent SMEs' successful implementation of electronic commerce activities and to discuss sample cases unique to several SMEs operating in different sectors.

THE EFFECTS OF ELECTRONIC COMMERCE APPLICATIONS IN SMES

Electronic commerce provides important opportunities to SMEs in reaching new markets and competing with rivals. Virtual shops on internet enable SMEs to reach distant markets by offering an effective and economical marketing channel. Therefore SMEs obtain a chance to enter global markets without necessitating high investments and expenditures and offer inexpensive, fast, and high quality products in these markets (Evans and Wurster, 1997:77). On the other hand product development and marketing processes are shortened in SMEs, where electronic commerce is actively used. In the past, thanks to the application of information technologies, SMEs that followed / copied large scale enterprises, obtained critical time advantages in product development and marketing processes (Heijden, 2000, p. 41; Walczuch et al., 2000, p. 570; Levy et al., 1999, p. 252; Coppel, 2000, p. 17; Porter, 2001, p. 67).

Regardless of the fact that electronic commerce contains in itself various advantages for SMEs, still it is hardly possible to assert that SMEs make enough use of electronic commerce. Researches on this issue reveal that SMEs generally use Internet as a basic communication means and regard it as an alternative communication tool that cuts off costs more than traditional communication mediums such as fax and telephone (Kleindl, 2000, p. 78; Fisher, 2000, p. 61; Soliman and Yousef, 2003, p. 548).

It is clear that job opportunities for electronic commerce provided to SMEs vary at different levels for each sector. Among the reasons, there are the type of commerce, technological infrastructure of the country, Internet utilization ratio, and cognitive literacy. Within this scope it is crucial that SMEs take into consideration several factors effective in their investments for electronic commerce. These factors can be outlined in general as the following issues (Liew, 2009, p. 25):

Target market and geographical region where business is concentrated: Today a great majority of SMEs produce for national markets and most of the exporting enterprises also have domestic market oriented commercial expansion. Orienting towards foreign markets by using electronic tools and methods renders it a requisite for an enterprise to change its basic job performance applications such as product marketing, managing customer relations, and securing after-sales customer assistance (MacGregor, 2008, p. 47).

Products and services offered through electronic channels: Enterprises in developed countries have required infrastructure and sufficient experience in selling products and services through electronic commerce. Electronic commerce can be effectively activated particularly in service industries, where information provides significant added value.

Internet based commerce opportunities and compatibility of production chain systems as business development method: A good deal of industrial products may not be suitable for direct sales on Internet. The reasons may be specified such that seller has a limited number of buyers with web page access, physical contents of product, specific features of product, or restrictions for marketing. Considering the fact that enterprises will keep on using traditional marketing and distribution methods, holding a position on web and catalogues, being a part of commercial opportunities and presentation chain webs can be valued as supportive services for commerce (Van Beveren, 2002, p. 253).

A research - Digital Marketing Compass - conducted in the beginning of 2009 focused on substantial investments, budget plans for future, and attitudes concerning electronic marketing of the total 783 decision makers. In Digital Marketing Compass, unlike many studies on electronic marketing, it has been pointed out that not only "large scale" companies, but also SMEs increased their electronic marketing investments a significant amount. According to the research, various opportunities provided through electronic marketing is generally known well by SMEs and used appropriately. In 2008 web based marketing utilization was 32%. The most striking outcome of this research is related to the orientation of SMEs towards international markets. Electronic based marketing activities of export-oriented SMEs were ahead of traditional marketing methods in 2008 (http://www.ogilvy.com.tr/digitalmarketingcompass/).

Cost and suitability of Internet access / hosting services: Under the condition that Internet access costs are reasonable, enterprises will more extensively use electronic mail, which is faster and less expensive than communication by telephone and fax. Besides, the costs of creating and supporting a website increase in line with the contents of site and the level of applied technology (Sadowski, 2002, p. 80; Quayle, 2002, p.1151).

The cost of accessing data for the market and potential partners: Private websites offering commercial data perform this mission in return for a certain price, which may be unaffordable for some SMEs. However, most public institutions provide supportive information for commerce free on Internet. Sustaining these services and reducing the cost of paid services in the long run will help SMEs to detect their target markets, access reliable data concerning their partners, determine the correct distribution channels, learn legal and regulative rules, reach financial sources, risk management, and logistic services (Colombo, 2001, p. 179).

Moreover particularly for SMEs with a unique product and operation model, it will be possible to finance electronic commerce investments in a short period. Because the extensive size of the market achieved through electronic commerce provides a market these enterprises can never reach with the help of traditional methods. Freeing themselves from the obligation of being local can create a global-scale breakthrough for companies with the best product and business performance (Stansfield and Grant, 2003, p. 17)

THE PROBLEMS AFFECTING ELECTRONIC COMMERCE ACTIVITIES OF SMES

The basic problems affecting electronic commerce applications of SMEs are inadequacy of cognitive learning and organizational strategy, financial and distribution problems specific to SMEs, restrictions in supply chain management, reluctance of organizational culture for electronic transformation, problems in the application of information technologies, lack of qualified personnel, resistance of top management against organizational transformation necessitated by applying information technologies, integration problem of new technologies with available systems, customers' lack of trust towards electronic commerce, and their worries concerning privacy (Vinberg, et al. 2000; Oyelaran-Oyeyinka and Kaushalesh Lal, 2006).

Janenko (2003) believes that one of the most important problems SMEs face in electronic commerce activities is "automatic success deception". According to Janenko, many SMEs have automated several aspects of their work processes through websites and are convinced that success will come automatically (2003). Varianini and Vaturi (2000) have found out similar causes for the problems affecting digitalizing process of SMEs such as to sustain a fixed market information flow, not possessing a flexible organization structure, not detecting clear targets, and lack of safety and integration. Farhoomand and Lovelock (2001) also, has discovered numerous negative elements affecting electronic commerce in SMEs such as poor income / outcome / profit model, lack of competition advantage, insufficiency in providing benefits to customer, organizational problems, and the conflict between website and current business partners.

As stated by Kshetri problems affecting electronic commerce negatively are mostly concentrated on economic and social areas (2007, p. 446). Economic problems can be outlined as low level of information technology applications, inadequacy of Telecom infrastructure, lack of capital, low level of credit card usage. The social problems are low level of cognitive literacy, foreign language (mainly English) insufficiency, promotion and marketing problems of local websites.

According to Kshetri the problems affecting electronic commerce can be categorized under three groups such as pre-electronic commerce, in electronic commerce processes, and post-electronic commerce (2007, p. 447). Pre-electronic commerce problems are mostly related to the adequacy of a country's cognitive infrastructure. Credit card usage nationwide and financial problems are observed in the electronic commerce process phase. Post-electronic commerce problems are distribution infrastructure and after-sales services. Within a macro point of view, Kshetri bases this grouping mostly to the technical problems associated with information infrastructure of countries. Peterson et al. (1997, p. 337) classify problems in electronic commerce as financial, legal, infrastructure, safety, customer privacy, protection of intellectual and industrial rights, problems faced during delivery, and customs operations. Dornan (2001, p. 27) on the other hand groups problems affecting electronic commerce just like Peterson et al.

While some authors point out that in electronic management activities of SMEs, efficiency of non-commercial based transformation will increase, traditional commerce will at the same time affect / delay / repress the development of electronic commerce activities (Heinen, 1996; Chaffey, 2007, Li, 2006; Chen and Siems, 2001; Sadowski, 2002). Some authors advocate that the development of electronic commerce in the entire organization will be experienced faster at the end of e-commerce based transformation process (Jelassi and Enders, 2008; Bayles, 2001; Strader and Ramaswami, 2002).

According to McGregor and Vrazalic in terms of adopting electronic commerce, SMEs can be categorized into two groups such as potential adopters and non-adopters. The non-adopter group cannot use electronic commerce due to internal causes of enterprises and external causes related to technological, economic, politic, legal, social, and cultural problems (2006, p. 7). Kapurubandara

Table 1. Review of literature

High cost of electronic commerce tools, hardware/software cost of Internet technology.	Jacovou (1995), Quayle (2002), Puaro and Campbell (1998), Lawrance (1997), Riquelme (2992) and Van Akkeren and Cavaye (1990)
Problems originating from size of small enterprises.	Webb and Sayer, (1998), Van Beveren, (2002)
Closeness to innovation and information technologies.	Van Beveren, (2002), (Davis, 2000), Dandridge, (2000)
Adoption problems to electronic commerce.	Walczuch et al., (2000), Webb and Sayer, (1998)
Complex structure of electronic commerce.	Quayle (2002), Chaston, (2001).
SMEs' family company structure and lack of institutionalism.	Dandridge, (2000), Sadowski, (2002), Colombo, (2001).
While SMEs have development necessity in a short term, the fact that electronic commerce acquires its feedbacks only in the long run.	Lawrance (1997)and McGowan and Madey (1998)
Low level of cognitive literacy among employees and resistance.	Lawrance (1997), Van Akkeren and Cavaye (1999)
Preferring traditional methods such as telephone, fax, and face-to-face communication.	Lawrance (1997), Vankatesan and Fink (2002) and Poon and Swatman (2000)
Safety problem of electronic commerce.	Quayle (2002), Puaro and Campbell (1998), Riquelme (2002), Van Akkeren and Cavaye (1999), Poon and Swatman (2000) and Hadjimonolis (1999).
Lack of integration among customers, suppliers and business partners who all have critical roles in implementing electronic commerce.	Hadjimonolis (1999), McDonagh, (2000)
Lack of adequate trust towards external consultancy firms	Lawrance (1997), Van Akkeren and Cavaye (1999), Chau and Turner (2001).
Deficiency of electronic commerce standards.	Tuunainen (1998), Dandridge, (2000), Webb and Sayer, (1998).

Source: Robert C.MacGregor, Lejla Vrazalic, "A Basic Model of Electronic Commerce Adoption Barriers", School Of Economics and Information Systems, University of Wollongong, Australia, p. 515

and Lawson advocate that in overcoming these obstacles methodologically "decision taking" and "adoption" processes take place (2006, p.2). Stockdale and Standing categorize all the factors under four main groups such as "lack of resources and data, skill levels of employees, safety issues and preparation of small enterprises" (2004). Kurnia and Johnson include supply chain structure in this grouping as well (2000). In Table 1, it is possible to summarize the different views mentioned above.

In this study, we evaluate the problems affecting successful electronic commerce applications of SMEs – as it is widely accepted in relevant literature; under two groups such as cultural and technical problems (Rowley, 2002; Warren and Hutchinson, 2005; Gottschalk, 2005; Combe, 2006).

CULTURAL PROBLEMS

Top Management Support

Management support is the driving force in electronic commerce applications in corporations. According to Delone top management support is the most crucial factor for information technology applications in SMEs (1988). In particular, without the support of top management in decision-making process, it is not possible for SMEs to realize structural and technological transformation in electronic commerce by making required decisions and moreover without their support, any initiative regarding this matter may become unsuccessful (Grandon and Pearson, 2004).

Imperfect Entrepreneurship

Social habits originating from the past of a country are among the main factors determining the implementation speed and form of new technological developments. These habits, which determine the confidence of people to their environment and economy, particularly to money earning process, are also basic causes lying behind economic differences among countries.

Unsuitability of Organizational Culture for Electronic Commerce

One of the potential problems almost any organization aiming electronic commerce implementation is that organizational culture may not be suitable for organizational transformation necessitated by electronic management. Technological transformation and electronic business environment as required by electronic commerce will cause vital changes such as developing infrastructure and training activities compulsory particularly for organizations where bureaucratic work is dominant (Chen, 2004).

Ambiguity of Benefits

Another problem for SMEs is the ambiguity of benefits that will be gained through electronic commerce implementation. Since electronic commerce is a recent phenomenon, it is hard to compare successful examples of SMEs. Small enterprises in particular are inclined to be more influenced by tangible practice results rather than theoretical knowledge.

On the other hand, although it can be possible for almost any field, electronic commerce may have high success in certain products but low in others. For instance in intangible goods such as music, software etc. that can be easily transmitted from one place to another through websites, electronic commerce provides numerous advantages. However, for products which are hard to be transmitted physically, the advantages of electronic commerce are relatively limited (Levy et al., 1999, p. 244).

Innovativeness and Insufficiency of Innovation Management

According to Zhao, similar electronic management applications that have become widespread in companies decrease the effectiveness of competition tools. They seriously differ from traditional business models, and their advantages and similarities reduce benefits of suppliers and customers (2006). Since innovation strategies in electronic management applications will provide quick and flexible dynamism necessitated by the demands of shareholders and electronic transformation, SMEs will have to prioritize their innovative activities (Singh and Waddell, 2006).

Difficulty of Changing Shopping Habits

This problem is particularly valid in countries where traditional life style is dominant. Transformation in shopping habits takes place at a slower pace than electronic commerce development of any country. It is common that people prefer to buy from people they already know after seeing and touching goods. Shopping from a virtual environment, not knowing the nature of the product or its delivery conditions may not be quite acceptable for some people.

On an Internet shoe seller zappos.com established in 1999, there are more than 3 million pairs of shoes. One of the most important features of this company which ensures 365 day refund guaranty is its free cargo service for both customer deliveries and returns. Seventy-five percent of all orders come from satisfied customers. Following his / her first shopping a customer makes 2.5 times more shopping in the next 12 months after the first order. Forty-three percent of the recently gained customers are from WOMM (word of mouth marketing) process. They provide a toll-free call line. Unlike other big e-commerce sites (Amazon, overstock, e-bay etc.) they place their number on each page. If their product does not meet the requirements of customers, they recommend other competitor sites. So far none of its customers, by providing their name or no name, has made any complaints (www.zappos.com).

Locality

For enterprises, one of the most significant economic developments introduced by Internet is the expansion of local markets to a global scale. Economic activities such as web-based advertisements, promotions, job offers, marketing activities, and sales are accessible for any Internet user enterprise and customers. Thus, it becomes easier for enterprises expanding towards foreign markets to sustain and enlarge their activities. Besides it is regarded as an opportunity not to be missed for medium and small sized enterprises, which have fully utilized foreign market potential (Reynolds and Mofazali, 2000; Combe, 2006).

TECHNICAL PROBLEMS

Inadequacy of Human Resources

Human resources management approach and its applications have now become effective in a new field described as electronic human resource by the influence of information technologies. Basically electronic human resource concept means supporting human resources management approach by a new structuring in the electronic environment. It is viewed as a way to support human resource oriented strategies, policies, and applications through Internet based channels (Williamson et al., 2003, p.247).

As an outcome of current use of information technologies in enterprises, new employment opportunities emerge in the relevant sectors, and demand for expert technology personnel increases in return. However, throughout the world parallel to the fast development of electronic commerce, new job opportunities and demand for human resource increase, but the supply of qualified human resource does not grow at the same pace (Lai and Chen, 2009).

Electronic commerce applications require changes in the commercial and organizational structures and qualifications of personnel. In several countries, lack of information personnel has turned out to be a critical problem. Although it is early to make a guess on the future demand for qualified labor force, it can be regarded as an indicator that of all the personnel working in electronic commerce related enterprises, an average of 45-50% are employed in sales and marketing, 25-35% in research-development, and the rest in management, finance, and other areas (Zerenler, 2007, p. 223).

Insufficient Marketing Strategies

The popularity of electronic commerce as a business medium is related to the capacity of Internet, namely its future potential, its attractive qualities, its dynamism in providing global share of information and resources, and Internet's power in offering an effective channel of advertisement, marketing and direct distribution of certain products and / or services. In his book titled "Supra-Competition" Edward de Bono states "despite everything you must not fall behind your rivals otherwise you cannot sustain your presence. Price, quality, product differentiation and setting special markets are all traditional mediums serving this objective" (1994, p. 27). Indeed, enterprises competing in today's modern world are obliged to implement electronic based marketing activities, which have turned out to be a necessity rather than an advantage in competition that is becoming increasingly violent and different. Thus in such an environment where even electronic commerce is dedifferentiated, followed, and imitated by rivals, differentiating electronic marketing to adapt them to the basic qualities of enterprise would reply to the predictions of Bono, namely being supra-competition.

Electronic marketing is regarded as a revolutionary tool transforming all business processes of enterprises. Electronic marketing also, causes transformation of the traditional market structures (Calin et al., 2001, p. 36). The central role of this transformation belongs to Internet. Internet's progress is the most vital determinant of electronic marketing development. In addition, electronic marketing transforms purchase decision process of buyers as well. As buyers get involved in electronic marketing, they catch a chance to examine more options than traditional markets and thus able to make quicker decisions.

The fact that electronic commerce is full of opportunities for enterprises and it has risk minimizing quality account for the reasons not to be used. The answer for the question how to use and how to make the best of it, is related to strategy formulation. Fearing that other enterprises will seize their own markets through Internet and planning the cost of not using Internet as a defense reflex, several enterprises choose to find methods to use Internet more effectively. To achieve this end, conscious application and marketing strategies unique to Internet use should be developed (Zerenler, 2007, p. 267). If electronic commerce or cognitive business processes are, above all, established on the information bases of sector and markets, then these enterprises starting business without sufficient pre-researches may face failure. To make a right start, it is a must that enterprises planning to operate in this field should conduct pre-researches and also forms the required information infrastructure.

The Size of Enterprise and Lack of Knowledge

Parallel to the phase of entering information based economy, for the purpose of adapting SMEs to the new work conditions introduced by this economic system, both national governments and international corporations initiated activities to inform enterprises about electronic commerce.

A great majority of relevant literature points out the fact that in most countries, except USA, a great portion of SMEs is not yet totally aware of electronic commerce benefits (Coppel, 2000, p. 71). On the other hand, some authors hold the view that enterprise size also, has an effect over cognitive literacy and electronic commerce competency. As the enterprises get smaller in size, it is witnessed that Internet use that constitutes the base of electronic commerce falls backward. According to a research conducted by Levy et al., in enterprises with more than 1000 workers Internet usage ratio reaches to a level of 42%, whereas this ratio decreases to 14% for SMEs employing 1-49 workers (2001, p. 135).

Inability of Managing Technology

Selecting the technology required by SMEs to achieve their strategic and short-term goals, planning the required technology applications, deciding for transfer or manufacturing and realizing the activities for implementing this decision within the framework of a plan and program are among the basic activity issues of technology management. Strategic technology selection and goal-oriented work planning will ensure successful application of technology management.

Although electronic commerce offers wider range of opportunities for enterprises where information technologies are intensively implemented or manufactured, the very same advantage is hard to be viewed in the sectors far away from these technologies. In short, sector features may be restrictive in electronic commerce applications (Zhao, 2006, p.47).

Language and Cultural Elements

In the Internet environment, making it possible to access resources from all over the world, it is observed that language and cultural elements also demonstrate significant effects. Although 70% of Internet contents are in English, half of Internet users do not understand English. Still as stated by Coppel, even without this language problem, customers are more eager to shop from websites in their native tongue (2000, p.21).

English that is spoken like a native language in almost any international activity is dominant in electronic management operations as well. Yet companies marketing to regions where Spanish, Chinese, and Urdu languages are common should direct their marketing activities by taking regional languages into account.

Aside from the language problem, cultural elements also greatly affect electronic commerce activities of SMEs. Since many visual elements from colors to symbols present cultural differences among societies, many SMEs willing to benefit from global nature of Internet encounter difficulties.

Infrastructure and Environmental Problems

The foundation of electronic commerce is structured over communication infrastructures and information technologies. Particularly in developing countries communication costs are high and technological infrastructure falls short. High communication cost is one of the most important problems in electronic commerce applications. Generally, it is possible to comment the following suggestions for solving infrastructure problems (Reynolds and Mofazali, 2000, p.81-83; Chen, 2004, p.161):

- Telecommunication infrastructure should be improved; and it should be possible for SMEs to benefit from these services in private.
- All forms of electronic commerce; particularly commerce through Internet, can be conducted by providing information flow through communication infrastructure. In cases where only Internet centered structuring is an issue, potential cutbacks

and problems on Internet may cease commerce. Hence, alternative connection forms should be structured.

- The obstacles keeping communication and markets of information technologies away from competition should be abolished.
- Technical standards in communication should be determined.
- Environment of confidence should be established for service providers, users, and consumers taking place in electronic systems and operations.

Connection Problems

Connection problems are among the most frequently faced obstacles on Internet in electronic commerce applications. This problem, which does not merely restrict electronic commerce but all types of Internet use, is a deficiency causing information access efforts to become fruitless (Nusair and Hua, 2009).

There are attempts to simplify Internet connection and increase the access speed of countries. Failure to provide an effective infrastructure and telecom activities, which are public in many countries, restrict the operations of private sector. Restricted activities introduce high costs, poor quality yet costly access options. Recently the attempts to enable access through satellite and improving the present options by using high quality cables have been speeded up by private sector.

Legal Problems

Legal problems are the foremost reason critically determining the transformation of electronic commerce implementation into a global structure. Many issues such as the validity and binding of a computer based contract, validity of data kept in computer environment and their power of evidence, validity and applicability of digital signature, protection of intellectual and artistic works on Internet environment, legal recognition of information based crimes and prevention of unfair competition affect SMEs greatly. The main legal problems in electronic commerce applications can be outlined as the following (Kalakota and Whinston, 1997, p. 33):

a. Intellectual ownership rights,
b. Taxation,
c. Approval procedures,
d. Deficiencies in international laws,
e. Privacy rights of people,
f. Validity of electronic documents problem,
g. Validity of digital signature problem,
h. Determining responsibilities of service providers,
i. Necessity to review laws by considering electronic environments,

Although so far insignificant developments have been achieved in universalizing legal infrastructure of electronic management operations among countries in areas such as digital signature, reliable third party, information management and safety, information crimes and coordination of electronic commerce, still some critical legal expansions have been achieved.

Safety Problems

Just as in traditional commerce, the basic condition in electronic commerce is the users' trust to the system. In a commercial procedure necessitating any contract or electronic communication even just for information transfer, the users (individuals or companies) on rightful grounds do not want third parties accessing to their private personal / corporate information, namely commercial, financial. Besides in communication that is open to third parties aside from privacy of personal data, integrity of transferred information (or in other words receiving the knowledge as it is originally) and confirmation of the identities of parties should also be guaranteed. The condition, which is being discussed in terms of technique and basic human rights, is to utilize which technique, administrative and legal tools to guarantee desired levels of privacy, information integrity and identity confirmation. Unless they are provided in sufficient levels, global development of electronic commerce will be affected significantly (Sadowski, 2002, p. 81).

Safety problems SMEs can face in commercial activities during electronic commerce operations can be expressed as indicated below (Palvia and Palvia, 1999):

- Access to web sources, which have no access authority,
- Damaging information and web resources,
- Changing, mixing or making additions to information,
- Transferring information to unauthorized personnel,
- Stealing information and web sources,
- Denying purchased services, transmitted or received information,
- Claiming to have received or transferred information, not received or transferred at all (Kraemer and Carayon, 2007).

According to the estimations in U.S.A., the value of the data stolen in one year is above 10 billion US dollars. As stated in a research conducted in 1996 on 1320 firms; 78% of participants declared to have lost money due to safety break, 63% asserted to have faced loss due to viruses, and 20 users stated to have lost at least 1 million US dollars (Singh and Frolick, 2000, p. 58).

GENERAL REVIEW

Developments in electronic commerce provide brand new advantages in terms of SMEs information technologies usage and access to global markets. However, SMEs have many problems including lack of technological infrastructure and locality, language, infrastructure, environment, legal, safety as categorized under two groups namely technical and cultural. Except U.S.A. and Singapore, which are developed countries regarding information technologies and electronic commerce, SMEs stick to the "wait and see" policy in many other countries. Governments and certain international organizations concerned with this issue have been working on comprehensive projects on a global scale to enable active participation of SMEs in electronic commerce. Furthermore, the fact that SMEs free themselves from traditional commerce practices and adopt new methods thoroughly seems to be closely related to the drive in market conditions and transformation in current business culture.

Prospective contributions that will emerge with electronic commerce implementations in SMEs are presented below (Burgess, 2002, p. 79; Kotler, 2000, p. 519; Mehrtens et al., 2001, p. 169):

Improved customer base: Enterprises may implement their electronic commerce activities without any regional boundaries, time or country limits. Hence, they may obtain important advantages in global activity by carrying their operations across the borders of region and country.

Time saving in delivery of product and services: Industrial market movement of goods and delivery time may cause great commercial problems. Since almost any enterprises avoids keeping stocks and thus order only when necessary, delivery time gains more attention. Web-based orders, compared to traditional orders, are provided and processed more quickly.

Increased sales: An increase trend in the sales of enterprises is observed at the end of electronic commerce process. Increased sales incomes are even more important for small enterprises. Online sales to customers, order chances and online check of the status of orders would add to customer satisfaction and sales.

Deactivation of mediators: The spread of Internet based electronic commerce has deactivated the mediators operating from producer to customer in the supply chain. Hence, producers offer cheaper, quicker goods and services to customers. Continuous and more appropriate information flow is attained.

Increased customer satisfaction: One of the most important outcomes of electronic commerce is increased customer satisfaction and service level. Because of electronic commerce, customers receive products and services on time; acquire online information, are connected directly to a customer based communication system. The needs of customers are determined by customers themselves and thus increase customer satisfaction.

Improved efficiency and reduced costs: Decreased use of paper and manual operations, automation of electronic commerce, news, business and operation processes play vital roles in reducing operation costs of enterprises.

Increased competition: Because of Internet, all enterprises regardless of their size, acquire equal conditions while accessing their customers. By electronic commerce, SMEs will be able to compete against large-scale enterprises with their recognized trademarks, purchase power, and mature structure (Poon and Swatman, 2000, p. 247).

Decrease in Order Processes and Bureaucracy: It is inevitable that once orders are transferred to the Internet, the size of personnel will decrease as compared to the traditional method of receiving and registering orders. In the same way, due to electronic works in place of paper work, enterprises will focus on stocks and inventory and search new ways to develop more creative cooperation with their suppliers. In this way, simplification occurs in routine orders processes and repeated works are automated. Thus, unnecessary applications are eliminated.

Trained customers: Electronic commerce will enhance cognitive literacy of customers and thus they become intellectually more capable. In order to make use of electronic commerce, customers are expected to possess Internet knowledge and computer skills.

Trained employees: Electronic commerce has positive effects on knowledge accumulation of employees as well. To ensure the success of electronic commerce, continuous training programs should be implemented and employees should adapt to the organizational transformation introduced by electronic commerce.

Basic economic effect of electronic commerce is that it creates an economic activity area where handicaps are less in number. This particular effect is basically an outcome generated by rapidly developing information technologies. Since electronic commerce uses this rapidly developing infrastructure, it will have such a great effect on economic life as well. Electronic commerce integrates potentially all the producers, suppliers, users and customers. Hence, it may be acknowledged that it is endowed with capabilities providing many forms of satisfaction that has been dreamed ever since the beginning of industrial revolution.

A STUDY OF THE TURKISH AUTOMOTIVE SUPPLIER INDUSTRY

A. Scope of the Research

The purpose of this research is to study the influencing factors, obstacles, and reasons for initiating electronic commerce in SMEs that are active in 2008 as suppliers of the Automotive Industry in Turkey. Population being too large in size, the sample of the research is arbitrarily chosen from the data base of TAYSAD, which is the Association of Automotive Suppliers in Turkey. The reasons of referring to the TAYSAD data base are as follows:

a. All organizations active in the industry are legally required to become a member of the Association,
b. its data base is frequently updated, and
c. information about the member profiles is easily accessed.

Examination of the TAYSAD data base has revealed that 268 organizations are currently registered. The suppliers not fitting the criteria or scale, or currently inactive have been eliminated and thus only 192 organizations are included in the research.

TAYSAD established in 1978 and a member of CLEPA - the European Association of Automotive Suppliers (www.clepa.be) - is the only authorized association representing the suppliers in the Turkish Automotive Industry. The Association is creditable in all automotive part and component transactions by the foreign and domestic organizations.

The product range of the TAYSAD members is sufficient to create 85-90 percent of the Turkish Automotive Industry production locally. The 268 registered members of the Association provide parts and components for the Turkish Automotive Industry and create 65% of the production and 70% of the exports. Eighty-five percent of the members are active in the Marmara region, 10% in the Aegean, and 5% in the others. The registered 268 companies of TAYSAD employ 72 000 workers and provide employment for 127 000 people including its suppliers. Fifty-eight registered companies have foreign partners with varying degrees of capital share.

The questionnaires were distributed to 268 companies as e-mail attachments, surface mail, face-to-face interviews, or by invitation to visit the website www.selcuk.edu.tr/zerenler/anket.01.html in the months of May and June 2009. As 31st of July 2009, 192 responses have been received(a response rate of 71.6); but twenty-four of the organizations registered in the data bank of TAYSAD could never be reached. Eighty-five responses were received as e-mail attachments, 42 by surface mail, 36 face-to-face interviews, and 29 by website visits.

B. Findings of the Research

As it is seen in Table 2, 33.6% of the organizations involved in the study have been active in the last 10 years. The companies with employment 200 and above are not included in the research. Hence, the study encompasses only small and medium size enterprises. The results illustrate that most of the respondents in the survey are top level professionals.

Table 2. Characteristics of the companies

Operation period	Frequency	Percentile
Between 6-10 years	79	41.2
Between 11-25 years	73	38.0
More than 26 years	25	13.0
Between 1-5 years	15	7.8
Total	**192**	**100.0**
Status of the respondent	**Frequency**	**Percentile**
General manager	51	26.6
Information center manager	47	24.5
Marketing manager	32	16.7
Public relations manager	22	11.5
Owner	17	8.9
Information expert	14	7.3
Board member	9	4.5
Total	**192**	**100.0**

Table 3. Implementation level of electronic commerce instruments

Electronic commerce instruments	Three years ago		*Current*		Change	Wilcoxon Test	
	Average	Std. Dev.	Average	Std. Dev.		Z	P
Internet	4.36	0.68	4.83	0.84	0.47	-2.172	<.001
Telephone (deck)	3.92	0.72	4.02	0.90	0.1	-3.264	<.001
Electronic mail	3.87	0.88	4.76	0.72	0.89	-4.634	<.001
Fax	3.76	0.64	3.28	0.94	-0.48	-3.268	<.001
Electronic data interchange	3.41	0.82	3.56	0.88	0.15	-4.264	<.001
Electronic payment and money transfer systems	3.29	0.90	3.85	0.73	0.56	-3.825	<.001
Television	1.63	0.74	1.72	0.96	0.09	-4.106	<.001
Telephone (mobile)	1.18	0.62	2.23	0.58	1.05	-3.634	<.001

The implementation level of the electronic commerce instruments in the companies involved in the study is illustrated in Table 3. Comparing the current level to the level three years ago indicates an increase in the implementation of electronic commerce instruments. As is it discussed in the previous sections, significant increases of implementation are expected in the near future as the SMEs gain more awareness. SMEs may gain competitive advantage against large scale enterprises and access to markets at low cost performance through increasing their electronic commerce abilities. As it is known, one of the major obstacles constraining electronic commerce activities of SMEs is distribution systems. However, it is possible to overcome this obstacle through utilizing distribution chains of large scale companies or outsourcing from the service suppliers in this field.

The results in Table 4 indicate that the companies aim to utilize time advantage of electronic commerce for accessing new markets. In general, SMEs face problems in accessing new markets because of reasons such as limited financial resources, insufficiency of qualified labor, and locality of marketing and distribution systems. Electronic commerce seems to provide advantages to overcome these problems. If compared to traditional commerce, SMEs obtain significant benefits of electronic commerce implementation against large scale companies as they move from local markets to global competition. Indeed, SMEs have acquired important advantages against large

Table 4. Importance level of electronic commerce implementation

Opinion	Arithmetic average	Standard deviation
Accessing new markets	4.68	0.90
Achieving competitive advantage	4.43	1.04
Gaining extra revenues	4.19	0.78
Cost reduction	3.95	0.92
Impact of rivals	3.76	1.07

Note: (i) n=143; (ii) In the scale, 1 indicates no impact, 5 definite impact; (iii) Friedman two way ANOVA test (χ^2=482.256 and $p<.001$), the results are statistically significant.

Table 5. Impact of electronic commerce

Impact	Arithmetic average	Standard deviation
Enhancement of business activities	4.17	0.92
Better access to global markets	4.02	0.90
Improvement of customer services	3.86	1.02
Increase of competitiveness	3.77	0.84
Increases in future revenues through creating new products and services	3.55	1.06
More options to provided customers at cheaper prices	3.19	1.10
Increase of delivery speed	3.12	0.76
Better inventory performance	3.04	0.88
Better understanding of customer demands and expectations	2.93	1.02
Better distribution performance	2.85	0.94
Achievement of more effective knowledge management	2.72	0.98

Note: (i) n=173; (ii) In the scale, 1 indicates no impact, 5 definite impact; (iii) Friedman two way ANOVA test (χ^2=386.721 and $p<.001$), the results are statistically significant.

scale companies through electronic commerce despite the differences among industrial sectors.

The results in Table 5 reveal that the most important impact of electronic commerce is enhancement of business activities. In addition, issues such as better access to global markets, improvement of customer services, increase of competitiveness, increases in future revenues through creating new products and services, increases in future revenues through creating new products and service, more options provided to customers at cheaper prices, increase of delivery speed, and better inventory performance have provided benefits to companies in their electronic commerce activities. On the other hand, better understanding of customer demands and expectations, better distribution performance, and achievement of more effective knowledge management seem to influence less than the other factors. However, overall all factors being above average indicates that electronic commerce generate some significant effects on SMEs. In fact, electronic commerce implementation has created some positive major impact on areas, which face many problems and limitations. The automotive suppliers industry provides parts to the major industry. Hence, it has a significant value because of its volume of transactions, but limited in terms of its customers. The automotive suppliers industry utilizes the benefits of electronic commerce implementation in order to enhance business, to facilitate business processes, and access to customers.

In Table 6, the importance level of obstacles constraining electronic commerce activities is shown. The companies point out that lack of three dimensional visual, touch effects, and test drives for automobiles and parts is the major obstacle constraining electronic commerce activities. As stated in the previous sections of the study, commodities such as automobile and real estate are not the goods that can be easily purchased because of their value and consumption. Hence, their purchasing process is more complicated and requires longer time as compared to non-durable goods purchased and consumed more frequently. In the light of these circumstances, the situation is quite the same for the products of automotive supplier industry. Even though the model, type, price, and other characteristics of the demanded products are well known by customers and providers, the lack of three dimensional visual, touch

Table 6. Importance level of obstacles constraining electronic commerce activities

Obstacle	Arithmetic average	Standard deviation
Lack of three dimensional visual, touch effects, and test drives for automobiles and parts	4.43	1.88
Lack of customization for automobile parts	4.29	0.94
Internet not being reliable	3.86	0.86
Requirement of Internet address for the companies	3.71	1.04
Lack of technological infrastructure of the major industry	3.58	0.90
Major industry preferring traditional commerce	3.36	1.12
Lack of face-to-face communication with sales people	3.09	0.76
Insufficiency of Internet payment methods	2.91	0.81
Small number of product varieties	2.85	1.02
Poor designed websites	2.62	1.13
Insufficiency of websites	2.57	1.06

Note: (i) n=192; (ii) In the scale, 1 indicates no impact, 5 definite impact; (iii) Friedman two way ANOVA test (χ^2=724.363 and $p<.001$), the results are statistically significant.

effects, and test drives significantly influence electronic commerce just like in traditional commerce activities. However, companies nowadays can easily monitor the products they want to purchase in the Internet and place their orders.

Lack of customization for automobile parts is another major obstacle to foster electronic commerce. However, as mentioned in the previous sections, mass customization practices are increasingly employed in many industrial sectors, including the automotive industry. In the automotive industry, it is extremely important to meet and even exceed customer expectations and needs. Lack of customization for automobile parts as pointed out by the companies may be attributed to an important limitation of technological capability. Hence, the Industry is required to develop its technological infrastructure, qualified manpower, and sophisticated information systems.

Table 7 exhibits the opinions of the companies about the future of electronic commerce. The companies have pointed out that organizations will become more dependent on electronic commerce in the future. In addition, it is generally agreed that electronic commerce will increasingly provide strategic competitive advantage. SMEs generally consent that electronic commerce will impact organizational structure of the companies

Table 7. Opinions about the future of electronic commerce

Opinion	Arithmetic average	Standard deviation
Organizations will become more dependent on electronic commerce.	4.62	1.06
Electronic commerce will provide strategic competitive advantage.	4.31	1.02
Electronic commerce will impact organizational structure of the companies radically.	4.17	1.08
Electronic commerce will be a part of conversion for our business.	3.79	0.92
Currently, electronic commerce is part of our business.	3.38	0.90

Note: (i) n=192; (ii) In the scale, 1 indicates not accept, 5 definitely accept; (iii) Friedman two way ANOVA test (χ^2=682.136 and $p<.001$), the results are statistically significant.

radically, be a part of conversion for our business, and already plays a significant role in today's business.

CONCLUSION

Globalization and intensive influence of information technologies renders it indispensable to carry out commercial activities in electronic ways. Small and medium enterprises (SMEs) are increasingly utilizing the electronic commerce for their commercial activities. Hence, electronic commerce is developed almost in every industrial sector as witnessed by the increasing number of examples. It provides too many advantages and benefits to companies and other organizations.

Electronic commerce has significantly transformed the way in which firms conduct business, allowing them to gain more business opportunities and competitive advantage. However, the results from the study have revealed a lack of or slow uptake of electronic commerce technologies among the local SMEs. The objectives of this study were to understand and determine the importance of internal and external barriers; and thus provide support to overcome their problems. Among the different variables studied, technical, financial and social/ cultural barriers have been reported to create significant influence in the context of electronic commerce development in the SMEs.

The study conducted in the Turkish Automotive Supplier Industry has revealed that electronic commerce has been adopted and its benefits are accepted by the companies. However, the industry has to overcome some of the difficulties to implement it more efficiently and effectively.

REFERENCES

Bayles, D. (2001). *E-Commerce Logistics and Fulfillment: Delivering the Goods*. Upper Saddle River, NJ, U.S.A.: Prentice Hall PTR.

Burgess, S. (2002). Information Technology in Small Business: Issues and Solutions. In Burgess, S. (Ed.), *Managing Information Technology in Small Business: Challenges and Solutions*, 1-17. Hershey, PA: Idea Group Publishing.

Calin G. Ranchhod, A. & Hackney, R. (2001). Internet Transactions and Physical Logistics: Conflict or Complementary. *Internet Research: Electronic Networking Applications and Policy*, 14 (½, s. 36).

Chaffey, D. (2007). *E-business and E-commerce Management–Strategy, Implementation and Practice* (3rd ed.). Harlow: Pearson Education.

Chaston, I. (2001). The Internet and E-Commerce: An Opportunity to Examine Organisational Learning in Progress in Small Manufacturing Firms? *International Small Business Journal*, *19*(2), 13–30. doi:10.1177/0266242601192001

Chen, A. H., & Siems, T. (2001). *B2B eMarketplace Announcements and Shareholder Wealth. Economic and Financial Review*. First Quarter.

Chen, S. (2004). *Strategic Management Of E-business*. New York: John Wiley.

Colombo, M. G. (2001). Technology-Based Entrepreneurs: Does Internet Make a Difference? *Small Business Economics*, *16*(3), 177–190. doi:10.1023/A:1011127205758

Combe, C. (2006). *Introduction To E-business: Management And Strategy*. New York: Butterworth-Heinemann Inc.

Coppel, J. (2000). E-commerce: Impacts and Policy Challenges. *OECD Economics Department Working Papers*, no.252

Dandridge, T. (2000). High-Tech Potential? An Exploratory Study Of Very Small Firms' Usage of the Internet. *International Small Business Journal*, *18*(2), 81–91. doi:10.1177/0266242600182004

Daniel, E., Wilson, H., & Myers, A. (2002). Adoption of Ecommerce by SMEs In The UK: Towards a Stage Model. *International Small Business Journal*, *20*(3), 253–270. doi:10.1177/0266242602203002

Dans, E. (2001). IT Investment in Small and Medium Enterprises:Paradoxically Productive? *The Electronic Journal of Information Systems Evaluation*, 4 (1).

Davis, P. S. (2000). Internationalization and Organizational Growth: The Impact of Internet Usage and Technology Involvement Among Entrepreneur-Led Family Businesses. *Family Business Review*, *13*(2), 107–120. doi:10.1111/j.1741-6248.2000.00107.x

De Bono, E. (1994). *Sur/petition*. New York: HarperCollins Publishers Ltd.

Delone, W. H. (1988). Determinants of Success for Computer Usage in Small Business. ***MIS Quarterly***, 12(1) 1988, 51-61.

Digital Marketing Compass. (n.d.). Retrieved from http://www.ogilvy.com.tr/digitalmarketing-compass/ Access date: 07.08.2009.

Dornan, A. (2001). *The Essential Guide to Wireless Communications Applications*. Upper Saddle, New Jersey: Prentice Hall.

Eikebrokk, T. R., & Olsen, D. H. (2007). An Empirical Investigation of Competency Factors Affecting e-business Success in European SMEs. *Information & Management*, *44*, 364–383. doi:10.1016/j.im.2007.02.004

Evans, P. B., & Wurster, B. S. (1997). Strategy and the new Economics of Information. *Harvard Business Review*, *75*(5), 70–83.

Farhoomand, A., & Lovelock, P. (2001). *Global E-commerce: Text and Cases*. New York: Prentice Hall.

Fischer, M. (2000). Using E-commerce to Deliver High Productivity. *Work Study*, *49*(2), 59–62. doi:10.1108/00438020010311188

Gottschalk, P. (2005). *E-Business Strategy, Sourcing and Governance*. Hershey, PA: Idea Group Publishing.

Hawkins, R., & Prencipe, A. (2000). *Business-to-Business E-Commerce in the UK: A Synthesis of Sector Report*. London: Department for Trade and Industry.

Heijden, H. d. (2000). The Inclusion of E-commerce Metrics in Strategic Planning: Results from an Exploratory Empirical Study. *Proceedings of the Americas Conference on Information Systems*, Long Beach, CA.

Heinen, J. (1996). Internet Marketing Practices. *Information Management & Computer Security*, *4*(5), 7–14. doi:10.1108/09685229610153120

Janenko, P. M. (2003). E-business: The Illusion of Automated Success. *The TQM Magazine*, *15*(3). doi:10.1108/09544780310469307

Jelassi, T., & Enders, A. (2008). *Strategies for e-business:Creating Value through Electronic and Mobile Commerce: Concepts and Cases*. Harlow: FT Prentice Hall.

Kalakota, K., & Whinston, A. (1997). *Electronic Commerce*. New York: Addison Wesley Longman, Inc.

Kapurubandara, M., & Lawson, R. (2006). *Barriers to Adopting ICT and e-commerce with SMEs in Developing Countries: an Exploratory Study in Sri Lanka. Collecter, (Collaborative Electronic Commerce Technology and Research), December 2006*. Adelaide: UniSA.

Kleindl, B. (2000). Competitive Dynamics and New Business Models For SMEs in the Virtual Marketplace. *Journal of Developmental Entrepreneurship*, *5*(1), 73–85.

Kotler, P. (2000). *Marketing Management, The Millenium Edition*. Upper Saddle River, NJ: Prentice Hall.

Kraemer, S., & Carayon, P. (2007). Human errors and violations in computer and information security: The viewpoint of network administrators and security specialists. *Applied Ergonomics, 38*(2), 143–154. doi:10.1016/j.apergo.2006.03.010

Kshetri, N. (2007). Barriers to e-commerce and competitive business models in developing countries: A case study. *Electronic Commerce Research and Applications, 6*, 446. doi:10.1016/j.elerap.2007.02.004

Kurnia, S., & Johnston, R. B. (2000). The Need for a Processual view of Inter-Organizational Systems Adoption. *The Journal of Strategic Information Systems, 9*(4), 295–319. doi:10.1016/S0963-8687(00)00050-0

Lai, J., & Chen, W. (2009). Measuring E-business Dependability: The Employee Perspective. *Journal of Systems and Software, 82*(6), 1046–1055. doi:10.1016/j.jss.2009.02.029

Levy, M., Powell, P., & Galliers, R. (1999). Assessing Information Systems Strategy Development Frameworks in SMEs. *Information & Management, 36*(5), 247–261. doi:10.1016/S0378-7206(99)00020-8

Levy, M., Powell, P., & Yetton, P. (2001). SMEs:Aligning is and the Strategic Context. *Journal of Information Technology, 16*, 133–144. doi:10.1080/02683960110063672

Li, J. (2006). Chinese Entrepreneurship and Small Business Development: An Overview and Research Agenda. *Journal of Small Business and Enterprise Development, 13*(2). doi:10.1108/14626000610665953

Liew, V. (2009). *E-Commerce Usage by the SMEs in Northern Malaysia: Analysis of the State of E-Commerce Adoption by the SMEs in Northern Malaysia and Factors that Might Hinder its Adoption: An Empirical Study*. VDM Verlag.

MacGregor, R. C. (2004). The Role of Strategic Alliances in The Ongoing Use of Electronic Commerce Technology in Regional Small Business. *Journal of Electronic Commerce in Organizations, 2*(1), 1–14.

MacGregor, R. C. (2008). *The Adoption of E-commerce in SMEs: The Role of Strategic Alliances*. VDM Verlag.

MacGregor, R. C., & Vrazalic, L. (2005). *A Basic Model of Electronic Commerce Adoption Barriers. School Of Economics and Information Systems* (pp. 515–529). Australia: University of Wollongong.

Mehrtens, J., Cragg, P. B., & Mills, A. M. (2001). A model of Internet Adoption by SMEs. *Information & Management, 39*(3), 165–176. doi:10.1016/S0378-7206(01)00086-6

Nusair, K., & Hua, N. (2009). Comparative Assessment of Structural Equation Modeling and Multiple Regression Research Methodologies: E-commerce Context. *Tourism Management, xxx*, 1–11.

Online Marketing Blog. (n.d.). Retrieved from http://www.theblognote.com/zapposcom-ornek-bir-e-ticaret-basari-hikayesi.html Access date: 10.06.2009.

Oyelaran-Oyeyinka, B., & Kaushalesh, L. K. (2004). *Internet Diffusion in sub-Saharan Africa: a cross-country Analysis*. Telecommunications Policy.

Palvia, P. C., & Palvia, S. C. (1999). An examination of the IT Satisfaction of Small-Business Users. *Information & Management, 35*, 127–137. doi:10.1016/S0378-7206(98)00086-X

Peterson, R. A., Balasubramanian, S., & Bronnenberg, B. J. (1997). Exploring the Implications of the Internet for Consumer Marketing. *Journal of Academy of Marketing Science,* 25(4. Poon, S. & Swatman, P. (2000). Internet-based Small Business Communication: seven Australian cases. *Electronic Markets*, *7*(2), 241–259.

Porter, M. (2001). Strategy and the Internet. *Harvard Business Review*, (March): 63–78.

Quayle, M. (2002). E-Commerce: the challenge for UK SMEs in the twenty-first century. *International Journal of Operations & Production Management*, *22*(10), 1148–1161. doi:10.1108/01443570210446351

Reynolds, J., & Mofazali, R. (2000). *The Complete E-commerce Book: Design, Build and Maintain a Successful Web-based Business.* New York: McGraw-Hill Inc.,US.

Rowley, J. (2002). *E-business: Principles and Practice*. New York: Palgrave.

Sadowski, B. M. (2002). Strategic Use of the Internet by Small and Medium-Sized Companies: an Exploratory Study. *Information Economics and Policy*, *14*(1), 75–93. doi:10.1016/S0167-6245(01)00054-3

Singh, C., & Frolick, M. N. (2000). Ibuttons: Building the Infrastucture for more Secure E-commerce. *Information Systems Security*, Winter, 8 (4), ss. 56-59.

Singh, M., & Waddell, D. (2006). *E-business Innovation and Change Management*. Hershey, PA: Idea Group Publishing.

Soliman, F., & Youssef, M. A. (2003). Internet-Based E-Commerce and Its Impact On Manufacturing and Business Operations. *Industrial Management & Data Systems*, *103*(8), 546–552. doi:10.1108/02635570310497594

Stansfield, M., & Grant, K. (2003). An Investigation Into Issues Influencing the use of the Internet and Electronic Commerce among Small–Medium Sized Enterprises. *Journal of Electronic Commerce Res*, *4*(1), 15–28.

Stockdale, R. & Standing, C. (2004). Benefits and barriers of electronic marketplace participation: an SME perspective.*Journal of Enterprise Information Management, 17*(4), pp, 301-311.

Strader, T. J. & Ramaswami, S. N. (2002).The Value of Seller Trustworthiness in C2C Online Markets.*Communications of the ACM*, 45:12(December), 45-49.

Van Beveren, J. (2002). The Use of Electronic Commerce by SMEs in Victoria, Australia. *Journal of Small Business Management*, *40*(3), 250–253. doi:10.1111/1540-627X.00054

Varianini, V., & Vaturi, D. (2000). Marketing Lessons from e-failures. *The McKinsey Quarterly*, 4.

Vinberg, S., Gelin, G., & Sandberg, K. (2000). Information Technology Levels, Competence Development and Performance in Swedish Small Business Enterprises. *Behaviour and Information Technology*, C:19, S:3.

Walczuch, R., Van Braven, G., & Lundgren, H. (2000). Internet Adoption Barriers for Small Firms in the Netherlands. *European Management Journal*, *18*(5), 561–572. doi:10.1016/S0263-2373(00)00045-1

Warren, M., & Hutchinson, W. (2005). A Systems Approach to Security. In Kurt a Richardon, Wendy J Gregory & Gerald Midgley (eds). *Systems Thinking and Complexity Science: Insights for Action Proceedings of the 11th Annual ANZSYS / Managing the Complex V conference,* New Zealand: ISCE Publishing.

Webb, B., & Sayer, R. (1998). Benchmarking Small Companies on the Internet. *Long Range Planning*, *31*(6), 815–827. doi:10.1016/S0024-6301(98)80018-6

Williamson, I. O., Lepak, D. P., & King, J. (2003). The effect of company recruitment web site orientation on individuals' perceptions of organizational attractiveness. *Journal of Vocational Behavior*, *63*(2), 242–263. doi:10.1016/S0001-8791(03)00043-5

Zerenler, M. (2007). *Dijital İş Yaşamı: Tüm Boyutlarıyla Elektronik Ticaret* (Digital BusinessLife: Electronic Commerce with all its Dimensions), (in Turkish), Ankara, Gazi Kitabevi (Gazi Bookstore).

Zhao, F. (2006). *Entrepreneurship and Innovations in E-business: An Integrative Perspective*. Hershey, PA: Idea Group Publishing.

Chapter 19
Constrains Associated to E-Business Evolution

Elisabete Paulo Morais
Instituto Politécnico do Bragança, Portugal

José Adriano Pires
Instituto Politécnico do Bragança, Portugal

Ramiro Gonçalves
Universidade de Trás-os-Montes e Alto Douro, Portugal

ABSTRACT

Technological advance of the last decades created an atmosphere in which the organizations are forced to look actively for new options for the cost reduction, in addition to, simultaneously, seeking to compete more effectively in their markets. This context requires focused, swift, more flexible and more competitive organizations which are forced, many times, to implement radical changes in the way they conduct business, employ people and use technology. Despite the recognition and the attention given to electronic business (or e-business) over the last years, this type of business hasn't yet achieved a desirable maturity stage. This problem, current and stated over the last years, demands research efforts so that a solution can be found to solve it. In this chapter, the authors explore a range of constraints which are suggested by the literature to influence e-business evolution, so that organizations could be better equipped in anticipating any difficulties while in progress through their e-business initiatives.

INTRODUCTION

New economy, new tools, new rules. Few concepts have revolutionized business more profoundly than e-business. To compete effectively in the e-business world, a company must structurally transform its internal foundation. This structural change requires a company to develop an innovative e-business strategy, focusing on speed to market and breakthrough execution (Kalakota and Robinson, 2001).

Since the introduction of computer technology into organizations in the 1960s, there have been numerous attempts to develop models of Information Systems/Information Technology (IS/IT) maturity (Nolan, 1973; Gibson and Nolan, 1974; Nolan, 1979; McFarlan et al., 1983; Earl, 1989; Hirschheim, 1996; Galliers and Sutherland, 1991;

DOI: 10.4018/978-1-61692-880-3.ch019

Auer, 1995; Zachman et al., 1997; Khandelwal and Ferguson, 1999). All of these models are premised on the idea that organizations pass through stages of maturity with respect to the way they use and manage IS/IT to support and facilitate business activities, processes and operations.

New maturity models, better adapted to the realities of e-business, have been developed by other researchers and practitioners. Recent research on growth stages and e-business has shown the usefulness of these models in describing the company position in terms of e-business development and of its possible development in the future (McKay et al. 2000; Earl 2000; Prananto et al. 2001; Rayport and Jaworsky 2002; Rao et al. 2003).

Achieving a high level of maturity of e-business is desirable, meaning that the e-business would be deeply embedded in all aspects of the organization, as with all business partners. Therefore, it is crucial for an organization to identify potential constraints to e-business in order to minimize the risk derived from its e-business initiative. The objective of this chapter is to explore the constraints that could act as a barrier to the development of e-business. Environmental, organizational and technological constraints were identified.

E-BUSINESS AND MATURITY MODELS

The terminology involved within the field of Information Communication Technology (ICT) usage on the Internet is vast and contradictory. Two frequently used terms are e-commerce and e-business.

Kalakota and Whinston (1996) define electronic commerce as the "… buying and selling of information, products and services via computer networks". Laudon and Travel (2006) define electronic commerce as the "use of the Internet and the Web to transact business". Sewell and McCarthey (2001) identify e-business as business facilitated by ICT. Others argue that e-business encompasses the entire world of internal and external electronically based activities, including electronic commerce (Kalakota and Robinson, 2003). In the scope of this chapter, electronic commerce will be regarded as a subset of e-business.

Based on various types of trading partners, there are many categories of e-business, for example: Business to Business (B2B), Business to Consumer (B2C), Consumer to Business (C2B), Business to Government (B2G), Consumer to Consumer (C2C), Pear to Pear (P2P), Government to Citizen (G2C), Citizen to Government (C2G) and Business to Employee (B2E). Without the use of face to face operations, all e-business transactions are performed electronically by using computer and communication networks.

The rules of business game are being rewritten to become the rules of e-business, as listed in Table 1.

In (Morais et al., 2007) was used a comparative framework to evaluate e-business stages of growth models. This comparative framework contained the following eight elements (Jones et al., 2006): perspective, development, emphasis, verification, barriers, focus, source and stages. Eight maturity models (KPMG, Grant's Model, McKay's Model, Earl's Model, SOG-e, Rayport and Jaworski's Model, Rao's Model and Chan and Swatman's Model) were compared.

After comparing the models, the authors concluded that none of the models considers constraints on development and strategic development within the framework, but it is obvious that enterprise growth is inhibited by barriers to development such as limited skills and finance.

CONSTRAINTS TO E-BUSINESS EVOLUTION

After conducting an exploratory study, we identified a set of constraints, which were then grouped into organizational, technological and environment constraints.

Table 1. Ten rules of e-business (adapted by (Kalakota and Robinson, 2001))

Rule 1	Technology is no longer an afterthought in forming business strategy but rather the cause and driver.
Rule 2	The ability to streamline the structure of information and to influence and control its flow is a dramatically more powerful and cost effective service than is that of moving and manufacturing physical products.
Rule 3	Inability to overthrow the dominant, outdated business design often leads to business failure.
Rule 4	Using e-commerce, companies can listen to their customers and became "the cheapest", "the most familiar", or "the best".
Rule 5	Do not use technology just to create the product. Use technology to innovate, entertain, and enhance the entire experience surrounding the product: from selecting and ordering to receiving and service.
Rule 6	The business design of the future increasingly uses reconfigurable e-business models to best meet customers' needs.
Rule 7	The goal of new business designs is for companies to create flexible outsourcing alliances that not only off-load costs but also make costumers ecstatic.
Rule 8	For urgent e-business projects, it is easy to minimize application infrastructure needs and to focus on the glitzy front-end applications. The oversight can be costly in move ways than one.
Rule 9	The ability to plan an e-business infrastructure course swiftly and to implement it ruthlessly are key to success. Ruthless execution is the norm.
Rule 10	The tough task management is to align business strategies, processes, and applications quickly, correctly, and all at once. Strong leadership is imperative.

Thus, from the analysis of literature, we set up the following conceptual model which graphically emphasizes the relations between their variables (dimensions) presented in Figure 1.

Various factors that inhibit the e-business development were identified, and were consequently grouped in technological, organizational and environmental constraints. In the next sections, these factors will be described in detail.

Technological Constraints

The following technological constraints were identified.

Inadequate Technology

There are several constraints that affect the e-business maturity of an organization, one being the existing technology (or nonexistent) in the organization. One can explain this type of constraint based on the evidence that there is in fact some inadequate technology, that is, the technology that does not back up the necessary tools for e-business.

According to Gouveia and Gaio (2004) one of the characteristics of the information society is the intensive use of ICT which assumes a mediating role.

The e-business fulfils its potential when the IT transforms processes, products and business methods.

IT companies are the generators of the e-business technology which enables e-business activities to take place. Therefore the success of these activities would depend on the success of the e-business technology products and services provided by the IT companies.

Obviously, without the technology and the technical talent, no company is going to get its e-business plan off the ground. And in this regard, companies often face considerable challenges.

Lientz and Rea (2001) presented nine principles for the implementation of an e-business, which condense the original position that an organization must have to start its own business electronically. In these principles, they mention that the balance of the infrastructure to support e-business is crucial. Many technologies, even if relevant, do not reach their potential automatically. A new technology

Figure 1. The conceptual model

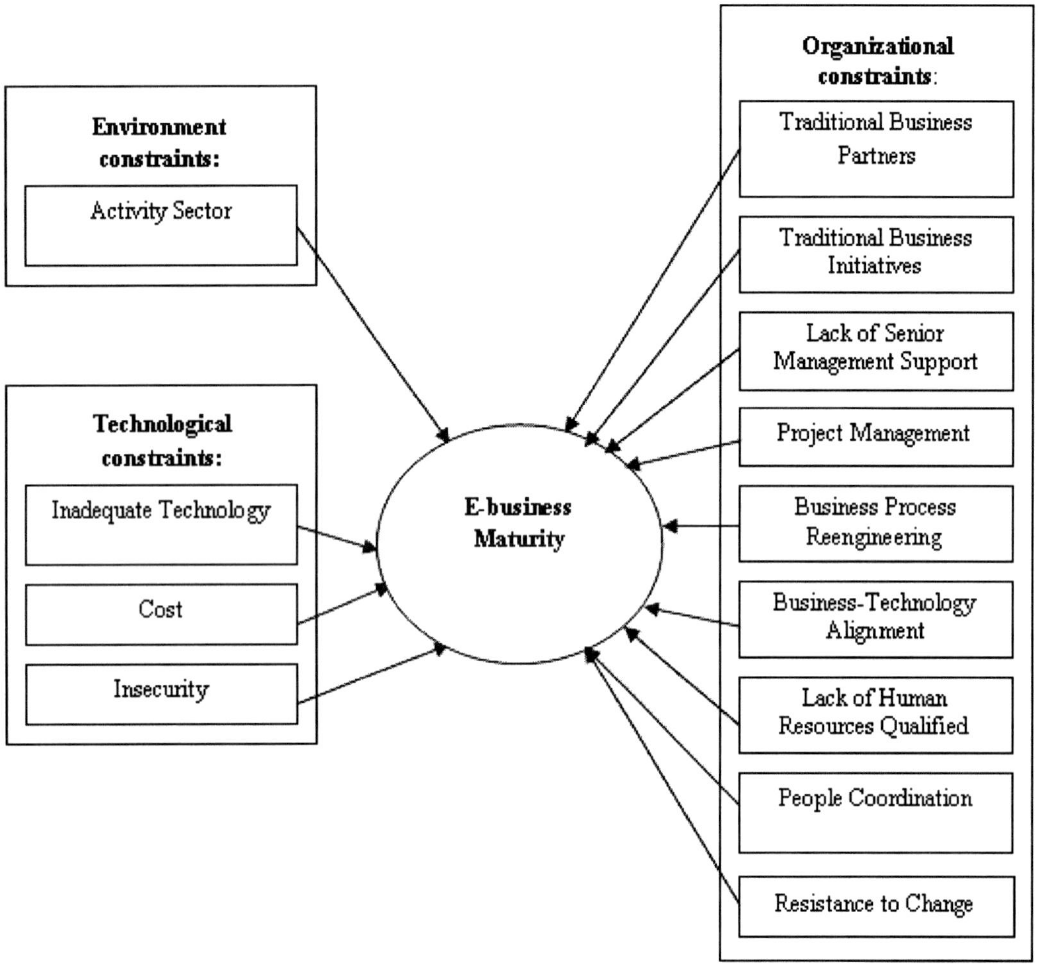

can create imbalance in the organization by not integrating easily.

The technology is, of course, the enabler of e-business (Bakry and Bakry, 2001), as such, the inadequate technology can be a constraint to the development of e-business.

Cost of E-Business Solutions

The contemporary history is permanently marked by technological advances. The development of information technologies, including Internet and everything that relates to hardware and software, has changed the model that was designed in the past for different economic activities.

Investments in IT / IS involve considerable intangible costs difficult to identify. The problem becomes even more complex when we try to evaluate, in a financial perspective, all the benefits of investments in IT / IS (Serrano and Caldeira, 2001).

O'Brien (2003) lists five levels that describe how companies can design and use IT:

- **Strategy:** The IT / IS are seen as differentiated, supporting the processing of transactions, decision making and collaboration;

- **Offensive:** The IT / IS are seen more as a point of influence than differential;
- **Defence:** growth of the IT / SI is controlled at a rate lower than the growth of business and investment in technology keeping up with the general behaviour of the sector.
- **Justified by the cost:** it maintains a strict control on IT / IS, there is no general plan of the spread of technology. Applications and platforms are ageing.
- **Held:** IT / IS are seen as an expense and administration is not prepared to invest in IT / IS.

The cost of technology is enormous (Grover et al., 1998, Legris et al., 2003), so this could be one of the constraints of the e-business and it is expected that the maturity will be adversely affected by the cost of solutions for e-business.

Insecurity

There are six key dimensions to e-business security: integrity, non-repudiation, authenticity; confidentiality; privacy and availability (Laudon and Traver, 2006).

Integrity refers to the ability to ensure that information displayed on a web site, or transmitted or received over the Internet, has not been altered in any way by any unauthorized part.

Non-repudiation refers to the ability to ensure that e-business participants do not deny their online actions.

Authenticity refers to the ability to recognize the identity of a person or entity with whom you are dealing with on the Internet.

Confidentiality refers to the ability to ensure that messages and data are available only to those who are authorized to view them. Confidentiality is sometimes confused with privacy, which refers to the ability to control the use of information a customer provides about himself or herself to an e-business merchant.

Security is one aspect of the utmost importance, if not the most important in relation to e-business. It is important to the user since he is provided with data and financial implications and it is also important to the entity that provides the service because it must ensure the credibility of the data sent, as well as ensure the confidentiality of information relating to their customers.

Availability refers to the ability to ensure that an e-business site continues to function as intended.

huge success factor in any business initiative is the electronic security (Worner, 2002). The uncertainty regarding the security aspects, the lack of trust in virtual relationships may affect the success of e-business (Liu, 2000; Neus, 2000; Trappey and Trappey, 2000; Chepaitis, 2002), influencing negatively its development.

Organizational Constraints

The following organizational constraints were identified.

Conflicts with Traditional Business Partners

In a scenario simultaneously cooperative and competitive, suppliers and customers, although they have very substantial powers, are considered business partners in the stabilization of a network of companies taking into account the interest they have in the joint creation of value (logical supply chain).

In times of change in the strong markets and globalization, which easily copy products / services and solutions, one should promote not only parts of the value but the value as a whole, integrating solutions for creating products / services more difficult to imitate. Supply chains are thus, increasingly, temporal training, which depend on the desirability of a given network of partners, typically large and complex. These chains also depend on the market services needs, whose demands, as we know, change according the circumstances.

The e-business offers an environment with great potential for collaboration within and between the organizations. Cooperation strategies are extremely important to the success of e-business, such as working with other companies to help gain competitive advantage within an industry. A strategy of cooperation typically involves a strategic alliance through the value chain of partners. This can be achieved through consortia or e-marketplaces (Ray, 2003).

If the traditional business partners do not adhere to this new way of doing business, conflicts with it could be a constraint to the development of e-business. One of the first steps in the development of e-business is to improve relations with key traditional business partners (Eisenmann, 2007).

Conflicts with Traditional Business and E-Business

The e-business use electronic means to reinvent the practice of traditional business. There are three types of approaches (Gouveia, 2006):

- The e-business as a separate activity. It is the establishment of a new business. If there is a traditional organization to sponsor the initiative, the new organization inherits most of the activities of business. Therefore the analysis of current activities is crucial to define the new activities and make improvements in the processes involved;
- The e-business is implemented over the traditional business, replacing it. Adopting this strategy, there is the e-business in the core of current work. As a result, some of the current activities of business will be reused;
- The e-business is integrated with regular business. In this case, usually there is a fixed intervention term and human and material resources already determined. This is the most common for an existing organization so that it synchronizes its activities taking into account the coexistence of traditional business and e-business. This approach requires more effort to implement, support and manage.

Porter (2001) considers a mistake the fact that a company with a history of success in the real world do not take advantage of its brand and its other assets to become stronger in the digital world. In defining a strategy based on e-business, it is essential to define how it will manage the conflict between the online business and offline business (or traditional). For this, it will prevent the new channel (online) to compete directly with the businesses already established in the same group of customers (the cannibalization effect). As such, the existence of conflicts between these two channels may be a constraint to the development of e-business.

Lack of Senior Management Support

The main problem that caused the failure of many initiatives in e-commerce was the apparent lack of support from top management as a lack of general understanding of the fundamental characteristics that constitute an environment of success for e-commerce (Schmid et al, 2001).

The participation and support of top management to the efforts of IS / IT have been highlighted as important factors for successful planning and implementation of IS in organizations (Kannabiran and Ranganathan, 2004).

The role of top management is related to the knowledge and understanding that this has on the strategic potential of IT, its involvement in IT initiatives and providing resources for IT.

The support of top management has been identified as a factor positively associated with the success of strategic IS planning, and essential, given the importance and strategic nature of technological IS (Kearns, 2006).

The vision of the company is the point of departure in developing a strategy and should reflect the company's strategic intent and define what it wants for the future. The top management must be involved in its definition to ensure that it is followed and implemented. According to Ware et al. (1998) the definition, development and implementation of a strategy for e-business includes seven stages, in which one of them is communication of vision from the top management to encourage the initiatives of the Internet. The support of top management is generally accepted as being critical to the success of e-business. This is because the leader of the company is usually the main decision maker because of the influence it has on the allocation of key resources (Lertwongsatien and Wongpinungwatana, 2003, Martin and Matlay, 2003; Rai and Patnaykuni, 1996, Thong and Yap, 1995). Sorenson (2000) also found a positive association between a participatory leadership and performance of the leading e-business. The lack of support from top management can influence in a negative way the stage of maturity of e-business.

E-Business Project Management

The project management has been consolidating itself as a key activity in any organization, whether their goals are economic, financial, social or political. The integral parts of any project, including human resources and/or materials, the cost, time available and activities to develop, need to be managed as efficiently and effectively as possible. The e-business projects, as all other projects of the organization, need to be assessed and monitored (Grembergen and Amelinckx, 2002).

The planning and implementation of e-business differs from traditional planning in the following aspects (Gouveia, 2006):

- **Scope:** the scope of an e-business project is the organization itself. Influence its systems, its activities, altering the processes that are critical;
- **Policies:** the implementation of e-business projects are of greater political sensitivity, and generally behaving more risk than a traditional project;
- **Coordination:** the e-business implementation requires more human resources, which involves more coordination for the reason that of the possibility of increased confusion of roles and responsibilities of employees;
- **Subprojects:** by their own characteristics of e-business, its implementation is complex since that involves a number of interdependent sub-projects, which must be conducted in parallel and in an integrated way.

We believe that a poor management of projects of e-business can be act as a constraint to the development of e-business.

Business Process Reengineering

In the globalized world in which the companies are inserted, the changes appear to be increasingly complex, characterized by increasing demands for speed, quality, low cost, flexibility and customer satisfaction.

In this context, to ensure high levels of business competitiveness, companies have to act quickly and flexibly, in a pro-active attitude, innovating their services, processes and technology, focused on customer needs and market. The reengineering of business processes promotes the realization of competitive advantage and creates value by improving organizational processes, using the full potential of IT to improve the performance of an organization.

Despite differences in definition, vision, concepts and methodologies of reengineering approach, by different authors, mainly Davenport (1993) and Hammer and Champy (1993) could be said that reengineering is the junction of three sciences (Joia,1994):

- Organization and Methods, which is linked to the mapping and monitoring the performance of the process;
- IT, which is the technological component;
- Management of change, which has the task of dealing with the organization, its culture and its professionals;

The e-business should be seen less and less as a phenomenon of online business and more as a change in the redesign of the organization (Wang, 2000).

We believe that the reengineering of business processes, although it is fundamental in an e-business project, may be a constraint to this evolution.

Business-Technology Alignment

The evolution of technologies and its requirements has forced the development of own resources, to ensure greater alignment between the needs of business and what the technological infrastructure can provide. Thus, the expansion in the use of new channels of information such as Internet, Intranet and Extranet is required to incorporate new equipment and new solutions. Since standard protocols for communication, through the firewall to reach the URL (Uniform Resource Locator), the whole technology of the telecommunications infrastructure has suffered during this last decade a rapid and continuous change.

Kearns and Lederer (2000) define strategic alignment of IT as a link between the company's business plan and the plan for IT. The strategic alignment between IT/IS and the business is one of the critical success factors for organizations to obtain the benefits and satisfactory performance for its business (Moura, 2004).

According to (Kearns and Lederer, 2000) the alignment between IT and the business plan is necessary to achieve the objectives of the business and capitalize the use of IT, helping and ensuring that investments in IT are used properly to support these goals and increase competitive advantage through the use of IT.

In some companies the bad alignment of business and IT strategy is weak because there is a small relationship between the business' processes planning and IT planning (King and Teo, 2000). A poor alignment between technology and business could adversely affect the maturity of e-business.

Lack of Human Resources Qualified

In the Knowledge Society, human resources are the most important asset of companies and organizations.

Competition for attracting skilled human resources, base of the knowledge economy, tends to aggravate the inequalities between developed and developing countries, the migration of students, many of whom completed their courses, not returning to their countries of origin.

The new market conditions and operation of organizations require an increase level of qualification of its employees, for one side can move from a system in intensive work to a knowledge-intensive system that allows optimum use of IT recently acquired or updated processes of change, and secondly, to extend the range of activities undertaken by the same developer to allow a functional flexibility that adjusts rapidly to changing skills needed for a competitive organizational performance.

In a context of high competition, uncertainty and constant change, the ability of organizations to learn and innovate, to interact and cooperate it is very important. The role of human resources has a preponderant role. The availability of qualified human resources supports the company's competitiveness, the adoption of new technologies and new forms of organization, innovation and productivity.

The report led by Wim Kok (2004), in which the European Council of 2004 used to establish priorities in employment, indicates as priorities the increased adaptability of workers and investment in human capital and education and training to lifelong learning, among others.

According to the OECD report, the lack of qualified human resources is a barrier to the development of e-business (OECD, 1999), especially when there is lack of experience and knowledge in the e-business (Mehrtens et al., 2001).

People Coordination

The prospects for development are always a concern (and hence also constitute one of the interests) of who conducts a business. The case of e-business is no exception. It is also necessary to consider more factors associated with the nature of e-business, including aspects related to technology and technological developments and new services and applications of ICT, whose innovations occur at a speed up. It is clear that this concern is not new, efforts to forecast the potential of a business were (and are) a central concern of their responsible, for more specific to the business is. Thus, the various attempts to predict the ways to take advantage of ICT in the context of human activity and business are limited and require an additional effort at all responsible for the design, the entrepreneurs and other introducers of e-business.

A business model is a mediated construction between technologies and business (Chesbrough and Rosenbloom, 2002), such as, a poor coordination between the heads of these two areas may be a constraint to the development of e-business in the organization.

Resistance to Change

Several studies have emerged in recent decades to capture, analyze and understand the phenomenon of organizational change. The review of these studies shows the attitude of resistance to change, considered as natural and inevitable (Kurtz and Duncan, 1998) and popularized as a major barrier to implementation of change processes (Braver, 1995).

The popularization of the concept of resistance to change as a major barrier in implementation of change processes and innovations have been disseminated to overcome many forms of overcome it. Although using different terminology, several authors have suggested various strategies to deal with general resistance to change (Iskatt and Liebowitz, 1996; Boyle, 1995; Poe and Viator, 1990). One way or another, all these formulas can be summarized in six broad strategies outlined by Kotter and Schlesinger (1979) to overcome resistance to change: a) education and communication, b) participation and involvement, c) facilitation and support d) negotiation and agreement, e) handling and cooperation f) explicit and/or implied coercion.

Innovation is one of the main drivers of a firm's competitive advantage. Innovation, however, has often a disruptive effect on the organization, because it is associated to or induces organizational change and adaptation. A new technology, a new product, or a new marketing method often imply the reshaping of relevant resources and expertise, the change of established norms and routines, and the rapid obsolescence of accumulated learning (Tushman and Anderson, 1986).

Resistance to change is inevitable, even when it represents growth and development. Managers should be prepared to deal with resistance to change (Fine, 1986).

Environment Constraints

The following environment constraints were identified.

Activity Sector

The business model is the main guarantor of the mission of the organization, because it identifies how to act within their environment, making it one of the main instruments of the strategic evaluation of the business. The definition of business model results from an integrated observation of the value chain of the organization with their value system, which characterizes the sector in which the organization belongs. The value chain, define the fundamental processes of business, while the value system is to make the characterization of the industry, not only in regard to relationships between the various value chains that make up that activity sector, but also with regard to competitive influences that affect the performance of each. The value chain can vary from company to company, depending on the specifics of your industry.

According to Porter (1985), each firm belongs to a generic value chain of the industry in which it operates and may seek position itself in one or more stages in the chain that believes that competitive advantage to create more value than its competitors, should not break the business model of the structure of the business in which it is inserted.

It has been proven in literature that the characteristics of each activity sector influence the adoption of e-business (Kwon and Zmud, 1987; Mehrtens et al., 2001, Raymond, 2001), with benefits for companies that take it (Premkumar and Roberts, 1999; Saxowski et al., 2002).

It is expected that the e-business maturity may be affected (positively or negatively) by the intrinsic characteristics of each activity sector.

The Most Problematic Constraints

A study was conducted with the objective to identify the constraints associated to e-business development. This study, oriented to the biggest Portuguese companies, concluded that the most problematic constraints were *conflict with traditional business and e-business initiatives*, *conflict with traditional trading partners* and *reengineering business processes*. The less problematic is the *lack of senior management support* (Morais et al, 2009a; Morais et al, 2009b).

The same study carried out in Small and Medium Enterprises (SME) (Santos, 2009), verified that for this type of companies the most problematic constraints are *inadequate technology*, *cost of e-business solutions* and *e-business project management*, despite many of the constraints associated with change being also considerable.

The constraints associated with change are normally the most problematic. Gibbs et al. (2003) conclude that for many European countries, cultural resistance to change and innovation are at the root of resistance to e-business.

Solutions and Recommendations

Although there are constraints more problematic than others, the studies found that since 2005 the constraints have become less problematic (Morais et al, 2009a; Morais et al, 2009b; Santos, 2009).

Each organization has its specific features and as such its own difficulties. However, the studies found that the most common way of solving the constraints outlined in the previous sections are the listed in the table below (Morais, 2009; Santos, 2009).

FUTURE RESEARCH DIRECTIONS

Despite the recognition and the attention given to e-business over the last years, this type of business hasn't yet achieved a desirable maturity stage. This problem, current and stated over the last years, demands research efforts so that a solution can be found to solve it.

As future work the perspective is the achievement of new studies, in companies of different size, and also by activity sector, since this variable may lead to quite different results.

The development of a maturity model for e-business which includes the constraints associated with each of the stages of the model and how to overcome them will also be useful for organizations to be able to avoid any difficulties.

Table 2. Ways of solving the constraints

Constraint	Ways of solving the constraint
Inadequate Technology	• Technological updating • Migration to other technological platforms
Cost of e-business solutions	• Own investment
Insecurity	• Use of security protocols • Systems for data protection • Implementation of security services
Conflicts with traditional business partners	• Integration with the value chain of business partners
Conflicts with traditional business and e-business	• E-business integrated with the regular business
Lack of Senior Management Support	• E-business seen as an opportunity
E-business Project Management	• creation of a multidisciplinary team to manage projects
Business Process Reengineering	• Analysis and management of business processes • Motivation of employees to the need to do reengineering
Business-Technology Alignment	• Awareness among employees about the importance of alignment between technology and business • involvement of the technology responsible when creating a new model / business process
Lack of Human Resources Qualified	• Training of employees • Recruitment
People Coordination	• Awareness among employees about the importance of both • Training of employees
Resistance to change	• Involvement and awareness of employees throughout the process • Training of employees

CONCLUSION

The use of ICT is not guaranteed to improve productivity, reducing costs and innovation. The organizations' success is related to a correct management of IS (Varajão, 2002) as well as with a proper management of ICT projects.

Since ICT is relatively recent, if compared, for example, with construction, management of projects in this area has evolved significantly over recent decades. Despite this progress, there are still quite significant levels in the failure of ICT projects (Rijo, 2008).

To contribute to the success of e-business initiatives, possible constraints to their development were identified. These constraints were grouped into technological, organizational and environment constraints.

It was thus possible to identify and characterize thirteen constraints associated with the development of e-business: Inadequate Technology; Cost of e-business solutions; Insecurity; Conflicts with traditional business partners; Conflicts with traditional business and e-business; Lack of senior management support; E-business project management; Business process reengineering; Business-Technology alignment; Lack of human resources qualified; People coordination; Resistance to change and the Activity sector.

The conceptual model (Figure 1) was validated through the construction of hypotheses, where each constraint has been tested to verify their influence in the maturity of e-business (Morais, 2009).

Of the thirteen constraints identified only the constraint *cost of e-business* and *insecurity* did not affect the maturity. Probably, because there are constraints that are present in all maturity stages of e-business (Morais, 2009).

REFERENCES

Auer, T. (1995). Beyond IS Implementation: a skill-based approach to IS use. In Proceedings of the 3rd *European Conference on Information Systems*, Athens, Greece.

Bakry, S., & Bakry, F. (2001). A strategic view for the development of e-business. *International Journal of Network Management, 11*, 103–112. doi:10.1002/nem.395

Boyle, R. D. (1995). Avoiding common pitfalls of reengineering. *Management Accounting, 77*(4), 24–30.

Braver, N. (1995). Overcoming resistance to TQM. *Research Technologic Management, 38*(5), 40–44.

Chepaitis, E. (2002). Soft barriers to ICT application in development: trust and information quality in Russia. *Journal of International Development, 14*, 51–60. doi:10.1002/jid.871

Chesbrough, H., & Rosenbloom, R. S. (2002). The role of the business model in capturing value from innovation: Evidence from Xerox Corporation's technology spin-off companies. *Industrial and Corporate Change, 11*(3), 529–555. doi:10.1093/icc/11.3.529

Davenport, T. H. (1993). *Process Innovation: Reengineering Work through Information Technology*. Boston: Harvard Business School Press.

Earl, M. J. (1989). *Management Strategies for Information Technology*. Upper Saddle River, NJ: Prentice Hall.

Earl, M.J. (2000). Evolving the E-Business. *Business Strategy Review*, 11(2).

Eisenmann, T. (2007). *Managing Networked Businesses: Course Overview for Educators*. Boston: Harvard Business School Press.

Fine, S. F. (1986). Technological innovation, diffusion and resistance: A historical perspective. *Journal of Library Administration, 7*, 83–108. doi:10.1300/J111V07N01_09Galliers, R. D., & Sutherland, A. R. (1991). Information systems management and strategy formulation: the 'stages of growth' model revisited. *Journal of Information Systems, 1*(2), 89–114. doi:10.1111/j.1365-2575.1991.tb00030.x

Gibbs, J., Kraemer, K., & Dedrick, J. (2003). Environment and Policy Factors Shaping Global E-Commerce Diffusion: A Cross-Country Comparison. *The Information Society, 19*(1), 5–18. doi:10.1080/01972240309472

Gibson, C., & Nolan, R. (1974). Managing the four stages of EDP growth. *Harvard Business Review*, (January-February): 76–88.

Gouveia, L. (2006). *Negócio Electrónico - conceitos e perspectivas de desenvolvimento*. SPI - Sociedade Portuguesa de Inovação.

Gouveia, L., & Gaio, S. (2004). *Readings in Information Society*. UFP University Press.

Grembergen, W., & Amenlinckx, I. (2002). Measuring and managing e-business projects through the balanced scorecard. In Proceedings of the *35th Hawaii International Conference on System Sciences*: 258-266.

Grover, V., Teng, J., Segars, A., & Fiedler, K. (1998). The influence of information technology diffusion and business process change on perceived productivity: The IS executive's perspective. *Information & Management, 34*(3), 141–15. doi:10.1016/S0378-7206(98)00054-8

Hammer, M., & Champy, J. (1993). *Reengineering the Corporation: A Manifesto for Business Revolution*. New York: Harper Business.

Hirschheim, R., Klein, H., & Lyytinen, K. (1996). Exploring the Intellectual Structures of Information Systems Development: A Social Action Theoretic Analysis. *Accounting. Management and Information Technologies*, *6*(1), 1–64. doi:10.1016/0959-8022(96)00004-5

Iskatt, G. J., & Liebowitz, J. (1996). What to do when employees resist change. *Super Vision*, *57*(8), 3–5.

Joia, L. (1994). *Reengenharia e Tecnologia da Informação: O Paradigma do Camaleão*. São Paulo: Pioneira.

Jones, P., Muir, E., & Beynon-Davies, P. (2006). The proposal of a comparative framework to evaluate e-business stages of growth models. *International Journal of Information Technology and Management*, *5*(4), 249–266. doi:10.1504/IJITM.2006.012039

Kalakota, R., & Robinson, M. (2001). *E-Business 2.0. Roadmap for Success*. Reading, MA: Addison Wesley.

Kalakota, R., & Robinson, M. (2003). *E-business 2.0: Roadmap for Success* (2nd ed.). Reading, MA: Addison-Wesley.

Kalakota, R., & Whinston, A. (1996). *Frontiers of Electronic Commerce*. London: Addison-Wesley.

Kannabiran, G., & Ranganathan, C. (2004). Effective management of information systems function: An exploratory study of Indian organizations. *International Journal of Information Management*, *24*, 247–266. doi:10.1016/j.ijinfomgt.2004.02.005

Kearns, G., & Lederer, A. (2000). The effect of strategic alignment on the use of IS based resources for competitive advantage. *The Journal of Strategic Information Systems*, *9*, 265–293. doi:10.1016/S0963-8687(00)00049-4

Khandelwal, V., & Ferguson, J. (1999). Critical Success Factors (CSFs) and the Growth of IT in Selected Geographic Regions. In Proceedings of the 32nd Hawaii *International Conference on System Sciences*, USA.

King, W., & Teo, T. (2000). Assessing the impact of proactive versus reactive modes of strategic information systems planning. *Omega*, *28*, 667–679. doi:10.1016/S0305-0483(99)00079-1

Kotter, J. P., & Schlesinger, L. A. (1979). Choosing strategies for change. *Harvard Business Review*, 106–114.

Kurtz, P., & Duncan, A. (1998). Shared service centres: overcomimg resistance to implementation of a shared services centre. *Management Accounting*, *76*(7), 47–48.

Kwon, T. H., & Zmud, R. W. (1987). Unifying the fragmented models of information systems implementation. In Boland, R. J., & Hirschheim, R. A. (Eds.), *Critical Issues in Information Systems Research* (pp. 247–252). New York: JohnWiley.

Laudon, K., & Traver, C. (2006). *E-commerce Business, Technology, Society*. Upper Saddle River, NJ: Prentice Hall.

Legris, P., Ingham, J., & Collerette, P. (2003). Why do people use information technology? A critical review of the technology acceptance model. *Information & Management*, *40*, 191–204. doi:10.1016/S0378-7206(01)00143-4

Lertwongsatien, C., & Wongpinunwatana, N. (2003). Ecommerce Adoption in Thailand: An Empirical Study of Small and Medium Enterprises (SMEs). *Journal of Global Information Technology Management*, *6*(3), 67–83.

Lientz, B., & Rea, K. (2001). *Comece bem no E-Business – Guia Passo a Passo para a Implementação do E-Business*. Market Books.

Liu, L. (2000). A measurement model to trust in electronic commerce. In *INFORMA* Proceedings 2000. San Antonio: Texas; TA26.

Martin, L. M., & Matlay, H. (2003). Innovative Use of the Internet in Established Small Firms, *Qualitative Market Research. International Journal (Toronto, Ont.)*, *6*(1), 18–26.

McFarlan, F. W., McKenney, J. L., & Pyburn, P. (1983). The information archipelago - plotting a course. Boston. *Harvard Business Review*, (January-February): 145–156.

McKay, J., Prananto, A., & Marshall, P. (2000). E-business Maturity: The SOG-e Model. In *Proceedings of the 11th Australasian Conference on Information Systems (ACIS)*, Australia.

Mehrtens, J., Cragg, P. B., & Mills, A. M. (2001). A model of Internet adoption by SME's. *Information & Management*, *39*, 165–176. doi:10.1016/S0378-7206(01)00086-6

Morais, E. (2009). Maturidade do Negócio Electrónico – Constrangimentos associados à sua evolução, Doctoral dissertation, University of Trás-os-Montes e Alto Douro, Portugal.

Morais, E., Gonçalves, E., & Pires, J. (2007). Electronic Commerce Maturity: A review of the principal models, In *Proceedings of IADIS International Conference - E-Society 2007*, Lisbon, Portugal, 463-466.

Morais, E., Pires, J., & Gonçalves, R. (2009a). Exploring the Constraints to the evolution of Electronic Business: The Portuguese reality. In *Proceedings of 11th IBIMA Conference*, Cairo, Egypt.

Morais, E., Pires, J., & Gonçalves, R. (2009b). An exploratory investigation of e-business constraints among large organizations in Portugal. In Proceedings of *International Conference on E-Business – ICEB 2009*, Milan, Italy.

Moura, R. (2004). *O papel da tecnologia e informação. Tecnologia de Informação. São Paulo: Atlas.Neus A. (2000). The quality of online registration information: factors influencing user decisions* (pp. 109–129). MA: Ridge.

Nolan, R. (1973). Managing the Computer Resource: A Stage Hypothesis. *Communications of the ACM*, *16*(7), 399–405. doi:10.1145/362280.362284

Nolan, R. (1979). Managing the crisis in data processing. *Harvard Business Review*, *57*(2), 115–126.

O'Brien, A., 2003. *Sistemas de Informação e as decisões gerenciais na era da Internet.* São Paulo, Saraiva.OECD, 1999. SMEs and Electronic Commerce: Proposals for Work, Working Party on Small and Medium-Sized Enterprises, DSTI/IND/PME (99)11/REV1, Paris.

Poe, C. D., & Viator, R. E. (1990). What to do when employees resist automation. *Journal of Accounting and EDP*, *5*(4), 9–14.

Porter, M. (1985). *Competitive Advantage: Creating and Sustaining Superior Performance*. Nova Iorque, The Free Press.

Porter, M. (2001). *Strategy and the Internet*. Harvard Business Review.

Prananto, A., McKay, J., & Marshall, P. (2001). Frameworks to Support E-Business Strategy, In *Global CoOperation in the New Millennium, The 9th European Conference on Information Systems*, 2001, Bled, Slovenia.

Premkumar, G., & Roberts, M. (1999). Adoption of new information technologies in rural small businesses. *Omega, International Journal Management. Science*, *27*, 467–484.

Rai, A., & Patnayakuni, R. (1996). A Structural Model for CASE Adoption Behaviour. *Journal of Management Information Systems*, *13*(2), 205–234.

Rao, S., Metts, G., & Monge, C. (2003). Electronic Commerce Development in Small and Medium Sized Enterprises: A Stage Model and its Implications. *Business Process Management Journal*, *9*(1), 11–32. doi:10.1108/14637150310461378

Ray, P. (2003). Integrated management from e-business perspective: concepts, architectures, and methodologies. Pradeep Kumar Ray New York: Kluwer Academic/Plenum Publishers.

Raymond, L. (2001). Determinants of web site implementation, small business. Int. Res. *Electronic Network Appl. and Policy*, *11*, 411–422.

Rayport, J., & Jaworski, B. (2002). *Introduction to E-Commerce*. Boston: McGraw Hill.

Rijo, R. (2008). *Framework para a Gestão de Projectos de Sistemas de Informação de Contact Centers*. Doctoral dissertation, Universidade de Trás-os-Montes e AltoDouro, Portugal.

Santos, S. (2009). *Maturidade do Negócio Electrónico nas Pequenas e Médias Empresas Portuguesas*.Master dissertation, University of Trás-os-Montes e Alto Douro, Portugal.

Saxowsky, D., & Duncan, M. (1998). *Understanding agriculture's transition into the 21st century: challenges, opportunities, consequences and alternatives, Report 181*. Department of Agricultural Economics, North Dakota State University.

Schmid, B. F., Stanoevska-Slabeva, K., & Tschammer, V. (2001). *Towards the E-Society: E-commerce, E-business, and E-government*. Boston: Kluwer Academic Publishers.

Serrano, A., & Caldeira, M. (2001). Gestão de Investimentos em Sistemas e Tecnologias de Informação – uma revisão critica. *Sistemas de Informação*, *15*, 99–107.

Sewell, M., & McCarthey, I. (2001). E-business and its role in small business networks. In Proceedings of the *Manufacturing Information Systems, 4th SMESME International Conference*, 214-221.

Sorenson, R. L. (2000). The Contribution of Leadership Style and Practices to Family and Business Success. *Family Business Review*, *13*(3), 183–200. doi:10.1111/j.1741-6248.2000.00183.x

Thong, J. Y. L., & Yap, C. S. (1995). CEO Characteristics, Organizational Characteristics and Information Technology Adoption in Small Business. *Omega international Journal of Management Science, 23*(4), 429–42.

Trappey, C., & Trappey, A. (2000). Great China e-commerce trends and development. In *INFORMS* Proceedings, San Antonio: Texas; TE07.

Tushman, M. L., & Anderson, P. (1986). Technological Discontinuities and Organizational Requirements. *Administrative Science Quarterly*, *31*, 439–465. doi:10.2307/2392832

Varajão, J. (2002). Função de Sistemas de Informação - Contributos para a melhoria do sucesso da adopção de tecnologias de informação e desenvolvimento de sistemas de informação nas organizações, Doctoral dissertation, Universidade do Minho, Portugal.

Wang, S. (2000). Managing the Organizational Aspects of Electronic Commerce. *Human Systems Management*, *9*(1), 49–59.

Ware, J., Gebauer, J., Hartman, A., & Roldan, M. (1998). *The Search for Digital Excellence*. New York: McGraw-Hill.

Wim K. (2004). *Facing the challenge: The Lisbon strategy for growth and employment*. Report from the High Level Group chaired by Wim Kok.

Worner, B. (2002). Choosing the right security infrastructure for E-Business Success. *Information Security Journal: A global Perspective*, 11(1), 51-56.

Zackman, J., Inmon, W., & Geiger, J. (1997). *Data Stores, Data Warehousing and the Zachman Framework: Managing Enterprise Knowledge*. New York: McGraw-Hill.

Chapter 20
An Integrative Framework on the Psychological Variables Explaining the Consumers' Use of E-Commerce-Based Recommendation Systems

Francisco J. Martínez-López
University of Granada, Spain

Juan Carlos Gázquez-Abad
University of Almería, Spain

Inma Rodríguez-Ardura
Open University of Catalonia, Spain

Claudia C. Cabal-Cruz
University of Quindío, Colombia

ABSTRACT

A conceptual model to understand the consumer's adoption and use of certain website recommendation system is presented; the research problem is tackled from a psychological perspective. The authors base on, adapt and integrate classical theories of consumer behavior with particular theories developed in the framework of computer-mediated environments. The model proposed, along with the relations analyzed among the variables considered (a total of 16 research propositions), should be of help for recommendation systems designer and website managers, in order to work with systems more aware of the psychological process experienced by consumers when interacting with them.

DOI: 10.4018/978-1-61692-880-3.ch020

INTRODUCTION

Recommendation systems (RS) represent a very useful tool to be applied in e-commerce based Business-to-Consumer relations. Such systems, if well designed and applied, should contribute to efficiently apply a mass-customization approach to manage the relationships with customers. Doubtless, their study is very necessary. However, research efforts have been usually characterized by a technical orientation, coming from areas as information systems and computer science (Xiao and Benbasat, 2007). Thus, proposals and solutions that can be found in regard to this question, though numerous and rich, have not paid enough attention to other perspectives which deserve analysis. In particular, a key perspective is that which help to understand why consumers get into interactive process with recommendation systems of websites. Reviewing the literature, few and notable attempts to model the consumers' adoption and use of these systems can be found (Wang and Benbasat, 2005; Xiao and Benbasat, 2007), though they present diverse weaknesses, depending on the case; for instance, a lack of enough attention to psychological variables or, if so, development of models not detailed enough to explain it in a more complete manner. Anyhow, recommendation systems' adoption, use and other related questions which help to know their influence in the online consumption behaviours are elements of an area of research with many opportunities for future studies yet in the e-marketing arena.

This paper is a theoretical attempt to model the consumer's process related with the adoption, use, main psychological and buying-related outcomes, and future use of a website recommendation system. The conceptual model presented here works mainly with psychological constructs, and it is product of a reflected integration of diverse general consumption theories, as well as specific approaches, to explain the acceptation of information technologies. In particular, the Technology of Acceptance Model (TAM), the integrated Trust-TAM model for online shopping the Theory of Planned Behaviour, an evolution of the Theory of Reasoned Action, and the theories of Flow in online environments. A total of 16 theoretical propositions are introduced and discussed.

Finally, the paper is structure as follows. First, we present diverse questions related with the general framework of the recommendation systems and with their interest from a marketing perspective in particular. Next, we introduce the basis of our conceptual model, its constituent variables/constructs, and the relations set between them. Lastly, the paper is closed with some concluding ideas.

BACKGROUND

Overall Overview

Recommendation systems –also known as "recommendation agents", "recommender systems", "recommendation systems", "shopping agents", "shopping bots", "comparison shopping agents", "product RAs", "e-commerce RAs" and "e-commerce product" (Xiao and Benbasat, 2007)– belong to impersonal sources providing personal information to consumers. This is a particular type of source highlighted for its potential for consumer research in the near future (Senecal and Nantel, 2004).

Notwithstanding, even though recommendations provided by these systems are observed to be less trustworthy or expertise than other sources (e.g.: human experts' and other consumers' evaluations), they seem to be the most influential in consumers' online choices (Senecal and Nantel, 2004). Besides, if it is considered that RS are able to articulate recommendations through diverse alternatives, their potential to stimulate and drive the consumers' selection of items in certain website is evident. In particular, it should not be only considered recommendations of products provided by intelligent agents, but also the collaboration with users for them to assess products; it is interesting RS to adequately integrate different sources when aiding the online consumption processes (Ansari, Essegaier and Kohli, 2000). In this regard, Schafer, Konstan and Rield (2001) point out three perspectives that should be taken into account: recommendations made by RS, predictions on users' preferences, and other community members' opinions. The following definition on RS they provide is illustrative of these questions:

"RS are used by E-commerce sites to suggest products to their customers and to provide consumers with information to help them decide which products to purchase. [...] recommended based on the top overall sellers on a site, on the demographics of the consumer, or on an analysis of the past buying behavior of the consumer as a prediction for future buying behavior. The forms of recommendation include suggesting products to the consumer, providing personalized product information, summarizing community opinion, and providing community critiques" (p. 116).

RS has been recently classified in three main types, depending on which is the approach followed to make recommendations (Adomavicius and Tuzhilin, 2005) approaches: (1) *Content-based filtering*, which bases recommendations on the similarity of items, considering the preferences of items shown by consumers in the past (e.g.; Balabanovic and Shoham, 1997; Herlocker and Konstan, 2001; Mooney and Roy, 2000; Pazzani and Billsus, 2007); (2) *Collaborative filtering*, which takes other people's choices, sharing profile with the user, to recommend items (e.g.: Canny, 2002; Cho and Kim, 2004; Goldberg et al., 1992; Goldberg et al., 2001; Konstan et al., 1997; Mild and Reutterer, 2003; Schafer et al., 2007). Nevertheless, it is a clear limitation being unable to combine, not only the type of data used by each of these two previous RS, but also their individual strengths (Ahn, 2006); and to overcome these shortcomings, a (3) hybrid approach to generate recommendations has been developed. It is characterized by combining several recommendation techniques, even from the same type (Burke, 2007).

Summarizing, RS are artificial intelligence-based tools that create users' profiles based on consumers' present and past preferences, characteristics or similarities between them, in order to do recommendations to customers.

Recommendation Systems and Online Consumption

The advantages of RS are notable when applied commercially. More than technological device, RS must be seen as tools that improve the conditions for both consumer and seller, tying business objectives to the interests of the consumer (Maes, 1994). Thus, aside from whether a specific online firm is characterized or not by applying a generalized relational focus (e.g.: Berry, 1983; Morgan and Hunt, 1994) to the management of its relations with customers, the use of RS clearly helps to improve the value of the company's client portfolio. In fact, due to the diversity of customers' profiles companies usually address, it is more convenient not using a general approach to electronic interchanges with a relational focus, but an approach adapted to what every customer really requires (Endo and Kincade, 2008). If we consider that Customer Relationship Management (CRM) takes care of the appropriate generation of market intelligence for companies, with the aim of strengthening the construction and maintenance of a "profit-maximizing portfolio of customer relationships" (Zablah et al., 2004, p. 481), RS act as a pillar of support for the e-CRM in a one-to-one basis (Kim et al., 2002).

The RS have been developed from a customer perspective. This starts when a current or potential customer accesses a particular website for information on a service or product, finding a large quantity of information that is impossible to process in its entirety. Therefore, it is worth applying a filter process to offer the visitor the most relevant information consumer-wise. The RS are based on huge banks of data with characteristics of interest or items sometimes defined by the user to provide a personalized list of recommended options (Haübl and Trifts, 2000). These personalized recommendations have recently become essential element in e-commerce. Some of the main reasons explaining this are (Ying, Feinberg and Wedel, 2006): (1) RS enable online firms attending individual preferences; (2) RS allow making recommendations to customers based on previous purchases, preferences shown by other customers with similar profiles, etc.; (3) online consumption processes are more efficient as recommendations provide by RS gain in accuracy, a valuable benefit taking into account the charge of information consumers have to deal with in electronic environments. In this regard, Maes (1999) remarks that the reduction of the effort in purchasing decisions is reflected in the favourable impact that the RS have on most of stages of consumer purchase behaviour; and finally, even more interesting, (4) as commented above, RS can be a very useful tool to support both the acquisition and retention of customers.

In sum, RS may clearly contribute to the increase in the added value offered to customers, via an improvement in the processes of mass online personalization. This has a subsequent positive effect on cost reduction, assistance in retaining customers, creation of an environment conducive to profitable exchanges, etc. (e.g.: Ansari, Essegaier and Kohli, 2000; Schafer, Konstan and Rield, 2001). All these likely uses of RS should definitively help to improving the company's competitiveness (Kim et al., 2005). Well-known and famous examples of companies that implemented RS to achieve improvements and consolidate products and services offered online are Amazon.com, eBay, Rhapsody, or Netflix, among others.

CONCEPTUAL MODEL

Brief Motivation and Justification

Based on the literature review, there seems to be a lack of specific research, with a clear user/customer focus orientation, on the psychological aspects explaining the use of a website recommendation system. A recent and notable attempt to model the effects of diverse aspects related to RS (e.g. use, characteristics and other factors) on consumer decision making, to the best of our knowledge the only one till the date, was that of Xiao and Benbasat (2007). However, though they proposed a very detailed model, it is a clear research opportunity yet to analyse the antecedents and outcomes of the RS use from a consumer's subjective (psychological variables) perspective; this perspective was weakly cover by said study. Furthermore, we pay also attention to the relationships among the psychological outcomes of the website RS, as well as to the plausible determinants of the future use of a website RS.

In essence, regardless other variables also considered, our proposed model is based on the adaptation and integration of several theoretical approaches developed to understand the consumer's behaviour in traditional and online shopping contexts: (1) the Technology of Acceptance Model (TAM) (Davis, 1989); the integrated Trust-TAM model for online shopping (Gefen, Karahanna and Straub, 2003; Wang and Benbasat, 2005); (3) the Theory of Planned Behaviour (TPB) (Ajzen, 1985; Ajzen, 1989; Ajzen, 1991), an evolution of the Theory of Reasoned Action (Ajzen and Fishbein, 1980; Fishbein and Ajzen, 1975); and (4) the theories of Flow in online environments (Hoffman and Novak, 1996; Novak, Hoffman and Yung, 2000). In Figure 1 we show a representation of the full model, distinguishing by blocks of variables, depending on the theories we have based on to establish the relations.

Figure 1. Conceptual model

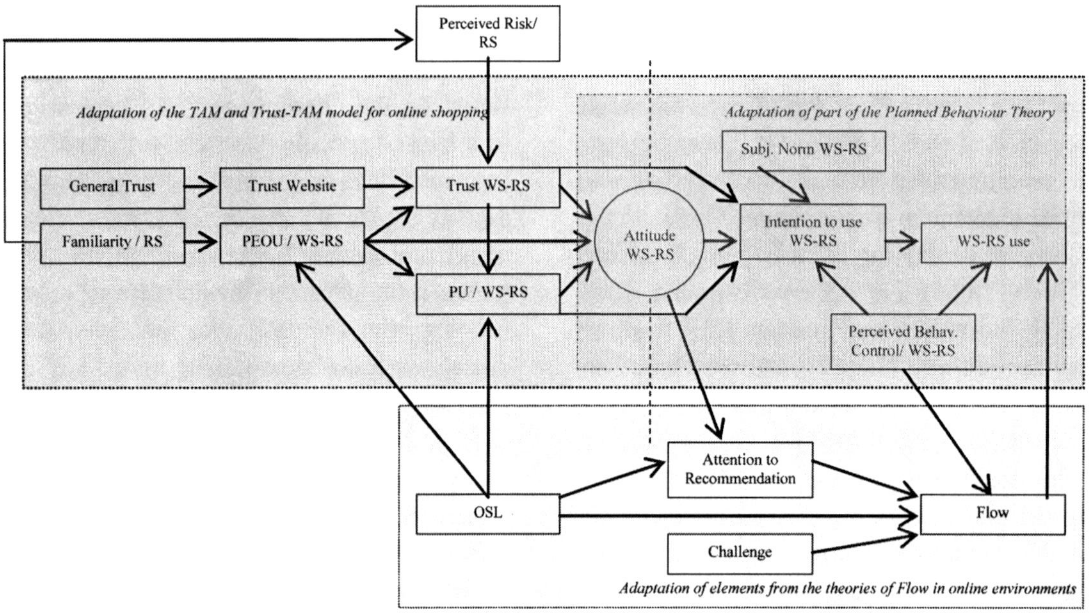

Construct/Variables

Our conceptual model is composed by a total of 15 variables. In Table 1, we synthetically show a brief description of them.

Theoretical Analyis of the Relations among Variables

Here, we synthetically introduce and justify the relations of the conceptual model by means of propositions. In order to follow a coherent sequence of analysis, this section is structured on the base of the blocks of relations shown in the model.

1. Adaptation of the TAM and Trust-TAM Model

The TAM model was originally introduced by Davis (1989) and Davis, Bagozzi and Warshaw (1989), and it has been successfully applied by later studies to explain diverse aspects related to Internet adoption. The TAM model has similarities to the classic Theory of Reasoned Action (Ajzen and Fishbein, 1980; Fishbein and Ajzen, 1975), and it has shown to be more suitable for tackling the understanding of the acceptance and use of new computer-based technologies (Gefen and Straub, 2000). However, recent studies have emphasized the convenience of extending the TAM model to other constructs. In particular, trust highlights a key factor for e-commerce-based technologies/applications (McKnight and Chervany, 2001; Urban, Sultan and Qualls, 2000), whose integration with Perceived Ease of Use (PEOU) and Perceived Usefulness (PU), the two main constructs of the TAM model, could be interesting. In this regard, the general integrated Trust-TAM model proposed by Gefen, Karahanna and Straub (2003) presents a solid solution for this question.

Our conceptual model focuses on the adoption and use of, not general, but a particular website RS (e.g. Amazon, Alibris, CDnow, etc.). This is why most of the constructs of our model refer to a certain website recommendation system; in these cases, we add the acronym RS-WS. Also, as can

Table 1. Description of the constructs/variables of the model

Construct/Variable	Brief Description
General Trust	Consistent tendency to trust across a broad variety of situations and persons (McKnight, Cummings and Chervany, 1998, p. 477)
Trust Website	Individual's belief in certain website/the e-vendor's trustworthy (see Gefen, 2000).
Trust WS-RS	Individual's beliefs of trust in certain website recommendation system (RS-WS)
PEOU WS-RS	Individual's perceived ease of use of certain RS-WS
PU WS-RS	The individual's perceived usefulness of certain RS-WS
Familiarity RS	Individual's understanding of recommendation systems (RS), based on prior and direct experiential exchanges with them (Komiak and Benbasat, 2006, p. 946)
Perceived Risk RS	Individual's perceived risk in the use of recommendation systems.
Attitude WS-RS	Indiviual's overall opinion (affective response) towards certain RS-WS.
Subj. Norm WS-RS	The individual's perception about others' opinions regarding the use of RS in general and certain RS-WS in particular.
Intention Use WS-RS	The indivdual's willingness to use certain RS-WS
Perceived Behav. Control WS-RS	The individual's perception on how easy or difficult is using certain RS-WS.
Use WS-RS	The fact of using certain RS-WS by the individual.
OSL	Degree of sensory stimulation that an individual regards as adequate for himself
Attention to Recommendation	The individual's level of attention to the recommendations of the RS-WS
Flow	An individual's mental state of optimal experience when deeply involved in the process of navigation in the Web

be seen in Figure 1, we adapt the key elements of the TPB to complement the central theories (i.e. TAM and Trust-TAM) on which we primarily base to explain the consumer's RS-WS intention to use and usage. But, this block of the model will be discussed in the next section. First, let us centre on the determinants, direct or indirect, of the consumer's attitude towards the RS-WS; one of the key constructs of the model.

The general Trust-TAM model (Gefen, Karahanna and Straub (2003), and also a particular Trust-TAM model to explain the intention to use RS [38], omits the user's attitude from the model, maybe for simplicity. Although, we think it is a necessary construct which should be explicitly considered. So, regardless of the direct effects caused by Trust RS-WS and PU RS-WS on the consumer's willingness to make use of a certain RS-WS, also considered in the conceptual model, a relationship framework for PEOU WS- RS, PU WS- RS, Trust WS-RS and Attitude WS-RS, inspired in the traditional TAM models, is proposed:

P1: The consumer's perceived ease of use of a certain website recommendation system will positively influence his/her: (a) perceived usefulness; and (b) attitude toward said particular RS.

P2: The consumer's perceived usefulness of a certain website recommendation system will positively contribute to his/her attitude toward said system.

Likewise, we add and work with the construct of trust WS-RS. There exist many attempts to conceptualize trust, though most of them consider it as a multidimensional concept. In marketing, a psychological widely accepted approach is that which follows a similar reasoning to that traditionally followed to structure the dimensions of attitude (Kenning, 2008): cognitive, affective and behavioural. Here, we focus on the cognitive dimension of trust. In particular, based on Wang and Benbasat (2005), Trust WS-RS in our conceptual model represents the user's starting trusting beliefs about a certain website recommendation system. Also, if we base, as in previous Business-to-Consumer (B2C) studies (Jarvenpaa, Tractinsky and Vitale, 2000), on the sequence of components of the TRA, then the user's trust in a certain website recommendation system can be considered a belief with influence on his/her attitude towards said WS-RS. Thus, adapting the conclusions of previous studies which successfully analyzed the consumer's trust-attitude relation to online stores, websites and B2C in general (Elliott and Speck, 2005Lim et al., 2006; Teo and Liu, 2007), it is proposed that:

P3: The consumer's trusting starting beliefs in a certain website recommendation system is positively related to his/her attitude towards said system.

We also consider a construct usually omitted by the trust-based studies in marketing, general trust. There is a recent work by Kenning (2008) which highlights this question, and theorizes and tests the relation between general trust and specific trust. The former represents the individual's structural willingness to trust, thus related to a psychological trait in the individual, while the latter refers to a particular object of trust. In our case, this specific object of trust is a certain website. Also, the user's trust in said website is expected to condition the set of particular objects of trust belonging to this framework, as it may be the recommendation system of the website. Therefore, it is proposed that:

P4: The consumer's general trust is positively related to specific objects of trust, as in the consumer's trust in a certain website.

P5: The consumer's trust in a certain website is expected to have a positive and direct influence on his/her trust in the website recommendation system.

Regarding the triangular relation between the constructs consumer's PEOU WS-RS, PU WS-RS on the one hand, and Trust WS-RS on the other, we base on the adaptation of the hypothesized relations analyzed and tested with success by Gefen, Karahanna and Straub (2003) in their general Trust-TAM model in online shopping. Such relations were later analyzed by Wang and Benbasat (2005) by means of an experimental study applied to a sample of 120 students in the context of a laboratory recommendation agent that provided advice for digital cameras.

Basically, when a consumer surfs a particular website–if behavioural patterns characterizing the process of personal interaction between people (see Blau, 1964) are extrapolated– he/she, more or less consciously, looks for cues which help them to know how reliable said website might be. In this regard, adapting the Gefen, Karahanna and Straub' (2003) reflections, an easy to use RS should be positively valued by users; it is also considered a sign that the online firm cares about its visitors, so facilitating the development of their navigational online consumption process with the firm. This is why, in particular, it is proposed that:

P6: The consumer's perceived ease of use of a certain website recommendation system will positively contribute to his/her trust in said system.

Also, when a consumer experiences a state of trust in a certain WS-RS, it is plausible to think that such trust may generate higher perceptions with respect to its utility as a supporting tool of his/her online consumption process in said website. In the end, a trusted website recommendation system increases the user's perceptions regarding its capability to provide benefits, through reliable and suitable recommendations. On the contrary, when trust is deficient, a user will have difficulties in deriving clear benefits from the use of a certain website recommendation system (Wang and Benbasat, 2005). Hence, it is proposed that:

P7: The consumer's trust in a certain website recommendation system will positively affect his/her perceptions about the usefulness of said system.

Finally, the Trust-TAM model for online shopping considers several antecedents, prior to the three key constructs PEOU, PU and Trust in the online vendor. Those could be grouped into the set of variables labelled by Davis, Bagozzi and Warshaw (1989) as "external variables", which can exert an effect on PEOU and PU. In our model, based on the Trust-TAM model's reasoning in this respect, and adapting it to our specific framework, we consider the user's familiarity with recommendation systems, in general, a condition that should influence the user's perception on the ease of use of a certain WS-RS. So, it is proposed that:

P8: The consumer's familiarity with recommendation systems, in general, will positively contribute to his/her perceived ease of use of a certain website recommendation system.

Likewise, when consumers are not familiarized enough with recommendation systems, it is expected that they present higher levels of perceived risk with its use (Wang and Benbasat, 2005), which will in turn negatively influence his/her starting trust beliefs about a certain website recommendation system. Consequently, it is proposed that:

P9: The consumer's familiarity with recommendation systems, in general, will positively influence his/her perceived risk with the use of recommendation systems.

P10: The consumer's perceived risk with the use of recommendation systems, in general, will negatively affect his/her starting trusting beliefs toward a certain website recommendation system.

2. Adaptation of the TPB

Most of the studies focused on the explanation of the adoption and use of information technologies have based on the TAM model and, most recently, as commented above, on the Trust-TAM model. However, such approaches missed interesting variables to explain more exhaustively the user's intention to use and usage of such technologies. In this way, the TPB (Ajzen, 1985; Ajzen, 1989; Ajzen, 1991), as an extension of the TRA, considers the consumer's subjective norms and perceived behavioural control as key elements to explain such intention and use. Recent studies apply the TPB model with good results to understand and predict e-commerce adoption (George, 2004; Pavlou and Fygenson, 2006). Thus, we propose to integrate the elements and relational sequence, from attitude to use, to our conceptual model. Consequently, it acts as a prolongation of the Trust-TAM model we have previously adapted to the specific framework we analyze. Therefore, it is proposed that:

P11: The consumer's intention to use a certain website recommendation system will be positively influenced by, on the one hand [Trust-TAM model elements], his/her (a) trust WS-RS, (b) PU WS-RS and, on the other [TPB elements], his/her (c) subjective norms about the use and, (d) perceived behavioural control of said system.

P12: The consumer's actual usage of a certain website recommendation system will be positively influenced by his/her (a) intention to use it, and (b) the perceived behavioural control of said system.

3. Adaptation of Elements of Flow in Online Environments

The flow concept originally comes from the field of psychology (Csikszentmihalyi, 1975: 1977). It is a mental state that individuals sometimes experience when they are deeply immersed in certain events, objects or activities. This concept has been adapted and widely applied to the Web environment since the mid-90s. In this specific environment, flow state is achieved when the consumer is so deeply involved in the process of navigation that "nothing else seems to matter" (Hoffman & Novak, 1996, p. 57). So, the flow state represents a mental state experienced by an individual during the process of navigation.

In particular, from the seminal paper Hoffman and Novak' (1996) on flow in computer-mediated environments, we have taken and adapted four key constructs to be integrated in our conceptual model: flow, the individual's optimum stimulation level (OSL), his/her level of attention and, finally, his/her perception of how challenging is using a certain WS/RS.

First, the construct OSL could be associated with both cognitive and sensory stimulation that an individual considers as adequate for him/herself (Baumgartner and Steenkamp, 1996). When individuals feel that they have not achieved such desired levels of stimulation, they then tend to develop exploratory behaviours with the aim of fulfilling that mental state by increasing their stimulation (Steenkamp and Baumgartner, 1992). Hence, it is expected that users of a recommendation system will perceive less difficulties in using them, so they would feel less uncomfortable with their use, as they need more stimulation when developing the online consumption process. Likewise, as individuals present higher OSL, their levels of curiosity, variety-seeking, risk taking and exploratory behaviour increase (Baumgartner and Steenkamp, 1996; Steenkamp and Baumgartner, 1992). On the contrary, individuals with low OSL are expected to experience anxiety when navigating (Hoffman and Novak, 1996), especially when they are exposed to a variety of stimuli and information provided by a recommender agent. So, they should see more benefits in the use of recommendation systems when shopping online. Thus, it is proposed that:

P13: The consumer's optimum stimulation level will positively contribute to his/her (a) perceived ease of use and (b) perceived usefulness of a certain website recommendation system.

In psychology, an individual experiences focused attention when his/her attention is centred on a limited stimulus field (Csikszentmihalyi, 1977). In the context of computer mediated environments, it is related to an individual's state of attention to the stimuli of the online navigational process (Hoffman and Novak, 1996). We adapt such a concept to our model as the consumer's attention to the recommendations made by the website recommender agent. Next, let us briefly justify its direct antecedents in the conceptual model. First, as commented above, higher OSL in individuals arouse their curiosity, need for cognitive and sensory stimuli, etc. Consequently, it is expected that consumers will be more willing to accept recommendations, so paying more attention to them, as they experience higher OSL, and vice versa. Second, it is also reasonable to think that the user's attitude toward a certain website recommendation system, as an overall opinion an affective response to said system, should also partially determine his/her degree of attention to its recommendations. Therefore, it is proposed that:

P14: The consumer's level of attention to the recommendations of a certain website recommendation system will be positively influenced by his/her (a) need for cognitive and sensory stimuli (OSL) and (b) overall attitude toward said system.

Let us centre on the direct antecedents and effects of Flow in our model. With respect to the antecedents, two of them, the individual's OSL and his/her level of attention, based on the theoretical analyses made by Hoffman and Novak' (1996), are expected to induce a state of flow in individuals when navigating. Also, it is plausible to think that consumers with high OSL will present higher levels of implication in searching for consumption experiences which satisfy their desired psychological stimulation level (Martínez-López, Luna-Huertas and Martínez, 2006).

With respect to the two other antecedents of Flow, the consumer's perceived behavioural control, one of the particular elements of the TPB model, and the consumer's perceived challenge related to a certain website recommendations system, it is also expected that they positively contribute to his/her flow state when exploring said system. This is an adaptation of the relations hypothesized and tested by previous studies for these variables in the context of human-computer interactions (Ghani and Deshpande, 1994; Ghani, Supnick and Rooney, 1991) and in Web-based environments (Hoffman and Novak, 1996; Novak, Hoffman and Yung, 2000). In essence, the idea is that when a user of a certain website recommendation system feels his/her degree of perceived control of such a system is congruent with the challenge it implies using it, then flow is probably to be experienced. Furthermore, it is more likely to experience flow when both perceived control and challenge are in high states (Ghani and Deshpande, 1994). So, it is proposed that:

P15: The consumer's state of flow when browsing a certain website recommendation system will be positively influenced by his/her (a) need for cognitive and sensory stimuli (OSL), (b) level of attention to the recommendations, (c) perceived behavioural control and (d) challenge with said system.

Finally, flow state has been initially related to the development of exploratory (Ghani and Deshpande, 1994) and experiential behaviours (Hoffman & Novak, 1996; Korzaan, 2003). However, Novak, Hoffman & Duhachek (2003) recently noted that flow state can generate both exploratory/experiential and goal-directed behaviours; though, of course, it is likely to expect a higher degree of influence with experiential behaviours. Thus, it is expected that users who experience flow when developing an online consumption process will interact with the recommender agent. This is why it is proposed that:

P16: An eventual experience of flow state by a consumer when consuming online at a certain website will contribute towards him/her interacting with the recommendation system of said website.

CONCLUSION

This paper presents and discusses a conceptual model to approach, with especial attention to the psychological, subjective dimension of consumer behaviour, the key elements related to the consumer's adoption and use of a particular website recommendation system. Diverse classic consumer theories (TRA and TPB), and particular theories on the adoption of information technologies (TAM, Trust-TAM) and consumer behaviour in a computer-mediated environment (Flow theories) have been integrated in a full model.

Several ideas on RS have been presented and discussed throughout the paper, from which diverse implications can be highlighted. Companies should pay attention to some psychological issues of their websites recommendation systems. First, said systems have to be designed in such a way that customers perceive them as useful and easy to use. So, though website RS may be designed with different levels of technical complexity, it should be considered that customers are not usually characterized by a homogeneous level of Internet expertise. This is an important issue if the role played by PEOU and PU in the use of a website recommendation system is taken into account, which is expected to positively influence the likelihood of shopping. Then, procedures should be clear and easy to understand, in order to facilitate its use. Anyhow, customer's familiarity with the use of recommendation systems to assist online shopping is expected to also positively influence how certain website RS is primarily perceived. It would be recommendable, in this regard, taking as a reference the design of successful and/or broadly used recommendation systems by consumers in the Internet, in order to foster the plausible positive influence of customer's familiarity in PEOU.

Also, the importance of customer's trust in a website RS adoption has been pointed out. In particular, two related questions are needed. First, it is unusual a customer use certain website RS if s(h)e does not present a general state of trust in said website. Thus, online companies should develop brand and website policies which promote customers' trust. This is expected to produce a positive halo effect in their website recommendation systems' trust, the second element to be stressed here.

Likewise, design of website RS should be some challenging for customers, in order to generate certain state of flow when using it to support an online consumption process; this is expected to increase customers' likelihood to use said system. Although, level of stimuli provided by a website RS, in the form of potential interesting choices associated with the primary item sought, should be congruent with the customer's interests and not surpass a threshold of intensity where customers begin to feel anxiety. On the contrary, website RS adoption would not be only negatively affected, but also, by extension, shopping in a company online site. In this regard, it is of help designing recommendation systems which could be easily used and controlled by customers.

In sum, RS can be an important tool to improve online sales of companies, as a consequence of fostering both planned and unplanned shopping in customers. But, it is important firms to pay attention to diverse questions related with the design of said systems, with the aim of getting the customers into a state of favourable mental predisposition to adopt them. This paper has presented and discussed a variety of psychological elements, with an integrative approach, which help to better understand this process. In future researches, we plan to empirical analyze the theoretical propositions presented here.

REFERENCES

Adomavicious, G., & Tuzhilin, A. (2005). Towards the next generation of recommender systems: a survey of the state-of-the art and possible extensions. *IEEE Transactions on Knowledge and Data Engineering, 17*(6), pp- 734-749.

Ahn, H. (2007). Utilizing Popularity Characteristics for Product Recommendation. *International Journal of Electronic Commerce*, *11*(2), 59–80. doi:10.2753/JEC1086-4415110203

Ajzen, I. (1985). From intentions to actions: A theory of planned behaviour. In Kuhl, J., & Beckman, J. (Eds.), *Actioncontrol: From cognition to behaviour.New York* (pp. 11–39). Heidelberg: Springer.Ajzen, I. (1989). Attitude Structure and Behavior. In Pratkanis, A. R., Breckler, S. J., & Greenwald, A. G. (Eds.), *Attitude Structure and Function* (pp. 241–274). Hillsdale, NJ: Lawrence Erlbaum Associates.

Ajzen, I. (1991). The theory of planned behaviour. *Organizational Behavior and Human Decision Processes*, (50): 179–211. doi:10.1016/0749-5978(91)90020-T

Ajzen, I., & Fishbein, M. (1980). *Understanding Attitudes and Predicting Social Behaviour*. Upper Saddle River, NJ: Prentice Hall.

Ansari, A., Essegaier, S., & Kohli, R. (2000). Internet recommendation systems. *JMR, Journal of Marketing Research*, *37*(3), 363–375. doi:10.1509/jmkr.37.3.363.18779

Balabanovic, M., & Shoham, Y. (2007). FAB: Content-based, collaborative recommendation. *Communications of the ACM*, *40*(3), 66–72. doi:10.1145/245108.245124

Baumgartner, H., & Steenkamp, J.-B. E. M. (1996). Exploratory consumer behavior: conceptualization and measurement. *International Journal of Research in Marketing*, *13*, 121–137. doi:10.1016/0167-8116(95)00037-2

Berry, L. L. (1983). Relationship Marketing. In L.L. Berry, G.L. Shostack, and G.D: Upah (eds), *Emerging Perspectives on Services Marketing*, American Marketing Association, Chicago, 25-38.

Blau, P. M. (1964). *Exchange and Power in Social Life*. New York: John Wiley & Sons.

Canny, J. (2002). Collaborative filtering with privacy via factor analysis. *Proceedings of the 25th annual international ACM SIGIR conference on Research and development in information retrieval* (Session: Collaborative Filtering), 238-245.

Cho, Y. H., & Kim, J. K. (2004). Application of Web usage mining and product taxonomy to collaborative recommendations in e-commerce. *Expert Systems with Applications*, *26*(2), 233–246. doi:10.1016/S0957-4174(03)00138-6

Csikszentmihalyi, M. (1975). Play and intrinsic rewards. *Journal of Humanistic Psychology*, *15*(3), 41–63. doi:10.1177/002216787501500306

Csikszentmihalyi, M. (1977). *Beyond boredom and anxiety* (2nd ed.). San Francisco: Jossey-Bass.

Davis, F. D. (1989). Perceived Usefulness. Perceived Ease of Use and User Acceptance of Information Technology. *Management Information Systems Quarterly*, *13*(3), 319–340. doi:10.2307/249008

Davis, F. D., Bagozzi, R. P., & Warshaw, P. R. (1989). User acceptance of computer technology: A comparison of two theoretical models. *Management Science*, *35*(8), 982–1003. doi:10.1287/mnsc.35.8.982

Elliot, M.T., & Speck, P.S. (2005). Factors that affect attitude toward a retail website. *Journal of Marketing Theory and Practice*, Winter, 40-50.

Endo, S., & Kincade, D. H. (2008). Mass customization for long-term relationship development: Why consumers purchase mass customized products again. *Qualitative Market Research: An International Journal*, *11*(3), 275–294. doi:10.1108/13522750810879011

Fishbein, M., & Ajzen, I. (1975). *Belief, Attitude, Intention, and Behavior: An Introduction to Theory and Research*. Reading, MA: Addison-Wesley.

Gefen, D. (2000). E-Commerce: the role of familiarity and trust. *Omega*, *28*(6), 725–737. doi:10.1016/S0305-0483(00)00021-9

Gefen, D., Karahanna, E., & Straub, D. W. (2003). Trust and TAM in Online Shopping: An Integrated Model. *Management Information Systems Quarterly*, *27*(1), 51–90.

Gefen, D., & Straub, D. W. (2000). The Relative Importance of Perceived Ease-of-Use in IS Adoption: A Study of E-Commerce Adoption. *Journal of the Association for Information Systems*, *1*(8), 1–30.

George, J. K. (2004). The theory of planned behavior and Internet purchasing. *Internet Research*, *14*(3), 198–212. doi:10.1108/10662240410542634

Ghani, J. A., & Deshpande, S. P. (1994). Task characteristics and the experience of optimal flow in human-computer interaction. *The Journal of Psychology*, *128*(4), 383–391. doi:10.1080/00223980.1994.9712742

Ghani, J. A., Supnick, R., & Rooney, P. (1991). The experience of flow in computer mediated and in face-to-face groups. In J.I. DeGross, I. Benbasat, G. DeSanctis & C.M. Beath (Eds.), *Proceedings of the 12th International Conference on Information Systems* (pp. 16-18), New York.

Goldberg, D., Nichols, D., Oki, B. M., & Terry, D. (1992). Using collaborative filtering to weave an information tapestry. *Communications of the ACM, 35*(12), 61–70. doi:10.1145/138859.138867

Goldberg, K., Roeder, T., Gupta, D., & Perkins, C. (2001). Eigentaste: A Constant-Time Collaborative Filtering Algorithm. *Information Retrieval, 4*(2), 133–151. doi:10.1023/A:1011419012209

Häubl, G., & Trifts, V. (2000). Consumer Decision Making in Online Shopping Environments: The Effects of Interactive Decision Aids. *Marketing Science, 19*(1), 4–21. doi:10.1287/mksc.19.1.4.15178

Herlocker, J. L., & Konstan, J. A. (2001). Content-independent task-focused recommendation. *IEEE Internet Computing, 5*(6), 40–47. doi:10.1109/4236.968830

Hoffman, D., & Novak, T. (1996). Marketing in hypermedia computer-mediated environments: conceptual foundations. *Journal of Marketing, 60*(July), 50–68. doi:10.2307/1251841

Jarvenpaa, S. L., Tractinsky, N., & Vitale, M. (2000). Consumer trust in an internet store. *Information Technology Management, 1*(1–2), 45–71. doi:10.1023/A:1019104520776

Kenning, P. (2008). The influence of general trust and specific trust on buying behaviour. *International Journal of Retail & Distribution Management, 36*(6), 461–476. doi:10.1108/09590550810873938

Kim, J. K., Cho, Y. H., Kim, W. J., Kim, J. R., & Suh, J. H. (2002). A personalized recommendation procedure for Internet shopping support. *Electronic Commerce Research and Applications, 1*, 301–313. doi:10.1016/S1567-4223(02)00022-4

Kim, Y. S., Yum, B.-J., Song, J., & Kim, S. M. (2005). Development of a recommender system based on navigational and behavioral patterns of customers in e-commerce sites. *Expert Systems with Applications, 28*(2), 381–393. doi:10.1016/j.eswa.2004.10.017

Komiak, S., & Benbasat, I. (2004). Understanding Customer Trust in Agent-Mediated Electronic Commerce, Web-Mediated Electronic Commerce, and Traditional Commerce. *Information Technology Management, 5*(1-2), 181–207. doi:10.1023/B:ITEM.0000008081.55563.d4

Konstan, J. A., Miller, B. N., Maltz, D., Herlocker, J. L., Gordon, L. R., & Riedl, J. (1997). Grouplens: Applying collaborative filtering to usenet news. *Communications of the ACM, 40*(3), 77–87. doi:10.1145/245108.245126

Korzaan, M. L. (2003). Going with the flow: predicting online purchase intentions. *Journal of Computer Information Systems*, (Summer): 25–31.

Lim, K., Sia, C. L., Lee, M. K. O., & Benbasat, I. (2006). Do I Trust You Online, and If So, Will I Buy? An Empirical Study of Two Trust-Building Strategies. *Journal of Management Information Systems, 23*(2), 233–266. doi:10.2753/MIS0742-1222230210

Maes, P. (1994). Agents that reduce work and information overload. *Communications of the ACM, 37*(7), 31–40. doi:10.1145/176789.176792

Maes, P. (1999). Smart commerce: The future of intelligent agents in cyberspace. *Journal of Interactive Marketing, 13*(3), 66–76. doi:10.1002/(SICI)1520-6653(199922)13:3<66::AID-DIR5>3.0.CO;2-C

Martínez-López, F. J., Luna-Huertas, P., & Martínez, F. J. (2006). Motivations for consumption behaviours on the web: a conceptual model based on a holistic approach. *International Journal of Electronic Marketing and Retailing*, *1*(1), 3–20. doi:10.1504/IJEMR.2006.010092

McKnight, D. H., & Chervany, N. L. (2001). What Trust Means in E-Commerce Customer Relationships: An Interdisciplinary Conceptual Typology. *International Journal of Electronic Commerce*, *2*(6), 35–59.

McKnight, D. H., Cummings, L. L., & Chervany, N. L. (1998). Initial trust formation in new organizational relationships. *Academy of Management Review*, *23*(3), 472–490. doi:10.2307/259290

Mild, A., & Reutterer, T. (2003). An improved collaborative filtering approach for predicting cross-category purchases based on binary market basket data. *Journal of Retailing and Consumer Services*, *10*(3), 123–133. doi:10.1016/S0969-6989(03)00003-1

Mooney, R. J., & Roy, L. (2000). Content-based book recommending using learning for text categorization. *Proceedings of the fifth ACM Conference on Digital Libraries*, 195-204.

Morgan, R. M., & Hunt, S. (1994). The Commitment-Trust Theory of Relationship Marketing. *Journal of Marketing*, *58*(3), 20–38. doi:10.2307/1252308

Novak, T., Hoffman, D., & Duhachek, A. (2003). The influence of goal-directed and experiential activities on online flow experiences. *Journal of Consumer Psychology*, *13*(1/2), 3–16.

Novak, T., Hoffman, D., & Yung, Y. (2000). Measuring the customer experience in online environments: A structural modelling approach. *Marketing Science,* 19 (1: Special Issue), 22-42.

Pavlou, P. A., & Fygenson, M. (2006). Understanding and predicting electronic commerce adoption: an extension of the Theory of Planned Behaviour. *Management Information Systems Quarterly*, *30*(1), 115–143.

Pazzani, M. J., & Billsus, D. (2007). Content-based recommendation systems. In P. Brusilovsky, A. Kobsa, & W. Nejdl (Eds.): *The Adaptive Web*. (LNCS 4321, pp. 325-341) New York: Springer

Schafer, J. B., Frankowski, D., Herlocker, J., & Sen, S. (2007). Collaborative filtering recommender systems. In P. Brusilovsky, A. Kobsa, & W. Nejdl (Eds.), The Adaptive Web. LNCS 4321, Springer-Verlag, 291-324.

Schafer, J. B., Konstan, J. A., & Riedl, J. (2001). E-Commerce Recommendation Applications. *Data Mining and Knowledge Discovery*, *5*, 115–153. doi:10.1023/A:1009804230409

Senecal, S., & Nantel, J. (2004). The influence of online product recommendation on consumers' online choices. *Journal of Retailing*, *80*, 159–169. doi:10.1016/j.jretai.2004.04.001

Steenkamp, J.-B. E. M., & Baumgartner, H. (1992). The role of optimum stimulation level in exploratory consumer behavior. *The Journal of Consumer Research*, *19*, 434–488. doi:10.1086/209313

Teo, T. S. H., & Liu, J. (2007). Consumer trust in e-commerce in the United States, Singapore and China. *Omega*, *35*, 22–38. doi:10.1016/j.omega.2005.02.001

Urban, G. L., Sultan, F., & Qualls, W. J. (2000). Placing Trust at the Center of Your Internet Strategy. *Sloan Management Review*, *42*(1), 39–48.

Wang, W., & Benbasat, I. (2005). Trust in and adoption of online recommendation agents. *Journal of the Association for Information Systems*, *6*(3), 72–100.

Xiao, B., & Benbasat, I. (2007). E-commerce product recommendation Agents: Use, Characteristics, and Impact. *Management Information Systems Quarterly*, *31*(1), 137–209.

Ying, Y., Feinberg, F., & Wedel, M. (2006). Leveraging missing ratings to improve online recommendation systems. *JMR, Journal of Marketing Research*, *XLIII*(August), 355–365. doi:10.1509/jmkr.43.3.355

Zablah, A. R., Bellenger, D. N., & Johnston, W. J. (2004). An evaluation of divergent perspectives on customer relationship management: towards a common understanding of an emerging phenomenon. *Industrial Marketing Management*, *33*(6), 475–489. doi:10.1016/j.indmarman.2004.01.006

Chapter 21
Fairness in Virtual Teams: A Construct of E-Organizational Justice

Constant D. Beugré
Delaware State University, USA

ABSTRACT

Using organizational justice as a conceptual framework, this chapter discusses the importance of fairness in managing virtual teams. It introduces a new construct, e-organizational justice, defined as employee perceptions of fairness in virtual work environments. The chapter also posits that fairness is essential to building and maintaining the cohesiveness and effectiveness of virtual teams. The chapter ends with a discussion on e-organizational justice's implications for further research and management practice.

INTRODUCTION

The phenomenon of managing work that is distributed over geographical distance is not new but is increasing in both frequency and intentionality as a function of globalization and knowledge-centric strategies (MacDuffie, 2007, p. 549). Distributed work entails the loss of physical proximity (Alexander, 1997; MacDuffie, 2007). This lack of physical proximity often leads to reduced social interactions that may result in feelings of isolation and change the interactions and relationships between the parties involved (Alexander, 1997). One of the challenges that such work environments pose to managers is how to effectively manage employees when they are not 'at home' or when they do not physically interact with them.

DOI: 10.4018/978-1-61692-880-3.ch021

More than a decade ago, Charles Handy (1995) posed an intriguing question related to managers' ability to supervise employees in a virtual work environment. He asked specifically: "How do you manage people whom you don't see?" This question is still relevant today to the extent that virtual work is an important and growing phenomenon in modern organizations (Wiesenfeld, Raguram, & Garud, 2001). To illustrate the ubiquity of virtual work in today's organizations, Goldsborough (2000) notes that more than 51% of North American companies have virtual programs and almost two-thirds of Fortune 1000 companies offer employees an opportunity to work virtually. For example, PricewaterhouseCoopers, which has 45,000 employees in 120 countries, uses virtual teams to bring employees from around the globe 'together' for a week or two to prepare for a particular client (Bell & Kozlowski, 2002, p. 15).

The management of virtual teams faces two main challenges: (a) developing trust and (b) establishing and maintaining effective communication patterns. Trust is an antecedent of justice defined as employee perceptions of fairness (Greenberg, 1987, 1990). When employees are fairly treated by their supervisors, they are likely to trust them. However, when employees are unfairly treated by their supervisors, they are less likely to trust them. Likewise, effective patterns of communication create a sense of fair treatment. Thus, managing virtual work represents one of the key challenges facing managers in the information age (Wiesenfeld et al., 2001). A particularly important aspect that organizational researchers and managers have yet to address is how to ensure that employees are treated fairly when they do not interact face-to-face with their managers and/or peers? Moreover, what does it mean to be fair in a virtual work environment? And, if fairness is important in virtual work environments, how can virtual teams develop a collective sense of fairness?

The purpose of this chapter is to address these questions. In so doing, the chapter proposes a new construct, *e-organizational justice*—defined as *employee perceptions of fairness in virtual work environments*. Assessing fairness in virtual teams has both theoretical and practical implications. From the theoretical standpoint, such a perspective could expand the study of organizational justice to virtual work environments. Although much attention has been devoted to the study of trust, less research has focused on fairness in virtual work environments (Kurkland & Egan, 1999, Hakonen & Lipponen, 2008, being an exception). While Hakonen and Lipponen (2008) analyzed the relationship between procedural justice and identification within virtual teams, Kurland and Egan (1999) focused on fairness in telecommuting, a particular form of distributed work but quite different from work in a virtual team environment. The vast majority of the research on organizational justice has occurred at the individual level, leading Colquitt, Noe, and Jackson (2002) to note that the failure to consider team contexts represents an important gap in the justice literature. It is only recently that it has moved to the team level (see Mossholder, Bennett, & Martin, 1998; Naumann & Bennett, 2000). Expanding the concept of justice to virtual teams is particularly important because team justice is likely to lead to positive outcomes, such as team member satisfaction (Philips et al., 2001) and team performance (Dayan & Colak, 2008).

From the practical standpoint, an e-organizational justice perspective could provide guidelines for managers on how to effectively ensure fairness in a work environment where they can't observe and/or physically interact with employees. Very often, managers believe that working in virtual environments does not require interpersonal skills. This is particularly important because information and communication technologies often open the possibility of less cohesion in the work environment (Chudoba, Wynn, Lu, & Watson-Manheim, 2005). The chapter is organized as follows. First, I review the extant literature on virtual teams with a particular emphasis on elements that could prove useful for the present analysis. Next, I discuss fairness in co-located teams. I then introduce the construct of e-organizational justice. I close the chapter with a discussion on the implications of the construct of e-organizational justice for further research and management practice.

UNDERSTANDING VIRTUAL TEAMS

Expressions, such as distributed teams, global virtual teams, and technology-supported distributed teams are used to characterize virtual teams. The most widely used definition of virtual teams is the one proposed by Townsend, DeMarie, and Hendrickson (1998) more than a decade ago. They define virtual teams as "groups of geographically dispersed coworkers that are assembled using a combination of telecommunications and information technologies to accomplish an organizational task" (Townsend et al., 1998, p. 18). Virtual teams also consist of cross-functional members working on highly interdependent tasks and sharing responsibility for team outcomes (Malhotra, Majchrzak, & Rosen, 2007). In defining virtual teams, the most commonly noted boundaries are those of geography, time, and organization (Martins, Gilson, & Maynard, 2004).

In this chapter, I expand the definition of virtual teams to include both *global virtual teams* (teams whose members are located in different countries) and *domestic virtual teams* (teams whose members operate within the same country). A company may rely on both global virtual teams (teams dispersed across countries) and domestic virtual teams (teams dispersed across cities, regions, or states within the same country). Maznevski and Chudoba (2000) defined global virtual teams as groups that (a) are identified by their organization(s) and members as a team; (b) are responsible for making and/or implementing decisions important to the organization's global strategy; (c) use technology-supported communication substantially more than face-to-face communication; and (d) work and live in different countries (p. 473). In virtual teams, spatial distance between organizations and their members may reduce individuals' contact with the organization, the visibility of their organizational membership, and their exposure to the organizational structures and processes that facilitate self-categorization as organizational members (Wiesenfeld et al., 2001).

Research on virtual teams, shows that they have both advantages and disadvantages. By using information and communication technologies, virtual teams provide several advantages, such as saving time, travel expenses, providing access to experts, enabling organizations to hire and retain the best people regardless of their physical location (Cascio, 2000). Virtual teams can also help to reduce team process losses associated with stereotyping, personality conflicts, power, politics, and cliques commonly experienced by face-to-face teams (Kirkman, Rosen, Gibson, Tesluk, & McPherson, 2002). Because of these advantages, virtual teams are ubiquitous in today's work environment. A recent survey by the Gartner Group found that more than 60% of professional employees in the United States work in virtual teams (Kanawattanachai & Yoo, 2002). Virtual teams provide an effective structural mechanism for handling the increased travel, time, coordination, and costs associated with bringing together geographically, temporally, and functionally dispersed employees to work on a common task (Martins et al., 2004).

The advantages offered by virtual teams, however, should not preclude the various challenges that they pose to managers and organizations. As distance increases, both communication and social interactions decrease. Although this may also be true for co-located teams, it is exacerbated by 'virtualness.' Virtualness refers to the degree to which the team uses computer-mediated communications to perform its main tasks. A team's extent of virtualness may vary depending on the nature of the task, technological resources, and members' skills and capabilities (Martins et al., 2004). Physical proximity in the workplace has some advantages including improved performance, positive attitudes, commitment, team contributions, and face-to-face social interactions. "Information and communication technologies eliminate nonlinguistic cues that put people at ease or draw out their ideas and restricts spontaneous social activities" (McDuffie, 2007, p. 562). Loss of proximity implies the potential loss of these benefits. The lack of physical interaction is the major disadvantage of virtual teams (Cascio, 2000). Hence, organizations should develop alternative strategies to make distributive work effective. Before discussing justice or fairness in virtual teams, (I use the two terms interchangeably as is often the case in the organizational justice literature), I review the extant literature on fairness in co-located teams.

FAIRNESS IN CO-LOCATED TEAMS

The concept of organizational justice has been primarily studied as an individual-level concept. It is only recently that it has been expanded to the group-level of analysis (Mossholder et al., 1998; Naumann & Bennett, 2000; Colquitt et al., 2002, Roberson & Colquitt, 2005, Roberson, 2006a, 2006b; Li & Cropanzano, 2009). Mossholder et al. (1998) were the first to explore fairness perceptions at the group-level of analysis. This concept was further expanded by Naumann and Bennett (2000) who found that group cohesion contributed to the formation of justice climate defined as shared perceptions of a work unit treatment by organizational authorities (Mossholder et al., 1998; Naumann & Bennett, 2000, Colquitt et al., 2002). Roberson (2006b) suggests that group members' perceptions of justice are subject to social influence through social comparisons and collective sense making about their experiences.

Applied to groups or teams, fairness refers to distinct group-level cognitions about how a work group as a whole is treated (Naumann & Bennett, 2000). Mossholder et al. (1998) and Nauman and Bennett (2000) equate the formation of a group-level sense of justice to the development of justice climate. They specifically argue that because group members have the opportunity to be exposed to the same policies and procedures as well as to the same leader, they tend to develop a shared sense of how they are treated. Roberson and Colquitt (2005) note that shared team justice refers to the shared perceptions of team members about how the team as a whole is treated (p. 596). These shared experiences serve to form a common sense of fairness. Naumann and Bennett (2000) found that work group cohesion and the visibility of supervisors in demonstrating procedural justice each contributed significantly to the development of procedural justice agreement.

Virtual teams share a number of properties commonly associated with traditionally conceived teams (Hinds & Bailey, 2003). Hence, the study of fairness within virtual teams could benefit a great deal from research and knowledge accumulated in analyzing traditional teams. Organizational justice is generally construed as a tri-dimensional concept including distributive justice (Adams, 1965), procedural justice (Thibaut & Walker, 1975; Lind & Tyler, 1988) and interactional justice (Bies & Moag, 1986; Cropanzano & Greenberg, 1997). Whereas distributive justice refers to the fairness of outcomes distribution, procedural justice concerns the fairness of the formal procedures underlying outcomes distribution (Lind & Tyler, 1988). Interactional justice refers to the fairness of interpersonal treatment (Bies & Moag, 1986).

Greenberg (1993), Beugré (1998) and Colquitt (2001) introduced a fourth dimension of justice—*informational justice,* which is in fact a sub-dimension of interactional justice. Greenberg (1993) considers informational justice as a social determinant of procedural justice. Informational justice refers to the social determinants of procedural justice, the adequacy of the information used to explain how decisions are made, and the thoroughness of the account (Beugré, 1998, p. 38). The benefits of information in fostering feelings of fairness have been underscored by several authors, such as Bies and Moag (1986) and Greenberg (1994). Bies and Moag (1986) found that providing clear and speedy feedback to rejected job applicants reduced the pain of the rejection and created a sense of fairness. Likewise, Greenberg (1994) demonstrated that the provision of information about a smoking ban eased the effect of this measure and elicited a sense of fairness from the recipients. These positive effects of informational justice could be replicated in virtual teams. In such settings, employees do not often have the opportunity to engage in face-to-face social interactions with one another. However, effectively sharing information with other team members and team leaders could help create a sense of fairness.

Recent research on fairness at the team level has demonstrated the benefits of shared perceptions of justice. Phillips, Douthill, and Hyland (2001) note that if a team member perceives leader behaviors to be fair, the member is less likely to feel attached to and want to remain a member of that team. The authors also found that procedural justice perceptions were positively related to both attachment to the team and satisfaction with the leader independent of the level of team decision accuracy. These findings are consistent with previous conceptualizations of justice as a symbol of one's standing within a group (Lind & Tyler, 1988). Fair treatment indicates that the person is a valued member of the group, whereas unfair treatment indicates otherwise. Following this line of reasoning, Lind and Tyler (1988) hypothesized that "procedural justice judgments should have strong effects on group cohesiveness and loyalty because fair procedures will reassure members that their interests will be protected and advanced through group membership" (p. 227).

However, shared perceptions of fairness in teams may be impeded by several factors, such as team diversity and team dispersion. Roberson and Colquitt (2005) note that team member diversity may constrain the development of shared team justice. Likewise, Colquitt and Jackson (2006) note that when a team is diverse, consistency and bias suppression, two of the six principles of procedural justice identified by Leventhal (1980) become more important. Colquitt et al. (2002) found that team diversity was associated with more disagreements over procedural justice levels. In this chapter, I use the four dimensions of distributive, procedural, interactional, and informational justice to explain the role of fairness in virtual teams.

THE CONSTRUCT OF E-ORGANIZATIONAL JUSTICE

Justice in virtual teams may concern three levels of analysis: (1) how individual members are treated by their managers and other team members, (2) how the team as an entity is treated by the team leader, and (3) how the team as a collective is treated by other teams of the same organization. Thus, it may occur at both the intra and interunit levels. In virtual teams, members do not interact face-to-face with managers or peers. Yet, they may experience the sense of fairness when they consider their electronic interactions with their managers or other team members. For instance, team members may wonder whether they receive fair outcomes based on their contributions. They may also wonder whether the processes underlying the distribution of these outcomes are fair and whether they are treated with respect and dignity, and receive accurate and timely information. Virtual team members may consider the effectiveness of their electronic communications with managers and peers as a means to judge the fairness of these computer-based interactions.

There is relatively little theory regarding the effects of virtual work and even less empirical research exploring this phenomenon (DeSanctis & Monge, 1999). Kurkland and Egan (1999) found that employees were concerned that their physical absence from their office's social network impeded the fairness of their organizational outcomes (distributive justice), the fairness of the processes governing their work (procedural justice) and the interpersonal relationships with colleagues and/or managers (interactional justice). This is consistent with Conner's (2003) contention that workers in virtual work environments do not have readily available referents who can be used as comparison others. Thus, the process of social comparison is more problematic in virtual work environments than in traditional ones.

Studying fairness in virtual teams calls for an important question that I examine in this section.

How can virtual team members develop a collective sense of fairness? Answering this question is important if one is to study fairness in virtual teams. The existence of a team requires sharing common values and having a sense of identity as a team. In virtual teams, communication is essential to the formation of shared perceptions of justice. All virtual team members are likely to be exposed to the same policies, procedures and practices. They are also likely to be exposed to the same type of information. Hence, they could overtime develop a sense of fairness of these processes and procedures. Figure 1 illustrates the importance of fairness in virtual teams. Three types of computer-mediated communications provide clues to team members' perceptions of fairness: (a) computer-mediated communications involving the virtual team leader and the virtual team members, (b) computer-meditated communications among virtual team members, and (c) computer-mediated communications between virtual teams. Because the virtual team context limits physical social interactions, computer-mediated communications help to gauge virtual team members' perceptions of fairness. These shared perceptions of fairness are observed at four levels, distributive, procedural, interactional, and informational. Justice considerations are important because they lead to attitudinal responses that are conducive to virtual team performance. Such attitudinal responses include identification with the virtual team, helping behavior and team cohesion to name but a few.

Figure 1 also indicates the existence of moderating variables, such as the degree of geographical dispersion, team diversity, the degree of virtualness and team interdependence. To the extent that team members are geographically dispersed, they may have few opportunities for social interactions. Limited social interactions may reduce the likelihood of forming shared perceptions of justice. Another moderating variable, team diversity as accentuated by cultural differences, especially for global teams, may influence the relationship between computer-mediated communications and shared perceptions of fairness. For instance, members of a virtual team located in India may have different views about what fairness entails compared to members located in the United States. Such cultural differences may impede the formation of shared perceptions of justice. In such circumstances, what is fair for an Indian team member may be entirely different from what is fair for his or her American counterpart. In the following lines, I explore the extent to which fairness may occur at the distributive, procedural, interactional and informational justice levels in virtual teams.

Distributive Justice in Virtual Teams

As defined earlier, distributive justice refers to the fairness of outcomes distribution. In the context of virtual teams, how can such fairness issues arise? To answer this question, one needs to look at the outcomes that are at stake when employees work in virtual teams. In a virtual team environment, employees still need to perform their tasks and receive outcomes dependent on their performance and contribution to the team. This is not different from working in co-located teams. Such outcomes may include compensation, opportunities for promotion as well as recognition for a job well done. How then, do fairness issues arise at this level? There are at least three areas in which distributive justice may be of concern to virtual team members: (1) compensation, (2) performance evaluation, and (3) opportunities for promotion. In virtual teams, assessing the direct link between an employee's contribution and the team's performance may be cumbersome to the extent that the manager may not be able to have adequate information related to team members' effective contributions. He or she may then rely on imperfect information to assess an employee's compensation.

Such limited information could have detrimental effects on promotion decisions. If tracking individual performance is difficult in virtual teams,

Figure 1.

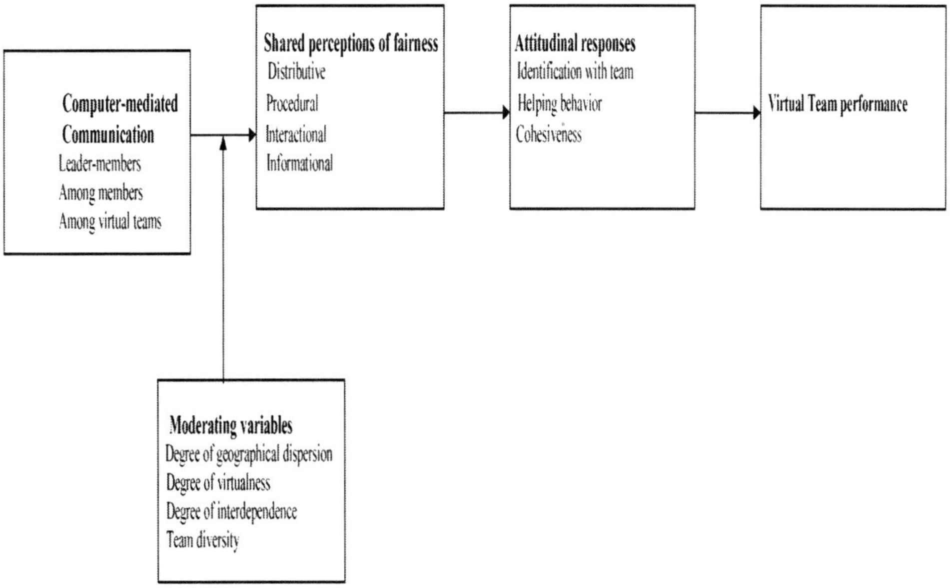

then it may prevent adequate recognition of personal efforts thereby diluting individual achievements. Thus, decisions related to performance evaluation and promotion may be challenging in virtual teams. Compensation is an important issue in co-located teams. In an empirical study conducted on self-management work teams, Kirkman, Shapiro, Novelli, and Brett (1996) found that 97% of distributive justice concerns revolved around issues of compensation, performance, and career. Specifically, employees expressed great concern about working hard and not being adequately rewarded for their efforts. These concerns may be expanded to virtual teams. However, managers may devise strategies, such as considering the output of each team member or allowing team members to rate each other on important goals to measure their performance.

Procedural Justice in Virtual Teams

Procedural justice in virtual teams entails an understanding of the processes governing team functioning. When virtual teams are formed, managers should ensure that all members understand the procedures and policies governing their functioning. The fairness of the process may start at the team formation, particularly when team members are selected and assigned their specific tasks. Criteria related to selection and assignments should be clear and unequivocal. Overall, procedures and policies affect employees simultaneously. As Mossholder et al. (1998, p. 132) put it, "depending on the demands of their particular environments, units may feel that policies and procedures thwart their attempts to service internal or external customers, constrain innovation within the unit, or increase social and economic costs to the unit." A lack of understanding of this process may lead to procedural injustice. This process should also allow opportunities for team members to voice their opinions. Voicing one's opinions in virtual teams would involve the use of technology. Hence, virtual team members could be allowed to express their disagreements by sending e-mail messages to their managers or other team members. Team members could also be allowed to voice their opinions by using appropriate websites developed in advance by the manager or the organization.

Leventhal (1980) suggested that procedures should have the following six characteristics to be considered fair: (1) consistent across people and time, (2) based on accurate information, (3) unbiased, (4) correctable, (5) representative of all groups' concerns, and (6) ethical. Applying these rules in virtual teams would require the use of computer-mediated communications. Fostering procedural justice in virtual teams is important because meta-analytical evidence and empirical research show that procedural fairness is positively associated with organizational outcomes, such as job satisfaction, organizational commitment, trust, citizenship behavior and job performance (Korsgaard, Schweiger, & Sapienza, 1995; Colquitt, Conlon, Wesson, Porter, & Ng, 2001; Colquitt et al., 2002, Phillips et al., 2001; Roberson, 2006a, 2006b). Korsgaard et al. (1995) demonstrated that procedural justice led to team decisions and trust in the leader. Likewise, recent research shows positive effects of procedural justice on the organizational outcomes described above at the group level (Colquitt, 2004; Colquitt et al., 2002, Phillips et al., 2001; Roberson, 2006a, 2006b). In assessing the role of procedural justice in new product development processes, Dayan and Colak (2008) found that climate level—defined as team members' perceptions of procedural justice was significantly related to new product creativity and speed to market. In other words, teams treated fairly were able to develop more creative products in a relatively faster time than teams that did not receive fair treatment.

Interactional Justice in Virtual Teams

Because of geographical dispersion, social interactions are very limited in virtual teams. Thus, virtual team members should devise strategies to compensate for the lack of physical proximity. Thus, to assess interactional fairness, team members would use technological cues, such as the speed with which their messages are answered and the tone used in these messages. There are some unique features of e-mail communication that may influence the dynamics of interaction between individual group members (Naquin, Kurtzberg, & Belkin, 2008). Because e-mail is text only and does not include body language as well as oral communication clues, it is difficult to assess how one is interpersonally treated using this medium of communication. However, the tone used in an e-mail message may serve as a cue that may reveal whether a team member is treated with respect and dignity by the team leader or peers. The tone of an e-mail message can be used as a heuristic to gauge interactional justice.

Organizations often used virtual teams that are geographically dispersed and yet communicate with one another on common tasks. Such relations between teams may elicit a sense of fairness to the extent that team members located in one country may feel unfairly treated by those located in another country. For example, team members located in an emerging country may express feelings that their counterparts in a developed one act in a condescending manner. Metiu (2006) found that status was both an input and an output in intergroup relations. In studying the relationships between US and Indian software development teams, the author found that the US high status team often refused to fully engage with the low-status Indian team. Such reluctance can reduce communication between geographically distributed teams and lead to perceptions of unfairness.

Informational Justice in Virtual Teams

Providing information is a key aspect of virtual work environments. Thus, informational justice is an important component of e-organizational justice. Information is fair when it is timely, accurate, and relevant. Providing outdated, inaccurate or irrelevant information may be considered unfair. Thus, informational justice in a virtual team may relate more to the characteristics of the information than to issues of policies and procedures. Informational justice would also occur in virtual teams when members rely on past electronic interactions with the team leader and/or other team members. In discussing traditional team building, Jarvenpaa, Knoll, and Leidner (1998) note that team members make their assessment of others on the basis of past history, namely, others' track record or recent performance in a team. Such assessment is highly important in virtual teams because of the reduced level of 'physical' social interactions. Virtual team members must be cognizant of the importance of providing timely accounts of work deliverables and offer feedback on the contributions of others (Bergiel, Bergiel, & Blasmeier, 2008). The authors argue that daily communications between the team leader and individual team members is the glue that holds a virtual team together.

DISCUSSION/IMPLICATIONS

The construct of e-organizational justice developed in this chapter has implications for both research and management practice. I discussed these implications in the following lines.

Directions for Future Research

Expanding the concept of organizational justice to virtual teams can pave the way for empirical investigations and further theorizing. Three interesting research areas could derive from this conceptual analysis: (1) How do virtual team members form justice judgments? (2) How do virtual team members form a collective sense of justice and (3) Are shared perceptions of justice more prevalent within intraunit virtual teams than between interunit virtual teams? Addressing these three questions requires empirical investigations. Organizational scholars could assess the conditions and factors influencing justice judgments within virtual teams. For example, they could survey virtual team members to identify the factors that they consider in making judgments of fairness or unfairness. The model presented in Figure 1 indicates that computer-based communications could facilitate the emergence of shared perceptions of justice. The extent to which this is so could be empirically tested. For instance, researchers could determine the impact of the frequency of computer-based communications on virtual team members' identification with the teams, virtual team cohesiveness or helping behavior.

Organizational scholars could also ascertain whether virtual team members are able to develop shared perceptions of fairness. They could determine whether there is some degree of consensus among virtual team members concerning what is fair or unfair. One may anticipate that homogeneity in regard to what constitutes fair treatment may be more prevalent in domestic virtual teams as compared to global virtual teams. The extent to which variables, such as the degree of virtualness, the degree of interdependence between virtual team members, the degree of geographical dispersion and team diversity act as moderators of the relationship between computer-mediated communications and shared perceptions of justice in virtual teams, warrants empirical inquiry. Knowledge gleaned from such research could provide valuable guidelines for the effective use of virtual teams in organizations.

Implications for Management Practice

The construct of e-organizational justice considers fairness as a strategy to counter the negative impact of distance on virtual team effectiveness. Treating virtual team members fairly could help achieve shared understanding, which in turn could lead to shared identity. Managers would need to set expectations about the communication process in virtual teams. They should determine what types of tone are appropriate in sending electronic messages to other members. Once such norms are set, they should be adequately communicated to virtual team members. Managers should themselves pay particular attention when communicating with team members. Team leaders need to communicate effectively with team members and provide detailed responses to their electronic messages.

Managers could also use a balanced scorecard in assessing the performance of virtual team members. Building such a balanced scorecard requires that expectations for each team member be made clear. The balanced scorecard could provide a relatively objective and standardized basis for the allocation of team-level rewards (Malhotra et al., 2007). In a study aimed at exploring leadership in virtual teams, Malhotra et al. (2007) report the observation of a virtual team member in the following terms. "The quickest way to build trust in a virtual team is to play fair and deliver on your promises." This quote highlights the role of fairness as an important element for the cohesiveness and performance of virtual teams. Fairness is also important because virtual teams are composed of individuals representing a rich diversity of stakeholders, experiences, functions, organizations, decision making styles, and interests (Malhotra et al., 2007, p. 63).

CONCLUSION

In the present chapter, I have introduced and discussed the construct of e-organizational justice. This construct can be used to study fairness in virtual teams, telecommuting and other work environments that span over geographical distances and rely mostly on information and communication technologies. Although previous research has discussed the role of trust, identification and leadership on the effectiveness of virtual teams, very few empirical investigations as well as conceptual frameworks on the role of fairness have been undertaken. Thus, this chapter contributes to the extant literature on the development of strategies to enhance the effectiveness of virtual work environments. The examination of justice in teams contributes to the evolution of justice theory and provides an opportunity for a more comprehensive knowledge of the meaning and operation of justice (Roberson & Colquitt, 2005, p. 604).

REFERENCES

Adams, S. J. (1965). Inequity in social exchange. In Berkowitz, L. (Ed.), *Advances in Social Experimental Psychology* (*Vol. 2*, pp. 267–299). New York: Academic Press. doi:10.1016/S0065-2601(08)60108-2

Alexander, M. (1997). Getting grips with the virtual organization. *Long Range Planning*, *30*(1), 122–124. doi:10.1016/S0024-6301(96)00122-7

Bell, B. S., & Kozlowski, S. J. (2002). A typology of virtual teams: Implications for effective leadership. *Group & Organization Management*, *17*(1), 14–46. doi:10.1177/1059601102027001003

Bergiel, B. J., Bergiel, E. B., & Balsmeier, P. W. (2008). Nature of virtual teams: A summary of their advantages and disadvantages. *Management Research News*, *31*(2), 99–110. doi:10.1108/01409170810846821

Beugré, C. D. (1998). *Managing fairness in organizations*. Westport, CT: Quorum Books.Bies, R. J., & Moag, J. S. (1986). Interactional justice: Communication criteria of fairness. In Lewicki, R. J., Sheppard, B. H., & Bazerman, M. H. (Eds.), *Research on negotiation in organizations* (*Vol. 1*, pp. 43–55). Greenwich, CT: JAI Press.

Cascio, W. F. (2000). Managing a virtual workplace. *The Academy of Management Executive*, *14*, 81–90.

Chudoba, K. M., Wynn, E., Lu, M., & Watson-Manheim, M. B. (2005). How virtual are we? Measuring virtuality and understanding its impact in a global organization. *Information Systems Journal*, *15*, 279–306. doi:10.1111/j.1365-2575.2005.00200.x

Colquitt, J. A. (2001). On the dimensionality of organizational justice: A construct validation of a measure. *The Journal of Applied Psychology*, *86*, 386–400. doi:10.1037/0021-9010.86.3.386

Colquitt, J. A. (2004). Does the justice of the one interact with the justice of the many? Reactions to procedural justice in teams. *The Journal of Applied Psychology*, *89*(4), 633–646. doi:10.1037/0021-9010.89.4.633

Colquitt, J. A., Conlon, D. E., Wesson, M. J., Porter, C. O. L. H., & Ng, K. Y. (2001). Justice at the millennium: A meta-analytic review of 25 years of organizational justice research. *The Journal of Applied Psychology*, *86*, 425–445. doi:10.1037/0021-9010.86.3.425

Colquitt, J. A., & Jackson, C. L. (2006). Justice in teams: The context sensitivity of justice rules across individual and team contexts. *Journal of Applied Social Psychology*, *36*, 868–899.

Colquitt, J. A., Noe, R. A., & Jackson, C. L. (2002). Justice in teams: Antecedents and consequences of procedural justice climate. *Personnel Psychology*, *55*, 83–109. doi:10.1111/j.1744-6570.2002.tb00104.x

Conner, D. S. (2003). Social comparison in virtual work environments: An examination of contemporary referent selection. *Journal of Occupational and Organizational Psychology*, *76*, 133–147. doi:10.1348/096317903321208925

Cropanzano, R., & Greenberg, J. (1997). Progress in organizational justice: Tunneling through the maze. In Cooper, C. L., & Robertson, I. T. (Eds.), *International Review of Industrial and Organizational Psychology* (pp. 317–372). New York: John Wiley & Sons.

Dayan, M., & Colak, M. (2008). The role of procedural justice in the new product development process. *European Journal of Innovation Management*, *11*(2), 199–218. doi:10.1108/14601060810869866

DeSanctis, G., & Monge, P. (1999). Communication processes for virtual organizations. *Organization Science*, *10*, 693–703. doi:10.1287/orsc.10.6.693

Goldsborough, R. (2000). Making telecommuting work. *Commercial Law Bulletin*, *15*, 34–35.

Greenberg, J. (1987). A taxonomy of organizational justice theories. *Academy of Management Review*, *12*, 9–22. doi:10.2307/257990

Greenberg, J. (1990). Organizational justice: Yesterday, today, and tomorrow. *Journal of Management*, *16*, 399–432. doi:10.1177/014920639001600208

Greenberg, J. (1993). The social side of fairness: Interpersonal and informational classes of organizational justice. In Cropanzano, R. (Ed.), *Justice in the workplace* (pp. 79–103). Mahwah, NJ: Lawrence Erlbaum Associates.

Greenberg, J. (1994). Using socially fair treatment to promote acceptance of a work site smoking ban. *The Journal of Applied Psychology*, *79*, 288–297. doi:10.1037/0021-9010.79.2.288

Hakanen, M., & Lipponen, J. (2008). Procedural justice and identification with virtual teams: The moderating role of face-to-face meetings and geographical dispersion. *Social Justice Research*, *21*(2), 164–178. doi:10.1007/s11211-008-0070-3

Handy, C. (1995). Trust and the virtual organization. *Harvard Business Review*, (May-June): 40–50.

Hinds, P. J., & Bailey, D. E. (2003). Out of sight out of sync: Understanding conflict in distributed teams. *Organization Science*, *14*, 615–632. doi:10.1287/orsc.14.6.615.24872

Jarvenpaa, S., Knoll, K., & Leidner, D. (1998). Is anybody out there? Antecedents of trust in global virtual teams. *Journal of Management Information Systems*, *14*(4), 29–64.

Kanawattanachai, P., & Yoo, Y. (2002). Dynamic nature of trust in teams. *The Journal of Strategic Information Systems*, *11*, 187–213. doi:10.1016/S0963-8687(02)00019-7

Kirkman, B. L., Rosen, B., Gibson, C. B., Testluk, P. E., & McPherson, S. O. (2002). Five challenges of virtual team success: Lessons from Sabre, Inc. *The Academy of Management Executive*, *16*(2), 67–79.

Kirkman, B. L., Shapiro, D. L., Novelli, L. Jr, & Brett, J. M. (1996). Employee concerns regarding self-managing work teams: A multidimensional justice perspective. *Social Justice Research*, *9*, 47–67. doi:10.1007/BF02197656

Korsgaard, M. A., Schweiger, D. M., & Sapienza, H. J. (1995). Building commitment, attachment, and trust in strategic decision-making teams: The role of procedural justice. *Academy of Management Journal*, *38*, 60–84. doi:10.2307/256728

Kurkland, N. B., & Egan, T. D. (1999). Telecommuting: Justice and control in the virtual organization. *Organization Science*, *10*(4), 500–513. doi:10.1287/orsc.10.4.500

Leventhal, G. S. (1980). What should be done with equity theory? In Gergen, K. J., Greenberg, M. S., & Willis, R. H. (Eds.), *Social Exchange: Advances in Theory and Research* (pp. 27–55). New York: Plenum Press.

Li, A., & Cropanzano, R. (2009). Fairness at the group level: Justice climate and intraunit justice climate. *Journal of Management*, *35*(3), 564–599. doi:10.1177/0149206308330557

Lind, E. A., & Tyler, T. R. (1988). *The social psychology of procedural justice*. New York: Plenum Press.

Malhotra, A., Majchrzak, A., & Rosen, B. (2007). Leading virtual teams. *The Academy of Management Perspectives*, *21*(1), 60–70.

Martins, L. L., Gilson, L. L., & Maynard, M. T. (2004). Virtual teams: What do we know and where do we go from here? *Journal of Management*, *30*(6), 805–835. doi:10.1016/j.jm.2004.05.002

Maznevski, M. L., & Chudoba, K. M. (2000). Bridging space over time: Global virtual team dynamic and effectiveness. *Organization Science*, *11*(5), 473–492. doi:10.1287/orsc.11.5.473.15200

McDuffie, J. P. (2007). HRM and distributed work. *Academy of Management Annals*, *1*, 549–615. doi:10.1080/078559817

Metiu, A. (2006). Owning the code: Status closure in distributed groups. *Organization Science*, *17*, 418–436. doi:10.1287/orsc.1060.0195

Mossholder, K. W., Bennett, N., & Martin, C. L. (1998). A multilevel analysis of procedural justice context. *Journal of Organizational Behavior*, *19*, 131–141. doi:10.1002/(SICI)1099-1379(199803)19:2<131::AID-JOB878>3.0.CO;2-P

Naquin, C. E., Kurtberg, T. R., & Blekin, L. Y. (2008). E-mail communication and group cooperation in mixed motive contexts. *Social Justice Research*, *21*, 470–489. doi:10.1007/s11211-008-0084-x

Naumann, S. E., & Bennett, N. (2000). A case for procedural justice climate: Development and test of a multiple model. *Academy of Management Journal*, *43*, 881–889. doi:10.2307/1556416

Phillips, J. M., Douthill, E. A., & Hyland, M. M. (2001). The role of justice in team member satisfaction with the leader and attachment to the team. *The Journal of Applied Psychology*, *86*(2), 316–325. doi:10.1037/0021-9010.86.2.316

Roberson, Q. M. (2006a). Justice in teams: The activation and role of sensemaking in the emergence of justice climates. *Organizational Behavior and Human Decision Processes*, *100*, 177–192. doi:10.1016/j.obhdp.2006.02.006

Roberson, Q. M. (2006b). Justice in teams: The effects of interdependence and identification on referent choice and justice climate strength. *Social Justice Research*, *19*(3), 323–344. doi:10.1007/s11211-006-0010-z

Roberson, Q. M., & Colquitt, J. A. (2005). Shared and configural justice: A social justice network model of justice in teams. *Academy of Management Review*, *30*(3), 595–607.

Thibaut, J. W., & Walker, L. (1975). *Procedural Justice: A psychological analysis*. Hillsdale, NJ: Erlbaum.

Townsend, A. M., DeMarie, S. M., & Hendrickson, A. R. (1998). Virtual teams: Technology and the workplace of the future. *The Academy of Management Executive*, *12*(3), 17–29.

Wiesenfeld, B. M., Raghuram, S., & Garud, R. (2001). Organizational identification among virtual workers: The role of need for affiliation and perceived work-based social support. *Journal of Management*, *27*, 213–229. doi:10.1016/S0149-2063(00)00096-9

Chapter 22
Open Innovation in SMEs:
From Closed Peripheries to Networked Paradigm

Hakikur Rahman
University of Minho, Portugal

ABSTRACT

Successful innovation is a key to business growth. In the realm of technological development, innovation processes have been transformed into various forms, like open innovation, crowdsourcing innovation, or collaborative innovation. This research would like to focus on open innovation processes to reach out to the common stakeholders in the entrepreneurship system through small and medium enterprises. It has been observed that to provide innovative services or products to the outer periphery of the customer chain, SMEs play an important role. Hence, focusing innovation for SMEs would lead to a newer dimension of innovation research for better business and economic growth. It could be applied to both ways in terms of value gain to the participants. This applies to all sorts of entrepreneurships, though often corporate business houses seem to be the most beneficiaries of innovation researches. This research will emphasize open innovation for SMEs at the outset by focusing transformation of innovation leading to a networked paradigm in spite of being in closed periphery, and try to provide some overview on innovation strategies, including various challenges.

INTRODUCTION

Innovation, in general sense may be seen as a process of designing, developing and implementing a novel product or service to improve economic, physical and logical parameters in the process. Open innovation, on the other hand, incorporates joint efforts from in-house capabilities and possible outsourcing or combination of several input paths during the product or service development.

However, innovation is not just any sort of change in an entity. It focus on qualitative changes, and especially targeted to enhance knowledge gain that would lead to economic gain. It is not just adapting someone's novelties, but it creates something of its own as a new, at least not existed

DOI: 10.4018/978-1-61692-880-3.ch022

Figure 1. Innovation process (Adopted from Christensen, 2007)

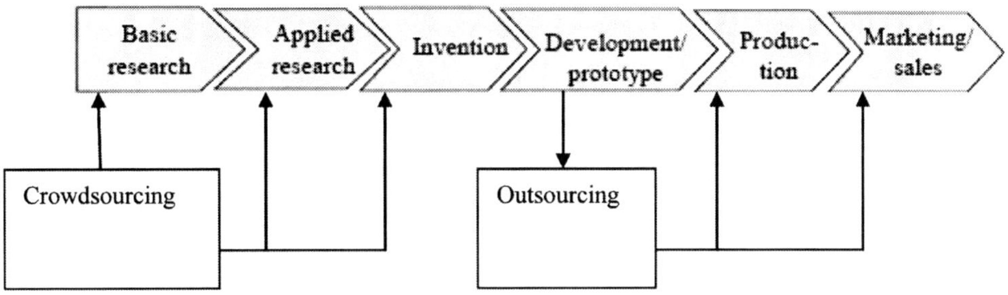

in exactly in such form before. Innovation may incorporate product specialization, or targeted commercialization, or an invention deliberately attempting to enhance the product value.

There could be product, service, process or technological innovation at the organizational level, or organizations at the grass roots, and be it fostered collaboratively. In the paradigm of opening the innovation process adaptable to the global environment to be termed as open innovation by incorporating knowledge flux from inside or outside (crowdsourcing), leading to unilateral development or outsourcing incorporates several stages of development (see Figure 1). It could follow any of these separate channels, or accommodate more than one channel to produce an innovative product.

Innovation could be driven by technology, supply, demand, process, design, value, sustainability, economy, culture, or regulation. The product may range from basic health support, inter-personal communications, equipment or accessories of specific nature, or supply driven items, as such targeting electronic and communication products, fashion industries, household items, constructions, or items of creative in nature.

Moreover, innovation is the nimbleness to adapt with the dynamic trend of the global market, and especially capable of growing, adjusting, modifying, or innovating at the same speed or faster than the ambient economic environment (Clark & Gottfredson, 2008). In addition to these, the organization must have the competency to undertake the challenges of today, else today's problems will accumulate tomorrow to become more complex task that may lead to become insurmountable (West, Vanhaverbeke & Chesbrough, 2006).

In the context of open innovation (OI), it is seen as utilization of inbound and outbound knowledge flows converting to economic values, and acceleration of product development and marketing accumulated ideas leading to added value chain (De Jong, Vanhaverbeke, Kalvet & Chesbrough, 2008). Diversified factors affect the open innovation process (see Figure 2), in addition to an organization's inherent entity. It incorporates management, governance, skills, technology and policy matters. It also integrates relationship of open innovation factors with other interrelated organizations, institutions and agencies. However, the fact is that in the arena of open innovation, much have not been researched in these aspects. Above all, at the policy making level, not enough work have been carried out to facilitate familiarization of positive aspects and impact of open innovation to the policy initiators, especially at the socio-economic strata. Furthermore, the role of government remains unchartered in many facets in the decision making process of open innovation at the national level.

Till date, most studies have examined open innovation at the organizational level, basically for two reasons. Firstly, innovation is tradition-

Figure 2. Factors effecting open innovation (Adopted from Beije, 2005)

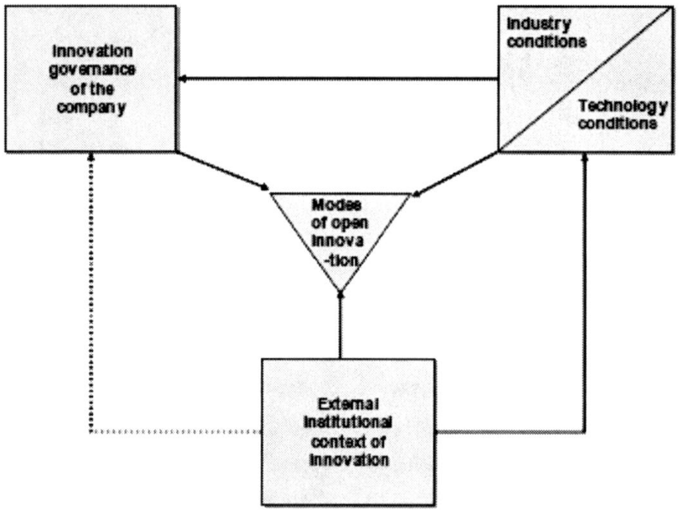

ally conceived as the outcome of deliberate actions of a single entrepreneur, and thus R&D competition has also been styled as an innovation race between two or more entrepreneurs. Secondly, the value of a technological invention is realized only through a business model of the enterprise (Chesbrough & Rosenbloom, 2002). While it is very natural that the business model may easily spill over the boundaries of an enterprise or even an industry (West, Vanhaverbeke & Chesbrough, 2006).

Most of the researches in open innovation remain restricted towards targeting common stakeholders through major global entrepreneurs or their alliances. In addition, a few of those global business houses are controlling the entire market or system of open innovation development through process modification and or diversification of resources. Despite immense potentiality to reach out the stakeholders at the grass roots through open ended demand, diversity of product variation, and scale of economic capacity major contemporary researches are confined towards generic pattern-oriented clients.

By far, the small and medium enterprises (SMEs[1]) who always deals with the clients at the grass roots the most and they have to satisfy the client base, though seldom they produce the product. Moreover, despite the globalization that offers unprecedented opportunities and challenges for SMEs, but seemingly they are thinking of mere survival in the context of global economy, marketing, value promotion, job creation and expansion (CSR Europe, 2008a; b). SMEs in Europe comprises of about 23M€ investment market that account for 99% of all businesses and represent 2/3rd of the total employment (Renaud, 2008). However, in spite of being key contributor to the global economy accounting for approximately 50% of local and national GDP, 30% of export and 10% of FDI[2] most of the SMEs communities are lagging behind promoting their products at the national level, and at the global level (OECD, 2006).

This research argues that, time has come to transform the process of innovation system (through organized deregulation, wider knowledge distribution, focused training, and capacity development) to put SMEs at the heart of the technology transfers as they represent a privileged source for the innovations in a competitive context in which large companies prefer to concentrate on their core competencies. So, SMEs play an important role and distinct part in the innovative activity whereas many large firms are acting as just a systems integrator. However, the challenge remains, particularly as delicate as before, because SMEs do not exists in this global environment by themselves, they require stronghold interoperability to larger entrepreneurs for better opportunities, to intermediaries for improving their capacities, and to the grass roots clients for offering better services. Hence, there are scope of promoting OI to reach out the grass roots, not only through the SMEs, but also through a combination of SMEs, agencies of corporate entrepreneurs, research centres, team of university researchers, and other catalytic factors.

The research focuses on innovation strategies initiating from closed innovation, open innovation leading to networked innovation (networked paradigm) improvising challenges faced by SMEs on the way of establishing collaborative innovation. It will categorize various aspects of open innovation in terms of reaching out the broad based clientele through SMEs, synthesize various operational models that are found in the contemporary arena, and try to framework a sustainable business model. The research outlines a discourse of SMEs within the OI models by establishing a network of SMEs, agents of corporate business groups, and team of university researchers targeting client base at the grass roots through the process of open innovation. Before conclusion, the study hints on a few aspects of future research.

BACKGROUND

Innovation, by definition could be termed as the creation, development and implementation of a new product, process or service, aiming at improving efficiency, effectiveness or competitive advantage. The term may apply to products, services, manufacturing processes, managerial processes or the design of an organization. It is most often viewed at a product or process level, where product innovation satisfies a customer's needs and process innovation improves efficiency and effectiveness of the organization. Innovation links to creativity and the creation of new ideas, and involves taking those new ideas and turning them into reality through invention, research and new product development[3]. Furthermore, innovation can be seen as the process that translates knowledge into economic growth and social well-being. It encompasses a series of scientific, technological, organizational, economic and commercial activities. Researches in the context of innovation are targeted towards one of these activities and may be carried out at different phases of the innovative process[4].

Open Innovation[5], a term recently added to the industries and organizations to promote open ended ideas, thoughts, processes, and researches to improve the product development, provide better services to the clients, increase efficiency and enhance value-addition. In terms of process dynamics, it incorporates accumulation of ideas, knowledge, licenses, intellectual properties, patents, and inventions (through licensing, joint ventures, spin-offs); and in terms of concept dynamics, user innovation, market innovation, cumulative innovation and distributed innovation.

Open innovation emerges on issues like, in the diverse world of widely distributed knowledge, solitary enterprises cannot afford (economically and organizationally) to rely entirely on their own research and resources, but may instead collaborate, buy, lease-out or license processes or inventions (patents, intellectual properties) from other companies, organizations or institutions. In addition, internal inventions that are not being used in a company's business process should be taken outside the company (through licensing, joint ventures, spin-offs). Currently, many companies are promoting open innovation and among them IBM, InnoCentive, InnovationXchange, Nerac, NineSigma, Nokia, Procter & Gamble, and Yet2.com[6] are widely renowned.

For sake of this research, literature review will be limited to only challenges that are being faced by SMEs on the way of establishing innovation, development of a sustainable business model, and inclusion of SMEs into a possible discourse within the process. However, before referring to the issues of challenges, a few strategies on open innovation will be described next.

STRATEGIES

Despite being a relatively new field as it has been introduced very recently, many of the concurrent researchers and organizations are active in making progressive researches on open innovation, and therefore, several strategies on OI prevail. Focused to open innovation for SMEs, this research entails a few of them those eventually lead to the proposed strategy of this research, which is networked and collaborative innovation.

From 'Closed Innovation' to 'Open Innovation'

Closed innovation refers to processes that restrict the use of internal knowledge solely within a company and make little or no use of external knowledge[7]. On the other hand, open innovation assumes that enterprises can and should use external ideas as well as internal ideas, and internal and external paths to market (concurrently, and successively) to discover and realize innovative opportunities. The open innovation model can be compared with the conventional, closed model in which enterprises generate, develop and market their own ideas, usually prepared in an internal R&D department (see Figure 3). This closed model has become outdated due to increased mobility of workers, better education, growing presence of venture capital, increasingly shortened product life cycles, growing competition, globalization of economy, improved use of information technology, and wide availability of knowledge from multiple sources. The better portion of the fact is that, in the open innovation model, enterprises can still initiate and nurture innovations within the boundaries of their organizations, but at the same time they may also draw on alternative pathways to bring ideas to the market and to benefit from external knowledge (De Jong, Vanhaverbeke, Kalvet & Chesbrough, 2008).

From 'Research and Development' to 'Connect and Develop'

Along the progress of development with concept of open innovation, majority of the entrepreneurs are shifting towards connecting their own R&D department to the outside of their boundaries and develop their products or services. This is termed as shifting from research and development (R&D) to

Figure 3. Comparison of open innovation with closed innovation (Adapted from Höllmüller, 2008)

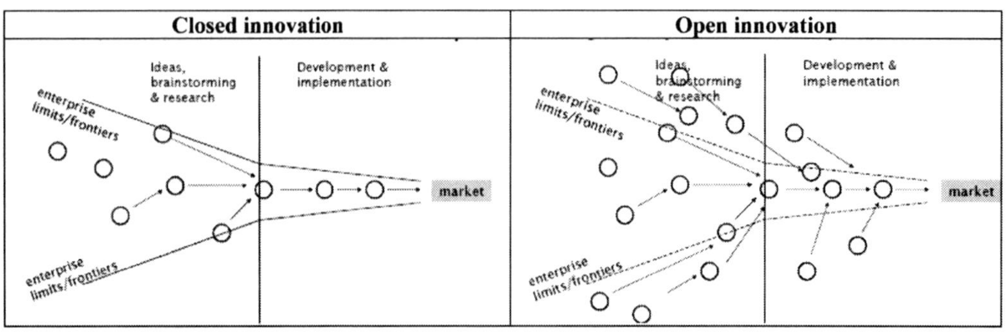

connect and develop (C&D). As stated by Huston & Sakkab (2006) that, two senior executives from Procter & Gamble have studied outside sources of innovation, and estimated that for every P&G researcher there were 200 scientists or engineers elsewhere in the world (around a total of 1.5 million people) who were just as good as talents the company could potentially use. But tapping into the creative thinking of potential inventors and others on the outside would require massive operational changes. Therefore, they needed to move the company's attitude from resistance to innovations "not invented here" to enthusiasm for those "proudly found elsewhere"; and needed to change how it was defined, and perceived, their R&D organization from 7,500 people inside to 7,500 *plus* 1.5 million outside, with a permeable boundary between them.

Huston & Sakkab (2006) further revealed that by 2006, more than 35 percent of their new products in market had elements that originated from outside P&G, up from about 15 percent in 2000. And 45 percent of the initiatives in their product development portfolio had key elements that were discovered externally. Through connect and develop strategy, along with improvements in other aspects of innovation related to production cost, design, and marketing their R&D productivity has increased by nearly 60 percent. Their innovation success rate raised to more than doubled, while the cost of innovation has fallen. R&D investment as a percentage of sales was down from 4.8 percent in 2000 to 3.4 percent in 2006. And, during 2004-2006, they launched more than 100 new products for which some aspect of execution came from outside the company. Furthermore, five years after the company's stock collapse in 2000, they doubled their share price with a portfolio of twenty-two billion-dollar brands.

From Competition to Cooperation

Challenging the increasing global competition and coping the rising R&D costs, companies can no longer survive on their own R&D efforts but look for new, and more open modes of innovation. Nowadays, companies' innovation activities are increasingly becoming international, and they are day by day embracing strategies of collaboration, rather than competition. Most of the successful OI entrepreneurs are collaborating with external partners, whether suppliers, customers or universities, to keep ahead of the game and get new products or services to market before their competitors (OECD, 2008)

Enterprises consider innovations as a major engine to augment their performance and to reinforce their competitive position in the market. Many firms have paid most of their management attention to an extended focus on internal efficiencies of the development process, team structures, decision making and cross functional interactions. However, as more and more entrepreneurs are bringing innovation straight to the heart of their corporate strategies, developing internal innovation capabilities is no longer adequate to gain and sustain competitive advantage. Since innovation strategies look increasingly similar and commoditized, increasing numbers of organizations are trying to further improve their innovation performance through intensifying collaboration and partnership across industry rather than competition (Chesbrough 2003, 2006; EIRMA, 2004; De Vrande, De Jong, Vanhaverbeke & De Rochemont, 2008). Figure 4 portrays a decade of cooperation at the international level in the area of science and technology, and figure-5 shows cooperation strategies among SMEs at the regional level.

From 'Closed Peripheries' to 'Networked Paradigm'

In this strategy, open innovation encompasses different dimensions of hypothesis ranging from in-house knowledge exploration and partnership among similar organizations to establishing networking among organizations, agencies and

Figure 4. Cooperation in the fields of science and technology at international level (Adopted from OECD, 2000)

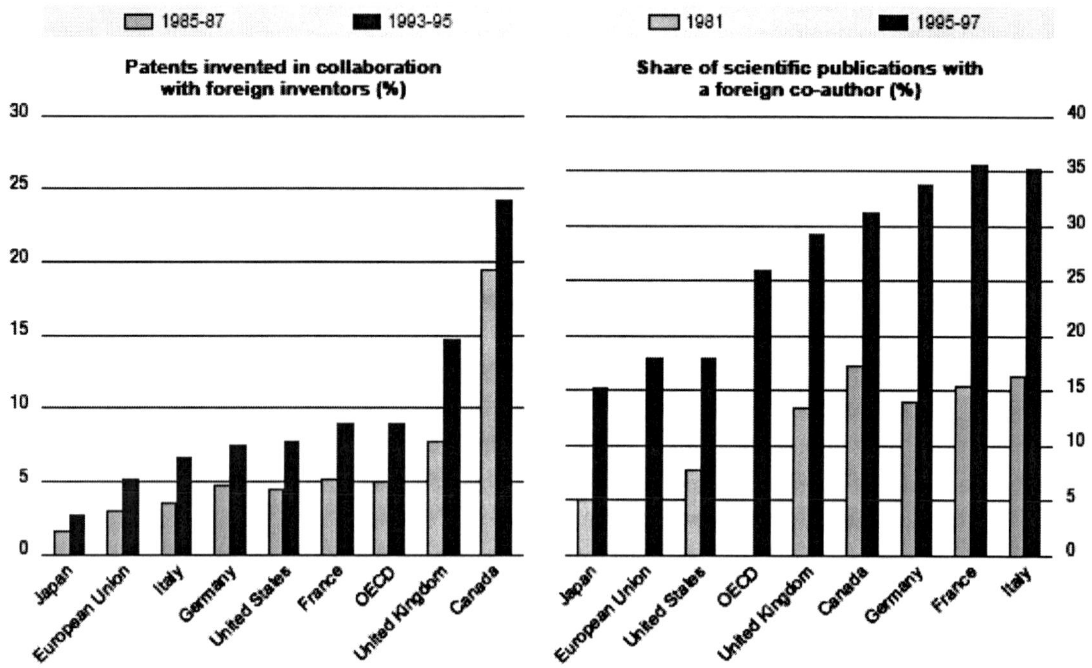

institutions. However, De Vrande, De Jong, Vanhaverbeke & De Rochemont (2008) emphasized on two aspects. Firstly, there is the inside-out movement (or technology exploitation), in which existing technological capabilities are leveraged outside the boundaries of the firm. Secondly, there is also an outside-in movement (or technology exploration), in which external sources of innovation are used to enhance current technological developments. Hence, in a comprehensive open

Figure 5. Cooperation among SMEs at the regional level (Wolf, 2009)

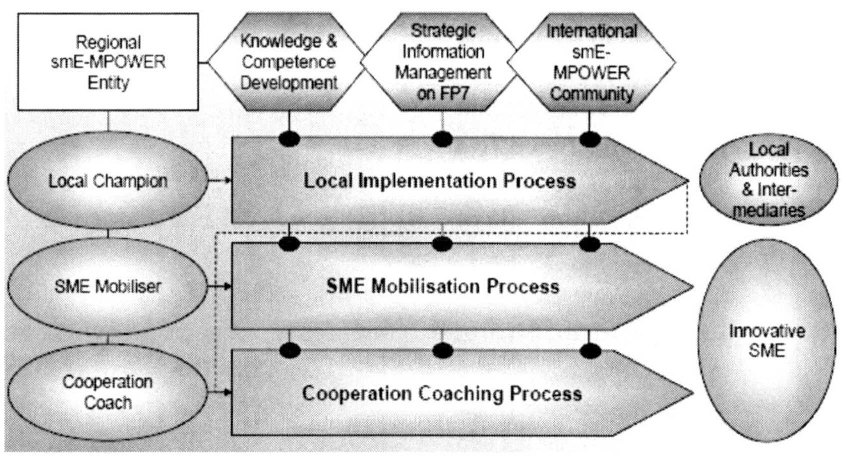

Figure 6. From closed towards open innovation (Adopted from Pullen, De Weerd-Nederhof, Groen & Fisscher, 2008)

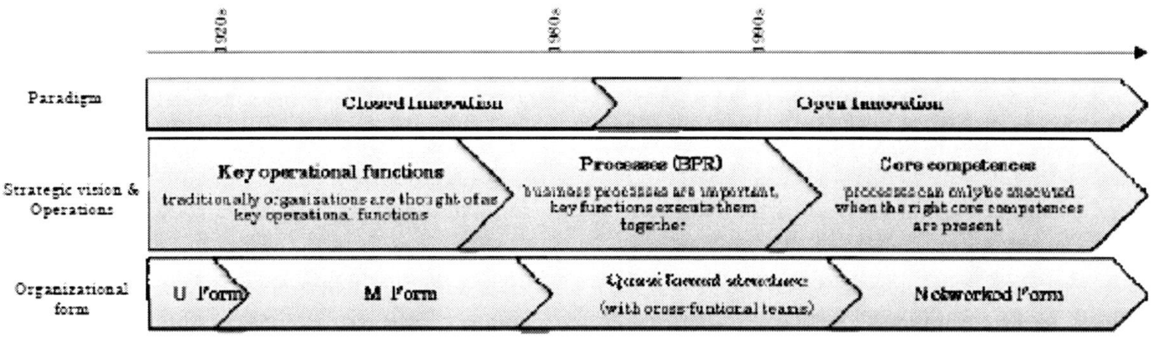

innovation setting, companies combine both technology exploitation and technology exploration in order to create maximum value from their technological capabilities or other competencies.

However, in order to successfully develop and commercialize new products, and achieve high innovation performance SMEs need to collaborate with external networks (Pullen, De Weerd-Nederhof, Groen & Fisscher, 2008). In this aspect, one may focus on the following four approaches of open innovation, such as collective or pooled R&D, spinouts or collaborative development, promoting products in partnerships and attracting similar actors to come forward for creating a positive ambient through crowdsourcing (West & Gallagher, 2006).

Furthermore, as West & Gallagher (2006) argued that, a central concern will remain there as how to best utilize the internal R&D capabilities of SME to maximize advantages through this form of open innovation. Those capabilities could include generation of innovations for internal commercialization similar to the traditional model; building of absorptive capacity and utilize that capacity to identify other external innovations; generation of innovations that promote value chain through external commercialization; and generation of intellectual property (IP) that may not produce direct economic benefit, but indirectly generates return through spillovers or sale of related products and services. It has been observed that successful approaches often combine a variety of strategies. Figure-6 shows how an organization may turn from U form (top-to-bottom/ up-to-down management), via M form (multi-divisional management) to networked form (ubiquitous management) (Pullen, De Weerd-Nederhof, Groen & Fisscher, 2008).

Despite various strategies taken by entrepreneurs, research houses, and institutions, there remain diverse challenges in the arena of open innovation for SMEs. These could be, What drives open innovation for SMEs?; How global innovation networks have developed incorporating SMEs?; How do global innovation networks operate to promote SMEs at the grass roots?; How big are global innovation networks as compared to networks comprised of SMEs?; What are the potential challenges for framing out a global innovation networks incorporating SMEs?; and What role a national policy should take to promote SMEs in the value chain? (OECD, 2008). The next section has been devoted to discuss more on these challenges and issues related to the promotion of open innovation for SMEs at the grass roots.

CHALLENGES

As mentioned above, a successful open innovation strategy for SMEs should find creative ways to exploit internal innovation by incorporating external innovation into internal development, and able to motivate external actors to sustain an ongoing stream of external innovations. However, while approaching the global market, it can be observed that large industries, especially the high tech ones, are already involved in open innovation scheme, and competing each other. In terms of SMEs with high tech facilities, often generated from universities or research center, would like to maintain good links to larger organizations, rather than reaching out at the grass roots. On the contrary, SMEs at the local level, equipped with low tech facilities are loosely motivated to promote research, and may not have sufficient resources to identify their needs for innovation through appropriate market analysis, and act accordingly to a defined innovation scheme. The problem aggravates further due to an appropriate adaptive business model (West & Gallagher, 2006).

Along this context, isolated SMEs are also in lack of adequate resources, so that they can at least take a medium term planning, if not a longer-term projection, to sensitize their demand and obtain an access to better research output. Majority of the SMEs fall under this category. To be more specific, SMEs in this category always find it difficult to enter a sustainable value chain market, as they only focus on short term market promotion; lack of even medium term demand due to mere limited resources; and lack of an authenticated contact network. Furthermore, most of the academic world are often lack vision and perspective of real life situation at the ground level while conducting researches in the field of open innovation, and therefore, there are question of reliability may arise. Foremost, the time frame of research output from the research team at universities may not always coincide with the actual time scale of SMEs to be ready to aggressively enter into the market at the right time and with the right product (CSR Europe, 2008b).

Furthermore, new product development always remain at the top of the agenda for both large and small- and medium sized organizations. However, compared to large firms, SMEs have a number of typical problems with regard to their innovation process, especially during the period of the development stages to the commercialization stages (Hanna & Walsh, 2002). In those stages, they are more challenged by financial constraints, in addition to other bottlenecks such as lack of qualified personnel and low possibility to substitute relevant products in the market and sufficient fixed asset in terms of cash (Kaufmann & Tödtling, 2002). On the other side, however, SMEs have some advantages with regard to new product development that makes them suitable as network partner, as they are usually less bureaucratic, and in general they may have greater incentives to be successful than large firms (Michael & Palandjian, 2004). But, as the SME desires to be included in the network to achieve high innovation performance at the individual level, the question arises of how to organize new product development within the network (Pullen, De Weerd-Nederhof, Groen & Fisscher, 2008).

In addition to these, a primary factor that relates to innovation in SMEs are the vision of innovation as perceived by the top management of the firms. Sometimes they may not act as the facilitators, and this perception is rather difficult to measure and motivate them (Hadjimanolis, 1999). There are internal barriers and external barriers to innovation for SMES (see Table 1).

Inclusive of above challenges, open innovation for SMEs, deserves further emphasize in resolving issues, like sales, licenses, cash flow, and trust in business relationship; to fulfill the grass roots clientele base by understanding their demand; to develop a transparent business process that add value to it; and to combine knowledge and technology for building a pipeline of opportunities, enabling a broad-based B2B networking through sustainable organic growth.

Table 1. Barriers of open innovation for SMEs (Piatier, 1984; Rush & Bessant, 1992; Hadjimanolis, 1999)

External barriers			**Internal barriers**		
Supply	**Demand**	**Environment**	**Resource**	**Culture/ human nature**	**System**
Technological information	Customer needs	Government regulations	Lack of internal funds	Attitude of top management to risk	Out-of-date accounting system
Raw materials	Customers' perception of the risk of innovation	Anti-trust measures	Technical expertise	Employee resistance to innovation	
Finance	Domestic market limitation	Policy actions	Management time		
	International market limitation				

DEVELOPMENT OF THE BUSINESS MODEL

A business model may be seen as the totality of how a company selects its clients, defines and differentiates its responses; classifies those tasks it will perform itself and those it will outsource; configures its resources, goes to market, creates utility for clients; and get hold of profits. It is the entire system for delivering utility to clients and gaining a profit from that activity (Pourdehnad, 2007). Figure 7 shows a relationship diagram with the various actors or stakeholders involved in a business model.

Triple Helix Model (see Figure 8) is another highly discussing model in this arena. According to this model, a spiral of innovation involves government, university, and industry in multiple reciprocal relationships, to create a flexible overlapping innovation system (CSR Europe, 2008b).

This research would like to point out to another business model that may be utilized in SMEs

Figure 7. Relationship with the stakeholders in a business model (Adopted from Pourdehnad, 2007)

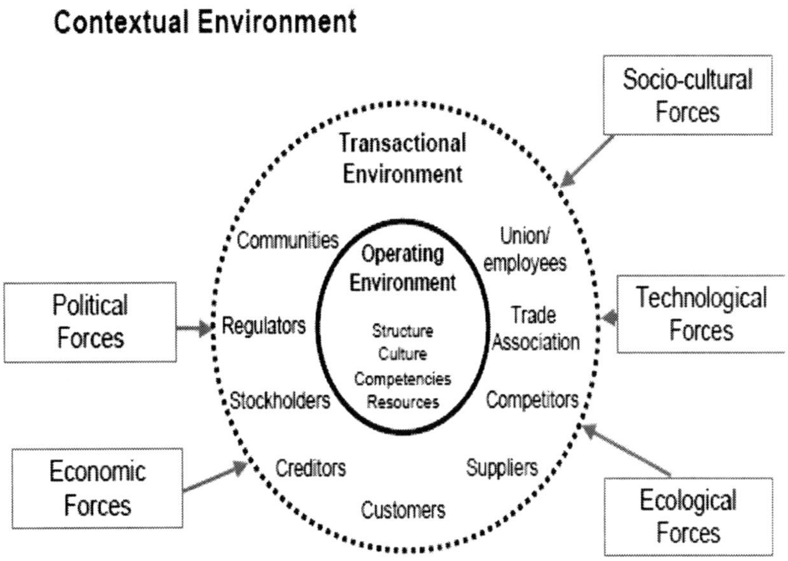

Figure 8. The triple helix model (Adopted from CSR Europe, 2008b)

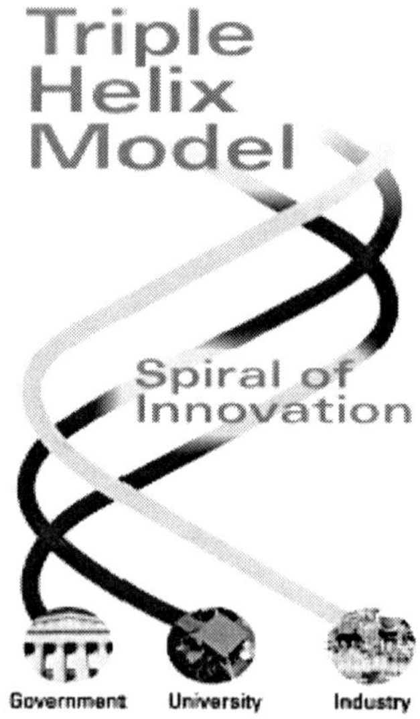

OI process, which has been developed incorporating mixed approach (Shorthouse, 2008). Figure 9 shows a mixed approach (closed and open innovation) business model.

However, to attain a sustainable business model in SMEs open innovation, one need to follow the flowchart indicated below:

Educate and raise SME awareness

⇩

Identify SME needs

⇩

Facilitate interactions between SMEs & Research Orgs

⇩

Identify & source partners / opportunity

⇩

Prepare SME for collaboration

Furthermore, a sustainable business model should also follow to:

Introduce both the closed and open innovation paradigms as optimized

⇩

Facilitate drivers of changes in the innovation process

⇩

Undo the possibilities of open innovation paradigm

⇩

Obtain better understanding of niche markets

⇩

Properly handle challenges of innovation management

Figure 9. A mixed approach business model (Adopted from Shorthouse, 2008)

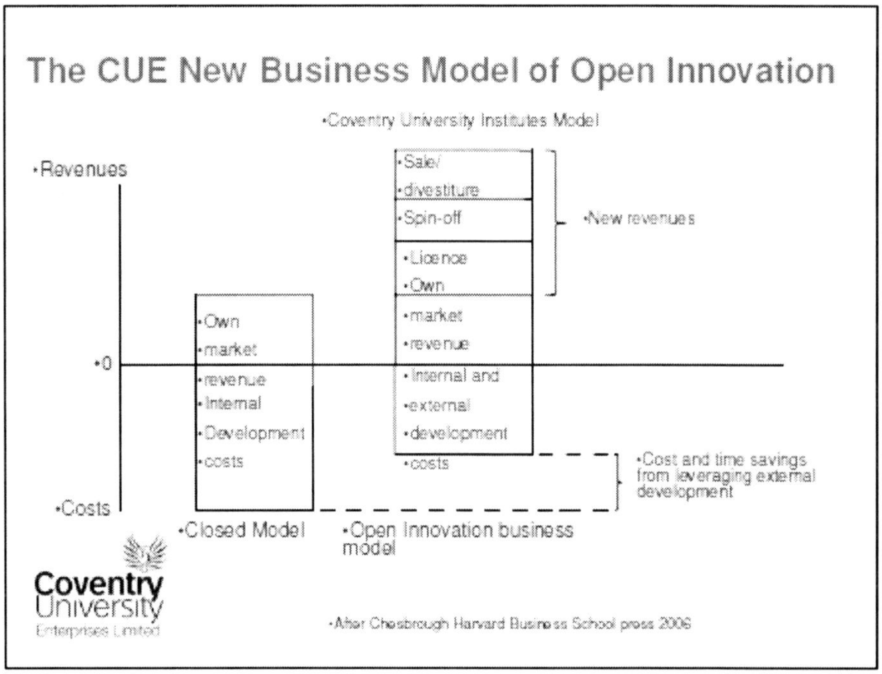

The business model should incorporate inclusion of SMEs inclusive in the dimension in Figure 10.

RECOMMENDATIONS AND FUTURE DISCOURSES

This has been observed that, in terms of improving their efficiency SMEs need to focus on improving their core competences. Furthermore, they need to cooperate with external partners to recompense for other competences and resources, especially in case of new product development. Therefore, recognizing the increasing importance of collaboration and partnership, new research may emerge as how to organize these external networks (Pullen, De Weerd-Nederhof, Groen & Fisscher, 2008).

Considering that the typical management challenges for SME managers that are quite different from those of managers of large enterprises, which would like to expedite the sustained growth engine in their company, would be an interesting uncharted area for future research (Chesbrough, Vanhaverbeke & West, 2006). However, the proximity of universities, research teams, brokering houses or intermediaries, large companies and lead users may play a key role in the deployment of open innovation in SMEs. Similarly, an optimized innovation policy fostering transactions among these innovation partners may also play a significant role in the longer run (De Vrande, De Jong, Vanhaverbeke & De Rochemont, 2008).

In terms of economic sustainability, cluster development is gaining importance in the economic policy debate. Despite, the globalization and evolution of information technologies, the phenomena of clusters, regional specialization of enterprises and institutions in common economic aspects are attracting potential researchers in this field (Ketels & Sölvell, 2006). As Chesbrough (2003; 2006) mentioned, future research on open innovation should foresee innovative clusters around enterprises, and this research foresee that especially

Figure 10. Building block of the proposed business model (Authors)

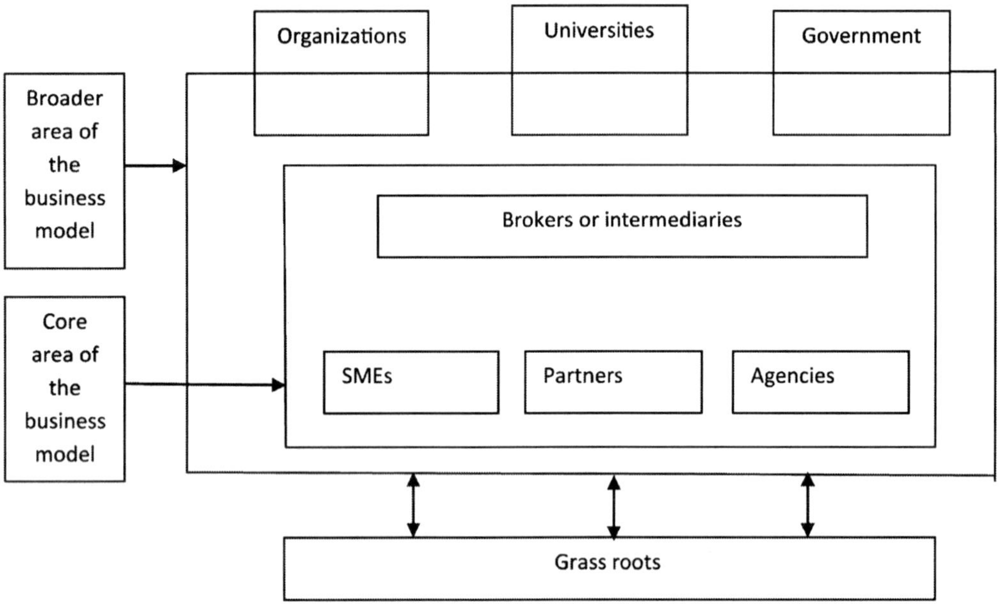

SMEs would be able to tap into the newest ideas needed to succeed in the contemporary market.

Future research in this aspect, should also incorporate establishment of national and regional policies to promote open innovation among the SMEs, not limiting them to the administrative borders. SMEs within a region should open themselves to others if the product or service are not locally available. Similarly, dedicated tools to access unified information, recognize accepted patterns, follow management chain, reduce physical distance, and add economic value in terms of open innovation deserves further research discourses.

CONCLUSION

Innovation is seen as the development and commercialization of knowledge, transforming ideas and research into value-added products, processes or services (EEDA, 2008). Innovation, may lead to higher performance, but the process is not solely automatic. The process need to be focused more attentively to obtain the final outcome. Sometimes, many company's R&D efforts remain unfocused. Money is wasted for "reinventing wheels" that others may have already rolled out. On the other hand, good ideas get stuck in developmental bottlenecks. Moreover, most of the time promising innovations never get to market because of flawed understanding of customer's needs, poor marketing and investment planning (Jaruzelski, Dehoff & Bordia, 2006).

Furthermore, increasing global competition and rising research and development (R&D) costs are pressurizing entrepreneurs to reach for new, more open modes of innovation, and to collaborate with external partners, whether suppliers, customers or universities or research centers, to keep ahead of the game and get new products or services to market before their competitors. At the same time, innovation is being generalized as users of products and services, both firms and individual consumers, are increasingly becoming involved within the innovation process by themselves (OECD, 2008). Therefore, open innovation for

SMEs has become a process of open, collaborative and networked model than the process of closed, classified and segmented model.

REFERENCES

Beije, P. (2005). *Open Innovation: the European Challenge*. A report submitted to Rotterdam School of Management / Erasmus University

Chesbrough, H. (2003). *Open Innovation: The New Imperative for Creating and Profiting from Technology*. Boston: Harvard Business School Press.

Chesbrough, H. (2006). *Open business models: How to thrive in a new innovation landscape*. Boston: Harvard Business School Press.

Chesbrough, H., & Rosenbloom, R. S. (2002). The role of the business model in capturing value from innovation: Evidence from Xerox corporation's technology spin-off companies. *Industrial and Corporate Change*, *11*(3), 529–555. doi:10.1093/icc/11.3.529

Chesbrough, H., Vanhaverbeke, W., & West, J. (2006). *Open innovation: Researching a new paradigm*. London: Oxford University Press.

Christensen, J. F. (2007). *Innovation concepts, processes and strategies*. Presentation in PhD Course, Copenhagen Business School.

Clark, T. R., & Gottfredson, C. A. (2008). In Search of Learning Agility: Assessing Progress from 1957 to 2008, A report submitted to TRCLARK LLC

De Jong, J. P. J., Vanhaverbeke, W., Kalvet, T., & Chesbrough, H. (2008).*Policies for Open Innovation: Theory, Framework and Cases, Final report for a Research project funded by VISION Era-Net*. Helsinki: Finland.

De Vrande, V.V., De Jong, J.P.J., Vanhaverbeke, W. & De Rochemont, M. (2008). Open innovation in SMEs: Trends, motives and management challenges, a report published under the SCALES-initiative (SCientific AnaLysis of Entrepreneurship and SMEs), as part of the 'SMEs and Entrepreneurship programme' financed by the Netherlands Ministry of Economic Affairs, 2008

EEDA. (2008). *ERDF Regional Workshops – Autumn 2008 Review Report*. UK: East of England Development Agency.

EIRMA. (2004). *Technology Access for open innovation*. Working Group Report WG63, Eirma: Paris.

Europe, C. S. R. (2008a). *The European Alliance for CSR Progress Review 2007: Making Europe a Pole of Excellence on CSR,* European Commission, Brussels, 4 March 2008

CSR Europe (2008b). *R&D Open Innovation: Networks with SME*, Open Innovation Network, 6 November 2008

Hadjimanolis, A. (1999). Barriers to innovation for SMEs in a small less developed country (Cyprus). *Technovation*, *19*, 561–570. doi:10.1016/S0166-4972(99)00034-6

Hanna, V., & Walsh, K. (2002). Small firm networks: a successful approach to innovation*? R & D Management*, *32*(3), 201–207. doi:10.1111/1467-9310.00253

Höllmüller, C. (2008*). Chances for Small and Medium-sized Enterprises (SME) in International Innovation Networks*, a presentation at the Innovation Day Swiss Texnet, Dübendorf, 28 August 2008

Huston, L. & Sakkab, N. (2006). *P&G's New Innovation Model*, An excerpt from Connect and Develop: Inside Procter & Gamble's New Model for Innovation. *Harvard Business Review, 84*, (3), March 2006.

Jaruzelski, B., Dehoff, K. & Bordia, R. (2006). *Smart Spenders: The Global Innovation, Special feature at Smart Spenders: The Global Innovation.* Strategy+Business, 45, 46-61.

Kaufmann, A., & Tödtling, F. (2002). How effective is innovation support for SMEs? An analysis of the region of upper Austria. *Technovation, 22*(3), 147–159. doi:10.1016/S0166-4972(00)00081-X

Ketels, C., & Sölvell, Ö. (2006). *The Baltic Sea Region – Top of Europe in Global Competition, State of the Region Report*. Denmark: Baltic Development Forum.

Michael, S. C., & Palandjian, T. P. (2004). Organizational learning in new product introductions. *Journal of Product Innovation Management, 21*, 268–276. doi:10.1111/j.0737-6782.2004.00078.x

OECD. (2000). *OECD Science Technology and Industry Outlook 2000*. France: OECD.

OECD. (2006). *The Athens Action Plans for Removing Barriers to SME Access to International Markets,* OECD Report, France.

OECD. (2008). *Open Innovation in Global Networks, a policy brief.* France: OECD.

Piatier, A. (1984). *Barriers to Innovation*. London: Frances Pinter.

Pourdehnad, J. (2007). *Idealized Design - An Open Innovation*.Process, a presentation from the annual W. Edwards Deming Annual Conference, Purdue University, West Lafayette, Indiana, October 2007

Pullen, A., De Weerd-Nederhof, P., Groen, A., & Fisscher, O. (2008). Configurations of External SME Characteristics to Explain Differences in Innovation Performance, a proceedings of the *High Technology Small Firms Conference 2008*: Twente University, Netherlands.

Renaud, P. (2008).*Open Innovation at Oseo Innovation: Example of the Passerelle Programme.* a presentation at the OECD Business Symposium on Open Innovation in Global Networks, Copenhagen, 25-26 February, 2008

Rush, H., & Bessant, J. (1992). Revolution in three-quarter time: lessons from the diffusion of advanced manufacturing technologies. *Technology Analysis and Strategic Management, 4*(1), 3–19. doi:10.1080/09537329208524075

Shorthouse, S. (2008). Innovation and Technology Transfer, a presentation from the International Conference DISTRICT 2008. *International Conference Centre*, Dresden, 29 May 2008.

West, J. & Gallagher, S. (2006). Open Innovation: The Paradox of Firm Investment in Open Source Software, R&D Management Special Issue on "*Opening-up the innovation process*", 36, 3 (June 2006).

West, J., Vanhaverbeke, W., & Chesbrough, H. (2006). Open Innovation: A Research Agenda. In Henry Chesbrough, Wim Vanhaverbeke and Joel West (Eds.) (2006). *Open Innovation: Researching a New Paradigm*.Oxford, UK: Oxford University Press.

Wolf, A. (2009). *smE MPOWER Outlook: Empowering SMEs for long-term research interest and increased participation in EU RTD activities!* Retrieved March 15, 2009 from http://www.sme-mpower.net/Presentations/11%20Andreas%20Wolf%20on%20smE-MPOWER-Community.pdf

ENDNOTES

1 There is no single agreed definition of a SME. A variety of definitions are applied among OECD and APEC economies, and employee number is not the sole defined criterion. SMEs are considered to be non-

subsidiary, independent firms which employ less than a given number of employees.

[2] This refers to firms in the formal sector only.

[3] http://www.digitalstrategy.govt.nz/Resources/Glossary-of-Key-Terms/

[4] http://www.arc.gov.au/general/glossary.htm

[5] a term promoted by Henry Chesbrough, a professor and executive director at the Center for Open Innovation at Berkeley

[6] http://en.wikipedia.org/wiki/Open_Innovation

[7] http://en.wikipedia.org/wiki/Open_innovation

Compilation of References

Abell, W., & Limm, L. (1996). *Business Use of the Internet in New Zealand: An Exploratory Study*. Retrieved August 22, 2009, from http://ausweb.scu.edu.au/aw96/business/abell/paper.htm

Abernethy, M. (2002). SMEs: Small world order. *The Bulletin, 120*(34). Retrieved September 1, 2009, from http://bulletin.syd.ninemsn.com.au/article.aspx?id=131748

ACCA. (2008). *Director's Briefing: Strategy*. UK: BHP Information Solutions Ltd.

ACS. (2002). *Annual Report 2002. WWW [On-line]*. Retrieved from http://www.acs-giz.si/pic/pdf/Letno-porocilo-(Annual-report)-2002.pdf.

Adams, S. J. (1965). Inequity in social exchange. In Berkowitz, L. (Ed.), *Advances in Social Experimental Psychology* (*Vol. 2*, pp. 267–299). New York: Academic Press. doi:10.1016/S0065-2601(08)60108-2

Adams, J. E. (2003). Seven Leadership Strategies for IT Success. *IQ Magazine*. Retrieved September 1, 2009, from http://www.xynomedia.com/media/Seven_Leadership_Strategies.pdf

Adeoti-Adekeye, W. (1997). The importance of management information systems. *Library Review, 46*(5), 318–327. doi:10.1108/00242539710178452

Adler-Milstein, J. (2009). Health Care Requires Big Changes to Complement New IT. *Harvard Business Review*, (April): 2009.

Adomavicious, G., & Tuzhilin, A. (2005). Towards the next generation of recommender systems: a survey of the state-of-the art and possible extensions. *IEEE Transactions on Knowledge and Data Engineering, 17*(6), pp- 734-749.

Afsarmanesh, H., & Camarinha-Matos, L. M. (2009). On the classification and management of Virtual Organisation Breeding Environments. *International Journal of Information Technology and Management, 8*, 234–259. doi:10.1504/IJITM.2009.024604

Afsarmanesh, H., & Camarinha-Matos, L. M. (2008). The ARCON Modelling Framework. In Camarinha-Matos, L. M., & Afsarmanesh, H. (Eds.), *Collaborative Networks: Reference Modelling* (pp. 67–82). New York: Springer.

Afuah, A., & Tucci, C. (2000). *Internet Business Models and Strategies: Text and Cases*. New York: McGraw-Hill.

Age, N. M. (2009). Press Release: Some Retailers see site traffic almost double. July 2009

Ahn, H. (2007). Utilizing Popularity Characteristics for Product Recommendation. *International Journal of Electronic Commerce, 11*(2), 59–80. doi:10.2753/JEC1086-4415110203

Ahoy, C. (2008). *Customer driven operations management*. New York: McGraw-Hill.

Ahrweiler, P., Gilbert, N., & Pyka, A. (2005) Institutions matter, but ...: Organizational alignment in knowledge-based industries, the case of German and British bio-pharmaceuticals. A paper presented at the EMAEE conference in Utrecht 2005.

Ajzen, I. (1991). The theory of planned behaviour. *Organizational Behavior and Human Decision Processes*, (50): 179–211. doi:10.1016/0749-5978(91)90020-T

Ajzen, I., & Fishbein, M. (1980). *Understanding Attitudes and Predicting Social Behaviour*. Upper Saddle River, NJ: Prentice Hall.

Ajzen, I. (1985). From intentions to actions: A theory of planned behaviour. In Kuhl, J., & Beckman, J. (Eds.), *Actioncontrol: From cognition to behaviour.New York* (pp. 11–39). Heidelberg: Springer.

Ajzen, I. (1989). Attitude Structure and Behavior. In Pratkanis, A. R., Breckler, S. J., & Greenwald, A. G. (Eds.), *Attitude Structure and Function* (pp. 241–274). Hillsdale, NJ: Lawrence Erlbaum Associates.

Alexander, M. (1997). Getting grips with the virtual organization. *Long Range Planning*, *30*(1), 122–124. doi:10.1016/S0024-6301(96)00122-7

Al-Mashari, M. (2002). Electronic commerce. *Benchmarking*, *9*(2), 182–189. doi:10.1108/14635770210421845

Amit, R., & Zott, C. (2001). Value Creation in E-Business. *Strategic Management Journal*, *22*, 493–520. doi:10.1002/smj.187

Amor, D. (1999). *E-business (R)evolution*. New York: Prentice Hall.

Anderson, D. (2000). *Managing Information Systems*. New York: Prentice Hall.

Anderson, C. (2006). *The Long Tail*. New York: Hyperion.

Andrews, K. (1980). *The concept of corporate strategy*. Homewood, USA: Dow-Jones - Irwin.

Ansari, A., Essegaier, S., & Kohli, R. (2000). Internet recommendation systems. *JMR, Journal of Marketing Research*, *37*(3), 363–375. doi:10.1509/jmkr.37.3.363.18779

Argyris, C., & Schön, D. (1978). *Organizational Learning: A theory of action perspective*. Reading, MA: Addison-Wesley.

Asia-Pacific Economic Cooperation. (2000). *APEC E-Commerce Readiness Assessment Guide*. APEC Telecommunications and Information Working Group. Retrieved September 3, 2009, from http://publications.apec.org/publication-detail.php?pub_id=647

Aspin, D., & Chapman, J. (2000). Lifelong learning: concepts and conceptions. *International Journal of Lifelong Education*, *19*(1), 2–19. doi:10.1080/026013700293421

Aspinall, D., & MacKenzie, K. (2006). Mobile resource guarantees and policies. *Construction and Analysis of Safe, Secure, and Interoperable Smart Devices (*LNCS series, Vol. 3956,pp. 16–36). New York: Springer.

ASTD. (2009). *2008 state of the industry report*. Alexandria, VA: American Society for Training and Development.

ASTD. (2009). *Learning in tough economic times*. Alexandria, VA: American Society for Training and Development.

ASTD, & Booz Allen Hamilton (2009). *Executive development: Strategic and tactical approaches*. Alexandria, VA: American Society for Training and Development.

Auer, T. (1995). Beyond IS Implementation: a skill-based approach to IS use. In Proceedings of the *3rd European Conference on Information Systems*, Athens, Greece.

Auger, P., BarNir, A., & Gallaugher, J.M. (2003). Strategic Orientation, Competition, and Internet-Based Electronic Commerce. *Information Technology Management*, *4*(2), 139–164. doi:10.1023/A:1022942026706

Australian Bureau of Statistics. (2003). Business use of Information Technology. Canberra.

Baccarini, D. (1996). The concept of project complexity – a review. *International Journal of Project Management*, *14*, 201–204. doi:10.1016/0263-7863(95)00093-3

Baier, A. (2007). *High Performance in der Automobilzulieferindustrie. WWW [On-line].* Retrieved from http://www.automotive-rheinland.de/content/P5_accenture_270307_kurzfassung.pdf.

Baker and McKenzie. (2001). *Doing E-Commerce in Europe*. Hong Kong: Baker and McKenzie.

Bakos, J. Y. (1991). A strategic analysis of electronic marketplaces. *Management Information Systems Quarterly*, *15*(3), 295–310. doi:10.2307/249641

Bakos, J. Y. (1997). Reducing buyer search costs: implications for electronic marketplaces. *Management Science*, *43*(12), 1676–1692. doi:10.1287/mnsc.43.12.1676

Bakos, Y., Lucas, H. C. Jr, Oh, W., Simon, G., Viswanathan, S., & Weber, B. W. (2005). The impact of E-Commerce on competition in the retail brokerage industry. *Information Systems Research*, *16*(4), 352–371. doi:10.1287/isre.1050.0064

Bakos, J.Y. (1998) The emerging role of electronic marketplaces on the Internet. *Common ACM*, 41 (8).35–42.

Bakry, S., & Bakry, F. (2001). A strategic view for the development of e-business. *International Journal of Network Management*, *11*, 103–112. doi:10.1002/nem.395

Balabanovic, M., & Shoham, Y. (2007). FAB: Content-based, collaborative recommendation. *Communications of the ACM*, *40*(3), 66–72. doi:10.1145/245108.245124

Bansal, P., & Roth, K. (2000). Why Companies Go Green: A Model of Ecological Responsiveness. *Academy of Management Journal*, *43*(4), 717–736. doi:10.2307/1556363

Barba-Sánchez, V., Martínez-Ruiz, M., & Del, P. (2007). Jiménez-Zarco, A.I. (2007). Drivers, Benefits and Challenges of ICT Adoption by Small and Medium Sized Enterprises (SMEs): A Literature Review. *Problems and Perspectives in Management*, *5*(Issue 1), 103–114.

Barker, J.E. (2008). The Foundations of Innovation, Transformation and Change, a WiKi book from the AussieInvention dot com

Barnard, L., & Wesson, J. L. (2003). Usability issues for E-commerce in South Africa: an Empirical Investigation. *In Proceedings of SAICSIT 2003*, 258 – 267.

Barnes, J. (2001). Developing manufacturing competitiveness in South Africa. *Technovation*, *21*(5). doi:10.1016/S0166-4972(00)00047-X

Barney, J. (1995). Looking inside for competitive advantage. *The Academy of Management Executive*, *9*(4), 49–61.

Barney, J. B. (1991). Firm Resources and Sustained Competitive Advantage. *Journal of Management*, *17*(1), 99–120. doi:10.1177/014920639101700108

Bascuñana, H., Blanco, B., Rivero, Y., Monguet, J., Muñoz, J., & Sampieri, M. (March 2009). A telehealth approach to oropharyngeal dysphagia therapy; Paper presented at the 5th World Congress of International Society of Physical Medicine and Rehabilitation, Istanbul, Turkey, June 14, 2009.

Bathe, G., & Fournet, C. (2007). *Trustworthy Global Computing*. (LNCS: Vol. 4912)New York: Springer-Verlag.

Baumgartner, H., & Steenkamp, J.-B. E. M. (1996). Exploratory consumer behavior: conceptualization and measurement. *International Journal of Research in Marketing*, *13*, 121–137. doi:10.1016/0167-8116(95)00037-2

Bayles, D. (2001). *E-Commerce Logistics and Fulfillment: Delivering the Goods*. Upper Saddle River, NJ, U.S.A.: Prentice Hall PTR.

Beacham, J. (2006). *60 Minute Guide to Innovation: Turning Ideas Into Profit. Succeeding Through Innovation, Department of Trade and Industry*. UK: Published by TSO.

Beard, J., & Sumner, M. (2004). Seeking strategic advantage in post-net era. *The Journal of Strategic Information Systems*, *13*(2), 129–150. doi:10.1016/j.jsis.2004.02.003

Becker, H. (2006). *High Noon in the Automotive Industry*. Berlin, Heidelberg: Springer.

Begley, S., & Check, E. (12/27/99-1/3/2000). Rewiring your gray matter. *Newsweek 135* (1), 89-31.

Beig, L., Montazer, G. A., & Ghavamifar, A. (2007). Adoption a proper tool for e-readiness assessment in developing countries (case studies: Iran, Turkey and Malaysia). *Journal of Knowledge Economy & Knowledge Management*, *2*, 54–69.

Beije, P. (2005). *Open Innovation: the European Challenge*. A report submitted to Rotterdam School of Management / Erasmus University

Bell, B. S., & Kozlowski, S. J. (2002). A typology of virtual teams: Implications for effective leadership. *Group & Organization Management*, *17*(1), 14–46. doi:10.1177/1059601102027001003

Benbunan-Fich, R. (2001). Using Protocol Analysis to Evaluate the Usability of a Commercial Web Site. *Information & Management*, *39*, 151–163. doi:10.1016/S0378-7206(01)00085-4

Beneton, E. J., Balloni, A. J., & Bacic, M. J. (n.d.). Information security in small and medium Brazilian companies. *Annals of International joint conferences on computer, information and systems, sciences and engineering*. Available at http://cisse2007online.org/ accessed on July, 2009.

Bensaou, M., & Venkatraman, N. (1995). Configurations of inter-organization relationships: A comparison between US and Japanese automakers. *Management Science*, *41*(9), 1471–1492. doi:10.1287/mnsc.41.9.1471

Berge, Z.L. (1998). Barriers to online teaching in post-secondary institutions. *Online Journal of Distance Education Administration, 1(2)*.

Bergiel, B. J., Bergiel, E. B., & Balsmeier, P. W. (2008). Nature of virtual teams: A summary of their advantages and disadvantages. *Management Research News*, *31*(2), 99–110. doi:10.1108/01409170810846821

Bernal, C. Jairo (2005). Diseño conceptual de productos asistido por ordenador: Un estudio analítico sobre aplicaciones y definición de la estructura básica de un nuevo programa. Doctoral dissertation, Universitat Politècnica de Catalunya, Spain.

IFIP/IFAC Task Force on Architectures for Enterprise Integration. (2003). The Generalized Enterprise Reference Architecture and Methodology. In Bernus, P., Nemes, L., & Schmidt, G. (Eds.), *Handbook on Enterprise Architectures* (pp. 21–63). Berlin: Springer-Verlag.

BERR. (2007). *The 2007 R&D Scoreboard, The top 850 UK and 1250 global companies by R&D investment. Department for Business Enterprise and Regulatory Reform*. UK: BERR.

BERR. (2008). *The 2008 Value Added Scoreboard, The top 800 UK and 750 European companies by Value Added: Commentary & Analysis. Department for Business Enterprise and Regulatory Reform*. UK: BERR.

Berry, L. L. (1983). Relationship Marketing. In L.L. Berry, G.L. Shostack, and G.D: Upah (eds), *Emerging Perspectives on Services Marketing*, American Marketing Association, Chicago, 25-38.

Bertot, Y., & Casteran, P. (2004). *Interactive theorem proving and program development: Coq'Art: the calculus of inductive constructions. Texts in theoretical comp. science*. New York: Springer-Verlag.

Beugré, C. D. (1998). *Managing fairness in organizations*. Westport, CT: Quorum Books.

Beynon-Davies, P. (2004). *E-Business*. Basingstoke: Palgrave.

Bhatia, S. (2001). *e-ASEAN Readiness Assessment*. Retrieved August 15, 2009, from http://www.itu.int/asean2001/documents/pdf/Document-28.pdf

Bies, R. J., & Moag, J. S. (1986). Interactional justice: Communication criteria of fairness. In Lewicki, R. J., Sheppard, B. H., & Bazerman, M. H. (Eds.), *Research on negotiation in organizations* (*Vol. 1*, pp. 43–55). Greenwich, CT: JAI Press.

Billig, A., Blomqvist, E., & Lin, F. (2007) Semantic Matching based on Enterprise Ontologies, In *Proc. of the 6th International Conference on Ontologies, DataBases, and Applications of Semantics, ODBASE 2007* (pp. 1161 – 1168)Vilamoura, Algarve, Portugal.

Bingley, S., Sellitto, C., & Burgess, S. (2009). The importance of third party websites: A study of small accommodation providers in Australia. *4^Th International Scientific Conference "Planning for the Future - Learning from the Past: Contemporary Developments in Tourism, Travel & Hospitality"*. Rhodes Island, Greece.

Bjorklund, B., & Bee, H. (2007). *Journey to adulthood* (6th ed.). Upper Saddle River: Prentice Hall.

Blau, P. M. (1964). *Exchange and Power in Social Life*. New York: John Wiley & Sons.

Bleeke, J., & Ernst, D. (1993). *Collaborating to Compete*. New York: John Wiley & Sons.

BlessingWhite. (2006). *Leading Technical Professionals 2006 Report*. Princeton, NJ: BlessingWhite, Inc.

Blog, P. S. (2009), Get Ready for a new Economic Era – The Creator Economy Beckons. Retrieved from http://whatmatters.mckinseydigital.com/internet/get-ready-for-a-new-economic-era, *consultation made in December 2, 2009*

Bloomberg, J., & Schmelzer, R. (2006). *Service Orient or Be Doomed!: How Service Orientation Will Change Your Business*. Hoboken, NJ: Wiley.

Blum, N., Magedanz, T., & Stein, H. (2007). Service creation & delivery for SME based on SOA/IMS. In *Proceedings of the 2007 Workshop on Middleware for next-generation converged networks and applications*. ACM: New York.

Bode, S., & Burn, J. M. (2002). Strategies for consultancy engagement for e-business development - a case analysis of Australian SMEs. In Burgess, S. (Ed.), *Managing Information Technology in Small Business: Challenges and Solutions*. Hershey, PA: Idea Group.

Bonsiepe, G. (2000). Una Tecnología Cognoscitiva - De la producción de conocimientos hacia la presentación de conocimientos. Simposium Ricerca+Design, Milano, 2000.

Botkin, J. (1999). *Smart Business: How Knowledge Communities Can Revolutionize Your Company*. Washington, DC: Free Press.

Bove, L. L., & Johnson, L. W. (2001). Customer relationships with sales associates: an opportunity for retailers. *International Quarterly Journal of Marketing*, *1*(1), 135–150.

Bovet, D., & Martha, J. (2000). *Value Nets: Breaking the Supply Chain to Unlock Hidden Profits*. Chichester, UK: John Wiley.

Bowersox, D. J., Closs, D., & Cooper, M. B. (2002). *Supply chain logistics management*. New York: Mc Graw Hill.

Boyle, R. D. (1995). Avoiding common pitfalls of reengineering. *Management Accounting*, *77*(4), 24–30.

Brandl, D. (2007). SOA explained. *Control Engineering*, *54*(8), 22–22.

Brasil. (2009). Portal do Governo Brasileiro. At www.brasil.gov.br, accessed on July, 2009.

Braver, N. (1995). Overcoming resistance to TQM. *Research Technologic Management*, *38*(5), 40–44.

Bridges.org. (2005). *Comparison of e-readiness assessment models and tools (updated).* Retrieved August 29, 2009, from www.bridges.org/publication/128

Brin, S., & Page, L. (1998). The Aanatomy of a Large-scale Hypertextual Web Search Engine, Proceedings of the Seventh International World Wide Web Conference, 30(1-7), p. 107-117.

Brocke, J., Schenk, B., & Sonnenberg, C. (2009) Organizational implications of implementing service oriented ERP systems: an analysis based on new institutional economics. In Abramowicz, W. (Ed.) *12th International Conference Business Information Systems*, Poznan, Poland (252–263). Berlin, Germany: Springer-Verlag.

Brodkin, J. (2007). Are SOAs saving anyone money? *New World (New Orleans, La.)*, *24*(28), 24–25.

Brown, D. H., & Lockett, N. (2004). Potential of critical e-applications for engaging SMEs in e-Business: A provider perspective. *European Journal of Information Systems*, *13*(1), 21–38. doi:10.1057/palgrave.ejis.3000480

Brun, M. H., & Lanng, C. (2006). Reducing barriers for e-business in SME's through an open service oriented infrastructure. In Proceedings of the 8th international conference on Electronic commerce: The new e-commerce: innovations for conquering current barriers, obstacles and limitations to conducting successful business on the internet (pp. 403-410). ACM: New York.

Bruun, P., Jensen, M., & Skovgaard, J. (2002). e-Marketplaces: Crafting A Winning Strategy. *European Management Journal*, *20*(3), 286–298. doi:10.1016/S0263-2373(02)00045-2

Bubenko, J. A., Jr., Persson, A., & Stirna, J. (2001). User Guide of the Knowledge Management Approach Using Enterprise Knowledge Patterns, *IST Programme project Hypermedia and Pattern Based Knowledge Management for Smart Organisations: Delivery 3*, Royal Institute of Technology (KTH) and Stockholm University, Sweden. Published October 01, 2001, at http://www.dsv.su.se/~js/ekd_user_guide.html.

Budd, L., & Harris, L. (2004). *E-Economy: Rhetoric or Business Reality*. New York: Routledge.

BUGHIN. Jacques, MANYIKA, James, ROBERTS, Roger (2009), Beyond the Sloan Age. at http://whatmatters.mckinseydigital.com/internet/beyond-the-sloan-age, McKinsey, February, consulted at September 2009.

Bui, T. X., Sankaran, S., & Sebastian, I. S. (2003). A framework for measuring national e-readiness. *International Journal of Electronic Business*, *1*(1), 3–22. doi:10.1504/IJEB.2003.002162

Burgess, S. (2008). Determining website content for small businesses: Assisting the planning of Owner/Managers. *International Journal of Knowledge Management Studies*, *2*(1), 143–161. doi:10.1504/IJKMS.2008.016449

Burgess, S., Bingley, S., & Sellitto, C. (2007). A model for website content decisions in micro businesses. *Global Business & Economics Anthology*, *1*, 474–487.

Burgess, S., & Schauder, D. (1999). *Assisting small businesses to identify internet opportunities* (pp. 121–128). San Deigo, California: Millenial Challenges in Management Education, Cybertechnology and Leadership.

Burgess, S., Sellitto, C., & Karanasios, S. (2009). *Effective web presence solutions for small businesses: Strategies for successful implementation*. Hershey, PA: Information Science Reference.

Burgess, S. (2002). Information Technology in Small Business: Issues and Solutions. In Burgess, S. (Ed.), *Managing Information Technology in Small Business: Challenges and Solutions*, 1-17. Hershey, PA: Idea Group Publishing.

Burgess, S. (2006). A model for B2C customer interactions on the web by small businesses: Adjustments for the 'Extended web'. *Grand Challenges in Technology Management: Proceedings of ISOneWorld 2006.* Las Vegas, Nevada.

Busen, D. (2004). The ACS to Co-Operate in Establishing the Serbian Auto Cluster. *ACS News*, *1*, 7.

Caffarella, R. (2001). *Planning programs for adult learners* (2nd ed.). San Francisco: Jossey-Bass.

Calin G. Ranchhod, A. & Hackney, R. (2001). Internet Transactions and Physical Logistics: Conflict or Complementary. *Internet Research: Electronic Networking Applications and Policy*, 14 (½, s. 36).

Callegati, E., & Grandi, S. (2005). Cluster dynamics and innovation in SMEs: the role of culture, Working paper No. 03/2005, International Centre for Research on the Economics of Culture, Institutions, and Creativity (EBLA), Università di Torino, Turin, Italy

Camarinha-Matos, L. M., & Afsarmanesh, H. (2005). Collaborative Networks: A New Scientific Discipline. *Journal of Intelligent Manufacturing*, *16*, 439–452. doi:10.1007/s10845-005-1656-3

Camarinha-Matos, L. M., & Afsarmanesh, H. (2007). A Framework for Virtual Organization Creation in a Breeding Environment. *Annual Reviews in Control*, *31*, 119–135. doi:10.1016/j.arcontrol.2007.03.006

Camarinha-Matos, L., Afsarmanesh, H., Garita, C., & Lima, C. (1999). Hierarchical Coordination in Virtual Enterprise Infrastructures. *Journal of Intelligent & Robotic Systems*, *26*, 267–287. doi:10.1023/A:1008137110347

Camarinha-Matos, L. M., & Afsarmanesh, H. (2008). Classes of Collaborative Networks. In G.Putnik & M. M. Cunha (Eds.), *Encyclopedia of Networked and Virtual Organizations* (pp. 193-198). Hershey, PA: Information Science Reference (IGI Global).

Canada (2009). Government of Canada Internet Portal. At http://canada.gc.ca/, accessed on July, 2009.

Canadian e-Business Initiative. (2003, May). *Fast forward 4.0 growing Canada's digital economy*, pp. 1-25.

Canadian e-Business Initiative. (2004, September). *Net impact study Canada. Strategies for increasing SME engagement in the e-economy*, Retrieved August 1, 2009, from http://www.netimpactstudy.com/ca/pdf/canada-en.pdf.

Canny, J. (2002). Collaborative filtering with privacy via factor analysis. *Proceedings of the 25th annual international ACM SIGIR conference on Research and development in information retrieval* (Session: Collaborative Filtering), 238-245.

Cao, M., Zhang, Q., & Seydel, J. (2005). B2C E-Commerce Web Site Quality: An Empirical Examination. *Industrial Management & Data Systems*, *105*(5), 645–661. doi:10.1108/02635570510600000

Caridi, M., Cigolini, R., & De Marco, D. (2005). Improving supply-chain collaboration by linking intelligent agents to CPFR. *International Journal of Production Research*, *43*(20), 4191–4218. doi:10.1080/00207540500142134

Carliner, C. (2002). Tips for Conducting Level 1 Evaluations of Asynchronous e-Courses. *American Society for Training and Development publication What Works, March*.

Carlsson, B., & Eliasson, G. (2002). Industrial dynamics and endogenous growth. *Industry and Innovation*, *10*(4), 435–455. doi:10.1080/1366271032000163676

Caron, A. (2003). *Inovações tecnológicas nas pequenas e médias empresas industriais em tempos de globalização: o caso do estado do Paraná.* Doctoral thesis, approved at Federal University of Santa Catarina, Brazil.

Carstensen, A., Holmberg, L., & Sandkuhl, K. (2008). Supporting collaboration in an Extended Enterprise with the Connector View on Enterprise Models. In *Proceeding of First IFIP WG 8.1 Working Conference, PoEM 2008* (pp. 111 - 126). Stockholm, Sweden.

Carstensen, A., Holmberg, L., & Sandkuhl, K. (2009). Modelling Interoperability in Networked Organisations with the Connector Concept. In *Proceedings of the 13th IFAC Symposium on Information Control Problems in Manufacturing* (pp. 916 - 921). Moscow, Russia.

Carstensen, A., Sandkuhl, K., & Holmberg, L. (2008). Towards a Methodology for Modeling Interoperability Between Collaborating Enterprises. In *Proc. of the 10th International Conference on Enterprise Information Systems* (pp. 333 - 338). Barcelona, Spain.

Cascio, W. F. (2000). Managing a virtual workplace. *The Academy of Management Executive*, *14*, 81–90.

Caussanel, J., & Chouraqui, E. (1999) Model and methodology of knowledge capitalization for small and medium sized enterprises. In *Proc. of the 12th Workshop on Knowledge Acquisition, Modeling and Management.* Banff, Alberta, Canada.

Cavallo, R. (2006). Optimal decision-making with minimal waste: strategy-proof redistribution of VCG payments. In Nakashima, H. (Eds.), *Autonomous Agents and Multi-Agent Systems 2006* (pp. 882–889).

CEC. (2009). *Internet of Things - An Action Plan for Europe. WWW [On-line].* Retrieved from http://ec.europa.eu/information_society/policy/rfid/documents/commiot2009.pdf.

Cervantes, M. (2009). *Open Innovation in Global Networks: Recent OECD work*, Policy issues and Open questions, a paper from Trade and Development Board Investment, Enterprise and Development Commission Multi-year expert meeting on enterprise development policies and capacity-building in science, technology and innovation, Geneva, 20–22 January 2009

CGI. BR – Comitê Gestor da Internet no Brasil. (2009). *Pesquisa sobre o uso das tecnologias da Informação no Brasil.* Retrieved from http://www.cetic.br/tic/2008/index.htm on July, 2009.

Chaffey, D. (2006). *E-business and E-commerce Management.* New York: Financial Times.

Chaffey, D. (2007). *E-business and E-commerce Management–Strategy, Implementation and Practice* (3rd ed.). Harlow: Pearson Education.

Chason, M. (2008). [Center, MA, USA.]. *The Innovator, 1*(1), IXL.

Chaston, I. (2001). The Internet and E-Commerce: An Opportunity to Examine Organisational Learning in Progress in Small Manufacturing Firms? *International Small Business Journal, 19*(2), 13–30. doi:10.1177/0266242601192001

Chau, S., & Pedersen, S. G. (2000). Small is Beautiful: The Emergence of New Micro Business Utilising Electronic Commerce. [Brisbane: Australia.]. *Proceedings of the Australian Conference on Information Systems, 2000*, 1–8.

Chau, S. B., & Turner, P. (2004). An SME Experience of E-Commerce: Some Considerations for Policy Formulation in Australia. In B.J. Corbitt and NAY. Nl-Qirim (eds), *E-Business, E-Government & Small and Medium-Sized Enterprises: Opportunities and Challenges* (91-111). Hershey, PA: Idea Group Publishing.

Chen, D., Doumeingts, G., & Vernadat, F. (2008). Architectures for enterprise integration and interoperability: Past, present and future. *Computers in Industry, 59*, 647–659. doi:10.1016/j.compind.2007.12.016

Chen, I., Long, J., & Yan, T. (2004). E-Supply chain implementation strategies in a transitional economy. *International Journal of Information Technology and Decision Making, 3*(4), 563–574. doi:10.1142/S0219622004001240

Chen, A. H., & Siems, T. (2001). *B2B eMarketplace Announcements and Shareholder Wealth.Economic and Financial Review*. First Quarter.

Chen, S. (2004). *Strategic Management Of E-business*. New York: John Wiley.

Chen, J. (2009). *The Impact of Aesthetics on Attitudes Towards Websites*. Retrieved from July 24, 2009 from http://usability.gov/articles/062009news.html.

Chen, X., & Deng, X. (2006) Settling the complexity of two-player Nash equilibrium. In FOCS 2006, 47th Annual IEEE Symposium on Foundations of Computer Science (pp. 261–272), IEEE Computer Society.

Chen, X., & Deng, X.(2005). 3-NASH is PPAD-complete. *Electronic Colloquium on Computational Complexity*, No 139.

Chepaitis, E. (2002). Soft barriers to ICT application in development: trust and information quality in Russia. *Journal of International Development, 14*, 51–60. doi:10.1002/jid.871

Chesbrough, H. (2003). *Open Innovation: The New Imperative for Creating and Profiting from Technology*. Boston: Harvard Business School Press.

Chesbrough, H. (2006). *Open business models: How to thrive in a new innovation landscape*. Boston: Harvard Business School Press.

Chesbrough, H. W. (2003b). The era of open innovation. *MIT Sloan Management Review, 44*(3), 35–41.

Chesbrough, H., & Rosenbloom, R. S. (2002). The role of the business model in capturing value from innovation: Evidence from Xerox Corporation's technology spin-off companies. *Industrial and Corporate Change, 11*(3), 529–555. doi:10.1093/icc/11.3.529

Chesbrough, H. (2003). *Open Innovation: The New Imperative for Creating and Profiting from Technology*. Boston: Harvard Business School Press.

Chesbrough, H., Vanhaverbeke, W., & West, J. (2006). *Open innovation: Researching a new paradigm*. London: Oxford University Press.

Chesbrough, H., Vanhaverbeke, W., & West, J. (2006). (Eds.). *Open innovation: Researching a new paradigm.* London:Oxford University Press.

Cho, Y. H., & Kim, J. K. (2004). Application of Web usage mining and product taxonomy to collaborative recommendations in e-commerce. *Expert Systems with Applications, 26*(2), 233–246. doi:10.1016/S0957-4174(03)00138-6

Christensen, J. F. (2007). *Innovation concepts, processes and strategies*. Presentation in PhD Course, Copenhagen Business School.

Chuan Jun Su. (2007). *Mobile multi-agent based, distributed information platform (MADIP) for wide-area e-health monitoring; Science Direct*. Elsevier.

Chudoba, K. M., Wynn, E., Lu, M., & Watson-Manheim, M. B. (2005). How virtual are we? Measuring virtuality and understanding its impact in a global organization. *Information Systems Journal*, *15*, 279–306. doi:10.1111/j.1365-2575.2005.00200.x

Ciravegna, F., & Petrelli, D. (2006). Annotating document content: a knowledge management perspective. *The Indexer*, *25*(1), 23–27.

Claesson, A. (2006). *Product Design by Configurable Components*. Unpublished PhD dissertation, Chalmers Technical University, Sweden. Retrieved December 19, 2009, from http://www.variant.se/acthesis/

Clark, T. R., & Gottfredson, C. A. (2008). In Search of Learning Agility: Assessing Progress from 1957 to 2008, A report submitted to TRCLARK LLC

Cloete, E., Courtney, S., & Fintz, J. (2002). Small Businesses' Acceptance and Adoption of E-Commerce in the Western-Cape Province of South-Africa. *Electronic Journal on Information Systems in Developing Countries*, *10*(4), 1–13.

Collins, E., Lawrence, S., Pavlovich, K., & Ryan, C. (2007). Business networks and the uptake of sustainability practices: the case of New Zealand. *Journal of Cleaner Production*, *15*(8-9), 729–740. doi:10.1016/j.jclepro.2006.06.020

Colombo, M. G. (2001). Technology-Based Entrepreneurs: Does Internet Make a Difference? *Small Business Economics*, *16*(3), 177–190. doi:10.1023/A:1011127205758

Colquitt, J. A. (2001). On the dimensionality of organizational justice: A construct validation of a measure. *The Journal of Applied Psychology*, *86*, 386–400. doi:10.1037/0021-9010.86.3.386

Colquitt, J. A. (2004). Does the justice of the one interact with the justice of the many? Reactions to procedural justice in teams. *The Journal of Applied Psychology*, *89*(4), 633–646. doi:10.1037/0021-9010.89.4.633

Colquitt, J. A., Conlon, D. E., Wesson, M. J., Porter, C. O. L. H., & Ng, K. Y. (2001). Justice at the millennium: A meta-analytic review of 25 years of organizational justice research. *The Journal of Applied Psychology*, *86*, 425–445. doi:10.1037/0021-9010.86.3.425

Colquitt, J. A., & Jackson, C. L. (2006). Justice in teams: The context sensitivity of justice rules across individual and team contexts. *Journal of Applied Social Psychology*, *36*, 868–899.

Colquitt, J. A., Noe, R. A., & Jackson, C. L. (2002). Justice in teams: Antecedents and consequences of procedural justice climate. *Personnel Psychology*, *55*, 83–109. doi:10.1111/j.1744-6570.2002.tb00104.x

Combe, C. (2006). *Introduction To E-business: Management And Strategy*. New York: Butterworth-Heinemann Inc.

Commonwealth of Australia (2009). *Powering Ideas: An Innovation Agenda for the 21st Century*. Commonwealth of Australia 2009

Computers System Policy Project. (1998). *The CSPP Readiness Guide: For living in the Networked World.* Retrieved September 3, 2009, from http://www.cspp.org/documents/NW_Readiness_Guide.pdf

Conceição, P., & Heitor, M. (2000). *Engineering and Technology for Innovation in PORTUGAL: a study on the dynamics of technological change*, A Preliminary Summary, Center for Innovation, Technology and Policy Research, Instituto Superior Tecnico, Technical University of Lisbon, available at http://in3.dem.ist.utl.pt/et2000/

Conner, D. S. (2003). Social comparison in virtual work environments: An examination of contemporary referent selection. *Journal of Occupational and Organizational Psychology*, *76*, 133–147. doi:10.1348/096317903321208925

Constantinides, E. (2002a). The 4S Web-Marketing Mix Model. *Electronic Commerce Research and Applications*, *1*, 57–76. doi:10.1016/S1567-4223(02)00006-6

Constantinides, E. (2002b) From Physical Marketing to Web Marketing: The Web-Marketing Mix.*Proceedings of the 35th Hawaii International Conference on System Science (HICSS)*, 7, 205-216.

Coppel, J. (2000). E-commerce: Impacts and Policy Challenges. *OECD Economics Department Working Papers*, no.252

Cosh, A., Fu, X., & Hughes, A. (2005). *Management Characteristics, Collaboration and Innovative Efficiency: Evidence from UK Survey Data.* Working Paper no. 311 (Cambridge: Centre for Business Research, 2005), p. 8.

Covin, J. G., & Slevin, D. P. (1991). A Conceptual Model of Entrepreneurship as Firm Behaviour. *Entrepreneurship Theory and Practice.*, *16*, 7–25.

Covin, J. G., & Slevin, D. P. (1986). The development and testing of an organization-level entrepreneurship scale. In Ronstadt, R. (Ed.), *Frontiers of Entrepreneurship Research* (pp. 628–639). Wellesley: Babson College.

Cox, C., Burgess, S., Sellitto, C., & Buultjens, J. (2008). *The influence of user-generated content on tourist travel behaviour*. Lismore, NSW, Australia: Australian Regional Tourism Research Centre.

Cox, G. (2008). Defining innovation: what counts in the University of Cape Town landscape? A proceedings of ascilite Melbourne 2008, Melbourne

Cragg, P. B., & King, M. (1993). Small-firm computing: Motivators and inhibitors. *Management Information Systems Quarterly*, *17*(1), 47–60. doi:10.2307/249509

Cramton, P., Shoham, Y., & Steinberg, R. (Eds.). (2006). *Combinatorial Auctions*. Cambridge, MA: MIT Press.

Cropanzano, R., & Greenberg, J. (1997). Progress in organizational justice: Tunneling through the maze. In Cooper, C. L., & Robertson, I. T. (Eds.), *International Review of Industrial and Organizational Psychology* (pp. 317–372). New York: John Wiley & Sons.

Csikszentmihalyi, M. (1975). Play and intrinsic rewards. *Journal of Humanistic Psychology*, *15*(3), 41–63. doi:10.1177/002216787501500306

Csikszentmihalyi, M. (1977). *Beyond boredom and anxiety* (2nd ed.). San Francisco: Jossey-Bass.

CSR Europe (2008b). *R&D Open Innovation: Networks with SME*, Open Innovation Network, 6 November 2008

Culler, A., & Webster, M. (2007). A model of B2B e-commerce, based on connectivity and purpose. *International Journal of Operations & Production Management*, *27*(2), 205–235. doi:10.1108/01443570710720621

Cunha, M., & Putnik, G. (2006). *Agile virtual enterprises: implementation and management support*. Hershey, PA: Idea Group Publishing.

Curran, K. (2004). Tips for Achieving High Positioning in the Results Pages of the Major Search Engine. *Information Technology Journal*, *3*(2), 202–205. doi:10.3923/itj.2004.202.205

Currie, W. (2000). *The global information society*. New York: John Wiley and Sons.

Dada, D. (2006). E-Readiness for Developing Countrie: Moving the Focus from the Environment to the Users. *The Electronic Journal of Information Systems in Developing Countries*, *27*(6), 1–14.

Daft, R. (2000). *Management*. Orlando, FL: The Dryden Press.

Daft, R. (2009). *The New Era of Management*. Cincinnati, OH: South-Western College.

Daft, R. (2003). *Organization Theory and Design*. Mason: Thomson South-Western.

Daft, R. (2006). *Understanding the theory and design of organizations.* Mason: Thomson South-Western.

Dai, Q., & Kauffman, R. J. (2002a). Business Models for Internet-Based B2B Electronic Markets. *International Journal of Electronic Commerce*, *6*(4), 41–72.

Daimler (2009). Daimler Supplier Network. WWW [On-line].

Dale, E. (1969). *Audiovisual Methods in Teaching*. New York: The Dryden Press.

Dandridge, T. (2000). High-Tech Potential? An Exploratory Study Of Very Small Firms' Usage of the Internet. *International Small Business Journal*, *18*(2), 81–91. doi:10.1177/0266242600182004

Daniel, E., Wilson, H., & Myers, A. (2002). Adoption of Ecommerce by SMEs In The UK: Towards a Stage Model. *International Small Business Journal*, *20*(3), 253–270. doi:10.1177/0266242602203002

Dannenberg, J., & Kleinhans, C. (2005). The Coming Age of Collaboration in the Automotive Industry. *Mercer Management Journal*, *17*, 88–94.

Dans, E. (2001). IT Investment in Small and Medium Enterprises:Paradoxically Productive? *The Electronic Journal of Information Systems Evaluation*, 4 (1).

Darch, H., & Lucas, T. (2002). Training as an e-commerce enabler. *Journal of Workplace Learning*, *14*(4), 148–156. doi:10.1108/13665620210427276

Daskalakis, K., & Papadimitriou, C. H. (2005) Three-player games are hard. *Electronic Colloquium on Computational Complexity, No 139.*

Data Monitor. (2004). *SME Banking in Australia 2004*. Retrieved August 15, 2009, from http://www.researchandmarkets.com/reports/219039

DataMonitor (2009). Global Hypermarkets & Super Centers, Industry Profile. March 2009

Davenport, C. (2006). *In Beacham (2006), 60 Minute Guide to Innovation: Turning Ideas Into Profit* (p. 3). UK: Succeeding Through Innovation, Department of Trade and Industry, Published by TSO.

Davenport, T. H. (1993). *Process Innovation: Reengineering Work through Information Technology*. Boston: Harvard Business School Press.

Davis, P. S. (2000). Internationalization and Organizational Growth: The Impact of Internet Usage and Technology Involvement Among Entrepreneur-Led Family Businesses. *Family Business Review*, *13*(2), 107–120. doi:10.1111/j.1741-6248.2000.00107.x

Davis, F. D. (1989). Perceived Usefulness. Perceived Ease of Use and User Acceptance of Information Technology. *Management Information Systems Quarterly*, *13*(3), 319–340. doi:10.2307/249008

Davis, F. D., Bagozzi, R. P., & Warshaw, P. R. (1989). User acceptance of computer technology: A comparison of two theoretical models. *Management Science*, *35*(8), 982–1003. doi:10.1287/mnsc.35.8.982

Dayan, M., & Colak, M. (2008). The role of procedural justice in the new product development process. *European Journal of Innovation Management*, *11*(2), 199–218. doi:10.1108/14601060810869866

De Bono, E. (1994). *Sur/petition*. New York: HarperCollins Publishers Ltd.

De Jong, J. P. J. (2006). *Open Innovation: Practice, Trends, Motives and bottlenecks in the SMEs (Meer Open Innovatie: Praktijk, Ontwikkelingen, Motieven en Knelpunten in het MKB)*. Zoetermeer: EIM.

De Jong, J. P. J., & von Hippel, E. (2009). Transfers of user process innovations to process equipment producers: A study of Dutch high-tech firms. *MIT Sloan School of Management Research Paper No. 4724-09,* March, 2009

De Jong, J. P. J., Vanhaverbeke, W., Kalvet, T., & Chesbrough, H. (2008), Policies for Open Innovation: Theory, Framework and Cases, Research project funded by VISION Era-Net, Helsinki: Finland.

De Jong, J.P.J. & von Hippel, E. (2005). *User Innovation in SMEs: Incidence and Transfer to Producers, SCALES-initiative (SCientific AnaLysis of Entrepreneurship and SMEs)*. the Netherlands Ministry of Economic Affairs.

De Vrande, V.V., De Jong, J.P.J., Vanhaverbeke, W. & De Rochemont, M. (2008). Open innovation in SMEs: Trends, motives and management challenges, a report published under the SCALES-initiative (SCientific AnaLysis of Entrepreneurship and SMEs), as part of the 'SMEs and Entrepreneurship programme' financed by the Netherlands Ministry of Economic Affairs, 2008

Del Brío, J. Á., & Junquera, B. (2003, December). A review of the literature on environmental innovation management in SMEs: implications for public policies. *Technovation*, *23*(12), 939–948. doi:10.1016/S0166-4972(02)00036-6

Dellaert, B. G. C., & Kahn, B. E. (1999). How Tolerable is Delay? Consumer's Evaluation of Internet Web Sites after Waiting. *Journal of Interactive Marketing*, *13*, 41–54. doi:10.1002/(SICI)1520-6653(199924)13:1<41::AID-DIR4>3.0.CO;2-S

Delone, W. H. (1988). Determinants of Success for Computer Usage in Small Business. *MIS Quarterly*, 12(1) 1988, 51-61.

Denis, M., Lessard, P., van der Werf, P., Vitello, C., Duplessis, J., Desgagnes, N., et al. (2003). Waste Mangement Guide for Small and Medium Enterprises – Canadian Version. Editions Ruffec. http://entreprisescanada.ca/servlet/ContentServer?cid=1184867843697&lang=en&pagename=CBSC_QC%2Fdisplay&c=InfoResources. Last Verified: 2007-12-21.

Department for Business. Enterprise & Regulatory Reform. (2008). *Small and Medium-sized Enterprise (SME) Statistics for the UK and Regions 2007*, UK.

DeSanctis, G., & Monge, P. (1999). Communication processes for virtual organizations. *Organization Science*, *10*, 693–703. doi:10.1287/orsc.10.6.693

Deshpande, Y., Chandrarathna, A., & Ginige, A. (2002). Web site auditing: First step towards re-engineering. *Proceedings of the 14th International Conference on Software Engineering and Knowledge Engineering(pp.* 731-737), Italy.

Design Council. (2005). *National Survey of Firms*. London: Design Council.

Devine, D. A., Dugan, C. B., Semaca, N. D., & Speicher, K. J. (2001). Building enduring consortia. *McKinsey Quarterly Special Edition*, *2*, 26–33.

Dey, A. (2001). Understanding and Using Context. *Personal and Ubiquitous Computing Journal*, *5*(1), 4–7. doi:10.1007/s007790170019

Dholakia, N., Dholakia, R. R., Laub, M., & Hwang, Y.-S. (1999). Electronic Commerce and the Transformation of Marketing, In Wolfgang, F., (Ed.), *Internet Marketing*, (pp. 55-80) Germany, Schaefer-Poeschel: Verlag.

Diário, I. O. L. (2008). Clientes do Continente Online crescem 35% ao Ano. Retrieved from http://diario.iol.pt/empresas/portugal-continente-sonae-internet-continente-online-distribuicao/1005286-1728.html*consultation made in September 9, 2009*

DIEESE – Departamento Intersindical de Estatística e Estudos Econômicos. (1999). *Aniversário do Real.* Retrieved on August, 2009, from http://www.dieese.org.br/esp/cju/jul99ptr.xml.

Digital Marketing Compass. (n.d.). Retrieved from http://www.ogilvy.com.tr/digitalmarketingcompass/ Access date: 07.08.2009.

Ding, L., Finin, T., Joshi, A., Pan, R., Cost, R. S., Pen, Y., et al. (2004). Swoogle: A Search and Metadata Engine for the Semantic Web. *Proceedings of the thirteenth ACM international conference on Information and knowledge management.*652 - 659.

Donner, R., Höfener, J., Lämmer, S., & Helbing, D. (2007). Dynamic Stabilization and Control of Material Flows in Traffic and Manufacturing Networks by Means of Phase Synchronization. In *Proceedings of the 3rd International Conference on Physics and Control (PHYSCON 2007)*. Potsdam, Germany. Retrieved June 02, 2009, from http://lib.physcon.ru/?item=1196.

Dornan, A. (2001). *The Essential Guide to Wireless Communications Applications*. Upper Saddle, New Jersey: Prentice Hall.

Doyle. Peter. (2008). eCommerce 2.0 – eCommerce next generation. Retrieved from *http://socialnetit.com*, in 25 September 2009.

Doz. Y. Santos, J., Williamson, P. (2001). *From global to Metanational: How Companies win in the knowledge economy*. Boston: Harvard Business School Press.

Drucker. P. (1995). Managing in a time of great change. *A Gestão numa Época de Grande Mudança*, translation made by Ana Paula Curado, Difusão Cultural, Lisboa.

Duan, Y., Mullins, R., Hamblin, D., & Stanek, S. (2002). Addressing ICT skill challenges in SMEs: Insights from three country investigations. *Journal of European Industrial Training*, *26*(8/9), 430–445. doi:10.1108/03090590210451524

Duin, H., Eschenbächer, J., & Thoben, K.-D. (2009). Strategische Planung in Unternehmensnetzwerken. *Industrie Management*, *25*, 9–12.

Duin, H. (2007b). In Camarinha-Matos, L. M., Afsarmanesh, H., Novais, P., & Abalide, C. (Eds.), *Causal Cross-Impact Analysis as Strategic Planning Aid for Virtual Organisation Breeding Environments* (pp. 147–154). New York: Springer.

Duin, H. (2008). In Camarinha-Matos, L. M., & Picard, W. (Eds.), *Systemic Strategic Managment for VBEs in the Manufacturing Sector* (pp. 25–32). New York: Springer.

Duin, H. (2007a). In Thoben, K.-D., Baalsrud Hauge, J., Smeds, R., & Riis, J. O. (Eds.), *Causal Cross-Impact Analysis as a Gaming Tool for Strategic Decision Making* (pp. 79–93). Aachen: Verlag Mainz.

Duin, H., Oliveira, M., & Saffarpour, A. (2007). A Simulation Model for Virtual Manufacturing Environments for Serious Games. In Proceedings from *13th International Conference on Concurrent Enterprising: Concurrent Innovation: An Emerging Paradigm for Collaboration and Competitiveness in the Extended Enterprise.*

Duncan, A. (2009, July 24). Education reform moon's shot. *The Washington Post.* Retrieved August 5, 2009, from http://www.washingtonpost.com/wp-dyn/content/article/2009/07/23/AR2009072302634.html.

Earl, T. (2005). *Service-oriented architecture: concepts, technology and design*. Upper Saddle River, NJ: Pearson Education.

Earl, T. (2008). *Principles of service design*. Boston: Pearson Education.

Earl, M. J. (1989). *Management Strategies for Information Technology*. Upper Saddle River, NJ: Prentice Hall.

Earl, M.J. (2000). Evolving the E-Business. *Business Strategy Review*, 11(2).

Eckersley, P., Harris, L., & Jackson, P. (2004). *E-business Fundamentals*. New York: Routledge.

Economist Intelligence Unit. (2009). *E-readiness rankings 2009: The usage imperative.* Retrieved September 3, 2009, from http://graphics.eiu.com/pdf/E-readiness%20rankings.pdf

EEDA. (2008). *ERDF Regional Workshops – Autumn 2008 Review Report*. UK: East of England Development Agency.

Egger, F. N. (2001). Affective Design of E-Commerce User Interfaces: How to Maximise Perceived Trustworthiness. *Proceedings of the International Conference on Affective Human Factors Design*, 317-324.

Eid, R., Trueman, M., & Ahmed, A. M. A. (2002). Cross-Industry Review of B2B Critical Success Factors. *Internet Research: Electronic Networking Applications and Policy*, *12*(2), 110–123. doi:10.1108/10662240210422495

Eikebrokk, T. R., & Dag, H. O. (2009). Training, competence, and business performance: Evidence in European small and medium-sized enterprises. *International Journal of E-Business Research*, *5*(1), 92–108.

Eikebrokk, T. R., & Olsen, D. H. (2007). An Empirical Investigation of Competency Factors Affecting e-business Success in European SMEs. *Information & Management*, *44*, 364–383. doi:10.1016/j.im.2007.02.004

EIRMA. (2004). *Technology Access for open innovation.* Working Group Report WG63, Eirma: Paris.

Eisenmann, T. R., Hallowell, R., & Tripsas, M. (2002). *Internet business models: Text and cases*. UK: McGraw-Hill Education-Europe.

Eisenmann, T. (2007). *Managing Networked Businesses: Course Overview for Educators*. Boston: Harvard Business School Press.

Elliot, M.T., & Speck, P.S. (2005). Factors that affect attitude toward a retail website. *Journal of Marketing Theory and Practice*, Winter, 40-50.

Ellsworth, J. H., & Ellsworth, M. V. (1995). *Marketing on the Internet*. Hoboken, NJ: John Wiley and Sons.

Elsammani, Z. A., Hackney, R., & Scown, P. (2004). SMEs Adoption and Implementation Process of Websites in the Presence of Change Agents. In Al-Qirim, N. A. Y. (Ed.), *Electronic Commerce in Small to Medium-Sized Enterprises: Frameworks, Issues and Implications* (pp. 146–163). Hershey, PA: Idea Group Publishing.

ENAPS Consortium. (2001). *ENAPS Indicator Model, Version 1.0*. Bremen, Germany: PRODUTEC Ingenieurgesellschaft mbH.

Endo, S., & Kincade, D. H. (2008). Mass customization for long-term relationship development: Why consumers purchase mass customized products again. *Qualitative Market Research: An International Journal*, *11*(3), 275–294. doi:10.1108/13522750810879011

Eng, T. Y. (2004). The role of e-marketplaces in supply chain management. *Industrial Marketing Management*, *33*, 97–105. doi:10.1016/S0019-8501(03)00032-4

Enriquez, J. (2001). *As the future catches you*. New York: Three Rivers Press.

Eschenbächer, J., & Duin, H. (2009). A Forecasting Concept for Virtual Organisations Supporting SMEs. In Cruz-Cunha, M. M. (Ed.), *Enterprise Information Systems for Business Integration in SMEs: Technological, Organizational and Social Dimensions* (pp. 76–101). Hershey, PA: IGI Global.

Etzioni, A. (1997). *Modern Organizations*. New York: Prentice-Hall.

EU. (2006) *Directive on services in the Internal Market*. Retrieved September 3, 2009, from http://ec.europa.eu/internal_market/services/services-dir/index_en.htm.

Europe, C. S. R. (2008a). *The European Alliance for CSR Progress Review 2007: Making Europe a Pole of Excellence on CSR,* European Commission, Brussels, 4 March 2008

European Commission (2002). Observatory of European SMEs 2002 / No 2, SMEs in Europe, including a first glance at EU candidate countries, Report submitted to the Enterprise Directorate-General of the European Commission by: KPMG Special Services and EIM Business & Policy Research in the Netherlands in co-operation with: European Network for SME Research (ENSR), and Intomart

European Commission, Enterprise & Industry Directorate General. (2008). ICT standards in the health sector: current situation and prospects. [A Sectoral e-Business Watch study by Empirica.]. *Special Study No.*, *1*, 2008.

European Commission. (2000). *The European Observatory for SMEs, Fifth Annual Report, Report submitted to the Enterprise Directorate-General of the Commission of the European Communities*. European Network for SME Research, European Commission.

European Commission. (2003a), Innovation Policy in Seven Candidate Countries: The Challenges. *Final Report* Volume 1, March, Brussels.

European Commission. (2003b), Innovation Policy in Seven Candidate Countries: The Challenges. *Volume 2.7, Innovation Policy Profile: Turkey,* Brussels.

European Commission. (2005). *SME definition: User guide and model declaration, Enterprise and Industry Publications*. Retrieved August 20, 2009, from http://ec.europa.eu/enterprise/enterprise_policy/sme_definition/sme_user_guide.pdf

European Communities. (2008). Antti Peltomäki. In *Foreword of Living Labs for user-driven open innovation: An overview of the Living Labs Methodology, Activities and Achievements.Directorate-General for the Information Society and Media, Unit F4 New Infrastucture Paradigms and Experimental Facilities, European Commission Information Society and Media, January 2009*. Luxembourg: Office for Official Publications of the European Communities.

Evangelista, R. (2000). Sectoral Patterns of Technological Change in Services. *Economics of Innovation and New Technology*, *9*, 183–221. doi:10.1080/10438590000000008

Evans, P. B., & Wurster, B. S. (1997). Strategy and the new Economics of Information. *Harvard Business Review*, *75*(5), 70–83.

Farell, J. (2008). What is the extended enterprise? Retrieved September 16, 2009, from http://jpfarrell.blogspot.com/2008/04/extended-enterprise.html.

Farhoomand, A., & Lovelock, P. (2001). *Global E-commerce: Text and Cases*. New York: Prentice Hall.

FEBRABAN – Federação Brasileira de Bancos. (2009). Retrieved from http://www.febraban.org.br on August,2009.

Feigenbaum, A. V., & Feigenbaum, D. S. (2009). *The power of management innovation*. New York: McGraw-Hill.

Feindt, S., Jeffcoate, J., & Chappell, C. (2001). Identifying Success Factors for Rapid Growth in SME E-Commerce. *Small Business Economics*, *19*, 51–62. doi:10.1023/A:1016165825476

Fernandes, D. H., & Santos, C. P. (2008). Orientação empreendedora: um estudo sobre as conseqüências do empreendedorismo nas organizações. Retrieved on May, 2009 from www.rae.com.br/eletronica*RAE – Revista de Administração de Empresas, 7*(1), Art. 6, January / June.

Ferreira, F. H. G., Leite, P. G., & Ravaillon, M. (2007). Poverty reduction without economic growth? Explaining Brazil's poverty's dyanimcs, 1985-2004. *World Bank Policy Research Paper,* retrieved on June, 2009, from http://econ.worldbank.org/external/default/main.

FFG. (2006). *SME Associations in Austria: an overview*. Austria: FFG Austrian Research Promotion Agency.

Fine, S. F. (1986). Technological innovation, diffusion and resistance: A historical perspective. *Journal of Library Administration*, *7*, 83–108. doi:10.1300/J111V07N01_09

Fischer, W. A. (1978). Follow-up strategies for technological growth. *California Management Review*, *21*(1), 11–20.

Fischer, M. (2000). Using E-commerce to Deliver High Productivity. *Work Study*, *49*(2), 59–62. doi:10.1108/00438020010311188

Fishbein, M., & Ajzen, I. (1975). *Belief, Attitude, Intention, and Behavior: An Introduction to Theory and Research*. Reading, MA: Addison-Wesley.

Flanagan, J. (1954). The Critical Incident Technique. *Psychological Bulletin*, *51*(4). doi:10.1037/h0061470

Folmer, E., & Bosch, J. (2004). Architecting for Usability: A Survey. *Journal of Systems and Software*, *70*(1-2), 61–78. doi:10.1016/S0164-1212(02)00159-0

Fong, M. (2005). *E-Collaborations and Virtual Organisations*. Hershey, PA: IRM Press.

Forrester Research. (2005). *US eCommerce forecast: Online retail sales to reach $329 billion by 2010*. Retrieved August 22, 2009, from http://www.forrester.com/Research/ Document/Excerpt/0,7211,3726,00

Fortina, D. R., Dholakia, R. R., & Dholakia, N. (2002). Emerging Issues in Electronic Marketing: Thinking Outside the Square. *Journal of Business Research*, *55*, 623–627. doi:10.1016/S0148-2963(00)00202-2

Fox, M.S., Barbuceanu, M., & Teigen, R. (2000). Agent-Oriented Supply-Chain Management. *International Journal of Flexible Manufacturing Systems*, 12(2.3), 165-188.

Frayret, J.-M., & Cloutier, L. Montreuil., B., & D'Amours, S. (2000). A Distributed Framework for Collaborative Supply Network Integration. In L. M. Camarinha-Matos, R. J. Rabelo, & H. Afsarmanesh (Eds.), *E-Business and Virtual Enterprises* (pp. 233 – 244). New York: Springer.

Fricke, E., & Schulz, A. (2005). Design for changeability (DfC): Principles to enable changes in systems throughout their entire lifecycle. *Systems Engineering*, *8*(4), 342–359. doi:10.1002/sys.20039

Gadenne, D. L., Kennedy, J., & McKeiver, C. (2009). An empirical study of environmental awareness and practices in SMEs. *Journal of Business Ethics*, *84*(1), 45–63. doi:10.1007/s10551-008-9672-9

Galliers, R. D., & Sutherland, A. R. (1991). Information systems management and strategy formulation: the 'stages of growth' model revisited. *Journal of Information Systems*, *1*(2), 89–114. doi:10.1111/j.1365-2575.1991.tb00030.x

Ganguly, A., Nilchiani, R., & Farr, J. (2009). Evaluating agility in corporate enterprises. *International Journal of Production Economics*, *118*(2), 410–423. doi:10.1016/j.ijpe.2008.12.009

Gardner, H. (2006a). *Five minds for the future*. Cambridge, MA: Harvard Business School Press.

Gardner, H. (2006b). *Multiple intelligences: New horizons in theory and practice*. New York: Basic Books.

Gartner, (2008).How to Determine Levels of Engagement for Generation Virtual. Retrieved from: http://www.gartner.com/DisplayDocument?ref=g_search&id=684508&subref=simplesearch*consultation made in September, 12, 2009.*

Gatti, R., & Honoratti, M. (2008). Informality among Formal Fims: Firm level, Cross-Country evidence on tax compliance and access to credit. *World Bank Policy Research Working Paper*, retrieved on June, 2009, from http://econ.worldbank.org/external/default/main.

Gausemeier, J., Fink, A., & Schlake, O. (1998). Scenario Management: An Approach to Develop Future Potentials. *Technological Forecasting and Social Change*, *59*, 111–130. doi:10.1016/S0040-1625(97)00166-2

Gefen, D. (2000). E-Commerce: the role of familiarity and trust. *Omega*, *28*(6), 725–737. doi:10.1016/S0305-0483(00)00021-9

Gefen, D., Karahanna, E., & Straub, D. W. (2003). Trust and TAM in Online Shopping: An Integrated Model. *Management Information Systems Quarterly*, *27*(1), 51–90.

Gefen, D., & Straub, D. W. (2000). The Relative Importance of Perceived Ease-of-Use in IS Adoption: A Study of E-Commerce Adoption. *Journal of the Association for Information Systems*, *1*(8), 1–30.

Gehrke, D., & Turban, E. (1999). Determinants of Successful Website Design: Relative Importance and Recommendations for Effectiveness. *Proceedings of the 32nd Hawaii International Conference on System Sciences (HICSSS-32)*, 1-8.

Geissler, G. L., Zinkhan, G. N., & Watson, R. T. (2006). The Influence of Home Page Complexity on Consumer Attention, Attitudes and Purchase Intent. *Journal of Advertising*, *35*(2), 69–80.

Gengatharen, D. E., & Standing, C. (2005). A framework to assess the factors affecting success or failure of the implementation of government-supported regional e-marketplaces for SMEs. *European Journal of Information Systems*, *14*(4), 417–433. doi:10.1057/palgrave.ejis.3000551

Geoffrion, M., & Krishnan, R. (2001). Prospects for Operations Research in the E-Business Era. *Interfaces*, *31*(2), 6–36. doi:10.1287/inte.31.2.6.10628

George, J. K. (2004). The theory of planned behavior and Internet purchasing. *Internet Research*, *14*(3), 198–212. doi:10.1108/10662240410542634

George, G., Wood Jr., R. D. & Khan, R. (2001).Networking strategy of boards: implication for small and medium-sized enterprises. *Entrepreneurship and regional development*, *13*(1), 269-285.

Ghani, J. A., & Deshpande, S. P. (1994). Task characteristics and the experience of optimal flow in human-computer interaction. *The Journal of Psychology*, *128*(4), 383–391. doi:10.1080/00223980.1994.9712742

Ghani, J. A., Supnick, R., & Rooney, P. (1991). The experience of flow in computer mediated and in face-to-face groups. In J.I. DeGross, I. Benbasat, G. DeSanctis & C.M. Beath (Eds.), *Proceedings of the 12th International Conference on Information Systems* (pp. 16-18), New York.

Ghemawat, P. (2006). *Strategy and the business landscape* (2nd ed.). Boston: Prentice Hall.

Gibbs, J., Kraemer, K., & Dedrick, J. (2003). Environment and Policy Factors Shaping Global E-Commerce Diffusion: A Cross-Country Comparison. *The Information Society*, *19*(1), 5–18. doi:10.1080/01972240309472

Gibson, C., & Nolan, R. (1974). Managing the four stages of EDP growth. *Harvard Business Review*, (January-February): 76–88.

Glanz, J. (1998). *Action research*. Norwood, MA: Christopher-Gordon.

Glassberg, C. B., & Merhout, W. J. (2007). Electronic markets hypothesis redux: Where are we now? *Communications of the ACM*, *50*(2), 51–55. doi:10.1145/1216016.1216020

Goeree, J. K., & HOLT, C. A. (2003). Stochastic game theory: For playing games not just for doing theory. *Proceedings of the National Academy of Sciences of the United States of America*, *96*(19), 10564–10567. doi:10.1073/pnas.96.19.10564

Gold, B. (1987). Approaches to Accelerating New Product Development. *Journal of Product Innovation Management*, *4*, 81–88. doi:10.1016/0737-6782(87)90054-3

Goldberg, D., Nichols, D., Oki, B. M., & Terry, D. (1992). Using collaborative filtering to weave an information tapestry. *Communications of the ACM*, *35*(12), 61–70. doi:10.1145/138859.138867

Goldberg, K., Roeder, T., Gupta, D., & Perkins, C. (2001). Eigentaste: A Constant-Time Collaborative Filtering Algorithm. *Information Retrieval*, *4*(2), 133–151. doi:10.1023/A:1011419012209

Goldman, S. L., Nagel, R. N., & Preiss, K. (1995). *Agile Competitors And Virtual Organizations: Strategies For Enriching The Customer*. New York: Van Nostrand Reinhold, International Thomson Publishing.

Goldsborough, R. (2000). Making telecommuting work. *Commercial Law Bulletin*, *15*, 34–35.

Golicic, S., Foggin, L. J., & Mentzer, T. J. (2003). Relationship Magnitude and Its Role in Interorganizational Relationship Structure. *Journal of Business Logistics*, *24*(1), 57–76.

Goode, S. (2002). Management attitudes toward the World Wide Web in Australian small business. *Information Systems Management*, (Winter): 45–48. doi:10.1201/1078/43199.19.1.20020101/31475.6

Google. (2009). Google Trends. Retrieved from http://www.google.com/trends*consultation made in August, 2009*

Gottschalk, P. (2005). *E-Business Strategy, Sourcing and Governance*. Hershey, PA: Idea Group Publishing.

Götze, U. (1993). *Szenario-Technik in der strategischen Unternehmensplanung*. Wiesbaden: Deutscher Universitäts-Verlag.

Gouveia, L. (2006). *Negócio Electrónico - conceitos e perspectivas de desenvolvimento*. SPI - Sociedade Portuguesa de Inovação.

Gouveia, L., & Gaio, S. (2004). *Readings in Information Society*. UFP University Press.

Govt. of UK. (2008). Accelerating the SME economic engine: through transparent, simple and strategic procurement, Government of UK., Crown copyright 2008

Grama, A., & Fotache, D. (2007). ICT and ERP Applications Challenges in Romanian SMEs, Analele Ştiinţifice Ale Universităţii „Alexandru Ioan Cuza" Din Iaşi. *Tomul LIV Ştiinţe Economice*, *2007*, 23–28.

Grant, K., Laney, R., & Pickett, B. (2002). A Process of Innovation in Marketing by SME's, ANZMAC 2002 Conference Proceedings, Deakin University, Australia, pp. 2531-2538

Greenberg, J. (1987). A taxonomy of organizational justice theories. *Academy of Management Review*, *12*, 9–22. doi:10.2307/257990

Greenberg, J. (1990). Organizational justice: Yesterday, today, and tomorrow. *Journal of Management*, *16*, 399–432. doi:10.1177/014920639001600208

Greenberg, J. (1994). Using socially fair treatment to promote acceptance of a work site smoking ban. *The Journal of Applied Psychology*, *79*, 288–297. doi:10.1037/0021-9010.79.2.288

Greenberg, J. (1993). The social side of fairness: Interpersonal and informational classes of organizational justice. In Cropanzano, R. (Ed.), *Justice in the workplace* (pp. 79–103). Mahwah, NJ: Lawrence Erlbaum Associates.

Grefen, P., Aberer, K., Hoffner, Y., & Ludwig, H. (2000). CrossFlow: Cross-Organizational Workflow Management in Dynamic Virtual Enterprises, *International Journal of Computer Systems. Science & Engineering*, *5*, 277–290.

Grefen, P., Mehandjiev, N., Kouvas, G., Weichhart, G., & Eshuis, R. (2009). Dynamic business network process management in instant virtual enterprises. *Computers in Industry*, *60*(2), 86–103. doi:10.1016/j.compind.2008.06.006

Grembergen, W., & Amenlinckx, I. (2002). Measuring and managing e-business projects through the balanced scorecard. In Proceedings of the *35th Hawaii International Conference on System Sciences*: 258-266.

Grieger, M. (2003). Electronic marketplaces: A literature review and a call for supply chain management research. *European Journal of Operational Research*, *144*, 280–294. doi:10.1016/S0377-2217(02)00394-6

Grieger, M. (2004). An empirical study of business processes across Internet-based electronic marketplaces. *Business Process Management Journal*, *10*(1), 80–100. doi:10.1108/14637150410518347

Griffin, J. (2004). Mapping the Diffusion of the Internet Technology Cluster: An Examination of Irish SMEs. In Al-Qirim, N. A. Y. (Ed.), *Electronic Commerce in Small to Medium-Sized Enterprises: Frameworks, Issues and Implications* (pp. 128–145). Hershey, PA: Idea Group Publishing.

Grigoroudis, E., Litos, C., Moustakis, V. A., Politis, Y., & Tsironis, L. (2008). The Assessment of User-Perceived Web Quality: Application of a Satisfaction Benchmarking Approach. *European Journal of Operational Research*, *187*, 1346–1357. doi:10.1016/j.ejor.2006.09.017

Grosz, A. (2008). *Intellectual Capacity Report for Pannon Automotive Cluster (PANAC). WWW [On-line]*. Retrieved from http://www.ricarda-project.org/downloads/ICR-panac.pdf.

Grover, V., Teng, J., Segars, A., & Fiedler, K. (1998). The influence of information technology diffusion and business process change on perceived productivity: The IS executive's perspective. *Information & Management*, *34*(3), 141–15. doi:10.1016/S0378-7206(98)00054-8

Guerin, F., & Tadjouddine, E. M. (2006) Realising common knowledge assumptions in agent auctions. *In The IEEE/WIC/ACM Int. Conf. on Intelligent Agent Technology (pp. 579–586)*, IEEE Computer Society.

Gulati, R., Nohria, N., & Zaheer, A. (2000). Strategic Networks. *Strategic Management Journal*, *21*(3), 203–215. doi:10.1002/(SICI)1097-0266(200003)21:3<203::AID-SMJ102>3.0.CO;2-K

Gulati, R., Nohria, N., & Zaheer, A. (2000). Strategic Networks. *Strategic Management Journal*, *21*(3), 203–215. doi:10.1002/(SICI)1097-0266(200003)21:3<203::AID-SMJ102>3.0.CO;2-K

Gullikson, S., Blades, R., Bragdon, M., McKibbon, S., Sparling, M., & Toms, E. G. (1999). The Impact of Information Architecture on Academic Web Site Usability. *The Electronic Library*, *17*(5), 293–303. doi:10.1108/02640479910330714

GzS/izGTM (2008). *Introduction to Innovative Groups of Slovenia. Innovative Clusters and Technology Networks*. Chamber of Commerce Slovenia (GzS) und National Center of Clusters and Technology Networks (izGTM).

Hadjimanolis, A. (1999). Barriers to innovation for SMEs in a small less developed country (Cyprus). Technovation, 19 (9), pp. 561-570. September 1999

Hage, J. T. (1999). Organizational Innovation and Organizational Change. *Annual Review of Sociology*, *25*, 597–622. doi:10.1146/annurev.soc.25.1.597

Hakanen, M., & Lipponen, J. (2008). Procedural justice and identification with virtual teams: The moderating role of face-to-face meetings and geographical dispersion. *Social Justice Research*, *21*(2), 164–178. doi:10.1007/s11211-008-0070-3

Hall, C. (2002). *Profile of SMEs and SME issues 1990-2000*. Singapore: Asia-Pacific Economic Cooperation.

Hall, B., & Snider, A. (2000). Glossary: The hottest buzz words in the industry. In Schreiber, D. A., & Berge, Z. L. (Eds.), *Distance training: How innovative organizations are using technology to maximize learning and business objectives*. San Francisco: Jossey-Bass.

Hamel, G. (1991), Competition for Competence and Inter-Partner Learning within International Strategic Alliances. *Strategic Management Journal*, no. 12 (special issue), 83-103.

Hamill, J. (1997). The Internet and International Marketing. *International Marketing Review*, *14*(5), 300–323. doi:10.1108/02651339710184280

Hammer, M. (2002). *The Agenda: What Every Business Must Do to Dominate the Decade*. New York: Three Rivers Press.

Hammer, M., & Champy, J. (1993). *Reengineering the Corporation: A Manifesto for Business Revolution*. New York: Harper Business.

Handy, C. (1995). Trust and the virtual organization. *Harvard Business Review*, (May-June): 40–50.

Hanna, V., & Walsh, K. (2002). Small firm networks: a successful approach to innovation*? R & D Management*, *32*(3), 201–207. doi:10.1111/1467-9310.00253

Harding, C. (2007). An Open Marketplace for Services. *DM Review*, *17*(9), 20–39.

Harker, D., & Akkeren, J. V. (2002). Exploring the Needs of SMEs for Mobile Data Technologies: the Role of Qualitative Research Techniques. *Qualitative Market Research: An International Journal*, *5*(3), 199–209. doi:10.1108/13522750210432002

Harris, M. D. S., Herron, D., & Iwanicki, S. (2008). *The Business Value of IT: Managing Risks, Optimizing Performance and Measuring Results*. New York: Auerbach Publications. doi:10.1201/9781420064759

Hartley, R. (2007). *Management Mistakes and Successes*. New York: Wiley.

Hartman, A., Sifonis, J., & Kador, J. (2000). *Net Ready: Strategies for Success in the E-conomy*. New York: McGraw Hill.

Hass, J., & Hochrinner, H. (2008). *Enhancing Product- and Process Innovation in SMEs through Cooperative Education, ASET Annual Conference 2008*, The Placement and Employability Professionals' Conference, 2-4 September 2008, Robbins Conference Centre, Plymouth, UK.

Hatch, M. (1997). *Organization theory: Modern, symbolic and postmodern perspectives*. Oxford: Oxford University Press.

Häubl, G., & Trifts, V. (2000). Consumer Decision Making in Online Shopping Environments: The Effects of Interactive Decision Aids. *Marketing Science*, *19*(1), 4–21. doi:10.1287/mksc.19.1.4.15178

Havey, M. (2005). *Essential business process modeling*. Sebastopol, CA: O'Reilly.

Hawk, S. (2004). A comparison of B2C e-commerce in developing countries. *Electronic Commerce Research*, *4*(3), 181–199. doi:10.1023/B:ELEC.0000027979.91972.36

Hawkins, R., & Prencipe, A. (2000). *Business-to-Business E-Commerce in the UK: A Synthesis of Sector Report*. London: Department for Trade and Industry.

Heide, J. B., & John, G. (1990). Alliances in industrial purchasing: the determinants of joint action in buyer–supplier relationships. *JMR, Journal of Marketing Research*, *27*, 24–36. doi:10.2307/3172548

Heijden, H. d. (2000). The Inclusion of E-commerce Metrics in Strategic Planning: Results from an Exploratory Empirical Study. *Proceedings of the Americas Conference on Information Systems*, Long Beach, CA.

Heinen, J. (1996). Internet Marketing Practices. *Information Management & Computer Security*, *4*(5), 7–14. doi:10.1108/09685229610153120

Helmer, O. (1977). Problems in Futures Research: Delphi and Causal Cross-Impact Analysis. *Futures*, *9*, 17–31. doi:10.1016/0016-3287(77)90049-0

Helmer, O. (1981). Reassessment of Cross-Impact Analysis. *Futures*, *13*, 389–400. doi:10.1016/0016-3287(81)90124-5

Hendrikse, M. (2008) *Search Engine Marketing 101: A Guide for Small Businesses and Not-For-Profits to Engage in Search Engine Marketing*. Retrieved from on July 25, 2009 from http://markhendrikse.com/storage/post-images/june-2009/SearchEngineMarketing101_MarkHendrikse.pdf.

Herber, J., Singh, J. V., & Useem, M. (2000). *The design of new organizational forms* (pp. 376–392). Wharton on Managing Emerging Techonologies.

Herlocker, J. L., & Konstan, J. A. (2001). Content-independent task-focused recommendation. *IEEE Internet Computing*, *5*(6), 40–47. doi:10.1109/4236.968830

Herring, T., & Job, R. (2008). The Next Generation of eLearning: Instructional Alternate Reality Games. *Online Forums*. Retrieved October 15, 2009 from http://www.elearningguild.com/olf/olfarchives/index.cfm?id=387&action=viewonly.

Herstad, S. J., Bloch, C., Ebersberger, B., & van de Velde, E. (2008). *Open innovation and globalisation: Theory, evidence and implications*. Eurostat.

Herzlinger, R. (2006). Why Innovation in Health Care Is So Hard. *Harvard Business Review*, (May): 2006.

Hevner, A., March, S., Park, J., & Ram, S. (2004). Design science in information systems research. *Management Information Systems Quarterly*, *28*(1), 75–105.

Heydon, A., & Najork, M. (1999). Mercator: A Scalable, Extensible Web Crawler. *World Wide Web (Bussum)*, *2*, 219–229. doi:10.1023/A:1019213109274

Hidalgo, D., Irusta, R., & Fermoso, J. (2008). Generation and management of industrial waste in Small and Medium sized Enterprises. *International Journal of Environmental Technology and Management*, *8*(4), 323–338. doi:10.1504/IJETM.2008.017505

Hill, J., & Wright, L. T. (2001). A Qualitative Research Agenda for Small to Medium-Sized Enterprises. *Marketing Intelligence & Planning*, *19*(6), 432–443. doi:10.1108/EUM0000000006111

Hillary, R. (2004). Environmental management systems and the smaller enterprise. *Journal of Cleaner Production*, *12*(6), 561–569. doi:10.1016/j.jclepro.2003.08.006

Hinds, P. J., & Bailey, D. E. (2003). Out of sight out of sync: Understanding conflict in distributed teams. *Organization Science*, *14*, 615–632. doi:10.1287/orsc.14.6.615.24872

Hirschheim, R., Klein, H., & Lyytinen, K. (1996). Exploring the Intellectual Structures of Information Systems Development: A Social Action Theoretic Analysis. *Accounting. Management and Information Technologies*, *6*(1), 1–64. doi:10.1016/0959-8022(96)00004-5

Hitchens, D., Clausen, J., Trainor, M., Keil, M., & Thankappan, S. (2003). Competitiveness, Environmental Performance and Management of SMEs. *Greener Management International*, *44*, 45–57.

Hitt, M., Black, S., & Porter, L. (2008). *Management*. New York: Prentice Hall.

Hitt, M., Bierman, L., Shimizu, K., & Kochhar, R. (2001). Directs and moderating effects of human capital on strategy and performance in professional service firms: a resource based perspective. *Academy of Management Journal*, *44*(1), 13–28. doi:10.2307/3069334

Hitt, M. A., Ireland, R. D., & Hoskisson, R. E. (2001). *Strategic Management: Competitiveness and globalization* (4th ed.). London, UK: Thomson Learning.

Hoeree, J. (2009) From Corporate Enterprise to Enterprise as a Service. *CTG Whitepaper*. Retrieved September 3, 2009, from http://www.ctg.com/PDF/From_CE_to_Eaas.pdf.

Hoffman, W., Keedy, J., & Roberts, K. (2002). The unexpected return of B2B. *The McKinsey Quarterly*, *3*, 97–105.

Hoffman, D., & Novak, T. (1996). Marketing in hypermedia computer-mediated environments: conceptual foundations. *Journal of Marketing*, *60*(July), 50–68. doi:10.2307/1251841

Hollanders, H., & Van Cruysen, A. (2009). *Design, Creativity and Innovation: A Scoreboard Approach*. Pro Inno. Innometrics.

Höllmüller, C. (2008*). Chances for Small and Medium-sized Enterprises (SME) in International Innovation Networks*, a presentation at the Innovation Day Swiss Texnet, Dübendorf, 28 August 2008

Holzl, W. (2006a). *Scoping Paper*. Gazelles, Europe Innova.

Hölzl, W. (2006b). Convergence of financial systems: Towards an evolutionary perspective, Journal of Institutional Economics-3

Hong, P., & Jeong, J. (2006). Supply chain management practices of SMEs: from a business growth perspective. *Journal of Enterprise Information Management*, *19*(3), 292–302. doi:10.1108/17410390610658478

Howard, M., Vidgen, R., & Powell, P. (2006). Automotive e-hubs: exploring motivations and barriers to collaboration and interaction. *The Journal of Strategic Information Systems*, *15*(1), 51–75. doi:10.1016/j.jsis.2005.06.002

Howarth 2002; Howarth, B. (2002). E-survivors: Get 'e' or get out. *Business Review Weekly*.

Hua, G. B. (2007). Applying the strategic alignment model to business and ICT strategies of Singapore's small and medium-sized architecture, engineering and construction enterprises. *Construction Management and Economics*, *25*, 157–169. doi:10.1080/01446190600827041

Hughes, M., Golden, W., & Powell, P. (2003). Interorganisational ICT systems: the way to innovative practice for SMEs. *Journal of Small Business and Enterprise Development*, *10*(3), 277–286. doi:10.1108/14626000310489754

Hughes, J., & Atwell, G. (2003). A Framework for the Evaluation of E-Learning. In *Proceedings of European Seminars – Exploring Models and Partnerships for E-Learning in SMEs*. Retrieved February 4, 2004 from http://www.theknownet.com/ict_smes_seminars/papers/Hughes_Attwell.html.

Huston, L. & Sakkab, N. (2006). *P&G's New Innovation Model*, An excerpt from Connect and Develop: Inside Procter & Gamble's New Model for Innovation. *Harvard Business Review, 84*, (3), March 2006.

Huth, M. R. A., & Ryan, M. D. (2000). *Logic in Computer Science: Modelling and Reasoning about Systems*. Cambridge, UK: Cambridge University Press.

Hüttenrauch, M., & Baum, M. (2008). *Effiziente Vielfalt. Die dritte Revolution in der Automobilindustrie*. Berlin, Heidelberg: Springer-Verlag.

IBGE – Instituto Brasileiro de Geografia e Estatística. (2003). *As micro e pequenas empresas comerciais e de serviços no Brasil - 2001*. Rio de Janeiro, Brazil: IBGE.

IBGE – Instituto Brasileiro de Geografia e Estatística. (2008). *Demografia das empresas. Estudos e Pesquisas – Informação econômica, número 10*. Rio de Janeiro, Brazil: IBGE.

IBGE – Instituto Brasileiro de Geografia e Estatística. (2009). At www.ibge.gov.br, accessed on August, 2009.

IBM. (2007). *Service Science: The next frontier in service innovation. IBM Singapore Pte Ltd.* IBM Corporation.

IBM. (2008). Global CEO Study: The Enterprise of the Future. *Ideias from IBM.* May 5, 2008, Retrieved September 3, 2009, from http://www.ibm.com/ibm/ideasfromibm/us/ceo/20080505/resources/IFI_05052008.pdf.

IDC. (2004). *IDC predicts double digit growth of Asia/Pacific Internet buyers from 2003 to 2008. IDC Australia.* Retrieved August 22, 2009, from http://www.idc.com.au/newsletters/ idcpulse/detail.asp?intID=43

IDC. (2009). IDC Retail Insights. Retrieved from http://www.globalretail-insights.com/GRI/index.jsp*consultation made in September 12, 2009*

IDC. (n.d.). Retrieved from http://www.idc.com

IFAD. (2007). *Country strategic opportunities programme, The Republic of Moldova, International Fund for Agricultural Development (IFAD)*, Executive Board — Ninety-second Session, Rome, 11-13 December 2007

Ignatiadis, I., Svirskas, A., Roberts, B., & Tarabanis, K. (2006). Promoting Trust in B2B Virtual Organizations through Business and Technological Infrastructures. *International Journal of Networking and Virtual Organizations, Special Issue on. Trust Development and Management in Virtual Organizations*, *3*(4), 395–411.

Ihlstrom, C., & Malin, N. (2003). E-business adoptions by SMEs – Prerequisites and attitude of SMEs in a Swedish network. *Journal of Organizational Computing and Electronic Commerce*, *13*(3), 211–223. doi:10.1207/S15327744JOCE133&4_04

Ihlström, C., Magnusson, M., Scupola, A., & Tuunainen, V. K. (2003). SME barriers to electronic commerce adoption: nothing changes-everything is new. In Gingrich, G. (Ed.), *Managing IT in Government Business & Communities* (pp. 147–163). Hershey: IGI Publishing.

ILIPT Project Description (2006). Retrieved June 02, 2009, from http://www.ilipt.org.

Ingenico. (n.d.). Retrieved from http://www.ingenico.com/.

Interact (2004). Project "Embrace" Preparation and Implementation: lessons learnt and recommendations to Potential Applicants, INNOSTART National Business and Innovation Centre, a project paper submitted to European Regional Development Fund, European Union and presented at Translational INTERREG IIIB CADSES Seminar, Katowice, Poland.

IPEA – Instituto de Pesquisas Econômicas Aplicadas. (2009). At www.ipea.gov.br, accessed on August, 2009.

Iskatt, G. J., & Liebowitz, J. (1996). What to do when employees resist change. *Super Vision*, *57*(8), 3–5.

ISO/IEC (2000). ISO/IEC JTC1/SC7/WG17, ISO/IEC 15414|ITU-T Recommendation X.911, Initial Committee draft; Information Technology-Open Distributed Processing-Reference Model-Enterprise Language. CD 15414.

ISO/IEC. (2007). IEEE Std 1471-2000 Recommended Practice for Architectural Description of Software Intensive Systems. ISO/IEC 42010. IEEE: 24.

Issa, R. R. A., Flood, I., & Caglasin, G. (2003). A Survey of e-Business Implementation in the US Construction Industry. In Bjork, B.(ed.), *Journal of Information Technology in Construction*, 8, 15-28.

It, S. N. (n.d.). Retrieved from http://www.socialnetit.com

Iyer, G. R. (2005). Global Internet Marketing Strategy: Framework and Managerial Insights. In Clarke, I. III, & Flaherty, T. (Eds.), *Advances in Electronic Marketing* (pp. 84–102). Hershey, PA: Idea Group Publishing.

Jackson, D. (2000). Automating first-order relational logic. In *SIGSOFT Foundations of Software Engineering* (pp. 130–139). New York: ACM Press.

Jagdev, H. S., Brennan, A., & Browne, J. (2004). *Strategic Decision Making in Modern Manufacturing*. Boston: Kluwer Academic Publishers.

Jaklic, M., Svetina, A. C., & Zagorsek, H. (2008). Specific Responses to Universal Pressures in the Industry - Comparing European Automotive Clusters. WWW [On-line]. Retrieved from http://miha.ef.uni-lj.si/_dokumenti/wp/paper_jaklic_cotic_zagorsek.doc.

Jamil, G. L. (2001). *Repensando a TI na empresa moderna.* Rio de Janeiro, Brasil: Axcel Books.

Jamil, G. L. (2007). Comércio Eletrônico no Brasil: Tendências e oportunidades. In *Balloni, A. J. (org.) (2007) Por que Gestão em sistemas e tecnologias da informação? Segurança, inovação e sociedade* (pp. 157–201). Campinas, Brasil: Komedi.

Janenko, P. M. (2003). E-business: The Illusion of Automated Success. *The TQM Magazine, 15*(3). doi:10.1108/09544780310469307

Jansson, K., & Thoben, K.-D. (2005). The Extended Products Paradigm, An Introduction. In Arai, E., Kimura, F., Goossenaerts, J., & Shirase, K. (Eds.), *Knowledge and Skill Chains in Engineering and Manufacturing. Information Infrastructure in the Era of Global Communications* (pp. 39–47). New York: Springer. doi:10.1007/0-387-23572-2_5

Jardim-Goncalves, R., Grilo, A., & Steiger-Garcao, A. (2006). Challenging the interoperability between computers in industry with MDA and SOA. *Computers in Industry, 57*(8), 679–689. doi:10.1016/j.compind.2006.04.013

Jaruzelski, B., Dehoff, K. & Bordia, R. (2006). *Smart Spenders: The Global Innovation, Special feature at Smart Spenders: The Global Innovation.* Strategy+Business, 45, 46-61.

Jarvenpaa, S. L., Tractinsky, N., & Vitale, M. (2000). Consumer trust in an internet store. *Information Technology Management, 1*(1–2), 45–71. doi:10.1023/A:1019104520776

Jarvenpaa, S., Knoll, K., & Leidner, D. (1998). Is anybody out there? Antecedents of trust in global virtual teams. *Journal of Management Information Systems, 14*(4), 29–64.

Jelassi, T., & Enders, A. (2005). *Strategies for e-Business: Creating Value though Electronic and Mobile Commerce.* Upper Saddle River, NJ: Pearson Education.

Jelassi, T., & Enders, A. (2008). *Strategies for e-business:Creating Value through Electronic and Mobile Commerce: Concepts and Cases.* Harlow: FT Prentice Hall.

Jennett, P., Yeo, M., Pauls, M., & Jennifer Graham, J. (2003). Organizational readiness for telemedicine: implications for success and failure. *Journal of Telemedicine and Telecare, 9*(Supplement 2), 27–30. .doi:10.1258/135763303322596183

Jennex, M. E., Amoroso, D., & Adelajun, O. (2004). E-Commerce Infrastructure Success Factors for Small Companies in Developing Economies. *Electronic Commerce Research, 4*, 263–286. doi:10.1023/B:ELEC.0000027983.36409.d4

Jensen, E. (2006). *Teaching with the brain in mind* (2nd ed.). Alexandria, VA: ASCD.

Jeon, B. N., Han, S. H., & Lee, M. J. (2006). Determining factors for the adoption of e-Business: The case of SMEs in Korea. *Applied Economics, 38*, 1905–1916. doi:10.1080/00036840500427262

Johnsen, S., et al. (2007). Model-based adaptive Product and Process Engineering. In M. Rabe, & P.Mihok (Eds.), *Ambient Intelligence Technologies for the Product Lifecycle: Results and Perspectives from European Research* (pp. 7 - 27). Fraunhofer: IRB Verlag.

Johnson, E., & Whang, S. (2002). E-business and supply chain management: An overview and framework. *Production and Operations Management, 11*(4), 413–423. doi:10.1111/j.1937-5956.2002.tb00469.x

Joia, L. (1994). *Reengenharia e Tecnologia da Informação: O Paradigma do Camaleão.* São Paulo: Pioneira.

Jones, P., Muir, E., & Beynon-Davies, P. (2006). The proposal of a comparative framework to evaluate e-business stages of growth models. *International Journal of Information Technology and Management, 5*(4), 249–266. doi:10.1504/IJITM.2006.012039

Joshi, A., & Motwani, R. (2006). Keyword Generation for Search Engine Advertising. *Sixth IEEE International Conference on Data Mining Workshops,* ICDM Workshops, 490-496.

Jutla, D., Bodorik, P., & Dhaliqal, J. (2002). Supporting the e-business readiness of small and medium-sized enterprises: approaches and metrics. *Internet Research: Electronic Networking Applications and Policy*, *12*(2), 139–164. doi:10.1108/10662240210422512

Kalakota, R., & Robinson, M. (2000). *E-Business 2.0: Roadmap for Success*. Boston: Addison-Wesley Professional.

Kalakota, R., & Robinson, M. (2001). *E-Business 2.0 – Roadmap for Success* (2nd ed.). Boston: Addison Wesley.

Kalakota, R., & Robinson, M. (2001). *E-Business 2.0: Road-map for Success*. Reading, MA: Addison-Wesley, Harlow.

Kalakota, K., & Whinston, A. (1997). *Electronic Commerce*. New York: Addison Wesley Longman, Inc.

Kalakota, R., & Robinson, M. (2001). *E-Business 2.0. Roadmap for Success*. Reading, MA: Addison Wesley.

Kalakota, R., & Robinson, M. (2003). *E-business 2.0: Roadmap for Success* (2nd ed.). Reading, MA: Addison-Wesley.

Kalakota, R., & Whinston, A. (1996). *Frontiers of Electronic Commerce*. London: Addison-Wesley.

Kambil, A., & van Heck, E. (2002). *Making markets. How firms can design and profit from online auctions and exchanges*. Boston: Harvard Business School Press. Kaplan, S. & Sawhney, M., (2000). E-hubs: the new B2B marketplaces. *Harvard Business Review,* 397-103.

Kanawattanachai, P., & Yoo, Y. (2002). Dynamic nature of trust in teams. *The Journal of Strategic Information Systems*, *11*, 187–213. doi:10.1016/S0963-8687(02)00019-7

Kang, K., Cohen, S., Hess, J., Novak, W., & Peterson, S. (1990). *Feature-oriented domain analysis (FODA) feasibility study*. Tech. Report CMU/SEI-90-TR-21, ADA235785. Software Engineering Institute, CMU, Pittsburgh, PA, November 1990.

Kannabiran, G., & Ranganathan, C. (2004). Effective management of information systems function: An exploratory study of Indian organizations. *International Journal of Information Management*, *24*, 247–266. doi:10.1016/j.ijinfomgt.2004.02.005

Kaplinsky, R., Morris, M., & Readman, J. (2003). The globalisation of product markets and immiserising growth: lessons from the South African furniture industry. *World Development*, *30*(7), 1159–1178. doi:10.1016/S0305-750X(02)00029-3

Kapurubandara, M., & Lawson, R. (2006). *Barriers to Adopting ICT and e-commerce with SMEs in Developing Countries: an Exploratory Study in Sri Lanka. Collecter, (Collaborative Electronic Commerce Technology and Research), December 2006*. Adelaide: UniSA.

Kartiwi, M., & MacGregor, R. C. (2007). Electronic commerce Adoption barriers in small to Medium-sized Enterprises (SMEs) in Developed and Developing countries: A cross-country comparison. *Journal of Electronic Commerce in Organizations*, *5*(3), 35–51.

Kaufmann, A., & Tödtling, F. (2002). How effective is innovation support for SMEs? An analysis of the region of upper Austria. *Technovation*, *22*(3), 147–159. doi:10.1016/S0166-4972(00)00081-X

Kaynak, E., Tatoglu, E., & Kula, V. (2005). An analysis of the factors affecting the adoption of electronic commerce by SMEs: Evidence from an emerging market. *International Marketing Review*, *22*(6), 623–640. doi:10.1108/02651330510630258

Kearns, G., & Shaberwal, R. (2007). Antecendents and consequences of information system planning integration. *IEEE Transactions on Engineering Management*, *54*(4), 628–643. doi:10.1109/TEM.2007.906848

Kearns, G., & Shaberwal, R. (2007a). Strategic alignment between business and information technology: a knowledge-based view of behaviors, outcome and consequences. *Journal of Management Information Systems*, *23*(3), 139–162. doi:10.2753/MIS0742-1222230306

Kearns, G. S., & Lederer, A. L. (2003). A resource based view of IT alignment: how knowledge sharing creates a competitive advantage. *Decision Sciences*, *34*(1), 1–29. doi:10.1111/1540-5915.02289

Kearns, G., & Lederer, A. (2000). The effect of strategic alignment on the use of IS based resources for competitive advantage. *The Journal of Strategic Information Systems*, *9*, 265–293. doi:10.1016/S0963-8687(00)00049-4

Keeble, D. (1997). Small Firms, Innovation and Regional Development in Britain in the 1990s. *Regional Studies*, *31*(3), 281–293. doi:10.1080/00343409750134692

Kenning, P. (2008). The influence of general trust and specific trust on buying behaviour. *International Journal of Retail & Distribution Management*, *36*(6), 461–476. doi:10.1108/09590550810873938

Ketels, C., & Sölvell, Ö. (2006). *The Baltic Sea Region – Top of Europe in Global Competition, State of the Region Report*. Denmark: Baltic Development Forum.

Khandelwal, V., & Ferguson, J. (1999). Critical Success Factors (CSFs) and the Growth of IT in Selected Geographic Regions. In Proceedings of the 32nd Hawaii *International Conference on System Sciences*, USA.

Kim, Y., Lee, Z., & Gosain, S. (2005). Impediments to successful ERP implementation process. *Business Process Management Journal*, *11*(2), 158–170. doi:10.1108/14637150510591156

Kim, J. K., Cho, Y. H., Kim, W. J., Kim, J. R., & Suh, J. H. (2002). A personalized recommendation procedure for Internet shopping support. *Electronic Commerce Research and Applications*, *1*, 301–313. doi:10.1016/S1567-4223(02)00022-4

Kim, Y. S., Yum, B.-J., Song, J., & Kim, S. M. (2005). Development of a recommender system based on navigational and behavioral patterns of customers in e-commerce sites. *Expert Systems with Applications*, *28*(2), 381–393. doi:10.1016/j.eswa.2004.10.017

King, K. P. (2003). *Keeping pace with technology: Educational technology that transforms* (*Vol. 2*). Cresskill, NJ: Hampton Press.

King, W., & Teo, T. (2000). Assessing the impact of proactive versus reactive modes of strategic information systems planning. *Omega*, *28*, 667–679. doi:10.1016/S0305-0483(99)00079-1

Kirkman, B. L., Rosen, B., Gibson, C. B., Testluk, P. E., & McPherson, S. O. (2002). Five challenges of virtual team success: Lessons from Sabre, Inc. *The Academy of Management Executive*, *16*(2), 67–79.

Kirkman, B. L., Shapiro, D. L., Novelli, L. Jr, & Brett, J. M. (1996). Employee concerns regarding self-managing work teams: A multidimensional justice perspective. *Social Justice Research*, *9*, 47–67. doi:10.1007/BF02197656

Kleinberg, J. M. (1999a). Authoritative Sources in a Hyperlinked Environment. *Journal of the ACM*, *46*(5), 604–632. doi:10.1145/324133.324140

Kleinberg, J. M. (1999b). Hubs, Authorities, and Communities [CSUR]. *ACM Computing Surveys*, *31*(4es), 1–3. doi:10.1145/345966.345982

Kleindl, B. (2000). Competitive Dynamics and New Business Models For SMEs in the Virtual Marketplace. *Journal of Developmental Entrepreneurship*, *5*(1), 73–85.

Koch, H. (2002). Business-to-business electronic commerce marketplaces: the alliance process. *Journal of Electronic Commerce Research*, *3*(2), 67–76.

Kok, W. (2004). *Facing the Challenge: The Lisbon strategy for growth and employment, report from the High Level Group*, available at http://europa.eu.int/growthandjobs/pdf/kok_report_en.pdf.

Kolb, D. A. (1984). *Experimental Learning – Experience as The Source of Learning and Development*. Upper Saddle River, NJ: Prentice Hall.

Komenar, M. (1997). *Electronic Marketing*. Hoboken: John Wiley and Sons.

Komiak, S., & Benbasat, I. (2004). Understanding Customer Trust in Agent-Mediated Electronic Commerce, Web-Mediated Electronic Commerce, and Traditional Commerce. *Information Technology Management*, *5*(1-2), 181–207. doi:10.1023/B:ITEM.0000008081.55563.d4

Kommers, P. A. M., Grabinger, S., & Dunlap, J. C. (1996). *Hypermedia Learning Environment: Introduction Design and Integration*. Mahwah, NJ: Lawrence Erlbaum Associates.

Konradt, U., Wandke, H., Balazs, B., & Christophersen, T. (2003). Usability in Online Shops: Scale Construction, Validation and the Influence on the Buyers' Intention and Decision. *Behaviour & Information Technology*, *22*(3), 165–174. doi:10.1080/0144929031000107072

Konstan, J. A., Miller, B. N., Maltz, D., Herlocker, J. L., Gordon, L. R., & Riedl, J. (1997). Grouplens: Applying collaborative filtering to usenet news. *Communications of the ACM*, *40*(3), 77–87. doi:10.1145/245108.245126

Korsgaard, M. A., Schweiger, D. M., & Sapienza, H. J. (1995). Building commitment, attachment, and trust in strategic decision-making teams: The role of procedural justice. *Academy of Management Journal*, *38*, 60–84. doi:10.2307/256728

Korzaan, M. L. (2003). Going with the flow: predicting online purchase intentions. *Journal of Computer Information Systems*, (Summer): 25–31.

Kotler, P. (2000). *Marketing Management, The Millenium Edition*. Upper Saddle River, NJ: Prentice Hall.

Kotter, J. P., & Schlesinger, L. A. (1979). Choosing strategies for change. *Harvard Business Review*, 106–114.

Kouzes, J. M., & Posner, B. Z. (2007). *The leadership challenge* (4th ed.). San Francisco: Jossey-Bass.

Kraemer, S., & Carayon, P. (2007). Human errors and violations in computer and information security: The viewpoint of network administrators and security specialists. *Applied Ergonomics*, *38*(2), 143–154. doi:10.1016/j.apergo.2006.03.010

Krauth, J., Duin, H., & Schimmel, A. (1998). A Comparison of Tools for Strategic Simulation and Scenario Generation with Special Emphasis on 'Soft Factors'. *Simulation Practice and Theory*, *6*, 23–33. doi:10.1016/S0928-4869(97)00005-0

Krogstie, J., & Jørgensen, H. D. (2004). Interactive Models for Supporting Networked Organizations. In [LNCS, Springer.]. *Proceedings of CAiSE*, *2004*, 307–332.

Kshetri, N. (2007). Barriers to e-commerce and competitive business models in developing countries: A case study. *Electronic Commerce Research and Applications*, *6*, 446. doi:10.1016/j.elerap.2007.02.004

Kurkland, N. B., & Egan, T. D. (1999). Telecommuting: Justice and control in the virtual organization. *Organization Science*, *10*(4), 500–513. doi:10.1287/orsc.10.4.500

Kurnia, S., & Johnston, R. B. (2000). The Need for a Processual view of Inter-Organizational Systems Adoption. *The Journal of Strategic Information Systems*, *9*(4), 295–319. doi:10.1016/S0963-8687(00)00050-0

Kurtz, P., & Duncan, A. (1998). Shared service centres: overcomimg resistance to implementation of a shared services centre. *Management Accounting*, *76*(7), 47–48.

Kürümlüoglu, M., Nostdal, R., & Karvonen, I. (2005). Base Concepts. In Camarinha-Matos, L. M., Afsarmanesh, H., & Ollus, M. (Eds.), *Virtual Organizations. Systems and Practices* (pp. 11–28). New York: Springer. doi:10.1007/0-387-23757-7_2

Kwon, T. H., & Zmud, R. W. (1987). Unifying the fragmented models of information systems implementation. In Boland, R. J., & Hirschheim, R. A. (Eds.), *Critical Issues in Information Systems Research* (pp. 247–252). New York: JohnWiley.

Lacoste, E., & Chalmin, P. (2006). FROM WASTE TO RESOURCE An abstract of 2006 "World Waste Survey". Retrieved July 29, 2009, from http://veoliaes.com/resource.php?id=566.

Lai, J., & Chen, W. (2009). Measuring E-business Dependability: The Employee Perspective. *Journal of Systems and Software*, *82*(6), 1046–1055. doi:10.1016/j.jss.2009.02.029

Lambert, T. (2002). *E-Commerce Answers: How to Turn Your Web Site into a Money Machine*. Upper Saddle River, NJ: Pearson Education Ltd, London.

Larrivee, B. (2007). SOA: No Governance Needed. Or Is It? *AIIM E-DOC*, *21*(5), 24–25.

Larsen, T. S., Kotzab, H., & Grieger, M. (2003). Electronic marketplaces and supply chain relationships. *Industrial Marketing Management*, *32*, 199–210. doi:10.1016/S0019-8501(02)00263-8

Laseter, T., Long, B., & Capers, C. (2001). *B2B benchmark: the state of electronic exchanges*. Booz Allen Hamilton.

Lau, T., & Sure, Y. (2002). Introducing Ontology-based Skills Management at a Language Insurance Company. In *Modellierung in der Praxis – Modellierung für die Praxis, 12*, LNI, 123 - 134.

Laudon, K., & Laudon, J. (2005). *Management Information Systems*. New York: Pearson-Prentice Hall.

Laudon, K., & Traver, C. (2008). *E-Commerce: Business, Technology, Society*. New York: Pearson/Prentice-Hall.

Laudon, K. C., & Laudon, J. P. (2010). *Management Information Systems: Managing the digital firm (11th Global edn.)*. Upper Saddle River, NJ: Pearson Education.

Laurent, W. (2007). The Importance of SOA Governance. *DM Review*, *17*(8), 38–38.

Lawrence, S. R., Collins, E., Pavlovich, K., & Arunachalam, M. (2006). Sustainability practices of SMEs: the case of NZ. *Business Strategy and the Environment*, *15*(4), 242–257. doi:10.1002/bse.533

Lawson, R., Alcock, C., Cooper, J., & Burgess, L. (2003). Factors affecting adoption of electronic technologies by SMEs: an Australian study. *Journal of Small Business and Enterprise Development*, *10*(3), 265–276. doi:10.1108/14626000310489727

Lazonick, W. (2007). The stock market and innovative enterprise. *Industrial and Corporate Change*, *16*(6), 983–1035. doi:10.1093/icc/dtm030

LBI. (n.d.). Retrieved from http://www.lbiiconnicholson.com/

Le, T. (2005). Business-to-business electronic marketplaces: evolving business models and competitive landscapes. *International Journal of Services Technology and Management*, *6*(1), 40–53. doi:10.1504/IJSTM.2005.006543

Lee, J. J., & Ben-Natan, R. (2002). *Integrating Service Level Agreements: Optimising your OSS for SLA Delivery*. New York: Wiley.

Lee, C. S. (2001). An Analytical Framework for Evaluating E-commerce Business Models and Strategies. *Internet Research. Electronic Network Applications and Policy*, *11*(4), 349–359. doi:10.1108/10662240110402803

Lefrere, P. (2007). Technology to support distance education. In proceedings from *Strategies for Global Manufacturing: a European view of IMS*. Available from ftp://ftp.cordis.europa.eu/pub/ims/docs/4-6-lefrere.pdf.

Legris, P., Ingham, J., & Collerette, P. (2003). Why do people use information technology? A critical review of the technology acceptance model. *Information & Management*, *40*, 191–204. doi:10.1016/S0378-7206(01)00143-4

Lemola, T., & Lievonen, J. (2008). *The role of innovation policy in fostering open innovation activities among Companies. a report from Vision Era.net*, Finland

Leonard-Barton, D. (1995). *Wellsprings of Knowledge – Building and sustaining the sources of innovation*. Cambridge, MA: Harvard Business School Press.

Leroy, X. (2006). Formal certification of a compiler back-end or: programming a compiler with a proof assistant. *ACM SIGPLAN Notices*, *41*(1), 42–54. doi:10.1145/1111320.1111042

Lertwongsatien, C., & Wongpinunwatana, N. (2003). Ecommerce Adoption in Thailand: An Empirical Study of Small and Medium Enterprises (SMEs). *Journal of Global Information Technology Management*, *6*(3), 67–83.

Lesser, E., & Butner, K. (2005)... *Knowledge and the Supply Chain, Inside Supply Management*, *16*(4), 12.

Levenburg, N. M., Schwarz, T. V., & Motwani, J. (2005). Understanding Adoption of Internet Technologies among SMEs. *Journal of Small Business Strategy*, *16*(1), 51–69.

Leventhal, G. S. (1980). What should be done with equity theory? In Gergen, K. J., Greenberg, M. S., & Willis, R. H. (Eds.), *Social Exchange: Advances in Theory and Research* (pp. 27–55). New York: Plenum Press.

Levi, M., Powell, P., & Yetton, P. (2001). SMEs: aligning IS and strategic context. *Journal of Information Technology*, *16*, 133–144. doi:10.1080/02683960110063672

Levy, M., Powell, P., & Worrall, L. (2005). Strategic intent and e-Business in SMEs: Enablers and inhibitors. *Resources Management Journal*, *18*(4), 1–8.

Levy, M., Powell, P., & Yetton, P. (2002). The Dynamics of SME Information Systems. *Small Business Economics*, *19*(4), 341–354. doi:10.1023/A:1019654030019

Levy, M., & Powell, P. (2005). *Strategies for growth in SMEs: the role of information systems*. Burlington, MA: Elsevier Butterworth-Heinemann.

Levy, M., Powell, P., & Galliers, R. (1999). Assessing Information Systems Strategy Development Frameworks in SMEs. *Information & Management*, *36*(5), 247–261. doi:10.1016/S0378-7206(99)00020-8

Lewis, R., & Cockrill, A. (2002). Going global - remaining local: the impact of e-commerce on small retail firms in Wales. *International Journal of Information Management*, *Vol.*, *22*, 195–209. doi:10.1016/S0268-4012(02)00005-1

Li, F. (2006). *What is e-business: How the internet transforms organizations*. New York: Wiley-Blackwell.

Li, J. (2006). Chinese Entrepreneurship and Small Business Development: An Overview and Research Agenda. *Journal of Small Business and Enterprise Development*, *13*(2). doi:10.1108/14626000610665953

Li, A., & Cropanzano, R. (2009). Fairness at the group level: Justice climate and intraunit justice climate. *Journal of Management*, *35*(3), 564–599. doi:10.1177/0149206308330557

Liao, J., Kickul, J. R., & Ma, H. (2009). Organizational dynamic capability and innovation: an empirical examination of Internet firms. *Journal of Small Business Management*, *47*(3), 263–286. doi:10.1111/j.1540-627X.2009.00271.x

Lientz, B., & Rea, K. (2001). *Comece bem no E-Business – Guia Passo a Passo para a Implementação do E-Business*. Market Books.

Liew, V. (2009). *E-Commerce Usage by the SMEs in Northern Malaysia: Analysis of the State of E-Commerce Adoption by the SMEs in Northern Malaysia and Factors that Might Hinder its Adoption: An Empirical Study*. VDM Verlag.

Lillehagen, F., & Krogstie, J. (2008). *Active Knowledge Modeling of Enterprises*. Springer Verlag. doi:10.1007/978-3-540-79416-5

Lillehagen, F. (2003). The Foundations of AKM Technology. In *Proceeding of 10th International Conference on Concurrent Engineering (CE) Conference* (pp. 619 - 629). Madeira, Portugal.

Lillehagen, F., & Karlsen, D. (1999). Visual Extended Enterprise Engineering embedding Knowledge Management, Systems Engineering and Work Execution. In *IFIP International Enterprise Modelling Conf.* Norway.

Lim, K., Sia, C. L., Lee, M. K. O., & Benbasat, I. (2006). Do I Trust You Online, and If So, Will I Buy? An Empirical Study of Two Trust-Building Strategies. *Journal of Management Information Systems*, *23*(2), 233–266. doi:10.2753/MIS0742-1222230210

Lin, G., Fu, D., Zhu, J., & Dasmalchi, G. (2009). Cloud Computing: IT as a Service. *IT Professional*, *11*(2), 10–13. doi:10.1109/MITP.2009.22

Lin, F., & Sandkuhl, K. (2007). A New Expanding Tree Ontology Matching Method. In *Proc. of OTM 2007: 3rd International IFIP workshop on Semantic Web & Web Semantic (SWWS2007)* (pp. 1329 - 1337). Vilamoura, Algarve, Portugal, November 25—30.

Lind, E. A., & Tyler, T. R. (1988). *The social psychology of procedural justice*. New York: Plenum Press.

Lindgaard, G., Fernandes, G., Dudek, C., & Brown, J. (2006). Attention Web Designers: You have 50 Milliseconds to Make a Good First Impression. *Behaviour & Information Technology*, *25*(2), 115–126. doi:10.1080/01449290500330448

Liu, C., & Arnett, K. P. (2000). Exploring the Factors Associated with Website Sucess in the Content of Electronic Commerce. *Information & Management*, *38*(10), 269–282.

Liu, L. (2000). A measurement model to trust in electronic commerce. In *INFORMA* Proceedings 2000. San Antonio: Texas; TA26.

Lovelock, C., & Wirtz, J. (2007). *Services marketing: people, technology, strategy*. Upper Saddle River, NJ: Pearson Prentice Hall.

Lu, H. (1995). Managerial behaviors over MIS growth stages. *Management Decision*, *33*(7), 40–46. doi:10.1108/00251749510090575

Lucas, H. C. Jr. (2005). *Information technology: strategic decision making for managers*. Hoboken: John Wiley and Sons.

Lumpkin, G. T., & Dess, G. G. (1996). Clarifying the entrepreneurial orientation construct and linking it to performance. *Academy of Management Review*, *21*(1), 135–172. doi:10.2307/258632

Lundqvist, M., Holmquist, E., Sandkuhl, K., Seigerroth, U., & Strandesjö, J. (2009). Information Demand Context Modelling for Improved Information Flow: Experiences and Practices. In *IFIP Working Conference PoEM, The Practices of Enterprise Modelling, 2* (pp. 8 - 22). LNBIP 39, Springer Verlag.

Lundvall, B.-Å. (1999). Innovation Policy and Economic Theory. In Schienstock, G., & Kuusi, O. (Eds.), *Transformation Towards a Learning Economy. The Finnish National Fund for Research and Development - Sitra. Report no. 213*. Helsinki.

Lybaert, N. (1998). The Information Use in a SME: its Importance and Some Elements of Influence. *Small Business Economics*, *10*(2), 171–191. doi:10.1023/A:1007967721235

Maamar, Z., Mostefaoui, S. K., & Yahyaoui, H. (2005). Toward an Agent-Based and Context-Oriented Approach for Web Services Composition. *IEEE Transactions on Knowledge and Data Engineering*, *17*(5), 686–697. doi:10.1109/TKDE.2005.82

MacGregor, R. C. (2004). The Role of Strategic Alliances in The Ongoing Use of Electronic Commerce Technology in Regional Small Business. *Journal of Electronic Commerce in Organizations*, *2*(1), 1–14.

MacGregor, R. C. (2008). *The Adoption of E-commerce in SMEs: The Role of Strategic Alliances*. VDM Verlag.

MacGregor, R. C., & Vrazalic, L. (2005). *A Basic Model of Electronic Commerce Adoption Barriers. School Of Economics and Information Systems* (pp. 515–529). Australia: University of Wollongong.

MacMillan, D. (2009, Mar 31). Hulu attracts crowds but not ads. *Business Week.* Retrieved August 4, 2009 from http://www.businessweek.com/print/technology/content/mar2009/tc20090330_571175.htm.

Madsing, D. (1997). *NCC presentation on the information technology initiative*. Manchester Metropolitan University, 1999

Maes, J. (2009). *SMEs' Radical Product Innovation: the Role of the Internal and External Absorptive Capacity Spheres, Job Market Paper July 2009*. Belgium: Katholieke Universiteit Leuven – Faculty of Business and Economics.

Maes, P. (1994). Agents that reduce work and information overload. *Communications of the ACM*, *37*(7), 31–40. doi:10.1145/176789.176792

Maes, P. (1999). Smart commerce: The future of intelligent agents in cyberspace. *Journal of Interactive Marketing*, *13*(3), 66–76. doi:10.1002/(SICI)1520-6653(199922)13:3<66::AID-DIR5>3.0.CO;2-C

Magazine, T. (2009). *The Best Inventions of the Year 2008*. Retrieved from http://www.time.com/time/specials/2007/article/0,28804,1677329_1678102_1678096,00.html#*consultation made in September 8, 2009*

Maguire, M. (2001). Methods to Support Human-Centered Design. *International Journal of Human-Computer Studies*, *55*, 587–634. doi:10.1006/ijhc.2001.0503

Maheu, M., Whitten, P., & Allen, A. (2001). *E-Health, Telehealth, and Telemedicine. A Guide to Start-up and Success*. New York: Jossey-Bass W. Wiley Company.

Mak, K-T & Ramaprasad, A. (2003). Knowledge Supply Network, *The Journal of the Operational Research Society, 54*(2), Palgrave, 175 – 183.

Malaga, R. A. (2008). Worst Practices in Search Engine Optimization. *Communications of the ACM*, *51*(12), 147–150. doi:10.1145/1409360.1409388

Malaga, R. A. (2007) The Value of Search Engine Optimization: An Action Research Project at a New E-Commerce Site. In Khosrow-Pour, M. (Ed.), *Journal of Electronic Commerce in Organizations*, 5(3), 68-82.

Malet, G., Munoz, F., Appleyard, R., & Hersh, W. (1999). A Model for Enhancing Internet Medical Document Retrieval with "Medical Core Metadata. *Journal of the American Medical Informatics Association*, *6*(2), 163–172.

Malhotra, A., Majchrzak, A., & Rosen, B. (2007). Leading virtual teams. *The Academy of Management Perspectives*, *21*(1), 60–70.

Malmström, M. (2002). *Acquiring Competence to Create and Sustain Competitive Advantages. A Study of four high technology firms*. Licentiate Thesis, Luleå University of Technology.

March, J. (2006). Ideas as Art. *Harvard Business Review*, (October): 83–89.

March, S., & Storey, V. (2008). Design science in the information systems discipline: An introduction to the special issue on design science research. *Management Information Systems Quarterly*, *32*(4), 725–730.

Marik, V., & McFarlane, D. (2005). Industrial Adoption of the Agent-based Technologies. *IEEE Intelligent Systems*, *20*(9), 27–35. doi:10.1109/MIS.2005.11

Marks, E. A., & Bell, M. (2006). *Service-Oriented Architecture: A Planning and Implementation Guide for Business and Technology*. Hoboken, New Jersey: Wiley.

Markus, M. L., & Christiaanse, E. (2003). Adoption and impact of collaboration electronic marketplaces. *Information Systems and E-Business Management*, *1*(2), 139–155. doi:10.1007/s10257-003-0001-7

Martin, L. M., & Matlay, H. (2003). Innovative Use of the Internet in Established Small Firms, *Qualitative Market Research. International Journal (Toronto, Ont.)*, *6*(1), 18–26.

Martínez-López, F. J., Luna-Huertas, P., & Martínez, F. J. (2006). Motivations for consumption behaviours on the web: a conceptual model based on a holistic approach. *International Journal of Electronic Marketing and Retailing*, *1*(1), 3–20. doi:10.1504/IJEMR.2006.010092

Martins, L. L., Gilson, L. L., & Maynard, M. T. (2004). Virtual teams: What do we know and where do we go from here? *Journal of Management*, *30*(6), 805–835. doi:10.1016/j.jm.2004.05.002

Mata, F. J., Fuerst, W. L. & Barney, J. B. (1995). Information technology and sustained competitive advantage: a resource-based analysis. *Management information science Quarterly,* pp. 487-505, December.

Matera, M., Rizzo, F., & Carughi, G. T. (2006). Web Usability: Principles and Evaluation Methods. In Mendes, E., & Mosley, N. (Eds.), *Web Engineering* (pp. 143–180). Berlin, Heidelberg: Springer. doi:10.1007/3-540-28218-1_5

Maur, J. C. (2008). Regionalism and trade facilitation: A primer. *World Bank Policy Research Working Paper*, retrieved on July, 2009, from http://econ.worldbank.org/external/default/main.

Maximilien, E. M., & Singh, M. P. (2005). *Multiagent System for Dynamic Web Services Selection.* Paper presented at The Workshop on Service-Oriented Computing and Agent-Based Engineering (SOCABE), Utrecht, The Netherlands.

Maznevski, M. L., & Chudoba, K. M. (2000). Bridging space over time: Global virtual team dynamic and effectiveness. *Organization Science*, *11*(5), 473–492. doi:10.1287/orsc.11.5.473.15200

McAdam, M., & McAdam, R. (2008). High tech start-ups in University Science Park incubators: The relationship between the start-up's lifecycle progression and use of the incubator's resources. *Technovation*, *28*, 277–290. doi:10.1016/j.technovation.2007.07.012

McBride, D. (1998). *Successful deployment of IT Service Management in the distributed enterprise*. Hewlett-Packard Company.

McBride, E. (2009). A special report on waste. The Economist.

McConnell International. (2000). *Risk E-Business: Seizing the Opportunity of Global E-Readiness*. Washington, DC: McConell International. Retrieved September 3, 2009 from http://whitepapers.zdnet.co.uk/0,1000000651,260019500p,00.htm

McConnell International. (2001). *Ready? Net. Go!Partnerships Leading the Global Economy*. Retrieved September 3, 2009 from http://www.witsa.org/papers/e-readiness2.pdf

McDuffie, J. P. (2007). HRM and distributed work. *Academy of Management Annals*, *1*, 549–615. doi:10.1080/078559817

McFarlan, F. W., McKenney, J. L., & Pyburn, P. (1983). The information archipelago - plotting a course. Boston. *Harvard Business Review*, (January-February): 145–156.

McGirt, E. (2009, Mar 17). How Chris Hughes helped launch Facebook and the Barack Obama campaign. *Fast Company.* Retrieved August 4, 2009 from http://www.fastcompany.com/magazine/134/boy-wonder.html

McKay, J., Prananto, A., & Marshall, P. (2000). E-business Maturity: The SOG-e Model. In *Proceedings of the 11th Australasian Conference on Information Systems (ACIS)*, Australia.

McKnight, D. H., & Chervany, N. L. (2001). What Trust Means in E-Commerce Customer Relationships: An Interdisciplinary Conceptual Typology. *International Journal of Electronic Commerce*, *2*(6), 35–59.

McKnight, D. H., Cummings, L. L., & Chervany, N. L. (1998). Initial trust formation in new organizational relationships. *Academy of Management Review*, *23*(3), 472–490. doi:10.2307/259290

McLeod, R., & Schell, G. (2007). *Management Information Systems*. New York: Pearson-Prentice Hall.

McNurlin, B. C., Sprague, P. H. Jr, & Bui, T. (2009). *Information systems management in practice* (8th ed.). Upper Saddle River, NJ: Pearson Education.

Meer, D., Romberger, T., Favaro, K. (2006). Five Rules for Retailing in a Recession. *Harvard Business Review*, Harvard Business School, April 2009

Mehrtens, J., Cragg, P. B., & Mills, A. M. (2001). A model of Internet Adoption by SMEs. *Information & Management*, *39*(3), 165–176. doi:10.1016/S0378-7206(01)00086-6

Meier, A., & Stormer, H. (2009). *eBusiness & eCommerce*. Berlin, Heidelberg: Springer-Verlag.

Metiu, A. (2006). Owning the code: Status closure in distributed groups. *Organization Science*, *17*, 418–436. doi:10.1287/orsc.1060.0195

Meyer, A., & Rose, D. H. (1998). *Learning to Read in the Computer Age*. Cambridge, MA: Brookline Books.

Meyer, J. H. F., & Land, R. (2003). Threshold concepts and troublesome knowledge: Linkages to ways of thinking and practising within the disciplines. In Rust, C. (Ed.), *Improving Student Learning: Improving Student Learning Theory and Practice – Ten Years On*. Oxford: Oxford Centre for Staff and Learning Development.

Mezegar, I., Kovacs, G., & Paganelli, P. (2000). Co-operative production planning for small- and medium-sized enterprises. *International Journal of Production Economics*, *64*, 37–48. doi:10.1016/S0925-5273(99)00032-8

Michael, S. C., & Palandjian, T. P. (2004). Organizational learning in new product introductions. *Journal of Product Innovation Management*, *21*, 268–276. doi:10.1111/j.0737-6782.2004.00078.x

Mild, A., & Reutterer, T. (2003). An improved collaborative filtering approach for predicting cross-category purchases based on binary market basket data. *Journal of Retailing and Consumer Services*, *10*(3), 123–133. doi:10.1016/S0969-6989(03)00003-1

Minges, M. (2002). Assessing e-readiness: A review of the Mosaic Methodology. *iNet Conference 2002*, Washington DC. Retrieved September 3, 2009, from http://www.itu.int/ITU-D/ict/papers/2002/inet02/MM.pdf

Mintzberg, H., Ahlstrand, B., & Lampel, J. (1998). *Strategy Safari. A Guided Tour through the Wilds of Strategic Management*. New York: The Free Press.

Mintzberg, H., Lampel, J., Quinn, J. B., & Ghoshal, S. (2003). *The strategy process: concepts, contexts, cases* (4th ed.). Upper Saddle River, NJ: Prentice Hall.

Minztberg, H., Ahlstrand, B., & Lampel, J. (1998). *Strategy safari: a guided tour through the wilds of strategic management*. Washington, DC: Free Press.

Mooney, R. J., & Roy, L. (2000). Content-based book recommending using learning for text categorization. *Proceedings of the fifth ACM Conference on Digital Libraries*, 195-204.

Morais, E. (2009). Maturidade do Negócio Electrónico – Constrangimentos associados à sua evolução, Doctoral dissertation, University of Trás-os-Montes e Alto Douro, Portugal.

Morais, E., Gonçalves, E., & Pires, J. (2007). Electronic Commerce Maturity: A review of the principal models, In *Proceedings of IADIS International Conference - E-Society 2007*, Lisbon, Portugal, 463-466.

Morais, E., Pires, J., & Gonçalves, R. (2009a). Exploring the Constraints to the evolution of Electronic Business: The Portuguese reality. In *Proceedings of 11th IBIMA Conference*, Cairo, Egypt.

Morais, E., Pires, J., & Gonçalves, R. (2009b). An exploratory investigation of e-business constraints among large organizations in Portugal. In Proceedings of *International Conference on E-Business – ICEB 2009*, Milan, Italy.

Moran, M., & Hunt, B. (2006). *Search Engine Marketing: Driving Search Traffic to Your Company's Web Site*. Upper Saddle River, NJ: IBM Press, Pearson PLC.

Morgan, R. M., & Hunt, S. (1994). The Commitment-Trust Theory of Relationship Marketing. *Journal of Marketing*, *58*(3), 20–38. doi:10.2307/1252308

Mosaic Group. (1998). *The Global Diffusion of the Internet Project: An Initial Inductive Study*. Retrieved September 3, 2009, from http://mosaic.unomaha.edu/GDI1998/GDI1998.html

Mosey, S. (2005). Understanding New-to-Market Product Development in SMEs. *International Journal of Operations & Production Management*, *25*(2), 114–130. doi:10.1108/01443570510576994

Mossholder, K. W., Bennett, N., & Martin, C. L. (1998). A multilevel analysis of procedural justice context. *Journal of Organizational Behavior*, *19*, 131–141. doi:10.1002/(SICI)1099-1379(199803)19:2<131::AID-JOB878>3.0.CO;2-P

Moura, R. (2004). *O papel da tecnologia e informação. Tecnologia de Informação. São Paulo: Atlas.Neus A. (2000). The quality of online registration information: factors influencing user decisions* (pp. 109–129). MA: Ridge.

Mulej, M. (2007). Systems Theory. *Systems Research and Behavioral Science*, *24*(3), 347–357. doi:10.1002/sres.810

Mulej, M. (et al.) (1992). *Systems Theory.* Maribor: FEB.

Müller, G., Eymann, T., Nopper, N., & Seuken, S. (2004). EMIKA System: Architecture and Prototypic Realization. In *Proc. of the IEEE Intl. Conf. on Systems, Man and Cybernetics (SMC), 6* (pp. 5621 – 5626). The Hague, The Netherlands, October 2004.

Mullins, L. (2007). *Management and Organisational Behaviour*. London: Prentice Hall.

Murphy, H. C., & Kielgast, C. D. (2008). Do Small and Medium-sized Hotels Exploit Search Engine Marketing? *International Journal of Contemporary Hospitality Management*, *20*(1), 90–97. doi:10.1108/09596110810848604

Nachira, F., Dini, P., & Nicolai, A. (2007). A Network of Digital Business Ecosystems for Europe: Roots, Processes and Perspectives. WWW [On-line]. Retrieved from http://www.digital-ecosystems.org/book/DBE-2007.pdf.

Nah, F. F.-H., & Davis, S. (2002). HCI Research Issues in E-commerce. *Journal of Electronic Commerce Research*, *3*, 98–113.

Nählinder, J. (2005). *Innovation and Employment in Services: The case of Knowledge Intensive Business Services in Sweden*, PhD Thesis, Department of Technology and Social Change, Linköping University, Sweden, Unitryck Linköping

Napier, G., Serger, S. S., & Hansson, E. W. (2004). *Strengthening Innovation and Technology Policies for SME Development in Turkey– Opportunities for Private Sector Involvement, International Organisation for Knowledge Economy and Enterprise Development*. IKED.

Naquin, C. E., Kurtberg, T. R., & Blekin, L. Y. (2008). E-mail communication and group cooperation in mixed motive contexts. *Social Justice Research*, *21*, 470–489. doi:10.1007/s11211-008-0084-x

Nath, R., Akmanligil, M., Hjelm, K., Sakaguchi, T., & Schultz, M. (1998). Electronic commerce and the internet: issues, problems, and perspectives. *International Journal of Information Management*, *18*(2), 91–101. doi:10.1016/S0268-4012(97)00051-0

Naumann, S. E., & Bennett, N. (2000). A case for procedural justice climate: Development and test of a multiple model. *Academy of Management Journal*, *43*, 881–889. doi:10.2307/1556416

Ndou V., Petti C., (2006) DMS Business Models Design and Destination Configurations: Choice and Implementation Issues, *Journal of Information Technology and Tourism,* 9.(1), New York: Congizant Comm. Corp.

Necula, G. C. (1997) Proof-carrying code. *In Annual Symposium on Principles of Programming Languages 1997 (pp. 106–119).New York:* ACM Press.

Nedelko, Z. (2008). The role and importance of groupware for teamwork. *Business Review (Federal Reserve Bank of Philadelphia)*, *10*(1), 211–217.

Nielsen, J. (1993). *Usability Engineering*. San Diego, CA: Academic Press.

Nielsen, J. (2000). *Designing Web Usability*. Indianapolis, USA: New Riders Publishing.

Nielsen, J., & Mack, R. L. (1994). *Usability Inspection Methods*. New York: Wiley.

Nielsen, J. (1994). Heuristic Evaluation. In Nielsen, J., & Mack, R. L. (Eds.), *Usability Inspection Methods*. New York: John Wiley & Sons.

Nielsen, J. (1994) *Usability Inspection Methods, Conference on Human Factors in Computing Systems*413-414.

Nielsen, J. (1998) *Failure of Corporate Websites*, Retrieved from July 21, 2009 from http://www.useit.com/alertbox/981018.html.

Nielsen, J. (1999) *Who Commits the Top Ten Mistakes of Web Design*?Retrieved from www.useit.com/alertbox/990307.html.

Nielsen, J. (2003) *Misconceptions About Usability*. Retrieved from July 20, 2009 from http://www.useit.com/alertbox/20030908.html.

Nielsen, J. (2003). *Usability 101: Introduction to Usability*. Retrieved from July 24, 2009 from http://www.useit.com/alertbox/20030825.html.

Nisan, N., & Ronen, A. (2000) Computationally feasible VCG mechanisms. *In the 2000 ACM Conference on Electronic Commerce (pp. 242–252),* New York: ACM Press.

Nissen, M. E. (2001). Agent-Based Supply Chain Integration. *Information Technology Management, 2*(3), 289–312. doi:10.1023/A:1011449109160

Nolan, R. (1973). Managing the Computer Resource: A Stage Hypothesis. *Communications of the ACM, 16*(7), 399–405. doi:10.1145/362280.362284

Nolan, R. (1979). Managing the crisis in data processing. *Harvard Business Review, 57*(2), 115–126.

Nonaka, I. (1994). A dynamic theory of organisational knowledge creation. *Organization Science, 5*(1), 14–37. doi:10.1287/orsc.5.1.14

Noran, O. (2003). A Mapping of Individual Architecture Frameworks (GRAI, PERA, C4ISR, CIMOSA, Zachman, ARIS) onto GERAM. In Bernus, P., Nemes, L., & Schmidt, G. (Eds.), *Handbook on Enterprise Architecture* (pp. 65–210). Berlin, Heidelberg: Springer-Verlag.

NOUS. (2007). Today's Knowledge Intensive SME: Where, Why and How? Discussion Paper, Department of Innovation, Industry and Regional Development, The Nous Group, Australia

Novak, T., Hoffman, D., & Duhachek, A. (2003). The influence of goal-directed and experiential activities on online flow experiences. *Journal of Consumer Psychology, 13*(1/2), 3–16.

Novak, T., Hoffman, D., & Yung, Y. (2000). Measuring the customer experience in online environments: A structural modelling approach. *Marketing Science,* 19 (1: Special Issue), 22-42.

Nusair, K., & Hua, N. (2009). Comparative Assessment of Structural Equation Modeling and Multiple Regression Research Methodologies: E-commerce Context. *Tourism Management, xxx,* 1–11.

O'Brien, A., 2003. *Sistemas de Informação e as decisões gerenciais na era da Internet.* São Paulo, Saraiva.OECD, 1999. SMEs and Electronic Commerce: Proposals for Work, Working Party on Small and Medium-Sized Enterprises, DSTI/IND/PME (99)11/REV1, Paris.

O'Connor, J., Galvin, E., & Evans, M. (2004). *Electronic Marketing: Theory and Practice for the Twenty-First Century*. London: Prentice Hall.

O'Sullivan, M. (2000). *Contests for corporate control*. Oxford, UK: Oxford University Press Oxford Business School (2008). Introducing the Oxford Centre for Entrepreneurship and Innovation, Retail Policy Issues, The Retail Digest, Oxford SAID Business School, pp. 30-31

Obama, B. (2009). President Obama on the race to the top. Retrieved August 5, 2009, from http://www.youtube.com/watch?v=VNbDv0zPBV4

Oberholzer-Gee. Felix (2006). Wal-Mart's Business Environment. *Harvard Business Review*, Harvard Business School, December 12, 2006.

OECD – Organisation for Economic Cooperation and Development. (2009). At www.oecd.org accessed on August, 2009.

OECD (2007). SME Policy Index 2007, Report on the Implementation of the European Charter for Small Enterprises in the Western Balkans, Prepared by: the European Commission Directorate General for Enterprise and Industry and the OECD Investment Compact for South East Europe. In consultation with: the European Bank for Reconstruction and Development and the European Training Foundation Published with the financial support of the European Commission and the OECD Investment Compact for South East Europe

OECD. (2000). *OECD Science Technology and Industry Outlook 2000*. France: OECD.

OECD. (2000b). *OECD Science Technology and Industry Outlook 2000*. France: OECD.

OECD. (2002). *OECD Science Technology and Industry Outlook 2002*. France: OECD.

OECD. (2008). *Open Innovation in Global Networks, a policy brief*. France: OECD.

OECD. (2008). *Open Innovation in Global Networks, a policy brief*. France: OECD.

OECD. (2000a). Enhancing the Competitiveness of SMEs in the Global Economy: Strategies and Policies Enhancing the Competitiveness of SMEs through Innovation, *Conference for Ministers responsible for SMEs and Industry Ministers, Bologna*, Italy, 14-15 June 2000

OECD. (2006). *The Athens Action Plans for Removing Barriers to SME Access to International Markets,* OECD Report, France.

OECD. (2006). *The Athens Action Plans for Removing Barriers to SME Access to International Markets,* OECD Report, France.

Öhgren, A. (2009). *Towards an Ontology Development Methodology for SME*. Unpublished PhD dissertation, Linköping University, Sweden.

Oliveira, O., Andersen, B., Oliveira, A., & Rolstadås, A. (2006). The Impact of Serious Games in the European Industry. In proceedings from the *10th Workshop on Experimental Interactive Learning in Industrial Management - IFIP WG5.7 SIG*, IFIP.

ONESource, (2009). eBay Inc One Stop Report. August 2009

ONESource, (2009a). *Marks & Spencer One Stop Report*August 2009

ONESource, (2009b). Amazon One Stop Report. August 2009

Online Marketing Blog. (n.d.). Retrieved from http://www.theblognote.com/zapposcom-ornek-bir-e-ticaret-basari-hikayesi.html Access date: 10.06.2009.

Oppenheim, C., & Ward, L. (2006). Evaluation of Web Sites for B2C E-commerce. *Aslib Proceedings: New Information Perspectives*, *58*(3), 237–260.

Ordanini, A., & Pol, A. (2001). Infomediation and Competitive Advantage in B2b Digital Marketplaces. *European Management Journal*, *19*(3), 276–285. doi:10.1016/S0263-2373(01)00024-X

Ordanini, A., Micelli, S., & Di Maria, E. (2004). Failure and Success of B-to-B Exchange Business Models: A Contingent Analysis of Their Performance. *European Management Journal*, *22*(3). doi:10.1016/j.emj.2004.04.013

Ordanini, A., & Pol, A. (2001). Informediation and competitive advantage in D2B digital marketplaces. *European Management Journal*, *19*(3), 276–285. doi:10.1016/S0263-2373(01)00024-X

Organisation for Economic Cooperation and Development. (1997). *Small Business, Job Creation and Growth: Facts*. Paris, France: Obstacles and Best Practices.

Organisation for Economic Cooperation and Development. (2005). *OECD SME and Entrepreneurship Outlook*. OECD Publishing.

Organisation for Economic Cooperation and Development. (2004). *SME Statistics; Towards a More Systematic Statistical Measurement of SME Behaviour*. Istanbul: Turkey.

Oroszi, A., Jung, T., Smirnov, A., Shilov, N., & Kashevnik, A. (2009). Ontology-Driven Codification for Discrete and Modular Products [Inderscience.]. *International Journal of Product Development*, *8*(2), 162–177. doi:10.1504/IJPD.2009.024186

Osman, N., & Robertson, D. (2007) Dynamic verification of trust in distributed open systems. *In International Joint Conference on Artificial Intelligence (pp. 1440–1445),* New York: ACM Press.

Ostergaard, K., & Summers, J. (2009). Development of a systematic classification and taxonomy of collaborative design activities. [London, England.]. *Journal of Engineering Design*, (February): 2009.

Oyelaran-Oyeyinka, B., & Kaushalesh, L. K. (2004). *Internet Diffusion in sub-Saharan Africa: a cross-country Analysis*. Telecommunications Policy.

Paas, F., & Firssova, O. (2004). Usability Evaluation of Integrated e-Learning. In Jochems, W., van Merrienboer, J., & Koper, E. J. R. (Eds.), *Integrated eLearning: Implications for Pedagogy, Technology and Organization* (pp. 112–125). London: RoutledgeFalmer.

Pahl, G., & Beitz, W. (1995). *Engineering Design: A systematic approach; Springer Science and Business media*. London: Springer Verlag.

Palmer, J. W. (2002). Web Site Usability, Design and Performance Metrics. *Information Systems Research*, *13*(2), 151–167. doi:10.1287/isre.13.2.151.88

Palvia, P. C., & Palvia, S. C. (1999). An examination of the IT Satisfaction of Small-Business Users. *Information & Management*, *35*, 127–137. doi:10.1016/S0378-7206(98)00086-X

Parish, A., Kibblewhite, G., Woodley, M., & Richardson, J. (2002). The UK electronics industry e-commerce initiative-a study of the adoption of e-commerce. Retrieved August 10, 2009, from www.intellectuk.org/publications/reports

Parker, D. (2009). *Microgeneration: low energy strategies for larger buildings*. Burlington, MA: Elsevier.

Parrilli, M. D. (2006). A Tripartite Innovation Framework for Small Firms in Developing Regions: Key Issues for Analysis and Policy, Paper Number 2007-01, *Institute for Economic Development Policy Discussion Paper Series,* University of Birmingham, UK

Partnership for 21st Century Skills. (2004). *Learning for the 21st century.* Retrieved July 23, 2009, from http://www.21stcenturyskills.org/images/stories/otherdocs/P21_Report.pdf.

Passmore, D. (1996). Setting performance expectations. *Business Communications Review*, *26*(12), 20–22.

Patten, K., Whitworth, B., Fjermestad, J., & Mahinda, E. (2005) Leading IT flexibility: anticipation, agility and adaptability. In Romano, N. (Ed.) *Proceedings of the 11th Americas Conference on Information Systems*, Omaha, NE, 11–14, Red Hook, NY: Curran Associates, Inc.

Pauly, M. (2005). Programming and verifying subgame-perfect mechanisms. *Journal of Logic and Computation*, *15*(3), 295–316. doi:10.1093/logcom/exi014

Pavic, S., Koh, S., Simpson, M., & Padmore, J. (2007). Could e-business create a competitive advantage in UK SMEs? *Benchmarking*, *14*(3), 1463–5771. doi:10.1108/14635770710753112

Pavlou, P. A., & Fygenson, M. (2006). Understanding and predicting electronic commerce adoption: an extension of the Theory of Planned Behaviour. *Management Information Systems Quarterly*, *30*(1), 115–143.

Pazzani, M. J., & Billsus, D. (2007). Content-based recommendation systems. In P. Brusilovsky, A. Kobsa, & W. Nejdl (Eds.): *The Adaptive Web*. (LNCS 4321, pp. 325-341) New York: Springer

Peet, S., Brindley, C., & Ritchie, B. (2002). The EC and SME support mechanisms for e-business. *European Business Review*, *14*(5), 335–341. doi:10.1108/09555340210444185

Pelham, A. M., & Wilson, D. T. (1996). A Longitudinal Study of the Impact of Market Structure, Firm Structure, Strategy, and Market Orientation Culture on Dimensions of Small-Firm Performance. *Journal of the Academy of Marketing Science*, *24*(1), 27–43. doi:10.1007/BF02893935

Peterson, R. A., Balasubramanian, S., & Bronnenberg, B. J. (1997). Exploring the Implications of the Internet for Consumer Marketing. *Journal of Academy of Marketing Science,* 25(4. Poon, S. & Swatman, P. (2000). Internet-based Small Business Communication: seven Australian cases. *Electronic Markets*, *7*(2), 241–259.

Petrie, C., & Bussler, C. (2003). Service agents and virtual enterprises: a survey. *IEEE Internet Computing*, *7*(4), 68–78. doi:10.1109/MIC.2003.1215662

Phillips, J. M., Douthill, E. A., & Hyland, M. M. (2001). The role of justice in team member satisfaction with the leader and attachment to the team. *The Journal of Applied Psychology*, *86*(2), 316–325. doi:10.1037/0021-9010.86.2.316

Piatier, A. (1984). *Barriers to Innovation*. London: Frances Pinter.

Pink, D. (2006). *A whole new mind: Why right-brainers will rule the future*. New York: Riverhead Trade.

PLASTIC. (2006). Retrieved June 2, 2009 from http://www.ist-plastic.org/.

Poe, C. D., & Viator, R. E. (1990). What to do when employees resist automation. *Journal of Accounting and EDP*, *5*(4), 9–14.

Pogue, D. (2009, May 27). Don't quit the Kindle yet. *The New Times*. Retrieved on August 7, 2009 from http://www.nytimes.com/2009/05/28/technology/personaltech/28pogue.html

Polanyi, M. (1967). *The Tacit Dimension*. Garden City, NY: Doubleday.

Poon, S. (2000). Business environment and internet commerce benefit - a small business perspective. *European Journal of Information Systems*, *9*, 72–81.

Poon, S., & Swatman, P. (1999). An exploratory study of small business Internet commerce issues. *Information & Management*, *35*, 9–18. doi:10.1016/S0378-7206(98)00079-2

Poon, S., & Swatman, P. M. C. (1999). An exploratory study of small business Internet commerce issues. *Information & Management*, *35*(1), 9–18. doi:10.1016/S0378-7206(98)00079-2

Poon, S. (1999). Small business and Internet commerce: What are the lessons learned? In Sudweeks, F., & Romm, C. (Eds.), *Doing business on the Internet: Opportunities and pitfalls* (pp. 113–124). London, UK: Springer-Verlag.

Poon, S., & Strom, J. (1997). Small businesses use of the Internet: some realities. *Association for Information Systems Americas Conference*, Indianapolis, IN, 15–17 August. Retrieved August 10, 2009, from http://www.isoc.org/INET97/proceedings/C2/C2_1.HTM

Poon, S., & Swatman, P. M. C. (1995). The Internet for Small Businesses: An Enabling Infrastructure for Competitiveness. *Proceedings of the Fifth Internet Society Conference*, (ed.) Chon K., Hawaii, 221-231.Retrieved August 10, 2009, from http://www.isoc.org/inet95/proceedings/PAPER/126/html/paper.html

Porter, M. E. (2001). Strategy and the internet. *Harvard Business Review*, *79*(3), 63–78.

Porter, M. (1980). *Competitive strategy*. New York: Free Press.

Porter, M. (1996). What is strategy? [November-December.]. *Harvard Business Review*, 61–78.

Porter, M. E. (1980). *Competitive Strategy*. New York: The Free Press.

Porter, M. (1985). *Competitive Advantage: Creating and Sustaining Superior Performance*. Nova Iorque, The Free Press.

Porter, M. (2001). Strategy and the Internet. *Harvard Business Review HBR OnPoint*. Boston, USA: Harvard Business School Publishing Corporation, pp. 62-78, March.

Porter, M. E., & Schwab, K. (2008). *The Global Competitiveness Report 2008–2009*. Geneve: World Economic forum.

Potocan, V. (2002). Business systems: Sustainable development and anticipatory system. *Management*, *7*(1), 67–77.

Potocan, V., & Kuralt, B. (2007). Synergy in business: Some new suggestions. *The Journal of Academy of Business*, *12*(1), 199–204.

Potocan, V., & Mulej, M. (2009). Business Cybernetics. *Kybernetes*, *38*(1/2), 93–112. doi:10.1108/03684920910930295

Pourdehnad, J. (2007). *Idealized Design - An Open Innovation.*Process, a presentation from the annual W. Edwards Deming Annual Conference, Purdue University, West Lafayette, Indiana, October 2007

Powell, W. W., Koput, K. W., & Smith-Doerr, L. (1996). Inter-organizational collaboration and the locus of innovation. Network learning in Biotechnology. *Administrative Science Quarterly*, *41*, 116–145. doi:10.2307/2393988

Prananto, A., McKay, J., & Marshall, P. (2001). Frameworks to Support E-Business Strategy, In *Global CoOperation in the New Millennium, The 9th European Conference on Information Systems*, 2001, Bled, Slovenia.

Pratt, J. H. (2002). *E-biz; Strategies for small business success*. US SBA Office of Advocacy. Retrieved August 10, 2009, from http://www.sba.gov/advo/research/rs220tot.pdf

Premkumar, G., & Roberts, M. (1999). Adoption of new information technologies in rural small businesses. *Omega, International Journal Management. Science*, *27*, 467–484.

Prensky, M. (2001). *Digital Game-Based Learning*. New York: McGraw Hill.

Pullen, A., De Weerd-Nederhof, P., Groen, A., & Fisscher, O. (2008). Configurations of External SME Characteristics to Explain Differences in Innovation Performance, a proceedings of the *High Technology Small Firms Conference 2008*: Twente University, Netherlands.

Purao, S; Baldwin, C.; Hevner, A; Storey, V.; Pries-Heje, J; Smith, B.; Zhu, Y. (2008). The Sciences of Design: Observations on an Emerging Field; Working Paper; Harvard Business School.

Putman, J. R. (2001). *Architecting with RM-ODP*. Upper Saddle River, NJ: Prentice Hall.

Putnik, G., & Sluga, A. (2007) Reconfigurability of manufacturing systems for agility implementation, part I: requirements and principles. In Cunha, P. & Maropoulos, P. (Eds.) *Digital Enterprise Technology: Perspectives and Future Challenges* (pp. 91-98). New York, NY: Springer Science+Business Media.

Quayle, M. (2002). E-Commerce: the challenge for UK SMEs in the twenty-first century. *International Journal of Operations & Production Management*, *22*(10), 1148–1161. doi:10.1108/01443570210446351

Quinton, S., & Khan, M. A. (2009). Generating web site traffic: a new model for SMEs. *Direct Marketing: An International Journal*, *3*(2), 109–123. doi:10.1108/17505930910964777

Qvortrup, L. (2006). *Knowledge, Education and Learning: E-Learning in the knowledge society*. Copenhagen: Forlaget Samfundslitteratur.

Rachman, Z. M. (2002). *ASEAN e-Readiness Assessment*. Retrieved August 22, 2009, from http://unpan1.un.org/intradoc/groups/public/documents/APCITY/UNPAN011274.pdf

Rai, A., & Patnayakuni, R. (1996). A Structural Model for CASE Adoption Behaviour. *Journal of Management Information Systems*, *13*(2), 205–234.

Raisch, W. D. (2001). *The e-Marketplace: Strategies for Success in B2B eCommerce*. New York: McGraw-Hill.

Raisinghani, M. S., Herwick, L. B., Pulamsetti, R., Gunther, T. H., Caisan, V., & Wang, A. (2005). E-Business in the Global Automotive Industry: Key Value Propositions. In Lan, Y.-C. (Ed.), *Global Information Society. Operating Information Systems in a Dynamic Global Business Environment* (pp. 240–264). Hershey, PA: Idea Group Publishing.

Ramsey, E., Ibbotson, P., Bell, J., & Gary, B. (2003). E-opportunities of service sector SMEs: An Irish cross-boarder study. *Journal of Small Business and Enterprise Development*, *10*(3), 250–264. doi:10.1108/14626000310489709

Ranganathan, C., & Ganapathy, S. (2002). Key Dimensions of Business-to-Consumer Web Sites. *Information & Management*, *39*(6), 457–465. doi:10.1016/S0378-7206(01)00112-4

Rao, S., Metts, G., & Monge, C. (2003). Electronic Commerce Development in Small and Medium Sized Enterprises: A Stage Model and its Implications. *Business Process Management Journal*, *9*(1), 11–32. doi:10.1108/14637150310461378

Rappa, M. (2001) *Managing the digital enterprise: Business models on the Web*. Retrieved from <http://ecommerce.ncsu.edu/business_models.html>

Rask, M., & Kragh, H. (2004). Motives for e-marketplace participation: Differences and similarities between buyers and suppliers. *Electronic Markets*, *14*(4), 270–283. doi:10.1080/10196780412331311720

Ray, P. (2003). Integrated management from e-business perspective: concepts, architectures, and methodologies. Pradeep Kumar Ray New York: Kluwer Academic/Plenum Publishers.

Raymond, L. (2001). Determinants of web site implementation, small business. Int. Res. *Electronic Network Appl. and Policy*, *11*, 411–422.

Rayport, J. F., & Jaworski, B. J. (2002). *Introduction to e-Commerce* (pp. 204–206). New York: McGraw-Hill.

Redon, R., Larsson, A., Leblond, R., & Longueville, B. (2007). Vivace context based search platform. In *Proceedings of the 6th International Conference CONTEXT-07*. LNCS (LNAI), *4635* (pp. 397–410). Heidelberg: Springer.

Reedy, J., & Schullo, S. (2004). *Electronic Marketing: Integrating Electronic Resources into the Marketing Process*. Florence, KY: Thompson Learning.

Renaud, P. (2008). Open Innovation at Oseo Innovation: Example of the Passerelle Programme, a presentation at the OECD Business Symposium on Open Innovation in Global Networks, Copenhagen, 25-26 February, 2008

Reserve Bank of India. (2009). *Master Circular-Lending to Micro, Small, & Medium Enterprises(MSME)*. Mumbai, India: Sector.

Reuters, (2009). *Web retail a bright spot in tepid U.S. holiday season*. Retrieved from http://www.reuters.com/article/internetNews/idUSTRE5B14AP20091202*consultation made in December 2, 2009*

Revell, A., & Rutherfoord, R. (2003). UK Environmental Policy and the Small Firm: Broadening the focus. *Business Strategy and the Environment*, *12*, 26–35. doi:10.1002/bse.347

Revell, A., Stokes, D., & Chen, H.(2009). Small businesses and the environment: turning over a new leaf? *Business Strategy and the Environment*. Published Online: 16 Feb 2009.

Reynolds, J., & Mofazali, R. (2000). *The Complete E-commerce Book: Design, Build and Maintain a Successful Web-based Business.* New York: McGraw-Hill Inc.,US.

Rijo, R. (2008). *Framework para a Gestão de Projectos de Sistemas de Informação de Contact Centers*. Doctoral dissertation, Universidade de Trás-os-Montes e Alto-Douro, Portugal.

Ring, P., & Vandeven, A. (1994). Development processes of cooperative interorganizational relationships. *Academy of Management*, *19*(1), 90–118. doi:10.2307/258836

Riquelme, H. (2002). Commercial internet adoption in China: comparing the experience of small, medium and large businesses. *Internet Research: Electronic Networking Applications and Policy*, *12*(3), 276–286. doi:10.1108/10662240210430946

Robbins, S. (2007). *Organization Theory: Structures, Designs, and Applications*. New Delhi: Dorling Kindersley.

Roberson, Q. M. (2006a). Justice in teams: The activation and role of sensemaking in the emergence of justice climates. *Organizational Behavior and Human Decision Processes*, *100*, 177–192. doi:10.1016/j.obhdp.2006.02.006

Roberson, Q. M. (2006b). Justice in teams: The effects of interdependence and identification on referent choice and justice climate strength. *Social Justice Research*, *19*(3), 323–344. doi:10.1007/s11211-006-0010-z

Roberson, Q. M., & Colquitt, J. A. (2005). Shared and configural justice: A social justice network model of justice in teams. *Academy of Management Review*, *30*(3), 595–607.

Roberts, B., Svirskas, A., & Matthews, B. (2005). Request Based Virtual Organizations (RBVO): An Implementation Scenario. In L. M. Camarinha-Matos, H. Afsarmanesh, A. Ortiz (Eds.) *Collaborative Networks and Their Breeding Environments: Sixth IFIP Working Conference on VIRTUAL ENTERPRISES IFIP International Federation for Information Processing Vol. 186, 6th IFIP Working Conference on Virtual Enterprises (PRO-VE'05)* (pp. p17-24). Valencia, Spain.

Roberts, B., Svirskas, A., & Ward, J. (2005). Implementation Options for Virtual Organizations: A Peer to Peer (P2P) Approach. In: Putnik, Goran and Cunha, Maria Manuela, (eds.) *Virtual enterprise integration: technological and organizational perspectives* (pp. 400-416). Hershey PA:Idea Group Publishing.

Rodgers, J., Yen, D., & Chou, D. (2002). Developing e-business. *Information Management & Computer Security*, *10*(4), 84–192. doi:10.1108/09685220210436985

Rolstadås, A. (2002). An Example of an E-Learning Solution for an International Curriculum in Manufacturing Strategy. In Proceedings from *e-2002 Conference.*

Rolstadås, A., & Hussein, B. (2002). Hybrid Learning in Project Management – Potentials and Challenges. In Proceedings from *PMI Research Conference*, PMI.

Romero Diaz, D. C. (2007). *An Instantiation Methodology for Virtual Breeding Environment Management.* Master Thesis. Campus Monterrey, Mexiko.

Romiszowski, A. (2004). How's the E-Learning Baby? Factors Leading to Success or Failure of an Education Technology Innovation. *Educational Technology*, *44*(1).

Roper, S., & Hewitt-Dundas, N. (2004). *Innovation, Networks and The Diffusion of Manufacturing Best Practice: A Comparison of Northern Ireland and the Republic of Ireland*, A report from Northern Ireland Economic Research Centre Queen's University of Belfast, UK.

Rose, C., & Nicholl, M. (1997). *Accelerated Learning for the Twenty-First Century*. New York: Delacote Press.

Rostro, F. R. & Grudzewski, W. M. (2008). Marketing Strategic Planning as a Source of Competitive Advantage for Mexican SMEs. *Institute of Organization and Management in Industry* ("ORGMASZ"), 1(1), 19-26.

Rowley, J. (2002). *E-business: Principles and Practice.* New York: Palgrave.

Rudberg, M., Klingenberg, N., & Kronhamn, K. (2002). Collaborative supply chain planning using electronic marketplaces. *Integrated Manufacturing Systems*, *13*(8), 596–610. doi:10.1108/09576060210448170

Ruggaber, R. (2006). ATHENA - Advanced Technologies for Interoperability of Heterogeneous Enterprise Networks and their Applications. In Konstantas, D., Bourrières, J.-P., Léonard, M., & Boudjlida, N. (Eds.), *Interoperability of Enterprise Software and Applications* (pp. 459–460). London: Springer. doi:10.1007/1-84628-152-0_45

Rush, H., & Bessant, J. (1992). Revolution in three-quarter time: lessons from the diffusion of advanced manufacturing technologies. *Technology Analysis and Strategic Management*, *4*(1), 3–19. doi:10.1080/09537329208524075

Rutherfoord, R., Blackburn, R. A., & Spence, L. J. (2000). Environmental management and the small firm: an international comparison. *International Journal of Entrepreneurial Behavior & Research*, *6*(6), 310–326. doi:10.1108/13552550010362750

Saabeel, W., Verduijn, T. M., Hagdorn, L., & Kumar, K. (2002). A Model Of Virtual Organization: A Structure And Process Perspective. *Electronic Journal Of Organizational Virtualness*, *4*(1), 1–17.

Sadowski, B. M. (2002). Strategic Use of the Internet by Small and Medium-Sized Companies: an Exploratory Study. *Information Economics and Policy*, *14*(1), 75–93. doi:10.1016/S0167-6245(01)00054-3

Sage Learning System. (2002). E-Learning Evaluation. Retrieved July 5, 2003 from http://www.sagelearning.com/papers/Evaluation%20Forms.pdf.

Sairamesh, J., Goh, S., Stanoi, I., Padmanabhan, S., & Li, C. S. (2004). Disconnected process, mechanisms and architecture for mobile e-Business. *Mobile Networks and Applications*, *9*, 651–662. doi:10.1023/B:MONE.0000042504.21014.61

Sako, M. (1992). *Prices, quality and trust—interfirm relations in Britain and Japan*. Cambridge, UK: Cambridge Univ. Press. doi:10.1017/CBO9780511520723

Salavou, H. E. (2006). Exploring Product Innovativeness Determinants in SMEs, PhD Thesis, Athens University of Economics & Business, 2006

Sandkuhl, K., & Billig, A. (2007). Ontology-based Artefact Management in Automotive Electronics [IJCIM]. *International Journal of Computer Integrated Manufacturing*, *20*(7), 627–638. doi:10.1080/09511920701566467

Sandkuhl, K. (2003). Information Logistics Support for Collaborative Engineering. In *Proceedings DDECS 2003*, Workshop CCE´03 (pp. 60 - 67). Poznan, Poland, April 2003.

Sandkuhl, K. (2008). Information Logistics in Networked Organizations: Selected Concepts and Applications. In *Proceedings of the 9th International Conference on Enterprise Information Systems – ICEIS 2008* (pp. 43 - 54). LNBIP, Springer.

Sandkuhl, K. (in press). Supporting Collaborative Engineering with Information Supply Patterns. *Euromicro PDP*. Pisa, Italy, February 2009.

Sandkuhl, K., & Lillehagen, F. (2008). The Early Phases of Enterprise Knowledge Modelling. In *Proc. 1st IFIP WG 8.1 Working Conference, PoEM 2008* (pp. 1 - 14). Stockholm, Sweden, November 2008. LNBIP, Springer.

Santoro, R., & Bifulco, A. (2005). Survey of Industriel Case Studies. In Camarinha-Matos, L. M., Afsarmanesh, H., & Ollus, M. (Eds.), *Virtual Organizations. Systems and Practices* (pp. 201–220). Berlin, Heidelberg, New York: Springer. doi:10.1007/0-387-23757-7_14

Santos, S. (2009). *Maturidade do Negócio Electrónico nas Pequenas e Médias Empresas Portuguesas.* Master dissertation, University of Trás-os-Montes e Alto Douro, Portugal.

Savole, M., & Raisinghani, M. (1999). Identifying future trends in information technology. *Industrial Management & Data Systems*, *99*(6), 247–250. doi:10.1108/02635579910253742

Sawyer, S., & Tapia, A. (2005). The sociotechnical nature of mobile computing work: Evidence from a study of policing in the United States. *International Journal of Technology and Human Interaction*, *1*(3), 1–14.

Saxowsky, D., & Duncan, M. (1998). *Understanding agriculture's transition into the 21st century: challenges, opportunities, consequences and alternatives, Report 181.* Department of Agricultural Economics, North Dakota State University.

Schafer, J. B., Konstan, J. A., & Riedl, J. (2001). E-Commerce Recommendation Applications. *Data Mining and Knowledge Discovery*, *5*, 115–153. doi:10.1023/A:1009804230409

Schafer, J. B., Frankowski, D., Herlocker, J., & Sen, S. (2007). Collaborative filtering recommender systems. In P. Brusilovsky, A. Kobsa, & W. Nejdl (Eds.), The Adaptive Web. LNCS 4321, Springer-Verlag, 291-324.

Schekkerman, J. (2006). *How to survive in the jungle of enterprise architecture frameworks*. Bloomington, IN: Trafford Publishing.

Schermerhorn, J. (2009). *Management*. New York: Wiley.

Schienstock, G., & Hämäläinen, T. (2001). Transformation of the Finnish innovation system. A network approach. The Finnish National Fund for Research and Development - Sitra. Report series No. 7. Helsinki.

Schmees, M. (2003). Distributed Digital Commerce. *Proceedings of the 5th International Conference on Electronic Commerce (ICEC2003)*, 131-137.

Schmid, B. F., Stanoevska-Slabeva, K., & Tschammer, V. (2001). *Towards the E-Society: E-commerce, E-business, and E-government*. Boston: Kluwer Academic Publishers.

Schön, D. (1983). *The reflective practitioner: How professionals think in action*. New York, NY: Basic Books.

Schrage, M. (2000). *Serious Play – How the Worlds Best Companies Simulate to Innovate*. Cambridge, MA: Harvard Business School Press.

Schulze, C., & Baumgartner, J. (2001). *Don't Panic, Do E-Commerce, A Beginner's Guide to European Law Affecting E-Commerce*. European Commission's Electronic Commerce Team.

Schwesig, M., Rolstadås, A., & Thoben, K.-D. (2005). An E-Learning experiment in manufacturing strategy. In proceedings from *8th IFIP World Conference on Computers in Education*, IFIP.

Searle, J. (2001). *UK Online for business*. Retrieved August 22, 2009, from www.ncc.co.uk/ncc/Jenny_Searle.pdf

SEBRAE – Serviço Brasileiro de apoio às pequenas e micro empresas. (2007). *Fatores condicionantes e taxas de sobrevivência e mortalidade de pequenas e médias empresas no Brasil: 2003-2005*. At http://www.biblioteca.sebrae.com.br/bds/ NT00037936.pdf accessed on March, 2009.

Segev, A., Gebauer, J., & Fäber, F. (1999). Internet-based Electronic Markets. *EM - International Journal of Electronic Markets*, 9 (3), 138-146.

Semantic Web. (2006). Retrieved June 2, 2009, from http://www.semanticweb.org.

Sen, R. (2005). Optimal Search Engine Marketing Strategy. *International Journal of Electronic Commerce*, *10*(1), 9–25.

Senecal, S., & Nantel, J. (2004). The influence of online product recommendation on consumers' online choices. *Journal of Retailing*, *80*, 159–169. doi:10.1016/j.jretai.2004.04.001

Sensis (2005). *The Online Experience of Small and Medium Enterprises*, Sensis e-business Report, Australia.

Sergio, R. S. G., Gomes, C. A. S., Rodrigues, C., & Boaventura, R. (2004). *Estratégias competitivas para pequenas e micro empresas: um estudo de caso*. Electronic anals of 4th Congresso de Controladoria e Contabilidade da USP, retrieved on May 2009, from http://www.congressousp.fipecafi.org/artigos42004/162.pdf.

Serrano, A., & Caldeira, M. (2001). Gestão de Investimentos em Sistemas e Tecnologias de Informação – uma revisão critica. *Sistemas de Informação*, *15*, 99–107.

Sewell, M., & McCarthey, I. (2001). E-business and its role in small business networks. In Proceedings of the *Manufacturing Information Systems, 4th SMESME International Conference*, 214-221.

Shabazz, D. (2004). Towards a Better Understanding of e-Marketing Strategy: Past and Present. *Services Marketing Quarterly*, *26*(2), 117–130. doi:10.1300/J396v26n02_08

Shen, W., Hao, Q., Wang, S., Li, Y., & Ghenniwa, H. (2007). An agent-based service-oriented integration architecture for collaborative intelligent manufacturing. *Robotics and Computer-integrated Manufacturing*, *23*(3), 315–325. doi:10.1016/j.rcim.2006.02.009

Sherer, S. (2003). Critical Success Factors for Manufacturing Networks as Perceived by Network Coordinators. *Journal of Small Business Management*, *41*, 325–345. doi:10.1111/1540-627X.00086

Sheth, J. N., & Sharma, A. (2005). International e-marketing: Opportunities and issues. *International Marketing Review*, *22*(6), 611–622. doi:10.1108/02651330510630249

Shorthouse, S. (2008). Innovation and Technology Transfer, a presentation from the International Conference DISTRICT 2008. *International Conference Centre*, Dresden, 29 May 2008.

Shrivastava, P. (1995). Environmental technologies and competitive advantage. *Strategic Management Journal*, *16*(1), 183–200. doi:10.1002/smj.4250160923

Silberberger, H. (2003). *Collaborative Business und Web Services*. Berlin, Heidelberg, New York: Springer-Verlag.

Silberschatz, A. (1996). Strategic Directions in Database Systems—Breaking Out of the Box. *ACM Computing Surveys*, *28*(4), 764–778. doi:10.1145/242223.242295

SILVERMAN. G. (2005). *The Secrets of Word-of-Mouth Marketing*, Culver, CA: Amacom

Simpson, M., & Docherty, A. J. (2004). E-Commerce Adoption Support and Advice for UK SMEs. *Journal of Small Business and Enterprise Development*, *11*(2), 315–328. doi:10.1108/14626000410551573

Simpson, M., Taylor, N., & Barker, K. (2004). Environmental responsibility in SMEs: Does it deliver competitive advantage? *Business Strategy and the Environment*, *13*, 156–171. doi:10.1002/bse.398

Singh, S. N., & Dalal, N. P. (1999). Web Home Pages as Advertisements. *Communications of the ACM*, *42*(8), 91–99. doi:10.1145/310930.310978

Singh, M., & Waddell, D. (2006). *E-business Innovation and Change Management*. Hershey, PA: Idea Group Publishing.

Singh, C., & Frolick, M. N. (2000). Ibuttons: Building the Infrastucture for more Secure E-commerce. *Information Systems Security*, Winter, 8 (4), ss. 56-59.

Smallbone, D., North, D., & Vickers, I. (2003). The role and characteristics of SMEs in innovation. In Asheim, B. T., Isaksen, A., Nauwelaers, C., & Todtling, F. (Eds.), *Regional innovation policy for small-medium enterprises, Edward Elgar Publishing, 2003* (pp. 3–20).

Smirnov, A., Levashova, T., & Shilov, N. (2009). Knowledge Sharing in Flexible Production Networks: A Context-Based Approach. In A. Graves, Mr. G. Stone, & Dr. J. Miemczyk (Eds.), *International Journal of Automotive Technology and Management (IJATM), 9*(1) (pp. 87-109). Onley, UK: Inderscience Publishers.

Snowden, D. J., & Boone, M. (2007). A Leader's Framework for Decision Making. *Harvard Business Review*, (November): 69–76.

SOA. (2007). *Service-oriented architecture (SOA) definition*. Retrieved June 2, 2009, from http://www.service-architecture.com/web-services/articles/service-oriented_architecture_soa_definition.html.

Soh, C., & Markus, L. M. (2002). B2B E-Marketplaces - Interconnection Effects, Strategic Positioning, and Perfor-mance. *Systemes d'Information et Management*, *7*(1), 77–103.

Soliman, F., & Youssef, M. A. (2003). Internet-Based E-Commerce and Its Impact On Manufacturing and Business Operations. *Industrial Management & Data Systems*, *103*(8), 546–552. doi:10.1108/02635570310497594

Song, H., Wang, Z., Song, Y., Zhang, Y., & Zhen, L. (2008). Exploring knowledge grid for knowledge supply in the collaborative design. In *Proceedings of the IEEE International Conference on Networking, Sensing and Control ICNSC 2008* (pp. 1663 – 1667). Hainan, China.

Sorenson, R. L. (2000). The Contribution of Leadership Style and Practices to Family and Business Success. *Family Business Review*, *13*(3), 183–200. doi:10.1111/j.1741-6248.2000.00183.x

Sousa, M. (2008). Open innovation models and the role of knowledge brokers, Inside Knowledge magazine, March 2008: 18-22

Spohrer, J., Vargo, S., Caswell, N., & Maglio, P. (2008) The Service System is the Basic Abstraction of Service Science. In Sprague Jr., R. (Ed.) *41st Hawaii International Conference on System Sciences*. Big Island, Hawaii, 104, Washington, DC: IEEE Computer Society.

Spremic, M., Jakovic, B., & Bach, M. P. (2008). Web metrics for managing quality and auditing croatian hotel web sites: Cluster analysis. *WSEAS Transactions on Systems*, *7*(3), 229–238.

SPVA. (n.d.). Retrieved from http://www.spva.org

Stair, R. M., & Reynolds, G. W. (2003). *Principles of information systems: a managerial approach* (6th ed.). Florence, KY: Cencage Learning.

Stamoulis, D., Panagiotis, K., & Martakos, D. (2002). An approach and model for assessing the business value of e-banking distribution channels: evaluation as communication services. *International Journal of Information Management*, *22*, 247–261. doi:10.1016/S0268-4012(02)00011-7

Stansfield, M., & Grant, K. (2003). An Investigation Into Issues Influencing the use of the Internet and Electronic Commerce among Small–Medium Sized Enterprises. *Journal of Electronic Commerce Res*, *4*(1), 15–28.

Stanworth, J., & Gray, C. (1991). *Bolton 20 years on: the small firm in the 1990s*. London: Paul Chapman.

Steenkamp, J.-B. E. M., & Baumgartner, H. (1992). The role of optimum stimulation level in exploratory consumer behavior. *The Journal of Consumer Research*, *19*, 434–488. doi:10.1086/209313

Stein, E. (2003). *Re-Engineering the Manufacturing System: Applying the Theory of Constraints*. New York, NY: Marcel Dekker, Inc.doi:10.1201/9780203912508

Stirna, J., Persson, A., & Sandkuhl, K. (2007). Participative Enterprise Modeling: Experiences and Recommendations. In *19th Intl Conference in Advanced Information Systems Engineering, CAiSE 2007* (pp.546 - 560). LNCS, Berlin / Heidelberg, Springer-verlag

Stockdale, R. & Standing, C. (2004). Benefits and barriers of electronic marketplace participation: an SME perspective.*Journal of Enterprise Information Management, 17*(4), pp, 301-311.

Stockdale, R., & Standing, C. (2003b). Increasing the adoption of electronic commerce by SMEs: Reflections from an empirical study.*4th International We-B Conference*, ECU, Perth, Australia.

Stone, G., Miemczyk, J., & Esser, R. (2005). Making Build to Order a Reality: The 5-Day Car Initiative. In *Strengthening Competitiveness through Production Networks. A prospective from European ICT research projects in the field of "Enterprise Networking"* (pp. 26 – 37). European Communities.

Storey, D. J. (1994). *Understanding the small business sector*. London: International Thomson Business Press.

Storey, D. J., & Sykes, N. (1996). Uncertainty, Innovation and Management. In Burns, P., & Dewhurst, J. (Eds.), *Small Business and Entrepreneurship* (pp. 73–93). London: Macmillan.

Strader, T. J. & Ramaswami, S. N. (2002).The Value of Seller Trustworthiness in C2C Online Markets.*Communications of the ACM*, 45:12(December), 45-49.

Strati, F., et al. (2002). *Short Paper on Sustainable District Logistics*, Retrieved June 2, 2009, from the Web-site of ENSDL – The European Network for Sustainable District Logic, http://www.districtlogistics.net/download/short-paper.pdf.

Stringer, E. T. (2007). *Action research* (3rd ed.). Thousand Oaks, CA: Sage.

Ströbel, M. (2000) Dynamic Outsourcing of Services, Report RZ 3236, IBM Research, Zurich Research Laboratory, Retrieved September 3, 2009, from http://www.zurich.ibm.com/~mis/publications/rz3236.

Studer, S., Tsang, S., Welford, R., & Hills, P. (2008). SMEs and voluntary environmental initiatives: a study of stakeholders' perspectives in Hong Kong. *Journal of Environmental Planning and Management, 51*(2), 285–301. doi:10.1080/09640560701865073

Sturm, F., Kemp, J., & Wendel de Joode, R. v. (2004). Towards Strategic Management in Collaborative Network Structures. In Camarinha-Matos, L. M., & Afsarmanesh, H. (Eds.), *Collaborative Networked Organisations. A Research Agenda for Emerging Business Models* (pp. 131–138). Boston: Kluwer Academic Publishers. doi:10.1007/1-4020-7833-1_16

Sullivan, A. (1998). Research outlays: the real bottom line: expenditures color a company's outlook. *Int. Herald Tribune* July 4-5th, pp. 15-17

Sumner, M. (2004). *Enterprise Resource Planning*. New York: Pearson-Prentice Hall.

Suresh, J. K., & Mahesh, K. (2008). Managing the Knowledge Supply Chain at Infosys, *Knowledge Management Review, 11*(4). Retrieved June 2, 2009, from http://findarticles.com/p/articles/mi_qa5362/is_200809/ai_n30991635/.

Svirskas, A., & Roberts, B. (2003). Towards business quality of service in virtual organisations through service level agreements and ebXML. In ISPE Conference (Ed.), *Concurrent Engineering: Vol. 1. Proceedings of the 10th ISPE International Conference on Concurrent Engineering: Research and Applications* (pp. 491-498). Taylor & Francis: Madeira, Portugal.

Swaminathan, M., & Tayur, R. (2003). Models for Supply Chains in E-business. *Management Science, 49*(10), 1387–1406. doi:10.1287/mnsc.49.10.1387.17309

Swaminathan, J. M., Smith, S. F., & Sadeh, N. M. (2007). Modeling Supply Chain Dynamics: A Multiagent Approach. [REMOVED HYPERLINK FIELD]. *Decision Sciences, 29*(3), 607–632. doi:10.1111/j.1540-5915.1998.tb01356.x

Sweller, J. (2005). Implications of cognitive load theory for multimedia learning. In Mayer, R. E. (Ed.), *Cambridge handbook of multimedia learning*. Cambridge, MA: Cambridge University Press.

Tadjouddine, E. M., Guerin, F., & Vasconcelos, W. (2008). Abstractions for model checking game-theoretic properties in auctions. In Padgham, L., Parkes, D. C., Müller, J., & Parsons, S. (Eds.), *Autonomous Agents and Multi-Agent Systems* (pp. 1613–1616). New York: ACM Press.

Tadjouddine, E. M. (2007) Complexity of verifying game equilibria. In B. Hans-Dieter et al (Ed.), *Vol. 4696, Lecture Notes in Artificial Intelligence (pp. 103–112).*New York: Springer.

Tadjouddine, E. M. (2008) On formal certification of AD transformations. In C. Bischof, M. Bucker, P. Hovland, U. Naumann, and J. Utke (Ed.), *Lecture Notes in Computational Science and Engineering, Vol. 64, Advances in Automatic Differentiation (pp. 23–34),* New York: Springer.

Tadjouddine, E. M., & Guerin, F. (2007) Verifying dominant strategy equilibria in auctions. In B. Hans-Dieter et al (Ed.), *Vol. 4696, Lecture Notes in Artificial Intelligence (pp. 288–297),* New York: Springer.

Takeuchi, H., & Nonaka, I. (2004). *Gestão do conhecimento*. Porto Alegre, Brasil: Bookman.

Tapscott, D., & Williams, A. D. (2006). *Wikinomics: How mass collaboration changes everything*. New York: Portfolio.

Tapscott, D., Lowi, A., & Ticoll, D. (2000). *Digital Capital: Harnessing the Power of Business Webs*. Boston: Harvard Business School Press.

Tatnall, A., Burgess, S., & Singh, M. (2004). Community and regional portals in australia: A role to play for small businesses? In Al-Qirim, N. (Ed.), *Electronic commerce in small to medium-sized enterprises: Frameworks, issues and implications* (pp. 304–320). Hershey, PA: Idea Group Publishing.

Taylor, M., & Murphy, A. (2004). SMEs and e-Business. *Journal of Small Business and Enterprise Development, 11*(3), 280–289. doi:10.1108/14626000410551546

Tedeschi, B. (1999). On-Line Merchants Find That a Well Designed Web Site can have a Big Impact on the Bottom Line. *E-Commerce Report, New York Times*, 30 August 1999, As accessed on August 10, 2009.

Tektonidis, D., Ignatiadis, I., Katriou, S. A., & Koumpis, A. (June, 2008). *PANDA: Enabling RBVOs for the ERP/CRM industry using a Service Oriented Approach.* Paper presented at the 5th International Conference on Information Technology and Applications, ICITA, Cairns, Australia.

Telemetica Institute. (2008). *Service innovation and ICT: Vision and ambition.* The Netherlands: Telemetica Institute.

Telstra Corporation. (2009). *Sensis E:Business report: The online experience of small and medium enterprises.* Australia: Sensis.

Teng, B. S., & Cummings, J. L. (2002). Trade-offs in managing resources and capabilities. *The Academy of Management Executive, 16*(2), 81–91.

Teo, T. S. H., & Liu, J. (2007). Consumer trust in e-commerce in the United States, Singapore and China. *Omega, 35*, 22–38. doi:10.1016/j.omega.2005.02.001

Tews, R. (2007). Beyond IT: The business value of SOA. *AIIM E-DOC, 21*, 14–17.

The Conference Board. (2009). *The ill-prepared U.S. workforce.* New York: The Conference Board.

Thibaut, J. W., & Walker, L. (1975). *Procedural Justice: A psychological analysis.* Hillsdale, NJ: Erlbaum.

Thome's Vincent. (2009). Social Retailing and Shoping, Virtual and Digital commerce Opportunities. Retrieved from http://www.thomevincent.com/blog/index.php?2007/08/15/349-social-retailing-and-shopping-virtual-and-digital-commerce-opportunities consultation made in September 12, 2009

Thong, J. Y. L., & Yap, C. S. (1995). CEO Characteristics, Organizational Characteristics and Information Technology Adoption in Small Business. *Omega international Journal of Management Science, 23*(4), 429–42.

Tidd, J., Bessant, J., & Pavitt, K. (2005). *Managing Innovation: Integrating technological, market and organizational change* (3rd ed.). John Wiley and Sons.

TIEKE. (2009). *ICT Cluster Finland Review 2009.* Finland: TIEKE Finnish Information Society Development Centre.

Tiessen, J. H., Wright, R. W., & Turner, I. (2001). A model of e-commerce use by internationalizing SMEs. *Journal of International Management, 7*(3), 211–233. doi:10.1016/S1075-4253(01)00045-X

Tilley, F., & Tonge, J. (2003). *Introduction.* In Jones, O. & Tilley, F. (Eds.). Competitive Advantage in SME's: Organising for Innovation and Change, John Wiley & Sons

Timmers, P. (1998). Business Models for Electronic Markets. *Journal on Electronic Markets, 8*(2), 3–8. doi:10.1080/10196789800000016

Timmers, P. (2000). *Electronic Commerce - strategies & models for business-to-business trading.* New York: Wiley.

Tiwana, A., & Willianms, M. (2000). *The Essential Guide to Knowledge Management: E-Business and CRM Applications.* New York: Prentice Hall.

Tödtling, F., & Kaufmann, A. (2001). The Role of the Region for Innovation Activities for SMEs. *European Urban and Regional Studies, 8*(3), 203–215. doi:10.1177/096977640100800303

Toivonen, M. (2004). Expertise as Business: Long-term development and future prospects of knowledge-intensive business services (KIBS), Laboratory of Industrial Management, Helsinki University of Technology, Doctoral dissertation series 2004/2

Tøle, M. & şi Zwegers, A. (2003). Virtual Enterprise Reference Architecture and Methodology, GLOBEMEN Joint D41/D43 Deliverable (technical report). Retrieved September 15, 2009, from http://cic.vtt.fi/projects/globemen/public.htm

Tølle, M., & Vesterager, J. (2003). Developing the Business Model – A Methodology for Virtual Enterprises. In Bernus, P., Nemes, L., & Schmidt, G. (Eds.), *Handbook on Enterprise Architectures* (pp. 291–308). Berlin, Heidelberg: Springer-Verlag.

Tonge, J. (2001). *A Review of Small Business Literature Part 1: Defining The Small Business*, Manchester Metropolitan University Business School Working Paper Series: WPS025, available at http://www.business.mmu.ac.uk/wps/

Townsend, A. M., DeMarie, S. M., & Hendrickson, A. R. (1998). Virtual teams: Technology and the workplace of the future. *The Academy of Management Executive*, *12*(3), 17–29.

Transactions, H. T. (n.d.). Retrieved from http://www.hypercom.com/.

Trappey, C., & Trappey, A. (2000). Great China e-commerce trends and development. In *INFORMS* Proceedings, San Antonio: Texas; TE07.

Trends, G. (n.d.). Retrieved from http://www.google.com/trends

Trienekens, J.J.M., & Bouman, J.J., & Zwan, Mvd. (2004). Specification of Service Level Agreements: Problems, Principles and Practices. *Software Quality Journal*, *12*, 43–57. doi:10.1023/B:SQJO.0000013358.61395.96

Trombly, R. (2000). E-Business Models. *Computerworld*, *34*(49), 61–62.

Turban, E., King, D., Lee, J., Warkentin, M., & Chung, H. M. (2002). *Electronic Commerce - A Managerial Perspective*. Upper Saddle River, New Jersey: Prentice Hall.

Turban, K., McKay, D., Marshall, J., Lee, P., & Vielhand, D. (2008). *Electronic Commerce: A Managerial Perspective*. Upper Saddle River, NJ: Pearson.

Turban, E., Mc Lean, E., & Wetherbe, J. (2002). *Information technology for management: transforming business in the digital economy* (3rd ed.). Hoboken, NJ: John Wiley and Sons.

Turban, E., Rainer, R. K. Jr, & Potter, R. E. (2007). *Introduction to information systems*. Hoboken, NJ: John Wiley and Sons.

Tushman, M. L., & Anderson, P. (1986). Technological Discontinuities and Organizational Requirements. *Administrative Science Quarterly*, *31*, 439–465. doi:10.2307/2392832

U.S. Department of Health and Human Services. (2006 ed.) Research-Based Web Design & Usability Guidelines. Retrieved September 10, 2009, from http://www.usability.gov/pdfs/guidelines.html.

U.S.I.G. (2003). Usability Special Interest Group: Usability checklist for E-Learning. Retrieved December 1, 2003 from http://www.stcsig.org/usability/resources/toolkit/E-Learning-checklist.doc.

UNESCO. (2009). *Improving education quality*. Retrieved July 23, 2009, from http://www.unesco.org/en/education_ar/themes/improving-education-quality/education-for-sustainable-development/strategy/learning-to-know/?0=.

UNITED NATIONS –. *Global E-government readiness report* (2005). United Nations Department of Public Affairs, division of public administration and development management, retrieved on July, 2009, from http://unpan1.un.org/intradoc/groups/public/documents/un/unpan021888.pdf.

Uram, M., & Stephenson, B. (2005). Services are the Language and Building Blocks of an Agile Enterprise. In Pal, N., & Pantaleo, D. (Eds.), *The Agile Enterprise*. New York, NY: Springer. doi:10.1007/0-387-25078-6_4

Urban, G. L., Sultan, F., & Qualls, W. J. (2000). Placing Trust at the Center of Your Internet Strategy. *Sloan Management Review*, *42*(1), 39–48.

Urdan, T. A., & Weggen, C. C. (2000). *Corporate E-Learning: Exploring a new frontier*. San Francisco, CA: WR Hambrecht & Co.

Urwin, S. (2000). The Internet as an Information Solution for the Small and Medium Sized Business. *Business Information Review*, *17*(3), 130–137. doi:10.1177/0266382004237647

US Department of Education. (2009, July 31). *Racing to the top of education*. Retrieved August 6, 2009, from http://www.ed.gov/programs/racetothetop/index.html.

Uschold, M., & Grüninger, M. (1996). Ontologies: Principles, methods and applications. *The Knowledge Engineering Review*, *11*(2), 93–155. doi:10.1017/S0269888900007797

Vaitheeswaran. V. (2007) Special Report: Innovation. *The Economist*. Retrieved from http://www.economist.com/specialreports/displaystory.cfm?story_id=9934754

Van Akkeren, J., & Cavaye, A. L. M. (1999). Factors affecting entry-level Internet technology adoption by small business in Australia - evidence from three cases. *Journal of Systems and Information Technology*, *3*(2), 33–48. doi:10.1108/13287269980000747

Van Beveren, J. (2002). The Use of Electronic Commerce by SMEs in Victoria, Australia. *Journal of Small Business Management*, *40*(3), 250–253. doi:10.1111/1540-627X.00054

Van de Vrande, V., de Jong, J. P. J., Vanhaverbeke, W., & de Rochemont, M. (2009, june-july). Open innovation in SMEs: Trends, motives and management challenges. *Technovation*, *29*(6-7), 423–437. doi:10.1016/j.technovation.2008.10.001

Van Hemel, C., & Cramer, J. (2002, october). Barriers and stimuli for ecodesign in SMEs. *Journal of Cleaner Production*, *10*(5), 439–453. doi:10.1016/S0959-6526(02)00013-6

VandenBos, G., Knapp, S., & Doe, J. (2001). Role of reference elements in the selection of resources by psychology undergraduates. [from http://jbr.org/articles.html]. *Journal of Bibliographic Research*, *5*, 117–123. Retrieved October 13, 2001.

Varajão, J. (2002). Função de Sistemas de Informação - Contributos para a melhoria do sucesso da adopção de tecnologias de informação e desenvolvimento de sistemas de informação nas organizações, Doctoral dissertation, Universidade do Minho, Portugal.

Varianini, V., & Vaturi, D. (2000). Marketing Lessons from e-failures. *The McKinsey Quarterly*, 4.

Venkatraman, N. (1989). Strategic orientation of business enterprises: the construct, dimensionality and measurement. *Management Science*, *35*(8), 942–962. doi:10.1287/mnsc.35.8.942

Verifone. (n.d.). Retrieved from http://www.verifone.com/.

Vernadat, F. B. (1996). *Enterprise Modelling and Integration*. Boca Raton, FL:Chapman & Hall. Wang, Q. & Rong, L. (2007). Agile Knowledge Supply Chain for Emergency Decision-Making Support. In Shi, Y., Dick van Albada, G., Dongarra, J., & Sloot, P. M. A. (Eds.), *Computational Science - ICCS 2007. Lecture Notes in Computer Science, 4490* (pp. 178–185). New York: Springer.

Vinberg, S., Gelin, G., & Sandberg, K. (2000).Information Technology Levels, Competence Development and Performance in Swedish Small Business Enterprises. *Behaviour and Information Technology*, C:19, S:3.

Vives, A. (2006). Social and Environmental Responsibility in Small and Medium Enterprises in Latin America. *Journal of Corporate Citizenship*, *21*, 39–50.

Vlaar, P., Van den Bosch, F., & Volberda, H. (2006). Coping with problems of understanding in interorganizational relationships: Using as a means to make sense. *Organization Studies*, *27*(11), 1617–1638. doi:10.1177/0170840606068338

Vokrinek, J., Biba, J., Hodik, J., Vybihal, J., & Volf, P. (2009). RBVO Formation Protocol. *International Journal of Agent-Oriented Software Engineering*, *3*(2/3), 135–162. doi:10.1504/IJAOSE.2009.023634

Walczuch, R, B, Van., G, & Lundgren, H. (2000). Internet adoption barriers for small firms in The Netherlands. *European Management Journal*, *18*(5), 561–572. doi:10.1016/S0263-2373(00)00045-1

Walczuch, R., Van Braven, G., & Lundgren, H. (2000). Internet Adoption Barriers for Small Firms in the Netherlands. *European Management Journal*, *18*(5), 561–572. doi:10.1016/S0263-2373(00)00045-1

Walters, D., & Lancaster, G. (1999). Using the Internet as a channel for commerce. *Management Decision*, *37*(10), 800–816. doi:10.1108/00251749910302908

Walton, J. S. (2008). Scanning Beyond the Horizon: Exploring the Ontological and Epistemological Basis for Scenario Planning. *Advances in Developing Human Resources*, *10*, 147–165. doi:10.1177/1523422307304101

Wang, V., & King, K. P. (Eds.). (2009). *Human performance models revealed in the global context*. Charlotte, NC: Information Age Publishing, Inc.

Wang, S. (2001). Designing information systems for electronic business. *Industrial Management & Data Systems*, *101*(6), 304–314. doi:10.1108/EUM0000000005580

Wang, S. (2000). Managing the Organizational Aspects of Electronic Commerce. *Human Systems Management*, *9*(1), 49–59.

Wang, W., & Benbasat, I. (2005). Trust in and adoption of online recommendation agents. *Journal of the Association for Information Systems*, *6*(3), 72–100.

Ware, J., Gebauer, J., Hartman, A., & Roldan, M. (1998). *The Search for Digital Excellence*. New York: McGraw-Hill.

Warren, M., & Hutchinson, W. (2005). A Systems Approach to Security. In Kurt a Richardon, Wendy J Gregory & Gerald Midgley (eds). *Systems Thinking and Complexity Science: Insights for Action Proceedings of the 11th Annual ANZSYS / Managing the Complex V conference,* New Zealand: ISCE Publishing.

Web services explained (2007). Retrieved June 2, 2009, from http://www.service-architecture.com/web-services/articles/web_services_explained.html.

Webb, H. W., & Webb, L. A. (2004). SiteQual: An Integrated Measure of Website Quality. *Journal of Enterprise Information Management*, *17*, 430–440. doi:10.1108/17410390410566724

Webb, B., & Sayer, R. (1998). Benchmarking Small Companies on the Internet. *Long Range Planning*, *31*(6), 815–827. doi:10.1016/S0024-6301(98)80018-6

Wei, Y., & Morgan, N. (2004). The Supportiveness of Organizational Climate, Market Orientation, and New Product Performance in Chinese Firms. *Journal of Product Innovation Management*, *21*, 375–388. doi:10.1111/j.0737-6782.2004.00092.x

Weideman, M. & Schwenke, F. (2006).The Influence that JavaScript™ has on the Visibility of a Website to Search Engines – A Pilot Study. *Information Research*, 11(4).

Weideman, M., & Mgidana, M. (2004). Website Navigation Architectures and their Effect on Website Visibility: A Literature Survey. Proceedings of SAICSIT, 292-296.

Wenger, E. (1999). *Communities of Practice: Learning, Meaning and Identity*. Cambridge, UK: Cambridge University Press.

Wernerfelt, B. (1984). The Resource-Based View of the Firm. *Strategic Management Journal*, *5*(2), 171–180. doi:10.1002/smj.4250050207

Wernerfelt (1984). A resource based view of a firm. *Strategic Management Journal.* 5, pp. 171-180.

West, J. & Gallagher, S. (2006). Open Innovation: The Paradox of Firm Investment in Open Source Software, R&D Management Special Issue on "*Opening-up the innovation process*", 36, 3 (June 2006).

West, J., Vanhaverbeke, W., & Chesbrough, H. (2006). Open Innovation: A Research Agenda. In Henry Chesbrough, Wim Vanhaverbeke and Joel West (Eds.) (2006). *Open Innovation: Researching a New Paradigm*.Oxford, UK: Oxford University Press.

Wheelen. T. L., Hunger, J. D. (2008). *Strategic Management and Business Policy*, Eleventh Edition. Upper Saddle River, NJ: Pearson International Edition, Pearson Prentice Hall.

White, A., Daniel, E., Ward, J., & Wilson, H. (2007). The adoption of consortium B2B e- marketplaces: An exploratory study. *The Journal of Strategic Information Systems*, *16*(1), 71–103. doi:10.1016/j.jsis.2007.01.004

White House. (2009). *United States of America Govern Internet Portal*. At www.whitehouse.gov, accessed on June, 2009.

Wiesenfeld, B. M., Raghuram, S., & Garud, R. (2001). Organizational identification among virtual workers: The role of need for affiliation and perceived work-based social support. *Journal of Management*, *27*, 213–229. doi:10.1016/S0149-2063(00)00096-9

Wiklund, J., Patzelt, H., & Shepherd, D. A. (2007). Building an integrative model of small business growth. *Small Business Economics*. Retrieved on June 2009 from http://www.springerlink.com/content/h0n5848j2330117p/fulltext.html.

Williamson, D., Lynch-Wood, G., & Ramsay, J. (2006). Drivers of Environmental Behaviour in Manufacturing SMEs and the Implications for CSR. *Journal of Business Ethics*, *67*, 317–330. doi:10.1007/s10551-006-9187-1

Williamson, I. O., Lepak, D. P., & King, J. (2003). The effect of company recruitment web site orientation on individuals' perceptions of organizational attractiveness. *Journal of Vocational Behavior*, *63*(2), 242–263. doi:10.1016/S0001-8791(03)00043-5

Willis, J. (2008, Feb.). Building a bridge from neuroscience to the classroom. *Phi Delta Kappan*, *89*(6), 424–427.

Wilson, S. G., & Abel, I. (2002). So You Want to Get Involved in E-Commerce. *Industrial Marketing Management*, *21*, 85–94. doi:10.1016/S0019-8501(01)00188-2

Wim K. (2004). *Facing the challenge: The Lisbon strategy for growth and employment*. Report from the High Level Group chaired by Wim Kok.

Wise, R., & Morrison, D. (2000). Beyond the Exchange - The Future of B2B. *Harvard Business Review*, (November-December): 86–96.

Witt, N., & McDermott, A. (2004). Web site accessibility: What logo will we use today? *British Journal of Educational Technology*, *35*(1), 45–56. doi:10.1111/j.1467-8535.2004.00367.x

Wlodkowski, R. (1998). *Enhancing adult motivation to learn: A comprehensive guide for teaching all adults* (Revised ed.). San Francisco: Jossey Bass.

Wlodkowski, R., & Ginsberg, M. (1995). *Diversity and motivation: Culturally responsive teaching*. San Francisco: Jossey Bass.

Wolf, A. (2009). *smE MPOWER Outlook: Empowering SMEs for long-term research interest and increased participation in EU RTD activities!* Retrieved March 15, 2009 from http://www.sme-mpower.net/Presentations/11%20Andreas%20Wolf%20on%20smE-MPOWER-Community.pdf

Woods, D. (2003). *Enterprise Services Architecture*. Sebastopol, CA: O' Reilly.

Worner, B. (2002). Choosing the right security infrastructure for E-Business Success. *Information Security Journal: A global Perspective*, 11(1), 51-56.

Wright, P., Kroll, M. J., & Parnell, J. A. (1998). *Strategic management: concepts*. Upper Saddle River, NJ: Prentice Hall.

Wu, J., & Hisa, T. (2008). Developing e-Business dynamic capabilities: An analysis of e-Commerce innovation from i – m, to u- commerce. *Journal of Organizational Computing and Electronic Commerce*, *18*(2), 95–111. doi:10.1080/10919390701807525

Wu, F., Mahajan, V., & Balasubramanjan, S. (2003). An Analysis of E-Business Adoption and Its Impact on Business Performance. *Journal of the Academy of Marketing Science*, *31*(4), 425–447. doi:10.1177/0092070303255379

Wu, L., & Park, D. (2009). Dynamic outsourcing through process modularization. *Business Process Management Journal, 15*(2), 255–244. doi:10.1108/14637150910949461

Xiao, B., & Benbasat, I. (2007). E-commerce product recommendation Agents: Use, Characteristics, and Impact. *Management Information Systems Quarterly, 31*(1), 137–209.

Xing, B., & Lin, Z. (2004).The Impact of Search Engine Optimization on Online Advertising Market. *Proceedings of the 8th international Conference on Electronic Commerce*, 519-529.

Xu, M., Rohatgi, R., & Duan, Y. (2007). E-Business Adoption in SMEs: Some Preliminary Findings from Electronic Components Industry. *International Journal of E-Business Research, 3*(1), 74–90.

Yahoo, (2008). "Marketing Promotion: Make me an offer", August 2009

Ying, Y., Feinberg, F., & Wedel, M. (2006). Leveraging missing ratings to improve online recommendation systems. *JMR, Journal of Marketing Research, XLIII*(August), 355–365. doi:10.1509/jmkr.43.3.355

Yolles, M. (2009). Competitive advantage and its conceptual development. *Business Information Review, 26*(2), 93–111. doi:10.1177/0266382109104411

Yorks, L. (2005). *Strategic human resource development*. Mason, OH: Thomson.

Young, M., & Jude, M. (2008). *iExec Enterprise Essentials Companion Guide*. San Jose, CA: Cisco Press

Yu, W. D., & Lin, A. (2007). The Design and Implementation of a Search Engine Marketing Management System (SEMMS) Based on Service-Oriented Architecture Platform. *IEEE International Conference on e-Business Engineering*, 513-519.

Zablah, A. R., Bellenger, D. N., & Johnston, W. J. (2004). An evaluation of divergent perspectives on customer relationship management: towards a common understanding of an emerging phenomenon. *Industrial Marketing Management, 33*(6), 475–489. doi:10.1016/j.indmarman.2004.01.006

Zackman, J., Inmon, W., & Geiger, J. (1997). *Data Stores, Data Warehousing and the Zachman Framework: Managing Enterprise Knowledge*. New York: McGraw-Hill.

Zahra, S. A. (1993). A conceptual model of entrepreneurship as firm behavior: A critique and extension. *Entrepreneurship: Theory and Practice*. Baylor University, USA. Summer.

Zerenler, M. (2007). *Dijital İş Yaşamı: Tüm Boyutlarıyla Elektronik Ticaret* (Digital BusinessLife: Electronic Commerce with all its Dimensions), (in Turkish), Ankara, Gazi Kitabevi (Gazi Bookstore).

Zhang, J., & Dimitroff, A. (2005). The Impact of Webpage Content Characteristics on Webpage Visibility in Search Engine Results (Part 1). *Information Processing & Management, 41*, 665–690. doi:10.1016/j.ipm.2003.12.001

Zhang, P. (2008) *Uniform price auctions and fixed price offerings in IPOs: an experimental comparison*. Tech. Rep. No. 200805, Centre for Decision Research and Experimental Economics, The University of Nottingham, UK.

Zhang, P., Small, R. V., von Dran, G. M., & Barcellos, S. (2000). A Two Factor Theory for Website Design. *Proceedings of the 33rd Hawaii International Conference on System Sciences (HICSS)*, 1, 1-10.

Zhao, F. (2006). *Entrepreneurship and Innovations in E-business: An Integrative Perspective*. Hershey, PA: Idea Group Publishing.

Zutshi, A., & Sohal, A. (2004). Adoption and maintenance of environmental management systems: critical success factors. *Management of Environmental Quality An International Journal, 15*(4), 399–419. doi:10.1108/14777830410540144

About the Contributors

Maria Manuela Cruz-Cunha is currently an Associate Professor in the School of Technology at the Polytechnic Institute of Cavado and Ave, Portugal. She holds a Dipl. Eng. in the field of Systems and Informatics Engineering, an M.Sci. in the field of Information Society and a Dr.Sci in the field of Virtual Enterprises, all from the University of Minho (Portugal). She teaches subjects related with Information Systems, Information Technologies and Organizational Models to undergraduated and post-graduated studies. She supervises several PhD projects in the domain of Virtual Enterprises and Information Systems and Technologies. She regularly publishes in international peer-reviewed journals and participates on international scientific conferences. She serves as a member of Editorial Board and Associate Editor for several International Journals and for several Scientific Committees of International Conferences. She has authored and edited several books and her work appears in more than 100 papers published in journals, book chapters and conference proceedings. She is the co-founder and co-chair of CENTERIS – Conference on ENTERprise Information Systems.

João Eduardo Varajão is professor of information systems management and software engineering at the University of Trás-os-Montes e Alto Douro and visiting professor at EGP – University of Porto Business School. He graduated in 1995, received his master degree in Computer Science in 1997 and, in 2003, received his PhD in Technologies and Information Systems, from University of Minho (Portugal). He currently supervises several Msc and PhD thesis in the information systems field. His current research includes information systems management, project management and enterprise information systems. He has over one hundred publications, including books, book chapters, refereed publications, and communications at international conferences. He serves as associate editor and member of editorial board for international journals and has served in several committees of international conferences. He is the co-founder and co-chair of CENTERIS – Conference on ENTERprise Information Systems. He is also a member of AIS, IEICE and APSI.

* * *

Bjorn Andersen is a Professor of Production and Quality Engineering at the Norwegian University of Science and Technology and research leader at SINTEF Technology and Society, Technology Management, Productivity and Project Management. He has been involved in various teaching and research efforts involving technology-enhanced learning during the last ten years, including being operational project manager for the European projects PRIME and TARGET. His publication list spans close to 200 papers and books, many within the field of e-Learning and technology-enhanced learning. He is also co-editor of the International Journal of Production Planning and Control and serves on several review boards of other journals and conferences.

Susana Badillo is a Ph.D student at the 'Project and Systems Engineering' program by the Polytechnic University of Catalonia. Degree in Graphic Design. Specialization and Master in Design by the Metropolitan Autonomous University, Mexico. Divisional Coordinator of Virtual Education. Teacher-Researcher in the Department of Research and Knowledge in the Division of Sciences and Arts for Design.

Antonio José Balloni is currently a researcher at the Center for Information Technology Renato Archer , working with MIS (Management of Information Systems) in the GESITI Project, Ph.D. in Experimental Plasma Physics/1988, by the Institute of Physics Gleb Wataghin – University of Campinas and Pos Doctor researcher/1992 at Interuniversity Microelectronics Centrum/Bélgica. Visiting professor at the Institute of Economy, at UNICAMP, lecturing about MIS. Author of the books: "Why GESITI? (Why management of system and information technology towards organizations?", and "Why GESITI? Security, Innovation and Society". Creator and Organizer of the Workshop GESITI, an workshop about MIS towards organizations, editions I to V. Has about 30 articles in international and national magazines. Since February 2008 is Coordinator of the GESITI Network, with about 2300 collaborators.

Ron Beckett's industry background is in R&D and manufacturing management associated with the aerospace industry. He has an ongoing interest in creative organisational change associated with inter-enterprise collaboration between firms and between sectors, managing innovation as a business process, and leveraging accessible knowledge and technology. Ron is continuing to research these topics with industry and university colleagues, and has published about 80 related articles or book chapters. He is currently the Managing Director of a management research and consultancy enterprise called the Reinvention Network that helps client firms during transitional growth periods, and is an Adjunct Professor at the University of Western Sydney, College of Business.

Constant D. Beugré (Ph. D. Rensselaer Polytechnic Institute) is a professor of management at Delaware State University, College of Business where he teaches courses in organizational behavior and strategic management at the undergraduate level and organizational leadership at the graduate level. Dr. Beugré also served as the chair of the department of business administration and acting associate dean of the college of business. Prior to joining Delaware State University, Dr. Beugré was an assistant professor of management and information systems at Kent State University, Tuscarawas Campus. Dr. Beugré was also a visiting fellow at Harvard University in 1996. His research interests include organizational justice, offshoring and neuroeconomics. Dr. Beugré has published three books and more than 70 refereed journal articles and conference proceedings. His publications have appeared in academic outlets, such as Organizational Behavior and Human Decision Processes, Decision Sciences, International Journal of Human Resource Management, International Journal of Manpower, Journal of Applied Behavioral Science, Journal of Applied Social Psychology, and Research in the Sociology of Organizations.

Stephen Burgess has research and teaching interests that include the use of ICTs in small businesses (particularly in the tourism field), the strategic use of ICTs, and B2C electronic commerce. He has received a number of competitive research grants in these areas. He has completed several studies related to website features in small businesses and how well websites function over time, including his PhD from Monash University, Australia (completed in 2002). He has authored/ edited three books and special editions of journals in topics related to the use of ICTs in small business and been track chair at the international ISOneWorld, IRMA, Conf-IRM and ACIS conferences in related areas. More recently, Stephen has extended his research interests to include the use of websites by community based organisations. He has published in journals such as the Journal of Information Science, Information Systems Frontiers, the International Journal of Tourism Research and the Journal of Hospitality, Marketing and Management.

Claudia C. Cabal-Cruz is a Lecturer in Finance at the Economic and Management Sciences Department, University of Quindio, Colombia. She is studying a doctorate in Social Economy at the International University of Andalucia, Spain. Her research area is e-marketing and consumer behavior.

Anders Carstensen, holds a Master of Science in Applied Physics and Electrical Engineering from Linköping Institute of Technology since1983. He is currently working as Subject teacher in computer science at Jönköping University since 1998, and is mainly teaching Database Management and Programming Methodology. He is also a Ph.D. student with main research interests in the area of enterprise modeling and interoperability problems in extended enterprises.

Bojan Cestnik is the general manager of the software company Temida and a researcher at the Department of Knowledge Technologies at the Jožef Stefan Institute in Ljubljana, Slovenia. He obtained his PhD in Computer Science at the Faculty of Electrical Engineering and Computer Science, University of Ljubljana. His professional and research interests include knowledge-based information systems and machine learning. His research work has been presented at several international conferences. He has been involved in several large-scale software development and maintenance projects.

Rodrigo Baroni de Carvalho is a professor in the Master in Business Administration of Fumec University, Minas Gerais, Brazil. He has a PhD in Information Science from the Federal University of Minas Gerais (UFMG). Part of his PhD was done at the Faculty of Information Studies, University of Toronto, Canada with the supervision of professor Chun Wei Choo. His master degree was in Information Science and the bachelor degree was in Computer Science both from UFMG. Before being a full-time professor, he has worked for 16 years as system analyst and IT project manager mainly in the financial industry. His main research interests are knowledge management, KM software, ERPs, portals, technology acceptance, software engineering and information science.

Ritesh Chugh lectures in the Faculty of Arts, Business, Informatics and Education at CQUniversity Melbourne, Australia. He teaches to both postgraduate and undergraduate students in the fields of Information Systems (IS) Management and Development, IS Project Management, and Electronic Commerce. Ritesh has been awarded CQUniversity's 2007 Faculty/Pro-Vice-Chancellors' portfolios/ AIC Tier One Award for teaching excellence and the CQUniversity's Melbourne teaching excellence award for 2008. Currently, he is working towards a doctoral degree that will develop a model to enhance tacit knowledge transfer and make knowledge ubiquitous. His range of interests includes project management, knowledge management, electronic commerce and developing varied teaching and learning practices on a formal note and philately and numismatics on a more casual note. Ritesh is a member of the Australian Computer Society, IEEE, and IEEE's Computer Society too.

José C. Delgado is an Associate Professor at the Computer Science and Engineering Department of the Instituto Superior Tecnico (Lisbon Technical University), in Lisbon, Portugal, where he earned the Ph.D. degree in 1988. He lectures courses in the areas of Computer Architecture, Information Technology and Service Engineering. He has performed several management roles in his faculty, namely Director of the Taguspark campus, near Lisbon, and Coordinator of the B.Sc. and M.Sc. in Computer Science and Engineering at that campus. He has been the coordinator of and researcher in several research projects, both national and European. As an author, his publications include one book and more than 40 papers in international refereed conferences and journals.

Heiko Duin, born in 1965, received his Master of Science in Computer Science in 1992 at the University of Bremen. He started as a research scientist at BIBA in1992. From 1997 to 2002 he was employed at the engineering company PRODUTEC Ingenieurgesellschaft. From 2000 until now he is one of the two managing directors of PRODUTEC Ingenieurgesellschaft. In 2002 he joined BIBA again. He participated in many European projects within the programmes RACE, ACTS, TEN-TELECON, ESPRIT, IST, ICT and NMP during his professional career. In some of them he performed in management functions, such as overall project manager or technical manager. Currently his main interests involve the development of tools to support strategic planning in enterprise networks, the development of serious gaming applications for educational purposes and the development of mobile applications.

Joaquín Fernández is a PhD in Computer Science by the Polytechnic University of Catalonia and Bachelor of Fine Arts by the University of Barcelona. Professor in the Department of Graphical Expression of Engineering, UPC. Has been Director of Design Superior Degree of UPC and Director of Laboratory of Multimedia Applications (LAM) of UPC. Research activity focuses in innovation in ICT applications in the fields of health and learning. Participating and directing several projects involving the application of multimedia and Internet technology.

Marco Ferruzca is a Professor at the Faculty of Design and Arts (Metropolitan Autonomus University) in Mexico City. Industrial Designer. Master in Hypermedia. He obtained in 2008 a Ph.D. degree at the Polytechnic University of Catalonia. His professional experience is focused on Applications, Products and Services of Web-based Systems. His research activity is related to collaborative design and knowledge management.

John J. Foley, III has an MBA in Finance from Hofstra University, Hampstead, New York and is pursuing his Master's Degree in Adult Education from Fordham University, New York City. He is currently a Senior Vice President in Global Risk Management at Citigroup, and is located in Manhattan. He has 25 years experience in lending, most recently in global capital markets, but commenced his career lending to small to mid-sized companies, such as those discussed in this book. As such, he understands the outlook of many of these entrepreneurs, and brings this understanding to the authorship of this chapter. He may be contacted at Jfoley22@nyc.rr.com

Manuel Fradinho holds a PhD in computer science from University College London. He is currently the R&D manager of Cyntelix, with six research verticals: semantic technologies, widgets, mobile services, collaborative work environments, serious games (competence development platforms) and social networking. He has about 12 years of experience in the industry, working on ICT solutions for

SMEs to improve their global competitiveness. He has over 70 publications. Fradinho is the scientific coordinator of the TARGET project, a multi-million Euros European project aimed at highly personalized competence development for e-professionals. He was also the technical coordinator of the PRIME European project.

Garyfallos Fragidis is Lecturer of Business Information Systems in the Department of Business Administration of the Technological Education Institute of Serres in Greece. He holds a M.B.A. from the University of Macedonia in Thessaloniki, Greece. His research is mostly related with the strategic and organizational aspects of electronic business. His current research interest focuses on the development of customer- centric business models. In the past he was engaged in research related to e-business models, service models, business ecosystems, e-government and knowledge management. He has working experience in information technology projects and participated in the implementation of several EU-sponsored research projects.

Luís Ganhão have a degree in Physics by Faculdade de Ciências de Lisboa, but developed is career in Information & Technology. In his more than 10 years of experience in IT he managed Projects in several countries (Portugal, Italy, Egypt, Saudi Arabia, Dubai) mainly in Extreme Performance. Since 2007 he Manages Oracle Portugal Solutions & Architecture Team. Luís Ganhão his an active lecturer in the most important IT events in Portugal.

Juan C. Gázquez-Abad (PhD. University of Almería) is Profesor of Marketing at the University of Almería (Spain). Moreover, he has been visiting professor at the University of Ghent (Department of Marketing), Belgium. His research program focus on issues related to retail management, brand management and consumer choice behaviour. Prof. Gázquez-Abad has published in the major Spanish Marketing Journals, as well as other international journals such as The Services Industries Journal, Managing Service Quality, Agribusiness and has presented papers in several conferences (e.g. EMAC, ICORIA, EAERCD, EIRASS).

Sıtkı Gözlü is a professor of production and operations management in the Faculty of Management at Istanbul Technical University. He holds a B.S. in Chemical Engineering from Bogazici University (June 1969), a M.A. in Management from Istanbul University (June 1981), and a Ph.D. in Management Engineering from Istanbul Technical University (June 1986). He became Associate Professor in October 1990 and full Professor in December 1996. He worked as a researcher for two years and as a plant and technical service engineer for more than four years. He lectures on Quality Management, Production Management, Technology Management, and Project Management. His research interests are in the areas of technology transfer and quality management. His works have been published in international and national journals and conference proceedings. He is a member of Turkish Chamber of Chemical Engineers, Production and Operations Management Society (U.S.A.), European Operations Management Association, and American Society for Quality.

Pramila Gupta has research and teaching interests in Information Modelling, Database Management Systems and e-business. Pramila started her academic career at CQUniversity Melbourne, Australia as a lecturer in 1998 and has progressed to be an Associate Professor providing academic leadership to a large team of about 100 academics at the university's Melbourne campus. Pramila's long tenure at the campus has helped her in acquiring sound knowledge about University's academic policies and processes and contributing to the efficient and positive support systems for students and staff at the Melbourne campus. Pramila has had substantial professional and industrial experience in India with major manufacturing and prestigious development corporations. Pramila is a member of the Australian Computer Society (MACS).

Eduardo Huerta is a Ph.D student at the 'Project and Systems Engineering' program by the Polytechnic University of Catalonia. Master in Interactive Systems by the Escola de Disseny ESDI, Barcelona. Professional designer by the Technological Metropolitan University, Chile. Doctoral thesis focuses on methods and processes of collaborative design for ICT artifacts and information systems in the fields of e-health and e-learning.

Ioannis Ignatiadis obtained a PhD degree in Information Systems from the University of Bath, School of Management, UK. He also holds Masters degrees in Information Technology and Technology Management from Imperial College and UMIST, UK. He worked in the industry as a software consultant in information technology projects for large European multinationals in UK, Germany and Greece. He also worked as an Information Systems researcher in the implementation of European Union-sponsored Information Society Technologies (IST) projects. His research interests evolve around the social, business and organizational aspects of Information Systems and E-business development and use. He is the author of a number of research publications in these areas.

George Leal Jamil is a professor in the Master in Business Administration of Fumec University, Minas Gerais, Brazil. He has a PhD in Information Science from the Federal University of Minas Gerais (UFMG). His master degree was in Computer Science (UFMG) and his graduate area was Electric Engineering (UFMG). He wrote 14 books in the information technology and strategic management areas. Yearly, he manages the doctoral consortium of the International Conference on Information Systems and Technology Management at the University of Sao Paulo (USP). His main research interests are information systems management, strategy, knowledge management, software engineering, marketing and IT adoption in business contexts.

Stamatia-Ann Katriou is a MSc student in Software Engineering at the University of Glasgow and holds an honors degree in Informatics from the Alexandreio Technological Institute (ATEI) of Thessaloniki. After working as a developer for a year on the EU-funded e-business PANDA project at the Research Programmes Division of ALTEC S.A. in Thessaloniki, Greece., she led ALTEC's development for the OneStopGov, SemantivGov and SCUBE-ICT EU-funded projects. Her research interests are in the fields of business computing, the semantic web and software engineering practices. She has traveled extensively concerning her collaborative work and research interests and also contributes at International Conferences.

Kathleen P. King, EdD, is professor of Adult Education and HRD at Fordham University's Graduate School of Education in New York City. King's major areas of research include professional development, transformative learning, instructional technology/distance learning, diversity and globalization. She is an award winning author (17 books), popular international keynote and conference speaker, editor, mentor, and private consultant. She enjoys international collaborations, appreciates multiple perspectives and dialogue. She is widely recognized for her research, service, and contribution to the fields of professional development, distance learning, and instructional technology. She may be reached by email at kpking@fordham.edu and her research website www.transformationed.com.

Adamantios Koumpis heads the Research Programmes Division of ALTEC S.A., which he founded at 1996 (then as independent division of Unisoft S.A.). His previous job position was at the Institute of Computer Science, FORTH, at Heraklio, Crete, where he worked at the Rehabilitation Tele-Informatics and Human-Computer Interaction Group on several EC RTD projects (RACE, ACTS and TAP). He is author of research papers, technical reports and Project deliverables and has successfully lead many industrial and European research projects in the areas of E-Commerce, the public sector and business enterprise re-organisation and information logistics, concerning linking of data/information repositories with knowledge management and business engineering models. Adamantios holds a PhD degree from the University of Kingston, UK and a Bachelor degree from the University of Crete, Greece. Together with Androklis Mavridis they have created the PACE toolkit and are responsible for this research activity in ALTEC.

Bojan Lalic, dipl ing during the course of working life over ten years spent working on projects at strategic and operational level in companies such as TESA SCG modeler Ltd., Beohemija Belgrade, Hotel Danube, Serbian Chamber of Commerce, etc. Currently, Manager of the International Graduate School of Engineering and Management, University of Novi Sad and an Institute Program Manager of Cisco Entrepreneur Institute Training Center Serbia. At the university teaches courses: Operations Management, E-Commercial, Strategic Project Management, Intelligent Enterprising and Effective Management. He is working on his doctoral dissertation on "Contribution to the development of conditions for the development of intelligent enterprises in Novi Sad, Maribor and New York". Dissertation is based on a set of real case studies.

Tatiana Levashova, PhD, received her ME degree at St.Petersburg State Electrical Engineering University, Russia, in 1986 and her PhD in computer science at SPIIRAS in 2009. She is a researcher at Computer Aided Integrated Systems Laboratory of SPIIRAS. Her current research is devoted to knowledge-related problems such as knowledge representation, ontology management, and context management.

Uglješa Marjanovic, MBA during the course of working life over five years spent working on projects at strategic and operational level in companies such as Bloomsburg Maintenance and Construction, University of Pennsylvania, Flat Rate Moving Systems in New York, Center for Competitiveness and Cluster Development, Faculty of Technical Sciences in Novi Sad. Currently, an assistant manager and facilitator at the Cisco Entrepreneur Institute, Training Center Serbia. At the Institute teaches course iExec Enterprise Essentials. Training iExec Ugljesa has performed in Belgrade, Novi Sad, Leskovac, and Kragujevac for over 120 participants with a positive response to the presented subject matter. Worked as a Teaching/Research Assistant during the course of pursuit of MBA at Bloomsburg University of Pennsylvania. He is working on his magister's thesis at the Faculty of Technical Sciences in Novi Sad where he teaches course E-Commerce.

Josep Maria Monguet, coordinator of the 'Project and Systems Engineering' Ph.D program (UPC). Has been: Vice Chancellor of Polytechnic University of Catalonia (UPC), Director of Design Superior Degree of UPC and Director of Laboratory of Multimedia Applications (LAM) of UPC. Director of the Audiovisual Department in the Education Sciences Institute, UPC. Since 1987, professor at the Industrial Engineering School of Barcelona. Businessman. Research activity focuses on innovation in ICT applications in the fields of health and learning. Since 1982, participating and directing several projects involving the application of multimedia and Internet technology.

Elisabete Paulo Morais is Professor of Computer Science in the Department of Informatics and Communications, in the Polytechnic Institute of Bragança. He received his PhD in Computer Science from Trás-os-Montes e Alto Douro University, Portugal. His current research focuses on electronic business and maturity models. It is a member of several scientific committees. Has several papers published in journals and proceeding of conferences.

Valentina Ndou, PhD is an assistant professor at eBusiness Management School, ISUFI, University of Salento. After graduating in 'Business Administration' at University of Scutari, she attended a master in marketing and development of territorial systems at ISUFI, eBusiness Management School. Then, she followed the PhD studies focusing her research on virtual networks applied to tourism enterprises and destinations. Her research specializes in analyzing the effectiveness of information systems for SME and their evolution over time, with particular emphasis on new solutions and approaches for business management, eBusiness models, internetworking approaches for SME, virtual clusters and training mechanisms.

Zlatko Nedelko, born 1983, is a researcher at Faculty of Economics and Business with the Department of Organization and Informatics, University of Maribor, Slovenia. He is also PhD student at same faculty. He published his papers at several scientific conferences, many of them abroad. He is also a member of scientific committees of several international conferences abroad. The fields of his research interests are organization and management. Recently he is involved heavily in researching personal values of managers.

Agustín Orfila is an Associate Professor at the Computer Science Department of the Universidad Carlos III de Madrid and a member of the Information Security Group of this department. He has a bachelor's degree in Physics from Universidad Complutense de Madrid and he obtained his Ph.D degree in Computer Science from Universidad Carlos III de Madrid in 2005. Dr. Orfila has several publications both in international conference proceedings and journals and he acts as a reviewer of different ISI journals. His interests are mainly focused on the security in information technologies, particularly on RFID and intrusion detection systems.

José Adriano Pires is Ph.D. in the technology and information systems field from the University of Minho. Professor Coordinator in the Department of Informatics and Communications, in the Polytechnic Institute of Bragança, where he served as director between 2001-2006. Currently, is Pro-President of IPB to the entrepreneurship area. It is a member of several scientific committees, guiding two PhD projects and has participated in several panels of the Master and Doctoral degree. Has several papers published in journals and minutes of meetings. Was coordinated of four projects resulting in the registration of two marks.

José Porfírio is Director of the Social Sciences and Management Department at Universidade Aberta in Portugal. He has a Phd in Strategic Management, a Master in Operational Research and a Degree in Management. He is currently responsible for the PhD in Management of Universidade Aberta. He is a professor in the MBA course of Universidade Aberta, which he coordinated until September 2009, being responsible for the scientific area of Strategy. Their research activities are mainly being done in the domain of Corporate Strategy, the role of Strategic Tools and MIS for the Strategic Management of Companies, and also in the area of Rural and Regional Development.

Vojko Potocan, born 1962, is an Associate Professor of organization and management on the Faculty of Economics and Business (FEB), Department of Organization and Informatics, University of Maribor, Slovenia. He teaches (on the graduate level, on the undergraduate level, and in doctoral program) in three universities in Slovenia and in three universities abroad (Germany, Croatia and Czech Republic). He takes part in different foreign scientific conferences and realized a number of study visits on abroad (University of Gent, Belgium; University of Greenwich, London, UK; University of Economics, Vienna, Austria). He was 3 times a visiting professor abroad and gave about eight further seminars at foreign universities. He has published +450 texts (+350 in foreign languages in 32 countries), including 8 books, and edited proceedings and textbooks. His research interests include Organization and Management.

Hakikur Rahman, PhD. is the Founder-Principal, Institute of Computer Management & Science (ICMS), and President of ICMS Foundation. He is currently serving as a Post-Doctoral researcher at the University of Minho, Portugal. He is an Adjunct Faculty of the Bangabandhu Sheikh Mujibur Rahman Agricultural University, and former Faculty of International University of Business, Agriculture and Technology, Bangladesh. He served Sustainable Development Networking Foundation (SDNF) as its Executive Director (CEO) from January 2007 to December 2007, the transformed entity of the Sustainable Development Networking Programme (SDNP) in Bangladesh where he was working as the National Project Coordinator (December 1999- December 2006). SDNP is a global initiative of UNDP and it completed its activity in Bangladesh on December 31, 2006. Before joining SDNP he worked as the Director, Computer Division, Bangladesh Open University. He also served as the Coordinator-Secretary of the South Asia Foundation Bangladesh Chapter (2001-2008); and Head Examiner (Computer), Bangladesh Technical Education Board (2000-2008). Graduating from the Bangladesh University of Engineering and Technology in 1981, he has done his Master's of Engineering from the American University of Beirut in 1986 and completed his PhD in Computer Engineering from the Ansted University, UK in 2001.

Inma Rodríguez-Ardura is an Associate Professor of Marketing in the Economic and Business Department of the Open University of Catalonia (Universitat Oberta de Catalunya or UOC), Spain. Currently she is serving as Director of the Doctoral Programme at the Internet Interdisciplinary Institute (IN3-UOC). She holds a doctorate in Economics and Business Studies from the University of Barcelona. Her research interests include e-commerce, consumer behaviour on the Internet, and marketing e-learning interfaces. She is the author of several books and articles on these areas.

Asbjorn Rolstadas is Professor of Production and Quality Engineering at the Norwegian University of Science and Technology and Vice Dean for research at the Faculty of Engineering Science and Technology. He has about 30 years of experience from education, research and consulting in project management. He has been much involved in continuing education for industry and has applied e-learning concepts since the early 1990ies. He has published more than 260 papers and books. Rolstadas is former president of the Norwegian Academy of Technical Sciences. He serves on the editorial board of number of journals. He is past president and honorary member of IFIP (International Federation for Information Processing).

Nezha Sadguy has collaborated with eBusiness Management Section working in projects related to eBusiness models for SME of Agrifood sector. After her graduation in Business Administration in Al Akhawayn University, Morocco - Major: Finance, Minor: International business, she followed the master ISUFI in Business Innovation Leadership. Her fields of research have been mainly concentrated in: Analysis and study of e-marketplace for Agrifood: e-business services, processes and attributes; supply chain management; Business Intelligence for e-Business Application in the Food Sector; Design and development of E-learning modules for Agrifood firms.

Kurt Sandkuhl, received his MSc and his PhD in computer science from Berlin University of Technology in Germany and his postdoctoral lecturing qualification from Linköping University in Sweden. He is full professor of information engineering in the School of Engineering at Jönköping University in Sweden. Before joining Jönköping University in 2002, he was department and division manager at Fraunhofer-Institute for Software and Systems Engineering in Berlin. His current research interests are in enterprise knowledge modeling, computer-supported collaborative work, information logistics and ontology engineering.

Nikolay Shilov, PhD, received his ME at St.Petersburg State Technical University, Russia, in 1998 and his PhD in computer science at SPIIRAS in 2005. He is a senior researcher at the Computer Aided Integrated Systems Laboratory of SPIIRAS. His current research interests belong to areas of virtual enterprise configuration, supply chain management, knowledge management, ontology engineering and Web-services.

Alexander Smirnov received his ME, his PhD and D.Sc. degrees at St.Petersburg, Russia, in 1979, 1984, and 1994 respectively. He is a Deputy Director for Research and a Head of Computer Aided Integrated Systems Laboratory at St.Petersburg Institute for Informatics and Automation of the Russian Academy of Sciences (SPIIRAS). He is a full professor of St.Petersburg State Electrical Engineering University. His current research interests belong to areas of corporate knowledge management, Web-services, group decision support systems, virtual enterprises, and supply chain management.

Emmanuel M. Tadjouddine is currently a lecturer in computer science at XJTLU (Xi'an Jiaotong-Liverpool University). He holds a Master in mathematics from the University of Limoges and a PhD in computer science from the University of Nice Sophia-Antipolis. Dr Tadjouddine's research is primarily concerned with issues between computer science, artificial intelligence, and economics. This includes designing electronic markets and verifying that these markets have some desired properties such as fairness, collusion-proofness, or strategy-proofness. He is also working on frontiers between computer science and applied mathematics focusing on Automatic Differentiation of algorithms and its application to computational engineering problems and to Financial Computing. Before Joining XJTLU, he was at Aberdeen University, and before that he was at Cranfield University (Defense Academy of the

UK formerly Royal Military College of Science, Shrivenham), and before that he was at INRIA Sophia Antipolis, where he earned his PhD in Computer Science.

Klaus-Dieter Thoben is professor in Production Engineering at the University of Bremen, Germany. He studied mechanical engineering at the TU Braunschweig. After finishing his studies, he became a staff member of the Faculty of Production Engineering (Department of Systematic Design) at the University of Bremen, where he received his Doctor of Engineering degree in CAD applications in 1989. In the same year he joined BIBA (Bremen Institute of Industrial Technology and Applied Work Science at the University of Bremen) as Manager of the CAD/CAM Lab. From 1991 until the end of 1996 he has headed the Department of Computer Aided Design, Planning and Manufacturing. Since 2003, he is head of "Information and Communication Technologies in Production". His special interests are organisational issues and applications of information and communication technologies in co-operative environments (including KM and e-leanings approaches).

Evangelos Tolias is a programmer and web developer interested in Semantic Web technologies, Web Services, Enterprise Application Integration and Evolutionary algorithms. He was born on 15 April 1985 and is completing a software engineering degree at the Alexandreio Technological Educational Institution (ATEI) of Thessaloniki. He has been working in the Research Programmes Division of ALTEC S.A since July 2008. He participated in the SemanticGov (Providing Integrated Public Services to Citizens at the National and Pan-European level with the use of Emerging Semantic Web Technologies), OneStopGov (A life-event oriented framework and platform for one-stop government), T-Seniority and SCUBE (Strategic Cooperation in Ukraine, Belarus and EU in Information and Communication Technologies) European Union projects.

Muammer Zerenler was born in 1975, in Konya. He earned his Bachelor of Science (B.Sc.) degree in 1996, his Master of Science (M. Sc.) degree in 1998, and PhD degree in 2003 from Selcuk University in Konya, Turkey. His doctoral thesis is titled "The Effect of Process Flexibility on the Businesses' Performance during the Crisis Period". He is Associate Professor of Production and Operations Management since 2009. He lectures courses such as Modern Production Systems, Strategic Production Management, and Electronic Commerce. He has published three books and co-authored many national and international articles and papers in the areas of Production Systems, Information Systems, and Electronic Commerce.

Index

D

E

K

L

M

N

O

U

V

W

Y

Breinigsville, PA USA
12 October 2010
247154BV00001B/5/P

Ethical Issues and Social Dilemmas in Knowledge Management:

Organizational Innovation

Gonçalo Jorge Morais da Costa
De Montfort University, UK

Information Science
REFERENCE

INFORMATION SCIENCE REFERENCE
Hershey · New York

Director of Editorial Content:	Kristin Klinger
Director of Book Publications:	Julia Mosemann
Acquisitions Editor:	Lindsay Johnston
Development Editor:	Joel Gamon
Publishing Assistant:	Milan Vracarich, Jr.
Typesetter:	Deanna Jo Zombro, Milan Vracarich, Jr.
Production Editor:	Jamie Snavely
Cover Design:	Lisa Tosheff

Published in the United States of America by
Information Science Reference (an imprint of IGI Global)
701 E. Chocolate Avenue
Hershey PA 17033
Tel: 717-533-8845
Fax: 717-533-8661
E-mail: cust@igi-global.com
Web site: http://www.igi-global.com

Library of Congress Cataloging-in-Publication Data

Ethical issues and social dilemmas in knowledge management : organizational innovation / Goncalo Jorge Morais da Costa, editor.
p. cm.
Includes bibliographical references and index.
ISBN 978-1-61520-873-9 (hardcover) -- ISBN 978-1-61520-874-6 (ebook) 1. Knowledge management. 2. Information society--Moral and ethical aspects. 3. Organizational change. I. Morais da Costa, Goncalo Jorge, 1979-
HD30.2.E85 2011
174'.4--dc22
2010041636

British Cataloguing in Publication Data
A Cataloguing in Publication record for this book is available from the British Library.

To the memory of my grandparents (João, Maria, José e Adelaide); and, to my princesses (Bianca and Ema), whose smiles fulfil my heart.

Editorial Advisory Board

List of Reviewers

Table of Contents

Detailed Table of Contents

The Japanese contribution to knowledge management results from the work of Ikujiro Nonaka and his colleagues, who developed an Organisational Knowledge Creation Theory. In fact, throughout the literature the importance of these scholars in knowledge management is evidently recognisable. However, it is important to understand this theoretical contribution in the context of the socio-cultural background that pervades it. For that reason, this chapter explores the relationship between the Japanese school of knowledge management and, the socio-cultural systems of Japan. Furthermore, the chapter also demonstrates that this relationship disrupts an organisation's ba (sense of place and structure), and as a consequence some social dilemmas arise, most importantly a degradation of trust.

In the same way that useful theory in knowledge management system leads us to rethink the nature of knowledge (Spender & Scherer, 2007) a theory of ethics that would be informed by current research in moral psychology will lead us to rethink the nature of ethical action. This chapter introduces a research program that has tracked ethical action among computer professionals and uses the insights from that research to make suggestions about how purposive moral action is undertaken and how it might be supported by knowledge management systems.

Section 2
Societal Knowledge Management

The main problem discussed in this essay is the question of compatibility between knowledge management in the knowledge economy and democracy in the ICT-driven global society. The assumption is made that democracy is the dominant form of organizing the global society on a variety of levels; and that it is regarded as desirable and morally superior in comparison with other such forms.

The term "knowledge management" is widely circumscribed to organizations, being considered fundamental at an institutional level (frequently within a specific corporate level). Hence, it is the domain of organizational and management theories, rational selection theories or, of various concepts related to economic efficiency. Nonetheless, this chapter will attempt to consider this issue from a holistic perspective, considering as a starting point the global dimension of this quandary. This overview falls back on analyses conducted by widely understood social studies, which use economic tools and methodologies. My opinion is that today the Internet evidently is a specific global knowledge warehouse. To be more specific, I mean the "ICT space" created by the Internet, which herein I will refer to as the cyberspace entails a global knowledge flux. As a result, this chapter is an overview of humanist discussions on cyberspace exploration and (more importantly) management.

Anti-Commons Theory is an interesting theme that is being developed in the area of property rights since the 80's. It intends to explain why an "anti-commons" emerges and why resources may be prone to under-use. In an anti-commons situation there are too many exclusion rights that lead to the under-use of resources. In Portugal, too many people (and institutions) have been involved in the approval processes of aquaculture projects. They may be involved in reaching a decision about the approval of a project which gives rise to the under-utilization of the resources that promoters aimed to exploit. Actually, it takes so long to approve a project that the time required for its implementation may be excessively delayed. This kind of problem results typically from bureaucratic environment. An ethical problem rises with this phenomenon. Projects may not go forward and all the amounts spent in the project will be lost. Besides, a viable project simply can be gone, with all the inherent losses of value.

Section 3
Organizational Knowledge Management

A key challenge that is emerging for organizations in nowadays is how to encourage knowledge sharing. Knowledge sharing is an activity through which knowledge is exchanged among people, a community or organization. Knowledge constitutes a valuable intangible asset for creating and sustaining competitive advantages. Knowledge sharing activities are generally supported by knowledge management systems. Nevertheless, technology comprises simply one of the several issues that influence organizational knowledge sharing, such as organizational culture, trust, and incentives. So, knowledge sharing entails a key challenge in the field of knowledge management because some individuals tend to resist sharing their knowledge with others (it may be an individual, a group, a community, or an organization). The aim of this chapter is to describe and discuss three emerging ethics of knowledge-sharing, namely: (i) hacker ethics, (ii) participatory culture ethics, and (iii) proselytization commons ethics. Future research directions are suggested and concluded the chapter.

This chapter analyzes some of the most relevant ethical issues and social dilemmas in knowledge management and organizational innovation, by focusing on a paramount feature of digital technology, which is "copying." The new ways in which information is produced, distributed, and shared in digital environments have in fact changed crucial aspects of human life. Whereas, most of the time, scholars consider such transformations in connection with the impact of digital copies on copyright law, the aim of the chapter is to widen this perspective by examining data protection as well as file sharing application systems. The new economical scenarios and business models proposed by this copy-based technology suggest new ways for balancing property rights and "the right to freely participate in the cultural life of the community."

Distance learning characteristics has been changing dramatically, namely since the fourth generation of distance learning. Moreover, e-learning impressive "evolution" enabled a trade-off between learning outcomes and ethical behaviour, which traditional learning theories do not embrace and that connectivism endeavours to illustrate. Although, two important queries arise: what challenges e-learning 2.0 and 3.0 impose? And, does connectivism promote ethical knowledge? Therefore, this chapter aims to endorse a theoretical debate regarding e-learning, as well as to understand if connectivism will act as 21st century learning theory, or if the quest for an ethical connective knowledge and e-learning fusion with knowledge management itself will require a novel contribution (connethionicism). Despite the assumption that connectivism has been promoting a reasonable debate, the author personal experiences highlight the need for ethicism.

Global networks through distributed systems technology granted a new meaning to knowledge creation, storage and distribution within higher education context. This global dimension imposes a considerable amount of ethical and social impacts concerning distributed knowledge because it is expressed within local contexts. Nonetheless, main stream literature highlights equity and cultural sensitivity as leading issues, and disregards the existent social dilemmas concerning organizational innovation in higher education. Therefore, this chapter aims to promote a philosophical and empirical argument within contextual determinants, in order to explore the ethical and social key dilemmas of distributed knowledge between global and local diversity in higher education. For that, under scrutiny will be a specific layer regarding first co-author e-University strategic implementation framework which interacts with ethics and culture, in order to, understand e-learning current practices in higher education, as well as, to nominate potential future guidelines concerning these trends.

Being knowledge management crucial to companies, it seems reasonable to understand an organisation intellectual capital. The three leading components of intellectual capital (human capital, structural capital and relational capital), are intrinsically bounded to the organisational ICT system, organisational structure, and to workers personal mastery. Nonetheless, in order to evolve organisational intellectual capital it is required a high level of personal mastery, which is clearly bounded to human resources.
Therefore, this chapter aims to promote a theoretical and empirical discussion in order to understand the diverse dimensions between renewal, personal mastery, and employee wellbeing within a knowledge-based organisation (Finnish ICT-company). For that, the chapter is divided into six major sections: the research questions; theoretical framework and main concepts; the case study organisation and research methods applied; findings; discussion; and future research.

Foreword

Long ago, in his classic work *Nicomachean Ethics*, Aristotle explored a number of significant connections between knowledge and ethics. For example, under some circumstances, *a lack of knowledge can excuse someone from blame*. Thus, suppose that a person had good reasons to believe that a certain chemical is medicine which can cure a given disease. In reality, however, that chemical is poison. The person in question did not know that the chemical is poison, so he gave it, with tragic consequences, to someone who was ill. If his lack of knowledge was not his own fault- if for example it was *not due to his own negligence-* and if he had excellent reasons to believe that the chemical actually is effective medicine- then the person *may be excused* for giving poison. On the other hand, if the person's lack of knowledge *was indeed due to his own negligence,* it would *not* excuse him from blame. This example is just one of many different important connections between knowledge and ethics.

According to Aristotle, because knowledge and ethics are significantly interrelated, a person must acquire appropriate knowledge- and apply it wisely- to be ethical. This includes knowledge about virtues and vices, as well as knowledge about the specific circumstances under consideration. It follows that *wisdom and excellent ethical judgment depend upon effective knowledge management*. Thus, among other things, parents, teachers and community leaders should take steps to make certain that their children can attain the knowledge needed to become virtuous. The amount of such knowledge is enormous, and Aristotle believed that a person must live for several decades before he or she could attain sufficient knowledge and experience to become ethically wise.

In the Western world, since the time of Plato, philosophers have offered a variety of theories of knowledge and have engaged in many debates about the fundamental nature of knowledge. Those debates continue to this day, and they often are interesting and helpful. Fortunately, however, we do not have to wait until all philosophers agree- if they ever do- about the fundamental nature of knowledge. Instead, our commonsense everyday understanding of knowledge is sufficient to explore some important connections between ethics and the management of knowledge. We know, for example, that knowledge can be created, stored, secured, copied, shared, applied, taught, learned, forgotten, lost, stolen, and managed in many other ways. Some of those ways are ethically reprehensible, some are ethically admirable, and some are ethically debatable. In the pages of the present book, a number of connections are explored between knowledge management and important ethical considerations.

All of the discussions in the book take for granted the fact that we are living in "the Information Age", and that we therefore have available to us a vast array of new information and communication technologies (ICTs), which can be used to create, compile, extract, store, retrieve, compare, filter, convey, disseminate, encode, hide, steal, scramble, erase, buy and sell information. And because knowledge and information are closely related, *the tools of the Information Age are having an enormous impact upon our ability to manage knowledge*. This book explores some aspects of that enormous ICT impact together with some related ethical issues.

A number of such issues can be viewed as questions of *fairness and distributive justice*. For example, in today's "knowledge economy" what is fair compensation for knowledge workers whose jobs and accomplishments are so central to the well being of society? Another issue of distributive justice concerns new knowledge being generated, in economically developed countries, by innovative companies and research laboratories. Doesn't justice require that this new knowledge- and related ICTs for managing it- be shared globally in ways that benefit poor countries as well as wealthy ones? Shouldn't knowledge and related ICTs be shared in ways that reduce "the digital divide" between the "haves" and the "have-nots"? And shouldn't that sharing include knowledge about the many diverse cultures of the world, as well as various ways to preserve and defend their cultural values, rather than merely disseminating knowledge and values of wealthy influential Western (i.e., America and European) countries?

One of the most effective ways to share knowledge globally- and also to spread cultural artifacts and values- is to use person-to-person (P2P) file sharing on the Internet. However, P2P distribution in the past has generated major worldwide ethical and legal questions involving, for example, ownership of intellectual property, privacy rights, security questions, and violations of personal freedom. These are fundamental issues that could take years- perhaps, even decades- to resolve. Since P2P knowledge sharing is here to stay- and it also provides new cultural, personal and business opportunities- many ethical, legal and cultural challenges lie ahead.

Knowledge sharing is related to a number of other ethical questions. For example, constant and rapid changes in the world economy make it necessary for businesses, if they are to remain competitive, to renew continually the knowledge resources that are embodied in their experts, their policies and their procedures. But sharing new knowledge that can help a business remain viable might also benefit its competitors and thereby threaten its own existence. On the other hand the economy generally and, therefore, the specific companies within the economy, depend upon new widely disseminated knowledge. There is tension, therefore, between knowledge protection and knowledge sharing.

A very special and important kind of knowledge sharing is the education of our children. Teaching involves the transfer of knowledge from teacher to student, as well as the facilitation, by teachers, of student self-learning. New ICTs have led to "distance learning" over the Internet, as well as ICT-enhanced teaching and learning in a traditional classroom. Pedagogical ethics requires that the new tools and teaching/learning techniques of the Information Age provide effective education. In addition, the new ICT teaching tools and methods require that teachers, if they are to remain effective, must acquire new knowledge themselves in order to be able to use the new tools and methods successfully. *Global* education issues are also ethically important, including an educational version of "the digital divide" in which distance learning and computer-assisted learning are concentrated in the developed world, thereby perpetuating the unjust distribution of knowledge between economically developed and underdeveloped countries.

Another global issue, of growing importance, is the possible development of a "global ethics" that could result from knowledge sharing among a wide diversity of the world's cultures. Access to the Internet in many different cultures has enabled a worldwide conversation about ethics and values. As part of that conversation, some philosophers have argued that the Internet is "inherently democratic"; and therefore, as more and more countries gain access to the Internet and to knowledge about democracy, respect for human rights and freedom will grow, and democracy could become the dominant form of governments worldwide. Other, more pessimistic, philosophers and social thinkers have argued, instead, that the powerful ICT tools of the Information Age might actually be used by politically and economically powerful people, companies, and governments to control and withhold knowledge and thereby dominate- perhaps even enslave- a vast majority of the world's population.

In addition to the above-mentioned knowledge-related ethical issues, there are *issues related directly to ethical knowledge itself.* For example, is knowledge about traditional ethical theories from philosophers, such as Aristotle, Bentham and Kant, sufficient to make a person ethically wise? Or does ethical wisdom require broader, tacit, and perhaps more intuitive kinds of knowledge? Can recent theories and experiments in moral psychology shed any light on the kinds of knowledge that wise persons actually use to make ethical judgments and to live ethical lives? These and related questions are also addressed in the pages below.

Terrell Ward Bynum
Southern Connecticut State University
New Haven, Connecticut, USA
29 November 2009

Terrell Ward Bynum *is Professor of Philosophy at Southern Connecticut State University, Director of the Research Center on Computing and Society there, and Visiting Professor at De Montfort University in Leicester, England. He is Past Chair of the Committee on Philosophy and Computers of the American Philosophical Association, a lifetime member of Computer Professionals for Social Responsibility, and Past Chair of the Committee on Professional Ethics of the Association for Computing Machinery. In 2005, he gave the Georg Henrik von Wright Ethics Lecture at the European Computers and Philosophy Conference in Sweden. In 2008, he won the Barwise Prize of the American Philosophical Association, and in 2009, he received the Weizenbaum Award of the International Society for Ethics and Information Technology.*

Preface

"All human situations have their inconveniences. We feel those of the present but neither see nor feel those of the future; and, hence we often make troublesome changes without amendment, and frequently for the worse." -- Benjamin Franklin

The editor at some extent agrees with Benjamim Franklin quotation, because hitherto main stream literature has been neglecting the ethical and social dilemmas that knowledge management enables. Nonetheless, if this handbook aims to alter the knowledge society *status quo* (mental and cultural revolution) through theoretical and practical solutions, it is reasonable to expect that these amendments will encourage a better society.

ABOUT THE SUBJECT

The philosophical dialogue as regards to "knowledge" is divided into four constructs:

"episteme (knowledge about common and collective agreements, hereby episteme means a concrete knowledge about something, which can be easily passed to the next generation), techne (ability or practical capacity, knowledge about how to handle tasks and exercises), phronesis (intuitive knowledge like wisdom, which is combined with personal experiences and with a specific social attitude, which cannot be easily passed to other people), métiers (knowledge, which is based on personal experiences and social practises; it means a specific type of cleverness and individual brilliancy, developed by a person in a specific context; obviously métiers also cannot be easily passed to other persons)" (Renzl 2004, p. 32).

This quotation emphasizes the process of creating, using and sharing knowledge despite the underlying level of knowledge management, which may vary according to literature. For example, Sinclair (2008) refers three levels: personally-based, community-based, and organizationally based.

Higgison (2005) describes personal knowledge management as the process of managing and supporting the knowledge that is significant and valuable to an individual through preserving its social networks. Community-based knowledge acknowledges the multiple configurations (communities of practices, virtual communities, etc) that technology supports in order to create, use and share knowledge (Sinclair, 2008). And, for instance Brelade & Harman (2003) argue that organizational knowledge management enables the acquisition and exploration of resources to generate an environment in which information is available to all organizational members. This environmental characteristic will allow individuals to acquire, share and use that information to develop their personal knowledge, as well as persuades them to apply their knowledge for the benefit of the organization.

Even so, the editor proposes another conception: personal, organizationally, and society-based. The disparity resumes two arguments:

- a perception of what is considered an organization, because the editor assumes community as a form of organizational taxonomy (broader perception);
- and, states possess their own knowledge management strategies (societal approach). For Wiig (2006), societal knowledge management entails the knowledge-related initiatives within a society, which is achieved through a blend of proactive and voluntary actions managed by personal and local contexts and public knowledge infrastructures.

Regardless the theoretical configuration, the relationship among these levels as well as the knowledge construct, induces ethical and social tensions never glimpsed before (the scope of *Ethical Issues and Social Dilemmas in Knowledge Management: Organizational Innovation*). Besides, these ethical and social dilemmas clearly reflect the need to rethink knowledge society fundamentals, or otherwise the positive and desirable legacy for future generations will be a mirage. If, the impact of knowledge society is economic, cultural, social, political and technological with intergenerational consequences, a multidimensional analysis is compulsory in order to promote a reliable and feasible discussion.

WHY THIS PUBLICATION

The underlying motivations for this handbook are the editor academic, professional and publishing background which IGI Global has recognized. From the array of these experiences, the editor has gain conscience that humans have a natural curiosity for understanding their world, which highlights dissimilar queries or means. On the other hand, it is also typical to query about the existing reality and until what extent we believe in the principles that guide mankind actions. In conclusion, this handbook attempts to demonstrate that knowledge management needs to change "its course", which is proven through brilliant theoretical and empirical contributions, as well it resumes the human reasoning: more we know, more we wonder about the right questions.

MISSION AND AIMS

The mission of this handbook is to provide an inclusive coverage of the latest and most relevant developments, solutions and problems related to this topic that has been systemically neglected by literature and given its overall impact in knowledge society and organizational knowledge management projects.

Thus, some significant objectives of this handbook embrace:

- to demonstrate the philosophical underpinnings concerning knowledge management, and the importance of ethics;
- to reveal the multiple facets of knowledge management;
- to illustrate the ethical and social dilemmas that occur in societal knowledge management;

- to exhibit the ethical and social dilemmas that arise in organizational knowledge management;
- to relate organizational innovation with these dilemmas;
- to introduce solutions that allow to minimize the ethical and social dilemmas;
- to promote a change for a truthful knowledge society (based on ethical and moral principles).

In conclusion, the resulting publication enables a valuable, challenging and multidisciplinary resource for Readers acquire excellent insights pertaining to the transformations and challenges that knowledge management is and will face.

ORGANIZATION

This handbook resumes a compilation of 15 contributions that discuss numerous dimensions: Knowledge Management- schools of thought and dimensions; "Societal" Knowledge Management- ethical and social dilemmas; "Organizational" Knowledge Management- ethical and social dilemmas; Organizational Innovation- dilemmas; and Trends. Hence, these chapters are written by 21 authors (20 authors and the editor), namely academic and practitioners related to the multiple dimensions that the handbook core enables: ICT experts, lawyers, ethicists, consultants, among others.

Ethical Issues and Social Dilemmas in Knowledge Management: Organizational Innovation is organized in five sections:

- **Section 1:** Knowledge Management, discusses the schools of thoughts and the contribution of moral psychology (critical dimension) to knowledge management;
- **Section 2:** "Societal Knowledge Management", acknowledges a macro perception of knowledge management and its ethical and social dilemmas;
- **Section 3:** "Organizational Knowledge Management", enables a meso perspective of these dilemmas within knowledge environments, namely within educational settings;
- **Section 4:** "Organizational Innovation", resumes a blend between organizational knowledge management and trends in order to the Reader understand the continuum process and bound between both realities;
- **Section 5:** Trends, debates practical solutions concerning the ethical and social dilemmas previously illustrated.

Nevertheless, at this point some additional remarks are mandatory: the handbook acknowledges the overlapping realities among the three levels and knowledge construct, as well as it might seems to assume a top-down analysis that disregards personal knowledge management (due to its sections, namely from section 2 to 5). Although, the personal dimension can be easily recognized within societal and organizational knowledge management, and section 1 is a "milestone" for what to expect (a non-traditional approach to knowledge management).

As a result, the following step is to articulate the aims and objectives of each section versus its content (chapters), and a graphical representation of the handbook's architecture. Section 1 includes 2 chapters, as well as it enables propaedeutic instructions about the philosophical underpinnings of knowledge management as a research field, as well as it introduces the contribution of moral psychology.

Kiyoshi Murata debates the SECI model, Japanese input to knowledge management, encompassing a double analysis: the explanation of the theoretical contribution of Nonaka and his colleagues given their importance to the research field; and, the socio-cultural background that pervades it. Chapter 1 investigates the bond between the Japanese school of knowledge management and, the socio-cultural systems of Japan. In addition, the Japanese socio-cultural features of *uchi/soto* awareness, insular collectivism and the *hon'ne/tatemae* tradition can disrupt an organisation's *ba* (sense of place and structure), leading to several social dilemmas, most importantly a degradation of trust.

Chapter 2 embraces the contribution of moral psychology to knowledge management, enabling the need to rethink the nature of ethical action by computer professionals given the importance of knowledge management systems in supporting knowledge creation, sharing and use. Chuck Huff introduces a research program that has tracked ethical action among computer professionals and uses the insights from that research to make suggestions. In that sense, the author has concluded that an ethical actor is not a passive recipient of a pre-packaged decision space, but shapes his or her decision according to the situation and goals of the system.

The second section, "Societal Knowledge Management", comprises 3 chapters that emphasize an overview of societal knowledge management, namely the conditions required to knowledge society flourish and be humanist, as well as the effect of bureaucracy in a national knowledge management project.

In chapter 3, *Knowledge management and democracy: A critical review of some moral issues and social dilemmas*, Krystyna Górniak-Kocikowska acknowledges the trade-off amid knowledge management economy and democracy in the ICT-driven global society. The assumption is that democracy is the prevailing structure of organizing the global society on a multiplicity of levels; and that it is regarded as desirable and morally superior in comparison with other political forms. This trade-off is "cyclical" (historical analysis) because it can benefit the humankind collectively and individually, or it merely benefits a select group of individuals. The outcome will depend on which ethical and social values would be accepted, however as Plato alleges the conception of good is the last assumption of knowledge.

Following up the previous chapter, Piotr Pawlak in chapter 4 approaches knowledge through a holistic viewpoint of the global dimension, which outlines the social studies approaches if we consider that Internet represents a specific global knowledge warehouse. This global warehouse enables global fluxes based on the cultural commodities as an extension of Western power, leading to an exchange of various cultural products. If this global flux detracts local culture, the recognition of an inclusive knowledge society is in danger or, if diasporic communities arise is essential to pose the following questions: how do equally ideas will be converted across cultures? Does the outcome depend on how components are demonstrated, or individuals' comprehension? It is possible to achieve infusion cultures that are neither isolationist or imperialistic? What will be the response of intellectual property rights?

Another potential approach to societal knowledge management is the effect of bureaucracy when managing environmental resources at a national level, namely in Portugal. The intention of chapter 5 is to describe why "anti-commons" appear and why resources may be prone to under-use. Anti-commons generate too many exclusion rights leading to the under-use of resources. In Portugal, the knowledge flux absorbs a wide spectrum of institutions as regards to the approval of aquaculture projects. The inflated interaction of knowledge responsibilities undermines the approval of a project which engages an inefficient utilization of the resources. Therefore, Filipe, Ferreira & Coelho refer that bureaucracy act as a constraint to national knowledge management projects, raising ethical issues like equity as a consequence of the anti-commons tragedy.

The third section, "Organizational Knowledge Management", covers 4 chapters and sheds some light over the ethical and social dilemmas that educational knowledge environments promulgate. Despite education be a transversal process and its key role in knowledge society, the editor has considered its focus and impacts at an organizational level as the following chapters will highlight.

In chapter 6, Masrom & Ismail debate the issues surrounding knowledge sharing, being this an action through which knowledge is exchanged among people, a community or organization. This sharing process is today based technological systems, although is only one of the features that influences organizational knowledge sharing. So, knowledge sharing entails a key challenge in the field of knowledge management because some individuals tend to resist sharing their knowledge with others (it may be an individual, a group, a community, or an organization) due to multiple reasons. The objective of this chapter is to portray and debate three emerging ethics of knowledge-sharing, namely: hacker ethics, participatory culture ethics, and proselytization commons ethics. In fact, this triangulated analysis reflects the need to change the mindset of people in line with common ethical norms in believing that "knowledge sharing is power".

On the other hand, Ugo Pagallo (chapter 7) demonstrates that knowledge sharing implies the need to debate the concept of copying in digital environments, meaning that novel ways for balancing property rights and "the right to freely participate in the cultural life of the community" are required. Therefore, it is remarkable that common thinking is that digital copy is solely related to copyright issues, and not a responsible or altruistic behaviour through trust or incentives in order to guarantee a fair compensation to the author. This perpetual "pursuit" attempts to weaken the potential of innovation that digital copies generate and its potential to permit a truly knowledge society, which is clearly contradictory.

Finally, chapters 8 and 9 highlight the ethical and social issues that learning environments have enhanced. In chapter 8, António dos Reis illustrates the differences among the e-learning generations and the trade-off about ethical behaviours. For this author, e-learning 2.0 and 3.0 will require novel learning theories despite the positive contribution of connectivism to achieve ethical knowledge. Hence, ethicism will facilitate the quest for an ethical connective knowledge in e-learning 2.0 environments, and "connethionicism" for e-learning 3.0 (linking connectivism, ethicism, connectionism). Silva, Alvarez & Rogerson in chapter 9 approach the global distributed knowledge systems in education and its ethical and social impacts in local contexts. So far, main stream literature points out equity and cultural sensitivity as leading issues, and ignores a systematic array of social dilemmas, as proven by these authors. For that, a theoretical and empirical argument within contextual determinants is exhibited in order to explore the arising dilemmas amid distributed knowledge, global and local diversity in higher education. Beyond these evidences, a wide range of empirical examples are depicted and analysed through Silva e-University strategic implementation framework which interacts e-learning with ethics and culture. As a final remark, the authors claim that to minimize the current and upcoming dilemmas novel educational systems must be: *localitas* (as a basic quality of bodies), *connectivitas* (blend status with reference to multi-glocal experiences), and *humanitas* (ability for self-consciousness).

Chapters 10, 11 and 12 are the components of the fourth section, "Organizational Innovation Dilemmas", which purpose is to portray the dialogue involving organizational knowledge management and trends. From this overlapping reality a more transparent analysis and outcomes will be achieved.

To Lohikoski, chapter 10, it is essential to realize organizational intellectual capital, and for that sheds some light over its three components: human capital, structural capital and relational capital, as well as how are these inherently bounded to the technological system, organizational structure, and to workers personal mastery. Even so, the importance of human resources in knowledge management is

Figure 1. Graphical representation of the handbook's architecture

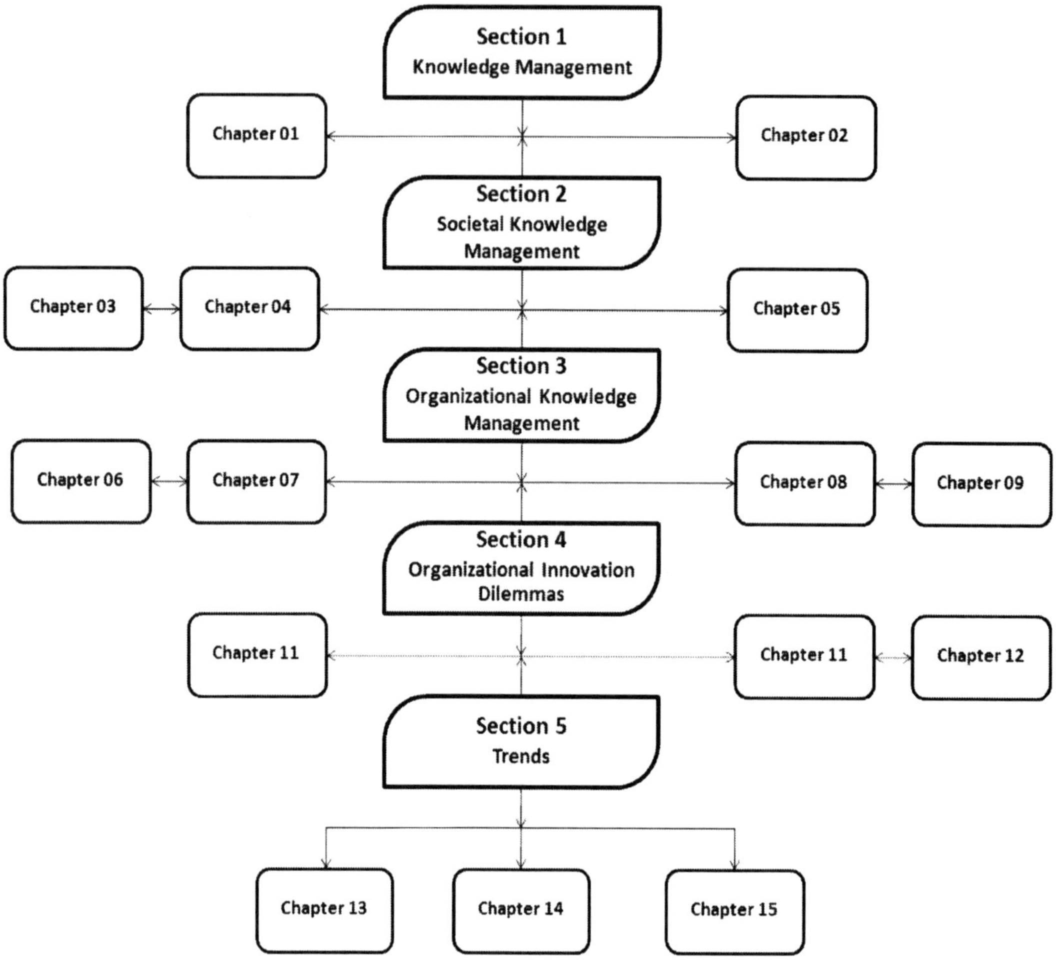

widely recognized in literature and the author promotes an academic and practical debate in order to identify the various dimensions connecting renewal, personal mastery, and employee wellbeing within a knowledge-based organisation (Finnish ICT-company). The conclusions of this contribution reveal that the transactional boundaries of interacting are obvious, generating change within communities that promote the integration of participants with unlike motivations.

Likewise, Takahashi in chapter 11 tries to acknowledge the challenge of protecting and interchange knowledge in organizations. Similarly to Lohikoski, this author claims that knowledge workers are an invaluable asset within organizational contexts; however, the problem relies on how to retain knowledge workers and their knowledge, and until what extent should be promoted access to the organizational body of knowledge. A not balanced trade-off may induce: the corrosion of working conditions, leading to a lack of attractiveness for future workers; lack of commitment and restraining knowledge sharing, so internal knowledge creation will be affected. Finally, the non-compete and non-disclosure agreements have a short term outcome, and despite increasing its length of time seem a practical hypothesis it entails a "mirror effect". The "mirror" effect acknowledges the lack of availability of knowledge workers at long term as a consequence of the previous procedure.

In chapter 12 is underlined the legitimacy of companies to increase profits but through moral knowledge. Furthermore, the chapter debates how it is possible to manage moral knowledge within organizational contexts having in consideration Blackler's assumptions. To become ethically competent, companies have to combine individuals and organizational ethical skills. Instead of focusing on what is supposed to be done, the authors bear in mind moral knowledge transference within the multiple organizational interactions. In order to help managers cope with these challenges Kostrzewa, Laaksoharju & Kavathatzopoulos introduce the Ethical Index ETHIX (questionnaire to describe how ethical issues are handled in the organization) and the IT system ETHXPERT (supports and structures the process of ethical decision making). The reason for this contribution derives from an empirical observation: the dominant approach toward ethics is normative, which does not accurately reproduce societal *status quo*, because norms are shaped and revised as a result of global information sharing.

Trends, the fifth section, aim to introduce practical explanations with reference to the ethical and social dilemmas highlighted throughout the handbook, and for that entail chapters 13, 14 and 15.

In his first contribution, the editor, questions the issue of fair compensation regarding knowledge workers. The recognition that human resources are a crucial asset in the knowledge economy is methodically documented in literature, as well as the underlying characteristics of knowledge workers and their responsibilities and duties. Furthermore, other leading focus is the human resources policies multiple features, as for instance: knowledge workers retention, personal mastery, intellectual property rights, etc. Despite this overall and continuous debate, literature seems to reveal lack of empirical studies with reference to the feeling of knowledge workers compensation fairness and what dimensions are valued as critical. So, in order to shed some light over this theme the editor resumes his PhD empirical results, as well as academic and professional experiences.

In chapter 14, Pullinger debates the current reality of UK government policy regarding knowledge management. Public knowledge management intends to create public value (outcomes, service quality and cost effectiveness) through trust. However, the author argues that the major constraint is to understand how it is possible that citizens shared knowledge become a source of value for public knowledge management, as well as the trade-off between personal data and shared knowledge. For that, Pullinger provides a comprehensive analysis of the ethical tensions in each stage of the SECI model in UK government. The empirical results allow us to conclude that cultural challenges need to develop consensus through social construction, which is enhanced by the relationship citizen-state in public knowledge management.

Last but not least, the editor presents the underlying assumptions of learning organizations namely its characteristics, dimensions, evolution, evaluation procedures, or ethical behaviour. In addition, Costa demonstrates that learning organization literature has been ignoring to the impacts of existing ethical and social dilemmas about knowledge creation, retention/use and sharing within organizational contexts (proven by the empirical outcomes of his PhD research project). So, in chapter 15 is acknowledged a conceptual framework that indicates the impacts of these dilemmas in organizational strategy and that certainly will produce feasible results when applied worldwide.

EXPECTATIONS

This handbook presents a comprehensive coverage of the theme, providing to a broad audience of researchers, scholars, practitioners and students with state of the art theoretical and practical developments and solutions on this domain. Some keen examples of potential Readers are people from management, human resources, organizational behaviour, information science, information technology, organizational sociology, computer ethics, and law, among others.

As a result, it is expectable several and interesting comments from the audience in order to promote an enhanced discussion with reference to the ethical and social dilemmas that knowledge management imposes. Moreover, the editor created an open forum about the handbook in order to promote a truly communitarian debate (http://www.goncalocosta.com/index/index.php?option=com_ccboard&view=forumlist&Itemid=66), as well as sincerely hopes that this stimulating and thought provocative work will allow future research and eloquence enough to change the guiding principles of the knowledge society.

Gonçalo Costa
Editor
Caldas da Rainha (Portugal), September 2010

REFERENCES

Brelade, S., & Harman, C. (2003). *A practical guide to knowledge management: A special commissioned report*. London: Thorogood Professional Insights.

Higgison, S. (2005). Your say: Personal knowledge management. *Insight Knowledge, 7(7)*. Retrieved September 20, 2010, from, http://www.ikmagazine.com/xq/asp/sid.0/volume.7/issue.7/qx/displayissue.htm.

Renzl, B. (2004). Zentrale aspekte des wissensbegriffs- Kernelemente der organisation von Wissen. In B. Wyssusek (Ed.), *Wissensmanagement Komplex- Perspektiven und Soziale Praxis* (pp. 27-42). Berlin: Erich Schmidt Verlag GmbH & Co. (in German).

Sinclair, N. (2008). The changing face of KM. *VINE: The Journal of Information and Knowledge Management Systems, 38(1)*, 22-29.

Wiig, K. M. (2006). Societal knowledge management in the globalised economy. *International Journal of Advanced Media and Communication, 1(2)*, 172-191.

Acknowledgment

This publication could not have been written without the support of several "actors", to whom I address my deepest regards. Similarly to the overall book configuration I advocate the existence of institutional/ organizational, groups and individual "actors", whose contributions assume different forms however with equal importance.

My sincere thanks to IGI Global for the unbelievable invitation and for believing in my work, as well as, guidance and support throughout the entire book editing process; nonetheless, I need to express my gratitude to my "personal assistant" at IGI Global, Mr. Joel Gamon, whose help was incomparable and far beyond my personal expectations.

I would like to acknowledge the support provided by all the educational institutions whose authors have contributed for this book. Likewise, I sincerely hope that these institutions recognize the tremendous effort of its researchers, in order to help me creating an innovative and critical publication concerning knowledge management *status quo*. Moreover, I want to thank to the Centre for Computing and Social Responsibility at De Montfort University, for its doctoral program experience, represented by my supervisors, Professor Mary Prior and Professor Simon Rogerson. Their intellectual guidance, judicious support, encouragement, and challenging ideas (some expressed in this book), have been the input of my evolution. Finally, it is essential to acknowledge the additional support that my lecturing institution in Portugal had provided me: to ISLA Leiria University my sincere esteem.

Moving forward, it is also necessary to remember the positive attitude of all the non-educational organizations that directly or, indirectly had contributed for this publication: to all my gratefulness. Therefore, I sincerely hope that the answers and new ideas presented in this book, become a useful tool for an ethical organizational innovation of their internal procedures.

Although, is time to scrutinize which were the various groups of actors that allowed the dream come true! Thus, the actors were:

- The Editorial Advisory Board: I am speechless, and as you all know it is not a ordinary situation. I felt deeply honoured with your marvellous support, comments, ideas and contributions, as well as, I had never expected that leading authors, whose knowledge and expertise I respect, could accept my challenging invitation. So: Nino, Bernd, Chuck, Kiyoshi, Krystyna, Mario, Mary, Simon, Terrell and Ugo, I am indebted to you.
- The contributors: A special regard is mandatory for all that believed that this publication could at some extent promote important changes. I am confident that those changes will occur, due to the high quality and unique contributions that you have produced. Therefore, without reasonable doubt I am a privileged editor.

- The reviewers: From a miscellaneous mixture of the Editorial Advisory Board and contributors a list of reviewers arose. And, once more the result was outstanding, because everyone understood the level of criticality regarding the reviewing process.
- Family: To my parents, brother, wife and daughters, I require their forgiveness due to my lack of time. Nonetheless, I know that you are proud of my achievements.
- and, my students: To my past and present students I thank their support and continuous challenges, because without them it was impossible to accomplish so different objectives. In fact, this book also represents our hopes and dreams concerning a more ethical knowledge society.

Finally, my thoughts go to a specific actor: Nuno Sotero Alves da Silva (my PhD comrade), and to Tiago Filipe Rodrigues da Fonseca (my honourable apprentice). Thank you to both for the continuous support, insightful comments and critics, and above all your friendship. It has been truly an honour to "serve" with both...

Gonçalo Costa
Editor
Caldas da Rainha (Portugal), September 2010

Section 1
Knowledge Management Social and Ethical Dimensions

"Morality, like art, means drawing a line someplace"
Oscar Wilde

If this manuscript's purpose is to rediscover knowledge management, namely knowledge as a process (people centred), it is crucial to understand its moral principles like Oscar Wilde argues. Therefore, it is reasonable to query if the founder and inspirational work of the SECI model imply moral issues given its recognition regarding the socio-cultural environment? Nonetheless, knowledge society is enabled through technology (knowledge management systems), leading to a relevant discussion as regards to the ethical actions that computer professionals should undertake without jeopardizing imaginative practices of knowledge workers.

Chapter 1
Knowledge Creation and Sharing in Japanese Organisations:
A Socio-Cultural Perspective on *ba*

Kiyoshi Murata
Meiji University, Japan

ABSTRACT

The Japanese contribution to knowledge management results from the work of Ikujiro Nonaka and his colleagues, who developed an Organisational Knowledge Creation Theory. In fact, throughout the literature the importance of these scholars in knowledge management is evidently recognisable. However, it is important to understand this theoretical contribution in the context of the socio-cultural background that pervades it. For that reason, this chapter explores the relationship between the Japanese school of knowledge management and the socio-cultural systems of Japan. Furthermore, the chapter also demonstrates that this relationship disrupts organisation's ba (a field of knowledge creation and sharing), and as a consequence some social dilemmas arise, most importantly a degradation of trust.

INTRODUCTION

Japanese business scholar Ikujiro Nonaka and his colleagues developed an organisational knowledge creation theory as a basic theory of knowledge-based management, rooted mainly in their observations of Japanese manufacturing firms such as Honda, Sony, Kao, Canon and NEC. They recognised that the competitive advantage of Japanese firms in the international market has derived from the skill and ability of these firms with regard to organisational knowledge creation. This theory is composed of four conceptual elements: a socialisation-externalisation-combination-internalisation (SECI) model, *ba* (spatial and time settings of organisational knowledge creation), knowledge assets, and knowledge leadership. The theory is based on a number of ideas such as tacit knowledge (Polanyi, 1966; 1958), the logic of *ba* or place (Nishida, 1933; 1911), teleonomic evolutionary theory (Imanishi, 1976), and holons, fluctuation, self-organisation and *ba* in bioholonics (Shimizu, 1992; 1978). Many of these ideas are based on Eastern thought.

DOI: 10.4018/978-1-61520-873-9.ch001

This chapter deals with knowledge creation and sharing in Japanese organisations, focusing on organisational knowledge creation theory (e.g., Nonaka & Konno, 1998; Nonaka & Takeuchi, 1995) and Japanese socio-cultural characteristics, including *uchi/soto* awareness, insular collectivism and the *hon'ne/tatemae* tradition (Adams, Murata & Orito, 2009). In particular, the nature of the *ba*/field, in which knowledge creation and sharing activities are made, is examined from a Japanese socio-cultural perspective. In that examination, the author explores how knowledge creation and sharing in Japanese organisations is enhanced or restricted by the cultural characteristics of Japanese society. Success and failure factors in organisational knowledge creation and sharing are the targets of the investigation in this chapter. This clarifies intrinsic Japanese elements embedded in the knowledge creation theory and could be useful for non-Japanese organisations in applying the theory.

The structure of the remainder of this chapter is as follows. The next section describes the ideas and the background of the organisational knowledge creation theory, based on the studies of Nonaka and his colleagues. The following section examines the relationships between the organisational knowledge creation theory and Japanese culture. The last section investigates how *ba*, as a field of knowledge creation and sharing, should be managed in Japanese business organisations to permit them to achieve successful knowledge creation and sharing in Japanese socio-cultural circumstances.

DEVELOPMENT OF THE ORGANISATIONAL KNOWLEDGE CREATION THEORY

Information Creation as a Self-Organising Activity

The organisational knowledge creation theory was originally developed as the antithesis of the scientific or analytical strategic planning theory (e.g., Abel & Hammond, 1979). Nonaka (1985) noted that the adoption of analytical strategic management methodologies such as product portfolio management in uncertain economic environments triggered the *paralysis by analysis syndrome* in many firms, in which strategic staff tend to exaggerate quantitative analysis and consequently design infeasible strategic plans. He also pointed out that modern organisational theory and contingency theory are useless in the ever-changing business environment, and stressed the necessity of evolution of business organisations by shifting their focus of strategic and organisational design from the analysis of market environments to the creation of information or new ways of thinking and behaving.

Nonaka's arguments are based on scientific research into areas such as dissipative structure (Nicolis & Prigogine, 1977), synergetics (Haken, 1983), teleonomic evolutionary theory (Imanishi, 1976) and bioholonics (Shimizu, 1978), among others. Bioholonics addresses life phenomena, and characterises a living system as a self-organising system where holons (autonomous components of a living system) create a new order for the whole system cooperatively, with each constituent, through fluctuation and entrainment. Applying the ideas of these scientific findings to the management of organisations, Nonaka described the nature of business organisation evolution and concluded that it essentially involves the creation of information through self-organising activities proactively conducted by organisational members in an intra-organisational environment designed to enhance the self-organising processes. According to his theory, typical evolutionary or self-innovative organisations have the following characteristics:

- they face rapidly changing business environments;
- they develop an organisational scheme to create internal fluctuation by generating chaos, diversity and/or uncertainty;

- internal individuals and groups are continually provided organisational support to behave autonomously to generate fluctuation;
- they develop a management scheme to enhance innovative destruction and self-transcendence;
- they develop an organisational mechanism to promote entrainment or synchronisation of fluctuation generated by internal individuals and/or groups;
- they enhance information/knowledge sharing among organisational members to develop learning organisations;
- their evolution is not random, but teleonomic.

Organisational Knowledge Creation and Management

Tacit and Explicit Knowledge

Scepticism about the practical effectiveness of the information processing paradigm (Galbraith, 1973; March & Simon, 1958; Simon, 1957), in which organisations are characterised as entities that process information to adapt to the uncertain environment surrounding them through solving problems given in the environment, and the belief that organisations are entities that proactively change their environment through creating information and knowledge motivated Nonaka (1990) to formulate the organisational knowledge creation theory. Based on the traditional theory of knowledge and Polanyi's concept of tacit knowing (Polanyi, 1966; 1958), he recognised that knowledge has two aspects or phases: explicit and tacit. The former is objective and rational knowledge that can be expressed in words and numerals, and shared among people in terms of formulae, data, procedures, universal principles and so on. The latter is subjective and experiential knowledge, and expressing this type of knowledge clearly in words and/or numerals is difficult.

Somewhat unlike Polanyi's definition, Nonaka's tacit knowledge, containing technical skills like know-how and cognitive skills like mental models (Johnson-Laird, 1983), is considered to have a cyclic and complementary relationship with explicit knowledge. Tacit knowledge can be converted into explicit knowledge in certain organisational settings using metaphor and analogy as a tool for the conversion. Polanyi, on the other hand, considered that tacit knowledge is hidden behind explicit knowledge and that it is impossible, or at least extremely difficult, to make tacit knowledge explicit. Once tacit knowledge is *articulated* or converted into explicit knowledge, it becomes sharable among members in an organisation. The converted knowledge can then be *internalised* to enrich the existing tacit knowledge possessed by individual members. Nonaka's knowledge creation theory was based on the belief that knowledge is created and expanded through the transition between tacit and explicit knowledge.

Nonaka also considered that someone's tacit knowledge could be transferred to others. This is typically observed in the process of training of an artisan or a martial artist. This transfer is called *socialisation*. Another type of knowledge creation is that of *combination*, which represents the process of creating new explicit knowledge through the combination of existing explicit knowledge.

Of the four modalities of knowledge creation, articulation, conversion of tacit knowledge into explicit knowledge, and internalisation, conversion of explicit knowledge into tacit knowledge, are fundamental because they deeply relate to self and subjectivity, and therefore enhance self-organisation. On the other hand, socialisation and combination create surface or phenomenological knowledge.

Individual and Organisational Knowledge Creation

Nonaka (1990) correctly recognised that an organisation cannot create knowledge. Instead, an organisation can create an environment or context for supporting and encouraging knowledge creation by individual members of the organisation. Individual knowledge creation in an organisation is the actual source of organisational knowledge creation.

Nonaka pointed out that intentional fluctuation and a certain level of autonomy on the part of individual organisational members in a well-designed organisational setting tends to enhance double loop learning (Argyris & Schön, 1978) and information/knowledge creation by organisational members. Knowledge creation performed by individuals in an organisation is social as well as personal in that knowledge creation generally occurs through interaction with others.

However, the tacit knowledge of individuals must be shared among organisational members to create organisational knowledge. According to Nonaka, setting up a field or *ba* for interaction among individuals in groups in an organisation is fundamental to enhancing tacit knowledge sharing. In this field, interaction with continual and candid dialogue among those who have strong mutual relationships makes it possible for each group member to relativise his/her own perspective and, therefore, any tacit knowledge the member has can be shared and verbalised or conceptualised among the members. This creative dialogue or concept development process in a group is supported by leadership which is the basis for constructive communication among the members and facilitates the development of useful concepts.

Concept development by groups is the basis of organisational knowledge creation. Concepts developed in groups often cause fluctuation in an organisation, which can be recognised as a non-equilibrium self-organising system or a living system. When the fluctuation is amplified through entrainment (Shimizu, 1992; 1978) or dynamic cooperation among groups as components of the organisation, a new order in the living system is formed. Then, if the order is fed back to each group, and the dynamic cooperation among the groups is enhanced, a new stable order of the organisation is formed. This newly created order or knowledge should be endorsed and justified by existing values shared among the organisational members. Therefore, the quality of the created knowledge tends to depend on the attitudes of the organisational leaders and members. In addition, created knowledge has to be materialised as products and services, for example. This enables the organisation to gain feedback information from individuals inside and outside the organisation, which enriches the organisational semantic network. The created knowledge and the revised organisational semantic network are resources for further knowledge creation in the organisation.

Organisational knowledge creation as *order formation from disorder or chaos* requires information redundancy in the organisation to enable dynamic cooperation among groups through the generation of mutual trust relationships. The organisation must also contain requisite variety (Ashby, 1956), which is internalised in individual members of the organisation to deal with information redundancy.

Middle-Up-Down Management

Based on the observation of Japanese firms that have been successful in organisational knowledge creation, Nonaka (1990) identified a new management style that these firms had developed, one that worked well in a fiercely competitive business environment with rapid changes in technology. He called it *middle-up-down management*. In this management style, top managers set out their vision or present grandiose, abstract concepts and values or grand theories (Nonaka & Takeuchi, 1995) that are, for example, embedded in the missions and domains of their companies. Lower managers in the same companies pragmatically face up to reality and generate realistic concrete concepts. When the concepts presented by top managers contradict, to some extent, those expressed by lower managers, middle managers then go on to create moderate concepts or mid-range theories (Nonaka &Takeuchi, 1995) to resolve the contradiction.

Here, unlike top-down or bottom-up management, organisational members from the top to the bottom commit organisational knowledge creation cooperatively. The top managers are catalysts of organisational knowledge creation who offer fundamental general directions or visions for information/knowledge creation in their organisations. They set up fields for knowledge creation, assign appropriate people to specific fields, and encourage them to engage in constructive communication with each other. They also fix deadlines for such creation when necessary.

Middle managers as knowledge producers (Nonaka, Toyama & Konno, 2000) are at the crossover point of macro/global and micro/local information provided by the top and lower managers, respectively, and are expected to play a central role in organisational knowledge creation. They develop their own information or concepts by integrating macro and micro information, and promote the realisation of organisational knowledge creation based on these concepts by generating and amplifying fluctuation. Thus, they occupy a strategic position and are required to demonstrate entrepreneurship. The decisions of top managers as to who should be assigned to middle management as entrepreneurs in a field of knowledge creation is extremely significant in organisational knowledge creation.

The lower managers are experts who respond to the dreams of top managers from the standpoints of their own specialties. Trust among members within a field of knowledge creation is necessary to successful middle-up-down knowledge creation because it is essential to this type of knowledge creation that the members in the field candidly discuss about concepts the middle managers propose.

Organisational Knowledge Creation Model

The SECI Model

In contrast with the Western definition of knowledge, as justified true belief, which has been strongly affected by Cartesian dualism, Nonaka & Takeuchi (1995) declared that knowledge is created in social interaction and is defined as a dynamic human process of justifying personal belief towards the truth. The observation of Japanese firms made them realise that these firms recognise knowledge as being primarily tacit. Based on this, and the Japanese intellectual tradition represented by terms of subject-object unity such as *oneness of humanity and nature*, *oneness of body and mind* and *oneness of self and other*, they considered that the organisational knowledge creation and sharing that were successful in the Japanese firms they observed could be described as an ordered spiral process of knowledge conversion between tacit and explicit knowledge. This process is embodied in the SECI model (Figure 1), where SECI stands for the four modalities of knowledge conversion (Nonaka & Konno, 1998). The SECI process can be interpreted as follows.

First, personal tacit knowledge is converted into group knowledge; i.e., tacit knowledge is shared among individuals in a group through physically proximal shared experiences. This conversion is called *socialisation*, as described above, and this creates *sympathised knowledge* such as shared mental models and know-how.

Second, shared tacit knowledge is converted into explicit or conceptual knowledge, typically through dialogue using metaphors, analogy and models, in that order. Nonaka & Takeuchi (1995) called this knowledge conversion *externalisation*, which includes *articulation*. Externalisation is crucial to successful knowledge creation in an organisation. Nonaka & Konno (1998) suggested that an individual commits to the group and thus

Figure 1. SECI model: Spiral evolution of organisational knowledge creation and sharing (Source: Nonaka & Konno, 1998, p. 43, Figure 1)

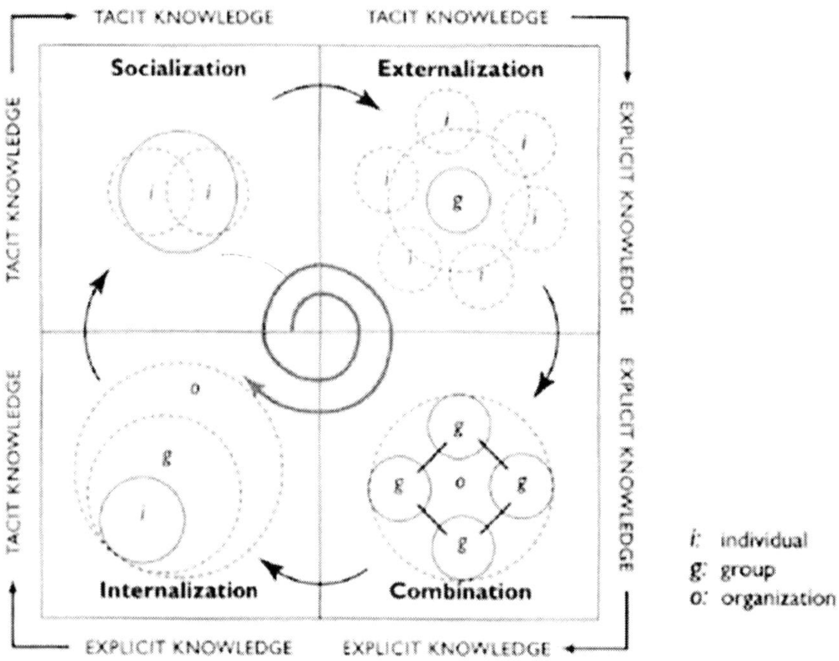

becomes one with the group during this stage of knowledge creation.

Third, explicit knowledge shared among members of a group is combined with explicit knowledge from other groups inside the organisation, and sometimes from outside the organisation, and is consequently converted into systematised explicit knowledge or *systemic knowledge*. This conversion or *combination* can be enhanced by the use of information and communication technology (ICT)-based facilities such as databases and email, and middle managers often play an important role as information editors for the realisation of the combination.

Finally, systemic knowledge is converted into organisational tacit knowledge in the form of, for example, organisational mental models and know-how. This *internalisation* brings about *operational knowledge*; it also enriches the personal tacit knowledge of individuals and, consequently, further enhances the higher-order knowledge creation started in the socialisation stage. Explicit knowledge should be verbalised or schematised as documents, manuals and stories, for example, to facilitate the internalisation.

ba as a Field of Knowledge Creation

To represent organisational settings that enable knowledge creation and sharing, Nonaka and his colleagues often use the Japanese term *ba*, which can be translated as field, place, space, playground, forum, agora or occasion. Nonaka & Konno (1998) explained that *ba* is a shared context or framework, made up of the borders of space and time in which knowledge is created, shared and used. Knowledge is embedded or resides in *ba* and is not isolable from it because knowledge is primarily personal and contextual. *ba* can be physical, virtual, mental or any combination of these. *ba* has a complex and ever-changing nature, and the creation of *ba* by design is a good way of motivating people in organisations to engage in creative activities.

Nonaka & Konno (1989) stated that there are four types of *ba* corresponding to the four modalities of knowledge creation in the SECI model; the *ba* terms were modified slightly by Nonaka, Toyama & Konno (2000) (Figure 2). *Originating ba*, where individuals in a group share feelings, emotions, experiences and mental models, is the primary *ba* from which the knowledge creation process begins. Physical face-to-face interaction is the key to sharing personal tacit knowledge among group members. Care, love, trust and commitment, which are the basis for knowledge conversion, emerge from this *ba*.

Tacit knowledge is converted into explicit knowledge in *interacting ba* or *dialoguing ba*. Dialogue with figurative language such as metaphors and analogies is helpful in actualising the conversion. This type of *ba* can be constructed more consciously than originating *ba*. *Cyber ba* or *systemising ba* is a framework of collective interaction in which the combination of existing explicit knowledge takes place. ICT-based systems provide this *ba* with efficient and effective support to enhance the combination. *Exercising ba* facilitates the conversion of explicit knowledge into organisational tacit knowledge. This type of *ba* synthesises transcendence and reflection through action such as on-the-job training.

Knowledge Assets and Leadership

ba is the platform for the resource concentration of organisational knowledge assets, which are the foundations of knowledge (Nonaka & Konno, 1998). During the spirally repeated knowledge creation processes conducted in the four types of *ba*, knowledge is accumulated and stored in the organisation as knowledge assets. Nonaka, Toyama & Konno (2000) defined knowledge assets as the input, output and moderating factors of the knowledge creation process. They recognised four types of knowledge assets: experiential, conceptual, systemic and routine.

Experiential knowledge assets are composed of tacit knowledge shared by organisational members as well as by people inside and outside the organisation through shared experience. The typical example of this type of knowledge asset is the skills and know-how acquired and accumulated by individuals through experience at work, and shared with other people in the workplace. Emotional knowledge like care, love and trust is another example of experiential knowledge assets.

Figure 2. Four types of ba (Source: Nonaka, Toyama & Konno, 2000, p. 16, Figure 6)

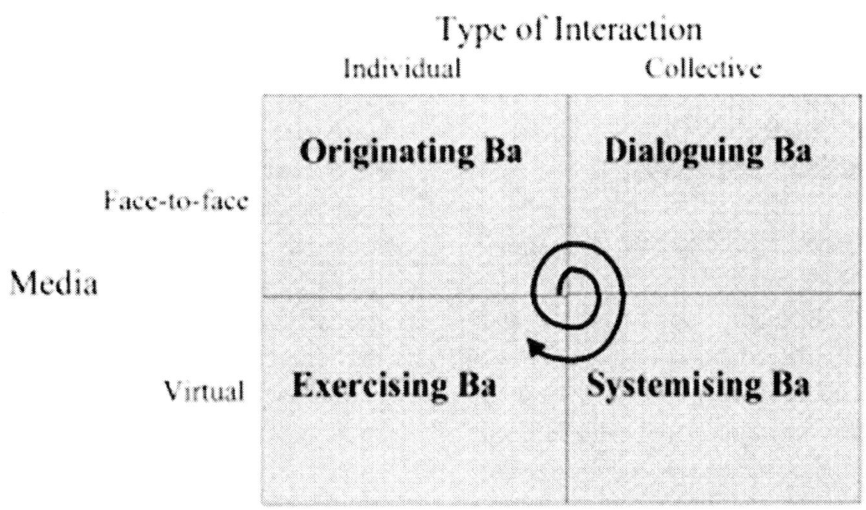

Conceptual knowledge assets are made up of explicit knowledge articulated with images, symbols and language, whereas systemic knowledge assets consist of systematised explicit knowledge. Routine knowledge assets are composed of tacit knowledge embedded in organisational routines of day-to-day operations, know-how and culture.

Nonaka, Toyama & Konno (2000) pointed out that to create knowledge successfully, the spiral knowledge creation processes should be well managed by knowledge producers or middle managers through the provision of proactive commitment and leadership in *ba*, and they should be properly supported by top managers. Top and middle managers should take a leadership role, not only by leading but also by *reading* the situation in terms of what kind of knowledge assets are available to their organisation, rather than in terms of what kind of knowledge they are lacking. Top managers are expected to articulate knowledge vision, which defines what kind of knowledge the organisation should create in what domain, and the value system that evaluates, justifies and determines the quality of the knowledge that the organisation creates. Top managers are also expected to communicate this throughout the organisation. Middle managers must break down the values and visions created by the top managers into concepts and images that can guide the knowledge-creation process in effective directions.

ORGANISATIONAL KNOWLEDGE CREATION AND JAPANESE CULTURE

Japanese Personal Identity and *ba*

Nonaka and his colleagues seem to consider that the actuality socially constructed by autonomous individuals in an organisation deeply influences what is created in the organisation as knowledge. However, as long as *ba* is composed of people, the human activities and interactions in *ba* are inevitably affected by the socio-cultural characteristics surrounding it.

Japanese ethicist Tetsuro Watsuji characterised ethics as a study area to investigate the order and logic that underlie human relationships and communities (Watsuji, 1934). He conducted an etymologic analysis of the Japanese term *ningen*, corresponding to the English concept of human beings. Watsuji concluded that *ningen* is a term used to express the world or *seken* a person lives in and, simultaneously, a person who lives in a *seken*. People can become human beings when they reside in a *seken* and are recognised as human beings because they represent the whole *seken*. Watsuji maintained that the principal problem of ethics is the fundamental dualistic structure of *ningen*. *Ningen* is self plus certain relationships with others or *aidagara*, and the inseparability of human existence from *aidagara* should be understood.

Watsuji's insistence of human existence in *aidagara* adequately represents a typical Japanese way of thinking and behaving. In fact, many other scholars have presented similar views. For example, the Japanese mentality of *amae* (Doi, 1973), which means an assumption of the good will of others, reflects Japanese people's realisation that their living is ruled by interdependent relationships with others. Kimura (1981) mentioned that the personal identity of an individual is usually determined based on his/her perception of relationships with others. Kimura called this *aida*, which has the same meaning as *aidagara*. Abe (1995) also pointed out that an ordinary Japanese person lives, at least mentally, not in society but in a *seken*, which is a small world defined by relationships with others whom the person recognises a present and/or future connection with and, therefore, considers the need to do his/her duty toward and to have human empathy with.

From the viewpoint of an Eastern mind-body theory, Yuasa (1987) interpreted existence in *aidagara* as human existence in a definite spatial *ba*. Instead of *ba*, he used the Japanese term *basho*, which has the same meaning as *ba*. Yuasa characterised Watsuji's *aidagara* as an intersubjective space or *ba*. Yuasa pointed out that Watsuji's view of a person emphasises space as the *ba* of human existence and hence stresses the spatial existence of the body, whereas the traditional Western view of humanity generally considers that time or historicity is more important than space, and that mind is more important than body. Yuasa identified the traditional Japanese and Eastern mode of thinking about the relationship between humanity and nature behind Watsuji's view as the inseparable unity of mind, body and nature.

ba in Shimizu's Bioholonics

Nonaka & Konno (1998) explained that the concept of *ba* was originally proposed by the Japanese philosopher Kitaro Nishida and has been further developed by Hiroshi Shimizu. Shimizu's bioholonics has exerted a considerable influence over theories of organisational knowledge creation.

Nishida's logic of *ba* involves identifying an authentic dimension of self. He contended that the self can reach correct knowledge of the Being of beings when it transforms itself from the everyday self grounded in *ba* of being to self as *ba* based on the *ba* of nothing (Yuasa, 1987). On the other hand, Shimizu's study was motivated by the question of "what is living?" He addressed this research subject from a natural scientific viewpoint and arrived at a recognition that the core of life phenomena is the macro living systems' spontaneous creation of order or information, through self-organisational and self-referencing processes, in order to survive and evolve in an unpredictably changing external environment (Shimizu, 1992; 1978). Contrary to the law of entropy increase, living systems, as non-equilibrium open systems, universally create dynamic order from chaos. They are hierarchy-like entities within which supersystems and subsystems usually exist. Micro living systems or *holons* that make up a macro system originally exhibit autonomous behaviour and fluctuate so that the macro system can survive in its changing environment. Once certain conditions are achieved to create a new but rudimentary order in the macro system as a consequence of the choice of a desirable outcome among the ones brought about by fluctuation, they react synergistically to create dynamic order cooperatively. Dynamic cooperation such as entrainment is directed by information concerning the place or location of each micro system in the macro system, provided by the rudimentary order, and the cooperative behaviour of the micro systems promotes the transformation of the rudimentary order into an established one.

A living system is controlled not by energy but by information, in terms of the necessity of continuing to create meaningful information for the system to survive and evolve in its environment. This occurs through information-feedforward and -feedback control, in processes of which information is exchanged between the living system and its supersystems and subsystems. In the feedforward and feedback processes, the semantic environment or *ba* surrounding the systems plays a role in providing each micro system with information about its semantic location in the whole system, or information about the *ba*, to enable dynamic cooperation among the micro systems.

Shimizu (2003) maintained that the nature of life or living is the functioning of a cyclical process of creation that develops *ba*, locates existence of self in *ba* and develops new *ba* through expressing self in existing *ba*. Life exists as *ba* or *globally existing self* and, simultaneously, as an individual substance located in that *ba* or *locally existing self*. Living things cannot exist independently of *ba*, because the function of life is to express itself. Based on these arguments, Nonaka & Konno (1998) defined *ba* as the world where the individual realises himself/herself as part of the environment on which his/her life depends.

Shimizu (2003) highlighted the oneness of a human being and *ba* by noting that no human being can be separable from *ba* and the others in *ba*.

He explained that when we attempt to undertake some action, we unconsciously envisage *ba* in which the action will be taken and those who will be involved in *ba*. Sharing of *ba* among people, therefore, is affected by the values and culture that people have. The greater the diversity in people's values and culture, the more that sharing of *ba* among them tends to be difficult.

Although Shimizu's conceptualisation of *ba* is basically derived from his natural scientific research, it is also strongly affected by Eastern thought, including Zen Buddhism and Nishida's philosophy (Shimizu, 2003), and is influenced by the ideas underlying the art and skill of the *Yagyu Shin-Kage-Ryu* Japanese swordplay tradition (Shimizu, 1996). He recognised that Japanese culture is characterised as the culture of *ba*, which was developed based on Buddhism, and that this culture has enabled co-creation in Japanese society (Shimizu, 2003). His recognition has similarities with views on Japanese culture provided by other researchers such as Abe (1995), Yamamoto (1983), Kimura (1981) and Nakane (1970).

Japanese Aspects of Organisational Knowledge Creation Theory

Both Nishida's and Shimizu's thoughts were affected by Zen Buddhism. This means that they were consciously or unconsciously influenced by the Daoist thought of Laozi and Zhuangzi, which constituted the foundation from which Zen and Jodo (Pure Land) Buddhism were developed during the Sui and Tang Dynasties. These Daoist gurus preached that everything in the universe is unity, and that language and letters are useless for perceiving or telling the truth. Only experiential intuition makes it possible for people to understand the truth. They contended that artificiality is an obstacle to knowing the world as it is (Mori, 1987). Daoism has influenced the Japanese way of thinking and behaving via Zen and Jodo Buddhism since the end of the 12th century, when these sects of Buddhism started to spread throughout Japan; thereafter, however, these separate sects combined with the tradition of spiritual life in Japan and developed independently (Suzuki, 1944). Thus, it is not surprising that we find the influence of Japanese and East Asian culture throughout the organisational knowledge creation theory that Nonaka and his colleagues have developed, whereas the theory also has aspects that are universally effective.

For example, many Japanese people can easily understand the paralysis by analysis syndrome because they tend to believe that the real world cannot be fully understood through logical analysis, according to Daoism. Socialisation, the conversion of personal tacit knowledge into tacit knowledge shared among group members, can be recognised as *ishin denshin* or knowing the details of another person's knowledge by telepathy among associates on the same wavelength. This relates to the characteristic of Japanese linguistic culture, where implication is often used when important things are communicated (Kindaichi, 1975) and also to Japanese collectivism or, more precisely, groupism culture where group members are expected to behave cooperatively based on common basic values.

The importance of the commitment of individuals to the group they belong to, and their becoming one with the group in the externalisation stage of organisational knowledge creation, is easily understood by Japanese people immersed in a groupism culture and the intellectual tradition of oneness of self and other. It is recognised in Japanese society that members of a group can be unified and that the group is essentially an indivisible social unit. This sort of group is typically composed of five to seven individual members who share a workplace and work cooperatively on a constant basis. This serves as the basis for the citizenship of its members (Nakane, 1978).

The meanings and nuances of *ba* as fields of knowledge creation activities, with spatial and time boundaries, may be comprehensible to Japanese people, at least in an obscure way, because they are living in a groupism culture. Nakane (1978) pointed out that Japanese people can behave animatedly as individuals and enjoy working and dealing with acquaintances when they are in their own small groups as the social units described above. They tend to have loyalty to their own groups and understand their responsibility only for those groups. Simultaneously, as Hamaguchi (1982) described, they are not totally ruled by the groups, but autonomously commit prosperity of the groups and attempt to accomplish symbiosis between the groups and the group members through the commitment. In fact, in a Japanese business organisation, people tend to be expected to behave as representatives of their own groups based on their recognition concerning their positions in the groups as well as in the organisation. If they forget their positions and behave in fully individualistic fashion, they are often branded incompetent employees.

In the context of knowledge creation in business organisations, this suggests the importance of the leadership exerted by middle managers, and their ability to edit information and knowledge. It is only they who are expected to be actually capable of behaving autonomously, even though they are also under the unification pressure from the groupism culture, among those who engage in knowledge creation in *ba*, in which organisational members from different groups can participate. Reading the situation or sensing the atmosphere in *ba* is an extremely important art that they are expected to develop, in order to avoid causing unnecessary friction among small groups, and to avoid discouraging participants in *ba*, thus ensuring that knowledge creation is not affected by a negative atmosphere. In fact, a situation in which some dominant atmosphere, for better or worse, shapes organisational decisions beyond dispute often exists in Japanese organisations (Yamamoto, 1983). *Nemawashi* or informal previous arrangements for consensus-building between leaders of groups from which participants attend *ba* is also a significant task middle managers have to do to make *ba* function well in Japanese business organisations because they are managed based not on individualistic but rather on communitarian principles (Yamada, 1985).

MANAGEMENT OF *ba* IN JAPANESE SOCIO-CULTURAL CIRCUMSTANCES

Characteristics of Japanese Communication Culture

Figure 3 shows the in-group/out-group or *uchi/soto* model describing the Japanese people's understanding of the relationship between self and others (Adams, Murata & Orito, 2009). The innermost regions are the individual self (*watashi*) and the close family (*miuchi*). The outermost region consists of *tanin*, those who can never be inside one of the individual's in-groups. The separation between *uchi* and *soto* is not a fixed measure but a sense of the relative psychological distance between people. In general, the further away one moves from the self, the less information is revealed. In speaking to members of one's *uchi* group, one uses *hon'ne* speech; that is, one speaks the bare truth or one's real intention. When speaking to members of one's *soto* group, one uses *tatemae* speech; that is, one communicates just what one politely says on the surface to casual acquaintances (Orito & Murata, 2008).

The *uchi/soto* awareness is directly related to Japanese insular collectivism (Adams, Murata & Orito, 2009). In a society characterised by insular collectivism, Japanese people tend to place more importance on the interests of the *uchi* group to which they belong than on their personal interests (Hendry, 2003; Benedict, 1946) or the good of society as a whole (Haitani, 1990). This Japanese form of groupism creates strong vertical hierarchies based on strong personal relationships with superiors and subordinates, weak horizontal relationships with fellow subordinates of a supe-

Figure 3. Uchi/soto model (Source: Adams, Murata & Orito, 2009, p. 334, Figure 2)

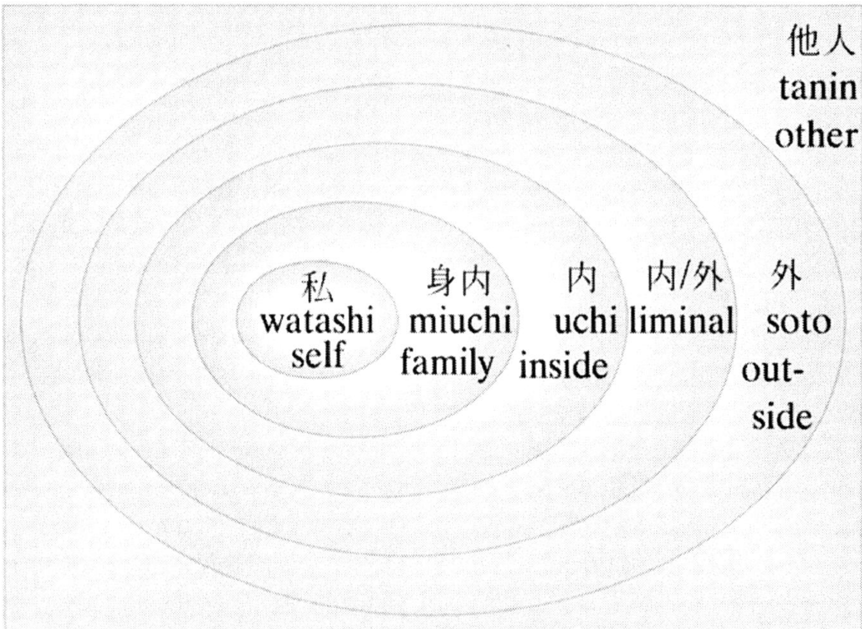

rior, and very weak ties to other members of the organisation.

Figure 4 shows a typical situation where *ba* is created in a Japanese organisation. Individuals in *ba* recognise a hierarchical human relationship between them. This relationship is not necessarily the same as the one described in the formal organisational structure of the organisation. Members at the same horizontal level of the hierarchy who have the same superior communicate with each other using *hon'ne* speech, whereas they use *tatemae* speech when talking with other members in *ba*. Subordinates behave carefully to prevent their superiors losing face and, therefore, they often hold back their true feelings in meetings held in *ba*. Instead, subordinates are sometimes required to express their superiors' views through reading the superiors' minds based on their words, expressions and gestures. Meanwhile, superiors are expected to give their support to their subordinates. Note that the basic human relationships between Japanese people are bilateral ones, constructed in *uchi* groups, which are recognised as unified, and not separate (Nakane, 1972).

Promotion of Organisational Knowledge Creation and Sharing in Japan

In the typical situation in *ba* in a Japanese organisation, individuals, except for those at the top of the hierarchy, usually find it difficult to behave autonomously and talk frankly. At the same time, individuals in *ba* consider that they should all take responsibility concerning knowledge created in *ba*. If some harm occurs due to the use of the knowledge, ambiguity regarding the locus of responsibility prevents loss of face on the part of the superiors and of the groups. However, this means that no one may take any responsibility regarding the knowledge.

On the other hand, due to a culture of insular collectivism, knowledge created in one insular group tends to be considered something *not invented here* by those in other insular groups. They sometimes hate to lose their own insulars' face as well as their superiors' face by easily accepting knowledge created by another insular. This can degrade the function of *ba* as a basis for knowledge creation

Figure 4. Vertical human relationship and communication

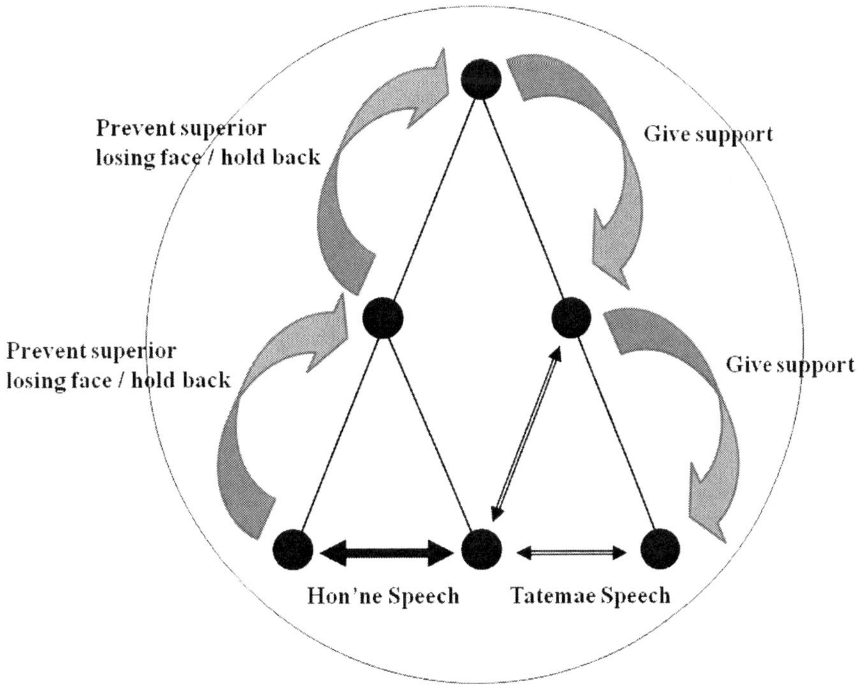

and sharing. When *ba* is composed of individuals from different insulars, the insular group to which a person at the top of the hierarchy in *ba* belongs tends to be recognised as an *owner* of knowledge created in that *ba*. It is not unusual that a person who committed knowledge creation but doesn't belong to the owner insular tells "actually, I was opposed to creating such knowledge" when the knowledge is used or shared. In addition, because any creation somewhat contains disavowal of the past and can become a threat to those who have vested interests, newly created knowledge is prone to be misconstrued in the externalisation stage and to be ignored or disallowed in the combination stage.

To avoid these difficulties, managers who are in charge of knowledge creation and sharing should remove invisible barriers between insular groups and shorten the mental distance between participants in *ba*. They are expected to show magnanimity to individuals in *ba* so as to develop a relaxed atmosphere in *ba* so that everyone in *ba* is encouraged to commit to knowledge creation. Fostering a sense of ownership of knowledge created in *ba* among participants in that *ba* is extremely important for successful sharing of created knowledge. In addition, *nemawashi* between relevant organisational members are usually necessary to be made by the mangers in order for created knowledge to be accepted in the organisation. Of course, these are not necessarily easy to do. Development of relationships based on trust between people, not assurance (Yamagishi & Yamagishi, 1994), should be recognised as an issue to be addressed in order to make organisational knowledge creation and sharing successful in Japanese society.

On the other hand, a high level of *ba* cohesiveness can be expected when *ba* is composed of individuals from the same insular group. This type of *ba* may be helpful for incremental or adaptive creation. However, sharing created knowledge from this *ba* across insular groups is difficult, as is innovative creation.

CONCLUSION

The organisational knowledge creation theory that Nonaka and his colleagues have developed includes useful concepts such as the SECI model, *ba*, middle-up-down management, knowledge assets and leadership for modern business organisations. Even though the theory is purported to be universally effective, these concepts have close relationships to Japanese culture and are therefore culturally bounded. Moreover, the Japanese socio-cultural characteristics of *uchi/soto* awareness, insular collectivism and the *hon'ne/tatemae* tradition can make it difficult for Japanese business organisations to create and share knowledge. These may cause malfunctions of *ba* as a field of organisational knowledge creation and sharing. Knowledge creation processes and *ba* should be properly managed to avoid these difficulties. Developing trust among people is a social issue that contributes to successful organisational knowledge creation and sharing in Japan.

REFERENCES

Abe, K. (1995). *What is "seken"?*Tokyo: Kodansha. (in Japanese)

Abel, D. F., & Hammond, J. S. (1979). *Strategic market planning*. Englewood Cliffs, NJ: Prentice-Hall.

Adams, A. A., Murata, K., & Orito, Y. (2009). The Japanese sense of information privacy. *AI & Society*, *24*(4), 327–341. doi:10.1007/s00146-009-0228-z

Argyris, C., & Schön, D. (1978). *Organizational learning: A theory of action perspective*. Reading, MA: Addison-Wesley.

Ashby, W. R. (1956). *An introduction to cybernetics*. London: Chapman & Hall.

Benedict, R. (1946). *The chrysanthemum and the sword: Patterns of Japanese culture*. Boston, MA: Houghton Mifflin.

Doi, T. (1973). *The anatomy of dependence*. Tokyo: Kodansha International.

Galbraith, J. R. (1973). *Designing complex organizations*. Reading, MA: Addison-Wesley.

Haitani, K. (1990). The paradox of Japan's groupism: Threat to future competitiveness? *Asian Survey*, *30*(3), 237–257. doi:10.1525/as.1990.30.3.01p03644

Haken, H. (1983). *Synergetics, an introduction: Nonequilibrium phase transitions and self-organization in physics, chemistry, and biology* (3rd ed.). New York: Springer-Verlag.

Hamaguchi, E. (1982). What is Japanese collectivism? In Hamaguchi, E., & Kumon, S. (Eds.), *Japanese Collectivism* (pp. 1–26). Tokyo: Yuhikaku. (in Japanese)

Hendry, J. (2003). *Understanding Japanese society*. Oxford, UK: Routledge.

Imanishi, K. (1976). *What is evolution?*Tokyo: Kodansha. (in Japanese)

Johnson-Laird, P. N. (1983). *Mental models*. Cambridge, UK: Cambridge University Press.

Kimura, B. (1981). *Self, relationship and time: Phenomenological psychopathology*. Tokyo: Kobundo. (in Japanese)

Kindaichi, H. (1975). *Japanese linguistic expression*. Tokyo: Kodansha. (in Japanese)

March, J. G., & Simon, H. A. (1958). *Organizations*. New York: John Wiley & Sons.

Mori, M. (1987). *Laozi and Zhuangzi*. Tokyo: Kodansha. (in Japanese)

Nakane, C. (1970). *Japanese society*. Berkley, CA: University of California Press.

Nakane, C. (1972). *Conditions for adaptation: The Japanese thought of continuation*. Tokyo: Kodansha. (in Japanese)

Nakane, C. (1978). *Dynamics of a vertical society*. Tokyo: Kodansha. (in Japanese)

Nicolis, G., & Prigogine, I. (1977). *Self-organization in non-equilibrium systems: From dissipative structures to order through fluctuations*. New York: John Wiley and Sons.

Nishida, K. (1911). *An enquiry into the good*. Tokyo: Kodokan. (in Japanese)

Nishida, K. (1933). *Fundamental problems of philosophy: The world of action and the dialectical world*. Tokyo: Iwanami Shoten. (in Japanese)

Nonaka, I. (1985). *Theory of corporate evolution*. Tokyo: Nihon Keizai Shimbun Sha. (in Japanese)

Nonaka, I. (1990). *Theory of organisational knowledge creation: Epistemology of Japanese firms*. Tokyo: Nihon Keizai Shimbun Sha. (in Japanese)

Nonaka, I., & Konno, N. (1998). The concept of "*ba*": building a foundation for knowledge creation. *California Management Review*, *40*(3), 40–54.

Nonaka, I., & Takeuchi, H. (1995). *The knowledge-creating company: How Japanese companies create the dynamics of innovation*. New York: Oxford University Press.

Nonaka, I., Toyama, R., & Konno, N. (2000). SECI, ba and leadership: A unified model of dynamic knowledge creation. *Long Range Planning*, *33*(1), 5–34. doi:10.1016/S0024-6301(99)00115-6

Orito, Y., & Murata, K. (2008). Socio-cultural analysis of personal information leakage in Japan. *Journal of Information. Communication and Ethics in Society*, *6*(2), 161–171. doi:10.1108/14779960810888365

Polanyi, M. (1958). *Personal knowledge: Towards a post-critical philosophy*. Chicago: University of Chicago Press.

Polanyi, M. (1966). *The tacit dimension*. Garden City, NY: Doubleday.

Shimizu, H. (1978). *Reconsidering life: What is living?* Tokyo: Chuo Koron. (in Japanese)

Shimizu, H. (1992). *Life and place: Relational science creating meanings*. Tokyo: NTT Publisher. (in Japanese)

Shimizu, H. (1996). *The logic of ba as knowledge of life: The logic of co-creation of Yagyu Shin-Kage-Ryu*. Tokyo: Chuo Koron. (in Japanese)

Shimizu, H. (2003). *The thoughts of ba: Creative stages of life*. Tokyo: University of Tokyo Press. (in Japanese)

Simon, H. A. (1957). *Administrative behaviour* (3rd ed.). New York: Free Press.

Suzuki, D. (1944). *The Japanese spirits*. Tokyo: Daito Publishing. (in Japanese)

Watsuji, T. (1934). *Ethics as the study on human beings*. Tokyo: Iwanami Shoten. (in Japanese)

Yamada, Y. (1985). *Ringi and nemawashi*. Tokyo: Kodansha. (in Japanese)

Yamagishi, T., & Yamagishi, M. (1994). Trust and commitment in the United States and Japan. *Motivation and Emotion*, *18*(2), 129–166. doi:10.1007/BF02249397

Yamamoto, S. (1983). *The study on "atmosphere"*. Tokyo: Bungei Shunju. (in Japanese)

Yuasa, Y. (1987). *The body: Toward an Eastern mind-body theory*. Albany, NY: State University of New York Press.

KEY TERMS AND DEFINITIONS

***ba*:** Can be interpreted as field, place, space, playground, forum, agora or occasion. In organisations entails a shared context or framework, made up of the borders of space and time in which knowledge is created, shared and used.

Japan: Country located in the Pacific Ocean that comprises by 6,852 islands. A major economic world player belonging to the G8, and a non-permanent member of the UN Security Council. Regarding knowledge management theories is well known the work of Nonaka and his colleagues.

Organisational Knowledge Creation: Multi-level process (because it involves all levels of an organisation) that intends to combine personal with existing organisational knowledge (or vice-versa) in order to produce new knowledge. The process is unique in each organisation, and in Japanese organisations is bounded to *ba*.

Organisational Knowledge Sharing: Other multi-level process which aims to facilitate knowledge transfer/sharing between all the individuals, as well as between the individual and the organisation (or vice-versa). Again, due to organisational culture the procedure is distinctive in every organisation, and in Japan is circumscribed to *ba*.

Socio-Cultural Characteristics: Cultural and social norms or, traditions that guide our basic behaviours within different contexts.

Chapter 2
What Does Knowledge Have to do with Ethics?

Chuck Huff
St. Olaf College, USA

ABSTRACT

In the same way that useful theory in knowledge management systems leads us to rethink the nature of knowledge (Spender & Scherer, 2007) a theory of ethics that is informed by current research in moral psychology will lead us to rethink the nature of ethical action. This chapter introduces a research program that has tracked ethical action among computer professionals and uses the insights from that research to make suggestions about how purposive moral action is undertaken and how it might be supported by knowledge management systems.

PROBLEMS, PURPOSES AND KNOWLEDGE

There is a consensus concerning the subject-matter of ethics so general that it would be tedious to document it. It is that the business of ethics is with "problems", i.e. situations in which it is difficult to know what one should do; that the ultimate beneficiary of ethical analysis is the person who, in one of these situations, seeks rational ground for the decision he must make; that ethics is therefore primarily concerned to find such grounds, often conceived of as moral rules and the principles from which they can be derived (Pincoffs, 1971, p. 552).

After claiming that it would be tedious to do so, Edmund Pincoffs' classic article on "Quandary Ethics" documents the extensive philosophical agreement that ethics is primarily about giving rational principles and procedures for solving moral problems, or "quandaries." This agreement on the nature of ethics is also foundational to agreed-upon goals for the practical and professional ethics curriculum (Callahan, 1980).

DOI: 10.4018/978-1-61520-873-9.ch002

If ethics is primarily about applying principles and procedures to make decisions in response to problems then what does knowledge have to do with it? Presumably, one needs to know the problem and the principles and then to apply the procedures. In much ethics teaching the problems are predefined by the cases, designed to highlight particular ethical principles, (Huff & Frey, 2005) and so not much effort is expended in defining the problem itself. Both in the classroom and on the job, the recommended procedure to define the problem is stakeholder analysis. Many decision support systems (e.g. Gotterbarn, 2001) use this approach to guide decision-making regarding the design of software systems. Thus, a knowledge management system to support such decisions would need to contain information about stakeholders and provide access to procedures and principles that could be applied to the problem.

This classic approach to ethics treats the problem as static and locates the expertise in the correct application of principles to the problem at hand. And the sort of knowledge needed to support such a process is relatively unproblematic factual knowledge that can be indexed and straightforwardly combined. In this approach, a knowledge management system to support ethical decisions should in principle be relatively simple to design and implement. It would include a structure to help the decision maker collect and organize the relevant factual knowledge, some processes that led the decision maker to evaluate various options in the decision space, and perhaps a way to systematize value tradeoffs in making a decision. This approach focuses the knowledge management system on the task of providing *decision support*, which in turn presumes that ethics is about the decisions one makes when confronted with a relevant choice.

But Pincoffs' (1971) early essay casts doubt on this approach to ethics and insists that being ethical is more than responding appropriately to isolated decision problems. Likewise, our recent research on moral exemplars in computing (Huff, Barnard & Frey, 2008a; 2008b) provides a picture of ethical careers that are not primarily composed of a series of ethical decisions, but instead are constructed over time in response to life goals, organizational and social constraints, and idiosyncratic attachment to particular ethical goals (e.g. help the customer or the handicapped, reform privacy laws or software design standards) (Huff & Rogerson, 2005).

The purpose of this short essay is to introduce this alternative notion of ethics, a conception that is rooted in planned action over the life of a career and based in the goals of the individual actor in their organizational context. We might call this a *purposive-action* approach as opposed to the *deliberative-decision* approach described above. If this is a better picture of ethical action in the modern organization, what are its implications for knowledge management systems that aim to support this sort of ethical action?

THE COMPLEXITY OF PURPOSIVE MORAL ACTION

The picture of purposeful moral action we present is based on the most recent work in moral psychology (Haidt, 2008; Huff & Frey, 2005; Lapsley & Narvaez, 2005; Narvaez & Lapsley, 2005) and on an analysis of extensive "life-story" interviews with moral exemplars in computing (Huff & Rogerson, 2005). The picture is not narrowly focused on how the individuals made isolated ethical decisions in particular circumstances. Instead, it is focused on how each one became the sort of person who was able to recognize opportunities for moral action, to plan the steps to take advantage of the opportunities, and then to carry out those plans in complex and conflicting social and organizational contexts. In psychological terms we are interested in how individuals achieve sustained excellence in ethical behavior in the field of computing. In philosophical terms we are interested in how individuals attain the virtues needed to achieve the virtuous practice of computing.

This model arises from our study of moral exemplars in computing (Huff & Barnard, 2008; Huff & Rogerson, 2005). In this research we did extensive interviews with individuals in the UK and Scandinavia who had been nominated as moral exemplars in the field of computing. An international panel with expertise in computing ethics nominated and approved all the exemplars. Criteria for nomination were:

1. Either a) a sustained commitment to moral ideals or ethical principles in computing that include a generalized respect for humanity, or b) sustained evidence of moral virtue in the practice of computing;
2. A disposition to make computing decisions in accord with one's moral ideals or ethical principles, implying also a consistency between one's actions and intentions and between the means and ends of one's actions;
3. A willingness to risk one's self-interest for the sake of one's moral values;
4. A tendency to be inspiring to other computing professionals and thereby to move them to moral action.

The final sample consisted of 24 individuals, including men and women, academics and those in industry and government, and people at the beginning and ends of their careers. Interviews ranged from 2 to 5 hours in length, spread across 2 days. Interviewees were asked to tell stories from their professional career (ranging from 19 to 30 stories each). These stories provide extensive detail about characters, goals, organizational contexts, personal feelings, strategic planning, and problem solving in the careers of people with a wide range of professional moral and ethical commitments.

Several striking findings from that work have shaped the theoretical position we outline here. First, we found that there was not a unitary profile of the way moral exemplars went about their work. There were, at least, two types: *reformers* who tried to change social systems and *craftspersons* who designed systems to help individuals. A significant number of the exemplars did not cleanly fit into either category. We expect that two types is not enough complexity to capture the variety of way our exemplars are pursuing moral goals. This leaves the likelihood that there are more types or forms of good computing. Each individual had a history of specific, even idiosyncratic, ethical commitments and purposes they were pursuing. From their perspective they were not trying to "make ethical decisions," but instead, they were designing systems for the handicapped, or designing privacy-enhancing software to change business-customer relationships, or supporting women in engineering, or changing the way safety-critical software was designed and evaluated, or supporting openness in software design. These purposes were the motivations for their actions and they varied dramatically from person to person. It was these purposes that organized and energized their moral action over their careers.

Occasionally they would talk of ethical deliberation at particular choice points in their careers (e.g. to take a job offer, accept a contract, to leave an organization). But most of their stories were about the pursuit of their purposes over time: forming goals and plans, gathering support from others in their networks, finding creative solutions to difficulties, regrouping when plans went awry. The skills and knowledge usually associated with ethical deliberation over choices were not often essential to these endeavors. Instead, we found that social skills (e.g. understanding other people) and technical skills (e.g. understanding database structures) more often featured as central in these stories.

Purposive moral action, undertaking long-term projects with ethical goals in mind, involves far more than simple decision making. It can take a variety of forms, have a variety of goals, and is supported by a variety of influences.

Influences on Purposive Ethical Action: PRIMES

This more complex picture of the moral actor as engaged in purposive action over time, within a social context, has lead us to construct a model of sustained moral action in social context (PRIMES). The model we present here (1) grounds moral action in relatively stable Personality characteristics, (2) guides moral action based on the Integration of Morality into the self-system, (3) shapes moral action by the context of the surrounding Moral Ecology, and (4) facilitates moral action with morally relevant Skills and knowledge (thus the PRIMES acronym). The model seeks to explain the daily performance of moral action of computing professionals and to illuminate ways that this ethical action might be supported and encouraged.

Personality

Personality clearly influences both the kinds of jobs that people undertake and the ways they go about their work (John & Srivastava, 1999). In our work, we have found that it influences the moral goals of our exemplars (Huff & Barnard, 2009). For instance, those who were more extraverted were more likely to choose goals that involved influencing organizations and systems in order to reform them. Thus, personality can serve as an anchoring point for moral inclination. Even so, personality can in turn be influenced by appropriate life experiences. New work in personality theory (Roberts, Walton, & Viechtbauer, 2006) suggests that personality can change over time, particularly when such change is reinforced by social roles (that is, moral ecology). Thus personality grounds, but does not solely determine moral character and action.

Integration of Morality into the Self

Much has been made of the centrality of moral commitment. But few theorists have spoken carefully about the components of moral commitment, how it is cultivated and achieved, and the ways that it influences moral action. Recent work in psychology can help us build a multi-faceted view of moral commitment as one component that guides moral action, but still is not solely determinative of it. Our picture of moral action among computing exemplars shows moral commitment appearing more like strategic goals that guide action over time, and less like isolated acts of willpower. These strategic goals are set apart from other goals in our exemplars by being so central to the individual's conception of who they are that they take precedence over many other goals. But they are not static. These strategic goals both influence and are influenced by the social and organizational surround and are themselves open to change over time.

Moral Ecology

Moral action is embedded in a social surround that can either support or thwart it. We call this social surround a moral ecology (Huff, Barnard, & Frey, 2008b), or more accurately, a system of interlinked moral ecologies. Countries, cultures, industries, companies, divisions, workgroups, mentorship networks, and professional organizations all have morally relevant expectations and pressures that constrain and sometimes support moral action. These values, expectations, and influences are embodied in rules, guidelines, and mission statements, but also in the structure of software, the design of buildings, the requirements of procedures, and the roles individuals in the organization adopt or are assigned. Individuals can enter and leave moral ecologies, can influence them, and can even act in defiance of them (Greene & Latting, 2004; van Es & Smit, 2003; Marnburg, 2000; Trevino, 1986). Knowing how to navigate in the relevant moral ecologies is a crucial skill for purposive moral action in an organization. But many of the moral exemplars told stories of significant time spent influencing moral ecologies in organizations or professional societies or in building smaller networks of "local climate" to support their plans. Moral ecologies thus constrain and support, but do not solely determine moral action.

Moral Skills and Knowledge

Much of what we call virtue is based in skills and knowledge of how to act in particular worlds (Lapsley & Narvaez, 2005). The highest praise we might summon for the morally committed incompetent would be "well intentioned" but certainly not "virtuous." Without these skills and knowledge, moral commitment would be impotent. Some of the skills and knowledge associated with successful moral action among our computing exemplars are listed in Table 1. The categories of skill and knowledge are based on a simplified version of the waterfall model of software design, and thus represent the kinds of tasks typically associated with the work of computer professionals. They encompass framing the work to be done, constructing creative solutions, testing those solutions, and finally implementing the solution. It is important to remember that the list in each set is composed of examples of relevant skills and knowledge. The particular skills and knowledge needed for any specific task can vary widely. As one might expect, the more abstract the description of the skill (e.g. "projecting oneself into the perspective of others") the more it will broadly apply. So the category labels are useful guides in understanding the structure of skills and knowledge in computing professionals, but less helpful in predicting the specific knowledge or skill needed in one application (e.g. understanding the privacy and job security concerns of Swedish union workers when designing a medical information system). In software design, where one might work on a range of different applications, some of the skills involve knowing how to seek out, acquire, and test the needed knowledge.

SKILLS, KNOWLEDGE, AND PURPOSEFUL MORAL ACTION

With the addition of the skills and knowledge component of the PRIMES model we can see where

Table 1. Skills and knowledge to support moral action (Adapted from Huff & Rogerson, 2005)

	Moral Imagination	**Moral Creativity**
Skills	Constructing the relevant stakeholders in a socio-technical system; data collection about stakeholders; understanding stakeholder perspectives	Identifying value conflicts in a socio-technical system; constructing and evaluating solutions under constraint
Knowledge	Specific knowledge about the domain (e.g. privacy, safety, equity); knowledge of socio-technical systems; knowledge of methods to investigate stakeholder perspectives	Specific knowledge about domains (e.g. privacy, safety, equity); technical knowledge of constraints and opportunities; knowledge of socio-technical systems
	Reasonableness	**Perseverance**
Skills	Constructing data-based and reasoned arguments; engaging in reasoned dialogue, gathering relevant evidence, listening to others, giving reasons, changing plans/positions based on reason	specific knowledge about domain (e.g. privacy, safety, equity); technical knowledge of constraints and opportunities; knowledge of ethical argumentation
Knowledge	Constructing and revising implementation plans based on organizational constraints. Negotiation within complex organizational environments	Specific knowledge about domain (e.g. privacy, safety, equity); knowledge of socio-technical systems; knowledge of ethical dissent and whistleblowing

Moral Imagination: projecting oneself into the perspective of others;
Moral Creativity: generating solutions to moral challenges while responding to multiple constraints;
Reasonableness: engaging in reasoned dialogue with openness;
Perseverance: planning moral action and responding to unforeseen circumstances while keeping moral goals intact.

the management of knowledge and the design of knowledge management systems might fit in the picture of purposive moral action. The PRIMES model delineates at least two categories where support could be helpful: not surprisingly, skills and knowledge, but also moral ecology.

Identifying Skills and Knowledge for Ethical Action

If we could compile an agreed upon list of skills and knowledge that aid the expression of moral decision making and performance, then it would be relatively straightforward to determine the sort of support they require and to include this support in knowledge management systems. But compiling a useful, generalizable list has proven more difficult than it sounds. Many have recently contributed to the discussion concerning moral skill sets, and their respective lists of skills differ from one another both in structure and content, despite many common themes (see Huff, Barnard & Frey, 2008b for several lists). Blasi (2005, pp. 70) notes that lists of skills tend to be "invariably long ... easily extended, and are largely unsystematic." Even where two authors agree on some of the same skills, they categorize them differently and use different terminology to describe the same skill.

This difficulty in determining a canonical set of skill sets is understandable, once one recognizes the variety of moral goals and moral ecologies that influence moral action. Different people with different moral goals and in different ecologies will need different skills and knowledge to achieve their goals. Thus, it is doubtful that a canonical list of skill sets could be created or that it should even be attempted. We can take some solace in the knowledge that as one is more concrete in specifying goals (e.g. protecting the privacy of the Swedish hospital workers mentioned above), the specific kinds of support that would be needed to accomplish those goals become more clear (e.g. knowledge of Swedish privacy law, empirical methods to understand the role of Swedish hospital workers, etc.).

Thus, though there may be a more general subset of skills and knowledge that support ethical action broadly, it is likely that skills and knowledge (and even commitment) are more domain specific. This domain specificity helps us to understand how individuals can carry out worthy ethical projects in one domain, and yet be found wanting in others.

Thus the success and structure of purposive moral action in one domain may well differ from those in other domains. In addition, the local moral ecology can alter the structure of moral action from one ecology to another. Work by Frey & O'Neill-Carillo (in press) suggests, for example, that in Caribbean countries where significant corruption is found, even individuals who simply want to adopt the goal of being good *craftspersons* may well find themselves of necessity engaging in reform of the system (in the form, for example, of whistleblowing). In addition, the structure of work in a profession or organization may well alter the kind of skills (and certainly the knowledge) required for successful moral action in that profession or organization. The work of our computing moral exemplars consists, for the most part, of planning, creating, testing, and implementing particular products. This is design work and requires something like the skill and knowledge sets listed in Table 1. The organization of table one is based on a simplified "waterfall design" from software development, and thus both the structure and content of the skills and knowledge are tailored to the context of design work. However, individuals in other occupations are engaged in differently structured work (e.g. the direct provision of service). We expect that inductive approaches to compiling a skills and knowledge inventory will find these differently structured professions to have different sets of skill and knowledge.

Again this has implications for the design of KM systems. If the skills and knowledge in moral action in software design are different from those required for moral action in direct service, then a KM system would have to reflect those differences, perhaps even in the structure of work flow and the kinds of knowledge indexed. This is not a trivial task. The idea is that there may well be no general-purpose KM system for ethical/moral action within a profession (since there are different goals even within the profession) and most likely no general-purpose KM system that would work across professions.

Swimming Upstream: Whistleblowing and Reform in Organizations

Another issue for the construction of knowledge management systems to support purposive moral action is the variety of purposes that the moral actor can adopt. One of the moral exemplars in our sample characterized the theme of his career as "swimming upstream." Invariably, the positions he adopted in organizations and in research direction were initially unpopular, but his persistence and skill in building supportive networks often allowed him to successfully challenge the received wisdom. This story of working within an organization to influence, adapt, and even challenge an organization' goals are not uncommon among our exemplars. This kind of moral excellence, then, often consists in going against the grain of at least the proximate goals of an organization. As the director of an academic program, our "upstream swimmer" shared higher order goals (e.g. designing and delivering good education) with his organization. But his vision for his program was substantially different (and ultimately successful). How can an organization (or a knowledge management system) anticipate and support such excellence when it occasionally runs counter to proximate organizational goals?

There are harder cases than the successful internal entrepreneur. The classic hard case is that of whistleblowing. Here, the proximate goal of the individual (exposing wrongdoing or changing organizational policy) runs explicitly counter to that of the organization. There are arguments to be made that supporting whistleblowing, or ethical dissent, is in fact in the interest of the organization (Near & Miceli, 1995). And there are recommendations for the construction of support systems for whistleblowing (Greene & Latting, 2004). But this kind of support consists less of providing static information to the individual and more of providing access to organizational networks, procedures, and resources. Ethical dissent in an organization requires support to be successful, and the support is consists not of traditional access to information, but rather what one might call *instrumenting the Moral Ecology*.

Designers of knowledge management systems are not, of course, ignorant of the need to provide access to people and procedures (Spender & Scherer, 2007). But it is interesting to note that in the moral domain as well as in other organizational support domain, access to static knowledge is not enough to support the complexity of action. Thus the greatest benefit that might come from KM systems in organizational life might be to instrument the moral ecology to provide support for ethical dissent.

CAN WE MANAGE SUPPORT FOR ETHICAL PERFORMANCE?

Thus we now find two places to anchor knowledge management for purposive moral action: (1) the skills and knowledge associated with a profession or goal set and (2) access to the moral ecology to support purposive moral action. This is a substantially different picture of the moral actor from that of "quandary ethics." It is not limited to decision-making or judgment and is as complex and long term in structure and goals as most other organizational activity. We thus need to think anew about moral action in organizations to discover how to support it with knowledge management systems. Useful knowledge management approaches derive their usefulness, at least in part, from the extent to which they make us think anew about knowledge (Spender & Scherer, 2007). And in this case, we need to think anew about the knowledge that supports ethical/moral action.

What knowledge management systems do, in fact, is help to support practice *in the absence of knowledge*, or "supporting imaginative practice" in knowledge workers (Spender & Scherer, 2007). This is also what moral exemplars do, act with skill in the face of a lack of knowledge. To support this imaginative practice, knowledge management systems should provide access to explicit and implicit knowledge, social relationships, organizational processes, and relatively straightforward things like standards and best practices. The variety of skills and knowledge in Table 1 corresponds to the similar variety in the sorts of things identified as knowledge in current theory on Knowledge management systems. And KM systems that support the acquisition, indexing, and access to knowledge that supports moral action could indeed be thought of as ethical KM systems.

CONCLUSION: RECONSTRUCTING ETHICAL ACTION AND ETHICAL KNOWLEDGE

It seems hopeful that in thinking carefully about ethics and knowledge management systems, we have had to rethink purposive moral action. This parallels the rethinking that knowledge management theorists have been doing about the nature of knowledge and work (see, for example, Spender & Scherer, 2007; or, Nonaka, 1991). The ethical actor is not a passive recipient of a pre-packaged decision space. Instead he or she must shape the decision, and the organization, in light of proximate and long-term goals and imaginatively construct and implement solutions, often in the absence of explicit knowledge about the right course of action. It is this more complex view of moral action that should be our guide in thinking about the role of knowledge management systems in supporting moral action.

We may well find that KM systems that support moral action in an application area are, indeed, simply those that best support the actors in doing their work well. The implication is that acting morally is not a general-purpose thing one does while doing other work. It is a thing that is inherent in the way one goes about the work itself, and the goals one chooses and skills one possesses. If so, then we are unlikely to see any useful generic "ethics knowledge management system" that can be applied in any profession or organization. Instead, we will need KM systems to incorporate a concern for the ethical aspects of action within each of the areas. In this respect, we might then say that "all ethics is local."

REFERENCES

Blasi, A. (2005). Moral character: A psychological approach. In Lapsley, D. K., & Power, F. C. (Eds.), *Character Psychology and Character Education* (pp. 67–100). Notre Dame, IN: University of Notre Dame.

Callahan, D. (1980). Goals in the teaching of ethics. In Callahan, D., & Bok, S. (Eds.), *Teaching Ethics in Higher Education* (pp. 61–74). New York: Plenum.

Frey, W., & O'Neill-Carillo, E. (in press). Engineering ethics in Puerto Rico: Issues and narratives. *Science and Engineering Ethics*.

Gotterbarn, D. (2001). Reducing software failures using software development impact statements. *Australasian Journal of Information Management Systems*, *9*(2), 155–165.

Greene, A. D., & Latting, J. K. (2004). Whistleblowing as a form of advocacy: Guidelines for the practitioner and organization. *Social Work*, *49*(2), 219–230.

Haidt, J. (2008). Morality. *Perspectives on Psychological Science*, *3*(1), 65–72.

Huff, C. W., & Barnard, L. (2008). Good computing: Life stories of moral exemplars in the computing profession. *IEEE Computers and Society*, *28*(3), 47–54.

Huff, C. W., Barnard, L., & Frey, W. (2008a). Good computing: A pedagogically focused model of virtue in the practice of computing (part 1). *Journal of Information. Communication and Ethics in Society*, *6*(3), 246–278. doi:10.1108/14779960810916246

Huff, C. W., Barnard, L., & Frey, W. (2008b). Good computing: A pedagogically focused model of virtue in the practice of computing (part 2). *Journal of Information. Communication and Ethics in Society*, *6*(4), 284–316. doi:10.1108/14779960810921114

Huff, C. W., & Frey, W. (2005). Moral pedagogy and practical ethics. *Science and Engineering Ethics*, *11*(3), 1–20. doi:10.1007/s11948-005-0008-1

Huff, C. W., & Rogerson, S. (2005). Craft and reform in moral exemplars in computing. In Collste, G. (Eds.), *ETHICOMP 2005: Looking Back to the Future (CD: paper 30)*. Linkoping, Sweden: Linkoping University.

John, O. P., & Srivastava, S. (1999). The big five trait taxonomy: History, measurement, and theoretical perspectives. In Pervin, L. A., & John, O. P. (Eds.), *Handbook of Personality: Theory and Research* (pp. 139–153). New York: Guilford.

Lapsley, D. K., & Narvaez, D. (2005). Moral psychology at the crossroads. In Lapsley, D. K., & Power, F. C. (Eds.), *Character Psychology and Character Education* (pp. 18–35). Notre Dame, IN: University of Notre Dame.

Marnburg, E. (2000). The behavioral effects of corporate ethical codes: Empirical findings and discussion. *Business Ethics (Oxford, England)*, *9*(3), 200–210. doi:10.1111/1467-8608.00191

Narvaez, D., & Lapsley, D. (2005). The psychological foundations of everyday morality and moral expertise. In Lapsley, D. K., & Power, F. C. (Eds.), *Character Psychology and Character Education* (pp. 140–165). Notre Dame, IN: University of Notre Dame.

Near, J., & Miceli, M. P. (1995). Effective whistle-blowing. *Academy of Management Review*, *3*(20), 679–708. doi:10.2307/258791

Nonaka, I. (1991). The knowledge creating company. *Harvard Business Review*, *69*(November-December), 96–104.

Pincoffs, E. L. (1971). Quandary ethics. *Mind*, *80*(320), 552–571. doi:10.1093/mind/LXXX.320.552

Roberts, B. W., Walton, K., & Viechtbauer, W. (2006). Patterns of mean-level change in personality traits across the life course: A meta-analysis of longitudinal studies. *Psychological Bulletin*, *132*(1), 1–25. doi:10.1037/0033-2909.132.1.1

Spender, J.-C., & Scherer, A. G. (2007). The philosophical foundations of knowledge management: Editors Introduction. *Organization*, *14*(1), 5–28. doi:10.1177/1350508407071858

Treviño, L. K. (1986). Ethical decision making in organizations: A person-situation interactionist model. *Academy of Management Review*, *11*(3), 601–617. doi:10.2307/258313

van Es, R., & Smit, G. (2003). Whistleblowing and media logic: A case study. *Business Ethics (Oxford, England)*, *12*(2), 144–150. doi:10.1111/1467-8608.00314

KEY TERMS AND DEFINITIONS

Craftspersons: Individuals who design systems to help others (e.g. to help the handicapped or to help clients).

Moral Action: How individuals achieve sustained excellence in ethical behavior within a domain (e.g. the domain of computing).

Moral Exemplars: Individuals that dedicate a significant amount of their resources to fulfill their moral obligations, follow their enthusiasm for service, and inspire others to do the same.

Moral Skills: Skills directly related to the ability of an individual to take moral action.

Reformers: Individuals who try to change social systems.

Whistleblowing: Premeditated, intentional disclosure of personal or organizational misconduct by a person who has or had access to data, events or information.

Section 2
Societal Knowledge Management

"He who exercises government by means of his virtue may be compared to the north polar star, which keeps its place and all the stars turn towards it"
Confucius

"Societal" knowledge management has been widely recognized, however the democratic concern for the people, by the people was been neglected. This is consistent with the supremacy of economic and cultural knowledge management (Western society). As a result, instead of embracing a "north polar star" (humanist and democratic), the global knowledge flux has become a "black hole" (nothing escapes and enables a deformation on knowledge society). These ethical and social dilemmas are even enhanced when bureaucracy resumes the political environment.

Chapter 3
Knowledge Management and Democracy:
A Critical Review of Some Moral Issues and Social Dilemmas

Krystyna Górniak-Kocikowska
Southern Connecticut State University, USA

ABSTRACT

The main problem discussed in this chapter is the question of compatibility between knowledge management in the knowledge economy and democracy in the ICT-driven global society. The assumption is made that democracy is the dominant form of organizing the global society on a variety of levels; and that it is regarded as desirable and morally superior in comparison with other such forms.

INTRODUCTION

When seen from a certain perspective, the problem of knowledge management and democracy- which is the chief subject of this essay- has a long history. However, I will discuss it mainly as it occurs in its most recent form, i.e., as it occurs in today's ICT-driven *global* society. Unfortunately, I will explore this problem almost exclusively from the "western" point of view due to both my inadequate familiarity with "non-western" societies as well as the restrictions to the length of this text. Nevertheless, I would like the Reader to be aware of the fact that a truly global context brings to this matter a richness of issues not mentioned in this essay, both important and interesting, which certainly need a thorough inquiry and which could shed new light on many aspects of the subject of knowledge management and democracy in the ICT-driven global society.

DOI: 10.4018/978-1-61520-873-9.ch003

There are certain concepts that are perceived as quite obvious and self-explanatory today, although they would be highly doubtful or controversial a few years ago. Twenty, or even just ten years back, some of them might not have even been in existence. For instance, the term *knowledge economy* gained popularity only as recently as the second half of the 1990s, apparently first in New Zealand, according to the World Bank website (The World Bank, 2009). Today, knowledge economy is almost a household name. Likewise, it seems that there isn't much doubt anymore that humankind entered the phase of *global society*. Yet, the global society is still not even well established; rather, it is in the process of becoming. It moves through its own formative period; its final shape is presently hard to predict.

The same applies to one of the foundations of the global society, namely *Information and Communication Technology* (or Technologies, as some prefer), hereafter referred to as ICT. It too is a relatively new phenomenon in its present form, although information and communication belong to the most ancient forms of human activity (Górniak-Kocikowska, 2008; 2007; 2005). Computers and other forms of digital technology which became the main components of ICT changed it so profoundly that the change can be safely declared as revolutionary, and ICT of today is justifiably seen as a very powerful *new* technology.

Knowledge management and several other concepts and processes which will be the subject of this essay have an even more recent presence in our "collective consciousness". Some of them are still "fuzzy"- their exact meaning has not been fully agreed upon yet. It is possible that the meaning ascribed to them today will not last; either because they will change to the point that the present understanding will cease to be correct, or because a better way of describing them will be found.

The definition of *democracy* used in this chapter covers notions like "government by the people" as well as "a state of society characterized by formal equality of rights and privileges", and also "political and social equality, democratic spirit" (Webster's Dictionary, 1996). A democratic global society would be, therefore, truly of the people, by the people, and for the people; whereas "the people" would include all humans.

The idea of democracy, unlike knowledge management and knowledge economy, has been a "staple" of western civilization for a very long time, although its definition evolved over the ages to take its present-day form as quoted above. There is a general agreement that it originated in Ancient Greece; and it had its devoted supporters and fierce opponents ever since. Although there have always been groups which were functioning on the principles of democracy they usually did not play a dominant role in society at large (one of the exceptions has been the *nobles' democracy* in Polish-Lithuanian Commonwealth which lasted several centuries and had a profound, not always positive, impact on the history of these nations). Most of the time, communities organized on the principle of democracy were treated as utopian social experiments. This situation started to change rapidly by the end of the 18th century, especially after the founding of the United States of America. Since then, democracy both as a theoretical concept and in its practical function progressed in the field of politics and in many other areas of public life worldwide. This progress accelerated in recent years due largely to the wide-spread use and rapid advance of ICT, which serve as news, information, knowledge, and opinion-sharing devices. Today, democracy can be rightfully regarded as a dominant form of social organization in the global society, especially with regard to political structures and organizations. In the area of political and social theory, too, democracy is favored as the best form of social organization, especially from the ethical standpoint. It is widely believed that democracy serves best the flourishing of human beings who treasure individual freedom, dignity, and actively practice self-perfection while believing that all their fellow humans should have the same rights as they do.

One of the questions emerging from what I have written above is the question of *compatibility* between knowledge management and democracy. When considering the title of the book this essay was written for, *Ethical Issues and Social Dilemmas in Knowledge Management: Organizational Innovation*, it seemed to me that one of the most urgent and daunting tasks regarding organizational innovation within knowledge management is making sure that knowledge management is built on the principle of democracy. Not fulfilling this task would almost certainly result in the emergence of several quite serious "ethical issues and social dilemmas", or in the deepening of the ones already in existence (Costa & Silva, 2007). For this reason, the question of compatibility of knowledge management and democracy is the question which I will primarily focus my attention to in this text. In order to establish the foundation of this endeavor, I shall first refer to definitions of some crucial terms used in this essay. I think it is necessary to do so because some of these terms are defined in a variety of ways. I would like the Reader to follow my train of thought knowing which definition I have in mind when I use a particular term.

KNOWLEDGE MANAGEMENT

There are quite a few definitions of *knowledge management*; they differ in details but the differences do not matter much for this essay. I selected- rather arbitrarily, I have to admit- for the purpose of this paper the definition according to which knowledge management is understood as an "integrated, systematic process for identifying, collecting, storing, retrieving, and transforming *information* and *knowledge assets* (including previously unarticulated expertise and experience held by individuals) into *knowledge* that is readily accessible in order to improve the performance of the organization" (Competitive Intelligence Glossary, 2009).

Knowledge management, defined in the way presented above is a fairly recent phenomenon, generated mostly by the shift from industrial (or agrarian-industrial) to post-industrial mode of production of wealth which took place in some societies in the second half of the 20th century. Presently, knowledge management is associated mostly with the field of business activities. One has to remember, though, that as long as there has been knowledge- whether organized, institutional, or otherwise- there were some forms of knowledge management exercised for public/institutional (in the sense of societal institutions and organizations) or private/individual purposes. In the past, knowledge management only very rarely was used directly in business enterprises in a conscious, purposeful and methodical way.

Today, unlike in the past, knowledge management is of great interest to the world of business. From the business perspective, one can be interested in knowledge management for two main reasons:

a. when knowledge is a tool used to manage particular business procedures (this is the reason indicated in the above quoted definition of knowledge management). In this case, the concept of knowledge management applies to already existing knowledge (and information); the definition quoted earlier is quite clear about it;
b. when knowledge itself is a commodity- a commodity that needs to be managed. In this case, the situation in more complicated. The management of *knowledge as a commodity* involves all three main processes the subject of which is knowledge namely, production (creation), storage (preservation) and distribution (dissemination).

This overlaps partly with knowledge management described in point A, where the basic goal is- according to the definition quoted earlier- "to improve the performance of the organization", which most often means: to maximize the organization's profits; but the scope of the entire process is much more complex and wide-spread than that. The management of knowledge as a commodity belongs also to the area of *knowledge economy*. Knowledge management as part of knowledge economy is of primary interest in this chapter.

KNOWLEDGE ECONOMY

Although Francis Bacon had already claimed in 1597 that "knowledge itself is power", and although at the time of the industrial revolution not only the economists but even poets were well aware of knowledge as an economic factor ("Grace is given of God, but knowledge is bought in the market", Arthur Hugh Clough, *The Bothie of Tober-na-Vuolich*), this was still quite a marginal factor. "For the last two hundred years, neo-classical economics has recognized only two factors of production: labor and capital" (Riley, 2003). It was only in the late 20th century that the commoditization of knowledge became fully and openly recognized. In the words of Luc Soete, "since the early 1980s, the economic profession has started to recognize the fact that knowledge accumulation can to a large extent be analyzed like the accumulation of any other capital good. That one can apply economic principles to the *production* and *exchange* of knowledge; that it is intrinsically endogenous to the economic and social system (…)" (Soete, 2002, pp. 36).

There are many definitions of knowledge economy. According to the same source which supplied the definition of knowledge management quoted earlier, *knowledge economy* (or, as it is sometimes called, knowledge-based economy or knowledge-driven economy) "is based on the production, distribution, and use of *knowledge* as the main driver of growth, wealth creation, and employment across all industries. It does not rely solely on a few advanced-technology industries but is applicable to traditional industries, such as mining and agriculture" (Competitive Intelligence Glossary, 2009). Another definition, similarly, claims that knowledge economy is an economy "in which the generation and exploitation of knowledge play the predominant part in the creation of wealth" (Ministry of Economical Development, 2006).

Let me quote just one other source because it is defining knowledge economy more bluntly than the above-quoted definitions do, namely as an "economy based on creating, evaluating, and trading knowledge" (Business Dictionary, 2009).

As I mentioned earlier, and as the above-quoted definitions show quite clearly, in the case of terms like this, that is for instance, knowledge management or knowledge economy, the definitions are more often than not still not "set in stone". They vary from source to source. Sometimes, the differences between these definitions are insignificant, but sometimes they are quite substantial. Case in point: Martin Boddy (2005) discusses not only a variety of existing definitions of knowledge economy, but he also presents the criteria for including an industry's activity into belonging- and to what degree- to knowledge economy. He relies heavily on the data provided by the Organization for Economic Co-operation and Development (OECD), one of the primary "movers and shakers" in the post-World War II economy [Boddy cites as his source: OECD (2003)]. Boddy notices that as recently as 2003, the OECD's definition of knowledge economy *excluded* "both higher education and hospital-based activities, both of which are considered to represent knowledge-intensive sectors in terms of both skills and the application of knowledge and outputs" (Boddy, 2005, pp. 7). Further in his text Boddy specified: "OECD (2003) does not include education or health in *knowledge-based services* as such on the basis that data are not available for all countries. It does however; include education and health separately in its country tables of technology and knowledge-intensive industries- indicative of the importance of these two sectors in this context" (Boddy, 2005, pp. 16). The exclusion of higher education as well as health care from the category of knowledge-based industries by an organization as influential and as "trend-setting" as OECD is very interesting from the point of view of the subject of this essay. Even more important are the reasons: "data are not available for all countries". Depending on the kind of criteria accepted for the decision-making process, this may make perfect sense- or not (Boddy himself changed the selection criteria for his own report into which he included *Higher Education* and *Hospital Activities* on the grounds of "the availability of data for the UK" (Boddy, 2005, pp. 17).

The above paragraph supports the argument that:

a. knowledge economy is presently a very important phenomenon; but it is still in its infancy;
b. the concept of knowledge economy is quite "fluid", its boundaries are "fuzzy", and it is sometimes re-defined to suit the purpose of a particular agent (researcher, administrator, politician, etc.);
c. institutions of production (creation), storage (preservation) and distribution (dissemination) of knowledge, e.g., institutions of higher education are not always included in the concept of knowledge economy. This may happen- as the case of the decision made by OECD shows- for reasons which are arbitrary and "bureaucratic" rather than theoretical, or conceptual. Yet, decisions like this may have a big impact on the theory of knowledge economy, and on the research in this area.

KNOWLEDGE

Thus far, neither knowledge management nor knowledge economy has turned out to be easy to define, to "pinpoint". There are many "gray areas" in the definitions which mean that a cautious treatment of both phenomena is advisable. But there is yet another difficulty in dealing with knowledge management and knowledge economy in a conceptual way. This difficulty is caused by the concept of *knowledge*, in particular, the difficulty with defining knowledge itself; a difficulty often acknowledged by authors who write about knowledge management and knowledge economy.

For the purpose of this essay, I have chosen to use one of the standard definitions of knowledge (unsurprisingly, there are many). According to this definition, knowledge is a "justified and true belief" (Quinton, 1972). This is a very basic and general definition, and as such, it is not very helpful in a detailed investigation. On the other hand, exactly because it is so general, this definition gives quite a clear image of how vast the area is denoted by the term "knowledge". Moreover, while the authors of definitions of "knowledge management" and "knowledge economy" often notice the difference between knowledge and *information* (see, e.g., the definition of knowledge management quoted earlier in this essay) they rarely pay attention to the difference between knowledge and *belief*; unlike Anthony Quinton (1972) in his definition of knowledge and in the text from which this definition was quoted. There are, of course, other important problems related to this issue, like, for example, the problem of knowledge and *certainty*, the problem of *truth* and the like. They may all have substantial influence on issues within knowledge management and knowledge economy; sometimes without the experts in these areas even being aware of them. As interesting and important as these problems are, however, I will not focus on them here due to the lack of space.

Like democracy, the phenomenon of knowledge has been an object of interest to scholars, especially philosophers, for a very long time- in western civilization at least since Ancient Greece. With time, especially after the Scientific Revolution, the problem of knowledge actually gained in importance to the point that epistemology (philosophical theory of knowledge) eventually became the leading branch of philosophy. Knowledge is also a very prominent subject of investigation in some other disciplines, like psychology, sociology and linguistics, to name but a few.

Such a wide range of disciplines investigating the problem of knowledge is due largely to the fact that knowledge is both a personal (private) as well as a societal (public) phenomenon; and that the two areas, far from being identical, overlap. Within personal knowledge, two types of knowledge could be of interest here: self-knowledge (or, as John Locke called it, consciousness) and private knowledge (knowledge kept to oneself, not revealed to others). Again, these two areas partly overlap; there are also other types of personal knowledge, and they are all interconnected and stimulate each other. Likewise, the societal knowledge (part of which what was sometimes called the "collective consciousness") is a tremendously complex phenomenon. The dynamics of the relations between these two areas of knowledge, personal and societal, heavily influence most of the social, political and economic phenomena, and also individual human lives. In organized social structures, among others in business organizations, these two basic types of knowledge with all their complexities meet in dynamic interaction, sometimes to the point of dramatic clashes.

One of the foundations of the modern concept of knowledge, and certainly the theoretical underpinning of modern science is the idea of democracy- understood in terms of the equality of human individuals *qua* humans- and the problem of personal (individual) knowledge. Ever since René Descartes, the "proper" method of scientific inquiry with its requirement of careful, thorough, rational verification assumes the equality of humans in this sense: it assumes the ability of every single human individual with a normally functioning brain to think rationally, and to be capable of learning to think according to certain rules, notably, the rules of logical reasoning, and to use this kind of thinking skillfully in a problem-solving process. Once equipped with the right set of tools (the mastery of rational/logical thinking) an individual should also be able to follow and/or to re-create the thinking of another human individual; a thinking which would be based on the same rules. This way, they can all participate in the process of creation, preservation, and dissemination of knowledge. Verifying the correctness of the thought-process of other individuals engaged in the solving of the same problem allows validation and acceptance of the results of the said process. This concept of "democracy of knowledge" purposefully excluded human emotions and individual characteristics, and today it is largely outdated for this exact reason. However, the idea that every human individual (except for individuals with no cognitive functions of the brain and no motor functions of the body) is capable of some form of knowledge is widely accepted based on studies done by psychologists, physiologists, neuroscientists and other scholars.

As interesting as the problem of knowledge is, however, this essay is not devoted to the subject of knowledge (or scientific knowledge for that matter) *per se*; therefore, I will not develop it any further. The point I am making here by bringing the issue of knowledge to the Reader's attention is that both knowledge management and knowledge economy in their present form can only apply to a very restricted area of the vast phenomenon called knowledge. This alone makes them both vulnerable to all kinds of criticism, unless they deal with a rather restricted field of human activities and use a very clear and narrow definition of knowledge. In this case, however, to define them as *knowledge* economy and *knowledge* management would be rather presumptuous, wouldn't it?

The problem of knowledge is obviously an important one; not only for the issue of knowledge management (don't we want to know what is to be managed?), but for humankind in general. Knowledge is fundamental to humankind's flourishing. Even this statement, however, could be questioned; some would say that only the *right kind* of knowledge is fundamental to humankind's flourishing. Not all knowledge is equally valuable.

Some philosophers (for instance, Plato, Friedrich Nietzsche, Roderick Chisholm, and others) claimed, explicitly or implicitly, that epistemology could be reduced to ethics. The reasoning for this case can be presented in a very simplified way in the following manner. Truth is a value;

generally speaking, truth is a "positive" value ("truth is *good*")- this is an ethical judgment. If knowledge is about truth (if it is a "justified and true belief" as claims the definition quoted earlier), seeking knowledge means seeking, identifying, and promoting the good. If one continued this reasoning the next step would be to ask the question: Does it mean, then, that *knowledge economy* and *knowledge management* are about seeking, identifying, and promoting the good? Does it mean, further, that knowledge economy and knowledge management belong to the field of *ethics*? Is this what their purpose is- to contribute to the moral betterment of humankind? They both belong in the field of business. Would it mean that spreading ethics is the purpose of business? What *is* the purpose of business?

WHAT IS THE PURPOSE OF BUSINESS?

Richard Field wrote, "in my job as a university professor, the question sometimes arises in class discussions about the purpose of business. One usual answer is *to make money*, but I don't think that is right" (Field, 2002). This quotation, it seems to me, encapsulates the core of the problem we are dealing with here. Is the purpose of business to make money? Or are there some values other than money which should be the fundamental goal of business? (I mean business in general, not the purpose one points to in answer to the question, "What is the purpose of *your* business?" An answer to this particular question should be corollary to the answer about the purpose of business in general).

Rakesh Khurana of Harvard Business School in Boston, Massachusetts and Herb Gintis of the Central European University in Budapest, Hungary, present a view similar to the view of Richard Field of the University of Alberta, Canada, quoted earlier in the essay. They argue that- although a wide-spread view among the business students is that the purpose of business is to make money- this is not what the primary goal of business *should* be (Khurana & Gintis, 2008). Moreover, this is not what used to be the purpose of business, at least in business theory. They cite Joseph Wharton, the founder of The Wharton School at the University of Pennsylvania in Philadelphia. Wharton expected that those who graduate from the school will "aid in maintaining sound financial *morality*" (Khurana & Gintis, 2008, pp. 55). He founded his school in 1881. But, the authors continue, "over the last century, however, business schools have placed less emphasis on a socially driven objective" (Khurana & Gintis, 2008, pp. 55).

It seems there are many people today (I don't want to say a "majority"), not only business school students, who think the purpose of business is to make money. Some people think this is the only purpose of business. And there are people (I don't want to say a "minority") who think that making money is not- or should not- be the only purpose of business; some even think that making money shouldn't be the most important part of business. Who is right? Who is wrong? Whose view will prevail? Who of these people has or will have the power to make decisions in the area of knowledge management? Who makes and will make the decisions in the knowledge economy and thus will be shaping the future of the global society?

Things are further complicated by the fact that often the same phrases are used to express quite different thoughts (this, of course, happens everywhere, not only in the world of business). Case in point: Lord John Browne, the Chief Executive Officer of British Petroleum said in his speech given at MIT in 2006: "I don't think that a business which just generated money would be a very good business". And further: "I believe that a good successful business is part of society, and exists to meet society's needs. That is the purpose of business at the highest level" (Browne, 2006). This sounds quite similar to the words spoken in 1925 by Wallace B. Donham, the dean of Harvard Business School. According to Khurana & Gintis, "Donham noted that the world's problems would not be solved through governmental or police intervention, but from within on a higher ethical plane" (Khurana & Gintis, 2008, pp. 55). The topic of Donhan's speech was *The Social Significance of Business*. But Lord Browne- after making his statement about meeting society's needs being the "purpose of business at the highest level"- proceeded in justifying BP's project to build a pipeline to transport oil (and another one for natural gas) from Baku, Azerbaijan, through Iran and Turkey, and emphasizing the need of security (military security) related to this project. Would that be an action taken "from within on a higher ethical plane" like Donhan wanted a business action to be? For my part, I have some doubts.

I would like to remind the Reader that, as mentioned earlier in this essay, the powerful multinational organization OECD excluded from its 2003 definition of knowledge economy the sectors of health care and higher education. Let's juxtapose this with the- rhetorical, I think- question asked by Khurana & Gintis (2008): "when business schools produce graduates who are unsure of the primary objective of business in society, how can society know exactly what role business schools play in the world?" (p. 54).

Now the problem I see here is this. OECD does not include higher education in knowledge economy. Business schools are part of the higher education system. Business schools are supposed to educate people for the knowledge economy- assuming, as I do, that knowledge economy will dominate the economy of the ICT-driven global society- but they are not part of this economy, according to OECD. Moreover, business schools "produce graduates who are unsure of the primary objective of business in society" (Khurana & Gintis, 2008, pp. 54). So now the graduates of business schools, "unsure of the primary objective of business in society" will make decisions about *knowledge* (i.e., about the production, storage, and distribution of knowledge in society). They will have to if they are to be active in the knowledge economy, and they will make these decisions- if it is true that knowledge economy is the economy of the future. What will they be guided by while making decisions? How will they *manage* knowledge? What a mess (The Reader is most likely not surprised to know that Khurana & Gintis rejoice at the fact that "a few business schools have returned to the *socially constructive* objectives set out by Joseph Wharton, Wallace Donham, and other founders of business education" (Khurana & Gintis, 2008, pp. 55). The objectives they have in mind are the ones cited earlier in this essay; the ones which focus on the ethical aspect of business.

So where are we at this point? The definitions of knowledge management and knowledge economy are not satisfactory enough; knowledge is such a vast issue that it can only be defined either very broadly or- if specified- with large parts of it left out; and there is no agreement as to what the purpose of business is. What about knowledge in society at large?

KNOWLEDGE ECONOMY VERSUS KNOWLEDGE SOCIETY: THE PROBLEM OF SHARING

Today, one almost takes it for granted that ICT is global. Therefore, the society of the ICT era can be rightly called the Global ICT-driven Society- a global society supported by a technology which is applied universally all over the world.

This new, global society is also often called the *knowledge society* (and its economy- the knowledge economy). The knowledge society is sometimes called the "knowledge and information society" as well. Knowledge society will be understood here as "a society endowed with the ability and capacity to generate and capture new knowledge and to access, absorb and use effectively information and ICTs" (d'Orville, 2000).

At times, "knowledge society" and "knowledge economy" seem almost to be synonymous, but they are not. It does matter whether we use the term "knowledge society" or "knowledge economy", even though sometimes it might be difficult to notice the difference between these two terms because at least since the time of Adam Smith and later Karl Marx there is a tendency to identify a society with its economy or- more precisely- with the society's leading mode of production of wealth. Therefore, if knowledge becomes the leading mode of the production of wealth, it is no surprise that a society in which it happens is "naturally" called a knowledge society. Yet, it is important to see the difference in the meaning of these two terms.

The roots of this difference go back to what in Ancient Greece was perceived as the difference between *episteme* and *techne*; roughly the equivalent of theoretical and practical knowledge or- as Joel Mokyr calls it- the propositional knowledge and the prescriptive knowledge (Mokyr, 2002). One could call the propositional knowledge the "what" knowledge, and the prescriptive knowledge the "how" knowledge (it seems that scholars who are more interested in the theoretical, propositional knowledge are inclined to favor the idea of the knowledge *society*, whereas those involved with the prescriptive knowledge, favor the concept of knowledge *economy*).

It is worthwhile to ask whether it would be possible to build a bridge between knowledge society and knowledge economy; and if so, what kind of ethical problems could be solved that way. It seems to me that ICT could be helpful here, since ICT, the universal technology, is used for the advancement of both propositional and prescriptive knowledge. Moreover, the presence of the communication component in ICT blurs the line somewhat between the technology understood as "the manipulation of nature for human material gain" (Mokyr, 2002, pp. 3) and human sciences. There seems to be, therefore, a hope that the new global society in which ICT plays a pivotal role can become a knowledge society based on knowledge economy.

Despite the relatively insignificant economic position of knowledge in the past, there has been a struggle over the *ethics* of the commoditization of knowledge throughout the history of western civilization ever since the famous controversy between Socrates and the Sophists. All that time- in theory, at least- the Socrates/Plato position, namely, that the production and distribution of knowledge should not be "polluted" with a market attitude (opposite of the "knowledge for sell" motto of the Sophists) seem to have been victorious in the West. Other civilizations generally supported similar views. The realm of ideas was supposed to be a common good, free for anyone bright enough, determined enough, brave enough, and patient enough to seek it. This accessibility of knowledge/ideas according to the above-listed criteria was supposed to even apply to some very lucky women and slaves. In other words, in the Socratic/Platonic theory, societal knowledge took precedence over personal knowledge. It had a higher value, including the ethical value, than the personal knowledge had. Plato makes it clear in the most famous part of his book *The Republic*, i.e., in the allegory of the den (or cave, depending on the translator's choice of word) that an individual who possesses personal knowledge of the kind that could alter the societal knowledge has the *moral duty* to share this knowledge with his fellow humans, even if this would bring him in danger of his own demise.

Almost since its beginnings, ICT became the battleground between two approaches to knowledge which mirror the Socrates-Sophists controversy. One of them is to see knowledge as a commodity and an individual property; the other- to treat knowledge as collective/communal property which should be freely shared (i.e., with no restrictions of any kind). At present, it is hard to imagine that a compromise between these two positions could be reached anytime soon or that it could be achieved easily. Intellectual property rights defendants are as fiercely convinced about the moral value of their position as are the shared knowledge advocates. In the context of this essay, the line between Socratic/Platonic "free knowledge" and the Sophists' "knowledge for sale" positions could be drawn- very imprecisely- in this way: at the present time, the concept of knowledge society fits in with the idea of shared knowledge, whereas the knowledge economy embraces the idea of knowledge as property and commodity.

A problem which could possibly tip the scale is the issue of the digital divide, and especially digital exclusion of certain segments of the global human population along economic, gender, geographic, racial and other lines. This is a problem addressed frequently by numerous authors. Digital exclusion is, among others, the result of the policy of denying certain groups in various societies, or even entire societies, access to societal/public knowledge. The arguments used by the critics of digital exclusion (some works of Richard Stallman, 2004; Helen Richardson, 2002; and, Andrzej Kocikowski, 1996 would be a fitting example) usually express the general philosophy of the knowledge society as presented in this paper.

One should notice that digital exclusion plays a negative role in an ICT-driven global society whose economy is the knowledge economy as a whole; and it has a negative impact on the knowledge economy itself, if only by restricting the number of users, i.e., consumers of ICT. Admittedly, there is an inherent tension- some may even say- contradiction between the capitalist knowledge economy in its present form and actions leading to the eradication of the digital exclusion, but only if the accepted definition of the purpose of business is that the purpose of business is to make money. Otherwise, the societal benefits of the abolishment of the digital exclusion are pretty obvious, including the economic benefits to the society as a whole. On the other hand, a strictly (business) organization-based, competition-focused approach to this problem not only will contribute to the strengthening of the digital divide and to the increase in the number of those discriminated by digital exclusion, but it will eventually have a negative impact (including an *economically negative* impact) on the global society. This said, one needs to add that the most obvious way to eradicate- or at least diminish- the digital exclusion, is through free and unrestricted access to societal knowledge the production, storage and distribution of which is today almost unimaginable without ICT.

Due to the dynamic changes taking place in the economy (as mentioned earlier, transition to knowledge economy is not a finished process yet), there are indicators- as shown by W. Chan Kim & Renée Mauborgne (2003) later in this essay- that the concept of shared knowledge will have to be adopted by the knowledge economy at least in the area of management, including knowledge management. This is a very interesting prospect; but it also means the emergence of hard-to-solve contradictions which the *economic theory* will have to deal with. In doing so, scholars will most likely have to reach to the fundamentals. Perhaps, even the theoretical foundation of the capitalist mode of production and the concept of capitalism itself will have to be re-examined and possibly modified.

Now let me share some thoughts on the ethics of the ICT-driven global society whose economy is the knowledge economy. Obviously, technology as well as knowledge can be used for ethical or unethical purposes. "Athena's gifts were many: she gave King Cecrops the olive tree, but she also gave the city of Troy the wooden horse that led to its destruction" (Mokyr, 2002, pp. 297). In the case of ICT the importance of this ambivalence was acknowledged very early on, even before the power of the new technology could be truly appreciated. One of the creators of computer technology, Norbert Wiener, paid great attention to the ethical problems this technology might generate. He was also exceptionally interested in the ethical aspect of science, his firm position being that science should *serve* the wellbeing of humankind. The following quotation indicates that he would also be a proponent of knowledge sharing. He wrote,

...we (Mexican physiologist Arturo Rosenblueth & Wiener) believed that the divisions between the sciences were convenient administrative lines for the apportionment of money and effort, which each working scientist should be willing to cross whenever his studies should appear to demand it. Science, we both felt, should be a collaborative effort (Wiener, 1956, p. 171).

Collaboration in a scientific endeavor without sharing knowledge is rather impossible. Today, scores of scholars examine ethical issues caused by and/or related to ICT, and ICT is now pretty much everywhere, and has an impact on everyone's life, not being dealt with by any single profession exclusively. Therefore, the ethics of ICT (earlier known as computer ethics) becomes more and more the ethics of the ICT-driven global *society*; it cannot be treated as just one of the types of professional ethics.

Another phenomenon that needs to be addressed with regard to further development of global ICT ethics (especially in the area of the social status of knowledge) is the shift in the interpretation of the definition of humans as *social animals*.

Throughout the history of western thought, several major changes occurred regarding this concept. When Aristotle brought it up while speaking of humans as "political animals," or when the Stoics, like Seneca, called humans "social animals" they did so mainly to emphasize that it is the presence of "the animal in us" that makes us social. Aristotle's definition of a human being placed humans within the category of animals. Living in society, or as Nietzsche much later derogatively called it, in a herd, has been seen as our natural condition. A human being was regarded as a member of a society first (usually with a fixed place and role in it), and a unique individual second.

With time, however, and especially since Descartes, a reversal of this order gradually took place in western societies. It became almost a paragon of humanness to suppress this "natural condition" part of which were the "herd instinct" and "herd mentality"; instead, one was supposed to regard oneself as a (rational) individual apart from society and ideally above it. This way, humans could elevate themselves above nature- a desirable process from the point of view of the value hierarchy accepted in those days. Consequently, the problem of the *individual self* and of one's own identity *as* an individual became of great interest to scholars and ordinary people alike.

However, when later philosophers, sociologists, and other scholars from George Herbert Mead and John Dewey (1960) through Peter Berger (1967) to Alasdair MacIntyre examined this problem, they concluded that it is indeed the social character of human nature that makes us truly human- if we define humans as rational beings. In their view, human rationality was not featuring which attested individual's uniqueness but rather the social character of human beings. In the words of G. H. Mead (1934), "minds and selves are essentially social products, products or phenomena of the social side of human experience" (p. 1). According to MacIntyre, the acknowledgement and cultivation of the social character of human nature is necessary for humans to flourish as humans (MacIntyre, 2002). He further writes: "for we cannot have a practically adequate understanding of our own good, of our own flourishing, apart from and independently of the flourishing of that whole set of social relationships in which we have found our place" (MacIntyre, 2002, pp. 107-108).

As a result, we seem to have arrived at some sort of synthesis because at present neither MacIntyre nor any other serious scholar who accepts the definition of humans as "social animals" would negate the individuality of each human being. To be fully human today means to flourish *as* an individual *within* human society; and to be not only a member of this society but to define oneself as such.

There are several other unsolved problems which would need to be dealt with from the perspective of both knowledge economy and knowledge management like, e.g., the problem of freedom- freedom of information, freedom of speech, even freedom of thought. The problem of freedom is closely related to the issue of intellectual property. Therefore, it has been raised for some time by scholars in the area of computer/ICT ethics. On the surface, the guarantees for freedom as worked out within the democratic societies organized in nation-states with capitalist free market economy remain undisturbed. But the very nature of knowledge economy as it is perceived today has to put the various kinds of freedom under scrutiny and make them questionable at best, and possibly even in danger of being suppressed. The commoditization of knowledge, if it becomes total, would also mean the commoditization of thought. A commodity is by definition not there to be shared freely- it is there to be traded for a profit. Therefore, as was so often in the past, freedom could once again become a luxury only attainable to few individuals, if any; but this time it would be because only a few could *afford* it. This would also mean that democracy in its present form would lose its credibility. All this could happen, but it does not mean that it will; it does not need to happen. Among other things, making ethics a foundation of knowledge economy is of the important conditions for protecting both freedom and democracy.

KNOWLEDGE ECONOMY AND KNOWLEDGE MANAGEMENT IN THE DEMOCRATIC ICT-DRIVEN GLOBAL SOCIETY

Obviously, it is impossible to exhaust the issue of the knowledge management and democracy in a short essay. It is even hard to present it adequately. Nevertheless, I hope the information I presented to the Reader shows that the task of preparing the global society for the transition to knowledge economy with a proper knowledge management is enormous, and that the business world at large is not yet ready to make this transition successfully.

As pointed out by one of the most prominent contemporary American ethicists, Alasdair MacIntyre, in the history of Western moral philosophy "from Plato to [George Edward] Moore and since" very little attention has been paid to the problem of "human vulnerability and affliction and to the connections between them and our dependence on others" (MacIntyre, 2002, pp. 1). At present, the structure and management of the majority of business enterprises still follows the theories (scientific and philosophical) created as a result of the scientific revolution and reinforced by the technological revolution. Consequently, the situation as characterized by MacIntyre didn't change much. Nevertheless, many of these theories need to be revised and the relations between them rearranged. ICT and globalization not only brought this process in motion; they also contributed to its acceleration. In the knowledge economy, these changes will have to be acknowledged. They will also have to be adopted in practice, which means, among others, in knowledge management.

In business circles, there seems to be a growth in awareness of the necessity to revise the old approaches to business which is based on outdated theories; an article by W. Chan Kim & Renée Mauborgne (2003) may serve to support this statement. I wrote earlier in this essay (in the part about knowledge) that the modern concepts of knowledge (science, in particular) as well as democracy rest on the view that human beings are first and foremost rational individuals. This view was so strong that one of the most prominent philosophers of the 20th century, Karl Popper (in Miller, 1985), made the *rationality principle* into one of the fundamental principles of scientific inquiry. The influence of his views is visible in what Kim & Mauborgne (2003) write about the business world: "for the purposes of their theories, economists assume that people are maximizers of utility, driven mainly by *rational* calculations" (p. 3-4) of their own self-interest. That assumption has migrated into much of the management theory and practice. It has, for instance, become embedded in the tools managers traditionally use to control and motivate employees' behavior- from incentive systems to organizational structures" (Kim & Mauborgne, 2003, pp. 3-4). The authors proceeded to present some cases which substantiated the claim that this approach is not only outdated but even harmful to management in the knowledge economy. Kim & Mauborgne (2003) do not "blame" Karl Popper for the present-day problems in management. Rather, they focus on Frederick Winslow Taylor (1911), who about a century ago created the concept of *scientific management*. Yet Taylor's views were firmly rooted in the modern (i.e., post-scientific revolution) theory of knowledge. Problem is, that in Taylor's interpretation, the rationality of a human being became the *only* characteristic that mattered (Taylor was by no means an exception; these views were wide spread). Moreover, Taylor followed in his theory the procedures of scientific inquiry with its clean cut "yes-no" answers (in Popper's terminology, the falsification-verification procedure). He also perceived productivity as an outcome of rational procedures which assigned each individual a precise, rather restricted role in the production process. Remembering this helps to understand why Taylor's "scientific management" promoted autocracy not democracy in the workplace.

"Scientific management" with its authocratic style relies, as Kim & Mauborgne (2003) point out, on the idea of "distributive justice". Yet, the factors which are necessary for an enterprise to thrive in knowledge economy and in knowledge management are "procedural justice" (or "fair process", as the authors call it), democratic approach to management ("voluntary cooperation"), and appreciation of all types of human intelligence (see Gardner, 1999) as well as all the knowledge an individual- no matter what his/her job description- brings to the table. Needless to say his type of management is hard, if not impossible, to envision in a situation where strict rules regarding *intellectual property* are observed. On the other hand, the principle of *knowledge sharing* is very advantageous to knowledge management based on the principles described above. Seen in this light, knowledge sharing seems to be the winning approach to the problem of ownership of ideas in the knowledge economy. Here, the other views of the human being which was mentioned earlier in this text needs to be remembered, the view that humans are *social* animals. In light of this view, *willing readiness to share* (in this case, to share knowledge) is regarded as part of the human nature. The problem, of course, remains whether it is in the best interest of the *flourishing* global society to follow the human nature, or rather to overcome and subdue it.

CONCLUSION

In the ICT-driven global society of today, knowledge management, like ICT, can be used to benefit the humankind collectively as well as the individual human being; or it can be used to benefit a select group of individuals while a large part or even the majority of the global population might not benefit from it at all. In the worst-case scenario, knowledge management could even have a harmful effect on a large segment of humanity. Much depends on which ethical and social values would be accepted by those who set the rules for knowledge management and by those who practice it, and how these values would be respected.

At present, the problem is further complicated by the fact that there seem to be no real agreement as to *what* is actually beneficial and what is harmful to humans (beyond the obvious like the claim that to live is beneficial while to die is not; but even this is debatable in some cases). Being fully aware of this difficulty, I adopted the concept of a "flourishing society" based on "flourishing ethics" proposed independently by two philosophers, Alasdair MacIntyre (2002) and Terrell Bynum (2006). Keeping in mind Alasdair MacIntyre's reflection on some of the basic flaws in the most influential theories within the western moral philosophy of the past, it seems to me that one of the fundamental moral rules should be the flourishing (both in MacIntyre's and Bynum's sense) of every human individual. And further, as MacIntyre writes, "for a human being to flourish unqualifiedly *qua* human being, it is her or his life as a whole that must flourish (...)" (MacIntyre, 2002, pp. 113) remembering that humans are "social animals" will help to see that individuals can truly flourish in a flourishing *society*.

This concept of flourishing does not contradict Kant's stipulation that a human should always be the goal, never a mere means, or Wiener's appeal for the human use of human beings; but it adds a new dimension to them. The human flourishing, perceived as the fullest development of the human potential towards the Good can actually stop being a utopia, and it can become a realistic goal for the global society.

The "flourishing ethics" is still not a fully satisfactory solution to all of the above-described problems, and it is still being worked on and refined, but it seems to me that there won't be anything better for some time to come; and possibly not for as long as the humankind (global society) will be composed of *unique individuals* because the human uniqueness dictates the diversity of goals, values, and actions. From my point of view, the uniqueness of each human being is definitely a positive value; one of the values which should- no, must- be preserved if there is to *be* a humankind. If this causes a disagreement as to what is harmful and what is beneficial to humans so be it, as long as humans know how to resolve their differences through a democratic process and according to the best of their knowledge (again, the importance of knowledge).

Moreover, the concept of human flourishing does not need to be in conflict with knowledge economy. Even if "useful knowledge" (Mokyr, 2002) is the backbone of knowledge economy, other types of knowledge and other human activities that contribute to human flourishing will also play a vital role in knowledge economy if they are to contribute to the greater productivity of the minds engaged in the production, trade, and application of knowledge. With the assistance of ICT, humans *can* accomplish this. What is now needed most is for knowledge economy to gear up for the pursuit of this goal. In the global society in which knowledge has the leading economic role and value, every human mind should be regarded as a potential source of economic growth, and it can contribute to the flourishing of humans. Therefore, every human being should have the opportunity and the conditions to develop his/her mind's potential to the fullest. This should be one of the most important tasks for knowledge management.

The task for moral philosophers would be to see to it that the goal towards which humans would *want* to develop their minds would be the wellbeing of the global society in which every individual could live in conditions of freedom, equality, and democracy. This is a very important point considering the fact that the two dominant positions, or cultures as some call it (Costa, Prior & Rogerson, 2008), in the world today are collectivism and individualism. More often than not they are regarded as antagonistic towards each other and mutually excluding. This would mean that the simultaneous occurrence and comparable strength of both of them would turn the global society into a deeply divided one. It would, therefore, mean also that the flourishing of humankind the way McIntyre and Bynum have envisioned it would be all but impossible. However, it needs not be so. The solution lays likely in the dialectic approach to this duality which would permit reaching a synthesis of individualism and collectivism through the process of changes. In order to make this process a successful one, i.e., to achieve a desirable result of a flourishing global, ICT-driven knowledge society, (which economy would be the knowledge economy) one would have to set the goal for a global effort; for purposeful actions towards the creation of the kind of society I mentioned above: a society in which every individual could live in conditions of freedom, equality, and democracy. Instead of treating collectivism and individualism as perennial antagonists, and the relationship between them as combative and aimed at the destruction of the other, humankind could follow the thought expressed by the German philosopher Karl Jaspers in his acceptance speech after receiving the Peace Prize from the German Book Trade he was awarded in 1958. Jaspers said: "a violent struggle gets extinguished in communication. The result is a collective truth, instead of superiority in victory" (Jaspers, 1958, pp. 10, my translation from German).

I believe the economy of the global society will increasingly be a knowledge economy. I also believe that the importance of knowledge management will increase not only in the business sector of society but in society at large. This essay was supposed to demonstrate, among other things, that the future character of the global society will depend very much on which direction both knowledge management and knowledge economy takes. My hope is that the new global society will become a *knowledge society* in the sense described earlier in this text; and that the economy of this society, the knowledge economy, will support the flourishing of knowledge society and all individuals in it. It will be based on principles of democracy aiming at the flourishing of all humans.

Right now there is still time to make crucial decisions about the direction the knowledge economy should take and to find the determination to execute them. One of the most important among these decisions will be the decision regarding the value of democracy for the ICT-driven global society whose economy will be the knowledge economy and whose knowledge management will be competent and skillful.

Should the value of democracy be determined as low then knowledge economy and knowledge management would become a very powerful tool for destroying democracy. If the value of democracy turns out to be high, then it seems to me that there will have to be some very serious work done before compatibility between knowledge economy (and within it knowledge management) and democracy as well as between individualism and collectivism in the ICT-driven global society could be achieved. It would be worth the trouble, though. As Plato claimed, "in the world of knowledge the idea of good appears last of all" (Plato, 1986, pp. 257), but it does appear nevertheless.

ACKNOWLEDGMENT

Some parts of this text were published in Górniak-Kocikowska, K. (2007). From computer ethics to the ethics of the global ICT society. K. E. Himma (Ed.), *Special Issue: Information Ethics* (pp. 47-57). Library Hi Tech: Emerald.

REFERENCES

Berger, P. L. (1967). *The sacred canopy: Elements of sociological theory of religion*. New York: Doubleday.

Boddy, M. (2005). The knowledge-driven economy. *South West of England Regional Development Agency*. Retrieved March 17, 2009, from http://download.southwestrda.org.uk/res/general/KE%20Final%20Report%20190705.pdf

Browne, J. (2006). The purpose of business. *Beyond Petroleum*. Retrieved July 27, 2009, from http://www.bp.com/genericarticle.do?categoryId=98&contentId=7017837

Business Dictionary. (2009). Knowledge economy. *Business Dictionary*. Retrieved August 2, 2009, from http://www.businessdictionary.com/definition/knowledge-economy.html

Bynum, T. W. (2006). Flourishing ethics. *Ethics and Information Technology*, *8*(4), 157–173. doi:10.1007/s10676-006-9107-1

Competitive Intelligence Glossary. (2009). The language of competitive business intelligence. *Quantumiii- the solutions people*. Retrieved August 2, 2009, from http://www.quantum3.co.za/CI%20Glossary.htm

Costa, G. J. M., Prior, M., & Rogerson, S. (2008). Individual ethics and knowledge management: arising Conflicts. In Bynum, T. W. (Eds.), *ETHICOMP 2008: Living, Working and Learning Beyond Technology* (pp. 117–129). Mantua, Italy: University of Pavia.

Costa, G. J. M., & Silva, N. M. A. (2007). Knowledge management: how ethical is your organization's knowledge? In Bynum, T. W., Rogerson, S., & Murata, K. (Eds.), *ETHICOMP 2007: Glocalisation: Bridging the Global Nature of Information and Communication Technology* (*Vol. 1*, pp. 123–136). Tokyo: Meiji University.

d'Orville, H. (2000). Towards the global knowledge and information society- The challenges for development cooperation. *United Nations Development Programme*. Retrieved March 15, 2009, from http://www.undp.org/info21/public/pb-challenge.html

Dewey, J. F. (1960). *The quest for certainty*. New York: Minton, Balch & Co.

Field, R. (2002). What is the purpose of business? *University of Alberta*. Retrieved May 23, 2009, from http://www.business.ualberta.ca/rfield/PurposeofBusiness.htm

Gardner, H. (1999). *Intelligence reframed: Multiple intelligences for the 21st Century*. New York: Basic Books.

Górniak-Kocikowska, K. (2005). Problemy z nazwaniem nowego spoleczenstwa. *Ethos (Berkeley, Calif.)*, *18*(1-2), 77–99.

Górniak-Kocikowska, K. (2007). From computer ethics to the ethics of the global ICT society. K. E. Himma (Ed.), *Special Issue: Information Ethics* (pp. 47-57). Boca Raton, FL: Library Hi Tech: Emerald.

Górniak-Kocikowska, K. (2008). ICT and the tension between old and new: The human factor. *Journal of Information. Communication & Ethics in Society*, *6*(1), 4–27. doi:10.1108/14779960810866774

Jaspers, K. (1958). *Wahrheit, freiheit und friede*. München, Germany: Piper & Co. Verlag.

Khurana, R., & Gintis, H. (2008). What is the purpose of business? *BizEd Magazine, January-February*, 54-55.

Kim, W. C., & Mauborgne, R. (2003). Fair process: Managing in the knowledge economy. *Harvard Business Review*, *81*(1), 127–136.

Kocikowski, A. (1996). Geography and computer ethics: An Eastern European perspective. T. W. Bynum & S. Rogerson (Guest Eds.). *Special Issue: Global Information Ethics. Science and Engineering Ethics*, *2*(2), 201–210. doi:10.1007/BF02583554

MacIntyre, A. (2002). *Dependent rational animals: Why human beings need the virtues*. IL, Peru: Open Court.

Mead, G. H. (1934). *Mind, self, & society: From the standpoint of a social behaviorist*. Chicago: University of Chicago Press.

Miller, D. (Ed.). (1985). *The rationality principle- Popper selections*. Princeton, NJ: Princeton University Press.

Ministry of Economical Development. (2006). What is knowledge economy? *New Zealand Government*. Retrieved June 11, 2009, from http://www.med.govt.nz/pbt/infotech/knowledge_economy/knowledge_economy-04.html

Mokyr, J. (2002). *The gifts of Athena: Historical origins of the knowledge economy*. Princeton, NJ: Princeton University Press.

OECD. (2003). OECD science, technology and industry scoreboard 2003. *Organization for Economic Co-operation and Development*. Retrieved June 11, 2009, from http://www.oecd.org/document/21/0,2340,en_2649_33703_16683413_1_1_1_1,00.html

Plato,. (1986). *The republic. (Transl. B. Jowett)*. Amherst, NY: Prometheus Books.

Quinton, A. (1972). Knowledge and belief. In P. Edwards (Ed.), *The Encyclopedia of Philosophy: Vol. 4* (pp. 345-352). New York: Macmillan Publishing & The Free Press. Richardson, H. (2002). Exercising different choices- The gender divide and government policy making in the "global knowledge economy". In I. M. S. B. Alvarez *et al.* (Eds.), *ETHICOMP 2002: The Transformation of Organisations in the Information Age: Social and Ethical Implications* (pp. 471-484). Lisbon: Lusíada University of Lisbon.

Riley, T. B. (2003). An overview of the knowledge economy. *e-Gov monitor*. Retrieved June 1, 2009, from http://www.egovmonitor.com/features/riley07.html

Soete, L. (2002). The challenges and the potential of the knowledge-based economy in a globalised world. In Rodrigues, M. J. (Ed.), *The New Knowledge Economy in Europe. A Strategy for International Competitiveness and Social Cohesion* (pp. 28–53). Northampton, MA: Edward Elgar Publishing.

Stallman, R. (2004). Why software should be free. In Bynum, T. W., & Rogerson, S. (Eds.), *Computer Ethics and Professional Responsibility* (pp. 294–310). Malden, MA: Blackwell Publishing.

Taylor, F. W. (1911). *The principles of scientific management*. New York: Harper Bros.

The World Bank. (2009). ICT Glossary Guide. *The World Bank*. Retrieved August 1, 2009, from http://web.worldbank.org/wbsite/external/topics/extinformationandcommunicationandtechnologies/0,contentMDK:21035032~menuPK:282850~pagePK:210058~piPK:210062~theSitePK:282823~isCURL:Y,00.html

Webster's Dictionary. (1996). *Webster's new universal unabridged dictionary*. New York: Barnes & Noble Books.

Wiener, N. (1956). *I am a mathematician: The later life of a prodigy*. Cambridge, MA: Doubleday & Day.

KEY TERMS AND DEFINITIONS

Democracy: A state of society characterized by formal equality of rights and privileges.

Knowledge: A non-linear commodity that needs to be managed. Therefore, involves three key processes, namely production (creation), storage (preservation) and distribution (dissemination).

Knowledge Economy: Economy based on creating, evaluating, and trading knowledge.

Knowledge Management: Integrated, systematic process for identifying, collecting, storing, retrieving, and transforming *information* and *knowledge assets* (including previously unarticulated expertise and experience held by individuals) into *knowledge* that is readily accessible in order to improve the performance of the organization.

Knowledge Sharing: Willing readiness to share (in this case, to share knowledge) as a component of the human nature, in order to promote a *flourishing* global knowledge society.

Knowledge Society: A society endowed with the ability and capacity to generate and capture new knowledge and to access, absorb and use effectively information and ICTs.

Chapter 4
Global "Knowledge Management" in Humanist Perspective

Piotr Pawlak
Adam Mickiewicz University of Poznan, Poland

ABSTRACT

The term "knowledge management" is widely circumscribed to organizations, being considered fundamental at an institutional level (frequently within a specific corporate level). Hence, it is the domain of organizational and management theories, rational selection theories or, of various concepts related to economic efficiency. Nonetheless, this chapter will attempt to consider this issue from a holistic perspective, considering as a starting point the global dimension of this quandary. This overview falls back on analyses conducted by widely understood social studies, which use economic tools and methodologies. The author's opinion is that today the Internet evidently is a specific global knowledge warehouse. To be more specific, he means the "ICT space" created by the Internet, which herein the author will refer to as the cyberspace entails a global knowledge flux. As a result, this chapter is an overview of humanist discussions on cyberspace exploration and (more importantly) management.

INTRODUCTION

This chapter aims to present a non-standard, a slightly different approach to knowledge management as a result of the inspiring work of Godzic (2001). Taking into account this novel approach, that can be characterized as more academic than practical in its essence, it is time to outline its basic definitions, as well as the scale within which the problem is being discussed. These matters must be elaborated on prior to further reading about the underlying topic of this contribution.

Traditionally, knowledge management is perceived by contemporary companies as one of the key elements for competitive advantage. The ever-changing world economy makes companies and other organizations permanently enhance their operation methods. The abrupt transformations occurring in all areas of corporate operations are the "signs of our time", because these amend-

DOI: 10.4018/978-1-61520-873-9.ch004

ments frequently challenge current trends and principles. The problem that most companies face is how to manage its assets in this new era: it is the proper use of knowledge, information and data that assumes a key relevance. According to Peter Drucker (1999) traditional resources, such as work, land, and capital have become more an obstacle than a driving force for corporate growth. Furthermore, creativity in all fields of life is born out of knowledge.

Knowledge management is a relatively new concept, which particular authors date it back to 1987. In this year the first conference about *Managing the Knowledge Assets into 21st Century* was held in the United States. It was jointly organized by Purdue University and DEC. Additionally in the same year in Sweden, the so called Konrad Group was established and it commenced its work on intellectual capital management. Consultancies were the first to identify the need for new management area, because for them knowledge itself was a product. They quickly got down to establishing repositories with their consultants' knowledge and experience.

Knowledge management grew rapidly in the late 1990's and the idea was disseminated by Ikujiro Nonaka, a Japanese researcher. In 1995 together with Hirotaka Takeuchi he published *The Knowledge - Creating Company- How Japanese Companies Create the Dynamics of Innovation.* To their minds knowledge is created to a smaller extent by collecting, processing and using the existing knowledge within a given organization. For them it is more about creating new knowledge. It is their belief that the overriding objective of knowledge management is about creation and not about its effective circulation within an organization. Their ideas shed new light on both theories: knowledge management and innovation.

Nonaka & Takeuchi (1995) emphasize the importance of using "tacit" knowledge (the idea of "tacit knowledge" was introduced by Michael Polanyi much earlier), embedded in the employees' heads, for a company's success. This led to another theory, which encompasses knowledge creation through contacts within teams and not in the heads of individual persons (Grudzewski & Hejduk, 2005; Rheingold, 1994).

Both in theory and in practice there are numerous definitions of knowledge management. This is the result of the popularity of the theory and a relatively short time of its use. Hence, knowledge management can be defined as a totality of formalized methods of collecting and using formal and tacit knowledge of the participants of an organization, as an attempt of its preeminent utilization and being available throughout the organization as new knowledge, and its increasing understanding.

Knowledge management is a multi-faceted process. It can be analysed from various points of view: particular entities (business ones- public and private- in particular), as well as particular states (knowledge management policy could even be elaborated on) and last but not least, in the context of international arena. From the following discussion it will be demonstrated that knowledge management is a specific element of international and supranational administration. At this point, the author constructs another singularity- on one hand exists knowledge management, which is understood as an element of a defined policy developed by particular international community (as for instance, the European Union); and, on the other hand, entails management of knowledge, which is understood as an element of wide-ranged global processes that are common for all international communities. This chapter investigates the issue from this global perspective.

The underlying topic is closely connected with various research fields: political science, law, economy, sociology, cultural studies, etc. For example, public administration research seeks to uncover answers as regards to knowledge management issues. Furthermore, the intrinsic characteristics of this research field (multidisciplinary and interdisciplinary), implies a valuable methodological to knowledge management analysis. Finally, social researchers have been continuously scrutinizing the global information flow, leading to multiple concepts and categorizations. Therefore, this chapter attempts to demonstrate several key concepts with reference to global knowledge flows. These concepts will reveal the mechanisms behind the world information and knowledge flow, which are subsumed under various theories.

GLOBAL KNOWLEDGE MANAGEMENT

Mapping the Global Knowledge Management "Territory"

Knowledge, as an expression, is used frequently. Despite this scenario encompasses a generic sense, or configures more or less abstract perceptions. In the classic definition by Plato (e.g. Jowett, 1899), which is featured in one of his dialogues, *Socrates* and *Theaetetus* concluded that knowledge is justified and is a true belief. According to the Oxford English Dictionary (2008), knowledge is expertise and skills acquired by a person through experience or education; the theoretical or practical understanding of a subject. Or, the Nowa Encyklopedia Powszechna (2004) (Polish Universal Encyclopedia) defines knowledge as all reliable information about reality together with the ability to use it.

The title of this chapter features a concept, which can be broken down into two basic items: "knowledge" and "management". For the purpose of this analysis "knowledge" is perceived as the totality of information to be found in cyberspace (Rheingold, 1992). Consequently, by information management I mean the activities of the dominating businesses (among others), which are to a different extent involved in filling the Internet with content (for further details concerning the differences between knowledge and content, e.g. Costa & Silva, 2010). Media (mass media in particular) are carriers of a substantial portion of human knowledge. Electronic media have a unique role to play, because practically almost every existing piece of information can be saved as hypertext or in any other electronic form (text, graphic, sound, video file, etc.) (Mróz, 2005). All data accumulated and saved data by this method fill up the global computer network and constitute a large and ever-expanding global knowledge base. It is currently the most popular compendium of knowledge about research, culture, tourism, education and even commercial institutions around the world. Furthermore, it features comprehensive information about almost all subjects (OCDE, 2008).

The other titular item is "management", which can be defined as all actions taken in order to use human and material resources effectively and attain the set out objectives. For the purpose of this analysis, management is viewed as a process of establishing objectives and streamlining their attainment in organizations subjugate to the manager with the use of own production capacity (possibilities) or own knowledge sources or resources (Drucker, 1999). Thus, the chapter will seek to describe the entities wielding the monopoly on information, as well as the knowledge management mechanisms at work at supranational scale.

I reckon that the Internet is clearly perceived as another mass medium (a relatively young one), which is influenced by similar (but not always identical) factors as the traditional mass media. Powerful businesses that is, international media corporations, have always impacted mass media market organization (inclusive the Internet) (Manovich, 2000). Together with various political determinants, the conglomerates decide about the worldwide flow of information and hence their operations and politics can be seen as a specific form of knowledge management at a global level (Golding & Harris, 1997). The above mentioned political determinants, which are particularly significant (especially under previous historical periods), as factors for providing or denying access to the widely considered knowledge, presently lose foothold against economic factors. As a result, their role is currently less essential and typically is economic factors that compel them to act in the context of global knowledge management.

Knowledge management at a global level has been inextricably connected to the monopolization of information flows, which has pestered traditional mass media from their onset and currently pervading the Internet. An analysis of the sector-specific problems illustrates that the largest global information production and distribution companies must be scrutinized (Lister *et al.*, 2003). The companies in question include: Time Warner (owner of CNN), Disney (owner of ABC), Sony, General Electric (owners of NBC, AT&T, The News Corporation, Seagram- music and movies), Viacom (owner of CBS and Bertelsmann).

Besides, the discussed problem is also strictly related to an additional global issue, which scholars from different fields of studies frequently refer to as the "ICT revolution". The revolution-related transformations, which occur in the context of ever-present globalization, substantially affect global knowledge management. The problem was relatively quickly recognized by various social studies researchers (Appadurai, 2005; Huntington, 2004; Castells, 2003; Mattelart, 2003; Rifkin, 2003; Chomsky & McChesney, 2000; Chomsky, 1999; Soros, 1998; McLuhan, 1962; and others), who have sought to address it and account for it in a number of ways. Eventually the researchers came up with several interesting concepts, which for the purpose of this chapter will be analysed in reference to the titular issue.

Framing the Discussion

McLuhan's Work

The exchange of electronic information is also related to establishment of a new qualitative social structure, which is variously referred to (for instance, "global society", "information society" or "information-based society"). At the turn of the 20th century Marshall McLuhan projected the creation of a global society. In *The Gutenberg Galaxy* he inferred that electronic media, television in particular, will create a global village, where "medium is a message" and communication tools exert a more tangible influence on people than the message itself. Nevertheless, in most cases the term "information society" is contextualized through contemporary societies that acknowledged highly developed capitalist countries. It illustrates technological transformations (advancement of information and communication technologies), as well as economic and social changes which occurred within the societies. The term "information society" was coined in 1963 by Tadao Umesao, a Japanese researcher and economist, in reference to the Japanese society.

Evidently, the titular issue must be analysed in connection with globalization-related matters. The comprehensive literature provides numerous interesting conclusions, which I tentatively called "global knowledge management". The prevalence of globalization triggers changes in societal structures and world economy. The transformations are induced by the abrupt boost in international trade and cultural exchange, which translates into an increased global interdependence between countries. From the economic point of view, the term is mainly linked with trade deregulation or "free trade". In a wider context it refers to the ever-spreading integration and co-dependence between global businesses on social, political and economic platforms (Gilpin, 2001). Three chief dimensions of globalization (economic, cultural and political) must be highlighted. Considering the focal point of the chapter, the cultural and economic aspects seem to be of particular significance; nevertheless we must also remember that all three dimensions are interconnected.

Cultural aspects of globalization are best evidenced in the high-profile commercialization of selected cultural products. The process appears to gain momentum in line with the advancement of mass communication tools, which, in turn are utilized by international corporations for marketing activities. When characterizing the dynamic growth of the advertising market, Marshall McLuhan (1962) concluded that never before such a high employment rate was reported in a sector which aims to manipulate other people. Globalization creates numerous problems, which some have a key significance for the discussed issue. Most importantly, globalization leads to creating and gapping of global disproportions in access to the widely understood knowledge. Disproportions in global communication and world information exchange can be categorized as dark sides of ICT revolution (Floridi, 2006).

Armand Mattelart Perception

Armand Mattelart (2003) puts forward to analyze the terms communication and information separately. Communication designates construction (reconstruction) of culture, which among others, aims to tighten ties between people by reinforcement of personal identity. Information, on the other hand, means identified evidences, acknowledgement of which involves our beliefs, queries and denies to-date acquired knowledge, make us review it, testing our readiness to take actions and, finally, separates people (Mattelart, 2003). Consequently, by this token, global knowledge management is perceived as a disbalanced flow of information. Hence, a small group of people has access to information, which next (selectively or after "reprocessing") is made available to others as, for instance, media information. According to Mattelart (2003) the idea of "information society" dates back to 1648 (date of the Peace of Westphalia, which ended the Thirty Years' War). The new order introduced by the Peace of Westphalia meant the beginning of a new state, where the rulers (who believed to be God anointed to rule) had a monopoly on information, which facilitated power-wielding. Monopoly on information was first recorded to be used in the Ancient times. The Egyptian elites restricted access to astronomy and resorted to it to corroborate its God-given right to rule (for example, Sun eclipse). The state used information to exert "symbolic pressure" and consequently to create state identity. According to Mattelart (2003), the so called "universal" culture, which is recognized by people worldwide, originates from the state-owned information.

The idea of "state information" is in fact an alternative (to be exact, it is the third solution) which came to light in the times of global competition between military and ideological blocks. It can be deemed as a kind of a compromise proposal. It was interesting for Mattelart (2003) to characterize the world communication and information situation (that is to depict two systems) in the 1970's and 1980's. Mattelart (2002) inferred that it was at that time that the planetary awareness in society was born. As a result, societies came to a conclusion that the "cultural dependence was not triggered by any conspiracy or plots, but stemmed from structural transformations. The domination was born out of a disproportionate exchange between the centre and its peripheries" (Mattelart, 2000, pp. 66-67). When it comes to communication discrepancies in both ideological blocks, information was more widely accessible in the West (in the countries of the "free world" as referred to by the author) as there were hardly any restrictions. Thus, information was consolidated and culturally affected by the US: "information society means a collective with access to information, yet it does not necessarily designate a society, which receives and processes information in a uniform way" (Mattelart, 2002, pp. XV).

It is with great reluctance that Mattelart (2003) describes the ultraoptimistic visions of the society of tomorrow (including the information society) as well as the far-reaching demands, which form its basis and promises born with it. He emphasizes that the idea of a society with unrestricted access to information is either a utopia or a romanticized vision enjoyed by a small society of hackers [society of hackers as defined by Castells (2003)], because the state still monopolizes information. It is thought that if the power is taken over by the widely understood economy (which in fact has already been underway) can be considered a viable alternative. Mattelart (2003) claims that information has a great economic significance, in particular all economic activities, because the free market can be seen as a game where the best informed wins (as referred by Bourdieu, 2003). At this point, it is worth noting that culture is crucial for attaining economic objectives. When it comes to defining "culture", I refer to the concept by Jerzy Kmita (1985), according to whom culture (to be more exact to one of its elements, which is composed of a collective of normative and directive judgments) motivates an individual to take specific actions, which as subjectively seen by him/her, will help to achieve the previously set-out goals (directive judgments). What must also be born in mind is the fact that the goal of an action (not only market action) is also culture-dependent (normative judgments), and thus culture infuses economic activities.

The vision of information society is subtly tainted by a kind of totality notion "bestsellers about the promised society of tomorrow forecast that we enter the *era of optimism*, and a failure to conform to the trend of positive thinking is instantly named *technological phobia* or *antimodren*. The old demons of anti-intellectual populism surface" (Mattelart, 2003, pp. 133). Technological revolution does not eradicate old problems and is not free from ever-present (frequently undesired) tendencies. At the same time, culture is shaped more quickly and intensively than ever before (as a consequence of advancement of communication technologies). Moreover, this author suggests that "for the sake of speed, the slow cumulative historical process of culture construction is thoroughly transformed, as it was the case ages ago in so called primitive societies, when heralds of the incessant progress imposed a strenuous march towards modernity" (p. 134). Information technology advancement sped up and consequently various societies began to be inter-linked. The technology reached more and more new fields and engaged more and more new countries. As a result, more and more entities became involved in shaping Web topology on the basis of diverse ideas, as for instance Mattelart (2000) points out:

- the universalism of predestined civilization;
- religious ecumenism (frequently in extreme forms);
- interdependence of nations for the sake of joint security;
- inflexible imperative of international work distribution;
- joint fight against domination.

Mattelart (2003) warns against forgetting history, which can be the consequence of unquestioned belief in numerous myths bounded to the future society. Recapitulating, a media expert of Belgian origin, makes a point that the present situation (for which implementation of new ICT technologies and appearance of "information society" is characteristic) stems from (yet not ultimately) a long-term process of knowledge management, which dates a long way back to transformations in social structures and forms of communication (flow of information). The reality, which is described by the researcher, represents a certain stage of the process and does not supersede the well-ingrained unchanged tendencies and processes and consequently does not create an entirely new cognitive category, the analysis of which would require a substantial review of so far applied tools and concepts.

Appadurai's Work under Scrutiny

A different point of view is shared by Arjun Appadurai (2005), to whom, the cultural aspects of globalization enable mankind to enter in a novel phase of development. What is characteristic about this stage is that, it distances itself from acquired experience and cuts itself off from the past. Before observe the postmodern reality under scrutiny, the central categories of cultural anthropology must be re-defined, which means that an entirely new approach to research on numerous aspects of globalization must be worked out (inclusive changes in culture and the role of mass media in the transformations). Otherwise, the erosion of our knowledge as regards to the world becomes obsolete and insignificant.

Appadurai (2005) suggests that we should stop to perceive the world as a totality of cultures separated by borders (geographically). With globalization in place, the borders of the cultures get blurred (disappear). The author pays attention to the process of deterritorialization, which is directly connected with two important factors- electronic media and mass migration of people. Thanks to deterritorialization, modern cultures are location-free and are subject of remote factors (fragments of other cultures) in their reproduction. In fact, culture is produced through soft political assumptions rather than contained by pre-determined boundaries, jeopardizing cultural reproduction. What cannot be ignored is the growing intensity of the process of culture shaping, which, according to the author is connected with the advancement of information and communication technologies. These technologies promoted an interrupt and continuous flow of miscellaneous cultural objects that defy geographical boundaries. As our media became omnipresent numerous cultural phenomena become fluid (specific fragments, ideas are detached from their original cultures and are taken away by ever-present electronic media and mass migration), while the entire process is free from domination of any prevailing culture and in its form resembles rather a diffusion of five basic spheres of culture-ethnic, media, technical, financial and ideological.

If the present transformations are diffusion-like, knowledge management on a global level becomes less vital or even inexistent. The author proposes to perceive global cultural economy though a prism of disjuncture, where economy, culture and politics are part ways. So, to Appadurai (2005) global cultural economy is intricate given its multiple overlaps, which traditional center-peripheries models cannot elucidate. This criticism is legitimate even in models that account multiple centers and peripheries. Disjuncture cultural content circulates globally in five "imaginary" cultural spheres (specific dimensions), which include: ethnoscapes, mediascapes, technoscapes, finanscapes and ideoscapes. Appadurai (2005) explains the use of the suffix "scape" in the following manner:

The terms with "scape" suffixes show it is not about objective accounts, which are the same from any point of view, but rather about perspective-sensitive constructs, which are either modified by historical, linguistic and political situations of various actors from different national states, international concerns, societies in diasporas, and also sub-national groups and movements (religious, political and economic ones) (Appadurai, 2005, p. 52).

Consequently, it is believed that globalization does not lead to a common homogenization of cultures around the world, as well as an incoherent global knowledge management (process or processes), or information restriction. Hence, the fear of a destructive influence of a given dominating culture (American or any other) is groundless.

Thus, various contents originated from a variety of cultures, incessantly circulate in a global flow of people and information connecting with other contents and cultures. What is particularly important for this analysis- their free economic assumption. Following Friedman (1999), it is feasible to claim these constant movements, not simply in terms of *migrating egos*, imposes chaos and cumulative disruptions in our lives. By this token the aforementioned five culture dimensions are diffuse. Yet, Appadurai (2005) appears to ignore the fact that the global flow of information in a contemporary world is not (has never been) totally unidirectional, even considering the most sceptical arguments (e.g. Schiller, 1976; Nordenstrang & Varis, 1974). Contents and values specific to particular cultures, just like "raw materials", are selected, properly treated, and afterwards sold on a global information market as a result of knowledge management. Although, they core characteristic is to become worldwide free dissemination commodities, because cultural representatives scarcely enjoy their economic profits.

The truth is that peculiar values are not sufficiently popular or appealing to pervade the postmodern global reality as described by Appadurai (2005). Theoretically speaking, these would catch on if mass media pluralism was at work (traditional and new mass media). Meanwhile, cultural contents are given a "tag", which is frequently concealed so as not to belittle the traditional "exotic" element of a unique culture. As a consequence, it is possible to buy a dangerous-looking mask of an African warrior, which inside hides its genuine place of origin- "made in China. Or, a traditional amulet utilized by Indian tribes living in North America, which is commonly known as the "dream catcher", exemplifies how an element of a culture is anchored off from its traditional port. In both cases, the proprietary cultures at some extent acknowledge an economic profit, which Appadurai (2005) also debates. At this point it is worth stressing one issue- the amulet is referred to by its English name all around the world, while most of its present owners do not have the faintest idea what the original name of the artifact is.

Similarly, large US film production companies popularize less known images from local productions or, various literary works on a global scale (just to mention the "Lord of the Rings" trilogy by J. R. R. Tolkien, or the film adaptation of the mythological tale of the Trojan War). Last but not least, would people all around the world try the "traditional" delicious Mexican tacos, if there were no McDonald's, or KFC chains? Media (particularly the new electronic media) tend to create a spacious mosaic of images and contents from pieces from a range of cultures. Appadurai (2005) makes the following point: individuals practically have unrestricted access to knowledge, which in turn makes it possible to create new identities. Nevertheless, we must bear in mind two issues: the several forms of access restriction in place typically referred as "digital exclusion"; the discussion about information flow in all sorts of media ought to consider an important context, which pertains to the cultural identification of the communication tool (as regards to content and form).

Furthermore, Appadurai (2005) discusses the concept of *habitus* as defined by the French sociologist Pierre Bourdieu. For Bourdieu (1996; 1993), *habitus* is a result of interiorization of trends, attitudes, values, cultural patterns, as well as social norms acquired by individuals. Thus, it covers the entire set of features which affect human behaviour- on one hand, personal beliefs of individuals and his/her inclinations, as well as a wide spectrum of behavioural patterns socially accepted in particular situations; which Appadurai (2005) concludes is devalued in the postmodern world. This is the result of abrupt transformations, due to transnational and deterritorized events commonly triggered by mass media.

The new power of imagination to create forms of social life is inextricably connected with images, ideas and possibilities, which flow in from everywhere and often are transmitted by mass media. Therefore, standard cultural reproduction is currently in peril (similarly as standard English). It is successful only in those places, where it is planned, pre-determined and supported by political will (Appadurai, 2005, p. 85).

This cultural reproduction introduces a new quality that allows to an individual to broaden his/her possibilities, which in turn, increases the likelihood of leading a life beyond the pre-defined strict patterns rooted in the *habitus*. Although Bordieu's (1996; 1993) concept of *habitus* remains partially topical, it is important to emphasize the concept of improvisation. Therefore, Appadurai (2005) remarked that in places that improvisation can be managed, it is compulsory to observe cold *habitus* trends, as well as *habitus* reinforcement against shifting life systems.

Paradoxically, an explanation of the role of *habitus* in the contemporary world is in accordance with certain elements of symbolic violence (e.g. Bourdieu & Wacquant, 1992). Appadurai (2005) concludes that is a result of dynamic processes taking place in the postmodern reality (with destructive features) the form of *habitus* evolved and turned global. Nevertheless, it is essential to remember that *habitus* is changed (removed) and replaced by a dissimilar one (pertinent to a legitimate culture), which is characteristic of symbolic violence (being its ultimate objective). If we realize that an individual in fact has abundance and a variety of choices, this soft form of violence will appear clandestine and secretive. Finally, Bourdieu's *habitus* can be seen as a shrewd knowledge management (locally and globally).

Debating Jeremy Rifkin Analysis

The problem of knowledge management at a global level is discussed by several authors, who scrutinize the crucial issues of late 20th century and early 21st century (social, civilization, cultural, political, economic issues, among others). These authors' tend to express their concerns with the interpretation of the present transformations, as well as prospects of global reality.

Appaduraj (2005) seems reluctant to discuss the economic aspects of cultural information and content circulation in media, which in turn is recognized by Jeremy Rifkin (2003). Rifkin infers that the production of information and cultural items is the most lucrative economic sector, being cultural contents transformed into commercial activities. The old giants of the industrial era- Exxon, General Motors, USX and Sears- lose grounds in favour of new giants of cultural capitalism- Viacom, Time Warner, Disney, Sony, Seagram, Microsoft, News Corporation, General Electric, Bertelsmann AG and PolyGram. "These super-state media companies use digital revolution for communication purposes and connect the entire world. Consequently, they engage culture to commercial activities, which transform culture into commercial experience tailored to the needs of particular clients" (Rifkin, 2003, pp. 11).

Therefore, Rifkin (2003), Appadurai (2005), Mattelart (2003), as well as many other scholars (not only from cultural studies) acknowledge certain global processes and try to describe them (resorting to various terminologies), leading to pinpoint the potential consequences (which for instance in the case of Rifkin take the form of changes in consciousness).

Combining Soros, Chomsky and Huntington Ideas

In his projections regarding world capitalism crisis, George Soros perceives the world as one gigantic circulation system which is composed by a centre and its peripheries, where "links between the centre and the peripheries are far from equivalent" (Soros, 1998, pp. 140). Any actions within the system can be characterized by absorption of global capital by financial markets, and centre institutions. Then, the capital is injected back to periphery countries (through investments or, activities of international corporations).

Noam Chomsky & Robert McChesney (2000) mention the chief institutions, which make possible to centre countries to wield their power (G-7 Group) over the world. These include- the International Monetary Fund, the World Bank, and the General Agreement on Tariffs and Trade (GATT). The institutions constitute a new ruling class (with global power), which adopts neoliberalism as its governing ideology- "the fundamental political and economic paradigm of our times, which pertains to procedures and processes, by which a small group of people can control, to the extent it is possible, the social life in order to maximize their proceeds" (Chomsky & McChesney, 2000, pp. 5).

Additionally, these authors plead that the United States are privileged in the core and use this standing to disseminate (to export) American values worldwide. These "*American values* are well visible in the trends of the future: in ICT, the Internet, in advanced computer technologies and other creations of the American entrepreneurship bulging on the market, which since Regan times has been free from political influences" (Chomsky & McChesney, 2000, pp. 53). Both realities, the advancement of new technologies and the extensive marginalization of social masses facilitate "the *centre* to wield power with the meagre intervention of common people, who anyway have no influence on the decisions of those in power, (the rudimentary rule of capitalist autocracy) and are oblivious of the fact" (Chomsky, 1999, pp. 104).

Another example of a power tool, which is enumerated by Chomsky is the "Davos people" as defined by Samuel Huntington (2004). By Davos people the author means businessmen, bank officers, state officials, intellectuals, journalists from numerous countries, who create the world elite, which convenes every year at the World Economic Forum in the Swiss town of Davos.

Almost all of them are holders of M. Sc. titles in physics, social studies, business or law. They deal in words or figures (or one and the other), speak fluent English, are employed by governments, corporations, colleges with international contacts, frequently travel the world. What they all have in common is individualism. They all believe in free economy and democracy, which are prevalent in the Western civilization. The Davos people are in charge of all international institutions, they rule many countries and are in control of a substantial part of economic and military resources (Huntington, 2004, p. 79).

Despite the fact that Huntington (2004) does not acquiesce to the idea of cultural homogenization and the existence of a "universal civilization", the author is also very sceptical about the role of media and information (knowledge) in culture creation. Nevertheless, it recognizes the unquestionable hegemony of the United States in mass media, and consequently in global knowledge management. Beyond this claim, Huntington concludes that mass communication tools currently are an evidence of Western power: "the American hegemony in film, television and video production is larger than in air industry. (...) Two American and two European organizations enjoy almost an equal monopoly to collect and disseminate topical information worldwide" (Huntington, 2004, pp. 81).

The Non-Forecasting of Hardt & Negri (2005)

Michael Hardt & Antonio Negri (2005) forecast (to be more precise- announce) the establishment of a new global order, which they refer to as the "empire". The authors do not associate it with the United States in spite of the country play a key role within the system. The empire enables a transformation from the modern to the postmodern world, which produces a mixture of deterritorized capital and decentralized sovereignty on the basis of a network (a new information infrastructure which is incorporated in the production of new processes and totally inherent). The power is self-governing without any headquarters and any specific location.

The empire is made up from a number of processes combined with political, economic and cultural interdependencies. It seems to parasitize humanity, divide it (in a novel way) and segregate it into different social layers. Next, it seeks to maintain the state of balance (order), to allow a feasible control regarding the divided and segregated layers. The imperial control is enforced by three global absolute tools: bombs, money and airwaves. Airwaves, as a tool of imperial control cover communication, which is clearly demonstrated by these authors:

communication management, the educational system and culture control are now more than ever before prerogatives of sovereignty. However, this all is dispersed by airwaves. Contemporary communication systems are not subject to sovereign power. Quite the opposite, sovereignty is subject to communication (Hardt & Negri, 2005, p. 366).

These authors still recognize the power behind communication and mass media, perceiving them as one of three elements topping the global structure. Their condition for structure endurance (existence) relies on the elements advancement: "the advancement of communication networks is somehow connected with establishment of a new world order. Another words, it is the consequence and reason, product and producer. Communication not only expresses, but also organizes globalization" (Hardt & Negri, 2005, pp. 48). The advancement and expansion of cutting-edge technologies (both computers and cell phones and evidently the Internet) led to a radical proliferation and popularization (larger mobility- for instance, telephones or portable computers) of web communication points (on the structure of which the empire is based), translating a more comprehensive deterritorization. In conclusion, despite promising democracy and equality information communication technologies have enhanced the disparities between countries.

CONTROVERSY

"Cultural Imperialism": History Repeats Itself?

The idea of "cultural imperialism" can be very helpful for understanding the complexities and interdependencies around knowledge management in a global context. It stems from the theory of unilateral acculturation, which endorses the prevalence of a dominating culture, as well as a subjugate minority, which by rule, is technologically less advanced. These sort of intercultural relations in the above-mentioned area leads to a focal interest by some researchers and publicists. Under scrutiny is the relationship with the concept of "cultural imperialism" by Herbert Schiller (1976), an American sociologist, who introduced the idea to the scientific arena.

Initially, the term was adopted to define inequalities in the global information flow, as well as in order to pinpoint their negative consequences for specific cultures and economies. Or, to exhibit the relationships between rich, developed countries (United States, in particular) and then newly-established so called developing countries. In the light of both concepts media and entertainment are key aspects of the economy, as well as operate in accordance with competition market rules, profitability and efficiency- similarly to all other industries and products. For historical reasons, which are commonly known- Western civilization (North Atlantic civilization) has at its disposal a substantial part of all financial and technological resources- material ones in particular- which are necessary to generate all media products, including global ones, such as big movie productions. Thus, the remaining countries are the recipient for those products, because it is cheaper and more cost-effective than launching own production.

Schiller (1976) proposed a model approach to debate these trends. The author connotes a biological expression of a "core" and a "circumference", that is the periphery. If the model is applied for analysing international relations, the dominating countries are the "core" and the dominated countries are the "circumference" (periphery). Both elements create a system, the objective laws of which set the core in motion. In return, the core motion- as a centrifugal reaction- reaches the circumference. By this token, culture is circulated together with all other values formed under the "root" countries' dominance. Hence, these are transported to the circumference, which is to the Third World countries. Despite the fact the Schiller's concept dates back to the 1970's and that it was mostly related to traditional mass media, it appears that it can also be of relevance today. It can be applicable for the purpose of analysis of knowledge management matters in the globalized world, which heavily relies on the omnipresent computer network.

Today information and knowledge are commodities and systematically adopted in order to boost production and consumption worldwide. Free access to information becomes restricted due to the dynamic advancement of new technologies, the substantial costs which must be incurred to implement them and the need of acquiring new skills to use them (Rifkin, 2003). Low income and low level of education, so characteristic of the Third World countries, only reinforce the negative trend.

The "Cultural imperialism on the Internet" is an interesting publication from 1998 by Seongcheol Kima, then a PhD from the Information Technology Communications Institute at the University of Michigan. It elaborates a cultural imperialist analysis with reference to the cutting-edge information technology communications. The author poses two questions: will the Internet become an additional tool for cultural imperialism; and, what can be the advantages and disadvantages of adopting the cultural imperialism premises for analysing the Internet's influence on the society.

Kim (1998) is argues that if mass communication researchers continue to disregard the Internet as an area of research, their theories will become useless. The author discusses several factors, which could potentially impede the adoption of cultural imperialism concepts for the analysis of the Internet. First of all, the difference between a recipient of traditional media and an Internet user (an Internet user is not passive- he/she actively searches for information); and second of all, there is no centralized power of control which would administer the Internet decentralization. Finally, in contrast to traditional media products, which are developed by TV stations or information agencies, in the Internet anyone can create information. Furthermore, Kim claims that thanks to the Internet users can participate in their cultures, despite their geographical location in a given moment. Consequently, it is feasible to stay in touch with their families and friends.

Nonetheless, it is important to acknowledge why the author adopted the ideas of cultural imperialism for research the Internet. Kim (1998) infers that the core reasons are: the unchallenged dominance of English in the cyberspace, Internet's basic infrastructure is located in the US, as well as the majority of Web navigation software is manufactured in the US or in English. Recapitulating, the author implies that the notion of cultural imperialism can be valuable to examine the irregular global flow of information.

Ethical Issues and Social Dilemmas

For a prompt and meaningful discussion as regards to ethical and social challenges the author acknowledges two leading arguments: knowledge flux characteristics in cultural commodities; and, cultural imperialism.

Given the previous sections it is possible to consider that globalization reinforced local inequalities despite enabling worldwide access (Cloete & Moja, 2005). As Quéau (2002) refers: the crux of globalization is to magnify the global divide! This global flux assumes ambiguous features since cyberspace promotes an innovative space-time configuration, as well as is filled with content. According to Costa & Silva (2010) content entails a collective representation and utilization of knowledge, which cultural commodities (movies, TV series, novels, etc) promulgate. This argument is reinforced throughout Nonaka's (1994) contribution: information is a flow of messages which schemas and mental models of each "actor" influence. In addition, this influence can be divided into three layers of actors: micro (individuals), meso (organizations) and macro (states) (Stahl, 2002). Therefore, the holistic and global perception of this manuscript will induce to shed light simply upon macro considerations.

According to Crystal (2003, pp. 12) "without a strong power-base, of whatever kind, no language can make progress as an international medium of communication"; however, this blend configures economic, technological, and cultural power. Moreover, this author argues that the utilization of a *lingua franca* is well documented throughout history, as well as English is an "open" language (etymological roots of several English words entail influences from Latin, Anglo-Saxon, French, etc). Even so, information media technology has distorted the existence of other languages, as will endanger 50% of the world languages during this century (Harrison, 2007), namely native dialects. For that, some organizations have trying to preserve this precious cultural heritage (e.g. The Foundation for Endangered Languages), because as Crystal (2000) refers most of these languages entails an oral tradition. Despite this effort the outcomes are unpredictable, which is crucial to question cultural media dominance. As a response, local regions have attempted to assume two dissimilar responses: a proactive; and, a reactive. At a first glimpse a reactive strategy seems more adequate (e.g. Cuba), but empirical results acknowledge otherwise (Eriksen, 2006).

On the other hand, as this chapter demonstrate Western civilization possess all the technological and financial resources to generate these cultural commodities. As De Laurentis (2006) demonstrates, cultural industries in knowledge economy are clearly uneven in geographically and economic terms. Still following De Laurentis (2006), regional cultural diversity could play an important role for peripheral regions reply to this cultural imperialism, leading to some key dilemmas:

- inequality: despite the effort of the UNESCO projects in funding cultural content productions of indigenous people (e.g. Salazar, 2009), in order to allow self-determination and maintain cultural heritage, the truth is that so far these efforts have been insufficient. Another interesting project that is worthwhile to acknowledge is *How Latitudes Become Forms: Art in a Global* (Dietz, 2003). Dietz (2003) engaged a translocal media art culture that gathers artists from Brazil, China, Croatia, India, Japan, Mexico, Singapore, South Africa, Turkey, and United States. This media art culture is enabled simply by cyberspace (virtual art);
- intellectual property rights: cultural imperialism corrupts indigenous cultural rights, as well as defends the dominant culture (Broude, 2007). This author still claims that international intellectual property laws are an allegory given the concept of culture, despite recognizing that are required at some extent in order to support the process of cultural production. Nevertheless, the author expresses that the current legislation is contrary to the UNESCO Convention on Cultural Diversity (UNESCO, 2005). This argument is even detailed by the work of Gruber (2008; 2006).

FUTURE RESEARCH DIRECTIONS

Bearing in mind the complexity for a comprehensive debate with reference to the underlying topic of this chapter, it is truly challenging to predict future outcomes, or to scrutinize any dominating tendencies. This is the aftermath of current world developments (present events which we are witnessing), since this cultural global flux is shaping non-Western cultures and societies. So far, researchers, as for instance ethnologists, observed the influence of Western culture on various local and regional cultures and its profound consequences. In order to describe these effects concepts like "cultural clash", "cultural contact", "cultural diffusion", "acculturation", "transculturation" have been acknowledged, although its numerous ambiguities imposes a continuous and additional discussion.

Acting as an inspiring guide for this debate, is the sublime writing (literary, language and philosophical interpretations) of Chang (2007), as well as *Le Choc du Numérique* (Hervé Fischer, 2001) (note that I am not trying to develop paradoxical laws for the digital world similarly to Fischer!). Thus, some important remarks will be detailed: cyberspace neutrality; and, "cultural infusion".

Cyberspace is not neutral! This claim is justifiable throughout this contribution, but also if we acknowledge the contributions of Gailey (2009) or, Turilli, Vaccaro & Floridi (2008). Gailey (2009) argues that ICANN need to substantiate its actions resumes the cultural battle (imperialism), because bureaucracy or indecision concerning cyberspace will continue, as well as United States argument (duty to the rest of the world) is simple deontological. Therefore, in order to understand network neutrality is needed to address the following questions (Turilli, Vaccaro & Floridi, 2008):

- what is the ethical nature of cyberspace neutrality?;
- should cyberspace neutrality endorse when considering its ethical implications?;
- what ethical framework should be endorsed for regulating Internet traffic?

Therefore, it is crucial to develop regulatory models that respect market power (resources and influence), and cultural and legal issues. Besides, it should congregate representatives from all groups (United Nations, World Trade Organization, UNESCO, etc) (for a first draft proposal based on similar principles examine Costa, Silva & Pawlak, 2010).

As regards to "cultural infusion" is a personal conceptualization to explore the dialogue between imperialist and remaining cultures. According to the Free Dictionary (2010), infusion resumes the introduction of a solution into the body through a vein for therapeutic purposes. Through a metaphorical interpretation, it is reasonable to consider: solution (Western cultural media), body (worldwide cultures), vein (cyberspace- information and communication technologies), and therapeutic purposes (imperialism). Although, contrarily to the medical perception, this cultural infusion entails an *explanans* and an *explanadum* bidirectional process, which is just starting due to mobility, connectivity and communication (Tsagarousianou, 2004). Moreover, this author claims that Benedict Anderson "imagined communities" will become a reality, which at some extent is explained by Pieterse (2009) layers of global multiculture. Therefore, Dietz (2003) raises the following questions: if cyberspace "non-space" can potentially create a diasporic community, what commons interests will be held? How do equally ideas will be translated across cultures? Does the outcome depend on how components are illustrated, or how individuals comprehend them? It is possible to achieve infusion cultures that are neither isolationist or imperialistic? What will be the response of intellectual property rights?

CONCLUSION

If the notion of knowledge management is adopted worldwide as an attempt to cover all Internet information, then a vast majority of the discussed ideas will be elements of the mass culture. The theory of cultural imperialism is occasionally referred to as a critical theory (Mattelart & Mattelart, 2001; Goban-Klass, 1999), which is connected (loosely) to the perception of culture claimed by the Frankfurt school (particularly by M. Horkheimer or T. W. Adorno). These authors suspected that media uses symbolic violence and are instruments of power or dominance. On the basis of the cultural industry, their analysis demonstrated that culture is a commodity, that is, a product produced and distributed by an industry. The dissemination of a cultural industry (its spreading on new areas and more and more effective production methods) resulted in an inevitable bankruptcy of culture. Cultural imperialism, which grew out of these theories, considers international relations in culture and communication and underscores the unequal exchange of various cultural products. Thus, this theory is yet another critical approach to mass culture, which concentrates on revealing the characteristic methods of production, as well as production objectives. "In accordance with this definition of pop culture, it is composed of works produced in a mechanical, planned, mass manner by specialized groups of people for profit-making only" (Krajewski, 2003, pp. 26). This organization of culture production (subject to market economy) is oriented towards maximum profit-making by producers and mass manipulation, that is, towards wielding control over production and consumption.

REFERENCES

Appadurai, A. (2005). *Modernity at large: Cultural dimensions of globalization* (2nd ed.). Minneapolis, MN: University of Minnesota Press.

Bourdieu, P. (1993). *The field of cultural production*. Cambridge, MA: Polity.

Bourdieu, P. (1996). *The rules of art*. Cambridge, MA: Polity.

Bourdieu, P. (2003). Participant objectivation. *The Journal of the Royal Anthropological Institute*, *9*(2), 281–294. doi:10.1111/1467-9655.00150

Bourdieu, P., & Wacquant, L. J. D. (1992). *An invitation to reflexive sociology*. Chicago: University of Chicago Press.

Broude, T. (2007). *Conflict and complementarity in trade, cultural diversity and intellectual property rights (Paper No. 11)*. Jerusalem: International Law Forum of the Hebrew University of Jerusalem Law Faculty.

Castells, M. (2003). *The internet galaxy: Reflections on the internet, business and society*. New York: Oxford University Press.

Chang, H.-H. (2007). *Fake globalization*. Taipei: Unitas Publishing.

Chomsky, N. (1999). *Year 501: The conquest continues*. Cambridge, MA: South End Press.

Chomsky, N., & McChesney, R. W. (2000). *Profit over people: Neoliberalism and global order*. Toronto, ON: Seven Stories Press.

Cloete, N., & Moja, T. (2005). Transformation tensions in higher education: Equity, efficiency, and development. *Social Research: An International Quarterly*, *72*(3), 693–722.

Costa, G. J. M., & Silva, N. S. A. (2010). Knowledge versus content in e-learning: A philosophical discussion. *Information Systems Frontiers*, *12*(4), 399–413. doi:10.1007/s10796-009-9200-1

Costa, G. J. M., Silva, N. S. A., & Pawlak, P. (2010). Controlling informational society: A Google error analysis! In Portela, I. M., & Cruz-Cunha, M. M. (Eds.), *Handbook of Information Communication Technology Law, Protection and Access Rights: Global Approaches and Issues* (pp. 466–495). Hershey, PA: IGI Global.

Crystal, D. (2000). *Language death*. Cambridge, UK: Cambridge University Press.

Crystal, D. (2003). *English as a global language* (2nd ed.). Cambridge, UK: Cambridge University Press. doi:10.1017/CBO9780511486999

De Laurentis, C. (2006). Digital knowledge exploitation: ICT, memory institutions and innovation from cultural assets. *The Journal of Technology Transfer*, *31*(1), 77–89. doi:10.1007/s10961-005-5014-6

Dietz, S. (2003). How latitudes become forms: Art in a global village. *Walker Art Center*. Retrieved December 15, 2009, from, http://latitudes.walkerart.org/

Drucker, P. F. (1999). *Management challenges for the 21st century*. Burlington, MA: Butterworth-Heinemann.

Eriksen, T. H. (2006, March). *Nations in cyberspace*. Paper presented at the ASEN Conference, London, UK.

Fischer, H. (2007). *Le choc du numérique*. Montréal, QC: VLB Éditeur. (in French)

Floridi, L. (2006). Information technologies and the tragedy of the good will. *Ethics and Information Technology*, *8*(4), 253–262. doi:10.1007/s10676-006-9110-6

Friedman, J. (1999). Indigenous conflicts and discreet bourgeois appeal. *The Australian Journal of Anthropology*, *10*(1), 1–14. doi:10.1111/j.1835-9310.1999.tb00009.x

Gailey, B. (2009). *ICANN, cultural imperialism, and democratization of internet governance*. Unpublished doctoral dissertation, Bryant University, Rhode Island.

Gilpin, R. (2001). *Global political economy- Understanding the international economic order*. Princeton, NJ: Princeton University Press.

Goban-Klass, T. (1999). *Media I komunikowanie masowe. Teorie i analizy prasy, radia, telewizji i Internetu*. Krákow, Poland: Wydawnictwo Naukowe PWN. (in Polish)

Godzic, W. (Ed.). (2001). *Humanista w cyberprzestrzeni*. Krákow, Poland: Wyd Rabid. (in Polish)

Golding, P., & Harris, P. (Eds.). (1997). *Beyond cultural imperialism: Globalization, communication and the new international order*. London: Sage Publications.

Graber, C. B. (2006). The new UNESCO convention on cultural diversity: A counterbalance to the WTO? *Journal of International Economic Law*, *9*(3), 553–574. doi:10.1093/jiel/jgl018

Graber, C. B. (2008). Substantive rights and obligations under the UNESCO convention on cultural diversity. In Schneider, H., & van den Bossche, P. (Eds.), *Protection of Cultural Diversity from an International and European Perspective* (pp. 141–162). Antwerp, The Netherlands: Intersentia.

Grudzewski, W. M., & Hejduk, I. (2005). Zarządzanie wiedzą w organizacjach (in Polish). *E-mentor*. Retrieved June 13, 2009, from http://www.e-mentor.edu.pl/artykul_v2.php?numer=8&id=115

Hardt, M., & Negri, A. (2005). *Empire*. Boston: Harvard Business Press.

Harrison, K. D. (2007). *When languages die: The extinction of the world's languages and the erosion of human knowledge*. London: Oxford University Press.

Horkheimer, M., & Addorno, T. W. (2002). Dialectic of enlightenment: Philosophical fragments (Cultural memory in the present). In Noerr, G. S. (Ed.), *trans. E. Jephcott*. Palo Alto, CA: Stanford University Press.

Huntington, S. P. (2004). *Who are we? The challenges to America's national identity*. New York: Simon & Schuster, Inc.

Jowett, B. (1899). *Protagoras: Dialogues of Plato*. Michigan, MI: The Colonial Press.

Kim, S. (1998), Cultural imperialism on the internet. *The Edge: E-Journal of Intercultural Relations, 1(4)*. Retrieved January 10, 2009, from http://interculturalrelations.com/v1i4Fall1998/f98kim.htm

Kmita, J. (1985). *Kultura i poznanie*. Warszawa, Poland: Wydawnictwo Naukowe PWN. (in Polish)

Krajewski, M. (2003). *Kultury kultury popularnej*. Poznań, Poland: Wydawnictwo Naukowe UAM. (in Polish)

Lister, M. (2003). *New media: A critical introduction*. New York: Routledge.

Manovich, L. (2000). *The language of new media*. Cambridge, MA: MIT Press.

Mattelart, A. (2000). *Networking the world, 1794-2000*. Minneapolis, MN: University of Minnesota Press.

Mattelart, A. (2002). *História da utopia planetária*. Porto Alegre, Portugal: Sulina. (in Portuguese)

Mattelart, A. (2003). *Information society: An introduction*. London: Sage.

Mattelart, A., & Mattelart, M. (2001). *Teorie komunikacji: Krótkie wprowadzenie*. Krákow, Poland: Wydawnictwo Naukowe PWN. (in Polish)

Matteo, T., Vaccaro, A., & Floridi, L. (2008). Network neutrality: Ethical issues in the Internet era. In Bynum, T. (Eds.), *ETHICOMP 2008: Living, Working and Learning Beyond Technology* (pp. 773–774). Mantua, Italy: University of Pavia.

McLuhan, M. (1962). *The Gutenberg galaxy*. London: Routledge & Kegan Paul.

Mróz, A. (2005). From Gutenberg to ICT: New lingua doctus. In Collste, G. (Eds.), *ETHICOMP 2005: Looking Back to the Future (CD: paper 48)*. Linkoping, Sweden: Linkoping University.

Nonaka, I. (1994). A dynamic theory of organizational knowledge creation. *Organization Science*, *5*(1), 14–37. doi:10.1287/orsc.5.1.14

Nonaka, I., & Takeuchi, H. (1995). *The knowledge-creating company*. New York: Oxford University Press.

Nordenstreng, K., & Varis, T. (1974). *Television traffic a one-way street (UNESCO Reports and Papers on Mass Communication, 70)*. Paris: Les Éditions UNESCO.

Nowa Encyklopedia Powszechna. (2004). *Nowa Encyklopedia Powszechna T. 8*. Warszawa, Poland: Wydawnictwo Naukowe PWN. (in Polish)

OCDE. (2008). *OCDE information technology outlook 2008*. Paris: Les Éditions OCDE.

Oxford English Dictionary. (2008). *Oxford English Dictionary*. Oxford, UK: Oxford University Press.

Pieterse, J. N. (2009). Global multiculture: Cultures, transnational culture, deep culture. In Baraldi, C., Borsari, A., & Carli, A. (Eds.), *Hybrids, Differences, Visions: On the Study of Culture* (pp. 1–14). Aurora, CO: Davies Group.

Polanyi, M. (1966). *The tacit dimension*. London: Routledge.

Quéau, P. (2002). Global governance and knowledge societies. *Development*, *45*(4), 10–16. doi:10.1057/palgrave.development.1110398

Rheingold, H. (1992). *The virtual reality*. New York: Touchstone.

Rheingold, H. (1994). *Virtual community: Finding connection in a computerized world*. London: Secker & Warburg Publishers.

Rifkin, J. (2003). *The age of access: The new culture of hypercapitalism where all of life is a paid-for experience* (2nd ed.). New York: Jeremy P. Tarcher/Putman.

Salazar, J. F. (2009). Self-determination in practice: The critical making of indigenous media. *Development in Practice*, *19*(4/5), 504–513. doi:10.1080/09614520902866397

Schiller, H. I. (1976). *Communication and cultural domination*. White Plains, NY: International Arts and Sciences Press.

Soros, G. (1998). *The crisis of global capitalism: Open society endangered*. New York: Public Affairs.

Stahl, B. C. (2002). Ethics and e-teaching: the students' perspective. *Communications of the IIMA*, *2*(3), 51–62.

The Free Dictionary. (2010). Infusion. *TheFreeDictionary.com*. Retrieved November 30, 2009, from, http://www.thefreedictionary.com/infusion

Tsagarousianou, R. (2004). Rethinking the concept of diaspora: Mobility, connectivity and communication in a globalised world. *Westminster Papers in Communication and Culture*, *1*(1), 52–65.

Umesao, T. (1963). Joho sangyo ron. *Chuo-kohron*, 46-58 (in Japanese).

UNESCO. (2005). Convention on the protection and promotion of the diversity of cultural expressions. *UNESCO*. Retrieved November 25, 2009, from http://unesdoc.unesco.org/images/0014/001429/142919e.pdf

KEY TERMS AND DEFINITIONS

Cultural Clash: Acknowledges the influence of Western culture on local and regional cultures, as well as its deep consequences. Nevertheless, social studies refer an array of synonymous of this concept: "cultural contact", "cultural diffusion", "and acculturation, among others.

Cultural Commodities: Concept that recognizes the importance, as well as the similar features of culture as an economical commodity.

Cultural Imperialism: Analysis concerning the unequal impacts of international relations and communication in cultural products distribution.

Cultural Infusion: Author metaphorical analysis for explaining the unequal cultural dialogue between Western culture (centre) and worldwide remaining cultures (peripheral).

Cyberspace: Informational flux between computer networks that allow an interactive experience despite the geographical location. These informational fluxes are filled with cultural content, leading to a global knowledge warehouse.

Humanism: A philosophical approach that refers to human behaviour, namely personal reasoning, experiences and values. Moreover, it claims that individuals should act according to socially accepted patterns.

Knowledge Management: Total of formal methods of collecting and using formal and tacit knowledge organizational participants, as an attempt of its preeminent utilization and being available throughout the organization as new knowledge, and its increasing understanding.

Mass Media: Technologies that enable massive communication, and which influence individuals at various levels. Although, cyberspace has deepen these influences with unforeseen consequences.

Chapter 5
Utilization of Resources: An Ethical Issue — The Anti-Commons and the Aquaculture Case

José António Candeias Bonito Filipe
UNIDE/ISCTE-IUL, Portugal

Manuel Alberto Martins Ferreira
UNIDE/ISCTE-IUL, Portugal

Manuel Francisco Pacheco Coelho
SOCIUS/ISEG-UTL, Portugal

ABSTRACT

Anti-Commons Theory is an interesting theme that is being developed in the area of property rights since the 80's. It intends to explain why an "anti-commons" emerges and why resources may be prone to under-use. In an anti-commons situation there are too many exclusion rights that lead to the under-use of resources. In Portugal, too many people (and institutions) have been involved in the approval processes of aquaculture projects. They may be involved in reaching a decision about the approval of a project which gives rise to the under-utilization of the resources that promoters aimed to exploit. Actually, it takes so long to approve a project that the time required for its implementation may be excessively delayed. This kind of problem results typically from bureaucratic environment. An ethical problem rises with this phenomenon. Projects may not go forward and all the amounts spent in the project will be lost. Besides, a viable project simply can be gone, with all the inherent losses of value.

DOI: 10.4018/978-1-61520-873-9.ch005

INTRODUCTION

Ethics, first of all, discusses matters related to human behaviour and character. If the objective is to discuss ethical issues, human values must not be neglected. In the discussion of ethics in resources exploitation area, particularly in aquaculture field when anti-commons are considered, some questions are posed primarily on resources environment and conservation but also on the violation of the basic rights of individuals and companies. Above all it happens when they propose to create value and to contribute to the improvement of the welfare of the society as a whole. Complex and bureaucratic administrative structures and procedures make these projects unviable.

This chapter has three main parts:

- commons and anti-commons discussion;
- anti-commons, ethics and aquaculture analysis;
- conclusions and final notes and remarks.

First, some ideas are presented on property rights, specifically on commons and anti-commons. The discussion about the concepts is not an objective of the present study. The main objective is to show how anti-commons may represent a problem when agents want to exploit resources and some impediments are posed, objecting to an efficient use of resources. So, in sections 1 and 2, commons and anti-commons conceptualization are presented and the discussion about how anti-commons tragedy happens is introduced. Ethical problems derived from these different situations are discussed.

In the second part (sections 3 and 4), the aquaculture sector in Portugal is approached to develop a case study in which we evaluate the possibility of using the hypothesis suggested by Buchanan & Yoon (2000) that the bureaucracy can be studied with the help of the anti-commons conceptualization. In this context, we approach some questions about ethics in the live resources exploitation, particularly in fisheries and aquaculture projects and raised the legal problems in the Portuguese case. An economic analysis is made to show how under-defined property rights can originate an important loss of value. These two sections comport a rich report on anti-commons tragedies and the relation with the aquaculture problem.

In the third and last part (sections 5, 6 and 7), conclusions of the study are made, highlighting the results of the analysis, specially the fact of the hypothesis of Buchanan & Yoon (2000) is considerably consistent with the problems of Portuguese aquaculture. Important considerations are made about the close connection between ethics, anti-commons in the aquaculture projects and effects over organization's structure, ethics and values. These conclusions are preceded by some solutions and recommendations that remark the importance of overcoming some impediments and barriers posed to the development of projects in the area of aquaculture. At the same time some future directions for the research are suggested.

The objective of this chapter is to show first how the utilization of common resources can carry important ethical problems, but mainly to stress that the many attempts to solve tragedies in the fisheries, by creating interesting projects in aquaculture, are confronted with many obstacles and barriers in the approval process. These obstructions conduct to inefficiencies and carry out also an important ethical problem. In situations in which projects are not approved, there are resources that are invested in the project and considering bureaucracies the projects become not exploited and many financial (and other) resources of investors are lost. Besides, promoters cannot profit with the project and their contribution to replace common fisheries for private aquaculture becomes not successful.

"COMMONS" TRAGEDIES AND ETHICS

Usually, commons are presented first, because commons and anti-commons may be viewed as the two faces of the same coin. According to this, follows a short introduction of the commons case.

Commons have long been a central theme in natural resources economics (Scott, 1979). The second half of the 20th century demonstrated the great problems caused by under-defined property rights for commons (Alchian & Demsetz, 1973; Demsetz, 1967). This kind of situations may represent an inefficient use of the resources (Filipe, Coelho & Ferreira, 2006b) and has generated tragedies around the world (Filipe, Coelho & Ferreira, 2007). The Hardin's metaphor "tragedy of the commons" (Hardin, 1968) is a reference to study the problem of commons in several areas, such as the overexploitation and extinction of species, the problems about human overpopulation, prices externalities, oligopoly behaviour, global warming or air pollution. The problem is that people usually have no incentives to preserve the common areas and common resources and often overuse them (Bjorndal & Conrad, 1987). A resource is prone to be overused when too many people have the privilege of using it and no one has the right to exclude others (Filipe, 2006).

The lack of property rights implies that no one can exclude others to access to a given resource. The existence of many agents to use the resource, in these conditions, causes an inefficient level for the resource use and causes a special motivation for agents over-using it. The real level of utilization for the resource will take place at a higher level compared with the optimal level for the society as a whole (Neher, 1990).

In a situation regarding the "Tragedy of the Commons" very important ethical problems are created. The overexploitation of resources is discarding the availability of the resources for the next generations because resources may collapse or they may get exhausted. Many examples can be presented, studied from the historical reality of the last decades. The collapse of the fishing stocks of several species or the disintegration of many forests in the world are cases that can be showed.

The conservation of natural resources is an ethical issue that is relevant to study. Besides, when some agents propose themselves not to exploit a resource because they are worried with resources preservation, if one agent considers that there is an opportunity to gain advantages to exploit the resources that another agent has left and he does it, the tragedy comes and an ethical question is posed. The agent that is concerned about the future has lost the rents for not exploiting the resource and, as a consequence, the other agent has won the short run rents for exploiting it.

This problem represents very well the traditional formal issue "Dilemma of the Prisoner" that is relevant in the Game Theory analysis (Filipe, 2007; Filipe, Coelho & Ferreira, 2005). This problem is posed in the Game Theory for situations in which the two players in the game have dominant strategies, what makes that the solution of the game is a dominant strategies' equilibrium. This equilibrium is stable and the players will not change their choices. What is a problem is that this kind of solution implies a total payoff that is under the result one that the players could have, if they had some form of cooperation between them. In these situations, the players will choose the dominant strategy (which in the case of the natural resources is always the strategy of non conservation) and they will not have incentives to use efficiently and conserve the resource. The players are compelled to switch this strategy because they are functioning in competition conditions. So, this puts the players in a situation that represents a dilemma with ethical boundaries. By one side, the fisherman really thinks that is important to have a proper management policy for the use of the resource in the long term but by the other side he is compelled to have an egoistic and myopic view of the resource use and exploit it too much compared with the ideal inter-temporal production level.

The problem of over-fishing has long been claiming for good practices coming from international cooperation and coming from a preserving approach on the processes of decision making of resource management institutions. This may be some kind of a contribution to solve some of the multiple problems in the ethical area of commons. So, to solve the problem of maintaining the biodiversity, the preservation and related ethical issues in this area it is necessary to pose questions about how to use environment and Earth resources and how to treat other species, plant or animal.

This problem raises a central question in resources economics. What should be the level of the inter-temporal discount rate, that is, the time preference rate? This discount rate allows making the evaluation of projects. In this sense, its level is a form of highlighting the relation between present and future consumption. It gives an idea about the way present generation gives importance to the resources left to the future generations and their level of welfare. This choice has also important ethical resonances.

Law is the first pillar for a rational exploitation of commons resources and the support on the preservation of resources, like fishing resources. Illegal fishing has been traditionally a big problem on this matter. Therefore it covers a wide range of behaviours. Any violation of national laws or international regulations, or any failure to comply with the recommendations of international bodies, especially those of Regional Fisheries Organisations, constitutes an infringement. The fundamental problem in fisheries management is to obviate the tendency towards overexploitation of the resources under common waters in the regime of open access. Regulation methods used to curb this tendency of overfishing and overcapacity includes gear restrictions, area and seasonal closures, TACs, ITQs, limiting entry and other forms of reducing fishing effort (Coelho & Lopes, 2000; Clark, 1980). So, public enforcement of law, that is, the use of public agents to detect and sanction violators of legal rules, is important for fighting illegal fishing (Polinsky & Shavell, 2000).

To give an idea of ethical issues that are posed in such a situation, a formal model of fisheries law enforcement is introduced to show how fishing firms behave and fisheries policies are affected by costly, imperfect enforcement of fisheries regulation (Sumaila, Alder & Keith, 2006; Sutinen & Anderson, 1985). This model combines standard Gordon/Schaefer fisheries model (Clark & Munro, 1975) with the theory of crime and punishment of Becker (1968).

Let's assume that, whatever means are applied to reduce catch rates, any catch level above the level of the permitted quota for a certain fishing, q^*, is illegal. If we suppose a system of individual non-transferable quotas, the amount of the individual firm catch above its quota $(q_i - q_i^*)$ is illegal. If detected and convicted, a penalty fee is imposed on the firm in an amount given by f,

Equation 1. Fee total amount

$$f = f(q_i - q_i^*),$$

where $f > 0$, if $q_i > q_i^*$; and $f = 0$, otherwise;

Equation 2. First derivative

$$\frac{\partial f}{\partial q} \geq 0$$

and,

Equation 3. Second derivative

$$\frac{\partial^2 f}{\partial q^2} \geq 0;\ \forall\ q_i > q_i^*.$$

An individual firm's profit before penalty is given by:

Equation 4. Individual firm profit

$$\prod{}^i (q_i x) = p * q_i - c^i (q_i x)$$

where p denotes the price of fish, x is the size of fish stock and $c(.)$ is the cost function. Let's assume that firms are price takers. In an imperfect law enforcement regime not every violator is detected and convicted. Let the probability of detection and conviction be given by θ, and, to simplify, presume that all firms face the same probability. If detected and convicted of a violation, a firm's profit will be:

Equation 5. Firm profit after a convicted violation

$$\prod^{i}(q_i x) = f(q_i - q_i{}^*)$$

If not:

Equation 6. Firm profit after non-convicted violation

$$\prod^{i}(q_i x).$$

So, expected profits are:

Equation 7. Expected profits

$$\theta\left[\prod^{i}(q_i x) - f(q_i - q_i^*)\right] + (1-\theta)\prod^{i}(q_i x)$$

Assuming that firms are risk neutral and maximizing expected profits, each q_i is determined by the first order condition (subscripts other than i denote partial derivatives)

Equation 8. Risk neutral and maximizing expected profits

$$\prod^{i}_{q}(q_i x) \geq \theta^{f_q(q_i - q_i^*)}$$

This solution has a clear economic meaning. For a given stock size (x), the firm sets its catch rate at a level in excess of its quota, where marginal profits equals the expected marginal penalty. If there were no penalty for fishing beyond legal quota, or if there were no probability of being detected and convicted ($f = 0$ or $\theta = 0$) the firm would set its catch at the open access catch rate. This approach reveals the importance of empirical studies trying to estimate the factors that ensure compliance with the regulation (Sutinen & Gauvin, 1989). These studies give important basis for public authority decision about the actions to be implemented. Stigler (1970) argues that public authorities have four basic means to improve compliance:

- minimizing the chances that violations will go undetected;
- maximizing the probability that sanctions will follow the detection of violations;
- speeding up the process from time to detection to assignment of sanction;
- making the sanctions larger.

There is a dispute among experts about the best alternatives. Some scholars have argued that the probability of being detected is more important than the size or magnitude of the sanction, while others argue that making the charging time follow as closely as possible to the detection of illegal behaviour is the most important factor in enhancing compliance. Others, also, put in evidence the level of expenditure oriented to monitoring activities (Tietenberg, 2003). An ethical vision is seen as a reflex of the model. That is, the authority practices of enforcement have an ethical reason. Governments can impose measures to create fairness and trust between the players and raise the compliance of fishermen because it is the only way to assure that the sacrifices of some fishermen in the recovery of the stocks are not in vain because of the irresponsible action of others.

ETHICS AND LIVE RESOURCES EXPLOTATION: FISHERIES AND AQUACULTURE PROJECTS, HOW "ANTI-COMMONS" HAPPEN?

There are other ways to offer fish in the market without producing wild fish. An entrepreneurial way to profit with the imposition of lower catches is to arrange alternatives to fisheries, particularly through the development of projects of aquaculture, friends of sea live resources. In the fishing area, this allows authorities to deal with the problem of overexploitation creating alternatives to fisheries, approving projects to be implemented in aquaculture sector. The aim is to reduce the fishing activity and to create artificially conditions for sea recovering. So, aquaculture may be seen as a possible part of the solution for the problem of fisheries overexploitation.

Some of the conflicts that result from ethical relationship between private agents and public agents or also some ones that result from environmental policies deal with the rights of individuals versus the rights of the state and with the rights of property owners versus those of the community. The ways of dealing with the environmental issues may vary according the organizations that intend to protect the environment and some conflicting situations may result from the way environment is faced. Often, a private agent intending to exploit a resource for self interest is contributing also with the project for the public good. This fact for itself permits to solve some ethical issues. When a private agent intends to implement an aquaculture project his interest is to make profit. Anyway, this will allow that sea live resources may be conserved. Aquaculture fish offer in the market is increased, given an existing demand. This means that aquaculture can give a strong contribution for reducing sea fisheries. This situation raises an important discussion on property rights. In the last decades, there has been an innovative approach to the issues generated by the excessive fragmentation of property rights, in order to solve this kind of problems. It has been classified as anti-commons tragedies (Filipe, Coelho & Ferreira, 2006a).

Michelman (1982) presented the anti-commons as "a type of property in which everyone always has rights respecting the objects in the regime, and no one is ever privileged to use any of them except as particularly authorized by others". Heller (1998) states that in an anti-commons problem there is a property regime in which numerous owners hold effective exclusion rights over a scarce resource. Therefore, the coexistence of multiple exclusion rights creates conditions for the suboptimal use of the common resource. The idea is that too many property rights lead to a sub-exploitation (a sub-utilization) for a given resource.

Heller brought a powerful tool for the analysis of property rights, which global implications are not known yet. Property rights are under-defined in many situations (Heller, 2008). In relation to anti-commons, the undefined limits for property rights trigger several problems that are expressed by the under-use of the resources as well as by loss of value. Indeed, an anti-commons problem produces tragedies that are presented as the mirror effect when it is compared with the tragedies of the commons (Parisi, Depoorter & Schulz, 2005). In fact, a "tragedy of the anti-commons" occurs when multiple agents have the right to exclude others from the use of a scarce resource but none of them has an effective privilege for its use.

When several agents take decisions about how to use a specific resource which is jointly held and exploited by all of them, and when one of them impose his/her own decision on the others, imposing his/her veto power, we face an anti-commons problem. In such a situation, all the agents must agree on the utilization given to the jointly used resource otherwise the resource may simply not be used or will be underused. We find the "Tragedy of the Anti-commons" when resources remain idle even in the economic region of positive marginal productivity. Acting under conditions of individualistic competition, exclusion rights will be exercised even when the use of the common resource by one part could yield net social benefits. One way of overcoming the inherent problems of anti-commons situations is to gather all the rights in a usable private property. However, this is often slow and complex.

Buchanan & Yoon (2000) have created a model in which commons and anti-commons are viewed as symmetrical. They used the same framework for the analysis of both theories and have suggested that this kind of conceptualization could be used to study the problems generated by bureaucracy. In a situation of anti-commons, once more there are several cases in which ethical questions may be posed. For example, each agent's veto power makes that a resource may rest idle or sub-utilized. Often, this resource is important for one specific agent that is co-proprietary of the resource but has not the right of using it without the consent of the others. In aquaculture, an investment of a private investor in a project may collapse because several public agents, each one with a veto power, make it unviable since they delay the approval or reject it.

In the case of aquaculture, valuable projects promoted by individual private companies can face the authorities' arms and their veto power when their own interests are contradictory with those of the project or even when the will of the agencies representatives diverge from the interest of the submitted project. Sometimes, some entities that must evaluate the project are more interested in discussing some particular non relevant issues than to promote the discussion of the real interest of the project and often their position is to say no or to delay the process approval. This situation leads to the anti-commons situation in which some entities have the power to impose their position to the others and consequently the viable project approval is rejected. The multiple rights to decide about the project, some with veto power, conduct to the suboptimal use of the resource or to its non utilization and, in this sense, the tragedy of the anti-commons happens.

In aquaculture private projects, considering that they can contribute to solve the problem of the "tragedy of the commons" in the world oceans with the problem of the overexploitation of fisheries resources, it is essential that practice change and projects are approved in a more rational basis. In the same way that we were reflecting about the tragedy of the commons in the case of anti-commons, regulation is also an important reflex of the implicit ethical issues. Law is fundamental to conserve and protect environment and so it is in this area of fishing resources. Rules should be precise and simple enough to be implemented and to be fulfilled. In aquaculture projects law often seems to arise too many procedures and to generate too many public agents involved in the decision process that complicate the final decision. An anti-commons problem can emerge from this complex situation. The multiple agencies and their work frequently frustrate worthwhile projects and economic growth (Filipe *et al.*, 2008).

LOSING VALUE IN AQUACULTURE PROJECTS IN PORTUGAL DUE TO "ANTI-COMMONS" ISSUE?

The General Problem

As it can be seen, the anti-commons problem can be studied in Portugal for projects in aquaculture area. Many entities must give their approval for a project to be implemented. All administrative procedures may motivate a situation of delayed global authorization. There can be no doubt that many interesting projects which are profitable, fishing-friendly and viable will simply not begin to be exploited because there are just too many exclusion rights. Even though there is an agent that wants to exploit a resource with important economic, biological and social consequences, bureaucracy and administrative procedures simply make the project unviable.

It can be anticipated an important loss of value. If there is a project to be launched (which requires financial resources) and the project has a delayed approval there will be no created value or even there will be a destruction of value. The agent who supports the project loses an important period of time to implement it and he loses money because there is an important period without producing. In many situations, projects are not implemented because the favourable and the appropriate time have simply gone.

Sometimes, government agencies are so complex that decision processes are not efficient. This leads to situations in which private entrepreneurs loose resources with projects that get lost just because government agencies make them unviable. A very pertinent ethical matter is born with the fact that the State, that should protect its companies and citizens, breaks the rules making a subversive process destroying the project by wasting time and making disparate decisions. This view is consistent with the suggestion of Buchanan & Yoon (2000) that the anti-commons construction offers an analytical means of isolating a central feature of "sometimes disparate institutional structures". That is, the bureaucracy. The persistence of bureaucratic circuits of approval and implementation of projects can difficult the entrepreneurship activities and it diminishes the potential of regional and coastal development.

The Portuguese Experience: And the Emergence of "Anti-Commons"

To show how we can speak about the emergence of an "anti-commons tragedy" in the aquaculture sector of Portuguese fisheries we must analyze the results of previous fisheries management plans in Portugal and the perspectives and aims of the new Portuguese Fisheries Program 2007-2013. In the last years, the impacts of investments in the aquiculture sector have been of little relevance and directed just for traditional species. Investments have not allowed significant productions. This situation is the reflex of:

- the insufficient dimension of economies of scale and the technical and organizational inadequacies of the project promoters;
- the emergency of the problem of the "tragedy of the anti-commons", in the sense that Buchanan & Yoon (2000) have designated. This reflects an excessive partition of the property rights and the existence of multiple bureaucratic circuits that create an enormous complexity and administrative slowness of processes of approval and implementation of the projects;
- the dimension of the environmental issues that are involved and the lack of a plan that regulates the coastal areas and that establish the territories to be used in the aquaculture sector, constitutes impediments equally significant.

The new Program for fisheries (the Fisheries Operational Program for the period 2007-2013) involves some particular risks in the aquaculture area to be highlighted (DGPA, 2007), such as:

- the experience has been demonstrating that the involved companies do not have the dimension, the economies of scale and the technical and organizational capacities to be involved in these projects;
- these developments involve an additional risk, larger periods of return of the investment and an additional competition in this area, particularly from the productions of the countries in the South of Europe.

The Portuguese Program for the Fisheries for 2007-2013 evidences a strong expectation from the private sector. However, the financial participation of the Fisheries European Fund is lower than the usual rates of co-participation. This problem gets a major dimension because of the "tragedy of the anti-commons".

The Legal and Procedures Problem

This aquaculture problem is fitted under the control and supervision of *Ministério da Agricultura, do*

Desenvolvimento Rural e das Pescas (see *Decreto Regulamentar nº 14/2000*- September, 21st, 2000), that is the Ministry for Agriculture, Fishing and Agriculture sector. This decree specifies the requisites and conditions needed to install and exploit a plant on this area. The *Decreto Regulamentar nº 9/2008* (March, 18th, 2008) defines a set of rules specifically for installations offshore. The responsible Department for Aquaculture is specifically DGPA (*Direcção Geral das Pescas e Agricultura*, that is General Board for Fishing and Agriculture), which is responsible for supervising and controlling the activity of aquaculture sector. The initial steps for a project approval are (*Decreto Regulamentar nº 14/2000*):

1. Request to DGPA;
2. The request must have the following elements attached (Art 10º- nº 3):
   a. copy of ID card of the requester;
   b. authorization to use the aquatic domain, issued by the competent authority;
   c. property documents for the land;
   d. technical description of the productive process;
   e. topographic plant of the local (1:25000);
   f. design layout of the facilities (1:5000);
   g. detailed project of the infra structures, at 1:200;
   h. coordinates of the area referred to a central country reference point;
   i. plant and detail drawings of the infra structures at 1:50 or 1:100;
   j. sea sign project, depending on the type of installation.

The competent authority for this specific kind of activity is named *Administração da Região Hidrográfica* (in English, Board for the Hydrographical Region) and has a huge power, demanding an aquatic tax and controls all the activities within 500 meters from the coast line. This decree refers that (art. 12º) whenever the site is located on an area under maritime jurisdiction, DGPA along with *Capitania do Porto* (Captaincy of the Port), promotes the following two actions within the next 30 days after having received the whole process:

a. writes an edict (edital) with the authorization request, which must be visible for 30 days on a few legal buildings, so that third parts can claim against the request;
b. call the survey committee.

If there are reactions against the project, it may be enough to block the project. Moreover, Art. 10º- nº 7 states that the project referred on j) of the number 3, is sent by DGPA to *Capitão do Porto* (Captain of the Port) of the area, with the objective of emitting a binding opinion, within 60 days, after consulting the *Instituto Hidrográfico* (Hydrographical Institute) and the *Direcção de Faróis* (Lighthouse Direction). The process is sent now by DGPA to each of the 10 entities involved in the survey that are described in the 13th article- see art 11º- nº 4. This part of the process may have already consumed 2 to 3 months. The referred entities that compose the survey committee are the following:

a. *Capitão do Porto* or another officer who may replace him;
b. DGPA representative;
c. IPIMAR representative;
d. Maritime public domain representative;
e. ICN representative (today ICNB);
f. DRA representative (*Direcção Regional do Ambiente*, which means Regional Board for the Environment);
g. *Instituto Português de Arqueologia* (Portuguese Institute for Archaeology) representative;
h. *Direcção Geral de Veterinária* (General Board for Veterinary);
i. Direcção Geral de Saúde (in English, General Board for Health);

j. Municipalities' representatives (all involved areas).

Gathering all these representatives on a certain date is quite difficult. The committee only works with the presence of the majority of its members. There are at least 3 members of this committee whose starting point is usually against:

a. *Capitão do Porto*, because he predicts more work and trouble in the future if the project is installed;
b. Maritime public domain representative, for the same reason;
c. ICN because they are always against everything in advance.

All the other members do not even care about the subject and their participation is not pleasant at all for them. The survey has to be scheduled within the next 30 days after the end of the edict term (art 14º). The result of the survey is considered favourable just if the whole committee members agree (art 15º). DGPA informs the requester about the result of the survey within the next 30 days. If the result is favourable under restrictions the requester has 30 days to correct the project according to these restrictions (art 16º). So, the edict is usually published 2 or 3 months after the request demand. It has to be published for 30 days before the survey is set up and the scheduled date for the survey may still take 30 days more to be set. All this may have taken more than 5 months, which clearly reveals how "disparate institutional structures" may lead to an irrational ending.

This study for Portugal reinforces the idea of anti-commons. There are just few empirical studies on this conceptualization and most of them focus on the pharmaceutical industry. Our attempts are directed to the fisheries sector and natural resources management. However it is not a unique case. Buchanan & Yoon (2000) also encountered other applications of the anti-commons tragedy, which represent an important step in the research of the relation between this conceptualization and ethics in economics. It shows how practices affect competence management and must rely on a systematic evaluation and planning of competences of public agents. This is the form of reducing the problems derived from bureaucracy when there are too many property rights involved in the organization decision process.

In the paper of Buchanan & Yoon (2000), the authors make reference to the case of Sardinia, Italy; here they were informed that a potential entrepreneur wanted to invest in a combined seaside/hunting-preserve resort. This action was inhibited by the necessity of getting permits of several regional agencies (tourist board, hotel-restaurant agency, wildlife protection agency), each one of which holds effective exclusion rights to the project. If the project was implemented it would be productive of value, but overlapping and intrusive regulatory bureaucracy introduced inefficiencies and provoke a loss of value.

The Economic Problem

A significant loss of value may result with this process. This leads to a problem of value destruction because financial resources are required for the project but no value is created due to the delay on the approval. The inefficiencies introduced by overlapping and intrusive regulatory bureaucracies are widely recognized and may be studied with the help of anti-commons conceptualization. When an entrepreneur seeks to invest in an aquaculture project and the action is inhibited by the need to obtain permits from various national and regional agencies, each of which holds effective exclusion rights on the project, we encounter the mirror effect of the "tragedy of the commons". Therefore, the Portuguese case suggests that all the authorities involved in the approval process (environmental, territorial, health, etc.) have prevented some value-reducing development but also value-enhancing development.

Economists and environmentalists usually concentrate too much attention on the commons side of natural and environmental resources and neglect the anti-commons side. This debate also raises another interesting issue. Neither the motivation of the bureaucratic authorities nor the constraints on their exclusion rights is captured by a simple one-dimensional theoretic model. Those who have the power to issue permits may not seek to maximize rents and, perhaps of greater importance, may be authorized to refuse permits only with cause. These agencies cannot or may not wish to acquire pecuniary gains. Therefore, the allowance for such non economic motivation on the part of the excluders also suggests that the potential conflict may not be primarily distributional but also reflect different objectives to facilitate welfare development.

The economic view may bring the discussion of an ethical perspective as well. Sometimes, the different visions of a project from economists or environmentalists' points of view may be different just because they have different forms and grids for analysis and not just because of self interest. There may be different kind of values and specific contextualization for their approaches. In this sense, we have also an ethical question.

SOME ADDITIONAL CONSIDERATIONS ABOUT ETHICS

The ethical problems in environment issues were greatly influenced by Thomas Malthus (1798). He questioned about how many human beings could be supported by Earth ecosystems. He stressed, like some others like Robert Owen (Latham, 1987), the need of controlling human population growth. Other authors like William Godwin (1793) defended that the progress would allow improving living standards of people. In fact, environmental issues continuously involved conflicts and opposite ideas.

In the natural resources area, by the end of the 19th century some natural resources were already threatened and a strong opposition between conservation movements and economic interests has appeared.

Conflicts are arisen between those who want to protect the natural environment and its species and those who think that this is not worrying or simply those who are not perturbed or sensible to environmental protection problems. These conflicts usually are centered on economic issues. Population increase and economic growth are the two most important factors that affect the demand for food fish. This permit to pose the following questions:

- the pressure posed to live sea resources oblige that viable solutions are developed to overpass the overexploitation of fish stocks?;
- aquaculture is a part of the solution? Or other ethical problems, for example, on environmental area emerge with big aquaculture projects? Particularly, aquaculture projects exploitation contributes for the environmental degradation of the aquatic environment?

A sustainable and responsible aquaculture is needed and must conduct, in other aspects, to the:

- increasing of the fish stocks offer in the market;
- increasing of the biomass levels of species in the sea;
- improvement of the quality of waters in the aquaculture plants;
- guarantee of safe levels of medical use in the aquaculture products.

Frequently, aquaculture projects do not consider a sustainable and a responsible exploitation, what poses several ethical questions. The importance of a responsible aquaculture may dictate the difference between the success of sea stocks development and the collapse of the stocks of several species. The combination of increasing demand for food and other goods from the finite natural resource base need that aquaculture projects are approved with diligence and with fast authorities' responses in order to allow an important increasing of the fish stocks in the market through this means. The efforts of fishing producers, researchers, national governments and development assistance agencies may contribute to solve emergent problems that are resulting from the development of non responsible projects.

Some important ethical implications are involved when we discuss this kind of phenomena. If there is a project for aquaculture and the project has to be submitted to an approval process, a collective group (administrative entities) has to analyze it. Often many interests are involved and the project can be delayed in terms of approval and implementation or even rejected. Frequently the time of implementation has gone. Two main ethical points must be analyzed about this subject:

a. there are too many regulators, and projects must be analyzed by every one of them. Too much time to overpass all the steps and when ready for implementation it may be too late. Too many resources were spent on the project and the project simply is now unviable. An ethical question is posed. The project is viable and creates value for the investor and for the community but all the time wasted in bureaucratic analysis made the project unviable. A considerable amount was spent in the project for nothing;
b. sometimes there are conflicting interests considering the promoters of the project (investors) and entities who are analyzing the project. These entities make things to slow down. And projects rest too long in the cabinets to be studied. Projects got unviable because a conflicting problem of interests. Again an ethical question is posed.

SOLUTIONS AND RECOMMENDATIONS

Aquaculture exploitation in Portugal, like it happens in other countries, involves many bureaucratic questions (Buchanan & Yoon, 2000) and with this, some ethical questions rise. Some important measures are needed and it is necessary to change structures and behaviours. Legislation must be recovered to avoid this kind of procedures and clean up this kind of obstruction structures and lobby organizations. A need to reduce the number of participants in the decision process seems to be clear.

Due to the importance that aquaculture activity has for Portugal and owing to the confusion of entities involved in the approval process, maybe the best solution is to create a High Authority, which would be the only responsible for the approval of the processes. The other entities nominated would be strictly consultant entities of the High Authority. Besides, the binding consultant entities should be reduced to three: DGPA, Health Authorities and IPIMAR.

The evaluation of these entities is fundamental in the process of approval of a project in this area. DGPA is the agency that regulates all the activities in the fisheries sector. Health Authorities must determine the health conditions for the projects and the accompanying process in this area. IPIMAR is the institution for the sea resources investigation. Other entities should create departments for fast answers in the non binding consultant process, as a way to create the best conditions for a sustainable and responsible project, as a whole.

Another important ethical matter results from the fact that aquaculture production may replace the sea production of fish and so it contributes for the preservation of sea stocks. The stocks dimension often determines the evolution of biomass for the stocks of given specie. The role of aquaculture as a part of a solution for the problem of exploitation is really relevant. It is important to note that there is a specific need of regulation for the public maritime domains, what is yet misregulated for aquaculture area in open sea. Public deciders must introduce maritime territorial physical definition of areas according to several requirements, particularly: areas for aquaculture, areas for fishing, areas for nature conservation, and so on. At the same time, authorities' competences must be defined and bounded.

The fisheries management requires the stakeholders' expertise and experience and gives good insights for knowledge management. In general, knowledge management comprises a set of interesting practices. Portuguese Authorities can identify and work on these practices. Such insights and experiences comprise knowledge, either embodied in individuals or embedded in organizational practice. These efforts focuses on the improvement of the organizations, which are subject of public policies and this kind of studies are very important to highlight the motivations leading the organizations to undertake a knowledge management approach. Making available increased knowledge in the development of products and services, increasing network between internal and external agents, solving complex problems as it is the case of bureaucracy, facilitating and managing innovation and organizational learning; all of these subjects are important forms of developing knowledge management.

FUTURE RESEARCH DIRECTIONS

In this context, Chaos Theory may be involved to explain the importance of keeping the health of ecosystems (Scones, 1999). It is important to analyze the behaviour of stocks when they reach certain bounds. In these cases, small changes in ecosystems may cause the complete deterioration of stocks and the final collapse of ecosystems, which in extreme cases can lead to extinction. This is particularly important for schooling species (Clark, 1985; Clark, 1974), which are concentrated in high density areas in small space. These are species that tend to live in large schools.

This can be extremely dangerous due to poor biotic potential of the species subject to this kind of pressure (Smith, 1968). The reproductive capacity requires a minimum value below which the extinction is inevitable. Since the efficiency of the school is proportional to its size, the losses due to the effects of predation are relatively high for low levels of stocks. This implies non-feedback in the relation stock-recruitment, which causes a break in the curves of income-effort, so that an infinitesimal increase on fishing effort leads to an unstable condition that can lead to its extinction (Filipe *et al.*, 2009).

The analysis of Chaos Theory has already been developed with some interesting results in Fisheries (Filipe, Ferreira & Coelho, 2005) and it is very relevant when we want to study the effective risks of some species. Anyway, some developments are necessary to get new effective results to the study of these problems. This analysis brings the necessity of a deeper treatment of data to reveal some important trends for some Portuguese species, what highlights the importance of aquaculture programs as a contribution to preserve species in risk of severe degradation of stocks or even is risk of extinction. This analysis reinforces the importance of a fast approval process of projects in aquaculture, even as a contribution to understand the thematic of ethical discussion on this approach.

An important point to discuss about this matter in Portuguese sector of fisheries is the relation between the traditional fisheries activities and the new aquaculture subsector. In this area, many things have to be researched in order to provide further practical measures. In this sense, we must discuss the trade off and complementarities between these two activities in terms of employment, competitiveness and entrepreneurship. Some important statistical developments about aquaculture are determinant in order to bring a stronger and robust analysis of the sector problems. At the same, an investigation of the relation between the economic side of this problematic and the biologic dynamics of the resources is required. There are a lot of issues to research in the area of the illness, growth capacity of the species, carrying capacity of the environment and the possible irreversibility that can result from the specific decisions made in an uncertain ambience.

CONCLUSION

Studies about anti-commons require innovative approaches to research. In fact, anti-commons considerations may result not only from taking problems of the real world into account but also from the new methodologies used to analyze them in research.

The anti-commons conceptualization seems to have an impressing capacity to be used in the analysis of the effects of bureaucracy. Empirical studies have been concentrated in the pharmaceutics industry. Our proposal of studying the aquaculture with the help of this framework suggests that the Buchanan & Yoon (2000) proposal satisfies the purposes of our study. Of course, this is just a working hypothesis but the results seem to be consistent with their suggestion. The analysis in this study is consistent with the idea that the existence of an extensive group of government agencies has a veto power that create impediments to good projects, the ones that can contribute to increase offer of fish in the market, instead to fish it in the sea banks, and contribute to maintain the health of oceanic ecosystems, preserving resources and guarantee the biodiversity for future generations.

At the same time, we can highlight the specific ethical problems that the situation brings out. Consequently, we consider that our aim of investigation has been reached. Anyway, this perspective of analysis was intended to complement other points of view on the resource utilization issue. More discussion is needed about the boundaries of the concept to clarify its precise meaning in the broader context of property rights.

Another important aspect of our research resides in the effects of the organizations and their ethics when they are confronted with the emergence of an anti-commons tragedy. This implies an important research about the values and principles of the organizations structures, rules of the game, human resources, the hierarchical relations in the organizations, the management and administrative circuits and processes.

REFERENCES

Alchian, A. A., & Demsetz, H. (1973). The property rights paradigm. *The Journal of Economic History*, *33*(1), 16–27. doi:10.1017/S0022050700076403

Becker, G. S. (1968). Crime and punishment: An economic approach. *The Journal of Political Economy*, *76*(2), 169–217. doi:10.1086/259394

Bjorndal, T., & Conrad, J. M. (1987). The dynamics of an open access fishery. *The Canadian Journal of Economics. Revue Canadienne d'Economique*, *20*(1), 74–85. doi:10.2307/135232

Buchanan, J. M., & Yoon, Y. J. (2000). Symmetric tragedies: Commons and anticommons. *The Journal of Law & Economics*, *43*(1), 1–13. doi:10.1086/467445

Clark, C. W. (1974). Possible effects of schooling on the dynamics of exploited fish populations. *Journal du Conseil Internatinal pour L'Exploration de la Mer*, *36*(1), 7–14.

Clark, C. W. (1980). Towards a predictive model for the economic regulation of commercial fisheries. *Canadian Journal of Fisheries and Aquatic Sciences*, *37*(7), 1111–1129. doi:10.1139/f80-144

Clark, C. W. (1985). *Bioeconomic modelling and fisheries management*. New York: John Wiley & Sons.

Clark, C. W., & Munro, G. R. (1975). The economics of fishing and modern capital theory: A simplified approach. *Journal of Environmental Economics and Management*, *2*(2), 92–106. doi:10.1016/0095-0696(75)90002-9

Coelho, M. F. P., & Lopes, R. J. (2000). The common fisheries policy and the feasibility of ITQs. In Hatcher, A., & Robinson, K. (Eds.), *The Definition and Allocation of Use Rights in European Fisheries* (pp. 138–156). Portsmouth, UK: CEMARE/University of Portsmouth.

Demsetz, H. (1967). Toward a theory of property rights. *The American Economic Review*, *57*(2), 347–359.

DGPA. (2007). Programa operacional da pesca 2007-2013. *Direcção Geral das Pescas e Agricultura*. Retrieved August 1, 2009, from http://www.dg-pescas.pt/pls/portal/docs/folder/dgpa_content_area/noticias/destaques/po_pesca_22_5_07.pdf

Filipe, J. A. C. B. (2006). *O drama dos recursos comuns. Um caso de aplicação da teoria dos jogos aos comuns da pesca. Estudo da Cooperação aplicada à pesca da sardinha nas Divisões VIIIc e IXa do ICES*. Unpublished doctoral dissertation, ISCTE, Lisboa, Portugal.

Filipe, J. A. C. B. (2007). *The drama of fishing commons: Cournot-Nash model and cooperation* (Working Paper 03). Lisboa, Portugal: ISEG/DE.

Filipe, J. A. C. B. (2008). Anti-commons: How tragedies happen. Some cases and the evidences on fisheries. *China- USA. Business Review (Federal Reserve Bank of Philadelphia)*, *7*(11), 9–13.

Filipe, J. A. C. B. (2009). *Complexity, theory of chaos and fishing (Scientific Bi-Annual Magazine)*. Mainz, Germany: Wirtschaft FH Mainz, University of Applied Sciences.

Filipe, J. A. C. B., Coelho, M. F. P., & Ferreira, M. A. M. (2005). Sistemas dinâmicos, caos e os comuns da pesca. *Revista de Economia Global e Gestão*, *X*(2), 45–59.

Filipe, J. A. C. B., Coelho, M. F. P., & Ferreira, M. A. M. (2006a). *A tragédia dos anti-comuns: Um novo problema na gestão da pesca?* (Working Paper No. 15). Lisboa, Portugal: ISEG/UTL, Seminário do Departamento de Economia.

Filipe, J. A. C. B., Coelho, M. F. P., & Ferreira, M. A. M. (2006b, July). *The drama of the commons: An application of Cournot-Nash Model to the sardine in Portuguese waters*. Paper presented at the Thirteen Annual International Conference on Advances in Management (ICAM 2006), Lisboa.

Filipe, J. A. C. B., Coelho, M. F. P., & Ferreira, M. A. M. (2007). *O drama dos recursos comuns. À procura de soluções para os ecossistemas em perigo*. Lisboa, Portugal: Sílabo.

Godwin, W. (1793). *Enquiry concerning political justice and its influence on morals and happiness*. London: G. G. & J. Robinson.

Hardin, G. (1968). The tragedy of the commons. *Science*, *162*(3859), 1243–1248. doi:10.1126/science.162.3859.1243

Heller, M. A. (1998). The tragedy of the anticommons: property in the transition from Marx to markets. *Harvard Law Review*, *111*(3), 621–688. doi:10.2307/1342203

Heller, M. A. (2008). *The gridlock economy*. New York: Basic Books.

Latham, C. (Ed.). (1987). *New harmony collection: 1814-1884*. Indiana, IN: Indiana Historical Society.

Malthus, T. R. (1798). *An essay on the principle of population*. New York: Penguin Classics.

Maynard, J. S. (1968). *Mathematical ideas in biology*. Cambridge, UK: Cambridge University Press.

Michelman, F. I. (1982). Ethics, economics and the law of property. In Pennock, J. R., & Chapman, J. W. (Eds.), *Nomos XXIV: Ethics, Economics and the Law* (pp. 3–40). New York: New York University Press.

Neher, P. A. (1990). *Natural resource economics: Conservation and exploitation*. Cambridge, UK: Cambridge University Press.

Parisi, F., Depoorter, B., & Schulz, N. (2005). Duality in Property: commons and anti-commons. *International Review of Law and Economics*, *25*(4), 1–25. doi:10.1016/j.irle.2005.12.003

Polinsky, A. M., & Shavell, S. (2000). The economic theory of public enforcement of law. *Journal of Economic Literature*, (38): 45–76.

Scones, I. (1999). New ecology and the social sciences: What prospects for a fruitful engagement? *Annual Review of Anthropology*, *28*, 479–507. doi:10.1146/annurev.anthro.28.1.479

Scott, A. (1979). Development of economic theory on fisheries regulation. *Journal of the Fisheries Research Board of Canada*, *36*(7), 725–741.

Stigler, G. J. (1970). The optimum enforcement of laws. *The Journal of Political Economy*, *78*(3), 526–536. doi:10.1086/259646

Sumaila, U. R., Alder, J., & Keith, H. (2006). Global scope and economics of illegal fishing. *Marine Policy*, *30*(6), 696–703. doi:10.1016/j.marpol.2005.11.001

Sutinen, J. G., & Andersen, P. (1985). The economics of fisheries law enforcement. *Land Economics*, *61*(4), 387–397. doi:10.2307/3146156

Sutinen, J. G., & Gauvin, J. R. (1989). An econometric study of regulatory enforcement and compliance in the commercial inshore lobster fishery of Massachusetts. In Neher, P. A. (Ed.), *Rights Based Fishing* (pp. 415–428). New York: Kluwer Academic Publishers.

Tietenberg, T. (2003). *Environmental and natural resource economics* (6th ed.). Reading, MA: Addison Wesley.

KEY TERMS AND DEFINITIONS

Anti-Commons: Dilemmas that seem to arise when interest groups press on for choice rights, often making their arguments in philanthropic terms that appeal to the remaining voters.

Aquaculture: Rearing of fish, shellfish, and some aquatic plants to supplement the natural supply. Fish are reared in controlled conditions worldwide.

Ethics Resonances: Entails the trade-off between the tragedy of the anti-commons and projects present economical value. As a consequence, in order to promote societal welfare it is required a truly institutional knowledge management.

Tragedy of the Commons: Metaphor concerning coordination and payment of public goods.

Section 3
Organizational Knowledge Management Dilemmas

"Education's purpose is to replace an empty mind with an open one"
Malcolm Forbes

The words of Malcolm Forbes clearly resume the importance of education on the knowledge society; yet, to reflect upon the ethical challenges of a participatory culture entails novel approaches to the creative and sharing process of knowledge within ethical norms. These ethical norms will act as praxis for balancing property rights within digital environments without a dictatorial regime that denies the humanist principles of knowledge society. Despite this argument a prompt answer does not exist, because empirical analyses highlight major ethical and social dilemmas in distributed knowledge environments, leading to a proposal: connethionicism.

Chapter 6
The Emerging Ethics of Knowledge Sharing:
Hacker Ethics, Participatory Culture Ethics and Proselytization Commons Ethics

Maslin Masrom
University Teknologi Malaysia, Malaysia

Zuraini Ismail
University Teknologi Malaysia, Malaysia

ABSTRACT

A key challenge that is emerging for organizations in nowadays is how to encourage knowledge sharing. Knowledge sharing is an activity through which knowledge is exchanged among people, a community or organization. Knowledge constitutes a valuable intangible asset for creating and sustaining competitive advantages. Knowledge sharing activities are generally supported by knowledge management systems. Nevertheless, technology comprises simply one of the several issues that influence organizational knowledge sharing, such as organizational culture, trust, and incentives. So, knowledge sharing entails a key challenge in the field of knowledge management because some individuals tend to resist sharing their knowledge with others (it may be an individual, a group, a community, or an organization). The aim of this chapter is to describe and discuss three emerging ethics of knowledge-sharing, namely: (1) hacker ethics, (2) participatory culture ethics, and (3) proselytization commons ethics. Future research directions are suggested and concluded the chapter.

INTRODUCTION

Nowadays, knowledge sharing has become an important organizational activity. Many companies have come up with their own creative efforts to make knowledge sharing happen. Typically, the company will collect and categorize lessons learned, provide yellow pages to help employees locate colleagues who might have access to the knowledge needed, as well as conduct site visits to other businesses. Dixon (2002) stated that these practices allow teams and individuals to successfully develop solutions to difficult problems, thereby reducing the costly duplication of effort while creating new and innovative solutions

DOI: 10.4018/978-1-61520-873-9.ch006

through collaboration. Due to information and communication technology (ICT) advancement and knowledge transmission, knowledge sharing gets more and more important (Liu, 2008).

In today's knowledge era, knowledge sharing is important for success of organizations operating in turbulent and uncertain environment. Many organizations are starting to realize that knowledge shared is knowledge smartly used and leverage (Dixon, 2002). For example, Japanese industry could grow and develop in this knowledge era because of its ability in converting between personal, tacit knowledge of individuals who produce creative insight, and the shared, explicit knowledge which the organization needs to develop new products and innovations (Nonaka & Takeuchi, 1995).

However, the simple equation that knowledge sharing is good for organizations cannot be sustained. Knowledge can be augmented if it is shared, and in this respect knowledge sharing may also prove detrimental to knowledge. Perhaps the most prominent ICT tool for facilitating knowledge sharing is an Intranet. Related problems may occur when information systems, such as Intranets, distributed libraries, document management systems, or groupware applications are introduced to support knowledge sharing (Cheng, Hailin & Hongming, 2008). The common motivation to introduce these technologies is that they may empower the individual knowledge worker by providing the tools to support and boost his or her knowledge-sharing skills (Hendriks, 1999). Hendriks further pointed out that the motivation for knowledge sharing provides the appropriate focus for conceiving the difference such as personal preferences.

Ethics relates to codes of conduct regarded by a community as right and good (Land, Amjad & Nolas, 2006). They are based on values and faith which is determined by rules of proper conduct laid down by higher authority, notions of morality. However, conflicts generally will arise when values clash. Unacceptable, illegal, and unethical use of computers are concerns of information system (IS) and/or information technology (IT) professionals because of the potential harm to society and to the integrity of the IS/IT profession (Leonard & Cronan, 2005). Sharing requires knowledge. We are not sharing if we did not ask for permission or the other party does not accede to our request. Take for example, when library staff takes records without the knowledge or permission of the other library, they are not sharing. They are basically stealing the intellectual property of the other library. Generally, gathering knowledge is easy, but sharing it is difficult. Therefore, the purpose of this chapter is to describe and discuss three emerging ethics of knowledge-sharing, namely: (1) hacker ethics, (2) participatory culture ethics, and (3) proselytization commons ethics. This chapter is best classified as a discussion paper rather than as a research paper.

In this chapter, we would like to discuss the need to share knowledge, how to ethically manage knowledge, as well as how to foster and sustain healthy activities of knowledge sharing. The chapter is divided into four sections. First we provide an overview of the knowledge management, knowledge sharing and ethics. Then, we describe how hacker's participatory culture and, proselytization view of knowledge sharing regarding ethics. Finally, we give some future research directions and end the chapter with a conclusion.

OVERVIEW OF KNOWLEDGE MANAGEMENT, KNOWLEDGE SHARING AND ETHICS

The biggest challenge in fostering a virtual or even the non-virtual community is the supply of knowledge, namely the willingness to share knowledge with other members. Technology, having made rapid and extensive advances particularly in the area of communication, has opened opportunities for the gathering of information and providing a means through which knowledge can be shared

(Hock, 1999). It is obvious that with information and knowledge have an important bearing on where they are going in the future. With technologies as enablers, it facilitates the link functional areas providing effective conduit for information and the sharing of knowledge. Hence, it would be worthwhile to first distinguish knowledge management, knowledge sharing and ethics.

Knowledge Management

Knowledge management refers to how organizations create, use, share, and protect knowledge (Liu, 2008). Gurteen (1999) defined knowledge management as a business philosophy, and it is an emerging set of principles, processes, organizational structures, and technology applications that help people share and leverage their knowledge to meet their business objectives. Knowledge management is fundamentally about sharing knowledge and putting that knowledge to use. Generally, knowledge is kept in people's minds but not shared in an organization (Fong, 2006).

More recent, some accounts (Martin, 2006; Bellinger, Castro & Mills, 2004; Waltz, 2003) have been produced in order to highlight diverse features of the discrete wisdom, knowledge, information, data and measurement. From the blend of largely widespread aspects explained throughout literature (Ullman,2004; Defense Acquisition University, 2003; Vandergriff, 2001), it is possible to promulgate a pyramid with wisdom at the apex and measurement as the base, implies that to achieve each level something is added and the volume is reduced. Thus, each level reflects intellectual capital with different processing and application levels.

As a result, the Wisdom, Knowledge, Information, Data, and Measurement (WKIDM) layers are (Vandergriff, 2008, pp. 433-434):

1. measurement- is defined as physical readings of phenomena from scientific instruments (for example, photons), or event/object observations by individuals or groups;
2. data- are the symbols, numbers, textual clauses, and other descriptive phrases or displays of measurements (for example, evidence);
3. information- is built from the organization of data sets through quantitative and/or qualitative analysis that relate data sets, and can range from mathematic equations, paragraphs, graphical illustrations, or images;
4. knowledge is created by applying experience to available measurements, data, and information;
5. wisdom results from the application of cognitive capability and judgment.

Despite earlier management principles addressed organizational knowledge, Fong & Chu (2006) detected that only during the 20th century, individuals' become aware of this importance and significance for an forceful organizational growth as a consequence of today's market characteristics (competition and uncertainty). Nowadays, knowledge creation and appliance is vital to the endurance of businesses. Potential motives for this scenario, among others are (Gurteen, 1999):

1. intangible products including ideas, processes, and information that are taking a growing share of global trade from the traditional, tangible goods of the manufacturing economy;
2. increasingly the only sustainable competitive advantage is continuous innovation. In other words, the application of new knowledge;
3. increasing turnover of staff. People do not take a job for life any more. When someone leaves an organization their knowledge walks out of the door with them;
4. our problem as an organization is that we do not know what we know. Large global or even small geographically dispersed organizations do not know what they know.

Expertise learnt and applied in one part of the organization is not leveraged in another;

5. accelerating change including technology, business and social. As things change so does our knowledge base erode whereby in some businesses, as much of 50% of what you knew five years ago is probably obsolete today?

Hence, from the various views of knowledge management, in a nutshell it is obviously a significant resource in order to support creation, transfer and the application of the knowledge. Next we proceed in defining knowledge sharing.

Knowledge Sharing

Knowledge sharing can be seen as continuously emerging patterns of interactions between individuals. It particularly focuses on the nature of human organizations and how that nature affects the emergence of organizational knowledge. In today's business environment, competitive advantage increasingly requires the open sharing of knowledge by organizational members (Chow, Deng & Ho, 2000). Ives, Torrey & Gordon (2000) defined knowledge sharing as a critical human behaviour that organizations need to carefully cultivate and harvest. Examples of eight dimensions of knowledge sharing are as follows (The International Labour Organization, 2007).

Creating a Supportive Culture

If knowledge sharing is to be a genuinely organization-wide endeavour, it must become part of the organization's culture, namely the set of basic values, ideologies and assumptions which guide and fashion the norms of desirable individual and group behaviour of its members. This requires both a positive attitude to learning, a commitment by everyone to contribute to the process and a willingness to legitimize learning by providing adequate resources.

Gathering Internal Experience

The process of gathering experience needs to be one based on sharing and exchange. This requires awareness inside the organization of what it does and the impact of what it does, namely a clear role for monitoring, review and evaluation. There are particular *paper mechanisms* which can be used for this which may include: (a) evaluation studies, (b) annual reports, (c) documentary information systems, (d) policy documents strategic plans, and (e) research reports. Other *non-paper mechanisms* include meetings, workshops, debriefing and other forms of informal contact.

Accessing External Learning

There are two major sources of organizational learning: (a) what the organization does, and (b) what others do. It is not enough to be clear about what the organization itself is achieving, it must actively seek out learning from elsewhere. This requires a genuine openness and willingness to share its own learning (which means being willing to share the learning from failure as well as success). Organizations may learn a lot from looking at "best practice" in a wide range of organizations in the corporate, public, and even the multilateral and bilateral agency sectors, as well as the Non Government Organization (NGO) world.

Communication Systems

Learning is processed through communication, so in communication systems are crucial to promote its circulation. As a result, communication system design must balance efficiency and performance in order to guarantee information stability. In this continuum process organizational documents, training can be considered as *heavy* communication; and, informal conversations through social networks, e-mail platforms may be considered *light* communication (if no streaming video or documents are being shared). At this point another important remark must be referred: is being witnessed in organizations that *light* communication is enhancing its weight, as well as its importance given its intrinsic features.

Mechanisms for Drawing Conclusions

To learn implies to portray conclusions and recognize the learning outcomes, which is clearly different of a simple information exchange. In order to draw conclusions, an individual needs to reflect upon the information in order to produce knowledge, and its appliance entails wisdom. Nonetheless, it is important to refer that those decisions are collective responsible (organizational level), and therefore experience engages a crucial part.

Developing an Organizational Memory

It is a distinctive feature of organizational learning to remember or memorize. Moreover, it is feasible to argue that if an organization cannot learn will undoubtedly forget. If learning is an innate process to individuals, organizations become defenceless when these tend to leave or to not recall. Thus, a learning organization needs to create mechanisms that enable *downloading* individual's memory to an information system, in order to everybody obtain access to that person's experience. This attitude will allow an analysis of those experiences if the individual abandon the organization.

Integrating Learning into Strategy and Policy

One way of building lessons learned into the fabric of an organization is to develop policy and procedures which reflect organizational learning. This provides the organization with a framework for decision-making and resource allocation which is grounded in the organization's own experience and that of other agencies. If policy-development is seen as a participative learning process in itself, this strengthens the process of integration and builds commitment for implementation.

Applying the Learning

The ultimate test of learning is the ability to apply what has been learned. Only when learning is applied in the work setting can it be said that a continuous learning cycle has been created. The notion of a dynamic knowledge sharing creates competitive advantage needs that extend beyond any boundaries. Indeed, in creating and recombining knowledge leads to the diversity of knowledge that resides within any network.

Ethics

According to Schlick (2008), ethics is a system of knowledge and nothing else to which its goal is the truth. The ethical questions are bounded to morality, values, standards and norms. Those concerned with protecting the knowledge sharing generally focus on the seriousness of Falsification, Fabrication, and Plagiarism (FFP). Violations of FFP are obvious threats to work and environmental trust; however, "normal misbehaviours" are components of ordinary life that promote an understanding how individuals, communities and organizations generate compliance and deviance from ethical norms (De Vries, Anderson & Martinson, 2006).

To date, the heavy usage of information communication technology (ICT) in society is creating a rather unique set of ethical issues that requires the making of new moral choices on the part of society and has yielded special implications for its members (Mason, 1995). Due to the innovative development in science and philosophy, in the mid 1940s, "computer ethics" or "information ethics", a new branch of ethics had been created. All ethical questions arise initially out of human agency. The mission statement of computer ethics involves restricting the presence of selfishness or egoism of human nature and enabling harmonious human life in the ICT domain (Siponen, 1997).

Technology itself is not the only, nor necessarily the most responsible, cause of these issues. Potential ICT related harm maybe general categories as personal (privacy and integrity), or network (bandwidth and its availability). The hire of power-enhancing capabilities makes technology an inducer of sorts, a necessary but not sufficient underpinning to many of the ethical issues we face today. Recently, there has been an increased interest in ethical standards for computer users. Many studies have questioned whether today's ICT user is a responsible and an ethical user (Masrom & Ismail, 2008; Baase, 2008; Gan & Koh, 2006; Turner & Roberts, 2001).

Boomelaer & Shears (2007) pointed out that the Internet society has been guided by a primary principle that stresses the inclusive dimension of all its activities: "the Internet is for everyone". This is no trivial matter, and remains as powerful a statement today as it was when the Internet Society was created: "for everyone" commits the Internet society to a set of key drivers or core values that are principle driven and rights based.

In preparing the young generation towards the use of IT in gaining knowledge, Malaysia's Ministry of Education embedded ICT to its secondary school curriculum commencing since 2006. Although ICT is an elective subject, issues on knowledge and ethics are addressed in tandem. The aims of the ICT curriculum at the school level are to provide students with knowledge and skills in ICT, to enable them to solve problems and make informed decisions in everyday life based on positive attitudes and noble values, and to develop concerned, dynamic and progressive individuals with an ICT culture that values knowledge and ethics towards the technological advancement of the nation (Samah, 2005).

Computers and internet are powerful instruments that allow students to reach around the world and it is educator's responsibility to teach them how to use it responsibly and inculcate a culture of ethics. Schools and universities have been so absorbed in their efforts to bring technology into classrooms, but the issue of values and ethics as far as the general guide in e-learning usage has been neglected (Posiah & Kamaruzaman, 2008). Some frequently cited studies have reported that between 40 to 70 percent of all college students have reported cheating sometime during their academic career.

Researchers identified factors that unethical academic influence includes competition and pressures for good grades, instructional situations that are perceived as unfair or excessively demanding, lack of knowledge and attitude on the part of the faculty towards academic ethics, peer pressure to support or to share with a friend, and a diminishing sense of academic integrity and ethical values among students (Bramucci, 2003*)*. The statements to acquire knowledge and teach students to understand that the electronic community requires people to behave responsibly and use the resources beneficially have somewhat change the basic principle of ethical characteristics.

Code of ethics had been applied in many professional bodies, among others, those in the medical field, lawyers, engineers, journalists. In general, a code of ethics is a set of rules and rights that to be inviolable, and self-evident. It perhaps seems odd that self-evident rights need to be declared at all, except that it gives us a yardstick, a modern form by which we can see how well we are doing in protecting those rights, and how our technology and our culture is doing to live up to the expectations and ideals of our individual lives and society.

When organizations introduce knowledge management and wish employees to share knowledge, conflicts may arise owing to individual differences in self-interest and ethical considerations. If knowledge is controlled by individuals, then sharing knowledge with others is assumed to be an ethical behaviour. Wang (2004) questions whether employees are glad to share knowledge with others from self-interest concern. His study showed a significant positive relationship between ethical concerns and knowledge sharing intentions.

It also found that specifically, individuals who see sharing knowledge with colleagues as required by workplace ethics will share knowledge.

In another study, Long & Driscoll (2008) discussion based on codes of ethics as institutionalized organizational structures that extend some form of legitimacy to organizations. They analyzed a sample of codes to consider the question of whether a strategic, self-interested rationale lies behind the adoption of a code of ethics. They proposed that the process of employing codes of ethics in this strategic manner has become, through isomorphism, an institutionalized practice that itself confers a cognitive form of legitimacy to the organization and further distances the codes from their moral foundation. Organizations can indeed use a variety of legitimating mechanisms to increase their reputation as ethical enterprises.

As knowledge is information combined with experience, context, interpretation and reflection, with ethical management of knowledge, knowledge sharing will instigate a more ethical society. Also, with the guideline known as code of ethics, a specific set of professional behaviours and values the professional interpreter must know and must abide by, including confidentiality, accuracy, privacy, integrity then knowledge sharing can happen in a more agreeable manner.

The following section describes and discusses three emerging ethics of knowledge-sharing, namely: (1) hacker ethics, (2) participatory culture ethics, and (3) proselytization commons ethics.

HACKER ETHICS

Hacker ethics is a new relation to knowledge. The term "hacker" originally meant anyone who loved computing. The term carried different meanings through four generations (Muktar, 2002):

- 1st generation (1960s)- used the term for a creative programmer;
- 2nd generation (1970s)- used the term for computer evolutionaries;
- 3rd generation (1980s)- used the term for games and copyright breakers;
- 4th generation (1990 to date)- used the term for criminal and cyber criminal.

Hacker ethics involves the values and philosophy that act like praxis within the hacker community (Wikipedia, 2009). The roots of hacker ethics as a cultural movement or philosophy can be traced to the 50s and 60s, namely within the Massachusetts Institute of Technology (MIT). Historically, the expression "hacker ethics" was firstly coined by the journalist Steven Levy in 1984, in his masterwork, *Hackers: Heroes of the Computer Revolution.* Hacker ethics principles easily demonstrate how computers have developed, as well as their impact in our daily lives. Then, its key aims are: access, free information, and life quality improvement.

Levy (1984) detailed these principles and beliefs, which are clarified below:

- hands on imperative- in order to promote a reliable knowledge every technology should be totally available, allowing a practical approach. This hypothesis of Levy reflects his personal belief with reference to hackers' abilities: to learn, to repair, and to develop pre-existing ideas and systems. So, the cumulated knowledge from this experience would make possible to create and reinvent technology;
- information wants to be free- the existing information should be free, and for that it is required to have access to it. As a consequence, hackers would have the ability to fix, improve and reinvent systems, because a constant and unlimited informational flux enhances creativity. To a hacker, every system could benefit from this assumption;
- mistrust authority- in order to obtain a continuous and free flow of information an

open system is required. This is consistent with hackers "hands on imperative" (practical knowledge), as well as the statement that bureaucracy impose flaws;

- no bogus criteria- hackers should be judged by their actions despite degrees, age, race, or position. Hacker ethics assumes a meritocratic system in order to promote esteem about skills, and the remaining criteria are considered irrelevant within the community. In fact, skill is a decisive condition for acceptance;
- you can create truth and beauty on a computer- programming minimization is considered a game between early hackers. This aims to create codes that perform complicated tasks with few instructions;
- computers can change your life for the better- the hacker community truly believes that information systems deepen their lives through a constant discovery adventure. On the other hand, that society should enjoy this fruitful experience in order to spread hackers' ethics. The process of transforming dreams into reality was achieved: hackers have demonstrated the unlimited boundaries that computer technology engages.

Still following Levy (1984), *sharing* is the basic and expectable rule within the informal hacker culture. This principle stemmed from the existing organizational environment of the MIT and its resources, because in "computer infancy" MIT hackers produced and shared programs. If a hack was considered good quality, it should be posted into the computers room board. This condition would enable free and immediately utilization by other members of the community, which attempted to do "bumming" (process of making source code more concise for an equal outcome). However, the second generation promulgate sharing with the general public beyond the community. A particular and idealistic organization was the Community Memory, which made available a computer outside Leopold's Records in Berkeley, California.

Another sharing experience was provided by Bob Altrecht to the People's Computer Company (PCC) (Levy, 1984). This non-profit organization opened a computer center, being the cost of utilization per hour fifty cents. Moreover, this generation claimed free and open software and Bill Gates' version of BASIC was heavily shared, leading to considerable economic costs. As a response, Gates wrote an open letter to several hobbyists.

The moral principles of hackers are not that dissimilar of those that believe it is wrong (Denning, 2002). The claim for this argument relies on that hackers do not break into systems for producing harmful results, because for them damage implies critical operational systems, or even destroy data. Therefore, systems files modifications in order to gain privileged access entail regular behavioural patterns, as well downloads or resources utilization without paying; instead, their counter argument is that those resources would remain unused.

Despite justifying their actions as a quest to promote learning, as well that free information benefits society (systems under scrutiny promote their development); the truth is that society does not accepted as legitimate. Although, hackers retort that is managers' responsibility to prevent security breaches. On the other hand, some groups acknowledge these behaviours are a consequence of hackers' innate skills and extra free-time, so punishment or sanctions are perceived in a positive way.

In summary, although hackers violate laws and professional codes of ethics in the domain of computing, they essentially are computer enthusiasts who were accused of being perpetrators of the IT crimes. The moral principles of hackers differ is in their interpretation of what constitutes "hurt" and "damage," and thus in their particular ethical standards of behaviour in promote knowledge sharing rationalize that the files remain on the system and the resources would otherwise go unused. Hackers are of the opinion that hacking is done for the purpose of learning, in search of system vulnerabilities, typically for the excitement of challenges, thrill, and social fun.

PARTICIPATORY CULTURE ETHICS

A participatory culture is a culture with relatively low barriers to artistic expression and civic engagement, strong support for creating and sharing one's creations, and some type of informal mentorship whereby what is known by the most experienced is passed along to novices (Jenkins et al., 2006).

A customary knowledge management has always to create the infrastructure for knowledge sharing in the organization but its limits are the limits of understanding of the firm. Knowledge management assumption is that every employee or staff was prepared to share what they know.

In the meantime, these members truly believe in the importance of their contributions, as well as at some extent are socially bounded (others personal perception of their achievements is a core concern). Forms of participatory culture include (Jenkins *et al.*, 2006):

- affiliations: entails official and unofficial membership through virtual communities centered around a variety of media forms;
- expressions: the production of novel and artistic forms;
- collaborative problem-solving: team work, whatever its nature or structure, enables knowledge creation;
- circulations: it is decisive to determine how media flows.

Participatory culture reallocates literacy hub as regards to individuality within a certain community. Therefore, "the new literacies almost all involve social skills developed through collaboration and networking" (Jenkins et al., 2006, pp. 4) (i.e. the ability to search for, synthesize, and disseminate information). Participatory culture ethics is related with the involvement in information and knowledge. Technology may support a knowledge-sharing environment, but getting users to participate in effective ways is a key of success.

According to Delaforce (2009), the "participatory culture" has been defined as "a new way of life that lets people create and circulate self-made content such as images, video, audio, and text". The culture has been taking shape in the form of social networking such as Facebook, Twitter, MySpace, Flickr, Wikipedia, and Friendster which have stimulated large number of participation and collaboration. Social networks have been scrutinizing organizational interactions which characterize executives' informal connections, as well as the relationships between individual workers in dissimilar organizations. For example, an organizational power flux entail until what extent an individual enables or connects potential relationships than is real job title engages. Besides, social networks have become an instrument regarding organizational human resources policies, because those provide an instantaneous impact in gathering information about competitors, or setting up price policies.

Delaforce (2009) asserts that collaboration can overcome reluctance to participate by identifying who is contributing; measure what that means to the organization, its partners and customers, and reward it like any other contribution. In this context, the participatory culture embraces communication, coordination, community and social interaction.

In establishing knowledge sharing through technology, among others, Mindjet, whose interactive knowledge sharing software is used by over one million people, believes that the *shared community* is the future for work. Mindjet permits groups to cooperate throughout the latest applications and web services (Mindjet, 2010). Similarly, ANOVA is not a tool that creates just another answers website; it also helps to create an entire knowledge-sharing community. ANOVA allows the creation of a forum where people from worldwide can easily submit and share information in order to promulgate a revolution. Hence, this software promotes knowledge novelty through video and audio replies, interactive forums where users can come together to discuss and debate answers and keep up to date with all information on the site through the Rich Site Summary or Really Simple Syndication (RSS) feed option (ANOVA, 2010).

PROSELYTIZATION COMMONS ETHIC

Proselytization commons ethic includes promoting information and knowledge. It was associated with religious conversion. Proselytization can be defined as any activity or process in which a person is trying to convert another person or group of people from not believing and acting in accordance with a certain set of religious beliefs, to accepting them and acting accordingly (Thiessen, 2000). In general, proselytization is the practice of attempting to convert people to another opinion, usually another set of beliefs or religion.

Religious beliefs are very important part of people lives. The people values and morals actually derived from their religious beliefs. Therefore, it is not surprising that some people want to "share" their religious beliefs with others (Cline, 2009).

Below are the ten commandments of proselytizing that are listed by Thiessen (2000):

1. Proselytizing must always be done in such a way as to protect the dignity and worth of the person or persons being proselytized;
2. Proselytizing must therefore always be part of a concern for the whole person or persons;
3. The more personal the form of proselytizing, the more it must be preceded by personal investment in the person or persons being proselytized. The proselytizer must earn the right to engage in personal proselytizing;
4. When proselytizing, there should be sensitivity to the pain involved in the crisis of conversion;
5. Tolerance (properly defined) must accompany all attempts at proselytizing;
6. Proselytizers affirming the right to proselytize must at the same time affirm and uphold the right of others to do the same;
7. Proselytizing must always be done in such a way as to protect the ability of the person or persons being appealed to, to make a genuinely free choice. Coercion and psychological manipulation are wrong;
8. Proselytizing must enhance the making of informed choices. It must therefore always include an appeal to the mind;
9. The proselytizer must be scrupulously honest in portraying not only the benefits but also the costs of being converted;
10. An attitude of humility should characterize all attempts at proselytizing.

The presence of proselytization in open society cannot be avoided. There will be some people trying to convince other people to agree with some ideas. The proselytization can occur in the workplace, and it includes religion, political and social issues (Håkansson & Deer, 2006; Deer & Håkansson, 2005). Nevertheless, proselytization at the workplace will create uncomfortable environment because good social connection can be distracted once people attempt to defend their beliefs and ideas from attack by others. Hence, interfere with people productivity. In the proselytization context, sharing and explaining our beliefs to others is a good thing because it is in the nature of a human being to proselytize. John Stuart Mill also defended proselytizing on the basis of its benefits to society as a whole, namely, proselytizing stimulates thought and discussion, without which individuals and society are in danger of falling into the "the deep slumber of decided opinion" (Raeder, 2002).

FUTURE RESEARCH DIRECTIONS

At this point, it is reasonable to claim that complexity and multidimensionality are the characteristics of an unpredictable future. Nevertheless, is the authors' belief that to frame future research directions about hackers, participatory ethics and proselytizing, a metaphorical analysis will be crucial.

Dance resumes an art form that encompasses social and spiritual interaction through body movement, as well as entails a message through informal communication depending on the style (Daly, 2002). Moreover, it incorporates several biases (social, cultural, aesthetic and even moral) given its personal and collective participatory characteristics (Dils & Albright, 2001), leading to a continuously development. Therefore, the relationship between hackers, participatory culture and proselytizing commons encompasses rhythm, informal communication, and biases.

Despite these assumptions and its importance in knowledge sharing literature has been neglecting this discussion, because only Koulikov (2008) attempted to explain the dialogue between hacker ethics, participatory culture ethics, and proselytization commons ethics. Likewise this criticism is extensible to a two dimensional analysis (participatory culture and proselytization), since mainstream focus merely discusses effects on education (McCrickard & Chewar, 2004), religion (Pelkmans, 2009; Malhotra, 2000), cultural imperialism (Berg, Evans & Fuller, 2007), or personal and organizational reflexitivity (Sultana, 2007). Thus, is the authors' intention to portray some ethical and social issues that require an urgent response as regards to knowledge sharing by topic.

Warren (2008) argues that "hacker taggers", a novel subgroup, does not promote ethical hacking. This author claims that "ethical hacking" resumes the compliance with Levy's (1984) ethical guidelines, which this subgroup disregards due to a fundamentalist perception of hacking (pure competition). This scenario poses the following question: does not humanism produce transformative creation (Losh, 2010)? Will not this proselytization diminish creativity and consequently knowledge sharing?

On the other hand, knowledge society promotes an individual and collective participation (Thomas, 2010), which engaged a world of creativity (commons) and afterwards proselytization commons due to end-to-end principles (Lessig, 2002). Despite this claim, de Laat (2008) questions if knowledge commons-based will not resume an equal dilemma concerning profitability, which acts like praxis for a crucial answer: will be that profit ethical? Or, it will be again a fallacy with reference to profits and social responsibility (e.g. Solomon, 1992)? Besides, community expertise is based on two competing dynamics (David, 2007, pp. 181-182):

(1) the legitimation of "aggregate" opinion, as opinions tend toward an equilibrium, even on controversial issues; and (2) the openness of the community to dissenting opinions, with the potential to change the aggregate consensus. In successful online communities, these dynamics produce confidence in the knowledge-making process, rather than confidence in any particular instance of expert opinion. The system is legitimate to the degree that it represents a properly constituted authority in the eyes of the community of users.

Although, what mechanisms ensure knowledge transfer, as well as the individual benefits within the community? Will individuals value these benefits equally? Until what extent knowledge sharing is affected if trust is disrupted? All these questions are still enhanced due to organizational memory issues (for learning is essential to remember), since historical records containing all the social debates, revisions, etc. are hypothetically accessible (David, 2007). In addition, a societal participatory culture promotes further dilemmas as Wikipedia demonstrates: (1) authenticity (who produces content); (2) accountability (whose is responsible in case of rubbish knowledge); (3) liability/credibility (which criteria allow to evaluate credibility, and who is responsible for that choice); identity/privacy (tracking content producers may impose serious issues).

At last, it is compulsory to bearing in mind that proselytization commons ethics affects knowledge sharing. If knowledge embodies a social interaction, then implies a process of proselytization! Hence, a debate about the characteristics of a sensitive proselytizer is vital, and for that the authors acknowledge Cline (2005) argument: (1) ought to comprehend the significance of its role; (2) should avoid stylized conduct, as well as promote potential conversion; (3) be willing to adapt and acknowledge that proselytization is a bidirectional process; (4) understand informational needs of others; (5) understands linguistic possibilities regarding communication; (6) provide an inclusive world perception for the community; (7) must be aware that knowledge transfer (learning process) resumes individuality. Therefore, it is possible to relate Cline's (2005) work with the ethical issues and social dilemmas of knowledge creators (Costa & Silva, 2010).

To wrap up, a possible contribution for understanding these ethical and social dilemmas regarding such transversal topic, the authors acknowledge the conceptual framework for computer ethics of Patrignani (2008). This model encompasses six vertical layers (planet, biosphere, people, infosphere, cyberspace and ideas), as well as twelve horizontal layers (e-democracy, accessibility/universal access/digital divide, workplace, content/education, copyrights, hackers, privacy, computer crimes, computers (un)reliability, artificial intelligence, war and ecology/recycling).

CONCLUSION

This chapter examines the various emerging ethics of knowledge sharing, and each ethics portrays a different focus. Hackers demonstrate ethics through the use of computers, encompassing that information needs to be free for hackers to fix, improve, and reinvent systems. Therefore, the notion of intrusion to any system is assumed permissible, unlike participatory culture ethics belief in expressing literarily through community collaboration and networking, sharing self-made content example images. In this case interactions within the collaborators are mutual.

However, proselytization commons deals with the attempt to convert the other party have set of belief in religion, political or social issues. People values and morals are rooted from religion and social issues, thus knowledge sharing can be educating yet may cross the line if one over-proselytized. Instigating political stands can also be damaging if not handled properly in trying to proselytize the party concern.

Each of the mentioned ethics has different focus and motives in sharing knowledge. Thus each requires different approach, methodology and treatment in conducting further research pertaining to the nature of the context. To sum, due to globalization of economy, rapid growth in information technology, increase in knowledge based work and competition pressure the concept of knowledge management has gained momentum despite the dilemmas it holds in knowledge sharing. Regardless whether knowledge management means different things to different people, the biggest challenges is how to change mindset of people in line with common ethical norms in believing that "knowledge sharing is power".

REFERENCES

ANOVA. (2010). Discover how you can take advantage of the online knowledge revolution and start cashing in on other people's knowledge right now! *ANOVA*. Retrieved February 20, 2010, from, www.anova.tv.

Baase, S. (2008). *A gift of fire: Social, legal and ethical issues for computers and the internet* (3rd ed.). Princeton, NJ: Prentice-Hall.

Bellinger, G., Castro, E., & Mills, A. (2004). Data, information, knowledge, and wisdom. *Systems Thinking*. Retrieved November 30, 2009, from, http://www.systems-thinking.org/dikw/dikw.htm

Berg, L. D., Evans, M., & Fuller, D. (2007). Ethics, hegemonic witness, and the contested imagination of "aboriginal community" in social science research in Canada. *ACME- An International E-Journal for Critical Geographies, 6*(3), 395-410. Retrieved March 10, 2010 from, http://www.acme-journal.org/vol6/LDBetal.pd

Boommelaer, C., & Shears, M. (2007). Ethics and human rights in the information society. *Internet Society*. Retrieved January 22, 2010, from, http://www.isoc.org/pubpolpillar/governance/ethics.shtml

Bramucci, R. S. (2003). Incidence and prevalence of cheating. *Teachopolis.org*. Retrieved January 3, 2010, from, http://teachopolis.org/justice/cheating/cheating_incidence.htm

Cheng, W., Hailin, L., & Hongming, X. (2008). Does knowledge sharing mediate the relationship between trust and firm performance? In F. Yu & Q. Luo (Eds.), *International Symposium on Information Processing/International Pacific Workshop on Web Mining, and Web-Based Application* (pp. 449-453). Washington, DC: IEEE Computer Society.

Chow, C. W., Deng, F. J., & Ho, J. L. (2000). The openness of knowledge sharing within organizations: A comparative study of the United States and the People's Republic of China. *Journal of Management Accounting Research, 12*(1), 65–95. doi:10.2308/jmar.2000.12.1.65

Cline, A. (2009). Proselytization at work- feel pressured to convert? Atheists at work. *About.com*. Retrieved October 30, 2009, from http://atheism.about.com/od/atheistswork/a/pressure.htm

Cline, B. J. (2005). *Reaching others: The rhetoric of proselytizing and community of a Christian campus organization*. Unpublished doctoral dissertation, Graduate College of Bowling Green State University, Ohio.

Costa, G. J. M., & Silva, N. S. A. (2010). Knowledge authoring in e-learning: An ethicultural diagnosis! In P. Dondon & O. Martin (Eds.), *7th WSEAS International Conference on Engineering Education* (pp. 48-53), Aquis Corfu Holiday Palace Hotel, Corfu, Greece.

Daly, A. (2002). *Critical gestures: Writings on dance and culture*. Middletown, CT: Wesleyan University Press.

David, S. (2007). Toward participatory expertise. In Karaganis, J. (Ed.), *Structures of Participation in Digital Culture* (pp. 176–199). New York, NY: Social Science Research Group.

de Laat, P. B. (2008). Moving open source beyond software while maintaining the public spirit? In T. Bynum *et al.* (Eds.), *ETHICOMP 2008: Living, Working and Learning Beyond Technology,* (pp. 511-523). Mantua: University of Pavia.

De Vries, R., Anderson, M. S., & Martinson, B. C. (2006). Normal misbehaviour: Scientists talk about the ethics of research. *Journal of Empirical Research on Human Research Ethics; JERHRE, 1*(1), 43–50. doi:10.1525/jer.2006.1.1.43

Deer, K., & Håkansson, A.-K. (2005). Towards an indigenous vision of the information society. In van Weert, T. J. (Ed.), *Education and the Knowledge Society- Information Technology Supporting Human Development* (pp. 237–240). New York: Kluwer Academic Publishers.

Defense Acquisition University. (2003). *What is knowledge management?* Fort Belvoir, VA: Defense Acquisition University.

Delaforce, C. (2009). Exploiting the participatory culture. *Human Capital Management, January/February*, 26-28. Retrieved October 30, 2009, from, http://www.media-insertpr.com/Graham-Jarvis_MC2_HCM_Jan-Feb_2009.pdf

Denning, D. E. (2002, August). *Hacker ethics*. Paper presented at the National Conference on Computing and Values, New Haven, CT.

Dils, A., & Albright, A. C. (Eds.). (2001). *Moving history/dancing cultures: A dance history reader*. Middletown, CT: Wesleyan University Press.

Dixon, N. (2002). The neglected receiver of knowledge sharing. *Ivey Business Journal*, *66*(4), 35–40.

Fong, P. S.-W., & Chu, L. (2006). Exploratory study of knowledge sharing in contracting companies: A sociotechnical perspective. *Journal of Construction Engineering and Management*, *132*(9), 928–939. doi:10.1061/(ASCE)0733-9364(2006)132:9(928)

Gan, L. L., & Koh, H. C. (2006). An empirical study of software piracy among tertiary institutions in Singapore. *Journal of Business Ethics*, *43*(5), 640–647.

Gurteen, D. (1999). Creating a knowledge sharing culture. *Knowledge Management Magazine*, *2*(5).

Håkansson, A.-K., & Deer, K. (2006). Promoting the building of a people-centred, development-oriented and inclusive information society, with a view to enhancing digital opportunities for all people. *Indigenous ICT taskforce: The Panel of the United Nations Commission on Science and Technology for Development*. Retrieved December 5, 2009, from, http://www.unctad.org/sections/dite_dir/docs/dite_pcbb_stdev0033_en.pdf

Hendriks, P. (1999). Why share knowledge? The influence of ICT on the motivation for knowledge sharing. *Knowledge and Process Management*, *6*(2), 91–100. doi:10.1002/(SICI)1099-1441(199906)6:2<91::AID-KPM54>3.0.CO;2-M

Hock, D. W. (1999). *Birth of the chaordic age*. San Francisco, CA: Berret-Koehler Publisher.

Ives, W., Torrey, B., & Gordon, C. (2000). Knowledge sharing is a human behaviour. In Morrey, D., Maybury, M., & Thuraisingham, B. (Eds.), *Knowledge Management: Classic and Contemporary Works* (pp. 99–12). Cambridge, MA: MIT Press.

Jenkins, H. (2006). *Confronting the challenges of participatory culture: Media education for the 21st century*. Chicago: The John D. and Catherine T. MacArthur Foundation.

Koulikov, M. (2008). *Emerging problems in knowledge-sharing and the three new ethics of knowledge transfer (Selected works)*. New York: New York Law Institute.

Land, F., Amjad, U., & Nolas, S.-M. (2006). The ethics of knowledge management. *International Journal of Knowledge Management*, *3*(1), 1–9.

Leonard, L. N. K., & Cronan, T. P. (2005). Attitude toward ethical behaviour in computer use: A shifting model. *Industrial Management & Data Systems*, *105*(9), 1150–1171. doi:10.1108/02635570510633239

Lessig, L. (2002). *The future of ideas: The fate of the commons in a connected world.* New York: Vintage Books.

Levy, S. (1984). *Hackers: Heroes of the computer revolution.* Garden City, NY: Anchor Press/ Doubleday.

Liu, C. C. (2008). The relationship between Machiavellianism and knowledge sharing willingness. *Journal of Business and Psychology, 22*(3), 233–240. doi:10.1007/s10869-008-9065-1

Long, B. S., & Driscoll, C. (2008). Codes of ethics and the pursuit of organizational legitimacy: Theoretical and empirical contributions. *Journal of Business Ethics, 77*(2), 173–189. doi:10.1007/ s10551-006-9307-y

Losh, L. (2010). Will "hacking the academy" be understood as "backing the academy"? *Virtual Politik.* Retrieved March 20, 2010, from, http:// virtualpolitik.blogspot.com/2010_05_01_archive.html

Malhotra, R. (2000, October). *The ethics of proselytizing.* Paper presented at the Conference on Human Rights and Religion, Ithaca, NY.

Martin, J. N. (2006, July). *Using the knowledge pyramid to characterize systems.* Paper presented at the INCOSE Symposium, Orlando, Florida.

Mason, R. O. (1995). Applying ethics to information technology issues. *Communications of the ACM, 38*(12), 55–57. doi:10.1145/219663.219681

Masrom, M., & Ismail, Z. (2008). *Computer security and computer ethics awareness: A component of management information system.* In H. B. Zaman *et al.* (Eds.), *Proceedings of International Symposium on Information Technology 2008, Volume 3* (pp. 1920-1926). Malaysia: Kuala Lumpur Convention Centre.

McCrickard, D. S., & Chewar, C. M. (2004). Proselytizing pervasive computing: A strategy and approach influenced by human computer interaction. In B. Werner (Ed.), *Proceedings of the 2nd IEEE Annual Conference on Pervasive Computing and Communications Workshops* (pp. 257-262). Orlando, FL: IEEE Computer Society.

Mindjet (2010). Support- Knowledge base. *Mindjet.com.* Retrieved February 17, 2010, from, http:// www.mindjet.com/support/overview

Muktar, M. (2002). Computer crime: The new threat. *Crime-Research.org.* Retrieved October 13, 2009, from, http://www.crime-research.org/ library/Mudavi1.htm

Nonaka, I., & Takeuchi, H. (1995). *The knowledge-creating company.* Oxford, UK: Oxford University Press.

Patrignani, N. (2008). A conceptual framework for computer ethics. In T. Bynum *et al.* (Eds.), *ETHICOMP 2008: Living, Working and Learning Beyond Technology* (pp. 640-647). Mantua. Italy: University of Pavia.

Pelkmans, M. (2009). The "transparency" of Christian proselytizing in Kyrgzstan. *Anthropological Quarterly, 82*(2), 423–445. doi:10.1353/ anq.0.0058

Posiah, M. I., & Kamaruzaman, J. (2008). Sustenance of values and ethics in the Malaysian higher education e-learning drive. *Asian Social Science, 4*(6), 115–121.

Raeder, L. C. (2002). *John Stuart Mill and the religion of humanity.* Columbia, MO: University of Missouri Press.

Samah, D. A. A. (2005, March). *Rethinking Malaysian education: A brave new world?* Paper presented at the 9th Malaysian Education Summit, Kuala Lumpur, Malaysia.

Schlick, M. (2008). *Problems of ethics.* New York: Prentice-Hall.

Siponen, M. T. (1997). *The applicability of ethical theories to computer ethics- Selected issues*. Unpublished manuscript, United Kingdom.

Solomon, R. (Ed.). (1992). *Ethics and excellence: Cooperation and integrity in business*. New York: Oxford University Press.

Sultana, F. (2007). Reflexivity, positionality and participatory ethics: Negotiating fieldwork dilemmas in international research. *ACME- An International E-Journal for Critical Geographies, 6(3)*, 374-385. Retrieved March 10, 2010, from, http://www.acme-journal.org/vol6/FS.pdf

The International Labour Organization. (2007). ILO knowledge strategy. *ILO.org*. Retrieved October 29, 2009, from, http://www.ilo.org/public/english/support/lib/knowledgesharing/strategy.htm

Thiessen, E. J. (2000, November). *The ethics of proselytizing: A multi-faith conversation*. Paper present at the Chaplain's Association and the Department of Studies in Religion, Toronto, Ontario.

Thomas, B. K. (2010). Participation in the knowledge society: The free and open source (FOSS) movement compared with participatory development. *Development in Practice*, *20*(2), 270–276. doi:10.1080/09614520903566509

Turner, E., & Roberts, P. (2001). Teaching computer ethics to IT students in higher education: An exploration of provision, practice and perspective. *Centre for Computing and Social Responsibility*. Retrieved October 13, 2009, from, http://www.ccsr.cse.dmu.ac.uk/conferences/ccsrconf/ethicomp2001/abstracts/turner.html

Ullman, D. G. (2004). Decision management: Punctuating the process. *Incose Insight, 6*(2).

Vandergriff, L. J. (2001, May). *Role tailored decision support: An investigation of decision-making and implementation process state of the art*. Paper present at the Course 398 Lecturing, Washington, DC.

Vandergriff, L. J. (2008). Welcome to the Intelligence age: An examination of intelligence as a complex venture emergent behaviour. *Vine*, *38*(4), 432–444. doi:10.1108/03055720810917697

Waltz, E. (2003). *Knowledge management in the intelligence enterprise*. Norwood, MA: Artech House.

Wang, C.-C. (2004). The influence of ethical and self-interest concerns on knowledge sharing intentions among managers: An empirical study. *International Journal of Management*, *21*(3), 370–381.

Warren, M. (2008). The ethics of the hacker taggers: The new generation of hackers. In Bynum, T. (Eds.), *ETHICOMP 2008: Living, Working and Learning Beyond Technology* (pp. 787–793). Mantua, Italy: University of Pavia.

Wikipedia. (2009). Hacker ethic. *Wikimedia Foundation, Inc*. Retrieved October 23, 2009, from, http://en.wikipedia.org/wiki/Hacker_ethic#The_hacker_ethics

ADDITIONAL READING

Cabrera, E. F., & Cabrera, A. (2002). Knowledge-sharing dilemmas. *Organization Studies*, *23*(5), 687–710. doi:10.1177/0170840602235001

Gee, W. B., & Kim, Y.-G. (2002). Breaking the myths of rewards: An exploratory study of attitudes about knowledge. *Information Resources Management Journal*, *15*(2), 14–21.

Quinn, J. B. (1992). *Intelligent enterprise: A knowledge and service based paradigm for industry*. New York, NY: Free Press.

Truch, E. (2001). *Trust in knowledge sharing*. Knowledge Management, July/August.

Wong, K. Y. (2008). An exploratory study on knowledge management adoption in the Malaysian industry. *International Journal of Business Information Systems*, *3*(3), 272–283. doi:10.1504/IJBIS.2008.017285

KEY TERMS AND DEFINITIONS

Ethics: Knowledge system which aims the truth, and that incorporates moral procedures, values, standards and norms.

Hacker: Expression to designate everyone that truly aims computing. Moreover, hackers' generations are a consequence of technological evolution.

Hacker Ethics: Moral principles that act as guidance for hackers: (1) hands on imperative; (2) information wants to be free; (3) mistrust authority; (4) no bogus criteria; (5) you can create truth and beauty on a computer; (6) computers can change your life for the better.

Knowledge Sharing: Ability that is innate to humans; however, is essential for organizations to foster in order to survive in a competitive market.

Participatory Culture Ethics: Involvement of users in a successful way within a community, as well with information and knowledge. This participatory culture is a consequence of Web development.

Proselytization: Action or procedures in which an individual attempts to convert other individual or group as regards to religious beliefs.

Proselytization Commons Ethics: Global process that entails a reconversion of personal and group religious beliefs through a participatory culture.

Chapter 7
The Trouble with Digital Copies: A Short KM Phenomenology

Ugo Pagallo
University of Turin, Italy

ABSTRACT

This chapter analyzes some of the most relevant ethical issues and social dilemmas in knowledge management and organizational innovation, by focusing on a paramount feature of digital technology, which is "copying." The new ways in which information is produced, distributed, and shared in digital environments have in fact changed crucial aspects of human life. Whereas, most of the time, scholars consider such transformations in connection with the impact of digital copies on copyright law, the aim of the chapter is to widen this perspective by examining data protection as well as file sharing application systems. The new economical scenarios and business models proposed by this copy-based technology suggest new ways for balancing property rights and "the right to freely participate in the cultural life of the community."

INTRODUCTION

Both the structure and functioning of the Internet are founded upon distributed storage and replicated copies of the data to be transmitted among the nodes of the network. While such new ways in which information is produced, distributed, and shared in digital environments have transformed crucial aspects of human life, they have also changed the very notion of "copy," since, theoretically speaking, there would no longer be any difference between the original and the replica. In order to offer a short (but hopefully comprehensive) phenomenology of this paramount transformation, this chapter is presented in six sections.

First of all, I delineate the background from an economic viewpoint, emphasising how the

DOI: 10.4018/978-1-61520-873-9.ch007

traditional "long route" between creators/producers and consumers has been joined- and even replaced- by a "short route" (up to the point where we talk about the new category of "prosumers"). Even though the impact of such an impressive innovation was initially perceived in the field of intellectual property and, more specifically, in the realm of copyright law, the paradox of a copy-based technology which has changed the very notion of copy has quickly extended to other areas.

In particular, I analyse how legislators and courts have reacted (and even overreacted) to changes and challenges brought on by the technological revolution. By comparing the U.S. and EU legal systems, it should be clear that the trouble with digital copies does not only concern copyright but privacy as well.

Hence, I illustrate some ways for balancing the various fundamental rights involved in file sharing application systems- namely P2P networks- as proposed by some projects such as FairPeers. Whereas the troubles with digital copies affect a number of other relevant areas like open access to the public sector information, executable programs, or traditional publishing, P2P systems clearly show how it is possible to harness the new economical scenarios and business models of the "short route" by sharing profits (and not only files) among users, while reinforcing responsibility and protecting people's personal data.

Of course, as I explain in the section on future research directions, further work is required on pseudonymous systems, reputation modules, trusted management, or recommender schemes, to name but a few. Nonetheless, the conclusion is that sound workable ways of balancing the different interests which are at stake are already viable. The potential contrast between fair compensation and privacy rights, between knowledge creation and digital sharing, can represent in fact an opportunity for organizational innovation. The trouble with digital copies does not only concern copyright after all.

BACKGROUND

In order to understand what has changed with the introduction of digital copies on the market, let me shortly illustrate the diverse phases and services of the traditional value chain of a media object (e.g., a music album). As I proposed with Glorioso & Ruffo (2010), the different activities and services may be distinguished in four different steps.

First, we have the authoring phase in which an artefact is created. Sometimes this phase includes a pre-production stage as with the preparation of a demo tape to be presented to a content producer. Then, the production phase starts with individual contracts between authors and business organizations such as record companies, publishers, and the like. The artefact is usually refined by a team of professionals, and finally copied on a given physical support (e.g., a CD).

Thirdly, what has been produced needs distribution according to a marketing strategy. Physical objects are then shipped all around the world (or a single country), so that the cost of the item increases as it is delivered to the distributed network of malls and shopping centres by means of transportation service-suppliers. Finally, there are the clients or consumers: they ideally close the chain by paying a price that covers all of the costs of the work which increase with every single step of the cycle.

In a nutshell, this is the traditional "long route" known for decades and, in some cases, even centuries in the pre-digital world. Records had to be printed and, therefore, some sort of manufactory was indispensable to produce "fixed, stable, material or- as the expression now goes- *hard* copies of the work" (Ricolfi, 2007, pp. 285-286). Whereas such hard copies had to be stored, transported, and distributed before they could eventually be purchased by the public, it goes without saying that most of the authors could not engage in all these phases. The rule, on the contrary, was that "they preferred to resort to businesses to set up the characteristic trilateral relationship between creator, business, and the public, which is typical of primary exploitation of copyrighted works" (Ricolfi, 2007, pp. 286). Besides, the secondary exploitation of the artefacts required an even longer route, because further classes of businesses and markets should be added both to the manufacture and sale of the product, as in the case of its broadcast via radio and television networks.

The emergence of digital technology and of the Internet has literally disrupted this framework for, at least, three reasons.

The first one deals with the revolutionary fact that, at least theoretically speaking, there is no longer any difference between the original version of an artefact and the copy. As the copyright holders of sound recordings and phonograms quickly understood both in the U.S. and in Europe, this new scenario means that the conventional distinction between primary and secondary exploitation of a given work simply vanishes in digital environments.

The second reason concerns the difference between distribution and delivery of digital works which collapses in one single service. As it is illustrated by some popular on-line stores like Amazon or iTunes, there exist fully integrated information systems that are implemented by means of complex server architectures such as a CDN (Content Delivery Network).

Finally, the digital revolution involves the very idea of creativity and authorship, along with the "route" connecting producers and consumers. While some scholars like Toffler (1980) or Anderson (2008) talk about the new type of "prosumers", others insist on the difference between centralized and decentralized choices, between market and non market mechanisms, in order to stress the novelty of social exchange based upon reciprocity and cooperation rather than price (as in Benkler, 2006). The typical "long route" has in fact been joined- and sometimes substituted- by a "short route" where production and distribution tend to migrate from traditional business activities to the public via social sharing. This transformation of the value chain does not depend only on the possibility of harnessing the "distributed intelligence" of the Internet, but also on the computational resources available at each step of the digital interaction that dwarfs conventional investments and makes many traditional intermediaries redundant (as already pointed out by Tapscott, 1997).

Digital technology, however, does not imply that the traditional trilateral relationship between creator, business, and the public, is necessarily destined to disappear. For example, as I insist below, even file sharing application systems do not exclude "third parties" from the overall process: Rather, what they suggest is to reinvent many phases of the business model. This also occurs with the FLOSS (Free Libre Open Source Software) movement, in terms of legal safeguards (copyleft rather than copy-right), value chain (services rather than commodities), and development (Eric Raymond's (1999) "bazaar model" rather than the "cathedral model").

Yet, in the early 1990s, most of the corporations and businesses did not think this was the case by arguing that digital copies would have destroyed their bricks-and-mortar rights. Hence, the first step in lobbying policy makers and legislators involved the realm of intellectual property and, more particularly, the field of copyright. The exclusivity rights over public communication pursuant to art. 20 of the Berne Convention (1886) were complemented by two international copyright treaties, namely the WIPO's *Copyright Treaty* (WCT) and the *Performances and Phonograms Treaty* (WPPT), both from December 1996. According to the "making available" clause, the idea was to prevent "that members of the public may access these works (protected by copyright in sound recordings and phonograms) from a place and at a time individually chosen by them" (WCT's art. 8; WPPT's art. 14).

Then, it was the turn of national legislators to defend the "long route" by tackling some of the possible illegal uses of the "short" one. In 1998, the

U.S. Congress amended the *Digital Performance Rights in Sound Recordings Act* from 1995 with the *Digital Millennium Copyright Act* (DMCA) and the so-called *Sonny Bono Act*. Three years later, in 2001, the European Parliament and the Council adopted the first EU directive on "copyright and related rights in the information society". Next, the U.S. Congress passed the *Consumer Broadband and Digital Television Promotion Act* in 2002, the *Family Entertainment Copyright Act* in 2005, and the *Net Neutrality Bill* in 2006. Meanwhile, the IPRED saga developed in Europe: the first directive on the enforced intellectual propriety rights is from 2004 (n. 48), and on April 25th, 2007, the European Parliament supported a new version (IPRED-2).

In the light of this massive legal trend, a first conclusion can be drawn: whereas digital technology opened up new economical scenarios, as well as different business models for the novel "short route" between creators, producers, and the public, the main (if not the only) legal concern has for a while dealt with the claims of some copyright holders as music companies and movie producers. In the name of the noble right proclaimed by the second comma of art. 27 of the Universal Declaration of Human Rights, law makers have forgotten to reinforce the principle declared by the first comma. In other words, in the 1990s "the right to the protection of the moral and material interests resulting from any scientific, literary or artistic production of which he is the author" trumped "the right freely to participate in the cultural life of the community, to enjoy the arts and to share in scientific advancement and its benefits". Against this background, let us see what has changed more recently.

FROM COPYRIGHT TO PRIVACY AND DATA PROTECTION

The first generation of legal cases involving copyright issues and digital copies concerned some file sharing applications on the Internet known as peer-to-peer (P2P) systems, that have become (in) famous because they make it particularly easy for users to access copy(right)-protected files for free.

The foremost important decision came in July 2000, when the U.S. District Judge Marilyn Patel granted the *Recording Industry Association of America* (RIAA)'s request to stop making copyrighted recordings available for download through Napster services. Although the San Mateo company did not store any information, such as the recordings on its own computers, it was declared illegal to provide the information of where the songs were available on the computers of the community logged on. In fact, it was not considered enough to claim that the DMCA grants immunity to ISP providers for what their customers do. As a matter of law, this kind of protection would not include "contributory infringers" as the District Court of Appeals confirmed in its own decision on Napster, in February 2001.

Four years later, it was the turn of the U.S. Supreme Court in *MGM vs. Grokster* to present P2P systems as Steamcast or Grokster, as a kind of technology that promotes the "ease of infringing on copyrights", so that its producers "can be sued for inducing copyright infringement committed by their users". The unanimous holding of the Court, however, did not make clear the legal consequences on further developments of these systems because the Justices were divided between the need to protect every technology "capable of substantial non infringing uses" as they declared in *Sony vs. Universal City Studios* from 1984, and the necessity to provide remedies against new ways of copyright infringement. Therefore, at least in the U.S., there is still the problem to determine whether the software creates "shared files folders" making the information protected by copyright "available for distribution" and, hence, illegally shared via those "files folders".

For example, in *Elektra vs. Baker*, a judge from the Manhattan federal court, Kenneth Karas, rejected the RIAA's "making available"-theory in January 2008, although he admitted the sufficiency of the allegations of "downloading" and "distributing". Whereas Karas' idea was to grasp the whole issue with the legal hypothesis of "offering to distribute for purposes of redistribution", it is important to note that the suit in *Elektra vs. Baker* was based on the report of an Internet investigator who claimed to have detected the "shared files folders" which I mentioned above.

In fact, there is a second major legal issue that involves digital copies on the Internet, which is privacy. As it occurred with another highly controversial decision in the U.S. opposing an American ISP, Verizon, and the RIAA, scholars have pointed out how people's privacy on the Internet- specially when using P2P file-sharing applications- "is threatened under certain interpretations of the Digital Millennium Copyright Act (DMCA) in the United States (as) a new form of *panoptic surveillance* that can be carried out by organizations such as the RIAA" (as stressed by Grodzinski & Tavani, 2005).

The thesis was confirmed in 2007, when the *Motion Picture Association of America* (MPAA) required (lawfully, according to federal judge Florence-Marie Cooper) the IP addresses of those connecting to TorrentSpy files via their service in the U.S. The MPAA had in fact filed a lawsuit against the popular P2P system, alleging that the company violated copyright law by helping sharers find pirated movies. The dispute then overheated when TorrentSpy accused the MPAA of hiring a hacker (by the way an ex TorrentSpy employee) to pilfer the company's trade secrets. Judge Cooper's interpretation, however, did not favour the European company: By following the *Wiretap Act*, the word "intercept" would only mean that someone must intentionally obtain e-mails and not just acquire them from an electronic storage. Since TorrentySpy used to store e-mails on its server before they were copied and forwarded to the hacker's e-mail account, the result was therefore that no interception would have occurred! Forced to enable server logging against its own privacy policy, it is not a surprise that TorrentSpy, whose servers are physically located in the Netherlands, announced its decision to stop doing business in the U.S. on August 27th, 2007.

The peculiarities of the U.S. legal system as well as some key differences between the U.S. and EU law can be further illustrated with two cases debated in Europe.

The first one took place in Italy in 2006, when a German music company, Peppermint, commissioned the Swiss firm Logistep to raise the IP addresses of people making available copyrighted works by means of P2P systems on the Internet. On the basis of the claim that Peppermint would have been the only right holder, the plaintiff required a section of the Tribunal in Rome to obtain both the "real addresses", and names of 3000 allegedly illegal file sharers from the involved ISPs. Judges, at first, granted the request so that three thousand letters were sent by a lawyer from Bozen to the indicted P2P users, asking them for EUR 330 in order to settle the case and avoid any further inquiry (in this way, Peppermint would have received cash worth almost ten times its own annual revenues…). Later on, in April 2008, the Bar Association in Paris interdicted a lawyer who sent similar letters to other French P2P users. Yet, even the Tribunal in Rome changed idea: on June 16th, 2007, it declared that it was illegal spying on citizens on the Web in order to guarantee the protection of alleged copyright holders pursuant to articles 13, 23, and 37 of the Italian "code of privacy" (ICP), as well as articles 2 and 15 of the Italian Constitution. Neither articles 8 and 9 from D-2004/48/EC, nor the exceptions from articles 3.2 and 13 D-1995/46/EC, could eventually legitimate such a violation of P2P users' privacy.

The second important ruling that confirms the relevance of data protection laws in deciding lawsuits against P2P file sharing systems is in *Promusicae vs. Telefónica de España*, decided by the European Court of Justice on January 29th, 2008. According to the judges in Luxembourg, EU law does *not* require Member States to lay down "an *obligation to communicate personal data* in order to ensure effective protection of copyright in the context of civil proceedings". In addition, the Court warned that, when transposing directives into national legal systems, Member States must "take care to rely on an interpretation of them which allows a fair balance to be struck between the various fundamental rights protected by the Community legal order" (§ 70 of the decision).

So, in the light of these different legal outcomes between the U.S. and the EU, between copyright claims and privacy concerns, a second conclusion can be drawn: The new economical scenarios and different business models for the "short route" between creators, producers, and the public, cannot ignore the data protection issues raised by the technology of digital copies. Furthermore, we are invited to seriously reconsider "the right to freely participate in the cultural life of the community" by exploiting all the opportunities of the "short route" created by digital technology. Recent work on P2P systems shows how all this is possible.

A MATTER OF BALANCE

There are two reasons why I think P2P technology is a particularly useful example in order to deepen our analysis on the current troubles with digital copies.

First of all, by the end of 2007, these file sharing systems have surpassed the Web as the most bandwidth-consuming application in many parts of the Internet. This undoubted success highlights some relevant ethical issues, as well as social dilemmas in business management and organizational innovation that involve other kinds of knowledge. Along with the music industry, think of movies, books, newspapers, blogs, and so forth. Whereas knowledge management deals with the acquisition and use of resources to set up an environment where information is accessible to individuals, P2P systems are revolutionizing how individuals acquire, share, or utilise that information to develop their own knowledge (Brelade & Harman, 2003).

Secondly, notwithstanding its undoubted success, P2P technology has polarized the opinion of the scholars. Some, like Michael Bauwens (2005), claim that these systems represent the key to a new paradigm since sharing of information via strongly decentralized or distributed forms of coordination among geographically dispersed actors would be the paramount example of a social transformation that should be further encouraged. Others, as Andrew Keen (2008), stress the risks and threats of such new technologies and how they undermine vital elements of our societies for "digital piracy, enabled by Silicon Valley hardware and justified by Silicon Valley intellectual property communists (sic!) such as Larry Lessig, is draining revenue from established artists, movie studios, newspapers, record labels, and song writers".

The polarization of the debate should be understood in connection with the ways in which information is distributed and shared in P2P networks. On the side of the new paradigm-advocates, it must be said that these file sharing application systems have solved some relevant problems of the CDN architecture- which is used by some of the most popular Web sites like Amazon, CNN, Google, and You Tube- based upon the traditional (and very expensive) client/server design. By decentralizing the processes of storage distribution and copy-replication of the data to be transmitted among nodes of the network through its "servents"- that is, nodes that are client and server at the same time- P2P systems have created wider opportunities in digital environments, making the "short route" even shorter.

Nevertheless, on the side of P2P censors and opponents, we must pay attention to some of the serious problems still afflicting this technology as the free-riding phenomenon, the abovementioned copyright claims, along with issues of connectivity and availability of resources, or, to be pessimistic in some cases, the collapse of the entire system. Despite the determined and at times even aggressive ways in which copyright holders are trying to protect themselves against this file sharing technology, the problems related to P2Ps have suggested some politicians in Washington, D.C., like the Government Reform Committee Chairman, Henry Waxman (D-CA), Rep. Tom Davis (R-VA), and Rep. Paul Hodes (R-NH), that P2P systems represent such a serious threat for national security that the best way to deal with all of these risks would be to simply shut them down (as some U.S. campuses have already done).

So, is there a way to overcome this deadlock? Can technical solutions be developed for balancing the various fundamental interests involved in file sharing application systems? Can the new economical scenarios and business models of the "short route" be exploited in order to share profits (and not only files), while reinforcing responsibility and protecting people's privacy?

As I show in the next section, some technical solutions are already viable and, yet, they require that even industry music producers and movie managers understand why digital copies via P2P systems represent more an opportunity than a threat for business and economic development. Let aside ethical issues (Pagallo, 2010), it is a matter of content delivery and multimedia streaming, broadband and multicast services, distributed databases, and so forth. The new horizons of digital sharing suggest avoiding the typical opposition between "long route"- and "short route"- advocates so as to focus on their common challenges, e.g., knowledge creation and fair compensation through individual contribution to the exchange of information in some crucial areas of the industry and society. Whereas knowledge management involves the connection between people, content, culture, and technology (Phillips, 2000), it is time to shed some light on the ways in which P2P management of digital copies is deeply reshaping such a dynamics.

ORGANISING INNOVATION VIA P2P SYSTEMS

In order to approach the new horizons in digital sharing via P2P systems, we may start by casting light on a paradox: although those file sharing applications can be considered as a "mature technology" that promotes novel forms of coordination between owners and consumers, between developers and providers, P2P business model is still quite problematic.

A main reason concerns the free-riding phenomenon (as shown by Adar & Huberman, 2000). Most peers, indeed, tend to use these systems to find information and download their favourite files without contributing to the performance of the system. Whereas this selfish behaviour is triggered by many properties of P2P applications like anonymity and hard traceability of the nodes, scholars have proposed ways to tackle the issue as, say, with incentives.

Inducements may be based on trust (e.g., reputation mechanisms) or trade (e.g., services in return). This latter scheme implies that "the receiver can recompense the provider immediately, during or after the service provision, or she can promise a service in return" (Ruffo & Schifanella, 2007, pp. 358). In the first hypotheses, there is a sort of digital barter as with the "tit-for-tat" model in Bit Torrent, or the credit system of Emule. In the second case, a bond scheme which involves forms of digital money like Kazaa's "Alnet's points" is set in place. These economic transactions can be managed via a central authority like Elon Musk's online-banking company PayPal- which was sold to eBay in 2002 for $1.5 billion- or via distributed systems based on different ways of accounting (i.e., local, token, or remote).

Since incentives can produce value in terms of revenue, some interesting management proposals have thus been presented like the Market Management of Peer-to-Peer Services or MMAPPS project, upon which additional architectural concepts have been suggested as the Service Oriented Peer-to-Peer Service and the distinction between service, market, and peer models proposed by Gerke *et al.* (2003). On this basis, further research has pointed out new ways to tackle the "original sin" of this technology, namely its copyright-related legal issues. Among such work, let me briefly insist on Ruffo & Schifanella's (2007) FairPeers model, for this is the only proposal that- up till now- supports both copyright management and "fairness".

On the one hand, the idea is to include proper copyright management "without mitigating the technical benefits of a P2P system" (Ruffo & Schifanella, 2007, pp. 361). In order to regulate the distribution of copy-protected items such as movies, songs, executable programs and the like, it is introduced an Authority that certifies the identity of the users as well as the Copyright Grantor that stores the information- related to all of the items in the system- such as ownership, cost, and details about the content. While it is possible to add other mediators like, for example, payment brokers, the files to be shared in the system are issued with the Grantor's copyright certificate and the distribution license released by the owner of the object. Therefore, the provider can be any regular peer of the system that has got the license to distribute files.

On the other hand, both the owner and the provider- who contributes to the functioning of the system in terms of bandwidth, cpu cycles, and disk space- should be paid every time that a file is downloaded. As suggested by the authors, "we think that this property has been deeply underestimated and a proper implementation of fair mechanisms can strongly incentive users to behave legally and can bring success to a market" (Ruffo & Schifanella, 2007, pp. 362). In the typical case where a file is very popular and there are many providers, an Electronic Lottery Tickets scheme is adopted, so that only one provider will get the entire revenue for the distribution. As shown by Rivest (1997), the risk that only few peers could be the winners is counterbalanced by the law of large numbers, while maintaining "fairness without invalidating typical P2P efficiency" (Ruffo & Schifanella, 2007, pp. 379).

However, it is hard to imagine a technology immune to all kinds of abuse, so that, in terms of responsibility, it is critical that service providers can avoid prosecution by denying accountability for other users' behaviour.

In this sense, the different possible configurations of these systems are particularly relevant just as how the nodes are linked to each other at the overlay level. P2P networks can in fact be unstructured, as in the cases of Gnutella and Kazaa, in which overlay links are created by chance. Yet, these systems can also be structured, as Kademlia and Pastry, that are defined in terms of a topology- like a forest, a ring, and so forth- along with routing mechanisms and identifier spaces which allow nodes and resources in the network to be located. This difference has legal significance because structured models seem to better prevent legal claims as liability for actions committed by users of these systems. Besides, compared to centralized networks, these structured overlays do not seem to present single points of failure or problems of efficiency like the flooding search method adopted by Gnutella. In addition, they do not push legal responsibility over few superpeers as in the case of Kazaa. This is why "the first learned lesson which must be considered during the implementation of (a) given P2P service model" is that "structured overlays are to be preferred to unstructured P2P systems in order to let the community owners and/or the developers decline their responsibilities for users' actions" (Glorioso, Pagallo & Ruffo, 2010, pp. 65).

In the same way, topology matters when we address the problem of protecting users' privacy. Both anonymity and confidentiality in P2P interaction should be addressed at the lowest level of the technological platform since the use of the overlay network makes it possible to easily identify users inserting or storing information in the system.

Authentication protocols as well as identification policies should provide for use of pseudonyms, OpenID, and ways of ciphering content. This makes it safer to prevent both unauthorized access to the information stored at the overlay level, and legal liability of the content provider whom does not happen to be the source or the owner of that very information.

Furthermore, significant evidence suggests spontaneous clustering of users by content distribution: this is what occurs with both Gnutella and Kazaa networks as shown by Ruffo & Schifanella (2009) and by Iamnitchi, Ripeanu & Foster (2004). Whereas different models can be used in order to detect this phenomenon like "data-sharing graphs" or "affinity networks", what is extraordinary about these features is the possibility to develop interesting applications for recommender systems on the Internet, i.e., techniques for coping with the problem of overloading information. Besides short paths between couples of peers and high clustering factor, the existence of hubs- that is, users who share a large amount of items playing a significant role in providing connectivity- has a remarkable effect. As I stressed in previous work with Ruffo (2007a; 2007b), such topological features can be used to defend people's privacy via decentralized recommendation schemes based on spontaneous affinities. By using partnership degree and relationships among peers there is no need for retrieving people's profiles, and users are not required to give feedbacks to a data collector entity in order to avoid the problem of overloading information.

Of course, anonymity and confidentiality techniques, encrypted communication and plausible deniability can be used by criminal organizations: it is still a hot issue, after all, whether OpenID represents the best solution to these problems. However, the aim of this section is not to claim that P2P networks offer the key to a new paradigm in the history of human evolution as asserted by Bauwens (2005). Although this technology encourages organizational innovation via decentralized or distributed forms of coordination between owners and providers, between developers and consumers, what I want to suggest here is that rights and interests involved in the current debate can be feasibly balanced as in the case of knowledge creation and digital sharing, fair compensation and privacy rights. It should be clear that we do not need to ban P2P systems in order to tackle the trouble with digital copies: Nonetheless, further research is required.

FUTURE RESEARCH DIRECTIONS

I have insisted on the example of file sharing application systems because this technology sums up some relevant issues concerning digital copies in today's debate, as in the case of copyright claims and privacy worries (interestingly enough, on July 23rd, 2009, some advocacy groups as the American Civil Liberties Union and the Electronic Frontier Foundation asked Google to commit to protect the privacy of readers in its book search service. Furthermore, Google's project to build an expansive digital library has already attracted criticism and is being scrutinized for possible antitrust and copyright problems).

Besides, P2P networks are particularly interesting in both the fields of knowledge management and organizational innovation insofar as these application systems specify some of the new ways in which information is produced, distributed, and shared in digital environments through strongly decentralized and distributed forms of collaboration. This is why further research on this copy-based digital technology includes a panoply of different topics like the structured vs. unstructured debate, search efficiency, incentive mechanisms, trust and reputation management, broadcast and multicast services, content delivery and multimedia streaming, distributed databases, anonymity techniques, advanced computing, and the like.

Yet, before discussing some possible innovative trends and perspectives, it is indispensable to address a preliminary question. By considering some ethical problems (e.g., selfish vs. altruistic behaviour), as well as social dilemmas (e.g., intellectual property vs. social sharing) fostered by digital copies, it could be questioned whether this approach for balancing these different rights and interests is the proper one. Think for example of the "governmentally administered reward system" as proposed by Fisher (2004) or, the other way around, of the Digital Rights Management (DRM)-systems used by iTunes, FairPlay, or Napster to Go.

In the first case, the proposal of a national administered system seems however inconsistent with the international obligations established by both the Berne Convention and the TRIPs Agreement, letting aside the ubiquitous nature of the Internet which transcends traditional legal borders. All in all, as frankly admitted by the same proponent of the system, the Berne Convention "would seem to forbid the curtailment of copyright law necessitated by the proposed regime" (Fisher, 2004, pp. 44).

In the second case, by enabling right-holders both to monitor and regulate the use of copyright protected works, the employ of DRM techniques risks to severely curtail freedom as behaviour would unilaterally be determined on the basis of technology rather than by choices of the relevant political institutions. As stressed by Steve Jobs (2007), DRM compliant systems raise severe problems of interoperability and, hence, antitrust-related issues. In addition, they jeopardize people's privacy and responsibility that represent some of the ethical concerns which P2P research should focus on and, possibly, resolve. This is why, throughout this chapter, I have insisted on the societal constraints that determine the horizon of possible technological improvements: What about the consequences of the *Grokster* case in the light of that "fair balance" to be struck between fundamental rights, according to the ECJ ruling in *Promusicae vs. Telefónica*?

Here, let me emphasize three areas of research which I think are particularly relevant.

The first field is trust and reputation management in digital environments. As I pointed out in previous sections, the trouble with digital copies has not only involved copyright issues but people's privacy as well. Business models and organizational innovation should pay particular attention to personal data protection, especially when it is considered malicious behaviour such as cheating, colluding, protocol aborting, and the like. One way of tackling these problems is obviously defined by security measures and reputation schemes; so that users can be asked to submit feedbacks once a transaction is completed (or aborted). However, one of the most relevant aspects of the "short route" scenario is that content distribution greatly benefits from users' participation because the more they are stimulated to contribute to the system; the more resources are available on it. While there is extensive work on such topics as reputation and trust schemas as in Jøsang, Ismail & Body (2007), Marti & Garcia-Molina (2006), etc., it is clear that the problem is cultural, as well as computational and, therefore, it requires interdisciplinary approaches.

The second direction of future research concerns the connection between anonymity, security, and responsibility. After the legal misadventures of Napster- that presented a typical centralized architecture in which operators of the server used to index each peer's files and, thus, they could have intervened to stop copyright infringements pursuant to art. 512 of the DMCA- the following generation of P2P systems has developed a typical decentralized topology that provides plausible anonymity for its users. This, in return, has created new problems and original forms of uncertainty, because full anonymity may not only protect people's rights against those political regimes that have developed extensive monitoring infrastructures (Deibert *et al.*, 2008). Anonymity, in fact, may also encourage irresponsible acts. While I stressed that it is still an open question whether pseudonymous systems like OpenID represent the best solution to these problems, it is always hard to determine a clear-cut line between the necessity of a venue for political information-sharing activities in countries where surveillance is routine, and the prospect that such systems protect or even encourage criminal activities. After all, it is certain that, among other things, Al' Qaeda has been using encryption since 1993 that is, in their first and partially failed attack on the Twin Towers (Etzioni, 2004).

Finally, we have the problem of overloading information in digital environments. Along with the "paradox of choice" (and abundance) as suggested by Schwartz (2005)- let alone the risk that people endorse positions that are not necessarily the best ones but simply the less controversial or most accepted, as denounced by Keen (2008)- there is the possibility that the distributed topology of some networks can represent an obstacle to people's interaction. Therefore, while some scholars as Kaune (2008), Zhao (2004), and their colleagues, have been proposing to reorganize even the topology of some P2P networks on the very idea of geographical proximity, the domain of recommender systems is among the most active fields of current research. After centralized and content-based schemes as with *News Weeder* or *Syskill & Webert*, or collaborative filtering as *Tapestry*, or using demographic approaches, we need new strategies as those discussed in the previous section by exploiting the specific topological properties of networks such as Gnutella (as in Ruffo & Schifanella, 2009).

CONCLUSION

It is striking that, so often, people (and scholars) associate the trouble with digital copies exclusively with copyright issues. What is more, there are some associations like the RIAA or the MPAA in the U.S. or the collective rights management organizations (CRMOs) in Europe, that tend to present the whole issue as if it were merely a matter of "piracy".

So, the aim of this chapter was to show that things are quite more complex and interesting. In a sort of Hegelian phenomenology, it is possible to sum up this remarkable complexity in three moments.

First, in the early 1990s, we witnessed the eruption of copy-based digital technologies with the "short route" joining and even replacing the traditional long one between author, business, and the public. Both at legal and political levels, the reaction was swift and, occasionally, aggressive: After more than a century of the well-functioning provisions of the Berne Convention, intellectual property and copyright law-fields became the target of an intensive and even frantic intervention by law makers. It was as if the only right that mattered from art. 27 UDHR were "the right to the protection of the moral and material interests resulting from any scientific, literary or artistic production".

A decade later, the drawbacks of such a short-sighted legal policy became evident: the trouble with digital copies did not concern only copyright holders' interests but involved people's privacy as well. While the technological innovation opened up new horizons and opportunities for business innovation, and the so-called "digital economy", courts and tribunals, at least in Europe have reminded legislators of the need to strike a fair balance between the different fundamental rights at stake. Perhaps time has come to seriously take "the right freely to participate in the cultural life of the community, to enjoy the arts and to share in scientific advancement and its benefits".

Finally, a lesson should be learnt when addressing further developments and future research. In fact, I illustrated some of the ways in which we can viably mediate digital file sharing and fair compensation with forms of trusted management, as well as selfish behaviour and altruistic actions via incentives, or people's anonymity and social responsibility through architectural devices and recommender systems. So, it is important to recall not only the societal boundaries which limit or restrict the universe of possible technological scenarios, but also the values and principles that lie behind those societal boundaries while orientating and determining political choices. Digital copies are here to stay and they represent more an opportunity for innovation than a threat for economics, politics, or business management. This is why it is critical to further develop copy-based digital technologies in connection with that fair legal balance which should be struck between different fundamental rights. Those who do not know their own history will be forced to repeat the errors. Do we really want to go back to the 1990s?

REFERENCES

Adar, E., & Huberman, B. A. (2000). Free riding on gnutella. *First Monday, 5*(10). Retrieved April 20, 2009, from http://firstmonday.org/htbin/cgiwrap/bin/ojs/index.php/fm/article/view/792/701

Anderson, C. (2008). *The long tail, revised and updated edition: Why the future of business is selling less of more*. New York: Hyperion.

Bauwens, M. (2005). P2P and human evolution: placing peer to peer theory in an integral framework. *Integral Visioning*. Retrieved April 20, 2009, from http://integralvisioning.org/article.php?story=p2ptheory1

Benkler, Y. (2006). *The wealth of networks: How social production transforms markets and freedom*. New Haven, CT: Yale University Press.

Brelade, S., & Harman, C. (2003). *A practical guide to knowledge management*. London: Thorogood.

Deibert, R. J. (2008). *Access denied: The practice and policy of global internet filtering*. Cambridge, MA: MIT Press.

Etzioni, A. (2004). *How patriotic is the patriot act? Freedom versus security in the age of terrorism*. New York: Routledge.

Fisher, W. (2004). *Promises to keep: Technology, law and the future of entertainment*. Stanford, CA: Stanford University Press.

Gerke, J. (2003). An architecture for a service oriented peer-to-peer system (SOPPS). *Praxis der Informationsverarbeitung und Kommunikation, 26*(2), 90–95. doi:10.1515/PIKO.2003.90

Glorioso, A., Pagallo, U., & Ruffo, G. (2010). The social impact of P2P networks. In X. Shen *et al.* (Eds.), *Handbook of P2P Networking* (pp. 47-70). Heidelberg, Germany: Springer.

Grodzinski, F. S., & Tavani, H. T. (2005). P2P networks and the Verizon v. RIAA case: Implications for personal privacy and intellectual property. *Ethics and Information Technology, 7*(4), 243–250. doi:10.1007/s10676-006-0012-4

Iamnitchi, A., Ripeanu, M., & Foster, I. (2004). Small-world file-sharing communities. In *INFOCOM 2004: 23th Annual Joint Conference of the IEEE Computer and Communications Societies: Vol 2* (pp. 952-963). Hong Kong: IEEE Communications Society.

Jobs, S. (2007). Thoughts on music. *Apple*. Retrieved April 20, 2009, from http://www.apple.com/hotnews/thoughtsonmusic/

Jøsang, A., Ismail, R., & Boyd, C. (2007). A survey on trust and reputation systems for online service provision. *Decision Support Systems, 43*(2), 618–644. doi:10.1016/j.dss.2005.05.019

Kaune, S., Lauinger, T., & Kovacevic, A. (2008). Embracing the peer next door: Proximity in Kademlia. In K. Wehrle (Ed.), *P2P '08: Proceedings of the Eighth International Conference on Peer-to-Peer Computing* (pp. 343-350). Aachen, Germany: IEEE Press.

Keen, A. (2008). *The cult of the amateur: How blogs, MySpace, YouTube, and the rest of today's user-generated media are destroying our economy, our culture, and our values*. New York: Doubleday Business.

Marti, S., & Garcia-Molina, H. (2006). Taxonomy of trust: Categorizing p2p reputation systems. *Computer Networks*, *50*(4), 472–484. doi:10.1016/j.comnet.2005.07.011

Pagallo, U. (2010). Ethics among peers: From Napster to Peppermint and beyond. In D'Atri, A., & Saccà, D. (Eds.), *Information Systems: People, Organizations, Institutions, and Technologies* (pp. 297–304). Heidelberg, Germany: Springer.

Pagallo, U., & Ruffo, G. (2007a). On the growth of collaborative and competitive networks: Opportunities and new challenges. In S. Rogerson & H. Yang (Eds.), *Proceedings of ETHICOMP Working Conference 2007* (pp. 92-97). Yunnan: Yunnan University.

Pagallo, U., & Ruffo, G. (2007b). P2P systems in legal networks. Another 'small world' case. In R. Winkels (Ed.), *Eleventh International Conference on Artificial Intelligence and Law* (pp. 287-288). Stanford, CA: ACM Press.

Phillips, J. T. (2000). Will KM alter information managers' roles? *Information Management Journal*, *34*(3), 58–59.

Raymond, E. S. (1999). *The cathedral & the bazaar: Musings on Linux and open source by an accidental revolution*. Sebastopol, CA: O'Reilly Media.

Ricolfi, M. (2007). Individual and collective management of copyright in a digital environment. In Torremans, P. (Ed.), *Copyright Law: A Handbook of Contemporary Research* (pp. 283–314). Cheltenham, UK: Edward Elgar.

Rivest, R. L. (1997). Electronic lottery tickets as micropayments. In R. Hirschfeld (Ed.), *Proceedings of the First International Conference on Financial Cryptography* (pp. 307-314). London: Springer.

Ruffo, G., & Schifanella, R. (2007). FairPeers: Efficient profit sharing in fair peer-to-peer market places. *Journal of Network and Systems Management*, *15*(3), 355–382. doi:10.1007/s10922-007-9066-9

Ruffo, G., & Schifanella, R. (2009). A peer-to-peer recommender system based on spontaneous affinities. *ACM Transactions on Internet Technology*, *9*(1), 1–34. doi:10.1145/1462159.1462163

Schwartz, B. (2005). *The paradox of choice: why more is less* (2nd ed.). New York: Harper Perennial.

Tapscott, D. (1997). *The digital economy: Promise and peril in the age of networked intelligence*. New York: McGraw-Hill.

Toffler, A. (1980). *The third wave*. New York: Bantam.

Zhao, B. (2004). Tapestry: A resilient global-scale overlay for service deployment. *IEEE Journal on Selected Areas in Communications*, *22*(1), 41–53. doi:10.1109/JSAC.2003.818784

ADDITIONAL READING

Ardizzone, A. (2009). *Copyright digitale. L'impatto delle nuove tecnologie tra economia e diritto*. Torino: Giappichelli.

Benkler, Y. (2004). Sharing nicely: On shareable goods and the emergence of sharing as a modality of economic production. *The Yale Law Journal*, *114*(273), 273–358. doi:10.2307/4135731

Bynum, T. W., & Moor, J. H. (Eds.). (1998). *The digital phoenix: How computers are changing philosophy*. New York, NY: Blackwell.

Bynum, T. W., & Rogerson, S. (Eds.). (2004). *Computer ethics and professional responsibility*. Oxford: Blackwell.

Christensen, C. M., & Raynor, M. E. (2003). *The innovator's solution*. Boston, MA: Harvard Business School Press.

Drahos, P., & Braithwaite, J. (2002). *Information feudalism*. London: Earthscan.

Floridi, L. (2010). *A very short introduction to information*. Oxford: Oxford University Press.

Foray, D. (2004). *Economics of knowledge*. Cambridge, MA: The MIT Press.

Frank, R. H., & Cook, P. J. (1995). *The winner-takes-all society*. New York, NY: Martin Kessler Books at The Free Press.

Gervais, D. (2004). The price of social norms: towards a liability regime for file sharing. *Journal of Intellectual Property Law*, *12*(1), 39–73.

Ghosh, R. (Ed.). (2005). *Code- Collaborative ownership and the digital economy*. Cambridge, MA: The MIT Press.

Goldstein, P. (1994). *Copyright's highway*. New York, NY: Hill & Wang.

Greco, G. M., & Floridi, L. (2004). The tragedy of the digital commons. *Ethics and Information Technology*, *6*(2), 73–81. doi:10.1007/s10676-004-2895-2

Himma, K. E. (2007). The legitimacy of intellectual property rights: The irrelevance of two conceptions of an information commons. In L. Hinman *et al.* (Eds.), *Proceedings of CEPE 2007: The 7th International Conference of Computer Ethics- Philosophical Enquiry* (pp. 180-193). San Diego: Centre for Telematics and Information Technology.

Hummel, T., Muhle, S., & Schoder, D. (2005). Business applications and revenue models. In Steinmetz, R., & Wehrle, K. (Eds.), *Peer-to-peer Systems and Applications* (pp. 473–489). Berlin, Heidelberg: Springer. doi:10.1007/11530657_28

Kelling, D. T. (2003). *Intellectual property rights in EU law: Free movement and competition law*. Oxford: Oxford University Press.

Krishnamurthy, S. (2003). A managerial overview of open source software. *Business Horizons*, *46*(5), 47–56. doi:10.1016/S0007-6813(03)00071-5

Landes, W. M., & Posner, R. A. (2003). *The economic structure of intellectual property law*. Cambridge, MA: Harvard University Press.

Lerner, J., & Tirole, J. (2002). Some simple economics of open source. *The Journal of Industrial Economics*, *50*(2), 197–234. doi:10.1111/1467-6451.00174

Lessig, L. (2001). *The future of ideas: The fate of the commons in an interconnected world*. New York, NY: Random House.

Limpsey, R. G., Karlaw, K. I., & Bekar, C. T. (2005). *Economic transformations- General purpose technologies and long-term economic growth*. Oxford: Oxford University Press.

Miller, F. H. (Ed.). (2003). *Rights and resources*. Dartmouth: Ashgate.

Nicita, A., & Ramello, G. B. (2007). Property, liability and market power: the antitrust side of copyright. *Review of Law and Economics*, *3*(3), 767–791.

Pagallo, U. (2005). *Introduzione alla filosofia digitale*. Torino: Giappichelli.

Pagallo, U. (2008). *La tutela della privacy negli Stati Uniti d'America e in Europa*. Milano: Giuffrè.

Posner, R. (2005). Intellectual property: The law-and-economics approach. *The Journal of Economic Perspectives*, *19*(2), 57–73. doi:10.1257/0895330054048704

Reichman, J. H. (1994). Legal hybrids between the patent and copyright paradigms. *Columbia Law Review*, *94*(88), 2432–2558. doi:10.2307/1123143

Shapiro, C., & Varian, H. R. (1998). *Information rules: A strategic guide to the network economy*. Boston, MA: Harvard Business School Press.

Shirky, C. (2008). *Here comes everybody: The power of organizing without organizations*. New York, NY: Penguin Press.

Slobogin, C. (2007). *Privacy at risk: The new government surveillance and the fourth amendment*. Chicago, IL: University of Chicago Press.

Solove, D. J., Rotenberg, M., & Schwartz, P. M. (2006). *Privacy, information, and technology*. New York, NY: Aspen.

Tapscott, D., & Williams, A. D. (2006). *Wikinomics: How mass collaboration changes everything*. New York, NY: Porfolio.

Tavani, H. T. (2005). Locke, intellectual property rights, and the information commons. *Ethics and Information Technology*, *7*(2), 87–97. doi:10.1007/s10676-005-4584-1

Von Hippel, E. (2005). *Democratizing innovation*. Boston, MA: The MIT Press.

West, J., & Gallagher, S. (2006). Patterns of open innovation in open source software. In H. W. Chesbrough, W. Vanhaverbeke & J. West (Eds.), *Open Innovation: Researching a New Paradigm* (pp. 82-106). Oxford: Oxford University Press.

Zittrain, J. (2008). *The future of the internet and how to stop it*. New Haven, CT: Yale University Press.

KEY TERMS AND DEFINITIONS

Copy: Traditionally conceived as the secondary representation or replica of an original, its current digital dimension has dramatically changed the relation with the archetype. Whereas, theoretically speaking, there is no longer any difference between the original and the copy, many relevant legal, economical, and business-related distinctions have vanished as with the demarcation between primary and secondary exploitation of an author's work.

Copyright: The right to the protection of the interests involved in any artistic or scientific production. The author's exclusive right to exploit the benefits of her own work, with the drawbacks of such a monopolistic condition, has always been counterbalanced by determining a period after which the exclusivity expires. If the first copyright act, i.e., the Statute of Anne (1709), established a fourteen year term of protection, this period has now expanded to an average term of seventy-five years worldwide (the algorithm is equivalent to adding twenty years to Mickey Mouse's age).

Digital Rights Management (DRM): Systems that enable right-holders both to monitor and regulate the use of their copyright protected artefacts. On the assumption that digital technologies undermine legal provisions as commands enforced through physical sanctions, the goal is to achieve a perfect self-enforcement. Besides problems of interoperability and antitrust issues, the risk is however that DRM compliant systems can curtail freedom because behaviour would unilaterally be determined on the basis of technology rather than by choices of the relevant political institutions.

Incentive: A positive motivator that is extremely relevant in digital environments since anonymity and decentralization often trigger selfish behaviour. They are mainly based on trust or trade, that is, through reputation mechanisms implemented via forms of digital barter or through services in return, where a bond scheme involves forms of digital money. As incentives can produce value in terms of revenue, there have been some interesting management proposals like the MMAPPS project or FairPeers.

Information: A tricky concept that has divided even giants like Wiener and Shannon. While, for the former, information and entropy are inversely proportioned, for the latter it works the other way around, because the more a message is unexpected or random, the more the information we have. Luckily enough, despite this difference, a new sort of metaphysics has arisen, according to which everything can be conceptualized in terms of information and the universe in terms of an "info-sphere".

Peer-to-Peer: File sharing applications for the Internet that have become particularly infamous, at least among music companies and movie producers, for they make it easy for users to access copy(right)-protected files for free. These systems, however, have solved some relevant problems of the CDN architecture based upon the traditional (and very expensive) client/server design, by decentralizing the processes of distributed storage and replicated copies of the data to be transmitted among nodes of the network through its "servents" (that is, nodes that are client and server at the same time).

Privacy: The old "right to be let alone" that technology has combined with the novel need to protect people's personal data in digital environments. While, in the U.S., a property approach still prevails, so that consent represents most of the times the key legal notion of current debate, privacy is mostly associated in Europe with human dignity and presented as an inalienable right. Today's troubles with digital copies have made this very difference extremely relevant in connection with alleged copyright infringements.

Route: A metaphor which is used to illustrate the different phases and services making up the value chain of a given object. In the pre-digital world there was a traditional "long route" between an author and the public, in that several different steps were required to reach the potential buyer or consumer: production, storage, distribution, delivery, and the like. This value chain has been joined and even replaced by a "short route" in the digital era. Not only distribution and delivery have collapsed into a single service but boundaries between creators and consumers tend to blur.

Topology: The way in which systems are configured and information is created and distributed in a network. Its relevance has not only a technical meaning- see the debate between centralized vs. decentralized networks- but legal and political significance as well. Different levels of technological platforms for sharing files on the Internet have an impact on the liability and responsibility of the users and the providers.

Chapter 8
From "Connectivism" to "Ethicism"

António dos Reis
The Graal Institute, Portugal

ABSTRACT

Distance learning characteristics has been changing dramatically, namely since the fourth generation of distance learning. Moreover, e-learning impressive "evolution" enabled a trade-off between learning outcomes and ethical behaviour, which traditional learning theories do not embrace and that connectivism endeavours to illustrate. Although, two important queries arise: what challenges e-learning 2.0 and 3.0 impose? And, does connectivism promote ethical knowledge? Therefore, this chapter aims to endorse a theoretical debate regarding e-learning, as well as to understand if connectivism will act as 21st century learning theory, or if the quest for an ethical connective knowledge and e-learning fusion with knowledge management itself will require a novel contribution (connethionicism). Despite the assumption that connectivism has been promoting a reasonable debate, the author's personal experiences highlight the need for ethicism.

INTRODUCTION

Since e-learning become aware literature has been debating pedagogical theories or its generations. However connectivism as a learning theory has emerged (Siemens, 2006a), and the analytical focus shifted completely. Therefore, today's questions are: does educational technology itself fulfil good learning practices (Egbert, 2008)? Or, is simply "technological noise" in order to promote happiness and motivation to online generations, instead of offering good learning (Cornwell & Cornwell, 2009)?

It is a fact that the uprising of new information and communication technologies opens a large range to learners' engagement (Small & Vorgan, 2008), as well as to implement a connectivist perspective due to the existence of information and connections (Downes, 2005b). Nonetheless, these technologies also enhance the gap of pedagogical

DOI: 10.4018/978-1-61520-873-9.ch008

and didactical skills with reference to educational agents' ethical perception. Hence, is essential an urgent debate in order to ensure that appropriate pedagogical and methodological training is bounded to e-learning 2.0 and 3.0.

In that sense, this chapter aims to discuss: what challenges e-learning 2.0 and e-learning 3.0 impose? And, if connectivism reinforces the quest for an ethical knowledge? Furthermore, for analytical purposes the author refers that ethical knowledge management comprises the learning process outcome and educational agents' behaviour.

At last, the chapter structure considers: historical background (presence versus distance learning and online learning generations); shaping educational knowledge (knowledge versus learning and emerging technology); mapping the territory ("blowing up" the mind and connective knowledge); the quest (ethics for connective knowledge, ethical frameworks for connective knowledge and a proposal: "ethicism"); and, future research directions.

HISTORICAL BACKGROUND

Presence vs. Distance Learning

During an important fraction of 19th and 20th centuries distance learning was a supporting tool for starting education, post graduation, or professional training to those who lived in peripheral areas. Therefore, Holmberg (2005) identifies several generations of distance learning:

- 1st generation (1840 to 1970): acknowledged correspondence courses;
- 2nd generation (1970 to 1980): open universities era, in which universities have full degree programmes through new media, in a systematic way, and having evaluation systems in various parts of the world;
- 3rd generation (1980 to 1990): videotapes and TV were the key technological features;
- 4th generation (from the "90s" until now): online teaching/e-learning are learning enablers. Nevertheless, this generation encompasses various strands (see section online learning generations).

Despite each generation technological features a common characteristic arises: until the 21st century presence and distance learning prevailed in two dissimilar worlds (Holmberg, 2005). Although, the evolution of e-learning to blended learning due to technological evolution gathered both realities. As a result, a distinctive feature of knowledge society is content massive production and distribution in multiple forms in order to support lifelong learning in all learning environments (Commission of the European Communities, 2009; Tuomi, 2004). Therefore, Harris, Connolly & Feeney (2009) argue that for a successful learning process in nowadays blended learning is crucial. This resumes online learning features (content delivery, potential, aperture and versatility), as well as presence learning (formal contact), in spite of e-learning latest streams of the fourth generation allow purely e-learning, as well as learners' characteristics.

Online Learning Generations

E-learning definition has in itself undergone major changes since its first appearance, so the analogy as regards to information processing supported by computers and teaching exhibits this development. Initially, computational programs were referred as *Computer Based Instruction* or, simply *Computer Based Learning* which frames distance learning fourth generation. In fact, this mutual exclusive relationship and dependency on distance learning is pointed out by Rosenberg (2001), which even prophesied e-learning *terminus*. Furthermore, this author aimed to distinguish distance learning

Figure 1. Comparing e-learning generations (Source: Reis et al., 2009, Figure 1)

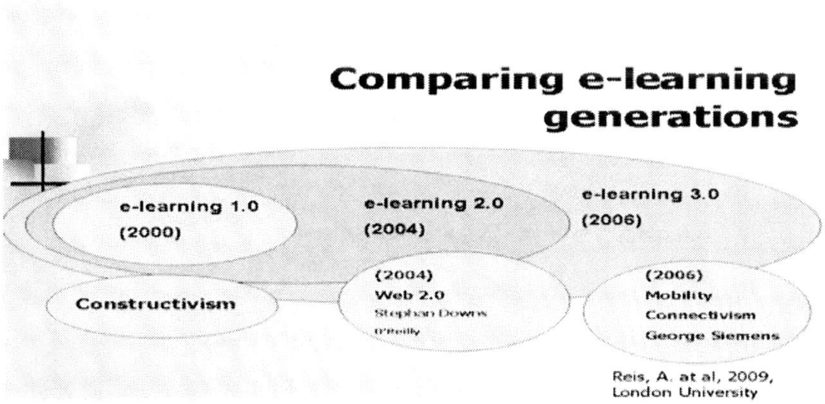

supported by information and communication technologies from the one supported by printed documents.

Nevertheless, today this theoretical debate is inadequate since it is common understanding that e-learning integrates all available means in order to support the learning process, whatever its key features (blended or pure distance learning). For example, Turban *et al.* (2006) define e-learning as the online delivery of information for purposes of education, training, or knowledge management, and is different from formal education, which occurs off campus, and usually, but not always, through online resources (distance learning). Or, for Abram (2003) is basically using the Internet, an intranet, extranet, or other Web technologies to provide training to individuals in a synchronous or asynchronous mode. As a result, a new arrangement of concepts and content is possible for e-learning (Reis, 2007):

- blended learning: includes formative multimedia contents (face-to-face or at a distance), online tutoring and online formative evaluation;
- distance learning: comprises auto study (contents and evaluation) and online tutoring (contents, tutoring and evaluation).

Likewise, at the moment mainstream debate focuses on e-learning generations: 1.0, 2.0 and 3.0. Although, how can we define them? E-learning 1.0 reflects the historical perception previously introduced; Downes (2005a) considers e-learning 2.0 as an "interlocking set of open-source applications, where learning is becoming a creative activity and that the appropriate venue is a platform rather than an application"; and, e-learning 3.0 corresponds to the introduction of semantic web technologies in order to provide contextual information and coordination with reference to text, voice or images through workflow tools as supporting infrastructure (Teten, 2007). In addition, for an easy perception of these generations the author introduces Figure 1.

Therefore, e-learning 1.0 acknowledges content distributed through asynchronous technologies, meaning unidirectional communication through top-down analysis; 2.0 engages interactive content through synchronous communication, leading to a bottom-up collaborative analysis; 3.0 resumes technologies for cooperation, enabling a transversal collaborative analysis (Ebner, 2007). Following Rossi (2008) it is still possible to denote that:

- e-learning 1.0: entails a prevalence of instructivist (learning objects design), socio-

Figure 2. Tools of e-learning generations (Source: Reis et al., 2009, Figure 2)

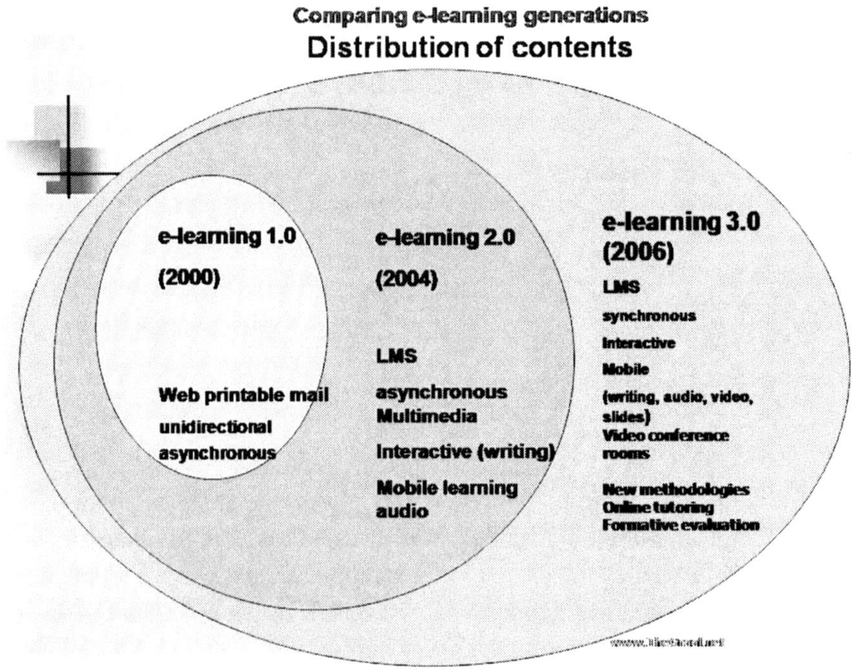

constructivist (peer review through e-mail, forum or chat) and cognitivist approach (consumption of information);

- e-learning 2.0: acknowledges a connectivist (distributed collaboration) dominance, despite a socio-cognitivist (social interaction observation) and socio-cultural (cultural competences) engagement;
- e-learning 3.0: remains in a "veil of ignorance" (e.g. Rawls, 2001; 1971), although artificial intelligence is bounded to this evolution.

As a result, it is time to shed some light as regards to the tools that allow content distribution in each e-learning, and for that the author pleads Figures 2 and 3.

If the Reader bears in mind the distinctive features of each generation, as well as Figures 2 and 3 easily recognizes that: (1) e-learning 1.0 (documents or videos) entails Web early version; (2) e-learning 2.0 is bounded to the rise of Web 2.0 (wikis, blogs, chats, games, among others), which O'Reilly (2005) describes as the evolution for a network platform given the possibility of users provide data and exercise some control over that data, as well as to participate; (3) and, last but not least e-learning 3.0 echoes Web 3.0 (video conference, e-meeting, webcasts, etc)! According to Hempel (2009), the Web 3.0 will configure novel information production through computers rather than humans.

In conclusion, today's learning process can be identified through the following table.

SHAPPING EDUCATIONAL KNOWLEDGE

Knowledge vs. Learning

According to Siemens (2006a), knowledge and learning are procedures that arise inside vague environments of variable core basics, which are

Figure 3. Content distribution in e-learning generations (Source: Reis et al., 2009, Figure 3)

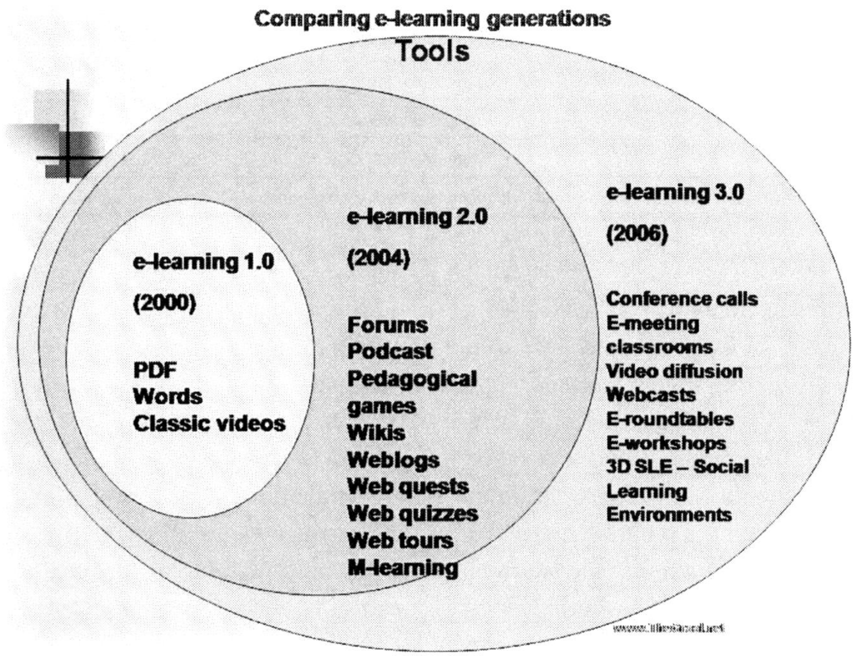

not totally under the control of the individual. However, given the overall argument of this manuscript it is fundamental to debate the underlying discrepancies between both concepts, because throughout literature both concepts are inconsistently used leading to a continuous conflict.

To Driscoll (2000, pp. 11) learning is "a persisting change in human performance or performance potential (…) as a direct result of the learner's experience and interaction with the world", or "a cognitive and/or physical process in which a person assimilates information and temporarily or permanently acquires or improves skills, knowledge, behaviours, and/or attitudes" (American Society for Training and Development, 2010). On the other hand, Stacey (2001) spotlights the paradoxical nature of knowledge, which is simultaneously a thing and a flow or, a process. Moreover, this author points out some key heuristics: knowledge can only be volunteered and values narrative in order to demonstrate knowledge context. And, the result or product of knowing; information or understanding acquired through experience; practical ability or skill; cognition (Oxford English Dictionary, 2008).

Hence the key remark is the notion of sense making, which Kurtz & Snowden (2003, pp. 466) describes as the "use patterns to order the world and make sense of things in complex situations". This scenario clearly outlooks present educational paradigm, because the aim is to analyse, interpret, and apply in order to obtain knowledge.

Emerging Technology

Regardless knowledge and learning dissimilarities, e-learning 2.0 and 3.0 is thrusting a technological fusion in order to enlarge e-learning scope. In fact literature has been discussing this blend (e.g. Haldane, 2004) although some open remarks continue to exist. Nonetheless, knowledge management in educational institutions is not a hype given the key characteristics that knowledge society encompasses (knowledge is a resource,

Table 1. E-learning processes (Adapted from Reis, 2008)

E-learning	Processes	Results
Content distribution	Synchronous technologies	Presence and virtual classroom
	Asynchronous technologies	Learning Management Systems (LMS)
Tutoring	Without tutoring	Self studying
	With tutoring	Presence and virtual classroom
Evaluation	Formative and summative evaluation	Presence and virtual classroom

and lifelong learning is compulsory) (Sedziuviene & Vveinhardt, 2009; Kidwell, Linde & Johnson, 2000). The reasons for this convergence are (Lytras, Pouloudi & Poulymenakou, 2002): (1) the connection to particular education requirements or problems; (2) the customization of content in order to reflect the needed learning circumstances; (3) promote learners' participation into the learning process; (4) improving commitment mechanisms, which will involve further sophisticated learning circumstances; (5) the establishment of tangible learning procedures in order to achieve unlike learning objectives; (6) the development of delivery modes able to support the daily business life of executives.

After debating this blend, is necessary to highlight LMS technological streams (Siemens, 2004a):

- Learning Knowledge Management Systems (LKMS)- acknowledges LMS social development, and involves Personal Learning Environments (PLEs) and Social Software (SS);
- Learning Oriented KM Systems (LOKMS)- LMS instructional evolution.

PLEs resume the ability to learners' manage their own learning environment ; and, SS gathers a mix of bounded technologies that allow a bidirectional process in creating and sharing information and knowledge, rather than simply accessing peripheral informational objects (Attwell, 2007). To conclude, Lytras & Pouloudi (2006) refer that LOKMS attempts to describe the required feedback loops that instructional design imposes to e-learning. Nevertheless, as Siemens & Tittenberger (2009, pp. 15) remind: "the choice to use a particular technology also reflects an accompanying world view or existing mindset". Consequently, this claim is consistent with recent e-learning literature regarding the importance of ethics within learning environments.

MAPPING THE TERRITORY

"Blowing Up" the Mind?

Several improvements in diverse scientific and social areas led to deep changes in the educational process: (1) technological evolution; (2) multichannel learning process; (3) and, socio-cultural revolution.

The 90's imposed a quality leap regarding information and communication technologies consolidation for educational purposes, as for example content generator software, video projectors, and easy presentation tools. Besides, computer chips evolution up to 2GHz, hard drives current speed (Nickerson & Bryner, 2002), as well as the idea that broadband distribution with affordable prices was essential to educational software and media (e.g. European Commission, 1996) allowed video processing and streaming leading to rich multimedia learning environments (present reality) (Handelzalts *et al.*, 2007). Simultaneously the open source movement enabled online tutoring and an effective cost reduction in all learning platforms (Online Education Database, 2007), as well as the possibility of to personalize the learning environments (examples of pure virtual lecturing platforms are Marratech, Adobe Connect, Elluminate, Saba, LiveLearning, among others).

As regards to multi-channel learning process the author draws his attention to psychology and neurobiology contributions to brain "mapping". In fact, Damasio and his colleagues' work (1984; 1985) established that the learning process involves concurrently several brain areas according to the existing *stimulus*, which empirical deductions during the 18th century seem to highlight (e.g. Brodmann, 1909). From this major discovery Joan Stiles-Davis (1988) identified the main physiological and psychological areas for each *stimulus*, namely two significant areas: rational and emotional. As a result, this discovery would be in the line of reasoning with Gardner's (1983) theory about learning styles, the VARK model (Fleming & Mills, 1992), and emotional intelligence (Goleman, 1995). The mix of these contributions gives emphasis to multi-channel formats in order to meet learning styles, as well as pedagogic principles bounded to motivation. In addition, Alcino Silva & Sheena Josselyn (2002) debated memorising processes from a neuropsychological perspective, which underlined dissimilar phases during learning. Once again, this discovery confirmed Moore's (1993), Lauzon's (1997), and Northrup's (2001; 2002) theories about interactivity aspects within the learning process (learner versus lecturer, learner versus learner, and learner versus contents and intra-personal interactivity).

The third reason, socio-cultural revolution, resumed lifelong learning that has been characterizing knowledge society (van Weert, 2005), and societal dependence on digital technologies (van der Velden *et al.*, 2009), which change dramatically education process for learners' and lecturers'.

Even so, in order to produce a more reliable argument the author will detail the overlapping dimension concerning e-learning generations. Neurobiology contributions, namely *spindle cells* and *mirror neurons*, legitimate socio-cultural interaction or collaboration (Goleman, 2006), because mirror-neuron system seems to be strongly bounded to the praxis of human culture (Rizzolatti & Craighero, 2004), to the evolution of language and other forms of expression (artistic and non-artistic) (Oztop, Kawato & Arbib, 2006), to cognitive skills involved in social groups (Erlhagen, Muskoysky & Bicho, 2006), and to emotional consciousness (Parr, Waller & Fugate, 2005). So, these arguments clearly reinforce e-learning 2.0 pedagogical features (connectivist, socio-cognitivist and socio-cultural), and justify the evolution from 1.0 to 2.0 since challenges 1.0 pedagogical theories (Chernigovskaya, 2007). Moreover, neurobiology and psychology scientific research on emotions and human computer interaction enables e-learning 3.0 (Gan & Wang, 2005), despite the nebulous scenario concerning pedagogical perceptions.

Connective Knowledge

Concept

From an etymological analysis it is possible to refer that "connective" derives from a combination of *connect* and the suffix *ive*, and *connect* suggests to establish a relationship or awaken meaningful emotions. Furthermore, a *connector* resumes a tube for connecting other materials, which entails a scientific perception (Online Etymology Dictionary, 2010). However, what is the meaning of connective knowledge? Downes (2005b) defines connective knowledge as the embryonic knowledge ensuing from connections, which in his own words, "a property of one entity must lead to or become a property of another entity in order to them be considered connected". Downes (2008) still points out that exist three types of knowledge: empirical (experiences); rationalist (quantitative); connective (derives from connections). Likewise, Downes' assumption engages a dissimilar perspective when compared to the work of Cromer (1997), *Connected Knowledge: Science, Philosophy and Education*, in which the author argues that connected knowledge demonstrates scientists and educators differences regarding scientific and philosophical principles. Regardless Cromer's (1997) argument, which etymology legitimizes at some extent, it is feasible to claim that today's educational reality does not reproduce these discrepancies.

Connectivism

Connectivism integrates principles explored by chaos, network complexity, and self-organization theories (Siemens, 2006a), as well as the tenets of connectivism is current educational technology (e-learning 2.0 and 3.0) instead of be simply a logistical vehicle that delivers information (Siemens & Tittenberger, 2009). Therefore, the principles of connectivism are (Siemens, 2004b):

- learning and knowledge relies in multiple beliefs;
- learning is a procedure of linking focused nodes or information sources;
- learning may be inherent to non-human applications;
- ability to know more is more important than what is presently known;
- fostering and preserving connections is obligatory to support continuous learning;
- talent to notice connections among fields, ideas and concepts is a core skill;
- existing or up-to-date knowledge is the aim of all connectivist learning activities;
- decision-making encompasses a learning process.

Additionally, Siemens (2005; 2004b) describes connectivism as a form of knowledge and a pedagogy based on distributed networks, in which learning entails the skill to construct and across those networks. Still following this author, learning versus knowledge is a dynamic, living and evolving state that depends on sharing environments characteristics (Siemens, 2003): informal, not structured, tool-rich, consistency and time, trust, and simplicity. In fact, for Downes (2007) connectivism implies pedagogy due to diversity, autonomy, openness and connectivity as key features of networks, as well as describes individual and societal procedures (learning is an individual and collective process). Thus the starting point of connectivism is the individual; nonetheless, it becomes an organizational and societal process. This is consistent with Siemens (2006b) argument that learners and organizations face numerous key challenges: societal changes, technology, globalization, information development, and decentralization. From this miscellaneous blend emerges some critical trade-offs: how knowledge is shared throughout educational organizations? Has everyone access to the organizational body of knowledge? Do connections promote learning?

THE QUEST

Ethics for Connective Knowledge

Ethics as a concept acknowledges an interchangeable distinction due to the continuous use of "morality" or "ethics" (Pojman, 1994). For the purpose of this manuscript ethics is centred on three basic concepts: good, self and the other (Rossouw, 2002), despite Stahl's (2008) perspective that a theoretical assumption is insufficient to discern on a latent issue, because our primary ideas must be considered moral conceptual instincts and require ethical legitimacy, which moral beliefs will admit or not. Therefore, due to information and communication technologies magnitude and overall impact in society computer ethics assumes a vital role, namely the underlying ethical issues in education. Issues like intellectual property, copyright violations, plagiarism, and open source versus open standards have been systemically under debate (Doha Development Agenda, 2008); or, power, privacy, monitoring, surveillance, access, opportunity cost, and awareness (Stahl, 2002).

Even so, is the author belief that the continuous debate around these issues, as well as computer ethics integration in curricula do not appear to diminish unethical practices. This conviction is based on some empirical evidences experienced by the author, as for instance the example of *Pedagogical Convention* in 2007. In this convention a speaker claimed that:

(...) Today we do not need to reinvent the wheel. We just need to use an Internet browser, find what we need, copy and paste it (...)

Of course that during the debate period the presenter was confronted namely the author of this manuscript through the following comments:

I totally agree with this idea, however I need to add three comments: always disclose the name of the author of the information, as well as always disclose the references where the information was extracted. This small attitude makes a difference between a plagiarist, intellectual property and copyright violator into a researcher (a credible person acting morally)... The key problem is that many educational actors, like lecturers and learners do not fully understand these ethical issues and its consequences.

And,

as a result of finding easily all types of information, a permanent temptation to anonymous copy and paste exists. It is absolutely necessary a clear and open debate covering the ethical and legal issues concerning plagiarism and copyright violations. This is the only way to teach our learners a proper behaviour.

Ethical Frameworks for Connective Knowledge

Jefferies & Stahl (2005) analyse the relationship among pedagogy, ethics and technology. These authors consider the overlaps about the three domains:

- e-learning- resumes the interaction between technology and pedagogy;
- computer ethics- is the relationship among technology and ethics;
- theories of learning- refers to the interface between pedagogy and ethics.

Although as Figure 4 exhibits the core overlapping domain remains unknown, despite Sarmento & Costa (2006) first proposal: ethics should be simultaneously a key domain and the overlap. This argument was further detailed by Silva *et al.* (2009): the "e" highlights lecturer's ethics, learner's ethics, and organizational ethics.

These contributions entail a follow-up of Stahl's (2002) work, *Ethical issues in e-teaching: A theoretical framework*. This author introduces a tridimensional matrix for e-learning ethical quandaries: the awareness of the ethical impact;

Figure 4. Pedagogy, ethics and technology model (Source: Jefferies & Stahl, 2005, Figure 1)

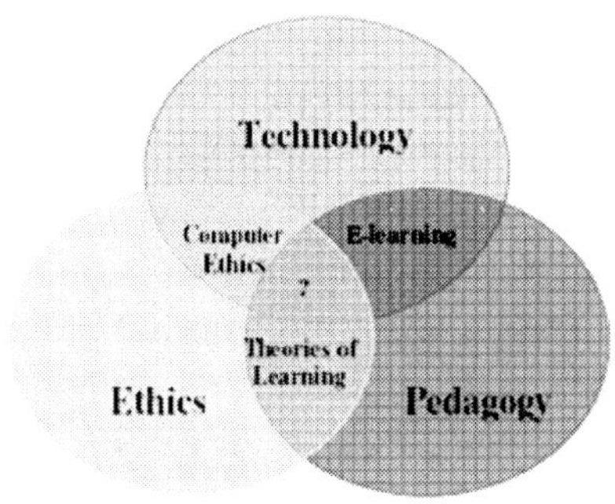

who is involved; and whether it is a hypothetical or practical problem. On the other hand, these dimensions engage three potential scales: micro-level (individuals); meso-level (organizations); and, macro-level (the educational institution, or society). The explanation for this assumption according to Stahl (2002) is that, ethical theories over time denote to be a characteristic associated to the micro-level, the e-learning project is inseparable from the organization, and the educational institution decisions have a tremendous impact in society.

A Proposal: "Ethicism"

According to The Free Dictionary (2010), "ethicism" is a conscious tendency to moralize, and a doctrine that ethics and ethical ideas are valid and important. Or, "is the thesis that the ethical assessment of attitudes manifested by works of art is a legitimate aspect of the aesthetic evaluation of those works" (Gaut, 2004, pp. 283).

Likewise, a considerable debate about strong or weaker versions of moralism exists in literature; however, given the nature of this manuscript the author pleads a less strong version of moralism (Carroll, 2000; 1996), as well as that e-learning entails an aesthetic perception (Stenalt & Godsk, 2006). Therefore Gaut (2007, pp. 10) claims that "an artwork is aesthetically flawed in so far as it possesses an ethical flaw that is aesthetically relevant, and conversely that an artwork has an aesthetic merit in so far as it possesses an ethical merit that is aesthetically relevant" due to ethicism features, which Halwani (2009) contradicts through five reasons: (1) artworks have no moral content; (2) that do have moral content but whose prescribed responses are non-moral; (3) whose prescribed moral responses do not ask the audience to accept or reject the moral claim but merely to contemplate or entertain it; (4) whose prescribed moral responses assert moral claims that are indeterminate; and (5) whose prescribed moral responses are embodied in equally plausible or true but incompatible interpretations. Nevertheless, Halwani (2009) assumes that all artwork encompasses similar features to a film which is clearly controversial. Besides e-learning 2.0 and 3.0 aim to engage people, and imply a trade-off between formal and informal education, which can be related to the claim of Conolly (2000) that education is a form of art, because: (1) aims to involve people in order to promote learning through pleasure; (2) and, pleasure engages subjectivity due to personal preferences which constraints an objective evaluation.

FUTURE RESEARCH DIRECTIONS

Revolutions affect all parts of society and education is not exempt from the ongoing technological revolution. Moreover, it is necessary to bear in mind that future predictions are a challenging discussion and for that three main assumptions ought to be underline:

- connectivism may not be the 21st century thinking as regards to pedagogy (Kerr, 2007), although it clearly enhanced a necessary dialogue concerning learning theories in network collaboration (Ally, 2008);
- the quest for a ethical connective knowledge is a long term scenario, because it is crucial to educate all future educational agents like the empirical evidences demonstrate;
- ethicism highlights a "natural" process that education as an artwork needs to integrate (Stenalt & Godsk, 2006).

Yet an important query arises: will e-learning 3.0 enhance these challenges? Will connectivism be able to cope with these challenges in e-learning 3.0? And if not, what theoretical contribution will emerge? If e-learning 3.0 "basic idea is to use the knowledge embedded within the web and include possible web elements on top to begin to extract greater meaning" (Kerr, 2006), is the author belief that connectivism will not highlight a full response to the new learning environments because educational agents have different learning styles, as well as that ethical challenges concerning connective knowledge will be enhanced due to the e-learning 3.0 appliances that will try to discover or extract knowledge. Summing up, a new theory for e-learning 3.0 is vital.

On the other hand, Downes (2009) explains through neurobiology contributions how cloud collaboration will enhance agents distributed cognition and learning, which is consistent to Stelarc's (2005) argument that our informational objects are our own body extensions. This is consistent with connectivism and the problem of moral judgment regarding non-human agents that ethicism imposes, which summarizes e-learning 3.0 challenges. Thus, e-learning 3.0 will shape a massive global neural learning network!

Despite the consideration that neural learning network discussion is not novelty (e.g. Roth, 2005); the truth is that connectionism may regain a new impulse with this global neural learning network. However, what is the meaning of connectionism? According to the Stanford Encyclopedia of Philosophy (2010) is a:

"movement in cognitive science which hopes to explain human intellectual abilities using artificial neural networks (...). Neural networks are simplified models of the brain composed of large numbers of units (the analogs of neurons) together with weights that measure the strength of connections between the units".

In this case, the author alleges that a potential pedagogical or learning theory for e-learning 3.0 will be "connethionicism". This concept resumes an overlap between connectivism (pedagogy and learning theory for collaborative environments), ethicism (the demand for ethical ideas) and connectionism (human and non-human learning agents). In conclusion, the author argues that Plato's *Allegory of the Cave* provides an interesting response to future research directions, because the shadows are a casual awareness of the omni-presence of light which illustrates educational agents' amendment to this challenging environment, and the rising of "connethionicism".

CONCLUSION

E-learning can be a powerful support tool to presence and distance learning; however, it is vital to remember that online learning stands on four structural pillars, as follows: (1) new learning technologies (generation 2.0 and 3.0); (2) novel lecturing methodologies (connectivism); (3) educational agents' ethical principles (ethicism); (4) and, context (societal circumstances).

Besides, connectivism contribution for understanding pedagogy, learning, and knowledge in nowadays educational environments is evident; although, it tends to disregard ethical issues as regards to connective knowledge. For that, ethicism will enable the quest for an ethical connective knowledge in e-learning 2.0 environments, since 3.0 learning environments characteristics and challenges will compel a further debate. Therefore a possible retort for e-learning 3.0 outcomes is "connethionicism", which will emphasize Sarmento & Costa (2006) argument that the "e" of e-learning implies ethics/ethical behaviours, instead of Rosenberg (2001)*terminus*. This is consistent with the four structural pillars in order to e-learning be globally accepted as a prerequisite for future social and economic development, providing basis for knowledge management in a truthfully education (Richards, 2004). Concluding, Machiavelli's comic play, *Mandragola*, it is possible to feel the spirit of modern science without any of its apparatus.

ACKNOWLEDGMENT

The author would like to appreciate the insightful comments of Nuno Sotero Alves da Silva to the earlier versions of this manuscript, as well as to the editor for its endeavour, support and guidance throughout the writing process.

REFERENCES

Abram, S. (2003). A primer on e-learning... The framework, the market, the players. *KM World, 12(2)*.

Ally, M. (2008). Foundations of educational theory for online learning. In Anderson, T. (Ed.), *The Theory and Practice of Online Learning* (2nd ed., pp. 15–44). Edmonton, Canada: AU Press.

American Society for Training and Development. (2010). E-Learning glossary. *ASTD.org*. Retrieved September 9, 2009, from, http://www.astd.org/LC/glossary.htm

Attwell, G. (2007). Personal learning environments- The future of elearning? *eLearning Papers, 2*(1), 1-8.

Atzori, P., & Woolford, K. (2005). Extended body: Interview with Stelarc. *Stanford*. Retrieved January 21, 2010, from, http://www.stanford.edu/dept/HPS/stelarc/a29-extended_body.html

Brodmann, K. (1909). *Vergleichende lokalisationslehre der grosshirnrinde in ihren prinzipien dargestellt auf grund des zellenbaues*. Leipzig, Germany: Barth. (in German)

Carroll, N. (1996). Moderate moralism. *British Journal of Aesthetics, 36*(3), 223–238. doi:10.1093/bjaesthetics/36.3.223

Carroll, N. (2000). Art and ethical criticism: An overview of recent directions of research. *Ethics, 110*(2), 350–387. doi:10.1086/233273

Chernigovskaya, T. V. (2007). The mirror brain, concepts, and language: The price of anthropogenesis. *Neuroscience and Behavioral Physiology, 37*(3), 293–302. doi:10.1007/s11055-007-0014-7

Commission of the European Communities. (2009). Commission Recommendation on media literacy in the digital environment for a more competitive audiovisual and content industry and an inclusive knowledge society. *European Commission*. Retrieved November 25, 2009, from, http://ec.europa.eu/culture/media/literacy/docs/recom/c_2009_6464_en.pdf

Conolly, O. (2000). Ethicism and moderate moralism. *British Journal of Aesthetics, 40*(3), 302–316. doi:10.1093/bjaesthetics/40.3.302

Cornwell, W. R., & Cornwell, J. (2009). Signal and noise: The power of n-dimensional query and education. In I. Gibson *et al.* (Eds.), *Proceedings of Society for Information Technology & Teacher Education International Conference 2009* (pp. 2505-2511). Chesapeake, VA: AACE.

Cromer, A. H. (1997). *Connected knowledge: Science, philosophy and education*. New York: Oxford University Press.

Damasio, A., & Geschwind, N. (1984). The neural basis of language. *Annual Review of Neuroscience, 7*(1), 127–147. doi:10.1146/annurev.ne.07.030184.001015

Doha Development Agenda. (2008). Negotiations, implementation and development. *World Trade Organization*. Retrieved August 1, 2009, from http://www.wto.org/english/tratop_e/dda_e/negotiations_summary_e.htm

Downes, S. (2005a). E-learning 2.0. *eLearn Magazine*. Retrieved October 29, 2009, from http://www.elearnmag.org/subpage.cfm?section=articles&article=29-1

Downes, S. (2005b). An introduction to connective knowledge. *Stephens's Web*. Retrieved November 28, 2009, from, http://www.downes.ca/cgi-bin/page.cgi?post=33034

Downes, S. (2007). What connectivism is. *Half an Hour*. Retrieved September 17, 2009, from, http://halfanhour.blogspot.com/2007/02/what-connectivism-is.html

Downes, S. (2008). Types of knowledge and connective knowledge. *Half an Hour*. Retrieved October 27, 2009, from, http://halfanhour.blogspot.com/2008/09/types-of-knowledge-and-connective.html

Downes, S. (2009). The cloud and collaboration. *Half an Hour*. Retrieved January 20, 2010, from, http://halfanhour.blogspot.com/2009/06/cloud-and-collaboration.html

Driscoll, M. (2000). *Psychology of learning for instruction* (2nd ed.). Needham Heights, MA: Allyn & Bacon.

Ebner, M. (2007, April). *E-learning 2.0 = E-learning 1.0 + Web 2.0?* Paper presented at the Second International Conference on Availability, Reliability and Security, Vienna, Austria.

Egbert, J. L. (2008). *Supporting learning with technology: Essentials of classroom practice*. Upper Saddle River, NJ: Prentice Hall.

Erlhagen, W., Muskovskiy, A., & Bicho, E. (2006). A dynamic model for action understanding and goal-directed imitation. *Brain Research, 1083*(1), 174–188. doi:10.1016/j.brainres.2006.01.114

European Commission. (1996). Educational software and multimedia (Report of the Task Force). *European Commission*. Retrieved October 2, 2009, from http://aei.pitt.edu/5651/01/001851_1.pdf

Fleming, N. D., & Mills, C. (1992). Not another inventory, rather a catalyst for reflection. *To Improve the Academy, 11*, 137-149.

Gan, Y. C., & Wang, W. (2005). Analysis and study on the multiple implications of virtual learning community strategies based on social constructivism. *Modern Distance Education Study, 5*, 10–16.

Gardner, H. (1983). *Frames of mind: The theory of multiple intelligences*. New York: Basic Books.

Gaut, B. (2004). The ethical criticism of art. In Lamarque, P., & Olsen, S. H. (Eds.), *Aesthetics and the Philosophy of Art: The Analytical Tradition: An Anthology* (pp. 283–294). Oxford, UK: Blackwell Publishing.

Gaut, B. (2007). *Art, emotion and ethics*. New York: Oxford University Press. doi:10.1093/acprof:oso/9780199263219.001.0001

Goleman, D. (1995). *Emotional intelligence*. New York: Bantam Books.

Goleman, D. (2006). *Social intelligence: The new science of human relationships*. London: Hutchinson.

Haldane, A. (2004). The convergence of e.learning and knowledge management: Fusion or confusion? *European Consortium for the Learning Organisation*. Retrieved October 14, 2009, from http://www.eclo.org/pages/uploads/File/The%20Convergence%20of%20e-learning%20and%20Knowledge%20Management%20-%20Andrew%20Haldane.pdf

Halwani, R. (2009). Ethicism, interpretation, and Munich. *The Journal of Applied Psychology, 26*(1), 71–87.

Handelzalts, A. (2007). Preservice teachers' perceptions of an ICT-rich learning environment: Development of an instrument. *Learning Environments Research, 10*(2), 131–144. doi:10.1007/s10984-007-9024-1

Harris, P., Connolly, J., & Feeney, L. (2009). Blended learning: Overview and recommendations for successful implementation. *Industrial and Commercial Training, 41*(3), 155–163. doi:10.1108/00197850910950961

Hempel, J. (2009). Web 2.0 is so over. Welcome to web 3.0. *CNN Money*. Retrieved September 22, 2009, from, http://money.cnn.com/2009/01/07/technology/hempel_threepointo.fortune/index.htm

Holmberg, B. (2005). *The evolution, principles and practices of distance education*. Oldenburg, Sweden: BIS-Verlag der Carl von Ossietzky Universität Oldenburg. http://halfanhour.blogspot.com/2008/09/types-of-knowledge-and-connective.html

Jefferies, P., & Stahl, B. C. (2005). Some ethical considerations regarding the relationship of e-learning and pedagogy. In Collste, G. (Eds.), *ETHICOMP 2005: Looking Back to the Future (CD: paper 31)*. Linköping, Sweden: Linköping University.

Kerr, B. (2006). Web 3.0- E-learning 3.0? E-learning technology. *E-learning Tech*. Retrieved January 21, 2010, from, http://elearningtech.blogspot.com/2006/11/web-30-elearning-30.html#ixzz0zfMkSsKW

Kerr, B. (2007). Which radical discontinuity? *Bill Kerr*. Retrieved January 20, 2010, from, http://billkerr2.blogspot.com/2007/02/which-radical-discontinuity.html

Kidwell, J. J., Linde, K. M. V., & Johnson, S. L. (2000). Applying corporate knowledge management practices in higher education. *EDUCAUSE Quarterly*, *23*(4), 28–33.

Kurtz, C. F., & Snowden, D. J. (2003). The new dynamics of strategy: Sense-making in a complex and complicated world. *IBM Systems Journal*, *42*(3), 462–483. doi:10.1147/sj.423.0462

Lauzon, A. C. (1997). Postmodernism, interactive technologies and the design of distance education. In M. Koble & E. Wagner (Eds.), *Distance Education Symposium 3: Course Design, ACSDE Research Monograph Number 14* (pp. 6-21). University Park, PA: The American Centre for Distance Education, PA, The Pennsylvania State University.

Lytras, M. D., & Pouloudi, A. (2006). Towards the development of a novel taxonomy of knowledge management systems from a learning perspective: An integrated approach to learning and knowledge infrastructures. *Journal of Knowledge Management*, *10*(6), 64–80. doi:10.1108/13673270610709224

Lytras, M. D., Pouloudi, A., & Poulymenakou, A. (2002). Knowledge management convergence- Expanding learning frontiers. *Journal of Knowledge Management*, *6*(1), 40–51. doi:10.1108/13673270210417682

Machiavelli, N. (1981). *Mandragola. Transl. M. J. Flaumenhaft*. Long Grove, IL: Waveland Press Inc.

Moore, M. G. (1993). Theory of transactional distance. In Keegan, D. (Ed.), *Theoretical Principles of Distance Education* (pp. 22–38). New York: Routledge.

Nickerson, M., & Bryner, J. (2002). From video tutors to electronic portfolios: Using advanced screen capture in support of educational technology instruction. In D. Willis *et al.* (Eds.), *Proceedings of Society for Information Technology & Teacher Education International Conference* (pp. 430-431). Chesapeake, VA: AACE.

Northrup, P. T. (2001). A framework for designing interactivity into web-based instruction. *Educational Technology*, *41*(2), 31–39.

Northrup, P. T. (2002). Online learners' preferences for interaction. *Quarterly Review of Distance Education*, *3*(2), 219–226.

O'Reilly, T. (2005). What is web 2.0. *O'Reilly Network*. Retrieved September 17, 2009, from, http://www.oreillynet.com/pub/a/oreilly/tim/news/2005/09/30/what-is-web-20.html

Online Education Database. (2007). How the open source movement has changed education: 10 success stories. *OEDB*. Retrieved September 22, 2009, from http://oedb.org/library/features/how-the-open-source-movement-has-changed-education-10-success-stories

Online Etymology Dictionary. (2010). Connective. *Online Etymology Dictionary*. Retrieved January 30, 2010, from, http://www.etymonline.com/index.php?search=diversity&searchmode=none

Oxford English Dictionary. (2008). *Oxford English Dictionary*. Oxford, UK: Oxford University Press.

Oztop, E., Kawato, M., & Arbib, M. (2006). Mirror neurons and imitation: A computationally guided review. *Neural Networks*, *19*(3), 254–271. doi:10.1016/j.neunet.2006.02.002

Parr, L. A., Waller, B. M., & Fugate, J. (2005). Emotional communication in primates: Implications for neurobiology. *Current Opinion in Neurobiology*, *15*(6), 716–720. doi:10.1016/j.conb.2005.10.017

Pojman, L. (1994). *Ethical theory: Classical and contemporary readings* (2nd ed.). Belmont, CA: Thomson Wadsworth.

Rawls, J. (1971). *A theory of justice*. Cambridge, MA: Belknap Press.

Rawls, J. (2001). *Justice as fairness: A restatement*. Cambridge, MA: Belknap Press.

Reis, A. D. (2007). *Media, knowledge & education (digital media ecologies)*. Innsbruck, Austria: Innsbruck University Press.

Reis, A. D. (2008). Support documentation for post graduation on pedagogic and didactic skills on e-learning and ICT. *The Graal Institute*. Retrieved August 1, 2009, from, http://thegraal.ccems.pt/

Reis, A. D., et al. (2009). To be or not to be m-learning (that it is the question). In P. Norbert & S. Judith (Eds.), *3rd WLE Mobile Learning Symposium, Mobile Learning Cultures across Education, Work and Leisure* (pp 75-80). London: WLE Centre.

Richards, C. (2004). From old to new learning: global dilemmas, exemplary Asian contexts, and ICT as a key to cultural change in education. *Globalisation, Societies and Education*, *2*(3), 337–353. doi:10.1080/1476772042000252470

Rizzolatti, G., & Craighero, L. (2004). The mirror-neuron system. *Annual Review of Neuroscience*, *27*(1), 169–192. doi:10.1146/annurev.neuro.27.070203.144230

Rosenberg, M. J. (2001). *E-learning: Strategies for delivering knowledge in the digital age*. New York: McGraw-Hill.

Rossi, P. G. (2008). *Intelligent learning environment (ILE). Learning environment with AI support tools for teachers and tutors*. Unpublished paper, Università degli Studi di Macerata, Marcerata.

Rossouw, D. (2002). *Business ethics in Africa* (2nd ed.). Cape Town, South Africa: Oxford University Press.

Roth, M. (2005). Program execution in connectionist networks. *Mind & Language*, *20*(4), 448–467. doi:10.1111/j.0268-1064.2005.00295.x

Sarmento, M. M., & Costa, G. J. M. (2006). E-learning: does the "e" also means ethics? In Reis, A., & Piecha, J. (Eds.), *DLCW 2006 (CD: paper 4)*. Lisbon, Spain: ISEG.

Sedziuviene, N., & Vveinhardt, J. (2009). The paradigm of knowledge management in higher educational institutions. *Inzinerine Ekonomika-Engineering Economics*, *5*(65), 79–90.

Siemens, G. (2003). Learning ecology, communities, and networks. Extended the classroom. *Elearnspace*. Retrieved August, 21, 2009, from, http://www.elearnspace.org/Articles/learning_communities.htm

Siemens, G. (2004a). Learning management systems: The wrong place to start learning. *Elearnspace*. Retrieved August 19, 2009, from, http://www.elearnspace.org/Articles/lms.htm

Siemens, G. (2004b). Connectivism: A learning theory for the digital age. *Elearnspace*. Retrieved August 21, 2009, from, http://www.elearnspace.org/Articles/connectivism.htm

Siemens, G. (2005). Connectivism: Learning as network-creation. *Elearnspace*. Retrieved August 21, 2009, from, http://www.elearnspace.org/Articles/networks.htm

Siemens, G. (2006a, October). *Connectivism: Learning and knowledge today*. Paper presented at the Education.au Global Summit 2006: Technology connected futures, Sydney, Australia.

Siemens, S., & Tittenberger, P. (2009). *Handbook of emerging technologies for learning*. Winnipeg, Manitoba, Canada: University of Manitoba.

Siemens (2006b). Knowing knowledge. *Elearnspace*. Retrieved August 21, 2009, from, http://www.elearnspace.org/KnowingKnowledge_LowRes.pdf

Silva, A. J., & Josselyn, S. A. (2002). Cognitive neuroscience: The molecules of forgetfulness. *Nature*, *418*(6901), 929–930. doi:10.1038/418929a

Silva, N. S. A., et al. (2009). *The evolution of e-learning management systems- An ethical approach*. Paper presented at the Network Ethics 2009, Lisbon, Portugal.

Small, G. W., & Vorgan, G. (2008). *iBrain: Surviving the technological alteration of the modern mind*. New York: Harper Collins.

Snowden, D. (2000). The paradox of story: Simplicity and complexity in strategy. *Journal of Scenario and Strategy Planning*, *1*(5), 16–20.

Stacey, P. (2001). E-learning value chain and market map. *New Media BC e-Learning SIG*. Retrieved August 17, 2009, from http://www.bctechnology.com/statics/bcelearning.swf

Stahl, B. C. (2002). Ethical issues in e-teaching- A theoretical framework. In King, G. (Eds.), *Proceedings of Inspire VII, Quality in Learning and Delivery Techniques* (pp. 135–148). Limerick, Ireland: The British Computer Society.

Stahl, B. C. (2008). Researching ethics and morality in information systems: Some guiding questions. In Te'eni, D. (Eds.), *ICIS 2008 (paper 175)*. Paris, France: University of Montpellier II.

Stanford Encyclopedia of Philosophy. (2010). Connectionism. *Stanford Encyclopedia of Philosophy*. Retrieved January 21, 2010, from http://plato.stanford.edu/entries/connectionism/

Stenalt, M. H., & Godsk, M. (2006). *The pleasure of e-learning- Towards aesthetic e-learning platforms*. In T. Lillemaa (Ed.), *Proceedings of the 12th International Conference of European University Information Systems* (pp. 201-212). Tartu, Finland: University of Tartu & EUNIS.

Stiles-Davis, J. (1988). Spatial dysfunctions in young children with right cerebral hemisphere injury. In Stiles-Davis, J., Kritchesvky, M., & Bellugi, U. (Eds.), *Spatial Cognition- Brain Bases and Development* (pp. 251–272). Hillsdale, NJ: Lawrence Erlbaum Associates, Inc.

Teten, D. (2007, June). *Web 3.0: Where are we headed?* Paper presented at the Web 2.0 New York Conference, New York, NY.

The Free Dictionary. (2010). Ethicism. *The Free Dictionary*. Retrieved January 15, 2010, from, http://www.thefreedictionary.com/ethicism

Tranel, D., & Damasio, A. (1985). Knowledge without awareness: An autonomic index of facial recognition by prosopagnosics. *Science*, *228*(21), 1453–1454. doi:10.1126/science.4012303

Tuomi, I. (2004, December). *Innovation, growth and competitiveness in the knowledge society*. Paper presented at the Foro de la Innovación y Modernización en Andalucía, Malaga, Spain.

Turban, E. (Eds.). (2006). *Electronic commerce: A managerial perspective*. Thousand Oaks, CA: Prentice Hall.

van der Velden, M., et al. (2009). *Autonomy and automation in an information society for all*. Paper presented at the Information Systems Research Seminar in Scandinavia, Molde, Norway.

van Weert, T. (2005). Lifelong learning in the knowledge society- Implications for education. *International Federation for Information Processing, 161*, 15–25.

ADDITIONAL READING

Bednar, A. (2010). Theory into practice: How do we link. In Anglin, G. (Ed.), *Instructional Technology: Past, Present and Future* (3rd ed., pp. 100–112). Denver, CO: Libraries Unlimited.

Costa, G. J. M., & Silva, N. S. A. (2010). Knowledge versus content in e-learning: a philosophical discussion! *Information Systems Frontiers, 12*(4), 399–413. doi:10.1007/s10796-009-9200-1

Costa, G. J. M., Silva, N. S. A., & Rogerson, S. (2008). Knowledge versus content in e-learning: A philosophical discussion! In T. Bynum *et al.* (Eds.), *ETHICOMP 2008: Living, Working and Learning Beyond Technology* (pp. 143-155). Mantua: University of Pavia.

Iacoboni, M. (2008). *Mirroring people: The new science of how we connect with others*. New York, NY: Farrar, Straus and Giroux.

Jones, A., & Mercer, N. (2003). Theories of learning and information technology. In Scrimshaw, P. (Ed.), *Language, Classroom and Computers* (pp. 11–26). London: Routledge.

Kelly, M. (Ed.), *Encyclopedia of aesthetics*. New York, NY: Oxford University Press.

Ravenscroft, A. (2001). Designing e-learning interactions in the 21st century: Revisiting and rethinking the role of theory. *European Journal of Education, 36*(2), 133–156. doi:10.1111/1467-3435.00056

Silva, N. S. A., et al. (2009). Knowledge or content? The philosophical boundaries in e-learning pedagogical theories! In A. M. Vilas *et al.* (Eds.), *m-ICTE 2009 - V International Conference on Multimedia and ICT in Education* (pp. 221-225). Lisbon: University of Lisbon.

Stiles-Davis, J., & Nass, R. (2004). Spatial grouping activity in young children with congenital right or left hemisphere brain. *Brain and Cognition, 15*(2), 201–222. doi:10.1016/0278-2626(91)90026-5

Trappl, R., Petta, P., & Payr, S. (Eds.). (2002). *Emotion in humans and artifacts*. Cambridge, MA: MIT Press.

KEY TERMS AND DEFINITIONS

Connecticism: A theoretical proposal that endeavours to be e-learning 3.0 future pedagogy. For that, it bonds connectivism, ethicism and connectionism features.

Connective Knowledge: Knowledge that arises through network collaboration, in which individual is a nodule that produces connections.

Connectivism: Form of knowledge and pedagogy that resumes network collaboration.

E-Learning 1.0: The first generation of learning through computational technology. It resumes a static and non bidirectional communication between all educational agents. Instructivism, constructivism and cognitivism characterize this generation.

E-Learning 2.0: Entails the evolution concerning synchronous technologies (podcast, wikis, blogs, etc) that promote bidirectional communication and total collaboration among the educational agents. For that, assumes the following pedagogical streams. connectivist, socio-cognitivist and social-cultural.

E-Learning 3.0: The ultimate generation of e-learning! It acknowledges the possibility of coordinate and generate contextual information through semantic appliances (artificial intelligence). At a pedagogical level it remains a mystery.

Ethicism: Philosophical system in which ethics and ethical ideas are legitimate and crucial.

Chapter 9
Glocality, Diversity and Ethics of Distributed Knowledge in Higher Education

Nuno Sotero Alves da Silva
De Montfort University, UK

Isabel Maria Surdinho Borges Alvarez
Lusíada University of Lisbon, Portugal

Simon Rogerson
De Montfort University, UK

ABSTRACT

Global networks through distributed systems technology granted a new meaning to knowledge creation, storage and distribution within higher education context. This global dimension imposes a considerable amount of ethical and social impacts concerning distributed knowledge because it is expressed within local contexts. Nonetheless, main stream literature highlights equity and cultural sensitivity as leading issues, and disregards the existent social dilemmas concerning organizational innovation in higher education. Therefore, this chapter aims to promote a philosophical and empirical argument within contextual determinants, in order to explore the ethical and social key dilemmas of distributed knowledge between global and local diversity in higher education. For that, under scrutiny will be a specific layer regarding first co-author e-University strategic implementation framework which interacts with ethics and culture, in order to, understand e-learning current practices in higher education, as well as, to nominate potential future guidelines concerning these trends.

INTRODUCTION

To debate XXI century high education is essential to investigate the key features that characterize informational society: communication, interaction, automation, post-industrial, specialist, service, immaterial needs, postmodern, or learning society (Webster, 2006; Castells, 2000). As a result, it is comprehensible that governments or organizations (namely universities), do not intend to mislay this opportunity related to information society (Lallana, 2004), because as Richards (2004) suggests:

DOI: 10.4018/978-1-61520-873-9.ch009

e-learning is globally accepted as a prerequisite for future social and economic development, providing a new essential style, as a base level for accessible education. This claim is justified by the e-learning concept itself: acquisition and use of knowledge distributed and facilitated primarily by electronic means, which incorporates synchronous or asynchronous access and may be distributed geographically with varied limits of time (Hall & Snider, 2000).

Therefore, the emergence of a global education marketplace can be understood as a consequence of informational society and globalization (Friedman, 2005). Despite this global awareness, education is inevitably expressed within local dimensions (Altbach, 2004), or at least focusing a certain global region (the European Bologna Process is an example), in which is feasible to distinguish different local perspectives regarding the process itself, as well as concerning the main issues that illustrate education in that region: cultural diversity, ethics and values, mobility, intercultural communication, organizational cooperation, economical value, and government's education policy. Thus, following Meyrowitz (2005) "glocality" (global dimension with multiple local dimensions) engages a whole new range of ethical and social issues in education. This line of reasoning is consistent with the work of Audrestch, Lehmann & Warning (2005): "local regions" exhibit an increasing importance in the era of globalization. In addition, diversity plays a progressively role in shaping the relationship between local and global (Gaspay, Legorreta & Dardan, 2009).

Furthermore, beyond the characteristic dialog concerning global and local dimensions in higher education, main stream literature focus as primary analysis the subsequent differentiated ethical issues: learner's diversity in various educational settings (Berge, 2001); highly sophisticated educational settings in distributed interactive versus learning experiences (Vrasidas & Glass, 2002); learner's versus ethical norms (Stahl, 2002); the relationship between ethics, technologies and pedagogy (Jefferies & Stahl, 2005), and in different local contexts (see for example: Heyneman, Anderson & Nuraliyev, 2008); or, how virtual universities may impact on cherished values, such as liberty, justice, privacy and sociality (Brey, 2004); equity issues (Patrick & Gaële, 2007); or even cultural sensitivity (Uzuner, 2009). However, it is interesting that e-learning literature seems to pay little regard to the current ethical and social key trends regarding distributed knowledge (creation, sharing and distribution), and diversity within globalized higher educational contexts.

Against this backdrop, the chapter structure considers: the contemporary scenario concerning higher education; knowledge in education (concept and systems evolution); globalization versus glocality (globalization, glocality and emergent trends); globalization versus glocality in higher education (overview, ethical issues, social dilemmas, and eureka); empirical evidences (overview, a cross-cultural diagnosis, lecturing experiences, and others testimonials); discussion; and finally, future trends. As a final remark, the authors point out that to understand the ethical and cultural issues trade-off between global and local in distributed knowledge, this contribution focuses upon the knowledge/content management layer regarding e-University strategic implementation conceptual framework (Silva, 2007).

HIGHER EDUCATION STATUS QUO

Higher education mission can be referred as teaching and research in order to promote societal development. Although 21st century manifestations enhance some of these fundamental roles of creating, preserving, integrating, transmitting and applying knowledge, which leads to a plausible conclusion: contemporary universities are "knowledge servers" (Duderstadt, 2001). Nonetheless, the key focus of this chapter impels an approach to the idea and purpose of a university.

Throughout literature it is possible to acknowledge dissimilar perceptions of this long standing debate: for example, Newman (1976) has debated the role and impact of universities in society during the latter half of the 20th century, namely concerning science, logic, lecturing, research, academic authority and national culture. However, the global movement concerning educational massification embraced a whole new perspective (Scott, 1995), in spite of the existing debate surrounding if education it is a private or, public good due to public expenditure constraints (Musial, 2007). Other authors like Gibbons *et al.* (1994) pointed out the shifting ideas with reference to knowledge universality, communication, and application. In fact, this scenario has produced an analogous outcome to organizational theory evolution: an assessment culture concerning organizational mission (Lucas, 2006). As a result, other scholars have debated higher education governance, as well as its allegations (Deem, Hillyard & Reed, 2007). Even so, since the last decade of the 20th century educational challenges enabled a tremendous shift regarding universities existence and purpose. Despite this finding, for Barnett (2003) universities multiple conceptions are often neglected which can be related to: the changing roles of the welfare state (Kwiek, 2006); or, the interference of supra-national organisations (Dewatripont, Thys-Clement & Wilkin, 2002); still, how novel technologies outline universities (Sakai, Kuriyama & Miyahara, 2007; Arias-Oliva, González & Santiago, 2004; Bygholm & Nyvang, 2004); and finally, the impact of globalization or else transnationalization (Santos, 2006).

In conclusion, the following sections of this chapter will reveal that Nowotny, Scott & Gibbons (2001) argument regarding the preservation of university values is insufficient and innocuous. The reason for this claim encompasses the leading aim of this chapter: the emergent ethical and social trends between global and local contexts, and the role of diversity in higher education.

KNOWLEDGE IN EDUCATION

From Praxis to Distributed Knowledge

Knowledge structure in academic organizations has changed over time, reflecting normative perceptions concerning its significance or educational conception, which knowledge sociology examines. For example, to Plato in his work "Protagoras", knowledge is "the food of the soul" (Jowett, 1899) given that academic knowledge embraced a non-formal structure; however, formal higher education have required formal knowledge categories. Therefore, traditional knowledge sociology tried to understand the bound between the development of ideas and the exact social setting, as well as individuals and groups interests (for further detail see Weber, 1946; Mannheim, 1936). Nevertheless, knowledge society represented a new leap about academic knowledge categories, requiring a feasible understanding on how social organization ordering leads to knowledge (Swidler & Arditi, 1994), specifically due to network connectivity (Cavanagh, 2007; Dron, 2007). In fact, in 1983 Clark had already argued the need to change the conservative approach to knowledge categories within higher education. In spite of these considerations it is imperative to discuss the overall concept of knowledge in education.

To Karl Popper (1972) objective knowledge resumes the result of synchronized research procedures, and that is written down in science communication processes. Gergen (1995) investigates the utilization of a dialogue as an allegory to evaluate a number of educational practices. So, these "knowledgeable tellings" are embedded on an ongoing relationship, which is analogous to the expression "just-in-context" with reference to knowledge (cultural bound) (Budin, 2002; Snowden, 2000). Thus, knowledge can be considered as a body of understanding and skills which is constructed by people (Standards Australia, 2003); or, the result or product of knowing;

information or understanding acquired through experience; practical ability or skill; cognition (Oxford English Dictionary, 2008).

Although modern forms of educational technology offer a great potential to act as an enabler for novel categories of knowledge, namely distributed knowledge (Hardaker & Smith, 2002; Gibbons, 2000), and also distributed learning experiences (McPherson & Nunes, 2006; Scardamalia & Bereiter, 2003), it is fundamental not disregard particular cultural attributes: language, discourse, and former peculiar forms of expression that learner's use to interpret and build knowledge (Anderson, 2008; Cheung, 2008; Nowotny, Scott & Gibbons, 2001). Nonetheless, it is interesting to acknowledge that literature suggests the concept of pedagogic content knowledge (Koppelman 2008; Kanuka, 2006; Wilson, Shulman & Richért 1987), even when a systematic methodology is under debate (Chu *et al.*, 2006; Rushkof, 2005; Davis *et al.*, 2001), which network learning environments seem to challenge regarding "knowledge" and "content" as concepts (Costa and Silva, 2010; Silva *et al.*, 2009; Costa, Silva & Rogerson, 2008).

Moving forward, distributed knowledge is supported by two generic principles (Bonifacio, Bouquet & Cuel, 2002):

- autonomy- each individual should have a high level of autonomy to manage its local knowledge (similar to personal knowledge management. See Efimova, 2005);
- coordination- each individual must be allowed to share knowledge with other individuals, not through imposition of a solo diagram, but making possible to each person understand other individuals context. According to Foss & Foss (2008), coordination it is possible without possessing much knowledge of the other elements.

Apart for this reasoning, various authors (for example: Coombs *et al.*, 2003; Coombs & Metcalfe, 2000) merely contemplate officially structured distributed activity (knowledge and learning) as a result of joint ventures, strategic alliances, conscious outsourcing, and other well-defined organizational forms, which the authors of this contribution do not agree due to the following reasons: due to uneven distributions of knowledge, it is often difficult to know where to look for appropriate knowledge (Robertson & Smith, 2007); and, the increasing and exponential importance of social media in distributed knowledge systems (see next sub-section of this contribution).

From Knowledge Management Systems to Distributed Knowledge Systems

In order to identify, capture, store, preserve and disseminate knowledge, higher education organizations have incorporated technological systems to promote continuous feedback and adjustment to their knowledge strategy (Handzic & Hasan, 2003). Nonetheless, recent evidence demonstrates a convergence between traditional Knowledge Management Systems (KMS) and e-learning (Mihalca *et al.* 2008); due to a mutual feedback process that entails two levels of analysis: the influence of e-learning on KM processes, and their common characteristics. The reasons for this alliance are expressed through two arguments: networks, are a essential foundation structure of social organization (Castells, 2009) which political actors seem to recognize (Bonifacio, Bouquet & Traverso, 2002); and, the new educational paradigm encompasses a certain intellectual affiliation between learner's and technologies (Small & Vorgan, 2008), and it is required to enquire whether if individualised and collective acquisition of knowledge, content and skills, is likely to support the development of competences needed to flourish in these environments (Castells, 2009). Therefore, networks encourage a collective contribution, and not individual ownership through distributed intelligence, which Jenkins (2006) emphasizes as the key role that technologies engage during the process, although it is closely bounded to the social production of knowledge. As a consequence e-learning (see for example Hall & Snider, 2000) is converted into distributed learning, or in distributed knowledge (Gâlea, Leon & Zaharia, 2003), meaning that course components are distributed across multiple media, as well as exhibits a tendency for a student-centred learning approach and evokes a collective contribution (Mason & Rennie, 2008).

Despite the previous acknowledgements it is compulsory to approach Distributed Knowledge Systems (DKS), which literature introduces as the evolution of Learning Management Systems (LMS) (Siemens, 2004). According this author LMS engages two different concepts:

- Learning Knowledge Management Systems (LKMS)- LMS evolution due to social interaction, which entails into Personal Learning Environments (PLEs) and Social Software (SS);
- Learning Oriented KM Systems (LOKMS)- LMS evolution at an instructional level.

PLEs are a recent feature of LKMS, as an alternative to the structured model of an LMS. PLEs are defined as: systems that help students to take control and manage their own learning (Hall, Paradice & Courtney, 2003). SS is "a conceptual shift that acknowledges the reality of distributed learning practices and the range of learner preferences" (van Harmelen, 2006). Finally LOKMS it is an evolution concerning instructional design, including feedback loops concerning KMS underlying inquiring systems (Hall, 2005).

Nevertheless, it is important to remember the discussion surrounding knowledge versus content, as well as student's content creation (see previous sub section), leading to a necessary approach regarding Learning Content Management Systems (LCMS). For Shaw (2008), these systems facilitate the subsequent features:

- separating content from presentation- authors need to be focused on delivering their content and not be anxious concerning layout reflection, except if it is relevant to understand the article itself;
- enforcing workflow processes- articles sent in by the authors are primary accepted by editors prior to publication.

GLOBALIZATION VS. GLOCALITY

Globalization

Globalization may bear a multiplicity of significances, which the final outcome can be considered as positive or, as negative. In spite of the previous argument, the authors believe that in order to understand this phenomenon an etymological, historical analysis can provide some important clues regarding the concept itself, as well as its contemporary dimensions.

Etymologically globalization derives from a combination between *globalize* and *action* (Online Etymology Dictionary, 2010a). Accordingly, *globalize* means global economic systems, and *action* the mode of doing it, which is not surprising due to the countless interpretations as a largely economic phenomenon (Friedman, 2005; Stiglitz, 2002). Nonetheless, this perception seems to unforeseen that globalization is a concept that goes far beyond the expansion of multinational and other transnational corporations, as well as the growth of information and communication technologies. In fact, throughout literature it is possible to acknowledge an overwhelmingly disagreement concerning the concept itself, and it dimensions.

A plausible reason for this controversy can be found into the book *Globalization and the Margins* (Grant & Short, 2002), whose authors demonstrate that to comprehend globalization is required a multidisciplinary approach. This is clearly consistent with other perspectives, namely focusing cosmopolitan ethics (Beck, 2006; Held, 2004), or the power discourses that construct globalization as a process of systemic marginalization (Steger, 2004; Kofman & Youngs, 2003), and finally as a general process of homogenization regarding Western culture and capitalism (Ferguson, 2005; Balakrishnan, 2003). Therefore, Benyon, & Dunkerley (2000) notes that exists a crude dichotomy between global and local, which requires an intermediate concept: *glocality*. As a result global and local are "negating but complementary reciprocation that erodes the major institutional and cultural framework of the nation-state" (Shafir & Peled, 2000, pp. 218).

As a final remark, the authors claim that metaphorically the dialog between global and local has its historical roots in the Roman Empire, which authors like Hitchner (2008), or Geraghty (2007) have demonstrated. Due to possible critics, the authors acknowledge two different arguments: the "tools" were the roots and bridges that characterized the Roman Empire, as well as due to the spatial conception of the Earth during that period. Later on, the second wave was the Portuguese Discoveries (for further detail see Friedman, 2005), and finally, ICT (distributed knowledge systems) the third (Toffler, 1980).

Glocality

In order to preserve a high level of analytical consistency, the authors will equally approach glocality through an etymological and historical analysis. Therefore, according to Meyrowitz (2005) it resumes a convergence between the terms: *global* and *local*, due to an increasing distinction of a synthesised existence among participating within a global village, and the preservation of local traditions and influences. In an etymological sense *global* is bounded to *globe* or *globalize* (see previous sub-section), and *local* encompasses the Latin words *localis* (pertaining to position or a place, as well as belonging to a place), or else *localitas* (as a necessary quality of bodies) (Online Etymology Dictionary, 2010b). Once again, the etymological root is reliable with the modern *status quo*.

Nevertheless, authors like Dirlik (1998), or Medeni (2004) argue that *glocality* has acquired various meanings and connotations, as well as resumes an artificial combination of concepts leading a lack of meaning. For that, these authors acknowledge this dilemma through a new expression: *lobal*. Following Medeni (2004), *lobal* results from a combination of the words *lobe* (lung or brain, which can be used through a metaphor), and its derivatives *lobalization* and *lobalism*. However, this present contribution will neglect that argument due to the following line of reasoning: the allegedly non-natural combination of *global* and *local* is similar to other several words, as for example: *biotechnology* and *nanotechnology* lead to *bionanotechnology*; *meme* and *genetics* give origin to *memetics*; or simply, *cybernetic* and *organism* were the praxis for *cyborg* (so neologisms like *glocality* are quite common); and, the contradictory claim of Medeni (2004), which points out that for some specific contexts with specific meanings attached, *glocal* can be a useful term.

Moving forward within the chapter analysis, Eric Gordon (2009) claims that local information access is no longer restricted to the geographic location, due to the network configuration or distributed fluxes of information, in spite of the undefeatable cultural barriers that glocality imposes (Meyrowitz, 2004). Although, this author recognizes that we are increasingly sharing information with individuals who reside in localities dissimilar from our own, as well as the dissociation involving physical position and experimental space encourages the maturity of what might be entitled as "glocal morality". Therefore, this "glocal morality" is a fusion between global and local identities, where diversity shapes the relationship between local and global (Poster, 2005).

Emergent Trends

Given the nature of this essay it is necessary to assess the relationship between globalization and glocality. Therefore, using as a starting point the following question: would be glocality be overlapped by the global process? Or, as Boyd (2006) criticizes is an ugliness that ensures that both concepts are propelled comfortably within a unique idea? For King & Heltne (2007) it is undeniably a process that is taking place, encompassing a dual movement with bidirectional consequences. Nonetheless, for Grixti (2006) this process is paradoxically reinforcing, as well as symbiotically transforming each dimension (for a practical example see Grixti, 2008).

World culture does not present itself as uniform, but can be rather described as "organised diversity", that is, a web of various local cultures (which are not necessarily anchored to a geographical territory): "glocalities". Particular articulations of global versus local in contemporary societies give life to new, modern and plural cultural forms. In fact, Welsch (1999) emphasize that cultural fertilisation on a multiplicity of levels, from the macro-level (whose cultural shapes are characterised today by a rising inner differentiation, intricacy and hybridisation), to micro-level (individual experiences), where personal and cultural uniqueness hardly ever, if ever, corresponds to civic and national identity and is instead gradually more influenced by multiple cultural connections. Therefore, we disregard Eriksen (2001) claim that it is not necessary to utilize the concept of culture in order to respect local conditions in development work: it is only sufficient to be sensitive to the fact that local realities are always locally constructed. However, Poster (2005) argue that if the concept of "culture" is dismissed, it is unfeasible to comprehend why the majority of local cultures embraces technoscience, but tries to negotiate a "cultural exception" to control the admission of foreign cultural products. This scenario obscure social space and reconfigures the relationship.

GLOBALIZATION VS. GLOCALITY IN HIGHER EDUCATION

Overview

Educational organizations are shifting their priorities to an emergent global education marketplace through the use of ICT (Richards, 2004). However, the internationalization of campus and community is simultaneously a chance and a challenge that higher education institutions ought to deal today. According to a study conducted by Wood (2006) that encompassed 110 U.S. institutions of higher education, university leaders comprehend and embrace this trade-off. This major conclusion reflected the input questions that Wood (2006) posed during the interviews:

- what kind of careers are emerging in today's interconnected world, where are they emerging and how do we prepare our students and communities for them?
- how can our departments, schools and university as a whole achieve an enhanced international presence?
- how can institutions of higher education be positioned for success in today's global environment, and what role should local, regional, national and international partners play?
- what global trends, developments and related research topics are most important to our scholarly disciplines today, and how can we take advantage of such to create new knowledge in the future?

Despite the comprehension of this phenomena, chronological data with reference to knowledge transfer in higher education exhibits a wide array of unequal results, namely when it concerns cultural restrictions (Altbach, 2004). For example, during the Colonial Period, it was common policy to set up colonial campus sponsored by metropolitan universities, forgetting significant aspects of local cultures (Bhabha, 1994). Nevertheless, in spite of the end of Colonialism over 50 years ago it is needed to criticize current practices, because as Coraggio (2001) claims: it is compulsory to understand global knowledge as local knowledge, whose meaning is regenerated as part of every other local knowledge system, not as local knowledge made globally accessible. Thus, the contemporary concept of a university (or a higher education institution), needs to reproduce this cosmopolitanism and recognize the substance of different cultures, which will permit a flexible separation of diverse categories of universities (Peters, 2007). This argument is consistent with the work of Lobera & Escrigas (2009) multiversity; the post-historical university of Peters (2007); or still, Santos (2006) that pleads the concept of pluriversity.

As a result, the existing and essential role that universities have in social context (Altbach, 2008), is reinforced by glocality in order to promote sustainability and intercultural dialogue. Yet, a decisive re-examine concerning the human development agendas imply that universities have been "followers" instead of "influencers" (proactive agents) (Tandon, 2008).

Ethical Issues

According to Cecez-Kecmannovic (2001) systemic aspects of a University involves: material and intellectual production, economical foundations, administrative and management structure, rules and regulations, etc. This contextual environmental is mostly determined by Government regulations, policies and funding; however, organizational model, curriculum, administrative policies, etc., should be considered as an essential component. Although, Brey (2004) claims that cross-cultural virtual universities need to understand the role of culture and language, which the authors believe to be an insufficient argument: it is compulsory that all cross-cultural higher education institutions acknowledge it. Moreover, Margison (2007) argues that higher education institutions are limited to two domains of meta-institutional practice, in order to produce a distinctive social "character" when approaching values and ethics:

- communicative association- owes somewhat to established beliefs to the insights of Jurgen Habermas about communicability within public sphere. Hence, it includes the right to speak, to conduct a dialogue based on honesty and mutual respect, as well as intra-institutional and inter-institutional relationships grounded in justice, solidarity, compassion, cosmopolitan tolerance and empathy for the other;
- secular intellectual practices- include sustaining actions for freedom and productive intellectual activity.

Nonetheless, as Stahl (2002) points out the relationship of ethics and e-learning is a complex one, as well as to achieve a responsible use regarding distributed learning, and for that, the participants need to recognize a considerable amount of "life facts". Consequently, it is fundamental to embrace a multidisciplinary perception (professionals, practitioners and users), in order to minimize unethical practices (Nagi, 2006). Moving forward, Laudon & Laudon (2004) identifies some moral dimensions regarding generic information systems (information rights and obligations; property rights and obligations; system quality; and, control); and, Stahl (2002) also acknowledges several moral problems in e-teaching (power; privacy; monitoring; surveillance; access; opportunity cost; and, awareness). Despite, these perceptions is necessary to debate the arising ethical issues in distributed knowledge.

In some ways globalization opens access, however existing local inequalities are only reinforced and new barriers erected, which is an emerging trend between equity and efficiency (Cloete & Moja, 2005). A clear example is developing countries, or smaller academic systems, because powerful universities have always dominated the production and distribution of knowledge, while weaker institutions and systems with fewer resources and lower academic standards have tended to follow in their wake (Altbach, 2004). This scenario is still enhanced due to the tightening copyright and other ownership restrictions through international treaties and regulations, which limit access to information sources, such as: databases, electronic journals, e-books, and related knowledge products (Correa, 2000). In fact, these arrangements were created to protect sellers and providers, not buyers and users, and once again negative implications arise (Raikhy, 2002). Nevertheless, if education plays a crucial role regarding the achievement of sustainable development, it is reasonable to agree with the critics of Solomon (1992) to the Aristotelian approach to business ethics, given false antagonism between profits and social responsibility.

Additionally, distributed knowledge systems current developments comprise also several ethical issues, including:

- privacy- standardize formats that allow learner's access to distributed knowledge, also require maintaining learner's profiles and activity records. Although, if this records are freely exchanged, without consent or learner's knowledge, their privacy is severely compromised (Harada *et al.*, 2002);
- plagiarism- language translation services enhance non detected digital plagiarism (Jia & Zhou, 2005). For Brey (2004), digital plagiarism had become one of the major forms of academic dishonesty;
- copyright violation- file sharing services allows other users to have access to stored files within a central server without permission (Kallinikou, 2009).

Social Dilemmas

At the turn of the millennium, the Task Force on Higher Education (World Bank, 2000) recommended a more generalized formal education as an alternative to the existing largely specialized curriculum in higher education; however, this report have tremendously failed in several social aspects that led to dilemmas, which distributed knowledge networks have enhanced. Even so, it is essential to debate these social dilemmas in order to the authors claim do not seem futile.

Almost a decade after, according to Patrick & Gaële (2007) is still fundamental to develop a programme of comparative research which focuses on the social characteristics of students who are enrolled in higher education. Recalling Anderson (2008), distributed learning environments must respect and accommodate particular cultural attributes, particularly language and particular forms of expression, which the learner uses to interpret and build knowledge, as well as lecturer's should be educated to get intellectually or, emotionally accustomed to unlike learning ways (for a cultural example see Schulte & Al-Fehaid, 2004). And, these socio-cultural realities also encompasses challenges to instructional designers regardless the technological platform (Rogers, Graham & Mayes, 2007).

Following Goertzel (2008a) it is possible to understand the features of distributed knowledge: local (abstract logical relationships stored in explicit logical form), and global (large-scale patterns of network activity). Hence, without local input and merely re-fashioning global knowledge distribution can be inappropriate, misconceived and perverse; because as Stone (2003) points out, when distributed knowledge is spread is not inevitably inclusive, legitimate or progressive. This dilemma is a corollary that resumes the extreme boundaries of knowledge (codified or, tacit) (Stone, 2003), as well as the perception how knowledge is transferred (as a process or, as a product) (Costa & Silva, 2007).

As a consequence, successful mechanisms are required in order to local communities share their indigenous knowledge; nonetheless, some tensions arise regarding intellectual property rights. For Tarasofsky & House (2005), in spite of not literally be "under the umbrella" of intellectual property rights, indigenous knowledge is collective and ignores power issues. Despite the authors agree at some extent with this argument; believe that this default or "gap" concerning intercultural communication cannot act as a constraint, due to two reasons: Universal Declaration of Human Rights (article 27, paragraph 2) (1948), and the International Covenant on Economic, Social and Cultural Rights (article 15, paragraph 1c) (UNHCHR, 1966). From the mishmash of these articles is possible to conclude that any scientific, literary or artistic production has the moral right to protection in spite of the author, and indigenous knowledge typically assumes literary or artistic forms. Even if some detractors exploit the default or gap, local knowledge should be fairly compensated (Castle & Gold, 2007; Norchi, 2000).

On the other hand, if the Reader observes the "other face of Janus" is obligatory to discuss content in its different levels:

- transnational or regional: enables questions like recognition and accreditation as for instance the Bologna Process. For example, Augusti (2006) have demonstrated that in spite of the process is difficult to recognize and acknowledge accreditation due to: the absence of legislative competence regarding education by the European Union, higher education institutions conflicting autonomy, and the process covers 40 countries, but is only valid in 25. Another critical dilemma is the global dominance of English-speaking academic systems, which leads to a global content homogenised market (Stewart, 2004), so disregarding local needs (educational that will have consequences into the local market labour), as well as posing once again a dilemma about human rights (Watson, 2007);
- national: high quality distributed learning implies content aligned to national curriculums, and so Governments are responsible for defining or approve national/regional core curriculum, (Stahl, 2002). The problem is that in present times, for example in Europe, the actual content delivered to students is regulated by the Bologna Process meaning that local needs are not embraced;
- local: students believe that introduce local content within the curriculum is a key issue (Dunn & Wallace, 2004), being an ideal example Korean learners: the top ten sites visited by them are all Korean (Retzer, 2005). However, in distributed learning it is usually the course coordinator that decides if this inclusion is relevant (Davis, Olson & Bohm, 2000), which according to Pyis & Chapman (2005), frequently not fully meet student expectations (and prior experiences) due to exaggerated Western frameworks.

In conclusion, this scenario is a clear signal of inertia concerning higher education institutions and stakeholders, in spite of distributed knowledge networks being widely recognized as a new and fascinating field of research (Stahl, 2004; Sorensen, 2002).

Eureka!

Despite some perceptions shed some light as regards to ethical issues, or social dilemmas in distributed knowledge, the truth is that main stream literature does not present a conceptual framework that allow a feasible and simultaneously analysis. As a consequence, a crucial evolution is first co-author e-University strategic implementation

Figure 1. e-University strategic implementation conceptual framework (Source: Silva, 2007, p. 59, Figure 2)

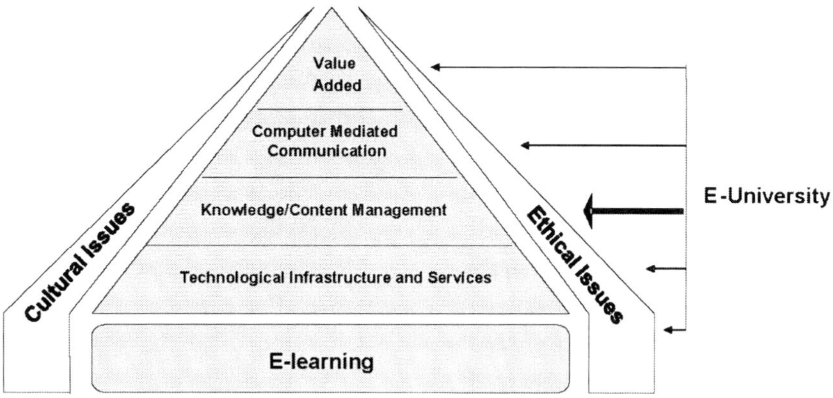

conceptual framework (Silva, 2007), which Figure 1 depicts.

The authors also inform that under scrutiny will be the *Knowledge/Content Management* layer; however, it is virtually impossible to detach distribute knowledge without acknowledging the other layers, because the framework engages an interactive process of bottom-up and top-down feedbacks in order to allow a real time comparison. Therefore, the following step of this chapter is to characterize the remaining layers:

- *Value Added*: a transversal cost/benefit ethical analysis, which aims to provide information regarding the e-University project, and each layer individually;
- *Computer Mediated Communication*: is transforming education making learning more interactive, diverse and enjoyable experience. This layer is prosperous in social interactions;
- *Technological Infrastructures and Services*: encompasses all technological means that support the distributed knowledge systems, as well as back-office or administrative services.

EVIDENCES

Overview

In order to portrait and match up empirical evidences with the theoretical background, the authors highlight some keen contextual examples that have detected through their academic experience, which reinforces the substance of this contribution. For that, under analysis will be three distinct analytical dimensions, nevertheless complementary among them:

- a cross-cultural diagnosis: underlines several conclusions that the first co-author has been noticing at an empirical level, due a cross-cultural project that he has been involved (related to his PhD research project);
- lecturing experiences: concerns to the lecturing experiences of the second co-author, namely with reference to the necessary preliminary work using e-learning, as well as lecturing process for divergent learner's background;
- other testimonials: emphasize some interesting and common testimonials that have been experienced by the first co-author,

throughout his participation in a recent conference (Network Ethics 2009).

A Cross-Cultural Diagnosis

This sub-section reproduces the empirical work that has been conducted by a global higher education institution with campuses in Europe (Portugal), and Africa (Angola, St. Thomas and Prince). These educational institutions share their name, as well as technology and knowledge, due to a cooperation protocol between all the autonomous entities that manage each local campus. Throughout data analysis it is possible to recognize some ethical issues and social dilemmas that glocality imposes to distributed knowledge.

For instance, if we draw our attention to common curricula and courses in each university some interesting conclusions arise. The intended consequence of Bologna Process in Europe, which is not being pursued in Africa, engages a tremendous social issue: the current curriculums and programs require a resynchronization in order to allow truly knowledge sharing and distribution. Despite the possible resynchronization another important social dilemma occurs: curriculums and programs do not attend the local labour market structure and its requirements.

Beyond these social dilemmas, it is remarkably important to stress an ethical issue that results from the misuse of incorrect information, in spite of its implicit authorization (African culture). This issue is enabled by the non-existence of an official website concerning the multiple African campuses, as well as the proliferation of multiple non-authorized websites of these universities. Likewise, when an African student access to these websites does not obtain reliable institutional information; as a result, searches the Portuguese website and download the existent curricula and programmes, which are applied in his *curriculum vitae*. Although, as previously acknowledged Portuguese educational process reflects the Bologna process leading to a contradictory reality.

Concerning the educational process, some important social dilemmas can be reported: inequality about regulatory procedures; and, inequality regarding knowledge sharing. Inequality about regulatory procedures is a consequence of the Portuguese content development, namely syllabus design in accordance with Bologna process. Contrarily, in Africa the regulatory procedures are reduced, and constantly not controlled: an example is the absence of a syllabus, or even class summaries. These differences promote a lower level of certainty concerning the educational process.

Moreover, from the standpoint of knowledge sharing, it is reasonable to attend the subsequent reciprocally dependent issues: linguistic interpretation; learner's cognitive skills; content cultural sensitivity; technological infrastructure liability and adoption. Regarding linguistic interpretation plentiful of inconveniences has been occurring because lecturers are primarily non-African natives. The most common nationalities are: Portuguese, Brazilians, Cubans, Russians, and even Eastern Europeans. Some cases of linguistic interpretation are: the use of *pandilha* (Brazilian) instead of *folha de cálculo* (Portuguese) regarding Excel sheets; Cubans do not pronounce correctly or, in a distinctive way some Portuguese vocabulary derived from Arab language, such as *algarismo* versus *algoritmo*. These evidences are enhanced by the 42 different native dialects that exist in Angola (Lewis, 2009), in spite of Portuguese be the official language; however, learner's communication is based on their own dialects. This quandary is enhanced because Portuguese content development is only in Portuguese and replicating the Bologna Process; therefore, ignoring local needs (absence of cultural sensitivity). In addition, this social dilemma is enhanced because local managers consider it a minor question, which is the main reason for sharing curricula and programmes. Beyond these claims, lecturers are confronted with an ethical issue: the use of global references (even digital), or instead a combination of global and local didactical references? The authors claim that this situation exposes the theme under debate: homogeneity or heterogeneity in distributed knowledge.

Finally, the core for all these linkages is ICT infrastructure liability and adoption, leading to a necessary comparison between both countries. For that, the authors introduce the World Bank (2009) report concerning *Information and Communications for Development*:

- Portugal: with reference to Internet subscribers (per 100 people) in 2007 is referred 15.2, and infrastructure liability (international Internet bandwidth (bits/second/person)) encompassed 4.790;
- Angola: as regards to Internet subscribers (per 100 people) in 2007 the integer was 0.3, and infrastructure liability (international Internet bandwidth (bits/second/person)) coverage was 17.

This reality is easily perceived throughout the field work as the following examples demonstrate: Internet connection through satellite is extremely difficult to obtain in Angola campus, and even its liability is easily questioned.

Lecturing Experiences

In this sub-section the second co-author reproduces her lecturing experiences concerning e-learning in two dissimilar settings: a higher education institution, located in Lisbon; and within a local publisher that enables lifelong learning. Despite their different organizational structures both organizations acknowledged an equal technological platform, but reporting considerable unlike outcomes.

In the university, the platform aimed to act as an auxiliary tool for lectures in classes (face to face contact) allowing: to post documentation, exercises and essays; online discussions through forums; virtual working groups; and possibly to perform online exams. This user friendly tool, however has reported low levels as regards to lecturer's adherence. This phenomenon, which is widely recognized in literature, was anticipated and foreseen by the ICT department. So, this department have organized some introductory open training sessions showing the usefulness of a DKS, its basic functions, and how to interact with the system. Nevertheless it was a failed attempt to target lecturer's population, because merely five per cent have attended these open training sessions.

Likewise, the second co-author noted during some informal conversations with her peers, in order to understand their level of adherence and found out that lecturer's scientific background had a major impact in their behaviours and attitudes towards this system. Therefore, it was possible to conclude that those with a technological background evidenced a higher level of adherence and understanding; although, an interesting transversal remark was the bound between lecturers' appetence to adhere and fear that e-learning would cause unemployment and so the negative reaction. A probable solution would be personalized training sessions to the different background groups in order to decrease their fears, as well as help to understand the systems usefulness. With reference to students, their usage was broader and acknowledged primarily the following issues: access to documentation, glimpse essays results, lab work to be done. However, it was clear that forums and online group discussion are not being utilised.

The second organizational setting is a publisher located in Lisbon, and specialized in publishing accounting and engineering/production books. They had already some experience in organizing training or seminar sessions for their customers (companies), under the scope of various business subjects. In 2006 they decided to start online lifelong training courses, because the majority of their customers are in remote areas. After some preliminary considerations about project implementation and characteristics, the choice was to exploit the same e-learning platform. For content creation (and literature seems to disregard how to develop proper content for an e-learning course), as well as to clarify format and layout it was decided to organize each course in sessions (ranging from 7 to 15 depending on the course complexity). Furthermore, each session should acknowledge: maximum 10 A4 pages with light colours, simple text and an individual practical exercise to be solved in the end of each session. Afterwards, it was outlined rules for lecturers and participants: lecturers should respond to participant's solicitations maximum within a timeline of 48 hours; and for participants, beyond the weekly essay is also compulsory to participate in forums in a weekly basis, as well as is impossible to download more than a session per week in order to enhance their level of understanding. Finally, it was also taken into account participant's organizational structure, namely technological infrastructure and ICT literacy of its human resources.

Contrarily to the previous scenario, e-learning courses participants are keen users of a distributed learning system. The adherence for these e-learning courses has been extremely high and exhibits positive comments. The participants claim that this is an excellent opportunity for lifelong learning, even for professional duties, without extra travelling costs due to their diverse geographical locations, and feeling that could manage their own learning depending on their availability.

From the above experiences it also important to denote that obligatory behaviours allow minimizing glocal barriers, as well the effects of diversity! From this assumption is possible to conclude that cultural change implies personal effort; even so, it raises an important ethical issue: self determination or info-exclusion?

Others Testimonials

As an introductory remark, the authors would like to present a more indulgent argument that justifies their choice concerning Network Ethics 2009: first, it was recently held in Portugal, from June 23 to 25, due a joint organization between: Carnegie Mellon University, Catholic University of Portugal, and the University of Northern Iowa; second, its intention was to debate ethical issues and social dilemmas that network society poses at three levels: social responsibility, business ethics, and education. Given the nature of this chapter the authors will focus their attention into the educational track, namely the contributions of Boyd & Newton (2009); Kenon (2009); and, Nicholas & Lewis (2009).

Boyd & Newton (2009) have shared the experience of Southern Cross University (a regional university) regarding the design of small courses within a global context. These authors have exposed a discrepancy involving curriculum aim and assessment principles, due to the effect of pedagogy in online re-design. Additionally, ethical issues become gradually more visible, especially regarding equity of access and embedding ethical practices in student learning.

Kenon (2009) has presented a case study concerning Transnational High School-University Bridge programs, which consent the student to adjust to a novel culture and work to develop their second language skills. In this particular case, the similarities were concerned linguistic interpretation regarding the delivered content for Chinese schools within the distributed knowledge platform: some schools have reported a considerable amount of problems due to the existing hundreds dialects only in Continental China, despite the initial translation for Chinese. The reason is simple: usually Chinese dialects are mutually unintelligible (Hearne, 2009).

Finally, Nicholas & Lewis (2009) from Salve Regin University conducted a study concerning the acceptance, usage and satisfaction of learner's concerning e-text books. It was interesting that the report demonstrates that 85% had never previously used an e-book; nonetheless, when questioned 100% claimed that their main motivation to buy an e-book was the price (usually half). In spite of these considerations the authors question an important ethical issue: it is an expenditure saving characteristic for students to use an e-text book, or an adversity for the ones that do not own a computer?

DISCUSSION

After introducing the theoretical background and empirical evidences, the authors truly believe that in order to produce a more fluid and indulgent argument is rather important to resume the chief findings. For that, ethical issues and social dilemmas will interact with the e-University strategic implementation framework as Table 1 demonstrates.

Going deeper with reference to the argument, and if the Reader consider the previous table as a "target" (metaphorical perception), in its inner centre or core it will be diversity! This is reliable with multiple distributed knowledge networks, as well as the contemporary awareness concerning multicultural higher education institutions.

Table 1. Glocal ethical issues and social dilemmas in higher education

Framework Level	Issue	Local	Global	Dilemmas
1	Organization	Economical foundations, organizational practices	Academic cooperation	Innovation, constraints, profitability, efficiency, governance, social responsibility
	Curriculum	Adapted to local labour needs, interests, social development	Transnational recognition and accreditation, enhanced educational market regulation	Equity, inequality, academic cultural responsibility
	Digital objects	Local access, price, delivering, copyright and other ownership restrictions, sustainable development	Global cost reduction (production and distribution), ecological value	Equity, homogeneity, local development needs, interoperability
2	Human Communications	Psycho-cultural constraints, group socialization, learner's profiles and activity records	Cultural sensitivity, high levels of community connectedness, time perception	Distance, information flux control, distributed multiple media, educational games use, privacy
3	Content	Cultural adaptation, language translation services	Public domain, digital library, file sharing, commons	Design, usability, interoperability, cultural concept of intelligence, cultural compatibility, digital plagiarism
	Knowledge	Dialects, cultural heritage, learning predisposition, psycho-cognitive competences	Dominant languages, international knowledge production and distribution	Autonomy, ethicultural sensitivity, international training for lecturers
	Pedagogy	Cultural influences, dissonant practices, psycho-cognitive-emotional competences	Connectivism, self- regulated learning, openness	Culturally sensitive instructional practices, lecturer cultural competences, distributed cognition
4	Network	Infrastructure, technological adaptation	Distributed environment, connectivity, international internet bandwidth	Cost, access, liability, digital literacy, market introduction time-frame according to local development

Level 1: Value Added;
Level 2: Computer Mediated Communications;
Level 3: Knowledge/Content Management;
Level 4: Technological Infrastructures and Services.

Nevertheless, several questions arise: how can we define diversity? What is its level of importance? What is its relationship with "glocal morality"?

Diversity derives from the Latin word *diversitatem* (contrariety, contradiction, or disagreement), that in a secondary sense is bounded to *diversus* (turned in different ways) (Online Etymology Dictionary, 2010c). The importance of diversity has been recognized throughout countless fields of research: literature, economics, sociology, anthropology, biology, etc., which is easily acknowledged. An example is the magnificent poem of Edgar Allan Poe, *The Raven* (1845):

"(...) Open here I flung the shutter, when, with many a flirt and flutter,
In there stepped a stately Raven of the saintly days of yore.
Not the least obeisance made he; not a minute stopped or stayed he,
But, with mien of lord or lady, perched above my chamber door
Perched upon a bust of Pallas just above my chamber door
Perched, and sat, and nothing more. (...)
(...) Then the ebony bird beguiling my sad fancy into smiling,
By the grave and stern decorum of the countenance it wore,
Though thy crest be shorn and shaven, thou, I said, art sure no craven,
Ghastly grim and ancient Raven wandering from the Nightly shore
Tell me what thy lordly name is on the Night's Plutonian shore!
Quoth the Raven: Nevermore. (...)
(...) Much I marvelled this ungainly fowl to hear discourse so plainly,
Though its answer little meaning- little relevancy bore;
For we cannot help agreeing that no living human being
Ever yet was blessed with seeing bird above his chamber door
Bird or beast upon the sculptured bust above his chamber door,
With such name as Nevermore." (...)

Furthermore, diversity implies a continuous intercultural communication which globalization has enhanced, and this glocal dialogue produced "glocal moralities" (see section 4). According to Roudometof (2005), glocalization leads to two dissimilar accounts of cosmopolitanism: a thick and a thin. Despite the existence of two options this author supports a thin account of cosmopolitanism, because it operationalizes the different degrees of attachment of an individual regarding the global and local predispositions. Therefore, a possible criterion for understanding this "glocal individual morality" is an existential criterion, since is simultaneously universal (global) and flexible (local) (see for example Dewey's (1938) criteria for experience). For, Taylor (2002) a genuine assessment requires a virtue of willingness to change, leading to a self-understanding and mutually understanding, which should be a characteristic of all educational "actors", as well as stakeholders.

FUTURE TRENDS

In spite of being under debate possible future trends, the authors argue that is necessary to shed some light regarding some contradictory contemporary assumptions with reference to 21st century education reality. In fact, it is interesting that modern literature encompasses two analytical levels for higher education institutions (Knight, 2006):

- recognized: includes public non-profit, private non-profit and private for-profit institutions, usually as a component of national educational systems and accredited;

- non-recognized: includes profit oriented domestically and internationally institutions, that typically are not a formal part of national educational systems.

Likewise, it is feasible to introduce potential critics: higher education as been seen in an economical sense (educational market) encouraged by political actions (Scott, 2008), leading to some ethical issues and social dilemmas presented throughout this contribution. This is consistent with the claim of ESU (2004) about cultural sensitivity and transnational recognition issues, as a mixed consequence of higher education taxonomies along with political actions.

Other key feature to point out is the significance surrounding diversity within 21st century educational context, which distributed knowledge has enhanced dramatically. This argument is justified through the concept of distributed universities: could mean that each learner is located in a different location, without any face-to-face interaction (Levin, 2002); however, this definition is reductionist given that lecturers can be also in different geographical locations, and not within the physical environment of the university. Despite this new educational scenario, researchers, practitioner's and stakeholders have focused their attention merely into policies and models for diversity management within the physical location (as for instance Davis, 2009; Inglis, 2008), instead of "distributed diversity" in order to identify intercultural dimensions of learning theories and teaching models (Bélisle, 2007; De Vita, 2003; De Vita, 2002), as international responsible governance imposes (Dominese, 2009; Morin, 1999). Even so, the authors argue that is crucial to develop international normative rules for ethical education knowledge distribution, which is in line of reasoning with Olsen's (2009) political glocalism: humanity's collective requirements ahead of vested interests' short term desires; humanity's collective priorities forward to politicians' short term ambitions; and, humanity's local needs and priorities equally balanced with global.

This dialectical-ethical relationship between local and global ethical systems ("glocal ethics") evokes a reciprocal and symmetrical recognition, which stresses the regulative principles of self-respect and justice (Zirfas, 1999). Moreover, distributed knowledge networks are ICT-based which can be referred as the most human technology (Górniak-Kocikowska, 2007), leading computer ethics to become a global ethics with different mindsets (Górniak-Kocikowska, 2004).

Thus, higher education institutions have a social responsibility to promote "glocal knowledge"; so, the authors believe that ultimately is required a deeper understanding of "glocal morality". Is the author's opinion, that "glocal morality" implies a fusion of competences that permit ethical decisions within different cultural diasporas (glocal), which is bounded to the degree of attachment claimed by Roudometof (2005). For that, is feasible to understand each individual moral intensity (degree of issue-related moral imperative in a circumstance) (Jones, 1991), and sensibility (individual cognitive process) (Jones, 1991), in which moral psychology may be considered a new paradigm (Huff & Frey, 2005). In addition, this "glocal self" implies that an individual mind is distributed across the social, natural and cultural environment ("glocal memory") as pointed out by Goertzel (2008a), which engages a whole new perspective of distributed knowledge or distributed cognition (Goertzel, 2008b).

Despite these novel perceptions the authors believe that noetic sciences as "explorations into the nature and potentials of consciousness using multiple ways of knowing- including intuition, feeling, reason, and the senses" (IONS, 2009), will allow further developments concerning "glocal morality". In conclusion, as Lewin Thomas (1995, pp. 150) has referred: "science will...produce the data..., but never the full meaning. For perceiving real significance, we shall need...most of all the brains of poets, (and) also those of artists, musicians, philosophers, historians, writers in general".

CONCLUSION

Distributed knowledge networks indeed facilitate knowledge sharing; however, its globality imposes serious ethical issues and social dilemmas, which generates critical dimensions for 21st century universities. This is reliable with the claim of Arias-Oliva, González & Santiago (2004) that higher education institutions and its stakeholders should consider the advantages and disadvantages of ICT, pertaining to educational practices, as a way to ensure openness, equity and international understanding. Nonetheless, as the authors have proved throughout this chapter this discourse is hitherto merely rhetoric or, in a non-fundamentalist perception is a very premature phenomenon.

Furthermore, education aims to embody "the beliefs, traditions, customs, rituals and sensibilities along with the knowledge of why these things must be maintained" (Maison, 2007, pp. 28), because is a dynamic flux where diversity engages an essential ingredient. In fact, the magnitude of diversity is recognized in the Declaration of Principles of the World Summit on the Information Society (2003), or in to UNESCO's Universal Declaration on Cultural Diversity (2002): "culture takes diverse forms across time and space. This diversity is embodied in the uniqueness and plurality of the identities of the groups and societies making up humankind. As a source of exchange, innovation and creativity, cultural diversity is as necessary for humankind as biodiversity is for nature." Therefore, the leading quandary (authors assumption to reproduce the sum of ethical issues and social dilemmas) underlying distributed knowledge and diversity in higher education, relies on the trade-off between homogeneity and heterogeneity in education leading to "glocality".

In conclusion, the authors argue that to minimize the existent and future dilemmas new educational systems must be: *localitas* (as a necessary quality of bodies), *connectivitas* (fusion status about multi-glocal experiences), and *humanitas* (capacity for self-consciousness, self-exploration, and self-determination as the Roman philosopher Cicero describes).

ACKNOWLEDGMENT

The authors would like to thank the insightful comments of Goncalo Costa (editor).

REFERENCES

Altbach, P. G. (2004). Globalization and the university: Myths and realities in an unequal world. Tertiary Education and management, 10(1), 3-25.

Altbach, P. G. (2008). The complex roles of universities in the period of globalization. In Global University Network for Innovation (Ed.), Higher Education in the World: New Challenges and Emerging Roles for Human and Social Development (pp. 30-35). London: Palgrave Macmillan.

Anderson, T. (2008). Towards a theory of online learning. In Anderson, T. (Ed.), *Theory and Practice of Online Learning* (2nd ed., pp. 45–74). Edmonton, AB: AU Press.

Arias-Oliva, M., González, L., & Santiago, R. (2004). University challenges in Information Society. In Bynum, T. W. (Eds.), *ETHICOMP 2004: Challenges for the Citizen of the Information Society* (*Vol. 1*, pp. 38–48). Syros, Greece: University of the Aegean.

Audretsch, D., Lehmann, E., & Warning, S. (2005). University spillovers and new firm location. *Research Policy*, *34*(7), 1113–1122. doi:10.1016/j.respol.2005.05.009

Augusti, G. (2006). Transnational recognition and accreditation of engineering educational programmes in Europe: Perspective in a global framework. *European Journal of Engineering Education*, *31*(3), 249–260. doi:10.1080/03043790600644370

Balakrishnan, G. (Ed.). (2003). *Debating empire*. London: Verso.

Barnett, R. (2003). *Beyond all reason: Living with ideology in the university*. Buckingham, UK: Open University Press.

Beck, S. E. (2006). The good, the bad & the ugly or, why it's a good idea to evaluate web sources. New Mexico State University. Retrieved July 1, 2009, from http://lib.nmsu.edu/instruction/evalcrit.html

Bélisle, C. (2007). Elearning and intercultural dimensions of learning theories and teaching model. Elearning Europa. Retrieved July 31, 2009, from http://www.elearningeuropa.info/files/media/media13022.pdf

Benyon, J. H., & Dunkerley, D. (Eds.). (2000). *Globalization: The reader (an anthology)*. New York: Routledge.

Berge, Z. (Ed.). (2001). *Sustaining distance training: Integrating learning technologies into the fabric of the enterprise*. San Francisco, CA: Jossey-Bass.

Bhabha, H. (1994). *The location of culture*. New York: Routledge.

Bonifacio, M., Bouquet, P., & Cuel, R. (2002). Knowledge nodes: The building blocks of a distributed approach to Knowledge Management. *Journal of Universal Computer Science*, *8*(6), 652–661.

Bonifacio, M., Bouquet, P., & Traverso, P. (2002). Enabling distributed knowledge management. Managerial and technological implications. Informatique, (1), 23-29.

Boyd, D. (2006, March). G/localization: When global information and local interaction collide. Paper presented at the O'Reilly Emerging Technology Conference, San Diego, CA.

Boyd, W. E., & Newton, D. (2009, June). Times of change, times of turbulence: Seeking an ethical framework for curriculum development during critical transition in higher education. Paper presented at the Conference Network Ethics 2009: The New Challenge in Business, ICT and Education, Lisbon, Portugal.

Brey, P. (2004). Ethical issues for the virtual university. In T. W. Bynum et al. (Eds.), ETHICOMP 2004: Challenges for the Citizen of the Information Society: Vol. 1 (pp. 170-187). Syros: University of the Aegean.

Budin, G. (2002). Global content management-challenges and opportunities for creating and using digital translation resources. University of Vienna. Retrieved August 1, 2009, from http://www.ifi.unizh.ch/cl/yuste/postworkshop/repository/gbudin.pdf

Bygholm, A., & Nyvang, T. (2004). Human centered informatics: The emergence of an educational infrastructure. In Dirckinck-Holmfeld, L. (Eds.), *Conditions for Productive Learning in Networked Learning Environments* (pp. 84–95). Aalborg, Germany: Kaleidoscope.

Castells, M. (2000). *The rise of the network society: The information age: economy, society and culture* (2nd ed., *Vol. 1*). Malden, MA: Blackwell.

Castells, M. (2009). *Communication power*. Oxford, UK: Oxford University Press.

Castle, D., & Gold, R. E. (2007). Traditional knowledge and benefit sharing: From compensation to transaction. In Peter, W. B., & Onwuekwe, C. B. (Eds.), *Accessing and Sharing the Benefits of the Genomics Revolution* (pp. 65–79). Amsterdam: Springer. doi:10.1007/978-1-4020-5822-6_4

Cavanagh, A. (2007). *Sociology in the age of the internet*. Buckingham: Open University Press.

Cecez-Kecmanovic, D. (2001). What enables and what prevents knowledge sharing via computer-mediated communications? *Journal of Systems and Information Technology*, *5*(1), 115–134. doi:10.1108/13287260180000762

Cheung, L. (2008). Collaborative knowledge building through the lens of paraphrasing. In B. Chang & H.-J. So (Eds.), ICCE 2008 Workshop Proceedings (pp. 70-79). Tapei: National Central University.

Chu, H., et al. (2006). A structured methodology for digital knowledge content development: Knowledge of mathematics teaching for students with mild disabilities as an example. In E. Pearson & P. Bohman (Eds.), Proceedings of World Conference on Educational Multimedia, Hypermedia and Telecommunications 2006, (pp. 935-940). Chesapeake, VA: AACE.

Clark, B. R. (1983). *The higher education system: Academic organization in cross-national perspective*. Berkeley, CA: University of California Press.

Cloete, N., & Moja, T. (2005). Transformation tensions in higher education: Equity, efficiency, and development. *Social Research*, *72*(3), 693–722.

Coombs, R., & Metcalfe, S. (2000). *Universities, the science base and the innovation performance of the UK (CRIC Briefing Paper No. 5)*. Manchester, UK: The University of Manchester & UMIST.

Cooms, R. (2003). Analysing distributed processing of provision and distribution. *Industrial and Corporate Change*, *12*(6), 1125–1155.

Coraggio, J.-L. (2001). Universities as sites of local and global (re)production. *Norrag News*, *28*(July), 66–67.

Correa, C. M. (2000). *Intellectual property rights, the WTO and developing countries*. London: Zed Books.

Costa, G. J. M., & Silva, N. M. A. (2007). Knowledge management: How ethical is your organization's knowledge? In Bynum, T. W., Rogerson, S., & Murata, K. (Eds.), *ETHICOMP 2007: Glocalisation: Bridging the Global Nature of Information and Communication Technology* (*Vol. 1*, pp. 123–136). Tokyo: Meiji University.

Costa, G. J. M., & Silva, N. S. A. (2009). Knowledge versus content in e-learning: a philosophical discussion! Information Systems Frontiers. Retrieved August 1, 2009, from http://www.springerlink.com/content/t2351vvn15686321/?p=68d64067302e4509a2d3daf97df75aa9&pi=6.

Costa, G. J. M., Silva, N. S. A., & Rogerson, S. (2008). Knowledge versus content in e-learning: A philosophical discussion! In Bynum, T. (Eds.), *ETHICOMP 2008: Living, Working and Learning Beyond Technology* (pp. 143–155). Mantua, Italy: University of Pavia.

Davis, D., Olsen, A., & Bohm, A. (Eds.). (2000). *Transnational education providers, partners and policy: Challenges for Australian institutions offshore*. Canberra: IDP.

Davis, D. J. (2009). The future and diversity in higher education. *Equal Opportunities International*, *28*(4), 351–353. doi:10.1108/02610150910954809

Davis, J. (2001). Creating shared information spaces to support collaborative design work. *Information Systems Frontiers*, *3*(3), 377–392. doi:10.1023/A:1011469727367

De Vita, G. (2002). Cultural equivalence in the assessment of home and international business management students: A UK exploratory study. *Studies in Higher Education*, *27*(2), 221–231. doi:10.1080/03075070220120038

De Vita, G. (2003). Rethinking the internationalisation agenda in UK higher education. *Journal of Further and Higher Education*, *27*(4), 383–398. doi:10.1080/0309877032000128082

Deem, R., Hillyard, S., & Reed, M. (2007). *Knowledge, higher education and the new managerialism: The changing management of UK universities*. Oxford, UK: Oxford University Press. doi:10.1093/acprof:oso/9780199265909.001.0001

Dewatripont, M., Thys-Clement, F., & Wilkin, L. (Eds.). (2002). European universities: Change or convergence? Bruxelles: Editions de L' Universities de Bruxelles.

Dewey, J. (1938). *Experience and education*. New York: The Macmillan Company.

Dirlik, A. (1998). Globalism and the politics of place. *Development*, *41*(2), 7–14.

Dominese, G. (2009). Global governance and innovation 2020: How to govern the complexities of the future. *Transition Studies Review*, *16*(2), 229–232. doi:10.1007/s11300-009-0096-8

Dron, J. (2007). *Control and constraint in e-learning: Choosing when to choose*. Hershey, PA: Information Science Pub.

Duderstadt, J. J. (2001). Technology. EDUCAUSE Review, January/February, 48-56.

Dunn, L., & Wallace, M. (2004). Australian academics teaching in Singapore: Striving for cultural empathy. *Innovations in Education and Teaching International*, *41*(3), 291–304. doi:10.1080/14703290410001733285

Efimova, L. (2005). *Understanding personal knowledge management: A weblog case*. Enschede, The Netherlands: Telematica Instituut.

Eriksen, T. H. (2001). Between universalism and relativism: A critique of the UNESCO concepts of culture. In Cowan, J. K., Dembour, M.-B., & Wilson, R. A. (Eds.), *Culture and Rights: Anthropological Perspectives* (pp. 127–148). Cambridge, UK: Cambridge University Press.

ESU. (2004). Transnational Education. European Students Union. Retrieved July 31, 2009, from http://www.esib.org/index.php/documents/policy-papers/326-policy-paper-qtransnational-education

Ferguson, N. (2005). Sinking globalization. *Foreign Affairs (Council on Foreign Relations)*, *84*(2), 64–77.

Foss, K., & Foss, N. F. (2008). Authority in the context of distributed knowledge (Working Paper No. 03-08). Aalborg: Danish Research Unit For Industrial Dynamics.

Friedman, T. L. (2005). *The world is flat: A brief history of the twenty-first century*. New York: Farrar, Straus and Giroux Publisher.

Gâlea, D., Leon, F., & Zaharia, M. H. (2003). E-learning distributed framework using intelligent agents. In M. Craus, D. Gâlea & A. Valachi (Eds.), New Trends in Computer Science and Engineering (Anniversary Volume) (pp. 159-163). Asachi, Iaşi: Polirom Press.

Gaspay, A., Legorreta, L., & Dardan, S. (2009). Flexibility of asynchronous distance learning: Reaching diverse cultures. *Journal of Knowledge Globalization*, *2*(2), 47–67.

Geraghty, R. M. (2007). The impact of globalization in the Roman Empire, 200bc-ad100. *The Journal of Economic History*, *67*(4), 1036–1061. doi:10.1017/S0022050707000484

Gergen, K. J. (1995). Social construction and the educational process. In Steffe, L. P., Gale, J. E., & Gale, J. (Eds.), *Constructivism in Education* (pp. 17–39). Hillsdale, MI: Lawrence Erlbaum.

Gibbons, M. (2000). Mode 2 society and the emergence of context-sensitive science. *Science & Public Policy*, *27*(3), 159–163. doi:10.3152/147154300781782011

Gibbons, M. (1994). *The new production of knowledge: The dynamics of science and research in contemporary societies*. London: Sage.

Goertzel, B. (2008a). Glocal memory: A new perspective on knowledge representation, neurodynamics, distributed cognition, and the nature of mind. Dynamical Psychology: An International, Interdisciplinary Journal of Complex Mental Processes. Retrieved July 25, 2009, from http://www.goertzel.org/dynapsyc/2008/glocal_memory.pdf

Goertzel, B. (2008b). Glocality of self and memory as a possible foundation for understanding psi. Dynamical Psychology: An International, Interdisciplinary Journal of Complex Mental Processes. Retrieved July 25, 2009, from http://www.goertzel.org/dynapsyc/2008/glocal_psi.pdf

Gordon, E. (2009). Redefining the local: The distinction between located information and local knowledge in location-based games. In Silva, A. S., & Sutko, D. M. (Eds.), *Digital Cityscapes: Merging Digital and Urban Playspaces* (pp. 21–36). New York: Peter Lang Publishing.

Górniak-Kocikowska, K. (2004). The computer revolution and global ethics. In Bynum, T. W., & Rogerson, S. (Eds.), *Computer Ethics and Professional Responsibility* (pp. 319–327). Malden, MA: Blackwell Publishing Ldt.

Górniak-Kocikowska, K. (2007). From computer ethics to the ethics of global ICT. *Library Hi Tech*, *25*(1), 47–57. doi:10.1108/07378830710735858

Grant, R., & Short, J. R. (Eds.). (2002). *Globalization and the margins*. New York: Palgrave Macmillan. doi:10.1057/9781403918482

Grixti, J. (2006). Symbiotic transformations: Youth, global media and indigenous culture in Malta. *Media Culture & Society*, *28*(1), 105–122. doi:10.1177/0163443706059295

Grixti, J. (2008). Glocalised youth culture as linguistic performance: Media globalisation and the construction of hybrid identities. Noves SL. Revista de Sociolingüística, Hivern, 2-8. Retrieved July 1, 2009, from http://www6.gencat.net/llengcat/noves/hm08hivern/docs/grixti.pdf.

Hall, B., & Snider, A. (2000). Glossary: The hottest buzz words in the industry. *Learning*, *44*(4), 85–104.

Hall, D. J. (2005). Philosophical foundations for a learning-oriented knowledge management system for decision support. *Decision Support Systems*, *39*(3), 445–461. doi:10.1016/j.dss.2004.01.005

Hall, D. J., Paradice, D. B., & Courtney, J. F. (2003). Building a theoretical foundation for a learning-oriented knowledge management system. *Journal of Information Technology Theory and Application*, *5*(2), 63–89.

Handzic, M., & Hasan, H. (2003). The search for an integrated KM framework. In Hasan, H., & Handzic, M. (Eds.), *Australian Studies in Knowledge Management* (pp. 3–34). Wollongong: UOW Press.

Harada, Y. (2002). Liberty, equity, and security in network-mediated learning and testing. In Bynum, T. W. (Eds.), *ETHICOMP2002: The Transformation of Organisations in the Information Age: Social and Ethical Implications* (pp. 575–588). Lisbon: Lusíada University of Lisbon.

Hardaker, G., & Smith, D. (2002). E-learning communities: Virtual markets and knowledge creation. *European Business Review*, *14*(5), 342–350. doi:10.1108/09555340210444194

Hearne, C. E. (2009). Chinese dialects. Suite101.com. Retrieved August, 5, 2009, from http://china.suite101.com/article.cfm/chinese_dialects#ixzz0csCvgDev

Held, D. (2004). *Global covenant: The social democratic alternative to the Washington consensus*. Cambridge: Polity.

Heyneman, S., Anderson, K., & Nuraliyev, N. (2008). The cost of corruption in higher education. *Comparative Education Review*, *52*(1), 1–25. doi:10.1086/524367

Hitchner, R. B. (2008). Globalization avant la lettre: Globalization and the history of the Roman Empire. New Global Studies, 2(2). Retrieved July 15, 2009, from http://www.bepress.com/ngs/vol2/iss2/art2

Huff, C., & Frey, W. (2005). Moral pedagogy and practical ethics. *Science and Engineering Ethics*, *11*(3), 389–408. doi:10.1007/s11948-005-0008-1

Inglis, C. (2008). *Planning for cultural diversity*. Paris: Les Éditions UNESCO.

IONS. (2009). What is noetic? Institute of Noetic Sciences. Retrieved July 15, 2009, from http://www.noetic.org/about/what_is.cfm

Jefferies, P., & Stahl, B. C. (2005). Some ethical considerations regarding the relationship of e-learning and pedagogy. In Collste, G. (Eds.), *ETHICOMP 2005: Looking Back to the Future (CD: paper 31)*. Linkoping, Sweden: Linkoping University.

Jenkins, H. (2006). *Convergence culture: Where old and new media collide*. New York: New York University Press.

Jia, W., & Zhou, W. (2005). *Distributed network systems: From concepts to implementations*. New York: Springer.

Jones, T. M. (1991). Ethical decision making by individuals in organizations: An issue-contingent model. *Academy of Management Review*, *16*(2), 366–395. doi:10.2307/258867

Jowett, B. (1899). *Protagoras: Dialogues of Plato*. Michigan, MI: The Colonial Press.

Kallinikou, D., et al. (2009, September). Alternative system for non-commercial use of intellectual property in consideration of free P2P file-sharing. Paper presented at the IASA 2009 Annual Conference, Athens, Greece.

Kanuka, H. (2006). Instructional design and e-learning: A discussion of pedagogical content knowledge as a missing construct. The e-Journal of Instructional Science and Technology, 9(2). Retrieved August 1, 2009, from http://www.usq.edu.au/electpub/e-jist/docs/vol9_no2/papers/full_papers/kanuka.htm

Kenon, V. K. (2009, June). Global education access utilizing high school-university partnerships and networked global learning communities. Paper presented at the Conference Network Ethics 2009: The New Challenge in Business, ICT and Education, Lisbon, Portugal.

King, A. H., & Heltne, M. M. (2007). Glocalization and ICT: Presuppositions, tensions and ethical possibilities. In Bynum, T. W., Rogerson, S., & Murata, K. (Eds.), *ETHICOMP 2007: Glocalization: Bridging the Global Nature of Information and Communication Technology and the Local Nature of Human Beings* (*Vol. 1*, pp. 288–301). Tokyo: Meiji University.

Knight, J. (2006). Crossborder education: An analytical framework for program and provider mobility. In Smart, J., & Tierney, W. (Eds.), *Higher Education: Handbook of Theory and Research* (*Vol. 21*, pp. 345–396). Dordrecht: Springer Academic Publishers.

Kofman, E., & Youngs, G. (Eds.). (2003). *Globalization: Theory and practice*. New York: Continuum.

Koppelman, H. (2008). Pedagogical content knowledge and educational cases in computer science: An exploration. Informing Science. Retrieved August 5, 2009, from http://proceedings.informingscience.org/InSITE2008/InSITE08p125-133Koppel450.pdf

Kwiek, M. (2006). *The university and the state*. New York: Peter Lang.

Lallana, E. C. (2004). *An overview of ICT policies and e-strategies of select Asian economies*. New Delhi: APDIP.

Laudon, K., & Laudon, J. (Eds.). (2004). *Managing the digital firm* (8th ed.). Upper Saddle River, NJ: Prentice Hall.

Levin, J. (2002). A 2020 vision: Education in the next two decades. *Quarterly Review of Distance Education*, *3*(1), 105–114.

Lewis, M. P. (Ed.). (2009). *Ethnologue: Languages of the world* (16th ed.). Dallas, TX: SIL International.

Lobera, J., & Escrigas, C. (2009). The glocal multiversity: New roles and emerging challenges for human and social development. Global University Network for Innovation. Retrieved July 15, 2009, from http://www.guni-rmies.net/news/detail.php?id=1464

Lucas, L. (2006). *The research game in academic life*. Maidenhead, UK: Open University Press & The Society for Research into Higher Education.

Maison, K. B. (2007). A case for professional studies in education for teachers in higher educational institutions. In Amenumey, D. E. K. (Ed.), *Challenges of Education in Ghana in the 21st Century* (pp. 248–256). Accra, Ghana: Woeli.

Mannheim, K. (1936). *Ideology and utopia: An introduction to the sociology of knowledge, (Transl. L. Wirth & E. Shils)*. New York: Harcourt Brace & World.

Marginson, S. (2007). Globalisation, the "idea of a university" and its ethical regimes. *Higher Education and Management Policy*, *19*(1), 31–45.

Mason, R., & Rennie, F. (2008). *E-learning and social networking: Handbook of resources for higher education*. New York: Routledge.

McPherson, M., & Nunes, M. B. (2006). Organizational issues for e-learning: Critical success factors as identified by HE practitioners. *International Journal of Educational Management*, *20*(7), 542–558. doi:10.1108/09513540610704645

Medeni, T. (2004, March). Lobal: A new dimension beside global, local and glocal. Paper presented at the International Workshop on Business and Information, Taipei, Taiwan.

Meyrowitz, J. (2005). The rise of glocality: New sense of place and identity in the global village. In Nyíri, K. (Ed.), *A Sense of Place: The Global and the Local in Mobile Communication* (pp. 21–30). Vienna: Passagen Verlag.

Mihalca, R. (2008). Knowledge management in e-learning systems. *Revista Informatica Economică*, *2*(46), 60–65.

Morin, E. (1999). *Seven complex lessons in education for the future*. Paris: Les Éditions UNESCO.

Musial, K. (2007, June). The public good function of universities in recent Nordic higher education reforms. Paper presented at the Conference of Higher Education Researchers, Dublin, Ireland.

Nagi, K. (2006). Solving ethical issues in e-learning. Special Issue of the International Journal of the Computer, the Internet and Management, 14(SP1), 7.1-7.6.

Newman, J. H. (1976). The idea of the university, (Modern ed.). Oxford, UK: Clarendon Press.

Nicholas, A. J., & Lewis, J. K. (2009, June). The net generation and e-text books. Paper presented at the Conference Network Ethics 2009: The New Challenge in Business, ICT and Education, Lisbon, Portugal.

Norchi, C. H. (2000). Indigenous knowledge as intellectual property. *Policy Sciences*, *33*(3-4), 387–398. doi:10.1023/A:1004835300774

Nowotny, H., Scott, P., & Gibbons, M. (2001). *Re-thinking science: Knowledge and the public in the age of uncertainty*. Cambridge, UK: Polity Press.

Olsen, L. T. (2009, July). Seattle 10 years on: Go glocal. Club of Amsterdam Journal, 119. Retrieved July 13, 2009, from http://www.clubofamsterdam.com/press.asp?contentid=799

Online Etymology Dictionary. (2001). Diversity. Online Etymology Dictionary. Retrieved July, 30, 2009, from http://www.etymonline.com/index.php?search=diversity&searchmode=none

Online Etymology Dictionary. (2001). Globalization. Online Etymology Dictionary. Retrieved August, 5, 2009, from http://www.etymonline.com/index.php?term=globalization

Online Etymology Dictionary. (2001). Local. Online Etymology Dictionary. Retrieved August, 5, 2009, from http://www.etymonline.com/index.php?term=local

Oxford English Dictionary. (2008). *Oxford English Dictionary*. Oxford: Oxford University Press.

Patrick, C., & Gaële, G. (2007). Exploring access and equity in higher education: Policy and performance in a comparative perspective. *Higher Education Quarterly*, *61*(2), 136–154. doi:10.1111/j.1468-2273.2007.00343.x

Peters, M. (2007, February). Reimagining the university in the global era. Paper presented at the World University Network Seminar, Bristol, United Kingdom.

Poe, E. A. (1845). The raven. Project Gutenberg. Retrieved July, 30, 2009, from http://www.gutenberg.org/etext/14082

Popper, K. R. (1972). *Objective knowledge: An evolutionary approach*. London: Oxford University Press.

Poster, M. (2005). Digitally local: Communications technologies and space. In Nyiri, K. (Ed.), *A Sense of Place: The Global and the Local in Mobile Communication* (pp. 31–41). Vienna: Passagen Verlag.

Pyvis, D., & Chapman, A. P. (2005). Culture shock and the international student "offshore". *Journal of Research in International Education*, *4*(1), 23–42. doi:10.1177/1475240905050289

Raikhy, P. S. (2002). Trade in education under the WTO policy regime: Implications for India. In Powar, K. B. (Ed.), *Internationalization of Higher Education* (pp. 127–133). New Delhi: Association of Indian Universities.

Retzer, J. (2005). The economical value of information networks. NWAX. Retrieved July 31, 2009, from http://www.nwax.net/documents/economic_value_of_networks.v2-3.pdf

Richards, C. (2004). From old to new learning: global dilemmas, exemplary Asian contexts, and ICT as a key to cultural change in education. *Globalisation, Societies and Education*, *2*(3), 337–353. doi:10.1080/1476772042000252470

Robertson, P. L., & Smith, K. H. (2007, March). Technological upgrading and distributed knowledge bases. Paper presented at the Workshop on Low and Medium Technology Industries, Dortmund, Germany.

Rogers, P. C., Graham, C. R., & Mayes, C. T. (2007). Cultural competence and instructional design: Exploration research into the delivery of online instruction cross-culturally. *Educational Technology Research and Development*, *55*(2), 197–217. doi:10.1007/s11423-007-9033-x

Roudometof, V. (2005). Transnationalism, cosmopolitanism and glocalization. *Current Sociology*, *53*(1), 113–135. doi:10.1177/0011392105048291

Rushkoff, D. (2005). Renaissance now! The gamers' perspective. In Raessens, J., & Goldstein, J. (Eds.), *Handbook of Computer Game Studies* (pp. 415–421). Cambridge, MA: MIT Press.

Sakai, K., Kuriyama, K., & Miyahara, T. (2007). The e-learning strategy of organizational design: Emerging the new university education for the next generation. In Bynum, T. W., Rogerson, S., & Murata, K. (Eds.), *ETHICOMP 2007: Glocalization: Bridging the Global Nature of Information and Communication Technology and the Local Nature of Human Beings* (*Vol. 1*, pp. 38–48). Tokyo: Meiji University.

Santos, B. S. (2006). The university in the 21st Century: Towards a democratic and emancipatory university reform. In Rhoads, R., & Torres, C. A. (Eds.), *The University, State, and Market. The Political Economy of Globalization in the Americas* (pp. 60–100). Stanford, CA: Stanford University Press.

Scardamalia, M., & Bereiter, C. (2003). Knowledge building environments: Extending the limits of the possible in education and knowledge work. In DiStefano, A., Rudestam, K. E., & Silverman, R. (Eds.), *Encyclopedia of distributed learning* (pp. 269–272). Thousand Oaks, CA: Sage Publications.

Schulte, W. D., & Al-Fehaid, A. (2004). National culture and knowledge management in the middle East: A cross-cultural comparison of Saudi Arabia and the US. In O. Yau (Ed.), Academy of International Business Southeastern United States Annual Meeting (pp. 279-290). Macau: Academy of International Business.

Scott, P. (1995). *The meanings of mass higher education*. Buckingham, UK: Open University Press.

Scott, P. (2008, November). Beyond the market: Higher Education in 2020. Paper presented at the Univeristies Association for Lifelong Learning Conference, Barcelona, Spain.

Shafir, G., & Peled, Y. (Eds.). (2000). *The new Israel: Peacemaking and liberalization*. Boulder, CO: Westview Press.

Shaw, S. (2008). Collaboration in the world of ISD. ASTD. Retrieved August, 5, 2009, from http://www.astd.org/LC/2008/0108_shaw.htm

Siemens, G. (2004). Learning management systems: The wrong place to start learning. Elearnspace. Retrieved August 1, 2009, from http://www.elearnspace.org/Articles/lms.htm

Silva, N. S. A. (2007). An investigation on the impact of culture and ethics on the implementation of e-university. MPhil/PhD unpublished dissertation, De Montfort University, Leicester.

Silva, N. S. A. (2009). Knowledge or content? The philosophical boundaries in e-learning pedagogical theories! In Vilas, A. M. (Eds.), *m-ICTE 2009: Research, Reflections and Innovations in Integrating ICT in Education* (pp. 221–225). Lisbon: Formatex.

Small, G. W., & Vorgan, G. (2008). iBrain: Surviving the technological alteration of the modern mind. New York: Harper Collins Publishers.

Snowden, D. J. (2000). The paradox of story. *Journal of Scenario and Strategy Planning*, *1*(5), 16–20.

Solomon, R. (Ed.). (1992). *Ethics and excellence: Cooperation and integrity in business*. New York: Oxford University Press.

Sorensen, E. (2002). Part of the online teacher's curriculum: Designing for collaborative knowledge building online. In D. Willis et al. (Eds.), Society for Information Technology and Teacher Education International Conference (pp. 995-999). Chesapeake, VA: AACE.

Stahl, B. C. (2002). Ethics and e-teaching: the students' perspective. *Communications of the IIMA*, *2*(3), 51–62.

Stahl, G. (2004). Building collaborative knowing: Elements of a social theory of learning. In Strijbos, J.-W., Kirschner, P., & Martens, R. (Eds.), *What We Know About CSCL in Higher Education* (pp. 53–85). Norwell, MA: Kluwer. doi:10.1007/1-4020-7921-4_3

Standards Australia. (2003). Interim Australian Standard- Knowledge management. Standards Australia Limited. Retrieved August 10, 2009, from http://www.standards.com.au

Steger, M. B. (Ed.). (2004). *Rethinking globalism*. Lanham, MD: Rowman & Littlefield Publishers.

Stewart, S. (2004). The A.I. web game. Sean Stewart. Retrieved July 30, 2009, from http://www.seanstewart.org/beast/intro/

Stiglitz, J. E. (2002). *Globalization and its discontents*. New York: Norton.

Stone, D. (2003). Knowledge in the global agora: Production, dissemination and consumption. In Krizsán, A. (Ed.), *Reshaping Globalization: Multilateral Dialogues and New Policy Initiatives* (pp. 41–62). Budapest, Hungary: Central European University Press.

Swidler, A., & Arditi, J. (1994). The new sociology of knowledge. *Annual Review of Sociology*, *20*, 305–329. doi:10.1146/annurev.so.20.080194.001513

Tandon, R. (2008). Civil engagement in higher education and its role in human and social development. In Global University Network for Innovation (Ed.), Higher Education in the World: New Challenges and Emerging Roles for Human and Social Development (pp. 65-66). London: Palgrave Macmillan.

Tarasofsky, R., & House, C. (2005). Report on trade, environment, and intellectual property rights. Intellectual Property Rights Organization. Retrieved July 25, 2009, from http://www.iprsonline.org/resources/docs/Tarasofsky-CATE-IPRs.pdf

Taylor, C. (2002). Gadamer on the human sciences. In Dostal, R. J. (Ed.), *The Cambridge Companion to Gadamer* (pp. 126–142). Cambridge, UK: Cambridge University Press. doi:10.1017/CCOL0521801931.007

Thomas, L. (1995). *Late night thoughts on listening to Mahler's ninth symphony*. New York: Penguin Books.

Toffler, A. (1980). *The third wave*. New York: Bantam Books.

UN. (1948). The universal declaration of human rights. United Nations. Retrieved July 25, 2009, from http://www.un.org/en/documents/udhr/

UNESCO. (2002). Universal declaration on cultural diversity. UNESCO. Retrieved August 10, 2009, from http://unesdoc.unesco.org/images/0012/001271/127160m.pdf

UNHCHR. (1966). International covenant on economic, social and cultural rights. United Nations High Commissioner for Human Rights. Retrieved July 27, 2009, from http://www2.ohchr.org/english/law/cescr.htm

Uzuner, S. (2009). Questions of culture in distance learning: A research review. *International Review of Research in Open and Distance Learning*, *10*(3), 1–19.

van Harmelen, M. (2006). Personal learning environments. University of Manchester. Retrieved August 2, 2009, from http://octette.cs.man.ac.uk/jitt/index.php/Personal_Learning_Environments

Vrasidas, C., & Glass, G. V. (2002). A conceptual framework for studying distance education. In Vrasidas, C., & Glass, G. V. (Eds.), *Current Perspectives in Applied Information Technologies: Distance Education and Distributed Learning* (pp. 31–56). Greenwich, CT: Information Age Publishing, Inc.

Watson, K. (2007). Language, education and ethnicity: Whose rights will prevail in the age of globalisation? *International Journal of Educational Development*, *27*(3), 252–265. doi:10.1016/j.ijedudev.2006.10.015

Weber, M. (1946). The social psychology of the world religions. In Gerth, H. H., & Mills, C. W. (Eds.), *From Max Weber: Essays in Sociology* (pp. 267–301). New York: Galaxy.

Webster, F. (2006). *Theories of the information society* (3rd ed.). London: Routledge.

Welsch, W. (1999). Transculturality- The puzzling form of cultures today. In Featherstone, M., & Lash, S. (Eds.), *Spaces of Culture: City, Nation, World* (pp. 194–213). London: Sage.

Wilson, S. M., Schulman, L. S., & Richért, A. E. (1987). 150 different ways of knowing: Representations of knowledge in teaching. In Calderhead, J. (Ed.), *Exploring Teacher's Thinking* (pp. 104–124). London: Cassell Education.

Wood, V. R. (2006). Globalization and higher education: Eight common perceptions from university leaders. IIE Network. Retrieved July 15, 2009, from http://www.iienetwork.org/page/84658/

World Bank. (2000). *Higher education in developing countries: Peril and promise. The Task Force on Higher Education and Society*. Washington, DC: World Bank Publications.

World Bank. (2009). *Information and communications for development 2009: Extending reach and increasing impact*. Washington, DC: World Bank Publications.

World Summit on the Information Society. (2003). Declaration of principles. International Telecommunications Union. Retrieved July 25, 2009, from http://www.itu.int/wsis/docs/geneva/official/dop.html

Zirfas, J. (1999). *Die lehre der ethik, zur moralischen begründung pädagogischen denkens und handelns*. Weinheim, Germany: Deutscher Studien Verlag.

KEY TERMS AND DEFINITIONS

Distributed Knowledge: Encompasses the new categories of knowledge that network learning environments consent. It assumes as fundamental principles: autonomy (is manageable at a local level by each individual), and coordination (each individual must be allowed to share knowledge, not through obligation, but through his personal context).

Diversity: In a cultural sense refers the collection of local cultures within a cultural setting (which is not necessarily anchored to a geographical territory). It resumes the multiple interactions that occur from the macro-level to a micro-level within a particular culture. In contemporary cultural forms, can be considered the referee between global and local (glocality).

Globalization: A complex and multidisciplinary phenomenon. In an early stage was considered as a consequence of the international economical movement, as well as the growth of ICT; however, today encompasses a tremendous challenge for researchers due to its cultural, social, ethic, artistic, etc dimensions, and how they interact.

Glocality: Refers to the growing peculiarity of a synthesised existence amongst participants within a global village, and the preservation of local cultural traditions and influences.

Higher Education: Includes all the organizations or institutions that devoted their work to teaching and research in order to promote human development. Nonetheless, its characteristics and impact have changed in accordance to the evolutionary stage of mankind.

Section 4
Organizational Innovation Dilemmas

"Imagination is more important than knowledge..."
Albert Einstein

What have in common personal mastery, knowledge protection versus interchange, and moral knowledge? The response is imagination! Imagination is decisive to create models that benefit organizations and workers concerning knowledge protection versus knowledge interchange, because it will allow an effective personal mastery. For that, it is vital for managers the existence of a support system that promotes an overall stakeholder analysis within these imaginative business models.

Chapter 10
Renewal and Personal Mastery in Knowledge-Based Organisations:
The Case of a Finnish ICT-Company

Päivi Lohikoski
University of Oulu, Finland

ABSTRACT

Being knowledge management crucial to companies, it seems reasonable to understand an organisation intellectual capital. The three leading components of intellectual capital (human capital, structural capital and relational capital), are intrinsically bounded to the organisational ICT system, organisational structure, and to workers personal mastery. Nonetheless, in order to evolve organisational intellectual capital it is required a high level of personal mastery, which is clearly bounded to human resources. Therefore, this chapter aims to promote a theoretical and empirical discussion in order to understand the diverse dimensions between renewal, personal mastery, and employee wellbeing within a knowledge-based organisation (Finnish ICT-company). For that, the chapter is divided into six major sections: the research questions; theoretical framework and main concepts; the case study organisation and research methods applied; findings; discussion; and future research.

INTRODUCTION

Powerful technological development in society and the Internet has changed world business structures and communication infrastructure massively since the 1990s. The Internet, which enables global activities and enhances globalization, has caused an ever-faster changing business infrastructure in which knowledge at all levels plays a more crucial role than ever before. Knowledge and the ability to renew are therefore among an organisation's key assets (Harrison & Kessels, 2004).

Plentiful research exists in many scientific fields on the organisation of learning, quality management, and change management. However, general wellbeing at work is current particularly in technology, economics, psychology, and social science research. A common understanding is that work environments must become more people-friendly for organisations to continue to innovate,

DOI: 10.4018/978-1-61520-873-9.ch010

creating better products and services for changing markets in a growing, knowledge-based economy (Torvi & Kiljunen, 2005). As everything in the world connects and changes, the ability to adapt and to renew becomes crucial to organisations and individuals (Ståhle & Laento, 2000). *Learning* and *change* always go hand in hand: change prompts learning and learning is a way to change. *Change management* means- among other tasks- managing team learning, individual learning, and learning at an organisation level (Otala, 2002; Argyris & Schön, 1996). It is the starting point to studying renewal. This study aims to recognise the state of an organisation's *intellectual capital* (IC). When weaknesses and strengths are acknowledged, processes and procedures can be developed from the results.

This article is based on a study carried out in spring 2005 in a Finnish ICT-company supplying information services to a large ICT company. The study looked to increase empirical knowledge of the *renewal ability of knowledge-based organisations*, and of *employee wellbeing* in a changing work environment. The purpose was principally to investigate the state of IC in that organisation. The theoretical background for the investigation stands on principle elements of a learning organisation and IC. Research methods were qualitative; the empirical data consisted of interviews within the case study organisation. Experts, it was assumed, to possess qualities of personal mastery, and a personal responsibility for learning. It was interesting therefore to examine how an organisation's culture and structure support or inhibit the expert's renewal ability and contribution to the organisation's ability to innovate and work effectively. In order to perform well, it is crucial to evaluate employees' personal mastery, in relation to the organisation's culture, values, goals, structure, and management practises. Performing well is also a question of power and how it is shared between employees, management and partners. In further sections the theoretical background of the study is presented, the research methods applied are described, and the main findings of the study reported. The chapter concludes by discussing the findings and further studies.

THE RESEARCH QUESTIONS

Traditionally, human resource (HR) managers have been responsible for enhancing and developing the organisational knowledge that resides in people. IC, however, belongs to the organisation as a whole. Organisational structures should support the development of organisational knowledge and competencies based on it, transforming those competencies into the property of the entire organisation. Before IC can be measured or developed, its present state must be investigated: existing processes and structures and their effects must- for instance- be known. By acknowledging the present state of competencies and their related renewal ability, the present state of an organisation's IC can be investigated and its commitment issues shared. To understand developing activities is part of investigating the present state of IC, because an organisation must balance economical objectives and intangible resources (Rastas & Einola-Pekkinen, 2001). In this study, the author examines organisational renewal through the central issues of its IC, including knowledge management (KM), relations with business partners, and structural capital, a critical factor between the human capital and the customer capital of an organisation. The research questions were set out as follows:

1. How does the IC renews itself?;
2. How does the renewal support achievement of the organisational goals?;
3. How does the renewal affect the organisation´s intellectual capital?;
4. How does the renewal support relations with the customers?;
5. What is the present state of the organisation´s IC?.

The first research question investigates whether the renewal of IC is in different areas: proactive or reactive, and if the channels are communicating the need for change and renewal. The second question approaches the meaning of renewal in relation to organisational goals. The third question clarifies how renewal supports individual and organisational learning, and how staff perceives the customer relationship. The last question, the most significant, elucidates about the present state of the IC.

THEORETICAL FRAMEWORK AND MAIN CONCEPTS

The theoretical framework of this article comprises the concepts of renewal ability, personal mastery, and IC, including the components of an organisation. These ideas and their relations are displayed in Figure 1.

Renewal Ability

Renewal ability evolves at an individual level and at a collective level. A quality of managers and other staff, renewal ability can be seen in practical procedures, and it directly influences an organisation's ability to carry out strategy and to adjust to changes in environment (Ståhle *et. al.*, 2002). Theories of learning organisation identify cumulative learning and constant self-renewal as the keys to success: a successful organisation combines flexibility and effectiveness. Mobilising knowledge, a high priority in a learning organisation, requires knowledge sharing and an open door policy that encourages staff members and managers to bring problems to the attention of top management (Minzberg, Ahlstrand & Lampel, 2005).

Renewal ability, a quality of an organisation's members, can be seen in the way those members work. The ability to renew directly impacts an organisation's ability to carry out strategy and adapt to changes in society, and is based on

Figure 1. The key elements of organisational renewal

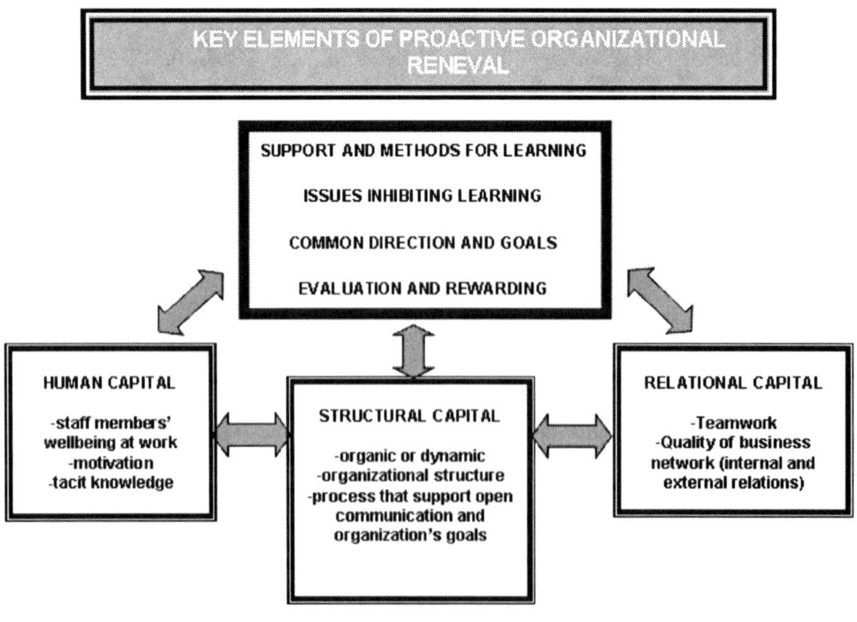

proactive learning and on efficiency in "taking advantage of new possibilities" (Ståhle *et. al.*, 2002, pp. 10). According to the organic growth principle, all members of an organisation must share common goals and a common vision, so that they can take responsibility for developing IC in the right direction. Employees must know what skills they will need to add value to the IC (Brooking, 1996).

An organisation can adapt easily to changes within a society by developing, planning, and managing information resources and processes. Just as it is important to be able to learn new things, it is equally important to unlearn old ways of thinking and old patterns of behaviour (Choo, 1998). Commonly, people only see their own place within an organisation and the positive sides of their behaviour and work. The impact of the work of other people, however, cannot be seen on a large scale. It also is typical to scapegoat and blame the system without trying to identify underlying reasons behind the existing problems (Senge, 1990). All people are different and all have their own limitations to sharing and receiving information (Choo, 1998). By applying the concept of *KM*, one may remove old patterns of thinking, leaving room to learn new things. Innovation and creativity can be enhanced through learning, and efficient decision-making can occur (Choo, 1998).

Personal Mastery

Personal mastery evolves mostly at an individual level, relating to personal responsibility for learning, and suggesting a special level of proficiency: personal and professional. Those with personal mastery live in a mode of continual learning (Senge, 2006), with a totally new attitude to life, an openness to new things, and a strong will to develop and grow as a human being. Furthermore, those with personal mastery, have a strong vision and a clear mission for where they are going, and what they want to become. They are often found in changing environments, because people with personal mastery do not use their energy to resist change. They also actively seek to change their environment without trying to control it (Senge, 1990).

Himanen, Torvalds & Castells (2001) also describe the importance of personal responsibility in learning. With personal responsibility they describe *self programming*, often called personal development (PD) in literature. They separate seven different characteristics for personal development that help people to get ahead in life and cope with change in society (Himanen, Torvalds & Castells, 2001). Growth as a human being, an essential part of personal mastery, starts with a commitment to something that truly matters. A commitment to personal growth is important, particularly for managers. Through the theory of personal mastery it is easier to understand that an organisation or a team is a social system and that there are more integrated ways of looking at problems (Senge, 2006).

Intellectual Capital

Interest in IC has grown steadily since Stewart introduced IC as a concept at the beginning of the 1990s. According to Stewart (1997), IC is the sum of everything people know that gives a competitive advantage in the market. IC consists of three components: human, structural, and customer capital. It has been defined, moreover, as a set of knowledge that creates value for the organisation, or can create value in the future (Castellanos, Rodriquez & Ranguelov, 2004). Common to these two definitions is the understanding that IC adds value to existing outcomes by producing, for instance, a competitive advantage (see Iivonen & Huotari, 2007).

Intellectual capital has become a popular concept as the number of knowledge-base organisations has increased. While the expert is the most important element of knowledge-based organisations, only a few companies can tell the value of an expert's intellectual capital. According to a survey carried out in the UK, companies use only around twenty percent of employee competence. The use of intellectual capital is valuable for the company and for motivating and rewarding the expert (Brooking, 1996).

IC involves *human capital* (HC), *structural capital* (SC), *customer capital* (CC) or, *relational capital* (RC). HC is knowledge, skills, know-how, experience, creativity, education, and the capability to innovate. RC is relations to customers, stakeholders, and also of image, brands, and contracts with business partners. SC is patents, technology, information systems, processes and procedures, values, organisational culture, and management philosophy (Lönnqvist & Mettänen, 2003). Iivonen & Huotari (2007) considered that the IC components of a university library indicate the potential contribution of that library to the overall performance of the university IC. Iivonen & Huotari (2007) referred to Seetharaman, Sooria & Saravanan (2002), who claim that even at the end of the last millennium, too much about the nature of IC remained unknown and was difficult to capture it in explicit terms. They contributed to this discussion by presenting summaries of the major components of IC, as displayed in Table 1.

Human Capital

HC is a component of IC whose content most often describes employee competence (see Table 1).

HC includes the explicit and tacit knowledge of employees and relates strongly to the cultural aspects of organisational knowing. Tacit knowledge is crucial to HC; because, personal and private knowledge is difficult to communicate to others. Tacit knowledge grows in time through experiences and can be seen as intuition, vision, and know-how (Choo, 1998). The concept of tacit knowledge can be traced to Michael Polanyi (1891-1976), a Hungarian researcher of medicine who identified tacit knowledge and explicit knowledge as concepts, and to Ikujiro Nonaka, who popularised the concepts in the mid-1990s. However, according to many authors, tacit knowledge has been used too superficially as a term in certain cases (Huotari & Iivonen, 2004; Yates-Mercer & Bawden, 2002; Cook & Brown, 1999). Tacit knowledge plays a vital role in HC, and manifests as the implicit knowledge of employees, crucial to promoting organisational learning and innovations (see Choo, 1998). Tacit knowledge can be transferred by teamwork and by learning-by-doing methods (Sveiby, 1997). As much as tacit knowledge is deeply rooted in organisational practices and culture, it may also have a negative impact by causing change resistance among staff members (Stewart, 1997). Embedded tacit knowledge may sometimes reduce the ability to enhance organisational performance.

Structural Capital

The SC of IC, its internal processes, may be organisational and include, for example: learning, management, and business processes; culture; and technological processes consisting of databases,

Table 1. A description of HC (Source: Iivonen & Huotari, 2007, pp. 85)

Components of IC	Edvisson & Malone (1997)	Magic Project (Seetharaman, Sooria & Saravanan, 2002)	Castellanos, Rodriquez & Ranguelov (2004)	Johannessen, Olsen & Olaisen (2005)
HC	All the individual capabilities, knowledge, skill, and experiences of the company's employees and managers	The basic potentials of an organisation	The set of explicit and tacit knowledge of the people in the organisation, shared or not amongst them, that has value to the organisation	The sum of internal and external knowledge bases in a system

licenses, and information systems. For the study this article reports on, SC is a crucial component of IC that includes an organisation's capability for continuous improvement, often called "innovation capital". Also, SC encompasses the ability of an organisation to adjust to environmental change and to create its own future, which in turn is entitled "systemic capital". According to Johannessen, Olsen & Olaisen (2005), SC consists of organisational learning and innovation. Explicit knowledge, state Castellanos, Rodriquez & Ranguelov (2004), relates to the internal processes of SC, both organisational and technological.

Edvinsson & Malone (1997) have separated a specific innovation capital that consists of renewal capability and of the results of innovation in the form of protected commercial rights, intellectual property, and other intangible assets and talents. Johannessen, Olsen & Olaisen also separate systemic capital, which they regard as an ability to adjust to changes in the environment demonstrated by social systems, and also an ability to create one's own future (Iivonen & Huotari, 2007).

Personnel development processes are necessary for an organisation to perform in changing business environments; they make learning possible at all times. Effective communication, supported by a strong structure of teams, is needed to secure continuous functioning and a flow of information on current issues, future changes, and new goals. Technology is needed to spread information about changes and new goals. By evaluating areas of knowledge and expertise, we can discover what goals must be reached and what is needed to achieve them in the future. Career plans are also required to develop learning processes, motivate employees, and simply to add knowledge and motivation. Also, a rewarding economic reflection of the work- and processes of reward in general- are crucial to structural capital in a knowledge-based organisation. Open feedback processes and their evaluation are needed. Learning, training, and developing competence is especially important, allowing supervisors and managers to lead teams, services, and products (Harrison & Kessels, 2004). It has been suggested that the nature of the reward is essential: the research shows that public recognition of skill and contribution, rather than plain economic reflection of the input measured, motivates the expert to work harder and stay longer with a company (Lee-Kelley, Blackman & Hurst, 2007).

Processes, the glue that keeps the components of an organisation together, should reflect its (the organisation's) values and management philosophy. The values of top management will not be visible in an organisation if middle management is not committed to working according to the values, mission, and strategy of the organisation; to quality processes, information management, change management and a continuous striving to work better. Among these strategies, communication methods are significant (Brooking, 1996). Structural capital can also help managers to build fences, support weak communication processes, or weaken the flow of information and learning in organisation. By simplifying and lowering organisational structure, processes can become even more effective, adding value for the customer. Well-formed structures support an efficient information flow between customers, stakeholders, and organisations. If they do not, an invisible informal structure can develop beside the formal structure, stronger than the "actual" formal structure. Different structures, upon analysis, either support or inhibit the successful work of an organisation (Rastas & Einola-Pekkinen, 2001).

Relational Capital

The RC (also called *customer capital*, *market capital*, or *network capital*) of IC comprises an organisation's relationships and includes the explicit and tacit knowledge of how an organisation deals with its external agents (Castellanos, Rodriquez & Ranguelov, 2004). In today's turbulent, networked environment, an organisation cannot survive without relations to stakeholders

(Iivonen & Huotari, 2007). Success in a relationship is based on quality: in an inter-organisational collaboration, quality means shaping cooperation, trust, mutuality, and joint learning. Supporting the building of such relationships is not easy, given the competitive culture and transactional relationships usual to "organisational" life (Senge *et al.*, 2007). Organisations usually have customers and stakeholders, but according to Schein (2004) definitions may be vague.

Is the customer, for instance, the person who ultimately buys the product; or the career occupant's peers in a neighbouring department, dependent on the department he or she is in; or the boss; or subordinates; or the community? "Client" and "customer" vary as concepts by function and by occupational community. Each community has norms for how to "get along", for information that can be passed or withheld, and for interests that must ultimately be protected (Schein, 2004).

An organisation's internal relations are essential to RC, being also essential to RC is the ability to network, to create and maintain relations beyond internal and external organisational boundaries. Success in collaboration stands, therefore, on an organisation's strategic-linking capability; RC indicates a capacity to build partnerships (see Iivonen & Huotari, 2007). Guiding ideas develop when people share values, vision, and general guidelines, resulting in a network of people working together, everything connected and renewed constantly through learning and change. In such a network, people share a common language by which to interpret their experiences to create something new and investigate shared values and beliefs (Choo, 2002). Partners have a joint interest in value creation and in mutual success, and must learn to trust in a joint future despite occasional mistakes and shortcomings, without looking for new service providers when dissatisfied (Iivonen & Huotari, 2007).

Modern organisational networks usually consist of teams, groups that share a common goal and vision. A team employs a variety of processes, procedures, and systems to achieve that goal and vision. Managers encourage employees to work towards a shared aim, and reorganise people to make teams (Scholtes, 1997). Team learning correlates the highest with resource adequacy. Simply being a team member may possibly give some employees greater job satisfaction. The independent nature of experts in a knowledge organisation is reflected in a low correlation of relations to co-workers. Experts value colleagues, but personal reward does not result from being with them; teamwork may not come naturally to experts. Knowledge workers tend to see development and learning as a personal thing. If team work is vital to a project, it needs to be managed carefully (Lee-Kelley, Blackman & Hurst, 2007).

Organisational Culture

Organisational culture and the ideas behind an organisation change constantly due to changes in society. Organisational culture defines how people should act and work within an organisation (Hofstede, 1993). A power that affects everything, it takes organisation and fragments it, knitting a collection of individuals into an integrated entity. Culture is what is unique about the way we do all things. It is interpretations shared collectively in a social process. No private cultures exist. There might be individual activities, but their significance is always collective (Minzberg, Ahlstrand, & Lampel, 2005).

According to Schein (1996), a culture can be a set of basic tacit assumptions about how the world is and ought to be. Culture is a group of people that share and determines their perceptions, thoughts, feelings, and, to some degree, their overt behaviour. Cultures arise within organisations based on their own histories and experiences. It manifests itself at three levels: the level of deep tacit assumptions that are the essence of the culture. Also the level of espoused values reflecting group's wishes to be ideally and what it wants to be publicly. Finally there is the day-to-day behaviour that represents a complex compromise among the espoused values, the deeper assumptions, and the immediate requirements of the situation. Different kinds of organisations exist, but common to all of them is that their internal functions have to be in balance with their mission, techniques, external functions, and their member needs and expectations (Aula & Hakala, 2000).

THE CASE STUDY ORGANISATION AND RESEARCH METHODS APPLIED

The Case Study Organisation

The case study organisation reported on in this article is a knowledge-based organisation specialising in engineering work, in the environmental sciences, and in information sciences. The case study organisation is located in five major cities in Finland and also in "international" locations: in China, India, Russia, and in Sweden. The study was conducted within the Information Services branch of the organisation, which produces a variety of information technology services that demand a high level of expertise based on a high level of education, a strong practical knowledge of the work, and on excellent English skills. Most of the employees work as technical writers, as the main users of databases, as information designers, or in other "information support" functions within customer organisations.

The Qualitative Approach

It is typical of qualitative research that its empirical results can be observed from many different angles. It is also typical of qualitative research that its data is expressive, rich, multileveled, and even complicated to understand (Alasuutari, 1995). Qualitative research is part of the examined organisation's world, a type of sample about language and culture of the organisation under investigation (Alasuutari, 1995). This research aims to explain certain phenomenon within the case study organisation, which is quite common in qualitative research, rather than to expose or prove phenomenon (Alasuutari, 1995).

The data was collected by applying the "theme interview" method, a half-structured interview method. In this type of interview, the form of the themes discussed is the same for all interviewees, but the interviewer can state the themes in a different order if necessary (Hirsjärvi & Hurme, 2000). Applying the theme interview method, all individual experiences can be studied, including thoughts, beliefs, feelings, and experiences (Hirsjärvi & Hurme, 2000). The theme interview method is excellent for situations and circumstances in which, a deeper and increasing understanding of the research is needed (Hirsjärvi & Hurme, 2000).

Collecting and Analysing the Empirical Data

The basis for the empirical study was formed from thirty-seven organisational members in two teams. The team managers also had members in other cities and in other location. The staff members to be interviewed were selected randomly, though, as the personnel in the case study organisation were homogeneous, the backgrounds of the study subjects displayed no variation when compared to the backgrounds of the rest of the staff. Features common to those interviewed included an age of around thirty, a master's degree at university level, and three years' work experience. Of the study subjects, seventy percent were women and thirty percent men. The services this company offered were outsourced from services provided by a larger technology company: a significant factor in employee backgrounds. Some of the subjects of the study had worked in the large company, which was their customer now, while others were new employees.

Some significance to the findings concerning the SC and RC of the case study organisation was caused also by the arrangement, where some of the interviewees were working in the customer's premises, while others worked in the company's own premises and were in contact with the customer mainly by e-mail or by phone.

The data was collected by interviewing the members of two teams in March and April 2005. The themes of the interview were divided into three main categories, namely HC, SC, and RC. Fourteen staff members altogether, from two separate teams, were invited for interviews. The researcher interviewed eleven study subjects either in a company meeting room or staff members' own offices. Each interview was recorded, and took from thirty-five minutes to an hour and fifteen minutes, depending on the interviewee. The recordings were transcribed within a few days after the interviews, and the researcher had the atmosphere and the details clearly in mind when analysing the data. The theme interview proved a suitable method for studying issues also of a more intangible nature, since it was possible in the interaction between the researcher and the study subjects to discover so-called "grey areas" connected to the subject. As a final remark, the author points out that Figure 2 shows the main themes of the study, which form the basis for both interviews and analysis.

FINDINGS

The Renewal of Intellectual Capital

IC is renewed mainly through customer orders, through changes in employees, and through the joint learning of employees. In the case study, renewal occurred principally by adjusting to new customer processes, new IT tools, and to new projects. The values, goals, and strategies of the case study organisation itself were unknown to employees; all those employees interviewed said that most important to the organisation was economic profit.

We are here only to make money for the company, that's it (Person A on the theme of values)

Well, a company can have all kinds of values, but you see the actual values in how things are done. There can be anything on paper. Those values have been presented to us in info sessions, but to

Figure 2. The central themes of an interview based on the theory of learning organisation

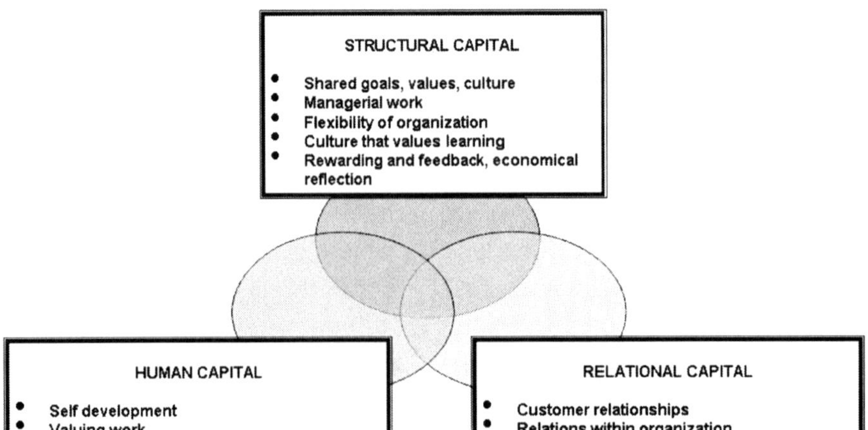

tell you the truth, I can't recall them. (Person H to the question about values)

The organisational structure showed signs of inflexibility at work, binding frames and processes so tightly together in certain procedures that employees found them almost impossible to change. This was evident even in situations in which personal competence and knowledge would suggest change. Staff learning together- one aspect of renewal activities- was possible due to good team spirit, due in part to the similar educational background and age structure of the staff. While top management were seen as distant and almost invisible, ten out of eleven study subjects found their nearest project managers easy to get along with and regarded them as equally important colleagues. However, six out of the ten staff members interviewed found it almost impossible to influence their own work environment.

Many of us have the competence to develop our services; we actually could do documents of excellent quality, but the company doesn't want that, they are missing common sense in all the decisions. The bureaucracy is too thick. It just isn't this company's thing to do excellent documentation. The customer has seen that also: when busy, we are trying to let out all kinds of crap (Person D to the question can you use your own full competence in your work?)

Managers promise to deliver whatever the customer asks. They don't know how to be strict about what can be ordered. They can't negotiate (Person H to the question about structural capital theme 'managerial work')

To achieve proactive renewal and enable better, innovative practices, an organic or even a dynamic organisational structure is needed. Managers require new competencies and qualities in this type of environment, including an ability to motivate people, to support learning and insight, and to motivate staff members and skills for KM (Rastas & Einola-Pekkinen, 2001). Those staff members interviewed wanted- in addition to nice managers- increased proactivity for change, better planning abilities, better negotiation skills, sturdiness, and better managing skills in general. According to Kessels (2001), managers can also be helpful facilitators who create the necessary environment for knowledge work. At worst, traditional managers who organise work in obedience to bureaucratic rules are a hindrance to the development of knowledge networks, which are a prerequisite for knowledge productivity (Kessels, 2001).

Renewal and Goals

Goals are an important foundation and motivating factor at individual, team, and organisational levels of decision making. A shared vision can be a goal that all members of an organisation can recognize. To achieve that vision, all members of an organisation must be committed to it and want it to work. It is extremely difficult for an organisation to succeed in a changing world without long term goals that all the members' share (Senge, 1990).

Organisations should have a plan for learning and renewal: not an educational program tied to a certain time or place, but a culture of learning visible in every-day work practises. Routine, work, and learning should mesh naturally in the everyday life of an organisation, creating an environment that supports and encourages the ability of staff to adopt changes and new procedures and to innovate (Harrison & Kessels 2004, 155). When an organisation has a clear goal, employees do not need to be pushed to change, but want to change of their own will, and look consciously to improve the quality of their work and of their work environment (Senge, 1990).

In the case study organisation, the biggest problems connected to a lack of goals were: insufficient commitment to work, and a lack of processes for evaluation and reward. All the staff members, ten out of eleven interviewees, did not have clear goals in their work. This was stated for example as follows:

There aren't any goals. Life goes on only by ongoing work orders. If something new suddenly comes up, they quickly try to train us for that. We just need to jump into new things with our head up. Whoever happens to have most time gives advice and trains as much as they possibly can, while taking care of their own projects. Work duties are tied too much to one person here. (Person A to the question what kind of goals do you have?)

Moreover, all the interviewed (11/11) thought the evaluation, reward, and feedback processes were inadequate or even poor:

There isn't a formal feedback channel. Feedback comes when it comes, just by accident sometimes. By e-mail, for example. Appreciation for work is not shown in the salary. It doesn't give any economical feedback about how well or poorly you do your job. It just doesn't matter. (Person I to the question: on salary, feedback and rewarding practices, what thoughts come to mind?)

Goals of the case study organisation other than economic were unknown to the staff, who were also without any personal goals or career plans. Work and training was planned according to customer orders. Also, lack of evaluation, reward, and feedback processes decreased motivation and the level of performance at work. The company did have regular "development discussions" between managers and staff members once a year, but these were considered inadequate and even useless.

The Effects of Renewal on Intellectual Capital

People find it rewarding to use their competencies at the highest level, which for an employer means taking risks instead of maximizing security and giving the freedom to innovate, even sometimes to fail. New methods should therefore be preferred to actions that have become routine. How beneficial new information is depends on the structure of the organisation. A mechanical structure aims to save organisational knowledge, an organic structure to renew knowledge, and a dynamic structure to innovate new, better practices (Ståhle *et al.*, 2002).

In the case study organisation, in-service training was regarded as inadequate and lacking in consensus as to priorities. However, employees learned by doing, by guiding each other at work and finding solutions together. This is a practical way of transferring tacit knowledge between employees and of generating new information or knowledge through shared experiences and meanings (Nonaka & Takeuchi, 19955). An unwillingness to share one's knowledge or a lack of shared time- among other hindrances- may obstruct the transfer of tacit knowledge. An organisation geographically scattered or under constant change has poor chances to benefit from the tacit knowledge its members have gained at work (Grönroos, 2003).

In the present study, all eleven interviewees regarded a heavy workload and even burnout as a significant problem in their organisation. Among factors causing burn-out stated in answers, the most common were those connected to the SC. A lack of resources was mentioned by all interviewees in all answers as the culprit causing burnout; employees had been overburdened with work for a long time. Changes in personnel or sick-leaves due to burnouts resulted in a need for those remaining to work overtime, as expressed, for example, as follows:

Burnout, it exists. People have taken other jobs. Meaningless work causes exhaustion; week after week you don't know what you are doing, you can't plan your work, contracts regulate everything, there are too many crisis situations, resourcing is below judgement. It is hard to feel any professional pride; working at a cash desk in a shop wouldn't make any difference to this.

Although good, skilful people, we feel humiliated and treated as slaves. (Person D to the question if they had found burnout in their job).

Customer demands and strictly-restricted assignments were regarded as obstacles to work. Eight out of the eleven study subjects felt that employees could not benefit from their capabilities in their work because of too many strict contracts. All the interviewees were prepared for more challenging tasks. Guiding others was not allocated any resources, and was supposed to happen along with one's own tasks. The most common reasons for exhaustion at work are overburdening, illegibilities, conflicts between aims and roles, a lack of independence and options, boredom at work, and problems connected to interaction (Hakanen, 1999). This study concludes, on the basis of the interviews, that reactive renewal in an organisation increases exhaustion among workers, and in that way has a negative impact on the IC of the organisation.

Proactive Renewal and Wellbeing at Work Close to the Customer

Of those interviewed in the present study, two were working on customer premises, while the remainder worked geographically apart from their customers. These two persons present an interesting exception: they appeared more satisfied with their jobs than the rest, having more freedom to develop their modes of action with customers and make arrangements and interact face-to-face as the following comment shows:

I work quite freely. I use my own relationships for taking care of things. (Person X answers a question about their chance to effect on own tasks).

The majority of those interviewed, by contrast, seemed regulated by agreements and strictly restricted tasks. One of the interviewees also pointed out a deterioration of customer relations after moving away from the customer´s premises. His view of this customer partnership was as follows.

I don´t know, really. The relationship has deteriorated after we moved away from their premises. (Person K answers the question about partner relationships)

In summarising the renewal of customer relations, it can be said that they are still mostly renewed by different requirements and agreements- as the following comment shows:

You really can´t be creative here; we should have more time and better knowledge of the products. If average or even poor quality has been accepted earlier, there really isn´t much motivation to improve the quality later either. In most tasks everything is really boring and strictly specified; all the orders come ready, like, "Do this, and do it exactly like this!" (Person H to the question about using one's full competence at work.)

Unfortunately this type of renewal supports a non-active culture in the organisation, characterised by a lack of confidence with no prospect of active participation to develop working conditions. According to the study, change was possible, but required face-to-face communication with the customer in confidential relationships.

Trust between partners is the key to strategic partnerships. Changes in surroundings put the endurance of the partnerships in a permanent test situation. Two out of three started partnerships fail, according to researchers. A strategic partnership requires- in addition to joint strategy- a shared goal and open actions towards achieving that goal. Everything is based on trust. A successful partnership results in efficiency in costs, predictability, and innovativeness, and benefits all partners (Vihma, 2005). According to Bradley & Vozikis (2004) (cited in Huotari, Hurme & Valkonen, 2005) when building confidence, the emphasis must be on creating an atmosphere for communication that is open and encourages co-operation. For individual skills, of equal importance is a positive attitude towards communication, as well as participation in decision making, and attentiveness. Building confidence requires that versatile abilities communicate. Good practises in co-operation indicate deep trust between partners (Huotari, Hurme & Valkonen, 2005).

The Current State of Intellectual Capital

At the end of the analysis, empirical findings were collected through a SWOT (Strengths, Weaknesses, Opportunities and Threats) analysis, and the organisational strengths, weaknesses, opportunities, and threats could be analysed easily, based on investigation of the interview data. The findings of the study show the principles of a mechanical organisational structure at work, attempting to control an ever-changing environment through typical methods, namely strictly specified work tasks, an excessive amount of reporting, and formal methods of communication with the customer. Moreover, when customer orders are the only input for renewal, an organisation cannot not produce its own goals or proactively renew, which in turn causes a lack of motivation, stress, and even cases of burnout among highly educated personnel. According to many interviewees, the prominent reasons for burnout were the lack of possibility to affect the work environment, a lack of goals, fragmented project work, and inadequate and improper processes for reward and feedback. Stress occurs, states Ek, when individual interests and ambitions do not meet the challenges or possibilities the environment has to offer (Ek, 2000). Threat can also be *reactive renewal* in itself. Knowledge and competence based on customer processes is not the same as the organisation's own competence, and can even be a risk to a business. It is also very likely that professionals will leave the organisation in the long run to seek better opportunities, better financial satisfaction, more respect, and above all a more internally rewarding job. A high level of sick leaves and of experts leaving an organisation should be considered as a warning that the organisation is losing IC and ultimately its competitive advantage (Sveiby, 1997).

Strengths of the case study organisation included a highly educated staff; endeavour towards self-development and developing the work community appeared as strengths in the SWOT analysis. The stuff had- furthermore- homogeneous backgrounds and good relations with co-workers and project managers. A clear opportunity exists for the organisation to utilise personnel more effectively in planning and developing services. Besides the possibility of better services, this would earn the company more profitable results in the long run, not to mention personnel happier about their work. According to Siltala (2004), workers who feel pleasure at work stay healthy, have fewer periods of sick leave, and produce a better outcome than workers continuously on overtime and overburdened.

Figure 3 illustrates the present state of the intellectual capital of the case study organisation, in the frame of the SWOT analysis. The key issues in renewal of the intellectual capital have been taken into account, namely human, structural, and relational capital. Figure 3 summarises the results of the present study in intellectual capital.

DISCUSSION

The findings of this study are based on empirical data from a Finnish ICT company operating in a constantly and rapidly changing environment, in which, tasks and organisation were based on a very strong customer orientation totally determining the sequence, nature, and speed of the experts' work. This study concludes that while it may seem easy to attempt to control a changing work environment with methods familiar from a mechanical organisation structure, such as: strictly regulated tasks; formal reporting; and manager control of

Figure 3. SWOT analysis on the present state of IC

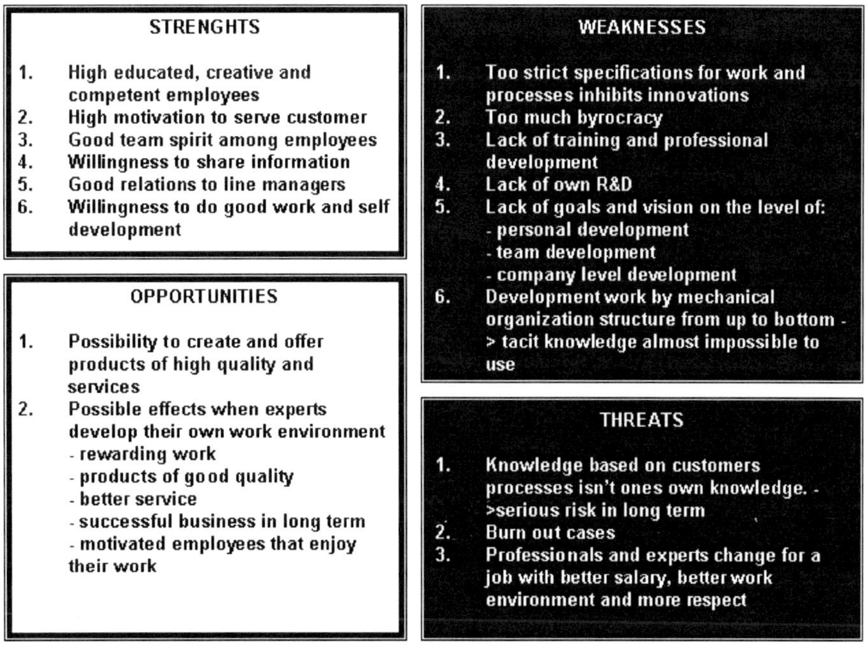

communication and development work. And, this approach does not work in a knowledge-based organisation.

In a knowledge-based organisation, mechanical structural methods cause *reactive renewal* of IC, not *proactive renewal*. They engender a lack of aims in the personal development of highly educated, creative employees, arriving at exhaustion and an absence of motivation. The material studied shows that employees working in customer's premises were more satisfied with their work, because they could regulate their working conditions and content of work and also had an opportunity to learn more effectively. In addition, employees working in customer premises felt that they could benefit the partnership more by better customer contact. Interpersonal communication is the starting point for the renewal of intellectual capital. The key to successful renewal is to support interaction between the customer and the team serving the customer. In-service training is required, and clear short and long-term objectives; also, possibilities to develop the content of the work, and processes producing incentive, processes of evaluation, feedback, and reward. Building a shared strategy and goals is crucial to working with partners (Harrison & Kessels, 2004).

An organisation's culture is a shared reality, is assumptions and unrecorded rules; these either encourage or slow learning. To gain the new, constructive ways of thinking and acting that are necessary to make justifiable decisions, you must also consciously give up old attitudes and beliefs. In the case study organisation, the customer had considerable influence on every facet of activity. The interviews demonstrate that the company's attitude to the customer was an essential part of its culture, but appeared unfavourable to human capital and structural capital, and especially to relational capital.

The interviews indicate, however, that proactive change may be produced when it is seen as valuable, and that it is possible to allocate resources to that change. Two persons working on customer premises felt that they were treated as experts and that their expertise was in full use and appreciated. As experts they also enjoyed appreciation of the customer, who asked for their advice. One employee working on customer premises said she could find better methods of working and could improve actions, meaning that she made the effort to introduce and justify those new ideas to the customer. In these cases, the integration of the IC produced added value for the customer, while mutual confidence in their co-operation increased. This type of activity should be rewarded consistently, giving more employees endurance and a willingness to develop co-operation towards proactive procedures. As a phenomenon this can be called *social intelligence*, meaning good negotiation skills, a deep knowledge of one's own competence, and excellent communication skills (Choo, 2002).

Among the management and personnel department, the outcomes of the study raised interest and they were unaware of the current situation of the IC. Details of the employees' working day had remained unknown to the distant top management and even to middle management. The renewal of intellectual capital among management and its expansion to the borderlines of customer contact would make a fruitful subject for further study, the outcomes of which may contribute to mutual understanding, and lead to better partnerships. So, Figure 4 shows recommendations for actions in the case study organisation.

An organisation reaching towards successful development has its basis of functions in different elements of learning. The keys to the renewal of an organisation are: developing competence management; problem solving abilities; social and communication skills; capability of creating new information; and creating and encouraging an atmosphere for learning. Creative-chaos-producing innovations are also needed, while on the other hand stability and time is necessary for finding and adopting new solutions and practical judgement in routines. The situations in which practical judgement is missing are easily detected, but it seems more complex to define the meaning of practical judgement where routines and learning are concerned (Harrison & Kessels, 2004).

FUTURE RESEARCH

The current situation within global financial markets affects all organisations, even in Finland. General wellbeing at work is an important issue that has been examined within the fields of technology, economics, psychology, and social sciences. This research expands the scope of KM and related Information Management (IM) to wellbeing at work in knowledge-based organisations. In this context, IM is crucial to providing information for the knowledge-based work of

Figure 4. Recommendations for actions in the case study organisation

RECOMMENDATIONS FOR ACTIONS

- Staff should be considered an investment
- Long and short term goals should be clear to everybody
- The Human resource department need to support managers in managing learning and in coordinating the organization´s goals and its needs for learning.
- Evaluation and reward processes that support learning are needed.
- Management that supports learning
- A proactive and goal oriented relationship to the customer
- Shared strategy with the customer
- Better negotiation skills and partnership skills are required.

experts, for which information is seen- among other things- as an input to knowledge processes (Huotari & Iivonen, 2005).

Personal mastery has been used frequently as a concept in organisational learning, in innovations, and in expert organisations. An organisation needs the commitment of employees with personal mastery to achieve its goals, mission, and vision. García-Morales *et al.* (2007) have examined the affect of personal mastery on organisational performance by calculating and analysing the correlations between personal mastery, innovation constructs, and organisational learning. Significant and positive correlations between personal mastery and organisation's performance exist directly and indirectly through organisational learning and innovation, state these authors. Further, organisational learning influences organisational performance positively, both directly and indirectly through organisational innovation (García-Morales, 2007). Also, Lee-Kelley, Blackman & Hurst (2007) demonstrate in their research a relationship between learning organisation theory and the potential to retain knowledge workers. By breaking down the elements of learning organisation, including personal mastery, managers are provided with a better insight on how a learning organisation´s disciplines impact knowledge workers. According to Lee-Kelley, Blackman & Hurst (2007), HR managers should adapt personal mastery to link HR strategies pertaining to challenge, sharing vision and developing holistic systems throughout the organisation (Lee-Kelley, Blackman & Hurst, 2007).

The talents of knowledge workers are put to optimal use through material provisions and especially through an educational environment that furthers personal expertise. This type of climate enhances and stimulates the participation of talented employees in interesting and useful projects in professional networks. Employee surroundings should enhance the development of individual perspective within opportunities for the organisation's strategic objectives (Kessels, 2001). According to Hamel, in every human being are innovation genes that managers and HR leaders simply do not know how to turn on; for that, the theory of innovation is required. Some individuals at certain points in time see opportunities that are invisible to everyone else (Hamel, 2009).

This research aims to increase our understanding of personal mastery in relation to wellbeing at work and to the renewal ability of an information-intensive, knowledge-based organisation. This includes, for example, the following aspects:

- increasing understanding of the relation between effective IM and experts' wellbeing and satisfaction at work;
- indicating the factors including communication and information competencies that affect personal mastery and wellbeing at work;
- increasing understanding of organisational change when communicating internal information processes

Through these aspects the study will contribute to our understanding of the nature of innovative knowledge- based work and its management. Therefore, Figure 5 describes the connection between personal mastery and the organisation.

CONCLUSION

While the limits of transactional ways of interacting are apparent, generating change at a scale that matters often requires engaging large communities of diverse participants with different motivations. All members should share a strong commitment to the success of the organisation as a whole (Senge *et al.*, 2007). On the basis of the attributes of personal mastery, power, and intellectual capital in relation to renewal ability, the following questions can be stated:

Figure 5. The link between personal mastery and the organisation

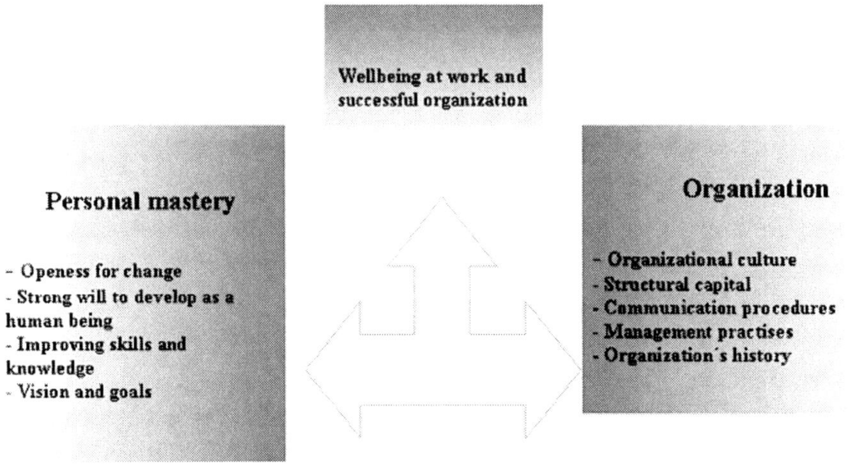

1. What are the main perceived qualities of personal mastery of the experts in case study organisations?;
2. What is the relation of wellbeing at work to carrying out personal mastery in practise?;
3. How are experts able to influence their work environment and tasks at work?;
4. What kind of factors, for instance culture, climate, and structure, affect experts' ability to renew?;
5. What kind of communication infrastructure supports individual and organisational renewal?;
6. How does management philosophy support experts' personal mastery?;
7. What is the difference between change-related formal documentation and face-to-face communication?

An expert's knowledge is power, but the key problem is how to utilise all this potential knowledge within an organisation (Castrén, 2001). This new research project will add knowledge of managing information for knowledge-based work within the fields of technology and health care. Growing interest lies in experts in the ICT field and in medical doctors who are specialists within their fields. My future study will pursue comparisons of the personal mastery of those professionals within their organisations and its management.

Due to the interdisciplinary nature of KM, the results of future research will contribute to the fields of Information Studies, Management Information Systems (MIS), Organisational Communication and Administrative or, Management Sciences. The results will be scrutinised in the most significant domestic and international scientific journals and conferences within these fields.

ACKNOWLEDGMENT

I would like to thank my supervisor, professor Maija-Leena Huotari who gave me help, suggestions, advice and who encouraged me to go ahead with my article. I furthermore would like to thank the Faculty of Humanities in Oulu University for partial funding for this article. Also, I would like to thank Matti McCambridge for correcting English style and grammar of this article. Especially, I would like to give special thanks to my husband Veikko Lohikoski who enabled me to complete this work.

REFERENCES

Alasuutari, P. (1995). *Researching culture: Qualitative method and cultural studies*. Thousand Oaks, CA: Sage Publications.

Argyris, C., & Schön, D. A. (1996). *Organizational learning II. Theory, method, and practise*. Reading, MA: Addison-Wesley Publishing Company.

Aula, P., & Hakala, S. (2000). *Kolmet kasvot. Näkökulmia organisaatioviestintään*. Helsinki: Lokikirjat. (in Finnish)

Bradley, W. E., & Vozikis, G. S. (2004). Trust in virtual teams. In Godar, S. H., & Ferris, S. P. (Eds.), *Virtual and Collaborative Teams: Processes, Technologies and Practice* (pp. 99–113). Hershey, PA: Idea Group Publishing.

Brooking, A. (1996). *Intellectual capital, core asset for the third millennium enterprise*. Boston: International Thomson Business Press.

Castellanos, A. R., Rodriquez, J. L., & Ranguelov, S. Y. (2004). University R&D&T capital: What types of knowledge drive it? *Journal of Intellectual Capital*, *5*(3), 478–499. doi:10.1108/14691930410550417

Castrén, A.-M. (2001). *Perhe ja työ helsingissä ja pietarissa- Elämänpiirit ja yhteiskunta opettajien sosiaalisissa verkostoissa*. Helsinki: Suomalaisen Kirjallisuuden Seura. (in Finnish)

Choo, C. W. (1998). *The knowing organization: How organizations use information to construct meaning, create knowledge and make decisions*. New York: Oxford University Press.

Choo, C. W. (2002). *Information management for the intelligent organization: The art of scanning the environment* (3rd ed.). Medford, NJ: Information Today Inc.

Cook, S. D. N., & Brown, J. S. (1999). Bridging epistemologies: The generative dance between organizational knowledge and organizational knowing. *Organization Science*, *10*(4), 381–400. doi:10.1287/orsc.10.4.381

Edvinsson, L., & Malone, M. S. (1997). *Intellectual capital: Realizing your company's true value by finding its hidden roots*. New York: Harper Business.

Ek, E. (2000). Vaikutusmahdollisuudet työhön ja stressinhallintakeinot- Yhteys psyykkiseen toimintakykyyn. *Työ ja Ihminen, 1*, 15-26 (in Finnish).

García-Morales, V. J., Lloréns-Montes, F. J., & Verdú-Jover, A. J. (2007). Influence of personal mastery on organizational performance through organizational learning and innovation in large firms and SMEs. *Technovation*, *27*(9), 547–568. doi:10.1016/j.technovation.2007.02.013

Grönroos, M. (2003). *Mahdollisuuden aika- Kohti virtuaalista organisaatiota*. Vammala, Finland: Transatlanta. (in Finnish)

Hakanen, J. (1999). Ketkä uupuvat? Miesten ja naisten työuupumus tutkimusten valossa. [in Finnish]. *Työterveiset*, *S2*, 16–18.

Hamel, G. (2009). Innovation masters. *Leadership Excellence, January*, 26-33.

Harrison, R., & Kessels, J. (2004). *Human resource development in a knowledge economy- An organizational view*. New York: Palgrave Macmillan.

Himanen, P., Torvalds, L., & Castells, M. (2001). *Hacker ethic and the spirit of the information age*. New York: Random House.

Hirsjärvi, S., & Hurme, H. (2000). *Tutkimushaastattelu. Teemahaastattelun teoria ja käytäntö*. Helsinki, Finland: Yliopistopaino. (in Finnish)

Hofstede, G. (1993). Cultural constrain in management theories. *The Academy of Management Executive*, *7*(1), 81–94.

Huotari, M.-L., Hurme, P., & Valkonen, T. (2005). *Viestinnästä tietoon. Tiedon luominen työyhteisössä*. Helsinki, Finland: WSOY. (in Finnish)

Huotari, M.-L., & Iivonen, M. (2004). Managing knowledge-based organizations through trust. In Huotari, M.-L., & Iivonen, M. (Eds.), *Trust in Knowledge Management and Systems in Organizations* (pp. 1–29). Hershey, PA: Idea Group Publishing.

Huotari, M.-L., & Iivonen, M. (2005). Knowledge processes: A strategic foundation for the partnership between the university and its library. *Library Management*, *25*(6/7), 324–335. doi:10.1108/01435120410609743

Iivonen, M., & Huotari, M.-L. (2007). The university library's intellectual capital. *Advances in Library Administration and Organization*, *25*, 85–95.

Johannessen, J.-A., Olsen, B., & Olaisen, J. (2005). Intellectual capital as a holistic management philosophy: A theoretical perspective. *International Journal of Information Management*, *25*(2), 151–171. doi:10.1016/j.ijinfomgt.2004.12.008

Kessels, J. W. M. (2001). Learning in organizations: A corporate curriculum for the knowledge economy. *Futures*, *33*(6), 497–506. doi:10.1016/S0016-3287(00)00093-8

Lee-Kelley, L., Blackman, D. A., & Hurst, J. P. (2007). An exploration of the relationship between learning organisations and the retention of knowledge workers. *The Learning Organization*, *14*(3), 204–221. doi:10.1108/09696470710739390

Lönnqvist, A., & Mettänen, P. (2003). *Suorituskyvyn mittaaminen- Tunnusluvut asiantuntijaorganisaation johtamisvälineenä*. Helsinki: Edita. (in Finnish)

Nonaka, I., & Takeuchi, H. (1995). *The knowledge creating company- How Japanese companies create the dynamics of innovation*. New York: Oxford University Press.

Otala, L. (2000). *Oppimisen etu- Kilpailukykyä muutoksessa*. Porvoo, Finland: WSOY. (in Finnish)

Rastas, T., & Einola-Pekkinen, V. (2001). *Arvoa aineettomasta pääomasta*. Tampere, Finland: Tammer-Paino Oy. (in Finnish)

Schein, E. H. (1996). Three cultures of management: The key to organizational learning. *Sloan Management Review*, *38*(1), 9–20.

Schein, E. H. (2004). Learning when and how to lie: A neglected aspect of organizational and occupational socialization. *Human Relations*, *57*(3), 260–273.

Scholtes, P. R. (1997). Tiimit järjestelmien aikakaudella. [in Finnish]. *Yritystalous*, *2*, 59–66.

Seetharaman, A., Sooria, H. H. B. Z., & Saravanan, A. S. (2002). Intellectual capital accounting and reporting in the knowledge economy. *Journal of Intellectual Capital*, *3*(2), 128–148. doi:10.1108/14691930210424734

Senge, P. M. (1990). *The fifth discipline: The art and practice of the learning organization*. New York: Doubleday Business.

Senge, P. M. (2006). *The fifth discipline: The art & practise of the learning organization* (2nd ed.). New York: Doubleday Business.

Senge, P. M. (2007). Collaborating for systemic change. *MIT Sloan Management Review*, *48*(2), 44–53.

Siltala, J. (2004). *Työelämän huonontumisen lyhyt historia. Muutokset hyvinvointivaltioiden ajasta globaaliin hyperkilpailuun*. Keuruu, Finland: Otavan kirjapaino Oy (in Finnish).

Ståhle, P. (2002). *Epävarmuus hallintaan- Yrityksen uudistumiskyky ja vaihtoehdot*. Jyväskylä, Finland: Gummerus Kirjapaino Oy. (in Finnish)

Ståhle, P., & Laento, K. (2000). *Strateginen kumppanuus- Avain uudistumiskykyyn ja ylivoimaan*. Porvoo, Finland: WS Bookwell Oy. (in Finnish)

Stewart, T. A. (1997). *Intellectual capital. The new wealth of organizations*. New York: Currency Doubleday.

Sveiby, K.-E. (1997). *The new organizational wealth- Managing & measuring knowledge based assets*. San Francisco, CA: Berret-Koehler Publishers, Inc.

Torvi, K., & Kiljunen, P. (2005). Onnellisuuden vaikea yhtälö. *Elinkeinoelämän valiokunnan (EVA)*. Retrieved July 30, 2009, from http://www.eva.fi/files/1110_onnellisuuden_vaikea_yhtalo.pdf (in Finnish).

Vihma, P. (2005). Kaikki etsivät kumppaneita. Yritysten yhteistyön hallinta on johtajien päällimmäinen puheenaihe. [in Finnish]. *Talouselämä*, *5*, 22–27.

Yates-Mercer, P., & Bawden, D. (2002). Managing the paradox: the valuation of knowledge and knowledge management. *Journal of Information Science*, *28*(1), 19–29. doi:10.1177/016555150202800103

ADDITIONAL READING

Aro, A. (2001). *On niin kiire, ettei ehdi tehdä mitään*. Helsinki: Edita. (in Finnish)

Mintzberg, H., Lampel, J., & Ahlstrand, B. (2005). *Strategy safari: A guided tour through the wilds of strategic management*. New York, NY: Free Press.

Siess, J. A. (2003). *The visible librarian: Asserting your value with marketing and advocacy*. Chicago, IL: American Library Association.

Ståhle, P., & Grönroos, M. (2000). *Dynamic intellectual capital- Knowledge management in theory and practise*. Vantaa: Tummavuoren Kirjapaino Oy. (in Finnish)

KEY TERMS AND DEFINITIONS

Human Resources: It includes all the existing personnel inside an organisation. Is the most important asset within a learning organisation, because personal mastery is commonly an individual feature, however human resources management policies seem to neglect this reality.

Intellectual Capital: A set of knowledge that creates, or might create value for the organisation in a near future. Its components are: human capital (encompasses workers explicit and tacit knowledge); structural capital (characterizes internal processes); and, customer capital (includes an organisation's relationships).

Learning Organisation: An organisation that in which all systems, processes, and structures- at all levels (individual, group, department, system-as-a-whole)- constantly seek data on system performance, and use it at all levels to make the organization more productive/creative now (integration), as well as simultaneously allows it to achieve a successful organisational position in an uncertain environment (adaptation).

Organisational Culture: Can be resumed as the way organisations recognize themselves. It is based on history and structure, giving a sense of identity: "who we are"; "what we stand for"; "what we do". It determines the existing organisational procedures.

Personal Mastery: Enables an individual feature, and implies a high level of proficiency: personal and professional.

Renewal Ability: Encompasses two levels: an individual; and, a collective. Related to the ability to people execute practical procedures or, how an organisation executes its strategy and adjusts to the changing environment.

Chapter 11
The Importance of Balancing Knowledge Protection and Knowledge Interchange

Yutaka Takahashi
Senshu University, Japan

ABSTRACT

Business organisations are aware of the importance of knowledge to keep and acquire competitiveness, so willing to find and keep knowledge holders in their organisations. However, employees in many developed countries have freedom to choose what to do for their living; it is possible a suddenly leave regarding their current jobs and get a new job elsewhere. This is a great loss for the former employer, because it means that not only the knowledge holders themselves but also their knowledge leaves the former business. Moreover, this knowledge would be beneficial for the new employers which are often competitors of the former employers. In order to avoid this kind of brain drain, employers often require that employees sign non-disclosure and non-compete agreements. Nevertheless, this request can cause some trouble in the long run. This chapter shows the structures causing this trouble and how to deal with it using the systems thinking approach.

INTRODUCTION

Knowledge and knowledge holders are crucial resources for competitive business organisations. Baskerville & Dulipovici (2006) indicate two classifications for knowledge: organizational knowledge and personal knowledge. If knowledge is dealt with as organizational knowledge, the rights concerning knowledge of the organization, knowledge acquirer, should be protected as the organization's property. On the other hand, the rights of a person, the knowledge holder, would be protected when the knowledge is classified into personal knowledge. Teece (2000) defines organizational knowledge as information being incorporated in organizations' activities. Naturally, such knowledge can be either articulated or tacit (Hedlund, 1994). Griffith, Sawyer & Neale (2003) give more detailed classification; organizational knowledge should be articulated and captured by

DOI: 10.4018/978-1-61520-873-9.ch011

some systems like information technology, and on the other hand, tacit knowledge in an organization would be called social knowledge. Myers (1996) illustrates that personal knowledge should be recognized as an attribute of its knowledge holder. Fahey & Prusak (1998) define knowledge as something known by someone. They stress the points that knowledge is produced only by knowledge holders and that knowledge acquired by organizations and embedded to task routines is always incomplete. Davenport & Prusak (1998) define knowledge as a mixture of experience, values based on contextual information, and insights. This thought is clearly based on the idea that knowledge is produced, matured, and used in knowledge holders' heads (Gottschalk, 2005).

The current ubiquitous computing society provides free or low cost access to various kinds of information; information is stored in computer devices, and these are mutually connected as a network. Such online information can be accessed by anyone with a computer. Besides, information can be accessed by ones who are not authentic creators, nor-owners of the information, and such access can also stimulate someone to create new value. This means that just storing or collecting much information no longer improves competitiveness of business players. This is completely different from tangible properties. Knowledge, which is the form of "a fluid mix of framed experience, values, contextual information, and expert insight that provides a framework for evaluating and incorporating new experiences and information" (Davenport & Prusak, 1998, p. 5), needs "a constant renewal through the accumulation process" (Costa & Silva, 2007, p. 125). Recently, knowledge is still more important in order for business people and organizations to be competitive than ever. The highly uncertain current situation requires us to solve new problems one after another using knowledge. Knowledge is not a product itself; using knowledge can produce something. Hiding or limiting use of knowledge does not earn anything. Rather, it would simply waste resources. Knowledge comprises information, and information reveals itself when being used (Arrow, 1962). Dealing with knowledge like a tangible or scarce resource may lead organisations to inefficient knowledge use and result in lowering organisations' competitiveness for obtaining consumers' advocacy.

Although managers and organizations are aware of the importance of knowledge, they often fail in knowledge management; companies lose knowledgeable employees despite the attempt to keep them within the organisations, or companies cannot see innovations despite the introduction of knowledge management software packages. One of the reasons that knowledge is lost within their organisations is the lack of balance between knowledge protection and knowledge interchange; they deal with knowledge like old physical assets, such as machinery. Indeed, precious, physical commodities should be safely kept in order not to be stolen. These commodities are valuable only for the current owners. Holding the commodities is important in being competent. However, knowledge does not disappear when being used. Rather, the use of knowledge yields profit. If knowledge is captured by other people, the original owner of the knowledge can still use the knowledge. It is possible that the relative personal competitiveness of the original knowledge owner might be temporarily damaged. However, how knowledge is utilized depends on the knowledge acquirers' ability. Tacit knowledge is often regarded as important knowledge, but at the same time, such knowledge would be hard to use soon after its acquisition. This means knowledge sharing does not directly lead to invalidation of the original knowledge holders' personal competitiveness.

Nevertheless, many organisations still only pay attention to how to protect knowledge. One of the most clearly described forms of knowledge protection is the non-compete and non-disclosure agreements, and these contracts are commonplace (Gayton, 2008). Non-compete agreement forbids employees to leave for the current employers' competitors, and non-disclosure means that employees must not disclose information obtained in their jobs. These agreements are comprehensive contracts to ensure that employees never use their knowledge for their employers' competitors. The agreements impose too stringent limitations on employees; it is possible that employees may not be able to work for another company in the future even when a former employer stops the business. They make employees feel anxious about their lives, although many developed countries secure rights for citizens to be free from fear and to choose one's job based on one's volition. Gayton (2008) argues that the agreements are now of a "one size fits all" design and should be "tailored to economic realities of both" (p. 181), employers and employees. In addition, economic situations and interests are diverse among people, organisations, and industries, and change over time.

Simple applications of past solutions do not always work well again because of changes in conditions and circumstances. Moreover, our intervention might cause counterintuitive behaviour (Forrester, 1971), and sometimes "yesterday's solutions become today's problems" (Sterman, 2001, p. 13). These unsuccessful interventions bring about further unexpected or unappreciated reactions or resistances (Meadows, 1982). This means that cumulative data or information cannot suffice in coping with real problems. Contextual meaning and understanding causality are important. People usually focus on events, as opposed to causality. One does something with a certain expectation. However, outcomes may differ from the expectation. In such cases, one feels that investment or effort is insufficient or that the circumstances are "complex." Nevertheless, it is not always true; everything is not always complicated with uncertainty and untraceable causal connections. Although structures around the object are simple, the performance of systems can be unexpected when they contain feedback loop structures (Sterman, 1989). Indeed, causalities often, or almost always, move in circular ways, called feedback loops. For example, the difficulty in holding the balance comes from the facts that every action and its influence change employees' decisions made in future, and these decisions also influence managers' and employees' decisions, attitudes, learning, and self-confidence in the further future; they comprise feedback loops around knowledge protection activities.

In this chapter, feedback loops mean circular sequences of causalities with a consistent direction, not advice or critique transactions. One change brings about another element's change, and this change consequently leads to a status change of the element which triggered the original change. A feedback loop is a powerful structure that influences or regulates performance of whole objective systems. Systems' structures comprising feedback loops have strong influences on their performance. Feedback systems steadily resist interventions or pressure produced by elements outside the systems; systems often seem to change their performance reflecting an intervention but soon go back to their original courses, although someone intervenes in the system. It is often difficult to understand feedback structures and make appropriate decisions for people who are inside systems including feedback structures or people whose research interests have feedback loops, as "cause and effect are often distant in time and space" (Sterman, 2000, p. 11) in such systems.

Employers have enjoyed significant rights over their employees' future because employers would be able to forbid them using any knowledge for any future employers because of the non-disclosure and non-compete agreements (Gayton, 2007). Nevertheless, these agreements would reduce their companies' competitiveness. Managers' experience in maintaining conditions which help to generate knowledge is important. However, it is not enough to have rich experience; managers and corporate governors need to understand the effect of feedback loops behind knowledge management in order to "hit the spot" when hoping for continuous growth. Otherwise, any policy which keeps people inside, encourages them to generate knowledge with great effort, and is in defiance of the effect of feedback loops, is only wasted.

Computer software packages, such as knowledge management systems, cannot currently offer full functions for knowledge interchange. In other words, there are possibilities that human managers are requested to do many things concerning knowledge management, including making sound agreements and contracts.

This chapter shows the causal loop structures which consist of knowledge protection through the agreements and knowledge interchange activities and then analyses them using the systems thinking (qualitative system dynamics) method. Observing this structure, one can understand elements which should be really controlled and the importance of balancing the influences of feedback loops to promote knowledge creation and utilisation. The analyses support the idea of relaxing this kind of strong restriction for knowledge workers in order to obtain and keep whole competitiveness of business organisations. This would be particularly effective in fast "clockspeed" (Fine, 1998) industries, such as information technology industry.

The systems thinking method is independent of one's sense of value. This is important in proposing generic ideas. Existing debates or guidelines have different standpoints, most of which employ normative theories. Knowledge management activities are naturally business activities. Thus, knowledge management should need to pay great attention to business ethics. Schmidt (2000) points out the fact that most business ethics textbooks deal with teleology and deontology. Teleology is the theory that states one always has a certain purpose so that one ought to choose the most rational and reasonable methods to serve the purpose. Deontology is another theory that one should conduct everything in reference to moral and ethics regardless of the purposes or results.

These normative ethics theories help one to choose a correct or appropriate activity when one is in a problematic or dilemmatic situation. Even in the field of knowledge management, it is not uncommon that normative theories sometimes give different answers to the same question because the ethical criteria are completely different between people and situations. For example, how much knowledge should employees share in private (inside organization) using a Social Network System (SNS)? Suppose that one faces a dilemmatic situation. One accepts the idea that an employer requests all employees to share their knowledge through SNS, a deontological answer would be that one should post all knowledge online. One is a member of a project team and sincerely hopes for the growth of the company. At the same time, one knows that some knowledge is also craved by other project teams. However, one believes that other teams might poorly deal with the information. In this situation, keeping the information secret would be correct from a teleological viewpoint.

Deontology might look less flexible than teleology because deontological suggestions set rigid criteria and teleological suggestions depend on the people and circumstances concerned. Nevertheless, there is no difference of rigidness between deontology and teleology. Norms, which provide bases for deontological ideas, are contingent on one's belief. Different religions, different geographical areas, and different positions in an organization contribute to setting different norms.

These normative theories are mainly implemented when one faces a dilemma (Schmidt, 2000). Now, one question arises: what kind of dilemmatic situations do knowledge holders or, knowledge acquirers' face when contracting the non-compete and non-disclosure agreements? One needs no decision process in reference to ethics when one is in situations with not only explicit personal rules nut also public legislation. In this situation, everyone must obey the rules. Otherwise, one can face the risk of accusation, or even dismissal.

Indeed, there is no explicit dilemma before nor after signing the agreements; an organisation maintains its knowledge workers and their knowledge in order to continue to be competitive for longer, and an employee would hope for the success of his or her employer organisation while he or she is hired. After signing the agreements, there are clearly contracts which should be complied with. However, there are no contracts, common senses of value, and common purposes before signing the agreements. In this situation, both employers and employees face no dilemma; they can pursue their own interests.

On the other hand, there is a significant difference in attitudes between employers and employees. As knowledge acquirers, organisations naturally hope to maintain their rights indefinitely. As knowledge holders, employees hope to terminate the agreement after their resignation. Normative theories cannot answer the question whether organisations should maintain the strict agreement thereafter or not because there is no dilemma. Therefore, this chapter employs no normative theories as tools to clarify and solve problems around the agreements. There is a quantitative difference in preferable length of time of agreements between employers and employees, so this chapter employs logical approach, systems thinking.

BACKGROUND

Because of the importance of knowledge, it is generally accepted that business organisations require knowledge workers to sign non-disclosure and non-compete agreements when hiring them. These contracts, or restrictions for employees' conducts, are bases of business organisations' knowledge management in order to keep and increase the business organisations' competitiveness. This employers' behaviour would look unethical because they eliminate their employees' right to choose and freely change their jobs or employers, although right to freely choose employments is secured for many employees in many developed countries. Moreover, at the time of recruitment, potential employees are not in a strong position, compared with their employers (Gayton, 2008). If they are unwilling to miss out on imminent job opportunities, their practical choice is to sign the agreement regardless of their thought on the agreements. This unbalanced condition between employers and employees can be also regarded as unethical.

UN (2005) indicates the importance of personal privacy protection when knowledge holders negotiate their labour conditions without worrying over privacy rights. On the other hand, prospective employers also have their reason to be cautious in evaluating knowledge holders highly; this may increase the cost of human resource, often the most expensive resource to employers. In addition to the inflexible agreement, some job applicants accept low remuneration despite their specialism. Arrow (1962) points out a fundamental paradox that the value of information and knowledge is not clear for potential information buyers so that potential buyers would estimate the value of incompletely appropriable information less than optimal evaluation. This situation gives managers a reason not to pay high remuneration to their knowledge workers.

Thus, both sides have their reasons to dislike and prefer the non-compete and non-disclosure agreements. However, if the agreements are unethical or at least problematic, employees and some employers might gradually feel more stress and change their attitudes and strategies to obtain and keep knowledge profitable for business. This might lead to the situation that employer's who prefer the agreements might lose excellent knowledge holders due to tough competition from other employers to hire high quality knowledge workers in the human resource market. Consequently, such employers might face difficulties in business growth.

However, regardless of the decision whether the agreements' effects on employers' behaviours are ethical or not, the agreements actually cause problems for knowledge workers throughout their careers. There have been many lawsuits concerning non-compete and non-disclosure agreements. This chapter introduces two examples that have appeared in the existing research. In order to show what kind of troubles can happen, both cases are ones that employees face relatively unbalanced, unfair, or unethical, from some viewpoints, conditions. Readers should notice that a country or region has its own restrictions to enforce or invalidate non-compete and non-disclosure agreements. The variety of restrictions is shown afterwards.

One case is referred to in Gayton (2008), which is a court case in the United States, *Advanced Marine Enterprise, Inc versus PRC, Inc.* in 1998. In this case, PRC employees were laid off due to PRC reason that PRC was going to sell one of its business sections to another company, and consequently, some of employees in the section were recruited by Advanced Marine Enterprise. After Advanced Marine Enterprise offered jobs to former PRC employees, PRC brought a suit against Advanced Marine Enterprise and former PRC employees. The original reason of the lay-off was that the PRC decided to abandon the business. When the employees were fired, PRC was no longer business which could compete with American Marine Enterprise. Nevertheless, PRC ultimately won the trial.

Another case is shown in Baskerville & Dulipovici (2006), a court case of Evan Brown versus DSC Communications and Alcatel USA, two parties was later merged. While Brown was working for DSC Communications, he developed a new idea. DSC (Alcatel, afterward) filed a suit against Brown after his resignation because he refused to relinquish his rights to the ideas he developed. He insisted that the idea was mainly drawn up in his vacation time, so his idea was his own property and not DSC Communications. Eventually, the DSC won the case.

These examples show that knowledge workers are actually restricted in choosing an appropriate job when they want to change employment while under the agreement. This is natural because the agreement is a contract and should be complied with after signing it even if it looks (partly) unethical. It would be also supported from a contractualism viewpoint. Contractualism gives importance on contracts and agreements more than circumstances, and Scanlon (1998) expresses contractualism's attitude like that "an act is wrong if it would be disallowed by any *principle* that no one could reasonably reject" (p. 197). Nevertheless, it could be also considered unethical both because the condition is unbalanced between employers and employees at the time of signing and because employers deny the freedom of job choice to employees with normative criteria, as mentioned above. Of course, knowledge workers might leave or choose less severe working conditions, which would be disagreeable situation for former employers. To avoid this situation, employers emphasise the importance of the non-compete agreement.

Even if they stay in their current jobs, the agreements paradoxically injure companies' performance. Under the non-compete agreement, knowledge workers' attitudes would be also self-protective regarding their companies and colleagues, or at least secretive. The reason for this is that employees want to be competitive in their organisations in order to secure their jobs, because they do not have a choice to go to another company. Otherwise, they might be fired because their specialism is no longer exclusive to them, and they are therefore not required by the company. Wang (2004) explains that severe competition among employees makes them self-protective, and the possibility of generating new knowledge is lowered. This means the whole competitiveness of the business organisation might be damaged in the long run. In order to extract knowledge from protective knowledge workers, it would be possible to introduce rules and systems to share forcibly knowledge in an organisation. However, it means to let people do "free ride" on another's efforts. This would be considered as an unethical attitude. Without sufficient respect for knowledge creators and practical sanctions against knowledge free-riders, no knowledge resource would be offered. The morale needs to be integrated into institutional rules and systems (Costa, Prior & Rogerson, 2008). Likewise, any cause of unethical attitude should be eliminated from rules and systems. Thus, forcible knowledge sharing would not function.

Moreover, new knowledge has a characteristic that it can be generated when existing knowledge is mixed with or stimulated by other knowledge or information. Making employees self-protective might prevent knowledge generation and sharing inside organisations. This means that the overprotective human resource control might lead to a decline in business competitiveness. Besides, Arrow (1962) indicates the fact that legal constraints on knowledge holders might lead to under-investment in innovation. Employers need to recognize the weak points of the non-disclosure and non-compete agreements.

One might consider that this protective policy is still reasonable for most managers because current merits look over-important. However, an overprotective policy on knowledge management results in reducing knowledge interchange between people inactive. Indeed, active interchanges of ideas are important for knowledge workers because they need opportunities not only to learn new ideas but also to build and maintain relationships with other people. As Bock *et al.* (2005) explain organisations' performance depends on their own employees' abilities to share their knowledge.

Whittaker, Burns & Bereven (2003) noted that social capital enables knowledge transfer. One of the tangible forms of such social capital would be information technology, such as knowledge management systems. However, simply retrieving information is different from knowledge transfer. It is important that knowledge givers and receivers share a common intellectual background, or "redundancy" (Nonaka & Takeuchi, 1995).

The non-disclosure agreement would be effective in increasing temporary competitiveness. However, the attitude behind this agreement would reduce the chance of collaborations, such as what O'Reilly (2005) refers to as "mash up" in Web 2.0 situation. In the current business situation where all conditions are changing with bewildering rapidity, such short term competitiveness is less important in the long run. In addition, using information brings about the situation that users or recipients know all or part of the information and knowledge; Arrow (1962) explains that a characteristic of information is that its use necessitates it to be revealed, so that legal restrictions, such as intellectual property rights, can only work partly. Rather, knowledge should be raised not only by people in an organisation but also by people outside the organisation, in order to catch up with the speed of changes in society.

Information technology businesses and World Wide Web services face difficulties brought about by old and current style of overprotective ideas behind the non-compete and non-disclosure agreements. In almost the whole history of commercial software, programs' source codes are proprietary and secret information, because they are an integration of engineers' knowledge. Companies invest many resources in order to release their software. They believe their business cannot continue unless they keep the contents of their software secret because no one buys their software when someone reproduces it and distribute it at a lower price or free of charge. Thus, software vendors and service providers protect their knowledge.

Nonetheless, in the age of Web 2.0 (O'Reilly, 2005), making source codes partially available publicly has begun to have a good effect on business. Many software packages and web services have opened their application programming interface (API) and rich sample codes in uncomplicated scripting languages. Users and other companies make their own interface or additional services for existing Web 2.0 services, which leads to an enrichment of the existing sites' services. Then, users increasingly depend on original service providers; sites using other existing service providers contribute to the original existing sites. These phenomena are achieved by offering free access to part of the source code which used to be hidden in proprietary software distribution. It might be different from the completely free circumstances around software. Rather, it can be a modern "feudalism" as Lessig (2004) indicated. Nevertheless, the conditions around software and knowledge related products and services are now changing from overprotective to open. There are also other ideas about software coding and distribution. In contrast to proprietary software, The Free Software Foundation (2009), led by Richard Stallman, proposes "free software" and "copyleft." It is possible that these different streams of ideas for knowledge usage can affect a major protective commercial stream. Von Hippel (2005), states that innovation and knowledge are democratized. Indeed, offering free access to the source codes by software developers has begun, and this has helped companies achieve significant business success. Successful new service providers are likewise opening up some of their API, and this is having a positive effect on business.

The trouble is that it is difficult to control or adjust the degree of "knowledge protection." First of all, it is doubtful to state that weakening knowledge protection is possible. The examples shown above are the cases in the situation which completely enforces the non-competence and non-disclosure agreements. Yet, there are some countries and regions which limit the efficacy of the agreements in order to protect employees' rights concerning their lives and jobs. For example, In Germany, the duration of the agreements is restricted to at most two years, and employers need to pay compensation for the agreements to employees in accordance with German Law, HGB 74.

Japan has no substantive enactment of the duration limit and compensation rules for the non-compete and non-disclosure agreements. However, Japan's courts use criteria based on judicial precedents. One model case was the "Foseco Japan Limited" case (Nara District Court, Japan, 23 October 1970). The court supported subsequently the validity of the agreements. The importance of this judgement is that it set limits practically on the valid duration and geographic area of the agreements. Moreover, this judgement indicated the fundamental idea that workers whose activities are restricted, such as looking for a new job, by the agreements must be a specialist, such as a person who knows trade secrets or other critical information, and that workers should be compensated for the inconvenience caused by the limitation of his or her activities. In the Foseco Japan Limited case, the company paid compensation for keeping the agreements during employment. Therefore, the court supported the company's argument.

After this judgement, Japanese courts have consistently returned verdicts similar to the Foseco Japan Limited case. Indeed, some former employees and board members have won their cases. A former auditor of Tokyo Legal Mind K.K. won his lawsuit (Tokyo District Court, 6 October 1995); the agreement was invalid because the compensation was too small. In another case, Tokyo District Court decided to deny the validity of the agreements between Tau Corporation and its former employees because the former workers' knowledge was not very critical to the company and the duration of the agreements was relatively too long (9 October 2002). On the other hand, there have been also judgements supporting the validity of the agreements. Tokyo District Court ordered that a former board member of French F&B Co., Ltd. must keep the agreement because the compensation was sufficient (4 October 1993). In another case, Yamada Denki Co., Ltd won a lawsuit against its former store manager because the court decided that the manager held trade information and related knowledge; the judgement resulted from the idea that the manager was recognised as a knowledge worker (Tokyo District Court, 24 April 2007).

Limiting the agreements' duration, geographic areas, and occupational categories is basically helpful and meaningful to protect knowledge workers. However, it is still unclear whether restrictions by the agreements are necessary and beneficial for businesses or not. The law and court decisions are currently still based on the existence of the agreements and separate, individual conditions. As a result, knowledge workers are often unsure whether they are free from constraints of agreements or not. Besides, courts in Japan seem to be still seeking the best criteria for issues concerning the agreements.

Indeed, knowledge is an advantage, more so than technology (Davenport & Prusak, 1998). Companies naturally tend to protect their knowledge and keep it proprietary. Nevertheless, for example in the computer science field, protection of source code is not compatible with the current situation, including the success of open source software and World Wide Web (WWW) services, as shown above.

Therefore, this chapter shows the causal structures which support the ideas that setting an appropriate degree of knowledge protection is profitable, and also those companies need to stop excessively tightening knowledge protection to keep their competitiveness. Observing these structures also allow us to discuss the pertinent issues in promoting knowledge cultivation, beyond simple protection. This is not a maverick opinion. Indeed, the agreements are invalid in California, the United States, in accordance with Business and Professions Code, section 16600-16607. Moreover, some researchers and business people have indicated the disadvantage of strict enforcement of the non-compete and non-disclosure agreements. Lessig (2006, p. 181) states "the balance of rights with intellectual property differs from the balance with ordinary real or personal property." Spinello & Tavani (2005) introduces the example that the United States court stated that "intellectual property rights do not give copyright holders immunity from obeying antitrust law" (p. 56); the court expects that the intellectual property rights should not prevent sound business activities and market competition. Moreover, in the panel discussion at Harvard University on 19th June 2008, panellists concluded that the agreements would stifle innovations and make hesitate to start new business (Berkman Center for Internet & Society, 2008). In this panel discussion, it is pointed out that the empirical data concerning the agreements' effects should be accumulated more. Although such empirical data are still being collected, the structure causing troubles not only with knowledge workers but also with organisations can be illustrated using systems thinking diagrams. The diagrams shown afterwards assist us to consider the power or rights balance between knowledge workers and employers with the agreements.

Of course, as Gayton (2007) points out, the importance of legislation on current intellectual property rights in most developed countries should be respected. Nevertheless, she proposes the need for a new scheme to protect intellectual property and knowledge not only for knowledge holders but also for knowledge acquirers. In order to achieve this, balancing knowledge protection and cultivation is crucial. This chapter provides evidence that suggests that there are common structures concerning issues related to the agreements and the importance of relaxing the agreements. Of course, the evidence is consistent with the purpose of the property legislations.

THE NON-COMPETE AND NON-DISCLOSURE AGREEMENT STRUCTURE

The non-compete and non-disclosure agreements are not only simply contracts but also catalysts that influence knowledge workers' attitudes. The agreements shackle knowledge workers to their current jobs. This means that knowledge workers are increasingly unwilling to concentrate on their jobs under the agreements. Rather, their devotion to their jobs declines. This would naturally adversely affect knowledge acquirers' performance in the long run. This process is caused not by laziness of employers or employees but by the causal structure among people involved in the agreements.

In this section, the non-compete and non-disclosure agreements structure is analysed using the system dynamics method. System dynamics is "a rigorous method for qualitative description, exploration and analysis of complex systems in terms of their processes, information, organisational boundaries and strategies" (Wolstenholme, 1990, p. 3). The following analyses use causal loop diagrams which allow an examination of the object system's characteristics using a qualitative method of system dynamics. Causal structures work logically without exception. When systems are stimulated, causal structures continuously drive systems in a consistent direction. Even if an element within the system tries to adjust or intervene in the systems' transitions, the system's consistent changing direction cannot be controlled because the change is caused not by lack of deontological or teleological ethics of people within the system but by physical causalities. This approach, based on physical causalities, is independent of any sense of value so that its analyses are generally acceptable regardless of the culture of organisations.

Securing Job Positions

The non-compete and non-disclosure agreements restrain employees from using their knowledge to seek another job. In order to express this, the model here employs the variable "length of time of the agreements". As illustrated above, there would be a gap in preferred length of time of the agreements between knowledge holders and knowledge acquirers; knowledge holders prefer the length of time to be shorter, whereas knowledge acquirers prefer it to be longer. This gap is one of switches bringing about change of states. Relatively longer agreements time reduce employees' opportunities for future job changes. When employees believe that they have the potential to be hired by another employer at the time they lose their current jobs, they might not be committed to current jobs. Still, under the agreements, employees might hope to secure their positions and try to get promoted inside their companies. This attitude brings about each knowledge worker's knowledge protection because they do not want lose their personal competitiveness. Trauth (1999) points out the possibility that employees are reluctant to share knowledge in order to protect their professional value. In the long run, companies would fail to accumulate knowledge within companies. This causes companies to lose their competitiveness. Consequently, lower performance of companies has a bad effect on job security. This leads to stronger "temporary commitments to current jobs" of employees. Temporary commitments are based not on the devotion to current jobs but on fear of dismissal, so these commitments are temporary. When knowledge workers recognise one of the above conditions, this structure makes companies' performance suffer. The causal loop diagram is shown in Figure 1. It has a reinforcing loop so that the organisations' performance changes are consistent once started.

Figure 1. Securing job position structure

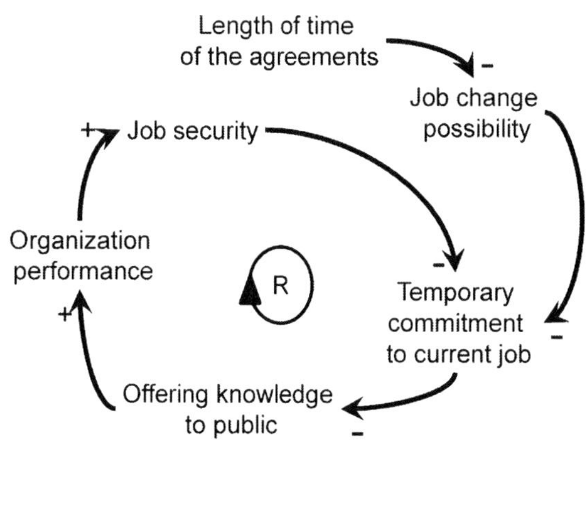

Working Conditions

When employees tend to stay in their current jobs and not to seek other better working conditions, employers would have little or no incentive to improve working conditions. Of course, there are many employers who have a strong belief that they shall treat employees well, which is an attitude based on deontological reasons. On the other hand, many other employers control their employees working conditions in order to make them focus on their work targets, which is an attitude from teleological reasons. However, these micro, person-oriented reasons for dealing with personnel might be easily changed by factors, such as recessions or senior managers' opinions.

Working conditions influence organisations' attractiveness to current employees. Therefore, this structure has a balancing (adjusting) process, shown in Figure 2. This adjustment does not always work. If there are sufficient applicants for vacant posts, working condition improvement might not appear. Nevertheless, this chapter deals with only knowledge workers; such workers are relatively limited. There are many talented people on the earth, but people who have a certain knowledge which contributes to a certain problem in a company are limited by practicalities. Thus, knowledge workers have a relatively stronger power or higher chance of adjusting their working conditions, compared with non-knowledge workers.

Figure 2. Working conditions and temporary commitment to current job

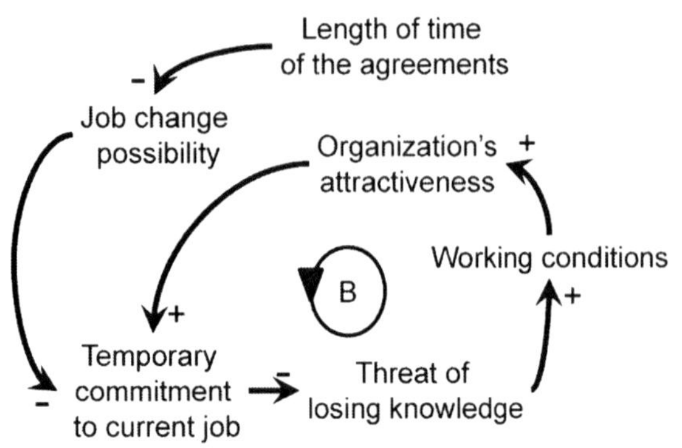

Attractiveness to Outside People

Figure 2 expresses the working environment around current employees. But, organisations' attitudes also change their own attractiveness to people outside the company at the same time. One possibility of such people is prospective employees. They might not apply for a vacant post at the present, but companies' cumulative reputations and performances influence the attitudes of knowledge holders in the human resource markets.

As illustrated in the previous subsection, knowledge workers who match the requirement of a company in a certain knowledge requiring situation are actually limited in number. If a company hopes to hire appropriate knowledge holders, its reputation and performance should be well maintained. Otherwise, really competitive people would not give the slightest attention even if offered higher salaries. Knowledge holders often have networks across organisational borders, and inside circumstances, such as working conditions, also influence the people outside their companies. This structure is shown in Figure 3.

Figure 3. Influence across organisational borders

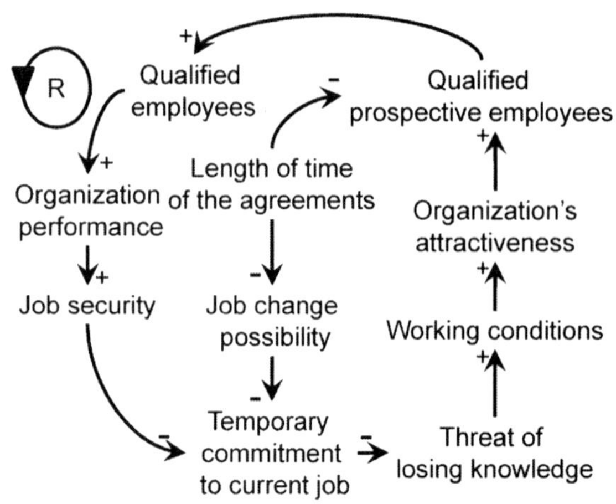

Holding Qualified Employees

Organisations' performances directly determine the stability of their businesses. Skilled and well experienced knowledge workers could not ignore their companies' performance, even if they have significant potential to be hired after quitting their current job. Unstable conditions around employees do not allow employees to plan their futures and they are concerned about their future careers so that their devotion for and concentration on, current jobs might be lost. This is not particular to knowledge workers but the general situation for people regardless of their job type. Figure 4 expresses this structure.

Whole System

All causal loop diagrams above are interconnected (Figure 5). The system has three reinforcing loops, shown in Figure 1, 3, and 4, and one balancing loop, shown in Figure 2.

All reinforcing loops bring one of two results: a continuous growth or inevitable crash. Both are generated by the same structure. This depends on a trigger, stimulus, or a change of state in the elements of a system. If an element slightly changes when the system is stable, a system moves as if it is a train on rails. After starting the movement, ordinary impacts cannot change the direction of movement, nor stop it.

The difficult point shown in this diagram (Figure 5) is that all reinforcing loops are impacted on by the same one element "length of time of the agreements". Moreover, the direction of change on each element is the same. This means that the controllability of the whole system is very limited because an intervention to all loops is difficult and intervention to each loop in turn is ineffective.

The most serious problem is that the source of impact on the reinforcing loops is only to recognise longer "length of time of the agreements". This leads organisations to lose their competitiveness: both in terms of good performance and qualified knowledge workers. One balancing loop (Figure 2) might be a control lever; the balancing loop can seek a goal. Nevertheless, this loop's efficacy is limited. The reason is that job seekers and employees are in a relatively weak position to state their opinion or, negotiate their working conditions than are the employers (Gayton, 2008). Therefore, this system has no realistic brake when the system starts to rush into a crash.

During the time when almost all companies are employing this system structure, one company does not face such severe conditions because its competitors are also struggling in the same situa-

Figure 4. Job security and the stability of employees

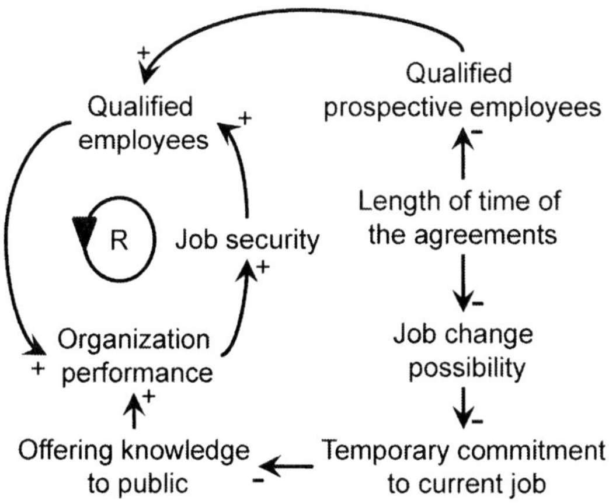

Figure 5. Whole systems

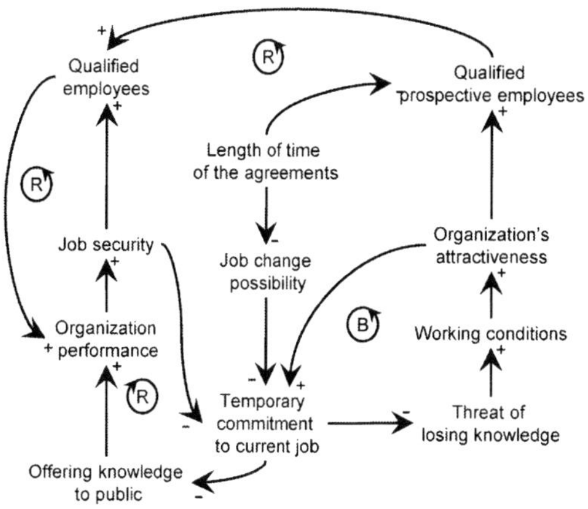

tion. However, if companies start to increasingly change their protective attitudes; other companies that might not be aware of the need for change might face severe competition, especially in the R & D area and human resource markets.

DISCUSSION

In order to eliminate some aspects of the agreements damaging companies' competitiveness, it is necessary to lessen loops' effect. For this purpose, there are two options: cutting the loop and inserting a new loop with the opposite direction.

In this case, cutting reinforcing loops is challenging; each reinforcing loop has an aspect that works as an engine for growth. Nonetheless, the link from "temporary commitment to job" to "offering knowledge" in Figure 1 is one of the keys to this. If a manager repeatedly assert that one's specialism and superiority cannot be easily removed, it is possible that employees could start opening their mouths and offer their knowledge. Knowledge transfer is always challenging because knowledge cannot be acquired without cumulative real experience. As Cohen & Prusak (2001, p. 66) indicate, "knowledge tends to be local, sticky, and contextual". This means that the common background, which is called "redundancy" by Nonaka & Takeuchi (1995), is required to share and transfer knowledge. Therefore, building and keeping social relationships is important and an inevitable aspect of knowledge creation and utilization. Cohen & Prusak (2001) also explain that providing such opportunities and places, which is "Ba" explained by Nonaka & Konno (1998), for knowledge workers means that they "earn their keep as social capital investments" (p. 47). There is another view about knowledge; Teece (2000) explains that some of this knowledge is useful only in particular circumstances, whose conditions are the same as those of knowledge working. Therefore, this kind of tacit knowledge would not be very important for organizations, because each circumstance has its own conditions. Supporting this view is the idea that simple knowledge transfer is naturally unrelated to job security issues.

Wasko & Faraj (2005) point out the roles of computer networks and services on knowledge and people; some computer networks provide a place for discussion and knowledge sharing. One can sometimes obtain profitable knowledge, which can often be found nowhere in one's own workplace, from such a virtual place. However, introducing a knowledge management system in order to help employees offer their knowledge should be done with great care. If employees feel that their knowledge is "abducted", they might become self-protective and secretive again. Some employees believe that an introduction of knowledge management systems increases knowledge acquirers' power over knowledge holders (Bryant, 2006). As Bryant (2006) maintains, knowledge management is simply another expression for downsizing. Thus, there are many "worries" about conducting knowledge management.

Nevertheless, information technology can attract managers who believe that it can improve companies' performance. Nahapiet & Ghoshal (1998) illustrate the roles of modern information technology as functions serving knowledge workers with collecting, systematizing, building structures of, storing, combining, distributing, and presenting knowledge. Knowledge workers seem to use communication technologies as a tool for solving problems or creating something new. These experiences are seen even online so that it is natural that they also communicate offline. Florida (2005) shows that creativity can be stimulated in cities where people naturally gather in the real (physical) world. Besides, this real world relationship is more important than a virtual one. Knowledge management systems can work both desirably and undesirably. It depends on the real office atmosphere and relationships of mutual trust. The protective tendency of humans depends naturally on the atmosphere in an organization; a supportive or reciprocal atmosphere could encourage employees to share their knowledge (Constant, Kiesler & Sproull, 1994); nonetheless, severe competition might let employees to be protective (Wang, 2004). Wasko & Faraj (2005) report that legal professionals share their experience when they recognise that sharing activities enhance their professional reputations and sharing is one way to maintain the status of a member of these expert societies. Knowledge sharing does not always entail monetary rewarding. For example, the Open Source Software community often succeeds in development of software without financial reward (Hertel, Niedner & Hermann, 2003). The situation that people feel free from worry about the possibilities of job loss seems to make knowledge sharing more dynamic.

Inserting opposite loops is possible. For example, giving learning opportunities to employees who offer their knowledge to the public can ensure that they are competitive and have high self-esteem so that the power of the reinforcing loop shown in Figure 1 might be weakened, or move in the opposite direction, namely, work as a growth engine. However, it might take a long time to show the effect of learning, and recognising longer length of time of the agreements might occur more frequently. Even inserting a new opposite loop is not a definitive solution. Managers should consider an appropriate agreement time in order to keep their organisations competitive.

The most important thing is knowledge, not knowledge management tools or methods. Nonaka, Toyama & Konno (2000) consider that organizational knowledge is, for organizations, not only an asset but also essential resources in order to be creative. This definition should include tacit, or personal, knowledge inside knowledge holders' brains. The reason for this is that the inevitability of this kind of knowledge is originated by the fact that one cannot easily produce such knowledge again. Knowledge captured by information systems can be stored and copied at a low cost. Nevertheless, transferring knowledge from one brain to another is difficult. Squeezing and storing knowledge make people protective and does not lead to successful knowledge management. Helping people generate knowledge is successful. This difference must be always remembered by on-site managers.

CONCLUSION

Since people have regarded knowledge as an invaluable asset to organisations, the non-compete and non-disclosure agreements are signed almost without exception by knowledge workers. They have been working to help companies be competitive, especially during the manufacturing industry era; innovations were brought about at relatively longer intervals than they are today, and having knowledge exclusively has been an important advantage for business. However, the situation is changing drastically. Innovations and version up of software and services occurs very frequently. This is rendering the agreements' efficacy relatively low.

Today's rapidly changing situation means that the expiry date of acquired knowledge is sooner than ever. Not all knowledge needs to be strictly protected. Under the protective agreements that not only forbid employees from using their knowledge with other companies in the future but also eliminate subsequent chances of job change, employers may believe that they are free of worry of losing good employees. This might also lead to worsening working conditions compared with other companies. When the deterioration of working conditions becomes clear, the company loses high quality knowledge workers and attractiveness to prospective future good employees. This adversely affects companies' competitiveness. Moreover, employees' temporary commitment to their current job might make themselves protect their knowledge in order to secure their positions; the internal knowledge creation might badly affect.

From a macro point of view, employers sometimes need to hire new employees who have newer, competent knowledge. Nevertheless, employers face difficulties in hiring new knowledge workers because external knowledge workers might be under non-compete and non-disclosure agreements of other companies. The non-compete and non-disclosure agreements are still meaningful in the short term. The important point is that the length of time of the agreements should be practical both for knowledge acquirers and knowledge holders.

REFERENCES

Arrow, K. J. (1962). Economic welfare and the allocation of resources for invention. In Groves, H. M. (Ed.), *The Rate and Direction of Inventive Activity: Economic and Social Factors* (pp. 609–626). Cambridge, MA: The National Bureau of Economic Research.

Baskerville, R., & Dulipovici, A. (2006). The ethics of knowledge transfers and conversions: Property or privacy rights? In K. VanLehn (Ed.), *Proceedings of the 39th Hawaii International Conference on System Sciences* (pp. 144b-144b). Washington, DC: IEEE Computer Society.

Berkman Center for Internet & Society. (2008). Employee non-compete agreements: Protecting innovation or stifling it? *Harvard University*. Retrieved August 31, 2009, from http://cyber.law.harvard.edu/node/4440

Bock, G., Zmud, R. W., Kim, Y., & Lee, J. (2005). Behavioural intention formation in knowledge sharing: examining the roles of extrinsic motivators, social-psychological forces, and organizational climate. *Management Information Systems Quarterly*, *29*(1), 87–111.

Bryant, A. (2006). Knowledge management: The ethics of the agora or the mechanisms of the market? In K. VanLehn (Ed.), *Proceedings of the 39th Hawaii International Conference on System Sciences* (pp. 144c-144c). Washington, DC: IEEE Computer Society.

Cohen, D., & Prusak, L. (2001). *In good company: How social capital makes organizations work*. Cambridge, MA: Harvard Business School Press.

Constant, D., Kiesler, S., & Sproull, L. (1994). What's mine is ours, or is it? A study of attitudes about information sharing. *Information Systems Research*, *5*(4), 400–421. doi:10.1287/isre.5.4.400

Costa, G. J. M., Prior, M., & Rogerson, S. (2008, September). *Free ride in knowledge management? Ethical and moral dilemmas!* Paper presented at the ETHICOMP 2008, Mantua, Italy.

Costa, G. J. M., & Silva, N. M. A. (2007). Knowledge management: How ethical is your organization's knowledge? In Bynum, T. W., Rogerson, S., & Murata, K. (Eds.), *ETHICOMP 2007: Glocalisation: Bridging the Global Nature of Information and Communication Technology* (*Vol. 1*, pp. 123–136). Tokyo: Meiji University.

Davenport, T. H., & Prusak, L. (1998). *Working knowledge: How organizations manage what they know*. Cambridge, MA: Harvard Business School Press.

Fahey, L., & Prusak, L. (1998). The eleven deadliest sins of knowledge management. *California Management Review*, *40*(3), 265–276.

Fine, C. H. (1998). *Clockspeed: Winning industry control in the age of temporary advantage*. New York: Perseus Books.

Florida, R. (2005). The world is spiky. *Atlantic Monthly*, *296*(3), 48–51.

Forrester, J. W. (1971). Counterintuitive behaviour of social systems. *Technology Review*, *73*(3), 52–68.

Gayton, C. M. (2007). Legal issues for the knowledge economy in the twenty-first century. *VINE: The Journal of Information and Knowledge Management Systems*, *36*(1), 17–26.

Gayton, C. M. (2008). Business ethics, restrictions on employment and knowledge management. *VINE: The Journal of Information and Knowledge Management Systems*, *38*(2), 174–183.

Gottschalk, P. (2005). *Strategic knowledge management technology*. Hershey, PA: Idea Group Publishing.

Griffith, T. L., Sawyer, J. E., & Neale, M. A. (2003). Virtualness and knowledge in teams: Managing the love triangle of organizations, individuals, and information technology. *Management Information Systems Quarterly*, *29*(2), 265–287.

Hedlund, G. (1994). A model of knowledge management and the N-form corporation. *Strategic Management Journal*, *15*(S2), 73–90. doi:10.1002/smj.4250151006

Hertel, G., Niedner, S., & Herrmann, S. (2003). Motivation of software developers in open source projects: An Internet-based survey of contributors to the Linux kernel. *Research Policy*, *32*(7), 1159–1177. doi:10.1016/S0048-7333(03)00047-7

Lessig, L. (2004). *Free culture: How big media uses technology and the law to lock down culture and control creativity*. New York: Penguin Group Inc.

Lessig, L. (2006). *Code: Version 2.0*. New York: Basic Books.

Meadows, D. H. (1982). Whole earth models and systems. *The Coevolution Quarterly*, *34*(Summer), 98–108.

Myers, P. S. (1996). Knowledge management and organizational design: An Introduction. In Myers, P. S. (Ed.), *Knowledge Management and Organizational Design* (pp. 1–6). Newton, MA: Butterworth-Heinemann. doi:10.1016/B978-0-7506-9749-1.50004-1

Nahapiet, J., & Ghoshal, S. (1998). Social capital, intellectual capital, and the organizational advantage. *Academy of Management Review*, *23*(2), 242–266. doi:10.2307/259373

Nonaka, I., & Konno, N. (1998). The concept of "Ba": Building a foundation for knowledge creation. *California Management Review*, *40*(3), 40–54.

Nonaka, I., & Takeuchi, H. (1995). *Knowledge-creating company: How Japanese companies create the dynamics of innovation*. New York: Oxford University Press.

Nonaka, I., Toyama, R., & Konno, N. (2000). SECI, ba and leadership: A unified model of dynamic knowledge creation. *Long Range Planning*, *33*(1), 5–34. doi:10.1016/S0024-6301(99)00115-6

O'Reilly, T. (2005). What is web 2.0. *O'Reilly*. Retrieved January 23, 2009, from http://www.oreillynet.com/pub/a/oreilly/tim/news/2005/09/30/what-is-web-20.html

Scanlon, T. M. (1998). *What we owe to each other*. Cambridge, MA: Harvard University Press.

Schmidt, D. P. (2000). Ethics for knowledge management. In Srikantaiah, T. K., & Koenig, M. E. D. (Eds.), *Knowledge Management for the Information Professional* (pp. 115–131). Medford, NJ: American Society for Information Science.

Spinello, R. A., & Tavani, H. T. (2005). Intellectual property rights in a network world: Theory and Practice. In Spinello, R. A., & Tavani, H. T. (Eds.), *Intellectual Property Rights in a Network World: Theory and Practice* (pp. 1–66). Hershey, PA: Information Science Publishing.

Sterman, J. D. (1989). Modeling managerial behaviour: Misperceptions of feedback in a dynamic decision making experiment. *Management Science*, *35*(3), 321–339. doi:10.1287/mnsc.35.3.321

Sterman, J. D. (2000). *Business dynamics: Systems thinking and modelling for a complex world*. Homewood, IL: Irwin/McGraw-Hill.

Sterman, J. D. (2001). System dynamics modelling: Tools for learning in a complex world. *California Management Review*, *43*(4), 8–25.

Takahashi, Y. (2008). Dynamics simulation modelling using descriptive information in natural language. *International Journal of Simulation and Process Modelling*, *4*(3/4), 215–222. doi:10.1504/IJSPM.2008.023683

Teece, D. J. (2000). Strategies for managing knowledge assets: The role of firm structure and industrial context. *Long Range Planning*, *33*(1), 35–54. doi:10.1016/S0024-6301(99)00117-X

The Free Software Foundation. (2009). Free software definition. *The Free Software Foundation*. Retrieved January 23, 2009, from http://www.fsf.org/licensing/essays/free-sw.html

Trauth, E. M. (1999). Who owns my soul? The paradox of pursuing organizational knowledge in a work culture of individualism. In R. Agarwal & J. Prasad (Eds.), *Proceedings of the 1999 ACM SIGCPR Conference* (pp. 159-163). New Orleans, LA: CM Press.

UN. (2005). *Understanding knowledge societies*. New York: United Nations.

Von Hippel, E. (2005). *Democratizing innovation*. Cambridge, MA: The MIT Press.

Wang, C.-C. (2004). The influence of ethical and self-interest concerns on knowledge sharing intentions among managers: An empirical study. *International Journal of Management*, *21*(3), 370–381.

Wasko, M. M., & Faraj, S. (2005). Why should I share? Examining social capital and knowledge contribution in electronic networks of practice. *Management Information Systems Quarterly*, *29*(1), 35–57.

Whittaker, J., Burns, M., & Beveren, J. V. (2003, September/October). *Understanding and measuring the effect of social capital on knowledge transfer within clusters of small-medium enterprises*. Paper presented at The Small Enterprise Association of Australia and New Zealand 16th Annual Conference, Ballarat, Australia. Retrieved January, 23, 2009, from http://www.cecc.com.au/programs/resource_manager/accounts/seaanz_papers/57Whittakeretal.pdf

Wolstenholme, E. F. (1990). *System enquiry*. Chichester, UK: Wiley.

ADDITIONAL READING

Alter, S. (2006). Goals and Tactics on the dark side of knowledge management. In K. VanLehn (Ed.), *Proceedings of the 39th Hawaii International Conference on System Sciences* (pp. 144a-144a). Washington, DC: IEEE Computer Society.

Anderson, C. (2008). *The long tail, revised and updated edition: Why the future of business is selling less of more*. New York, NY: Hyperion.

Anderson, V., & Johnson, L. (1997). *Systems thinking basics: From concepts to causal loops*. Waltham, MA: Pegasus Communication.

Cheng, E. Y., & Liu, Y. L. (2008). Adoption of knowledge management technologies and organisational culture: An exploratory study. *Journal of Information & Knowledge Management*, *7*(1), 15–29. doi:10.1142/S0219649208001944

Christensen, C. M. (1997). *The innovator's dilemma: When new technologies cause great firms to fail*. Cambridge, MA: Harvard Business School Press.

Christensen, C. M., & Raynor, M. E. (2003). *The innovator's solution: Creating and sustaining successful growth*. Cambridge, MA: Harvard Business School Press.

Forrester, J. W. (1961). *Industrial dynamics*. Waltham, MA: Pegasus Communications.

Frohmann, B. (2008). Subjectivity and information ethics. *Journal of the American Society for Information Science and Technology*, *59*(2), 267–277. doi:10.1002/asi.20742

Garrick, J., & Clegg, S. (2000). Knowledge work and the new demands of learning. *Journal of Knowledge Management*, *4*(4), 279–286. doi:10.1108/13673270010379821

Gick, E. (2003). Cognitive theory and moral behaviour: The contribution of F. A. Hayek to business ethics. *Journal of Business Ethics*, *45*(1/2), 149–165. doi:10.1023/A:1024141017104

Gordon-Till, J. (2002). Applied ethics in business information units. *Business Information Review*, *19*(2), 48–54. doi:10.1177/026638202321036231

Kim, D. H. (1999). *Introduction to systems thinking*. Waltham, MA: Pegasus Communication.

Land, F., Amjad, U., & Nolas, S.-M. (2007). The ethics of knowledge management. *International Journal of Knowledge Management*, *3*(1), 1–9.

Lin, C. P., & Ding, C. G. (2003). Modeling information ethics: The joint moderating role of locus of control and job insecurity. *Journal of Business Ethics*, *48*(4), 335–346. doi:10.1023/B:BUSI.0000005745.63324.79

López-Huertas, M. J. (2008). Some current research questions in the field of knowledge organization. *Knowledge Organization*, *35*(2/3), 113–136.

Maani, K. E., & Cavana, R. Y. (2000). *Systems thinking and modelling: Understanding change and complexity*. 2nd ed. Zug: Pearson Education.

Mooradian, N. (2005). Tacit knowledge: Philosophic roots and role in KM. *Journal of Knowledge Management*, *9*(6), 104–113. doi:10.1108/13673270510629990

Murray, F., & Stern, S. (2007). Do formal intellectual property rights hinder the free flow of scientific knowledge? An empirical test of the anti-commons hypothesis. *Journal of Economic Behavior & Organization*, *63*(4), 648–687. doi:10.1016/j.jebo.2006.05.017

Northcutt, S. (2004). *IT ethics handbook: Right and wrong for IT professionals*. Rockland, MA: Syngress Media Inc.

Richardson, G. P. (1986). Problems with causal-loop diagrams. *System Dynamics Review*, *2*(2), 158–170. doi:10.1002/sdr.4260020207

Senge, P. M. (1990). *The fifth discipline: The art & practice of the learning organization*. New York, NY: Doubleday Business.

Senge, P. M., Kleiner, A., Roberts, C., Ross, R., & Smith, B. (1994). *The fifth discipline fieldbook: Strategies and tools for building a learning organization*. New York, NY: Broadway Business.

Sullivan, P. H. (2000). *Value driven intellectual capital: How to convert intangible corporate assets into market value*. New York, NY: John Wiley & Sons.

Sussman, L. (2002). Organizational politics: Tactics, channels, and hierarchical Roles. *Journal of Business Ethics*, *40*(4), 313–329. doi:10.1023/A:1020807700478

Tapscott, D., & Williams, A. D. (2006). *Wikinomics: How mass collaboration changes everything*. New York, NY: Portfolio.

Widén-Wulff, G., & Ginman, M. (2004). Explaining knowledge sharing in organizations through the dimensions of social capital. *Journal of Information Science*, *30*(5), 448–458. doi:10.1177/0165551504046997

Wilson, T. D. (2002). The nonsense of knowledge management. *Information Research*, 8(1). Retrieved September 25, 2009, from http://informationr.net/ir/8-1/paper144.html.

KEY TERMS AND DEFINITIONS

Balancing Loop: A feedback loop with an odd number of negative causal relationships. Elements in this kind of loop perform goal seeking or oscillation.

Causal Loop Analysis: The detailed examination focusing on feedback loop structures. The concept of this method is generated in the development of system dynamics. Using this, systems' broad performance can be predicted, like exponential growth, goal seeking, or oscillation. This is also called qualitative analysis of system dynamics.

Causality: Relationship between cause and effect (result). In system dynamics, there are two types of causality: positive and negative. Positive causality means a result element changes to the same direction as its cause element changes to. Negative causality indicates a result element changes to the opposite direction to its cause element's change. This is also called a causal relationship.

Feedback Loop: Circulations which consist of causalities between elements in subject systems. Feedback loops are classified into reinforcing loops and balancing loops.

Non-Compete and Non-Disclosure Agreements: The contract that an employer and an employee exchange. Under these agreements, an employee must not work for competitors in the future and disclose information acquired and generated in business.

Reinforcing Loop: A feedback loop with an even number of causal relationships. Elements in this kind of loop perform exponential growth or decay.

System Dynamics: Originally developed as a computer simulation method for social systems. It focuses on the causalities between systems' elements and uses diagrams (stock flow diagrams and causal loop diagrams). Stock flow diagrams precisely express accumulation, delay, or other complex processes. The modellers eventually simulate dynamic models generated by system dynamics software from stock flow diagrams.

Systems Thinking: An analysis method based on system dynamics. It focuses on feedback loop structure in order to forecast the direction of performance and find pertinent elements for controlling systems. This is also called qualitative system dynamics.

Chapter 12
Management of Moral Knowledge and Ethical Processes in Organizations

Agata Kostrzewa
Uppsala University, Sweden

Mikael Laaksoharju
Uppsala University, Sweden

Iordanis Kavathatzopoulos
Uppsala University, Sweden

ABSTRACT

Moral knowledge is necessary for organizational functioning in order to get legitimacy and increase profits. Given Blackler's assumptions about organizations, the authors discuss managing moral knowledge in organizations as a set of organizational processes with a time point and in a certain environment. They argue that to become ethically competent, organizations have to combine individuals and organizational ethical skills. Instead of on what is supposed to be done, the authors focus on what is done: interactions within the organization and with its environment, structured by practical routines, bearing main responsibility for transferring moral knowledge. The means facilitating this are organizational roles and structures, trainings, formal and informal support systems along with rules and guidelines. Further, the authors suggest two tools to assist managing moral knowledge: Ethical Index ETHIX (questionnaire to describe how ethical issues are handled in the organization) and the IT system ETHXPERT (supports and structures the process o ethical decision making).

INTRODUCTION

In order to avoid raising the reader's expectations we feel urged to state already from the start that we, in this chapter, will not give any clues to what a correct decision in an ethical matter is. We will focus only on the process of handling moral problems, disregarding the normative content of them. Without doubt, it is necessary that the solution of the problem at hand becomes satisfactory, but if the process is correct then the result will be appropriate (Kant, 1997). If we compare with baking

DOI: 10.4018/978-1-61520-873-9.ch012

a cake it seems obvious that the result, the cake, would be what we judge the quality of the baker by. Nevertheless, if we would like to reproduce an excellent result it seems better to investigate exactly how the baker did when producing it instead of fooling ourselves to believe that the daintiness and aroma of the outcome are results of just using the right ingredients. We would correctly assume that a delicious cake requires both good ingredients and suitable processing. Moral problems are on the other hand often treated as "good in- good out", i.e. if good values are guiding the solution then the result will be good.

Psychological studies have shown that this is not always enough; the process is often complicated by the strong emotions involved (Sunstein, 2005; Baron & Spranca, 1997). An explicit process when handling real-life problems, in situations where we can assume to be naturally constrained by moral boundaries, does not mean that the results will risk becoming immoral. More likely, a systematic structuring will widen the problem scope and help discover other important aspects. Consequently, we will discuss how ethical issues are handled in organizations, where we treat moral knowledge as latent in the ability to manage moral problems, i.e. knowledge as a process.

Moral knowledge about what is right and what is wrong is not always offered ready to use. Neither is it easy to have awareness of the moral problems an organization is facing, or of the moral problems that might be coming. And, of course, the ability to handle moral problems, to find solutions and to make decisions is not located explicitly in a certain group or in a specific person. Both moral knowledge in the form of suitable solutions, and ethical competence in the form of skills and processes are spread in the organizations.

One might think that the aim for a decision maker always should be to establish a conception, as complete as possible, about the problem at hand. However, one easily realizes that such a conception is often hard to achieve for many reasons. If we for a moment disregard the apparent difficulties in the actual information gathering and instead focus on the mental process of decision making, we can identify unawareness about possible implications, inattention, preconceptions and cognitive biases about the problem as some of the obstacles to overcome in the pursuit of a wide problem understanding. The decision maker thus seems to need help to block tendencies to biased decision making apart from the obvious call for help with widening the understanding of a problem (Kunsch, Kavathatzopoulos & Rauschmayer, 2009). From a knowledge management perspective we also consider it to be important to make a decision process explicit and formalized; the organization as a whole should benefit from the experiences made in specific problem situations. The usual strategy to facilitate organizational learning about moral problems is to codify implications into codes of ethics and ethical guidelines. These assemblies of ethical considerations tend to have a more or less general and normative approach, addressed more to the public at large than to the decision maker facing a difficult situation. They are purposeful, because are telling to the public what to expect from the organization, and thus also for setting up moral boundaries for the people in the organization. Nonetheless, for a specific decision maker in a specific situation, or for a group during a process of creating ethical rules or policies, it would be more valuable to have some kind of support when structuring the problem, in order to be better able to judge which of the codified principles to consider relevant for the specific case and which to disregard. The most important issue is to understand why choices are made and to have good explicit arguments supporting the final decision. Therefore we seek to codify the actual process of ethical decision making rather than the outcomes of it.

Moral problems, the way they are posed, often depict the world in a black-and-white dichotomy, which can give the impression that there do not exist any satisfactory solutions to the problem. It is the nature of such problems; since they occur when conflicting values or interests cannot all be satisfied at the same time. For many real-life moral problems it can also be asserted that a common-sense solution most of the time leads to the "best" result, be it neither completely satisfactory nor sustainable. Given these preconditions, there is, from the member's point of view, little incentive to *not* act according to a standard protocol. Also from an organizational perspective, acting according to standards has mostly positive features: the actions of individuals become predictable by anyone aware of the protocol and the organization can better control and regulate the behaviour of its members. A side effect of strong organizational control is that it leaves the individual, to a large degree, free from responsibility in situations where misjudgements have occurred. Whenever a scandal with moral implications has occurred, it does not come as a surprise when a spokesperson from the responsible organization makes some fuzzy statements about policies that need revising. Even though the problem is caused by professional misconduct it is often hard to point out a responsible individual. First, it has to be proven that the member who committed the misconduct did it knowingly and second, the organization has to judge how other members, not to mention the public, will view such scapegoatism. The unclear distribution of ethical responsibility often leads to the impression that moral problems are owned by organizations rather than by its representatives. There thus seems to be a need for procedures and tools to identify and handle possible moral issues and also to make clear what responsibilities each member has. Ethical awareness on an organizational level requires an inventory of the ethical competence of its members and processes to share moral knowledge between these.

The use of IT systems has revolutionized many fields of knowledge management, but within the field of ethics, technology has yet not had the same breakthrough. In our research we have come to suspect that this is likely to be a result of an interpretation of ethical choices as something different than usual decisions; moral problems as something greater and vaguer than ordinary problems; ethical decision- making as something dependent on secrets "out there"- something indescribable- something more than mere reality.

This interpretation might be true, but it still does not reduce the need for systematizing of the ethical decision process. One may wonder why this field has not yet been widely approached. The catch seems to be the lack of strategies for how to approach the seemingly volatile character of ethics in a computerized support system. In our research we have found strong indications for our hypothesis that the most purposeful and general method to treat moral problems is to do just like philosophers do, namely to focus on the specific interests and needs of the stakeholders that are involved in the problem. If this identification of interests is carried out in a systematic, reflective and holistic way, it will help to identify and include considerations about previously neglected stakeholders (Rauschmayer *et al.*, 2009).

In this chapter we will therefore present two tools for organizations to handle moral issues in a competent way. One of them is the Ethical Index ETHIX, a survey that describes the way the organization manages those in a given point of time, and thus can be used as a starting point for development. The other tool, ETHXPERT, is an IT system to support ethical decision making through making the process a conscious one. We begin, though, by discussing the theoretical basis on how moral knowledge can be viewed upon.

BACKGROUND

Recent decades have shown an increasing recognition for knowledge management as a success factor, also within traditional fields of trade. With the emergence of new technologies, requiring a substantial knowledge input, understanding sources of knowledge and learning how to handle it has become an issue of central importance.

Both practitioners and scholars seem to agree that knowledge offers competitive advantages (Empson, 2003; Davenport & Prusak, 1998; Reich, 1991; Sveiby & Lloyd, 1987; etc). As Davenport & Prusak (1998) put it: knowledge (…) can provide a substantial advantage. Eventually, competitors can almost always match the quality and the price of a market leader's current product or service. By the time that happens, though, the knowledge-rich, knowledge-managing company will have moved on to a new level of quality, creativity or efficiency. The knowledge advantage is sustainable because it generates increasing returns and continuing advantage. Unlike material assets, which decrease as they are used, knowledge assets increase with use: "ideas breed new ideas, and shared knowledge stays with the giver while it enriches the receiver" (Davenport & Prusak, 1998, pp. 17).

The view on knowledge presented above is dynamic: the greatest advantage is granted to the first mover; yet, even the subsequent users can benefit from it. Moreover, using it promotes its growing, as new ideas are being born.

The above paragraphs give an image of knowledge being distributed (and to some extent shared) among different actors on the market. Similarly, there is a common conception that the actors within a company- the CEO, the HR department, the R&D department, etc- possess knowledge that is unique to them and act in accordance to it. Yet, we would rather subscribe to the viewpoint as presented by Styhre (2003), i.e. that process of decision-making cannot be limited to certain areas and departments. Instead, it "takes place everywhere all the time and often on basis of collective discussions and agreements" (Styhre, 2003, pp. 34). Therefore, it is of vital importance to make the process of coordinating decision making based on the possessed knowledge a conscious one.

Whereas the above-mentioned ideas apply to organizational knowledge, with regard to the company's daily operation within the area of manufacturing or innovations, it should be stressed that they apply even more too moral knowledge due to the special nature of ethics. Nowadays, it is hardly sufficient to concentrate on making business- and profit- without taking into account the ethical aspects of the company's operation. The two areas, making business and ethics, are intertwined; an organization neglecting the latter may lose legitimacy and, as a consequence, face decreased profits.

The above-discussed, growing interest in and stress on managing knowledge in organizations and companies, due to an ongoing technology development, has resulted in an emergence of two research streams; one accentuating knowledge as an asset, or "objectively definable commodity", while the other one emphasizing knowledge as processes, "a social construct" defining what proper knowledge is (Empson, 2001, pp. 812). For the former conceptual model, the unit of analysis is the firm or organization perceived as a set of competencies and capabilities used to add competitive advantage (Grant, 1996; Szulanski, 1996). Within this model, knowledge is viewed as static, a commodity to be identified and effectively managed. The latter model, on the other hand, presents knowledge as a social process, "created, articulated, disseminated, and legitimated within organizations" (Empson, 2001, pp. 813). Below we will discuss the two models with regard to how they apply to managing moral knowledge.

Knowledge as an Asset

The viewpoint that knowledge is a commodity among others to provide competitive advantage can be observed within a range of research areas. Knowledge can be treated as any other resource; it can be generated, stored, managed and transferred.

For strategic management theory, the focus lies in analyzing how firms generate competitive advantage and position themselves on the market (Powell, 2001; Ghemawat, 1986). The firm can either by its superior position on the market create competitive advantages (Porter, 1985; 1980; Bain,

1968); or, it is the firm-specific resources that are the origin of heterogeneity on the market, which in turn help the firm outperform its competitors (Penrose, 1959). As one of the resources, knowledge is looked upon with regard to its attributes ("valuable", "costly to imitate or substitute", etc), as a way of assessing how it contributes to the success of a firm, its role being instrumentally limited to dealing with achieving goals (Kalling & Styhre, 2003; Styhre, 2003). Knowledge can, and often is, created as a joint effort by companies, either in networks (Teece, 1998) or in co-operation with other companies (Simonin, 1999). Some researchers argue that firms and organizations often experience difficulties when relocating knowledge since it is "sticky" (von Hippel, 1998) as it requires effort and is costly to transfer.

Moral knowledge, like technology knowledge, contributes to competitive advantage of a firm, its efficiency and profit. The view on moral knowledge as a resource is however inapplicable in our opinion. Certainly, written or unwritten rules like ethical guidelines can be regarded as assets. Nevertheless, they have to be created, interpreted, applied and revised in an ongoing process. In most cases static moral knowledge is purposeful to reach satisfactory solutions in an automatic, knee-jerk way, but in new or special situations, when new thinking is necessary, such knowledge can best contribute by promoting awareness about known moral issues. On the other hand, it can obstruct critical thinking by luring people into believing that what is not included in the knowledge base is morally accepted. This can also lead to insensitivity to nuances and misinterpretation of how guidelines should be applied (Fairweather, 2004).

Furthermore, moral knowledge does not, unlike technology knowledge, in itself increase production rates, but it can legitimize the firm and in the long run improve revenues. Even though it can in parts be branch-specific due to the special requirements of the industry type in question, it should in general be shared across the markets. The flow of it is accomplished more easily and is less cost-intensive. In addition, the view is static and neglects the fact that knowledge (be it moral or technological) is subject to constant changes in the process of using it.

Knowledge as a Process

"As a socially constructed phenomenon", Alvesson (2001) writes, "knowledge does not exist on its own, but is dependent on social recognition, without being perceived and recognized by others, for all practical matters, knowledge does not appear as such" (Alvesson, 2001, pp. 872). Knowledge demands a social context, an interaction between individuals or groups of people, inside and outside the firm. As such, it emerges, and undergoes changes during the activities of a firm in operation. As a consequence, it is subjected to a constant process of becoming an alteration; its nature is fluid and amorphous (Styhre, 2003).

The same is valid for moral knowledge. It cannot exist without human interactions, and is spread on all levels of the hierarchy in a firm or organization, even though, as there are differences in between the ranks, persons of the higher hierarchical rank being more aware of the process of ethical decision-making (Kavathatzopoulos, Kostrzewa & Berg, 2008; Kavathatzopoulos & Rigas, 2006; 1998) (see below, section ETHIX: A tool describing moral knowledge management). It comes into expression not just in what is said in ethical codices, guidelines or rules; it rather shows itself and develops through what is done practically. It affects the course of the firm's operation, i.e. in action; and, on the other hand, action creates new moral knowledge as well. The process is never-ending, due to the constant influences from the environment (on a normative level as new laws and regulations and on a processual level as new awareness of how moral issues can be managed more effectively) as well as, from inside the firm where novel approach to handling moral problems can emerge.

But, how can moral knowledge be processed in the best way? We believe that in order to answer this question it is important to see firms and organizations as activity systems, which enables an analysis of the relationship between intentions behind and the context of action, and of the thought process leading to an activity. Based on the theory of Vygotsky (1978; 1962) and his followers, and furthermore developed by Engström (1987), activity theory in the form provided by Blackler (1993) provides information about the society-based motives of action, discusses mediation processes in performing activities, participation and the role of tensions and inconsistencies in activity systems.

In Blackler's model of organizations, the unit of analysis is collective activity, not thoughts of individuals. Knowledge management in organizations is placed on a time trajectory, since concepts and approaches change and develop over time. Organizations learn from previous methods of action that did not necessarily fit their goal and either apply minor changes in the old ones or, create new ones. These social and economic histories of organizations consist of normative and ideological constraints, choice of technology and core competence, etc. They are also dependent on the social context of learning: as a result of inconsistencies, tensions and ambiguities within and around them, organizations have to revise old approaches and develop new methods to cope with the changing requirements of the environment. As a way of managing social interactions, mediating is used on three levels: of tools and concepts that regulate the interaction between the individual and their context, of traditions, rituals and rules mediating the interaction between the individual and the organization they are active in, as well as of division of labour that regulates the interaction between the organization and the activities of its members. The most important role in unifying of the system is played, however, by practical organizational routines, promoting co-operation rather than conflict. Routines are often tacit, entrenched in the system, chosen automatically until some unusual events make the users to consciously examine their choice. As a consequence, in case routines are changed, even rethinking of the activities of the individual members of the organization might be needed (cf. Grant, 1996).

The active participation of the individual is thus essential, as a bearer of knowledge, or rather expertise. Keeping in mind the influence of the organization's history and social context, it can be concluded that expertise can be of diverse kind due to the origin of the issue at hand. Furthermore, the expert acts in response to specific situations, employing information gathered from the activity system he or she works in. Becoming an expert, i.e. making knowledge explicit, is a process in itself since people sometimes perform more than they are aware of being able to. This motivates an interpretation of individual ethical competence as a process of self-critical systematizing and structuring of problem situations and as a way to increase the awareness about these. As an organizational process, ethical competence is about creating roles and processes that formalize and utilize its members' ability to handle moral issues.

Lastly, we would like to draw the reader's attention to the fact that the emergence of thinking of knowledge as a process seems to coincide with the IT revolution during the last decades of the previous century. We agree that IT has affected the operation of organizations, as well as created new threats and problems which have to be addressed (Gotterbarn, 2004; Maner, 2004), but we think that it is rather the complex and changing world of today with its ambiguities and conflicts, to which IT has also contributed, that makes it more suitable to regard knowledge more as a process than as an asset.

Formal and Informal Processes

In our view, the process-based activity theory answers the question of how to create, store, transfer and deploy moral knowledge. The actual processes can be both formal and informal. Formal processes and structures reflect the goals of an organization in order to make it efficient (Simon, 1997; Taylor, 1911). The organization regulates explicitly, through its organizational scheme, the behaviour and the nature of relationships of its members and makes them standardized and predictable. As a result, if the goals are changed, the organizational structure can easily be remodelled. However, there are two serious disadvantages with this approach. First, the organization does not adapt to changing conditions on the market without operational control, and second, the approach does not take into consideration real internal organizational dynamics. At the same time, formal structures and standardized procedures call for a stable environment that is a seldom-observed state in today's world. Moreover, efficient operation of an organization depends on the interactions between its members, as well as cooperation processes and support relationships. Therefore, informal processes and structures are needed for an efficient operation of an organization.

Informal processes develop their own goals and activities, which, nevertheless, support the accomplishment of the organization's formal goals. They make the organization respond better to internal as well as external influences since they focus on what in reality happens rather than on controlling how well structures and operations fit formal goals. This is also explained by the fact that the behaviour and activities of the individuals and groups within the organization are not only a result of economical considerations but also other factors not necessarily determined by the organization. In sum, informal structures and processes should complement formal ones in order to enhance the efficiency of the organization (Kavathatzopoulos, 2001).

Management and Moral Knowledge

According to our opinion, it does not suffice to treat moral knowledge as a commodity. Naturally, it can be seen as part of the intellectual capital, something to be created, acquired, stored and deployed by the organization. It is, on the other hand, spread between the individuals and groups in the organization and has to be coordinated so that the whole organization can profit from it. We subscribe here to Grant's (1996) words, when he concludes: "… the organizational problem common to all forms of social organizations is that of cooperation: reconciling the conflicting goals of organizational members" (Grant, 1996, pp. 121). It is, however, important to mention that the notion of members, beside individuals, include groups (teams), departments, etc.

We view moral knowledge rather as a process, with the whole organization participating in managing it. It is an ongoing process of learning, since the organization has to adapt to the changing moral demands of the surrounding environment, as well as to internal changes. New issues become valid and thus a new approach to handle them has to be created. The organization is then an arena of activity (Blackler, 1993), coordinating interactions between its members and between the organization and its stakeholders. Each organization has to develop practical routines to be able to do it. Frequently, the routines are not explicit; instead, things are "done just the usual way". To facilitate the interactions, in addition, a set of three mediating factors is used: division of labour, tools and concepts along with explicit and implicit rules.

On a practical level, these mediating factors are represented by four categories of processes in managing moral knowledge:

- education for training all aspects of ethical competence, e.g. ethical problem solving, argumentation and rule construction;
- personal support where the decision maker works together with an expert in ethical competence, who is supporting the analysis and structuring of the ethical decision-making process;

- organizational support where the organization cooperates with an expert in ethical competence when handling moral problem situations and crises or when constructing ethical rules and guidelines for the organization;
- formal roles and structures, routines and informal support structures among organizational members.

Formal roles and structures developed for handling ethics account for Blackler's factor *division of labour* and can include ethical officers and/or boards. Education as well as support structures both on the personal and organizational levels provide *tools* for improving the members' ethical competence and confidence. Most of the processes listed above are of formal nature, initiated by the organization to promote the efficient handling of moral issues. In the instable world of today, organizations need additional structures beside the formal ones, in order to respond properly to what is happening inside as well as outside their venues. The informal support among the members is such a complement to the formal processes, contributing with additional expertise, strengthening the interactions in the organization and enhancing the process of its members becoming ethical experts. Given that we focus on organizational and personal processes of handling and producing moral knowledge we can build reliable tools that can describe, evaluate and support ethical problem solving and decision making. Last but not least, Blackler's *explicit and implicit rules* can be found partly in codes of ethics and ethical guidelines and partly in the corporate culture.

ETHIX: A TOOL FOR DESCRIBING MORAL KNOWLEDGE MANAGEMENT

Ethical Index (ETHIX) is a survey constructed to describe ethical competence in organizations, both at personal and organizational levels (Kavathatzopoulos, Kostrzewa & Berg, 2008). It is aimed to identify organizational ethical strengths and weaknesses, to map needs, to plan, follow-up and evaluate organizational changes, in addition to assessing the effect of certain measures such as personnel training, introduction of ethical processes and roles, etc. ETHIX describes how an organization manages moral knowledge, i.e., ethical processes, on both a group and personal levels.

Personal ethical competence is an indispensable condition for organizational ethical competence. There is a need for ethically competent individuals so that organizational structures and procedures, aimed at answering to the demands of ethical competence can work properly. Ethical competence on personal level in our opinion includes: high ethical awareness, ethical problem-solving abilities, ethical argumentation skills, and ethical confidence. The above-mentioned factors constitute a good method for handling moral issues and are necessary for members, officers and decision makers. With the conditions of personal ethical competence fulfilled, for organizational ethical competence suitable processes and roles are needed, both for managing moral issues and problems, and for providing satisfactory support to the members confronting those. Both these two levels of ethical competence, personal and organizational, are mutually dependent: the ethical development of an (already ethically competent) individual progresses faster in an organization which demands it from them, and an organization can function ethically only if the persons working there are able to run it in an ethically competent way.

As mentioned above, parameters of ethical competence at personal level include awareness, problem-solving and decision-making skills, argumentation skills, training, and confidence. At organizational level important parameters are organizational profile and concern in moral issues, adoption of special processes and roles, and support to the members. Another important aspect are ethical guidelines, the way they are constructed, revised and applied as well as what impact they have on organizational effectiveness, member support, work environment, and customer/stakeholder satisfaction.

The approach is process-oriented, seeing the organization as a place of activity. The interaction between the individual workers is inquired- both on formal and informal levels in form of training possibilities, perceived support from co-workers and own opportunities to affect ethical processes. The system of informal support that is included in the formal structure of the organization is a complement to other processes. The parameters mediating the ethical activities include organizational structures and roles promoting ethics (e.g. ethical boards and officers), explicit and implicit traditions and rules (ethical guidelines, codices, etc), as well as training tools. The questionnaire gives an image of the implicit routines for handling moral issues, as a unifying factor for the efforts the organization makes to manage ethics.

The questionnaire in its full version consists of 37 questions of Likert-type with six alternatives (see Appendix). The survey has already been tested on two organizations- a university department and a manufacturing company. At that time, it contained only two subscales, Personal Competence and Organizational Processes. In future versions of the instrument, however, a subscale about the construction, revision and application of ethical rules and guidelines will be included.

The results of the pilot study proved to be encouraging, confirming the reliability of the questionnaire, as assessed by Cronbach's alpha, correlations and factor analysis. The levels of acceptance were high, pointing at one main factor, in this case, ethical competence. ETHIX did not only show high internal reliability; it also revealed differences between persons, as indicated by the respondent's hierarchical position in the organization, as well as between organizations, depending on their organizational structure. Persons at higher levels of organizational hierarchy, on one hand, as well as working in expert organizations such as a university department, on the other hand, scored higher. This can be explained by the fact that persons working independently and taking more responsibility, at higher hierarchical levels or in the flat structure of university department, tend to perceive themselves and their organization as more ethically competent. Moreover, organizations like the university, with a flat structure and responsibility taking members, encourage their members to become more ethically conscious. This said, we are quite aware, though, that even the university world faces sometimes cases of plagiarism and fraud. We do not claim scientists to be morally superior in general. We just notice that there is a difference in the way the members of various organizations treat moral problems.

Although subjective, an ETHIX report provides valuable knowledge on the state of affairs in organizations and is an important starting point in the process of acquiring and/or enhancing ethical competence.

ETHXPERT: A TOOL FOR SUPPORTING ETHICAL PROCESSES

ETHXPERT (Kavathatzopoulos & Laaksoharju, 2010; Laaksoharju & Kavathatzopoulos, 2009) is an IT system to support the process of structuring and gathering information. It is based on the assumption that moral problems are best understood through identification of interests and values of stakeholders affected by and affecting a decision. It is important to point out that this kind of system does not, and should not, make any assertions of the normative correctness in any decisions or statements. The system's sole purpose is to *support* the decision maker, irrespective of whether this is a person, a group or the whole organization, when analyzing, structuring and reviewing choice situations- not to make any decisions for the user.

In the ETHXPERT procedure options and interests of each imaginable stakeholder are identified; gains and risks in the relationships between stakeholders are scrupulously assembled and studied. The user interface of the system presents relational data in three different ways depending on which part of the process that is undertaken. These different views have specific purposes. The first view is intended for identifying and establishing relationships between stakeholders and organizations. It represents stakeholders as nodes in a network, where each stakeholder and organization is initially assumed to have an interest relationship towards other stakeholders and organizations. Some of these relations might appear unnecessary at first thought, but the purpose of implying them is to provoke the user into widening the scope of attention and countering selective search for evidence and choice-supportive bias. People generally choose the easiest way to handle problems, which means that, apart from limiting the number of aspects to consider by neglecting "irrelevant" information, they will try to avoid having to justify decisions. The reverse approach to forming relations shifts the need for justification from adding to removing relations. Choosing which relationships to dismiss thus becomes an action that requires attention. The second and the third views are somewhat similar. These feature a visually optimized matrix intended to support a holistic overview of the problem. The purpose is to block biases about selective search for evidence and choice-support through reminding the user of the complexity of the information. If the matrix becomes unbalanced it will alert the user to investigate the reasons for it. One of these views is intended for management and revision of relationship information and the other for determining the effects of optional decisions. The process of adding stakeholders and interests, identifying how interests affect other stakeholders and how stakeholders are affected by optional solutions, is central in the process and much care has been put on to make this process lean. The procedural simplicity combined with a systematic, associative process reduces the risk for oversimplification of the problem.

Somewhat ironically, this kind of widening of moral problems does not always make the choice easier. More likely it makes it harder to determine what is "right"; such is the downside of ethical awareness. When preconceptions about what is right and what is wrong have been rightfully questioned, the decision maker, whether this is a person or an organizational process, is left to the own ability to make a good judgment based on known facts. This of course creates stress and anxiety, and puts a lot more responsibility on the decision maker, but it can increase the chances to make sustainable decisions.

Many decision makers already use this kind of mental process, even though they are not explicitly aware of it (Kavathatzopoulos & Rigas, 2006; 1998). Organizations can, however, benefit from a more systematic sharing of the experiences made in specific situations. ETHXPERT is constructed so that several users can work independently with the same decision problem- analyzing stakeholders, interests and options- and then share the insights through the system. The system, thus, becomes a platform for collaborative work and knowledge sharing.

Even in this case, a process of managing knowledge in the activity area of the organization is in focus. Active participation in using the tool is required. The users are trained to identify different actors, internal and external for the organization, who take part in the process as well as to recognize the underlying interactions between them. The roles and different interests of the actors are highlighted and reflected upon, both on the formal and informal levels. The tool can be used in a process of training the organizational members to consider various situational outcomes and their impact on the stakeholders.

FUTURE RESEARCH DIRECTIONS

Knowledge management has faced a shift in interest during the last few decades: from viewing knowledge as a commodity to be created, stored, managed and transferred to perceiving it as a process, where the focus rests on the longitudinal relations between the organizational members and with the environment, as well as on the factors to facilitate these interactions (Empson, 2001). This shift is not as apparent when it comes to managing moral knowledge. The dominant approach toward ethics is normative, which does not properly reflect the current society where ethics is in a constant state of flux; where norms are created and recreated as a result of global information sharing. However, even in this area, a change of focus is eventually likely to be expected. In our opinion, this is a necessary development in order to adapt to the demands of an evolving information society. We can expect more tools and methods to approach moral issues arising from the recognition of new, previously unexpected stakeholders and values. Even the tools described in this chapter, ETHIX and ETHXPERT, need further development to better serve their goal of codifying ethical processes in organizations and supporting the acquisition and the use of personal ethical skills and suitable organizational processes.

CONCLUSION

Both knowledge about facts and knowledge about skills have to be managed in suitable ways. Access to knowledge could otherwise prove to be very difficult if not impossible to get; organizations therefore have to find ways to handle this problem. However, in the case of moral knowledge this is absolutely necessary. Moral knowledge in the form of values, interests, stakeholders etc, as well as in the form of personal skills and organizational procedures, is almost exclusively distributed, shared and tacit. Although the main issue when facing a moral problem is its solution, the focus of our approach is on the processes leading to the solutions.

Viewing the organization as an arena of activity, where moral knowledge is managed in a conscious way, we see that both ETHIX and ETHXPERT address the interactions between the various actors within and outside the organization. Moreover, they give us a longitudinal image of the organization in its environment. ETHIX enables us to describe the formal and informal ethical processes on personal and organizational levels present (or sometimes absent) in the examined organization, the way the survey participant perceives them. It also gives an idea of which underlying routines lie behind the management of moral knowledge. ETHXPERT, on the other hand, is a dynamic tool to support the processes of making ethical decisions. Instead of merely describing the processes for the researcher, it highlights and makes them conscious to the tool user in order for him or her to find a solution to a given moral issue.

Supported theoretically by knowledge management as well as by research in social sciences, carefully constructed tools, using the advances and the advantages of IT, this chapter can contribute to a more efficient and effective management of ethical processes and moral knowledge in organizations.

REFERENCES

Alvesson, M. (2001). Knowledge work: Ambiguity, image and identity. *Human Relations*, *54*(7), 863–886. doi:10.1177/0018726701547004

Bain, J. S. (1968). *Industrial organizations*. New York: Wiley.

Baron, J., & Spranca, M. (1997). Protected values. *Organizational Behavior and Human Decision Processes*, *70*(1), 1–16. doi:10.1006/obhd.1997.2690

Blackler, F. (1993). Knowledge and the theory of organizations: Organizations as activity systems and the reframing of management. *Journal of Management Studies*, *30*(6), 863–884. doi:10.1111/j.1467-6486.1993.tb00470.x

Davenport, T. H., & Prusak, L. (1998). *Working knowledge: How organizations manage what they know*. Boston, MA: Harvard School Press.

Empson, L. (2001). Introduction: Knowledge management in professional service firms. *Human Relations*, *54*(7), 811–817. doi:10.1177/0018726701547001

Engström, Y. (1987). *Learning by expanding: An activity-theoretical approach to developmental research*. Helsinki, Finland: Orienta-Konsultit.

Fairweather, N. B. (2004). No, PAPA: Why incomplete codes of ethics are worse than none at all. In Bynum, T. W., & Rogerson, S. (Eds.), *Computer Ethics and Professional Responsibility* (pp. 142–157). Malden, MA: Blackwell Publishing.

Ghemawat, P. (1986). Sustainable advantage. *Harvard Business Review*, *86*(5), 53–58.

Gotterbarn, D. (2004). Informatics and professional responsibility. In Bynum, T. W., & Rogerson, S. (Eds.), *Computer Ethics and Professional Responsibility* (pp. 107–118). Malden, MA: Blackwell Publishing.

Grant, R. M. (1996). Toward a knowledge-based theory of the firm. *Strategic Management Journal, 17*(Winter Special Issue), 109-122.

Kalling, T., & Styhre, A. (2003). *Knowledge sharing in organizations*. Malmö, Sweden: Liber Ekonomi.

Kant, I. (1997). *Grundläggning av sedernas metafysik*. Göteborg, Sweden: Daidalos. (in Swedish)

Kavathatzopoulos, I. (2001). IT user learning: the role of informal processes. In Makrakis, V. (Ed.), *New Technologies in Education and Distance Education* (pp. 337–345). Athens, Greece: Atrapos.

Kavathatzopoulos, I., Kostrzewa, A., & Berg, K. (2008, October). *Measuring ethical competence of organizations*. Paper presented at the 21st Annual European Business Ethics Network, Antalya, Turkey.

Kavathatzopoulos, I., & Laaksoharju, M. (2010). Computer aided ethical systems design. In M. Arias-Oliva et al. (Eds.), *The "backwards, forwards, and sideways" changes of ICT* (332-340). Universitat Rovira i Virgili: Tarragona, Spain.

Kavathatzopoulos, I., & Rigas, G. (1998). A Piagetian scale for the measurement of ethical competence in politics. *Educational and Psychological Measurement*, *58*(5), 791–803. doi:10.1177/0013164498058005005

Kavathatzopoulos, I., & Rigas, G. (2006). A measurement model for ethical competence in business. *Journal of Business Ethics Education*, *3*, 55–74.

Kunsch, P. L., Kavathatzopoulos, I., & Rauschmayer, F. (2009). Modelling complex ethical decision problems with operations research. *Omega- The International Journal of Management Science, 37*(6), 1100-1108.

Laaksoharju, M., & Kavathatzopoulos, I. (2009). Computerized support for ethical analysis. In M. Botti et al. (Eds.), *Proceedings of CEPE 2009 – Eighth International Computer Ethics and Philosophical Enquiry Conference*. Ionian University: Kerkyra, Greece.

Maner, W. (2004). Unique ethical problems in information technology. In Bynum, T. W., & Rogerson, S. (Eds.), *Computer Ethics and Professional Responsibility* (pp. 39–59). Malden, MA: Blackwell Publishing.

Penrose, E. T. (1959). *The theory of the growth of the firm*. Oxford, UK: Blackwell.

Porter, M. E. (1980). *Competitive strategy*. New York: Free Press.

Porter, M. E. (1985). *Competitive advantage, creating and sustaining superior performance*. New York: The True Press.

Powell, T. C. (2001). Competitive advantage: Logical and philosophical considerations. *Strategic Management Journal*, *22*(9), 875–888. doi:10.1002/smj.173

Rauschmayer, F. *et al.* (2009). Why good practice of OR is not enough- Ethical challenges for the OR practitioner. *Omega- The International Journal of Management Science, 37*(6), 1089-1099.

Reich, R. B. (1991). *The work of nations: Preparing ourselves for the 21st century capitalism*. New York: Alfred A. Knopf, Inc.

Simon, H. A. (1997). *Administrative behaviour* (4th ed.). New York: McMillan.

Simonin, B. L. (1999). Ambiguity and the process of knowledge transfer in strategic alliances. *Strategic Management Journal*, *20*(7), 595–623. doi:10.1002/(SICI)1097-0266(199907)20:7<595::AID-SMJ47>3.0.CO;2-5

Styhre, A. (2003). Knowledge management beyond codification: Knowing as practice/concept. *Journal of Knowledge Management*, *7*(5), 32–40. doi:10.1108/13673270310505368

Sunstein, C. R. (2005). Moral heuristics. *The Behavioral and Brain Sciences*, *28*(4), 531–573.

Sveiby, K. E., & Lloyd, T. (1987). *Managing knowhow: Add value by valuing creativity*. London: Bloomsbury.

Szulanski, G. (1996). Exploring internal stickiness: Impediments to the transfer of best practice within the firm. *Strategic Management Journal, 17*(Winter Special Issue), 27-43.

Taylor, F. W. (1911). *The principles of scientific management*. New York: Harper.

Teece, D. J. (1998). Capturing value from knowledge assets: The new economy, market for know-how and intangible assets. *California Management Review*, *40*(3), 55–79.

von Hippel, E. (1998). Economics of product development by users: The impact of "sticky" local information. *Management Science*, *44*(5), 629–644. doi:10.1287/mnsc.44.5.629

Vygotsky, L. S. (1962). *Thought and language*. Cambridge, MA: The MIT Press. doi:10.1037/11193-000

Vygotsky, L. S. (1978). *Mind in society: Development of Higher Psychological Processes* (14th ed.). Cambridge, MA: Harvard Press.

ADDITIONAL READING

Blackler, F. (1995). Knowledge, knowledge work and organizations: An overview and interpretation. *Organization Studies*, *16*(6), 1021–1046. doi:10.1177/017084069501600605

Bynum, T. W. (2004). Ethical decision-making and case analysis in computer ethics. In Bynum, T. W., & Rogerson, S. (Eds.), *Computer Ethics and Professional Responsibility* (pp. 60–88). Malden, MA: Blackwell Publishing.

Kavathatzopoulos, I. (2004). Making ethical decisions in professional life. In Montgomery, H., Lipshitz, R., & Brehmer, B. (Eds.), *How Professionals Make Decisions* (pp. 277–288). Mahwah, NJ: Lawrence Erlbaum Associates Inc.

Styhre, A. (2003). *Understanding knowledge management- Critical and postmodern perspectives*. Malmö: Liber Ekonom.

KEY TERMS AND DEFINITIONS

Ethics: The authors include into ethics all the matters that arise from conflicting values and interests of stakeholders. Ethics is not just about specific nameable core values like right to life, justice, privacy, etc. Rather it regards all the needs, values and interests of individuals and groups.

Ethical Competence: Not the ability to always act according to guidelines or predefined principles; not the ability to act in a manner that is consistent with the most number of normative philosophies; but the ability to use purposeful ethical problem-solving and decision-making methods when handling moral problems.

Ethical vs. Moral: The distinction between these two terms is not always clear and it is not uncommon to use them as synonyms. We use the word ethical when we write about ethics from a metaphilosophical perspective and, moral when we write about personal values or interpretations of ethical topics. An expression "moral decision making" would for instance suggest that a person is well acquainted with contextual moral values and readily prepared to do "good" in any given situation. The expression "ethical decision making" does not address the substance of morality but instead the procedural competence of handling moral problems.

APPENDIX

Ethical Index: ETHIX

Person

1. Have you received education in sufficient extensiveness and quality for you to be able to deal with moral conflicts and problems in a satisfying way?
2. How do you find predicting moral conflicts and problems before they arise or develop into bigger conflicts?
3. How do find handling and solving concrete moral problems you face upon in your work?
4. How do you find arguing for, explaining and defending your ethical decisions and procedures in a convincing way?
5. Do you feel certain or uncertain when dealing with moral problems?

Organization

1. Does your organization show an ethical profile outwards and inwards; does it present itself as an organisation that cares about ethical issues?
2. Do you find your organization taking a real interest in ethical issues, or does it only pretend?
3. How do you find your organization dealing with the ethical issues?
4. Does your organization have special processes and routines for handling moral problems, for example, plan meetings, discussion groups etc.?
5. If your organization has ethical processes and routines, how do find them working?
6. Are there in your organization formally responsible individuals, groups or committees dealing with ethical issues?
7. If your organization has formally responsible individuals or groups, how do you find them working?
8. Do find your organization supportive when you face ethical issues?
9. Do you find support in your colleagues if and when you face ethical issues?

Section 5
Trends

"Action is eloquence"
William Shakespeare

In order to be an eloquent manuscript, the following chapters will "unlock" ideas and practical proposals to approach the ethical and social issues in private and public knowledge management environments. The future is starting despite a "long road ahead"... Therefore, is challenging to expect a multiple critics and comments from scholars and practitioners from a broad range of research disciplines, in order to improve these proposals as well as to introduce new ones.

Chapter 13
Knowledge Worker Fair Compensation:
Ethical Issues and Social Dilemmas

Gonçalo Jorge Morais Costa
De Montfort University, UK

ABSTRACT

One of the key characteristics in knowledge management is the importance of human resources. Therefore, main stream literature has been discussing the concept of knowledge worker, its characteristics, and duties versus rights, and human resources policies in its dissimilar perspectives (knowledge workers retention, personal mastery, intellectual property rights, among others). Although, empirical studies seem to disregard if knowledge workers feel that are well compensated, or what dimensions entail faire compensation. Hence, this chapter aims to recognize knowledge workers feeling about faire compensation, and what elements are essential to achieve it through a conceptual framework. For that, the chapter is divided into six sections: the research questions; knowledge worker (key characteristics and responsibilities versus rights); fairness (etymology and the contribution of Rawls); linking the theoretical basis; empirical results (methodological remarks, findings and discussion); future research directions (the surrealist assumption, Dali surrealism and the metaphorical assumption).

INTRODUCTION

The last decades have witnessed production of research on knowledge work, due to a conviction that economic achievement of post-industrial societies progressively depends on skills to utilize knowledge (Stehr, 2001; Castells, 2000). Therefore, beyond manage knowledge organizations need to realize that human resources are essential to promote knowledge creation, utilization and sharing. In spite of this level of criticality that human resources introduce the concept of "knowledge worker" entails an ambiguous perception (Pyöriä, 2005; Alvesson, 2004; 2001). This is a consequence of an attempt to resume its distinctive features, as for instance: processes information (Davenport, Järvenpää & Beers, 1996); utilizes information and communication technologies

DOI: 10.4018/978-1-61520-873-9.ch013

(Garavelli *et al.*, 2003); has problem-solving skills (Tsoukas & Vladimirou, 2001); produces non-routine work (Lillrank, 2002); has increasing levels of autonomy (Darr, 2003); and, is collaborative (Kristensen & Kijl, 2008).

Furthermore, in order to attract these workers (Gayton, 2008) with high levels of personal mastery (Senge, 2006) it is essential to create an effective Human Resources policy. Literature has been recognizing this quandary and assumes that human resource management practices need to be internally consistent so that they mutually reinforce each other, namely career structure and reward systems (Currie & Kerrin, 2003). In that sense, an array of organizational incentives can be highlighted: monetary and non-monetary rewards, as well as intrinsic and extrinsic (Bartol & Srivastava, 2002); despite dissimilar motivation strategies for knowledge workers (Petroni & Colacino, 2008).

As a result, this contribution endeavours to discuss knowledge workers feeling about faire compensation, and what elements are essential to achieve it through a conceptual framework based on the theory of justice (Rawls, 1971). The author still refers that the argument will consider the concept of fairness about compensation as a combination of three dimensions of organizational justice: distributive, procedural, and interactional (e.g. Cropanzano & Randall, 1992).

THE RESEARCH QUESTIONS

Since this contribution is not promoting a traditional approach to human resources managing, namely knowledge workers. Despite the novelty of the subject it entails a minor component of the author PhD research project (for further details chapter 16), leading to the following research questions:

1. Do you consider that knowledge creation, management and sharing into the organizational environment are fairly rewarded?
2. State what is meant to be a fair compensation regarding knowledge creation, management and sharing in an organizational environment?

The initial research query examines if knowledge workers feel that are fairly rewarded, as well as the question was also posed to middle managers and top managers in order to understand each group perception. Yet, it is compulsory to notify the potential Readers that is an open choice question with the subsequent answering possibilities: never, rarely, usually, often, always, and I do not respond. On the other hand, the second question seeks to recognize fair compensation dimensions through an ask for agreement option.

KNOWLEDGE WORKER

Key Characteristics

Following Kelloway & Barling (2000) it is possible to illustrate knowledge workers as investors, because these choose when they want to use their knowledge. So, knowledge workers are likely to employ their knowledge as an extension of their skills, motivation and opportunity. Or, Davenport & Prusak (2000) define knowledge workers as those who create knowledge, or the prevailing component of their work is knowledge. Although, this definition was enhanced in order to include the ones who also distribute and employ knowledge (Davenport, 2002). Concluding, the author will follow Horvath (2001) definition: "anyone who works for a living at the tasks of developing or using knowledge". Additionally, for Efimova (2003) knowledge work can be explained through the iceberg metaphor: unlike traditional work its interactions seem invisible, because informal circumstances may represent until 80%.

Thus, knowledge workers impose a shift in the balance of organizational power, because power in social contexts assumes three primary sources (Nickols, 2003, pp. 5): "politics (i.e., power derived from relationships among people); position (i.e., power derived from formally constituted authority); and profession (i.e., power derived from specialized knowledge)."

Responsibilities Versus Rights

Bearing in mind that every worker is bounded to duties and rights, it is reasonable to claim that a trade-off arises. For The Free Dictionary (2010a), trade-off can be defined as an exchange of one thing in return for another, especially relinquishment of one benefit or advantage for another regarded as more desirable.

For the purpose of this analysis the author introduces the work of Storey (2005) as regards to knowledge worker requirements:

- behaviour: resumes the organizational expectation that workers have the ability to be creative and proactive instead of complying with repeated custom actions. Another prerequisite is to present educational qualifications along with pertinent professional experiences, as well as the possess the ability to learn constantly;
- capabilities: ability to deal with large amount of complex data or information, as well as to learn from it in order to respond to the external environment challenges through semi-structured organizational routines;
- motivations: knowledge workers need to be motivated in order to enhance their personal mastery, and for that the organizational values, culture and climate are vital.

FAIRNESS

Etymology

According to the Wiktionary (2010) fairness is the property of being fair; and fair means free of bias, which evolved from an earlier meaning "morally pure" (Online Etymology Dictionary, 2010). Moreover, fairness or fair entail a similar definition in nowadays: having or exhibiting a disposition that is free of favouritism or bias; impartial: a fair mediator; just to all parties; or even, equitable: a compromise that is fair to both factions (The Free Dictionary, 2010b).

The Contribution of Rawls

John Rawls (1971) defined justice as fairness: "it conveys the idea that the principles of justice are agreed to in an initial situation as fair." (p. 12). Rawls still claims that individuals decide under the veil of ignorance, meaning that are not entirely aware of their personal features and role in society. Hence, this assumption leads us to conclude that people do not pursue personal interests, and by that mean assuring equality. In addition, this author refers three psychological factors that sustain the principle of justice: morality of authority, morality of association, and morality of principles. Therefore, Okin (1989) criticizes Rawls moral development assumptions namely the duty to teach morals and gender neutrality. Although, the author will disregard Okin criticism as pointed out by Hartline (Hartline, 2008).

LINKING THE THEORETICAL BASIS

After framing the theoretical components it is time to understand how these variables interact, and most importantly which key issues promote the existence of a fair compensation within knowledge environments.

Remembering Horvath (2001), "anyone who works for a living at the tasks of developing or using knowledge" is considered a knowledge worker. This statement induces to the following assumption: knowledge process (creation, retention/utilization, and sharing), meaning that Rawls (1971) macro analytical guidelines will be:

- justice and knowledge creation and sharing;
- justice and fair protection and retribution;
- justice and fair compensation;
- justice and recognition of human dignity and autonomy.

Justice and Knowledge Creation and Sharing

According to Hurley (2005), knowledge workers are morally accountable with reference to knowledge production and sharing within the organizational environment. In addition, that moral accountability is also bounded to organizations (Costa, Prior & Rogerson, 2008a), because it is compulsory the existence of a knowledge sharing environment. Nevertheless, to promote ethical environments concerning knowledge sharing is extremely difficult, and not utopian like Wilson (2002) points out. The answer relies on balancing the ethics of self-interest versus knowledge sharing (Wang, 2004).

Justice and Fair Protection and Retribution

Lambert *et al.* (2005) defends that exclusively spotlighting upon employee rewards or outcomes, is expectable to deal with sanction in a fair and just manner, which is consistent with the claim of Costa, Prior & Rogerson (2008). The focus on fairness should act for rewarding and sanctioning, because workers have a moral responsibility not simply to be productive but also share the produced organizational knowledge (O'Neill & Adya, 2007). The following example resumes the previous arguments:

an employee might compare the pay and benefits received by their fellow employee and make a comparison of their effort at work with their rewards. As a result of this comparison, individuals decide to exert more or less effort, or change their perceptions of inputs or outcomes. Equity is perceived when the input/outcome ratio of the individual is equal to those of others compared with. Perceived inequality, for example, an employee who perceives rewards are inequitably distributed among employees in their organization, might react with seeking employment elsewhere. (Haar & Spell, 2009, p. 1829)

Justice and Fair Compensation

Distributive justice principles would acknowledge that a worker deserves additional compensation, however does not portray the reasons to such claim. In fact, distributive justice frequently evaluates job satisfaction and workers intentions to continue working (Greenberg & Cropanzano, 2001). Although, workers are also concerned with the fairness of procedures that enable compensation systems, which according to these authors are: be a consistent process, free from bias, correct, participative and ethical.

On the other hand, procedural justice will shed some light over the impact of organizational values and mutual trust, because workers that are fairly treated easily accept if necessary a decreasing in their payment (Turillo *et al.*, 2002). Furthermore, fair compensations must reproduce desirable values and ways of achieving organizational goals (Verplanken & Holland, 2002), since compensation systems structure typically reflects the underlying organizational ideology. Therefore, these systems must entail acceptable ethical and moral values (Cropanzano *et al.*, 2001), which for example CEOs exorbitant wages are an example (Lavelle, 2002).

Justice and Recognition of Human Dignity and Autonomy

Miller (1999) refers that a core component of any theory of justice embraces human rights, which in this case configures the following dimensions:

- the right to life- includes the right to feel secure and safe, which means that organizations ought to inform society about potential harm (Ryan, 2002);
- the right to the freedom of expression of ideas- is bounded to the moral accountability of knowledge workers produce knowledge, as well as organizations create a knowledge environment (du Plessis, Britz & Davel, 2007);
- the right of access to those ideas- debates the existing trade-off between personal effort and benefit (Ford & Staples, 2005);
- the right to protect and control expressed ideas- resumes the trade-off among workers faire compensation, and the organizational moral right to protect its economic interests (Blyth, 2005);
- the right to privacy recognizes the autonomy and dignity of individuals- knowledge environments must respect individual privacy rights (Baskerville & Dulipovici, 2006), which leads to a necessary discussion about privacy (Stahl, 2007).

Intermediate Conclusion

The quotation of O'Reilly III & Pfeffer (2000, pp. 3) summarizes in an interesting way the overall discussion: "great people want to work at great places where they can actually use their talents, where they are treated with dignity, trust, and respect, and where they are engaged by the values and culture of the organization."

Theoretical Framework

As a final remark, the author refers that figure 1 depicts these concepts and their relationships (theoretical framework).

EMPIRICAL RESULTS

Methodological Remarks

Creswell (2003) refers that a qualitative research may induce several angles of analysis. For that, in order to explore an event from an in-depth insight the researcher might choose a diminutive but informative case, or might perform a simple inferential numerical analysis. On the other hand, Miles & Huberman (1994) denote that descriptive research intends to make complex issues logical by reducing them to their fundamentals; or, if the researcher is not entirely conscious of the facts, in

Figure 1. Theoretical framework

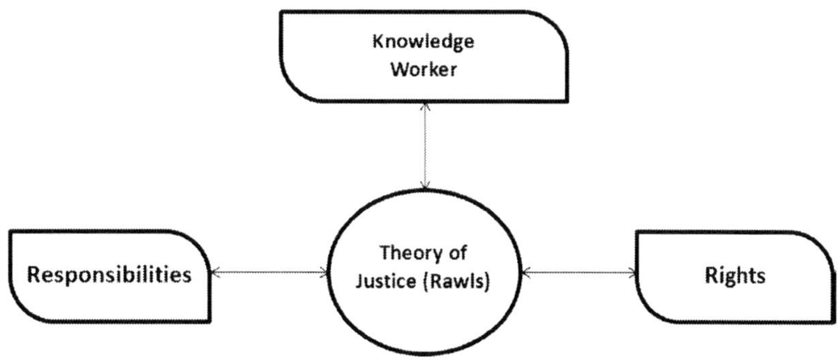

spite of recognizing the research issue (Zikmund & Zikmund, 2000). And, explanatory research endeavours to exemplify certain phenomena from contrasting insights (Yin, 1994), which entails the research problem.

In addition, to consent subjective and inquisitive outcomes a blend of interpretative and critical theory is consistent with look for meaning in context. So, to identify how a reality appeared is imperative to analyse the social and historical environment (Klein & Myers, 1999), regardless the possibility to question the output (Sandberg, 2005). Likewise, the study of social reality is inner to critical research as acknowledged in numerous narratives of critical research (Hirschheim & Klein, 1994).

Finally, empirical data was collected throughout questionnaires and interviews (PhD research project- see chapter 16), and informational conversations. Semi-structured interviews sponsor a method to acquire the informants beliefs and opinions through a verbal exchange (Burns, 2000); a questionnaire can serve as an inductive method with the aim to formulate new theory with higher or lower levels of validity according to the type of questions (Gill & Johnson, 2002); and, informational conversations intend to discover, understand and gain insight of people experiences (Paton, 1980).

Findings

PhD Results

The empirical outcomes highlighted in this section involve two levels of analysis: pre-tests and pilot studies results. In short, pre-tests were performed to 50 individuals with divergent professional and educational backgrounds during February 2009; and, the pilot studies have occurred in June 2009 within a learning organization that operates in Portugal, being their sample size objective 25 per cent of the organizational population. Moreover, for further details as regards to the methodological and analytical procedures read chapter 16; although, an important remark is: the results for each procedure will be divided into simple inferential numerical analysis (global and by focus group- top management, middle management, and workers) for research question 1, and content analysis for research question 2 (just focus groups).

The results demonstrate the denial of a fair compensation, and it is interesting to denote that middle managers seem to share workers perspective with reference to this topic. Nonetheless, a higher detail of analysis is decisive for understanding these results (observe the following sections), and the dimensions of faire compensation (content analysis). Hence, some keen examples of fair compensation and its dimensions are illustrated in table 2, as well as translation was not performed in order to avoid the lost of sensitive meanings.

Academic Experiences

This subsection endeavours to shed some light over the author personal experiences in his lecturing or participation in worldwide conferences, and a major conclusion seems to arise: fair compensation tends to demonstrate extreme positions! The expression "extreme positions" intends to portray the existing gigantic gap about faire compensation: managers' assumption is that workers are often fairly rewarded; and, workers acknowledge the absence of a fair compensation. For instance, during IIRH 2010 Conference in Setúbal, Portugal, devoted to *Research in Human Resources* it was interesting to denote that despite literature refer that people are the "core", and what stimulus managers need to produce to engage a knowledge environment the empirical results demonstrate that these policies do not engage personalization, compensation features resume traditional approaches which are not suitable for a knowledge economy, or even that managers actions do not match their discourse. An example was the keynote speech of Francisco Cesário, CEO of PT Contact:

Table 1. Research question 1 results

Pre-tests		Results
Global		The generic results were: never (8%), rarely (50%), usually (22%), often (16%), always (4%)
Group	Top management	More than 80% believed that workers are fairly compensated (combining usually, often and always)
	Middle management	60% referred never and rarely
	Workers	The combination never and rarely entailed over 85%
Pilot studies		**Results**
Global		52% acknowledged rarely, 24% usually and 20% often
Group	Top management	100% argued that workers were fairly compensated
	Middle management	65% combining never and rarely
	Workers	62% claimed rarely

Nós apostámos em transferir parte dos nossos call centers para zonas do país com elevadas taxas de desemprego (interior), pelo que se prova a nossa responsabilidade social (...) (transfer of "production" to areas with high rates of unemployment, as a sign of moral responsibility)

However, when confronted about the true reasons for this movement the answer was:

Razões económicas! Por exemplo, as entidades públicas locais cederam um espaço para permitir a instalação da empresa, assim como efectivamente os salários auferidos pelos colaboradores destas regiões são inferiores aos praticados em Lisboa ou no Porto (..) (economic reasons! Being examples, the local government support, and these workers lower salaries when compared with Lisbon or Oporto)

These arguments clearly demonstrate that beyond rich literature is vital to educate managers to be open-minded and ethical! In fact, this corroborates the numerous informal dialogues undertaken with the editor learners about the perception of faire compensation in knowledge environments. Their responses, representing professional experiences, demonstrate that two additional critical issues seem to arise: the Human Resources policies shortcomings about intellectual property rights (personal versus organizational), as well as the gap amid managers and workers compensation.

Eu rejeito por complete que as experiências pessoais vivenciadas pela minha pessoa na organização sejam propriedade intelectual desta (personal experiences as intellectual organization property- a explicit denial)

É inacreditável a diferença existente entre os valores auferidos pelos colaboradores e a gestão, até porque esta comete erros de palmatória! (gap between managers and workers compensation, as well as knowledge workers have the ability to question about strategic options)

Professional Experiences

While as a Key Account (before embracing lecturing), or acting today as a consultant the author has observed that faire compensation is an extremely complex issue in organizational contexts, namely in small and medium enterprises (SME's). Despite this observation a detailed analysis will be underlined in subsection discussion; so, about

Table 2. Research question 2 results

Pre-tests	Results	Analysis
Top management	*"Justa compensação: o retorno (pessoal e profissional) pela participação individual nos processos de criação, gestão e partilha do conhecimento"*	The importance of knowledge creation, use and sharing
	"Justa compensação não assenta em princípios meramente economicistas, mas também de reconhecimento e valorização do colaborador"	The recognition of the financial and non-financial dimensions
	"Justa compensação: quando alguém recebe algo em troca do seu trabalho ou esforço por ter conseguido um feito com relevância para a organização, sendo partilhado por toda a equipa"	The identification of the financial and non-financial elements
Middle management	*"Justa compensação pode ser monetária, ou melhores condições no ambiente organizacional"*	The acknowledgment of financial and non-financial realities
	"Todas as pessoas na organização quando partilham ideias ou colaboram devem ser reconhecidas, ou monetariamente ou através de novos cargos, etc"	Primacy regarding recognition for those who create, use and share knowledge
	"Compensação: plano de carreira e promoção de acordo com o desempenho, assim como, prémios monetário"	The traditional perspective: pure economic
Workers	*"Acho que se deve recompensar de forma justa aqueles que contribuem para a criação, gestão e partilha do conhecimento"*	Again, the significance of knowledge as a process
	"A justa compensação poderá mostrar-se pela análise, validação e quiçá adaptação e partilha de novas ideias, podendo assim ser um contributo positivo para a empresa"	The importance of knowledge sharing
	"Justa compensação pode ser monetária, flexibilidade de horários, aumento da autonomia"	A interesting bound: enhanced autonomy as a way of fair compensation
Pilot studies	**Results**	**Analysis**
Top management	*"Justa compensação é o reconhecimento a todos os colaboradores que fazem parte da organização"*	The evidence of an organizational transversal process
	"Justa recompensa surge através de factores monetários e não monetários"	Economic and non-economic factors
	"Tudo depende do impacto e das próprias pessoas em causa"	Personalization as a fact
Middle management	*"Entendo os valores financeiros associados (salário e/ou promoções), e os não financeiros (reconhecimento)"*	The combination of economic and non-economic principles
	"Compensação pode resumir-se apenas ao reconhecimento verbal do esforço no desenvolvimento do conhecimento. Não tem que se reflectir obrigatoriamente em valores monetários"	Recognition as a crucial factor
	"Em termos pessoais uma perfeita compensação é saber qual o meu trabalho e papel organizacional, e através dele respeitarem a minha autonomia e privacidade"	Autonomy and privacy as basics for faire compensation
Workers	*"O conhecimento que o colaborador possa partilhar e que o vá afectar positivamente ou negativamente na evolução dentro da empresa"*	Knowledge sharing substance
	"Justa compensação é a partilha de conhecimento sustentada na confiança mútua"	Sharing knowledge and trust as keys for faire compensation
	"As nossas organizações ainda não estão adaptadas à realidade de que as empresas são as pessoas e não o contrário, isto é, o mérito deve trazer mais valias, apesar do objecto de trabalho ser raramente recompensado seja por estímulo oral ou por valores compensatórios (financeiros ou outros)"	The claim that Human Resources policies are inadequate

of empirical evidences at a professional level is the author intention to highlight two essential quotations: the first occurred during a meeting with a CEO of a medium learning organization;

Table 3. Professional experiences as regards to question 2

Professional experience	Context	Results	Analysis
Meeting	Discussion about innovation in rewarding workers	*"Os colaboradores não necessitam de incentivos adicionais, pois já auferem o salário (...) Além disso, autonomia significa que não podemos controlar o seu trabalho"*	Ignoring literature recommendations
Conference about organizational innovation	Human Resources Manager speech	*"Nós temos uma verdadeira política de recursos humanos, pois valorizamos o conhecimento dos nossos colaboradores (...). Um exemplo foi a atribuição de um prémio de produtividade de 400€ a um colaborador por ter criado um produto financeiro totalmente novo que vai ser introduzido nos mercados financeiros"*	The quandary of fair compensation

the second happened in a conference organized by a major financial institution on the topic organizational innovation. Nevertheless, it is vital to detail the context of each quotation, as well as to understand the content of these quotations (observe table 3). Once again, translation was not executed in order to avoid the lost of insightful connotations.

Discussion

More people feel that are treated fairly, more reasons will have to identify with that group. This assumption is also recognized in organizational environments, because empirical data demonstrate that workers are less worried their absolute income (Adams, 1963). In fact, Cohen (2008) highlights that Rawls social requires benefits and burdens distribution by individuals, as well as inequalities concerning incentive payments are indeed fair. The reason for his claim relies on the following argument: workers with higher levels of productivity will benefit the organization, and as consequence all organizational members will benefit from that situation. Even so, a CEO salary when compared to the remaining organizational members is a social dilemma. For instance, Söderström *et al.* (2003) have demonstrated tremendous gaps between CEOs and other professions; Piketty & Saez (2006) study acknowledges that CEO salaries between 1980-1998 raised 9 per cent average and workers just 3,7; and, the major problem is the historical data of unethical and fraudulent behaviours as regards to corporate performance for CEOs personal gain (Meyer, 2003). The knowledge economy has enhanced this dilemma because knowledge workers possess enough competencies, skills and knowledge to question managers' strategic decisions as well as their consequences. In addition, it is common to observe that knowledge workers academic and professional background is higher than the CEO, namely in small medium companies, which enhances this dilemma. Thus, the author disregards Nichols & Subramaniam (2001) claim that CEO compensation is a matter of personal judgment.

On the other hand, procedural fairness is related to the process of distributive fairness and can be summarized through:

- participation: reflects the opportunity of knowledge workers express their knowledge, which bounded to a tangible and intangible reward as regards to knowledge sharing will promote a truthful sharing environment (Cabrera, Collins & Salgado, 2006). This is consistent with the recognition that sharing activities improves and sustains knowledge professionals (Wasko & Faraj, 2005), as well as if knowledge workers feel that their knowledge is "snatched" tend to become self-protective and secretive;

- neutrality- a precondition to achieve it the conviction that rules do not allow personal advantages to enter their decision-making. Fehr & Rochenbach (2003) also demonstrate that sanctions that serve the punisher's self-interests disable cooperative behaviour, whereas sanctions perceived as pro-socially;
- and dignity/respect/autonomy- empirical evidences highlight that knowledge workers treated with dignity and respect enhance their levels of sharing behaviour and altruism (Moorman, Niehoff & Organ, 1993). Furthermore, autonomy encompasses for managers the following actions: acknowledge the knowledge worker understanding, afford it significant information in a non-manipulative way, offering decision making, and encouraging proactivity (Baard, Deci & Ryan, 2004), because a supportive management style to autonomy is crucial to promote knowledge sharing (Vansteenkiste *et al.*, 2004).

FUTURE RESEARCH DIRECTION

The Surrealist Assumption

According to the Merriam-Webster Dictionary (2010), surrealism resumes the principles, ideals, or generating fantastic or inconsistent imagery or effects in art, literature, film, or theater through deviant juxtapositions and blends. As such, it reproduces quite well the proposals to be introduced by the author for future research.

Dali Surrealism

Dali through is *Paranoia Critical Method* assumed a way to observe reality in order to reflect double images in the same composition (Salvador Dali Art Gallery, 2010). Moreover, his artwork is not merely used in artistic creation, but equally in scientific work because surrealist theory of automatism was transformed in a method. For Ruffa (2005), by linking surrealist actions and scientific research Dali demonstrates that we systemically have partial or total lack of understanding regarding a subject, meaning that reflection upon existing models is required. As a result, "Dalí draws our attention to the fact that there is no ontological difference between the scientific and artistic spheres, and nor is one superior to the other in terms of their approach to reality" (Ruffa, 2005, pp. 12).

The Metaphorical Assumption

After a careful research with reference to Salvador Dali paintings, the author has decided to illustrate *The Ship* (1943). In his painting, Dali inspires us to question ourselves instead of being slaves ("tied up to the strings of life"), as well as to promote change ("go by the wind"). The wind is seen as the life flow which people may dare (Coelho, 2009). In fact, the aim of these proposals is to acknowledge the need to challenge the established principles with reference to knowledge workers without ignoring compensation systems literature (e.g. Scott *et al.*, 2007) despite the several critics that will arise.

Therefore some proposals that organizations should entail are:

- personalize the compensation systems: as Cohen (2008) demonstrates it is possible to sustain equity and fairness;
- creative rewarding systems: personalization will promote creative rewarding systems. From the author professional experience, typically too many constraints are imposed in designing novel ways of acknowledging the topic. For some ideas the author suggests the work of Zairi, Jarrar & Aspinwall (2010), or Petroni & Colacino (2008);
- protect tacit and explicit knowledge: is common that organizational tacit and ex-

plicit knowledge is not entirely protected. Explicit knowledge encompasses a simple resolution; however, organizational tacit knowledge is bounded to workers personal knowledge which resumes the trade-off between self-interest and versus knowledge sharing (Wang, 2004). A potential solution is to "draw a moral flexible rule" that acknowledges personal experiences as non-organizational property. Through this assumption knowledge workers will feel treated with fairness and dignity leading to a truly knowledge sharing environment;

- acknowledge intellectual property rights: as previously referred Human Resources policies do not address this issue. Define a Solomonic decision, meaning to acknowledge workers intellectual property rights as for instance, offer a percentage over the market outcome of the product or service for a period of time which can be diminished if the worker leaves the organization. Bearing in mind the second example of professional experiences, the financial institution ought to reward the worker with a percentage of the market result during a year!;
- create a knowledge sharing environment: despite the existing backgrounds and competences of knowledge workers, it is vital to be aware of the existing relationships in knowledge sharing amid "those who know" and the "know-notes" (Wang & Noe, 2010);
- assume that knowledge workers values maybe contradictory to organizational values: organizational culture is "a spherical concept (metaphorical symbolism for perfect and constant), and therefore does not reproduces the existing challenges that knowledge management enables" (Costa, Prior & Rogerson, 2010, pp. 84). Although, to recognize values diversity and knowledge workers autonomy will allow to enhance knowledge sharing (Berg, 2010), and ultimately a growing identification with the organization ethical values;
- actions versus discourse ethics: managers primary responsibilities inherent in the organizational ontology through discursive ethics resumes two assumptions: normative claims in order to be valid require a cognitive meaning and can be treated *like* claims to truth; the justification of norms involves a real discourse be carried out and thus cannot occur in a strictly monological form, i.e., in the form of a hypothetical process of argumentation occurring in the individual mind (Rhen, 2002).

As a final remark, the author reveals the following thought for managers: do not question the financial value of increasing compensations if knowledge workers demonstrate higher levels of productivity, because it would be a sign of a competitive organization as well as additional profits. Besides, the economic approach skews any changing attitude as regards to non-monetary compensation, which is sometimes far more important than the monetary one.

CONCLUSION

Changing traditional compensation systems enable several theoretical constraints namely "psychological and cultural", however neglecting that possibility induces to a lack of organizational retention concerning knowledge workers. Knowledge workers have distinctive characteristics that require a novel approach to its rewarding as the empirical results clearly demonstrate, which top management continues to ignore. A potential justification for today's organizational reality might be the novelty of the topic, but clearly depicts the *status quo* of knowledge society and managers lack of moral reasoning. In fact, despite the introduction of ethics in business the truth is that managers still ignore it, or use it as a marketing tool (similar to corporate social responsibility) which will endanger organizational survival. The assumption for this resumes the lack of recognition about justice in knowledge creation and sharing, fair protection and retribution, fair compensation, and the recognition of human dignity and autonomy. As a final remark, the author argues that the conceptual framework also enables a positive and feasible response to the research questions; yet, is urgent to enhance the number of empirical studies and novel approaches to the topic.

ACKNOWLEDGMENT

The editor would like to thank the insightful comments of Nuno Sotero Alves da Silva to the earlier versions of this chapter, as well as to all that shared their insights with the editor with reference to fair compensation in knowledge environments.

REFERENCES

Adams, J. S. (1963). Toward an understanding of inequity. *Journal of Abnormal and Social Psychology*, *67*(5), 422–463. doi:10.1037/h0040968

Alvesson, M. (2001). Knowledge work: Ambiguity, image and identity. *Human Relations*, *54*(7), 863–886. doi:10.1177/0018726701547004

Alvesson, M. (2004). *Knowledge work and knowledge intensive firms*. Oxford, UK: Oxford University Press.

Baard, P. P., Deci, E. L., & Ryan, R. M. (2004). Intrinsic need satisfaction: A motivational basis of performance and well-being in two work settings. *Journal of Applied Social Psychology*, *34*(10), 2045–2068. doi:10.1111/j.1559-1816.2004.tb02690.x

Bartol, K. M., & Srivastava, A. (2002). Encouraging knowledge sharing: The role of organizational reward systems. *Journal of Leadership & Organizational Studies*, *9*(1), 64–76. doi:10.1177/107179190200900105

Baskerville, R., & Dulipovici, A. (2006). The ethics of knowledge transfers and conversions: Property or privacy rights. In K. VanLehn (Ed.), *Proceedings of the 39th Hawaii International Conference on System Sciences* (pp. 144-152). Hawaii: IEEE.

Berg, A. M. (2010, September). *"Lean and mean or fat and good?" - On organizational redundancies and diversity*. Paper presented at the 32nd EGPA Annual Conference, Toulouse, France.

Blyth, A. (2005). Business behaving responsibly. *Director (Cincinnati, Ohio)*, *59*(1), 30.

Burns, R. B. (2000). *Introduction to research methods*. London: Sage Publishers.

Cabrera, A., Collins, W. C., & Salgado, J. F. (2006). Determinants of individual engagement in knowledge sharing. *International Journal of Human Resource Management*, *17*(2), 245–264.

Castells, M. (2000). *The rise of the network society*. Oxford, UK: Blackwell Publishers.

Coelho, P. (2009). Salvador-Dali. *Paulo Coelho's Blog*. Retrieved September 2, 2010, from, http://paulocoelhoblog.com/2009/03/13/my-favorite-painters-salvador-dali/

Cohen, C. A. (2008). *Rescuing justice and equality*. Cambridge, MA: Harvard University Press.

Costa, G. J. M., Prior, M., & Rogerson, S. (2008a). Individual ethics and knowledge management: Arising conflicts. In Bynum, T. (Eds.), *ETHICOMP 2008: Living, Working and Learning Beyond Technology* (pp. 117–129). Mantua, Italy: University of Pavia.

Costa, G. J. M., Prior, M., & Rogerson, S. (2008b, September). *Free ride in knowledge management? Ethical and moral dilemmas!* Paper presented at the ETHICOMP 2008: Living, Working and Learning Beyond Technology, Mantua, Italy.

Costa, G. J. M., Prior, M., & Rogerson, S. (2010). Individual ethics and knowledge management: Arising conflicts. In Bynum, T. (Eds.), *ETHICOMP 2010: The "Backwards, Forwards and Sideways" Changes in ICT* (pp. 117–129). Tarragona, Italy: University of Rovira i Virgili.

Creswell, J. W. (2003). *Research design: Qualitative, quantitative and mixed methods approaches* (2nd ed.). Thousand Oaks, CA: Sage Publications.

Cropanzano, R. (2001). Moral virtues, fairness heuristics, social entities, and other denizens of organizational justice. *Journal of Vocational Behavior*, *58*(2), 164–209. doi:10.1006/jvbe.2001.1791

Cropanzano, R., & Randall, M. L. (1992). Injustice and work behavior: A historical review. In Cropanzano, R. (Ed.), *Justice in the Workplace: Approaching Fairness in Human Resource Management* (pp. 3–20). Hillsdale, NJ: Lawrence Erlbaum.

Currie, G., & Kerrin, M. (2003). Human resource management and knowledge management: Enhancing knowledge sharing in a pharmaceutical company. *International Journal of Human Resource Management*, *14*(6), 1027–1045. doi:10.1080/0958519032000124641

Darr, A. (2003). Control and autonomy among knowledge workers in sales: An employee perspective. *Employee Relations*, *25*(1), 31–41. doi:10.1108/01425450310453508

Davenport, T. (2002). Can you boost knowledge work's impact on the bottom line? *Management Update*, *7*(11), 3–5.

Davenport, T., & Prusak, L. (2000). *Working knowledge: How organizations manage what they know*. Boston, MA: Harvard Business School Press.

Davenport, T. H., Järvenpää, S. L., & Beers, M. C. (1996). Improving knowledge work processes. *Sloan Management Review*, *37*(4), 53–65.

du Plessis, J. C., Britz, J. J., & Davel, R. (2007). Slave or sibling: A moral reframing the corporate knowledge sharing community. *University of Pretoria*. Retrieved August 25, 2010, from, http://ol.up.ac.za/upspace/bitstream/2263/1808/1/DuPlessis_Slave%282006%29.pdf

Efimova, L. (2003). Knowledge worker paradox. *Knowledge Board*. Retrieved August 28, 2010, from, https://doc.novay.nl/dsweb/Get/Version-12745/knowledge_worker_paradox.pdf

Fehr, E., & Rockenbach, B. (2003). Detrimental effects of sanctions on human altruism. *Nature*, *422*(13), 137–140. doi:10.1038/nature01474

Ford, D. P., & Staples, D. S. (2005). Perceived value of knowledge: Shall I give you my gem, my coal? In W. Arbeitspapiere (Ed.), *Proceedings of 38th Hawaii International Conference on Systems Sciences* (pp. 247-256). Hawaii: IEEE.

Garavelli, A. C., et al. (2003). How motivating knowledge workers. *European KM Forum*. Retrieved August 25, 2010, from, http://www.knowledgeboard.com/download/480/Theme2-Synthesis_Report-_public_.v03.2003-02-06.pdf

Gayton, C. M. (2008). Business ethics, restrictions on employment and knowledge management. *VINE: The Journal of Information and Knowledge Management Systems*, *38*(2), 174–183.

Gill, J., & Johnson, P. (2002). *Research methods for managers* (3rd ed.). Thousand Oaks, CA: Sage Publications.

Greenberg, J., & Cropanzano, R. (2001). *Advances in organizational justice*. Stanford, CA: Stanford University Press.

Haar, J. M., & Spell, C. S. (2009). How does distributive justice affect work attitudes? The moderating effects of autonomy. *International Journal of Human Resource Management*, *20*(8), 1827–1842. doi:10.1080/09585190903087248

Hartline, T. (2008). Rawls's a theory of justice: Addressing the criticisms of Okin and Pateman. In Wolf, M. P., & Musselman, L. (Eds.), *Voicing Ideas* (*Vol. 3*, pp. 59–63). Fresno, CA: California State University.

Hirschheim, R., & Klein, H. K. (1994). Realizing emancipatory principles in information systems development: The case for Ethics. *Management Information Systems Quarterly*, *18*(1), 83–109. doi:10.2307/249611

Horvath, D. (2001). Knowledge worker. *SearchCRM*. Retrieved August 28, 2010, from, http://searchcrm.techtarget.com/definition/knowledge-worker

Hurley, T. A., & Green, G. W. (2005). Knowledge management and the nonprofit industry: A within and between approach. *Journal of Knowledge Management Practice, 6*. Retrieved September 15, 2010, from, http://www.tlainc.com/articl79.htm

Kelloway, E. K., & Barling, J. (2000). Knowledge work as organizational behavior. *International Journal of Management Reviews*, *2*(3), 287–304. doi:10.1111/1468-2370.00042

Klein, H. K., & Myers, M. D. (1999). A set of principles for conducting and evaluating interpretive field studies in information systems. *Management Information Systems Quarterly*, *23*(1), 67–93. doi:10.2307/249410

Kristensen, K., & Kijl, B. (2008). Productivity in collaboration-intensive knowledge work: The collaboration management imperative. In K.-D. Thoben, K. S. Pawar & R. Gonçalves (Eds.), *Proceedings of the 14th International Conference on Concurrent Enterprising*. Lisbon: Nova University. Retrieved August 25, 2010, from, http://www.ice-proceedings.org/default.asp?P=408&obj=B1

Lambert, E. G. (2005). The impact of distributive and procedural justice on social service workers. *Social Justice Research*, *18*(4), 411–427. doi:10.1007/s11211-005-8568-4

Lavelle, L. (2002). Executive pay. *Business Week*. Retrieved August 29, 2010, from, http://www.businessweek.com/magazine/content/02_15/b3778012.htm

Lillrank, P. (2002). The broom and nonroutine processes: A metaphor for understanding variability in organizations. *Knowledge and Process Management*, *9*(3), 143–148. doi:10.1002/kpm.145

Linking the theoretical basis- justice and knowledge creation ahd sharing

Merriam-Webster Dictionary. (2010). Surrealism. *Merriam-Webster Dictionary*. Retrieved September 2, 2010, from, http://www.merriam-webster.com/dictionary/surrealism

Meyer, P. (2003). From halos to horns: Demonizing the American CEO. *Directorship*. Retrieved September 10, 2010, from, http://www.allbusiness.com/marketing-advertising/branding-brand-development/972067-1.html

Miles, M. B., & Huberman, M. (1994). *Qualitative data analysis: An expanded source book* (2nd ed.). Thousand Oaks, CA: Sage Publications.

Miller, D. (1999). *Principles of justice*. London: Harvard University Press.

Moorman, R. H., Niehoff, B. P., & Organ, D. W. (1993). Treating employees fairly and organizational citizenship behavior: Sorting the effects of job satisfaction, organizational commitment, and procedural justice. *Employee Responsibilities and Rights Journal*, *6*(3), 209–225. doi:10.1007/BF01419445

Nichols, D., & Subramaniam, C. (2001). Executive compensation: Excessive or equitable? *Journal of Business Ethics*, *29*(4), 339–351. doi:10.1023/A:1010764828523

Nickols, F. (2003). The shift to knowledge work. *Distance Consulting*. Retrieved August 28, 2010, from, http://www.nickols.us/shift.pdf

O'Neill, B. S., & Adya, M. (2007). Knowledge sharing and the psychological contract: Managing knowledge workers across different stages of employment. *Journal of Managerial Psychology*, *22*(4), 411–436. doi:10.1108/02683940710745969

O'Reilly, C. A. III, & Pfeffer, J. (2000). *Hidden value: How great companies achieve extraordinary results with ordinary people*. Boston, MA: Harvard Business School Press.

Okin, S. M. (1989). *Justice, gender and the family*. New York, NY: Basic Books.

Online Etymology Dictionary. (2010). Fair. *Online Etymology Dictionary*. Retrieved September 10, 2010, from, http://www.etymonline.com/index.php?term=fair

Patton, M. Q. (1980). *Qualitative evaluation methods*. Thousand Oaks, CA: Sage Publications.

Petroni, A., & Colacino, P. (2008). Motivation strategies for knowledge workers: Evidences and challenges. *Journal of Technology Management & Innovation*, *3*(3), 21–32.

Piketty, T., & Emmanuel, S. (2006). The evolution of top incomes: A historical and international perspective. *The American Economic Review*, *96*(2), 200–205. doi:10.1257/000282806777212116

Pyöriä, P. (2005). The concept of knowledge work revisited. *Journal of Knowledge Management*, *9*(3), 116–127. doi:10.1108/13673270510602818

Rawls, J. (1971). *A theory of justice* (4th ed.). Cambridge, MA: Belknap Press.

Rhen, A. (2002). Good times, bad times: The moral discourse of time and management. *Revista Comportamento Organizacional & Gestão*, *8*(1), 49–59.

Ruffa, A. (2005). Dalí's surrealist activities and the model of scientific experimentation. *Papers for Surrealism*, *4*, 1–14.

Ryan, C. (2002). The reputation wars. *Australian Financial Review Boss Magazine, March*, 300-305.

Salvador Dali Art Gallery. (2010). Paranoia critical method. *Dali-Gallery.com*. Retrieved September 2, 2010, from, http://www.dali-gallery.com/html/dali.php

Sandberg, J. (2005). How do we justify knowledge produced within interpretative approaches? *Organizational Research Methods*, *8*(1), 41–68. doi:10.1177/1094428104272000

Scott, D. (2007). Reward programs: What works and what needs to be improved. *WorldatWork Journal*, *16*(3), 6–21.

Senge, P. M. (2006). *The fifth discipline: The art & practise of the learning organization* (2nd ed.). New York: Doubleday Business.

Söderström, H. T. (2003). *Corporate governance and structural change: European challenges*. Stockholm: SNS Förlag.

Stahl, B. C. (2007). Privacy and security as ideology. *IEEE Technology and Society Magazine*, *26*(1), 35–45. doi:10.1109/MTAS.2007.335570

Stehr, N. (2001). *The fragility of modern societies: Knowledge and risk in the information age*. Thousand Oaks, CA: Sage Publications.

Storey, J. (2005). Human resources and organizational structures. In Stephen, L., Quintas, P., & Ray, T. (Eds.), *Managing Knowledge- An Essential Reading* (pp. 349–355). London: Sage Publications.

The Free Dictionary. (2010a). Trade-off. *The Free Dictionary*. Retrieved September 12, 2010, from, http://www.thefreedictionary.com/trade-off

The Free Dictionary. (2010b). Fairness. *The Free Dictionary*. Retrieved September 12, 2010, from, http://www.thefreedictionary.com/Fairness

Tsoukas, H., & Vladimirou, E. (2001). What is organizational knowledge? *Journal of Management Studies, 38*(7), 973–993. doi:10.1111/1467-6486.00268

Turillo, C. J. (2002). Is virtue its own reward? Self-sacrificial decisions for the sake of fairness. *Organizational Behavior and Human Decision Processes, 89*(1), 839–865. doi:10.1016/S0749-5978(02)00032-8

Vansteenkiste, M. (2004). Motivating learning, performance, and persistence: The synergistic effects of intrinsic goal contents and autonomy supportive contexts. *Journal of Personality and Social Psychology, 87*(2), 246–260. doi:10.1037/0022-3514.87.2.246

Verplanken, B., & Holland, R. W. (2002). Motivated decision making: Effects of activation and self-centrality of values on choices and behavior. *Journal of Personality and Social Psychology, 82*(3), 434–447. doi:10.1037/0022-3514.82.3.434

Wang, C.-C. (2004). The influence of ethical and self-interest concerns on knowledge sharing intentions among managers: An empirical study. *International Journal of Management, 21*(3), 370–381.

Wang, S., & Noe, R. A. (2010). Knowledge sharing: A review and directions for future research. *Human Resource Management Review, 20*(2), 115–131. doi:10.1016/j.hrmr.2009.10.001

Wasko, M. M., & Faraj, S. (2005). Why should I share? Examining social capital and knowledge contribution in electronic networks of practice. *Management Information Systems Quarterly, 29*(1), 35–57.

Wiktionary (2010). Fairness. *Wiktionary*. Retrieved September 10, 2010, from, http://en.wiktionary.org/wiki/fairness

Wilson, T. D. (2002). The nonsense of knowledge management. *Information Research, 8*(1). Retrieved August 28, 2010, from, http://informationr.net/ir/8-1/paper144.html

Yin, R. K. (1994). *Case study research: Design and methods* (3rd ed.). Thousand Oaks, CA: Sage Publications.

Zairi, M., Jarrar, Y. F., & Aspinwall, E. (2010). A reward, recognition, and appraisal systems for future competitiveness: A UK survey of best practices. *European Centre for Best Practice Management*. Retrieved September 10, 2010, from, http://www.ecbpm.com/files/Talent%20-%20People%20Management/A%20Reward,%20Recognition,%20and%20Appraisal%20System%20for%20Future%20Competitiveness.pdf

Zikmund, W. G., & Zikmund, E. G. (2000). *Business research methods* (6th ed.). London: Dryden Press.

KEY TERMS AND DEFINITIONS

Compensation: Something given or received as a counterpart for actions taken. Compensation systems in organizational systems assume two major dimensions: monetary and non-monetary.

Equity Theory: The perception of fairness in allocating resources within social and professional realities.

Fairness: Inexistence of favouritism or bias, impartiality, or equity.

Human Resources Policies: Formal rules and guiding principles that organizations need to encompass for hiring, training, evaluating, and rewarding its organizational members.

Knowledge Workers: Everyone who works that needs to create, manage and share knowledge.

Chapter 14
Mobilizing Knowledge in the UK Public Sector:
Current Issues and Discourse

David Pullinger
London, UK

ABSTRACT

Knowledge management supports the key goals of an organization. For government this is creating public value, through trust, outcomes, service quality and cost effectiveness. These are vital matters for the UK government, and the need to mobilize knowledge is essential in delivering them. Knowledge management has tended to be about corporate knowledge inside an organization. This is important for government, not least in joining up its many parts to deliver more effective services and outcomes to citizens. However, citizens also have knowledge that can help deliver public value. How citizens and government share knowledge forms a second exploration. Citizens are also concerned about the use made by the state of personal data and knowledge about them; this forms the third strand. The issues that arise are mapped as ethical tensions onto Nonaka's SECI model, providing both a framework for exploring ethics and for examining the space for organizational innovation.

INTRODUCTION

A group of us were gathered to discuss aspects of delivering the UK government's new information and knowledge strategy (HM Government, 2008a). Who exactly is in this group, and for what is it responsible, I was asked by someone the group meeting. It's an informal group of people who meet occasionally to exchange information and build each other's knowledge, I replied, continuing that it had no formal authority, governance or reporting, although we did so through various routes. The initial reaction of my colleague civil servant seemed to be one of unease. This encapsulates and illustrates a feeling in the government's administration about the need to follow processes that can be monitored and for which it should be accountable. There are

DOI: 10.4018/978-1-61520-873-9.ch014

very good reasons for state administration being consistent, process-driven and open to scrutiny but meetings are consequently often representative, hierarchic and proceduralised. Sharing knowledge is not like that. Access to, and engaging with, the knowledge that people have, whatever their role and seniority, requires a major cultural shift from a procedure-based approach. The first section of this chapter looks at some of the aspects that need to be addressed in mobilizing knowledge within government.

The work of government in setting strategy, policy and implementation extends widely. The knowledge that is required to do each well does not only reside in public service officials. This is one reason for the large number of independent advisory bodies set up by the government in the UK. Beyond this more formal means of sharing knowledge from expert to government, is a move towards citizens communicating what they experience and sharing their knowledge through feedback mechanisms (HM Government, 2009c). To deliver the maximum benefit for society, everyone needs to be involved. This may be done, perhaps, through social media tools. The public, however, cannot get fully involved if they do not know what is going on, so there is also a major move in the UK to release data about public services and more generally to allow others to analyze and communicate (Cabinet Office, 2009). In release of data and use of social media, there are issues about data control, rights to use and re-use and intellectual property. The second part of the chapter explores what knowledge mobilization looks like when including people external to an organization into the delivery of its goals.

Individuals, whatever their role, expect that increased transparency should not lead to personal information being shared. With the increasing ability to analyze information, security and protection of data is essential. What is considered personal is itself a social construction. In the UK, people are astonished that Norwegians can put a name into a government website and discover how much they declared in earnings to the tax authorities. Or, that in USA one can type the name of a realtor and see if there has ever been a court case associated with that person. What is personal and what is not is yet to be clearly defined in the UK. Moreover, we can be double-minded about the use of data in the delivery of public services. When we need to report the death of a family member to the authorities, there can be 44 contacts in the UK (Varney, 2006) and people would like to be able to do it just once, as in Sweden, and all the public bodies know about it. But there is a strong and consistent reaction against the idea that information might be shared between public bodies. The third section of the chapter examines this aspect of information and knowledge about an individual.

In summary, we look at mobilizing knowledge in government, mobilizing the knowledge in the citizenry and sharing it with government, and the knowledge that the state has about individuals and how that should be treated. We explore a number of issues and then consider the ethical aspects more specifically in the final fourth section. First, we begin with scoping the work of government that makes knowledge sharing critical and the ways in which knowledge management (KM) can contribute to its outcomes.

WHY LOOK AT KNOWLEDGE MANAGEMENT?

Why does an organization such as a government want to look at the mobilization and management of knowledge? KM is more usually associated with competitive business advantage (Liebowitz, 1999).

There are a number of drivers for UK government looking at how to mobilize and manage its knowledge more effectively. First it is recognized that some implementation of government policy cannot take place without a broader integration of information and knowledge. For example, the welfare of children was highlighted through a major incident where a child died (Laming, 2003). Poor record-keeping and exchange of knowledge among different parts of the organization were given as contributory reasons. One result was the integration of some local government functions covering social and educational care. In that case organizational development was considered to be part of the overall solution. Another example is dealing with the context that gives rise to drug use, which can often involve policing, health and education policies. Traditionally these are in different sections of government. Recognizing this, for the first time, the UK government set all its targets for its three-year outcomes so that policies and actions across the various parts of government had to be joined up (McNabb, 2006). Many of the benefits to nations come when policies and practices are integrated. Mobilizing knowledge within and across different parts of a complex organization becomes critical.

In parallel, there is a strand that seeks to make implementation of policies more effective, in delivery and cost efficiencies. This includes delayering of the traditional staffing structures, outsourcing to new public bodies and outsourcing to commercial companies independent of government. Each requires better exchange of knowledge. Delayering means that the organization is much more sensitive to the movement of staff, who hold much of the knowledge. Outsourcing policy implementation to new public bodies, while strategy is retained within central government, can mean lack of access to knowledge on feedback. Specifically, is what is enacted what was intended, with consequent input to forming strategy. Outsourcing from the public to private sector can mean a similar lack of knowledge transfer, but one that is even more established through contract, custom and practice.

Such issues are common to all governments and most large organizations. They have the need for effective and efficient delivery units while finding ways to join up services around customers. Information management and knowledge mobilization can be seen as glue between the tensions of forming delivery units that are sufficiently focused to implement the required outcomes and yet delivering an overall integrated service to a customer. The difference between governments and other organizations is moving beyond shareholder value to something that can be judged to be in the public interest (HM Government, 2005).

PUBLIC VALUE

If the purpose of KM is to support the outcome of government, what exactly is that outcome? The benefit of KM is usually described in terms of using corporate knowledge as a competitive advantage to businesses (for example McElroy, 2000). For the public sector the outcome can be described as public value. Work is underway to define this further in order to measure it and assess efficiencies and value for money. For example Jones (2003), Kaplan (1999), and others have examined public value from the perspective of balanced scorecard approaches. Kelly, Mulgan & Muers (2002) identified three main factors as service quality, outcomes and trust. In a recent review of the different approaches to public value, Lusk, Roberts & Mackie (2008) note that the different approaches coalesce around three main categories:

- public value is that which the public values- understanding what individuals in society need and transforming public services to meet those needs with clear marketing and communication;
- public value as a system of mandates- delivering public goods through the unique authority of government, for example to levy taxes, to administer justice and imprison people or to provide welfare benefits, where each depends on the endorsement of

elected representatives and expressions of public support;
- public value as equivalent to shareholder value- the government acting as a good corporate body in delivering efficiently, effectively and doing what is perceived by society as the right thing.

They believe that when looking at outcomes, all three should be considered in combination. Public value should deliver services that people need, that are endorsed and which are done efficiently and effectively. Clearly managing data and information well is essential to delivering on each of these categories of public value, but so is managing knowledge and, which we will consider in the second section, the engagement of citizens in the generation of public value. Before turning to how government can organize itself to mobilize knowledge, we clarify what we mean by knowledge in this context.

KNOWLEDGE IN THE PUBLIC SECTOR

We will use the increasingly standard distinctions between data, information and knowledge. Following Improvement and Development Agency (2004), data (using the term for both singular and plural forms) is something given, a discrete, specific or limited bit of communication. For example 3.000, 4.000, and "this care home has 100 beds". Information is the result of asking a question and (quite literally) being in-formed, with the asker being different as a result of knowing it. For example, 3.000m is the height of this aircraft, 4.000m is the height of that mountain; or "these figures represent the bedding capacity of a care home, calculated as a theoretical capacity based on floor space or actually number of physical beds available at the home, or number of beds that the home is resources to support, backing on staff levels, health and safety, etc.". Knowledge is about something in addition that is either not or, not easily capable of being codified, as for example: "aircraft that have got within 20 miles of that mountain at this height have often crashed" or, "this is a large care home that is likely to be difficult to manage because of the known staffing difficulties in this area of the city and tends to be the place where people go if they cannot afford private care".

UK Government has tended to focus on two complementary types of knowledge strategy: connection and codification (Improvement and Development Agency, 2004). Connection strategies focus on interactions and communications among people, while codification strategies seek to make explicit knowledge available, usually on some form of IT-based service. What is apparent is the most of the focus hitherto has been on the codification approach (see also McElroy, 2000, on this for businesses). Examining some models may help move knowledge strategies on.

Nonaka & Takeuchi (1995) researched the value of distinguishing between two kinds of knowledge: explicit and tacit. Explicit knowledge either has been or is capable of being captured somewhere, perhaps in a document or as notes attached to data. Tacit knowledge tends to be personal and rooted in experience, ideals and values, and is difficult, or found to be impossible, to articulate in a way that is codifiable. As those working in expert systems discovered to their frustration, what is done by top experts was often found not to be describable. This could either be because the models and language do not yet exist, or perhaps because knowledge is not processed in the conscious and rationalizing brain. These are closely related, and one way to develop the needed models and language is through group work. Nonaka's SECI model describes a way of moving from a single person's knowledge to others through discourse and internalization within a group, rather than seeking to extract from someone as if they were a data store, and then codifying that for the benefit of others to internalize and use. Nonaka's SECI model appears to be the most referenced in UK government documents, however there are other approaches that are valuable to consider because their classifications encompass elements that transcend internal organization development.

Costa & Silva (2007) review the major classifications of knowledge that lie in the different models. Boisot's (2002) classifies knowledge assets into three dimensions: uncodified to codified; concrete to abstract; undiffused to diffused. This is a helpful approach in determining progress in the process of sharing knowledge and making it sufficiently explicit to enable it to be shared. Antonelli (2005), considers the different kinds of knowledge from which it is useful to determine which one is being considered in managing knowledge, whether as a public good, as a proprietary good or complex path dependent activity. This would be a valuable exploration for governments to make about their knowledge. In Costa, Prior & Rogerson (2008a) it is suggested that the different types of knowledge can be viewed in two dimensions: an individual to system embedding and a market to non-market embedding. This could be fruitful for governments to explore since much of their knowledge is embedded in the administrative processes of government with specific areas of expertise in individuals. The process of delayering, noted above, changes the intrinsic knowledge of process and, potentially, ready access to tacit knowledge. Moreover, government actions affect markets, even without direct policy intervention. For example through release of data that can encourage development of new commercial services (Newbury, Bently & Pollock, 2008). Other models include a customer-focused knowledge strategy. Given that one of the main drivers for government is to support its policies for citizens, this kind of strategy may also be worth exploring.

MOBILIZING KNOWLEDGE WITHIN GOVERNMENT

Towards a Culture Change

KM has been a recurrent theme across national and local UK government over the past 15 years (for example, Hovland, 2003). Although some of the work could be described as closer to information management (codification strategy), there is growing momentum to address the culture that is required for sharing knowledge (connection strategy).

There are various parts of government: the elected representatives who form the House of Commons and set the direction including through legislation; the senior civil service who develop policies on how to deliver required outcomes; and, a set of delivery bodies ranging from school education, health and policing through to administrative functions. The process of government in UK is based on a Cabinet of Ministers of which one is (s)elected as the Prime Minister, but each runs their brief and Department separately. Only in 2008 was it established that outcome targets would be shared across the Departments in the Public Sector Agreements and Service Transformation Agreement (Comprehensive Spending Review 2007 for period 2008-11) (National Audit Office, 2009). Right from the top, there is separation of responsibilities with a consequent wide variety in organization. This results in state departments with very different cultures, that now need to begin to work together to deliver their targets. Mobilizing the expertise and knowledge of each has become a critical necessity.

Into this context, a review of knowledge and information management has pointed to how the success of technological approaches to data and information has tended to encourage people towards similar ones for managing knowledge. The much more important task is to develop a culture to mobilize the knowledge that exists among people (HM Government, 2008a). This strategy proposes some actions, ranging from the informal to very formal, as follows: harness the enthusiasm for sharing knowledge that goes on via social networking sites and look for ways to establish profession and vibrant communities of interest within government; enable teams and communities to achieve common business purposes, with simple support toolkits; integrate KM into core competencies as a priority so that senior staff adopt the appropriate behaviours; and review each Department's capability in managing knowledge. These recommendations essentially constitute a culture change around connection strategies.

There are some early innovative approaches to connecting people. For example the Government Communications Headquarters (GCHQ) new building was explicitly designed to encourage the informal contact that leads to exchange of knowledge (HM Government, 2008a). Internal wikis are being used to build knowledge bases, and to identify those with knowledge through their contributions. Other social networking tools are in use within and across public bodies, for example the forums run by Improvement and Development Agency for local government that are now being used by central government. When in 2008 we wanted to build a community of experts in digital communication instead of the hierarchic council structure adopted by the IT profession (appropriate for them), we chose a free grouping approach, supplying some tools and encouraging others into trying out what might work and be useful. It looks as if it lacks general authority and might appear anarchic to some, but mirrors the loosely and constantly re-forming groups found on the Internet. It is working well, but the reaction of senior policy-makers to people forming and declaring new groups is sometimes instructional about how far the public sector needs to move culturally to mobilize knowledge!

Just as challenging are those aspects that are more sociopsychological: willingness to display differences of opinion and thought about what to do; to be prepared to say "I don't know"; to give up individual reward for ideas.

Sociopsychological Factors Inhibiting Knowledge Mobilization

The wish to give the appearance of unanimity is a driving force in some organizations. For example, Coyle (2001) examined policy-making in the World Bank and International Monetary Fund. There she found that policy-making in both institutions was characterised by a tension between consensus and dissent, in which it proved difficult to incorporate dissenting knowledge into programmes and decision-making because of the need to present an image of the organization having the right answers and maintaining a consensual official line. My experience is that this is as true, if not more so, of government activities. The UK media, in particular, enjoys headlining disagreement and controversy; any hint of that within policy-making is aired as some kind of failure. In a knowledge-sharing environment, however, it is essential that different views are heard, recorded, accessible and used to inform work as appropriate (HM Government, 2009a).

For this kind of reason, public bodies can also be reluctant to record lessons learned, case studies, and discussions or expressions of views in the policy-making process, particularly as these are open to Freedom of Information requests. The fear is that they might be used in a misrepresentative way to illustrate incompetence, whether directly from things that could have been done better, or merely from expressing a need for expertise from others. To address this concern, ways need to be found to ensure that the detail of case studies and lessons learned is not lost, while at the same time generalizing and anonymising to the extent that individuals and suppliers, for example, are not identifiable, even while the salient facts are communicated and those with knowledge able to be accessed. The codified knowledge may be sufficient, but often it is the start of access to tacit knowledge. Last year I was invited to respond to a Parliamentary Public Accounts Committee report and its recommendations, including making a public statement in response to their press release. I was advised that this had to follow certain rules. I looked up the rules, but their interpretation and the usual practice was what I then wanted to know. I could not find anyone who had actually gone through the process, dealing with all the necessary Ministers and briefing the Prime Minister. Indeed, I and the press office had a long discussion about interpretation that could probably have been circumvented by identification of a person with knowledge through experience. This is a typical need in large complex organizations.

Another cultural issue is the nature of expertise in government. Recently there has been a strategy of qualification and professionalization for specific corporate functions of public bodies that support policy-making, for example, financial, HR, IT and project management, to add to the long-established legal, statistical and communication professions. This is a shift within UK government, and introduces the idea of specialists working in partnership with the policy-making generalist whom can turn their brains and work to any subject required by the elected political party (Public Management and Policy Association & National School of Government, 2007). This gives scope for knowledge sharing that has hitherto not come easily to those familiar with generating new ideas and policies. New knowledge strategies are needed to encompass these aspects within a connection perspective.

Codification strategies assume that knowledge can be captured, distributed and managed primarily through IT systems in the form of documents and other digital media. Their focus is therefore on making knowledge explicit wherever possible and doing so in such a way that people are rewarded for contributing, and that others can easily find it and use it and are rewarded for doing so.

When the strategy has been restricted to putting codified knowledge into structured databases, without the ease of process for finding it and any reward mechanisms for using or contributing, then little use appears to be made of it. New tools may offer a better approach to storing, accessing and retrieving stories, lessons learned, ideas and case studies. For example they might be stored in the discussions, comments and Question and Answer exchanges stored in social media, whether in forums, blogging or networking applications. Rather than structured databases as found in previous IT-based approaches, another means to facilitate retrieval is to mark up unstructured text in some way that enables findability. For example one might use the new W3C standards for semantic web to identify aspects in which others may be interested. This approach is already used by UK government for unpublished research reports, facilitating access and access control, in addition to some published information restructured for re-use (for example The London Gazette). In particular, marking up the individuals connected with lessons-learned document would be valuable, so that the knowledge searcher can ask the questions of the type “what other projects has this person worked on?”

These examples illustrate that what is needed in a codified approach is ease of contribution and ease of findability. Social media offers a natural way of contributing story, experience and expertise at point of need (i.e. there is known value for investment of time and effort). Explicit effort, however, towards use of new search and monitoring tools because of the many services supporting discourse and the different languages used to talk about a particular subject. Where knowledge is held on known services then semantic web mark-up offers a natural way of handling unstructured data. Neither, however, will ensure that any knowledge will be used unless there is also a culture in which there is a reward system for contribution and usage. Some measures will need to be found that members of the public sector recognize as fair and equitable. They may include, for example, such measures as the number of contribution made, the number of times the contribution is accessed, and the number of contributions used.

MOBILIZING KNOWLEDGE ACROSS ORGANISATIONAL BOUNDARIES

Mobilizing Citizen Knowledge

The work of the public sector cannot be easily bounded. The knowledge to set strategy, propose policy and implement effectively also engages many others beyond public sector officials, including experts, stakeholders, voluntary sector and citizens. The value given to expertise among specialists can be seen in, for example, the hundreds of government-funded independent advisory bodies and the solicitation of stakeholder views during public consultations. The public sector also works in partnership with the voluntary sector, who are also lobbyists for change. And citizens have experience of public services that can provide information for improvement or new strategies, and the UK Government is keen to gather this experience through feedback processes, conversation and collaboration (for example HM Government, 2009c; Parker & Gallagher, 2007). Public value cannot be delivered without some meaningful interaction with citizens. What does KM look like when it includes people external to an organization into delivery of its goals? Introducing a new dialogue to share knowledge present throughout society can be done through a variety of face to face or digital means, with varying degrees of direct, representational or mediated contact. These include citizen juries and forums, summits and wikis, workshops and petitions, feedback and public meetings, blogs and webchats, to name some of the available mechanisms. To deliver the maximum benefit for society, everyone needs to be involved (Graham, 1992).

There have already been successful initiatives in improving services at a local level through local engagement, in improving medical care through patients being able to comment on their experience of doctors and hospitals (through feedback opportunities in Patient Opinion and www.nhs.uk), and through the introduction of some schemes such as Children's Trusts that formalize inclusion of citizens. Parker & Gallagher (2007), point to four different means of encouraging such collaboration between government and the citizen: by incentivise with money or recognition; by force through introduction of new structures by law and funding mechanisms; by augmenting what government can do by working with partners and the voluntary sector; and by a small number of prioritized goals for a limited time. A propos this last, I argue in Pullinger (2001), that both culture and online tools encourage this kind of short-term political engagement by citizens.

Conversely, civil servants have been given permission and encouraged to participate in online forums and respond to blogs as individuals. Previously any contact with the public was either routed through the press office or similar formal procedures, or designated as part of their frontline job. Commenting and participating in citizen discourse is a new departure for government as an organization and is being closely watched by other governments to see where this innovation might lead. The person can speak on their own behalf, instead of representing an elected representative, provided they are clear about their role and limit commentary to agreed positions (HM Government, 2009b).

Since most dialogues occur on commercial web-interfaced Internet services, there are some interesting tensions around who owns what and who has the rights of re-use and under what conditions, who can delete content and under what national jurisdiction would decisions be made. To give one small example, some online services have sought to claim that they own the copyright on whatever is stored in their service. Sometimes this may be Crown Copyright, but there is no recognized means for legally transferring of Crown Copyright in this way. The UK Government is therefore exploring how to enable appropriate use of individual contributions and re-use of government content that has previously been automatically Crown Copyright (Cabinet Office, 2009).

Enabling Citizen Engagement through Data Release

The public cannot get fully involved if they don't know what is going on, so there is also an important parallel move in the UK to release data (Cabinet Office, 2009) and, specifically, data about public service performance (HM Government, 2009c).

It is a major cultural change to release data and information in a form that others can use to create new analyses and services. In the UK, it was considered radical in 2000 when the then Prime Minister Tony Blair launched National Statistics, following the Labour Party Manifesto (1997). Prime Minister Gordon Brown made it completely independent of government in 2008, in the form of the United Kingdom Statistics Authority. The first step was a process whereby information about what was happening was issued even if it was inconvenient to the government. The potential discomfort was either its content, perhaps showing something different to what the government wanted to announce, or its timing, for example bad figures appearing on the eve of a party conference. The second step was to put a distance between productions of statistics about what is happening in UK to political comment upon it (HM Government, 2008b).

Systematically releasing data and information explicitly structured to enable others to use and re-use it in analysis, new services and commercial use is a further step. It has been routine in US, where there is a strong consensus that public data belongs to the public. There are however many concerns among the public bodies, including the following:

- risks and liabilities on the use of the data, whether, for example, on listing all schools with their locations, or releasing the results of health inspections of restaurants, which might damage their business. In what way might the public body be responsible for third party use?;
- worry about misuse, for example of giving a list of all schools that removes all those of a particular type, for example faith schools. In what way might the public body be responsible when not monitoring all uses?;
- apprehension over analyses that might come to a different conclusion about the policy that should be adopted to those of the public body releasing the data, for example on catchment areas for local schooling. Will the role and identity of the public body need to change?;
- loss of revenue, where previously the data had been sold to cover some costs. What will have to stop being done if revenue is no longer forthcoming?;
- lack of resources in making data available in a form that others can use, which go beyond the requirements of the public body itself. Why spend money making things possible for others (especially given the fears listed above)?;
- uncertainty over whether there is any value in the data, when none has been demanded. Why spend if there might be no takers?.

It is agreed that no personal data will be released, but the power of information processing means that some unexpected combinations of data can amount to data being identified to particular individuals. For example, crime statistics are being mapped so that people can see hotspots. A search of local newspapers is likely to retrieve the victim's name and even place of residence and any conviction will also result in that information being public. Although all this data is already available, it can be brought together into a service that might not have been anticipated, and transgress what might be perceived as victims' rights, even though that information is already in the public domain. This debate was aired in the national media (for example, Edwards, 2008). So there is a tension about deciding how to release the data. Where crimes are low in number, do you anonymise and place the incident anywhere in a large area to avoid all possible information processing and so deliver a service close to the point of uselessness, or do you say that it is already in the public domain and so should not be an issue? Both government and individuals have reason to be cautious while exploring these new data releases.

KNOWLEDGE THROUGH PERSONAL DATA

A common reaction to my writing this chapter has been for friends to launch into discussions of personal data. This appears to be in the context of the danger of the state "knowing too much about me". Further exploration identified this as a feeling of being known, but not having the reciprocal knowledge to what use the impersonal knower, the state, may put the knowledge "about me". The question then is about power and its potential.

This has, of course, been widely analyzed and is reflected in Dahrendorf's sociological definition of power: "is the ability to reduce, limit or eliminate alternatives for the social action of one person or group by another person or group" (Dahrendorf, 1959, pp. 89). Boguslaw (1965) explicitly applied the idea to computer programmers and designers of computer equipment and languages, with Robins & Webster (1999) claiming that the information revolution does not lie in technical innovation as much as in "differential (and unequal) access to, and control over information resources" (p. 91).

This is of particular concern to individuals in regards to the state, which has need to gather data and information on its citizens in order to promote social, economic and welfare goals, for example through a census to plan for schools and hospitals, and the individual's need to protect personal data as far as possible. This is part of the three-way relationship that individual citizens have with the state (Offe, 1996). Note that two of the three share commonality with the main strands in public value identified by Lusk, Roberts & Mackie (2008), but the middle one, with which we are concerned, is different:

- creators of state authority through the democratic voice;
- potentially threatened by state force or coercion, but protected by rule of law;
- dependent on the services and provision for welfare organised by the state.

Data and information about individuals are required to run the administrative function of the state. There is also non-codified knowledge about individuals. In UK this is at the interface between citizens and officials (for example, welfare and benefit officers) and service delivery agents (for example, nurses, police and teachers). Their knowledge is used for specific cases and increasingly so for the care of children. However, it is rarely documented or codified and so open for others to use except when explicitly and legally required, for example when doctors suspect that patients are addicted drug users and for suspicions about the welfare of children (Recommendation 16) (Laming, 2003). In order to improve public services, the expertise of these frontline workers is being encouraged to grow through knowledge sharing of observations and experience without an intention to discuss details of individual people except in exceptional circumstances (HM Government, 2009c). In particular, citizens want to ensure that their options for manoeuvre are not reduced by the state bringing data together in such a way that disadvantages them, either by painting an inaccurate picture through losing contextual and clarifying information ("this person lives on a boat") or by identifying inaccuracies to which the state may want answers, thereby imposing additional burdens of proof. Citizens also want free-loaders and criminal activity in relation to the state to be caught.

This leads to an interesting situation perhaps peculiar to the UK government: the history of public services has led to departments or agencies focusing on the supply of specific products rather than taking a citizen or business-led approach. Departments' and agencies' services are all developed independently of each other. It is leaving the citizen or business to join up the public service island economy to meet their needs (Varney, 2006, p. 4). As in the example recounted in the introduction to the chapter of a citizen needing to contact government 44 times following a bereavement, it is often the most vulnerable citizens who have to do the most joining-up between the public service islands; much of it could be avoided with more collaborative service delivery. Although people don't want their information shared across the government, they also want the benefit of services that can only result from doing so. Why this might be is currently being explored, but ideas include: it might build up too comprehensive a picture (too much knowledge); contain errors that affect other services (inaccurate data); or be misapplied in situations other than the one for which it was given (contextual misapplication).

One approach is to identify what is reasonable to be shared across the whole public sector, what should not be shared, except with express permission of the individual concerned, and what falls into the middle ground where what is shared is a matter of consensus. Thomas & Walport (2008) began to explore these different categories. In the first category lies the registration and updating of records associated with births, deaths and name changes by choice or on marriage. The registration of citizens has been the most basic form of government because of the state's role to protect and seek the well-being of its, and not that of others', people along with rights of abode. Such registration answers the question about whom the state should be responsible for.

Despite some appearances to the contrary, there is often no need to share data in order to provide the services needed. For example, it is possible to interrogate data by asking if it meets certain criteria, without ever having access to that data or knowing what it contains. Thus to provide a free school meal at lunchtime for a child whose parents have no income, requires checking status of parents and their receipt of welfare benefits as an indicator. Data does not need to be transferred for this, only establishing if a condition is met. This approach means that there need not be the concatenation of data that might lead to knowledge that individuals consider inappropriate. Through a social consensus, it may therefore be possible to start to map a series of interactions with personal data that can be used to deliver services people want that is:

- able to be shared and updated (for example the death of someone);
- shareable but not changed;
- used and viewed for specific tasks but no transfer or recording made;
- interrogated with certain criteria with no viewing of the data;
- not accessible at all.

The Institute for Public Policy Research is beginning a series of qualitative discussions with citizens on such matters. This presumes we know what we mean by personal data and what should and should not be in the public arena. In fact there is little consensus over this. It varies considerably across nations as our examples from Norway, Sweden and USA have illustrated. That this information is socially constructed and varies widely in practice can be seen from comparison with other countries. Germany, for example, does not publish the names of its company directors. USA makes data about many events concerning individual's public.

There is publication by statute of some individual data in the UK as it is deemed important for the overall welfare of citizens. These include, for example, names of those who are insolvent and so unable to pay bills, names of directors of companies, and those convicted of criminal offences. In some areas citizens would like to go further, for example have published the location of people on the child sex register or convicted paedophiles. The state has obligations for their protection too, so arrangements are in place for ensuring protection of all parties. So to our former list, we can also add those data that are associated with being made public:

- that is published by law (statutory notices);
- that is published by custom (e.g. honours list);
- that is published routinely but was previously difficult to get hold of and so is perceived to be newly available;
- that may be made available upon request (either set up to do so, or through Freedom of Information requests);
- for which there is public clamour that should be made available, but where the government has responsibilities to individuals (paedophile locations);
- which is used only in exceptional circumstances with explicit legal powers (for example in counter terrorism actions in protection of citizens);
- for which the state is guardian and should never release (personal data);
- for which the state declares it will not itself use other than in aggregation (Census data).

Identification of individual data that is personal and falls into all these different categories is an urgent task in order to deliver the trust in the state that citizen wants in the context of the three-way relationship. There is no simple means for this, as the differences between nations exemplify. Rather there is a social construction leading to a consensus about what is and what is not acceptable to that society at that time. That acceptability or otherwise is usually described as ethics, to which we know turn, focusing on the KM issues.

ETHICAL TENSIONS

Most people are prepared to share if they get something back- if there is some perceived reciprocity in making contributions. This appears to be part of the human condition in that the size of community groups are claimed to be created around reciprocity and avoiding freeloading, or freeriding as it is also described (Dunbar, 2007). The need to encourage sharing through some return has always been part of the problem about KM, and various attempts have been made to address it. For example, one might say that you cannot get information unless you give it (Thimbleby, Witten & Pullinger, 1995) or that there is a financial reward to the contributor for its use (for example the knowledge-trading IQPort, Skyrme, 2001). This is the exchange model that is found in all human societies, however old. Intellectual property is an outworking of this as the right to be associated with a contribution and get some return for it. This has been described as contribution justice (Mason, Mason & Culnan, 1995) and explored in Costa, Prior & Rogerson (2008b).

Nonaka's SECI framework where externalization phase follows socialization identifies an associated problem with intellectual property- that it is often generated in a group. This is the converse of the freerider, being where people may be contributing but not getting the recognition for doing so. The redactor may be writing up a group activity and some members of the group might look for credit for their contribution to the process and feel aggrieved if it is not there. New practices are required to encourage knowledge sharing and externalization by the identification of all players within recognition and reward structure. Contribution justice is as applicable a term here.

A second theme to emerge is access to knowledge. First in changing the culture so as to encourage its mobilization and then in finding ways to get access to people and knowledge in documents that cannot be fully codified in the same way as information, stored often in the form of stories, case studies, experiences, and lessons learned. The ethical tension comes in whether there is a presumed right of no access, or presumed right of access to others' knowledge (and its associated data), and under what terms. The former has prevailed both within government and for the citizen about what the government does. There are moves to a presumed right of access, but this is still contested and requires more than an individual reward and recognition- it is the interplay between the corporate task of building public value and the individual delivery components of the organization. The clarity of the business proposition about impact on the bottom line has yet to be developed in the public sector.

A specific tension for government, that may not be applicable to all organizations, is one that lies between three groups of people: the generalist policy-makers who need to be able to turn to any policy; the specialist corporate support functions; and the process-driven government administrative function. Public value cannot be delivered without joining these up across government. Moreover it is also necessary to include citizens and other stakeholders. Thus the process for sharing is challenging and requires a new recognition of the role and value of each within the overall purpose of delivering public value.

Another tension, related to the first, is the individual need to develop and be recognized for one's knowledge at the very time one is subsuming it for the greater good into the group. There are tensions over the time and effort in sharing knowledge that frequently conflicts with that for building on and developing further knowledge. Space is required to develop knowledge, either through accomplishing tasks and responsibilities or through reflection and learning, but it is only recognized when shared and released. In other words, reward is delayed relative to the cost and so can be hard to justify.

In summary, in mobilizing the knowledge from inside people's heads and documentary evidence there are a number of tensions that must be resolved in any organization. For government this can pose a particular challenge as the public sector is extensive and includes many different organizations, as well as citizens in the process of delivering value for the nation. In examining the issues that arise around mobilizing and managing knowledge, one way of viewing the tensions is the use of Nonaka's SECI framework:

Each of those tensions relates in some way to balancing our needs to pursue our own self-interest with duties to make the best possible decisions for all parties concerned. If there were no such tensions, then we wouldn't need to establish practices of what is acceptable and what is not. If our actions fitted naturally into what everyone else expected and wanted, then there would be no need. Conversely, if we could act as we wished purely on the basis of our own desires, then there would be social chaos.

Whereas there have been many broad treatments of ethics in information management over the past two decades, for example Mason, Mason & Culnan (1995) and the reader Dunlop & Kling (1991), there has not been the same focus on doing the same for mobilizing and managing knowledge. Using UK Government as a case study, this chapter has looked at some of the issues for government and the ethical tensions that arise. Many of these will be applicable to other large complex organizations.

FUTURE RESEARCH DIRECTIONS

In exploring the issues for government and its citizens in mobilizing knowledge, we have identi-

Table 1. Ethical tensions displayed using Nonaka's SECI framework

SECI Point	Conversion Process	Examples of Organisational Innovation	Ethical Tensions
Externalization	Conversion of tacit knowledge into a form accessible to others	Use of wikis, forums, and other social media inside government; citizens sharing their experience of public services through online feedback mechanisms	Contribution justice: the right to be recognized and rewarded for contributions and reciprocal contributions
Combination	Conversion into new sets of explicit knowledge that can be shared	Introduction of semantic web applications into government (using RDFa); reorganization of Local Authorities to integrate welfare for children	Development of individual knowledge
Internalization	Conversion of new explicit knowledge into individual (or organization) tacit knowledge		Development of individual knowledge
Socialization	Sharing tacit knowledge; converting individual knowledge into other people's tacit knowledge	Permission for civil servants to blog and participate in forums and respond to blogs; construction of GCHQ building explicitly to encourage sharing of knowledge	Individual development of knowledge and being recognized as source to go to, while at the same time giving it to others; finding means to share knowledge across organizational boundaries

fied a number of ethical tensions and mapped them onto Nonaka's SECI model. Building on this model and frameworks that have been developed from it, may be a fruitful way to uncover more issues and present a structure for discussing them in a coherent way. The SECI model has been used, as it is the one most cited by government documents looking at KM. However there is other with classifications that could prove fruitful for examining ethical issues. Throughout, we have also noted some organizational innovation. Again future research may wish to take the different models and ask more specifically how organizational innovation could be used at various parts to support the mobilization and use of knowledge. Finally, we have implied throughout the chapter that the ethical tensions should be resolved by consensus, pointing to national differences as evidence that these are socially constructed (Burr, 2003). Further research might usefully be done in identifying effective means to do this and so directly address the issues that arise in mobilizing knowledge.

CONCLUSION

Public value is driving many of the initiatives in the UK Government. This can be seen particularly when expressed as trust, outcomes, service quality and cost effectiveness, (Lusk, Roberts & Mackie, 2008; Kelly, Mulgan & Muers, 2002) which are all vital issues for UK society in relation to government. The financial constraint initiated by the collapse of the banking sector in 2007 has further driven the need to deliver public value, and this was one genesis for UK Government's strategy (HM Government, 2009c). It sets out the development of delivering professionalism and efficiencies through joining up and sharing across government and engaging citizens in a new dialogue to reform public services and give them information on public service performance to enable them to do so. The cultural challenges and need to develop consensus through social construction on the issues identified in the chapter suggest that such an agenda might take some time and may have to survive several political changes in order to be driven through. There are examples of organizational innovation and we have identified them through the chapter. These should be considered experiments to see what further questions are raised and if sufficient numbers can be drawn into their use to make a real difference. In each area there are ethical issues that need to be made explicit as choices, so that a process of deliberation can be created in order to ascertain what will be acceptable and what will not in terms of mobilizing and sharing knowledge. This is true whether in terms of behaviour inside the public sector itself, in the citizen-state relationship and in what the state knows about individuals as persons. Nonaka's SECI model has been much developed from the time when it was first published and alternatives proposed, nevertheless it has proved a useful structure for the initial identification and articulation of some core ethical issues.

DISCLAIMER

The author works at the Central Office of Information, part of the UK Government, but writes in an individual capacity; nothing written here constitutes or should be taken to constitute UK Government policy, unless published as such in the documents referenced.

ACKNOWLEDGMENT

With appreciation to the UK Government Head of Profession for Knowledge Management, Natalie Ceeney, and to Kevin McLean for discussions on key issues facing government in KM. However, all responsibility for the content is the author's.

REFERENCES

Antonelli, C. (2005). Models of knowledge and systems of governance. *Journal of Institutional Economics*, *1*(1), 51–73. doi:10.1017/S1744137405000044

Boguslaw, R. (1965). *The new utopians, a study of system design and social change*. Englewood Cliffs, NJ: Prentice-Hall.

Boisot, M. (2002). The structuring and sharing of knowledge. In Choo, C. W., & Bontis, N. (Eds.), *Strategic Management of Intellectual Capital and Organization Knowledge* (pp. 65–78). New York: Oxford University Press.

Burr, V. (2003). *Social constructionism* (2nd ed.). New York: Routledge.

Cabinet Office. (2009). Power of information task force report. *Cabinet Office*. Retrieved August 5, 2009, from http://www.cabinetoffice.gov.uk/reports/power_of_information.aspx

Costa, G. J. M., Prior, M., & Rogerson, S. (2008a, September). *Free ride in knowledge management? Ethical and moral dilemmas!* Paper presented at the ETHICOMP 2008, Mantua, Italy.

Costa, G. J. M., Prior, M., & Rogerson, S. (2008b). Individual ethics and knowledge management: Arising conflicts. In Bynum, T. W. (Eds.), *ETHICOMP 2008: Living, Working and Learning Beyond Technology* (pp. 117–129). Mantua, Italy: University of Pavia.

Costa, G. J. M., & Silva, N. M. A. (2007). Knowledge management: How ethical is your organization's knowledge? In Bynum, T. W., Rogerson, S., & Murata, K. (Eds.), *ETHICOMP 2007: Glocalisation: Bridging the Global Nature of Information and Communication Technology* (*Vol. 1*, pp. 123–136). Tokyo: Meiji University.

Coyle, E. (2001). *Consensus and dissent in Washington: Negotiating change in the World Bank and IMF*. MPhil thesis, University of Cambridge, Cambridge, UK.

Dahrendorf, R. (1959). *Class and class conflict in industrial society*. Stanford, CA: Stanford University Press.

Dunbar, R. (2007). *Grooming, gossip, and the evolution of language* (2nd ed.). Cambridge, MA: Harvard University Press.

Dunlop, C. E. M., & Kling, R. (Eds.). (1991). *Computerization and controversy: Value conflicts and social choices*. Boston: Academic Press.

Edwards, R. (2008). Crime maps to show offences for every street. *Telegraph*. Retrieved August 2, 2009, from www.telegraph.co.uk/news/newstopics/politics/lawandorder/2466325/Crime-maps-to-show-offences-for-every-street.html

Government, H. M. (2005). Transformational government: Enabled by technology. *Cabinet Office*. Retrieved August 7, 2009, from http://www.cabinetoffice.gov.uk/media/141734/transgov-strategy.pdf

Government, H. M. (2008a). Information matters: Building government's capability in managing knowledge and information. *National Archives*. Retrieved July 31, 2009, from http://www.nationalarchives.gov.uk/documents/information-matters-strategy.pdf

Government, H. M. (2008b). Data handling procedures in government: Final report. *Cabinet Office*. Retrieved August 1, 2009, from http://www.cabinetoffice.gov.uk/media/65948/dhr080625.pdf

Government, H. M. (2009a). The United Kingdom report on the re-use of public sector information 2009. *Office of Public Sector Information*. Retrieved August 5, 2009, from http://www.opsi.gov.uk/advice/psi-regulations/uk-report-reuse-psi-2009.pdf

Government, H. M. (2009b). How the civil service code applies to online participation. *Civil Service*. Retrieved August 7, 2009, from www.civilservice.gov.uk/about/work/codes/participation-online.aspx

Government, H. M. (2009c). Working together: Public services on your side. *HM Government*. Retrieved August 7, 2009, from http://www.hmg.gov.uk/media/15556/workingtogether.pdf

Graham, G. (1992). *The internet- A philosophical enquiry: The Gifford Lectures*. London: SCM Press.

Hovland, I. (2003). Knowledge management and organizational learning: An international development perspective. *ODI Working Paper 224*. Retrieved August 5, 2009, from http://www.odi.org.uk/resources/download/143.pdf

Improvement and Development Agency. (2004). *An introduction to knowledge management: Topic briefing*. London: Improvement and Development Agency.

Jones, R. (2003). Measuring the benefits of knowledge management at the financial services authority. *Journal of Information Science*, *29*(6), 475–487. doi:10.1177/0165551503296005

Kaplan, R. (1999). The balanced scorecard for public-sector organizations. *Harvard Business Review*, (January/February): 3–4.

Kelly, G., Mulgan, G., & Muers, S. (2002). Creating public value: An analytical framework for public service reform. *Cabinet Office*. Retrieved July 31, 2009, from http://www.cabinetoffice.gov.uk/media/cabinetoffice/strategy/assets/public_value2.pdf

Laming, H. (2003). The victoria climbie inquiry report. *House of Commons- Health Committee*. Retrieved August 7, 2009, from http://www.publications.parliament.uk/pa/cm200203/cmselect/cmhealth/570/570.pdf

Liebowitz, J. (1999). *Knowledge management handbook*. Boca Raton, FL: CRC Press.

Lusk, S., Roberts, T., & Mackie, J. (2008). Strategy: What place in government. Summary of research findings. *National School of Government*. Retrieved July 31, 2009, from http://virtual.nationalschool.gov.uk/StrategyExchange/News/NSG%20strategy%20project%20-%20research%20summary%20paper%20July%2008.doc

Mason, R. O., Mason, F. M., & Culnan, M. J. (1995). *Ethics of information management*. Thousand Oaks, CA: Sage Publications.

McElroy, M. H. (2000). Integrating complexity theory, knowledge management and organizational learning. *Journal of Knowledge Management*, *4*(3), 195–203. doi:10.1108/13673270010377652

McNabb, D. E. (2006). *Knowledge management in the public sector: A blueprint for innovation in Government*. New York: M. E. Sharpe, Inc.

National Audit Office. (2009). *Helping government learn*. London: The Stationary Office.

Newbury, D., Bently, L., & Pollock, R. (2008). Models of public sector information provision via trading funds. *UK Department for Business, Innovation and Skills*. Retrieved August 1, 2009, from www.berr.gov.uk/files/file45136.pdf

Nonaka, I., & Takeuchi, H. (1995). *The knowledge-creating company: How Japanese companies create the dynamics of innovation*. New York: Oxford University Press.

Offe, C. (1996). *Modernity and the state: East, West*. Cambridge, UK: Polity Press.

Parker, S., & Gallagher, N. (Eds.). (2007). *The collaborative state: How working together can transform public services. Cabinet Office*. Retrieved August 1, 2009, from http://www.cabinetoffice.gov.uk/media/cabinetoffice/strategy/assets/collaborative_state_report.pdf

Public Management and Policy Association & National School of Government. (2007). Evidence based policy-making: Making the most of academic-practitioner exchange. *The Chartered Institute of Public Finance & Accountancy*. Retrieved August 3, 2009, from http://www.cipfabusiness.com/pmpa/news/past_news.cfm

Pullinger, D. (2001). *Information technology and cyberspace: Extra-connected living*. London: Darton, Longman and Todd.

Robins, K., & Webster, F. (1999). *Times of the technoculture: From the information society to the virtual life*. London: Routledge.

Skyrme, D. J. (2001). *Capitalizing on knowledge: From e-business to k-business*. Wobunr, MA: Butterworth-Heinemann.

Thimbleby, H. W., Witten, I. H., & Pullinger, D. J. (1995). Concepts of cooperation in artificial life. *IEEE Transactions on Systems, Man, and Cybernetics*, *25*(7), 1166–1171. doi:10.1109/21.391298

Thomas, R., & Walport, M. (2008). Data sharing review report. *Ministry of Justice*. Retrieved August 3, 2009, from http://www.justice.gov.uk/reviews/docs/data-sharing-review-report.pdf

Varney, D. (2006). *Service transformation: A better service for citizens and businesses, a better deal for the taxpayer. HM Treasury*. Retrieved August 5, 2009, from www.hm-treasury.gov.uk/d/pbr06_varney_review.pdf

KEY TERMS AND DEFINITIONS

Codification Strategy: A knowledge management strategy that focuses on making knowledge explicit, usually through an IT-based service.

Connection Strategy: A knowledge management strategy that focuses on interactions and communications between people.

Contribution Justice: The perception of fairness and reciprocity in giving and receiving contributions, for example, knowledge.

Data Release: Free communication of non-personal data for others to use and re-use.

Data Sharing: Communication of data to third parties.

Ethical Tension: The ongoing interplay between two goals about what is acceptable and not acceptable practice and behaviour.

Knowledge Mobilization: A preferred term to Knowledge management as it describes getting knowledge moving around and across organizations.

Personal Data: Data specific to an individual.

Public Value: The purpose of government activity, equivalent to the competitive advantage in commercial organizations.

Social Construction: The idea that concepts and agreements are not delivered from outside a society but constructed through discourse within it.

Chapter 15
Ethical Evaluation of Learning Organizations:
A Conceptual Framework

Gonçalo Jorge Morais Costa
De Montfort University, UK

ABSTRACT

A key assumption for recognizing knowledge society is the existence of learning organizations. As a result, literature has been fruitful in engaging a wide debate concerning its characteristics, dimensions, evolution, evaluation procedures, or ethical behaviour. Likewise, it is interesting to denote that research appears to pay little regard to the impacts of existing ethical and social dilemmas about knowledge creation, retention/use and sharing within organizational contexts. Therefore, the key purpose of this manuscript is to present a conceptual framework that denotes these dilemmas and their impacts in organizational strategy.For that, this contribution resumes an ongoing research project which intends to approach ethical and social dilemmas in learning organizations. Moreover, it suggests that these dilemmas impact on organizational strategy, as well as that existing evaluation models for learning organizations do not promote the ethical evaluation.

INTRODUCTION

Complexity is probably the most significant distinctive feature of our civilization (Pinha e Cunha, Fonseca & Gonçalves, 2001). As technical and economic progresses allow production, transportation and communication to be further efficient, individuals interrelate with a growing number of other individuals, institutions, systems and objects. Concurrently, while this network of connections develops and spreads around the world, the miscellaneous systems become reciprocally dependent.

Accordingly, 21st management requirements compel a collaborative approach in order to capitalize dissimilar workers perceptions, instead of the traditional authoritarian, command and control philosophies. People are considered as a "natural" resource and an organizational asset to promote sustainable competitive advantage. Hence, the

DOI: 10.4018/978-1-61520-873-9.ch015

novel managing orientation is also embracing innovation as a key element for success and competitiveness (Liyanage & Poon, 2002). This involves expanding the innovative potential of the organization by nurturing new ideas, harnessing people's creativity and keenness, tapping the innovative potential of workers, and encouraging the dissemination of autonomy and entrepreneurship (Black & Porter, 2000).

Nevertheless, new ideas (knowledge) creation, retention/use and sharing in organizations have simultaneously shaped crucial dilemmas for managers given their key role in promoting creativity and innovation inside an organization. Despite Roth & Kleiner (1998) argument that learning organizations have been recognized for decades, the truth is that knowledge society have strengthen several inner ethical and social dilemmas that impact organizational strategy. Thus, this manuscript suggests that these dilemmas, as well their impacts have been neglected as regards to evaluate learning organizations ethical behaviour.

DISCLOSURE INFORMATION

Following The Free Dictionary (2010), disclosure is the act or process of revealing or uncovering, as well as to make a revelation. Given the overall argument of this chapter, is the author intention to shed some light as regards the concept of an ethical learning organization. For analytical purposes, refers to the recognition of the ethical and social dilemmas that resume knowledge creation, retention/use and sharing within organizational contexts (access to organizational knowledge, autonomy, dignity, privacy, intellectual property, faire compensation and trust). In spite of being a complex reality, because it depends on the moral values of each agent (Moraga, 2006) it is reasonable to claim that managers need to identify and develop idiosyncratic virtues strategically recognized by the society (Gowri, 2007). As a result, to promote an ethical learning organization is necessary that managers recognize these existing dilemmas in order to minimize their organizational impacts.

LEARNING ORGANIZATIONS: "WHO", "WHAT", "HOW" AND "WHY"!

Literature, at least main stream, is approaching managers' latest responsibilities' within organizations ("who"), "what" is a learning organization or even its dimensions ("how"). However, the "why" has been almost neglected which resumes a paradox, due to the importance of the ethical and social dilemmas that arise throughout the knowledge flow (Costa & Silva, 2007). So, the author argues that the "why" is the missing link!

Managers Responsibilities' ("Who")

CEO character is an imperative because these enable organizational values, culture, and performance. The range of outcomes in a virtuous or vicious cycle may be a function of the length of time that an individual is a CEO, which can influence positively or negatively an organization, depending on its character (Gowri, 2007). As a result, the CEO is a key "building block" for setting up an ethical climate. In addition a numerical constraint occurs in this process, since few individuals generate at some extent organizational commitment.

Furthermore, if an organization's unique features are aligned with ethical values will permit to differentiate from other competitors, and thereby produce competitive advantage (Chun, 2005), being a truthfully positive organization (Verbos *et al.*, 2007), as well as transparent one (Costa, Prior & Rogerson, 2008a). Although, to obtain an ethical corporate background is compulsory to verify the subsequent settings (Gilmartin, 2003): managers ought to "embrace the right tone"; formal guidance in ethics and standards of conduct is an organizational imperative; and, the organization should grant formal instruments, internal and external, in order to permit reporting any misconduct.

Concept ("What")

What is the meaning of learning organization? Some writers highlight the learning of all organizational members (Johnson, 2002; Pedler, Burgoyne & Boydell, 1996), whereas others focus on organizational competitiveness (Cavaleri, 2008; Moilanen, 2005; Dealtry, 2002; Slater & Narver, 1995), or even abilities and business purposes (Dusko *et al.*, 2006; Gilley & Maybunich, 2000; Lessem, 1990). At last, a number of authors like Senge (1996) adopt a broader approach, including all the preceding perspectives.

Therefore, since the expression "learning organization" was referred by Senge *et al.* (1994), explanations have prospered in management literature (Sankar, 2003; Loermans, 2002). Yet, literature seems to reveal a lack of accuracy about the concept itself. Ortenbald (2002) denotes that merely a few authors, as for example Argyris (1999), have attempted to produce groups of learning organizations. According to Ortenblad (2002), a learning organization can be recognized throughout four ontological dimensions: cultural values, leaders, communication, and workers.

Dimensions ("How")

Researchers and practitioners advocate that permanent learning is crucial to obtain novel skills allowing companies to achieve ever-changing client demands (Barkur, Varambally & Rodrigues, 2007; Addleson, 2000). With constant education and training, assigning resources is vital because the talent to learn is insufficient. An organization must also highlight its ongoing improvement procedure, and engaging a learning culture exhibits a substantial amount of features. Initially, the organization ought to clearly set its lifelong learning practices, from incessant learning and education to fostering and assisting workers learning (Yeo, 2005; Leitch *et al.*, 1996). Secondly, is necessary to maintain a learning environment, which is verified by free will in order to generate stuff and fail, and failure does not entail any organizational sanction (Bratton, 2001; Ahmed, Loh & Zairi, 1999). Thirdly, typically learning organizations do not encompass boundaries, in which members aspire to learn and are compelled to share knowledge (DiBella, 2001; Abernathy, 1999). Finally, permanent innovation is an idiosyncratic element of a learning organization (Cavaleri, 2004; Waldersee, 1997). Leaders embrace key roles given their importance for organizational change (Senge, 1996), however enhance workers' ability to learn. Therefore, leadership commitment and empowerment should be recommended.

Learning organizations managers have the duty to communicate organizational mission and goals to everyone within the company. Moreover, a communication network among organizational members requires being successful and proficient (Ortenblad, 2002; West III & Meyer 1997), because upward or downward communication allows knowledge creation and sharing within an organizational context (Nesan & Holt, 2002). Additionally, communication is the link amid workers' behaviour and organizational performance. In fact, an easy assumption can be illustrated: if more knowledge is communicated, the more it grows (Sunoo, 1999). For this reason, knowledge transfer is a significant characteristic of learning organizations, given that if more interactions involving individuals are encouraged, the higher level of knowledge transfer is achieved (Ortenblad, 2004; Bresman, Birkinshaw & Nobel, 1999); nevertheless knowledge growth is a non linear process due to some ethical and moral dilemmas (Costa & Silva, 2007).

Last but not least, some authors enquire about learning organizations values. For Otala (1995, pp. 163) a learning organization is

like a living organism, consisting of empowered, motivated employees, living in a clearly perceived symbiosis, sharing the feeling of a common destiny and profit, striving towards jointly defined goals, anxious to use every opportunity to learn from situations, processes and competition in order to adapt harmoniously to the changes in their environment and to improve continuously their own and their company's competitive performance?

It is an ambition frequently viewed cynically by people who do not consider this rhetoric (Garrat, 1999)? Does it suggest to individuals' liberation and empowerment to capitalize their full potential as inventive, intelligent workers (Dymock & McCarthy, 2006; Fenwick, 1995)? Or, it is a tool that can be changed into a "weapon" by managers in a competitive world (Grieves, 2008; Pandey & Gupta, 2008)?

Ethical and Social Challenges ("Why")

In order to approach the potential ethical and social dilemmas within learning organizations, it is crucial to embrace the unlike insights with reference to the knowledge creation, retention, and sharing. Following O'Neill & Adya (2007), workers have a moral duty not only to be productive (particularly regarding knowledge creation), as well as to share knowledge that benefits organizational body of knowledge. Nonetheless, tacit knowledge should be debarred from manageable knowledge within organizational contexts (KPMG, 2002). This is consistent with KPMG (2002) definition of intellectual property: not just patents, trademarks, copyrights, database rights and other pure intellectual property, or even other types of codified knowledge like business processes, methodologies and know how.

Despite this argument, it is important to clarify the reasons that promote this claim: organizational knowledge versus individual knowledge rights entails a trade-off between privacy, property rights (du Plessis, Britz & Davel (2007), and job security (Costa, Prior & Rogerson, 2008b). Thus, opinions that allege that personal knowledge is effortlessly managed, because it can be "more readily bought and sold" by hiring and firing individuals (Teece, 2000) is a social dilemma that requires an urgent answer. In fact, Ryan (2002) refers that is a personal social right to have right to security and safety.

Companies have a moral accountability to build a knowledge environment where workers can be productive, and engage a chance to generate, share and learn with other organizational members (Costa, Prior & Rogerson, 2008b); although, have the right of reasonably defend their economic moral interests (Blyth, 2005), without violating individual rights like autonomy, dignity, privacy (Baskerville & Dulipovici, 2006). On the other hand, a core query arises: how to sponsor ethical knowledge sharing environments? This paradox replicate two possible trade-offs: holding personal tacit knowledge for individual output versus sharing for organizational output (Trauth, 1999); and, personal effort versus benefit (Ford & Staples, 2005).

Finally, knowledge creators have the right to be fairly compensated for their work (Blyth, 2005), and typically employment contracts do not define in a proper and explicit way intellectual property rights and how these are compensated. Even so, as Davenport & Prusak (1998) recommend is necessary to combine monetary and non-monetary instruments.

In conclusion, Wilson (2002) declares that a truly knowledge environment is a utopian assumption, which at some extent is illustrated by ethics and self-interest act like counter-determinants for knowledge sharing (Wang, 2004). Thus, the ethics of knowledge transfers and conversions become extremely important due to the individual losing sole rights to knowledge (Baskerville & Dulipovici, 2006). Besides, it is intricate to detach divergent motivations versus the kind of social relations (Manski, 2000), since individual conduct is determined by various motives which may vary in similar contexts (Mooradian, Renzl & Matzler

2006). The identification of pre-conditions for successful cooperation engages a major challenge, as well as the role of trust to support knowledge sharing (Cabrera & Cabrera, 2002; Ostrom, 2000).

THE CLICHÉ OF EVALUATING

The expression "cliché" aims to resume the stereotype that is possible to measure, manage and evaluate everything. In fact, prior literature focuses on evaluating the subsequent characteristics of learning organizations: economic performance (e.g. Westover, 2006); organizational knowledge project (e.g. Ali & Ahmad, 2006; Collison & Parcell, 2001); auditing organizational knowledge flows (e.g. Bontis, Fearon & Hishon, 2003); organizational and individual learning (e.g. Sun & Scott, 2003; Simons, 1995). Hence, an ethical evaluation has been neglected! Although, is the author belief that is logical to portray the concept "evaluation" and its dimensions in order to promote a substantial argument.

Evaluation: An Overview

The traditional perception outlooks evaluation as a method that basically commences when capacity-building has happened, and overlooks historical data in order to guarantee that organizational demands about evaluation are being meet (Armitage *et al.*, 2003). The evaluation procedure must capitulate significant information permitting an incessant upgrading process, and for that needs to embrace the following topics:

- what is the organizational strategy and how does it assist in meeting its objectives?;
- what is the position of capacity-building in the overall structure and function of the organizational strategy?;
- how does capacity-building support the organization's strategy and its objectives?;
- what data does the organization need about the effectiveness of its capacity-building programmes?;
- how will this data be applied?

As a final remark, it is feasible to claim that transparency is crucial and the responses to these questions will act as guidance for the measurement procedure. If transparency do not occur, its results will not be relevant for the organization, because evaluation main purpose is to warrant organizational improvement and consequently organizational competitiveness (Armitage *et al.*, 2003).

Economic Performance

Westover (2006) work enables the following conclusion: none of the features that describe a learning organization affects its economical performance, which is consistent with the theoretical assumption of Kontoghiorghes, Awbre & Feurig (2005). For that, Westover (2006) firstly applied the learning organization assessment matrix of Kline & Saunders (1993) to determine if the organizations were learning organizations. Afterwards these results were gathered in ten primary categories, and finally constructed a table to exhibit the information about sector, size, ownership, share value or net profit and the average scores for each category. Finally, each individual score was graphed against share value and net profit in order to recognize the influence or not of each characteristic.

Organizational Knowledge Project

The Ali & Ahmad (2006) framework advocates that environmental forces and organizational resources are geographically disseminated; and an active response to the environmental forces imply a knowledge management project. Throughout a mix of human resources, ICT, information and energy is facilitated goods and services production. For that reason, the authors acknowledge three major components with reference to knowledge progress: creation, retention, and sharing. Furthermore, management literature pleads that decision making involves uncertainty and incomplete information, reinforcing the need for novel approaches. Time pressure demands that companies exploit historical data; hitherto, this approach indulges serious limitations as demonstrated by the current economic crisis. Therefore, it is important to embrace a refined level of know-how, know-what, know-who, know-where and know-why.

The knowledge management model has created about 700 virtual communities around the world including in public and private domains (Collison & Parcell, 2001). Collison & Parcell (2001) refer that during its implementation a myriad of processes require managers' attention: integration process, cultural barriers, and best practices. In fact, acquisitions and mergers are keen examples of cultural conflicts within organizational contexts which require a pro-active attitude by managers. Likewise best practices resume a critical praxis for managers in diverse organizational scenarios, because it promotes a culture of improvement and continuous learning without ignoring business ethics practices.

Organizational Knowledge Flows

Bontis, Fearon & Hishon (2003) in their work *The e-flow audit: An evaluation of knowledge flow within and outside a high-tech firm*, have evaluated through an auditing process the knowledge flow through e-mail. For that, the authors considered:

1. the e-mail flow inside and outside the company;
2. the flow map through a combined organizational chart;
3. how workers utilize the e-mail;
4. e-mail correspondents and senders;
5. which factors affect its usage.

The methodology is quite simple: an amount of internal and external e-mails is chosen and the following step is to categorize them by senders (individuals and departments), as well as the correspondents (individuals and departments). Additionally, the subject was analysed in order to understand if acknowledges the expected flow within the organizational context. Afterwards, a questionnaire provides information regarding the factors that affect its usage, as well as the motives about the correspondents' choice.

Individual and Organizational Learning

The theoretical model of Sun & Scott (2003) resumes an attempt to link individual and organizational learning. Despite individuals perform as prime learning agents (Huber, 1991; Argyris & Schön, 1978); their learning process is far from independent. In fact, Brodbeck & Greitemeyer (2000) demonstrate that when individuals act as a communal agent have a more steady and productive form of learning. Nonetheless, the nature of learning is related to the existing barriers, anxieties, and results in either single or double-loop learning, which acknowledges the quandary of learning transfer throughout the organization. In addition, the transfer itself hinders some disabling factors that require to be minimized. Sun & Scott (2003) still argue that single and loop-learning is the sphere of influence of learning theorists, while learning transfer is the field of learning organization practitioners. So, the extent of learning transfer, across its dissimilar stages, determines the gap amid both streams. This clearly highlights that learning barriers constantly enhance the gap as regards to descriptive and prescriptive organizational learning.

Simons (1995) examines the existing levels of learning: individual ability; groups' ability; and, organizational ability. All these levels configure objectives, actions, measuring, and feedback/ rewards. Objectives configuration entails the common influence of the external and internal environment, leading to an analysis of their sources: environment; individuals; groups; and management. What literature refers is that idealistic all these sources should engage a similar way, as well as individual objectives will be a component of group and organization learning throughout a mix of autonomy and freedom. Moreover, individual influence over group and organizational objectives reveals a blend among strict and broad boundaries, which allows maximizing autonomy within these limits.

RESEARCH PROTOCOL

Traditionally the main purpose is to portray a clear and a complete description concerning aims, objectives, methodological assumptions and data collection methods. In spite of this statement, the author will simply shed some light upon the aims and methodological assumptions. The motives are simple: data collection methods will be explained in section empirical procedures due to their importance, as well as to promote a more indulgent argument; in addition, it is vital to integrate the research project methodological assumptions and empirical procedures with analogous studies in order to consent a plausible and effective explanation.

Aims

The ongoing research project aims to debate the ethical and social dilemmas in learning organizations, as well as their overall impact in organizational strategy. For that, the analysis embraces three distinctive dimensions: knowledge management, organizational culture and ethics.

Methodology

Assumptions

Miles & Huberman (1994) refer that descriptive research aims to make complex issues logical by reducing them to their elements; or, when the researcher is not totally aware of the circumstances, despite acknowledging the research problem (Zikmund & Zikmund, 2000). On the other hand, explanatory research aims to illustrate certain phenomena from unlike perceptions (Yin, 1994), which resumes the research problem.

In order to permit subjective and inquiring results a mix of interpretative and critical theory is consistent with look for meaning in context. Therefore, Klein & Myers (1999) argue that to recognize how a reality emerged is vital to analyse the social and historical context, despite the output be discussable (Sandberg, 2005). Likewise, the observation of social reality is an imperative of critical research as documented in several narratives of critical research (Hirschheim & Klein, 1994).

Moving forward, a blend of a case study approach and grounded theory will generate reasonable outcomes. Hence, the author considers that an embedded multiple-case study (Yin, 1994), as well as Myers (1997) procedures as regards to case study method will assure a positive answer to the underlying research option. Plus, grounded theory enables a theoretical framework through data rather prior studies, as well as permits modify data collection through continuous penetrating questions (Glaser & Strauss, 1967).

Design Justification

As a consequence of being a recent discipline knowledge management studies do not engage a conceptual consensus, and this scenario is even enhanced due to an insignificant number of empirical research about its ethical dilemmas. Thus, the limitations of a positivist approach and the researcher's pre-understanding allow recognizing the validity of an interpretative approach (e.g. Senges, 2007), leading to a descriptive and explanatory analysis for organizational knowledge processes.

Regardless the existence of other theoretical contributions (e.g. Seppanen, 2008; Bajracharya & Masdeu, 2006), a novel one is required to promote an effective and realistic response to the underlying assumptions. So, to interpret managers' and workers' behaviours and decision making is essential through subjectivity and inquiring results (e.g. Senges, 2007). Additionally, two case studies and one pilot study will let a feasible comparison of organizational environments (e.g. Greig, 2008), and the emerging theory will disclose the complexity of human interactions throughout a permanent feedback process pertaining to the empirical results (e.g. Douglas, 2006; Fuchs & Hanning, 2001).

EMPIRICAL PROCEDURES

Data collection methods acknowledge five semi-structured interviews to organizational key managers, and web questionnaires comprising multiple choice and ask for agreement queries for workers. Semi-structured interviews promote a way to obtain the informants beliefs and opinions through a verbal exchange (Burns, 2000), and according to Macionis & Plummer (1998) these questionnaires are typically filled in by the respondents. Although, due to interviews or questionnaires multiple perils and the sensitive nature of the research project is advisable to conduct pre-tests and pilot studies (Yin, 1994).

Besides, for justifying data collection methods the author refers as examples the work of Squier (2003) and Kull (2002), who have reported semi-structured interviews as a way to be aware of managers' insights about organizational culture, and their decision-making process. This argument is still reinforced with Hariparsard (2005) multiple choice questionnaires for observing workers' awareness concerning organizational culture. As a final remark, analogous cases can be pointed for fine-tune the interview protocol or questionnaires in order to recognize managers' and workers' behaviours and values (Waldstrøm, 2003; Kull, 2002).

Pre-Tests Diagnosis

Pre-tests (simply questionnaires) have occurred throughout February 2009, and acknowledged various sampling constraints:

- sample size: 50 individuals from dissimilar professional and educational environments. Plus, to promote a high level of reliability it was determined the following weights for each focus group (top management: 30%; middle management: 30%; operational management: 40%);
- professional background: at least five years of professional experience, and working in learning organizations were also considered.

In order to proceed with the pre-tests some design procedures were required:

- sections: the questionnaires were divided in three sections (participant profiling, knowledge management and organizational culture). Participant profiling aimed to highlight respondents' characteristics, and the remaining sections to identify the ethical and social dilemmas because ethics is an unifying and transversal element;
- feedback process: a box for comments and suggestions was introduced for each query in order to obtain feedback about the question content, generated feelings (comfortable or uncomfortable), and if respondents answers were honest and sincere.

So, the next step is to report the existing questions, its category, as well as its aim of analysis (Table 1).

In order to understand the systematic procedures about pre-tests conclusions, it is vital to illustrate three milestones:

- comments and suggestions content analysis: reported respondents remarks, as well as the grounded theory procedures that allowed to gather and categorize them;
- answers content analysis: underlined a qualitative scrutiny for all questions, despite each query category had a dissimilar combination of methods. Multiple choice queries were revised using a numerical analysis to all results, as well as for each group analysis (top managers, middle managers and workers); on the other hand, the ask for agreement questions were authenticated through a blend of grounded theory and hermeneutics;
- framework versus results: described the interaction involving pre-tests results and the theoretical framework.

After the pre-tests results analysis, four leading conclusions were asserted:

- sampling constraints: sampling size and professional background were both achieved, in spite of a minor detail (two respondents had less than two years of professional experience). This was considered irrelevant due to sample features as well as pre-tests do not act as *modus operandi* for a research protocol;
- commentaries and suggestions content analysis: the queries revealed a high level of consistency, which was demonstrated by insignificant amendments in questions 2, 5 (instigated two dissimilar questions), 6, 8, 10 and 15 (observe Table 2);
- answers content analysis: the results indicated that the ethical and social challenges referred are factual, and managers tend to recurrently ignored them (Costa, Prior & Rogerson, 2010a);
- framework versus outcomes: justified the need for a novel approach, as well as the outlined framework (observe section "a proposal") engaged an encouraging reply.

Pilot Studies Diagnosis

After accomplishing the pre-tests, during June 2009 a series of pilot studies (questionnaires and interviews) were conducted within a learning organization in Portugal; nevertheless, at this point is decisive to emphasize the systematic procedures of both data collection methods.

In order to guarantee a feasible and consistent research, the author has produced similar sampling constraints for the questionnaires:

- sample size: 25 per cent of the population within the learning organization, representing each focus group the following weights: top management (30%), middle management (30%), and workers (40%);
- professional background: at least five years of professional practice within the pilot study organization.

Nonetheless, an important detail concerning pilot questionnaires design was the absence of a box for comments and suggestions in order to emphasize the results of pre-tests, and to confirm the queries reliability. Beyond these assumptions, the author acknowledged two interviews outside the learning organization prior to dialogue with the learning organization Human Resources Manager (HRM). Once again, these procedures validate the research protocol namely through recognizing potential differences among interviews in learning and non-learning organizations.

Table 1. Pre-tests questionnaire

Nr.	Question	Category	Aim of analysis
1	Organizational position: top manager, middle manager or worker?	MC	To understand which organizational perception is being covered
2	What you value most? (order from 1 to 3 your options)	MC	To perceive individual behaviour of managers and workers
3	How you mainly define your organizational role?	MC	To recognize the level of influence of managers and workers inside organizational culture
4	Do you consider that workers may express themselves and have free access concerning the organizational body of knowledge?	MC	To identify possible ethical dilemmas concerning organizational knowledge processes
5	Do you consider that worker's autonomy, dignity and privacy are recognized into the organizational body of knowledge?	MC	To identify ethical dilemmas concerning personal knowledge management
6	Do you consider that your personal experience is organizational intellectual property?	MC	To understand ethical dilemmas concerning personal knowledge management
7	Do you consider that knowledge creation, management and sharing into the organizational environment are fairly rewarded?	MC	A not faire compensation may undermine cooperation, therefore knowledge sharing can be seriously affected
8	Do you consider that workers who do not proceed to knowledge creation, management and sharing are fairly sanctioned?	MC	To perceive the relationship between behaviour and knowledge sharing
9	State what is meant to be a fair compensation or a fair sanction regarding knowledge creation, management and sharing in an organizational environment?	AfA	Allows the perception of possible contradictory answers regarding the two previous questions
10	In your opinion, does the organizational code of ethics or conduct clearly demonstrate the possible dilemmas concerning the process of knowledge creation, management and sharing, particularly at an individual level?	AfA	Allows a personal perception concerning existing organizational codes
11	Do you consider that employees feel that exists a culture of trust in the organizational environment?	MC	To comprehend the level of confidence concerning organizational culture is a key issue
12	Do you consider that a culture of trust is vital to allow knowledge creation, management and sharing into the organizational environment?	MC	Given the learning organization dimensions it is vital to realize this relationship
13	Do you consider that top management and workers feel confident in their mutually organizational relationship?	MC	To be aware of possible tensions concerning managers and workers
14	Do you consider that organizational values represent a culture of trust in the organizational environment?	MC	To grasp how organizational codes generate trust
15	In your opinion, in which ways can a culture of trust be promoted in the organizational environment? And, how could you individually generate trust in the organizational environment?	AfA	To understand how each focus group values trust
16	Refer if you consider that ethical decisions may change according to the role and the context of knowledge creation, management and sharing. And, in which way such decisions affect organizational trust?	AfA	A key question to understand individual decision making, as well as ethical intensity
17	In your opinion, does the organizational code of ethics or conduct allow a transparent relationship regarding all the stakeholders?	AfA	To realize how the framework responds
18	Practical examples (for managers only)	MC and AfA	Two practical examples in order to allow managers present and justify their personal beliefs

MC: multiple choice queries;
AfA: ask for agreement queries.

Table 2. Pre-tests revised queries

Nr	Question	Category	Aim of analysis
2	What you value most? (order from 1 to 3 your options, being 1 the most important. In case of evaluating the criteria in the same way choose that option)	MC	To perceive individual behaviour of managers and workers
5	Do you consider that worker's autonomy, dignity are recognized into the organizational body of knowledge?	MC	To identify ethical dilemmas concerning personal knowledge management
6	Do you consider that worker's privacy is recognized into the organizational body of knowledge?	MC	To identify ethical dilemmas concerning personal knowledge management
7	Do you consider that your personal experience lived within the organization is organizational intellectual property?	MC	To understand ethical dilemmas concerning personal knowledge management
9	Do you consider that workers who do not proceed to knowledge creation, management and sharing are sanctioned?	MC	To perceive the relationship between behaviour and knowledge sharing
11	In your opinion, does the organizational code of ethics or conduct (written or tacit) clearly demonstrate the possible dilemmas concerning the process of knowledge creation, management and sharing, particularly at an individual level?	AfA	Allows a personal perception concerning existing organizational codes
16	In your opinion, in which ways can a culture of trust be promoted in the organizational environment? What measures you individually take to generate trust in the organizational environment?	AfA	To understand how each focus group values trust

As a result, the underlying analytical procedures resumed the following remarks:

- answers content analysis: a qualitative enquire was performed, in spite of multiple choice embrace a generic and group numerical analysis and a mix of grounded theory with hermeneutics for ask for agreement queries;
- framework versus results: similar results were reported.

Given the overall arguments, it is mandatory to report the pilot studies results:

- sampling conditions: sample size and constraints intentions were reached, since the learning organization population was roughly 100 employees, being produced 28 questionnaires from which 25 were considered valid;
- answers content analysis: revealed queries reliability and corroborated the existence of ethical and social dilemmas, as well as an analogous awareness as regards to managers' (Costa, Prior & Rogerson, 2010b);
- framework versus results: similar conclusions were obtained.

"LIGHT REFRACTION"

"Light Refraction": An Understatement

According to the Wikipedia (2010a) "refraction is the change in direction of a wave due to a change in its speed", so dissimilar optical materials resume different refraction angles and levels of dispersion (refraction index). Likewise is reasonable to suggest multiple refraction (multidisciplinary analysis), as well the refraction index (each research discipline contribution) to describe the conceptual proposal.

Conceptual Tools

The theoretical contribution exploits instruments of four research fields: business strategy, maintenance management, e-learning, and ethics. It might appear complex and reckless to merge these four disciplines; nonetheless, the intricacy of an ethical evaluation justifies a multidisciplinary approach.

Business Strategy

According to Thompson & Strickland (2003), organizational strategy is a management game plan to reinforce the organization's competitive position, please customers, and achieve performance goals because through flexibility and adaptability. The conceptual tool that this discipline provides is the SWOT analysis, which aims to audit the organizational internal and external environment to determine its competitiveness and survival chances. Following Freire (2008) strengths and weaknesses are internal factors, and opportunities and threats are external factors. Given the nature of this manuscript the ethical and social dilemmas mainly influence organizational strengths and weaknesses.

Maintenance Management

Maintenance management acknowledges the industrial function or other that unites management, technical and economic activities, in order to optimize any organizational good life cycle (Campbell & Jardine, 2001), with the intention to achieve high levels of availability. In this case, under debate will be the Permanent Internal Auditing Process (PIAP), which is a diagnosis process supported by a sequence of questionnaires, with three analytical stages: data collection; information analysis; and to set up an improvement action plan when a quandary is recognized (Marimba & Farinha, 2003).

Each question introduces four possible answers pertaining to the organizational context: "always" (if always occur); "not always" (sometimes is not verified); "hardly ever" (occasionally takes place); and "never" (never happens within the organization). As a result, the questionnaire entails two components: answers about the performed enquiries; and, assess the obtained outcomes. In addition, to every potential reply is specified a scale of importance, representing three colours: green, yellow, and red. These retorts act as elimination criteria: green is the suitable answer (desirable answer); yellow implies an extraordinary reply (its existence must be squat, entailing an urgent upgrading); and finally, red designates a critical answer (under no circumstances should occur within the organization).

As a final remark, the author denotes that throughout PIAP will be possible to continuously monitor, diagnosis and improve action plans to minimize the ethical and social dilemmas that arise in knowledge creation, retention/use and sharing.

E-Learning

E-learning can be considered as the use of new multimedia technologies and the web, to develop learning throughout access to resources and services, as well as remote exchanges and cooperation (Commission of the European Communities, 2001). Or, basically is nothing more than the exploitation of electronic tools and technologies to support lecturing and learning. In addition, when compared to organizational knowledge management e-learning entails analogous ethical and social dilemmas, as for instance: intellectual property, privacy, autonomy, among others. Therefore, to explore the e-teaching model of Stahl (2002) is reasonable.

Stahl's (2002) theoretical matrix connects three analytical levels: ethical impact awareness, subject involved, and whether it is a hypothetical or practical problem. The insights concerning ethical impact exhibit the distinction between descriptive, normative and meta-theory philosophy. The next dimension represents the evolution of acting in a moral sense, because traditionally ethical theories symbolize an individual feature. Despite this argument, contemporary society has been replacing individual by collective agents (meso-level). This level causes numerous issues since the agent status is blurry; even so, its decisions encompass moral rights and duties. Apart from the previous levels state or society is also a moral subject (macro-level), given its influence over ethical issues. Moreover, the author believes that is not required to detail the divergences amid theoretical and practical ethical problems.

In conclusion, this contribution will allow to recognize the awareness, subject involved, and if the ethical issue is theoretical or practical.

Ethics

As a field of academic inquiry, ethics aims to differentiate among good or evil in more or less abstract terms, despite the lack of consensus regarding the concept itself (Pojman, 1994). However, since the mid 1990s a rising number of scholars and practitioners from diverse research fields considered as vital the introduction of ethics into their disciplines. Thus, this manuscript will focus two business ethics instruments: codes of ethics and codes of conduct, regardless Kaptein & Schwartz (2008) critics. These authors acknowledge the concept of "business codes" as a sum up of both codes, although codes of conduct act as an instrumental component of an organizational code of ethics. This argument resumes the non-unitary perspective of ethics, in which ethics embraces the "common good" and moral regulates our actions (Stahl, 2002).

It is broadly recognized that codes of conduct or behaviour attempt to predict and avoid certain particular behavioural patterns like conflicts of interest, self-dealing, bribery, and inappropriate actions. To Schneider & Baroux (2002), these refer principles and rules of conduct about individual's responsibility within organizational environments. These authors still argue that in spite their changes overtime (biological comparison), occasionally is valuable to reflect upon historical standards in order to identify related behavioural issues, bearing in mind the impacts of technological and social constraints. For that, the author does not agree that is possible to locate codes of conduct amid codes of ethics and of practice as Donald Gotterbarn (2000) refers, because codes of ethics are also used to express individual and collective purposes.

Examples of collective purposes are easily demonstrated throughout history, as well as their antagonism with reference to law (Bynum & Rogerson, 2003). Ethical codes rarely provide meticulous or precise prohibitions; instead, they refer a broader set of attitudes which endeavours to inform individuals pertaining to their behaviours (Gilman, 2005). Or, according to Pater & Van Gils (2003) ethical codes can be described as written, official and formal manuscripts which act as guide for employees and corporate behaviour. Nevertheless, in order to produce a fruitful debate surrounding codes of ethics is necessary to comprehend their efficiency. For authors like Seib & Fitzpatrick (2006), McNamara (2005), and Bivins (1993) an effective code of ethics must demonstrate to stakeholders that violators will be punished. Simultaneously, it must promote cooperation by working with offenders as a replacement for instant punishing (Ayers & Braithwaite, 1992).

Despite the impeccable logic of these theoretical contributions, Fairweather (2003) expresses a complex quandary: what constitutes an incomplete ethical code? And what constitutes a complete ethical code? The answer to the first question is acknowledged above. The second question leads to a further query: does the author of any ethical code or any other writing moral obligation foresee (mis)interpretations of this code? Hence, the option is to cover as many circumstances and issues as possible or not? The truth is simple: it is impossible for an author to determine the "completion" of a code of ethics or to foresee all probable behaviours. In spite of this claim, through the analysis of the organizational codes of ethics and conduct it will be possible to recognize the ethical practices and values, as well as how these

Figure 1. Theoretical framework, part

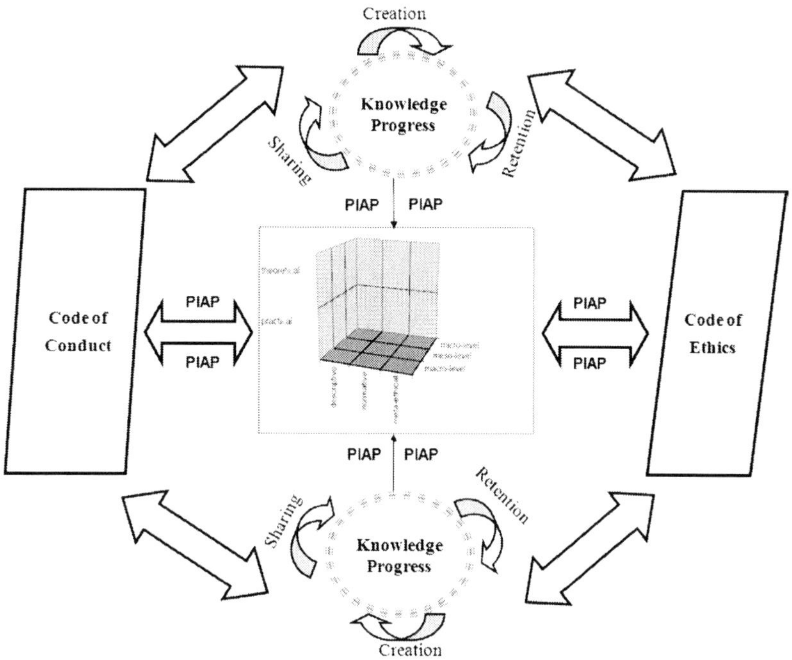

influence managers perception regarding the ethical and social quandaries.

A Proposal

As previously explained PIAP is a diagnosis method based on a sequence of enquiries, with three analytical stages: data collection; information analysis; and to elaborate an improvement action plan every time a dilemma is acknowledged. Accordingly, PIAP will continuously interact (feedback process) with the organizational code of ethics, organizational code of conduct, and also with the organizational knowledge management project. Besides, the questionnaire outcomes (by colours) will be reflected in Stahl's (2002) matrix, indicating an "intermediate status" on the topic of organizational ethical and moral behaviours, as Figure 1 exhibits.

The idea of "intermediate status" intends to express an incomplete analysis (stage 1), since organizational survival depends on how the market (society) comprehends these internal and external behaviours, leading to the "final status" (stage 2, which Figure 2 illustrates). For that reason, the SWOT analysis will evaluate the organization's ethical positioning despite potential critics (e.g. Deephouse & Carter, 2005). Nevertheless, in order to produce a reliable argument is vital to detail the interaction among the PIAP, Stahl's (2002) matrix and the SWOT analysis (Tables 3 and 4).

Table 3 displays the virtual weighting of every impact within the SWOT analysis, considering the probable scenarios of Stahl's (2002) matrix. The lowest value is 0% and the highest value is 100%, which for some readers may contradict the research design criteria (a qualitative analysis). Although, the author argues that such criticism is groundless due to the importance of the following reminders:

- SWOT analysis: the SWOT itself considers unlike impacts for each criteria within

Figure 2. Theoretical framework, part 2

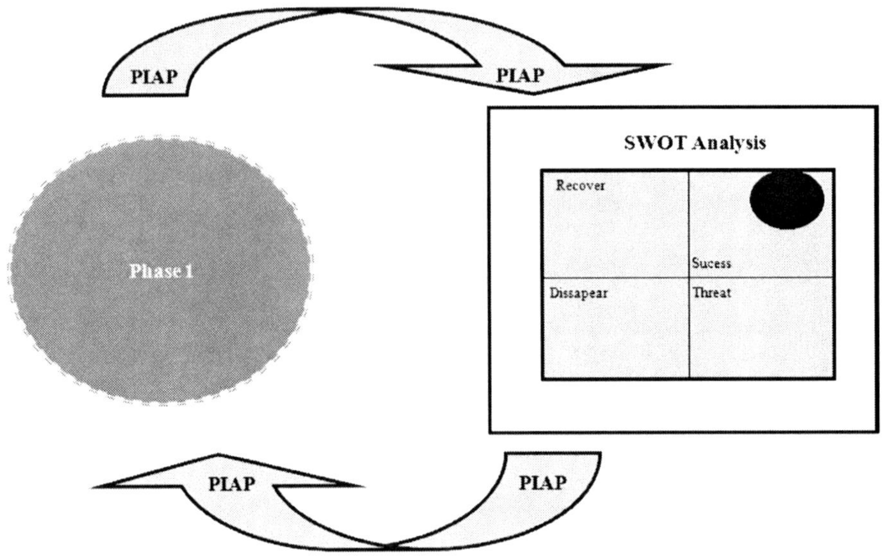

the different layers: strengths, weaknesses, opportunities and threats. These impacts reflect a combination of a relative and absolute scales, and are a pre-condition of constructing a SWOT analysis. Even so, the "value" given by individuals depends on their personal experiences, judgment and sensitivity;

- PIAP analysis: a pre-condition for constructing the PIAP framework is that the probable responses to the enquiries ("always", "not always", "hardly ever", and "never"), are transformed into a colour scale according to their historical data: "always" and "not always" (green); "hardly ever" (yellow); and "never" (red);
- descriptive research: resumes the author "blurry" perception about the organizational impacts for both analysis. This is consistent with the fact of the researcher is not entirely conscious of the situation (descriptive research).

Likewise, to avoid further negative comments the author introduces a novel table as regards to the organizational impact, by converting the numerical values into colour scales due to PIAP (read after Table 4 the empirical argument). Furthermore, in

Table 3. PIAP, Stahl's (2002) matrix, and the SWOT analysis interface (act 1)

		Subject Involved				
		Micro	Meso	Macro		
Ethical Impact	Meta-theory	5	10	15	Theory	Category
		20	25	30	Practice	
	Normative	70	75	65	Theory	
		85	90	80	Practice	
	Descriptive	45	40	35	Theory	
		60	55	50	Practice	

Table 4. PIAP, Stahl's (2002) matrix, and the SWOT analysis interface (act 2)

		Subject Involved				
		Micro	**Meso**	**Macro**		
Ethical Impact	**Meta-theory**	Green	Green	Green	**Theory**	**Category**
		Green	Green	Green	**Practice**	
	Normative	Yellow	Yellow	Yellow	**Theory**	
		Red	Red	Red	**Practice**	
	Descriptive	Yellow	Yellow	Yellow	**Theory**	
		Red	Red	Red	**Practice**	

section rigor and liability the author will proclaim and validate these procedures through research methods literature.

The conversion procedure reflects the absence of historical data, because the empirical results analysis undeniably reveal that top managers have been ignoring the reported ethical and social dilemmas (for further details see Costa, Prior & Rogerson, 2010a; Costa, Prior & Rogerson, 2010b). As a consequence, the following combinations arise:

- meta-theory/micro-level/theoretical- green, since it discusses theoretical issues an individual level, so no impact is verified;
- meta-theory/meso-level/theoretical- green, due to similar reasons in spite of being at a meso-level;
- meta-theory/macro-level/theoretical- green, because societal theoretical debates have no impact into the organization;
- meta-theory/micro-level/practical- green, in spite of analyzing practical issues because it is simply a theoretical subject;
- meta-theory/meso-level/practical- green, by analogy although at a meso-level;
- meta-theory/macro-level/practical- green, since macro issues have a inexistent impact within organizational context;
- normative/micro-level/theoretical- yellow, because normative ethics attempts to substantiate individual moral issues, as well as theoretical scenarios have a lower impact;
- normative/meso-level/theoretical- yellow, by equivalence in spite of a dissimilar ethical actor;
- normative/macro-level/theoretical- yellow, for the reason that societal moral issues have some impact into organizational strategies;
- normative/micro-level/practical- red, because it becomes a practical issue meaning higher impact;
- normative/meso-level/practical- red, due to analogous reasons although at a divergent level;
- normative/macro-level/practical- red, assuming the impact into organizational strategies;
- descriptive/micro-level/theoretical- yellow, regardless theoretical dilemmas promote lower impacts within organizational contexts. Moreover, descriptive ethics engages ethical practices and that is what justifies this colour;
- descriptive/meso-level/theoretical- yellow, due to comparable state of affairs although concerning meso-level;
- descriptive/macro-level/theoretical- yellow, because societal ethical and social practices have a gigantic impact in business strategy;

- descriptive/micro-level/practical- red, for assuming practical issues and individual's ethical behaviour;
- descriptive/meso-level/practical- red, in order to be consistent with the previous arguments concerning the relationship between micro and meso-level;
- descriptive/macro-level/practical- red, as a consequence regarding organizational strategy.

Is the author belief that these answers may be changed as a consequence of organizational dynamics (historical data interpretation), as for instance the next example highlights: if top management is having a conjectural debate pertaining to intellectual property rights throughout the use of its social network, the colour will be green (first interaction); however, if the dilemma becomes practical within the organizational context the colour is yellow (a non-regular issue that requires an intervention) (historical data because resumes a second interaction), or will become red if its level of frequency enhances tremendously (future interactions). Finally, this novel insight with reference to ethical and social dilemmas impacts promise to capture the richness of results that empirical data will produce.

"Shedding Extra Light": A Practical Example

This subsection aims to highlight two practical cases (similar to the existing ones in pre-tests and pilot studies), in order to display how the framework interacts. A critical assumption will be considered: the organizational code of conduct consents workers to explore the IT resources apart from their standard tasks: is legitimate to have private folders, receive personal e-mails, and utilise the social network for social or collaborative reasons. Despite these privileges, the code informs that is an organizational right to monitor employee's productivity throughout remote control systems.

The initial example is theoretical: managers are trying to classify potential content violation with reference to workers' personal folders or e-mails. This quandary is theoretical because it has no historical background within the organization, and a non-replication constraint is included. The second example can be labelled as practical: managers obtain an idea for an innovative product through the monitoring process of the social network, namely using a conversation amid two workers. The idea was non-work related, and non-related to the organizational core business or future strategies. In spite of these characteristics, this product became a worldwide market leader.

So, in order to achieve a clear and productive explanation concerning how the framework will interact the author introduces Table 5.

If the reader bears in mind the relative weights typified in table 4, the outcome for each example into the SWOT analysis will be similar to Figure 3 and Figure 4.

Table 5. Practical examples analysis

Case	Ethical and social dilemmas	Stage 1 (PIAP)	Stage 2 (Stahl's matrix)
1	Privacy	Answer: "never" due to the absence of similar past events	Answer: meta-ethics; meso-level; and, theoretical. Colour: green, in spite of being an attempt to categorize a possible event
2	Faire Compensation	Answer: "never" due to the absence of similar past events	Answer: normative; micro-level; and, practical. Colour: yellow, because it requires a intervention, because it is a practical situation

Figure 3. Example 1

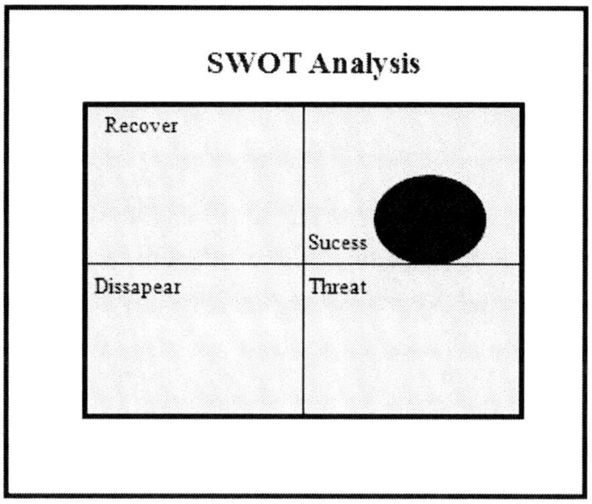

Rigor and Liability

Rigor and liability are key features of any empirical research, so the author has decided to shed some light regarding the following issues: methodological design, empirical procedures, and philosophical argument.

Numerous researchers plead the concept of methodological pluralism or "triangulation" (e.g. Cox & Hassard, 2005; Weber, 2004), as an opposite perspective to multi-site research (Audet & d'Amboise, 2001). According to Creswell & Clark (2007) mixed methods promote: triangulation (corroborate data and obtain convergent validity); complementarity (total explanation about the results); development (guide further data collection, sampling, or analysis). Even so, Ammenwerth, Ilber & Mansmann (2003) argue that different categories of data obtained through unlike sources cannot validate each other, which the empirical outcomes seem to contradict. This last claim is consistent with the philosophical, cultural and even psychological concern that Alaranta (2006) reports with reference to triangulation, because in spite of facilitating the phenomenon analysis engages multiple practical problems.

On the other hand, the empirical procedures promote two analytical dimensions: pre-tests and pilot studies design, and results analysis. The questionnaires "design" (sections and queries characteristics) intended to understand individual ethical behaviour and its impact within a system, which is similar to qualitative and numerical approach of Šuc, Vladušič & Bratko (2004). Regarding results analysis it is possible to acknowledge:

- answers reliability: the author has drawn a table that compares respondent's data profiling (organizational position, what you value most and organizational role) with their answers (multiple choice and ask for agreement) of each section, as well as this procedure was acknowledged with both sections to detect probable conflicting opinions and beliefs (interpretative flexibility) (Doherty, Coombs & Loan-Clarke, 2006);
- answers content analysis: multiple choice questions were analysed through a numerical analysis, which is defensible through Creswell (2003) argument: if a researcher asserts to acknowledge in-depth insight into an event, it might choose a diminutive however informative example, or might also exploit a simple inferential numerical analysis to detail the results. Nevertheless, the concept "numerical analysis" will surely induce criticism because in Anglo-Saxon culture numerical implies a quantitative research, which is consistent with the argument of Alaranta (2006). In addition, ask for agreement questions were analysed through a mix of grounded theory and hermeneutics which is consistent with Strauss & Corbin (1998, pp. 178) claim that "grounded theory will include its combination with other methodologies including phenomenology and hermeneutics", as well as that can interact as the missing link in interpretative research (Goulding,

Figure 4. Example 2

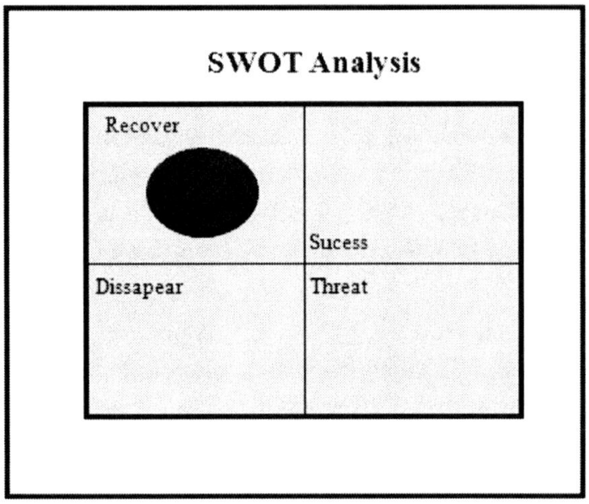

1998). This argument is enhanced because interpretative research limits are visibly diminished when methodological isolation does not occur (Williams, 2000);

- framework versus results: the pre-conditions to construct a PIAP and SWOT analysis, as well as the conversion process sums up the author judgment and sensitivity as regards to managers perception of the ethical and social dilemmas throughout the questionnaires and interviews (including the practical examples). Descriptive research features will help to cope with probable critics, and once again the visible limitations of interpretative research are diminished due to grounded theory "cycles", which is consistent with Williams (2000).

Finally, the philosophical argument refers to abduction (identical to inferation of a cause in order to explain a consequence), which acknowledges numerous explanations along with some erroneous outcomes (Zait & Zait, 2009). Peirce (1878) argues that is a method of experimentational mental reflection hospitable to forming hypotheses and conducive to testing them, whereas the abductive argument reaches beyond the limits of critical evidences (Calvert-Minor, 2009).

FUTURE RESEARCH DIRECTIONS

Bearing in mind light refraction, the author proposes to extend the metaphor to lighthouses lens to debate potential future research directions. Following the Wikipedia (2010b):

A lighthouse is a tower, building, or other type of structure designed to emit light from a system of lamps and lenses or, in older times, from a fire, and used as an aid to navigation for pilots at sea or on inland waterways.

Furthermore, their light refraction depends on several factors, like the power of the optical device, observer geographical position, etc. and its range is expressed in three levels (Instituto Hidrográfico, 2003):

- geographical: distance that the light can be seen from the lighthouse;
- light: maximum distance that light is observable;
- nominal: imposes to calculate its height (distance among the base and light) and altitude (difference amid the mean sea level and light focal plane).

Through a metaphorical explanation, it is reasonable to consider that geographical range (enables the ethical evaluation framework proposal), light range (potential organizations under scrutiny), nominal range (framework critical assessment). Yet, two important queries arise: what is the significance of potential organizations? And, what is a critical assessment?

The initial purpose of the conceptual framework is to evaluate learning organizations as regards to ethical avoidance, although some authors like Rowley & Gibbs (2008) argue that learning organizations will become wisdom organizations. The concept is related to the confrontation between neo-liberal tendencies and internal and external moral practices, so:

wise organization must create time for the virtues that allow wise, practical judgements to be made. An organization has a temporality where it remembers the past, accepts responsibility for it and uses that to devise a new space for itself in the future whilst acting now (Rowley & Gibbs, 2008, p. 364).

Hence, to grasp the veracity of this scenario the author claims that wisdom organizations fall under the "conceptual umbrella", despite the importance to initially assess the framework through worldwide applications in learning organizations given the specificity of organizational contexts. This process will generate an adequate amount of historical data (empirical results), allowing to determine if changes are required or not, in order to increase the level of reliability.

CONCLUSION

In spite of being an ongoing research project, the author will pinpoint some additional interesting conclusions through two macro arguments: research protocol analysis, and author future insights. Yet, research protocol analysis will be divided into the following issues: reseaarch protocol overall structure; data collection analysis; framework response; rigor and liability; author future insight.

First, the research design structure (including data collection methods) appears to respond positively to existing ethical and social dilemmas within learning organizations. Secondly, the empirical results confirm the existence of these dilemmas, being reasonable to argue that learning organizations are not ethical because managers neglect these dilemmas with reference to knowledge creation, retention/use, and sharing. This attitude is at some extent explained by the novelty of these dilemmas; nonetheless, is the author conviction that resumes managers' lack of moral reasoning and sensitivity. The second conjecture requires further focused empirical research despite numerous approaches to managers' moral sensitivity (e.g. Pedersen, 2009; Treviño & Weaver, 2003; Wittmer, 2000). On the other hand, it is important to emphasize that the conceptual framework also enables a positive response, allowing categorizing these dilemmas and analysing their impact in organizational strategy. Therefore, it is reasonable to argue that rigor and liability resume this ongoing research.

Regarding the second macro reason is the author conviction that future case studies will entail similar empirical results, which demonstrates the need for an ethical evaluation (permanent procedure that helps managers to recognize the outcomes of applying new strategies concerning moral and behavioural values in organizations). Therefore, wisdom organizations will require an analogous analysis despite Rowley's (2006) argument that these will act ethically in order to collective good be achievable.

REFERENCES

Abernathy, D. J. (1999). Leading-edge learning. *Training & Development*, *53*(3), 40–42.

Addleson, M. (2000). What is good organization? Learning organizations, community and the rhetoric of the bottom line. *European Journal of Work & Organizational*, *9*(2), 233–252. doi:10.1080/135943200397969

Ahmed, P. K., Loh, A. Y. E., & Zairi, M. (1999). Cultures for continuous improvement and learning. *Total Quality Management*, *10*(4), 426–434.

Alaranta, M. (2006). Combining theory-testing and theory-building analyses of case study data. *London School of Economics and Political*. Retrieved August 3, 2010, from, http://is2.lse.ac.uk/asp/aspecis/20060059.pdf

Ali, H. M., & Ahmad, N. H. (2006). Knowledge management in Malaysian banks: A new paradigm. *Journal of Knowledge Management Practice, 7*(3). Retrieved August 1, 2010, from, http://www.tlainc.com/articl120.htm

Ammenwerth, E., Ilber, C., & Mansmann, U. (2003). Can evaluations studies benefit from triangulation? A case study. *International Journal of Medical Informatics, 70*(2/3), 237–248. doi:10.1016/S1386-5056(03)00059-5

Argyris, C. (1999). *On organizational learning* (2nd ed.). Oxford, UK: Blackwell Publishing.

Argyris, C., & Schön, D. A. (1978). *Organizational learning: A theory of action perspective*. Reading, MA: Addison Wesley.

Armitage, A. (2003). *Teaching and training in post-compulsory education*. Maidenhead, UK: Open University Press.

Audet, J., & d'Amboise, G. (2001). The multi-site study: An innovative research methodology. *The Qualitative Report, 6*(2). Retrieved August 3, 2010, from, http://www.nova.edu/ssss/QR/QR6-2/audet.html

Ayres, I., & Braithwaite, J. (1992). *Responsive regulation: Transcending the deregulation debate*. New York: Oxford University Press.

Bajracharya, P., & Masdeu, N. R. (2006). *Tacit knowledge transfer in small segment of small enterprises*. Linköping, Sweden: Linköping University.

Barkur, G., Varambally, K. V. M., & Rodrigues, L. L. R. (2007). Insurance sector dynamics: Towards transformation into learning organization. *The Learning Organization, 14*(6), 510–523. doi:10.1108/09696470710825123

Baskerville, R., & Dulipovici, A. (2006). The ethics of knowledge transfers and conversions: Property or privacy rights. In K. VanLehn (Ed.), *Proceedings of the 39th Hawaii International Conference on System Sciences* (pp. 144-152). Hawaii: IEEE.

Bivins, T. H. (1993). Public relations, professionalism, and the public interest. *Journal of Business Ethics, 12*(2), 117–126. doi:10.1007/BF00871931

Black, S. J., & Porter, L. W. (2000). *Management: Meeting new challenges*. New York: Prentice Hall.

Blyth, A. (2005). Business behaving responsibly. *Director (Cincinnati, Ohio), 59*(1), 30.

Bontis, N., Fearon, M., & Hishon, M. (2003). The e-flow audit: An evaluation of knowledge flow within and outside a high-tech firm. *Journal of Knowledge Management, 7*(1), 6–19. doi:10.1108/13673270310463581

Bratton, J. A. (2001). Why workers are reluctant learners: The case of the Canadian pulp and paper industry. *Journal of Workplace Learning, 12*(7/8), 333–344. doi:10.1108/13665620110411120

Bresman, H., Birkinshaw, J., & Nobel, R. (1999). Knowledge transfer in international acquisitions. *Journal of International Business Studies, 30*(3), 439–462. doi:10.1057/palgrave.jibs.8490078

Brodbeck, F. C., & Greitemeyer, T. (2000). Effects of individual versus mixed individual and group experience in rule induction on group member learning and group performance. *Journal of Experimental Social Psychology, 36*(6), 621–648. doi:10.1006/jesp.2000.1423

Burns, R. B. (2000). *Introduction to research methods*. London: Sage Publishers.

Bynum, T. W., & Rogerson, S. (2003). *Computer ethics and professional responsibility*. Malden, UK: Blackwell Publishing.

Cabrera, A., & Cabrera, E. F. (2002). Knowledge sharing dilemmas. *Organization Studies*, *23*(5), 687–710. doi:10.1177/0170840602235001

Calvert-Minor, C. (2009). Commonsense realism and triangulation. *Philosophia*, *37*(1), 67–86. doi:10.1007/s11406-008-9160-6

Campbell, J. D., & Jardine, A. K. S. (Eds.). (2001). *Maintenance excellence: Optimizing equipment life cycle*. New York, NY: Marcel Dekker.

Cavaleri, S. A. (2004). Principles for designing pragmatic knowledge management systems. *The Learning Organization*, *11*(4/5), 312–321. doi:10.1108/09696470410538215

Cavaleri, S. A. (2008). Are learning organizations pragmatic? *The Learning Organization*, *15*(6), 474–485. doi:10.1108/09696470810907383

Chun, R. (2005). Ethical character and virtue of organizations: An empirical assessment and strategic implications. *Journal of Business Ethics*, *57*(3), 269–284. doi:10.1007/s10551-004-6591-2

Collison, C., & Parcell, G. (2001). *Learning to fly: Practical knowledge management from leading and learning organizations*. Chichester, UK: Capstone Publishing Limited.

Commission of the European Communities. (2001). *The e-learning action plan*. Brussels: Commission of the European Communities.

Costa, G. J. M., Prior, M., & Rogerson, S. (2008a). Will the evolution of ICT ethics engage organizational transparency? In Vaccaro, A., Horta, H., & Madsen, P. (Eds.), *Transparency, Information and Communication Technology- Social Responsibility and Accountability in Business and Education* (pp. 31–50). Chesapeake, VA: Softbound.

Costa, G. J. M., Prior, M., & Rogerson, S. (2008b). Individual ethics and knowledge management: Arising conflicts. In Bynum, T. (Eds.), *ETHICOMP 2008: Living, Working and Learning Beyond Technology* (pp. 117–129). Mantua, Italy: University of Pavia.

Costa, G. J. M., Prior, M., & Rogerson, S. (2010a). Why link knowledge management, organizational culture and ethics: Analysing empirical inquiry. In Arias-Oliva, M. (Eds.), *ETHICOMP 2010* (pp. 83–92). Tarragona, Spain: Rovira i Virgili University.

Costa, G. J. M., Prior, M., & Rogerson, S. (2010b). Linking knowledge management, organizational culture and ethics: Inquiring results. In E. Tomé (Ed.), *Proceedings of the 11th European Conference on Knowledge Management* (pp. 1144-1152). Vila Nova de Famalicão, Portugal: Lusiada University of Vila Nova de Famalicão.

Costa, G. J. M., & Silva, N. M. A. (2007). Knowledge management: How ethical is your organization's knowledge? In Bynum, T. W., Rogerson, S., & Murata, K. (Eds.), *ETHICOMP 2007: Glocalisation: Bridging the Global Nature of Information and Communication Technology* (*Vol. 1*, pp. 123–136). Tokyo: Meiji University.

Cox, J., & Hassard, J. (2005). Triangulation in organizational research: A representation. *Organizational Articles*, *12*(1), 109–133.

Creswell, J. W. (2003). *Research design: Qualitative, quantitative and mixed methods approaches* (2nd ed.). Thousand Oaks, CA: Sage Publications.

Creswell, J. W., & Clark, V. L. P. (2007). *Designing and conducting mixed methods research*. Thousand Oaks, CA: Sage.

Davenport, T. H., & Prusak, L. (1998). *Working knowledge: How organizations manage what they know*. Boston: Harvard Business School Press.

Dealtry, R. (2002). Configuring the corporate university- Managing the issue of learning relevance in the formulation of corporate learning strategies. *Journal of Workplace Learning*, *14*(5), 209–214. doi:10.1108/13665620210433909

Deephouse, D. L., & Carter, S. M. (2005). An examination of differences between organizational legitimacy and organizational reputation. *Journal of Management Studies*, *42*(2), 329–360. doi:10.1111/j.1467-6486.2005.00499.x

DiBella, A. J. (2001). *Learning practices: Assessment and action for organizational improvement*. Upper Saddle River, NJ: Prentice Hall.

Doherty, N. F., Coombs, C. C., & Loan-Clarke, J. (2006). A re-conceptualization of the interpretative flexibility of information technologies: Redressing the balance between the social and the technical. *European Journal of Information Systems*, *15*(6), 569–582. doi:10.1057/palgrave.ejis.3000653

Douglas, D. (2006). Intransivities of managerial decisions: A grounded theory case. *Management Decision*, *44*(2), 259–275. doi:10.1108/00251740610650238

du Plessis, J. C., Britz, J. J., & Davel, R. (2007). *Slave or sibling: A moral reframing the corporate knowledge sharing community*. University of Pretoria, Pretoria, South Africa. Retrieved August 1, 2010, from, http://ol.up.ac.za/upspace/bitstream/2263/1808/1/DuPlessis_Slave%282006%29.pdf

Dusko, U. (2006). System-organizational aspect of a learning organization in companies. *Systemic Practice and Action Research*, *19*(1), 81–99. doi:10.1007/s11213-005-9005-1

Dymock, D., & McCarthty, C. (2006). Towards a learning organization? Employee perception. *The Learning Organization*, *13*(5), 525–537. doi:10.1108/09696470610680017

Fairweather, N. B. (2003). No, PAPA: Why incomplete codes of ethics are worse that none at all. In Bynum, T. W., & Rogerson, S. (Eds.), *Computer Ethics and Professional Responsibility* (pp. 142–155). Malden, MA: Blackwell Publishing.

Fenwick, T. J. (1995). *Limits of the learning organization: A critical look*. Nova Scotia, Canada: St. Francis Xavier University.

Ford, D. P., & Staples, D. S. (2005). Perceived value of knowledge: Shall I give you my gem, my coal? In W. Arbeitspapiere (Ed.), *Proceedings of 38th Hawaii International Conference on Systems Sciences* (pp. 247-256). Hawaii: IEEE.

Freire, A. (2008). *Estratégia- Sucesso em Portugal*. Braga, Portugal: Verbo. (in Portuguese)

Fuchs, M., & Hanning, C. (2001). *Ethical capability as a competitive advantage- Three case studies within the Volvo corporation*. Luleå, Sweden: Luleå Tekniska University.

Garrat, B. (1999). The learning organization 15 years on: Some personal reflections. *The Learning Organization*, *6*(5), 202–207. doi:10.1108/09696479910299802

Gilley, J. W., & Maybunich, A. (2000). *Beyond the learning organization. Creating a culture of continuous growth and development through state-of-the-art human resource practices*. Cambridge, MA: Perseus Books.

Gilman, S. C. (2005). *Ethics codes and codes of conduct as tools for promoting an ethical and professional public service: Comparative successes and lessons*. Washington, DC: World Bank.

Gilmartin, R. V. (2003). Ethics and the corporate culture. *Bentley College*. Retrieved July 31, 2010, from, http://www.bentley.edu/cbe/documents/Gilmartin.pdf

Glaser, B. G., & Strauss, A. L. (1967). *The discovery of grounded theory*. New York: Aldine De Gruyter.

Gotterbarn, D. (2000). Virtual information and the software engineering code of ethics. In Langford, D. (Ed.), *Internet Ethics* (pp. 200–215). London: McMillan.

Goulding, C. (1998). Grounded theory: The missing methodology on the interpretivist agenda. *Qualitative Market Research: An International Journal*, *1*(1), 50–57. doi:10.1108/13522759810197587

Gowri, A. (2007). On corporate virtue. *Journal of Business Ethics*, *70*(4), 391–400. doi:10.1007/s10551-006-9117-2

Greig, G. (2008). *The role and importance of context in collective learning: Multiple case studies in Scottish primary care*. St. Andrews, Scotland: University of St. Andrews.

Grieves, J. (2008). Why should we abandon the idea of the learning organization. *The Learning Organization*, *15*(6), 463–473. doi:10.1108/09696470810907374

Hariparsad, I. D. (2005). *The work ethic of the principal as an aspect of management*. Johannesburg, South Africa: University of Johannesburg.

Hirschheim, R., & Klein, H. K. (1994). Realizing emancipatory principles in information systems development: The case for Ethics. *Management Information Systems Quarterly*, *18*(1), 83–109. doi:10.2307/249611

Huber, G. P. (1991). Organizational learning: The contributing process and the literatures. *Organization Science*, *2*(1), 88–115. doi:10.1287/orsc.2.1.88

Instituto Hidrográfico. (2003). *Ajudas à navegação: Lista de luzes, bóias, balizas e sinais de nevoeiro*, (6ª ed.). Lisboa: Instituto Hidrográfico (in Portuguese).

Johnson, J. R. (2002). Leading the learning organization: Portrait of four leaders. *Leadership and Organization Development Journal*, *23*(5), 241–249. doi:10.1108/01437730210435956

Kaptein, M., & Schwartz, M. S. (2008). The effectiveness of business codes: A critical examination of existing studies and the development of an integrated research model. *Journal of Business Ethics*, *77*(2), 111–127. doi:10.1007/s10551-006-9305-0

Klein, H. K., & Myers, M. D. (1999). A set of principles for conducting and evaluating interpretive field studies in information systems. *Management Information Systems Quarterly*, *23*(1), 67–93. doi:10.2307/249410

Kline, P., & Saunders, B. (1993). *Ten steps to a learning organization*. Arlington, VA: Great Ocean Publishers.

Kontoghiorghes, C., Awbre, S., & Feurig, P. (2005). Examining the relationship between learning organization characteristics and change adaptation, innovation, and organizational performance. *Human Resource Development Quarterly*, *16*(2), 185–212. doi:10.1002/hrdq.1133

KPMG. (2002). *Intellectual gold- KPMG's European Intellectual Property Survey reveals the value hidden in Europe's leading companies*. London: KPMG.

Kull, M. D. (2002). *Stories of knowledge management: Exploring coherence in a community of practice*. Washington, DC: The George Washington University.

Leitch, C. (1996). Learning organizations: The measurement of company performance. *Journal of European Industrial Training*, *20*(1), 31–44. doi:10.1108/03090599610105264

Lessem, R. (1990). *Developmental management principle of holistics business*. Oxford: Blackwell.

Liyanage, S., & Poon, P. S. (2002). Technology and innovation management learning in the knowledge economy. *Journal of Management Development*, *22*(7), 579–602. doi:10.1108/02621710310484740

Loermans, J. (2002). Synergizing the learning organization and knowledge management. *Journal of Knowledge Management*, *6*(3), 285–294. doi:10.1108/13673270210434386

Macionis, J. J., & Plummer, K. (1998). *Sociology: A global introduction*. Upper Saddle River, NJ: Prentice Hall Inc.

Manski, C. F. (2000). Economic analysis of social interactions. *The Journal of Economic Perspectives*, *14*(3), 115–136. doi:10.1257/jep.14.3.115

Marimba, A., & Farinha, T. (2003, May). *Controlo e monitorização da gestão da manutenção: Metodologia de auditoria interna permanente*. Paper presented at the 3as Jornadas de Organização e Gestão Industrial da ESTG, Leiria (in Portuguese).

McNamara, C. (2005). Complete guide to ethics management: An ethics toolkit for managers. *Management Help*. Retrieved August 2, 2010, from, www.managementhelp.org/ethics/ethxgde.htm

Miles, M. B., & Huberman, M. (1994). *Qualitative data analysis: An expanded source book* (2nd ed.). Thousand Oaks, CA: Sage.

Moilanen, R. (2005). Diagnosing and measuring learning organizations. *The Learning Organization*, *12*(1), 71–89. doi:10.1108/09696470510574278

Mooradian, T., Renzl, B., & Matzler, K. (2006). Who trusts? Personality, trust and knowledge sharing. *Management Learning*, *37*(4), 523–540. doi:10.1177/1350507606073424

Moraga, E. (2006). Cultural learning organizations: A model. *Cultural Learning Organizations*. Retrieved July 31, 2010, from, www.culturallearningorganizations.net/index_files/The%20 ethics%20of%20LO.pdf

Myers, M. D. (1997). Qualitative research in information systems. *Management Information Systems Quarterly*, *21*(2), 241–242. doi:10.2307/249422

Nesan, L. J., & Holt, G. D. (2002). Assessment of organizational involvement in implementing empowerment. *Integrated Manufacturing Systems*, *13*(4), 201–211. doi:10.1108/09576060210426903

O'Neill, B. S., & Adya, M. (2007). Knowledge sharing and the psychological contract: Managing knowledge workers across different stages of employment. *Journal of Managerial Psychology*, *22*(4), 411–436. doi:10.1108/02683940710745969

Ortenblad, A. (2002). A typology of the idea of learning organization. *Management Learning*, *33*(2), 213–230. doi:10.1177/1350507602332004

Ortenblad, A. (2004). The learning organization: Towards an integrated model. *The Learning Organization*, *11*(2), 129–144. doi:10.1108/09696470410521592

Ostrom, E. (2000). Collective action and the evolution of social norms. *The Journal of Economic Perspectives*, *14*(3), 137–158. doi:10.1257/jep.14.3.137

Otala, M. (1995). The learning organization: Theory into practice. *Industry and Higher Education*, *9*(3), 157–164.

Pandey, A., & Gupta, R. (2008). Perspective of collective consciousness of business organizations. *Journal of Business Ethics*, *80*(4), 889–898. doi:10.1007/s10551-007-9475-4

Pater, A., & Van Gils, A. (2003). Stimulating ethical decision-making in a business context: Effects of ethical and professional codes. *European Management Journal*, *21*(6), 762–772. doi:10.1016/j.emj.2003.09.016

Pedersen, L. J. T. (2009). See no evil: Moral sensitivity in the formulation of business problems. *Business Ethics (Oxford, England)*, *18*(4), 335–348. doi:10.1111/j.1467-8608.2009.01567.x

Pedler, M., Burgoyne, J., & Boydell, T. (1996). *The learning company* (2nd ed.). Maidenhead, UK: McGraw-Hill.

Peirce, C. S. (1878). Deduction, induction, and hypothesis. *Popular Science Monthly*, *13*, 470–482.

Pinha e Cunha, M., Fonseca, J. M., & Gonçalves, F. (Eds.). (2001). *Empresas, caos e complexidade-Gerindo à beira de um ataque de nervos*. Mem-Martins, Portugal: Editora RH. (in Portuguese)

Pojman, L. (1994). *Ethical theory: Classical and contemporary readings* (2nd ed.). Belmont, CA: Thomson Wadsworth.

Roth, G. L., & Kleiner, A. (1998). Developing organizational memory through learning histories. *Organizational Dynamics*, *27*(2), 43–60. doi:10.1016/S0090-2616(98)90023-7

Rowley, J. E. (2006). What do we need to know about wisdom? *Management Decision*, *44*(9), 1246–1257. doi:10.1108/00251740610707712

Rowley, J. E., & Gibbs, P. (2008). From learning organization to practically wise organization. *The Learning Organization*, *15*(5), 356–372. doi:10.1108/09696470810898357

Ryan, C. (2002). The reputation wars. *Australian Finance Review Boss, March*, 300-305.

Sandberg, J. (2005). How do we justify knowledge produced within interpretative approaches? *Organizational Research Methods*, *8*(1), 41–68. doi:10.1177/1094428104272000

Sankar, Y. (2003). Designing the learning organization as an information-processing system: Some design principles from the systems paradigm and cybernetic. *International Journal of Organization Theory and Behavior*, *6*(4), 501–521.

Schneider, S. C., & Baroux, J.-L. (2002). *Managing across cultures* (2nd ed.). Upper Saddle River, NJ: Prentice Hall.

Seib, P., & Fitzpatrick, K. R. (2006). *Public relations ethics*. Belmont, CA: Thomson.

Senge, P. M. (1996). Leading learning organizations. *Training & Development*, *50*(12), 36–37.

Senge, P. M. (1994). *The fifth discipline field book: Strategies and tools for building a learning organization*. New York: Doubleday/Currency.

Senges, M. (2007). *Knowledge entrepreneurship in universities: Practice and strategy in the case of Internet base innovation appropriation*. Barcelona, Spain: Universitat Oberta de Catalunya.

Seppanen, R. (2008). *Trust in organizational relationships*. Lappeenranta, Sweden: Lappeenranta University of Technology.

Simons, P. (1995). Learning in organizations. *Comportamento Organizacional e Gestão*, *1*(2), 173–186.

Slater, S. F., & Narver, J. C. (1995). Market orientations and the learning organization. *Sloan Management*, *59*(3), 7–23.

Squier, M. M. (2003). *The principles and practice of knowledge management*. Pretoria, South Africa: University of Pretoria.

Stahl, B. C. (2002). Ethical issues in e-teaching: A theoretical framework. In G. King *et al.* (Eds), *Proceedings of INSPIRE VII, Quality in Learning and Delivery Techniques* (pp. 135-148). Limerick, UK: The British Computer Society.

Strauss, A., & Corbin, J. C. (1998). *Basics of qualitative research: Grounded theory, procedures and techniques*. Newbury Park, CA: Sage Publications.

Šuc, D., Vladušič, D., & Bratko, I. (2004). Qualitatively faithful quantitative prediction. *Artificial Intelligence*, *158*(2), 189–214. doi:10.1016/j.artint.2004.05.002

Sun, P. Y. T., & Scott, J. L. (2003). Exploring the divide-organizational learning and learning organization. *The Learning Organization*, *10*(4), 202–215. doi:10.1108/09696470310476972

Sunoo, B. P. (1999). How human resources supports knowledge sharing. *Workforce, Crain Communications. Inc.*, *78*(3), 30–34.

Teece, D. J. (2000). Strategies for managing knowledge assets: The role of firm structure and industrial context. *Long Range Planning*, *33*(1), 35–54. doi:10.1016/S0024-6301(99)00117-X

The Free Dictionary. (2010). Disclosure. *The Free Dictionary*. Retrieved July 31, 2010, from, http://www.thefreedictionary.com/disclosure

Thompson, A. A., & Strickland, A. J. (2003). *Strategic management: Concepts and cases* (13th ed.). Boston: Irwin/McGraw-Hill.

Trauth, E. M. (1999). Who owns my soul? The paradox of pursing organizational knowledge in a work culture of individualism. In R. Agarwal & J. Prasad (Eds.), *Proceedings of the 1999 ACM SIGCPR Conference,* (pp. 159-163). New Orleans, LA: CM Press.

Treviño, L. K., & Weaver, G. R. (2003). *Managing ethics in business organizations: Social scientific perspectives*. Stanford, CA: Stanford University Press.

Verbos, A. K. (2007). The positive ethical organization: Enacting a living code of ethics and ethical organizational identity. *Journal of Business Ethics*, *76*(1), 17–33. doi:10.1007/s10551-006-9275-2

Waldersee, R. (1997). Becoming a learning organization: The transformation of the workforce. *Journal of Management Development*, *16*(4), 262–273. doi:10.1108/02621719710164544

Waldstrøm, C. (2003). *Understanding intra-organizational relations through social network analysis*. Aarhus, Denmark: Aarhus University.

Wang, C.-C. (2004). The influence of ethical and self-interest concerns on knowledge sharing intentions among managers: An empirical study. *International Journal of Management*, *21*(3), 370–381.

Weber, R. (2004). The rhetoric of positivism versus interpretivism: A personal view. *Management Information Systems Quarterly*, *28*(1), iii–xii.

West, G. P. III, & Meyer, G. D. (1997). Communicated knowledge as a learning foundation. *The International Journal of Organizational Analysis*, *5*(1), 25–58. doi:10.1108/eb028861

Westover, R. (2006). *Learning organizations: A preliminary investigation between the presence of a learning organization and profit*. Unpublished master thesis, Gonzaga University, Spokane.

Wikipedia (2010a). Refraction. *Wikipedia*. Retrieved August 2, 2010, from, http://en.wikipedia.org/wiki/Refraction

Wikipedia (2010b). Lighthouse. *Wikipedia*. Retrieved August 3, 2010, from, http://en.wikipedia.org/wiki/Lighthouse

Williams, M. (2000). Interpretivism and generalization. *Sociology*, *34*(2), 209–224.

Wilson, T. D. (2002). The nonsense of knowledge management. *Information Research, 8*(1). Retrieved August 1, 2010, from, http://informationr.net/ir/8-1/paper144.html

Wittmer, D. P. (2000). Ethical sensitivity in management decisions: Developing and testing a perceptual measure among management and professional student groups. *Teaching Business Ethics*, *4*(2), 181–205. doi:10.1023/A:1009866315139

Yeo, R. Y. (2005). Revisiting the roots of learning organization: A synthesis of the learning organization literature. *The Learning Organization*, *12*(4), 368–382. doi:10.1108/09696470510599145

Yin, R. K. (1994). *Case study research: Design and methods* (3rd ed.). Thousand Oaks, CA: Sage.

Zait, D., & Zait, A. (2009). Research anticipation: The methodological choice. *Review of International Comparative Management*, *10*(5), 902–909.

Zikmund, W. G., & Zikmund, E. G. (2000). *Business research methods* (6th ed.). London: Dryden Press.

KEY TERMS AND DEFINITIONS

Ethical Dilemmas: A situation that frequently engages an apparent conflict among moral imperatives. It is also considered an ethical paradox in which ethical decision enables conflicts.

Ethical Learning Organizations: Organizations that recognize the existing ethical and social dilemmas as regards to knowledge creation, retention/use, and sharing within their contexts, as well as their impacts in organizational strategy.

Evaluation: Method that aims to gather organizational historical data in order to give updated information feedback as regards to capacity-building versus strategy, objectives and effectiveness.

Learning Organizations: Organizations that recognize that knowledge will only flourish if: individual and collective learning occurs, an innovative environment exists, boundaries are not well defined, and how communication is essential among all members.

Social Dilemmas: Circumstances in which individuals reasoning leads to collective irrationality. Resumes interpersonal conflicts versus group reasoning.

Compilation of References

Abe, K. (1995). *What is "seken"?* Tokyo: Kodansha. (in Japanese)

Abel, D. F., & Hammond, J. S. (1979). *Strategic market planning*. Englewood Cliffs, NJ: Prentice-Hall.

Abernathy, D. J. (1999). Leading-edge learning. *Training & Development*, *53*(3), 40–42.

Abram, S. (2003). A primer on e-learning... The framework, the market, the players. *KM World, 12(2)*.

Adams, A. A., Murata, K., & Orito, Y. (2009). The Japanese sense of information privacy. *AI & Society*, *24*(4), 327–341. doi:10.1007/s00146-009-0228-z

Adams, J. S. (1963). Toward an understanding of inequity. *Journal of Abnormal and Social Psychology*, *67*(5), 422–463. doi:10.1037/h0040968

Adar, E., & Huberman, B. A. (2000). Free riding on gnutella. *First Monday, 5*(10). Retrieved April 20, 2009, from http://firstmonday.org/htbin/cgiwrap/bin/ojs/index.php/fm/article/view/792/701

Addleson, M. (2000). What is good organization? Learning organizations, community and the rhetoric of the bottom line. *European Journal of Work & Organizational*, *9*(2), 233–252. doi:10.1080/135943200397969

Ahmed, P. K., Loh, A. Y. E., & Zairi, M. (1999). Cultures for continuous improvement and learning. *Total Quality Management*, *10*(4), 426–434.

Alaranta, M. (2006). Combining theory-testing and theory-building analyses of case study data. *London School of Economics and Political*. Retrieved August 3, 2010, from, http://is2.lse.ac.uk/asp/aspecis/20060059.pdf

Alasuutari, P. (1995). *Researching culture: Qualitative method and cultural studies*. Thousand Oaks, CA: Sage Publications.

Alchian, A. A., & Demsetz, H. (1973). The property rights paradigm. *The Journal of Economic History*, *33*(1), 16–27. doi:10.1017/S0022050700076403

Ali, H. M., & Ahmad, N. H. (2006). Knowledge management in Malaysian banks: A new paradigm. *Journal of Knowledge Management Practice, 7*(3). Retrieved August 1, 2010, from, http://www.tlainc.com/articl120.htm

Ally, M. (2008). Foundations of educational theory for online learning. In Anderson, T. (Ed.), *The Theory and Practice of Online Learning* (2nd ed., pp. 15–44). Edmonton, Canada: AU Press.

Altbach, P. G. (2004). Globalization and the university: Myths and realities in an unequal world. Tertiary Education and management, 10(1), 3-25.

Altbach, P. G. (2008). The complex roles of universities in the period of globalization. In Global University Network for Innovation (Ed.), Higher Education in the World: New Challenges and Emerging Roles for Human and Social Development (pp. 30-35). London: Palgrave Macmillan.

Alvesson, M. (2001). Knowledge work: Ambiguity, image and identity. *Human Relations*, *54*(7), 863–886. doi:10.1177/0018726701547004

Alvesson, M. (2004). *Knowledge work and knowledge intensive firms*. Oxford, UK: Oxford University Press.

American Society for Training and Development. (2010). E-Learning glossary. *ASTD.org*. Retrieved September 9, 2009, from, http://www.astd.org/LC/glossary.htm

Ammenwerth, E., Ilber, C., & Mansmann, U. (2003). Can evaluations studies benefit from triangulation? A case study. *International Journal of Medical Informatics*, *70*(2/3), 237–248. doi:10.1016/S1386-5056(03)00059-5

Anderson, C. (2008). *The long tail, revised and updated edition: Why the future of business is selling less of more*. New York: Hyperion.

Anderson, T. (2008). Towards a theory of online learning. In Anderson, T. (Ed.), *Theory and Practice of Online Learning* (2nd ed., pp. 45–74). Edmonton, AB: AU Press.

ANOVA. (2010). Discover how you can take advantage of the online knowledge revolution and start cashing in on other people's knowledge right now! *ANOVA*. Retrieved February 20, 2010, from, www.anova.tv.

Antonelli, C. (2005). Models of knowledge and systems of governance. *Journal of Institutional Economics*, *1*(1), 51–73. doi:10.1017/S1744137405000044

Appadurai, A. (2005). *Modernity at large: Cultural dimensions of globalization* (2nd ed.). Minneapolis, MN: University of Minnesota Press.

Argyris, C., & Schön, D. (1978). *Organizational learning: A theory of action perspective*. Reading, MA: Addison-Wesley.

Argyris, C., & Schön, D. A. (1996). *Organizational learning II. Theory, method, and practise*. Reading, MA: Addison-Wesley Publishing Company.

Argyris, C. (1999). *On organizational learning* (2nd ed.). Oxford, UK: Blackwell Publishing.

Argyris, C., & Schön, D. A. (1978). *Organizational learning: A theory of action perspective*. Reading, MA: Addison Wesley.

Arias-Oliva, M., González, L., & Santiago, R. (2004). University challenges in Information Society. In Bynum, T. W. (Eds.), *ETHICOMP 2004: Challenges for the Citizen of the Information Society* (*Vol. 1*, pp. 38–48). Syros, Greece: University of the Aegean.

Armitage, A. (2003). *Teaching and training in post-compulsory education*. Maidenhead, UK: Open University Press.

Arrow, K. J. (1962). Economic welfare and the allocation of resources for invention. In Groves, H. M. (Ed.), *The Rate and Direction of Inventive Activity: Economic and Social Factors* (pp. 609–626). Cambridge, MA: The National Bureau of Economic Research.

Ashby, W. R. (1956). *An introduction to cybernetics*. London: Chapman & Hall.

Attwell, G. (2007). Personal learning environments- The future of elearning? *eLearning Papers, 2*(1), 1-8.

Atzori, P., & Woolford, K. (2005). Extended body: Interview with Stelarc. *Stanford*. Retrieved January 21, 2010, from, http://www.stanford.edu/dept/HPS/stelarc/a29-extended_body.html

Audet, J., & d'Amboise, G. (2001). The multi-site study: An innovative research methodology. *The Qualitative Report, 6*(2). Retrieved August 3, 2010, from, http://www.nova.edu/ssss/QR/QR6-2/audet.html

Audretsch, D., Lehmann, E., & Warning, S. (2005). University spillovers and new firm location. *Research Policy*, *34*(7), 1113–1122. doi:10.1016/j.respol.2005.05.009

Augusti, G. (2006). Transnational recognition and accreditation of engineering educational programmes in Europe: Perspective in a global framework. *European Journal of Engineering Education*, *31*(3), 249–260. doi:10.1080/03043790600644370

Aula, P., & Hakala, S. (2000). *Kolmet kasvot. Näkökulmia organisaatioviestintään*. Helsinki: Lokikirjat. (in Finnish)

Ayres, I., & Braithwaite, J. (1992). *Responsive regulation: Transcending the deregulation debate*. New York: Oxford University Press.

Baard, P. P., Deci, E. L., & Ryan, R. M. (2004). Intrinsic need satisfaction: A motivational basis of performance and well-being in two work settings. *Journal of Applied Social Psychology*, *34*(10), 2045–2068. doi:10.1111/j.1559-1816.2004.tb02690.x

Baase, S. (2008). *A gift of fire: Social, legal and ethical issues for computers and the internet* (3rd ed.). Princeton, NJ: Prentice-Hall.

Bain, J. S. (1968). *Industrial organizations*. New York: Wiley.

Bajracharya, P., & Masdeu, N. R. (2006). *Tacit knowledge transfer in small segment of small enterprises*. Linköping, Sweden: Linköping University.

Balakrishnan, G. (Ed.). (2003). *Debating empire*. London: Verso.

Barkur, G., Varambally, K. V. M., & Rodrigues, L. L. R. (2007). Insurance sector dynamics: Towards transformation into learning organization. *The Learning Organization, 14*(6), 510–523. doi:10.1108/09696470710825123

Barnett, R. (2003). *Beyond all reason: Living with ideology in the university*. Buckingham, UK: Open University Press.

Baron, J., & Spranca, M. (1997). Protected values. *Organizational Behavior and Human Decision Processes, 70*(1), 1–16. doi:10.1006/obhd.1997.2690

Bartol, K. M., & Srivastava, A. (2002). Encouraging knowledge sharing: The role of organizational reward systems. *Journal of Leadership & Organizational Studies, 9*(1), 64–76. doi:10.1177/107179190200900105

Baskerville, R., & Dulipovici, A. (2006). The ethics of knowledge transfers and conversions: Property or privacy rights. In K. VanLehn (Ed.), *Proceedings of the 39th Hawaii International Conference on System Sciences* (pp. 144-152). Hawaii: IEEE.

Bauwens, M. (2005). P2P and human evolution: placing peer to peer theory in an integral framework. *Integral Visioning*. Retrieved April 20, 2009, from http://integralvisioning.org/article.php?story=p2ptheory1

Beck, S. E. (2006). The good, the bad & the ugly or, why it's a good idea to evaluate web sources. New Mexico State University. Retrieved July 1, 2009, from http://lib.nmsu.edu/instruction/evalcrit.html

Becker, G. S. (1968). Crime and punishment: An economic approach. *The Journal of Political Economy, 76*(2), 169–217. doi:10.1086/259394

Bélisle, C. (2007). Elearning and intercultural dimensions of learning theories and teaching model. Elearning Europa. Retrieved July 31, 2009, from http://www.elearningeuropa.info/files/media/media13022.pdf

Bellinger, G., Castro, E., & Mills, A. (2004). Data, information, knowledge, and wisdom. *Systems Thinking*. Retrieved November 30, 2009, from, http://www.systems-thinking.org/dikw/dikw.htm

Benedict, R. (1946). *The chrysanthemum and the sword: Patterns of Japanese culture*. Boston, MA: Houghton Mifflin.

Benkler, Y. (2006). *The wealth of networks: How social production transforms markets and freedom*. New Haven, CT: Yale University Press.

Benyon, J. H., & Dunkerley, D. (Eds.). (2000). *Globalization: The reader (an anthology)*. New York: Routledge.

Berg, A. M. (2010, September). *"Lean and mean or fat and good?"- On organizational redundancies and diversity*. Paper presented at the 32nd EGPA Annual Conference, Toulouse, France.

Berg, L. D., Evans, M., & Fuller, D. (2007). Ethics, hegemonic witness, and the contested imagination of "aboriginal community" in social science research in Canada. *ACME- An International E-Journal for Critical Geographies, 6*(3), 395-410. Retrieved March 10, 2010 from, http://www.acme-journal.org/vol6/LDBetal.pd

Berge, Z. (Ed.). (2001). *Sustaining distance training: Integrating learning technologies into the fabric of the enterprise*. San Francisco, CA: Jossey-Bass.

Berger, P. L. (1967). *The sacred canopy: Elements of sociological theory of religion*. New York: Doubleday.

Berkman Center for Internet & Society. (2008). Employee non-compete agreements: Protecting innovation or stifling it? *Harvard University*. Retrieved August 31, 2009, from http://cyber.law.harvard.edu/node/4440

Bhabha, H. (1994). *The location of culture*. New York: Routledge.

Bivins, T. H. (1993). Public relations, professionalism, and the public interest. *Journal of Business Ethics*, *12*(2), 117–126. doi:10.1007/BF00871931

Bjorndal, T., & Conrad, J. M. (1987). The dynamics of an open access fishery. *The Canadian Journal of Economics. Revue Canadienne d'Economique*, *20*(1), 74–85. doi:10.2307/135232

Black, S. J., & Porter, L. W. (2000). *Management: Meeting new challenges*. New York: Prentice Hall.

Blackler, F. (1993). Knowledge and the theory of organizations: Organizations as activity systems and the reframing of management. *Journal of Management Studies*, *30*(6), 863–884. doi:10.1111/j.1467-6486.1993.tb00470.x

Blasi, A. (2005). Moral character: A psychological approach. In Lapsley, D. K., & Power, F. C. (Eds.), *Character Psychology and Character Education* (pp. 67–100). Notre Dame, IN: University of Notre Dame.

Blyth, A. (2005). Business behaving responsibly. *Director (Cincinnati, Ohio)*, *59*(1), 30.

Bock, G., Zmud, R. W., Kim, Y., & Lee, J. (2005). Behavioural intention formation in knowledge sharing: examining the roles of extrinsic motivators, social-psychological forces, and organizational climate. *Management Information Systems Quarterly*, *29*(1), 87–111.

Boddy, M. (2005). The knowledge-driven economy. *South West of England Regional Development Agency*. Retrieved March 17, 2009, from http://download.southwestrda.org.uk/res/general/KE%20Final%20Report%20190705.pdf

Boguslaw, R. (1965). *The new utopians, a study of system design and social change*. Englewood Cliffs, NJ: Prentice-Hall.

Boisot, M. (2002). The structuring and sharing of knowledge. In Choo, C. W., & Bontis, N. (Eds.), *Strategic Management of Intellectual Capital and Organization Knowledge* (pp. 65–78). New York: Oxford University Press.

Bonifacio, M., Bouquet, P., & Cuel, R. (2002). Knowledge nodes: The building blocks of a distributed approach to Knowledge Management. *Journal of Universal Computer Science*, *8*(6), 652–661.

Bonifacio, M., Bouquet, P., & Traverso, P. (2002). Enabling distributed knowledge management. Managerial and technological implications. Informatique, (1), 23-29.

Bontis, N., Fearon, M., & Hishon, M. (2003). The e-flow audit: An evaluation of knowledge flow within and outside a high-tech firm. *Journal of Knowledge Management*, *7*(1), 6–19. doi:10.1108/13673270310463581

Boommelaer, C., & Shears, M. (2007). Ethics and human rights in the information society. *Internet Society*. Retrieved January 22, 2010, from, http://www.isoc.org/pubpolpillar/governance/ethics.shtml

Bourdieu, P. (1993). *The field of cultural production*. Cambridge, MA: Polity.

Bourdieu, P. (1996). *The rules of art*. Cambridge, MA: Polity.

Bourdieu, P. (2003). Participant objectivation. *The Journal of the Royal Anthropological Institute*, *9*(2), 281–294. doi:10.1111/1467-9655.00150

Bourdieu, P., & Wacquant, L. J. D. (1992). *An invitation to reflexive sociology*. Chicago: University of Chicago Press.

Boyd, D. (2006, March). G/localization: When global information and local interaction collide. Paper presented at the O'Reilly Emerging Technology Conference, San Diego, CA.

Boyd, W. E., & Newton, D. (2009, June). Times of change, times of turbulence: Seeking an ethical framework for curriculum development during critical transition in higher education. Paper presented at the Conference Network Ethics 2009: The New Challenge in Business, ICT and Education, Lisbon, Portugal.

Bradley, W. E., & Vozikis, G. S. (2004). Trust in virtual teams. In Godar, S. H., & Ferris, S. P. (Eds.), *Virtual and Collaborative Teams: Processes, Technologies and Practice* (pp. 99–113). Hershey, PA: Idea Group Publishing.

Bramucci, R. S. (2003). Incidence and prevalence of cheating. *Teachopolis.org*. Retrieved January 3, 2010, from, http://teachopolis.org/justice/cheating/cheating_incidence.htm

Bratton, J. A. (2001). Why workers are reluctant learners: The case of the Canadian pulp and paper industry. *Journal of Workplace Learning*, *12*(7/8), 333–344. doi:10.1108/13665620110411120

Brelade, S., & Harman, C. (2003). *A practical guide to knowledge management*. London: Thorogood.

Bresman, H., Birkinshaw, J., & Nobel, R. (1999). Knowledge transfer in international acquisitions. *Journal of International Business Studies*, *30*(3), 439–462. doi:10.1057/palgrave.jibs.8490078

Brey, P. (2004). Ethical issues for the virtual university. In T. W. Bynum et al. (Eds.), ETHICOMP 2004: Challenges for the Citizen of the Information Society: Vol. 1 (pp. 170-187). Syros: University of the Aegean.

Brodbeck, F. C., & Greitemeyer, T. (2000). Effects of individual versus mixed individual and group experience in rule induction on group member learning and group performance. *Journal of Experimental Social Psychology*, *36*(6), 621–648. doi:10.1006/jesp.2000.1423

Brodmann, K. (1909). *Vergleichende lokalisationslehre der grosshirnrinde in ihren prinzipien dargestellt auf grund des zellenbaues*. Leipzig, Germany: Barth. (in German)

Brooking, A. (1996). *Intellectual capital, core asset for the third millennium enterprise*. Boston: International Thomson Business Press.

Broude, T. (2007). *Conflict and complementarity in trade, cultural diversity and intellectual property rights (Paper No. 11)*. Jerusalem: International Law Forum of the Hebrew University of Jerusalem Law Faculty.

Browne, J. (2006). The purpose of business. *Beyond Petroleum*. Retrieved July 27, 2009, from http://www.bp.com/genericarticle.do?categoryId=98&contentId=7017837

Bryant, A. (2006). Knowledge management: The ethics of the agora or the mechanisms of the market? In K. VanLehn (Ed.), *Proceedings of the 39th Hawaii International Conference on System Sciences* (pp. 144c-144c). Washington, DC: IEEE Computer Society.

Buchanan, J. M., & Yoon, Y. J. (2000). Symmetric tragedies: Commons and anticommons. *The Journal of Law & Economics*, *43*(1), 1–13. doi:10.1086/467445

Budin, G. (2002). Global content management-challenges and opportunities for creating and using digital translation resources. University of Vienna. Retrieved August 1, 2009, from http://www.ifi.unizh.ch/cl/yuste/postworkshop/repository/gbudin.pdf

Burns, R. B. (2000). *Introduction to research methods*. London: Sage Publishers.

Burr, V. (2003). *Social constructionism* (2nd ed.). New York: Routledge.

Business Dictionary. (2009). Knowledge economy. *Business Dictionary*. Retrieved August 2, 2009, from http://www.businessdictionary.com/definition/knowledge-economy.html

Bygholm, A., & Nyvang, T. (2004). Human centered informatics: The emergence of an educational infrastructure. In Dirckinck-Holmfeld, L. (Eds.), *Conditions for Productive Learning in Networked Learning Environments* (pp. 84–95). Aalborg, Germany: Kaleidoscope.

Bynum, T. W. (2006). Flourishing ethics. *Ethics and Information Technology*, *8*(4), 157–173. doi:10.1007/s10676-006-9107-1

Bynum, T. W., & Rogerson, S. (2003). *Computer ethics and professional responsibility*. Malden, UK: Blackwell Publishing.

Cabinet Office. (2009). Power of information task force report. *Cabinet Office*. Retrieved August 5, 2009, from http://www.cabinetoffice.gov.uk/reports/power_of_information.aspx

Cabrera, A., Collins, W. C., & Salgado, J. F. (2006). Determinants of individual engagement in knowledge sharing. *International Journal of Human Resource Management*, *17*(2), 245–264.

Cabrera, A., & Cabrera, E. F. (2002). Knowledge sharing dilemmas. *Organization Studies*, *23*(5), 687–710. doi:10.1177/0170840602235001

Callahan, D. (1980). Goals in the teaching of ethics. In Callahan, D., & Bok, S. (Eds.), *Teaching Ethics in Higher Education* (pp. 61–74). New York: Plenum.

Calvert-Minor, C. (2009). Commonsense realism and triangulation. *Philosophia*, *37*(1), 67–86. doi:10.1007/s11406-008-9160-6

Campbell, J. D., & Jardine, A. K. S. (Eds.). (2001). *Maintenance excellence: Optimizing equipment life cycle*. New York, NY: Marcel Dekker.

Carroll, N. (1996). Moderate moralism. *British Journal of Aesthetics*, *36*(3), 223–238. doi:10.1093/bjaesthetics/36.3.223

Carroll, N. (2000). Art and ethical criticism: An overview of recent directions of research. *Ethics*, *110*(2), 350–387. doi:10.1086/233273

Castellanos, A. R., Rodriquez, J. L., & Ranguelov, S. Y. (2004). University R&D&T capital: What types of knowledge drive it? *Journal of Intellectual Capital*, *5*(3), 478–499. doi:10.1108/14691930410550417

Castells, M. (2003). *The internet galaxy: Reflections on the internet, business and society*. New York: Oxford University Press.

Castells, M. (2000). *The rise of the network society: The information age: economy, society and culture* (2nd ed., *Vol. 1*). Malden, MA: Blackwell.

Castells, M. (2009). *Communication power*. Oxford, UK: Oxford University Press.

Castells, M. (2000). *The rise of the network society*. Oxford, UK: Blackwell Publishers.

Castle, D., & Gold, R. E. (2007). Traditional knowledge and benefit sharing: From compensation to transaction. In Peter, W. B., & Onwuekwe, C. B. (Eds.), *Accessing and Sharing the Benefits of the Genomics Revolution* (pp. 65–79). Amsterdam: Springer. doi:10.1007/978-1-4020-5822-6_4

Castrén, A.-M. (2001). *Perhe ja työ helsingissä ja pietarissa- Elämänpiirit ja yhteiskunta opettajien sosiaalisissa verkostoissa*. Helsinki: Suomalaisen Kirjallisuuden Seura. (in Finnish)

Cavaleri, S. A. (2004). Principles for designing pragmatic knowledge management systems. *The Learning Organization*, *11*(4/5), 312–321. doi:10.1108/09696470410538215

Cavaleri, S. A. (2008). Are learning organizations pragmatic? *The Learning Organization*, *15*(6), 474–485. doi:10.1108/09696470810907383

Cavanagh, A. (2007). *Sociology in the age of the internet*. Buckingham: Open University Press.

Cecez-Kecmanovic, D. (2001). What enables and what prevents knowledge sharing via computer-mediated communications? *Journal of Systems and Information Technology*, *5*(1), 115–134. doi:10.1108/13287260180000762

Chang, H.-H. (2007). *Fake globalization*. Taipei: Unitas Publishing.

Cheng, W., Hailin, L., & Hongming, X. (2008). Does knowledge sharing mediate the relationship between trust and firm performance? In F. Yu & Q. Luo (Eds.), *International Symposium on Information Processing/International Pacific Workshop on Web Mining, and Web-Based Application* (pp. 449-453). Washington, DC: IEEE Computer Society.

Chernigovskaya, T. V. (2007). The mirror brain, concepts, and language: The price of anthropogenesis. *Neuroscience and Behavioral Physiology*, *37*(3), 293–302. doi:10.1007/s11055-007-0014-7

Cheung, L. (2008). Collaborative knowledge building through the lens of paraphrasing. In B. Chang & H.-J. So (Eds.), ICCE 2008 Workshop Proceedings (pp. 70-79). Tapei: National Central University.

Chomsky, N. (1999). *Year 501: The conquest continues*. Cambridge, MA: South End Press.

Chomsky, N., & McChesney, R. W. (2000). *Profit over people: Neoliberalism and global order*. Toronto, ON: Seven Stories Press.

Choo, C. W. (1998). *The knowing organization: How organizations use information to construct meaning, create knowledge and make decisions*. New York: Oxford University Press.

Choo, C. W. (2002). *Information management for the intelligent organization: The art of scanning the environment* (3rd ed.). Medford, NJ: Information Today Inc.

Chow, C. W., Deng, F. J., & Ho, J. L. (2000). The openness of knowledge sharing within organizations: A comparative study of the United States and the People's Republic of China. *Journal of Management Accounting Research*, *12*(1), 65–95. doi:10.2308/jmar.2000.12.1.65

Chu, H., et al. (2006). A structured methodology for digital knowledge content development: Knowledge of mathematics teaching for students with mild disabilities as an example. In E. Pearson & P. Bohman (Eds.), Proceedings of World Conference on Educational Multimedia, Hypermedia and Telecommunications 2006, (pp. 935-940). Chesapeake, VA: AACE.

Chun, R. (2005). Ethical character and virtue of organizations: An empirical assessment and strategic implications. *Journal of Business Ethics*, *57*(3), 269–284. doi:10.1007/s10551-004-6591-2

Clark, C. W. (1974). Possible effects of schooling on the dynamics of exploited fish populations. *Journal du Conseil Internatinal pour L'Exploration de la Mer*, *36*(1), 7–14.

Clark, C. W. (1980). Towards a predictive model for the economic regulation of commercial fisheries. *Canadian Journal of Fisheries and Aquatic Sciences*, *37*(7), 1111–1129. doi:10.1139/f80-144

Clark, C. W. (1985). *Bioeconomic modelling and fisheries management*. New York: John Wiley & Sons.

Clark, C. W., & Munro, G. R. (1975). The economics of fishing and modern capital theory: A simplified approach. *Journal of Environmental Economics and Management*, *2*(2), 92–106. doi:10.1016/0095-0696(75)90002-9

Clark, B. R. (1983). *The higher education system: Academic organization in cross-national perspective*. Berkeley, CA: University of California Press.

Cline, A. (2009). Proselytization at work- feel pressured to convert? Atheists at work. *About.com*. Retrieved October 30, 2009, from http://atheism.about.com/od/atheistswork/a/pressure.htm

Cline, B. J. (2005). *Reaching others: The rhetoric of proselytizing and community of a Christian campus organization*. Unpublished doctoral dissertation, Graduate College of Bowling Green State University, Ohio.

Cloete, N., & Moja, T. (2005). Transformation tensions in higher education: Equity, efficiency, and development. *Social Research*, *72*(3), 693–722.

Coelho, M. F. P., & Lopes, R. J. (2000). The common fisheries policy and the feasibility of ITQs. In Hatcher, A., & Robinson, K. (Eds.), *The Definition and Allocation of Use Rights in European Fisheries* (pp. 138–156). Portsmouth, UK: CEMARE/University of Portsmouth.

Coelho, P. (2009). Salvador-Dali. *Paulo Coelho's Blog*. Retrieved September 2, 2010, from, http://paulocoelhoblog.com/2009/03/13/my-favorite-painters-salvador-dali/

Cohen, D., & Prusak, L. (2001). *In good company: How social capital makes organizations work*. Cambridge, MA: Harvard Business School Press.

Cohen, C. A. (2008). *Rescuing justice and equality*. Cambridge, MA: Harvard University Press.

Collison, C., & Parcell, G. (2001). *Learning to fly: Practical knowledge management from leading and learning organizations*. Chichester, UK: Capstone Publishing Limited.

Commission of the European Communities. (2009). Commission Recommendation on media literacy in the digital environment for a more competitive audiovisual and content industry and an inclusive knowledge society. *European Commission*. Retrieved November 25, 2009, from, http://ec.europa.eu/culture/media/literacy/docs/recom/c_2009_6464_en.pdf

Commission of the European Communities. (2001). *The e-learning action plan*. Brussels: Commission of the European Communities.

Competitive Intelligence Glossary. (2009). The language of competitive business intelligence. *Quantumiii- the solutions people*. Retrieved August 2, 2009, from http://www.quantum3.co.za/CI%20Glossary.htm

Conolly, O. (2000). Ethicism and moderate moralism. *British Journal of Aesthetics*, *40*(3), 302–316. doi:10.1093/bjaesthetics/40.3.302

Constant, D., Kiesler, S., & Sproull, L. (1994). What's mine is ours, or is it? A study of attitudes about information sharing. *Information Systems Research*, *5*(4), 400–421. doi:10.1287/isre.5.4.400

Cook, S. D. N., & Brown, J. S. (1999). Bridging epistemologies: The generative dance between organizational knowledge and organizational knowing. *Organization Science*, *10*(4), 381–400. doi:10.1287/orsc.10.4.381

Coombs, R., & Metcalfe, S. (2000). *Universities, the science base and the innovation performance of the UK (CRIC Briefing Paper No. 5)*. Manchester, UK: The University of Manchester & UMIST.

Cooms, R. (2003). Analysing distributed processing of provision and distribution. *Industrial and Corporate Change*, *12*(6), 1125–1155.

Coraggio, J.-L. (2001). Universities as sites of local and global (re)production. *Norrag News*, *28*(July), 66–67.

Cornwell, W. R., & Cornwell, J. (2009). Signal and noise: The power of n-dimensional query and education. In I. Gibson *et al.* (Eds.), *Proceedings of Society for Information Technology & Teacher Education International Conference 2009* (pp. 2505-2511). Chesapeake, VA: AACE.

Correa, C. M. (2000). *Intellectual property rights, the WTO and developing countries*. London: Zed Books.

Costa, G. J. M., & Silva, N. S. A. (2010). Knowledge versus content in e-learning: A philosophical discussion. *Information Systems Frontiers*, *12*(4), 399–413. doi:10.1007/s10796-009-9200-1

Costa, G. J. M., Prior, M., & Rogerson, S. (2010a). Why link knowledge management, organizational culture and ethics: Analysing empirical inquiry. In Arias-Oliva, M. (Eds.), *ETHICOMP 2010* (pp. 83–92). Tarragona, Spain: Rovira i Virgili University.

Costa, G. J. M., Prior, M., & Rogerson, S. (2008). Individual ethics and knowledge management: arising Conflicts. In Bynum, T. W. (Eds.), *ETHICOMP 2008: Living, Working and Learning Beyond Technology* (pp. 117–129). Mantua, Italy: University of Pavia.

Costa, G. J. M., Silva, N. S. A., & Rogerson, S. (2008). Knowledge versus content in e-learning: A philosophical discussion! In Bynum, T. (Eds.), *ETHICOMP 2008: Living, Working and Learning Beyond Technology* (pp. 143–155). Mantua, Italy: University of Pavia.

Costa, G. J. M., Prior, M., & Rogerson, S. (2010). Individual ethics and knowledge management: Arising conflicts. In Bynum, T. (Eds.), *ETHICOMP 2010: The "Backwards, Forwards and Sideways" Changes in ICT* (pp. 117–129). Tarragona, Italy: University of Rovira i Virgili.

Costa, G. J. M., & Silva, N. M. A. (2007). Knowledge management: How ethical is your organization's knowledge? In Bynum, T. W., Rogerson, S., & Murata, K. (Eds.), *ETHICOMP 2007: Glocalisation: Bridging the Global Nature of Information and Communication Technology* (*Vol. 1*, pp. 123–136). Tokyo: Meiji University.

Costa, G. J. M., Silva, N. S. A., & Pawlak, P. (2010). Controlling informational society: A Google error analysis! In Portela, I. M., & Cruz-Cunha, M. M. (Eds.), *Handbook of Information Communication Technology Law, Protection and Access Rights: Global Approaches and Issues* (pp. 466–495). Hershey, PA: IGI Global.

Costa, G. J. M., Prior, M., & Rogerson, S. (2008a). Will the evolution of ICT ethics engage organizational transparency? In Vaccaro, A., Horta, H., & Madsen, P. (Eds.), *Transparency, Information and Communication Technology- Social Responsibility and Accountability in Business and Education* (pp. 31–50). Chesapeake, VA: Softbound.

Costa, G. J. M., & Silva, N. S. A. (2010). Knowledge authoring in e-learning: An ethicultural diagnosis! In P. Dondon & O. Martin (Eds.), *7th WSEAS International Conference on Engineering Education* (pp. 48-53), Aquis Corfu Holiday Palace Hotel, Corfu, Greece.

Costa, G. J. M., & Silva, N. S. A. (2009). Knowledge versus content in e-learning: a philosophical discussion! Information Systems Frontiers. Retrieved August 1, 2009, from http://www.springerlink.com/content/t2351vvn156 86321/?p=68d64067302e4509a2d3daf97df75aa9&pi=6.

Costa, G. J. M., Prior, M., & Rogerson, S. (2008b, September). *Free ride in knowledge management? Ethical and moral dilemmas!* Paper presented at the ETHICOMP 2008: Living, Working and Learning Beyond Technology, Mantua, Italy.

Costa, G. J. M., Prior, M., & Rogerson, S. (2010b). Linking knowledge management, organizational culture and ethics: Inquiring results. In E. Tomé (Ed.), *Proceedings of the 11th European Conference on Knowledge Management* (pp. 1144-1152). Vila Nova de Famalicão, Portugal: Lusiada University of Vila Nova de Famalicão.

Cox, J., & Hassard, J. (2005). Triangulation in organizational research: A representation. *Organizational Articles, 12*(1), 109–133.

Coyle, E. (2001). *Consensus and dissent in Washington: Negotiating change in the World Bank and IMF*. MPhil thesis, University of Cambridge, Cambridge, UK.

Creswell, J. W. (2003). *Research design: Qualitative, quantitative and mixed methods approaches* (2nd ed.). Thousand Oaks, CA: Sage Publications.

Creswell, J. W., & Clark, V. L. P. (2007). *Designing and conducting mixed methods research*. Thousand Oaks, CA: Sage.

Cromer, A. H. (1997). *Connected knowledge: Science, philosophy and education*. New York: Oxford University Press.

Cropanzano, R. (2001). Moral virtues, fairness heuristics, social entities, and other denizens of organizational justice. *Journal of Vocational Behavior, 58*(2), 164–209. doi:10.1006/jvbe.2001.1791

Cropanzano, R., & Randall, M. L. (1992). Injustice and work behavior: A historical review. In Cropanzano, R. (Ed.), *Justice in the Workplace: Approaching Fairness in Human Resource Management* (pp. 3–20). Hillsdale, NJ: Lawrence Erlbaum.

Crystal, D. (2000). *Language death*. Cambridge, UK: Cambridge University Press.

Crystal, D. (2003). *English as a global language* (2nd ed.). Cambridge, UK: Cambridge University Press. doi:10.1017/CBO9780511486999

Currie, G., & Kerrin, M. (2003). Human resource management and knowledge management: Enhancing knowledge sharing in a pharmaceutical company. *International Journal of Human Resource Management, 14*(6), 1027–1045. doi:10.1080/0958519032000124641

d'Orville, H. (2000). Towards the global knowledge and information society- The challenges for development cooperation. *United Nations Development Programme*. Retrieved March 15, 2009, from http://www.undp.org/info21/public/pb-challenge.html

Dahrendorf, R. (1959). *Class and class conflict in industrial society*. Stanford, CA: Stanford University Press.

Daly, A. (2002). *Critical gestures: Writings on dance and culture*. Middletown, CT: Wesleyan University Press.

Damasio, A., & Geschwind, N. (1984). The neural basis of language. *Annual Review of Neuroscience, 7*(1), 127–147. doi:10.1146/annurev.ne.07.030184.001015

Darr, A. (2003). Control and autonomy among knowledge workers in sales: An employee perspective. *Employee Relations*, *25*(1), 31–41. doi:10.1108/01425450310453508

Davenport, T. (2002). Can you boost knowledge work's impact on the bottom line? *Management Update*, *7*(11), 3–5.

Davenport, T., & Prusak, L. (2000). *Working knowledge: How organizations manage what they know*. Boston, MA: Harvard Business School Press.

Davenport, T. H., Järvenpää, S. L., & Beers, M. C. (1996). Improving knowledge work processes. *Sloan Management Review*, *37*(4), 53–65.

Davenport, T. H., & Prusak, L. (1998). *Working knowledge: How organizations manage what they know*. Boston: Harvard Business School Press.

David, S. (2007). Toward participatory expertise. In Karaganis, J. (Ed.), *Structures of Participation in Digital Culture* (pp. 176–199). New York, NY: Social Science Research Group.

Davis, D., Olsen, A., & Bohm, A. (Eds.). (2000). *Transnational education providers, partners and policy: Challenges for Australian institutions offshore*. Canberra: IDP.

Davis, D. J. (2009). The future and diversity in higher education. *Equal Opportunities International*, *28*(4), 351–353. doi:10.1108/02610150910954809

Davis, J. (2001). Creating shared information spaces to support collaborative design work. *Information Systems Frontiers*, *3*(3), 377–392. doi:10.1023/A:1011469727367

de Laat, P. B. (2008). Moving open source beyond software while maintaining the public spirit? In T. Bynum *et al.* (Eds.), *ETHICOMP 2008: Living, Working and Learning Beyond Technology,* (pp. 511-523). Mantua: University of Pavia.

De Laurentis, C. (2006). Digital knowledge exploitation: ICT, memory institutions and innovation from cultural assets. *The Journal of Technology Transfer*, *31*(1), 77–89. doi:10.1007/s10961-005-5014-6

De Vita, G. (2002). Cultural equivalence in the assessment of home and international business management students: A UK exploratory study. *Studies in Higher Education*, *27*(2), 221–231. doi:10.1080/03075070220120038

De Vita, G. (2003). Rethinking the internationalisation agenda in UK higher education. *Journal of Further and Higher Education*, *27*(4), 383–398. doi:10.1080/0309877032000128082

De Vries, R., Anderson, M. S., & Martinson, B. C. (2006). Normal misbehaviour: Scientists talk about the ethics of research. *Journal of Empirical Research on Human Research Ethics; JERHRE*, *1*(1), 43–50. doi:10.1525/jer.2006.1.1.43

Dealtry, R. (2002). Configuring the corporate university- Managing the issue of learning relevance in the formulation of corporate learning strategies. *Journal of Workplace Learning*, *14*(5), 209–214. doi:10.1108/13665620210433909

Deem, R., Hillyard, S., & Reed, M. (2007). *Knowledge, higher education and the new managerialism: The changing management of UK universities*. Oxford, UK: Oxford University Press. doi:10.1093/acprof:oso/9780199265909.001.0001

Deephouse, D. L., & Carter, S. M. (2005). An examination of differences between organizational legitimacy and organizational reputation. *Journal of Management Studies*, *42*(2), 329–360. doi:10.1111/j.1467-6486.2005.00499.x

Deer, K., & Håkansson, A.-K. (2005). Towards an indigenous vision of the information society. In van Weert, T. J. (Ed.), *Education and the Knowledge Society- Information Technology Supporting Human Development* (pp. 237–240). New York: Kluwer Academic Publishers.

Defense Acquisition University. (2003). *What is knowledge management?* Fort Belvoir, VA: Defense Acquisition University.

Deibert, R. J. (2008). *Access denied: The practice and policy of global internet filtering*. Cambridge, MA: MIT Press.

Delaforce, C. (2009). Exploiting the participatory culture. *Human Capital Management, January/February*, 26-28. Retrieved October 30, 2009, from, http://www.media-insertpr.com/GrahamJarvis_MC2_HCM_Jan-Feb_2009.pdf

Demsetz, H. (1967). Toward a theory of property rights. *The American Economic Review*, *57*(2), 347–359.

Denning, D. E. (2002, August). *Hacker ethics*. Paper presented at the National Conference on Computing and Values, New Haven, CT.

Dewatripont, M., Thys-Clement, F., & Wilkin, L. (Eds.). (2002). European universities: Change or convergence? Bruxelles: Editions de L' Universities de Bruxelles.

Dewey, J. F. (1960). *The quest for certainty*. New York: Minton, Balch & Co.

Dewey, J. (1938). *Experience and education*. New York: The Macmillan Company.

DGPA. (2007). Programa operacional da pesca 2007-2013. *Direcção Geral das Pescas e Agricultura*. Retrieved August 1, 2009, from http://www.dg-pescas.pt/pls/portal/docs/folder/dgpa_content_area/noticias/destaques/po_pesca_22_5_07.pdf

DiBella, A. J. (2001). *Learning practices: Assessment and action for organizational improvement*. Upper Saddle River, NJ: Prentice Hall.

Dietz, S. (2003). How latitudes become forms: Art in a global village. *Walker Art Center*. Retrieved December 15, 2009, from, http://latitudes.walkerart.org/

Dils, A., & Albright, A. C. (Eds.). (2001). *Moving history/dancing cultures: A dance history reader*. Middletown, CT: Wesleyan University Press.

Dirlik, A. (1998). Globalism and the politics of place. *Development*, *41*(2), 7–14.

Dixon, N. (2002). The neglected receiver of knowledge sharing. *Ivey Business Journal*, *66*(4), 35–40.

Doha Development Agenda. (2008). Negotiations, implementation and development. *World Trade Organization*. Retrieved August 1, 2009, from http://www.wto.org/english/tratop_e/dda_e/negotiations_summary_e.htm

Doherty, N. F., Coombs, C. C., & Loan-Clarke, J. (2006). A re-conceptualization of the interpretative flexibility of information technologies: Redressing the balance between the social and the technical. *European Journal of Information Systems*, *15*(6), 569–582. doi:10.1057/palgrave.ejis.3000653

Doi, T. (1973). *The anatomy of dependence*. Tokyo: Kodansha International.

Dominese, G. (2009). Global governance and innovation 2020: How to govern the complexities of the future. *Transition Studies Review*, *16*(2), 229–232. doi:10.1007/s11300-009-0096-8

Douglas, D. (2006). Intransivities of managerial decisions: A grounded theory case. *Management Decision*, *44*(2), 259–275. doi:10.1108/00251740610650238

Downes, S. (2005a). E-learning 2.0. *eLearn Magazine*. Retrieved October 29, 2009, from http://www.elearnmag.org/subpage.cfm?section=articles&article=29-1

Downes, S. (2005b). An introduction to connective knowledge. *Stephens's Web*. Retrieved November 28, 2009, from, http://www.downes.ca/cgi-bin/page.cgi?post=33034

Downes, S. (2007). What connectivism is. *Half an Hour*. Retrieved September 17, 2009, from, http://halfanhour.blogspot.com/2007/02/what-connectivism-is.html

Downes, S. (2008). Types of knowledge and connective knowledge. *Half an Hour*. Retrieved October 27, 2009, from, http://halfanhour.blogspot.com/2008/09/types-of-knowledge-and-connective.html

Downes, S. (2009). The cloud and collaboration. *Half an Hour*. Retrieved January 20, 2010, from, http://halfanhour.blogspot.com/2009/06/cloud-and-collaboration.html

Driscoll, M. (2000). *Psychology of learning for instruction* (2nd ed.). Needham Heights, MA: Allyn & Bacon.

Dron, J. (2007). *Control and constraint in e-learning: Choosing when to choose*. Hershey, PA: Information Science Pub.

Drucker, P. F. (1999). *Management challenges for the 21st century*. Burlington, MA: Butterworth-Heinemann.

du Plessis, J. C., Britz, J. J., & Davel, R. (2007). *Slave or sibling: A moral reframing the corporate knowledge sharing community*. University of Pretoria, Pretoria, South Africa. Retrieved August 1, 2010, from, http://ol.up.ac.za/upspace/bitstream/2263/1808/1/DuPlessis_Slave%282006%29.pdf

Duderstadt, J. J. (2001). Technology. EDUCAUSE Review, January/February, 48-56.

Dunbar, R. (2007). *Grooming, gossip, and the evolution of language* (2nd ed.). Cambridge, MA: Harvard University Press.

Dunlop, C. E. M., & Kling, R. (Eds.). (1991). *Computerization and controversy: Value conflicts and social choices*. Boston: Academic Press.

Dunn, L., & Wallace, M. (2004). Australian academics teaching in Singapore: Striving for cultural empathy. *Innovations in Education and Teaching International*, *41*(3), 291–304. doi:10.1080/14703290410001733285

Dusko, U. (2006). System-organizational aspect of a learning organization in companies. *Systemic Practice and Action Research*, *19*(1), 81–99. doi:10.1007/s11213-005-9005-1

Dymock, D., & McCarthty, C. (2006). Towards a learning organization? Employee perception. *The Learning Organization*, *13*(5), 525–537. doi:10.1108/09696470610680017

Ebner, M. (2007, April). *E-learning 2.0 = E-learning 1.0 + Web 2.0?* Paper presented at the Second International Conference on Availability, Reliability and Security, Vienna, Austria.

Edvinsson, L., & Malone, M. S. (1997). *Intellectual capital: Realizing your company's true value by finding its hidden roots*. New York: Harper Business.

Edwards, R. (2008). Crime maps to show offences for every street. *Telegraph*. Retrieved August 2, 2009, from www.telegraph.co.uk/news/newstopics/politics/lawandorder/2466325/Crime-maps-to-show-offences-for-every-street.html

Efimova, L. (2005). *Understanding personal knowledge management: A weblog case*. Enschede, The Netherlands: Telematica Instituut.

Efimova, L. (2003). Knowledge worker paradox. *Knowledge Board*. Retrieved August 28, 2010, from, https://doc.novay.nl/dsweb/Get/Version-12745/knowledge_worker_paradox.pdf

Egbert, J. L. (2008). *Supporting learning with technology: Essentials of classroom practice*. Upper Saddle River, NJ: Prentice Hall.

Ek, E. (2000). Vaikutusmahdollisuudet työhön ja stressinhallintakeinot- Yhteys psyykkiseen toimintakykyyn. *Työ ja Ihminen*, *1*, 15-26 (in Finnish).

Empson, L. (2001). Introduction: Knowledge management in professional service firms. *Human Relations*, *54*(7), 811–817. doi:10.1177/0018726701547001

Engström, Y. (1987). *Learning by expanding: An activity-theoretical approach to developmental research*. Helsinki, Finland: Orienta-Konsultit.

Eriksen, T. H. (2001). Between universalism and relativism: A critique of the UNESCO concepts of culture. In Cowan, J. K., Dembour, M.-B., & Wilson, R. A. (Eds.), *Culture and Rights: Anthropological Perspectives* (pp. 127–148). Cambridge, UK: Cambridge University Press.

Eriksen, T. H. (2006, March). *Nations in cyberspace*. Paper presented at the ASEN Conference, London, UK.

Erlhagen, W., Muskovskiy, A., & Bicho, E. (2006). A dynamic model for action understanding and goal-directed imitation. *Brain Research*, *1083*(1), 174–188. doi:10.1016/j.brainres.2006.01.114

ESU. (2004). Transnational Education. European Students Union. Retrieved July 31, 2009, from http://www.esib.org/index.php/documents/policy-papers/326-policy-paper-qtransnational-education

Etzioni, A. (2004). *How patriotic is the patriot act? Freedom versus security in the age of terrorism*. New York: Routledge.

European Commission. (1996). Educational software and multimedia (Report of the Task Force). *European Commission*. Retrieved October 2, 2009, from http://aei.pitt.edu/5651/01/001851_1.pdf

Fahey, L., & Prusak, L. (1998). The eleven deadliest sins of knowledge management. *California Management Review*, *40*(3), 265–276.

Fairweather, N. B. (2004). No, PAPA: Why incomplete codes of ethics are worse than none at all. In Bynum, T. W., & Rogerson, S. (Eds.), *Computer Ethics and Professional Responsibility* (pp. 142–157). Malden, MA: Blackwell Publishing.

Fairweather, N. B. (2003). No, PAPA: Why incomplete codes of ethics are worse that none at all. In Bynum, T. W., & Rogerson, S. (Eds.), *Computer Ethics and Professional Responsibility* (pp. 142–155). Malden, MA: Blackwell Publishing.

Fehr, E., & Rockenbach, B. (2003). Detrimental effects of sanctions on human altruism. *Nature*, *422*(13), 137–140. doi:10.1038/nature01474

Fenwick, T. J. (1995). *Limits of the learning organization: A critical look*. Nova Scotia, Canada: St. Francis Xavier University.

Ferguson, N. (2005). Sinking globalization. *Foreign Affairs (Council on Foreign Relations)*, *84*(2), 64–77.

Field, R. (2002). What is the purpose of business? *University of Alberta*. Retrieved May 23, 2009, from http://www.business.ualberta.ca/rfield/PurposeofBusiness.htm

Filipe, J. A. C. B. (2008). Anti-commons: How tragedies happen. Some cases and the evidences on fisheries. *China- USA. Business Review (Federal Reserve Bank of Philadelphia)*, *7*(11), 9–13.

Filipe, J. A. C. B. (2009). *Complexity, theory of chaos and fishing (Scientific Bi-Annual Magazine)*. Mainz, Germany: Wirtschaft FH Mainz, University of Applied Sciences.

Filipe, J. A. C. B., Coelho, M. F. P., & Ferreira, M. A. M. (2005). Sistemas dinâmicos, caos e os comuns da pesca. *Revista de Economia Global e Gestão*, *X*(2), 45–59.

Filipe, J. A. C. B., Coelho, M. F. P., & Ferreira, M. A. M. (2007). *O drama dos recursos comuns. À procura de soluções para os ecossistemas em perigo*. Lisboa, Portugal: Sílabo.

Filipe, J. A. C. B. (2006). *O drama dos recursos comuns. Um caso de aplicação da teoria dos jogos aos comuns da pesca. Estudo da Cooperação aplicada à pesca da sardinha nas Divisões VIIIc e IXa do ICES*. Unpublished doctoral dissertation, ISCTE, Lisboa, Portugal.

Filipe, J. A. C. B. (2007). *The drama of fishing commons: Cournot-Nash model and cooperation* (Working Paper 03). Lisboa, Portugal: ISEG/DE.

Filipe, J. A. C. B., Coelho, M. F. P., & Ferreira, M. A. M. (2006a). *A tragédia dos anti-comuns: Um novo problema na gestão da pesca?* (Working Paper No. 15). Lisboa, Portugal: ISEG/UTL, Seminário do Departamento de Economia.

Filipe, J. A. C. B., Coelho, M. F. P., & Ferreira, M. A. M. (2006b, July). *The drama of the commons: An application of Cournot-Nash Model to the sardine in Portuguese waters*. Paper presented at the Thirteen Annual International Conference on Advances in Management (ICAM 2006), Lisboa.

Fine, C. H. (1998). *Clockspeed: Winning industry control in the age of temporary advantage*. New York: Perseus Books.

Fischer, H. (2007). *Le choc du numérique*. Montréal, QC: VLB Éditeur. (in French)

Fisher, W. (2004). *Promises to keep: Technology, law and the future of entertainment*. Stanford, CA: Stanford University Press.

Fleming, N. D., & Mills, C. (1992). Not another inventory, rather a catalyst for reflection. *To Improve the Academy*, *11*, 137-149.

Florida, R. (2005). The world is spiky. *Atlantic Monthly*, *296*(3), 48–51.

Floridi, L. (2006). Information technologies and the tragedy of the good will. *Ethics and Information Technology*, *8*(4), 253–262. doi:10.1007/s10676-006-9110-6

Fong, P. S.-W., & Chu, L. (2006). Exploratory study of knowledge sharing in contracting companies: A sociotechnical perspective. *Journal of Construction Engineering and Management*, *132*(9), 928–939. doi:10.1061/(ASCE)0733-9364(2006)132:9(928)

Ford, D. P., & Staples, D. S. (2005). Perceived value of knowledge: Shall I give you my gem, my coal? In W. Arbeitspapiere (Ed.), *Proceedings of 38th Hawaii International Conference on Systems Sciences* (pp. 247-256). Hawaii: IEEE.

Forrester, J. W. (1971). Counterintuitive behaviour of social systems. *Technology Review*, *73*(3), 52–68.

Foss, K., & Foss, N. F. (2008). Authority in the context of distributed knowledge (Working Paper No. 03-08). Aalborg: Danish Research Unit For Industrial Dynamics.

Freire, A. (2008). *Estratégia- Sucesso em Portugal*. Braga, Portugal: Verbo. (in Portuguese)

Frey, W., & O'Neill-Carillo, E. (in press). Engineering ethics in Puerto Rico: Issues and narratives. *Science and Engineering Ethics*.

Friedman, J. (1999). Indigenous conflicts and discreet bourgeois appeal. *The Australian Journal of Anthropology*, *10*(1), 1–14. doi:10.1111/j.1835-9310.1999.tb00009.x

Friedman, T. L. (2005). *The world is flat: A brief history of the twenty-first century*. New York: Farrar, Straus and Giroux Publisher.

Fuchs, M., & Hanning, C. (2001). *Ethical capability as a competitive advantage- Three case studies within the Volvo corporation*. Luleå, Sweden: Luleå Tekniska University.

Gailey, B. (2009). *ICANN, cultural imperialism, and democratization of internet governance*. Unpublished doctoral dissertation, Bryant University, Rhode Island.

Galbraith, J. R. (1973). *Designing complex organizations*. Reading, MA: Addison-Wesley.

Gâlea, D., Leon, F., & Zaharia, M. H. (2003). E-learning distributed framework using intelligent agents. In M. Craus, D. Gâlea & A. Valachi (Eds.), New Trends in Computer Science and Engineering (Anniversary Volume) (pp. 159-163). Asachi, Iaşi: Polirom Press.

Gan, L. L., & Koh, H. C. (2006). An empirical study of software piracy among tertiary institutions in Singapore. *Journal of Business Ethics*, *43*(5), 640–647.

Gan, Y. C., & Wang, W. (2005). Analysis and study on the multiple implications of virtual learning community strategies based on social constructivism. *Modern Distance Education Study*, *5*, 10–16.

Garavelli, A. C., et al. (2003). How motivating knowledge workers. *European KM Forum*. Retrieved August 25, 2010, from, http://www.knowledgeboard.com/download/480/Theme2-Synthesis_Report-_public_.v03.2003-02-06.pdf

García-Morales, V. J., Lloréns-Montes, F. J., & Verdú-Jover, A. J. (2007). Influence of personal mastery on organizational performance through organizational learning and innovation in large firms and SMEs. *Technovation*, *27*(9), 547–568. doi:10.1016/j.technovation.2007.02.013

Gardner, H. (1999). *Intelligence reframed: Multiple intelligences for the 21st Century*. New York: Basic Books.

Gardner, H. (1983). *Frames of mind: The theory of multiple intelligences*. New York: Basic Books.

Garrat, B. (1999). The learning organization 15 years on: Some personal reflections. *The Learning Organization*, *6*(5), 202–207. doi:10.1108/09696479910299802

Gaspay, A., Legorreta, L., & Dardan, S. (2009). Flexibility of asynchronous distance learning: Reaching diverse cultures. *Journal of Knowledge Globalization*, *2*(2), 47–67.

Gaut, B. (2007). *Art, emotion and ethics*. New York: Oxford University Press. doi:10.1093/acprof:oso/9780199263219.001.0001

Gaut, B. (2004). The ethical criticism of art. In Lamarque, P., & Olsen, S. H. (Eds.), *Aesthetics and the Philosophy of Art: The Analytical Tradition: An Anthology* (pp. 283–294). Oxford, UK: Blackwell Publishing.

Gayton, C. M. (2007). Legal issues for the knowledge economy in the twenty-first century. *VINE: The Journal of Information and Knowledge Management Systems*, *36*(1), 17–26.

Gayton, C. M. (2008). Business ethics, restrictions on employment and knowledge management. *VINE: The Journal of Information and Knowledge Management Systems*, *38*(2), 174–183.

Geraghty, R. M. (2007). The impact of globalization in the Roman Empire, 200bc-ad100. *The Journal of Economic History*, *67*(4), 1036–1061. doi:10.1017/S0022050707000484

Gergen, K. J. (1995). Social construction and the educational process. In Steffe, L. P., Gale, J. E., & Gale, J. (Eds.), *Constructivism in Education* (pp. 17–39). Hillsdale, MI: Lawrence Erlbaum.

Gerke, J. (2003). An architecture for a service oriented peer-to-peer system (SOPPS). *Praxis der Informationsverarbeitung und Kommunikation*, *26*(2), 90–95. doi:10.1515/PIKO.2003.90

Ghemawat, P. (1986). Sustainable advantage. *Harvard Business Review*, *86*(5), 53–58.

Gibbons, M. (2000). Mode 2 society and the emergence of context-sensitive science. *Science & Public Policy*, *27*(3), 159–163. doi:10.3152/147154300781782011

Gibbons, M. (1994). *The new production of knowledge: The dynamics of science and research in contemporary societies*. London: Sage.

Gill, J., & Johnson, P. (2002). *Research methods for managers* (3rd ed.). Thousand Oaks, CA: Sage Publications.

Gilley, J. W., & Maybunich, A. (2000). *Beyond the learning organization. Creating a culture of continuous growth and development through state-of-the-art human resource practices*. Cambridge, MA: Perseus Books.

Gilman, S. C. (2005). *Ethics codes and codes of conduct as tools for promoting an ethical and professional public service: Comparative successes and lessons*. Washington, DC: World Bank.

Gilmartin, R. V. (2003). Ethics and the corporate culture. *Bentley College*. Retrieved July 31, 2010, from, http://www.bentley.edu/cbe/documents/Gilmartin.pdf

Gilpin, R. (2001). *Global political economy- Understanding the international economic order*. Princeton, NJ: Princeton University Press.

Glaser, B. G., & Strauss, A. L. (1967). *The discovery of grounded theory*. New York: Aldine De Gruyter.

Glorioso, A., Pagallo, U., & Ruffo, G. (2010). The social impact of P2P networks. In X. Shen *et al.* (Eds.), *Handbook of P2P Networking* (pp. 47-70). Heidelberg, Germany: Springer.

Goban-Klass, T. (1999). *Media I komunikowanie masowe. Teorie i analizy prasy, radia, telewizji i Internetu*. Krákow, Poland: Wydawnictwo Naukowe PWN. (in Polish)

Godwin, W. (1793). *Enquiry concerning political justice and its influence on morals and happiness*. London: G. G. & J. Robinson.

Godzic, W. (Ed.). (2001). *Humanista w cyberprzestrzeni*. Krákow, Poland: Wyd Rabid. (in Polish)

Goertzel, B. (2008a). Glocal memory: A new perspective on knowledge representation, neurodynamics, distributed cognition, and the nature of mind. Dynamical Psychology: An International, Interdisciplinary Journal of Complex Mental Processes. Retrieved July 25, 2009, from http://www.goertzel.org/dynapsyc/2008/glocal_memory.pdf

Goertzel, B. (2008b). Glocality of self and memory as a possible foundation for understanding psi. Dynamical Psychology: An International, Interdisciplinary Journal of Complex Mental Processes. Retrieved July 25, 2009, from http://www.goertzel.org/dynapsyc/2008/glocal_psi.pdf

Golding, P., & Harris, P. (Eds.). (1997). *Beyond cultural imperialism: Globalization, communication and the new international order*. London: Sage Publications.

Goleman, D. (1995). *Emotional intelligence*. New York: Bantam Books.

Goleman, D. (2006). *Social intelligence: The new science of human relationships*. London: Hutchinson.

Gordon, E. (2009). Redefining the local: The distinction between located information and local knowledge in location-based games. In Silva, A. S., & Sutko, D. M. (Eds.), *Digital Cityscapes: Merging Digital and Urban Playspaces* (pp. 21–36). New York: Peter Lang Publishing.

Górniak-Kocikowska, K. (2005). Problemy z nazwaniem nowego spoleczenstwa. *Ethos (Berkeley, Calif.)*, *18*(1-2), 77–99.

Górniak-Kocikowska, K. (2008). ICT and the tension between old and new: The human factor. *Journal of Information. Communication & Ethics in Society*, *6*(1), 4–27. doi:10.1108/14779960810866774

Górniak-Kocikowska, K. (2004). The computer revolution and global ethics. In Bynum, T. W., & Rogerson, S. (Eds.), *Computer Ethics and Professional Responsibility* (pp. 319–327). Malden, MA: Blackwell Publishing Ldt.

Górniak-Kocikowska, K. (2007). From computer ethics to the ethics of the global ICT society. K. E. Himma (Ed.), *Special Issue: Information Ethics* (pp. 47-57). Boca Raton, FL: Library Hi Tech: Emerald.

Gotterbarn, D. (2001). Reducing software failures using software development impact statements. *Australasian Journal of Information Management Systems*, *9*(2), 155–165.

Gotterbarn, D. (2004). Informatics and professional responsibility. In Bynum, T. W., & Rogerson, S. (Eds.), *Computer Ethics and Professional Responsibility* (pp. 107–118). Malden, MA: Blackwell Publishing.

Gotterbarn, D. (2000). Virtual information and the software engineering code of ethics. In Langford, D. (Ed.), *Internet Ethics* (pp. 200–215). London: McMillan.

Gottschalk, P. (2005). *Strategic knowledge management technology*. Hershey, PA: Idea Group Publishing.

Goulding, C. (1998). Grounded theory: The missing methodology on the interpretivist agenda. *Qualitative Market Research: An International Journal*, *1*(1), 50–57. doi:10.1108/13522759810197587

Government, H. M. (2005). Transformational government: Enabled by technology. *Cabinet Office*. Retrieved August 7, 2009, from http://www.cabinetoffice.gov.uk/media/141734/transgov-strategy.pdf

Government, H. M. (2008a). Information matters: Building government's capability in managing knowledge and information. *National Archives*. Retrieved July 31, 2009, from http://www.nationalarchives.gov.uk/documents/information-matters-strategy.pdf

Government, H. M. (2008b). Data handling procedures in government: Final report. *Cabinet Office*. Retrieved August 1, 2009, from http://www.cabinetoffice.gov.uk/media/65948/dhr080625.pdf

Government, H. M. (2009a). The United Kingdom report on the re-use of public sector information 2009. *Office of Public Sector Information*. Retrieved August 5, 2009, from http://www.opsi.gov.uk/advice/psi-regulations/uk-report-reuse-psi-2009.pdf

Government, H. M. (2009b). How the civil service code applies to online participation. *Civil Service*. Retrieved August 7, 2009, from www.civilservice.gov.uk/about/work/codes/participation-online.aspx

Government, H. M. (2009c). Working together: Public services on your side. *HM Government*. Retrieved August 7, 2009, from http://www.hmg.gov.uk/media/15556/workingtogether.pdf

Gowri, A. (2007). On corporate virtue. *Journal of Business Ethics*, *70*(4), 391–400. doi:10.1007/s10551-006-9117-2

Graber, C. B. (2006). The new UNESCO convention on cultural diversity: A counterbalance to the WTO? *Journal of International Economic Law*, *9*(3), 553–574. doi:10.1093/jiel/jgl018

Graber, C. B. (2008). Substantive rights and obligations under the UNESCO convention on cultural diversity. In Schneider, H., & van den Bossche, P. (Eds.), *Protection of Cultural Diversity from an International and European Perspective* (pp. 141–162). Antwerp, The Netherlands: Intersentia.

Graham, G. (1992). *The internet- A philosophical enquiry: The Gifford Lectures*. London: SCM Press.

Grant, R., & Short, J. R. (Eds.). (2002). *Globalization and the margins*. New York: Palgrave Macmillan. doi:10.1057/9781403918482

Grant, R. M. (1996). Toward a knowledge-based theory of the firm. *Strategic Management Journal, 17*(Winter Special Issue), 109-122.

Greenberg, J., & Cropanzano, R. (2001). *Advances in organizational justice*. Stanford, CA: Stanford University Press.

Greene, A. D., & Latting, J. K. (2004). Whistleblowing as a form of advocacy: Guidelines for the practitioner and organization. *Social Work, 49*(2), 219–230.

Greig, G. (2008). *The role and importance of context in collective learning: Multiple case studies in Scottish primary care*. St. Andrews, Scotland: University of St. Andrews.

Grieves, J. (2008). Why should we abandon the idea of the learning organization. *The Learning Organization, 15*(6), 463–473. doi:10.1108/09696470810907374

Griffith, T. L., Sawyer, J. E., & Neale, M. A. (2003). Virtualness and knowledge in teams: Managing the love triangle of organizations, individuals, and information technology. *Management Information Systems Quarterly, 29*(2), 265–287.

Grixti, J. (2006). Symbiotic transformations: Youth, global media and indigenous culture in Malta. *Media Culture & Society, 28*(1), 105–122. doi:10.1177/0163443706059295

Grixti, J. (2008). Glocalised youth culture as linguistic performance: Media globalisation and the construction of hybrid identities. Noves SL. Revista de Sociolingüística, Hivern, 2-8. Retrieved July 1, 2009, from http://www6.gencat.net/llengcat/noves/hm08hivern/docs/grixti.pdf.

Grodzinski, F. S., & Tavani, H. T. (2005). P2P networks and the Verizon v. RIAA case: Implications for personal privacy and intellectual property. *Ethics and Information Technology, 7*(4), 243–250. doi:10.1007/s10676-006-0012-4

Grönroos, M. (2003). *Mahdollisuuden aika- Kohti virtuaalista organisaatiota*. Vammala, Finland: Transatlanta. (in Finnish)

Grudzewski, W. M., & Hejduk, I. (2005). Zarządzanie wiedzą w organizacjach (in Polish). *E-mentor*. Retrieved June 13, 2009, from http://www.e-mentor.edu.pl/artykul_v2.php?numer=8&id=115

Gurteen, D. (1999). Creating a knowledge sharing culture. *Knowledge Management Magazine, 2*(5).

Haar, J. M., & Spell, C. S. (2009). How does distributive justice affect work attitudes? The moderating effects of autonomy. *International Journal of Human Resource Management, 20*(8), 1827–1842. doi:10.1080/09585190903087248

Haidt, J. (2008). Morality. *Perspectives on Psychological Science, 3*(1), 65–72.

Haitani, K. (1990). The paradox of Japan's groupism: Threat to future competitiveness? *Asian Survey, 30*(3), 237–257. doi:10.1525/as.1990.30.3.01p03644

Hakanen, J. (1999). Ketkä uupuvat? Miesten ja naisten työuupumus tutkimusten valossa. [in Finnish]. *Työterveiset, S2*, 16–18.

Håkansson, A.-K., & Deer, K. (2006). Promoting the building of a people-centred, development-oriented and inclusive information society, with a view to enhancing digital opportunities for all people. *Indigenous ICT taskforce: The Panel of the United Nations Commission on Science and Technology for Development*. Retrieved December 5, 2009, from, http://www.unctad.org/sections/dite_dir/docs/dite_pcbb_stdev0033_en.pdf

Haken, H. (1983). *Synergetics, an introduction: Non-equilibrium phase transitions and self-organization in physics, chemistry, and biology* (3rd ed.). New York: Springer-Verlag.

Haldane, A. (2004). The convergence of e.learning and knowledge management: Fusion or confusion? *European Consortium for the Learning Organisation.* Retrieved October 14, 2009, from http://www.eclo.org/pages/uploads/File/The%20Convergence%20of%20e-learning%20and%20Knowledge%20Management%20-%20Andrew%20Haldane.pdf

Hall, B., & Snider, A. (2000). Glossary: The hottest buzz words in the industry. *Learning*, *44*(4), 85–104.

Hall, D. J. (2005). Philosophical foundations for a learning-oriented knowledge management system for decision support. *Decision Support Systems*, *39*(3), 445–461. doi:10.1016/j.dss.2004.01.005

Hall, D. J., Paradice, D. B., & Courtney, J. F. (2003). Building a theoretical foundation for a learning-oriented knowledge management system. *Journal of Information Technology Theory and Application*, *5*(2), 63–89.

Halwani, R. (2009). Ethicism, interpretation, and Munich. *The Journal of Applied Psychology*, *26*(1), 71–87.

Hamaguchi, E. (1982). What is Japanese collectivism? In Hamaguchi, E., & Kumon, S. (Eds.), *Japanese Collectivism* (pp. 1–26). Tokyo: Yuhikaku. (in Japanese)

Hamel, G. (2009). Innovation masters. *Leadership Excellence, January*, 26-33.

Handelzalts, A. (2007). Preservice teachers' perceptions of an ICT-rich learning environment: Development of an instrument. *Learning Environments Research*, *10*(2), 131–144. doi:10.1007/s10984-007-9024-1

Handzic, M., & Hasan, H. (2003). The search for an integrated KM framework. In Hasan, H., & Handzic, M. (Eds.), *Australian Studies in Knowledge Management* (pp. 3–34). Wollongong: UOW Press.

Harada, Y. (2002). Liberty, equity, and security in network-mediated learning and testing. In Bynum, T. W. (Eds.), *ETHICOMP2002: The Transformation of Organisations in the Information Age: Social and Ethical Implications* (pp. 575–588). Lisbon: Lusíada University of Lisbon.

Hardaker, G., & Smith, D. (2002). E-learning communities: Virtual markets and knowledge creation. *European Business Review*, *14*(5), 342–350. doi:10.1108/09555340210444194

Hardin, G. (1968). The tragedy of the commons. *Science*, *162*(3859), 1243–1248. doi:10.1126/science.162.3859.1243

Hardt, M., & Negri, A. (2005). *Empire*. Boston: Harvard Business Press.

Hariparsad, I. D. (2005). *The work ethic of the principal as an aspect of management*. Johannesburg, South Africa: University of Johannesburg.

Harris, P., Connolly, J., & Feeney, L. (2009). Blended learning: Overview and recommendations for successful implementation. *Industrial and Commercial Training*, *41*(3), 155–163. doi:10.1108/00197850910950961

Harrison, K. D. (2007). *When languages die: The extinction of the world's languages and the erosion of human knowledge*. London: Oxford University Press.

Harrison, R., & Kessels, J. (2004). *Human resource development in a knowledge economy- An organizational view*. New York: Palgrave Macmillan.

Hartline, T. (2008). Rawls's a theory of justice: Addressing the criticisms of Okin and Pateman. In Wolf, M. P., & Musselman, L. (Eds.), *Voicing Ideas* (*Vol. 3*, pp. 59–63). Fresno, CA: California State University.

Hearne, C. E. (2009). Chinese dialects. Suite101.com. Retrieved August, 5, 2009, from http://china.suite101.com/article.cfm/chinese_dialects#ixzz0csCvgDev

Hedlund, G. (1994). A model of knowledge management and the N-form corporation. *Strategic Management Journal*, *15*(S2), 73–90. doi:10.1002/smj.4250151006

Held, D. (2004). *Global covenant: The social democratic alternative to the Washington consensus*. Cambridge: Polity.

Heller, M. A. (1998). The tragedy of the anticommons: property in the transition from Marx to markets. *Harvard Law Review*, *111*(3), 621–688. doi:10.2307/1342203

Heller, M. A. (2008). *The gridlock economy*. New York: Basic Books.

Hempel, J. (2009). Web 2.0 is so over. Welcome to web 3.0. *CNN Money*. Retrieved September 22, 2009, from, http://money.cnn.com/2009/01/07/technology/hempel_threepointo.fortune/index.htm

Hendriks, P. (1999). Why share knowledge? The influence of ICT on the motivation for knowledge sharing. *Knowledge and Process Management*, *6*(2), 91–100. doi:10.1002/(SICI)1099-1441(199906)6:2<91::AID-KPM54>3.0.CO;2-M

Hendry, J. (2003). *Understanding Japanese society*. Oxford, UK: Routledge.

Hertel, G., Niedner, S., & Herrmann, S. (2003). Motivation of software developers in open source projects: An Internet-based survey of contributors to the Linux kernel. *Research Policy*, *32*(7), 1159–1177. doi:10.1016/S0048-7333(03)00047-7

Heyneman, S., Anderson, K., & Nuraliyev, N. (2008). The cost of corruption in higher education. *Comparative Education Review*, *52*(1), 1–25. doi:10.1086/524367

Himanen, P., Torvalds, L., & Castells, M. (2001). *Hacker ethic and the spirit of the information age*. New York: Random House.

Hirschheim, R., & Klein, H. K. (1994). Realizing emancipatory principles in information systems development: The case for Ethics. *Management Information Systems Quarterly*, *18*(1), 83–109. doi:10.2307/249611

Hirsjärvi, S., & Hurme, H. (2000). *Tutkimushaastattelu. Teemahaastattelun teoria ja käytäntö*. Helsinki, Finland: Yliopistopaino. (in Finnish)

Hitchner, R. B. (2008). Globalization avant la lettre: Globalization and the history of the Roman Empire. New Global Studies, 2(2). Retrieved July 15, 2009, from http://www.bepress.com/ngs/vol2/iss2/art2

Hock, D. W. (1999). *Birth of the chaordic age*. San Francisco, CA: Berret-Koehler Publisher.

Hofstede, G. (1993). Cultural constrain in management theories. *The Academy of Management Executive*, *7*(1), 81–94.

Holmberg, B. (2005). *The evolution, principles and practices of distance education*. Oldenburg, Sweden: BIS-Verlag der Carl von Ossietzky Universität Oldenburg. http://halfanhour.blogspot.com/2008/09/types-of-knowledge-and-connective.html

Horkheimer, M., & Addorno, T. W. (2002). Dialectic of enlightenment: Philosophical fragments (Cultural memory in the present). In Noerr, G. S. (Ed.), *trans. E. Jephcott*. Palo Alto, CA: Stanford University Press.

Horvath, D. (2001). Knowledge worker. *SearchCRM*. Retrieved August 28, 2010, from, http://searchcrm.techtarget.com/definition/knowledge-worker

Hovland, I. (2003). Knowledge management and organizational learning: An international development perspective. *ODI Working Paper 224*. Retrieved August 5, 2009, from http://www.odi.org.uk/resources/download/143.pdf

Huber, G. P. (1991). Organizational learning: The contributing process and the literatures. *Organization Science*, *2*(1), 88–115. doi:10.1287/orsc.2.1.88

Huff, C. W., & Barnard, L. (2008). Good computing: Life stories of moral exemplars in the computing profession. *IEEE Computers and Society*, *28*(3), 47–54.

Huff, C. W., & Frey, W. (2005). Moral pedagogy and practical ethics. *Science and Engineering Ethics*, *11*(3), 1–20. doi:10.1007/s11948-005-0008-1

Huff, C. W., & Rogerson, S. (2005). Craft and reform in moral exemplars in computing. In Collste, G. (Eds.), *ETHICOMP 2005: Looking Back to the Future (CD: paper 30)*. Linkoping, Sweden: Linkoping University.

Huntington, S. P. (2004). *Who are we? The challenges to America's national identity*. New York: Simon & Schuster, Inc.

Huotari, M.-L., Hurme, P., & Valkonen, T. (2005). *Viestinnästä tietoon. Tiedon luominen työyhteisössä*. Helsinki, Finland: WSOY. (in Finnish)

Huotari, M.-L., & Iivonen, M. (2005). Knowledge processes: A strategic foundation for the partnership between the university and its library. *Library Management, 25*(6/7), 324–335. doi:10.1108/01435120410609743

Huotari, M.-L., & Iivonen, M. (2004). Managing knowledge-based organizations through trust. In Huotari, M.-L., & Iivonen, M. (Eds.), *Trust in Knowledge Management and Systems in Organizations* (pp. 1–29). Hershey, PA: Idea Group Publishing.

Hurley, T. A., & Green, G. W. (2005). Knowledge management and the nonprofit industry: A within and between approach. *Journal of Knowledge Management Practice, 6*. Retrieved September 15, 2010, from, http://www.tlainc.com/articl79.htm

Iamnitchi, A., Ripeanu, M., & Foster, I. (2004). Small-world file-sharing communities. In *INFOCOM 2004: 23th Annual Joint Conference of the IEEE Computer and Communications Societies: Vol 2* (pp. 952-963). Hong Kong: IEEE Communications Society.

Iivonen, M., & Huotari, M.-L. (2007). The university library's intellectual capital. *Advances in Library Administration and Organization, 25*, 85–95.

Imanishi, K. (1976). *What is evolution?* Tokyo: Kodansha. (in Japanese)

Improvement and Development Agency. (2004). *An introduction to knowledge management: Topic briefing*. London: Improvement and Development Agency.

Inglis, C. (2008). *Planning for cultural diversity*. Paris: Les Éditions UNESCO.

Instituto Hidrográfico. (2003). *Ajudas à navegação: Lista de luzes, bóias, balizas e sinais de nevoeiro*, (6ª ed.). Lisboa: Instituto Hidrográfico (in Portuguese).

IONS. (2009). What is noetic? Institute of Noetic Sciences. Retrieved July 15, 2009, from http://www.noetic.org/about/what_is.cfm

Ives, W., Torrey, B., & Gordon, C. (2000). Knowledge sharing is a human behaviour. In Morrey, D., Maybury, M., & Thuraisingham, B. (Eds.), *Knowledge Management: Classic and Contemporary Works* (pp. 99–12). Cambridge, MA: MIT Press.

Jaspers, K. (1958). *Wahrheit, freiheit und friede*. München, Germany: Piper & Co. Verlag.

Jefferies, P., & Stahl, B. C. (2005). Some ethical considerations regarding the relationship of e-learning and pedagogy. In Collste, G. (Eds.), *ETHICOMP 2005: Looking Back to the Future (CD: paper 31)*. Linkoping, Sweden: Linkoping University.

Jenkins, H. (2006). *Confronting the challenges of participatory culture: Media education for the 21st century*. Chicago: The John D. and Catherine T. MacArthur Foundation.

Jenkins, H. (2006). *Convergence culture: Where old and new media collide*. New York: New York University Press.

Jia, W., & Zhou, W. (2005). *Distributed network systems: From concepts to implementations*. New York: Springer.

Jobs, S. (2007). Thoughts on music. *Apple*. Retrieved April 20, 2009, from http://www.apple.com/hotnews/thoughtsonmusic/

Johannessen, J.-A., Olsen, B., & Olaisen, J. (2005). Intellectual capital as a holistic management philosophy: A theoretical perspective. *International Journal of Information Management, 25*(2), 151–171. doi:10.1016/j.ijinfomgt.2004.12.008

John, O. P., & Srivastava, S. (1999). The big five trait taxonomy: History, measurement, and theoretical perspectives. In Pervin, L. A., & John, O. P. (Eds.), *Handbook of Personality: Theory and Research* (pp. 139–153). New York: Guilford.

Johnson, J. R. (2002). Leading the learning organization: Portrait of four leaders. *Leadership and Organization Development Journal*, *23*(5), 241–249. doi:10.1108/01437730210435956

Johnson-Laird, P. N. (1983). *Mental models*. Cambridge, UK: Cambridge University Press.

Jones, T. M. (1991). Ethical decision making by individuals in organizations: An issue-contingent model. *Academy of Management Review*, *16*(2), 366–395. doi:10.2307/258867

Jones, R. (2003). Measuring the benefits of knowledge management at the financial services authority. *Journal of Information Science*, *29*(6), 475–487. doi:10.1177/0165551503296005

Jøsang, A., Ismail, R., & Boyd, C. (2007). A survey on trust and reputation systems for online service provision. *Decision Support Systems*, *43*(2), 618–644. doi:10.1016/j.dss.2005.05.019

Jowett, B. (1899). *Protagoras: Dialogues of Plato*. Michigan, MI: The Colonial Press.

Kalling, T., & Styhre, A. (2003). *Knowledge sharing in organizations*. Malmö, Sweden: Liber Ekonomi.

Kallinikou, D., et al. (2009, September). Alternative system for non-commercial use of intellectual property in consideration of free P2P file-sharing. Paper presented at the IASA 2009 Annual Conference, Athens, Greece.

Kant, I. (1997). *Grundläggning av sedernas metafysik*. Göteborg, Sweden: Daidalos. (in Swedish)

Kanuka, H. (2006). Instructional design and e-learning: A discussion of pedagogical content knowledge as a missing construct. The e-Journal of Instructional Science and Technology, 9(2). Retrieved August 1, 2009, from http://www.usq.edu.au/electpub/e-jist/docs/vol9_no2/papers/full_papers/kanuka.htm

Kaplan, R. (1999). The balanced scorecard for public-sector organizations. *Harvard Business Review*, (January/February): 3–4.

Kaptein, M., & Schwartz, M. S. (2008). The effectiveness of business codes: A critical examination of existing studies and the development of an integrated research model. *Journal of Business Ethics*, *77*(2), 111–127. doi:10.1007/s10551-006-9305-0

Kaune, S., Lauinger, T., & Kovacevic, A. (2008). Embracing the peer next door: Proximity in Kademlia. In K. Wehrle (Ed.), *P2P'08: Proceedings of the Eighth International Conference on Peer-to-Peer Computing* (pp. 343-350). Aachen, Germany: IEEE Press.

Kavathatzopoulos, I., & Rigas, G. (1998). A Piagetian scale for the measurement of ethical competence in politics. *Educational and Psychological Measurement*, *58*(5), 791–803. doi:10.1177/0013164498058005005

Kavathatzopoulos, I., & Rigas, G. (2006). A measurement model for ethical competence in business. *Journal of Business Ethics Education*, *3*, 55–74.

Kavathatzopoulos, I. (2001). IT user learning: the role of informal processes. In Makrakis, V. (Ed.), *New Technologies in Education and Distance Education* (pp. 337–345). Athens, Greece: Atrapos.

Kavathatzopoulos, I., Kostrzewa, A., & Berg, K. (2008, October). *Measuring ethical competence of organizations*. Paper presented at the 21st Annual European Business Ethics Network, Antalya, Turkey.

Kavathatzopoulos, I., & Laaksoharju, M. (2010). Computer aided ethical systems design. In M. Arias-Oliva et al. (Eds.), *The "backwards, forwards, and sideways" changes of ICT* (332-340). Universitat Rovira i Virgili: Tarragona, Spain.

Keen, A. (2008). *The cult of the amateur: How blogs, MySpace, YouTube, and the rest of today's user-generated media are destroying our economy, our culture, and our values*. New York: Doubleday Business.

Kelloway, E. K., & Barling, J. (2000). Knowledge work as organizational behavior. *International Journal of Management Reviews*, *2*(3), 287–304. doi:10.1111/1468-2370.00042

Kelly, G., Mulgan, G., & Muers, S. (2002). Creating public value: An analytical framework for public service reform. *Cabinet Office*. Retrieved July 31, 2009, from http://www.cabinetoffice.gov.uk/media/cabinetoffice/strategy/assets/public_value2.pdf

Kenon, V. K. (2009, June). Global education access utilizing high school-university partnerships and networked global learning communities. Paper presented at the Conference Network Ethics 2009: The New Challenge in Business, ICT and Education, Lisbon, Portugal.

Kerr, B. (2006). Web 3.0- E-learning 3.0? E-learning technology. *E-learning Tech*. Retrieved January 21, 2010, from, http://elearningtech.blogspot.com/2006/11/web-30-elearning-30.html#ixzz0zfMkSsKW

Kerr, B. (2007). Which radical discontinuity? *Bill Kerr*. Retrieved January 20, 2010, from, http://billkerr2.blogspot.com/2007/02/which-radical-discontinuity.html

Kessels, J. W. M. (2001). Learning in organizations: A corporate curriculum for the knowledge economy. *Futures*, *33*(6), 497–506. doi:10.1016/S0016-3287(00)00093-8

Khurana, R., & Gintis, H. (2008). What is the purpose of business? *BizEd Magazine, January-February*, 54-55.

Kidwell, J. J., Linde, K. M. V., & Johnson, S. L. (2000). Applying corporate knowledge management practices in higher education. *EDUCAUSE Quarterly*, *23*(4), 28–33.

Kim, W. C., & Mauborgne, R. (2003). Fair process: Managing in the knowledge economy. *Harvard Business Review*, *81*(1), 127–136.

Kim, S. (1998), Cultural imperialism on the internet. *The Edge: E-Journal of Intercultural Relations, 1(4)*. Retrieved January 10, 2009, from http://interculturalrelations.com/v1i4Fall1998/f98kim.htm

Kimura, B. (1981). *Self, relationship and time: Phenomenological psychopathology*. Tokyo: Kobundo. (in Japanese)

Kindaichi, H. (1975). *Japanese linguistic expression*. Tokyo: Kodansha. (in Japanese)

King, A. H., & Heltne, M. M. (2007). Glocalization and ICT: Presuppositions, tensions and ethical possibilities. In Bynum, T. W., Rogerson, S., & Murata, K. (Eds.), *ETHICOMP 2007: Glocalization: Bridging the Global Nature of Information and Communication Technology and the Local Nature of Human Beings* (*Vol. 1*, pp. 288–301). Tokyo: Meiji University.

Klein, H. K., & Myers, M. D. (1999). A set of principles for conducting and evaluating interpretive field studies in information systems. *Management Information Systems Quarterly*, *23*(1), 67–93. doi:10.2307/249410

Kline, P., & Saunders, B. (1993). *Ten steps to a learning organization*. Arlington, VA: Great Ocean Publishers.

Kmita, J. (1985). *Kultura i poznanie*. Warszawa, Poland: Wydawnictwo Naukowe PWN. (in Polish)

Knight, J. (2006). Crossborder education: An analytical framework for program and provider mobility. In Smart, J., & Tierney, W. (Eds.), *Higher Education: Handbook of Theory and Research* (*Vol. 21*, pp. 345–396). Dordrecht: Springer Academic Publishers.

Kocikowski, A. (1996). Geography and computer ethics: An Eastern European perspective. T. W. Bynum & S. Rogerson (Guest Eds.). *Special Issue: Global Information Ethics. Science and Engineering Ethics*, *2*(2), 201–210. doi:10.1007/BF02583554

Kofman, E., & Youngs, G. (Eds.). (2003). *Globalization: Theory and practice*. New York: Continuum.

Kontoghiorghes, C., Awbre, S., & Feurig, P. (2005). Examining the relationship between learning organization characteristics and change adaptation, innovation, and organizational performance. *Human Resource Development Quarterly*, *16*(2), 185–212. doi:10.1002/hrdq.1133

Koppelman, H. (2008). Pedagogical content knowledge and educational cases in computer science: An exploration. Informing Science. Retrieved August 5, 2009, from http://proceedings.informingscience.org/InSITE2008/InSITE08p125-133Koppel450.pdf

Koulikov, M. (2008). *Emerging problems in knowledge-sharing and the three new ethics of knowledge transfer (Selected works)*. New York: New York Law Institute.

KPMG. (2002). *Intellectual gold- KPMG's European Intellectual Property Survey reveals the value hidden in Europe's leading companies*. London: KPMG.

Krajewski, M. (2003). *Kultury kultury popularnej*. Poznań, Poland: Wydawnictwo Naukowe UAM. (in Polish)

Kristensen, K., & Kijl, B. (2008). Productivity in collaboration-intensive knowledge work: The collaboration management imperative. In K.-D. Thoben, K. S. Pawar & R. Gonçalves (Eds.), *Proceedings of the 14th International Conference on Concurrent Enterprising*. Lisbon: Nova University. Retrieved August 25, 2010, from, http://www.ice-proceedings.org/default.asp?P=408&obj=B1

Kull, M. D. (2002). *Stories of knowledge management: Exploring coherence in a community of practice*. Washington, DC: The George Washington University.

Kunsch, P. L., Kavathatzopoulos, I., & Rauschmayer, F. (2009). Modelling complex ethical decision problems with operations research. *Omega- The International Journal of Management Science, 37*(6), 1100-1108.

Kurtz, C. F., & Snowden, D. J. (2003). The new dynamics of strategy: Sense-making in a complex and complicated world. *IBM Systems Journal, 42*(3), 462–483. doi:10.1147/sj.423.0462

Kwiek, M. (2006). *The university and the state*. New York: Peter Lang.

Laaksoharju, M., & Kavathatzopoulos, I. (2009). Computerized support for ethical analysis. In M. Botti et al. (Eds.), *Proceedings of CEPE 2009 – Eighth International Computer Ethics and Philosophical Enquiry Conference.* Ionian University: Kerkyra, Greece.

Lallana, E. C. (2004). *An overview of ICT policies and e-strategies of select Asian economies*. New Delhi: APDIP.

Lambert, E. G. (2005). The impact of distributive and procedural justice on social service workers. *Social Justice Research, 18*(4), 411–427. doi:10.1007/s11211-005-8568-4

Laming, H. (2003). The victoria climbie inquiry report. *House of Commons- Health Committee*. Retrieved August 7, 2009, from http://www.publications.parliament.uk/pa/cm200203/cmselect/cmhealth/570/570.pdf

Land, F., Amjad, U., & Nolas, S.-M. (2006). The ethics of knowledge management. *International Journal of Knowledge Management, 3*(1), 1–9.

Lapsley, D. K., & Narvaez, D. (2005). Moral psychology at the crossroads. In Lapsley, D. K., & Power, F. C. (Eds.), *Character Psychology and Character Education* (pp. 18–35). Notre Dame, IN: University of Notre Dame.

Latham, C. (Ed.). (1987). *New harmony collection: 1814-1884*. Indiana, IN: Indiana Historical Society.

Laudon, K., & Laudon, J. (Eds.). (2004). *Managing the digital firm* (8th ed.). Upper Saddle River, NJ: Prentice Hall.

Lauzon, A. C. (1997). Postmodernism, interactive technologies and the design of distance education. In M. Koble & E. Wagner (Eds.), *Distance Education Symposium 3: Course Design, ACSDE Research Monograph Number 14* (pp. 6-21). University Park, PA: The American Centre for Distance Education, PA, The Pennsylvania State University.

Lavelle, L. (2002). Executive pay. *Business Week*. Retrieved August 29, 2010, from, http://www.businessweek.com/magazine/content/02_15/b3778012.htm

Lee-Kelley, L., Blackman, D. A., & Hurst, J. P. (2007). An exploration of the relationship between learning organisations and the retention of knowledge workers. *The Learning Organization, 14*(3), 204–221. doi:10.1108/09696470710739390

Leitch, C. (1996). Learning organizations: The measurement of company performance. *Journal of European Industrial Training, 20*(1), 31–44. doi:10.1108/03090599610105264

Leonard, L. N. K., & Cronan, T. P. (2005). Attitude toward ethical behaviour in computer use: A shifting model. *Industrial Management & Data Systems, 105*(9), 1150–1171. doi:10.1108/02635570510633239

Lessem, R. (1990). *Developmental management principle of holistics business*. Oxford: Blackwell.

Lessig, L. (2002). *The future of ideas: The fate of the commons in a connected world*. New York: Vintage Books.

Lessig, L. (2004). *Free culture: How big media uses technology and the law to lock down culture and control creativity*. New York: Penguin Group Inc.

Lessig, L. (2006). *Code: Version 2.0*. New York: Basic Books.

Levin, J. (2002). A 2020 vision: Education in the next two decades. *Quarterly Review of Distance Education*, *3*(1), 105–114.

Levy, S. (1984). *Hackers: Heroes of the computer revolution*. Garden City, NY: Anchor Press/Doubleday.

Lewis, M. P. (Ed.). (2009). *Ethnologue: Languages of the world* (16th ed.). Dallas, TX: SIL International.

Liebowitz, J. (1999). *Knowledge management handbook*. Boca Raton, FL: CRC Press.

Lillrank, P. (2002). The broom and nonroutine processes: A metaphor for understanding variability in organizations. *Knowledge and Process Management*, *9*(3), 143–148. doi:10.1002/kpm.145

Linking the theoretical basis- justice and knowledge creation ahd sharing

Lister, M. (2003). *New media: A critical introduction*. New York: Routledge.

Liu, C. C. (2008). The relationship between Machiavellianism and knowledge sharing willingness. *Journal of Business and Psychology*, *22*(3), 233–240. doi:10.1007/s10869-008-9065-1

Liyanage, S., & Poon, P. S. (2002). Technology and innovation management learning in the knowledge economy. *Journal of Management Development*, *22*(7), 579–602. doi:10.1108/02621710310484740

Lobera, J., & Escrigas, C. (2009). The glocal multiversity: New roles and emerging challenges for human and social development. Global University Network for Innovation. Retrieved July 15, 2009, from http://www.guni-rmies.net/news/detail.php?id=1464

Loermans, J. (2002). Synergizing the learning organization and knowledge management. *Journal of Knowledge Management*, *6*(3), 285–294. doi:10.1108/13673270210434386

Long, B. S., & Driscoll, C. (2008). Codes of ethics and the pursuit of organizational legitimacy: Theoretical and empirical contributions. *Journal of Business Ethics*, *77*(2), 173–189. doi:10.1007/s10551-006-9307-y

Lönnqvist, A., & Mettänen, P. (2003). *Suorituskyvyn mittaaminen-Tunnusluvut asiantuntijaorganisaation johtamisvälineenä*. Helsinki: Edita. (in Finnish)

Losh, L. (2010). Will "hacking the academy" be understood as "backing the academy"? *Virtual Politik*. Retrieved March 20, 2010, from, http://virtualpolitik.blogspot.com/2010_05_01_archive.html

Lucas, L. (2006). *The research game in academic life*. Maidenhead, UK: Open University Press & The Society for Research into Higher Education.

Lusk, S., Roberts, T., & Mackie, J. (2008). Strategy: What place in government. Summary of research findings. *National School of Government*. Retrieved July 31, 2009, from http://virtual.nationalschool.gov.uk/Strategy-Exchange/News/NSG%20strategy%20project%20-%20research%20summary%20paper%20July%2008.doc

Lytras, M. D., & Pouloudi, A. (2006). Towards the development of a novel taxonomy of knowledge management systems from a learning perspective: An integrated approach to learning and knowledge infrastructures. *Journal of Knowledge Management*, *10*(6), 64–80. doi:10.1108/13673270610709224

Lytras, M. D., Pouloudi, A., & Poulymenakou, A. (2002). Knowledge management convergence- Expanding learning frontiers. *Journal of Knowledge Management*, *6*(1), 40–51. doi:10.1108/13673270210417682

Machiavelli, N. (1981). *Mandragola. Transl. M. J. Flaumenhaft*. Long Grove, IL: Waveland Press Inc.

MacIntyre, A. (2002). *Dependent rational animals: Why human beings need the virtues*. IL, Peru: Open Court.

Macionis, J. J., & Plummer, K. (1998). *Sociology: A global introduction*. Upper Saddle River, NJ: Prentice Hall Inc.

Maison, K. B. (2007). A case for professional studies in education for teachers in higher educational institutions. In Amenumey, D. E. K. (Ed.), *Challenges of Education in Ghana in the 21st Century* (pp. 248–256). Accra, Ghana: Woeli.

Malhotra, R. (2000, October). *The ethics of proselytizing*. Paper presented at the Conference on Human Rights and Religion, Ithaca, NY.

Malthus, T. R. (1798). *An essay on the principle of population*. New York: Penguin Classics.

Maner, W. (2004). Unique ethical problems in information technology. In Bynum, T. W., & Rogerson, S. (Eds.), *Computer Ethics and Professional Responsibility* (pp. 39–59). Malden, MA: Blackwell Publishing.

Mannheim, K. (1936). *Ideology and utopia: An introduction to the sociology of knowledge, (Transl. L. Wirth & E. Shils)*. New York: Harcourt Brace & World.

Manovich, L. (2000). *The language of new media*. Cambridge, MA: MIT Press.

Manski, C. F. (2000). Economic analysis of social interactions. *The Journal of Economic Perspectives*, *14*(3), 115–136. doi:10.1257/jep.14.3.115

March, J. G., & Simon, H. A. (1958). *Organizations*. New York: John Wiley & Sons.

Marginson, S. (2007). Globalisation, the "idea of a university" and its ethical regimes. *Higher Education and Management Policy*, *19*(1), 31–45.

Marimba, A., & Farinha, T. (2003, May). *Controlo e monitorização da gestão da manutenção: Metodologia de auditoria interna permanente*. Paper presented at the 3as Jornadas de Organização e Gestão Industrial da ESTG, Leiria (in Portuguese).

Marnburg, E. (2000). The behavioral effects of corporate ethical codes: Empirical findings and discussion. *Business Ethics (Oxford, England)*, *9*(3), 200–210. doi:10.1111/1467-8608.00191

Marti, S., & Garcia-Molina, H. (2006). Taxonomy of trust: Categorizing p2p reputation systems. *Computer Networks*, *50*(4), 472–484. doi:10.1016/j.comnet.2005.07.011

Martin, J. N. (2006, July). *Using the knowledge pyramid to characterize systems*. Paper presented at the INCOSE Symposium, Orlando, Florida.

Mason, R. O. (1995). Applying ethics to information technology issues. *Communications of the ACM*, *38*(12), 55–57. doi:10.1145/219663.219681

Mason, R., & Rennie, F. (2008). *E-learning and social networking: Handbook of resources for higher education*. New York: Routledge.

Mason, R. O., Mason, F. M., & Culnan, M. J. (1995). *Ethics of information management*. Thousand Oaks, CA: Sage Publications.

Masrom, M., & Ismail, Z. (2008). *Computer security and computer ethics awareness: A component of management information system*. In H. B. Zaman *et al.* (Eds.), *Proceedings of International Symposium on Information Technology 2008, Volume 3* (pp. 1920-1926). Malaysia: Kuala Lumpur Convention Centre.

Mattelart, A. (2000). *Networking the world, 1794-2000*. Minneapolis, MN: University of Minnesota Press.

Mattelart, A. (2002). *História da utopia planetária*. Porto Alegre, Portugal: Sulina. (in Portuguese)

Mattelart, A. (2003). *Information society: An introduction*. London: Sage.

Mattelart, A., & Mattelart, M. (2001). *Teorie komunikacji: Krótkie wprowadzenie*. Krákow, Poland: Wydawnictwo Naukowe PWN. (in Polish)

Matteo, T., Vaccaro, A., & Floridi, L. (2008). Network neutrality: Ethical issues in the Internet era. In Bynum, T. (Eds.), *ETHICOMP 2008: Living, Working and Learning Beyond Technology* (pp. 773–774). Mantua, Italy: University of Pavia.

Maynard, J. S. (1968). *Mathematical ideas in biology*. Cambridge, UK: Cambridge University Press.

McCrickard, D. S., & Chewar, C. M. (2004). Proselytizing pervasive computing: A strategy and approach influenced by human computer interaction. In B. Werner (Ed.), *Proceedings of the 2nd IEEE Annual Conference on Pervasive Computing and Communications Workshops* (pp. 257-262). Orlando, FL: IEEE Computer Society.

McElroy, M. H. (2000). Integrating complexity theory, knowledge management and organizational learning. *Journal of Knowledge Management*, *4*(3), 195–203. doi:10.1108/13673270010377652

McLuhan, M. (1962). *The Gutenberg galaxy*. London: Routledge & Kegan Paul.

McNabb, D. E. (2006). *Knowledge management in the public sector: A blueprint for innovation in Government*. New York: M. E. Sharpe, Inc.

McNamara, C. (2005). Complete guide to ethics management: An ethics toolkit for managers. *Management Help*. Retrieved August 2, 2010, from, www.managementhelp.org/ethics/ethxgde.htm

McPherson, M., & Nunes, M. B. (2006). Organizational issues for e-learning: Critical success factors as identified by HE practitioners. *International Journal of Educational Management*, *20*(7), 542–558. doi:10.1108/09513540610704645

Mead, G. H. (1934). *Mind, self, & society: From the standpoint of a social behaviorist*. Chicago: University of Chicago Press.

Meadows, D. H. (1982). Whole earth models and systems. *The Coevolution Quarterly*, *34*(Summer), 98–108.

Medeni, T. (2004, March). Lobal: A new dimension beside global, local and glocal. Paper presented at the International Workshop on Business and Information, Taipei, Taiwan.

Merriam-Webster Dictionary. (2010). Surrealism. *Merriam-Webster Dictionary*. Retrieved September 2, 2010, from, http://www.merriam-webster.com/dictionary/surrealism

Meyer, P. (2003). From halos to horns: Demonizing the American CEO. *Directorship*. Retrieved September 10, 2010, from, http://www.allbusiness.com/marketing-advertising/branding-brand-development/972067-1.html

Meyrowitz, J. (2005). The rise of glocality: New sense of place and identity in the global village. In Nyíri, K. (Ed.), *A Sense of Place: The Global and the Local in Mobile Communication* (pp. 21–30). Vienna: Passagen Verlag.

Michelman, F. I. (1982). Ethics, economics and the law of property. In Pennock, J. R., & Chapman, J. W. (Eds.), *Nomos XXIV: Ethics, Economics and the Law* (pp. 3–40). New York: New York University Press.

Mihalca, R. (2008). Knowledge management in e-learning systems. *Revista Informatica Economică*, *2*(46), 60–65.

Miles, M. B., & Huberman, M. (1994). *Qualitative data analysis: An expanded source book* (2nd ed.). Thousand Oaks, CA: Sage Publications.

Miles, M. B., & Huberman, M. (1994). *Qualitative data analysis: An expanded source book* (2nd ed.). Thousand Oaks, CA: Sage.

Miller, D. (Ed.). (1985). *The rationality principle- Popper selections*. Princeton, NJ: Princeton University Press.

Miller, D. (1999). *Principles of justice*. London: Harvard University Press.

Mindjet (2010). Support- Knowledge base. *Mindjet.com*. Retrieved February 17, 2010, from, http://www.mindjet.com/support/overview

Ministry of Economical Development. (2006). What is knowledge economy? *New Zealand Government*. Retrieved June 11, 2009, from http://www.med.govt.nz/pbt/infotech/knowledge_economy/knowledge_economy-04.html

Moilanen, R. (2005). Diagnosing and measuring learning organizations. *The Learning Organization*, *12*(1), 71–89. doi:10.1108/09696470510574278

Mokyr, J. (2002). *The gifts of Athena: Historical origins of the knowledge economy*. Princeton, NJ: Princeton University Press.

Mooradian, T., Renzl, B., & Matzler, K. (2006). Who trusts? Personality, trust and knowledge sharing. *Management Learning*, *37*(4), 523–540. doi:10.1177/1350507606073424

Moore, M. G. (1993). Theory of transactional distance. In Keegan, D. (Ed.), *Theoretical Principles of Distance Education* (pp. 22–38). New York: Routledge.

Moorman, R. H., Niehoff, B. P., & Organ, D. W. (1993). Treating employees fairly and organizational citizenship behavior: Sorting the effects of job satisfaction, organizational commitment, and procedural justice. *Employee Responsibilities and Rights Journal*, *6*(3), 209–225. doi:10.1007/BF01419445

Moraga, E. (2006). Cultural learning organizations: A model. *Cultural Learning Organizations*. Retrieved July 31, 2010, from, www.culturallearningorganizations.net/index_files/The%20ethics%20of%20LO.pdf

Mori, M. (1987). *Laozi and Zhuangzi*. Tokyo: Kodansha. (in Japanese)

Morin, E. (1999). *Seven complex lessons in education for the future*. Paris: Les Éditions UNESCO.

Mróz, A. (2005). From Gutenberg to ICT: New lingua doctus. In Collste, G. (Eds.), *ETHICOMP 2005: Looking Back to the Future (CD: paper 48)*. Linkoping, Sweden: Linkoping University.

Muktar, M. (2002). Computer crime: The new threat. *Crime-Research.org*. Retrieved October 13, 2009, from, http://www.crime-research.org/library/Mudavi1.htm

Musial, K. (2007, June). The public good function of universities in recent Nordic higher education reforms. Paper presented at the Conference of Higher Education Researchers, Dublin, Ireland.

Myers, M. D. (1997). Qualitative research in information systems. *Management Information Systems Quarterly*, *21*(2), 241–242. doi:10.2307/249422

Myers, P. S. (1996). Knowledge management and organizational design: An Introduction. In Myers, P. S. (Ed.), *Knowledge Management and Organizational Design* (pp. 1–6). Newton, MA: Butterworth-Heinemann. doi:10.1016/B978-0-7506-9749-1.50004-1

Nagi, K. (2006). Solving ethical issues in e-learning. Special Issue of the International Journal of the Computer, the Internet and Management, 14(SP1), 7.1-7.6.

Nahapiet, J., & Ghoshal, S. (1998). Social capital, intellectual capital, and the organizational advantage. *Academy of Management Review*, *23*(2), 242–266. doi:10.2307/259373

Nakane, C. (1970). *Japanese society*. Berkley, CA: University of California Press.

Nakane, C. (1972). *Conditions for adaptation: The Japanese thought of continuation*. Tokyo: Kodansha. (in Japanese)

Nakane, C. (1978). *Dynamics of a vertical society*. Tokyo: Kodansha. (in Japanese)

Narvaez, D., & Lapsley, D. (2005). The psychological foundations of everyday morality and moral expertise. In Lapsley, D. K., & Power, F. C. (Eds.), *Character Psychology and Character Education* (pp. 140–165). Notre Dame, IN: University of Notre Dame.

National Audit Office. (2009). *Helping government learn*. London: The Stationary Office.

Near, J., & Miceli, M. P. (1995). Effective whistleblowing. *Academy of Management Review*, *3*(20), 679–708. doi:10.2307/258791

Neher, P. A. (1990). *Natural resource economics: Conservation and exploitation*. Cambridge, UK: Cambridge University Press.

Nesan, L. J., & Holt, G. D. (2002). Assessment of organizational involvement in implementing empowerment. *Integrated Manufacturing Systems*, *13*(4), 201–211. doi:10.1108/09576060210426903

Newbury, D., Bently, L., & Pollock, R. (2008). Models of public sector information provision via trading funds. *UK Department for Business, Innovation and Skills*. Retrieved August 1, 2009, from www.berr.gov.uk/files/file45136.pdf

Newman, J. H. (1976). The idea of the university, (Modern ed.). Oxford, UK: Clarendon Press.

Nicholas, A. J., & Lewis, J. K. (2009, June). The net generation and e-text books. Paper presented at the Conference Network Ethics 2009: The New Challenge in Business, ICT and Education, Lisbon, Portugal.

Nichols, D., & Subramaniam, C. (2001). Executive compensation: Excessive or equitable? *Journal of Business Ethics*, *29*(4), 339–351. doi:10.1023/A:1010764828523

Nickerson, M., & Bryner, J. (2002). From video tutors to electronic portfolios: Using advanced screen capture in support of educational technology instruction. In D. Willis *et al.* (Eds.), *Proceedings of Society for Information Technology & Teacher Education International Conference* (pp. 430-431). Chesapeake, VA: AACE.

Nickols, F. (2003). The shift to knowledge work. *Distance Consulting*. Retrieved August 28, 2010, from, http://www.nickols.us/shift.pdf

Nicolis, G., & Prigogine, I. (1977). *Self-organization in non-equilibrium systems: From dissipative structures to order through fluctuations*. New York: John Wiley and Sons.

Nishida, K. (1911). *An enquiry into the good*. Tokyo: Kodokan. (in Japanese)

Nishida, K. (1933). *Fundamental problems of philosophy: The world of action and the dialectical world*. Tokyo: Iwanami Shoten. (in Japanese)

Nonaka, I. (1985). *Theory of corporate evolution*. Tokyo: Nihon Keizai Shimbun Sha. (in Japanese)

Nonaka, I. (1990). *Theory of organisational knowledge creation: Epistemology of Japanese firms*. Tokyo: Nihon Keizai Shimbun Sha. (in Japanese)

Nonaka, I., & Konno, N. (1998). The concept of "*ba*": building a foundation for knowledge creation. *California Management Review*, *40*(3), 40–54.

Nonaka, I., & Takeuchi, H. (1995). *The knowledge-creating company: How Japanese companies create the dynamics of innovation*. New York: Oxford University Press.

Nonaka, I. (1991). The knowledge creating company. *Harvard Business Review*, *69*(November-December), 96–104.

Nonaka, I. (1994). A dynamic theory of organizational knowledge creation. *Organization Science*, *5*(1), 14–37. doi:10.1287/orsc.5.1.14

Nonaka, I., Toyama, R., & Konno, N. (2000). SECI, ba and leadership: A unified model of dynamic knowledge creation. *Long Range Planning*, *33*(1), 5–34. doi:10.1016/S0024-6301(99)00115-6

Norchi, C. H. (2000). Indigenous knowledge as intellectual property. *Policy Sciences*, *33*(3-4), 387–398. doi:10.1023/A:1004835300774

Nordenstreng, K., & Varis, T. (1974). *Television traffic a one-way street (UNESCO Reports and Papers on Mass Communication, 70)*. Paris: Les Éditions UNESCO.

Northrup, P. T. (2001). A framework for designing interactivity into web-based instruction. *Educational Technology*, *41*(2), 31–39.

Northrup, P. T. (2002). Online learners' preferences for interaction. *Quarterly Review of Distance Education*, *3*(2), 219–226.

Nowa Encyklopedia Powszechna. (2004). *Nowa Encyklopedia Powszechna T. 8*. Warszawa, Poland: Wydawnictwo Naukowe PWN. (in Polish)

Nowotny, H., Scott, P., & Gibbons, M. (2001). *Re-thinking science: Knowledge and the public in the age of uncertainty*. Cambridge, UK: Polity Press.

O'Neill, B. S., & Adya, M. (2007). Knowledge sharing and the psychological contract: Managing knowledge workers across different stages of employment. *Journal of Managerial Psychology*, *22*(4), 411–436. doi:10.1108/02683940710745969

O'Reilly, C. A. III, & Pfeffer, J. (2000). *Hidden value: How great companies achieve extraordinary results with ordinary people*. Boston, MA: Harvard Business School Press.

O'Reilly, T. (2005). What is web 2.0. *O'Reilly*. Retrieved January 23, 2009, from http://www.oreillynet.com/pub/a/oreilly/tim/news/2005/09/30/what-is-web-20.html

OCDE. (2008). *OCDE information technology outlook 2008*. Paris: Les Éditions OCDE.

OECD. (2003). OECD science, technology and industry scoreboard 2003. *Organization for Economic Co-operation and Development*. Retrieved June 11, 2009, from http://www.oecd.org/document/21/0,2340,en_2649_33703_16683413_1_1_1_1,00.html

Offe, C. (1996). *Modernity and the state: East, West*. Cambridge, UK: Polity Press.

Okin, S. M. (1989). *Justice, gender and the family*. New York, NY: Basic Books.

Olsen, L. T. (2009, July). Seattle 10 years on: Go glocal. Club of Amsterdam Journal, 119. Retrieved July 13, 2009, from http://www.clubofamsterdam.com/press.asp?contentid=799

Online Education Database. (2007). How the open source movement has changed education: 10 success stories. *OEDB*. Retrieved September 22, 2009, from http://oedb.org/library/features/how-the-open-source-movement-has-changed-education-10-success-stories

Online Etymology Dictionary. (2010). Fair. *Online Etymology Dictionary*. Retrieved September 10, 2010, from, http://www.etymonline.com/index.php?term=fair

O'Reilly, T. (2005). What is web 2.0. *O'Reilly Network*. Retrieved September 17, 2009, from, http://www.oreillynet.com/pub/a/oreilly/tim/news/2005/09/30/what-is-web-20.html

Orito, Y., & Murata, K. (2008). Socio-cultural analysis of personal information leakage in Japan. *Journal of Information. Communication and Ethics in Society*, *6*(2), 161–171. doi:10.1108/14779960810888365

Ortenblad, A. (2002). A typology of the idea of learning organization. *Management Learning*, *33*(2), 213–230. doi:10.1177/1350507602332004

Ortenblad, A. (2004). The learning organization: Towards an integrated model. *The Learning Organization*, *11*(2), 129–144. doi:10.1108/09696470410521592

Ostrom, E. (2000). Collective action and the evolution of social norms. *The Journal of Economic Perspectives*, *14*(3), 137–158. doi:10.1257/jep.14.3.137

Otala, L. (2000). *Oppimisen etu- Kilpailukykyä muutoksessa*. Porvoo, Finland: WSOY. (in Finnish)

Otala, M. (1995). The learning organization: Theory into practice. *Industry and Higher Education*, *9*(3), 157–164.

Oxford English Dictionary. (2008). *Oxford English Dictionary*. Oxford, UK: Oxford University Press.

Oxford English Dictionary. (2008). *Oxford English Dictionary*. Oxford: Oxford University Press.

Oztop, E., Kawato, M., & Arbib, M. (2006). Mirror neurons and imitation: A computationally guided review. *Neural Networks*, *19*(3), 254–271. doi:10.1016/j.neunet.2006.02.002

Pagallo, U. (2010). Ethics among peers: From Napster to Peppermint and beyond. In D'Atri, A., & Saccà, D. (Eds.), *Information Systems: People, Organizations, Institutions, and Technologies* (pp. 297–304). Heidelberg, Germany: Springer.

Pagallo, U., & Ruffo, G. (2007a). On the growth of collaborative and competitive networks: Opportunities and new challenges. In S. Rogerson & H. Yang (Eds.), *Proceedings of ETHICOMP Working Conference 2007* (pp. 92-97). Yunnan: Yunnan University.

Pagallo, U., & Ruffo, G. (2007b). P2P systems in legal networks. Another 'small world' case. In R. Winkels (Ed.), *Eleventh International Conference on Artificial Intelligence and Law* (pp. 287-288). Stanford, CA: ACM Press.

Pandey, A., & Gupta, R. (2008). Perspective of collective consciousness of business organizations. *Journal of Business Ethics*, *80*(4), 889–898. doi:10.1007/s10551-007-9475-4

Parisi, F., Depoorter, B., & Schulz, N. (2005). Duality in Property: commons and anti-commons. *International Review of Law and Economics*, *25*(4), 1–25. doi:10.1016/j.irle.2005.12.003

Parker, S., & Gallagher, N. (Eds.). (2007). *The collaborative state: How working together can transform public services. Cabinet Office*. Retrieved August 1, 2009, from http://www.cabinetoffice.gov.uk/media/cabinetoffice/strategy/assets/collaborative_state_report.pdf

Parr, L. A., Waller, B. M., & Fugate, J. (2005). Emotional communication in primates: Implications for neurobiology. *Current Opinion in Neurobiology*, *15*(6), 716–720. doi:10.1016/j.conb.2005.10.017

Pater, A., & Van Gils, A. (2003). Stimulating ethical decision-making in a business context: Effects of ethical and professional codes. *European Management Journal*, *21*(6), 762–772. doi:10.1016/j.emj.2003.09.016

Patrick, C., & Gaële, G. (2007). Exploring access and equity in higher education: Policy and performance in a comparative perspective. *Higher Education Quarterly*, *61*(2), 136–154. doi:10.1111/j.1468-2273.2007.00343.x

Patrignani, N. (2008). A conceptual framework for computer ethics. In T. Bynum *et al.* (Eds.), *ETHICOMP 2008: Living, Working and Learning Beyond Technology* (pp. 640-647). Mantua. Italy: University of Pavia.

Patton, M. Q. (1980). *Qualitative evaluation methods*. Thousand Oaks, CA: Sage Publications.

Pedersen, L. J. T. (2009). See no evil: Moral sensitivity in the formulation of business problems. *Business Ethics (Oxford, England)*, *18*(4), 335–348. doi:10.1111/j.1467-8608.2009.01567.x

Pedler, M., Burgoyne, J., & Boydell, T. (1996). *The learning company* (2nd ed.). Maidenhead, UK: McGraw-Hill.

Peirce, C. S. (1878). Deduction, induction, and hypothesis. *Popular Science Monthly*, *13*, 470–482.

Pelkmans, M. (2009). The "transparency" of Christian proselytizing in Kyrgzstan. *Anthropological Quarterly*, *82*(2), 423–445. doi:10.1353/anq.0.0058

Penrose, E. T. (1959). *The theory of the growth of the firm*. Oxford, UK: Blackwell.

Peters, M. (2007, February). Reimagining the university in the global era. Paper presented at the World University Network Seminar, Bristol, United Kingdom.

Petroni, A., & Colacino, P. (2008). Motivation strategies for knowledge workers: Evidences and challenges. *Journal of Technology Management & Innovation*, *3*(3), 21–32.

Phillips, J. T. (2000). Will KM alter information managers' roles? *Information Management Journal*, *34*(3), 58–59.

Pieterse, J. N. (2009). Global multiculture: Cultures, transnational culture, deep culture. In Baraldi, C., Borsari, A., & Carli, A. (Eds.), *Hybrids, Differences, Visions: On the Study of Culture* (pp. 1–14). Aurora, CO: Davies Group.

Piketty, T., & Emmanuel, S. (2006). The evolution of top incomes: A historical and international perspective. *The American Economic Review*, *96*(2), 200–205. doi:10.1257/000282806777212116

Pincoffs, E. L. (1971). Quandary ethics. *Mind*, *80*(320), 552–571. doi:10.1093/mind/LXXX.320.552

Pinha e Cunha, M., Fonseca, J. M., & Gonçalves, F. (Eds.). (2001). *Empresas, caos e complexidade- Gerindo à beira de um ataque de nervos*. Mem-Martins, Portugal: Editora RH. (in Portuguese)

Plato,. (1986). *The republic. (Transl. B. Jowett)*. Amherst, NY: Prometheus Books.

Poe, E. A. (1845). The raven. Project Gutenberg. Retrieved July, 30, 2009, from http://www.gutenberg.org/etext/14082

Pojman, L. (1994). *Ethical theory: Classical and contemporary readings* (2nd ed.). Belmont, CA: Thomson Wadsworth.

Polanyi, M. (1958). *Personal knowledge: Towards a post-critical philosophy*. Chicago: University of Chicago Press.

Polanyi, M. (1966). *The tacit dimension*. Garden City, NY: Doubleday.

Polinsky, A. M., & Shavell, S. (2000). The economic theory of public enforcement of law. *Journal of Economic Literature*, (38): 45–76.

Popper, K. R. (1972). *Objective knowledge: An evolutionary approach*. London: Oxford University Press.

Porter, M. E. (1980). *Competitive strategy*. New York: Free Press.

Porter, M. E. (1985). *Competitive advantage, creating and sustaining superior performance*. New York: The True Press.

Posiah, M. I., & Kamaruzaman, J. (2008). Sustenance of values and ethics in the Malaysian higher education e-learning drive. *Asian Social Science*, *4*(6), 115–121.

Poster, M. (2005). Digitally local: Communications technologies and space. In Nyiri, K. (Ed.), *A Sense of Place: The Global and the Local in Mobile Communication* (pp. 31–41). Vienna: Passagen Verlag.

Powell, T. C. (2001). Competitive advantage: Logical and philosophical considerations. *Strategic Management Journal*, *22*(9), 875–888. doi:10.1002/smj.173

Public Management and Policy Association & National School of Government. (2007). Evidence based policy-making: Making the most of academic-practitioner exchange. *The Chartered Institute of Public Finance & Accountancy*. Retrieved August 3, 2009, from http://www.cipfabusiness.com/pmpa/news/past_news.cfm

Pullinger, D. (2001). *Information technology and cyberspace: Extra-connected living*. London: Darton, Longman and Todd.

Pyöriä, P. (2005). The concept of knowledge work revisited. *Journal of Knowledge Management*, *9*(3), 116–127. doi:10.1108/13673270510602818

Pyvis, D., & Chapman, A. P. (2005). Culture shock and the international student "offshore". *Journal of Research in International Education*, *4*(1), 23–42. doi:10.1177/1475240905050289

Quéau, P. (2002). Global governance and knowledge societies. *Development*, *45*(4), 10–16. doi:10.1057/palgrave.development.1110398

Quinton, A. (1972). Knowledge and belief. In P. Edwards (Ed.), *The Encyclopedia of Philosophy: Vol. 4* (pp. 345-352). New York: Macmillan Publishing & The Free Press.

Richardson, H. (2002). Exercising different choices- The gender divide and government policy making in the "global knowledge economy". In I. M. S. B. Alvarez *et al.* (Eds.), *ETHICOMP 2002: The Transformation of Organisations in the Information Age: Social and Ethical Implications* (pp. 471-484). Lisbon: Lusíada University of Lisbon.

Raeder, L. C. (2002). *John Stuart Mill and the religion of humanity*. Columbia, MO: University of Missouri Press.

Raikhy, P. S. (2002). Trade in education under the WTO policy regime: Implications for India. In Powar, K. B. (Ed.), *Internationalization of Higher Education* (pp. 127–133). New Delhi: Association of Indian Universities.

Rastas, T., & Einola-Pekkinen, V. (2001). *Arvoa aineettomasta pääomasta*. Tampere, Finland: Tammer-Paino Oy. (in Finnish)

Rauschmayer, F. *et al.* (2009). Why good practice of OR is not enough- Ethical challenges for the OR practitioner. *Omega- The International Journal of Management Science, 37*(6), 1089-1099.

Rawls, J. (2001). *Justice as fairness: A restatement*. Cambridge, MA: Belknap Press.

Rawls, J. (1971). *A theory of justice* (4th ed.). Cambridge, MA: Belknap Press.

Raymond, E. S. (1999). *The cathedral & the bazaar: Musings on Linux and open source by an accidental revolution*. Sebastopol, CA: O'Reilly Media.

Reich, R. B. (1991). *The work of nations: Preparing ourselves for the 21st century capitalism*. New York: Alfred A. Knopf, Inc.

Reis, A. D. (2007). *Media, knowledge & education (digital media ecologies)*. Innsbruck, Austria: Innsbruck University Press.

Reis, A. D. (2008). Support documentation for post graduation on pedagogic and didactic skills on e-learning and ICT. *The Graal Institute*. Retrieved August 1, 2009, from, http://thegraal.ccems.pt/

Reis, A. D., et al. (2009). To be or not to be m-learning (that it is the question). In P. Norbert & S. Judith (Eds.), *3rd WLE Mobile Learning Symposium, Mobile Learning Cultures across Education, Work and Leisure* (pp 75-80). London: WLE Centre.

Retzer, J. (2005). The economical value of information networks. NWAX. Retrieved July 31, 2009, from http://www.nwax.net/documents/economic_value_of_networks.v2-3.pdf

Rheingold, H. (1992). *The virtual reality*. New York: Touchstone.

Rheingold, H. (1994). *Virtual community: Finding connection in a computerized world*. London: Secker & Warburg Publishers.

Rhen, A. (2002). Good times, bad times: The moral discourse of time and management. *Revista Comportamento Organizacional & Gestão*, *8*(1), 49–59.

Richards, C. (2004). From old to new learning: global dilemmas, exemplary Asian contexts, and ICT as a key to cultural change in education. *Globalisation, Societies and Education*, *2*(3), 337–353. doi:10.1080/1476772042000252470

Richards, C. (2004). From old to new learning: global dilemmas, exemplary Asian contexts, and ICT as a key to cultural change in education. *Globalisation, Societies and Education*, *2*(3), 337–353. doi:10.1080/1476772042000252470

Ricolfi, M. (2007). Individual and collective management of copyright in a digital environment. In Torremans, P. (Ed.), *Copyright Law: A Handbook of Contemporary Research* (pp. 283–314). Cheltenham, UK: Edward Elgar.

Rifkin, J. (2003). *The age of access: The new culture of hypercapitalism where all of life is a paid-for experience* (2nd ed.). New York: Jeremy P. Tarcher/Putman.

Riley, T. B. (2003). An overview of the knowledge economy. *e-Gov monitor*. Retrieved June 1, 2009, from http://www.egovmonitor.com/features/riley07.html

Rivest, R. L. (1997). Electronic lottery tickets as micropayments. In R. Hirschfeld (Ed.), *Proceedings of the First International Conference on Financial Cryptography* (pp. 307-314). London: Springer.

Rizzolatti, G., & Craighero, L. (2004). The mirror-neuron system. *Annual Review of Neuroscience*, *27*(1), 169–192. doi:10.1146/annurev.neuro.27.070203.144230

Roberts, B. W., Walton, K., & Viechtbauer, W. (2006). Patterns of mean-level change in personality traits across the life course: A meta-analysis of longitudinal studies. *Psychological Bulletin*, *132*(1), 1–25. doi:10.1037/0033-2909.132.1.1

Robertson, P. L., & Smith, K. H. (2007, March). Technological upgrading and distributed knowledge bases. Paper presented at the Workshop on Low and Medium Technology Industries, Dortmund, Germany.

Robins, K., & Webster, F. (1999). *Times of the technoculture: From the information society to the virtual life*. London: Routledge.

Rogers, P. C., Graham, C. R., & Mayes, C. T. (2007). Cultural competence and instructional design: Exploration research into the delivery of online instruction cross-culturally. *Educational Technology Research and Development*, *55*(2), 197–217. doi:10.1007/s11423-007-9033-x

Rosenberg, M. J. (2001). *E-learning: Strategies for delivering knowledge in the digital age*. New York: McGraw-Hill.

Rossi, P. G. (2008). *Intelligent learning environment (ILE). Learning environment with AI support tools for teachers and tutors*. Unpublished paper, Università degli Studi di Macerata, Marcerata.

Rossouw, D. (2002). *Business ethics in Africa* (2nd ed.). Cape Town, South Africa: Oxford University Press.

Roth, M. (2005). Program execution in connectionist networks. *Mind & Language*, *20*(4), 448–467. doi:10.1111/j.0268-1064.2005.00295.x

Roth, G. L., & Kleiner, A. (1998). Developing organizational memory through learning histories. *Organizational Dynamics*, *27*(2), 43–60. doi:10.1016/S0090-2616(98)90023-7

Roudometof, V. (2005). Transnationalism, cosmopolitanism and glocalization. *Current Sociology*, *53*(1), 113–135. doi:10.1177/0011392105048291

Rowley, J. E. (2006). What do we need to know about wisdom? *Management Decision*, *44*(9), 1246–1257. doi:10.1108/00251740610707712

Rowley, J. E., & Gibbs, P. (2008). From learning organization to practically wise organization. *The Learning Organization*, *15*(5), 356–372. doi:10.1108/09696470810898357

Ruffa, A. (2005). Dalí's surrealist activities and the model of scientific experimentation. *Papers for Surrealism*, *4*, 1–14.

Ruffo, G., & Schifanella, R. (2007). FairPeers: Efficient profit sharing in fair peer-to-peer market places. *Journal of Network and Systems Management*, *15*(3), 355–382. doi:10.1007/s10922-007-9066-9

Ruffo, G., & Schifanella, R. (2009). A peer-to-peer recommender system based on spontaneous affinities. *ACM Transactions on Internet Technology*, *9*(1), 1–34. doi:10.1145/1462159.1462163

Rushkoff, D. (2005). Renaissance now! The gamers' perspective. In Raessens, J., & Goldstein, J. (Eds.), *Handbook of Computer Game Studies* (pp. 415–421). Cambridge, MA: MIT Press.

Ryan, C. (2002). The reputation wars. *Australian Financial Review Boss Magazine, March*, 300-305.

Sakai, K., Kuriyama, K., & Miyahara, T. (2007). The e-learning strategy of organizational design: Emerging the new university education for the next generation. In Bynum, T. W., Rogerson, S., & Murata, K. (Eds.), *ETHICOMP 2007: Glocalization: Bridging the Global Nature of Information and Communication Technology and the Local Nature of Human Beings* (*Vol. 1*, pp. 38–48). Tokyo: Meiji University.

Salazar, J. F. (2009). Self-determination in practice: The critical making of indigenous media. *Development in Practice*, *19*(4/5), 504–513. doi:10.1080/09614520902866397

Salvador Dali Art Gallery. (2010). Paranoia critical method. *Dali-Gallery.com*. Retrieved September 2, 2010, from, http://www.dali-gallery.com/html/dali.php

Samah, D. A. A. (2005, March). *Rethinking Malaysian education: A brave new world?* Paper presented at the 9th Malaysian Education Summit, Kuala Lumpur, Malaysia.

Sandberg, J. (2005). How do we justify knowledge produced within interpretative approaches? *Organizational Research Methods*, *8*(1), 41–68. doi:10.1177/1094428104272000

Sankar, Y. (2003). Designing the learning organization as an information-processing system: Some design principles from the systems paradigm and cybernetic. *International Journal of Organization Theory and Behavior*, *6*(4), 501–521.

Santos, B. S. (2006). The university in the 21st Century: Towards a democratic and emancipatory university reform. In Rhoads, R., & Torres, C. A. (Eds.), *The University, State, and Market. The Political Economy of Globalization in the Americas* (pp. 60–100). Stanford, CA: Stanford University Press.

Sarmento, M. M., & Costa, G. J. M. (2006). E-learning: does the "e" also means ethics? In Reis, A., & Piecha, J. (Eds.), *DLCW 2006 (CD: paper 4)*. Lisbon, Spain: ISEG.

Scanlon, T. M. (1998). *What we owe to each other*. Cambridge, MA: Harvard University Press.

Scardamalia, M., & Bereiter, C. (2003). Knowledge building environments: Extending the limits of the possible in education and knowledge work. In DiStefano, A., Rudestam, K. E., & Silverman, R. (Eds.), *Encyclopedia of distributed learning* (pp. 269–272). Thousand Oaks, CA: Sage Publications.

Schein, E. H. (1996). Three cultures of management: The key to organizational learning. *Sloan Management Review*, *38*(1), 9–20.

Schein, E. H. (2004). Learning when and how to lie: A neglected aspect of organizational and occupational socialization. *Human Relations*, *57*(3), 260–273.

Schiller, H. I. (1976). *Communication and cultural domination*. White Plains, NY: International Arts and Sciences Press.

Schlick, M. (2008). *Problems of ethics*. New York: Prentice-Hall.

Schmidt, D. P. (2000). Ethics for knowledge management. In Srikantaiah, T. K., & Koenig, M. E. D. (Eds.), *Knowledge Management for the Information Professional* (pp. 115–131). Medford, NJ: American Society for Information Science.

Schneider, S. C., & Baroux, J.-L. (2002). *Managing across cultures* (2nd ed.). Upper Saddle River, NJ: Prentice Hall.

Scholtes, P. R. (1997). Tiimit järjestelmien aikakaudella. [in Finnish]. *Yritystalous*, *2*, 59–66.

Schulte, W. D., & Al-Fehaid, A. (2004). National culture and knowledge management in the middle East: A cross-cultural comparison of Saudi Arabia and the US. In O. Yau (Ed.), Academy of International Business Southeastern United States Annual Meeting (pp. 279-290). Macau: Academy of International Business.

Schwartz, B. (2005). *The paradox of choice: why more is less* (2nd ed.). New York: Harper Perennial.

Scones, I. (1999). New ecology and the social sciences: What prospects for a fruitful engagement? *Annual Review of Anthropology*, *28*, 479–507. doi:10.1146/annurev.anthro.28.1.479

Scott, A. (1979). Development of economic theory on fisheries regulation. *Journal of the Fisheries Research Board of Canada*, *36*(7), 725–741.

Scott, P. (1995). *The meanings of mass higher education*. Buckingham, UK: Open University Press.

Scott, D. (2007). Reward programs: What works and what needs to be improved. *WorldatWork Journal*, *16*(3), 6–21.

Scott, P. (2008, November). Beyond the market: Higher Education in 2020. Paper presented at the Univeristies Association for Lifelong Learning Conference, Barcelona, Spain.

Sedziuviene, N., & Vveinhardt, J. (2009). The paradigm of knowledge management in higher educational institutions. *Inzinerine Ekonomika-Engineering Economics*, *5*(65), 79–90.

Seetharaman, A., Sooria, H. H. B. Z., & Saravanan, A. S. (2002). Intellectual capital accounting and reporting in the knowledge economy. *Journal of Intellectual Capital*, *3*(2), 128–148. doi:10.1108/14691930210424734

Seib, P., & Fitzpatrick, K. R. (2006). *Public relations ethics*. Belmont, CA: Thomson.

Senge, P. M. (1990). *The fifth discipline: The art and practice of the learning organization*. New York: Doubleday Business.

Senge, P. M. (2007). Collaborating for systemic change. *MIT Sloan Management Review*, *48*(2), 44–53.

Senge, P. M. (2006). *The fifth discipline: The art & practise of the learning organization* (2nd ed.). New York: Doubleday Business.

Senge, P. M. (1996). Leading learning organizations. *Training & Development*, *50*(12), 36–37.

Senge, P. M. (1994). *The fifth discipline field book: Strategies and tools for building a learning organization.* New York: Doubleday/Currency.

Senges, M. (2007). *Knowledge entrepreneurship in universities: Practice and strategy in the case of Internet base innovation appropriation.* Barcelona, Spain: Universitat Oberta de Catalunya.

Seppanen, R. (2008). *Trust in organizational relationships.* Lappeenranta, Sweden: Lappeenranta University of Technology.

Shafir, G., & Peled, Y. (Eds.). (2000). *The new Israel: Peacemaking and liberalization.* Boulder, CO: Westview Press.

Shaw, S. (2008). Collaboration in the world of ISD. ASTD. Retrieved August, 5, 2009, from http://www.astd.org/LC/2008/0108_shaw.htm

Shimizu, H. (1978). *Reconsidering life: What is living?* Tokyo: Chuo Koron. (in Japanese)

Shimizu, H. (1992). *Life and place: Relational science creating meanings.* Tokyo: NTT Publisher. (in Japanese)

Shimizu, H. (1996). *The logic of ba as knowledge of life: The logic of co-creation of Yagyu Shin-Kage-Ryu.* Tokyo: Chuo Koron. (in Japanese)

Shimizu, H. (2003). *The thoughts of ba: Creative stages of life.* Tokyo: University of Tokyo Press. (in Japanese)

Siemens, S., & Tittenberger, P. (2009). *Handbook of emerging technologies for learning.* Winnipeg, Manitoba, Canada: University of Manitoba.

Siemens (2006b). Knowing knowledge. *Elearnspace.* Retrieved August 21, 2009, from, http://www.elearnspace.org/KnowingKnowledge_LowRes.pdf

Siemens, G. (2003). Learning ecology, communities, and networks. Extended the classroom. *Elearnspace.* Retrieved August, 21, 2009, from, http://www.elearnspace.org/Articles/learning_communities.htm

Siemens, G. (2004a). Learning management systems: The wrong place to start learning. *Elearnspace.* Retrieved August 19, 2009, from, http://www.elearnspace.org/Articles/lms.htm

Siemens, G. (2004b). Connectivism: A learning theory for the digital age. *Elearnspace.* Retrieved August 21, 2009, from, http://www.elearnspace.org/Articles/connectivism.htm

Siemens, G. (2005). Connectivism: Learning as network-creation. *Elearnspace.* Retrieved August 21, 2009, from, http://www.elearnspace.org/Articles/networks.htm

Siemens, G. (2006a, October). *Connectivism: Learning and knowledge today.* Paper presented at the Education.au Global Summit 2006: Technology connected futures, Sydney, Australia.

Siltala, J. (2004). *Työelämän huonontumisen lyhyt historia. Muutokset hyvinvointivaltioiden ajasta globaaliin hyperkilpailuun.* Keuruu, Finland: Otavan kirjapaino Oy (in Finnish).

Silva, A. J., & Josselyn, S. A. (2002). Cognitive neuroscience: The molecules of forgetfulness. *Nature, 418*(6901), 929–930. doi:10.1038/418929a

Silva, N. S. A. (2009). Knowledge or content? The philosophical boundaries in e-learning pedagogical theories! In Vilas, A. M. (Eds.), *m-ICTE 2009: Research, Reflections and Innovations in Integrating ICT in Education* (pp. 221–225). Lisbon: Formatex.

Silva, N. S. A. (2007). An investigation on the impact of culture and ethics on the implementation of e-university. MPhil/PhD unpublished dissertation, De Montfort University, Leicester.

Silva, N. S. A., et al. (2009). *The evolution of e-learning management systems- An ethical approach.* Paper presented at the Network Ethics 2009, Lisbon, Portugal.

Simon, H. A. (1957). *Administrative behaviour* (3rd ed.). New York: Free Press.

Simon, H. A. (1997). *Administrative behaviour* (4th ed.). New York: McMillan.

Simonin, B. L. (1999). Ambiguity and the process of knowledge transfer in strategic alliances. *Strategic Management Journal, 20*(7), 595–623. doi:10.1002/(SICI)1097-0266(199907)20:7<595::AID-SMJ47>3.0.CO;2-5

Simons, P. (1995). Learning in organizations. *Comportamento Organizacional e Gestão, 1*(2), 173–186.

Siponen, M. T. (1997). *The applicability of ethical theories to computer ethics- Selected issues.* Unpublished manuscript, United Kingdom.

Skyrme, D. J. (2001). *Capitalizing on knowledge: From e-business to k-business.* Wobunr, MA: Butterworth-Heinemann.

Slater, S. F., & Narver, J. C. (1995). Market orientations and the learning organization. *Sloan Management, 59*(3), 7–23.

Small, G. W., & Vorgan, G. (2008). iBrain: Surviving the technological alteration of the modern mind. New York: Harper Collins Publishers.

Snowden, D. (2000). The paradox of story: Simplicity and complexity in strategy. *Journal of Scenario and Strategy Planning, 1*(5), 16–20.

Söderström, H. T. (2003). *Corporate governance and structural change: European challenges.* Stockholm: SNS Förlag.

Soete, L. (2002). The challenges and the potential of the knowledge-based economy in a globalised world. In Rodrigues, M. J. (Ed.), *The New Knowledge Economy in Europe. A Strategy for International Competitiveness and Social Cohesion* (pp. 28–53). Northampton, MA: Edward Elgar Publishing.

Solomon, R. (Ed.). (1992). *Ethics and excellence: Cooperation and integrity in business.* New York: Oxford University Press.

Sorensen, E. (2002). Part of the online teacher's curriculum: Designing for collaborative knowledge building online. In D. Willis et al. (Eds.), Society for Information Technology and Teacher Education International Conference (pp. 995-999). Chesapeake, VA: AACE.

Soros, G. (1998). *The crisis of global capitalism: Open society endangered.* New York: Public Affairs.

Spender, J.-C., & Scherer, A. G. (2007). The philosophical foundations of knowledge management: Editors Introduction. *Organization, 14*(1), 5–28. doi:10.1177/1350508407071858

Spinello, R. A., & Tavani, H. T. (2005). Intellectual property rights in a network world: Theory and Practice. In Spinello, R. A., & Tavani, H. T. (Eds.), *Intellectual Property Rights in a Network World: Theory and Practice* (pp. 1–66). Hershey, PA: Information Science Publishing.

Squier, M. M. (2003). *The principles and practice of knowledge management.* Pretoria, South Africa: University of Pretoria.

Stacey, P. (2001). E-learning value chain and market map. *New Media BC e-Learning SIG.* Retrieved August 17, 2009, from http://www.bctechnology.com/statics/bcelearning.swf

Stahl, B. C. (2002). Ethics and e-teaching: the students' perspective. *Communications of the IIMA, 2*(3), 51–62.

Stahl, B. C. (2007). Privacy and security as ideology. *IEEE Technology and Society Magazine, 26*(1), 35–45. doi:10.1109/MTAS.2007.335570

Stahl, G. (2004). Building collaborative knowing: Elements of a social theory of learning. In Strijbos, J.-W., Kirschner, P., & Martens, R. (Eds.), *What We Know About CSCL in Higher Education* (pp. 53–85). Norwell, MA: Kluwer. doi:10.1007/1-4020-7921-4_3

Stahl, B. C. (2008). Researching ethics and morality in information systems: Some guiding questions. In Te'eni, D. (Eds.), *ICIS 2008 (paper 175).* Paris, France: University of Montpellier II.

Stahl, B. C. (2002). Ethical issues in e-teaching: A theoretical framework. In G. King *et al.* (Eds), *Proceedings of INSPIRE VII, Quality in Learning and Delivery Techniques* (pp. 135-148). Limerick, UK: The British Computer Society.

Ståhle, P. (2002). *Epävarmuus hallintaan- Yrityksen uudistumiskykyja vaihtoehdot*. Jyväskylä, Finland: Gummerus Kirjapaino Oy. (in Finnish)

Ståhle, P., & Laento, K. (2000). *Strateginen kumppanuus- Avain uudistumiskykyyn ja ylivoimaan*. Porvoo, Finland: WS Bookwell Oy. (in Finnish)

Stallman, R. (2004). Why software should be free. In Bynum, T. W., & Rogerson, S. (Eds.), *Computer Ethics and Professional Responsibility* (pp. 294–310). Malden, MA: Blackwell Publishing.

Standards Australia. (2003). Interim Australian Standard- Knowledge management. Standards Australia Limited. Retrieved August 10, 2009, from http://www.standards.com.au

Stanford Encyclopedia of Philosophy. (2010). Connectionism. *Stanford Encyclopedia of Philosophy*. Retrieved January 21, 2010, from http://plato.stanford.edu/entries/connectionism/

Steger, M. B. (Ed.). (2004). *Rethinking globalism*. Lanham, MD: Rowman & Littlefield Publishers.

Stehr, N. (2001). *The fragility of modern societies: Knowledge and risk in the information age*. Thousand Oaks, CA: Sage Publications.

Stenalt, M. H., & Godsk, M. (2006). *The pleasure of e-learning- Towards aesthetic e-learning platforms*. In T. Lillemaa (Ed.), *Proceedings of the 12th International Conference of European University Information Systems* (pp. 201-212). Tartu, Finland: University of Tartu & EUNIS.

Sterman, J. D. (1989). Modeling managerial behaviour: Misperceptions of feedback in a dynamic decision making experiment. *Management Science*, *35*(3), 321–339. doi:10.1287/mnsc.35.3.321

Sterman, J. D. (2000). *Business dynamics: Systems thinking and modelling for a complex world*. Homewood, IL: Irwin/McGraw-Hill.

Sterman, J. D. (2001). System dynamics modelling: Tools for learning in a complex world. *California Management Review*, *43*(4), 8–25.

Stewart, T. A. (1997). *Intellectual capital. The new wealth of organizations*. New York: Currency Doubleday.

Stewart, S. (2004). The A.I. web game. Sean Stewart. Retrieved July 30, 2009, from http://www.seanstewart.org/beast/intro/

Stigler, G. J. (1970). The optimum enforcement of laws. *The Journal of Political Economy*, *78*(3), 526–536. doi:10.1086/259646

Stiglitz, J. E. (2002). *Globalization and its discontents*. New York: Norton.

Stiles-Davis, J. (1988). Spatial dysfunctions in young children with right cerebral hemisphere injury. In Stiles-Davis, J., Kritchesvky, M., & Bellugi, U. (Eds.), *Spatial Cognition- Brain Bases and Development* (pp. 251–272). Hillsdale, NJ: Lawrence Erlbaum Associates, Inc.

Stone, D. (2003). Knowledge in the global agora: Production, dissemination and consumption. In Krizsán, A. (Ed.), *Reshaping Globalization: Multilateral Dialogues and New Policy Initiatives* (pp. 41–62). Budapest, Hungary: Central European University Press.

Storey, J. (2005). Human resources and organizational structures. In Stephen, L., Quintas, P., & Ray, T. (Eds.), *Managing Knowledge- An Essential Reading* (pp. 349–355). London: Sage Publications.

Strauss, A., & Corbin, J. C. (1998). *Basics of qualitative research: Grounded theory, procedures and techniques*. Newbury Park, CA: Sage Publications.

Styhre, A. (2003). Knowledge management beyond codification: Knowing as practice/concept. *Journal of Knowledge Management*, *7*(5), 32–40. doi:10.1108/13673270310505368

Šuc, D., Vladušič, D., & Bratko, I. (2004). Qualitatively faithful quantitative prediction. *Artificial Intelligence*, *158*(2), 189–214. doi:10.1016/j.artint.2004.05.002

Sultana, F. (2007). Reflexivity, positionality and participatory ethics: Negotiating fieldwork dilemmas in international research. *ACME- An International E-Journal for Critical Geographies, 6(3)*, 374-385. Retrieved March 10, 2010, from, http://www.acme-journal.org/vol6/FS.pdf

Sumaila, U. R., Alder, J., & Keith, H. (2006). Global scope and economics of illegal fishing. *Marine Policy*, *30*(6), 696–703. doi:10.1016/j.marpol.2005.11.001

Sun, P. Y. T., & Scott, J. L. (2003). Exploring the divide-organizational learning and learning organization. *The Learning Organization*, *10*(4), 202–215. doi:10.1108/09696470310476972

Sunoo, B. P. (1999). How human resources supports knowledge sharing. *Workforce, Crain Communications. Inc.*, *78*(3), 30–34.

Sunstein, C. R. (2005). Moral heuristics. *The Behavioral and Brain Sciences*, *28*(4), 531–573.

Sutinen, J. G., & Andersen, P. (1985). The economics of fisheries law enforcement. *Land Economics*, *61*(4), 387–397. doi:10.2307/3146156

Sutinen, J. G., & Gauvin, J. R. (1989). An econometric study of regulatory enforcement and compliance in the commercial inshore lobster fishery of Massachusetts. In Neher, P. A. (Ed.), *Rights Based Fishing* (pp. 415–428). New York: Kluwer Academic Publishers.

Suzuki, D. (1944). *The Japanese spirits*. Tokyo: Daito Publishing. (in Japanese)

Sveiby, K.-E. (1997). *The new organizational wealth-Managing & measuring knowledge based assets*. San Francisco, CA: Berret-Koehler Publishers, Inc.

Sveiby, K. E., & Lloyd, T. (1987). *Managing knowhow: Add value by valuing creativity*. London: Bloomsbury.

Swidler, A., & Arditi, J. (1994). The new sociology of knowledge. *Annual Review of Sociology*, *20*, 305–329. doi:10.1146/annurev.so.20.080194.001513

Szulanski, G. (1996). Exploring internal stickiness: Impediments to the transfer of best practice within the firm. *Strategic Management Journal, 17*(Winter Special Issue), 27-43.

Takahashi, Y. (2008). Dynamics simulation modelling using descriptive information in natural language. *International Journal of Simulation and Process Modelling*, *4*(3/4), 215–222. doi:10.1504/IJSPM.2008.023683

Tandon, R. (2008). Civil engagement in higher education and its role in human and social development. In Global University Network for Innovation (Ed.), Higher Education in the World: New Challenges and Emerging Roles for Human and Social Development (pp. 65-66). London: Palgrave Macmillan.

Tapscott, D. (1997). *The digital economy: Promise and peril in the age of networked intelligence*. New York: McGraw-Hill.

Tarasofsky, R., & House, C. (2005). Report on trade, environment, and intellectual property rights. Intellectual Property Rights Organization. Retrieved July 25, 2009, from http://www.iprsonline.org/resources/docs/Tarasofsky-CATE-IPRs.pdf

Taylor, F. W. (1911). *The principles of scientific management*. New York: Harper.

Taylor, C. (2002). Gadamer on the human sciences. In Dostal, R. J. (Ed.), *The Cambridge Companion to Gadamer* (pp. 126–142). Cambridge, UK: Cambridge University Press. doi:10.1017/CCOL0521801931.007

Teece, D. J. (1998). Capturing value from knowledge assets: The new economy, market for know-how and intangible assets. *California Management Review*, *40*(3), 55–79.

Teece, D. J. (2000). Strategies for managing knowledge assets: The role of firm structure and industrial context. *Long Range Planning*, *33*(1), 35–54. doi:10.1016/S0024-6301(99)00117-X

Teten, D. (2007, June). *Web 3.0: Where are we headed?* Paper presented at the Web 2.0 New York Conference, New York, NY.

The Free Dictionary. (2010). Infusion. *TheFreeDictionary.com*. Retrieved November 30, 2009, from, http://www.thefreedictionary.com/infusion

The Free Dictionary. (2010). Ethicism. *The Free Dictionary*. Retrieved January 15, 2010, from, http://www.thefreedictionary.com/ethicism

The Free Dictionary. (2010a). Trade-off. *The Free Dictionary*. Retrieved September 12, 2010, from, http://www.thefreedictionary.com/trade-off

The Free Dictionary. (2010b). Fairness. *The Free Dictionary*. Retrieved September 12, 2010, from, http://www.thefreedictionary.com/Fairness

The Free Dictionary. (2010). Disclosure. *The Free Dictionary*. Retrieved July 31, 2010, from, http://www.thefreedictionary.com/disclosure

The Free Software Foundation. (2009). Free software definition. *The Free Software Foundation*. Retrieved January 23, 2009, from http://www.fsf.org/licensing/essays/free-sw.html

The International Labour Organization. (2007). ILO knowledge strategy. *ILO.org*. Retrieved October 29, 2009, from, http://www.ilo.org/public/english/support/lib/knowledgesharing/strategy.htm

The World Bank. (2009). ICT Glossary Guide. *The World Bank*. Retrieved August 1, 2009, from http://web.worldbank.org/wbsite/external/topics/extinformationandcommunicationandtechnologies/0,contentMDK:21035032~menuPK:282850~pagePK:210058~piPK:210062~theSitePK:282823~isCURL:Y,00.html

Thiessen, E. J. (2000, November). *The ethics of proselytizing: A multi-faith conversation*. Paper present at the Chaplain's Association and the Department of Studies in Religion, Toronto, Ontario.

Thimbleby, H. W., Witten, I. H., & Pullinger, D. J. (1995). Concepts of cooperation in artificial life. *IEEE Transactions on Systems, Man, and Cybernetics*, *25*(7), 1166–1171. doi:10.1109/21.391298

Thomas, B. K. (2010). Participation in the knowledge society: The free and open source (FOSS) movement compared with participatory development. *Development in Practice*, *20*(2), 270–276. doi:10.1080/09614520903566509

Thomas, L. (1995). *Late night thoughts on listening to Mahler's ninth symphony*. New York: Penguin Books.

Thomas, R., & Walport, M. (2008). Data sharing review report. *Ministry of Justice*. Retrieved August 3, 2009, from http://www.justice.gov.uk/reviews/docs/data-sharing-review-report.pdf

Thompson, A. A., & Strickland, A. J. (2003). *Strategic management: Concepts and cases* (13th ed.). Boston: Irwin/McGraw-Hill.

Tietenberg, T. (2003). *Environmental and natural resource economics* (6th ed.). Reading, MA: Addison Wesley.

Toffler, A. (1980). *The third wave*. New York: Bantam Books.

Torvi, K., & Kiljunen, P. (2005). Onnellisuuden vaikea yhtälö. *Elinkeinoelämän valiokunnan (EVA)*. Retrieved July 30, 2009, from http://www.eva.fi/files/1110_onnellisuuden_vaikea_yhtalo.pdf (in Finnish).

Tranel, D., & Damasio, A. (1985). Knowledge without awareness: An autonomic index of facial recognition by prosopagnosics. *Science*, *228*(21), 1453–1454. doi:10.1126/science.4012303

Trauth, E. M. (1999). Who owns my soul? The paradox of pursing organizational knowledge in a work culture of individualism. In R. Agarwal & J. Prasad (Eds.), *Proceedings of the 1999 ACM SIGCPR Conference*, (pp. 159-163). New Orleans, LA: CM Press.

Treviño, L. K. (1986). Ethical decision making in organizations: A person-situation interactionist model. *Academy of Management Review*, *11*(3), 601–617. doi:10.2307/258313

Treviño, L. K., & Weaver, G. R. (2003). *Managing ethics in business organizations: Social scientific perspectives*. Stanford, CA: Stanford University Press.

Tsagarousianou, R. (2004). Rethinking the concept of diaspora: Mobility, connectivity and communication in a globalised world. *Westminster Papers in Communication and Culture*, *1*(1), 52–65.

Tsoukas, H., & Vladimirou, E. (2001). What is organizational knowledge? *Journal of Management Studies*, *38*(7), 973–993. doi:10.1111/1467-6486.00268

Tuomi, I. (2004, December). *Innovation, growth and competitiveness in the knowledge society*. Paper presented at the Foro de la Innovación y Modernización en Andalucía, Malaga, Spain.

Turban, E. (Eds.). (2006). *Electronic commerce: A managerial perspective*. Thousand Oaks, CA: Prentice Hall.

Turillo, C. J. (2002). Is virtue its own reward? Self-sacrificial decisions for the sake of fairness. *Organizational Behavior and Human Decision Processes*, *89*(1), 839–865. doi:10.1016/S0749-5978(02)00032-8

Turner, E., & Roberts, P. (2001). Teaching computer ethics to IT students in higher education: An exploration of provision, practice and perspective. *Centre for Computing and Social Responsibility*. Retrieved October 13, 2009, from, http://www.ccsr.cse.dmu.ac.uk/conferences/ccsrconf/ethicomp2001/abstracts/turner.html

Ullman, D. G. (2004). Decision management: Punctuating the process. *Incose Insight*, *6*(2).

Umesao, T. (1963). Joho sangyo ron. *Chuo-kohron*, 46-58 (in Japanese).

UN. (2005). *Understanding knowledge societies*. New York: United Nations.

UN. (1948). The universal declaration of human rights. United Nations. Retrieved July 25, 2009, from http://www.un.org/en/documents/udhr/

UNESCO. (2002). Universal declaration on cultural diversity. UNESCO. Retrieved August 10, 2009, from http://unesdoc.unesco.org/images/0012/001271/127160m.pdf

UNESCO. (2005). Convention on the protection and promotion of the diversity of cultural expressions. *UNESCO*. Retrieved November 25, 2009, from http://unesdoc.unesco.org/images/0014/001429/142919e.pdf

UNHCHR. (1966). International covenant on economic, social and cultural rights. United Nations High Commissioner for Human Rights. Retrieved July 27, 2009, from http://www2.ohchr.org/english/law/cescr.htm

Uzuner, S. (2009). Questions of culture in distance learning: A research review. *International Review of Research in Open and Distance Learning*, *10*(3), 1–19.

van der Velden, M., et al. (2009). *Autonomy and automation in an information society for all*. Paper presented at the Information Systems Research Seminar in Scandinavia, Molde, Norway.

van Es, R., & Smit, G. (2003). Whistleblowing and media logic: A case study. *Business Ethics (Oxford, England)*, *12*(2), 144–150. doi:10.1111/1467-8608.00314

van Harmelen, M. (2006). Personal learning environments. University of Manchester. Retrieved August 2, 2009, from http://octette.cs.man.ac.uk/jitt/index.php/Personal_Learning_Environments

van Weert, T. (2005). Lifelong learning in the knowledge society- Implications for education. *International Federation for Information Processing*, *161*, 15–25.

Vandergriff, L. J. (2008). Welcome to the Intelligence age: An examination of intelligence as a complex venture emergent behaviour. *Vine*, *38*(4), 432–444. doi:10.1108/03055720810917697

Vandergriff, L. J. (2001, May). *Role tailored decision support: An investigation of decision-making and implementation process state of the art*. Paper present at the Course 398 Lecturing, Washington, DC.

Vansteenkiste, M. (2004). Motivating learning, performance, and persistence: The synergistic effects of intrinsic goal contents and autonomy supportive contexts. *Journal of Personality and Social Psychology*, *87*(2), 246–260. doi:10.1037/0022-3514.87.2.246

Varney, D. (2006). *Service transformation: A better service for citizens and businesses, a better deal for the taxpayer. HM Treasury*. Retrieved August 5, 2009, from www.hm-treasury.gov.uk/d/pbr06_varney_review.pdf

Verbos, A. K. (2007). The positive ethical organization: Enacting a living code of ethics and ethical organizational identity. *Journal of Business Ethics*, *76*(1), 17–33. doi:10.1007/s10551-006-9275-2

Verplanken, B., & Holland, R. W. (2002). Motivated decision making: Effects of activation and self-centrality of values on choices and behavior. *Journal of Personality and Social Psychology*, *82*(3), 434–447. doi:10.1037/0022-3514.82.3.434

Vihma, P. (2005). Kaikki etsivät kumppaneita. Yritysten yhteistyön hallinta on johtajien päällimmäinen puheenaihe. [in Finnish]. *Talouselämä*, *5*, 22–27.

von Hippel, E. (1998). Economics of product development by users: The impact of "sticky" local information. *Management Science*, *44*(5), 629–644. doi:10.1287/mnsc.44.5.629

Von Hippel, E. (2005). *Democratizing innovation*. Cambridge, MA: The MIT Press.

Vrasidas, C., & Glass, G. V. (2002). A conceptual framework for studying distance education. In Vrasidas, C., & Glass, G. V. (Eds.), *Current Perspectives in Applied Information Technologies: Distance Education and Distributed Learning* (pp. 31–56). Greenwich, CT: Information Age Publishing, Inc.

Vygotsky, L. S. (1962). *Thought and language*. Cambridge, MA: The MIT Press. doi:10.1037/11193-000

Vygotsky, L. S. (1978). *Mind in society: Development of Higher Psychological Processes* (14th ed.). Cambridge, MA: Harvard Press.

Waldersee, R. (1997). Becoming a learning organization: The transformation of the workforce. *Journal of Management Development*, *16*(4), 262–273. doi:10.1108/02621719710164544

Waldstrøm, C. (2003). *Understanding intra-organizational relations through social network analysis*. Aarhus, Denmark: Aarhus University.

Waltz, E. (2003). *Knowledge management in the intelligence enterprise*. Norwood, MA: Artech House.

Wang, S., & Noe, R. A. (2010). Knowledge sharing: A review and directions for future research. *Human Resource Management Review*, *20*(2), 115–131. doi:10.1016/j.hrmr.2009.10.001

Wang, C.-C. (2004). The influence of ethical and self-interest concerns on knowledge sharing intentions among managers: An empirical study. *International Journal of Management*, *21*(3), 370–381.

Warren, M. (2008). The ethics of the hacker taggers: The new generation of hackers. In Bynum, T. (Eds.), *ETHICOMP 2008: Living, Working and Learning Beyond Technology* (pp. 787–793). Mantua, Italy: University of Pavia.

Wasko, M. M., & Faraj, S. (2005). Why should I share? Examining social capital and knowledge contribution in electronic networks of practice. *Management Information Systems Quarterly*, *29*(1), 35–57.

Watson, K. (2007). Language, education and ethnicity: Whose rights will prevail in the age of globalisation? *International Journal of Educational Development*, *27*(3), 252–265. doi:10.1016/j.ijedudev.2006.10.015

Watsuji, T. (1934). *Ethics as the study on human beings*. Tokyo: Iwanami Shoten. (in Japanese)

Weber, R. (2004). The rhetoric of positivism versus interpretivism: A personal view. *Management Information Systems Quarterly*, *28*(1), iii–xii.

Weber, M. (1946). The social psychology of the world religions. In Gerth, H. H., & Mills, C. W. (Eds.), *From Max Weber: Essays in Sociology* (pp. 267–301). New York: Galaxy.

Webster, F. (2006). *Theories of the information society* (3rd ed.). London: Routledge.

Webster's Dictionary. (1996). *Webster's new universal unabridged dictionary*. New York: Barnes & Noble Books.

Welsch, W. (1999). Transculturality- The puzzling form of cultures today. In Featherstone, M., & Lash, S. (Eds.), *Spaces of Culture: City, Nation, World* (pp. 194–213). London: Sage.

West, G. P. III, & Meyer, G. D. (1997). Communicated knowledge as a learning foundation. *The International Journal of Organizational Analysis*, *5*(1), 25–58. doi:10.1108/eb028861

Westover, R. (2006). *Learning organizations: A preliminary investigation between the presence of a learning organization and profit*. Unpublished master thesis, Gonzaga University, Spokane.

Whittaker, J., Burns, M., & Beveren, J. V. (2003, September/October). *Understanding and measuring the effect of social capital on knowledge transfer within clusters of small-medium enterprises*. Paper presented at The Small Enterprise Association of Australia and New Zealand 16th Annual Conference, Ballarat, Australia. Retrieved January, 23, 2009, from http://www.cecc.com.au/programs/resource_manager/accounts/seaanz_papers/57Whittakeretal.pdf

Wiener, N. (1956). *I am a mathematician: The later life of a prodigy*. Cambridge, MA: Doubleday & Day.

Wikipedia (2010a). Refraction. *Wikipedia*. Retrieved August 2, 2010, from, http://en.wikipedia.org/wiki/Refraction

Wikipedia (2010b). Lighthouse. *Wikipedia*. Retrieved August 3, 2010, from, http://en.wikipedia.org/wiki/Lighthouse

Wikipedia. (2009). Hacker ethic. *Wikimedia Foundation, Inc*. Retrieved October 23, 2009, from, http://en.wikipedia.org/wiki/Hacker_ethic#The_hacker_ethics

Wiktionary (2010). Fairness. *Wiktionary*. Retrieved September 10, 2010, from, http://en.wiktionary.org/wiki/fairness

Williams, M. (2000). Interpretivism and generalization. *Sociology*, *34*(2), 209–224.

Wilson, S. M., Schulman, L. S., & Richért, A. E. (1987). 150 different ways of knowing: Representations of knowledge in teaching. In Calderhead, J. (Ed.), *Exploring Teacher's Thinking* (pp. 104–124). London: Cassell Education.

Wilson, T. D. (2002). The nonsense of knowledge management. *Information Research, 8*(1). Retrieved August 28, 2010, from, http://informationr.net/ir/8-1/paper144.html

Wittmer, D. P. (2000). Ethical sensitivity in management decisions: Developing and testing a perceptual measure among management and professional student groups. *Teaching Business Ethics*, *4*(2), 181–205. doi:10.1023/A:1009866315139

Wolstenholme, E. F. (1990). *System enquiry*. Chichester, UK: Wiley.

Wood, V. R. (2006). Globalization and higher education: Eight common perceptions from university leaders. IIE Network. Retrieved July 15, 2009, from http://www.iienetwork.org/page/84658/

World Bank. (2000). *Higher education in developing countries: Peril and promise. The Task Force on Higher Education and Society*. Washington, DC: World Bank Publications.

World Bank. (2009). *Information and communications for development 2009: Extending reach and increasing impact*. Washington, DC: World Bank Publications.

World Summit on the Information Society. (2003). Declaration of principles. International Telecommunications Union. Retrieved July 25, 2009, from http://www.itu.int/wsis/docs/geneva/official/dop.html

Yamada, Y. (1985). *Ringi and nemawashi*. Tokyo: Kodansha. (in Japanese)

Yamagishi, T., & Yamagishi, M. (1994). Trust and commitment in the United States and Japan. *Motivation and Emotion*, *18*(2), 129–166. doi:10.1007/BF02249397

Yamamoto, S. (1983). *The study on "atmosphere"*. Tokyo: Bungei Shunju. (in Japanese)

Yates-Mercer, P., & Bawden, D. (2002). Managing the paradox: the valuation of knowledge and knowledge management. *Journal of Information Science*, *28*(1), 19–29. doi:10.1177/016555150202800103

Yeo, R. Y. (2005). Revisiting the roots of learning organization: A synthesis of the learning organization literature. *The Learning Organization*, *12*(4), 368–382. doi:10.1108/09696470510599145

Yin, R. K. (1994). *Case study research: Design and methods* (3rd ed.). Thousand Oaks, CA: Sage.

Yuasa, Y. (1987). *The body: Toward an Eastern mind-body theory*. Albany, NY: State University of New York Press.

Zairi, M., Jarrar, Y. F., & Aspinwall, E. (2010). A reward, recognition, and appraisal systems for future competitiveness: A UK survey of best practices. *European Centre for Best Practice Management*. Retrieved September 10, 2010, from, http://www.ecbpm.com/files/Talent%20-%20People%20Management/A%20Reward,%20Recognition,%20and%20Appraisal%20System%20for%20Future%20Competitiveness.pdf

Zait, D., & Zait, A. (2009). Research anticipation: The methodological choice. *Review of International Comparative Management*, *10*(5), 902–909.

Zhao, B. (2004). Tapestry: A resilient global-scale overlay for service deployment. *IEEE Journal on Selected Areas in Communications*, *22*(1), 41–53. doi:10.1109/JSAC.2003.818784

Zikmund, W. G., & Zikmund, E. G. (2000). *Business research methods* (6th ed.). London: Dryden Press.

Zirfas, J. (1999). *Die lehre der ethik, zur moralischen begründung pädagogischen denkens und handelns*. Weinheim, Germany: Deutscher Studien Verlag.

About the Contributors

Gonçalo Jorge Morais da Costa is a PhD student in Knowledge Management and Ethics, through the doctoral programme of the Centre for Computing and Social Responsibility at De Montfort University, with supervision of Professor Mary Prior and Professor Simon Rogerson. In addition, he is a member of ILID Research Group at Lusíada University of Lisbon since 2006, and lecturer in several universities as an inherent consequence of its academic background (Degree in Economics, Master in E-Business and IT, and MBA in Management) along with its professional background (Key Account Manager in Finance and ICT). Beyond the challenging PhD, its current research areas are all the major appliances regarding ICT and ethics, which is demonstrated throughout his published work in several journals or books chapters, as well as presented in several conferences. Among other publications, he has published: *Knowledge versus content in e-learning: a philosophical discussion (2010), Knowledge authoring in e-learning: an ethicultural diagnosis! (2010), Why link knowledge management, organizational culture and ethics: analysing empirical enquiry (2010), Trustworthy and ethical environment in knowledge management: a dilemma to solve! (2009), Communities of practices- the future or return to the past- a sceptical approach (2008), Will the evolution of ICT ethics engage organizational transparency? (2008), Free ride in knowledge management: ethical and moral dilemmas! (2008), Individual ethics and knowledge management (2008), Knowledge management: how ethical is your organization's knowledge (2007).* Finally, the editor is also a reviewer of the following journals: Journal of Information, Communication and Ethics in Society, Journal of Ethics and Information Technology, IPSI Transactions Journal, and Energy- the International Journal. For further and continuously updated information, visit the editor's website at www.goncalocosta.com, namely this publication forum.

* * *

David Pullinger has worked on the interface between people and technology since 1979, focusing particularly on online information systems. His PhD was one of the first in the area of human-computer interaction, which, for him, has gone onto to include psychosocial aspects and so ethics. He contributed many firsts during the time the Internet and then the World Wide Web were growing, including the first academic journal onto the Web and conceiving and initiating the linking of references from one to another through CrossRef. He won awards for innovation and websites and has reflected ethically on this work through articles and books, including one for an ethics series, Information Technology and Cyberspace (2001). He now works for the UK Government to improve the user experience of public sector online services, ensuring that they are customer-focused by setting standards, describing best practice and giving advice and guidance.

Kiyoshi Murata is a director of Centre for Business Information Ethics and a professor of management information systems at School of Commerce, Meiji University, Tokyo, Japan. His research interest is in information quality management, e-business, knowledge management and information ethics in business organisations including privacy, ICT professionalism, surveillance, gender issues and online bullying. He is an international research associate at Centre for Computing and Social Responsibility, De Montfort University, Leicester, UK and an editorial board member of Journal of Information, Communication and Ethics in Society, Journal of the Japan Society for Management Information and Journal of Information and Management. He has organised an information ethics research project within the Japan Society for Information and Management since 2008.

Chuck Huff is Professor of Psychology at St. Olaf College, USA. He began doing research in social and ethical issues in computing in the mid-1980s at BellCORE and Princeton University. After a post-doc at Carnegie-Mellon University he moved to St. Olaf College where he has continued his research in moral psychology and in computing. His National Science Foundation funded work in moral exemplars in computing has taken him to Scandinavia and the UK to interview exemplars in those cultures. He most recently served on a US National Academy of Sciences and Engineering panel to survey the state of the art in teaching science and engineering ethics.

Krystyna Górniak-Kocikowska She published more than one hundred articles in scholarly journals and books in several languages mainly in the area of the history of philosophy, and social and ethical problems in the ICT-driven global society. Is also co-author of the books *On Selected Problems in Contemporary Ethics (*1979) and *The History of German Intellectual Culture* (1985), both published in Polish. Moreover, also co-edited several books, including *The Introduction to Information Ethics* (with Andrzej Kocikowski and Terrell Bynum), a CD-ROM collection of "milestone" papers on Computer Ethics translated from English into Polish; and translated works of German and American authors into Polish. Finally, is on the Editorial Advisory Board of the *Journal of Information, Communication & Ethics in Society.*

Piotr Pawlak Piotr holds a Ph.D. title at the Adam Mickiewicz University of Poznan, Poland. His specialization is political sciences, as well as cultural sciences. He studied at the Social Science Faculty, Adam Mickiewicz University of Poznan, obtaining during 2008 his doctorate title. Currently, his areas of interest are: cultural, social and also political aspects of modern mass-media, especially the Internet (his PhD thesis). One of his basic scopes is to try to give a response about the influence of Information and Communication Technologies at the lives of individuals, and societies.

José António Candeias Bonito Filipe has a PhD in Resource Management and Theory of Games by ISCTE. He is an investigator of UNIDE/ISCTE. His interests are directed to Theory of Games and Environmental and Natural Resource Economics. He is Assistant Professor in Quantitative Methods Department at ISCTE-IUL.

Manuel Alberto Martins Ferreira has a PhD in Management and an Aggregation in Quantitative Methods Area by ISCTE, where he is Full Professor. He was Chairman of the Board of Directors and Vice-President of ISCTE. He is an investigator of UNIDE/ISCTE, being his interests directed to the Stochastic Processes Area (Queues, Applied Probabilities) and to the Theory of Games and to their applications to management, finance and social problems.

Manuel Francisco Pacheco Coelho has a PhD in Economics by the Instituto Superior de Economia e Gestão, Universidade Técnica de Lisboa, where he is Assistant Professor. He is an investigator of SOCIUS/ISEG. His main field of research is Environmental and Natural Resource Economics.

Maslin Masrom is a Senior Lecturer in College of Science and Technology at University Technology Malaysia. She received her Bachelor in Computer Science (1989) at University Technology Malaysia, and Master in Operations Research (1992) at Western Michigan University. She pursued her Ph.D. in Management Information Systems, which was obtained in 2003 at University Putra Malaysia. Her current research interest includes information security and ethics, security management, and IS adoption using structural equation modelling. She has published, among others, in *Information & Management, Oxford Journal, International Journal of Cyber Society and Education, and ACM SIGCAS Computers and Society.*

Zuraini Ismail started her tertiary education with Diploma in Computer Science (1981) at University Technology MARA. She obtained her Bachelor in Computer Management Systems (1984) at Southern New Hampshire, and a Masters in Computer Management (1987) from University of New Haven. She further awarded PhD in Management Information System (2007) at International Islamic University Malaysia. Currently, she is a Senior Lecturer at College of Science and Technology (CST), University Technology Malaysia, as well as CST's IT Manager. Her present research interest includes information security- policy, awareness and ethics, physical and cyber security, knowledge management, IT outsourcing. Furthermore, has been publishing in *Journal of US-China Public Administration, and ACM SIGCAS Computers and Society.*

Ugo Pagallo is a full Professor at the Faculty of Law, University of Turin, since 2000, and visiting professor at Georgetown University Law School in Washington, D.C., and at the Center for Transnational Legal Studies in London. Member of the board in the PhD programs of the University of Turin, where he directed the research on "Computer Science and Law" (2004-2006), he has coordinated various national scientific projects and is current chief editor of the *Digitalica* series published by Giappichelli. In addition to numerous essays in scholarly journals, he is the author of eight monographs, among which *Introduzione alla filosofia digitale* (2005), *Teoria giuridica della complessità* (2006), and *La tutela della privacy negli Stati Uniti d'America e in Europa* (2008).

Nuno Sotero Alves da Silva is doing PhD in Computer Ethics and Education in De Montfort University with supervision of Professor Simon Rogerson and Dr. Bernd Stahl. Plus, he holds a Degree in Computer Science Engineering and a Pos-Degree in E-Business and IT. He is also a lecturer and IT Manager in Lusíada University of Lisbon, Portugal. His current research areas are e-learning, bionano-tecnhology, computer happiness bounded to ethics.

Isabel Maria Surdinho Borges Alvarez holds a Ph.D. title at the De Montfort University, United Kingdom. She is specialized into culture and electronic commerce, namely within the pharmaceutical sector, in which was IT Manager during 20 years. Beyond these achievements she is an IS lecturer since 1986 in Lusíada University of Lisbon, and was involved in several Portuguese governmental projects concerning IT implementation.

Professor Simon Rogerson is Director of CCSR. He is experienced in identifying the ethical issues related to new technologies. He is Europe's first Professor in Computer Ethics. He received the 2000 IFIP Namur Award for outstanding contribution to the creation of awareness of the social implications of ICT. In 2005 he was given the prestigious SIGCAS Making a Difference Award by the ACM. He is currently working on two European-funded projects PHM-Ethics; Personalized health monitoring (PHM): interdisciplinary research to analyse the relationship between ethics, law and psychosocial as well as medical sciences and ETICA; Ethical Issues of Emerging ICT Applications. He conceived and co-directs the ETHICOMP conference series on the ethical impacts of ICT and created the world's leading portal on computer ethics. He is Chair of Council and Vice President of the Institute for the Management of Information Systems (IMIS), and a member of the Ethics Strategic Panel of BCS.

MA Päivi Lohikoski is a Ph.D. student in Finnish, Information Studies, and Logopedics at the Centre of Excellence in Research in Faculty of Humanities in University of Oulu. An associated member of The Graduate School of Communication Sciences and a member of The Graduate School of Culture and Interaction, she has worked previously as a lecturer in Communication Studies at Oulu University. Before that she worked several years as a Documentation and Communication Coordinator in an ICT-company in Oulu, Finland. Päivi's interest is in expert engineers in the ICT field. Her future studies aim to compare the personal mastery of those professionals within their organisations and management. Financial crises add the need for education, training, and reorganisation of duties within organisations, and stress the importance of renewal ability in knowledge-based work. Moreover, an increasing need exists for better managerial skills to improve wellbeing at work in all organisations.

Yutaka Takahashi is a professor of computer simulation of business and social issues at School of Commerce, Senshu University in Japan. He is applying simulation methods, including system dynamics and systems thinking, to solving social science issues. His current interest is providing solutions to troubles related to use of information communication technology and designing policies of public and private sectors using modelling and simulation. Developing simulation methods which are convenient not only for engineers but also for management people to help their own decision making is also his interest. He earned PhD at Gakushuin University in Japan with a doctoral dissertation on a system dynamics modelling method focused on mental model expressions in 1999.

Agata Kostrzewa is a PhD student in Business Studies at the Department of Business Studies, Uppsala University. Agata's work focuses on how companies and organizations cope with ethical issues as well as how to enhance their ability to do it efficiently. Agata is now working on the construction and application of questionnaires and interviews to identify and evaluate ethical processes in organizations. She holds also a Master of Science in Business and Economics from Uppsala University. Before the Ph.D. studies she worked as a Research Assistant within the project "Between Public and Private: Democratic Governance in Healthcare Networks", the field of her interest being creating markets in healthcare.

Mikael Laaksoharju is a PhD student in Human Computer Interaction. He has a background as civil engineer and has as student been working with artificial intelligence in robots. His research is concentrated on developing computer tools to support and train ethical decision making. The tools are based on an assumption that structuring and presenting information in a suitable way can improve the handling of moral problems. They have been presented at several conferences and the procedural approach has impacted especially the field of Operations Research. Among his duties at the University is to ensure good usability in the development of a new web content management system.

Iordanis Kavathatzopoulos is Associate Professor of Psychology and Human-Computer Interaction at the Department of Information Technology, Uppsala University, Sweden. His main interests are in the areas of Business Ethics and Information Technology Ethics. He has created education programs for the development of ethical competence of professional decision makers, and constructed special tests for the assessment of ethical problem-solving and decision-making ability. His research is also in the areas of assessment and development of personal skills and organizational processes behind construction and running of usable IT Systems. He has constructed special instruments for the evaluation of IT systems usability and investigated the structure and dynamics of informal cooperation and cognitive support between IT systems users.

Index

T

U

V

W

Breinigsville, PA USA
23 November 2010
249730BV00005B/1-82/P

9 781615 208739